Dictionary of Literary Biography

Documentary Series

1 *Sherwood Anderson, Willa Cather, John Dos Passos, Theodore Dreiser, F. Scott Fitzgerald, Ernest Hemingway, Sinclair Lewis*, edited by Margaret A. Van Antwerp (1982)

2 *James Gould Cozzens, James T. Farrell, William Faulkner, John O'Hara, John Steinbeck, Thomas Wolfe, Richard Wright*, edited by Margaret A. Van Antwerp (1982)

3 *Saul Bellow, Jack Kerouac, Norman Mailer, Vladimir Nabokov, John Updike, Kurt Vonnegut*, edited by Mary Bruccoli (1983)

4 *Tennessee Williams*, edited by Margaret A. Van Antwerp and Sally Johns (1984)

5 *American Transcendentalists*, edited by Joel Myerson (1988)

6 *Hardboiled Mystery Writers: Raymond Chandler, Dashiell Hammett, Ross Mac-donald*, edited by Matthew J. Bruccoli and Richard Layman (1989)

7 *Modern American Poets: James Dickey, Robert Frost, Marianne Moore*, edited by Karen L. Rood (1989)

8 *The Black Aesthetic Movement*, edited by Jeffrey Louis Decker (1991)

9 *American Writers of the Vietnam War: W. D. Ehrhart, Larry Heinemann, Tim O'Brien, Walter McDonald, John M. Del Vecchio*, edited by Ronald Baughman (1991)

10 *The Bloomsbury Group*, edited by Edward L. Bishop (1992)

11 *American Proletarian Culture: The Twenties and The Thirties*, edited by Jon Christian Suggs (1993)

12 *Southern Women Writers: Flannery O'Connor, Katherine Anne Porter, Eudora Welty*, edited by Mary Ann Wimsatt and Karen L. Rood (1994)

13 *The House of Scribner, 1846-1904*, edited by John Delaney (1996)

14 *Four Women Writers for Children, 1868-1918*, edited by Caroline C. Hunt (1996)

15 *American Expatriate Writers: Paris in the Twenties*, edited by Matthew J. Bruccoli and Robert W. Trogdon (1997)

16 *The House of Scribner, 1905-1930*, edited by John Delaney (1997)

17 *The House of Scribner, 1931-1984*, edited by John Delaney (1998)

18 *British Poets of The Great War: Sassoon, Graves, Owen*, edited by Patrick Quinn (1999)

19 *James Dickey*, edited by Judith S. Baughman (1999)

Yearbooks

1980 edited by Karen L. Rood, Jean W. Ross, and Richard Ziegfeld (1981)

1981 edited by Karen L. Rood, Jean W. Ross, and Richard Ziegfeld (1982)

1982 edited by Richard Ziegfeld; associate editors: Jean W. Ross and Lynne C. Zeigler (1983)

1983 edited by Mary Bruccoli and Jean W. Ross; associate editor: Richard Ziegfeld (1984)

1984 edited by Jean W. Ross (1985)

1985 edited by Jean W. Ross (1986)

1986 edited by J. M. Brook (1987)

1987 edited by J. M. Brook (1988)

1988 edited by J. M. Brook (1989)

1989 edited by J. M. Brook (1990)

1990 edited by James W. Hipp (1991)

1991 edited by James W. Hipp (1992)

1992 edited by James W. Hipp (1993)

1993 edited by James W. Hipp, contributing editor George Garrett (1994)

1994 edited by James W. Hipp, contributing editor George Garrett (1995)

1995 edited by James W. Hipp, contributing editor George Garrett (1996)

1996 edited by Samuel W. Bruce and L. Kay Webster, contributing editor George Garrett (1997)

1997 edited by Matthew J. Bruccoli and George Garrett, with the assistance of L. Kay Webster (1998)

Concise Series

Concise Dictionary of American Literary Biography, 7 volumes (1988-1999): *The New Consciousness, 1941-1968; Colonization to the American Renaissance, 1640-1865; Realism, Naturalism, and Local Color, 1865-1917; The Twenties, 1917-1929; The Age of Maturity, 1929-1941; Broadening Views, 1968-1988; Modern Writers: Supplement, 1900-1998.*

Concise Dictionary of British Literary Biography, 8 volumes (1991-1992): *Writers of the Middle Ages and Renaissance Before 1660; Writers of the Restoration and Eighteenth Century, 1660-1789; Writers of the Romantic Period, 1789-1832; Victorian Writers, 1832-1890; Late-Victorian and Edwardian Writers, 1890-1914; Modern Writers, 1914-1945; Writers After World War II, 1945-1960; Contemporary Writers, 1960 to Present.*

Concise Dictionary of American Literary Biography
Supplement

Modern Writers, 1900–1998

Concise Dictionary of American Literary Biography
Supplement

Modern Writers, 1900–1998

A Bruccoli Clark Layman Book
Gale Research
Detroit, Washington, D.C., London

CONCISE DICTIONARY
OF AMERICAN LITERARY BIOGRAPHY

Matthew J. Bruccoli and Richard Layman, *Editorial Directors*
C. E. Frazer Clark Jr., *Managing Editor*

Manufactured by Braun-Brumfield, Inc.
Ann Arbor, Michigan
Printed in the United States of America

Library of Congress Cataloging-in-Publication Data

Modern Writers: Supplement, 1900–1998
(Concise dictionary of American literary biography
supplement; v. 7)
    "A Bruccoli Clark Layman book."
    Includes index.
    1. Authors, American–20th century–Biography–
Dictionaries 2. American literature–20th century–
Dictionaries. 3. American literature–20th century–
Bio-bibliography.
PS129.C66   1988   810'.9'0054   [B]   86-33657

ISBN 0-7876-1695-8 (vol. 7)
ISBN 0-8103-1818-0 (set)

Contents

Plan of the Work

The *Concise Dictionary of American Literary Biography* was developed in response to requests from high-school and junior-college teachers and librarians, and from small- to medium-sized public libraries, for a compilation of entries from the standard *Dictionary of Literary Biography* chosen to meet their needs and their budgets. The *DLB,* which comprises more than two hundred volumes as of the end of 1998, is moving steadily toward its goal of providing a history of literature in all languages developed through the biographies of writers. Basic as the *DLB* is, many librarians have expressed the need for a less comprehensive reference work that in other respects retains the merits of *DLB.* The *Concise DALB* provides this resource.

This series was planned by an advisory board, consisting primarily of secondary-school educators, who developed a method of organization and presentation for selected *DLB* entries suitable for high-school and beginning college students. Their preliminary plan was circulated to some five thousand school librarians and English teachers, who were asked to respond to the organization of the series and the table of contents. Those responses were incorporated into the plan described here.

Uses for the Concise DALB

Students are the primary audience for the *Concise DALB.* The stated purpose of the standard *DLB* is to make our literary heritage more accessible. *Concise DALB* has the same goal and seeks a wider audience. What the author wrote; what the facts of his life are; a description of his literary works; a discussion of the critical response to his works; and a bibliography of critical works to be consulted for further information: these are the elements of a *Concise DALB* entry.

The first step in the planning process for this series, after identifying the audience, was to contemplate its uses. The advisory board acknowledged that the integrity of *Concise DALB* as a reference book is crucial to its utility. The *Concise DALB* adheres to the scholarly standards established by the parent series. Thus, within the scope of major American literary figures, the *Concise DALB* is a ready reference source of established

value, providing reliable biographical and bibliographical information.

It is anticipated that this series will not be confined to uses within the library. Just as *DLB* has been a tool for stimulating students' literary interests in the college classroom—for comparative studies of authors, for example, and, through its ample illustrations, as a means of invigorating literary study—the *Concise DALB* is a primary resource for high-school and junior-college educators. The series is organized to facilitate lesson planning.

Organization

The advisory board further determined that entries from the standard *DLB* should be presented complete—without abridgment. Their feeling was that the utility of the *DLB* format has been proven and that only minimal changes should be made.

The advisory board further decided that the organization of the *Concise DALB* should be chronological to emphasize the historical development of American literature. Each volume is devoted to a single historical period and includes the most significant literary figures from all genres who were active during that time. The *Concise DALB* limits itself to major figures, but it provides the same coverage of those figures as the *DLB* does.

The seven period volumes of the *Concise DALB* are *Colonization to the American Renaissance, 1640–1865; Realism, Naturalism, and Local Color, 1865–1917; The Twenties, 1917–1929; The Age of Maturity, 1929–1941; The New Consciousness, 1941–1968; Broadening Views, 1968–1988;* and *Modern Writers: Supplement, 1900–1998.* This volume includes a cumulative index by proper names to the entire *Concise DALB.*

Form of Entry

The form of entry in the *Concise DALB* is substantially the same as in the standard series, with the following alterations:

1) Previously published entries have been updated or augmented to include a discussion of works published since the standard entry ap-

peared and to reflect recent criticism and research of interest to the high school audience.

2) The secondary bibliography for each entry has been selected to include those books and articles of particular interest and usefulness to high-school and junior-college students.

It bears repeating that the *Concise DALB* is restricted to major American literary figures. Users of this series will find it advantageous to consult the standard *DLB* for information about those writers omitted from the *Concise DALB* whose significance to contemporary readers may have faded but whose contribution to our cultural heritage remains meaningful.

Comments about the series and suggestions about how to improve it are earnestly invited.

A Note to Students

The purpose of the *Concise DALB* is to enrich the study of literature. In their various ways, writers react in their works to the circumstances of their lives, the events of their time, and the culture that envelops them. Writers provide a way to see and understand what they have observed and experienced. Besides being inherently interesting, biographies of writers provide a basic perspective on literature.

Concise DALB entries start with the most important facts about writers: what they wrote. We strongly recommend that you also start there. The chronological listing of an author's works is an outline for the examination of his or her career achievement. The biographies that follow set the stage for the presentation of the writings. Each of the author's important publications and the most respected critical evaluations of them are discussed in *Concise DALB*. If you require more information about the author or fuller critical studies of the author's works, the references section at the end of the entry will guide you.

Illustrations are an integral element of *Concise DALB* entries. Photographs of the author are reminders that literature is the product of a writer's imagination; facsimiles of the author's working drafts are the best evidence available for understanding the act of composition—the author in the process of refining his work and acting as self-editor; and dust jackets and advertisements demonstrate how literature comes to us through the marketplace, which sometimes serves to alter our perceptions of the works.

Literary study is a complex and immensely rewarding endeavor. Our goal is to provide you with the information you need to make that experience as rich as possible.

Acknowledgments

This book was produced by Bruccoli Clark Layman, Inc. Karen L. Rood is senior editor for the *Dictionary of Literary Biography* series. Tracy Simmons Bitonti and Penelope M. Hope were the in-house editors. They were assisted by Jan Peter F. van Rosevelt.

Administrative support was provided by Ann M. Cheschi, Tenesha S. Lee, and Shawna M. Tillman.

Bookkeeper is Neil Senol.

Copyediting supervisor is Phyllis A. Avant. The copyediting staff includes Brenda Carol Blanton, Jannette L. Giles, Thom Harman, Melissa D. Hinton, Raegan E. Quinn, and Audra Rouse. Freelance copyeditors are Brenda Cabra, Rebecca Mayo, Nicole M. Nichols, and Jennie Williamson.

Editorial associate is Jeff Miller.

Layout and graphics staff includes Janet E. Hill, Mark J. McEwan, and Alison Smith.

Office manager is Kathy Lawler Merlette.

Photography editors are Margo Dowling and Paul Talbot. Photographic copy work was performed by Joseph M. Bruccoli.

Production manager is Marie L. Parker.

SGML supervisor is Cory McNair. The SGML staff includes Linda Drake, Frank Graham, Jennifer Harwell, and Alex Snead.

Systems manager is Marie L. Parker.

Database manager is Javed Nurani. Kimberly Kelly performed data entry.

Typesetting supervisor is Kathleen M. Flanagan. The typesetting staff includes Karla Corley Brown, Pamela D. Norton, and Patricia Flanagan Salisbury. Freelance typesetters include Deidre Murphy and Delores Plastow.

Walter W. Ross and Steven Gross did library research. They were assisted by the following librarians at the Thomas Cooper Library of the University of South Carolina: Linda Holderfield and the interlibrary-loan staff; reference-department head Virginia Weathers; reference librarians Marilee Birchfield, Stefanie Buck, Stefanie DuBose, Rebecca Feind, Karen Joseph, Donna Lehman, Charlene Loope, Anthony McKissick, Jean Rhyne, and Kwamine Simpson; circulation-department head Caroline Taylor; and acquisitions-searching supervisor David Haggard.

Concise Dictionary of American Literary Biography
Supplement

Modern Writers, 1900–1998

Concise Dictionary of American Literary Biography

Maya Angelou

*This entry was updated by Darren Harris-Fain (Shawnee State University)
from the entry by Lynn Z. Bloom (Virginia Commonwealth University)
in DLB 38: Afro-American Writers After 1955: Dramatists
and Prose Writers.*

BIRTH: St. Louis, Missouri, 4 April 1928, as Marguerite (some sources say Marguerita) Johnson, to Bailey and Vivian Baxter Johnson.

EDUCATION: Attended public schools in Arkansas and California; studied music privately; studied dance with Martha Graham, Pearl Primus, and Ann Halprin; studied drama with Frank Silvera and Gene Frankel.

MARRIAGES: 1950 to Enistasious (Tosh) Angelos (divorced circa 1952); 1960s to an unnamed African official (divorced); December 1973 to Paul Du Feu (divorced circa 1981); child: Clyde Bailey "Guy" Johnson.

AWARDS AND HONORS: National Book Award nomination for *I Know Why the Caged Bird Sings,* 1970; Yale University fellowship, 1970; Pulitzer Prize nomination for *Just Give Me a Cool Drink of Water 'fore I Diiie,* 1972; Antoinette Perry ("Tony") Award nomination from League of New York Theatres and Producers for performance in *Look Away,* 1973; Rockefeller Foundation scholar in Italy, 1975; named Woman of the Year in Communications by *Ladies' Home Journal,* 1976; Emmy Award nomination for best supporting actress for *Roots,* 1977; named one of the top one hundred most influential women by *Ladies' Home Journal,* 1983; North Carolina Award in Literature, 1987; named Woman of the Year by *Essence* magazine, 1992; named Distinguished Woman of North Carolina, 1992; Horatio Alger Award, 1992; Grammy Award for best spoken-word or nontraditional album for recording of "On the Pulse of Morning," 1994; recipient of more than fifty honorary degrees.

Maya Angelou reading "On the Pulse of Morning" at the presidential inauguration of William Jefferson Clinton, 1993

BOOKS: *I Know Why the Caged Bird Sings* (New York: Random House, 1969; London: Virago, 1984); excerpt published as *Mrs. Flowers: A Moment of Friendship* (Minneapolis, Minn.: Redpath Press, 1986);
Just Give Me a Cool Drink of Water 'fore I Diiie: The Poetry of Maya Angelou (New York: Random House, 1971); published together with *Oh Pray*

My Wings Are Gonna Fit Me Well (London: Virago, 1988);

Gather Together in My Name (New York: Random House, 1974; London: Virago, 1985);

Oh Pray My Wings Are Gonna Fit Me Well (New York: Random House, 1975); published together with *Just Give Me a Cool Drink of Water 'fore I Diiie: The Poetry of Maya Angelou* (London: Virago, 1988);

Singin' and Swingin' and Gettin' Merry Like Christmas (New York: Random House, 1976; London: Virago, 1985);

And Still I Rise (New York: Random House, 1978; London: Virago, 1986);

The Heart of a Woman (New York: Random House, 1981; London: Virago, 1986);

Shaker, Why Don't You Sing? (New York: Random House, 1983);

All God's Children Need Traveling Shoes (Franklin Center, Pa.: Franklin Library / New York: Random House, 1986; London: Virago, 1987);

Poems: Maya Angelou (New York: Bantam, 1986)—includes *Just Give Me a Cool Drink of Water 'fore I Diiie, Oh Pray My Wings Are Gonna Fit Me Well, And Still I Rise,* and *Shaker, Why Don't You Sing?;*

Now Sheba Sings the Song, art by Tom Feelings (New York: Dutton/Dial, 1987; London: Virago, 1987);

I Shall Not Be Moved (New York: Random House, 1990; London: Virago, 1990);

Maya Angelou Omnibus (London: Virago, 1991);

Life Doesn't Frighten Me (New York: Stewart, Tabori & Chang, 1993);

On the Pulse of Morning (New York: Random House, 1993; London: Virago, 1993);

Lessons in Living (New York: Random House, 1993);

Soul Looks Back in Wonder, text by Angelou and others, art by Feelings (New York: Dial, 1993);

Wouldn't Take Nothing for My Journey Now (New York: Random House, 1993; London: Virago, 1994);

The Complete Collected Poems of Maya Angelou (New York: Random House, 1994; London: Virago, 1994);

My Painted House, My Friendly Chicken, and Me, text by Angelou, photographs by Margaret Courtney-Clarke (New York: Clarkson Potter, 1994; London: Bodley Head, 1994);

Phenomenal Woman: Four Poems Celebrating Women (New York: Random House, 1994);

A Brave and Startling Truth (New York: Random House, 1995);

Kofi and His Magic, text by Angelou, photographs by Courtney-Clarke (New York: Clarkson Potter, 1996);

Even the Stars Look Lonesome (New York: Random House, 1997; London: Virago, 1998).

PLAY PRODUCTIONS: *Cabaret for Freedom,* by Angelou and Godfrey Cambridge, New York, Village Gate Theatre, 1960;

The Least of These, Los Angeles, 1966;

Ajax, adaptation of play by Sophocles, Los Angeles, Mark Taper Forum, 1974;

And I Still Rise, Oakland, Cal., Ensemble Theatre, 1976.

MOTION PICTURES: *Georgia, Georgia,* Independent-Cinerama, 1972;

All Day Long, American Film Institute, 1974.

TELEVISION: *Blacks, Blues, Black* [series], National Educational Television, 1968;

Assignment America [series], 1975;

"The Legacy," 1976;

"The Inheritors," 1976;

I Know Why the Caged Bird Sings, adaptation by Angelou, Leonora Thuna, and Ralph B. Woolsey, CBS, 1979;

Sister, Sister, NBC, 7 June 1982.

RECORDINGS: *Miss Calypso,* Liberty Records, 1957;

The Poetry of Maya Angelou, GWP Records, 1969;

An Evening with Maya Angelou, Pacific Tape Library (BC 2660), 1975;

Women in Business, University of Wisconsin, 1981.

OTHER: Elliot Schneider, *The Women of the Regent Hotel: The Unheard Voices of the Homeless in Poems,* introduction by Angelou (New York: Child Development Center of the Jewish Board of Family and Child Services, 1987);

Margaret Courtney-Clarke, *African Canvas: The Art of West African Women,* foreword by Angelou (New York: Rizzoli International, 1991);

Zora Neale Hurston, *Dust Tracks on a Road: An Autobiography,* foreword by Angelou (New York: HarperPerennial, 1991);

Patricia Bell-Scott, ed., *Double Stitch: Black Women Write about Mothers and Daughters,* foreword by Angelou (Boston: Beacon, 1991);

"Arts and Public Policy," in *Culture and Democracy: Social and Ethical Issues in Public Support for the Arts and Humanities,* edited by Andrew Buchwalter (Boulder, Colo.: Westview, 1992), pp. 27–40;

"Cicely Tyson: Reflections on a Lone Black Rose,"
     in *Speech and Power: The African-American Essay
     and Its Cultural Content from Polemics to Pulpit,* ed-
     ited by Gerald Early (Hopewell, N.J.: Ecco,
     1992), pp. 348–353;
"M. F. K. Fisher," in *Conversations with M. F. K.
     Fisher,* edited by David Lazar (Jackson: Uni-
     versity Press of Mississippi, 1992), pp. 70–75;
Richard A. Long, *African Americans: A Portrait,* fore-
     word by Angelou (New York: Crescent,
     1993);
"Maya Angelou Interviews Amiri Baraka," in *Con-
     versations with Amiri Baraka,* edited by Charlie
     Reilly (Jackson: University Press of Missis-
     sippi, 1994), pp. 260–266;
Jontyle Theresa Robinson, ed., *Bearing Witness: Con-
     temporary Works by African American Women Art-
     ists,* foreword by Angelou (New York: Spel-
     man College/Rizzoli International, 1996).

Maya Angelou's literary significance rests primarily upon her exceptional ability to tell her life
story as both a human being and a black American
woman in the twentieth century. Five serial autobiographical volumes have been published to date (in
1969, 1974, 1976, 1981, and 1986), covering the period from 1928 to the mid 1960s; more may be expected. She asserts in *I Know Why the Caged Bird Sings*
(1969): "The fact that the adult American Negro female emerges a formidable character is often met
with amazement, distaste and even belligerence. It is
seldom accepted as an inevitable outcome of the
struggle won by survivors and deserves respect if
not enthusiastic acceptance." Yet Angelou's own
autobiographies and vivid lectures about herself,
ranging in tone from warmly humorous to bitterly
satiric, have won a popular and critical following
that is both respectful and enthusiastic.

As she adds successive volumes to her life
story, she is performing for contemporary black
American women—and men, too—many of the same
functions that escaped slave Frederick Douglass performed for his nineteenth-century peers through his
autobiographical writings and lectures. Both become articulators of the nature and validity of a collective heritage as they interpret the particulars of a
culture for a wide audience of whites as well as
blacks. As one critic said, Angelou illuminates "with
the intensity of lightning the tragedy that was once
this nation's two-track culture." As people who have
lived varied and vigorous lives, they embody the
quintessential experiences of their race and culture.

An account of the life and major writings of
Angelou is of necessity based largely on information
that she herself has supplied in her autobiographies;

*Dust jacket for Angelou's first autobiographical volume (1970),
the story of her childhood in Stamps, Arkansas,
and St. Louis, Missouri*

where lacunae exist, they do so because Angelou
herself has chosen not to discuss certain periods of
time, events, or people. "I will say how old I am
[53], I will say how tall I am [six feet], but I will not
say how many times I have been married," she told
an interviewer in 1981. "It might frighten them off."

Angelou's odyssey—psychological, spiritual,
and literary, as well as geographical—begins with *I
Know Why the Caged Bird Sings,* generally acceded to
be the best of her autobiographical volumes and the
almost exclusive focus, to date, of serious critical attention. Marguerite Johnson (she did not become
Maya Angelou until her debut as a dancer at the
Purple Onion cabaret in her early twenties) was
born in St. Louis on 4 April 1928 to Bailey and
Vivian Baxter Johnson. When she was three and her
brother Bailey was four, they were sent by their divorced parents to live in Stamps, Arkansas, which
was, she said, the same as "Chitlin' Switch, Georgia;
Hang 'Em High, Alabama; Don't Let the Sun Set on
You Here, Nigger, Mississippi." "High spots in

Angelou with a picture of her son, Clyde Bailey Johnson (photograph by Mary Ellen Mark)

Stamps were usually negative," she observes, "droughts, floods, lynchings and deaths."

There Angelou remained for a decade in the care of her maternal grandmother, Annie ("Momma") Henderson, who kept a country store and ruled her grandchildren with the same sense of "work, duty, religion," and morality with which she ruled her own life. Observes Angelou, "I don't think she ever knew that a deep-brooding love hung over everything she touched."

In Stamps, Angelou learned what it was like to be a black girl in a world whose boundaries were set by whites. She learned what it meant to wear for Easter a "plain ugly cut-down [dress] from a white woman's once-was-purple throwaway," her skinny legs "greased with Blue Seal Vaseline and powdered with the Arkansas red clay." As a young child she expected at any minute to wake from "my black ugly dream" and find her "Nappy black hair" metamorphosed to a long, blonde bob. She thought, then, that "God was white," but she wondered whether He would "allow His only Son to mix with this crowd of cotton pickers and maids, washerwomen and handymen." She learned the humiliation of being refused treatment by a white dentist who would "rather stick my hand in a dog's mouth than in a nigger's."

She learned, also, that blacks would not only endure, but prevail. Momma, head of one of the few black families "not on relief" during the Depression, was an honest but shrewd businesswoman who could turn aside the taunts of the "powhitetrash"

and beat the bigoted dentist at his own game. From her Angelou learned common sense, practicality, and the ability to control one's own destiny that comes from constant hard work and courage, "grace under pressure." She learned, sometimes forcibly, the literature of black writers: "Bailey and I decided to memorize a scene from *The Merchant of Venice,* but we realized that Momma would question us about the author and that we'd have to tell her that Shakespeare was white, and it wouldn't matter to her whether he was dead or not. So we chose 'The Creation' by James Weldon Johnson instead."

The pride in herself this new knowledge engendered took a devastating fall when she was eight, during a brief stay in St. Louis with her beautiful mother, Vivian Baxter, "light-skinned with straight hair." She was raped by her mother's boyfriend, a taciturn "big brown bear" who was found "dropped . . . [or] kicked to death" shortly afterward. In court she had not revealed that she had permitted him to fondle her on two earlier occasions. Therefore she felt responsible for his murder (committed by her uncles), and she decided that "I had to stop talking."

Back in Stamps, where she was sent perhaps because "the St. Louis family just got fed up with my grim presence," her burgeoning pride disappeared for nearly five years, along with her speech. Both were restored by delicious afternoons, "sweet-milk fresh" in memory, of reading and reciting great world literature with Mrs. Flowers, the educated "aristocrat of Black Stamps" who "acted just as re-

6

fined as whitefolks in the movies and books and . . . was more beautiful." Angelou adds that "she made me proud to be a Negro, just by being herself." Angelou later published as a children's book the section from *I Know Why the Caged Bird Sings* about their friendship.

She learned during this time the importance of self-expression, as well as communication, for "the wonderful, beautiful Negro race" survives "in exact relationship to the dedication of our poets (include preachers, musicians and blues singers)." She explained to an interviewer in 1981 that "there isn't one day since I was raped that I haven't thought about it . . . I have gotten beyond hate and fear, but there is something beyond that." Her multiple careers in the arts—singing, dancing, acting, and writing—have become ways of transcending her personal hates and fears, as well as of proclaiming her black identity and pride.

In 1940, after Angelou's graduation at the top of her eighth-grade class, her fun-loving mother, then a professional gambler, moved the children from Stamps to San Francisco, imposing experience on innocence, disorder upon order. Angelou's subsequent formal education consisted of attending George Washington High School in San Francisco throughout World War II while concurrently taking dance and drama lessons at the California Labor School. Her informal schooling, in the "fourteen-room typical San Franciscan post-Earthquake" rooming house her mother ran in the Fillmore District, was much more extensive. From her mother she learned "proper posture, table manners, good restaurants"; from her stepfather, how to play "poker, blackjack, tonk and high, low, Jick, Jack and the Game"; from the household, the ways of shipyard workers, "much-powdered prostitutes," and "the most colorful characters in the Black underground."

These people she accepted as honest in their own way, but she fled the hypocrisy of a summer vacation with her failed father and his nouveau bourgeois girlfriend in their tacky trailer in southern California. Unable to return to her mother for a month, she lived in a graveyard of wrecked cars, many inhabited by homeless children whose own natural brotherhood "set a tone of tolerance for my life."

The book ends with her determined rush toward maturity. With the perseverance that foreshadowed later civil rights work, she finally obtained a job, while still in high school, as the first black woman streetcar conductor in San Francisco. With equal determination to prove that she was a woman, she became pregnant and at sixteen gave birth to a son, one month after graduation from

summer school at Mission High School in 1945. She has since been awarded honorary degrees by more than fifty universities.

The next installment of Angelou's autobiography, *Gather Together in My Name* (1974), seems much less satisfactory than the first. The difference may result in large part because in this book Angelou is less admirable as a central character than she was in *I Know Why the Caged Bird Sings*. In instance after instance she abandons or jeopardizes the maturity, honesty, and intuitive good judgment toward which she had been moving in *I Know Why the Caged Bird Sings*. Her bold, headstrong temperament leads her to bluff her way into situations dangerous to herself and her infant son, Clyde Bailey Johnson, nicknamed Guy. When she cannot learn enough quickly enough to escape, she becomes dependent on others who too often exploit her naïveté and good will—when she is not exploiting theirs. As Angelou anatomizes her exploits, she makes it hard to tell whether she intends this segment of her life story to be emblematic of the lives of all other unwed, undereducated black teenage mothers, or for her misadventures to serve as a warning to others, or to demonstrate as she did in *I Know Why the Caged Bird Sings* the survival and staying power of black women in adverse circumstances. The wit and panache with which she narrates her picaresque tale prevent it from being a confessional; the writing of this volume itself may be the final exorcism of the flaws.

Angelou is determined to leave her mother's household, "take a job and show the whole world (my son's father) that I was equal to my pride and greater than my pretensions." As soon as she discovered that the Creole Café would pay $75 a week for a cook, "I knew I could cook Creole, whatever that was." She learned quickly, and with equal haste fell in love with a customer: "When he opened the steamy door to the restaurant, surely it was the second coming of Christ."

When the affair ended after two months (he was engaged to another woman), Angelou decided to make a new life in San Diego, buttressed by $200 and her mother's advice, unwittingly prophetic: "Be the best of anything you get into. If you want to be a whore, it's your life. Be a damn good one."

Angelou's gradual initiation into prostitution began with a job as a nightclub waitress. There she met a pair of lesbian lovers and, fearing seduction, conned them into letting her become their manager. At eighteen she had "managed in a few tense years to become a snob at all levels, racial, cultural and intellectual. I was a madam and thought myself morally superior to the whores. I was a waitress and believed myself cleverer than the customers I served. I

Angelou with James Baldwin and his mother at his sixtieth birthday party, 1984

was a lonely unmarried mother and held myself to be freer than the married women I met."

Seeking sanctuary in Stamps when her ten-week-old empire crashed brought no solace. She talked back to a "slack-butted" store clerk, and the threat of a reprisal by the Ku Klux Klan caused Momma Henderson to send Angelou back to San Francisco for safety. Then, rejected on the eve of her induction into the army because she lied on her application, she escaped into marijuana and sought solace in the dream that is an ironic leitmotiv of *Gather Together:* "I was going to have it made—and no doubt through the good offices of a handsome man who would love me to distraction."

Her artificial high was replaced by a natural one as she became part of a nightclub dancing act, with R. L. Poole as her partner, manager, mentor, and intermittent lover: "As a dancer, my instrument was my body. I couldn't just allow . . . anyone to screw my instrument." The emergence of Poole's drug-dependent "old lady" ended their liaison, and Angelou fled again into a restaurant kitchen and daydreams of the perfect husband.

Her romantic imagination, inspired by a naïveté that never ripened into wisdom during the three-year span of *Gather Together,* endowed the dapper L. D. Tolbrook, "an established gambler who had Southern manners and big city class," with the

means for her salvation. Prepared to be "an old man's darling," deluded by her wish to marry, she too willingly rationalized the virtues of life as a prostitute earning money for him: "Prostitution is like beauty. It is in the eye of the beholder. There are married women who are more whorish than a street prostitute because they have sold their bodies for marriage licenses, and there are some women who sleep with men for money who have great integrity because they are doing it for a purpose."

It took threats of violence from her brother, himself on the verge of drug addiction, to keep her from returning to the whorehouse after a week's dismal stint. She tried a few more legitimate jobs, but survival "didn't take hold." She rejected the traditional options for black women: hustling ("I obviously had little aptitude for that"), working as a housemaid ("I would keep my negative Southern exposures to whites before me like a defensive hand"), or "wrestling with old lady Welfare (my neck wouldn't bend for that)." Prepared to turn to hard drugs again because of an unrealistic romantic love, she was dragged from the edge of the addiction abyss by her lover, who forced her to watch him shoot up in a sewerlike "hit joint for addicts." She concludes her account of this sordid segment of her life with a plea for forgiveness devoid of moral reflection. She was seemingly neither sadder nor wiser: "As I watched the wretched nod and scratch, I felt my own innocence as real as a grain of sand between my teeth. I was pure as moonlight and had only begun to live. My escapades were the fumblings of youth and to be forgiven as such."

In the third volume of Angelou's saga, *Singin' and Swingin' and Gettin' Merry Like Christmas* (1976), her actions finally began to match her aspirations for maturity, though intermittently, as she lurched and ultimately strode through the years from 1950 to 1955. At about twenty-two (Angelou is usually vague about dates) she married Tosh Angelos, a former sailor who was "intelligent, kind and reliable"–and white. Her mother exploded in rage, anticipating "A hell of a wedding gift–the contempt of his people and the distrust of your own."

Although she experienced little of either, the fortress of bourgeois respectability for which she had longed soon became a prison, restrictive of her independence. Too free a spirit to remain fettered for long, she was divorced within three years and resumed her career as a dancer, entertaining customers as the first black dancer at a local bar with "a little rhumba, tango, jitterbug, Susy-Q, trucking, snake hips, conga, Charleston and cha-cha-cha."

Before long she attracted the notice of the much more skilled performers at the chic Purple Onion and was soon, to her amazement, offered a job there: "There whites were treating me as an equal, as if I could do whatever they could do. They did not consider that race, height, or gender or lack of education might have crippled me and that I should be regarded as someone invalided."

Stripped of these excuses for failure, Angelou had to succeed on her own, and she did. She turned down one of the lead roles in the Broadway production of *House of Flowers* to join the European touring cast of *Porgy and Bess,* leaving Guy in her mother's care. She devotes more than half the book to describing the tour–from Montreal to Paris, Zagreb, and Belgrade, from Greece to Egypt, Israel, and Italy: "Dancing and singing every night with sixty people was more like a party than a chore." She loved the ambience of the tightly knit, black professional community; she loved the freedom as well as the work, freedom from housework, "freedom from the constant nuisance of a small child's chatter," freedom from the mores of the bourgeois world she had only recently walked out on.

Duty to her child, nine and miserable without her, drove her home. Guilt over her neglect of him nearly drove her to suicide, but love of life and of motherhood and of dancing drove her instead to resume her career.

Dust jacket for Angelou's 1986 autobiographical volume, which chronicles her experiences in Ghana during the mid 1960s

In *The Heart of a Woman* (1981) Angelou intertwines an account of seven years of her own coming of age (1957–1963) with the coming of age of the civil rights movement and the beginning of the second wave of feminism in the 1960s. Her enlarged focus and clear vision transcend the particulars and give this book a fascinating universality of perspective and psychological depth that almost matches the quality of *I Know Why the Caged Bird Sings,* in contrast to the shallower and more limited intervening volumes. Its motifs are commitment and betrayal.

By the time she was thirty, Angelou had made a commitment to become a writer. Inspired by her friendship with the distinguished social-activist author John Killens, she moved to Brooklyn to be near him and to learn her craft. Through weekly meetings of the Harlem Writers Guild she learned to treat her writing seriously: "If I wanted to write, I had to be willing to develop a kind of concentration found mostly in people awaiting execution. I had to learn technique and surrender my ignorance." Although it was difficult, she learned to tolerate criticism, however harsh, and was accepted as a practic-

Angelou with artist Tom Feelings at a book signing for their 1987 collaboration, Now Sheba Sings the
Song *(photograph by Ted Pontiflet)*

ing member of a group of established writers that included John Henrik Clarke, Paule Marshall, and
James Baldwin. Recognizing that "trying to overcome was black people's honorable tradition," Angelou resolved to overcome the problems in her
writing until it met the exacting standards of her literary mentors.

At the same time Angelou made a commitment
to promote black civil rights. Her widening circle of
black intellectual friends was "persistently examining the nature of racial oppression, racial progress
and racial integration," excoriating "white men,
white women, white children and white history, particularly as is applied to black people." Through Killens and others she learned to acknowledge her kinship with blacks nationwide: "Georgia is Down
South. California is Up South. If you're black in this
country you're on a plantation."

As a result, when she met Martin Luther King
Jr., she was prepared to accept his challenge: "We,
the black people, the most displaced, the poorest,
the most maligned and scourged, we had the glorious task of reclaiming the soul and saving the honor
of the country." With comedian Godfrey Cambridge she organized a benefit, *Cabaret of Freedom,* for
King's Southern Christian Leadership Conference.
She was starring "on the stage of life," a "general in
the army" of fighters against legal discrimination,
and as a consequence was soon appointed by the
veteran civil rights activist Bayard Rustin to succeed
him as the northern coordinator of the Southern
Christian Leadership Conference. During her six

months in office she was grateful for the interracial
cooperation that was "new and old and dynamic,"
from children and adults alike, not only in Harlem
but also throughout the nation. The same dyna-
mism pervaded the black support of communists,
from Fidel Castro's Cuba to Russia. Angelou vividly captures the mood of the era with snatches of
song, dialogue, and slogans that dynamically
punctuate this book: "Castro never had called
himself white, so he was O.K. from the git . . .
and as black people often said . . . 'Wasn't no
Communist lynched my poppa or raped my
mamma.' 'Hey, Khruschev. Go on, with your bad
self.'"

Despite her increasing maturity as a writer and
her effective advocacy of black civil rights, Angelou
in her early thirties still retained the romantic notion of quiet suburban domesticity that had betrayed her repeatedly in her teens and early twenties. She, who by this time had performed with
Odetta and the revolutionary Clancy Brothers and
had gotten half of Harlem to demonstrate at the
United Nations to protest Patrice Lumumba's assassination, proposed marriage to a laconic bail bondsman she had met in a bar. As he plied her with engagement presents of stolen goods he had confis-
cated, she was preparing to "cook, clean house . . .
and join some local women's volunteer organizations."

In betraying her active, creative life, she could
only betray her fiancé. Indeed, she left him quickly
for the bulky, impeccably suave Vusumzi Make, a

South African freedom fighter who proposed to her instantly, claiming that their marriage would be "the joining of Africa and Africa-America!" Although despite their good intentions they were never legally wed, Make's initial adoration helped Angelou, ever romantic, to feel exactly the way she wanted to, like "a young African virgin, made beautiful for her chief." Make convinced her to accept a major theatrical role as the White Queen in Jean Genet's *The Blacks,* effectively countering her objection, "The play says given the chance, black people will act as cruel as whites," with, "Dear Wife, that is a reverse racism. Black people are human. No more, no less."

They left New York in the same flutter of unpaid bills that pursued them to Egypt. While Make stumped the world for South African freedom and shamelessly womanized on the side, Angelou violated an African prohibition against women working professionally and got a job to help pay the bills. Make met her announcement that she was associate editor of the English language *Arab Observer* (another type of work she, typically, had to learn on the job) with a tirade that vilified her "insolence, independence, lack of respect, arrogance, ignorance, defiance, callousness, cheekiness and lack of breeding." Angelou concluded, "He was right." This point marked the beginning of the end of their relationship as he continued to betray her sexually and she persisted in remaining true to her black American culture that ultimately could not bend to his African worldview.

Before a tribunal of the African diplomatic community, she defended, "with openness and sass," her decision to leave Make. The "African palaver" vindicated her and assured her an independent welcome in the African community. *The Heart of a Woman,* which has received consistent critical acclaim, ends with her arrival in Kwame Nkrumah's Ghana, her commitment to black freedom—as well as her own—intact.

The next installment of Angelou's autobiography, *All God's Children Need Traveling Shoes* (1986), focuses exclusively on her experiences in Ghana from 1963 to 1966. The narrative begins as dramatically as *The Heart of a Woman* ends: her son, Guy, recently graduated from high school, is involved in an automobile accident within a few days of their arrival in the West African nation. Though Angelou originally had intended to help him enroll at the University of Ghana and then move on to Liberia herself, she remained in the country through Guy's month-long recovery and found a job at the university in Accra.

Angelou worked as an assistant administrator in the School of Music and Drama in the Institute of African Studies at the university, and occasionally she coached dance and drama students; she also participated in a university production of Bertolt Brecht's *Mother Courage and Her Children.* Later she found additional work writing for the *Ghanaian Times* and serving as an editor for the *African Review.*

All of these experiences are related in *All God's Children Need Traveling Shoes,* but in addition to its account of the material facts of Angelou's life during these four years, the book devotes a considerable amount of space to her relationships with the small but closely knit community of African Americans drawn to Nkrumah's Ghana following its independence from Great Britain. Angelou describes this community as "a little group of Black folks, looking for a home." This portion of the autobiography thus connects to others throughout the series with its motif of the search for the balance between the individual and the community, self and society. Like other parts of Angelou's multivolume work, *All God's Children Need Traveling Shoes* is about the search for a place one can call home.

Angelou made Ghana her home for only four years, but as the book reveals, it was an exciting place to reside while she was there. She met the African-American novelist Julian Mayfield, who served as an adviser to Nkrumah's government between 1961 and 1966 and founded the *African Review.* She also met Malcolm X during his visit to Ghana in 1964. Her portraits of both men are among the high points of the book, and her presentation of a conversation with Malcolm X is similar to a conversation with King in *The Heart of a Woman.* In both instances her political awareness is expanded through contact with an important civil rights leader. In this case Malcolm X takes her to task for criticizing someone's brand of political activism, saying to her, "We need people on each level to fight our battle." Indeed, much of Angelou's activism since the 1960s has been less overtly political than in her youth, but nonetheless she has devoted considerable time and resources to various political causes. Perhaps her most significant contribution, in fact, has been the sharing of her life story, an act her autobiographies have yet to chronicle.

Another significant episode in *All God's Children Need Traveling Shoes* was her experience of being mistaken for a native African woman during a visit to a coastal village. When the women there realized she was an American, they publicly mourned for Angelou's ancestors who had been taken in slavery from West Africa—a moment described by Angelou as highly moving. Such moments of identification, however, were balanced by the awareness that in many cases Africans had sold other Africans as

Dust jacket for Angelou's 1993 collection of personal essays

slaves to Europeans and Americans: "Were those laughing people who moved in the streets with such equanimity today descendants of slave-trading families? Did that one's ancestor sell mine . . . ?"

Indeed, despite the many positive aspects of her sojourn in Ghana, Angelou reveals that she never truly felt at home in Africa—that to be African and to be African American were two different things. For one thing, despite Nkrumah's call to blacks around the world to move to Ghana and the optimism many African Americans felt at the time about the possibility of reclaiming their African roots, many Ghanaians resented the intrusion of foreign blacks into their national life. Angelou and other African Americans experienced no color prejudice in Ghana—a wonderful experience in contrast to what they had experienced at home—but they nonetheless felt another type of discrimination. Finally, for all their points of similarity, Africans and African Americans, according to Angelou, possessed separate cultures as the result of centuries of African-American slavery and oppression. Thus, in contrast to African courtesy, Angelou claims that African Americans had "developed a doctrine of resistance which included false docility, sarcasm . . .

and insouciance" in response to American racism. Ironically, then, Angelou felt the need to return to the place where she had gotten to know racism all too well, an "ache for home" that compelled her to leave Ghana, and the book ends with Angelou preparing to board an airplane for the United States.

Since her return Angelou has not only written five volumes of her autobiography but also been involved in many other projects. She first taught at the University of California, Los Angeles, where she began work on *I Know Why the Caged Bird Sings,* and its success led to a series of positions at universities across the country. She finally settled at Wake Forest University in Winston-Salem, North Carolina, in 1981, when she received a lifetime appointment as Reynolds Professor of Literary Studies. It is widely hoped that, in addition to her many projects, she is also continuing to write her life story. Many of the essays in recent collections such as *Wouldn't Take Nothing for My Journey Now* (1993) are also autobiographical.

In describing her development in her autobiographies, Angelou gives generous credit to the influences of dominant women during her childhood. *I Know Why the Caged Bird Sings* focuses on three impressive female role models: "Momma" Henderson, her powerful, enterprising, righteous, religious grandmother; Mrs. Flowers—beautiful, cultivated, and pridefully black; and her mother—the sexy, sassy, and savvy embodiment of black mores. The combined characteristics of these women became leitmotivs throughout the volumes of Angelou's autobiography.

Men, however, get little credit for who she is and how she got that way. During Angelou's childhood, adult black men were either absent (her father), weak (her crippled uncle), subservient to women (her uncle and her mother's boyfriends), sexually abusive (the man who raped her), or lazy and hedonistic (her father when she met him again in her teenage years). Of the men she had romantic relationships with as an adult (to the point at which *All God's Children Need Traveling Shoes* ends), the blacks are either stodgy (her bail bondsman fiancé) or unwilling to make a long-term commitment (Make). The man who treats her with greatest respect and affection is white (Angelos, her first husband).

The primary disruptive factor in all these relationships is Angelou's quest for identity, manifested through the assertiveness and the self-expression that come not only from her careers as a dancer, a singer, and a writer but also from being so good at these endeavors. As she matures, she becomes more and more her own person. Through her own efforts and innate talent, which she minimizes in concentrating on the results, she succeeds early and spectacularly in these highly competitive fields in which many fail. Her enjoyment of the freedom, mobility, independence, and acclaim that success makes possible is evident from the zestful assurance with which she writes her autobiographies.

Angelou's volumes of poetry are generally considered to possess less stature than her autobiographical writing, even though it was as a poet that Angelou participated in William Jefferson Clinton's 1993 presidential inauguration. Collections of her poetry include *Just Give Me a Cool Drink of Water 'fore I Diiie* (1971), *Oh Pray My Wings Are Gonna Fit Me Well* (1975), *And Still I Rise* (1978), *Shaker, Why Don't You Sing?* (1983), *Now Sheba Sings the Song* (1987), *I Shall Not Be Moved* (1990), and *Life Doesn't Frighten Me* (1993).

Much of Angelou's poetry, almost entirely short lyric works, expresses in strong, often jazzy rhythms some of the themes common to the life experiences of many American blacks—discrimination, exploitation, being on welfare. Some of her poems extol the survivors, those whose black pride enables them to prevail over the otherwise demeaning circumstances of their existence. Thus in "When I Think about Myself" she adopts the persona of an aging domestic to comment ironically about the phenomenon of black survival in a world dominated by whites: "Sixty years in these folks' world / The child I works for calls me girl / I say 'Yes ma'am' for workings' sake. / Too proud to bend / Too poor to break." In "Times-Square-Shoeshine Composition" the feisty black shoeshine boy defends, in dialect, his thirty-five-cent price against the customer who tries to cheat him out of a dime, his slangy remarks punctuated by the aggressive "pow pow" of the shoeshine rag.

Other poems deal with social issues and problems that, though not unique to blacks, are explored from a black perspective. In "Letter to an Aspiring Junkie" a street-smart "cat" cautions the prospective junkie to beware: "Climb into the streets, man, like you climb / into the ass end of a lion." Angelou sympathizes with the plight of abandoned black children, embodied in "John J," whose "momma didn't want him," and who ends up gambling in a bar with a "flinging singing lady." Her superficial look at "Prisoners" shows them predictably experiencing "the horror / of gray guard men"—"It's jail / and bail / then rails to run." At her most irritating, Angelou preaches. In language and hortatory tone reminiscent of popular turn-of-the-century poetry, she advises readers to "Take Time Out" to "show some kindness / for the folks / who thought that blindness / was an illness that / affected eyes alone." This persona of the writer as sage also pervades such nonfiction books as *Lessons in Living* (1993), *Wouldn't Take Nothing for My Journey Now,* and *Even the Stars Look Lonesome* (1997), all slim volumes dispensing moral truths and truisms.

When Angelou's lyrics deal with the common experiences of licit and illicit love, and of youth and aging, she writes from various female perspectives similar to those Dorothy Parker often used, sharing Parker's self-consciousness but not her wit. For example, in "Communication I" the love-lorn damsel, impervious to her wooer's quotations from Alexander Pope, George Bernard Shaw, and J. D. Salinger, "frankly told her mother / 'Of all he said I understood, / he said he loved another.'" In mundane imagery ("The day hangs heavy / loose and grey / when you're away") a comparable persona laments her lover's evasiveness ("Won't you pull yourself together / For / Me / ONCE"). In "Telephone" she screams at the silent instrument, "Ring. Damn you!" Her occasional vivid black dialect ("But forty years of age . . . / stomps / no-knocking / into the script / bumps a funky grind on the / shabby curtain of youth. . . .") enlivens expressions that seldom rise

Dust jacket for Angelou's 1997 collection of essays, in which she discusses topics such as growing older and African art

above the banal. Her poems seem particularly derivative and cloying when expressed in conventional language: "My pencil halts / and will not go / along that quiet path / I need to write / of lovers false. . . . "

Angelou's poetry becomes far more interesting when she dramatizes it in her characteristically dynamic stage performances. Angelou's statuesque figure, dressed in bright colors (and sometimes African designs), moves exuberantly and vigorously to reinforce the rhythm of the lines, the tone of the words. Her singing and dancing and electrifying stage presence transcend the predictable words and rhymes.

Perhaps the high point of Angelou's career as a poet was the opportunity to write and read a poem for the 20 January 1993 presidential inauguration of fellow Arkansas native Bill Clinton. The result, "On the Pulse of Morning," is a lyrically evocative poem filled with images of progress, affirmation, and the sense that people have more similarities than differences, even while the poem celebrates America's diversity. The closing stanza provides a good example of her mature poetic style:

Here on the pulse of this new day
You may have the grace to look up and out

And into your sister's eyes, and into
Your brother's face, your country
And say simply
Very simply
With hope
Good morning.

The poem received mixed reviews in the press. However, the fact that an African-American woman had been invited to participate in such an august event was nonetheless significant. In giving this inaugural reading, Angelou joined the company of Robert Frost, who read at the 1961 inauguration of John F. Kennedy, and James Dickey, who read at an inaugural ball the day before the 1977 inauguration of James Earl Carter. She was also invited to read from her poetry at the Million Man March, a political rally held in Washington, D.C. on 16 October 1995 in support of African-American men in American society.

In the 1990s Angelou wrote several short books of essays and children's books and became even more popular on the lecture circuit than she already was. Her popularity has also been bolstered by her public friendship with television talk-show hostess Oprah Winfrey. Angelou had not celebrated her birthday for years since it coincided with the day King was assassinated, but she did so for her seventieth birthday, on which occasion Winfrey chartered a cruise ship and paid for 150 of Angelou's friends to participate in a Caribbean birthday cruise.

In addition to writing and teaching, Angelou has remained active as a performer since the 1960s, appearing in plays on both coasts, narrating television documentaries, and doing other work in movies and television. Her work in these media as a writer has included *Georgia, Georgia* (1972), a motion picture about the career of a black singer (which also marked the first time a black woman had created an original script for a movie); an adaptation of *I Know Why the Caged Bird Sings* for television (1979); and *Sister, Sister* (1982), a television movie about the tensions ignited when three sisters are reunited. Angelou has also appeared as an actress in television movies such as *Roots* (1977) and *There Are No Children Here* (1993) and in motion pictures such as *Poetic Justice* (1993), which also incorporated her poetry, and *How to Make an American Quilt* (1995). In addition, she directed a 1998 motion picture titled *Down in the Delta*.

Because she continues to write, a final critical assessment of her work at this point is premature. Yet it is clear from the five-volume serial autobiography that Angelou is in the process of becoming a self-created Everywoman. In a literature and a culture where there are many fewer exemplary lives of women than of men, black or white, Angelou's autobiographical self, as it matures through successive volumes, is gradually assuming that exemplary stature. She has said, "I speak to the black experience but I am always talking about the human condition—about what we can endure, dream, fail at and still survive."

I Know Why the Caged Bird Sings begins with the words from a spiritual:

> What you lookin at me for?
> I didn't come to stay . . . [.]

Angelou's autobiographical volumes explain both why she is worth being looked at and why, like many blacks, both real and fictional, she "didn't come to stay" but is always moving on. She is forever impelled by the restlessness for change and new realms to conquer that is the essence of the creative artist and of exemplary American lives, white and black.

Interviews:

Jeffrey M. Elliot, ed., *Conversations with Maya Angelou* (Jackson: University Press of Mississippi, 1989);

George Plimpton, "The Art of Fiction CXIX: Maya Angelou," *Paris Review,* 32 (Fall 1990): 145–167;

Dannye Romine Powell, "Maya Angelou," in her *Parting the Curtains: Interviews with Southern Writers* (Winston-Salem, N.C.: J. F. Blair, 1994), pp. 2–13;

Cornel West, "Maya Angelou," in *Restoring Hope: Conversations on the Future of Black America,* edited by Kelvin Shawn Sealey (Boston: Beacon, 1997), pp. 187–208.

Bibliography:

Dee Birch Cameron, "A Maya Angelou Bibliography," *Bulletin of Bibliography,* 36 (January–March 1979): 50–52.

References:

Harold Bloom, ed., *Maya Angelou* (Philadelphia: Chelsea House, 1998);

Joanne M. Braxton, ed., *Maya Angelou's I Know Why the Caged Bird Sings: A Casebook* (New York: Oxford University Press, 1998);

Daniel D. Challener, *Stories of Resilience in Childhood: The Narratives of Maya Angelou, Maxine Hong Kingston, Richard Rodriguez, John Edgar Wideman, and Tobias Wolff* (New York: Garland, 1997);

Ekaterini Georgoudaki, *Race, Gender, and Class Perspectives in the Work of Maya Angelou, Gwendolyn Brooks, Rita Dove, Nikki Giovanni, and Audre Lorde* (Thessoloníki, Greece: Aristotle University of the Thessoloníki, 1991);

Lyman B. Hagen, *Heart of a Woman, Mind of a Writer, and Soul of a Poet: A Critical Analysis of the Writings of Maya Angelou* (Lanham, Md.: University Press of America, 1997);

Dolly A. McPherson, *Order out of Chaos: The Autobiographical Works of Maya Angelou* (New York: Peter Lang, 1990);

Claudia Tate, "Maya Angelou," in her *Black Women Writers at Work* (New York: Continuum, 1983), pp. 1–38;

Mary E. Williams, ed., *Readings on Maya Angelou* (San Diego: Greenhaven Press, 1997).

Toni Cade Bambara

This entry was updated by Katherine M. Mellen (Yale University) from the entry by Alice A. Deck (University of Illinois, Urbana–Champaign) in DLB 38: *Afro-American Writers After 1955: Dramatists and Prose Writers.*

BIRTH: New York, New York, 25 March 1939, as Miltona Mirkin Cade, to Walter and Helen Brent Henderson Cade.

EDUCATION: B.A., Queens College (now Queens College of the City University of New York), 1959; University of Florence, studied at Commedia del'Arte, 1961; student at Ecole de Mime Etienne Decroux in Paris, 1961, New York, 1963; M.A., City College of the City University of New York, 1964; additional study in linguistics at New York University and New School for Social Research; also attended Katherine Dunham Dance Studio, Syvilla Fort School of Dance, Clark Center of Performing Arts, 1958–1969, and Studio Museum of Harlem Film Institute, 1970.

CHILD: Karma (daughter).

AWARDS AND HONORS: Peter Pauper Press Award, 1958; John Golden Award for Fiction from Queens College (now Queens College of the City University of New York), 1959; Theatre of Black Experience Award, 1969; Rutgers University research fellowship, 1972; Black Child Development Institute service award, 1973; Black Rose Award from *Encore,* 1973; Black Community Award from Livingston College, Rutgers University, 1974; award from the National Association of Negro Business and Professional Women's Club League; George Washington Carver Distinguished African-American Lecturer Award from Simpson College; *Ebony* Achievement in the Arts Award; Black Arts Award from University of Missouri; American Book Award for *The Salt Eaters,* 1981; Best Documentary of 1986 Award from Pennsylvania Association of Broadcasters and Documentary Award from National Black Programming Consortium for *The Bombing of Osage Avenue,* both 1986; nominated for Black Caucus of the American Library Association Literary Award for *Deep Sightings and Rescue Missions: Fiction, Essays, and Conversations,* 1997.

Toni Cade Bambara (photograph © by Nikky Finney)

DEATH: Philadelphia, Pennsylvania, 9 December 1995.

BOOKS: *Gorilla, My Love: Short Stories* (New York: Random House, 1972);
The Sea Birds Are Still Alive: Collected Stories (New York: Random House, 1977);
The Salt Eaters (New York: Random House, 1980; London: Women's Press, 1982);
Deep Sightings and Rescue Missions: Fiction, Essays, and Conversations, edited by Toni Morrison (New York: Pantheon Books, 1996).

MOTION PICTURES: *The Bombing of Osage Avenue,* script and narration by Bambara, Scribe Video Center, 1986;
W.E.B. DuBois: A Biography in Four Voices, written and directed by Bambara, scriptwriter with Amri Baraka, Wesley Brown, and Thulani Davis, Scribe Video Center, 1996.

TELEVISION: *Zora,* WGBH, 1971;
"The Johnson Girls," *Soul Show,* National Educational Television, 1972;
The Long Night, ABC, 1981;
The Atlanta Child Murders, scriptwriter with Cecil B. Moore, 1985.

OTHER: "Black Theater," in *Black Expression: Essays by and about Black Americans in the Creative Arts,* edited by Addison Gayle Jr. (New York: Weybright & Talley, 1969), pp. 134–143;
The Black Woman: An Anthology, edited, with contributions, by Bambara (New York: New American Library, 1970);
Tales and Stories for Black Folks, edited, with contributions, by Bambara (Garden City: Zenith Books/Doubleday, 1971);
Southern Exposure 3 (Spring/Summer 1976), edited by Bambara;
Cecelia Smith, *Cracks,* preface by Bambara (Atlanta: Select Press, 1980);
"What It Is I Think I'm Doing Anyhow," in *The Writer on Her Work,* edited by Janet Sternburg (New York: Norton, 1980);
"Beauty is Just Care . . . Like Ugly is Carelessness" and "Thinking About My Mother," in *On Essays: A Reader for Writers,* edited by Paul H. Connolly (New York: Harper & Row, 1981);
Cherríe Moraga and Gloria Anzaldúa, eds., *This Bridge Called My Back: Radical Women of Color,* foreword by Bambara (Watertown, Mass.: Persephone Press, 1981);
The Sanctified Church: Collected Essays by Zora Neale Hurston, foreword by Bambara (Berkeley: Turtle Island, 1982);
"Salvation Is the Issue," in *Black Women Writers (Nineteen Fifty to Nineteen Eighty): A Critical Evaluation,* edited by Mari Evans (Garden City: Doubleday/Anchor, 1984), pp. 41–71;
Julie Dash, *Daughters of the Dust: The Making of an African American Woman's Film,* preface by Bambara (New York: New Press, 1992).

Toni Cade Bambara dedicated her life and her art to realizing positive change and healing in the black community. As writer, filmmaker, educator, and political organizer, she celebrated the power, beauty, and wisdom of African American culture and its storytelling traditions. Her fiction is distinguished by its emphasis on the African American community, its idiomatic expressions, interpersonal relationships, myths, music, and history. For Bambara art and politics were inseparable. As Toni Morrison once observed, "Any hint that art was over there and politics was over here would break her up into tears of laughter, or elicit a look so withering it made silence the only intelligent response." During the 1960s and 1970s Bambara, like her contemporaries in the Black Arts Movement, immersed herself in the cultural and sociopolitical activities of the urban community, lecturing and helping to organize rallies, while at the same time using these experiences as the nucleus of her essays and creative writings. In later decades Bambara devoted her attentions to independent filmmaking and encouraging others, especially women, to use video as a medium for their storytelling.

Born Miltona Mirkin Cade to Helen Brent Henderson Cade and Walter Cade II, Bambara and her brother, Walter, grew up with their mother in New York City (Harlem, Bedford-Stuyvesant, and Queens) and Jersey City. In what Bambara later described as the "old plantation tradition," her father named her after his employer, but while she was in kindergarten, the young Miltona announced to her mother that henceforward she would be known as Toni. She adopted Bambara in 1970 while searching for a name for her unborn child and remembered that "the minute I said it I immediately inhabited it, felt very at home in the world." When speaking of specific biographical details of her life, Bambara often chose to give enlarged impressions of a few individuals and events from her early life that she felt most influenced her. In September 1973 Bambara published an essay in *Redbook* explaining what she most appreciated about her mother, Helen. Typical of her tendency to enlarge upon reality as a means of emphasizing an important point, Bambara began the essay with an anecdote narrated, in a distinctly African American dialect, by a young girl who remembers the many occasions on which her mother visited her public-school classroom to set the teacher straight on a few facts about African American history and people. The mother would march in, plant herself firmly in front of the teacher, speak her mind loudly enough for the entire class to hear, and then march out. The scene mesmerized the children and terrified the apologetic teacher. The young narrator recalls the enormous pride that would well up in her own breast whenever her mother made her appearances. She could then walk home triumphantly as her schoolmates expressed their awe and gratitude for her mother's having fought their battle with the teacher. As the narrator says, "She was my mother, but she was everybody's champion."

The anecdote, replete with humor that does not belie the seriousness of the point Bambara is making, leads into a discussion of those less dramatic but equally heroic stances that, to Bambara's way of thinking, Helen Cade took in the course of raising her two children alone. Bambara remembers her mother as one who understood and respected her children's need to get in touch with their private selves. Thus, in the face of criticism from neighbors and friends who said she was overindulging her two children, Helen Cade allowed them to feel they had the right "to be cozy with ourselves." Bambara thanks her mother in this essay for nurturing, rather than thwarting, her habit of taking private inventory, of examining her feelings: ". . . she knew, I suspect, the value of the inner life." The essay shows a daughter who in retrospect realizes how much inner resolve it took for her mother to defend her children's right to be different and to be self-confident in following their inner urges. In a 1979 interview Bambara explained that in her mother's household both she and her brother were expected to be self-sufficient, competent, and "rather nonchalant about expertise in a number of areas." No distinction was made, Bambara insists, between how a girl and a boy should think and behave: both of the Cade children were expected to be sensitive, caring people who took responsibility for themselves and their own personal growth beyond the guidance that their working mother could provide.

The family moved frequently, and as a child Bambara's inquisitive nature led her out to explore each new neighborhood in which her family lived. "As a kid with an enormous appetite for knowledge and a gift for imagining myself anywhere in the universe, I always seemed to be drawn to the library or to some music spot or to 125th Street and Seventh Avenue, Speaker's Corner, to listen to Garveyites, Father Diviners, Rastafarians, Muslims, trade unionists, communists, Pan-Africanists." A woman she called "Grandma Dorothy," or "Miss Dorothy," or "M'Dear" was particularly influential in Bambara's girlhood days. Though they weren't related, the friendship between the older woman and the young girl and its lessons became the foundation of the artistic aesthetic of Bambara's fiction. Time and again Grandma Dorothy greeted her young friend's enthusiasm and inquiries with the question "What are we *pretending* not to know today?" based on the premise that "colored people on the planet earth really know everything there is to know. And if one is not coming to grips with the knowledge, it must mean that one is scared or pretending to be stupid." According to Bambara, Grandma Dorothy "trained me to understand that a story should be informed by the emancipatory impulse" of the African American storytelling tradition and that "a story should be grounded in cultural specificity and shaped by the modes of Black art practice" such as call-and-response, which "bespeaks a communal ethos." The

basic implication of Bambara's stories is that there is an undercurrent of caring for one's neighbors that sustains black Americans. The relationships between her characters speak to the interdependence of the community members, young and old, as the means for cultural transmission of values, guidance, and survival.

Two other types of women in the various neighborhoods where she grew up fascinated Bambara: the Miss Naomi types were those women who led a very exciting night life and who had "lots of clothes in the closet" and a shrewd method of dealing with men; the Miss Gladys types were the women who lived on the first floor of the tenement building, took part in the local gambling, and who, like the Miss Naomi types, were ready, willing, and able to give free advice on everything from "how to get your homework done" to which number you should play. These women, as Bambara describes them, cared about the young girls in the neighborhood and therefore took it upon themselves to advise them on how to avoid those things that could be harmful, such as "those cruising cars that moved through the neighborhood patrolling little girls." Bambara incorporated the Miss Naomis and the Miss Gladyses into her fiction as a means to "teach us valuable lessons of life" and to challenge prevailing stereotypes of black women in the larger American culture.

Bambara published her first short story, "Sweet Town," in *Vendome* magazine (as Toni Cade in January 1959). That same year she received her B.A. in Theater Arts/English and the John Golden Award for Fiction from Queens College. The *Long Island Star* awarded her its Peter Pauper Press Award for nonfiction that same year. While enrolled as a graduate student of modern American fiction at the City College of New York, Bambara worked as a social worker for the Harlem Welfare Center for the year 1959–1960. She published her second story, "Mississippi Ham Rider," in the Summer 1960 *Massachusetts Review*. In 1961 she studied at the Commedia del'Arte in Italy and worked there as a freelance writer. Between 1962 and 1965 she completed her master's degree and worked as program director at Colony House in Brooklyn and as the recreational and occupational therapist for the psychiatric division of Metropolitan Hospital.

During those years she also took on various positions as either coordinator or director of local neighborhood programs, such as the Equivalency Program, the Veteran Reentry Program, the 8th Street Play Program sponsored by the Lower Eastside Tenants Association, and the Tutorial Program at the Houston Street Public Library. After receiving her master's degree Bambara taught at the City College of New York from 1965 to 1969 and served as director/adviser for the Theater of the Black Experience and as an adviser for various types of publications sponsored by the City College SEEK program, such as *Obsidian, Onyx,* and *The Paper*. It was during this same four-year period that more of her stories began to appear in various journals and magazines, such as *The Liberator, Prairie Schooner,* and *Redbook*. Bambara was also involved in the black liberation and women's movement, and in 1970 she edited and published *The Black Woman,* an anthology of poetry, short stories, and essays by black women writers and women students in the City College SEEK program.

Bambara, still writing under the name of Cade, envisioned the collection as a response to all the male "experts," both black and white, who had been publishing articles and conducting sociological studies on black women. Even the leading white feminists of the 1960s, Bambara felt, were not equipped to understand, much less to explain, the feelings and the situation of the black female. Hence, as editor Bambara selected items that she felt best reflected the thoughts and feelings of the many black women she had met while attending and participating in discussion clubs, work-study group meetings, and workshops both on college campuses and in local black communities. While some of the poems and short stories aim to defuse and reject the popular myths and stereotypes of black women, some essays defiantly question the traditional roles assigned to women by males within both the black community and the larger American society. One of the three essays Bambara contributed to the anthology, "On the Issue of Roles," focuses on the fact that in many cases women working in black political action groups had not been allowed to participate on an equal footing with male workers in decision making. They had instead been relegated to "the unreal role of mute servant," a position that was causing needless tension between black men and women who presumably believed in the need to work toward social equality. Barbara argued that the solution was to "let go of all notions of manhood and femininity and concentrate on Blackhood."

Another of Bambara's contributions to the anthology, "The Pill: Genocide or Liberation?" outlines her opinion that birth control is not black genocide but a means of making black women less vulnerable to black males' idealistic notions of producing "warriors for the revolution." The pill could help black women maintain control of their bodies and give them the peace of mind needed to take on new social responsibilities. Bambara's third essay in the anthology was a reprint from *Obsidian* (October 1968). "Thinking About the Play 'The Great White Hope'" evaluates the production in terms of its positive portrayal of black women and how they interact with the male characters. Bambara found the production to be accurate historically but also relevant to the social situation of the 1960s.

In editing *The Black Woman,* Bambara cut across age, class, and occupational barriers to show that black women shared some of the same concerns about black men, social issues (such as education and housing), and their personal development as women. The readings in the anthology also reveal that black women were sharply divided along political lines, and this fact reflects Bambara's goal to provide the women with a public forum for discussing both their similarities and their differences. By dispelling the monolithic assumption that all blacks at this time were preoccupied with racial equality, *The Black Woman* offered an alternative view of African American women, one that voiced the multiple perspectives of their thoughts, experiences, and lives in the public sphere. Today, *The Black Woman* is recognized as one of the most significant early texts of contemporary black feminism.

From 1969 to 1974 Bambara taught in the English Department at Livingston College in New Jersey. She also served on the Livingston Black Faculty Organization and worked as the coadvisor for the Harmbee dancers, the Malcolm Players, and Sisters in Consciousness. During her tenure at Livingston, Bambara edited her second anthology, titled *Tales and Stories for Black Folks* (1971). The collection had broad appeal in the black community, but Bambara had an audience of high-school and college students in mind when she wrote it. As she explains in her introduction, the major intention of the volume was to teach young African Americans the historical value of one of their daily activities—telling stories. Bambara called it "Our Great Kitchen Tradition" or the common experience of hearing various family members tell stories about the "old times" or about the various experiences of individuals within the family. She urged her readers to take these folktales seriously as valuable lessons on human behavior and as examples of living history.

The first section of the collection consists of stories that Bambara said, "I wish I had read growing up," short stories by professional African American writers such as Langston Hughes, Alice Walker, Pearl Crayton, and Ernest J. Gaines. Bambara also included one of her own stories, "Raymond's Run," in this section. The second half of the collection begins with Bambara's "Rapping about Story Forms," which introduces her readers to the origins and

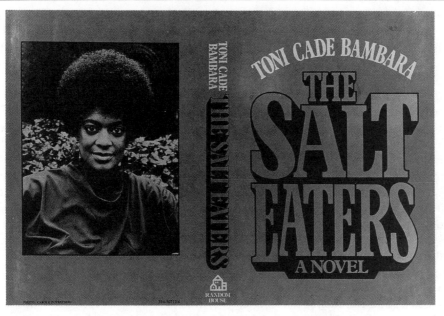

Dust jacket for Bambara's 1980 novel, in which she investigates the bonds between the African American community and other ethnic communities

characteristics of African American fables. This section includes an English translation of a fable by the Senegalese Birago Diop and one by the Ghanaian James Aggrey, as well as several selections written by students in a freshman composition course Bambara was teaching at Livingston College. Some of the students had been working with children in an independent community school, and Bambara had asked them to produce term papers that were useful to the community. She explains their reactions to the assignment: "A great many of them took traditional European tales and changed them so as to promote critical thinking, critical reading for the young people they were working with outside of the class." As was the case with her first anthology, Bambara's decision to include student writings with those by older professional writers shows her desire to give young writers a chance to make their talents known to a large audience. In *Tales and Stories for Black Folks* Bambara also aimed to inspire young adults to read, to think critically, and to write.

In following her own directives to her students, Bambara teamed with Geneva Powell, a black community worker from Newark, New Jersey, to write "The Three Little Panthers," which she included in *Tales and Stories for Black Folks*. The story concerns three urban panthers who, having been sent on a survival mission in "the forest called the suburbs," are continually harassed by antagonistic locals such as a rat, a vulture, a rabbit, an ostrich, an owl, and a fox. Refusing to conform to a suburban lifestyle, the only way they can peacefully reside

there, the panthers choose to return to their own neighborhood, where they can work to sustain their own culture. While the parallels to the original "Three Little Pigs" make the story predictable in terms of plot and dialogue, a cross burning and a bombing indicate the two authors' preoccupation with the racial violence African Americans have encountered historically and during the Civil Rights and Black Power movements of the 1960s and 1970s. The panthers' brandishing of guns when antagonists approach their house also speaks to a tradition of self-defense that had existed throughout African American history, but the Black Panther Party especially brought into the public discourse those blacks who chose to be assimilated in order to live in American suburbs. Bambara and Powell imply that the inner-city experience and environment are potentially more fulfilling for blacks. Not all stories in the collection carry an overtly political message. Others, such as "The Toad and the Donkey," can be read as the type of folktale intended to explain the reasons why humans and animals behave as they do. As a whole, *Tales and Stories for Black Folks* offers a balance between readings that are entertaining and others that are didactic, without losing sight of the instructive element in each.

Most of the stories Bambara wrote as Toni Cade between 1959 and 1970 were published in October 1972 in what was to become her most widely read collection–*Gorilla, My Love*. Though some of these stories are about adults, Bambara's concern with the relationship between the community and its children is the central focus of the collection. Eight of the fifteen stories in *Gorilla, My Love* are told from the perspective of young girls who become Bambara's vehicle for addressing the larger community. These characters are rebellious, tough, independent, and lovable little girls who often seek to assert their own identity in a world that would deny them power. As narrators, Bambara places them in a position to critically question their society in order that their answers will lead to an increased awareness and action in all members of the community.

One of the most appealing stories in *Gorilla, My Love,* and the one that is perhaps best representative of Bambara's style and technique, is the title story. Narrated in the first person by Hazel, a young girl who is completely fed up with "grown-ups messin over kids just cause they little and can't take 'em to court," the story describes the carelessness of adults who say things to Hazel and her brothers without realizing the effect of their words. The children are disappointed time and again because they expect adults to follow through on promises, no matter how long ago they were made. In each instance it is Hazel who shrewdly argues with adults, making them see just how much they are responsible for the chaos their words create. Hazel is resolved to defend herself and her brothers from the carelessness of the adult world, and her feisty nature enables her to triumph over her personal disappointments.

Another story that centers around a young girl and her disillusionment with the world outside of her immediate community is "The Lesson." In this story Miss Moore, an older woman who had been to college and is somewhat ostracized within the community because she does not attend church, leads a group of kids on an educational excursion to Fifth Avenue and F.A.O. Schwartz. Here the children see toys that range from a three-hundred-dollar microscope to a one-thousand-dollar sailboat. Sylvia, the main character, wonders "Who are these people that spend that much for performing clowns and $1,000 for toy sailboats? What kind of work they do and how they live and how come we ain't in on it?" The social message in "The Lesson" is obvious, but Miss Moore does not provide her students with the answers, merely the questions. The children must come to their own conclusions, and the lesson is lasting because they have to figure it out for themselves.

Yet another important story in *Gorilla, My Love* is "The Johnson Girls." Inez, the main character, who is going through an emotional crisis (her boyfriend has left town without indicating that he is coming back), is surrounded by a group of her closest female friends, each of whom offers a plan of ac-

tion to bring him back. While Inez obviously needs to have her friends around her and is listening to their advice, she has already made up her mind about what she will do and will not share her decision with her friends. The narrator is a much younger girl who sits on the sidelines listening to each woman state her philosophy of how to deal with men. She listens in the hope that when she "jumps into her woman stride," she will not "have all this torture and crap to go through." In this story Bambara focuses on a particular feature of the friendship among women: namely, the way in which intimate conversation with close friends (replete with confessions of past mistakes, hopes for future relationships, and lessons learned) can help one to get over a personal crisis. This is what Bambara has termed "drawing the wagons in a circle," a phrase she used to describe the protectiveness and sense of revitalization that can occur from such an encounter. Hence this story shows that the inner resolve, the resiliency, and the determination of her younger protagonists in *Gorilla, My Love* must be supplemented with the support of friends and family.

When *Gorilla, My Love* was published, it received enthusiastic reviews. Poet and writer Lucille Clifton said: "She has captured it all, how we really talk, how we really are; and done it with both love and respect." Poet Mari Evans claimed that the stories were "shavings off our Black experience—like chocolate. Bittersweet that is. . . . " In a review published in the July 1973 edition of *Black World* June Jordan acknowledged that Bambara allowed her readers to turn away momentarily from issues of genocide, poverty, and other "alien factors" to "concentrate on what we love and who loves us and how the family is and how the folks be managing, by our hilarious/sorrowing own self."

During the five-year span between 1972 and the publication in 1977 of her second collection of stories, *The Sea Birds Are Still Alive,* Bambara traveled to Cuba and Southeast Asia. Both trips had a profound influence on her thinking and writing. In 1973 she visited Cuba, where she met with the Federation of Cuban Women as well as with women working in factories, on farms, in markets, and in parks. She was impressed, she said in an interview, with how Cuban women were able to resolve many class conflicts as well as color conflicts and to coordinate a mass organization. Their success at this, Bambara felt, "says a great deal about the possibilities here." Another benefit she derived from her trip to Cuba was being made aware of how effective a creative writer can be in a political movement: "People made me look at what I already knew about the power of the word. . . . I think it

Bambara at the time of The Salt Eaters *(photograph © by Nikky Finney)*

was in 1973 when I really began to realize that [writing] was a perfectly legitimate way to participate in struggle."

Bambara visited Vietnam in the summer of 1975 as a guest of the Women's Union. On this trip she says she was impressed by "the women's ability to break through traditional roles, traditional expectations . . . and come together again in a mass organization that is programmatic and takes on a great deal of responsibility for the running of the nation." She summed up her Vietnam experience by saying: "I got a certain amount of miseducation behind me and got a more serious kind of self education. I got more deeply into community organizing." Hence, after having relocated with her daughter, Karma, to Atlanta, Georgia, in 1974, Bambara became more involved in those community activities that she had begun there before her trip to Southeast Asia. Concurrent with her teaching duties as writer in residence at Spelman College from 1974 to 1977, Bambara became a founding member of the Southern Collective of African-American Writers and the Neighborhood Cultural Arts Center, Inc. She was also director of the Pomoja Writers Guild, a founding member and officer of the Conference Committee on Black South Literature and Art, an associate/aide of the Institute of the Black World, and the

designer and program coordinator of the Arts-in-the-Schools Project sponsored by CETA. In 1984 she helped to organize the Conference on Black Literature and Art that was held at Emory University. For a short time she also served on the faculty of the English department at Duke University in Durham, North Carolina.

The effect of Bambara's travels abroad, her relocation to Atlanta, and her work in so many community art groups can be seen in the stories published in *The Sea Birds Are Still Alive*. At least five of the stories are set outside of an urban center; the title story takes place in Southeast Asia. The characters in many of these stories move across greater geographical distances than did those in her first collection, and their immediate concerns are not so much with their personal relationships as with their involvement in art groups, community centers, or sociopolitical organizations. "The Organizer's Wife," "The Apprentice," "Broken Field Running," "The Sea Birds Are Still Alive," and "The Long Night" all focus on the need for people in a community to organize and keep a spiritual faith in their efforts even during periods of major setbacks and "low consciousness." In line with her belief in the inherent resiliency of a people involved in social struggles, all of the central characters in these stories are combatants who have the strength not only to resist but also to inspire others in their circle to continue the fight.

In "The Organizer's Wife" Graham, the community leader, has been arrested by local authorities after being reported by a minister from the same community who opposed his power. The story focuses on Graham's wife, Virginia, who, with their infant son in her arms, is on the way to visit her husband in jail. Flashbacks explain how she first met Graham and fell in love with him and his ideals. Basically a quiet but hardworking and devoted woman, Virginia took on large responsibilities in community projects. After Graham's arrest she realizes that her personal strength and the strength of their relationship is being put to a test, especially when she sees that much of what they had worked for has gone to ruin. By the end of the story Virginia has paid a visit to the minister and vented her rage against what he had done, so that when she walks into the jail to see her husband, she is all the more determined that their work will continue and their marriage will endure.

The title story of the collection, "The Sea Birds Are Still Alive," is noteworthy because it focuses on the people of Southeast Asia and reveals how Bambara portrays an ethnic group other than her own. The story is set aboard a boat that is transporting people caught up in the war to a larger city. On the deck of the boat are a country peasant, an old schoolteacher, two women on their way to market their crafts, a soldier, refugees, and a couple of foreigners (a female French news correspondent and an American businessman), all of whom are thinking about the effect of war on their lives. The central characters are a young girl and her mother who had been tortured by the imperialist forces but who had been able to resist by chanting to themselves: "Nothing, I'll tell you nothing. You'll never break our spirits. We cannot be defeated." Once in the city, the little girl will be put to work, but she, like some of the little girls in *Gorilla, My Love,* has shown throughout the story a capability to survive, despite her size. The emphasis in the story is on resistance rather than on despair, and it dramatizes Bambara's belief in "the power of words, of utterances" to nourish one through trying situations.

The remaining five stories in *The Sea Birds Are Still Alive* focus on the relationships between African American men and women ("Medley," "A Tender Man," "Witchbird"), the fear and complete confusion a young girl feels when she first begins her menstrual cycle ("A Girl's Story"), and the loneliness a teenage daughter feels when she realizes that her father, now that he has remarried following his divorce from her mother, will not be coming to spend Christmas with her ("Christmas Eve at Johnson Drugs and Goods"). While defeat and despair are not the focus of these stories, there is less high-spirited humor than in *Gorilla, My Love.* The various neighborhoods described in *The Sea Birds Are Still Alive* do not offer the same sort of comfort or sense of belonging as in *Gorilla, My Love.* In "Broken Field Running," for example, the characters live in housing projects riddled with black-on-black crime and walk along sidewalks with broken pavement and glass bottles. "A Girl's Story" reveals the wide emotional and physical distances among those living in a crowded apartment. Even those stories that focus on the personal love between two individuals present a strained or exploitative situation.

Reviews of *The Sea Birds Are Still Alive* were mixed. Ruby Dee, the actress and social activist, highly praised the collection, saying that Bambara "writes like a fine poet who makes every word count because there's so much to say." On the other hand, Robie Macauley, in reviewing the book for *The New York Times,* saw Bambara's verbal dexterity as a flaw: "Some of the stories fail just because there is too much verbal energy, too much restless pursuit of random anecdote." He did, however, have much praise for the title story and for "Witchbird," the central character of which he assessed as "shrewd, cat-smart, and at the same time both sentimental and humane." The re-

viewer for *Choice* felt the first two stories in the collection, "The Organizer's Wife" and "The Apprentice," did not fulfill their promise of good character development: "Instead, the stories become tiresome with the excessive and heavy-handed effort to reproduce the black idiom. Furthermore, the reader seldom can determine where he is in time or place. The tale from whence the title comes is perhaps most frustrating in this regard." Mary Helen Washington extolled two of Bambara's stories, "Medley" and "Witchbird," as excellent dramatizations of the contemporary black American woman; however, she criticized all of the other stories for displaying too much political ideology: "The trouble with deliberately creating models is that they slip all too easily out of character (who they are) into being mouthpieces for the writer's ideology (who the writer would like them to be). It's not that politics does not belong in the realm of art, but that some of the models Bambara offers are too predictable (Naomi in 'The Apprentice')."

Bambara herself commented to an interviewer that she felt that the stories in *The Sea Birds Are Still Alive* were too long: "To my mind, the six-page story is the gem. If it takes more than six pages to say it, something is the matter. So I'm not too pleased with the new collection, *The Sea Birds Are Still Alive.* Most of these stories are too sprawling and hairy for my taste, although I'm very pleased, feel perfectly fine about them as pieces. But as stories they're too damn long and dense."

In several interviews and in an essay ("What It Is I Think I'm Doing Anyhow") Bambara emphasizes her preference for the short story as a convenient tool both for use in the classroom and in lecture engagements (she refers to them as "portable") and as an easier art form to produce than the novel. The brevity and its "modest appeal for attention" are what she finds most effective about the short story, but in Bambara's own figurative style of explaining it, she says, "Temperamentally, I move toward the short story because I'm a sprinter rather than a long-distance runner."

Nevertheless, in 1978 Bambara began working on her first novel. Prompted by what she saw as a split in the African American community among the "spiritual, political, and psychic forces" during the 1970s, she began working on a story that would reveal these splits and propose a fusion that could help get the community back in touch with its own "healing powers." *The Salt Eaters* (1980) grew out of this story and tries to specify the potential links or bridges not only among the various entities within the black community but also among the black community and other ethnic communities in the United States. To this end, the novel includes Asian Americans, Hispanic Ameri-

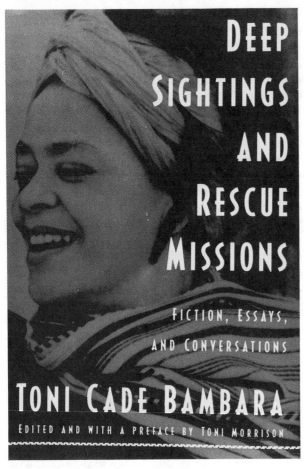

DEEP
SIGHTINGS
AND
RESCUE
MISSIONS

FICTION, ESSAYS,
AND CONVERSATIONS

TONI CADE BAMBARA
EDITED AND WITH A PREFACE BY TONI MORRISON

*Dust jacket for the 1996 posthumously published collection of
Bambara's prose writings and interviews*

cans, Native Americans, and Americans of West Indian descent.

Set in Claybourne, Georgia, during a spring carnival, *The Salt Eaters* focuses on Velma Henry, a heretofore indefatigable community organizer who is experiencing such a severe mental and emotional crisis that she has attempted suicide. She has been rushed to Southwest Community Infirmary, where the staff combines traditional folk remedies with modern medical techniques as part of its standard method of treatment. In the opening scene Velma Henry is perched on a stool facing Minnie Ransom, a faith healer, whose reputation for curing her patients is impeccable. Velma and Minnie are in turn surrounded by a circle of twelve senior citizens known collectively as The Master's Mind. Each member of the Mind represents a sign of the Zodiac, and their presence and continuous chanting and humming "in long meter" help create the proper atmosphere Minnie needs in order to effect her cure.

Velma's spiritual crisis symbolizes the chaos and confusion of the entire community, for she and her husband, Obie, have over the years been working

through the Academy of the Seven Arts (in effect, a community center in Claybourne) to bring all the various conservative and radical factions of the community to a point of reconciliation—a point at which they recognize and build on the items of commonality in their individual agendas. While the major cultural focus of the novel is African American, the introduction of other ethnic groups underscores Bambara's conviction that Third World people should overlook artificial barriers, such as language, and strive to link with one another on the basis of a common cosmology and the fact that they are all victims of the same threats to human existence. At various points in the novel, for example, these characters discuss the threat that the local nuclear power plant and chemical corporation pose to all of their lives and the need for all of them to join the antinuclear movement.

Minnie asks Velma in the beginning of the novel: "Are you sure, sweetheart, that you want to be well?" and she continues to ask this question throughout the story until Velma is able to respond. Minnie tries to tell Velma that in order to be well she must " . . . give it up, the pain, the hurt, the anger, and make room for lovely things to rush in and fill you full. Nature abhors a so-called vacuum, don't you know?" In order to "give it up" Velma relives her life through flashbacks, recalling all the physical and emotional pains she has been through during her life with Obie as a community worker.

Minnie's question is directed to the community as well. Velma's narrative is interlaced with those of several other characters: Fred Holt, a bus driver nearing retirement; Julius Matthews, a street hustler, pimp, and gambler now known as Doc Serge, who is also on staff at the Infirmary; Sophie Haywood, Velma's godmother and a member of The Master's Mind; and Velma's husband, Obie. Bambara's point is that collective action and collective well-being are necessary for spiritual renewal and cultural survival. She suggests that the characters can be healed by looking inward, centering themselves in their own cultural traditions, and then moving forward in a joint coalition to save humanity. The overriding question of *The Salt Eaters* is whether Velma Henry *and* her community desire to be healed, and if so, whether they can bear the responsibility of being well. Being well also means being committed to carrying on the struggle.

The implied question in all of the reviews of *The Salt Eaters* is whether or not a writer who had been such an artistic and commercial success with two collections of short stories could succeed at producing a novel. While most reviewers followed the basic story line, there was considerable criticism of the structure, the dialogue, and the general expansiveness of *The Salt*

Eaters. The entire narrative takes place in about one hour, but the breaks in the story line required to accommodate the various narrative strains became the sticking point for many who reviewed the novel. As one critic said in *First World,* " . . . the very act of reading *The Salt Eaters* through requires transformative agility." Reviewing the novel for the *Washington Post,* Anne Tyler commented that "too many people swarm by too quickly. Too much is described too elliptically, as if cutting through to the heart of the matter might be considered crude, lacking in gracefulness, not sufficiently artistic." Judith Wilson, in another review, noted that while the novel included much food for thought on all of the sociopolitical issues raised by the characters, "Bambara's facility for dialogue sometimes leads her astray. Too many snatches of conversation, though clever and convincing, repeat previously stated themes or offer trivial observations that disrupt the narrative." John Wideman was one of the few reviewers who sympathized with what Bambara was trying to do. In *The New York Times Book Review* he said that Bambara's narrator "shuttles backward and forward in time, plunges the reader into the middle of conversations, thoughts, and dreams . . . to accommodate her complex vision," which he understood to be comparable to concentric circles and the concept of "sacred space and sacred time of traditional African religion." Years after its publication, Bambara described her efforts in *The Salt Eaters:* "I was stretching, reaching, trying to do justice to that realm of reality that we all live in but do not acknowledge." She also admitted that she was still trying to come to grips with the novel herself: "When I look at that book now, I realize I'm not there yet. . . . It resonates, it chimes in my bones, but I don't understand it yet."

While in Atlanta, Bambara came to favor filmmaking over writing as the primary vehicle for her message. She began writing scripts and transferred her energies to the world of independent black filmmaking. Bambara's investigation of the Atlanta child murders became one of her first film projects. The project, cowritten by Cecil B. Moore and Bambara, became a television movie titled *The Atlanta Child Murders* and was produced in 1985. When she suggested to Louis Massiah, founder and director of the Scribe Video Center in Philadelphia, that he produce a movie on the 1985 police bombing of the radical MOVE activists, Massiah invited her to participate in the project. Bambara wrote the script and narrated *The Bombing of Osage Avenue* (1986). For the remainder of her life, Bambara lived in Philadelphia and called Scribe her base. She worked as a production facilitator for Scribe's Community Visions project, which encourages "community-based organizations to explore video as an instrument of social change." She envisioned a U.S. cinema that would "be characterized by an increased pluralistic, transcultural, and international sense and by an amplified and indelible presence of women" and labored to make this a reality. When not working on film, Bambara directed her energies toward establishing a memorial that would honor the African ancestors who died during the middle passage. Diagnosed with cancer in 1993, Toni Cade Bambara died in a Philadelphia hospital on 9 December 1995.

The hallmark of Bambara's fiction is her keen ear for the music of African American speech. With gentle humor and wisdom, her stories celebrate the African American storytelling tradition. Someone once asked her how she became a writer. Bambara replied, "I never thought of myself as a writer. I always thought of myself as a community person who writes and does a few other things." Her legacy emphasizes the inseparable bonds between the individual and the community, between art and politics, between storytelling and survival.

Interviews:
Beverly Guy-Sheftall, "Commitment: Toni Cade Bambara Speaks," in *Sturdy Black Bridges: Visions of Black Women in Literature,* edited by Bell Parker and Guy-Sheftall (Garden City, N.Y.: Doubleday/Anchor, 1979);

Kalamu ya Salaam, "Searching for the Mother Tongue: An Interview," *First World,* 2, no. 4 (1980): 48–52;

Kay Bonetti, "The Organizer's Wife: A Reading by and Interview with Toni Cade Bambara," American Audio Prose Library, 1982;

Deborah Jackson, "An Interview with Toni Cade Bambara," *Drum Magazine* (Spring 1982);

Claudia Tate, "Toni Cade Bambara," in *Black Women Writers at Work,* edited by Tate (New York: Continuum, 1983), pp. 12–38;

Zala Chandler, "Voices Beyond the Veil: An Interview With Toni Cade Bambara and Sonia Sanchez," in *Wild Women in the Whirlwind: Afro-American Culture and the Contemporary Literary Renaissance,* edited by Joanne M. Braxton and Andreé Nicola McLaughlin (New Brunswick, N.J.: Rutgers University Press, 1990), pp. 342–362.

Reference:
Nancy D. Hargrove, "Youth in Toni Cade Bambara's *Gorilla, My Love,*" in *Women Writers of the Contemporary South,* edited by Peggy Whitman Prenshaw (Jackson: University Press of Mississippi, 1984), pp. 215–232.

Pearl S. Buck

This entry was updated from the entries by Paul A. Doyle (Nassau Community College) in DLB 9: American Novelists, *1910–1945,* and by Pat Salomon (Bowling Green State University) in DLB 102: American Short-Story Writers, *1910–1945, Second Series.*

BIRTH: Hillsboro, West Virginia, 26 June 1892, to Absalom and Caroline Stulting Sydenstricker.

EDUCATION: B.A., Randolph-Macon Woman's College, 1914; M.A., Cornell University, 1926.

MARRIAGES: 30 May 1917 to John Lossing Buck (divorced); children: Carol, Janice. 11 June 1935 to Richard John Walsh (died May 1960); children: Richard, John, Edgar, Jean C., Henriette, Theresa, Chieko, Johanna.

AWARDS AND HONORS: Pulitzer Prize for fiction, 1932, and William Dean Howells Medal for the most distinguished work of American fiction published in the period 1930–1935, 1935, both for *The Good Earth;* elected to membership in the National Institute of Arts and Letters, 1936; Nobel Prize for literature, 1938; Women's National Book Association Skinner Award, 1960; Pennsylvania Governor's Award for Excellence, 1968; Philadelphia Club of Advertising Women Award, 1969. Recipient of several honorary degrees, including M.A. from Yale University, 1933; D.Litt. from University of West Virginia, 1940, St. Lawrence University, 1942, and Delaware Valley College, 1965; LL.D. from Howard University, 1942, and Muhlenberg College, 1966; L.H.D. from Lincoln University, 1953, Woman's Medical College of Philadelphia, 1954, and Rutgers University, 1969; D.H.L. from University of Pittsburgh, 1960, Bethany College, 1963, and Hahnemann Hospital, 1966; D.Mus. from Combs College of Music, 1962; and H.H.D. from West Virginia State College, 1963. Recipient of more than 300 humanitarian awards, including President's Committee on Employment of Physically Handicapped Citation, 1958, and Big Brothers of America Citation, 1962.

DEATH: Danby, Vermont, 6 March 1973.

BOOKS: *East Wind: West Wind* (New York: John Day, 1930; London: Methuen, 1931);
The Good Earth (New York: John Day, 1931; London: Methuen, 1931);

Pearl S. Buck, 1938 (The Pearl S. Buck Foundation)

Sons (New York: John Day, 1932; London: Methuen, 1932);
The Young Revolutionist (New York: Friendship, 1932; London: Methuen, 1932);
The First Wife and Other Stories (New York: John Day, 1933; London: Methuen, 1933);
The Mother (New York: John Day, 1934; London: Methuen, 1934);
A House Divided (New York: Reynal & Hitchcock, 1935; London: Methuen, 1935);
House of Earth (New York: Reynal & Hitchcock, 1935; London: Methuen, 1936);

26

The Exile (New York: Reynal & Hitchcock, 1936; London: Methuen, 1936);

Fighting Angel: Portrait of a Soul (New York: Reynal & Hitchcock, 1936; London: Methuen, 1937);

This Proud Heart (New York: Reynal & Hitchcock, 1938; London: Methuen, 1938);

The Chinese Novel (New York: John Day, 1939; London: Macmillan, 1939);

The Patriot (New York: John Day, 1939; London: Methuen, 1939);

Other Gods: An American Legend (New York: John Day, 1940; London: Macmillan, 1940);

Stories for Little Children (New York: John Day, 1940);

Today and Forever: Stories of China (New York: John Day, 1941; London: Macmillan, 1941);

Of Men and Women (New York: John Day, 1941; London: Methuen, 1942);

American Unity and Asia (New York: John Day, 1942); republished as *Asia and Democracy* (London: Macmillan, 1943);

China Sky (New York: Triangle, 1942);

The Chinese Children Next Door (New York: John Day, 1942; London: Methuen, 1943);

Dragon Seed (New York: John Day, 1942; London: Macmillan, 1942);

What America Means to Me (New York: John Day, 1943; London: Methuen, 1944);

The Promise (New York: John Day, 1943; London: Methuen, 1944);

Twenty-Seven Stories (Garden City, N.Y.: Sun Dial Press, 1943)—includes *The First Wife* and *Today and Forever;*

The Water-Buffalo Children (New York: John Day, 1943);

The Dragon Fish (New York: John Day, 1944; London: Methuen, 1946);

China Flight (Philadelphia: Triangle/Blakiston, 1945);

The Townsman, as John Sedges (New York: John Day, 1945; London: Methuen, 1946);

Portrait of a Marriage (New York: John Day, 1945; London: Methuen, 1946);

Talk About Russia, by Buck and Masha Scott (New York: John Day, 1945);

Tell the People: Talks with James Yen about the Mass Education Movement (New York: International Mass Education Movement, 1945);

Yu Lan: Flying Boy of China (New York: John Day, 1945);

Pavilion of Women (New York: John Day, 1946; London: Methuen, 1947);

The Angry Wife, as Sedges (New York: John Day, 1947; London: Methuen, 1948);

Far and Near: Stories of Japan, China, and America (New York: John Day, 1947); republished as *Far and Near: Stories of East and West* (London: Methuen, 1949);

How It Happens: Talk About the German People, by Buck and Erna von Pustau (New York: John Day, 1947);

Peony (New York: John Day, 1948); republished as *The Bondmaid* (London: Methuen, 1949);

The Big Wave (New York: John Day, 1948);

American Argument, by Buck and Eslanda Goode Robeson (New York: John Day, 1949; London: Methuen, 1950);

Kinfolk (New York: John Day, 1949; London: Methuen, 1950);

The Long Love, as Sedges (New York: John Day, 1949; London: Methuen, 1950);

The Child Who Never Grew (New York: John Day, 1950; London: Methuen, 1951);

One Bright Day (New York: John Day, 1950); enlarged as *One Bright Day and Other Stories for Children* (London: Methuen, 1952);

God's Men (New York: John Day, 1951; London: Methuen, 1951);

The Hidden Flower (New York: John Day, 1952; London: Methuen, 1952);

Bright Procession, as Sedges (New York: John Day, 1952; London: Methuen, 1952);

Come, My Beloved (New York: John Day, 1953; London: Methuen, 1953);

The Man Who Changed China: The Story of Sun Yat-sen (New York: Random House, 1953; London: Methuen, 1955);

Voices in the House, as Sedges (New York: John Day, 1953; London: Methuen, 1954);

Johnny Jack and His Beginnings (New York: John Day, 1954);

My Several Worlds, A Personal Record (New York: John Day, 1954; London: Methuen, 1955);

The Beech Tree (New York: John Day, 1954);

Imperial Woman (New York: John Day, 1955; London: Methuen, 1956);

Letter from Peking (New York: John Day, 1957; London: Methuen, 1957);

Christmas Miniature (New York: John Day, 1957); republished as *The Christmas Mouse* (London: Methuen, 1959);

American Triptych: Three "John Sedges" Novels (New York: John Day, 1958)—includes *The Townsman, The Long Love,* and *Voices in the House;*

Friend to Friend, by Buck and Carlos Romulo (New York: John Day, 1958);

Command the Morning (New York: John Day, 1959; London: Methuen, 1959);

Fourteen Stories (New York: John Day, 1961); republished as *With a Delicate Air and Other Stories* (London: Methuen, 1962);

A Bridge for Passing (New York: John Day, 1962; London: Methuen, 1963);

Hearts Come Home, and Other Stories (New York: Pocket Books, 1962);

Satan Never Sleeps (New York: Pocket Books, 1962);

The Living Reed (New York: John Day, 1963; London: Methuen, 1963);

Escape at Midnight, and Other Stories (Hong Kong: Dragonfly Books, 1964);

The Joy of Children (New York: John Day, 1964);

Welcome Child (New York: John Day, 1964);

The Big Fight (New York: John Day, 1965);

Children for Adoption (New York: Random House, 1965);

Death in the Castle (New York: John Day, 1965; London: Methuen, 1966);

The Gifts They Bring: Our Debt to the Mentally Retarded, by Buck and Gweneth T. Zarfoss (New York: John Day, 1965);

For Spacious Skies: Journey in Dialogue, by Buck and Theodore F. Harris (New York: John Day, 1966);

The Little Fox in the Middle (New York: Collier, 1966);

Matthew, Mark, Luke, and John (New York: John Day, 1966);

The People of Japan (New York: Simon & Schuster, 1966; London: Hale, 1968);

The Time Is Noon (New York: John Day, 1967; London: Methuen, 1967);

To My Daughters, With Love (New York: John Day, 1967);

The New Year (New York: John Day, 1968; London: Methuen, 1968);

The Good Deed, and Other Stories of Asia, Past and Present (New York: John Day, 1969; London: Methuen, 1970);

The Three Daughters of Madame Liang (New York: John Day, 1969; London: Methuen, 1969);

Mandala (New York: John Day, 1970; London: Methuen, 1971);

The Kennedy Women: A Personal Appraisal (New York: Cowles, 1970; London: Methuen, 1970);

China as I See It, edited by Harris (New York: John Day, 1970; London: Methuen, 1971);

The Chinese Story Teller (New York: John Day, 1971);

Pearl Buck's America (New York: Bartholomew, 1971);

The Story Bible (New York: Bartholomew, 1971);

China Past and Present (New York: John Day, 1972);

A Community Success Story: The Founding of the Pearl Buck Center, by Buck and Elisabeth Waechter (New York: John Day, 1972);

The Goddess Abides (New York: John Day, 1972; London: Eyre Methuen, 1972);

Once Upon a Christmas (New York: John Day, 1972);

Pearl Buck's Oriental Cookbook (New York: Simon & Schuster, 1972);

All Under Heaven (New York: John Day, 1973; London: Eyre Methuen, 1973);

A Gift for the Children (New York: John Day, 1973);

Mrs. Starling's Problem (New York: John Day, 1973);

The Rainbow (New York: John Day, 1974; London: Eyre Methuen, 1976);

Words of Love (New York: John Day, 1974);

East and West (New York: John Day, 1975);

Mrs. Stoner and the Sea, and Other Works (New York: Ace, 1976);

Secrets of the Heart (New York: John Day, 1976);

The Lovers and Other Stories (New York: John Day, 1977);

The Woman Who Was Changed, and Other Stories (New York: Crowell, 1979);

The Old Demon (Mankato, Minn.: Creative Education, 1982);

Little Red (Mankato, Minn.: Creative Education, 1987).

TRANSLATION: *Shui hu chuan* (Water Margin), translated as *All Men are Brothers* (New York: John Day, 1933).

OTHER: *China in Black and White: An Album of Woodcuts by Contemporary Chinese Artists,* compiled by Buck (New York: John Day, 1945);

Fairy Tales of the Orient, edited by Buck (New York: Simon & Schuster, 1965);

Pearl Buck's Book of Christmas, edited by Buck (New York: Simon & Schuster, 1974).

Pearl S. Buck's genius as a writer lay in her ability to portray her characters in a universal manner; their joys, sorrows, problems, and disillusionments transcend cultural barriers to become understandable to all readers. Buck's earlier works, most of them portrayals of Chinese characters and subjects, appropriately made her the bridge between the Eastern and Western worlds, China and America. She wrote more than sixty novels, several nonfiction essays and children's books, and many short stories.

Pearl Sydenstricker Buck was born on 26 June 1892 in Hillsboro, West Virginia, while her parents, Absalom and Caroline Stulting Sydenstricker, were on furlough from their missionary work in China.

The Sydenstricker family circa 1901: Pearl, Absalom, Grace, Caroline, and their governess, Wang
(The Pearl S. Buck Foundation)

Taken to the Orient during infancy, Buck grew up among Chinese families (her parents eschewed the formal religious compounds in which most missionaries lived) and spoke Chinese before she learned English. She was educated rigorously and proved a brilliant student. In addition to tutoring and private schooling, she was required by her mother to do written exercises. She was sent to Randolph-Macon Woman's College in Lynchburg, Virginia; after graduation in 1914 she returned to China.

On 30 May 1917 Pearl married John Lossing Buck, an American agricultural expert originally from upstate New York. He was employed by the Presbyterian Mission Board to teach American farming techniques to the Chinese. After their marriage the Bucks lived in remote northern China, where they often traveled, visiting the Chinese farmers and engaging them in conversation. In 1921 her only natural child, Carol, was born. (During this marriage a second daughter, Janice, was adopted.)

Later in 1921 the Bucks moved to Nanking, where he taught rural economics and she taught literature part-time at the University of Nanking, Southeastern University, and Chung Yang University. In Nanking modern ideas from the West had already begun to infiltrate the old traditional Chinese customs and ways. The young Chinese felt trapped between these opposing forces; this situation would become one of Buck's major themes in her early writing.

In 1922 she began to write essays on her impressions of a country caught in the throes of change. Her first published article, titled "In China, Too," appeared in the 23 January issue of *Atlantic Monthly*. She also wrote articles for *Forum* and *Nation*, began to write short stories, and planned her first novel.

In 1925 she brought Carol to the United States for medical treatment and discovered that her daughter would always be mentally handicapped. To distract herself, Buck enrolled at Cornell University in Ithaca, New York, for a master's degree in English. There she won the Laura Messinger Prize in history for her essay "China and the West" (later published in *Annals of the American Academy*, July 1933).

On the ship to America she had written the story that became her first novel. It appeared as "A Chinese Woman Speaks" in *Asia* magazine (April–May 1926). Kwei-lan, a traditionalist, tells of her marriage, which is unhappy until she can accept the Western ideas of her modern Chinese husband. Buck was solicited by a publisher to expand the story into a full-length novel, but thinking the framework too slight and delicate, she suggested two shorter narratives in one volume. She was refused but found another publisher, the John Day Company. The story was published as *East Wind: West Wind* (1930), with the first part concerning Kwei-lan and the second part her brother. In both parts the characters are caught in a dilemma between traditional and modern ideas. *East Wind: West Wind* was an immediate popular success.

In March 1927, having returned to China, Buck and her family, through the help of Chinese friends and servants, escaped Communist soldiers who had entered Nanking, looting and killing foreigners. Her observations on this event and other scenes of revolution are portrayed in the group of stories that make up the second section of her first short-story collection, *The First Wife and Other Stories* (1933).

The first section of the book, "The Old and the New," explores the clash between the traditions of the East and the modern ideas of the West. "The First Wife" (originally published in *Asia*, December 1931 and January 1932) tells of a traditional wife who is unable to change as her American-educated husband has. He divorces her to take a modern bride, and when he wants his first wife to leave his parents' household, she hangs herself. Another story in this section, "The Frill," communicates the

idea of American exploitation of the East. Mrs. Lowe, a well-to-do American, browbeats her Chinese tailor. He works for hours making an elaborate frill for her dress, is underpaid for his efforts, then is refused further work, though he urgently needs the money. Mrs. Lowe is unconscious of her cruelty and callousness. The last section of *The First Wife*, "The Flood," comprises four stories centered on the tragic Yangtze flood of 1931.

The First Wife is probably the best collection of Buck's short stories. They are realistic and free of the sentimentalism and romanticism of her later work. The 9 August 1933 review in the *Christian Century* states, "Here one feels, are not only the deep realities about the soul of China, but some of the basic truths about nature regardless of race." This collection was also significant in Buck's winning the Nobel Prize for literature in 1938; she was the third American to be so honored.

The second section of *The First Wife*, "Revolution," includes the story "Wang Lung," from which Buck took the title character and the looting scene and expanded them into her novel *The Good Earth* (1931). She won a Pulitzer Prize for fiction in 1932 with this book. *The Good Earth* traces the rise of simple farmer Wang Lung from destitution to wealth, portraying the complexities of marriage, parenthood, joy, pain, and human frailty, and emphasizing with a compelling realism that existence is "shaped by eternities." The value of fertile land and the virtues of hard work, thrift, and responsibility are implicitly stressed, and the universality of the experiences renders the Chinese setting an all-too-familiar part of all cultures. *The Good Earth* also succeeds stylistically because the frequent sentence parallelism, rhythmic word repetition, and archaic phrasing effectively blend the techniques of the King James Version of the Bible with the simplicity and directness of the old Chinese narrative sagas.

Hoping to capitalize on the success of *The Good Earth*, Buck wrote two sequels—*Sons* (1932) and *A House Divided* (1935). These books follow the careers of Wang Lung's three male heirs, all of whom give up their father's land and decline into decadence and irresponsibility. *Sons* presents a detailed portrait of a warlord, but lacks strength because Buck seems to have taken much of the material from secondhand sources rather than from personal observation. Further, she is unable to sustain the archaic beauty and pleasing melody that characterize the style of *The Good Earth*. Focusing mainly on Wang Lung's grandsons, *A House Divided* reveals the same difficulty. In 1935 this trilogy about Wang Lung and his family was published in one volume as *House of Earth*.

153 *152*

XV/10pt.

Today I am weary and spent, My Sister. In my
heart it is as though a harp string had been too tightly
drawn for many days and then suddenly relaxed, so that
music is dead in it.

The hour have dreaded is over! No, I will
not say how it went. I will tell you of the whole matter
and then you may judge of it for yourself. As for me -
but I will not tell of the end before the beginning.

We sent the messenger to our parents, bearing
our request that we be allowed to present ourselves the
next day at noon. He returned saying that our father
had left home for Tientsin as soon as he heard of my
brother's arrival. Thus did he avoid the difficult moment - thus has he ever avoided decisions! But Our mother signified her readiness to received my brother and me in her
room. room in the p of the womans courts
She made no mention of the foreign one, but after we had
talked of this together, we decided to ignore the omission.
although I doubted the wisdom of this. But my voice was
but a feeble one in opposition, when my husband and my
brother spoke together. Of the foreigner no mention was made, but
my brother cried "; If I go, my wife will go also."

I went first, therefore, the next day,
at the appointed hour, which was noon; and a servant bore the
gifts before me. My brother had chosen these gifts in

Page from a revised typescript for East Wind: West Wind *(1930), Buck's first book (Harry Ransom Humanities
Research Center, University of Texas at Austin)*

Appearing between the second and third books of the Wang Lung family saga was a novel titled *The Mother* (1934), which portrays a universal *mater dolorosa,* the sorrowful mother. Like *The Good Earth,* this novel derives immense power from its parable-like concentration on the common, shared experiences of life. A peasant wife, who tills the land as well as performing domestic chores, is deserted by her immature husband. She must then rear the children, one of whom is almost blind, and she suffers both the pains and joys of matriarchy. Her old age is brightened by grandchildren, and the difficulties of existence seem more balanced by her line being carried into a new generation.

Because of unsettled conditions in China, including the growing Communist influence, Buck came to the United States in 1934 to take up permanent residence. Her marriage to John Lossing Buck had proved unsuccessful, so on 11 June 1935 she divorced him and married Richard J. Walsh, the president of the John Day publishing firm, that same afternoon. During her marriage to Walsh, they adopted eight more children, some of them hard-to-place Asian-Americans.

Buck's writing career continued uninterrupted. She was awarded an honorary M.A. from Yale University in 1933; two years later she received the William Dean Howells Medal for the most distinguished work of American fiction published in the period 1930–1935; and she was elected to membership in the National Institute of Arts and Letters in 1936. That same year she published two penetrating biographies of her father and mother: *Fighting Angel: Portrait of a Soul* and *The Exile.* The Nobel Prize Committee called these works "masterpieces." Absalom Sydenstricker was obsessed with God and with spreading the message of the Bible. In *Fighting Angel,* Buck writes of his travels through the Chinese countryside facing continuous hardships and frustrations, frequently just managing to escape death. Yet he almost ignored his family, and his aloofness and otherworldliness make his portrait a sharp and taut etching. Buck respected her stern father but could not love him. Caroline Sydenstricker, on the other hand, was family-oriented, warm, loving, and outgoing, although occasionally homesick for America, wavering in religious belief, and pained by the deprivations caused by Absalom's vocation. In some passages *The Exile* becomes overly sentimental, but both volumes are so searching and frankly realistic that every facet of the parents' lives rivets the reader's attention.

This Proud Heart (1938), Buck's first serious novel with an American setting, is highly autobiographical. It portrays a woman sculptor marked by genius but caught in a conflict between total artistic dedication and the yearning for love and motherhood. While stylistically awkward because of excessive use of clichés and Buck's initial difficulty in handling American colloquialisms, *This Proud Heart* presents a stimulating commentary on genius and the burdens it brings.

When Buck received the Nobel Prize for literature in 1938, the Nobel Committee not only extolled her biographies but also applauded her "novels of Chinese peasant life" for their "authenticity, wealth of detail and rare insight with which they describe a region that is little known and rarely accessible to Western readers." Although most American literary critics resented the awarding of the prize to Buck, claiming she had written too few books, was too facile and unchallenging, and was not even an "American" writer, European and Far Eastern critics were far more enthusiastic. Buck has been widely read in Europe and in the Orient. She remains one of the most frequently translated authors in the history of American letters, challenged only by Mark Twain.

Buck was shaken by the hostility of American critics. She immediately defended her writings by tracing the literary roots of her work to the traditional saga, which emphasizes an interesting story above all else. She maintained that she sought to write not for academics but for the masses. A humanitarian note, which to this point had been muted, began to assert itself in her writing. This quality, derived from a personality shaped by her missionary upbringing and perhaps from a realization that she could not fulfill the demands of her more rigorous critics, commenced to dominate her work. Aside from *The Patriot* (1939), which is a perceptive study of the differences between Chinese and Japanese characteristics and attitudes as well as an analysis of the conditions that led to the Sino-Japanese War, Buck's novels became didactic. *Dragon Seed* (1942) and *The Promise* (1943) are blatant propaganda tracts supporting the "heroic struggle" of China against the "imperialistic" Japanese. She became active in humanitarian causes, joined various committees and groups, and started to write more magazine essays and short stories, arguing that she wished to reach ordinary people because "their senses are unspoiled and their emotions are free."

Buck's activities during World War II also included the writing of radio plays, some of which were written for the Office of War Information and broadcast to China, and the founding of the East and West Association, a nonprofit group dedicated to the promotion of greater understanding among the people of the world. Her later novels almost al-

King Gustavus V of Sweden presenting the Nobel Prize for literature to Buck in 1938
(The Pearl S. Buck Foundation)

ways emphasize an important message; thus, *Pavilion of Women* (1946) stresses the need for spiritual love and unselfish behavior; *The Hidden Flower* (1952) assails antimiscegnation laws; and *Command the Morning* (1959) denounces the use of atomic weapons. In these and other late novels, the message has become more important than artistry, and characters too often seem mere cutouts used to underscore the thesis.

Buck's second collection of stories, *Today and Forever* (1941), displays a special pattern of arrangement: the book begins with stories of old China, develops to stories illustrating the effect of new ways on the country, then follows China into the Sino-Japanese period. Buck states in the "Author's Note" that she wished to portray "the tough, resistant, indominable quality of the Chinese people." The in-

tent is good, but because of the exaggerated Hollywood-style quality of most of the stories, this second collection is not as successful as her first. In "Tiger! Tiger!" for example, character and plot are both fantastic and incredible: a bored, American-educated Chinese girl falls in love with a warlord who is heavily taxing the area. She convinces him not to attack a neighboring bandit headquarters, but then he is captured by the bandit leader. He escapes, and afterward is determined to lead his men against the Japanese.

The most effective story in this collection is "The Angel" (first published in *Women's Home Companion*, April 1937), a portrait of an American missionary, Miss Barry, who, although dedicated to her work, despises the Chinese people: they are unclean, lazy, and never live up to her expectations.

Buck in the 1960s with one of the children helped by her adoption agency, Welcome House (The Pearl S. Buck Foundation)

Out of frustration she commits suicide by leaping off a cliff. This story reveals a bleak realism in the same vein as "The First Wife."

Unlike Buck's first two collections, *Far and Near: Stories of Japan, China, and America* (1947) includes stories set in America. Though written in a cool, competent style, these American stories, except for one, are rather superficial. "The Truce," concerning a woman who realizes there is no love in her marriage, reaches the quality of sophistication of Buck's Chinese stories. The theme of disharmony in family life, or variations of it, is incorporated in all the American stories here. The best works in this collection, however, are the Chinese stories, especially "The Tax Collector" and "A Few People," because they depict the fundamental conflicts of Chinese village life. A critic for *The New York Times Book Review* (30 November 1947) summed it up: "Miss Buck's art thrives best on the Chinese scene; transplanted in America, it grows pale and artificial."

Buck's prolific output of two to three books a year interfered with the marketing of her works. To solve this difficulty she assumed the pseudonym John Sedges and published five novels between 1945 and 1953 under this nom de plume. Only the first of this group, *The Townsman* (1945), achieved success. A study of an early pioneering settlement in

nineteenth-century Kansas, the novel centers on an idealistic schoolmaster who helps build the community and brings law and order to the surrounding area. Painstakingly researched, although at times overplotted, *The Townsman* drew Ernest E. Leisy's praise in his study of the American historical novel. He observes that *The Townsman* is a significant contribution because it emphasizes that there was much more to the early West than sheriffs, outlaws, and dance-hall girls.

In addition to the John Sedges volumes, Buck continued to produce an unceasing stream of novels, short stories, essays, and works for young people. She wrote plays and collaborated with others such as Masha Scott, Eslanda Goode Robeson, and Carlos Romulo, composing books on Communism, racial discrimination against blacks and Asiatics, and similar timely topics. In 1949 she founded Welcome House, an agency designed to arrange the adoptions of Asian-American children who had been fathered by American servicemen overseas. In 1964 she established the Pearl S. Buck Foundation to give support to those children who had no opportunity to be adopted and thus were forced to live virtually as nonpersons in various Asian countries.

Much of the work in the collection *Fourteen Stories* (1961) is about love and marriage and is romantic in tone. The stories are easy to read and well written, yet they seem mechanical and too neatly worked out. "The Silver Butterfly" (which first appeared in *The Saturday Evening Post,* 14 May 1960), however, is worth mentioning. The story is about an episode among members of a Chinese Communist commune. An aged woman gives a piece of family jewelry to one of the commune children. Since no one is supposed to own personal items, she is punished for this transgression at a commune meeting. The story expresses the idea that, although many technological advances are being made in Communist China, the people still suffer; the intensity almost reaches that of her earlier Chinese stories, and the impact remains with the reader.

While her writing activity was untiring, only two of the twenty-three novels she produced after 1945 were better than average: *The Living Reed* (1963) and *The Time Is Noon* (1967). *The Living Reed* explores the history of the Kim family in Korea from 1883 to 1945 and analyzes the family in relation to the changing social, political, and economic conditions that Korea suffered while undergoing diplomatic pressures from Russia and China and eventual military occupation by Japan. At times more a textbook than a novel (hence reducing several characters almost to the level of puppets), the volume succeeds as dramatized history and gives the best overall view of Korea and its people ever presented in fictional form.

The Time Is Noon studies a talented woman who grows up in a minister's family in the early part of the twentieth century and who experiences marriage and childbirth and concomitant anxieties. Much of the novel is objectively presented with taut construction and sharply etched family portraits reminiscent of Buck's work in the *Good Earth* period, although the lyrical style is lacking. In fact, the novel was actually written between 1936 and 1939 but not published until thirty years later because it deals with Buck's and Richard Walsh's divorces in order to marry one another, a subject not considered favorable to her public image at that time.

Buck continued writing almost to the moment of her death from lung cancer on 6 March 1973. She left several collections of short stories and a novel, which were brought out gradually by her publishers, including *East and West* (1975), *Secrets of the Heart* (1976), *The Lovers and Other Stories* (1977), and *The Woman Who Was Changed, and Other Stories* (1979). These collections focus on such contemporary topics as maintaining both a home and a career; marrying for security; illegal abortion; nuclear research; and racial prejudice.

As her humanitarian preoccupations increased, Buck had exchanged the objectivity and realism that had made her early works significant for didacticism, sentimentality, and romanticism. In addition to these weaknesses, critics object to her method of old-fashioned storytelling. Her conventional technique, lack of penetration into her characters, and the absence of myth and symbolism leave little for her readers to think about. While Buck wrote too much and too hastily, thus producing many books that lack distinction, she will be remembered for creating the best portraits of life in China in the 1920s and 1930s ever drawn and for the brilliant biographies of her mother and father. Several of her later works are superior to mere best-seller ephemera because they deal realistically with such eternal topics as injustice, racial discrimination, clashing political philosophies, and conflicts between generations.

Bibliography:
Lucille S. Zinn, "The Works of Pearl S. Buck: A Bibliography," *Bulletin of Bibliography,* 36 (October–December 1979): 194–208.

Biographies:
Cornelia Spencer, *The Exile's Daughter: A Biography of Pearl S. Buck* (New York: Coward-McCann, 1944);

Theodore F. Harris, *Pearl S. Buck: A Biography,* 2 volumes (New York: John Day, 1969–1971);

Nora Stirling, *Pearl Buck: A Woman in Conflict* (Piscataway, N.J.: New Century, 1983);

Warren Sherk, *Pearl S. Buck: Good Earth Mother* (Philomath, Oreg.: Drift Creek Press, 1992);

Peter J. Conn, *Pearl S. Buck: A Cultural Biography* (Cambridge & New York: Cambridge University Press, 1996).

References:
Phyllis Bentley, "The Art of Pearl S. Buck," *English Journal,* 24 (December 1935): 791–800;

Oscar Cargill, *Intellectual America: Ideas on the March* (New York: Macmillan, 1941; New York: Cooper Square, 1968), pp. 146–154;

George A. Cevasco, "Pearl Buck and the Chinese Novel," *Asian Studies,* 5 (December 1967): 437–450;

Paul A. Doyle, *Pearl S. Buck* (New York: Twayne, 1965; revised, 1980);

Doyle, "Pearl S. Buck's Short Stories: A Survey," *English Journal,* 55 (January 1966): 62–68;

Ami Henchoz, "A Permanent Element in Pearl Buck's Novels," *English Studies,* 25 (August 1943): 97–103;

Ann LaFarge, *Pearl Buck* (New York: Chelsea House, 1988);

Ernest E. Leisy, *The American Historical Novel* (Norman: University of Oklahoma Press, 1950), p. 205;

Kang Liao, *Pearl S. Buck: A Cultural Bridge Across the Pacific* (Westport, Conn.: Greenwood Press, 1997);

Elizabeth J. Lipscomb, Frances E. Webb, and Peter Conn, eds., *The Several Worlds of Pearl S. Buck: Essays Presented at a Centennial Symposium, Randolph-Macon Woman's College, March 26–28, 1992* (Westport, Conn.: Greenwood Press, 1994);

Mamoru Shimizu, "On Some Stylistic Features, Chiefly Biblical, of *The Good Earth,*" *Studies in English Literature* (Tokyo), English Number (1964): 117–134;

Dody Weston Thompson, "Pearl Buck," in *American Winners of the Nobel Literary Prize,* edited by Warren G. French and Walter E. Kidd (Norman: University of Oklahoma Press, 1968), pp. 85–110.

Papers:
The primary collection of Buck materials is located at the Lipscomb Library, Randolph-Macon Woman's College, Lynchburg, Virginia.

Rita Dove

This entry was updated by Lotta M. Lofgren (University of Virginia)
from the entry by Kirkland C. Jones (Lamar University) in
DLB 120: American Poets Since World War II.

BIRTH: Akron, Ohio, 28 August 1952, to Ray A. and Elvira Elizabeth Hord Dove.

EDUCATION: B.A. (summa cum laude), Miami University of Ohio, 1973; attended Universität Tüebingen, West Germany, 1974–1975; M.F.A., University of Iowa, 1977.

MARRIAGE: 23 March 1979 to Fred Viebahn; child: Aviva Chantal Tamu Dove-Viebahn.

AWARDS AND HONORS: Fulbright fellow, 1974–1975; grants from National Endowment for the Arts, 1978, and Ohio Arts Council, 1979; International Working Period for Authors fellow State of Northrhine-Westphalia and University of Bielefeld, West Germany, 1980; Portia Pittman fellow at Tuskegee Institute from National Endowment for the Humanities, 1982; John Simon Guggenheim fellow, 1983; Peter I. B. Lavan Younger Poets Award, Academy of American Poets, 1986; Pulitzer Prize in poetry for *Thomas and Beulah,* 1987; General Electric Foundation Award for Younger Writers, 1987; Bellagio (Italy) residency, Rockefeller Foundation, 1988; Ohio Governor's Award, 1988; Mellon fellow, National Humanities Center, North Carolina, 1988–1989; Ohioana Award for *Grace Notes,* 1991; Literary Lion citation, New York Public Libraries, 1991; inducted Ohio Women's Hall of Fame, 1991; U.S. Poet Laureate and Consultant in Poetry at the Library of Congress 1993–1995; Women of the Year Award, *Glamour* magazine, 1993; NAACP Great American Artist Award, 1993; Harvard University Phi Beta Kappa lecturer, 1993; Distinguished Achievement medal, Miami University Alumni Association, 1994; Renaissance Forum Award for leadership in the literary arts, Folger Shakespeare Library, 1994; Carl Sandburg Award, International Platform Association, 1994; Golden Plate Award, American Academy of Achievement, 1994; Kennedy Center Fund for New American Plays grant, 1995; Charles Frankel Prize / National Medal in the Humanities, 1996; The Heinz Award in the Arts and Humanities, 1996; American Phil-

Rita Dove (photograph by Fred Viebahn)

osophical Society, 1996; Sara Lee Frontrunner Award, 1997; Barnes and Noble Writers for Writers Award, 1997; honorary doctorates: Miami University, 1988, Knox College, 1989, Tuskegee University, 1994, University of Miami, 1994, Washington University, St. Louis, 1994, Case Western Reserve University, 1994, University of Akron, 1994, Arizona State University, 1995, Boston College, 1995, Dartmouth College, 1995, University of Pennsylvania, 1996, Spelman College, 1996, Notre Dame University, 1997, University of North Carolina at Chapel Hill, 1997, Northeastern University, 1997, and Columbia University, 1998.

BOOKS: *Ten Poems* (Lisbon: Penumbra, 1977);
The Only Dark Spot in the Sky (Tempe, Ariz.: Porch, 1980);
The Yellow House on the Corner (Pittsburgh: Carnegie-Mellon University Press, 1980);
Mandolin (Athens: Ohio Review, 1982);
Museum (Pittsburgh: Carnegie-Mellon University Press, 1983);
Fifth Sunday (Lexington: University Press of Kentucky, 1985);
Thomas and Beulah (Pittsburgh: Carnegie-Mellon University Press, 1986);
The Other Side of the House (Tempe, Ariz.: Pyracantha, 1988);
Grace Notes (New York: Norton, 1989);
Through the Ivory Gate: A Novel (New York: Pantheon, 1992);
Selected Poems (New York: Vintage, 1993);
Lady Freedom Among Us (West Burke, Vt.: Janus Press, 1994);
The Darker Face of the Earth: A Verse Play in Fourteen Scenes (Brownsville, Oreg.: Story Line Press, 1994); revised as *The Darker Face of the Earth* (Brownsville, Oreg.: Story Line Press, 1996);
The Poet's World (Washington, D.C.: Library of Congress, 1995);
Mother Love: Poems (New York: Norton, 1995);
Evening Primrose (Minneapolis, Minn.: Tunheim, 1998);
On the Bus with Rosa Parks (New York: Norton, 1999).

PLAY PRODUCTION: *The Darker Face of the Earth,* Ashland, Oregon, Shakespeare Festival, 1996.

Rita Dove's poems began to appear in print as early as 1974, but until 1987, the year she won the Pulitzer Prize in poetry for *Thomas and Beulah* (1986), her name was mentioned only occasionally in college classrooms and at meetings of learned societies. Not long after she won the Pulitzer Prize, though, her name and works began to appear in college courses and academic panels on American literature, African American studies, and women's studies. Before Dove won the Pulitzer Prize, Gwendolyn Brooks was the only African American poet who had gained this coveted award.

Born in Akron, Ohio, to well-educated parents, Dove is the daughter of Ray A. Dove, the first African American chemist to break the racial barrier in the tire-and-rubber industry. Her mother is the former Elvira Elizabeth Hord. In 1970, shortly before her eighteenth birthday, Dove was invited to the White House as a "Presidential Scholar," indicating that she had ranked among the top one hundred high-school seniors in the nation for that year.

Dove earned a bachelor's degree from Miami University at Oxford, Ohio, where she enrolled as a National Achievement Scholar; in 1973 she graduated summa cum laude. During the year that followed, she studied at West Germany's Tubingen University on a Fulbright scholarship. Her study there led to graduate studies at the University of Iowa Writers' Workshop. She went on from there to begin publishing her impressive list of poems and short stories. In 1979 Dove married Fred Viebahn, a German-born novelist, and together they have a daughter, Aviva Chantal Tamu Dove-Viebahn. The family lives in Charlottesville, Virginia.

In 1974 Dove's poems began to appear in major periodicals. After two early chapbooks Dove's first full-length book of poems, *The Yellow House on the Corner,* was published by Carnegie-Mellon University Press in 1980. This publication was followed, after another chapbook, by *Museum* (1983), and in 1986 *Thomas and Beulah* appeared.

Dove's concept of poetry is akin to that of such other modern American poets as Robert Frost, Langston Hughes, and Gwendolyn Brooks, especially as to rhetorical structure. Dove's readers learn that she often melds several time-tested devices to shape an original idiom. Like Alice Walker in *Good Night, Willie Lee, I'll See You in the Morning* (1979) and like Zora Neale Hurston in virtually all of her fiction, Dove bridges the gap between orality and written text.

In 1977 Dove published *Ten Poems,* the first of her chapbooks of verse. Some of these poems are set in the turbulent 1960s, with one of the poems titled "1963." Characteristically combining narrative and lyric modes, the book may be described as Dove's apprentice work, but "Adolescence II," "Adolescence III," and "The Bird Frau" reveal hints of her later strength. Included in this initial chapbook is "Upon Meeting Don L. Lee, in a Dream." Dove was inspired by such revolutionary writers as Lee and LeRoi Jones (Imamu Amiri Baraka). Both the Lee poem and "The Bird Frau" reappear in *The Yellow House on the Corner.*

In 1980 another Dove chapbook of poems, *The Only Dark Spot in the Sky,* was published. This volume includes some poems that appeared again that year in *The Yellow House on the Corner.* Critics attempted to dismiss *The Yellow House on the Corner* as conventional and self-serving, but some evaluators were perceptive enough to praise Dove's sparkling voice, which is as polyphonic as an African dance or chant. Admittedly *The Yellow House on the Corner* is autobiographical, but as *Thomas and Beulah* revealed six years later, this autobiographical thread is the most profound source of meaning in her art. As early as her first book Dove's use of dramatic monologue

*Dust jacket for Dove's sequence of narrative poems about
her family, including her grandparents Thomas
and Beulah Hord*

and compressed narrative showed her cross-cultural perceptivity. Her keen sense of history and her well-disciplined use of rhetorical decorum set her apart; her characters and their voices move in and out of the centuries as they transcend the local and the mundane, becoming, as a result, decidedly inclusive in their view of the universe and of humanity. Moreover, Dove's allusions to the Psalms and to other Old Testament verses ("Teach us to number our days," "children of angels," and "some point true and unproven") provide a sense of community among the slaves, their masters, and the surrounding fields.

The poems in *The Yellow House on the Corner,* from which these biblical phrases are taken, set forth universal themes in fresh contexts. In "Adolescence III" Dove writes of the laying on of hands and of love's ennobling effects: "I dreamed how it would happen / . . . At his touch, the scabs would fall away." Frequently in Dove's verses the healing touch of healthful mating informs the imagery.

The publication of *Mandolin,* another chapbook, came in 1982. This seven-poem sequence presents more of Dove's narrative verses that a few years later functioned individually as segments of the opening episode of *Thomas and Beulah,* Dove's tale of her family's history. *Mandolin* shows Dove using music, musical instruments, and dance as metaphors for beauty, youth, and the power of sexuality, especially when she uses comparison to depict a dark maleness that is strong and irresistible: "with nothing to boast of but good looks and a mandolin, . . . / Heading North, . . . gold hoop / from the right ear jiggling / And a glass stud, bright blue in his left. The young ladies / saying he sure plays that tater bug like the devil!" Dove's poetry sings as she records significant events of the musician's life.

Museum, published in 1983, was Dove's most impressive work until *Thomas and Beulah.* Critical reaction to *Museum* was plentiful and frequently laudatory. This book presents a mature Dove, expert in the use of recurrent images of light and darkness. Most critics noticed the polish of these poems and their author's growth since the late 1970s. In this work the poet's voice is sometimes meditative, sometimes clairvoyant, then at other times peering "through a glass, darkly," as if through haze or smoke. The subject matter is as varied as that in *The Yellow House on the Corner,* if not more so.

Dove chose for the cover of *Museum* a painting by German artist Christian Shad. This painting presents a view of two sideshow entertainers, a white male figure naked to the waist and a black woman seated below him in the posture of creative dance. Such a cover design was inspired, no doubt, by the penultimate poem in part 2 of the book, "Agosta the Winged Man and Rasha the Black Dove," a poem of seven oddly shaped stanzas, suggesting through spatial configuration the snake imagery:

He could not leave his skin—once
he'd painted himself a new one,
silk green . . . turning slowly in place as the boa
constrictor coiled counter clock wise. . . .

The title of the poem is as complex and multitextured as its imagery. The appearance of the author's own last name as the last word of the title echoes the autobiographical suggestion of the portrait in the cover design as well as some of the poems, such as "November for Beginners," "Reading Holderlin on the Patio with the Aid of a Dictionary," "At a German Writer's Conference in Munich," "Sunday Night at Grandfather's," "My Father's Telescope," "To Bed," and "Why I Turned Vegetarian."

Although poetry is Dove's primary medium, she has also published *Fifth Sunday,* a 1985 collection of eight short stories. The subject matter of the stories in *Fifth Sunday* ranges from the onset of puberty and adolescent courtship–with growing awareness of the self and the selves of others–to the displacement and oddity that American blacks feel when they venture into Europe, to the flowering of womanhood and manhood in mature relationships, to sex and reproduction as the music of life played on the instruments of life.

Thomas and Beulah, her volume of narrative verse published in 1986, presents the saga of her family, depicting the generations descended from her maternal grandparents–Thomas Hord, born in Wartrace, Tennessee, and his wife Beulah, four years younger than Thomas and from the hamlet of Rockmart, Georgia. When Beulah was only two, her parents moved the family to Akron, Ohio, Dove's birthplace. Thomas, a virile young man full of wanderlust, arrived, as if by chance, in Akron in 1921. Three years later he married Beulah in a December wedding, and two years after that Rose (Dove's aunt), their first child, was born. This verse saga steadily unfolds until it ends with Beulah's death in 1969. Many of the poems in this prizewinning volume had been published previously. Appropriately Dove dedicated the book to her mother, Elvira Elizabeth, in recognition of both her mother and her "mother's garden," a la Alice Walker.

Thomas and Beulah, an eighty-page volume, includes forty-four poems arranged in two parts. The first part is titled "Mandolin," and the second part is titled "Canary in Bloom." "Mandolin" presents twenty-three poems, and "Canary" presents the remaining twenty-one. At the end of the volume is a chronology that offers more than a little help in following Dove's mythos. The epigraph to the first part of the book is this couplet from Melvin B. Tolson's *Harlem Gallery* (1965): "Black Boy, O Black Boy / is the port worth the cruise?" The quotation preceding the second part is from Anne Spencer's "Lines to a Nasturtium" (1926): "Ah, how the senses flood at my repeating, / As once in her fire-lit heart I felt the furies / Beating, beating." Both passages help the reader appreciate the permanence and depth of the love shared by Thomas and Beulah. Their love becomes a "fire" that they pass on to their children and grandchildren. They are a love-blessed pair whose marriage becomes the clan's bridge over the "troubled waters" of variance–a "viaduct," as Dove identifies it, that spans the differ-

ences between their families and carries them all across the river that sometimes divides the sexes.

Because Thomas and Beulah have become "one flesh," one spirit, they are able to impart, carefully and lovingly, this wholeness to their progeny. As a result the clan is capable of coping with pain, guilt, despair, bereavement, and the loss of illusion, as seen in "The Event" and "Straw Hat," two poems that appear in the first sequence. "The Event" boasts of Thomas's "silver falsetto," accompanied by the mandolin of his manhood. Then, in "Straw Hat," Thomas learns that he is not perfect, that "no one was perfect." During the 1930s Thomas lent his "sweet tenor" to the "gospel choir," a kind of chorus that rocks and sways and that only the black church possesses. In "Definition in the Face of Unnamed Fury," Thomas, in shame, threatens: "I'll just / let go." And in "Gospel" the tenor from "a fortress / of animal misery" gives vent to his "sorrow and his sacrifice." Eventually overcome by an intense mixture of emotions, Thomas "lets go" and quits the gospel choir of the African Methodist Episcopal Zion Church. Dove, in *Thomas and Beulah,* harmonizes history and human experience.

Critics praised *Thomas and Beulah* and its author. Helen Vendler, in the *New York Review of Books* (23 October 1986), described Dove as one who has "planed away unnecessary matter: pure shapes, her poems exhibit the thrift that Yeats called the sign of a perfected manner." None of Dove's many reviewers gave this volume a negative notice, and many were lavish in their praise. Emily Grosholz, in the *Hudson Review* (1987), wrote that "Rita Dove . . . understands the long-term intricacies of marriage, as the protagonists of her wonderful chronicle . . . testify." Critics have also described this work as wise and affectionate. Dove succeeds in treating two sides of her subject, and she warns her reader, at the bottom of the dedicatory page of the book, that these poems "tell two sides of a story and are meant to be read in sequence." Dove emphasizes the separateness and the individuality of her grandparents, who dealt with hostilities and the loss of love, as well as grief at the loss of life. Through good times and bad this ancestral pair never fell out of love, maintaining their devotedness, each to the other. All critics of the book, in their own ways, have celebrated this melding of biography and lyric, one of Dove's trademarks.

Following a chapbook, *The Other Side of the House* (1988), Dove's book of poems *Grace Notes* was published in 1989. Most of the forty-eight poems in *Grace Notes* had appeared previously, sometimes in varying versions, in some of the most prestigious poetry periodicals, including *Black Scholar, Boston Re-*

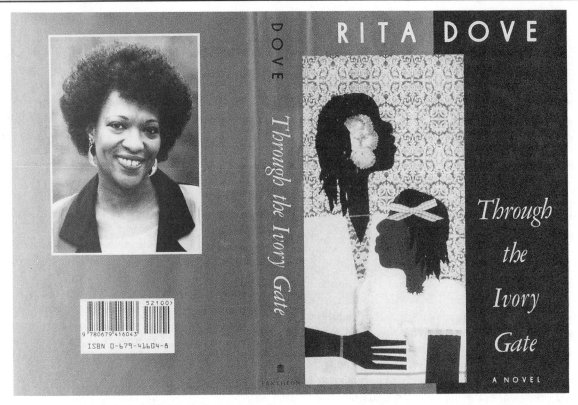

Dust jacket for Dove's 1992 novel that explores the isolation of a well-educated young black woman

view, *Georgia Review, Michigan Quarterly Review, Ars Poetica, Southwest Review,* and *Yale Review.* The arrangement of the poems appeals to sight, sound, and touch. Typical of Dove's manner are the first two poems, "Summit Beach" and "Silos," and the last poem, "Old Folk's Home, Jerusalem," one of her finest, a multispaced, fifteen-line poem that she has dedicated to Harry Timar. "Summit Beach" includes her earlier African maleness motif, frequently represented by images of an adult male singer who also dances to his own accompaniment or to another musician's tinkling on the xylophone or strumming on a mandolin—"masculine toys," as the poet describes them in "Silos." "Summit Beach" serves as a verse introduction to the entire volume, with "Silos" following it immediately as the first poem in the first of the five sequences in the book.

The poems in this volume are shaped into groups of lines that sometimes function as one sentence that ebbs and flows across the page. Her male dancer in "Silos" impresses his woman, "the rib of the modern world," as he struts, parades, marches to a rhythm, now marcato, now staccato, now swaying with the gospel chorus. Dove's use of color in this volume is brighter and more multifaceted than the more somber shades of *Thomas and Beulah,* ranging from yellow to orange, from red to indigo. A fa-

vorite refrain of her male dancer appears: "Man, she was butter just waiting to melt."

Through the Ivory Gate, Dove's only published novel, appeared in 1992. It tells the story of a young woman, Virginia, who returns to her hometown of Akron, Ohio, where she has not lived since she was a child, to teach art in an elementary school. This move allows her to tie up the threads of her past, through her own memories and through listening to stories recounted by elderly relatives she has not seen for years. She learns to find value even in those unpleasant stories that fester—because hidden—in her family's past. The novel meanders across her life as unfettered as memory: one memory leads to another in no particular order, and the reader follows along wherever they go. As in much of her poetry, Dove in this novel illustrates the need for understanding and communicating with both personal and cultural pasts. Virginia teaches her pupils and their parents about puppetry from other cultures but learns from her personal experiences that she must find richness in her own. At the end of the novel she tells an audience in a dream that a Black Sambo doll ought not to be an object of ridicule: "The first thing to bear in mind about Sambo . . . is that Sambo is all of us. We all want to make merry, to wear bright colors and sing in the sun all day."

40

She learns that the seductive power of music, which in part resides in its power to transcend history and culture ("That was the irresistible thing about music—it needed no intermediary of the mind; it was a direct infusion, straight to the bowels"), should not keep people from embracing that history and culture. Life, as she comes to believe, must be a wedding of fantasy and memory.

Though Dove seems to make the transition from poetry to prose with little effort, weaving together the threads of *Through the Ivory Gate* to create a satisfying whole, the voice of the poet is never far away. The novel includes passages of lyrical force, as in this excerpt, spoken by Aunt Carrie: "Did you ever notice how the air looks like it's full of feathers sometimes when it gets dark? Everything seems to come apart and float around, and heavy things like tables and chairs take on a grainy look, like old sugar." *Through the Ivory Gate* was generally well received by reviewers, though some found facile elements in it. In *The New York Times Book Review* (11 October 1992) Geoff Ryman objects to what he sees as Virginia's too likable qualities. Though the other characters respond positively to her, she is not without her own agonies. The novel baldly illustrates Virginia's debilitating isolation as a well-educated young black woman; as her mother tells her, the more educated she becomes, the more alone she will be. At the end of the novel Virginia still maintains her isolation, rejects a potential lover, and moves on to a new town: "Why did it seem like she was always running away?" It is a question the reader is left to ponder with Virginia.

Dove was named poet laureate of the United States in 1993, a post she held for two years. She became the youngest person, first African American, and second woman to hold the position. The appointment catapulted an already well-known and major author into the national spotlight. Many awards and degrees have followed: since 1993 Dove has garnered fourteen honorary degrees from institutions of higher learning throughout the country. Dove's main self-appointed task as poet laureate was to make the public, especially children and young people, more comfortable with poetry. She remarks in a *Washington Post* (24 April 1994) interview with Elizabeth Kastor: "Poetry may not change the world. But it can change a heart, and it can change a moment—a heart *in* a moment." To this end Dove used such opportunities as television spots and interviews, telecasts from classrooms, and visits to *Sesame Street*. Her collection of essays *The Poet's World* (1995), most of which originated as lectures at the Library of Congress, deals primarily with the difficulty of and yet necessity for poets to "find the right mix between the interior moment and the pulse of the

world." She decries both extremes of isolating oneself from the world and using poetry for the purpose of protest and slogans. In her own verse she moves from close observation of detail outward to a broader scope of social relevance. For example, in "Lady Freedom Among Us," which opens *The Poet's World,* Dove exhorts people to regard the statue closely and to be moved by it to adopt a social conscience:

> with her oldfashioned sandals
> with her leaden skirts
> with her stained cheeks and whiskers and heaped up trinkets
> she has risen among us in blunt reproach
> . . . .
> don't think you can ever forget her
> don't even try
> she's not going to budge
>
> no choice but to grant her space
> crown her with sky
> for she is one of the many
> and she is each of us

Now as earlier Dove writes about "the underside of history—its vanquished and oppressed peoples, its ordinary citizens and unsung heroes."

Dove's only play, *The Darker Face of the Earth,* has appeared in two editions, in 1994 and 1996. The play is written in free verse, not in blank verse as some early reviewers contended. The 1994 version, which Dove never expected to see performed, is the work of an accomplished poet and storyteller but a less experienced playwright. The 1996 version is more polished: in the interim the play went through four revisions (with editorial input from Derek Walcott, among others) while Dove guided it to its 1996 premiere at the Ashland, Oregon, Shakespeare Festival. It has since appeared at the Crossroads Theater in New Brunswick, New Jersey, and at the Kennedy Center in Washington, D.C. The play makes use of the Oedipus legend to create a story of miscegenation in antebellum South Carolina. Amalia, a plantation owner, has a child with Hector, a slave. To protect the child from the wrath of her husband, Louis, she agrees to have the child sold into slavery. Twenty years later her son, Augustus, returns to the plantation as a slave, his identity unknown to all. Even as he plots with a group of conspirators to free the slaves and kill Amalia and Louis, Augustus becomes Amalia's lover. When the time comes, he kills Louis (he has already killed Hector in a confrontation in the swamp); at the inevitable moment of recognition, he is spared the task of killing Amalia when she stabs herself with his knife. In the final scene Augustus, maddened by the truth, is carried offstage on the back of the conspirators, a hero in their eyes. Although critics often seem to miss this point, Dove

Dust jacket for Dove's 1995 collection of poems, which takes the Demeter-Persephone myth as its central theme

makes use of the Oedipus legend above all to explore the differences between the two stories, not their similarities. The curse that has settled over the plantation has its origins not in divine caprice but in social evil. Despite the attempts of the characters—both victims and perpetrators—to blame fate for their condition and thereby justify their passivity, the institution of slavery is the curse they cannot name. Dove explores, through Augustus's simultaneous goals to love Amalia and free his people, the conflicts in all individuals between personal desire and responsibility to the group. Augustus comes to understand that the concept of freedom is complex and multifaceted:

> everything was so simple before!
> hate and be hated.
> but this—love or freedom—
> is the devil's choice.

Dove's latest volume of poems, *Mother Love,* appeared in 1995. All poems have appeared previously in a wide range of journals (a testament to Dove's ever-rising stature), but many have been heavily reworked for this volume. Taking the Demeter-Persephone cycle as its central myth, the collection focuses on relationships between mothers and daughters through the generations. Dove explodes the traditional conception of the relationship among Demeter, Persephone, and Hades; she uncovers multiple levels of fragmentation, then works to resolve them, adding new complexity and finally new cohesion to the ancient myth. The volume also includes several poems not directly connected to the myth but thematically related to the others. In a review of *Mother Love* in *The New Yorker* (15 May 1995) Helen Vendler speaks with admiration for "Dove's willingness to slant the myth upward to sublimity, downward to the ordinary, and—at her best—outward to the uncanny." Dove gives each of the three main characters a chance to tell his or her side of the story, interweaving their disparate perspectives. The volume describes Demeter's nearly self-indulgent grief at losing her daughter to the underworld, as in "Demeter, Waiting": "I will drag my grief through a winter / of my own making and refuse / any meadow that recycles itself into / hope." She learns by the end of the volume that a mother's greatest gift to her daughter is to let her grow up, to let her go. Indeed, even before her abduction Persephone yearns to separate herself from her mother; she is "a young girl dying to feel alive, to discover / a pain majestic enough / to live by" ("Golden Oldie"). She welcomes Hades willingly into her life. Hades, though Demeter disapproves of him ("The Bistro Styx"), is seductive ("Hades' Pitch," "Persephone in Hell") but never brutal.

Ultimately, the volume cautions that what should mitigate the inevitable frictions in any relationship is a sense of self-sufficiency ("Lamentations," "Rusks"). Demeter must learn to get along without Persephone, and Persephone's journey to Hades cannot simply be a voyage toward Hades, for such a journey would merely replace dependence on the mother with dependence on Hades. Only if the journey is also one of self-knowledge can Persephone find a perspective that sustains her, even in the depths of hell. Dove speaks in "An Intact World," the volume's preface, of "mother-goddess, daughter-consort and poet . . . struggling to sing in their chains." In *Mother Love* Dove identifies not only with Demeter and Persephone but also with Hades—the "Great Artist" ("The Bistro Styx"). For what, after all, is a poet but a seductress coaxing readers toward a new understanding of life and art? From this perspective, *Mother Love* is a psychomachy illustrating the poet's own struggle with the disparate demands on mother, daughter, poet, and the imperfect yet sufficient truce between these warring roles.

As Dove explains in "An Intact World," the volume includes multiple and various experimentations with the sonnet form. She reflects, "I like how the sonnet comforts even while its prim borders (but what a pretty fence!) are stultifying: one is constantly bumping up against Order." The freedom Dove takes with the sonnet parallels Persephone's struggle for freedom and her ambivalence toward the security with the mother, who wants her relationship with Persephone to be fixed and immutable. Dove tantalizes the reader with seemingly endless variations on the sonnet once the traditional "prim borders" are pushed outward. This impulse reminds her readers of the many ways Dove has taught them throughout her career that they must blend tradition with individual expression to find a voice both personal and relevant. Since her first published volume of poetry, *The Yellow House on the Corner,* Dove has demanded the freedom to move unfettered across boundaries of personal history, African American history, and all facets of world culture. With the privilege of one who has had a cross-cultural perspective thrust upon her, she appropriates these elements and fashions them into new coherence.

Rita Dove is not the stereotypical woman writer, nor is she simply the traditional African American author. She appreciates the aesthetics of race and gender but does not feel the need to raise the color problem merely for the sake of color. Dove writes because she enjoys creating word impressions as she wrestles with significant ideas. Throughout her career music has been a force that sustains her and infuses her work in all genres. In a *Christian Science Monitor* interview (20 May 1993) with Steven Ratiner, she muses, "I think that music was one of those first experiences I had of epiphany, of something clicking, of understanding something beyond, deeper than rational sense." She defies the disabling pigeonhole or comfortable niche. Furthermore, Dove emulates what she admires in other great poets who have become her favorites—William Shakespeare, Melvin B. Tolson, Derek Walcott, Lucille Clifton, Langston Hughes, Don L. Lee, Amiri Baraka, and Anne Spencer—to name a few. Dove is not hampered by fragmentation nor by any defensive need to justify her own experiences. Dove sets most of her verse in the past, and she handles nostalgia well. In all of her works she presents a variety and richness of theme and structure found in fine poetry the world over. She remains steadfast in her belief that poetry can change the world for the better, for everyone. She told Ratiner, "I am interested in recovering a sense that we, as individual human beings, can connect to the universe." That is the task she sets for herself in all her writings.

References:

Robert McDowell, "The Assembling Vision of Rita Dove," *Callaloo,* 25 (Winter 1985): 61–70;

Arnold Rampersad, "The Poems of Rita Dove," *Callaloo,* 26 (Winter 1986): 52–60;

Lisa M. Steinman, "Dialogues Between History and Dream," *Michigan Quarterly Review,* 26 (Spring 1987): 428–438;

Peter Stitt, "Coherence Through Place in Contemporary American Poetry," *Georgia Review,* 40 (1986): 1021–1033;

Helen Vendler, *The Given and the Made: Strategies of Poetic Definition* (Cambridge, Mass.: Harvard University Press, 1995).

Louise Erdrich

P. Jane Hafen
University of Nevada, Las Vegas

See also the Erdrich entries in *DLB 152: American Novelists Since World War II, Fourth Series,* and *DLB 175: Native American Writers of the United States.*

BIRTH: Little Falls, Minnesota, 7 June 1954, to Ralph Louis and Rita Joanne Gourneau Erdrich.

EDUCATION: B.A., Dartmouth College, 1976; M.A., Johns Hopkins University, 1979.

MARRIAGE: 10 October 1981 to Michael Anthony Dorris (died 11 April 1997); children: Reynold Abel (died 1991), Jeffrey Sava, Madeline Hannah (all adopted), Persia Andromeda, Pallas Antigone, Aza Marion.

AWARDS AND HONORS: Johns Hopkins University teaching fellow, 1978; MacDowell Colony fellow, 1980; Yaddo Colony fellow, 1981; Dartmouth College visiting fellow, 1981; Nelson Algren Award for "The World's Greatest Fishermen," 1982; National Endowment for the Arts Fellowship, 1982; Pushcart Prize for "Indian Boarding School: The Runaways," 1983; National Magazine Fiction awards, 1983 and 1987; Virginia McCormack Scully Prize for best book of the year dealing with Indians or Chicanos in 1984, National Book Critics Circle Award for best work of fiction in 1984, *Los Angeles Times* Award for best novel, Sue Kaufman Prize from the American Academy and Institute of Arts and Letters for best first fiction, and American Book Award from the Before Columbus Foundation, all for *Love Medicine,* which was also named one of the best eleven books of 1985 by *The New York Times Book Review;* Guggenheim Fellowship, 1985–1986; O. Henry Award for "Fleur," 1987; Minnesota Book Award for *Tales of Burning Love,* 1996.

BOOKS: *Imagination* (Westerville, Ohio: Merrill, 1981);
Jacklight (New York: Holt, Rinehart & Winston, 1984; London: Abacus, 1990);

Louise Erdrich (photograph by Michael Dorris)

Love Medicine (New York: Holt, Rinehart & Winston, 1984; London: Deutsch, 1985; revised edition, New York: Holt, 1993; London: Flamingo, 1993);
The Beet Queen (New York: Holt, 1986; London: Hamilton, 1987);
Tracks (New York: Holt, 1988; London: Flamingo, 1994);
Baptism of Desire (New York: Harper & Row, 1989);
The Crown of Columbus, by Erdrich and Michael Dorris (New York: HarperCollins, 1991; London: Flamingo, 1992);
Route 2, by Erdrich and Dorris (Northridge, Cal.: Lord John, 1991);
The Bingo Palace (New York: HarperCollins, 1994; London: Flamingo, 1994);
The Blue Jay's Dance: A Birth Year (New York: HarperCollins, 1995);
Tales of Burning Love (New York: HarperCollins, 1996);
Grandmother's Pigeon (New York: Hyperion, 1996);
The Antelope Wife (New York: HarperCollins, 1998).

OTHER: "American Horse," in *Earth Power Coming: An Anthology of Native American Fiction,* edited by Simon Ortiz (Tsaile, Ariz.: Navajo Community College Press, 1984), pp. 59–72;

"Conversions," in *Day In, Day Out: Women's Lives in North Dakota,* edited by Bjorn Benson, Elizabeth Hampsten and Kathryn Sweney (Grand Forks: University of North Dakota, 1988), pp. 23–27;

Michael Dorris, *The Broken Cord: A Family's Ongoing Struggle with Fetal Alcohol Syndrome,* foreword by Erdrich (New York: Harper & Row, 1989; London: Futura, 1992);

The Best American Short Stories 1993, edited by Erdrich (Boston: Houghton Mifflin, 1993);

John Tanner, *The Falcon: A Narrative of the Captivity and Adventures of John Tanner,* introduction by Erdrich (New York: Penguin, 1994);

"The Preacher," in *Out of the Garden: Women Writers on the Bible,* edited by Christina Büchmann and Celina Spiegel (New York: Fawcett Columbine, 1994), pp. 234–237;

"Big Grass," in *Heart of the Land: Essays on Last Great Places,* edited by Joseph Barbato and Lisa Weinerman (New York: Pantheon, 1994), pp. 145–150.

SELECTED PERIODICAL PUBLICATIONS– UNCOLLECTED: "The True Story of Mustache Maude," *Frontiers,* 7 (Summer 1984): 62–67;

"Excellence Has Always Made Me Fill with Fright When It Is Demanded by Other People, But Fills Me with Pleasure When I Am Left to Practice It Alone," *Ms.,* 13 (January 1985): 84;

"Where I Ought to Be: A Writer's Sense of Place," *New York Times Book Review,* 28 July 1985, pp. 1, 23–24;

"Mister Argus," *Georgia Review,* 39 (Summer 1985): 379–390;

"Pounding the Dog," *Kenyon Review,* new series 7 (Fall 1985): 18–28;

"Who Owns the Land?" *New York Times Magazine,* 4 September 1988, pp. 32–35, 52–54, 57, 65;

"A Wedge of Shade," *New Yorker,* 65 (6 March 1989): 35–40;

"Mauser," *New Yorker,* 67 (8 April 1991): 38–42;

"Line of Credit," *Harper's,* 284 (April 1992): 55–61;

"A Woman's Work: Too Many Demands and Not Enough Selves," *Harper's,* 286 (May 1993): 35–46;

"Satan: Hijacker of a Planet," *Atlantic Monthly,* 279 (August 1997): 64–68.

The writings of Louise Erdrich not only reflect her multilayered, complex background but also con-found a variety of literary genre and cultural categories. Although she is known primarily as a successful contemporary Native American writer, Erdrich's finely polished writing reveals both her Turtle Mountain Chippewa and Euramerican heritages. Nevertheless, her diverse imageries, subjects, and textual strategies reaffirm imperatives of American Indian survival. In her essay "Where I Ought to Be: A Writer's Sense of Place" (1985) she prescribes the literary challenge for herself and other contemporary Native writers: "In the light of enormous loss, they must tell the stories of contemporary survivors while protecting and celebrating the cores of cultures left in the wake of the catastrophe."

Karen Louise Erdrich was born on 7 June 1954 in Little Falls, Minnesota, into a family of storytellers and survivors. Her mother, Rita Joanne Gourneau Erdrich, was a daughter of Turtle Mountain Chippewa tribal chair Pat Gourneau. Both her mother and her father, Ralph Erdrich, were teachers at the Indian school in Wahpeton, North Dakota, where Erdrich grew up. Mary Korll, her paternal grandmother, was of German descent and ran a butcher shop, much like Mary Adare in *The Beet Queen* (1986). Her parents' commitment to education led Erdrich to the first coeducational class at Dartmouth, where she won her first poetry prize and graduated in 1976. Also at Dartmouth, Erdrich first met Michael Dorris, then a professor of anthropology. After various jobs teaching poetry and editing a Boston Indian Council newspaper as well as earning a master's degree from Johns Hopkins University, Erdrich returned to Dartmouth in 1981 as writer-in-residence.

On 10 October 1981 Erdrich married Dorris and began a stellar literary union with a tragic end. Dorris had previously adopted three children from a reservation. After their marriage Erdrich also adopted them, and the couple later had three children of their own. Dorris's editorial suggestions helped launch Erdrich's career and led to his own literary pursuits. Their extensive writing collaboration, so close that the couple agreed on every word, went uncredited until the novel *The Crown of Columbus* (1991) and a collection of travel essays, *Route 2* (1991). Each of their books has a loving dedication to the other person: "To Michael—Complice in every word, essential as air" *(The Beet Queen)* and "For Louise—Who found the song and gave me the voice" *(Cloud Chamber,* 1997). Dorris eventually gave up his academic career to manage Erdrich's literary career and to write his own creative works. Dorris's books include two novels, *A Yellow Raft in Blue Water* (1987) and *Cloud Chamber,* both of which recount the story of a mixed African-American/American In-

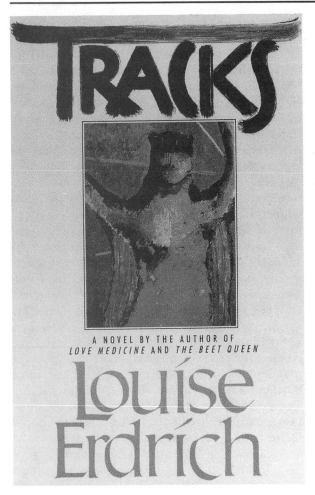

Dust jacket for Erdrich's 1988 novel, a tale of loss and survival narrated by two characters who are consummate storytellers

dian girl, Rayona, and her multigenerational family. A collection of short stories, *Working Men* (1993), has both Native and non-Native topics and characters. *Rooms in the House of Stone* (1993) recounts his humanitarian work in Africa. His influential scholarship in American Indian Studies and literary criticism was collected in *Paper Trails* (1994). Additionally, Dorris wrote several juvenile fiction books that depict events from a Native American point of view. *Morning Girl* (1992) tells the story of a young girl who meets and welcomes the 1492 Columbus expedition. *Guests* (1994) portrays a Thanksgiving feast, and *Sees Behind Trees* (1996) focuses on a blind Native youth.

Dorris chronicled the difficult life of their oldest child, Reynold Abel (called Adam in the book), in *The Broken Cord: A Family's Ongoing Struggle with Fetal Alcohol Syndrome* (1989), winner of the National Book Critics Circle Award for nonfiction. Although the book was highly praised for its compelling tragedy, it also received strong criticism for its harsh condemnation of drinking mothers. Erdrich confesses in the foreword:

love is inextricable from anger, and in loving Adam, the anger is mostly directed elsewhere, for it is impossible to love the sweetness, the inner light, the qualities that I trust in Adam, without hating the fact that he will always be kept from fully expressing those aspects of himself because of his biological mother's drinking.

When as an adult Abel was struck and killed by a car in 1991, Dorris's depressive tendencies escalated. The strain on the marriage intensified when another child was arrested in 1993 for attempting to extort money from the couple. Erdrich and Dorris separated in 1995. Two years later Dorris committed suicide.

Erdrich had made an impressive literary debut in 1982 with "The World's Greatest Fishermen," a short story that won the Nelson Algren Award. She submitted the story at Dorris's urging, writing and revising in a "barricaded" kitchen while Dorris, incapacitated with a bad back, encouraged her from the floor. The next year her story, "Scales," which incorporated her own job experience at a highway weigh station, was selected for *The Best American Short Stories 1983*. Both stories became chapters in Erdrich's stunning inaugural novel, *Love Medicine* (1984). The book received several awards, including the National Book Critics Circle Award. Although usually classified as a novel because of recurring characters and development, *Love Medicine* challenges the definition with independent nonlinear and multiple-voiced narratives. Erdrich expands the genre further with subsequent volumes that continue the story, themes, and characters: *The Beet Queen* (1986), *Tracks* (1988), *The Bingo Palace* (1994), and *Tales of Burning Love* (1996).

In 1984, the same year as *Love Medicine,* Erdrich published *Jacklight,* her first collection of poems. Most of the poems had been written in the late 1970s and without Dorris's collaborative assistance. The volume was generally well received and planted the seeds of Erdrich's later themes of "Abandonment and return. Pleasure and denial. Failure. Absurdity." The return is to tribal roots, place, and community, as with the lost Chippewa woman of "Walking in the Breakdown Lane" or the students in "Indian Boarding School: The Runaways," which won the Pushcart Prize in 1983. In this poem the escapees are running toward home, instead of away from it. Their sense of home is embedded in history, place, and traditions:

> Home's the place we head for in our sleep.
> Boxcars stumbling north in dreams
> don't wait for us. We catch them on the run.
> The rails, old lacerations that we love,
> shoot parallel across the face and break

just under Turtle Mountains. Riding scars
you can't get lost. Home is the place they cross.

The captured runaways are punished with humiliating manual labor and forced to wear green dresses. They persistently avoid the intended assimilation of the boarding school by "remembering the delicate old injuries."

"The Butcher's Wife," a section of fifteen poems in *Jacklight*, is a cycle of narratives with characters and setting that prefigure *The Beet Queen*. Many other poems in the volume are grounded in the Chippewa worldview, such as the title poem, "Jacklight," which depicts a dual hunting and flirting ritual. "Family Reunion" gathers the characters and circumstances that appear in the first chapter of *Love Medicine*. The concluding section comprises a rendering of Chippewa tales of trickster Potchikoo, forsaking poetic form for straight narrative.

After *Jacklight*, Erdrich claimed she would no longer publish poetry because the medium was too personal. Yet in 1989, after *The Beet Queen* and *Tracks*, she published a second collection, *Baptism of Desire*. Erdrich admits "most . . . poems in this book were written between the hours of two and four in the morning, a period of insomnia brought on by pregnancy." This volume continues the "Butcher's Wife" and Potchikoo cycles. The title section is a series of poems that reinterpret Catholic sacraments through Chippewa experience. A long poem at the center of the book is titled "Hydra" and incorporates imagery from Greek myth, Catholicism, popular culture, and Chippewa culture. Several reviewers suggested that Erdrich is a better storyteller than lyricist, but her poetic renderings of motherhood refute such criticism, as in "The Fence":

My body is a golden armor around my unborn child's body,
and I'll die happy, here on the ground.
I bend to the mixture of dirt, chopped hay,
grindings of coffee from our dark winter breakfasts.
I spoon the rich substance around the acid-loving shrubs.
I tear down the last year's drunken vines,
pull the black rug off the bed of asparagus
and lie there, knowing by June I'll push the baby out
as easily as seed wings fold back from the cotyledon.

Additionally, the poems in *Baptism of Desire* emphasize the intensity of spiritual experience, although not always in formal religious settings.

In anticipation of the Columbus Quincentenary, Erdrich and Dorris received an advance, reportedly more than $1 million, to write *The Crown of Columbus*. Principally narrated by Dartmouth professors Vivian Twostar, a Navajo-Coeur d'Alene, and Roger Williams, Puritan in heritage and spirit, the novel is a balancing of polar opposites. Both scholars search for the "truth" about Columbus. Vivian wishes to tell the story from a Native perspective; Roger wishes to make Columbus the hero of an epic poem. Their quests lead to love, a child, and a mystery plot that is resolved by a startling discovery.

Dorris originally conceived the character of the female professor, who, although he denied the autobiographical roots, shares such personal similarities with Dorris as being an Indian academic and a person of mixed blood. Vivian says: "I belong to the lost tribe of mixed bloods, that hodgepodge amalgam of hue and cry that defies easy placement . . . . 'Caught between two worlds,' is the way we're often characterized, but I'd put it differently. We are the *catch*." While Erdrich stated in a 29 April 1991 interview on the *Today* show that she researched the diaries of Columbus for the historical details in the plot, neither would take credit for specific passages, declaring that the novel was a complete collaboration. The crying infant, Violet, whose voice inhabits the background of the novel, was not unlike their own squalling child during the writing of the book. Together Erdrich and Dorris created characters who cross the boundaries of race, gender, religions, histories, and cultures to find their own human treasure.

Although the novel was widely criticized in reviews for its adventure plot and less-than-literary language, it became a best-seller. Such criticism generally overlooks the subtleties about urban professional Indians in the novel as well as such bold gestures as having Roger recite his epic Columbus poem at the climax of the story. In one of the few scholarly treatments of the book (in the *North Dakota Quarterly*, 1991), Thomas Matchie discusses Erdrich and Dorris's metaphor of discovery.

In *The Blue Jay's Dance: A Birth Year* (1995) Erdrich continued to reveal intimate aspects of her life and marriage. In this well-received memoir she details how she juggles her various responsibilities as wife, mother, and writer, and how those roles overlap. As she describes her writing process, she observes with poignancy (and with the lyrical detail of her fiction) the natural world around her. Although this narrative is self-revealing and includes private details, such as Dorris's thick hair and an intense range of emotional responses to a colicky baby, Erdrich preserves the anonymity of her three daughters by combining their identities into one representative infant and by never naming them. Lovingly written, the book echoes the themes in her fiction of survival and continuity and spans generations through recollections of Erdrich's grandparents.

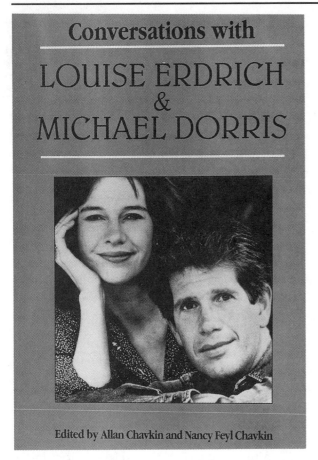

Conversations with
LOUISE ERDRICH
&
MICHAEL DORRIS

Edited by Allan Chavkin and Nancy Feyl Chavkin

*Dust jacket for a 1994 collection of interviews in which Erdrich
and her husband discuss their creative processes*

The "birth year" is divided according to the seasons and the development of mother and child. As the representative baby grows, Erdrich integrates her into the wider experiences of environment and family. Again expanding genre, Erdrich includes anecdotes, reminiscences, and recipes such as those used in an all-licorice dinner Dorris cooked to "saturate the senses." At the end of her first year, the infant is prepared gradually to spend some time outside the home with a caregiver: "As our baby grows more into her own life, so I recover mine, but it is an ambiguous blessing. With one hand I drag the pen across the page and with the other, the other hand, I cannot let go of hers." Yet Erdrich relinquishes her child to a new cycle of life.

Just as *The Blue Jay's Dance* is a cyclical telling of Erdrich's life with her infants, so the North Dakota cycle of novels is a fictive telling of twentieth-century Chippewa life. Epic in scope, *Love Medicine, The Beet Queen, Tracks, The Bingo Palace,* and *Tales of Burning Love* continue characters and themes, yet shift in narrative styles, overlap chronologically, and present a holistic view of modern American experience, both Indian and non-Indian. While some

characters are unforgettable, a lack of emphasis on a singular hero or heroine, together with the multiple narrators, establishes the communal voice as the protagonist in the series. These books, according to Thomas Disch (reviewing *Tracks* for the *Chicago Tribune,* 4 September 1988), create "a North Dakota of the imagination that, like Faulkner's Yoknapatawpha County, unites the archetypal and the arcane, heartland America and borderline schizophrenia." This inextricable connection between identity and place for both the Native and non-Native characters permeates these novels.

Although published third in the sequence, *Tracks* was conceived first and begins the saga of tribal endurance by chronicling events from 1912 through 1924. The harrowing story of land loss and cultural negotiation is placed around Matchimanito Lake. The narration unfolds alternately between Nanapush, a characterization of the Chippewa trickster *Nanabozho,* and Pauline Puyat. Both are consummate storytellers: Nanapush focuses on tribal strength and survival and directs his narrative toward Lulu Nanapush Lamartine, who inherits his name and spirit if not his genes; Pauline, however, is desperately trying to escape her mixed-blood confusion. Neither is a reliable narrator and each underscores the transmutability of perception and truth. Without her own narrative voice, but nonetheless a central presence, is the mythic Fleur Pillager, who repeatedly defies death.

With tragic allusions to Leslie Fiedler's concept of the Vanishing American, *Tracks* begins as Nanapush rescues Fleur from an influenza epidemic: "We started dying before the snow, and like the snow, we continued to fall. It was surprising there were so many of us left to die." Yet his story is of physical and cultural survival. As Nanapush hurriedly cares for the bodies of the dead, he must abbreviate the traditional mourning rituals. Such a gesture does not indicate a tragic loss of culture but a melding of pragmatism and redefining of Chippewa practices. In the second chapter, titled "Fleur," Pauline tells of Fleur's off-reservation survival against lecherous poker partners in the town of Argus. Inadvertently Pauline also reveals her own puerile voyeurism.

Although Nanapush is the traditionalist, guiding the last buffalo hunt and seeing the last bear shot, he recognizes the changes that must be made to preserve his people. Often he seems powerless to act, such as when he is unable to protect Margaret Kashpaw from the shears of Boy Lazarre and Clarence Morrissey. Nanapush overcomes his impotency through tricksterism and storytelling, as James Flavin notes in his discussion of performance and Erdrich's storytelling. Though instructing Fleur's daughter, Lulu, in the oral tradition, Nanapush acknowledges the power of literacy and the political power that comes from being tribal chair, much as Erdrich expresses indigenous orality through the literary novelistic tradition of Western civilization.

Pauline vainly grasps for acceptance through her outrageous stories and ritual manipulations. She appears to lose herself to the forces of the dominant culture by denying her Indianness in order to become a nun. Although critics Daniel Cornell and Lee Schweninger try to psychoanalyze Pauline in feminist terms, Sidner Larson is more sympathetic to her mixed-blood dilemma. Despite her extreme behaviors and self-mortifications, she will survive, transformed as Sister Leopolda, and appear in each subsequent novel through *Tales of Burning Love*.

The action centers around Fleur and her natural, mystical powers. According to Pauline, Fleur exacted nature's revenge upon her poker partners and rapists. Annette Van Dyke examines the power of the water monster, Missepeshu, rumored to be the father of Fleur's daughter, Lulu. Fleur endures the loss of a second child, but she cannot abide the loss of her land. Nanapush's parting description, like so many of Erdrich's characterizations, renders Fleur's indelible strength:

> Her black skirt and red blouse were worn so sheer that they clung like vapor to her breasts and waist, tied up with strips of floursacking. Her hair was thick, full of lights, falling in a wide arc. She wore no jewelry or feathers. Her legs were bare, her best moccasins, quilled in yellow swirls and flowers, were on her feet.

She cannot leave, however, without dispatching a destructive wind or without collecting emblems of her life in a small cart. Her figure and the cart become a recurring image in the later novels. Like Fleur, Pauline (as Sister Leopolda), Moses Pillager, Margaret (Rushes Bear) Kashpaw and her sons, Eli and Nector, appear in other novels as well.

Much of the critical response to this best-seller has focused on the historical aspects of *Tracks* and discusses colonial land-grabs and language mediations. James D. Stripes and Native critics Larson and Gloria Bird have challenged Erdrich's version of Chippewa history, while Nancy Peterson posits that Erdrich has written her own Chippewa counterhistory. Published independently, the second chapter, "Fleur," won an O. Henry Award in 1987. Despite the seemingly tragic denouement of *Tracks*, with loss of life, land, and place, the novel is a compelling story of Native survival.

The Beet Queen returns to the small town of Argus, North Dakota, and jumps ahead to events occurring between 1932 and 1972. In addition to several first-person narrators, Erdrich includes a third-person omniscient narrator to clarify and summarize. The novel begins and ends with images of airplanes. In an early episode, Adelaide Adare flies away with a barnstorming pilot, abandoning her three children, Karl, Mary, and their infant brother. The novel concludes with Adelaide's granddaughter, Dot, flying and being tempted by the same escape, yet returning to the familiar comfort of Argus.

The cast of characters is an array of displaced non-Indian and Chippewa individuals without binding tribal traditions. All are off-center, or as Gretchen M. Bataille suggests, literary grotesques: Chippewas Russell Kashpaw (confined to a wheelchair) and Celestine James are separated from the community by race; Mary Adare is obsessed with spiritualism and visually notable because of her squat physique; and her cousin Sita Kozka is psychotic. Karl Adare is bisexual and, with Celestine, fathers Wallacette, also known as Dot. Beet baron Wallace Pfef is a closet homosexual who acts paternally toward Dot. Because no adult character is "normal" and no "stable" traditional family structure exists, Erdrich extends the bounds of acceptability to the whole community, creating an environment of diversity which allows the characters to bond with one another despite traditional prejudices and barriers. Unity amid such diversity is furthered by their collective and individual interest in Dot.

Erdrich's sense of absurdity, strongly evident in this novel, suggests the heritage of a trickster worldview. The humor ranges from slapstick (with a spinning birthday cake) to black comedy (with a nearly dead Indian and really dead woman on parade). In an interview included in *Conversations with Louise Erdrich and Michael Dorris* (1994), Erdrich admits that an episode in which Dot is placed in the school naughty-box is autobiographical. Skillfully told, the comic events become survival mechanisms in bleak circumstances.

Although *The Beet Queen* was nominated for the National Book Critics Circle Award, Erdrich received harsh personal criticism from renowned Laguna writer Leslie Marmon Silko. Silko complained that the novel and Erdrich were not Indian enough and called the book a "strange artifact" that belonged on the shelf with fairy tales. Gerald Vizenor, Chippewa critic and author, defended Erdrich's style and content as postmodern. In an interview included in *Conversations with Louise Erdrich and Michael Dorris*, Erdrich graciously excused Silko for not reading the book carefully and for assuming that the

Dust jacket for Erdrich's 1996 story for children, which teaches that "nature is both tough and fragile"

German and Polish characters were Indians. Despite the number of non-Indian characters, the book centers on the mixed-bloods Celestine and Dot, whose thoughts of her mother close the book:

> I want to lean into her the way wheat leans into the wind. . . . It flows through the screens, slams doors, fills the curtains like sails, floods the dark house with the smell of dirt and water, the smell of rain. I breathe it in, and I think of her lying in the next room, her covers thrown back too, eyes wide open, waiting.

Published first, *Love Medicine* is the most complex of the North Dakota novels. Though the opening chapter sets the time as 1981, the narratives circle back to 1934. These stories depict contemporary reservation life with its grim realities and joys: alcoholism, suicide, abandoned children, and disrupted relationships as well as continuity in extended families, new life, escapes, and humor. The love medicine of the title heals and offers hope and forgiveness.

In this novel Erdrich established narrative techniques to which she returned in the subsequent books. As in William Faulkner's *As I Lay Dying* (1930), multiple narrators tell their stories, yet each voice remains distinct. Rather than emphasizing individualistic quests, the solo voices create a chorus of tribal storytelling. Both Julie Maristuen-Rodakowski and Margie Towery have attempted to construct family trees to illustrate the complex relationships among the many characters. Three of the principal characters—Marie Lazarre, Nector Kashpaw, and Lulu Lamartine—originated in *Tracks,* and as their adult lives intertwine in *Love Medicine,* they create ties to the future.

Marie Lazarre Kashpaw is the maternal center of the novel. She opens her home to abandoned children, including June Morrissey and her son, Lipsha. She understands the power of compassion and forgiveness. The daughter of Pauline, she unknowingly battles her mother in the convent: "But I wanted Sister Leopolda's heart. And here was the thing: sometimes I wanted her heart in love and admiration. Sometimes. And sometimes I wanted her heart to roast on a black stick." She absolves her husband, Nector, even after he had fully intended to leave her for Lulu: "So I did for Nector Kashpaw what I learned from the nun. I put my hand through what scared him. I held it out there for him. And when he took it with all the strength of his arms, I pulled him in." She even reconciles with Lulu after Nector's death.

Nector is torn between women and cultures. As a young man he sought his fortune in popular media, playing an extra in movies as a dying Indian and posing for an artist's rendering of the noble savage. Yet he returns to the reservation and eventually becomes tribal chair. He sees himself simultaneously as Ishmael and Ahab from Herman Melville's *Moby-Dick* (1851), an allusion that Matchie expands in analyzing Erdrich's style (*Midwest Quarterly*, 1989). Nector yells his prayers in church so the Christian God might hear him. Like the pair of wild geese he carries when he meets young Marie, they will mate for life. Still, he is always drawn to Lulu. Although he dies in a tragic misapplication of Chippewa love medicine, by choking on turkey hearts, his entrepreneurial legacy will live on through his and Lulu's son, Lyman Lamartine.

Lulu bequeaths her trickster heritage to another son, Gerry Nanapush, and her grandson, Lipsha Morrissey. She has eight children by eight men, a fact she uses to her political advantage when her home is endangered and she threatens to reveal the names of the fathers in a public meeting. While Marie extends community beyond bloodlines, Lulu unmasks the genetic ties. She reveals to Lipsha his true parentage, thus giving him a place in the community and a connection to Gerry Nanapush that will extend through the next novels.

Tracing the Chippewa image of the trickster in *Love Medicine* and *Tracks,* Catherine M. Catt shows how, along with Nanapush from *Tracks,* Gerry Nanapush is an obvious trickster manifestation. Falsely imprisoned, Gerry escapes. He frequently disappears, often depicted with the imagery of a rabbit (the Chippewa incarnation of trickster), but he is eventually caught. He has a relationship with Dot Adare, who gives birth to their daughter, Shawn. In the last chapter he and his son, Lipsha, are on the run for the Canadian border. In addition to these direct trickster references, *Love Medicine,* like the other novels, reflects a playful trickster heritage.

The chapter titles in *Love Medicine,* from "The World's Greatest Fishermen," "Saint Marie," and "The Beads," to "Flesh and Blood," "Crown of Thorns," and "Resurrection," reveal a Catholic undercurrent and suggest religious mediations between Native and Christian cultures. However, Erdrich, who was raised Catholic, privileges Chippewa tradition through the voice of Lipsha: "Now there's your God in the Old Testament and there is Chippewa Gods as well. . . . Our Gods aren't perfect, is what I'm saying, but at least they come around."

In 1993 Erdrich revised the already successful *Love Medicine,* adding material, a daring act which shows that storytelling is a living tradition. The new sections include a passage on childbirth, added after Erdrich had experienced the birth of her own children. The expanded material also more clearly links *Love Medicine* to the other novels in the series.

Early literary criticisms of *Love Medicine* addressed thematic elements, narrative strategies, and structural readings of Chippewa culture. Louis Owens offers the strongest interpretations of contemporary American Indian experience: "The seemingly doomed Indian[s] . . . hang on in spite of it all, confront with humor the pain and confusion of identity and, like a storyteller, weave a fabric of meaning and significance out of the remnants."

The Bingo Palace (1994) originated, Erdrich confessed in an interview included in *Conversations with Louise Erdrich and Michael Dorris,* from her "consistent failure to break even at the black jack tables." Erdrich continues to probe modern reservation issues, this time including tribal gaming and the powwow circuit. There are fewer characters in this novel, as Lipsha Morrissey, Lyman Lamartine, and their object of desire, Shawnee Ray Toose, take center stage.

Lyman develops his business talents, first in a tomahawk factory in *Love Medicine*—a manufacturing enterprise that produces museum-quality Indian artifacts—then with Indian gaming. The narrative voice describes the collective perception of Lyman:

> Here was a man everybody knew and yet did not know, a dark-minded schemer, a bitter and yet shaman-pleasant entrepreneur who skipped money from behind the ears of Uncle Sam, who joked to pull the wool down, who carved up this reservation the way his blood father Nector Kashpaw did, who had his own interest so mingled with his people's that he couldn't tell his personal ambition from the pride of the Kashpaws.

Lyman's systematic approach to success is virtually opposite to Lipsha's, who relies on luck and the spiritual guidance of his dead mother, June Morris-

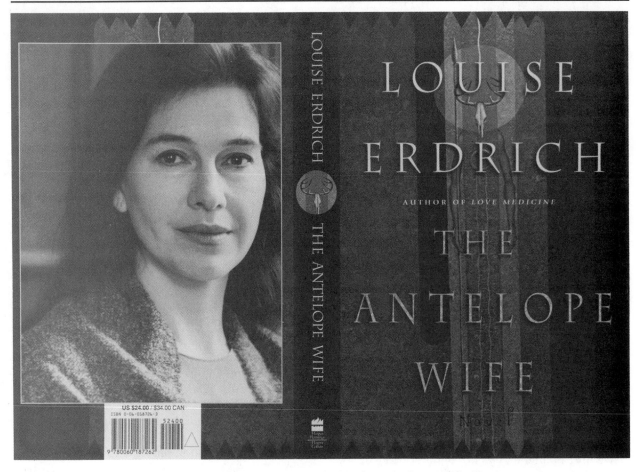

Dust jacket for Erdrich's 1998 novel, about love, marriage, and families

sey. Lipsha's luck pays off and he wins a bingo van, an emblem of material comfort: "a starter home, a portable den with front-wheel drive . . . a four wheeled version of North Dakota." Nevertheless, his good fortune does not last and he loses the van, along with his pride. Lipsha's stream-of-consciousness narration extends back to the elements and images of *Tracks,* and especially to Fleur Pillager.

Powwow dancer Shawnee Ray is a new character. Young, a single mother of Lyman's child and hopelessly attracted to Lipsha, she gracefully dances through their lives, teasing as she tries to carve her own future as a clothes designer. Shawnee Ray is contrasted by Albertine, whose character drifted in *Love Medicine,* but who is now a medical student. Much as Lyman and Lipsha are opposites, so Shawnee Ray and Albertine have varying and contrasting responses to their circumstances.

While the younger characters play out their lives, the backdrop is inhabited by the matriarchs Lulu Lamartine, Zelda Kashpaw, Fleur Pillager, and a new character, Josette Bizhieu, who may be the Jo-

sette from the Potchikoo stories. As the book opens, Lulu mails Lipsha a photocopy of Gerry's "Wanted" poster from the post office and takes home the original to frame. At the end of the book, she has returned to tribal traditions and is being led off by federal marshals. Lipsha is distracted from Shawnee Ray when he embarks once again on an escape adventure with his father, Gerry. Erdrich leaves the fate of Lipsha and Gerry ambiguous, stranded in a blizzard and being led by the spirit of June. Although the language is similar to the opening scene of *Love Medicine,* where June wanders off into the snow to freeze to death, Erdrich's theme of survival suggests that Lipsha and Gerry will not perish, as *Tales of Burning Love* confirms.

Not all characters can live forever, though. Fleur makes her final appearance, not necessarily dying but disappearing and transforming:

And yet on clear and brilliant days and nights of black stars they are sometimes again left among us, Fleur's tracks, once more, so it is said that she still walks. . . . For that day we heard the voices, the trills and resounding cries that greeted the old woman when she arrived

52

on the pine-dark island, and all night our lesser hearts beat to the sound of the spirit's drum, through those anxious hours when we call our lives to question.

Most reviewers suggested that *The Bingo Palace* did not explore new territory as the other novels had. Still, Erdrich continued to reap praises for her lyrical writing. Reviewers overlooked Erdrich's introduction of a first-person plural narrative voice. The tribal "we" becomes more than a chorus of simple observers or reporters as they encourage action and respond emotionally. When Lulu is arrested, for example, the narrative voice comments, "We told her, we reminded her that she'd done wrong. . . . What can we do? Drawing deep breaths, hearts shaking, we can't help join her."

In *Tales of Burning Love,* as with *The Beet Queen,* Erdrich seems to move off-reservation. However, the central character, Jack Mauser, is a mixed-blood Chippewa whom Lyman Lamartine rescues by returning him to tribal enterprises. Jack has been married at least four times, and after a funeral service for his faked death, the surviving wives are snowbound together. In the grand literary traditions of talespinning and in Native traditions of sacred recitations only in winter, they take turns storytelling to preserve their lives and to pass the time through the freezing night. Dot Adare Nanapush Mauser, Jack's current wife, whom he married to prevent her testimony against him in a fraud case, sets the parameters:

> Rule one . . . No shutting up until dawn. Rule two. Tell a true story. Rule three. The story has to be about you. Something that you've never told another soul, a story that would scorch paper, heat up the air!

Each wife tells of her differing relationship with Jack. In the beginning of the novel, Jack appears to be a scoundrel, yet as the wives reconstruct his life, he emerges as a complex human being. Each storyteller is self-revealing, discovering a little of herself as well as her life with Jack. Eleanor is a college professor, self-exiled to a convent after seducing a student. Candice is a dentist; Marlis has Jack's child; and these two women find love with each other. All of the women form a bond and are rescued in conjunction with the surprising appearance of Gerry and Lipsha. As usual, the novel garnered praise for Erdrich's eloquent style. It also won the 1996 Minnesota Book Award.

Erdrich and Dorris planned the North Dakota novels to be elemental: *Tracks* represents the earth; images of air elevate *The Beet Queen; Love Medicine* has watery baptisms and drownings; *The Bingo Palace* is illuminated with images of light; and *Tales of*

Burning Love has incendiary relationships. Characters recur in surprising ways when different narrators recount the same events from varying points of view. Although some characters, such as June Morrissey, perish, they keep living through storytelling or mythic appearance. Others, such as Nanapush, Lulu, Gerry Nanapush, and Lipsha Morrissey, survive through trickster escapades. Fleur has a continuing presence of power, while Pauline/Sister Leopolda maintains her perversions until her demise in *Tales of Burning Love.* While each novel features the death of a significant character, the survivors triumph. Nonlinear narratives represent mythic time, and all events are bound by the land, whether through its loss in *Tracks,* the fields of *The Beet Queen,* or the consuming blizzards in *Love Medicine, The Bingo Palace,* and *Tales of Burning Love.*

Erdrich's cycle of North Dakota novels is an extraordinary achievement. She has paradoxically created a Chippewa experience in the context of the Euramerican novelistic tradition. Yet she bends that tradition within the scope of storytelling, overlapping temporal and narrative techniques. Complemented by her other writings, the novels comprise an already significant career.

Grandmother's Pigeon (1996) is Erdrich's venture into storytelling for children. She dedicates the book to her daughter: "Gallant, funny, kind and always living the mystery—Love, Mom." A picture book, illustrated by Jim Lamarche, *Grandmother's Pigeon* tells the story of a family whose grandmother has hitched a ride to Greenland on the back of a porpoise. In her room she has left behind treasures, including three pigeon eggs. The eggs hatch, revealing passenger pigeons previously believed to be extinct. After excessive media and scientific attention, the children release the pigeons to nature, and the birds track down the missing grandmother. Erdrich explicitly states the moral of the story: "The lesson they teach is this—nature is both tough and fragile." The same could be said of Erdrich's finely crafted characters, of her language, and of her own life—tough yet fragile.

The toughness and survival emerge in *The Antelope Wife* (1998), the first novel published after Dorris's death. The prefatory note indicates: "This book was written before the death of my husband. He is remembered with love by all of his family." Erdrich departs from her familiar cast of North Dakota characters, yet with a typically complex narration and eloquence of language she creates a new community of Ojibwa survivors, urban Indians in Minneapolis. The Roy families and Shawano families intricately interweave histories, desires, and survivals. Among the narrators is Almost Soup, a clever windigo dog. Central nourishing metaphors of beadworking and cooking blend consuming and destructive loves. Tales of obsessive marriage between Rozin Roy and Richard Whiteheart Beads and of Richard's subsequent suicide in *The Antelope Wife* tempt comparisons with the drama of Erdrich's own life with Dorris. However, as Michiko Kakutani noted in *The New York Times Book Review* (23 March 1998), "The point is not that Ms. Erdrich's fiction, like that of many writers, mirrors some of her own experiences; the point is that *The Antelope Wife* stands as one of her most powerful and fully imagined novels yet."

Interviews:

Kay Bonetti, "An Interview with Louise Erdrich and Michael Dorris," *Missouri Review*, 11 (1988): 79–99;

Jan George, "An Interview with Louise Erdrich," *North Dakota Quarterly*, 56 (Winter 1988): 240–247;

Bill Moyers, "Louise Erdrich and Michael Dorris," *A World of Ideas,* videotape, Public Affairs Television, 1988;

Paul Bailey, "Louise Erdrich and Michael Dorris," *Roland Collection of Films on Art,* videotape, ICA Video, 1989;

Allan Chavkin and Nancy Feyl Chavkin, eds., *Conversations with Louise Erdrich and Michael Dorris* (Jackson: University of Mississippi Press, 1994).

Bibliographies:

"Louise Erdrich: A.S.A.I.L. Bibliography," *Studies in American Indian Literatures: Newsletter, Association for the Study of American Indian Literatures,* 9 (Winter 1985): 37–41;

Lillian Brewington, Normie Bullard, and Robert W. Reising, comps., "Writing in Love: An Annotated Bibliography of Critical Responses to the Poetry and Novels of Louise Erdrich and Michael Dorris," *American Indian Culture and Research Journal,* 10, no. 4 (1986): 81–86;

Mickey Pearlman, "A Bibliography of Writings by Louise Erdrich," in *American Women Writing Fiction,* edited by Pearlman (Lexington: University Press of Kentucky, 1989), pp. 108–112;

Debra A. Burdick, "Louise Erdrich's *Love Medicine, The Beet Queen,* and *Tracks:* An Annotated Survey of Criticism through 1994," *American Indian Culture and Research Journal,* 20, no. 3 (1996): 137–166.

References:

Gretchen M. Bataille, "Louise Erdrich's *The Beet Queen:* Images of the Grotesque on the Northern Plains," in *Critical Perspectives on Native American Fiction,* edited by Richard F. Fleck (Washington, D.C.: Three Continents, 1993), pp. 277–285;

Gloria Bird, "Searching for Evidence of Colonialism at Work: A Reading of Louise Erdrich's *Tracks,*" *Wicazo Sa Review: A Journal of Indian Studies,* 8 (Fall 1992): 40–47;

Susan Pérez Castillo, "Postmodernism, Native American Literature and the Real: The Silko-Erdrich Controversy," *Massachusetts Review,* 32 (Summer 1991): 285–294;

Catherine M. Catt, "Ancient Myth in Modern America: The Trickster in the Fiction of Louise Erdrich," *Platte Valley Review,* 19 (Winter 1991): 71–81;

Daniel Cornell, "Woman Looking: Revis(ion)ing Pauline's Subject Position in Louise Erdrich's *Tracks,*" *Studies in American Indian Literatures,* 4 (Spring 1992): 49–64;

James Flavin, "The Novel as Performance: Communication in Louise Erdrich's *Tracks,*" *Studies in American Indian Literatures,* 3 (Winter 1991): 1–12;

P. Jane Hafen, "Sacramental Language: Ritual in the Poetry of Louise Erdrich," *Great Plains Quarterly,* 16 (Summer 1996): 147–157;

Ellen Lansky, "Spirits and Salvation in Louise Erdrich's *Love Medicine,*" *Dionysos: The Literature and Addiction Tri-Quarterly,* 5 (Winter 1994): 39–44;

Sidner Larson, "The Fragmentation of a Tribal People in Louise Erdrich's *Tracks,*" *American Indian Culture and Research Journal,* 17, no. 2 (1993): 1–13;

Julie Maristuen-Rodakowski, "The Turtle Mountain Reservation in North Dakota: Its History As Depicted in Louise Erdrich's *Love Medicine* and *Beet Queen,*" *American Indian Culture and Research Journal,* 12, no. 3 (1988): 33–48;

Thomas Matchie, "Exploring the Meaning of Discovery in *The Crown of Columbus,*" *North Dakota Quarterly,* 59 (Spring 1991): 243–250;

Matchie, "*Love Medicine*: A Female *Moby-Dick,*" *Midwest Quarterly,* 30 (Summer 1989): 478–491;

James McKenzie, "Lipsha's Good Road Home: The Revival of Chippewa Culture in *Love Medicine,*" *American Indian Culture and Research Journal,* 10, no. 3 (1986): 53–63;

Louis Owens, *Other Destinies: Understanding the American Indian Novel,* edited by Gerald Vizenor, American Indian Literature and Critical Studies Series, volume 3 (Norman: University of Oklahoma Press, 1992), pp. 192–224;

Nancy Peterson, "History, Postmodernism, and Louise Erdrich's *Tracks*," *PMLA*, 109 (October 1994): 982–994;

Catherine Rainwater, "Reading between Worlds: Narrativity in the Fiction of Louise Erdrich," *American Literature*, 62 (September 1990): 405–422;

Greg Sarris, "Reading Louise Erdrich: *Love Medicine* as Home Medicine," in his *Keeping Slug Woman Alive: A Holistic Approach to American Indian Texts* (Berkeley: University of California Press, 1993), pp. 115–145;

Lissa Schneider, "*Love Medicine:* A Metaphor for Forgiveness," *Studies in American Indian Literatures,* 4 (Spring 1992): 1–13;

Lydia A. Schultz, "Fragments and Ojibwe Stories: Narrative Strategies in Louise Erdrich's *Love Medicine,*" *College Literature,* 18 (October 1991): 80–95;

Lee Schweninger, "A Skin of Lakeweed: An Ecofeminist Approach to Erdrich and Silko," in *Multicultural Literatures through Feminist/Poststructuralist Lenses,* edited by Barbara Frey Waxman (Knoxville: University of Tennessee Press, 1993), pp. 37–56;

Robert Silberman, "Opening the Text: *Love Medicine* and the Return of the Native American Woman," in *Narrative Chance: Postmodern Discourse on Native American Indian Literatures,* edited by Gerald Vizenor (Albuquerque: University of New Mexico Press, 1989), pp. 101–120;

Leslie Marmon Silko, "Here's an Odd Artifact for the Fairy-Tale Shelf," *Studies in American Indian Literatures,* 10 (Fall 1986): 177–184;

Jeanne Smith, "Transpersonal Selfhood: The Boundaries of Identity in Louise Erdrich's *Love Medicine,*" *Studies in American Indian Literatures,* 3 (Winter 1991): 13–26;

James D. Stripes, "The Problem(s) of (Anishinaabe) History in the Fiction of Louise Erdrich: Voices and Contexts," *Wicazo Sa Review: A Journal of Indian Studies,* 7 (Fall 1991): 26–33;

Margie Towery, "Continuity and Connection: Characters in Louise Erdrich's Fiction," *American Indian Culture and Research Journal,* 16, no. 4 (1992): 99–122;

Annette Van Dyke, "Questions of the Spirit: Bloodlines in Louise Erdrich's Chippewa Landscape," *Studies in American Indian Literatures,* 4 (Spring 1992): 15–27;

Gerald Vizenor, "Introduction," in *Narrative Chance: Postmodern Discourse on Native American Indian Literatures,* edited by Vizenor (Albuquerque: University of New Mexico Press, 1989).

John Gardner

This entry was updated from the entries by David Cowart (University of South Carolina)
in DLB 2: American Novelists Since World War II, First Series,
and by Carol A. MacCurdy (University of Southwestern Louisiana)
in DLB Yearbook 1982.

BIRTH: Batavia, New York, 21 July 1933, to John Champlin and Priscilla Jones Gardner.

EDUCATION: DePauw University, 1951–1953; A.B., Washington University, St. Louis, 1955; M.A., State University of Iowa, 1956; Ph.D., State University of Iowa, 1958.

MARRIAGES: 6 June 1953, Joan Louise Patterson (divorced 1976); children: Joel, Lucy; 1980, Liz Rosenberg (divorced).

AWARDS AND HONORS: Woodrow Wilson Fellowship, 1955–1956; Danforth Fellowship, 1972–1973; Guggenheim Fellowship, 1973–1974; National Education Association Award, 1972; *Grendel* named one of the best fiction books by *Time* and *Newsweek,* 1971; *October Light* named one of the ten best books of 1976 by *Time* and *The New York Times;* National Book Critics Circle Award for fiction for *October Light,* 1976; Armstrong Prize for *The Temptation Game,* 1980.

DEATH: Susquehanna, Pennsylvania, 14 September 1982.

BOOKS: *The Forms of Fiction,* by Gardner and Lennis Dunlap (New York: Random House, 1962);
The Resurrection (New York: New American Library, 1966);
The Gawain-Poet: Notes (Lincoln, Neb.: Cliff's Notes, 1967);
Le Morte DArthur: Notes (Lincoln, Neb.: Cliff's Notes, 1967);
The Wreckage of Agathon (New York: Harper & Row, 1970);
Grendel (New York: Knopf, 1971; London: Deutsch, 1972);
The Sunlight Dialogues (New York: Knopf, 1972; London: Cape, 1973);
Jason and Medeia (New York: Knopf, 1973);
Nickel Mountain (New York: Knopf, 1973; London: Cape, 1974);

John Gardner (photograph by Joel Gardner)

The King's Indian Stories and Tales (New York: Knopf, 1974; London: Cape, 1975);
The Construction of the Wakefield Cycle (Carbondale: Southern Illinois University Press, 1974; London & Amsterdam: Feffer & Simons, 1974);
The Construction of Christian Poetry in Old English (Carbondale: Southern Illinois University Press, 1975; London & Amsterdam: Feffer & Simons, 1975);
Dragon, Dragon and Other Tales (New York: Knopf, 1975);
Gudgekin the Thistle Girl and Other Tales (New York: Knopf, 1976);
October Light (New York: Knopf, 1976; London: Cape, 1977);
The Poetry of Chaucer (Carbondale: Southern Illinois University Press, 1977; London & Amsterdam: Feffer & Simons, 1977);
The Life & Times of Chaucer (New York: Knopf, 1977);
The King of the Hummingbirds and Other Tales (New York: Knopf, 1977);

A Child's Bestiary, with Lucy Gardner and Eugene Rudzewicz (New York: Knopf, 1977);

In the Suicide Mountains (New York: Knopf, 1977);

On Moral Fiction (New York: Basic Books, 1978);

Poems (Northridge, Cal.: Lord John, 1978);

Rumpelstiltskin (Dallas: New London, 1979);

Frankenstein (Dallas: New London, 1979);

William Wilson (Dallas: New London, 1979);

Vlemk the Box-Painter (Northridge, Cal.: Lord John, 1979);

Freddy's Book (New York: Knopf, 1980; London: Secker & Warburg, 1981);

The Temptation Game (Dallas: New London, 1980);

The Art of Living and Other Stories (New York: Knopf, 1981);

Death and the Maiden (Dallas: New London, 1981);

Mickelsson's Ghosts (New York: Knopf, 1982);

On Becoming a Novelist (New York & London: Harper & Row, 1983);

The Art of Fiction: Notes on Craft for Young Writers (New York: Knopf, 1984);

Stillness and Shadows, edited by Nicholas Delbanco (New York: Knopf, 1986; London: Secker & Warburg, 1987).

OTHER: *Papers on the Art and Age of Geoffrey Chaucer, Papers on Language and Literature, III,* edited by Gardner (Summer 1967);

MSS: A Retrospective, edited by Gardner and L. M. Rosenberg (Dallas: New London, 1980);

The Best American Short Stories 1982, edited by Gardner and Shannon Ravenel, introduction by Gardner (Boston: Houghton Mifflin, 1982).

TRANSLATIONS: *The Complete Works of the Gawain-Poet,* translated by Gardner (Chicago & London: University of Chicago Press, 1965);

The Alliterative Morte Arthure, translated by Gardner (Carbondale: Southern Illinois University Press, 1971; London & Amsterdam: Feffer & Simons, 1971);

Tengu Child: Stories by Kikuo Itaya, edited and translated by Gardner and Nobuko Tsukui (Carbondale & Edwardsville: Southern Illinois University Press, 1983);

Gilgamesh, edited and translated by Gardner and John Maier (New York: Knopf, 1984).

SELECTED PERIODICAL PUBLICATIONS—UNCOLLECTED:

FICTION

"The Music Lover," *Antaeus: Special Fiction Issue,* edited by Caniel Halpern, no. 13-14 (Spring-Summer 1974): 176-182;

"Trumpeter," *Esquire,* 86 (December 1976): 114-116, 182;

"Redemption," *Atlantic Monthly,* 239 (May 1977): 48-50, 55-56, 58-59;

"Stillness," *Hudson Review,* 30 (Winter 1977-1978): 549-559;

"Nimran," *Atlantic Monthly,* 244 (September 1979): 39-48;

"Come on Back," *Atlantic Monthly,* 24 (March 1981): 52.

NONFICTION

"The Way We Write Now," *New York Times Book Review,* 9 July 1972, pp. 2, 32-33;

"Moral Fiction," *Hudson Review,* 29 (Winter 1976-1977): 497-512;

"The Quest for the Philosophical Novel," review of *Lancelot* by Walker Percy, *New York Review of Books,* 20 February 1977, pp. 1, 16, 20;

"The Idea of Moral Criticism," *Western Humanities Review,* 31 (Spring 1977): 97-109;

"Death by Art; or, 'Some Men Kill You with a Six-Gun, Some Men with a Pen,'" *Critical Inquiry,* 3 (Summer 1977): 741-774;

"Moral Fiction," *Saturday Review,* 5 (1 April 1978): 29-30, 32-33;

"A Novel of Evil," review of *Sophie's Choice* by William Styron, *New York Times Book Review,* 27 May 1979, pp. 1, 16-17;

"What Johnny Can't Read," *Saturday Review,* 7 (1 March 1980): 35-37.

John Champlin Gardner Jr.—novelist, epic poet, and scholar—was born in Batavia, New York, on 21 July 1933 to John Champlin and Priscilla Jones Gardner. As a boy he lived in Batavia, attended the local schools, and worked on his father's farm. His mother was an English teacher, and his father, a lay preacher, had read deeply in the Bible and in Shakespeare; consequently their son was sensitive to language from the first. "Half-Welsh," he was also sensitive to music and grew up singing in various choirs. On excursions to nearby Rochester for concerts and opera he cultivated a taste for serious music, and on Saturdays his father gave him and the other hands the afternoon off to listen to the Metropolitan Opera broadcasts. Gardner loved opera enough to insult people who said they did not, and among his many literary productions were libretti for two operas by Joe Baber: *Frankenstein* (1979) and *Rumpelstiltskin* (1979).

In school he felt drawn to chemistry but did not care for the laboratory. Noticing that he always got A's in English, he decided that was his field. He attended DePauw University from 1951 to 1953, the year in which, a month shy of his twentieth

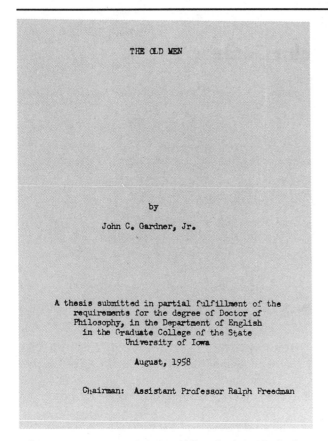

```
                    THE OLD MEN




                         by

                 John C. Gardner, Jr.






     A thesis submitted in partial fulfillment of the
        requirements for the degree of Doctor of
        Philosophy, in the Department of English
          in the Graduate College of the State
                  University of Iowa

                    August, 1958

      Chairman:  Assistant Professor Ralph Freedman
```

*Title page for the unpublished novel that Gardner submitted as
a dissertation at the State University of Iowa*

birthday, he married Joan Louise Patterson. They
had two children, Joel and Lucy. Gardner received
an A.B. at Washington University in St. Louis in
1955, and at the State University of Iowa he received an M.A. in 1956 and a Ph.D. in 1958. For his
doctoral dissertation he wrote a novel, "The Old
Men," which has not been published. He taught medieval literature and creative writing at many
schools, including Oberlin College, Bennington
College, Skidmore College, the University of Southern Illinois, Northwestern University, Chico State
College, the University of Detroit, San Francisco
State University, and the University of Rochester.
He spent at least three summers at Bread Loaf in
Vermont. In 1977 he accepted a position as writer in
residence at George Mason University and made,
according to a friend, "something like his twentieth
move in twenty-five years." The last school with
which Gardner was associated was the State University of New York at Binghamton. Joining its English
faculty in the fall of 1978, he returned to an area of
the country near Batavia, New York, where he was
born.

Gardner's first published novel, *The Resurrection* (1966), attracted little attention. In a waspish
dismissal in *Saturday Review* Granville Hicks declared it "pretty muddled," and said the novel
makes many demands on the reader because of a
good deal of technical experimentation. Gardner re-
produces, for example, an essay written on an ab-
struse subject by a man whose mind is deteriorating
due to the deadly effects of aleukemic leukemia.
The essay gradually becomes less and less coherent
as its author fades mentally. The writer is James
Chandler, a philosophy professor whose doctor has
given him only a few months to live. The book asks
the question Gardner would ask in every succeeding
novel: how can existential man—under sentence of
death—live in such a way as to foster life-affirming
values, regardless of how ultimately provisional
they may prove? *The Resurrection* is sensitive, poignant, and harrowing; it is also a good indication of
the startling literary abilities of its author.

During the 1960s those abilities were becoming increasingly evident in academic publishing circles. Prior to *The Resurrection* Gardner had collaborated with Lennis Dunlap on a textbook, *The Forms of
Fiction* (1962); his translation *The Complete Works of the
Gawain-Poet* (1965) also predates his appearance as a
novelist. Gardner had been writing since childhood,
and more than one of the books published in the
1970s, after he had gained recognition, was written
during the lengthy rejection-slip period that is the lot
of virtually every aspiring novelist. In a 1974 interview he hinted at the sequence in which he wrote his
novels: "When you're sitting writing for fifteen
years, and nobody liking you, you do build up a backlog. I've been publishing an early work, a late work,
an early work. . . . *The Sunlight Dialogues* is an early
work; *Grendel* is a late work; *Nickel Mountain* . . . is a
very early work. Right after that comes my newest
thing, *The King's Indian and Other Fireside Tales,* a very
jazzy technical thing. That and *Jason and Medeia* are
my two newest things." *October Light* (1976), he
would later comment, had occupied him "for
years." In the meantime he produced scholarly articles, Cliff's Notes, and books. With Nicholas Joost
he coedited *Papers on the Art and Age of Geoffrey Chaucer* (1967), and on his own he produced *The Alliterative Morte Arthure* (1971), *The Construction of the Wakefield Cycle* (1974), and *The Construction of Christian Poetry in Old English* (1975).

The remarkable thing about Gardner's fiction
is its consistent clarity of purpose and moral vision.
From the beginning of his career as a writer he has
looked for ways to confute or reshape the fiction of
exhaustion and despair then fashionable. He sought
ways to follow Faulkner's lead toward some kind of
credible, meaningful affirmation, something beyond
the mere fantasies of wish-fulfillment that he saw a
few novelists trying to offer as antidotes to de-

spair. Thus in his dissertation-abstract he describes "The Old Men" in terms that could be applied to such important and typical later productions as *The Sunlight Dialogues* (1972) and *October Light.* "'The Old Men' is a novel which takes as its general theme the place of man in the universe and attempts to work out the nature and ramifications of man's two essential choices, affirmation and denial." The characters of this novel are experimenting, he explains, with "responsible" and "irresponsible" modes of affirmation; some achieve "objectification of guilt" and become "morally responsible." In doing so they adumbrate major characters in all of Gardner's novels. The same confrontation with guilt, the same aspiration to moral responsibility, exercises Henry Soames in *Nickel Mountain* (1973), James Page in *October Light,* and the doomed Hodges in *The Sunlight Dialogues.*

Fourteen years after "The Old Men," in the essay "The Way We Write Now," Gardner would denounce black humor, nihilism, and "smartmouth satire," declaring that the novelist must present "thought-out values" by means of "empathy and the analysis of moral and psychological process." Whatever the subject, "it's in the careful scrutiny of clearly apprehended characters, their conflicts and ultimate escape from immaturity, that the novel makes up its solid truths, finds courage to defend the good and attacks the simple-minded." Gardner's desiderata point to a conception of the novel as essentially didactic or "philosophical," but always with the stipulation that philosophy must be "dramatized." "I think I'm a philosophical novelist," he told Joe David Bellamy, "but that doesn't mean a philosopher."

Nevertheless, there is perhaps too much philosophy in *The Wreckage of Agathon* (1970), Gardner's second published novel. The book attracted more attention than its predecessor, but though *Time* and *Newsweek* were kind, one reviewer lambasted it as "more hysterical than historical" and called it "a total bore." Thomas Edwards describes the book more judiciously as "an inventive if rather baroque meditation on the status of imaginative freedom within an oppressive political order." In ancient Sparta a disreputable old seer named Agathon and his sidekick, Demodokos, are jailed by Lykourgos, the tyrannical devotee of law and order. Gardner presents the philosophical impasse between the state and its laws and the individual and his freedom with high gusto, but since the narration is accomplished by Agathon and Demodokos in a series of monologues, it is hard to move beyond a kind of manic glee in disputation (Agathon has disputed even with the great Solon)—a delight in forensic and rhetorical

flashiness for its own sake. This philosophical argumentation is also central to *The Sunlight Dialogues,* but when an omniscient narrator can sympathetically examine arguments against the absolute but ultimately antisocial freedom of anarchism, the result is a finer novelistic performance, one that brings mutually exclusive philosophical positions into more instructive contrast. Gardner combines both Agathon and Lykourgos in himself. "I am on the one hand a kind of New York State Republican, conservative," he admitted in a 1977 interview in the *Atlantic.* "On the other hand, I am a kind of bohemian type. I really don't obey the laws. I mean to, but if I am in a hurry and there is no parking here, I park."

No doubt he also combines Beowulf and Grendel. His third novel, *Grendel,* which established him as an important literary figure, came out in 1971. In it he retells the Beowulf story from the monster's point of view, but he does so in a manner that violates neither the original tale nor the sensibilities of the twentieth-century reader. *Grendel* illustrates T. S. Eliot's dictum that the individual talent enriches and slightly modifies the literary tradition, for in this short novel Gardner burnishes the classic at the same time that he creates a new masterpiece.

The ghastly embodiment of the futility and meaninglessness of life, Grendel is the dark shape that has always waited in the shadows, the offspring of Chaos and Old Night. Wonderfully mythic, he represents "the brute existent," the unknown. An arch-nihilist, he knows that "the world is all pointless accident," and indeed, accident claims him in the end. In the time that Grendel observes humanity he witnesses the coming of one great cultural phase after another, beginning with the birth and growth of civilization itself. He sees how roving bands of hunters begin to unite, settle down, and develop agriculture and animal husbandry. Kings emerge; they build roads, collect taxes, raise armies, make war on other kings. Religion waxes and wanes, from crude and primitive animism to Christianity, in both its traditional and existential forms. At each phase the people define Grendel differently: at first he is the "oaktree spirit," later Cain, or Satan, or "the Great Destroyer." Grendel also witnesses the emergence of what Gardner describes in his interview with Bellamy as "the main ideas of Western Civilization," including the heroic and courtly love ideas, Hobbesian and Rousseauesque notions of human nature, materialism, hedonism, mysticism, and even *Realpolitik* and revolution-for-the-hell-of-it. Grendel recognizes the futility and absurdity of them all. None changes what he knows to be the existential truth, and he dismisses all of them as the desperate and pa-thetic illusions with which "pattern makers" attempt to clothe the world and their existence in meaning; but one of their activities, poetry, he finds hard to dismiss. He understands from the first that the Shaper, the Scop, is the one responsible for all the other dodges. If he sings of "the greatest of gods," man becomes monotheistic; if he sings of heroism, man becomes heroic; and if he sings of courtly love, man becomes chivalrous. The Shaper is at once the greatest liar and the most puissant staver-off of despair. Thus even Grendel, who denounces illusion in tones reminiscent of Sigmund Freud, Jean-Paul Sartre, and Lord Bertrand Russell, melts before the powerful magic of poetry.

The Shaper does not celebrate the glory and power of Hrothgar and the Scyldings after the fact. *He makes it happen,* and herein lies Gardner's own artistic credo, one he embraces in apostolic succession from Oscar Wilde. "Art leads, it doesn't follow," he told his *Atlantic* interviewers. "Art doesn't imitate life, art makes people do things. . . . if we celebrate bad values in our arts, we're going to have a bad society; if we celebrate values which make you healthier, which make life better, we're going to have a better world. I really believe that." Gardner's point in *Grendel* is that art is not merely our least pernicious illusion; it is our healthiest one. It can teach us ways to live and die with courage—and do so better than can other, less efficacious illusions such as religion (which the Shaper created anyway).

Gardner affirms more in *Grendel* than the primacy of art. The novel has twelve chapters, each devoted to one astrological house and each including references to the appropriate astrological symbol. The story begins and ends in spring—Aries to Pisces—and this circularity is important, as is the number of chapters. Twelve is a mystical number symbolic of the cosmos; it is the product of three and four, the numbers symbolic of godhead and earth (Gardner uses the same numerical symbolism in the prologue to *The Sunlight Dialogues*). The twelve months described in Grendel comprise the twelfth year of the monster's "idiotic war" on Hrothgar and the Scyldings. In numerology a number multiplied by itself represents an intensification of the original symbolism, and Gardner's implied structure in *Grendel,* twelve-times-twelve, emphasizes the cosmic significance of the story he presents.

The circular structure is significant because in the end, grappling with Beowulf, Grendel learns that he, too—death itself, symbolically—is mortal. Beowulf whispers to him: "*Though you murder the world . . . The world will burn green, sperm build again.*" It is Gardner's most beautiful way of saying "life goes on," a phrase that recurs in his novels. Life goes on, it

recycles, and death's ascendancy can never be more than temporary until the culmination of the entropic drift makes the very concept of life and death irrelevant. In other words, Gardner elects not to be distressed by the Parthian shot with which Grendel expires: "Poor Grendel's had an accident. . . . *So may you all.*" His defeat, Grendel maintains, has been by "mindless chance," pure "accident." The structure of *Grendel,* however, is in dynamic tension with the nihilism of its narrator, for Gardner means for his readers to recall that in medieval iconography the circle symbolizes faith. The faith Gardner adumbrates here is, of course, not religious faith, but faith, simply, in the wonderful regenerative properties of life—faith defined as the opposite of the despair that comes of brooding morbidly on the accidental, amoral nature of human life and of the universe that includes such an anomaly.

Gardner finds the horrors of chance harder to gainsay in his next novel, perhaps because it was written earlier than *Grendel.* The monumental scale of *The Sunlight Dialogues,* published in 1972, contrasts even more sharply with the economy of *Grendel.* With its intricate plot and its more than eighty characters, this is Gardner's most massive novel, and possibly his finest. In Batavia, New York, during a few weeks in 1966, Police Chief Fred Clumly stakes his career and his reputation on a bizarre and protracted duel with the most extraordinary criminal he has ever encountered: the Sunlight Man. Vagrant and vandal, polymath and prestidigitator, the Sunlight Man is arrested for painting LOVE across a road. Bearded, maimed, and more than half crazy, he babbles for days in the Batavia jail, like Ezra Pound in the stockade in Pisa. Then he escapes and quickly becomes implicated in several murders and kidnappings. The police chief devotes himself more and more obsessively to tracking down the Sunlight Man, convinced that he is "the sum total of all Clumly had been fighting all his life." The quarry reciprocates by going out of his way to humiliate the hunter.

Rather glum, dumb, and clumsy, as his name implies, Fred Clumly is a fearsome figure, with his obese, pallid, and completely hairless body, his red eyes, and his mole's nose. His single-minded and unimaginative devotion to law and order hardly endears him to the reader. In his life "there was only order, lifted against the world like rusty chickenwire. . . ." He takes a ghoulish delight in funerals and attends one after another in the course of the book, secretly pleased at their testimony to the "orderly" closure of human life. Yet even when Clumly acts viciously—smashing the jaw of a prisoner with a pistol butt—or deviously—taping, wiretapping, and eavesdropping–Gardner somehow makes readers sympathize with him, or at least refuses to allow him to degenerate into that familiar figure of pasteboard villainy, the fascist policeman. As a result of his encounters with the Sunlight Man, Clumly eventually comes to question himself, his values, and the cultural order of which he is a part. Towards the end of the book he passes up a funeral, a hopeful sign that is borne out when, dismissed from his post, he finally has the Sunlight Man in his power–and lets him go. When the Sunlight Man dies, in the end, as a result of what is described on his death certificate as "police action in pursuit of order," the chief eulogizes him and gives the impression that he has learned something from the dead man.

The Sunlight Man is really Taggert Hodge, prodigal son of a prominent but declining local family. Made frantic by the deaths of his children, by the insanity of his wife, and by the refusal of his father-in-law, a sadistic tyrant, to defray the cost of the one type of therapy that might help the sick woman, he returns to Batavia to murder the old man and to terrorize the community and its police chief. As the manic and protean Sunlight Man, he becomes something more than human, something beyond "the solemn judgements of psychiatry, sociology, and the like." He is a superb magician, a master pickpocket, and a prankster–a cross between Till Eulenspiegel and the Fiend Incarnate. Like the Trickster-god described by Jung, he modulates from cruel prankster to something like a savior. He calls himself the Sunlight Man for reasons never made entirely clear, but his impact on Clumly and others is nothing less than that of the sunlight outside Plato's cave: a blinding, overwhelming, and terrible epistemological revelation. The Sunlight Man knows that "the truth is always larger than you think"; thus to Clumly he narrates a fantastic version of Plato's parable and comments: "I doubt that anything in all our system is in tune with, keyed to, reality." On finding herself a widow, his mother-in-law is disgusted at the shabbiness of her husband's corpse and observes–with unconscious irony, since she is unaware of how the old man met his end–"Sunlight in the morning shows things as they are."

Although the police chief and the Sunlight Man destroy themselves in the course of their drawn-out and obsessive duel, they eventually come to recognize that each defines the other, the one viewing order as an absolute, the other espousing absolute freedom. Cop and robber become thesis and antithesis of a profound dialectic–order versus anarchy–that the two hammer out in a series of one-sided "dialogues" in which the Sunlight Man, a brilliant rhetorician, lectures the hapless police chief on the eternally warring principles for which they stand. Moreover, in a strange way, each is the other, for the conjurer "was once a policeman," and the policeman, alienated from other men by his profession, "meets the world and gets along with it by means of a conjuring trick inside his brain." By means of subplots that universalize the theme of the essential identity of hunter and quarry, Gardner at once expands and undercuts this dialectic. For example, a bill collector stalks–and begins to fear–a murderous swindler in whom, more and more, he recognizes himself. "We're somewhat alike, you and I," declares his quarry. Another character actually embodies this doubling, leading two lives as Walter Boyle, housebreaker, and Walter Benson, respectable citizen.

Despite Clumly's manic devotion to order, things gradually run down in the community of Batavia. Crimes multiply, from minor hooliganism to ghastly murders, and the police sense that things are getting away from them. Disorder increases, and in disorder the author resolves the dichotomy represented by robber and cop; the Sunlight Man's anarchy shadows forth not perfect freedom but perfect randomness, which also dooms the police chief's cherished orderliness. The thesis and antithesis represented by these two characters, in other words, have their synthesis in entropy, and neither Clumly's rusty chicken wire nor the Sunlight Man's patter about *l'acte gratuit* can obscure the terrible truth. Although "human consciousness" may be "the most fantastic achievement of the whole fantastic chronicle of time and space," as the Sunlight Man says, he comes closest to the truth when he asks: "What is there in this world but accident?"

Gardner's next published work was not a novel but an epic poem, *Jason and Medeia* (1973). In this extraordinary and eclectic performance he translates, borrows, and invents new material to retell several Greek myths and merge them into a great new whole. "Parts of this poem," the author writes in a preface, "freely translate sections of Apollonios Rhodios' *Argonautica* and Euripides' *Medeia,* among other things." It is as daring a venture, in literary terms, as Jason's own. Perhaps the poem should be regarded as a vast archaeological restoration project, the forging (in both senses of the word) of an epic the ancients neglected to write. In rectifying the oversight, Gardner resembles Wyatt Gwyon, the hero of William Gaddis's *The Recognitions,* who paints forgeries that no expert can distinguish from the real thing. Like Gaddis, Gardner means for his readers to ponder the paradox of authenticity inherent in literary artifice. Opinion on

THE COMPLETE WORKS OF
THE GAWAIN-POET

In a Modern English Version with a Critical Introduction
by John Gardner

Woodcuts by Fritz Kredel

THE UNIVERSITY OF CHICAGO PRESS
Chicago & London

Title page for Gardner's 1965 translation of the Middle English poems in a fourteenth-century manuscript

Jason and Medeia has been sharply divided, and it is still too early to say whether it will finally be viewed as a colossal miscalculation or as an example of the kind of literary risk-taking that reveals an artist of Robert Graves's or Ezra Pound's stature.

One can say, however, that *Jason and Medeia* is light years distant from *Nickel Mountain,* the book that appeared the same year. In this novel Gardner introduces Henry Soames, the middle-aged, lonely, and extremely fat proprietor of a dilapidated diner in the Catskills. Soames has had one heart attack and lives in dread of the little click in his chest that will announce a second, fatal one. Yet though he fears death, he feels "vaguely drawn" to the snow that surrounds and isolates him. Leading an empty life, he reads much of the night but cannot go south in the winter. Though he pretends to like solitude, he talks obsessively and irritatingly to his infrequent patrons—the drunks who heed the plea of the diner's neon name burning into the night: Stop Off. He broods over a few shabby memories: a one-night stand spoiled by violence, a grotesquely fat and inef-

fectual father despised by Henry's mother, and a high school crush—his nearest encounter with love—that came to nothing. The emptiness of his life and the imminence of death fill him with a panic that he cannot name; indeed, much of Gardner's accomplishment here is his rendering of the verbal inadequacies of people painfully inarticulate, people whose lives—outwardly "simple"—are in fact chaotic.

Yet Soames is capable of great love, and his "heart trouble" suggests the damming up of what he needs to give. He offers his love to Callie Wells, a pregnant sixteen-year-old who works for him. Desperate, she takes him, and they begin to make a life. She is a hard worker, and he is good-hearted and protective. The simplicity and decency of these people are important, for Gardner describes *Nickel Mountain* in a subtitle as "A Pastoral Novel." In pastoral, as George Stade remarked in *The New York Times Book Review,* rural characters, free of the city and its ills, embody and sometimes speak for simple human virtues and wisdom. Soames has seen the city and the appalling indifference of urbanites to each other. He is haunted by a

> vision of people as meaningless motion, a stream of humanity down through time, no more significant than rocks in a mountain slide. It was different in the country, where a man's life or a family's past was not so quickly swallowed up, where the ordinariness of thinking creatures was obvious only when you thought a minute, not an inescapable conclusion that crushed the soul the way pavement shattered men's arches.

Henry's embittered friend, George Loomis, believes that man's "pure meanness" underlies progress, but Henry will not accept this, believing in the possibility, at least, for human goodness. Though he recognizes the frangibility of his new family, of his happiness in it, and of his very existence, he does not allow the recognition to dampen his altruism and continually seeks, selflessly, to help his fellow-man, even to the point of taking in the crazed and dangerous Simon Bale, a religious fanatic whose wife has perished in a fire possibly of her husband's making. When Bale declares himself unwilling to have his wife properly buried, Henry quietly spends $600 on a funeral that no one attends. Henry resembles the unlikely heroes in Albert Camus's *La Peste* (1947), who persist in alleviating human misery, however hopeless the prospects. Henry's world picture, while hardly sophisticated, includes no illusions about religion. His father left him a Bible, but it has "a fermented, museum smell." While "the world was vastly more beautiful with angels than it was without," he knows that they and the transcendent order for which they stand are chimerical. "What was pleasant to believe was not necessarily true."

Nickel Mountain is filled with casually reported instances of violent death and dismemberment that are the more terrible for being so gratuitous, random, and "accidental." Truckers die plummeting from slick mountain roads; Soames's friend Kuzitski perishes in a flaming wreck; a homeowner's skull is crushed by intruders; a woman burns to death in the senseless arson of her home; a motorist dies crashing into a snowplow; a fourteen-year-old boy dies freakishly in the "dry lightning" of newly-gathered hay; George Loomis—already crippled in the Korean War—loses an arm to his corn binder; later, driving carelessly, he kills an old eccentric. These random deaths and accidents form a sinister ostinato to the exploration in the book of the frailty of human life. The ability of the soft and meek Henry Soames to defy the yawning void and provide sustenance not only to his little family, but also to incidental human strays like Simon Bale, should be viewed as a poignant way of depicting a humble but very real form of heroism.

When Simon Bale dies of a broken neck sustained as he recoiled from a Soamesian outburst and fell down a staircase, Henry is profoundly distressed. The death was accidental, but he believes obsessively that he caused it. Chagrined, he goes through a bad period in which he seems to be trying to eat himself to death. Though he cannot put it into words, he understands that in contributing, however slightly, to Bale's accident he has allied himself—a human being—to chance, and he can imagine no sin more terrible. It is one thing to accept chance, another thing to conspire with it against a humanity already playing against a stacked deck.

Soames eventually transcends his guilt and achieves serenity, becoming something of a mystic and believing in "the holiness of things." He emerges finally as an almost numinous figure, his meekness and ineffectuality paradoxically balanced by an inner strength and tranquility born of his recognition and acceptance of the natural scheme of things, including his own death. Though individual men perish, "life goes on." By the end of the book Soames has matured from a feckless fat man terrorized by intimations of his own mortality and "close to a nervous breakdown" into a rustic sage, a life-affirmer chastened by an awareness of accident and strengthened by the battle with guilt. Like so many modern fictional heroes, Henry Soames has had to learn to live with the horror of the random. Like all Gardner's books, *Nickel Mountain* explores the possi-

bilities for affirmation in the face of the absurdity of the world.

Before resuming his chronicling of the simple lives and passions of Yankee rustics in *October Light,* Gardner published *The King's Indian Stories and Tales* (1974), a collection of short stories, sketches, and the title novella. In "Sailing through the Universe with John Napper"—a sketch of the Gardner circle of home, family, and friends—as in *October Light,* the author describes himself in a state of inebriation, as if he means to cultivate the image of a hard-drinking latter-day Hemingway. The John Napper of the title, an artist, did the illustrations for *The Sunlight Dialogues.* (One of the extraordinary things about Gardner's novels is that they are always splendidly and copiously illustrated.) Gardner admires Napper because his good-natured insouciance never falters despite his awareness—as Grendel would put it—that "things fade."

The title of "The King's Indian" refers not to a redskin but to a chess opening; the deception is part of the hoaxing this story is about. The narrator of the story, Jonathan Upchurch, describes it as a thing that "has no purpose to it, no shape or form or discipline but the tucket and boom of its own high-flown language," but John Gardner, who breaks in to address the reader in *vox propria* toward the end, maintains that it is intended as "a celebration of all literature and life." The plot concerns a voyage of the whaler *Jerusalem,* which seems to be a sea-going version of John Barth's Funhouse, commanded by another Sunlight Man, and manned by a cast out of Samuel Taylor Coleridge, Herman Melville, Edgar Allan Poe, and Joseph Conrad. Basically the tale is a composite of every sea voyage in literature, from the *Odyssey* to *Moby-Dick* (1851). The narrator-hero is at once the Ancient Mariner, Ishmael, and Arthur Gordon Pym. He also bears more than a passing resemblance to Barth's Ebenezer Cooke, for he is an innocent who gains experience through a series of brutal and comic batterings.

From the initiation of youth in "The King's Indian" Gardner turns to the trials of age in *October Light,* which is actually two interlocking novels. The formal experimentation, like that of Grendel and "The King's Indian," indicates that this book does not come from Gardner's backlog—though apparently it was fairly long in the writing. In the frame story of *October Light,* an elderly brother and sister living together in Vermont have a falling-out. James Page, the seventy-two-year-old brother, holds irascible opinions on a variety of things: welfare, social security, unions, and television. Sally Page Abbot, his eighty-three-year-old sister, holds diametrically opposed opinions: she is for minority rights, the

ERA, government social programs, and nuclear re-actors. Worst of all, she belongs to the Democratic Party, and, of course, few Vermonters make any distinction at all between the Democrats and the Communists. The situation in the household recalls nothing so much as the skirmishing between Squire Western and his politically-opinionated, bluestocking sister in Henry Fielding's *Tom Jones* (1749). The real trouble starts when James blows Sally's television to smithereens with his shotgun. Shortly thereafter, irate at the very idea of a woman's holding opinions and defending them, and brandishing a piece of firewood as a club, he drives her upstairs and locks her in her room. A duel of wills ensues. Finding that she has a bedpan, a box of Kleenex, and access to the apples stored in the attic, Sally settles in for a long siege. Every bit as mulish as her brother, she locks the door from her side and refuses to leave the room, even when her niece, James's daughter, unlocks the door. Friends organize a party in hopes of luring her down, but she resists the entreaties and blandishments of everyone who comes to the door. Sally passes the time reading a "trashy" novel she finds on the floor: *The Smugglers of Lost Souls' Rock,* described in the jacket blurbs as "A Black-Comic Blockbuster" and "A sick book, as sick and evil as life in America." Though parts of the old paperback are missing, and though its text appears interwoven with the frame story, it proves easy to follow and immediately recognizable for what it is: a parody of the contemporary novel of Angst, black humor, emptiness, alienation, disenchantment, aridity, and despair. One of the first shocks of this production—at once melodramatic and heavily symbolic—is the reader's recognition of just how clichéd modern fiction has become with its modish bleakness and its "existentialist" or "absurdist" outlook.

The challenge of Gardner's double novel is somehow to integrate his homely tale of domestic squabbling with his trendy novel of modern emptiness. It is a formidable task, and he brings it off beautifully. The symbolism of *Smugglers* is quite transparent, and neither Sally nor the reader has any difficulty making it out. The chief of the smugglers, Captain Johann Fist, is Faustian man in league with the devil. He and his boat, the *Indomitable,* represent capitalism, while a rival boat, the *Militant,* represents the challenge posed by minorities and the third world. The crew of the *Militant,* needless to say, is composed entirely of minorities, and some members are highly articulate, a fact that makes for some wonderfully "dialectic" exchanges with Fist and his crew, who include an inventor named Mr. Nit (Technology), a good man named Goodman, a

ridiculously libidinous ingenue, and a world-despairer and would-be suicide—Peter Wagner—shanghaied into service aboard the *Indomitable*. The creator of this farrago (it is, of course, Gardner himself, assisted by his wife Joan) gets all the political and philosophical mileage he can out of a confrontation on the high seas, which is followed by an alliance between the two crews.

Sally not only "solves" the symbolism, she also begins to recognize people she knows in the novel. The odious Captain Fist, who seems beyond rapprochement with the crew of the *Militant,* is her nasty old Republican brother James. Mr. Nit becomes James's son-in-law, the handyman Lewis Hicks. Peter Wagner is Richard Page, James's son, whose suicide some years ago left the old man with an almost intolerable burden of guilt. The struggle between left and right in *Smugglers,* as well as the suicidal brooding, adumbrates or reflects the less baroque but no less bitter tensions in the Vermont household.

Sally's interpretations are ours as well. Gardner explains in his *Atlantic* interview: "As you read the inner and outer novels, you begin to recognize that that situation is exactly like this situation, that character is paralleled to this one." Ultimately the exotic world of *Smugglers* has been refined, so to speak, into terms at once more human and more credible, and Gardner makes—dramatically and novelistically—the points he made expositorily in his essay "The Way We Write Now." In that piece he took modern fiction to task for dwelling on bleakness and horror and for attempting occasionally to escape them by means of simple-minded and unrealistic "affirmation" (at the end of *Smugglers* a flying saucer appears to deliver the protagonists from apocalypse). Gardner is all for affirmation, but it must be reasoned and credible, growing out of "thought-out values—the solid formulations of character that Henry James or Jane Austen fictionally develop and recommend to the reader."

In the frame story of *October Light* Gardner lives up to his own exhortation. "Great novelists," he maintains, "build tight form out of singleminded psychological and moral analysis," and the reconciliation between James and Sally, when it comes, is as heartening as anything in literature. The old man, whose moral drama the book has come to emphasize, discovers that he has been guilty of a kind of inflexible righteousness that has poisoned the lives of those around him—most tragically the life of his son, driven to drink and finally suicide by the fecklessness his father had inadvertently fostered in him. *October Light,* then, includes a rustic world where the same horrors obtain as in the black-

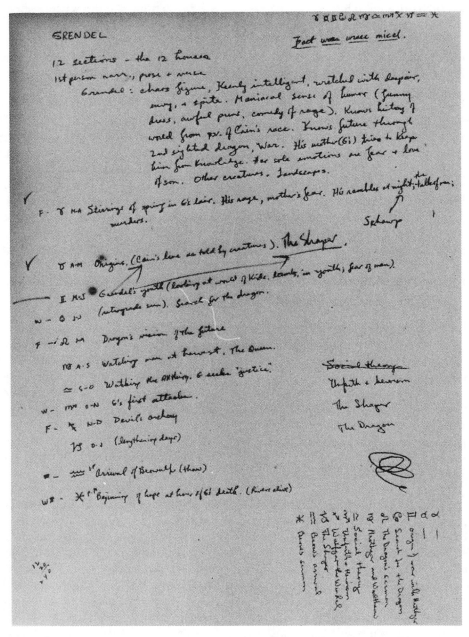

Gardner's outline for his 1972 novel, Grendel *(Morris Library, Southern Illinois University at Carbondale)*

comic, nihilistic, "smart-mouth satirical" novels typified by *Smugglers,* but Gardner convinces us that James Page can, at the age of seventy-two, come to self-knowledge—and that the thawing of this man's frozen heart holds much promise for all people who, bound in spiritual winter, have ever despaired of the spring.

In many ways the publication of *October Light* in 1976 was the highlight of Gardner's literary career. This novel not only garnered the National Book Critics Circle Award for fiction but also marked Gardner's biggest commercial success. The years following 1976, however, proved more difficult—both professionally and personally. A few months before winning the award Gardner and his wife of twenty-three years separated. Later, in 1977, doctors discovered and removed a cancer of the colon. Regularly tested for a cancer recurrence, he began to "feel pressed for time" and desired only time for reading and writing. Renting a large, century-old house in Lanesboro, Pennsylvania, he moved in with Liz Rosenberg, a young writer whom he married in February 1980. His books *In the Suicide Mountains* (1977), *On Moral Fiction* (1978), and *Mickelsson's*

Ghosts (1982) are all dedicated to her. Yet this marriage also ended in divorce. In fact, his fatal motorcycle accident came only four days before the twice-divorced Gardner planned to marry Susan Thornton, whom he had met at a writers' conference.

Gardner's professional problems also began in 1977. Following the publication of his biography *The Life & Times of Chaucer* (1977), he was accused of "borrowing passages" from other Chaucerian scholars. The controversy even sparked an article in *Newsweek* (10 April 1978) titled "Did John Gardner Paraphrase or Plagiarize?" He admitted to "paraphrasing" and remained somewhat defensive of the charge throughout his career. His post-1977 novels acknowledge sources and influences in an effort to fend off any further charges.

The publication of Gardner's critical manifesto *On Moral Fiction* generated an even more far-reaching controversy. His asserted purpose in this book is to analyze "what has gone wrong" in recent years with fiction—to explain why "most art these days is either trivial or false." Prior to its publication other contemporary writers were alerted to Gardner's assessments of their work because several of the book's essays were excerpted in literary journals (the title essay won the Pushcart Prize). Gardner further fanned the controversy over his criticism of contemporary fiction by reading papers on the subject at various universities. He also appeared on the "Dick Cavett Show" (PBS, 16 May 1978) to explain his position.

Early drafts of this book began evolving as early as 1965, before Gardner himself had published fiction. Society's need for truly moral art was a major concern for Gardner and one he felt a great conviction in espousing. He begins his book with the claim that "art is essentially and primarily moral—that is, life-giving." He is careful to clarify that, by the word *moral,* he does not mean didactic, for "didacticism and true art are immiscible." To Gardner "true art is moral" because it "clarifies life, establishes models of human action, casts nets toward the future, carefully judges our right and wrong directions, celebrates and mourns. It does not rant. It does not sneer or giggle in the face of death, it invents prayers and weapons. It designs visions worth trying to make fact. It does not whimper or cower or throw up its hands and bat its lashes. It does not make hope contingent on acceptance of some religious theory. It strikes like lightning, or is lightning; whichever."

Gardner finds fault with postmodernist writers "who disparage the pursuit of truth" and refers to them as "a gang of absurdist and jubilant nihilists." To explain why "our serious fiction is not much good," he points to the writers' emphasis on technique over truth. Such "performance" artists call attention to their fiction's linguistic fabric or to what Gardner calls "texture." The reason writers occupy themselves with surface is "that we tend to feel we have nothing to say. . . . Texture is our refuge, the one thing we know we're good at." Therefore, he explains, "Fiction as pure language (texture over structure) is *in,*" and writers who are concerned with pursuing truth, goodness, and beauty are "old-fashioned." The end result of focusing on language, Gardner argues, is a lack of communication: "linguistic opacity suggests indifference to the needs and wishes of the reader and to whatever ideas may be buried underneath all the brush."

Even those authors who are interested in ideas and arguments too often turn to outrage or propaganda, according to Gardner. Such a "fierce ethic," he says, is not "rooted in love," a requirement of truly great art. Gardner states, "Despite the labors of academic artists and those sophisticates who are embarrassed by emotion, it seems all but self-evident that it is for the pleasure of exercising our capacity to love that we pick up a book at all." For Gardner morality and love are inextricably bound. Artists, therefore, who assert only causes, those who have no love of character but only of style, and those who approach the world with cynical detachment are doomed to short literary lives.

For Gardner the morality of art is not a matter of "message" or doctrine but is a "process." "The writer discovers, works out, and tests his ideas in the process of writing. Thus at its best fiction is . . . a way of thinking, a philosophical method." Art's morality springs from this "process," which clarifies life and opposes chaos. Gardner warns, "Discursive thought is not fiction's most efficient tool."

Gardner's annoyance with the present state of the arts comes from his firm belief that art affects the way people behave. "Life follows art." In his view society is cynical and debased because its art is, not the other way around: "if we celebrate bad values in our arts, we're going to have a bad society." In this rather angry book Gardner sends out a cry for fiction that will bolster life, not undermine its value. To Gardner the literary artist is the conscious guardian of society; his message to the reader is clear: "Since bad art has a harmful effect on society, it should never go unchallenged." Gardner got the literary gunfight he wanted. Many prominent novelists fired back.

Many reviewers found the book to be an arrogant recitation of pronouncements in which Gardner magisterially dismisses other writers for the purpose of offering an extended apologia for his own

Two-page title for Gardner's novel about a duel of wills between an elderly brother and sister in Vermont

writing. Gardner's combativeness, his "bombastic exaggerations," according to Thomas LeClair in *Saturday Review,* simply "reveal a writer ill at ease with himself." Gardner's argument does seem to be defensive, for he puts most other current writers on the other side of his moral fence. In an *Atlantic Monthly* interview he says that "hardly anybody belongs with me" and then explains, "Very few people believe in fiction as exploration, as understanding."

Gardner's view of the artist as moral agent places him on old-fashioned, time-tested ground and aligns him with Tolstoy. His call for "moral fiction" appeals to disgruntled readers and critics alike who find current fiction too remote from their experience and devoid of sincere emotions. Although Gardner fired up some literary tempers, he also found a sympathetic audience. Julian Moynahan, for example, in *The New York Times Book Review* admits that, despite Gardner's "righteousness," "it's a positive pleasure to see various fashionable gloom spreaders and doomsday peddlers get it in the neck." In *Contemporary Literature* Thomas LeClair criticizes Gardner's "pride" and "militantly unimaginative" readings of recent fiction but finds it "still a necessary book. . . . Its earnest force requires even the reader who resists it page by page to examine his assumptions about fiction and because no

other writer . . . has reminded us recently that art is by and for human beings." LeClair concludes that the book "does not collapse through its many weaknesses because, ultimately, Gardner sides with great art. . . ."

Following the publication of *On Moral Fiction,* Gardner continued to demonstrate his versatility as a writer and his wide-ranging creative interests by writing poetry, opera libretti, children's tales, and radio plays. A small volume of his verse, titled *Poems,* was published in 1978. A broadside of the poem "Nicholas Vergette 1923–1974" coincided with the publication of *Poems.* Gardner first read the poem at a memorial service held for his friend Nicholas Vergette in Carbondale, Illinois, on 28 February 1974. The New London Press published three of his opera libretti–*Rumpelstiltskin, Frankenstein,* and *William Wilson* (1979). Gardner saw his *Rumpelstiltskin* performed by the Opera Company of Philadelphia. Gardner also began writing radio plays in 1979 and won the Armstrong Prize for *The Temptation Game* (1980).

Gardner's next novel, *Freddy's Book,* came out in 1980. It resembles in structure the widely praised *October Light,* since it too is composed of a novel within a novel. Beginning with "Freddy," a sixty-page prologue, the novel introduces Prof. Jack

Winesap, a "psycho-historian." Guest-lecturing at the University of Wisconsin (on "The Psycho-politics of the Late Welsh Fairytale: Fee, Fie, Foe—Revolution"), Winesap meets a strange old historian, Professor Agaard, at a reception. While Winesap holds forth on "the popular appeal of monstrosity," Agaard begins to twitch nervously and says, "I have a son who's a monster." Although the admission leads to rather awkward conversation, Winesap later accepts an invitation to the man's house. Arriving at the isolated, run-down estate in a blizzard, Winesap becomes snowed in for the night. After a suspenseful delay, Agaard takes his visitor upstairs to meet his "monster" son. A painfully shy, obese, eight-foot-tall adolescent, Freddy exiles himself in a locked room, which keeps the mocking world at bay. For two years he has been working on a book. A "fan" of Winesap's writing, Freddy sneaks down during the night to the visitor's room and deposits his book, called "Freddy's Book."

"Freddy's Book" is the tale "King Gustav and the Devil." A fablelike retelling of historical events in sixteenth-century Scandinavia, his story traces the rise to power of young Gustav Vasa (an authentic historical figure). After the Stockholm massacre of 1520, this new young leader emerges, and with the help of both his giant, country-bred cousin Lars-Goren and of the protean Devil who whispers in men's ears, he becomes King Gustavus I of Sweden. In the process he makes an ally and then an enemy of Bishop Brask, an intellectual cleric and cynical kingmaker.

Although Gustav is the king of Sweden, Lars-Goren is the hero of the story. This simple knight's only fear is the Devil, and toward the end of the story King Gustav sends his comrade Lars-Goren and Bishop Brask to Lapland to kill the Devil. Suspecting treachery brought on by his own injustices, Gustav betrays his friend by sending men out to kill him. In flight Lars-Goren and Bishop Brask ride to the northern-most top of the world through an arctic snowscape that obscures all form. In a powerful final scene they scale the Devil as if he were an ice-encrusted mountain:

> Even to Hans Brask it was a strange business, a kind of miracle. He had meant to cry out from despair, as usual, and he had reason enough: he was beyond pain, numb to the heart; yet what he felt was the wild excitement of a child or an animal. He would not be fooled by it. He was a sick old man, and he knew there was no chance of getting back ever, he had no faith in God. As surely as he knew he was alive he knew God was dead or had never existed. What was this euphoria but an animal pleasure in existence at the margin—the joy of the antelope when the tiger leaps? Yet the joy was real enough.

> Absurdly, for all his philosophy, he was glad to be alive and dying. . . . "This is poetry, this is love and religion!" he thought. He crawled closer to Lars-Goren, filled with excitement, almost laughing, though no sound came out and his cheeks were all ice from his tears.

Euphoric in the face of Lars-Goren's brave actions, Brask simultaneously mocks him: "What a stupid fool you are, Lars-Goren! You know as well as I do that all this means nothing!" Lars-Goren, nevertheless, succeeds in killing the Devil with his knife of bone. The mission is accomplished and Lars-Goren can return to his country home. Back in the city of Stockholm, however, the future appears anything but heroic. Gustav looks out from his window as "darkness fell. There was no light anywhere, except for the yellow light of cities."

The ending seems to suggest that evil cannot be conquered; that the Devil as dragon had been killed, but that he remains a human condition—"the evil is life itself." Because the close of the novel seems to substantiate fatalism, some critics point to the discrepancy between *Freddy's Book* and the moral values Gardner advocates in *On Moral Fiction*. Yet Lars-Goren's individual triumph over his personal nemesis seems life-affirming. As he rides toward his impossible quest and the confrontation with what he fears most, he identifies his fear as "the chaos" that is "in myself, as in everything around me." He then acts with the double knowledge that the Devil cannot be killed and that his striking out at evil is a necessity. Although Gardner laments civilization's moral failure, he embraces human aspiration for magnificence.

After publication of *On Moral Fiction*, critics tended to assess Gardner's fiction in the light of his critical theory. Many critics alienated by his argument were eager to attack *Freddy's Book;* others were eager to defend it. Many reviewers found the provocative opening of the book the most entertaining part and wished, as Paul Gray expressed in *Time,* that he had provided "the other half of the two-part structure, some critics accused Gardner of building Barthian funhouses for no purpose," a practice which *On Moral Fiction* criticizes.

An association between the book's two parts does, however, seem evident, with freakish Freddy transforming himself into the heroic Lars-Goren. As artist rather than misfit, Freddy is equipped to fight the hostile forces of the outside world. In the *Saturday Review* LeClair explains that Freddy's composing himself into Lars-Goren is an attempt to heal his wound—"his difference from others, the country-boy feeling of not being good enough." LeClair goes a step further in suggesting that "Gardner 'lives with' an analogous, perhaps quite similar wound—the sense of being a literary misfit," which "is quite explicitly suggested by the prologue." If LeClair's theory is correct, then Gardner's self-portrait as a writer may be partly responsible for the book's main flaw—his interjection of ideas at the expense of the story and its characters. At one point Lars-Goren and Brask become, in LeClair's phrase, "mouths on horseback," with one championing moral fiction and the other elegant rhetoric.

In *The New York Times Book Review* John Romano suggests that Gardner's two consuming interests—one, his love of "the fabulous, the enchanted" and the other, his philosophical commitment to a "moral scheme"—often work at cross-purposes. Romano explains: "Gardner's particular brand of morality, with its characteristic stress on strength of will, turns out to be incompatible in practice with the softer charms of storytelling. Gardner's problem, then, is that he is unwilling, on principle, to indulge the fabulistic for its own sake. In just the same way, he won't allow himself simply to revel in those Chinese-box structures that so strongly attract him." Romano implies that Gardner struggles against his own gifts and "is better modernist than he knows."

Gardner followed *Freddy's Book* with a collection of ten stories—his first since *The King's Indian*—titled *The Art of Living and Other Stories* (1981). Half the stories were published earlier in various journals and magazines. All the stories explore the relationship between art and life. For example, in "Nimran," dedicated to William Gass, a famous orchestra conductor meets a dying girl, who later goes to his stirring concert. Gardner's theme of art's transcending powers unites these stories. In a 1974 *New Fiction* interview he explained his approach to art: "Blake says a wonderful thing: 'I look upon the dark satanic mills; I shake my head; they vanish.' That's it. That's right. You *redeem* the world by acts of imagination. . . ." Unfortunately, in this short-story collection oftentimes the theme relating to art overpowers the simple story.

The short story "Redemption" is a truly fine one that carries much personal significance for its author. Originally published in the *Atlantic Monthly,* it was later chosen for *The Best American Short Stories 1978.* Based on the death of Gardner's younger brother, the story opens:

> One day in April—a clear, blue day when there were crocuses in bloom—Jack Hawthorne ran over and killed his brother, David. Even at the last moment he could have prevented his brother's death by slamming on the tractor brakes, easily in reach for all the shortness of his legs; but he was unable to think, or, rather, thought unclearly, and so watched it happen, as he would again and again watch it happen in his mind, with nearly undiminished intensity and clarity, all his life.

The accident described in the story took place when Gardner was almost twelve and his brother seven. Although the death shook the family, no one blamed John Gardner; his mother insisted, "only God could have stopped that tractor, and he doesn't work that way." Jack Hawthorne struggles with his belief that he could have prevented the death, and the story traces his resulting grief, rage, and guilt. Just as Gardner did, Jack begins playing the French horn and goes to Rochester's Eastman School of Music for lessons. Jack seeks redemption through art, yet learns from his crusty old Russian teacher, who survived the Bolshevik slaughter, that he must also plunge back into "the herd" of humanity.

The experience of writing the story proved cathartic for Gardner. In a 1979 *Paris Review* interview he described how, before he wrote "Redemption," he always, regularly, every day used

> to have four or five flashes of that accident. I'd be driving down the highway and I couldn't see what was coming because I'd have a memory flash. I haven't had it once since I wrote the story. You really do ground your nightmares, you *name* them. When you write a story, you have to play that image, no matter how painful, over and over until you've got all the sharp details so you know exactly how to put it down on paper. By the time you've run your mind through it a hundred times, relentlessly worked every tic of your terror, it's lost its power over you. That's what bibliotherapy is all about, I guess.

"Redemption" was praised for its pure power and its lack of self-conscious pyrotechnics. In a 1977 interview with Henry Allen, Gardner explains that he purposely shunned some of his early writing bravura, "I spent a lot of time evading the dark center of things by, usually, technical tricks." In "Redemption," however, "for once the techniques aren't showing. That's the important thing. I have spent all my life so far developing more and more techniques. . . . What I want to do now is start using them. And that's the moment when you change from a kind of good writer with a very serious mind and set of emotions into a really major writer. And whether or not I can make that transition, I don't know." He goes on to suggest that he is at the beginning of the transition and that he wants "to write great fiction."

Gardner obviously had ambitions for his next novel, *Mickelsson's Ghosts,* a lengthy work, and in that it resembles *The Sunlight Dialogues* with its immense

Gardner as Jonathan Upchurch, illustration by Herbert L. Fink for Gardner's 1974 novella "The King's Indian"

cast and labyrinthine story. At the center of this ambitious novel is Peter Mickelsson, a mid-fiftyish philosophy professor who teaches at the State University of New York in Binghamton. The novel of more than six hundred pages is an immersion into the emotional, intellectual, and psychic life of this beleaguered professor and his surrounding world. Separated, but not yet divorced, from an embittered, money-hungry wife, worried about his terrorist son who is fighting the nuclear-power industry, and unable to write, teach, or pay his bills, Mickelsson is in the grips of a terrible life crisis. "Once the most orderly of men, a philosopher almost obsessively devoted to precision and neatness (despite his love of Nietzsche), distrustful if not downright disdainful of passion," he has lost control of himself and his world.

In an effort to simplify his life, Mickelsson buys an old farmhouse outside of the depressed town of Susquehanna, Pennsylvania, and devotes himself to restoring the old house in a massive self-renewal project. Drinking and brooding as he works, he discovers that his Eden is more like hell. From the locals he learns his sanctuary is not only haunted but was also the former residence of Joseph Smith, the Mormon prophet, and the scene of a murder. Almost immediately, bizarre events begin to

happen. His house is ransacked, unlit trucks barrel down the dark mountain highway, mysterious burnt-out patches appear in the landscape, and rumors of unsolved murders, witchcraft, and UFO landings whisper through the community. These mysterious omens culminate in Mickelsson's house with the ghosts' eventual appearance—an old man with no teeth and an angry-looking woman. Trying to maintain his equilibrium, Mickelsson shares his house with the knowledge of their horror—his ghosts are an incestuous brother and sister who killed their child and eventually each other.

Interwoven with this gothic story line are Mickelsson's academic escapades in Binghamton. Commuting into this otherworld of academia, he faces his seemingly affable colleagues who are murderously competitive, his students—among them a possibly suicidal young man who looks to him for salvation—and a beautiful sociology professor, Jessica Stark, who is the victim of a campaign to oust her. Mickelsson is in love with this elegant Jewish widow but becomes shamelessly obsessed with a teenage prostitute named Donnie who lives in a Susquehanna tenement. When the teenager becomes pregnant and tells Mickelsson the baby is his, the anti-abortionist professor robs a man to pay Donnie to have the baby. During the robbery, the man (a former bank thief) is stricken with a heart attack, and Mickelsson watches him die. Under suspicion for murder, he hides out in his house only to learn that Donnie has escaped with the money and had an abortion. This crisis, along with the events at school and the presence of the ghosts, pushes him more deeply into self-loathing and despair.

Near the end when madness threatens, a violent crisis precipitates his eventual redemption. A Mormon fanatic (actually a member of the secret society known as Sons of Dan, which pursues apostate saints to their deaths) bangs on Mickelsson's door bearing arms. Threatening Mickelsson's life, the fanatic commands him to tear apart his newly renovated rooms piece by piece in order to uncover a church scandal that is hidden in the walls. As Mickelsson dismantles his entire house, tearing out the fresh plaster, the ending of the novel moves toward the apocalyptic. Saved from murderous destruction at the very last, Mickelsson is finally able to reach out for affirmation—his love for Jessica.

Many of Gardner's lifelong preoccupations are evidenced in *Mickelsson's Ghosts,* especially his philosophical bent and moral vision. The reader of this novel can hear Gardner's voice from *On Moral Fiction.* The author clearly cares about his central character—perhaps too much. He lovingly describes Mickelsson's every mood, nervous habit, or intellectual query. Always a lover of ideas, Gardner has difficulty maintaining his distance from his central character, especially as the novel progresses. In the *Saturday Review,* Robert Harris suggests that "too often Mickelsson is a garrulous spokesman for Gardner" and that, even though the author "may chastise Mickelsson for what he does," he is too "taken with Mickelsson's thought-processes (because they are so much his own)." Examples of such excesses occur when Gardner relates not only Mickelsson's philosophical conversations with his friends but also entire class discussions from his Philosophy 108 course.

Throughout his career Gardner referred to himself as a "philosophical novelist." In a *Paris Review* interview he explained that "when I write a piece of fiction I select my characters and settings and so on because they have a bearing, at least to me, on the old unanswerable philosophical questions. And as I spin out the action, I'm always very concerned with springing discoveries. But at the same time I'm concerned with what the discoveries do to the character who makes them, and to the people around him." Benjamin DeMott points out in the *The New York Times Book Review* that all of Gardner's novels to an extent are "the story of somebody's intellectual life" and that *Mickelsson's Ghosts,* in particular, demonstrates Gardner's engagement in the "genuinely challenging phiosophical theme" of "the mind's endless—and doomed—hunt for self-knowledge." Indeed, Gardner envelops the reader in Mickelsson's agonizing musings about life and offers him no other perspective. This feeling of entrapment suggests Mickelsson's own intellectual imprisonment. Gardner once commented to Ed Christian in a *Prairie Schooner* interview that "the real prison is the prison of the intellect. We're locked into logical systems, unwilling to have faith in the things that count, like love." Gardner's last novel, like many of his others, traces his central character's movement from such ordered restrictions toward a renewed faith in life's potentiality.

Gardner's hopes for this ambitious novel went unrealized, for the reviews were largely negative, some hostile. James Wolcott in *Esquire* called it "a whopping piece of academic bullslinging." In the *New York Review of Books,* Robert Towers offered a more evenhanded criticism of the novel: "My objection, of course, is not to the presence of significant ideas in a novel or to a protagonist who is an academic philosopher; rather, it is the indiscriminate, underdramatized parade of the ideas that makes this reader quail—that, and the verbal self-intoxication of the philosopher-protagonist."

Throughout his career Gardner's propensity for philosophical argumentation brought him criticism, and perhaps *Mickelsson's Ghosts* suffers the most from this inclination, making it all the more unfortunate that this novel is his last. Before his fatal accident Gardner was reportedly "badly hurt" at the poor reviews and blamed them on a critical backlash resulting from *On Moral Fiction.*

His last contributions to American letters is *The Best American Short Stories 1982,* which he edited. This collection, selected and introduced by Gardner, provides a clear statement of his artistic vision. In his selection he passes over many well-known writers, such as John Updike, Donald Barthelme, and Ann Beattie as well as most *New Yorker* pieces, in favor of many newcomers whose works appear in literary reviews, quarterlies, and little magazines. Acknowledging in the ten-page introduction that literary choice is mainly a matter of taste, he selected works that convey "a new seriousness"—not by chronicling manners or politics but by engaging "in serious personal concern."

Gardner's untiring commitment to the state of the art of fiction cannot be questioned. Even though his outspoken opinions alienated some critics and fellow novelists, his intellectual energy and devotion to fiction will be missed. His messianic voice is responsible for much of the literary discussion on the direction of contemporary fiction. His critical voice will be missed, but his fiction will be a greater loss. Even though his career was cut short, he left an impressive canon. Most impressive are his novels, which are inventive, witty, and extraordinarily varied. Many critics consider *Grendel* a modern classic, *The Sunlight Dialogues* an epic of the 1970s, and *October Light* a dazzling piece of Americana. Explaining his commitment to art, Gardner told Stephen Singular, "It's made my life, and it made my life when I was a kid. . . . Art has filled my life with joy and I want everybody to know the kind of joy I know."

Interviews:

Joe David Bellamy, *The New Fiction: Interviews with Innovative American Writers* (Urbana: University of Illinois Press, 1974), pp. 169–193;

C. E. Frazer Clark Jr., "John Gardner," in *Conversations with Writers I* (Detroit: Bruccoli Clark/Gale, 1977), pp. 82–103;

Don Edwards and Carol Polsgrove, "A Conversation with John Gardner," *Atlantic Monthly,* 239 (May 1977): 43–47;

Henry Allen, "John Gardner: 'I'm One of the Really Great Writers,'" *Washington Post Magazine,* 6 November 1977, pp. 22–23, 28, 33, 37;

Marshall L. Harvey, "Where Philosophy and Fiction Meet: An Interview with John Gardner," *Chicago Review,* 29 (Spring 1978): 73–87;

Daniel Laskin, "Challenging the Literary Naysayers," *Horizon,* 21 (July 1978): 32–36;

Thomas LeClair, "William Gass and John Gardner: A Debate on Fiction," *New Republic,* 180 (10 March 1979): 25, 28–33;

Paul F. Ferguson, John R. Maier, Frank McConnell, and Sara Matthieson, "John Gardner: The Art of Fiction LXXIII," *Paris Review,* 21 (Spring 1979): 36–74;

Joyce Renwick and Howard Smith, "Last of the Radio Heroes," *Horizon,* 22 (July 1979): 67–71;

Stephen Singular, "The Sound and Fury Over Fiction," *New York Times Magazine,* 8 July 1979, pp. 13–15, 34, 36–39;

Ed Christian, "An Interview with John Gardner," *Prairie Schooner,* 54 (Winter 1980–1981): 70–93;

Alan Burns and Charles Sugnet, *The Imagination on Trial: British and American Writers Discuss Their Working Methods* (London: Allison & Busby, 1981);

Benjamin DeMott, "A Philosophical Novel of Academe," *New York Times Book Review,* 20 June 1982, pp. 1, 26–27;

Allan R. Chavkin, ed., *Conversations with John Gardner* (Jackson: University Press of Mississippi, 1990).

Bibliographies:

John Michael Howell, *John Gardner: A Bibliographical Profile* (Carbondale: Southern Illinois University Press, 1980);

Robert A. Morace, *John Gardner: An Annotated Secondary Bibliography* (New York: Garland, 1984).

References:

Joe David Bellamy and Pat Ensworth, "John Gardner," *Fiction International,* 2/3 (1974): 33–49;

Thomas Edwards, "The Sunlight Dialogues," *New York Times Book Review,* 10 December 1972, pp. 1, 14;

W. P. Fitzpatrick, "John Gardner and the Defense of Fiction," *Midwest Quarterly,* 20 (Summer 1979): 405–415;

Paul Gray, "Devil's Due," *Time,* 155 (31 March 1980): 82;

Robert Harris, "What's So Moral About John Gardner's Fiction?" *Saturday Review,* 9 (June 1982): 70–71;

Jeff Henderson, *John Gardner: A Study of the Short Fiction* (Boston: Twayne, 1990);

Henderson, ed., *Thor's Hammer: Essays on John Gardner* (Conway: University of Central Arkansas Press, 1985);

John Michael Howell, *Understanding John Gardner* (Columbia: University of South Carolina Press, 1993);

Norma L. Hutman, "Even Monsters Have Mothers: A Study of Beowulf and John Gardner's Grendel," *Mosaic,* 9, no. 1 (Fall 1975): 19–31;

Thomas LeClair, "The Clatter of Moral Fiction," *Saturday Review,* 7 (29 March 1980): 53–54;

LeClair, "Moral Criticism," *Contemporary Literature,* 20 (Autumn 1979): 509–512;

Larry McCaffery, "The Gass-Gardner Debate: Showdown on Main Street," *Literary Review,* 23 (Fall 1979): 134–144;

Dean McWilliams, *John Gardner* (Boston: Twayne, 1990);

Robert A. Morace and Kathryn Van Spanckeren, eds., *John Gardner: Critical Perspectives* (Carbondale: Southern Illinois University Press, 1982);

Julian Moynahan, "Moral Fictions," *New York Times Book Review,* 17 May 1981, pp. 7, 27–28;

Judy Smith Murr, "John Gardner's Order and Disorder: *Grendel* and *The Sunlight Dialogues*," *Critique,* 18, no. 2 (1977): 97–108;

Ronald Grant Nutter, *A Dream of Peace: Art and Death in the Fiction of John Gardner* (New York: Peter Lang, 1997);

John Romano, "A Moralist's Fable," *New York Times Book Review,* 23 March 1980, pp. 1, 26–27;

Jay Rudd, "Gardner's *Grendel* and *Beowulf*: Humanizing the Monster," *Thoth,* 14, nos. 2–3, (1974): 3–17;

Roger Sale, "Banging on the Table," *New York Times Book Review,* 16 April 1978, pp. 10–11;

Elizabeth Spencer, "Experiment is Out, Concern is In," *New York Times Book Review,* 21 November 1982, pp. 7, 49;

George Stade, "Nickel Mountain," *New York Times Book Review,* 9 December 1973, p. 5;

Susan Strehle, "John Gardner's Novels: Affirmation and the Alien," *Critique,* 18, no. 2 (1977): 86–96;

Robert Towers, "So Big," *New York Times Book Review,* 24 June 1982, pp. 17–18;

Per Winther, *The Art of John Gardner: Instruction and Exploration* (Albany: State University of New York Press, 1992);

James Wolcott, "Core Curriculum," *Esquire,* 97 (June 1982): 134, 136.

Nikki Giovanni

This entry was updated by Mozella G. Mitchell (University of South Florida) from her entry in DLB 41: Afro-American Poets Since 1955.

See also the Giovanni entry in *DLB 5: American Poets Since World War II.*

BIRTH: Knoxville, Tennessee, 7 June 1943, as Yolande Cornelia Giovanni Jr., to Jones (Gus) and Yolande Cornelia Watson Giovanni.

EDUCATION: B.A. (with honors), Fisk University, 1967; postgraduate studies at University of Pennsylvania, School of Social Work, and Columbia University School of the Arts.

CHILD: Thomas Watson.

AWARDS AND HONORS: Grants from Ford Foundation, 1967, National Endowment for the Arts, 1968, and Harlem Cultural Council, 1969; Outstanding Achievement Award, *Mademoiselle,* 1971; Omega Psi Phi Fraternity Award for outstanding contribution to arts and letters, 1971; Woman of the Year Youth Leadership Award, *Ladies' Home Journal,* 1972; National Association of Radio and Television Announcers Award for *Truth Is on Its Way,* 1972; National Book Award nomination for *Gemini,* 1973; "Best Books for Young Adults" citation, American Library Association, for *My House,* 1973; elected to Ohio Women's Hall of Fame, 1985; "Outstanding Woman of Tennessee" citation, 1985; *Post*-Corbett Award, 1986; Ohioana Book Award, 1988; Jeanine Rae Award for the Advancement of Women's Culture, 1995; Langston Hughes Award, 1996; honorary degrees include Doctorate of Humanities, Wilberforce University, 1972, Fisk University, 1988; Doctorate of Literature, University of Maryland (Princess Anne Campus), 1974, Ripon University, 1974, and Smith College, 1978; Doctorate of Humane Letters, The College of Mount St. Joseph on the Ohio, 1985, Indiana University, 1991, Rockhurst College, 1991, Otterbein College, 1992, Widener University, 1993, Albright College, 1995, Cabrini College, 1995, and Allegheny College, 1997.

BOOKS: *Black Feeling, Black Talk* (New York: Black Dialogue Press, 1967);

Nikki Giovanni

Black Judgement (Detroit: Broadside Press, 1968);
Black Feeling, Black Talk/Black Judgement (New York: Morrow, 1970);
Re: Creation (Detroit: Broadside Press, 1970);
Gemini: An Extended Autobiographical Statement on My First Twenty-Five Years of Being a Black Poet (Indianapolis: Bobbs-Merrill, 1971);
Spin a Soft Black Song: Poems for Children (New York: Hill & Wang, 1971);
My House: Poems (New York: Morrow, 1972);
Ego-Tripping and Other Poems for Young People (New York: Lawrence Hill, 1973);
A Dialogue: James Baldwin and Nikki Giovanni, by Giovanni and James Baldwin (Philadelphia: Lippincott, 1973; London: Joseph, 1975);
The Women and the Men (New York: Morrow, 1975);
Cotton Candy on a Rainy Day (New York: Morrow, 1978);

Vacation Time: Poems for Children (New York: Morrow, 1980);
Those Who Ride the Night Winds (New York: Morrow, 1983);
Sacred Cows—and Other Edibles (New York: Morrow, 1988);
Knoxville, TN (New York: Scholastic Publications, 1994);
Racism 101 (New York: Morrow, 1994);
The Genie in the Jar (New York: Holt, 1996);
The Selected Poems of Nikki Giovanni (New York: Morrow, 1996);
The Sun Is So Quiet (New York: Holt, 1996);
Love Poems (New York: Morrow, 1997).

RECORDINGS: *Truth Is on Its Way,* Right-On Records, 1971;
Like a Ripple On a Pond, Nik Tom, 1973;
The Way I Feel, Atlantic Records, 1974;
Legacies, Folkways Records, 1976;
The Reason I Like Chocolate, Folkways Records, 1976;
Cotton Candy on a Rainy Day, Folkways, 1978.

OTHER: *Night Comes Softly: An Anthology of Black Female Voices,* edited by Giovanni (Newark, N.J.: Medic Press, 1970);
A Poetic Equation: Conversations Between Nikki Giovanni and Margaret Walker, by Giovanni and Margaret Walker (Washington, D.C.: Howard University Press, 1974);
Appalachian Elders: A Warm Hearth Sampler, edited by Giovanni and Cathee Dennison (Blacksburg, Va.: Pocahontas Press, 1991);
Shimmy Shimmy Shimmy like My Sister Kate: Looking at the Harlem Renaissance through Poems, edited by Giovanni (New York: Holt, 1996).

SELECTED PERIODICAL PUBLICATIONS—UNCOLLECTED: "Black Poems, Poseurs, and Power," *Negro Digest,* 18 (June 1969): 30–34;
"The Planet of Junior Brown," *Black World,* 21 (March 1972): 70–71;
"Celebrating the Human Species," *Encore,* 7 (18 December 1978): 20+;
"Why We Are Brokers at the Table of Peace," *Encore,* 8 (15 October 1979): 8–9;
"Root of the Matter," *Encore,* 9 (January/February 1981): 18–19;
"Root of the Matter," *Encore,* 10 (March/April 1981): 19;
"Root of the Matter," *Encore,* 10 (November 1981): 17–18;
"Communication," *Ebony,* 38 (February 1983): 48;
"I Wrote a Good Omelet," *Essence,* 14 (October 1983): 88;

"Mother-To-Mother: What Life Is Like Living with a 14-Year Old Son," *Essence,* 15 (September 1984): 154+;
"My Own Style," *Essence,* 16 (May 1985): 60+;
"They Clapped," *Essence,* 16 (May 1985): 226;
"Campus Racism," *Essence,* 21 (April 1991): 94;
"Shooting for the Moon," *Essence,* 23 (April 1993): 58–60;
"Racism 101: Academic Advice," *Jet,* 85 (4 April 1994): 29–30;
"Light the Candles," *Essence,* 26 (May 1995): 109–111.

Nikki Giovanni came into prominence on the American scene as one of the most noted poets of the new black renaissance that began in the 1960s. Since that time she has grown from the open, aggressive, and explosive revolutionary tendencies that characterized her early verses to expressions of universal sensitivity, artistic beauty, tenderness, warmth, and depth. Accompanying this steady growth in artistic quality as a poet has been her attainment of wide popularity and acclaim as a lecturer in the black community and on college campuses around the country and in other parts of the world. Especially popular among the generations of the 1960s, 1970s, and 1980s for her easy blending of curse words into her most elegant speeches, she has become somewhat of a folk hero and has been called the "Princess of Black Poetry." On her frequent speaking tours she attracts overflowing crowds. Addressing such a crowd at Wilberforce University in 1972, where she received an honorary Doctor of Humanities degree, she laughingly pointed out that her shocking language had helped bring her to that moment; the graduating seniors gave her a standing ovation. She has served as professor of English at Livingston College of Rutgers University in New Jersey, as professor of Black Studies at Queens College of City University of New York, visiting professor of English at Ohio State University, professor of creative writing at Mount St. Joseph's College, and visiting professor at Virginia Polytechnic Institute and State University, where she has remained since 1989. She has traveled in Africa, Europe, and the Caribbean and has received many honors and awards. Her recording *Truth Is on Its Way* (1971), in which she recites some of her poetry to the background of gospel music, was among the best-selling albums of that year. Her poetry also demands and has received much critical attention. In 1987 PBS produced a film about her life, titled *Spirit to Spirit: The Poetry of Nikki Giovanni.*

Giovanni was born Yolande Cornelia Giovanni Jr. in Knoxville, Tennessee, the younger of

BLACK
JUDGE
MENT

Cover for Giovanni's 1968 collection, which grew out of her political activism

the two daughters of Gus and Yolande Giovanni. Even as early as four years of age she was brave, assertive, and forceful and idolized her older sister, Gary, whom she was determined to "protect." When Giovanni was quite young, her family moved to Wyoming, Ohio, a suburb of Cincinnati. Her mother and father, who was from Cincinnati, had met while students at Knoxville College. In Cincinnati, Giovanni's mother served as a supervisor for the Welfare Department, and her father served as a social worker. Louvenia Terrell Watson, Giovanni's maternal grandmother, seems to have exerted a tremendous influence upon Nikki. She was assertive, militant, and terribly intolerant of white people. She and Giovanni's grandfather, John Brown ("Book") Watson, a schoolteacher in Albany, Georgia, were urged to leave that city for fear of Louvenia's being lynched for her outspokenness. They left hurriedly one night in a buggy, lying concealed under a blanket, and settled in Knoxville, where Giovanni's mother, Yolande, and two other daughters were born. Giovanni revered her grandmother, with whom she lived during her sophomore and junior years at high school. Louvenia Watson taught her responsibility to her own people.

Seriously disaffected with what she considered the trivial and insincere regard for humanness that seemed to exist in marital relations, Giovanni decided early that marriage was not for her, at least

not at that time. She then concentrated her energies on developing her career as a writer. She was deeply concerned about her own identity as a person—who she was and what her purpose in life should be. Her sister Gary was especially gifted in music, but Giovanni had a difficult time establishing herself as a poet. She was imaginative, given to fantasizing and intellectual speculation. She says that her fantasy life went on with a "different personality emerging all the time." This side of her was balanced by absorption in hearty reading—about fifty books a year, including Ezra Pound, T. S. Eliot, Richard Wright, and Greek and Roman mythology. She attended an Episcopal school, where she was not too fond of the white teaching nuns, who on one occasion called Richard Wright's *Black Boy* (1945), which she had read as a seventh grader, a trashy book. Her decision to become a writer was based on the recognition of and desire to develop her intellectual and imaginative gifts rather than to stifle them in a typically middle-class domestic situation. Therefore, having a strong affinity for family life but not desiring to be inhibited by a possibly inhospitable marriage, Giovanni made the conscious choice to have a child out of wedlock. Her son, Thomas (Tommy), was born to her while she was visiting her parents for Labor Day in 1969. He became the center of her life, and in 1971 she dedicated to him her first book of poems for children, *Spin a Soft Black Song*.

The 1960s were tumultuous for all of America. Producing many emotional highs and lows, they abounded in mass movements and rebellious demonstrations, as well as in shocking occurrences. In the area of civil rights there were sit-in demonstrations, freedom rides, and the Voting Rights Act, which was accompanied by many voter registration projects. The National Association for the Advancement of Colored People (NAACP), the Southern Christian Leadership Conference (SCLC), the Student Non-Violent Coordinating Committee (SNCC), the Congress of Racial Equality (CORE), and many other black-oriented groups were in full action, fighting for the liberation and equality of black people and competing for recognition in the black community and the nation. The 1960s were also an era of marches in Washington and other places under leaders such as Martin Luther King Jr., Stokely Carmichael, Floyd McKissick, and James Forman.

It was a time of transformation from this milder form of struggle to black power and liberation and black revolutionary efforts. Elijah Muhammad, Malcolm X, and the Nation of Islam stirred black people to move toward radical self-assertion and revolutionary change. Malcolm X, Medgar Evers, John F. Kennedy, Martin Luther King Jr., and Robert Kennedy were all felled by assassins' bullets. Riots and rebellion sprang up in Watts (Los Angeles), California; Newark, New Jersey; New York City; Nashville, Tennessee; Chicago, Illinois; Detroit, Michigan; Washington, D.C.; and in other cities across the nation. Antiwar demonstrations and rebellion erupted at colleges around the country. To say the least, it was an exciting time to be a student on a college campus.

At the beginning of this period of upheaval, Nikki Giovanni—a small, quick, sometimes harsh, sometimes gentle girl of seventeen—entered Fisk University in September 1960. Coming from a middle-class family residing in a suburb of Cincinnati, she was then a Goldwater supporter who had read much of, among other books, Ayn Rand, cheap novels, and fairy tales. Yet she was in a state of growth. She did not like Fisk, whose social life did not appeal to her. (During the early 1960s Fisk was widely known for its intelligent, relatively well-off young women who more than likely would marry the graduates of Meharry Medical College in the same Nashville area. Less privileged young women and men attended Tennessee State University in the same city.) Giovanni did not approve of the dean of women, whom she referred to as "bitchy," and the following Thanksgiving she rushed home to her grandmother's in Knoxville without getting the dean's permission. Upon her return to school, Gio-

vanni was placed on probation. Her attitude did not change, however, for in February she was released from the school for having attitudes that did not "fit those of a Fisk woman." Her grandfather died in April, and after the funeral Giovanni returned to Cincinnati with her mother, strongly regretting, however, having to leave her grandmother alone.

In 1964 Giovanni, true to her contradictory nature, returned to Fisk University and became respected as an ideal student. These were some of her most active years. She developed her literary talents and edited *Elan,* a campus literary magazine. She also became politically active; in 1964 she was sufficiently politically aware to found a chapter of SNCC on the Fisk campus. This activity is the first evidence of her interest in black power, for this act followed Stokely Carmichael's declaration of "Black Power" on a freedom march down a Mississippi highway in 1963. What marked the radical shift from the conservative Goldwater stance to that of black power is not quite clear. It might be conjectured, however, that her encounters in the Southern environment and her close observations of the progressive developments in the nation of the civil rights demonstrations, especially in the South, along with the great popularity of Malcolm X and the Nation of Islam around the country, among other things, captured the imagination and enthusiasm of this sensitive young woman.

While at the university Giovanni also took part in the Fisk Writers' Workshop under the direction of the celebrated author John O. Killens, who no doubt inspired her literary talents as well as contributed to her awakening as a black liberationist. On 4 February 1967 she graduated magna cum laude in history. Her grandmother's death followed closely upon this happy occasion— on 8 March of the same year. Spiritually, artistically, and politically awakened, Giovanni was profoundly affected by this incident. It stirred in her a sense of guilt and shame both for the way in which society had dealt with this strong, sensitive woman to whom she had been so close and who had deeply influenced her life and for the way she herself had left her grandmother alone to die. Presumably, this great attachment to Louvenia Terrell Watson made Giovanni cherish so much the friendship of women more than fifty years old and caused her to become quite sensitive to the needs and aspirations of the women who fill much of her poetry.

When Giovanni had gone home after graduation to Cincinnati, the news of her grandmother's death came as a shock, for Giovanni had been planning to drive down and bring her grandmother back to Cincinnati for a visit only two days later. When her father called and gave her the news, Giovanni became ill and remained so throughout the funeral. Weighing heavily on her conscience in addition to her own feeling that she had deserted her grandmother was the belief that "progress" had killed Louvenia Watson. Earlier, the street on which Louvenia Watson had lived, Mulvaney Street in Knoxville, had been located in a development area of a Model Cities project. Louvenia Watson had been forced to leave her home to make way for a new shopping mall, convention center, and expressway. Though the new house on Linden Avenue had a bigger backyard and no steps to climb, it was never home to her. Giovanni felt her grandmother died because "she didn't know where she was and didn't like it. And there was no one there to give a touch or smell." No doubt, her sensitivity to the reality of this situation aroused in Giovanni an awareness of the helplessness of other humans under similar social conditions and served as a significant cause of the anger evident in her early verse.

In June 1967 Giovanni planned and spearheaded the first Cincinnati Black Arts Festival, thus initiating an awareness of arts and culture in the black community and becoming a prime mover in the struggle for the awakening that was characteristic of the period. This effort evolved into The New Theatre, an indigenous black theater movement. Deeply engrossed in community organization and the concepts of black nation-building rather than advancing herself occupationally or professionally, Giovanni's mother told her daughter that she would either have to get a job or go to graduate school. Feeling that either of these alternatives would interfere with her black liberation activities, Giovanni tried every means to evade the issue. She consulted with her father, from whom she hoped to receive sympathy, but discovered the avenue of escape lay elsewhere; she resolved to attend graduate school.

With a Ford Foundation Grant she attended the University of Pennsylvania School of Social Work and later entered the School of Fine Arts at Columbia University. In 1968 she received a National Foundation for the Arts Grant and served as assistant professor of English in the SEEK Program of Queen's College. In the same year she lived for a time in Wilmington, Delaware, where she started a black history workshop in the black community, thereby continuing her activist involvement.

Out of these involvements grew her first two books, which were published successively, *Black Feeling, Black Talk* (1967) and *Black Judgement* (1968), later combined into one volume. The first book, *Black Feel-*

ing, Black Talk, consists mostly of black consciousness-raising, chatty lyrics, monologues, and ritual recitations, some relating to her personal experiences as a black liberation advocate and many of these dedicated to black persons and groups whom she felt contributed to her own development. These poems seem to represent a kind of ritualistic exorcism of former non-black ways of thinking and an immersion in blackness. Not only are they directed at other black people whom she wanted to awaken to the beauty of blackness but also at herself as a means of saturating her own consciousness. For instance, "Poem (No Name No. 2)," six lines long, reads like an incantation:

Bitter Black Bitterness
Black Bitter Bitterness
Bitterness Black Brothers
Blacker Yet Bitter
Get Black Bitterness
          NOW

This type of exorcistical chant is expanded in "The True Import of Present Dialogue, Black vs. Negro," which aims also for a psychological reversal of the state of one's mind:

Nigger
Can you kill
Can a nigger kill
Can a nigger kill a honkie
Can a nigger kill the Man
Can you kill nigger
Huh? Nigger can you
kill

The poem continues with daring questions, interspersed with ironic allusions to violent actions blacks have committed for the nation against their own color across the world and ends with the command: "Can you learn to kill WHITE for BLACK / Learn to kill niggers / Learn to be Black men."

Another poem, "A Short Essay of Affirmation Explaining Why (With Apologies to the Federal Bureau of Investigation)" is of a confessional nature. As the title suggests, it affirms blackness and ends on a humorous note: "I'm into my Black thing / And it's filling all / My empty spots / Sorry 'bout that, / Miss Hoover." One poem in this collection, "Word Poem (Perhaps Worth Considering)," goes beyond Giovanni's vision of violent change to a vision of rebuilding:

As things be/come
let's destroy
then we can destroy
what we be/come
let's build
what we become
when we dream

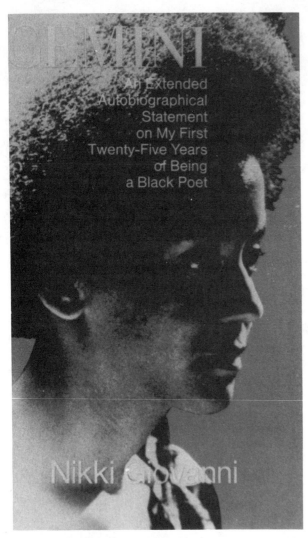

Dust jacket for Giovanni's 1971 collection of poems about significant experiences in her life

play with words to create humor, chagrin, or irony and to convey feelings of hatred, love, tenderness, and moods of loneliness, sadness, and joy. However, in this early stage of her commitment of her talent to the service of the black revolution, her creativity is bound by a great deal of narrowness and partiality from which her later work is free. The capacity for growth, incidentally, is a singular quality exhibited in her works as a whole. A steady progression toward excellence in craftsmanship is one of the key elements in her development.

Her second work, *Black Judgement,* published in 1968, is pivotal and includes the germs of later ideas. Already in it, for instance, is the tension between the private artistic self, which she masks by excessive revolutionary rhetoric, and the public, communal, political self. Later works show the partisanism fading into a universal outlook and identity along with the growth in individualistic artistic skill and perception. First, however, the revolutionary fire had to run its course. *Black Judgement* is an extremely important book in this regard, because it reflects what seems to be a kind of death and rebirth in the artist's life in which she is baptized in the revolutionary spirit and rhetoric and finally awakens later to a healthier self and world consciousness. This experience is marked by two great events of the 1960s: the assassinations of Martin Luther King Jr. and Robert F. Kennedy. The poems are dated, and some make direct reference to the events.

The tragic death of King on 4 April 1968 enraged and embittered her and stirred in her a deep desire for revenge, as the heavy-handed prose piece, "Reflections on April 4, 1968," exhibits. It was written the next day and records her initial reaction in such incendiary statements as "What can I, a poor Black woman, do to destroy America?"; "The Assassination of Martin Luther King is an act of war"; and "May his blood choke the life from ten million whites." These aggressive sentences are balanced by broader reflections scattered about on the deeper ironies of the situation, such as "Let us pray for the whole state of Christ's church"; "Let America's baptism be the fire this time" (an allusion to Baldwin's *The Fire Next Time* and to the black spiritual about the biblical flood); and "This is a thirsty fire they have created. It will not be squelched until it destroys them." Referring ironically to America's notion of itself as the promised land and its people as the chosen, she closes the piece with a call to black people for some form of saving action, reinforced by allusion to King's favorite hymn, "Precious Lord—Take Our Hands—Lead Us On." Giovanni obviously separated the man from his methods. Showing disrespect for his tactics in the earlier "Poem for

A few other poems in the volume are surprisingly full of pleasant remembrances of warm human contacts and feelings of personal intimacies, joys, and sorrows: "You Came, Too," "Poem (For TW)," "Poem (For BNC No. 1)," and "Poem (No Name No. 1)." The volume opens with a reminiscence of a black arts conference in Detroit. "Detroit Conference of Unity and Art (For HRB)" is dedicated to H. Rap Brown, a prominent revolutionary figure on the American scene during the time who was charged with inciting riots. The poem recalls the cherished topics of the conference (the possibility of blackness, inevitability of revolution, black leaders, black love, and black men and women); it climaxes with the revealing quatrain: "But the most / valid of them / All was that / Rap chose me."

Giovanni's genuine poetic talent is clearly exhibited in this first volume in her clever and skillful

Black Boys," written two days before his assassination, in "Reflections . . . " two days later she is plunged into deepest melancholy at the news of his murder. Several of the other poems reflect stages of religious melancholy Giovanni underwent as a result of the tragic occurrence. Five days later in "The Funeral of Martin Luther King, Jr.," after attending the funeral in Atlanta, she expresses chagrin at the words on King's headstone: "Free At Last, Free at Last / But death is a slave's freedom." And contrary to the claim of critics that her early poetry was lacking in a sense of hope for the future, she concludes the poem with, "We seek the freedom of free men / And the construction of a world / Where Martin Luther King could have lived and preached nonviolence." Three days after the funeral she moved deeper into spiritual despondency.

"A Litany for Peppe," written on 12 April 1968, is a perverted parody of genuine religious ritual, reminiscent of Christ's Sermon on the Mount, especially the Beatitudes. Its disconnected recitations mingled with a refrain are suggestive of mental distraction combined with a studied call for avenging actions. For instance, it begins with the lines "They had a rebellion in Washington this year / because white people killed Martin Luther King / Even the cherry blossoms wouldn't appear." This passage is followed by the refrain: "Black Power and Sweet Black Peace." Another section about riots is followed by "And sweet peace to you my child," juxtaposed ironically with "Blessed be machine guns in Black hands." The poem closes with the perverted beatific refrain, "Blessed is he who kills / For he shall control this earth."

This macabre vision is balanced by a rather pleasing and wholesome prose poem about the author's life while growing up. "Nikki-Rosa," which has long been Giovanni's most cherished creation, was written on the same day as "Litany." It focuses on the joys and pleasantries of growing up in a black home in spite of poverty and some unhappy occurrences. She recalls gratefully such things as:"how happy you were to have your mother / all to yourself and / how good the water felt when you got your bath"; "how much you / understood their feelings / as the whole family attended meetings"; "and though you're poor it isn't poverty that / concerns you"; "it isn't your father's drinking that makes any difference / but only that everybody is together and you / and your sister have happy birthdays and very good Christmases / and I really hope no white person ever has cause to write about me / because they never understand Black love is Black wealth and they'll probably talk about my hard childhood and never understand that / all the while I was quite happy."

Dust jacket for Giovanni's 1971 book dedicated to her son and exploring black children's feelings about their neighborhoods, American society, and themselves

A few weeks after King's funeral, still brooding in the same state of melancholy, Giovanni wrote "The Great Pax Whitie," a perversion of a black sermon and a parody of the Pax Romana. It opens with a parody of Genesis: "In the beginning was the word / And the word was / Death. / And the word was nigger / and the word was death to all niggers / And the word was death to all life." Punctuated with the refrains of "peace be still" and "ain't they got no shame," the poem catalogues America's sins of violence as well as those of the Western world in general, making allusions to the holocaust. It closes with a sense of horror at the same violence that took the lives of John Kennedy, Malcolm X, and Martin Luther King:

> So the great white prince
> Was shot like a nigger in Texas
> And our Black shining prince was murdered
> like that thug in his cathedral
> While our nigger in Memphis
> was shot like their prince in Dallas
> and my lord
> ain't we never gonna see the light.

A few days later Giovanni becomes the little girl again back home in Knoxville with "daddy," "grandmother," and "going to church and listening to gospel music" as she writes "Knoxville, Tennessee" (17 May 1968): "I always like summer / best / you can eat fresh corn / from daddy's garden / and okra / and greens / and cabbage / and lots of / barbecue / and buttermilk /

and homemade ice-cream. . . . " Like "Nikki-Rosa," it is a return to the source, to the beginning, to the mother's womb, so to speak, from which a glorious rebirth is to be expected.

Before that could take place another national tragedy occurred that only intensified Giovanni's despondency, the assassination of Robert F. Kennedy on 6 June 1968, a few weeks after "Knoxville" was written. The poem "Records" was written in response to this occurrence:

> how i feel about a
>   family
>   being wiped out
>   trying to explain
> that they have nothing
>   against bobby
>   he's white
>   millionaire
> several times over
>   so it must be me
>   they are killing

The subtlety of this assumption leads her to advocacy of retaliation as a means of self-protection:

> this country must be
>   destroyed
>   if we are to live
> must be destroyed if we are to live
> must be destroyed if we are to live.

"Adulthood," written on the same day, is a monologue detailing certain phases of the author's life up to that time. It is concentrated as well as comprehensive and may be looked upon as describing the evolution of a revolutionary. It begins with the girlhood stage of wonder ("i was meaningless / and i wondered if life / would give me a chance to mean") and records the changes in the teenage stage of dating, the young-adult stage of college, and commitment and black awareness. Then she cites her involvement in artistic pursuits and black cultural activities as a means of aiding black liberation:

> for a while progress was being
>   made along with a certain
>   degree
> of happiness cause i wrote a book and found
>   a love
> and organized a theatre and even
>   gave some lectures on
> Black history
> and began to believe all good
>   people could get
> together and win without bloodshed[.]

Then the author begins ritualistically to catalogue a series of tragic deaths and regretful happenings that shattered her faith and transformed her into an indignant revolutionary; "a for real Black person who must now feel / and inflict / pain." The events include the deaths of Dag Hammarskjöld, Patrice Lumumba, President Diem, President Kennedy, and other killings prior to and including King and the second Kennedy brother; the arrests of LeRoi Jones (Amiri Baraka) and H. Rap Brown; and the flight of Stokely Carmichael.

Giovanni's emergence from this "night-journey" is seen in later works, but hopeful signs of it appear in a few of the poems in this collection, especially those dealing with pleasant remembrances of her childhood days and wholesome family relations. The harshness of the revolutionary verses of some of these poems overshadows certain other more lyrical images such as in "Beautiful Black Men" and the personal, perceptive, and revealing monologue "Woman Poem." Both of these poems were written on 10 September 1968. A few lines from each should illustrate the point. "Black Men" sounds like a jazz song:

> i wanta say just gotta say someting
> bout those beautiful beautiful beautiful
> outasight
> black men
> with the afros
> walking down the street
> is the same ol danger
> but a brand new pleasure—.

"Woman Poem" is written in the chatty dialogue of an average woman:

> you see, my whole life
> is tied up
> to unhappiness
> its father cooking breakfast
> and me getting as fat as a hog
> or having no food
> at all and father proving
> his incompetence
> again
> i wish i knew how it would feel
> to be free.

Her first two books brought Giovanni to critical attention as one of the three leading figures of the new black poetry between 1968 and 1971 (the other two were Don L. Lee and Sonia Sanchez). Their works and the works of others were variously described as hate poetry by Arthur Davis in 1973; humanistic protest by Richard K. Barksdale in 1973; nation-building poetry by R. Roderick Palmer

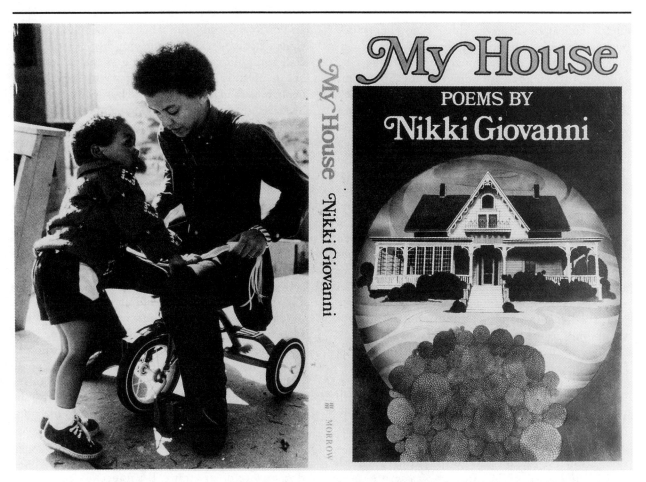

Dust jacket for Giovanni's 1972 collection, which turns from political and social issues to thoughts of home, family, and love

in 1971; positive in celebrating blackness and the need for dynamic change by A. Russell Brooks in 1971; rooted in the love of black people and an affirmation of life, posing a tension between hatred and love, life and death, thus constituting a real vitality; and, as Don L. Lee himself said in 1971, as reflecting awareness of the values of black culture and commitment to the revolution.

Having been awarded the Harlem Cultural Council on the Arts Grant and cited in the *Amsterdam News* as one of the ten most admired American women, Giovanni in 1969 began to emerge from her state of grief and shock. Before she became an associate professor at Rutgers University, Livingston College, Giovanni gave birth to her son, Thomas. The birth of her son constituted the turning point in her life; as she returned from her mother's house in Cincinnati where her son had been born, she began to center herself on her relationship with Tommy.

In 1970 Giovanni founded the publishing cooperative, NikTom, Limited, and collected, edited, and published a volume of poetry by black female poets, several of whom were prominent—Gwendolyn Brooks, Mari Evans, Jewel C. Latimore (Jo-

hari Amini), Carolyn Rodgers, and Margaret Walker.

Her third volume of poetry, *Re: Creation,* published in 1970, was not significantly different in tone, content, and style from the first two: it included black revolutionary verse. In 1970, also, her first two books were reissued in a combined volume by William Morrow Publishers. In the meantime, between 1969 and 1971 Giovanni had traveled to the Caribbean to such places as Haiti and Barbados. She wrote the autobiographical work *Gemini: An Extended Autobiographical Statement on My First Twenty-Five Years of Being a Black Poet* (1971), and her fourth book of poetry, *Spin a Soft Black Song: Poems for Children* (1971), dedicated to her son. With the publication of these two works a significant change took place in her as a person and as an artist.

In these two works there is evidence of a more developed individualism, greater introspection, and a sharpening of her creative and moral powers, as well as of her social and political focus and understanding. In *Gemini* it is obvious she now takes herself more seriously as a poet and a woman as well as a revolutionary. Giovanni attempts to clarify in poetic, polemical, descriptive, critical essays her stance on many issues. As her poetry is not traditional, neither is this book a conventional autobiography. She calls it "An Extended Autobiographical Statement on My First Twenty-Five Years of Being a Black Poet." Being a poet is what she is about; it has been a part of her very nature from infancy onward. Also important is that she is a black poet. Rather than a completely chronological report and clarification of her development, *Gemini* gives a piecemeal characterization of the author from the presentation of bits and pieces of her various experiences of growing up, going to college, working, getting involved with black liberation, having a baby, traveling, and so on. The book also characterizes the members of her family, including her grandmother and grandfather as well as her mother, father, sister, and nephew. In addition, essays and prose pieces, some previously published in magazines, explain and defend her views on various subjects and persons, including black literature, music, Angela Davis, and Lena Horne.

Of particular interest are the two articles "A Revolutionary Tale" and "Don't Have a Baby till You Read This," both of which are perceptive, half-humorous, sometimes rambling stories of incidents occurring in critical phases of her life—becoming a revolutionary, deciding to go to graduate school, and having a baby. The former was written and published in June 1968 in *Negro Digest,* and the latter appears for the first time in this volume. Both reveal warm, sensitive, charming sides of the artist's nature and the wholesome, loving, sharing family environment in which she was raised. The artist's ability to weave tales of her own life as though they were those of a fictional character and entertain and captivate her audience with humor and insight is remarkably displayed.

The first story reveals it was her roommate Bertha who was influential in the author's transformation from the Ayn Rand-Barry Goldwater mentality to black activist-revolutionary; subsequently she converted her mother and father by getting them to read Frantz Fanon, Stokely Carmichael, H. Rap Brown, John O. Killens, Amiri Baraka, Larry Neal, and others. In the second story she confesses that she did not discover that she was pregnant until she was in the fourth month, while visiting in Barbados; that her heart had stopped temporarily during the birth of her son by cesarean section; and that her newly born son was gladly welcomed into a supportive, loving, caring family.

Finally, in the chapter titled "It's a Case of . . . ," she reflects on her travels to California, Haiti, Barbados; on Angela Davis, among others; on groups; and on social and political issues. Giovanni shows signs of considerably modifying her personal, social, and political views, as well as the direction of her intellectual and emotional growth. For instance, being black did not help her in Haiti, for even in this black nation she was open to being preyed upon as a foreigner. She enjoyed Barbados much more but still realized she was not simply in a black country but also in a foreign land. As a result of pondering on subjects related to these journeys, she modified her views of West Indians in the United States as being exploited immigrants. "I bobbed up and down in the water and thought about how beautiful a people is at home. I would have hated West Indians had I not visited Barbados. I fully understood and agreed with Harold Cruse about that."

She began to formulate a humanist worldview and to see individuals, including herself, of course, in terms of their places in the scheme of things. "The state of the world we live in is so depressing. And this is not because of the reality of the men who run it but it just doesn't have to be that way. The possibilities of life are so great and beautiful that to see less wears the spirit down." Facing this reality, she begins to sort out meaningful responses to the situation: "It's like the more you move toward the possible, the more bitter you become toward the stumbling blocks. I can really understand why people don't try to do anything. It's not really easy, but if you have to deal with energy it's a much more realistic task to decide not to feel than to feel. It takes the same amount of time but not to feel is ultimately more rewarding because things always come back to that anyway. . . . You were a fool." Whether one agrees with her or not, one sees that she is figuring things out for herself, that she is preparing herself for tremendous personal growth. "The truth is that there is this shell around you, and the more you say, 'All right, you can come in' to someone, the more he questions the right of the shell to exist. And if you fall for that and take it away, he looks at your nakedness and calls you a whore. It's an awful thing when all you wanted was to laugh and run and touch and make love and really not give a damn." *Gemini* received mixed reviews.

Spin a Soft Black Song, published the same year and dedicated to her new son, includes some thirty poems recounting the feelings of black children about their neighborhoods, American society, and themselves. These poems well represent the tenor of the black experience and convey interesting insights into it and life in general. In spite of the author's attempt to emulate the language of childhood and convey the thoughts from a childlike point of view, however, the ideological bent of the works is anything but childish. One can see Giovanni's increase in skill and movement toward a wider and more humane ideal in her writing.

Also in 1971 Giovanni soared to national popularity and fame by the recording of her album *Truth Is on Its Way,* in which she reads some of her poetic creations against the background of gospel music provided by the New York Community Choir. Ellis Haizlip, producer and director of the WNET-TV show *Soul,* was instrumental in getting Giovanni to become involved in the venture. The earlier popularity of shows he had done with women writers reading their own poems induced him to experiment further and to suggest to Giovanni the possibility of combining gospel music with her work. In July she introduced the recording before a crowd of 1,500 during a free concert at Canaan Baptist Church in Harlem. Its reception was sensational and, surprisingly, converted listeners who otherwise had rejected the new black poetry as being offensive and antagonizing. In a May 1972 article in *Jet* she explained, "I wanted people to take not just my poetry, but something I thought was a valid comment on my poetry which was gospel music." Her desire to relate her poetry not to street music but to church music, she explained, was expressive of a new aim in her life, to get inside institutions and effect changes in and through them. For the same reason, she joined the National Council of Negro Women, founded by Mary McCleod Bethune.

Giovanni's album became a top-selling record and was popular on radio stations around the country. The author was in great demand for making personal appearances nationally, making the rounds especially on college campuses. *Mademoiselle* magazine presented her with an award for outstanding achievements; Omega Psi Phi fraternity presented her an award for her outstanding contribution to arts and letters. In November 1971 she became ill from too much travel.

In 1972 she was featured on the covers and within the pages of many magazines, including *Ebony, Jet, Harper's Bazaar,* and *Publishers' Weekly.* She was presented the keys to Gary, Indiana, and Lincoln Heights, where the mayor proclaimed 14 April Giovanni Day. It was "marked with a motorcade led by Mayor James E. Lowry and other elected city officials, a dinner at St. Simon's Church, and a ceremony before an overflow crowd at Lincoln Heights High School, where Mayor Lowry read the proclamation from the city fathers and citizens." The National Association of Radio and Television announcers presented her an award for the Best Spoken Word Album;

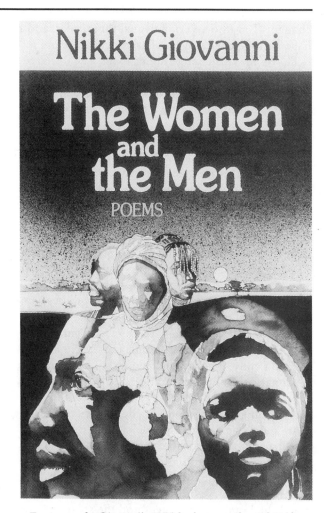

Front cover for Giovanni's 1975 book, poems devoted to ideas about human relationships and the art of poetry

Prince Matchabelli presented her its Sun Shower Award (for women who achieved new heights in their careers in 1971); the National Council of Negro Women granted her a life membership and scroll; and she became a part of the National Black Heroines for PUSH.

In April of the same year she was presented with an honorary doctorate of humanities degree by Wilberforce University. In an article in *Jet* she says she was startled by the Reverend Leon G. Sullivan's description of her as "this fine, young woman who walks in truth and who brought a measure of wisdom to all who've seen what she's written." As she walked to the podium, she thought to herself, "Now, all these graduating brothers and sisters are going to feel that I'm telling them that they could be honored just by saying mother. . . ."

In 1972 her new book of poetry *My House* also appeared, evidencing a remarkable change in her writing. She briefly commented on this change: "I'm into a very personal thing, now, and I have a two and a half-year-old-son, and I'm more settled." As for this change in her focus, she declared, "Only a fool doesn't change. Only the mass of the earth remains the same. It has not changed in weight since it was formed, but yet, it is a constantly changing thing."

Having visited Africa and Europe in July 1971 with Ida Lewis (who wrote the foreword to *My House*), Giovanni further modified her views of the world and herself. The individualism in her earlier works that was either separate from or in tension with her political ideology now came to the fore and blended with a modified political stance, and in most cases it supplanted the narrow revolutionary conception. Giovanni's creative genius abounds. Rhythmic, lyrical qualities; vivid imagery; shifting moods, tones, and atmospheres; and the liquid flow of words and phrases combine to reveal the author's enormous skill.

In *My House* Giovanni turns more from the outside issues to thoughts of home and family and extended family, love, and humanness. The poems are personal and autobiographical, all dated, written mostly in 1971 and 1972, and are grouped under the two headings "The Rooms Inside" (twenty-three poems) and "The Rooms Outside" (thirteen poems). In the first section the poems concentrate on the warmth, pleasures, and comforts of home and family, intimate relations, personal thoughts, and love. The second section is about people (mostly black) beyond the home environment and the struggles and issues they have to face. The predominant form is the monologue, revealing the mood and innermost thoughts of the personas in descriptive, rhythmic language.

The author's changing attitude is expressed in "Categories." Thinking back on occasions of seeing an "old white woman" and wanting to relate to her as a person but finding it impossible to because of the great psychological distance, the poet concludes:

> if she weren't such an aggressive
>   bitch she would see
> that if you weren't such a Black one
> there would be a relationship but
>   anyway–it doesn't matter
> much–except you started out to
>   kill her and now find
> you just don't give a damn cause
>   it's all somewhat of a bore
> so you speak of your mother or sister
>   or very good friend
> and really you speak of your feelings
>   which are too personal
>   for anyone else
>   to take a chance on feeling.

The "too personal" feelings, in fact, are often exposed in the poems of *My House*–for example, in the direct physical imagery of "When I Nap": "i lay at the foot / of my bed and smell / the sweat of your feet / in my covers / while I dream." In "Africa I" the reader is invited to share the creative exuberance of the persona: "on the bite of a kola nut / i was so high the clouds blanketing africa / in the mid morning flight were pushed / away in an angry flicker / of the sun's tongue." In contrast, the closing words display the delicacy of the speaker's interaction with her mother, "and something in me said shout / and something else said quietly / your mother may be glad to see you / but she may also remember why / you went away."

One of Giovanni's closest friends, Ida Lewis, comments in the foreword to *My House* on the author's focus on family and individualism: "one key to understanding Nikki is to realize the pattern of her conviction. The central core is always associated with her family: the family that produced her and the family she is producing. She has reached a simple philosophy more or less to the effect that a good family spirit is what produces healthy communities, which is what should produce a strong (Black) nation."

In 1973 Giovanni collected and edited a volume of her poems especially for young people, *Ego-Tripping and Other Poems for Young People*. It consists chiefly of poems appearing in previous volumes. The title poem characterizes the general tone of the rest in the volume. Proud, boasting, and filled with hyperbolic imagery, the poem fairly struts up and down the page. The speaker is an omniscient female god: "I was born in the congo / I walked to the fertile crescent and built / the sphinx"; she continues "I sat on the throne / drinking nectar with allah," "My daughter is nefertiti," "My son noah built new / ark and / I stood proudly at the helm." The poem ends in a sudden shift to the words of a popular blues song: "I am so perfect so divine so ethereal so surreal / I cannot be comprehended / except by my permission / I mean . . . I . . . can fly / like a bird in the sky. . . ."

Giovanni's popularity was still growing. She was cited in the *Ladies' Home Journal* as Outstanding Woman of the Year for Youth Leadership, and she received a National Book Award Nomination for *Gemini*. Her collaborative volume with James Baldwin, *A Dialogue,* was published. Two years earlier on 4 November 1971, in London, the two authors taped a conversation for the television program *Soul*. The videotape was shown in two installments on 15 and 22 December 1971. The two authors revised and edited the transcribed tape for this published volume. What is significant is that Giovanni and Baldwin represented two generations of black writers who were deeply affected by and involved in the black movement for liberation but who were of different ideologies and philosophies. It was a dynamic meeting of minds on such subjects as religion, black men and women and love, America and black people, junkies, the American society and hope, the black movement, literature, and criticism and the art of writing. All in all the dialogue is quite interesting and closes on a genuine note of hope.

One year after the successful dialogue with Baldwin, in October 1972, Giovanni appeared on the Paul Laurence Dunbar Centennial program at the University of Dayton in Ohio along with Margaret Walker and other writers reading from Dunbar's work. Giovanni and Walker had an almost electrifying effect on their audiences. During the occasion Giovanni accepted a challenge from a participant to do a "Conversation Book" with Margaret Walker. Giovanni had for many years had a great admiration for Margaret Walker, especially in appreciation for her poem, "For My People." Therefore, in Walker's home in Jackson, Mississippi, in November 1972 and in Washington, D.C., in January 1973, the two poets discussed a range of subjects, and the conversations were published in the volume *A Poetic Equation: Conversations Between Nikki Giovanni and Margaret Walker* (1974). This encounter was much more potentially explosive than the one with Baldwin, for although the two poets admired each other immensely, they came from sharply different settings and orientations.

The preface to the book defines the contrast between the two minds. "Margaret Walker had decided to sow her seeds in the South (her home is Jackson, Mississippi) after finding the northern soil of Chicago and New York interesting but not the kind of stuff from which her roots are grown. She is a woman who reflects the values of a generation of blacks steeped in scholarship (and proud of it), who experienced the Depression, World War II, the rise of the American Communist Party and McCarthyism, and a racial perspective which had its own particular kind of radical and conservative aspects." Giovanni, on the other hand, is "a virtual embodiment of the sixties and seventies: controversial, in constant physical and mental movement; not only unafraid to explore the dichotomies of the times and of herself, but determined to lay them bare. Her sensibility thrives in an urban world, and she has shored up her life forces to not only survive but direct it."

The resultant book consists of six chapters of exciting intellectual encounter between two women

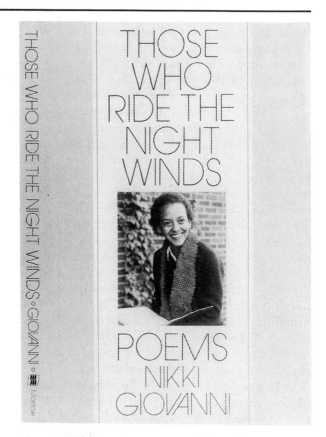

Dust jacket for Giovanni's 1983 book, poems written in a style suggesting the halting process of thought

of high intelligence. The subjects discussed include the methods of the black liberation movement, thoughts on writing and criticism, war, the black woman, and black people and their future in America. Clearly the differences come through in Walker's humanism and theological stance and Giovanni's more radical stance concerning violence and self-defense as opposed to degradation, the views the two have of each other's writing. On many issues the poets reached an agreement. Both especially endorsed the changes in society regarding sex roles and the role of the family. Giovanni expresses the belief that "sex-derived roles" do not work in the community. She recommends "getting rid of them!" The discussion ends on a hopeful note that stresses the need for black people to take responsibility in getting things straight in America.

The publication of *The Women and the Men* in 1975 marks another milestone in the life and career of Nikki Giovanni. In this collection of poems she has permitted to flower fully portions of herself and her perception that had been evident only in subdued form or in incompletely worked-through fragments. Ideas concerning women and men, universal human relatedness, and the art of poetry are seen here as being in the process of fuller realization in the psyche of the author. Furthermore, the delicate, charming, poetic expression they are given in these verses shows superior skill and mature creative development. The artist has evidently relaxed the revolutionary restraints on her artistic talents and has allowed her full creative powers to blossom.

The poems are included under three divisions: "The Women," "The Men," and "And Some Places." The first and second divisions are devoted to full poetic expression of the interests and insights she briefly dealt with in the pivotal work *Black Judgement* ("Beautiful Black Men" and "Woman Poem"), that were issues in her dialogues with Baldwin and Walker and that ran through (as a minor theme) most of her previous works. The first division, "Revolutionary Dreams" (a dramatic monologue), describes surrender to natural powers and sums up her shift in focus from "militant," "radical" dreams of political takeover to an emphasis on self-realization: "If I dreamed natural / dreams of being a natural / woman doing what a woman / does when she's natural / i would have a revolution."

In a review in *Best Sell* in January 1976 Robert McGeehin responded quite positively to this volume, especially to the poems in the first division. He referred to them as a "startling group of poems," primarily portraits, "clear and honest expressions and statements of Black womanhood and repetition that would make for easy musical scoring." McGeehin is right. For instance, "The Women Gather" is a dirge reflecting on the contradictions of life. "Each Sunday" tries to capture the serious philosophical thinking of a woman waist-deep in domestic affairs. "The Genie in the Jar (for Nina Simone)" is a beautiful song celebrating creativity. Also included are "A Poem for Aretha" and "Ego-Tripping."

In the second division, "The Men," the author's haunting desire to understand black men, strongly presented in her dialogue with James Baldwin, has seemingly dissolved in a submission to simply loving them in joy and appreciation. The imagery of this section is unusual and skillfully chosen and combined, often with musical word arrangements reflective of jazz and blues songs. "The Way I Feel" concludes, "in my mind's eye you're a clock / and I'm the second hand sweeping / around you sixty times an hour / twenty-four hours a day." "Kidnap Poem" declares, "if i were a poet / i'd kidnap you / put you in my phrases and meter / you to jones beach." "Poem" ends with the phrase "with the relief of recognition / i bend to your eyes / casually / raping me." "Autumn Poem" closes, after a reflection on an earlier love-making scene, with "i am a leaf / falling from your tree upon which i was / impaled."

The last division, "And Some Places," reveals a mellowed revolutionary revisiting some places and her former self and detailing new insights and new perceptions. "Africa" depicts a land describing itself as a "teller of tales / a dreamer of dreams" of freedom and hope and joy, the resolving of tensions between "blacks and Africans" who will walk "side by side in a new world / described by love and bounded by difference / for nothing is the same except oppression and shame." "A Very Simple Wish" expresses surprise at the simple fact "that it's easier to stick / a gun in someone's face / or a knife in someone's back / than to touch skin to skin / anyone whom we like." After summarizing the need for blending all the world's people and differences into one harmonious whole, the poem concludes "i want to make a quilt / of all the patches and find / one long strong pole / to lift it up / i've a mind to build / a new world / want to play." Finally, the author's simple, artistic view of her craft is summarized in "Poetry": "Poetry is motion graceful / as a fawn / gentle as a teardrop / strong like the eye / finding peace in a crowded room." A poem, she continues, "is pure energy / horizontally contained / between the mind / of the poet and the ear of the reader / if it does not sing discard the ear / for poetry is song."

By 1976 and 1977 America showed signs of turning inward, away from the raucous times of the 1960s and early 1970s. The me-generation limped to the foreground. Many black revolutionaries were simply overwhelmed by the sudden turn of events of a new era; old tactics of marches, demonstrations, riots, rhetoric, and burnings had lost their appeal. Some revolutionaries were able to change their tactics to suit the times of economic and energy crises and political repression. Some became more introspective and began to sort out a new, relevant approach to life. Nikki Giovanni survived this lull in the black liberation struggle because she had already begun to cultivate the inner resources she possessed and always remained open to spiritual, intellectual, artistic, ethical, as well as political growth. These years found her still traveling, writing, and developing and sharpening her skills and perceptions.

In 1978 she published *Cotton Candy on a Rainy Day,* perhaps her most sobering book of verse yet. It includes thoughtful and insightful lyrics on the emotions, fears, insecurities, realities, and responsibilities of living. The extended metaphor of the title poem is rather apt. The insubstantial, fleeting quality of life is cleverly depicted in relation to her personal growth and social involvement and the necessity for change occasioned by the 1970s. "Don't look now / I'm fading away / into the gray of my

No one asked us . . . what we thought of Jamestown . . . in
1619 . . . they didn't even say . . . "Welcome" . . .
"You're Home" . . . or even a pitiful . . ."I'm Sorry . . .
But We Just Can't Make It . . . Without You" . . . No . . .
No one said a word . . . They just snatched our drums . . .
separated us by language and gender . . . and put us on
blocks . . . where our beauty . . . like our dignity . . .
was ignored

No one said a word . . . in 1776 . . . to us about Freedom
. . The rebels wouldn't pretend . . . the British lied . . .
We kept to a space . . . where we owned our souls . . .
since we understood . . . another century would pass . . .
before we owned our bodies . . . But we raised our voices .
. . in a mighty cry . . . to the Heavens above . . . for the
strength to endure

No one says . . . "What I like about your people" . . . then
ticks off the wonder of the wonderful things . . . we've
given . . . Our song to God, Our strength to the Earth . . .
Our unfailing belief in forgiveness . . . I know what I like
about us . . . is that we let no one turn us around . .
not then . . . not now . . . we plant our feet . . . on
higher ground . . . I like who we were . . . and who we are
. . . and since someone has asked . . . let me say: I am
proud to be a Black American . . . I am proud that my people
labored honestly . . . with forbearance and dignity . . . I
am proud that we believe . . . as no other people do . . .
that all are equal in His sight . . . We didn't write a
constitution . . . we live one . . . We didn't say "We the
People" . . . we are one . . . We didn't have to add . . .
as an after-thought . . . "Under God" . . . We turn our
faces to the rising sun . . . knowing . . . a New Day . . .
is always . . . beginning

Nikki Giovanni
18 September 1993

*Typescript for Giovanni's poem "But Since You Finally Asked," commemorating the annual Slave Memorial
Wreath-Laying at Mt. Vernon (Collection of Nikki Giovanni)*

mornings / or the blues of every night," it begins.
Characterizing the 1970s as "loneliness," she calls it
"The sweetest soft essence / of possibility / never
quite maturing." Somehow, the incompleteness of
the liberation movement of which she was so intricately a part arouses a sense of loneliness, boredom,

and futility in which she sees herself as fragile and
incomplete: "I am cotton candy on a rainy day / the
unrealized dream of an unborn idea."

The fragile aspects of the human condition are
reflected in other poems such as "The New York-
ers," which describes scenes of men and women in

various troublesome stances of life. "Crutches" and "Boxes" reflect desperation: "emotional falls always are / the worst / and there are no crutches / to swing back on." "I am a box / on a tight string / subject to pop / without notice." "Age," "Because," "Their Fathers," and "Life Cycles" are examples of her philosophical reflections on life that are so prevalent in this volume. The author's new sober attitude toward life is aptly described in "Fascinations": "finding myself still fascinated / by the falls and rapids / i nonetheless prefer the streams / contained within the bountiful brown shoreline / i prefer the inland waters / to the salty seas / knowing that journeys end / as they begin."

Paula Giddings, who wrote the introduction to *Cotton Candy,* titled "A Woman of the Seventies," sees the volume as completing Giovanni's cycle of dealing with society, others, and finally herself. This pensive, introspective, plaintive work "speaks of loneliness, personal emptiness, and love which is not unrequited but, even worse, misunderstood and misbegotten."

In 1978, the same year of the publication of *Cotton Candy,* Giovanni's father suffered a serious stroke. Realizing the dilemma this put her family in, Giovanni and her son, Tommy, moved from their New York apartment back to Cincinnati to be with her parents, still, however, maintaining a small apartment in New York. Her father was moved to California to stay with her sister, Gary, for a convalescence. Giovanni proved her genius for home and family life by fixing up the basement of her family home to include a living area, work space, bedroom, and bathroom; she cooked, shopped, washed her car, and played football with her son.

In 1980 Giovanni published *Vacation Time: Poems for Children,* a delightful collection, totally free of ideology, full of bubbles, joy, animals, flowers, birds, sunshine, rainbows, stars, and the light fantastic. One may be dazzled by the smooth way she drops all political and personal concerns and completely enters the world of the child and brings to it all the fanciful beauty, wonder, and lollipopping.

In 1983 *Those Who Ride the Night Winds* was published by William Morrow. In this book Giovanni has adopted a new and innovative form, and the poetry reflects her heightened self-knowledge and imagination. Written in short paragraphs punctuated with ellipses reminiscent of telegraphic communication, most of the poems appear to be hot off the mind of the author. Yet the style also suggests the halting flow of perceptive thought. "If you want to share . . . a vision . . . or tell the truth . . . you pick up . . . your pen . . . and take your chances . . . ,"

she writes in "Lorraine Hansberry: An Emotional View." This is what she herself has done. Her vision concerns specifically those who have the courage to seek change and to take a risk; it is about those "who ride the night winds" and "learn to love the stars . . . even while crying in the darkness . . . ": Lorraine Hansberry, John Lennon, Billy Jean King, Martin Luther King Jr., Robert Kennedy, and Phillis Wheatley. In most cases the poems are meditation pieces that begin with some special quality in the life of the subject and with thoughtful, clever, eloquent, and delightful words amplify and reconstruct salient features of his or her character.

Such is the case with "The Drum," which invokes the Pied Piper, Kunta Kinte, and Henry David Thoreau in a rhythmic reflection upon Martin Luther King Jr.'s "Drum Major for Peace" speech. In "This Is Not For John Lennon" she contemplates the artist as "an astronaut of inner peace" who "celebrated happiness, gave word to the deaf . . . vision to the insensitive . . . sang a long low note when he reached the edge of this universe and saw the blackness . . . poetry. . . . " Not all of the poems are written in the telegraphic style; a few free verse pieces are more traditional. All the poems are not about famous persons. Some of the pieces are built upon everyday people and events: mothers, children, skydiving, love, anniversaries. In fact, the most impressive and delightful poem in the book is titled "I Wrote a Good Omelet":

> hot poem
> after loving you
> Buttoned my car . . . and drove
> my coat home . . . in the rain . . .
> after loving you
> I goed on red . . . and stopped on
> green . . .
> floating somewhere
> in between . . .
> being here and being there . . .
> after loving you.

As Giovanni has lived through the great transitional periods—from the passionate engagement with vital social, spiritual, economic, and literary issues in the 1950s and 1960s to lulls and downshifts in intellectual and social intensity and the conservative backlash and retrenchment of the 1970s and 1980s, along with the resurfacing of overt racist attitudes and attacks—she has managed to stay abreast of the issues and to expand her thinking and writing so as to remain a relevant interpreter and commentator on the moods, issues, and directions of the times. She has insight and wisdom to offer each age and speaks to the needs of the times with vision and

Dust jacket for Giovanni's 1997 collection, dedicated to slain rap star Tupac Shakur

perception. She has lived through evolutionary processes in which strong black groups have undergone changes of leadership and focus. For example, the militant and radical revolutionist H. Rap Brown, whom Giovanni revered in one of her first volumes of poetry in 1968, *Black Judgement,* dedicating her Detroit Conference of Unity and Art to him, has undergone steady transformation and radical conversion. He is presently called Jamil Abdullah Al-Amin and lives in Atlanta, where he is the Imam (spiritual head in the Islamic religion) of the Community Mosque of Atlanta and commands the respect of some ten thousand Muslims from around the country. All manner of other changes have taken place in these waning years of the twentieth century, including an explosion of diversity of ethnic and cultural groups in this country, along with the massive social, economic, and cultural problems of the times.

Artists and intellectuals such as Giovanni give definition to predicaments, attitudes, and reactions of the times. Giovanni still proves to be a decisive and insightful voice. She has five books that have appeared from 1988 to 1997 in addition to poems that have appeared in various periodicals. Of the five books, only two are poetry. The other three consist of prose writings: one that includes interviews of Giovanni in conversation with other thinkers and two that are composed of essays in which she comments and elaborates on issues in life and literature as she sees them.

In the mid 1980s Giovanni's career of teaching and lecturing advanced considerably both nationally and internationally. She accepted professorships at major universities within this period, serving as professor of English at Ohio State University (1984–1985) and professor of creative writing at Mount St. Joseph's College (1985–1987). After undergoing an intense battle in 1984 with leaders of TransAfrica over her refusal to participate in the boycott of South Africa, during which she was blacklisted and even received bomb threats for her independent actions, she showed signs of stress. However, she was able to recover her composure, strength, and courage, and in 1985 she made a European lecture tour for the USIA. (United States Information Agency). In the same year she received several honors, such as being inducted into the Ohio Women's Hall of Fame and named Outstanding Woman of Tennessee. Her career picked up even further when in 1986 she received the *Post*-Corbett Award from the *Cincinnati Post* and became Artist-in-Residence at the Taft Museum in Cincinnati.

Accepting a visiting professorship at Virginia Polytechnic Institute in Blacksburg in 1987, Giovanni produced another volume of prose, published in 1988, filled with short pieces on a multiplicity of subjects, from the most private and personal concerning her family life to the most public and universal. This book is aptly titled *Sacred Cows—And Other Edibles,* for it is a gold mine of wit and wisdom, down-to-earth and pointed criticism of almost every conceivable important subject. In all cases Giovanni presents challenging, provocative, original ideas that invite self-criticism, cultural criticism, and social, political, economic, and religious reexamination of values. The next to last essay, titled "Our Own House Is In Disorder," is expressive of the kind of matter-of-fact, honest assessment of society included in the other essays in the book. Giovanni cites the evidence of social disorder that has developed since the Civil Rights era, Black Power/Black Liberation movement, Women's Movement, Peace Movement, Voting Rights Act, Civil Rights Act, and others.

She received several other awards and recognitions during this period, including the PBS production of a film on her life and writings, titled *Spirit to Spirit: The Poetry of Nikki Giovanni* (1987), and being the featured poet of the Utrecht Literary Festival in Holland in 1991. In 1989 she received a permanent faculty appointment at the Virginia Polytechnic Institute, where she had been serving as a visiting professor. In 1992 Virginia C. Fowler, professor of English at Virginia Polytechnic Institute and author of *Nikki Giovanni: An Introduction to Her Life and Work,* edited a collection of dialogues with Giovanni titled *Conversations with Nikki Giovanni,* which includes discussions with a variety of intellectuals, artists, and journalists such as Margaret Walker, James Baldwin, Stephanie Stokes, Claudia Tate, and Fowler herself. The book reveals much not only about Giovanni but also about other persons, such as Baldwin, Margaret Walker, Toni Morrison, and Alice Walker, as well as a crucial period in American history. The dialogues, arranged chronologically over a twenty-year period from the late 1960s to the 1990s, show the development of Giovanni's thinking. She reveals herself as both prophet and historian. Lynn Litterine said in her 1973 dialogue with Giovanni that she seemed to be endlessly absorbing the world scene—digesting information from various sources such as television, newspapers, and the streets—and trying to make sense of the underlying structure. She believes people can spend only so much time disliking or fighting each other; they cannot get around that they all live in the United States—almost nobody is going back to Africa or Europe—and this fact, to her, strongly suggests trying to make the present situation work, not by exclusion but by inclusion, changing, improving, and working together.

In 1993 the author wrote the poem "But Since You Finally Asked" to commemorate the annual Slave Memorial Wreath-Laying at Mt. Vernon. This penetrating work recounts in sharp, pictorial imagery and phraseology the history of a people brought to this country in chains and never asked what they thought of Jamestown or told "Welcome . . . You're Home." Nevertheless, in spite of the brutalities, indignities, and inhumanity of slavery, they forged a brave and proud history. In her "Foreword" to Giovanni's *Selected Poems,* Fowler notes that the realities of life for African Americans are juxtaposed in the poem with the ideals expressed in the Declaration of Independence and the Constitution, strongly suggesting the irony that these people are practically the only Americans who have actually believed in and tried to practice those ideals that were never intended to include them.

Also in 1993 Giovanni published the twentieth-anniversary edition of *Ego-Tripping and Other Poems for Young People,* which was expanded to include additional poems. In her private life her son, Thomas, graduated magna cum laude from Morehouse College in Atlanta. Her mother and sister, Gary, moved from California (where her mother had lived with Gary since 1987, her father, having died of a lingering illness in 1982) to Virginia, which brought the family back together again geographically. Giovanni published another book of prose in 1994 titled *Racism 101,* which responds to the seemingly eternal reality and overt revival of racism in America. From her vantage point as an African American professor for the past six or seven years at the predominantly white Virginia Polytechnic Institute, a distinguished research university, she focuses criticism on the inequities of American higher education and provides a kind of freshman course ("101") for African American students in navigating the slippery seas of existence and survival on predominantly white campuses. Other subjects she addresses are W. E. B. DuBois, gardening, Toni Morrison, *Star Trek,* space exploration, the role of the African griot, and Spike Lee's film on Malcolm X, which she condemns (she writes her own ideas about what such a film should be like). Fowler comments in the "Foreword" to the book that Giovanni's voice in the work reflects the changes that have occurred in American culture over the past twenty-five years, but what remains constant in Giovanni herself over this period are the fundamental values that shape her vision of society, culture, and life. Fowler sums these up as a belief in the necessity to fight injustice wherever it appears and in whatever form; a commitment to an historical perspective, to looking at the present with a fully informed sense of the past; a respect, often even a reverence, for the past and present struggles of African American people; a desire to find underlying connections between and among people and events; and an abiding belief in the integrity and power of the individual.

In 1995 Giovanni underwent a successful operation for lung cancer. After recuperating she worked on a collection of her poetry, published in 1996 under the title *The Selected Poems of Nikki Giovanni.* Serving as writer-in-residence for the National Book Foundation's Family Literacy Program at the Family Academy in Harlem, she wrote the poem "Stardate Number 18628.190" (alternately titled "Light the Candles") for the twenty-fifth anniversary issue of *Essence* magazine. Since the magazine is a publication devoted to the lifestyle, culture, and beauty of black women, Giovanni's poem aptly focuses on a celebration of the history, culture, style, uniqueness, and beauty of African American women of all varieties, characters, personalities, classes, colors, and ages. It cites the songs, activities, involvements, survival mechanisms, and faith, among other things, that have contributed to the successful lives and characters of these women. She announces near the end of the poem:

> This is the Black woman . . . in all our trouble and glory . . . in all
> past history and future forbearance . . . in all that ever made
> love a possibility. . . . . .This is about us . . .
>   bleached and natural . . . braided and straightened hair . . .
>   made up . . . or . . . beaten up faces . . .
>   tall . . . short . . . stately . . . bent . . .
>   CC Riders . . . junkies . . . whores . . .
>   wives . . . mothers . . . grandmothers . . . aunts
>   working in the home or outside . . .
>   working in the system or outside . . .
>   working praying working to survive . . .
>   giving pride . . . giving succor . . . giving voice . . . giving
>   encouragement . . . giving whatever . . . we can give.

The two poems "Stardate 18628.190" and "But Since You Finally Asked" are respectively, the opening and closing poems of the 1996 book, implying that gender and race form the basis upon which the selections from her works were made from the nine volumes published during the previous twenty-five years. The first and last poems in the selection were not among those but frame the edition in a thematic perspective. Fowler notes in the "Foreword" to the work that when reading through the poems included, one cannot avoid recognizing that race and gender are inextricably intertwined as central concerns.

In 1997 the author published a selected volume of her poetry, titled *Love Poems,* which is dedicated to slain rap star Tupac Shakur, whom she describes as "a lover whose love was often deliberately misunderstood but who will live in the sun and rains and whose name will echo through all the winds whose spirit will flower and who like Emmett Till and Malcolm X will be remembered by his people for the great man he could have become and most especially for the beautiful boy that he was." Needless to say, this tribute is one of the most noble portrayals of the young rapper and movie star to be found anywhere. Many of the poems included in this volume have been published previously, though some are entirely new. The types of love covered are broad, ranging from friendship to romantic love to love of nature, family, country, and all facets of life. Having had a rapidly and steadily changing literary career over the past decade and a half, Nikki Giovanni has exhibited tremendous creative, intellectual, ethical, and political growth.

Interviews:
Virginia C. Fowler, *Conversations with Nikki Giovanni* (Jackson: University Press of Mississippi, 1992).

References:
Peter Bailey, "Nikki Giovanni: I Am Black, Female, Polite," *Ebony* (February 1972): 48–50;

Richard K. Barksdale, "Humanistic Protest in Black Poetry," in *Modern Black Poets: A Collection of Critical Essays,* edited by Donald B. Gibson (Englewood Cliffs, N.J.: Prentice-Hall, 1973), pp. 157–164;

Bernard W. Bell, "New Black Poetry: A Double-Edged Sword," *CLA Journal,* 15 (September 1971): 37–43;

A. Russell Brooks, "The Motif of Dynamic Change in Black Revolutionary Poetry," *CLA Journal,* 15 (September 1971): 7–17;

Arthur P. Davis, "The New Poetry of Black Hate," in *Modern Black Poets: A Collection of Critical Essays,* edited by Donald B. Gibson (Englewood Cliffs N.J.: Prentice-Hall, 1973), pp. 147–156;

Virginia C. Fowler, *Nikki Giovanni: An Introduction to Her Life and Work* (New York: Twayne, 1992);

Don L. Lee, *Dynamite Voices: Black Poets of the 1960s* (Detroit: Broadside Press, 1971), pp. 68–74;

Gwen Mazer, "Nikki Giovanni," *Harper's Bazaar* (July 1972): 50;

Jeanne Noble, *Beautiful, Also, Are the Souls of My Black Sisters; A History of the Black Woman in America* (Englewood Cliffs: Prentice-Hall, 1978), pp. 197–198;

R. Roderick Palmer, "The Poetry of Three Revolutionists: Don L. Lee, Sonia Sanchez, and Nikki Giovanni," *CLA Journal,* 15 (September 1971): 25–35;

Stephanie J. Stokes, "'My House': Nikki Giovanni," *Essence,* 12 (August 1981): 84–88;

Cordell M. Thompson, "Nikki Giovanni: Black Rebel with Power in Poetry," *Jet* (25 May 1972): 18–24;

E. B. Washington, "Nikki Giovanni: Wisdom for All Ages," *Essence,* 24 (March 1994): 67.

Papers:
A selection of Nikki Giovanni's public papers are at Mugar Memorial Library at Boston University.

Alex Haley

This entry was updated by Marilyn Kern-Foxworth (Florida A & M University) from her entry in
DLB 38: Afro-American Writers After 1955: Dramatists and Prose Writers.

BIRTH: Ithaca, New York, 11 August 1921, to Simon Alexander and Bertha George Palmer Haley.

EDUCATION: Attended Alcorn Agricultural & Mechanical College (now Alcorn State University); attended Elizabeth City State Teachers College, 1937–1939.

MARRIAGES: 1941 to Nannie Branch, (divorced 1964); children: Lydia Ann, William Alexander. 1964 to Juliette Collins (divorced 1972); child: Cynthia Gertrude. 1974 to Myran E. Haley.

AWARDS AND HONORS: special citations from National Book Award committee and from Pulitzer Prize committee, both for *Roots,* 1977; Spingarn Medal from NAACP, 1977; nominated to Black Filmmakers Hall of Fame for producing *Palmerstown, U.S.A.,* 1981; honorary degrees include Litt.D, Simpson College, 1971, Howard University, 1974, Williams College, 1975, and Capitol University, 1975; doctorate, Seton Hall University, 1974.

DEATH: Seattle, Washington, 10 February 1992.

BOOKS: *The Autobiography of Malcolm X* (New York: Grove, 1965; London: Hutchinson, 1966);
Roots: The Saga of an American Family (Garden City, N.Y.: Doubleday, 1976; London: Hutchinson, 1977);
A Different Kind of Christmas (New York: Doubleday, 1988);
Alex Haley's Queen: The Story of an American Family, by Haley and David Stevens (New York: Morrow, 1993; London: Macmillan, 1993);
The Playboy Interviews, edited by Murray Fisher (New York: Ballantine, 1993);
Mama Flora's Family, by Haley and Stevens (New York: Scribners, 1998).

TELEVISION: *Roots,* script consultant, ABC, January 1977;
Roots: The Next Generation, script consultant, ABC, February 1979;
Palmerstown, U.S.A., CBS, 20 March 1980.

Alex Haley (Gale International Portrait Gallery)

RECORDING: *Alex Haley Speaks,* Kinte Corporation, circa 1980.

OTHER: Marilyn Kern-Foxworth, *Aunt Jemima, Uncle Ben and Rastus: Blacks in Advertising, Yesterday, Today and Tomorrow,* foreword by Haley (Westport, Conn.: Greenwood Press, 1994).

SELECTED PERIODICAL PUBLICATIONS–
UNCOLLECTED: "My Search for Roots," *Reader's Digest,* 104 (May 1974): 73–78;
"In Search of the African," *American History Illustrated,* 8 (Fall 1974): 21–26;
"Alex Haley on Kids in Search of Their Roots," *Parents Magazine,* 52 (Spring 1977): 60–61;
"What Roots Mean to Me," *Reader's Digest,* 110 (May 1977): 73–76;

"Sea Islanders, Strong-Willed Survivors Face Their Uncertain Future Together," *Smithsonian,* 13 (October 1982): 88–97.

Alex Haley's reputation in the literary world rests upon his much-acclaimed historical novel, *Roots: The Saga of an American Family* (1976). Haley's tracing of his African-American ancestry back to a tiny village in Gambia, West Africa, spawned one of the most ambitious television productions ever undertaken, and it inspired a generation of ancestor-seeking Americans. Eleven years before the appearance of *Roots,* Haley had also gained fame for writing Malcolm X's "as told to" autobiography. Haley published four more books, two of which appeared after his death. He also wrote many articles for popular magazines, appeared on several television shows, and lectured throughout the country.

Alex Murray Palmer Haley was born 11 August 1921 in Ithaca, New York, and grew up in the small town of Henning, Tennessee. He was the oldest of three sons born to Bertha George Palmer and Simon Alexander Haley. When he was born, both parents were in their first year of graduate school, Bertha at the Ithaca Conservatory of Music and Simon at Cornell University. They took the young Alex to Henning, where he grew up under the influence of women who inspired his search for his past. He remembered listening for hours as his family reminisced about an African ancestor who refused to respond to the slave name "Toby": "They said anytime any of the other slaves called him that, he would strenuously rebuff them, declaring that his name was 'Kin-tay.'" These initial stories served as the basis from which the *Roots* saga grew.

Not a stellar student in high school, Haley graduated with a C average at the age of fifteen. He then entered Alcorn A & M College in Lorman, Mississippi. After a short period, he transferred to Elizabeth City State Teachers College in North Carolina, from which he withdrew at age seventeen.

His experiences after college contributed directly to his growth as a writer. In 1939 he enlisted in the U.S. Coast Guard as a mess boy. To alleviate the boredom he experienced while cruising in the southwestern Pacific aboard an ammunition ship, he began writing. His first venture included writing love letters for his shipmates. He expanded his range with articles that he submitted to several American magazines, but a series of rejection slips followed before his first article was accepted for publication by *This Week,* a syndicated Sunday newspaper supplement.

When Haley retired from the coast guard at the age of thirty-seven, he had attained the position of chief journalist. Although he had dutifully served twenty years in the coast guard, he was not permitted to collect his pension checks—those were given as child support to Nannie Branch, whom he had married in 1941. They had two children, William Alexander and Lydia Ann. They were separated for several years before getting divorced in 1964, the year he married Juliette Collins, whom he subsequently divorced and with whom he had one child, Cynthia Gertrude. Haley eventually remarried for a third time.

Determined to continue his avid interest in writing, Haley moved to New York City and rented a basement apartment in Greenwich Village, where, as a freelance writer, he lived a penurious existence. He was in debt and saw no brightness in his immediate future:

> I owed everyone. One day a friend called with a Civil Service job that paid $6000 per year. I turned it down. I wanted to make it writing. My friend banged the phone down. I owed him too. I took psychic inventory. I looked in the cupboard, and there were two cans of sardines, marked two for 21 cents. I had 18 cents in a sack and I said to myself that I'd keep them.

As a reminder of what he had to endure to achieve his goals, Haley framed the coins and cans and displayed them in his private library; he called them a symbol of his "determination to be independent," and vowed that they would always be on the wall.

Haley's life soon took a turn for the better. The day after taking inventory of his circumstances, Haley received a check for an article he had written. This small reward fell short of the recognition he desired, but it did establish the beginning of assignments from more magazines, including *Reader's Digest,* in which he later published the first excerpts from *Roots.*

Eventually, Haley's commitment to writing paid off in two significant ways. First, he received an assignment from *Playboy* in 1962 to interview jazz trumpeter Miles Davis, an assignment that led to the establishment of the "Playboy Interview," a new series for the magazine. (*The Playboy Interviews,* a collection of Haley's discussions with figures such as Martin Luther King Jr., Melvin Belli, and Quincy Jones, was published in 1993.) Second, he was asked to write a feature about Black Muslim leader Malcolm X. This interview was the impetus for Haley's writing the best-selling *The Autobiography of Malcolm X* (1965), which sold fifty thousand hardcover copies and about five million copies in paperback.

The Autobiography of Malcolm X traces Malcolm Little's transformation into Malcolm X, signifying his belief that black people in America had been de-

Dust jacket for Haley's 1976 novel, which made a significant impact in print and on television, and which led to charges of plagiarism

nied their true identities. The book depicts the poverty in which Malcolm grew up, his early bouts with authorities in social service agencies after his father was killed and his mother was slowly losing her sanity, and his wild life on the streets of Detroit following his mother's institutionalization and the separation of his family. The street life led to his imprisonment, during which he was converted to the Muslim faith. He quickly became a respected leader in the Muslim community until his disagreements with Elijah Muhammad, head of the Black Muslims. The book ends shortly after he makes a trip to Mecca and begins to redefine his conception of whites as "devils."

The book was well received and became required reading for many courses in colleges. It also had popular appeal; it was not uncommon to find young black men on street corners, in subways, or walking along the streets with copies of the book in their hands. The assassination of Malcolm X in 1965 contributed to the popularity of the book.

Two weeks after he completed the manuscript for the book on Malcolm X, Haley wandered into the National Archives Building in Washington, D.C., to begin researching his own genealogy. At the time,

Haley did not know that this initial search would eventually lead him to "50 or more archives, libraries and research repositories on three continents" before his curiosity would be satisfied, and that his efforts would culminate with the writing of *Roots,* published twelve years later on 1 October 1976.

Roots is the story of Kunta Kinte, a Mandinkan from the small village of Juffure, Gambia, in West Africa, and his American descendants; he was "the African" about whom Haley's grandmother and other relatives told stories. Haley imaginatively re-created his ancestor's life in Africa, his capture into slavery, and his experiences in the new world. Haley had been fascinated and intrigued by the story from childhood, because Kunta Kinte, he was told, refused to accept the ways and customs of his white masters and never forgot his African heritage.

Haley's relatives also spoke of how Kunta cherished his freedom and would not relinquish the thought of escaping until, upon his fourth attempt, he was caught, and his foot was severed. Eventually Kunta married the cook, Bell, in the big house, and they had a child named Kizzy. Kunta spent many hours telling Kizzy about her African ancestry. "When Kizzy became four or five . . . her father would point out to her various objects and name them in his native tongue. For example, he would point to a guitar and make a single-syllable sound, ko."

Kizzy gave birth to a son, George, who was fathered by her master. She, in turn, began teaching him African sounds and telling him folktales when he was four or five. Perhaps the most famous of Haley's ancestors after Kunta, George became a well-known gamecock trainer and acquired the pseudonym "Chicken George." George married Mathilda and fathered eight children. His fourth son, Tom, became a blacksmith, and when he reached adulthood and married, he was sold to the owner of a tobacco plantation in Alamance County, North Carolina. There he met and married a half-Indian girl named Irene, and she bore him eight children. Tom carried on the oral tradition of his family.

One of Tom's children, Cynthia (Haley's maternal grandmother), was the most immediate influence upon the writing of *Roots*. When Cynthia was two years old, she was taken to Henning, Tennessee, on a wagon train of freed slaves. In Henning she married Will Palmer and had a daughter named Bertha who married Simon Haley. Cynthia, along with Haley's aunts Viney, Mathilda, and Liz, perpetuated the traditional stories concerning the trials, tribulations, and successes of Kunta Kinte's family. Their front porch became their forum. Haley later continued the tradition of his family by sharing the stories with his own children, William, Lydia Ann, and Cindy.

Although it took Haley twelve years to research and write *Roots,* it did not take nearly that long for it to reach the pinnacle of success. Two years following its publication, the book had won 271 awards, including citations from the judges of the 1977 National Book Awards and the Pulitzer Prize. Hundreds of thousands of Americans identified vicariously with the story of *Roots* both in its book form and in the television adaptation. Within this short time, eight and one-half million copies of the book had been printed in twenty-six languages.

Much of the success of *Roots* can be attributed to the airing of two television miniseries which dramatically portrayed the saga outlined in the book. As a result of the television hit, *Roots* was one of the nonfiction best-sellers in 1977; it penetrated domestic, foreign, societal, cultural, geographical, racial, gender, age, and socio-economic barriers. Of its effect, Paul Zimmerman wrote: "Instead of writing a scholarly monograph of little social impact, Haley has written a blockbuster in the best sense—a book that is bold in concept and ardent in execution, one that will reach millions of people and alter the way

we see ourselves." Another testament to the phenomenon that *Roots* became is the fact that prior to the release of the book in paperback, it was used in 276 college courses.

The book was so broadly popular that a children's edition was published, as was a $75 special edition with gold trim. Vernon Jordan, former director of the National Urban League, remarked in a 1976 *Time* magazine article that the televised version of *Roots* was "the single most spectacular educational experience in race relations in America."

This reaction was a surprise to the producers of the miniseries. Produced by David L. Wolper for ABC, *Roots* was originally planned to be televised over a much longer period of time but was shown on eight consecutive nights because of an increased fear that it would be a monumental embarrassment. When the first part of the miniseries aired on 23 January 1977, it was universally acclaimed. Some one hundred thirty million Americans watched at least one of the episodes. Seven of the eight episodes ranked among the top ten shows in all TV ratings. At the end of its run, *Roots* had attained an average of sixty-six percent of the audience shares, which had been projected at thirty-one percent; it was nominated for thirty-seven Emmy awards.

Roots was such a phenomenal success that ABC produced a sequel, *Roots: The Next Generation.* "Roots II," as it was called, cost $16.6 million to make and ran for fourteen hours. The first episode was aired on 18 February 1979. The story line began in 1882, twelve years after the end of "Roots I," and it ended in 1967.

During the eighty-five-year span of "Roots II" Haley's family was dramatized against the backdrop of the activities of the Ku Klux Klan, world wars, race riots, and the Great Depression. As one critic noted in *Time* (19 February 1979), "Roots II" was also able to dramatize normal black middle-class life—at home, work, and college—and to show some of the heartbreaks, ambitions, and conflicts that blacks had in common with whites.

The *Roots* phenomenon turned Haley into an entrepreneur. He formed the Kinte Corporation in California and became involved in the production of movies and records. One of Haley's first productions was a record titled *Alex Haley Speaks;* it features tips from Haley on how to research one's genealogy. Through such ventures, and others tied to the success of *Roots,* Haley became a millionaire.

Haley's success was marked by relentless hours of autographing tours and press interviews on radio and television, as well as in newspapers. Although he was on the lecture tour constantly, he managed to find time to pursue other writing proj-

Haley with Maya Angelou and LeVar Burton during production of the 1977 television miniseries of Roots *(Schomburg Center for Research in Black Culture, New York Public Library, Astor, Lenox and Tilden Foundations)*

ects. In 1980 he teamed with Norman Lear to develop a limited television series, *Palmerstown, U.S.A.,* about the friendship of two young boys—one black and one white—who grew up in the rural South in the 1930s.

Despite fame and fortune, Haley remained reserved about his success. He commented in an article by Hans J. Massaquoi: "The funny thing is that all that money has almost no meaning to me. I was broke so long that I got used to being without money. The few things I do want, including a decent stereo set, don't cost more than $5,000. All I'm concerned with is just being comfortable, being able to pay my debts, and having a little to buy something or make a gift to somebody."

Haley's success brought some conflicts in addition to the fortune. Amid his newly acquired wealth, he found himself involved in two plagiarism suits. The first was brought by Margaret Walker Alexan-

der, author of *Jubilee* (1966), which had won the Houghton Mifflin Literary Fellowship Award; on 20 April 1977 she charged Haley with copyright infringement. Eventually the charges were dropped, but not before Haley had incurred $100,000 in lawyers' fees. The second accusation of plagiarism was brought by Harold Courlander, author of *The African* (1968). Courlander claimed that certain passages in his book were plagiarized in *Roots.* On 14 December 1977, Haley conceded that the charge was accurate and paid $500,000 in out-of-court settlement fees; Courlander had sued for half the profits of *Roots.* According to Haley, "there were three paragraphs from [*The African*] that appeared verbatim in my notes." He explained that during the course of writing his book he often accepted undocumented notes and information from other people and that some of what he used "turned out to be extracted from Courlander's book."

Haley attempted to authenticate as much of the material in *Roots* as possible. He was so obsessed with authenticity, especially from the emotional perspective, that he went to extremes to validate his re-creation of the emotional anguish that Kunta and others must have experienced on the middle passage. An *Ebony* interviewer recounted some of Haley's efforts: "He somehow scrounged up some money and flew to Liberia where he booked passage on the first U.S. bound ship. Once at sea, he spent the night lying on a board in the hold of the ship, stripped to his underwear, to get a rough idea of what his African ancestor might have experienced. . . . That same night, he says, he went back into the hold. 'Lying again on that board, it was as if some kind of catharsis had occurred. I felt for the first time that I was Kunta Kinte. From that moment on, I had no problem with writing what his senses had registered as he was crossing the ocean.'"

Haley's next book, *A Different Kind of Christmas* (1988), appeared twelve years after *Roots*. Set in 1855, this short novel depicts the moral conversion of Fletcher Randall, a nineteen-year-old white North Carolinian who comes to realize that slavery (including on his own family's plantation) is wrong. He joins the Underground Railroad, and together with Harpin' John, a neighboring farmer's slave who uses his harmonica to send signals to escapees, Fletcher helps several slaves get away and gives up his old life.

Another of Haley's books that evolved from his research into family genealogy was *Alex Haley's Queen: The Story of an American Family* (1993), completed by David Stevens from extensive materials, including Haley's seven-hundred-page outline, after Haley's death. This novel traces Haley's paternal ancestry, focusing particularly on his grandmother, Queen Haley, the daughter of a slave named Easter and her white master, "Jass" Jackson. In an afterword, Stevens quotes Haley's declared vision for the project: "This book will convey visceral America. For our land of immigrants is a testimonial to the merging of the cultures of the world, and of their bloodlines." *Queen* was also made into a miniseries in February 1993, starring Halle Berry and Danny Glover.

In 1998 another novel begun by Haley and finished by Stevens was published. *Mama Flora's Family* is the story of a woman who raises her son, Willie, and her orphaned niece, Ruthana, after her husband is shot and killed by whites. A critic for *Kirkus Reviews* (1 September 1998) judged this book to be "Not in the same class as *Roots,* but an affecting if superficial take on recent racial history." In a 19 August 1998 review in *Booklist,* Brad Hooper wrote that

Dust jacket for the posthumously published 1993 novel in which Haley chronicled the lives of his father's ancestors

"Haley's attempt to show 'the things [that] children do, the journeys they make,' may lack for artistry, but it is a heartfelt personalization of social conditions in the black community from the post-World War I period to the present." Like Haley's other sagas, *Mama Flora's Family* was made into a miniseries, televised on CBS in November 1998 and featuring Cicely Tyson as Flora.

One of Haley's last writing endeavors prior to his death was a foreword to *Aunt Jemima, Uncle Ben and Rastus: Blacks in Advertising, Yesterday, Today and Tomorrow* (1994), the first book to chronicle the history of blacks in advertising. In the foreword Haley wrote:

> On September 29, 1967, I stood on a dock in Annapolis, Maryland, where my great-great-great-grandmother had been taken ashore two hundred years earlier on September 29, 1767. It was one of the moments when I truly realized the importance of knowing one's history and the importance of documenting every fact of that history. Because for a long period of time it was against

the law to teach slaves to read and write, much of black American history had to be documented by people other than blacks. As a result, much of our history has either been lost or severely distorted.

Alex Haley, historian, master storyteller, and researcher, died unexpectedly on 10 February 1992. He was buried on the grounds of the Alex Haley Museum in Henning, Tennessee. His contributions to society and humanity were acknowledged with a bronze statue of his likeness, dedicated on 26 November 1997. The 12-foot-high, 4200-pound statue, created by internationally acclaimed artist Tina Allen, was placed in Morningside Park in Knoxville, Tennessee, where Haley resided at the time of his death. Evon Easley Milton, a community activist responsible for the honor given to Haley, stated in a 28 November 1997 Associated Press story, "It is about honoring an average-looking man of color who is famous because of his writing, not because he is an athlete with a good physique." The statue is the focal point of Haley Square, a spot offering a panoramic view of historic Knoxville, the downtown business district, and the Smoky Mountains the author loved. It depicts Haley as a man of the people, dressed in casual clothes, sitting beside a stream. His left hand holds a copy of *Roots,* while his right hand reaches out as though punctuating a story he is telling.

Haley emerged as the first black American to trace his ancestry back to Africa, as documented by *Roots.* He is also admired by many for helping to foster better race relations. Hence, his indelible mark on history will not only be as a creative writer but also as a great civil rights advocate. Haley bridged a part of the gap between the historical liaisons of Africans and African Americans, and his name has become synonymous with the desire to know about heritage and roots.

Interviews:

W. McGuire and M. S. Clayton, "Interview with Alex Haley," *Today's Educator,* 66 (September 1977): 45–47;

Jeffrey Elliot, "Alex Haley Talks to Jeffrey Elliot," *Negro History Bulletin,* 41 (January 1978): 782–785;

Marilyn Kern-Foxworth, "Beyond Roots: An Exclusive Interview with Alex Haley," *Black Collegian* (September–October 1985): 116–124, 186–188.

References:

Katrine Ames and Ronald Henkoff, "Uprooted," *Newsweek,* 93 (22 January 1979): 10;

H. Boyd, "Plagiarism and the *Roots* Suits," *First World,* 2, no. 3 (1979): 31–33;

Cheryl Forbes, "From These Roots: The Real Significance of Haley's Phenomenon," *Christianity Today,* 21 (6 May 1977): 19–22;

M. Granfield, "Uncle Tom's Roots," *Newsweek,* 89 (4 February 1977): 100;

W. Marmon, "Haley's RX: Talk, Write, Reunite," *Time,* 109 (14 February 1977): 72;

Hans J. Massaquoi, "Alex Haley in Juffure," *Ebony,* 32 (July 1977): 31–33;

Massaquoi, "Alex Haley: The Man Behind *Roots,*" *Ebony,* 32 (April 1977): 33–36;

Martin Rein and Jeffrey M. Elliot, "Roots," *Negro History Bulletin,* 40 (January 1977): 664–667;

Madalynne Reuter, "Doubleday Answers Haley: Denies All Charges," *Publishers Weekly,* 211 (25 April 1977): 34–35;

Reuter, "Haley Settles Plagiarism Suit, Concedes Passages," *Publishers Weekly,* 214 (25 December 1978): 22;

Reuter, "Why Alex Haley Is Suing Doubleday: An Outline of the Complaint," *Publishers Weekly,* 211 (4 April 1977): 25;

"A Super Sequel to Haley's Comet," *Time,* 113 (19 February 1979): 85–88;

"View from the Whirlpool," *Time,* 113 (19 February 1979): 88;

Harry F. Waters, "After Haley's Comet," *Newsweek,* 89 (14 February 1977): 97–98;

Waters and V. E. Smith, "One Man's Family," *Newsweek,* 87 (21 June 1976): 73;

Kenneth L. Woodward and Anthony Collings, "Limits of Faction," *Newsweek,* 89 (25 April 1977): 87;

Paul D. Zimmerman, "In Search of a Heritage," *Newsweek,* 88 (27 September 1976): 94–96.

Mark Helprin

*This entry was updated by Keith A. Morgan (North Carolina State University) from the entry by
William J. Scheick (University of Texas at Austin) in* DLB Yearbook 1985.

BIRTH: New York, New York, 28 June 1947, to Morris and Eleanor (Lynn) Helprin.

EDUCATION: B.A., Harvard University, 1969; M.A., Harvard University, 1972; postgraduate study at Magdalen College, Oxford University, 1976–1977.

MARRIAGE: 28 June 1980 to Lisa Kennedy; children: Alexandra Morris, Olivia Kennedy.

AWARDS AND HONORS: PEN/Faulkner Award, National Jewish Book Award, and American Book Award nomination, all for *Ellis Island and Other Stories,* all 1982; American Academy and Institute of Arts and Letters Prix de Rome, 1982; Guggenheim Fellowship, 1984.

BOOKS: *A Dove of the East and Other Stories* (New York: Knopf, 1975; London: Hamilton, 1976);
Refiner's Fire: The Life and Adventures of Marshall Pearl, a Foundling (New York: Knopf, 1977; London: Hamilton, 1977);
Ellis Island and Other Stories (New York: Delacorte Press/Seymour Lawrence, 1981; London: Hamilton, 1981);
Winter's Tale (New York: Harcourt Brace Jovanovich, 1983; London: Weidenfeld & Nicolson, 1983);
Swan Lake, illustrated by Chris Van Allsburg (Boston: Houghton Mifflin, 1989);
A Soldier of the Great War (New York: Harcourt Brace Jovanovich, 1991; London: Hutchinson, 1992);
Memoir from Antproof Case (New York: Harcourt Brace Jovanovich, 1995);
A City in Winter, illustrated by Van Allsburg (New York & London: Viking, 1996);
The Veil of Snows, illustrated by Van Allsburg (New York & London: Viking, 1997).

SELECTED PERIODICAL PUBLICATIONS– UNCOLLECTED:
FICTION
"Passchendaele," *New Yorker,* 58 (18 October 1982): 50–58;
"The Pacific," *Esquire,* 273 (March 1986): 74–80;

Mark Helprin (photograph © by Jerry Bauer)

"Waiting for the 20th Century," *Esquire,* 106 (November 1986): 239, 241;
"Mar Neuva," *New Yorker,* 64 (30 May, 1988): 28;
"Last Tea With the Armorers," *Esquire,* 124 (October 1995): 134–144.
NONFICTION
"American Jews in Israel," *New York Times Magazine,* 7 November 1982, 34–37;
"My Father's Life," *Esquire,* 99 (March 1983): 90–92;
"Drawing the Line in Europe: The Case for Missile Deployment," *New York Times Magazine,* 4 December 1983, 52–56;

"The Canon under Siege," *New Criterion,* 7 (September 1988): 33–40;

"Against the Dehumanization of Art," *New Criterion,* 13 (September 1994): 91–94;

"The Acceleration of Tranquility," *Forbes ASAP,* 229 (2 December 1996): 17–24;

"Revolution or Dissolution," *Forbes ASAP supplement,* 161 (24 February 1998): 87–103;

"Statesmanship and its Betrayal," *Imprimis,* 27 (April 1998): 1–5.

Born in New York City on 28 June 1947, Mark Helprin is the son of Eleanor Lynn and Morris Helprin. Morris Helprin, the son of émigrés, was a movie critic for *The New York Times* who later served in the publicity department of major film companies and still later became president of London Films. Mark Helprin grew up in New York City, the Hudson River Valley, and the British West Indies. He received a B.A. degree from Harvard University in 1969, and it was while he was an undergraduate that, at the age of twenty-one, he sold his first story to *The New Yorker.* Although he did not feel comfortable at Harvard, Helprin nonetheless speaks well of the sort of humanistic education he encountered there as an important preparation for coping with the contradictions and paradoxes of life. In 1972 he completed his studies at the Harvard Center for Middle Eastern Studies and was awarded an M.A.

Helprin served in the Israeli army and air force in 1972–1973, after which, in 1976–1977, he did postgraduate work under the direction of Hugh Trevor-Roper at Magdalene College, Oxford University. On 28 June 1980 (his birthday) he married Lisa Kennedy, a tax lawyer and a vice president of Chase Manhattan Bank.

Believing that his fiction speaks for itself, Helprin is hesitant to talk about it or about himself. Nevertheless, he has described himself as Jewish by birth and by faith, although not in the orthodox tradition. When asked in an interview in *Paris Review* why he writes, Helprin refused to "present" what he termed the generally expected "elaborate theoretical construct graced with ornaments of altruism that veer into politics." Instead he offered as a reason the epigram from *A Dove of the East and Other Stories* (1975): *amor mi mosse, che mi fa parlare.* Helprin translates this phrase, taken from Dante's *Inferno,* as "Love moved me, and makes me speak." In a further elaboration on the same question he states that "I write in the service of illumination and memory. I write to reach into 'the blind world where no one can help.' I write because it is a way of glimpsing the truth. And I write to create something of beauty." He has also remarked on his determined pursuit of exceptional experiences in life; he is, for example, a skilled mountain climber. He gained somewhat of a reputation for telling tall tales about himself, a fact that made some hesitate over the credibility of some of his personal revelations, such as his claim to have never tasted coffee and his account of meeting his wife by merely showing up at her door after learning who she was from employees of a bookstore where she purchased one of his works. This assumption reached new heights in 1991 in a profile in *The New York Times Magazine* in which Helprin's truthfulness was further impugned. Helprin attempted to correct the story with letters to *The New York Times.* When he was ignored, he took the unusual step of turning a publicity tour for *A Soldier of the Great War* (1991) into a fourteen-city, ten-thousand-mile camping trip with his wife and two daughters. He used many of his public appearances to publicly refute the story in *The New York Times* and offer documentary proof of his assertions. Although he now admits as fictional his account of how his father insisted that he tell an acceptable story before he was allowed to sit and eat at the dinner table, he brought copies of his medical history and British Merchant Navy service to his *Paris Review* interview.

He once called himself a "Roosevelt Republican," a description that he believed gave his political views some latitude. In recent years Helprin has more publicly asserted his political views. In 1987 he began writing an occasional political opinion column for the *Wall Street Journal,* to which he was appointed a contributing editor in 1991. In his columns he has discussed such varying international issues as the Gulf War, Bosnia, Russia, defense spending, and military preparedness as well as problems related to President Clinton's domestic agenda and troubles with the independent counsel. He is a senior fellow at the Hudson Institute, a private, nonprofit research organization founded in 1961 by the late Herman Kahn. During the 1996 U.S. presidential election campaign Helprin's name became more visible when it was revealed he had written Republican Party candidate Bob Dole's nomination acceptance speech. The experience soured for Helprin when further speeches were substantially rewritten; he left the Dole campaign before the November election. Despite the outcome, the Dole acceptance speech remains one of the more graceful and eloquent expressions of political oratory in recent times. Helprin has also written several serious nonfiction pieces for *Commentary, New Criterion,* and *Forbes ASAP.*

Most of Helprin's short fiction has appeared in *The New Yorker,* and many of his stories have been anthologized. Helprin has been awarded a Guggenheim Fellowship and nominated for the PEN/Faulkner Award and the American Book Award for fiction. In 1982 he won the National Jewish Book Award for *Ellis Island and Other Stories* (1981) and also received the Prix de Rome from the American Academy and Institute of Arts and Letters. Perhaps the most important comment Helprin has made about his fiction occurred during a 1984 interview for *The New York Times Book Review:* "Everything I write is keyed and can be understood as (although very few people see it as) devotional literature" concerned with beauty.

This concern, especially as related to the survivor, is prominent in Helprin's first book, *A Dove of the East and Other Stories,* a collection of twenty short stories. In many of the stories in this book the main characters have experienced the loss of someone they loved, and they somehow learn to cope with their loss. In "A Dove of the East," for example, Leon Orlovsky loses his parents and wife during World War II, but he is a survivor, someone who has been forced by life to enter "into quiet places" where he could "only reflect," someone who develops an internal strength. Leon balances the deep pain of his loss with a survivor's equally deep appreciation of the "savage beauty"of nature, seen for example when "sharp mountains of ice and rock rise suddenly out of soft green fields," an image that objectifies his cutting losses and his vernal hope. This profound appreciation of nature's harsh loveliness—its capacity to elicit hope in the midst of despair—informs Leon's effort, even at the risk of losing his job, to care for a beautiful, multicolored dove accidentally stepped on by Leon's horse. To Leon the beauty of the dove reflects the splendor of nature and life in general. Caring for the wounded dove, Leon engages with a regenerating natural beauty that helps balance the enervating grief over his dead parents and wife.

Just as Leon offsets grief with a survivor's new strength drawn from nature's resplendent beauty, Josie in "Mountain Dancing in Truchas" finds that after the loss of her husband "she valued her own life a little less, and life itself much more." Now (like Leon tending the wounded dove) she is more devoted to her children; "she was learning to change her sadness into tenderness" as "the pain . . . withered to a point of beauty." So too the protagonist in "The Legitimacy of Medium Beauty" discovers, like Leon, "quiet moments alone" and, like Josie, "a deep and beautiful sadness." Now "she drew from everything she saw enough to make her life a deep cool color, a medium beauty, that full wind which made the trees shudder, and draw breath, and seem

Dust jacket for Helprin's first collection of short stories (1975), in which the main characters learn to cope with the loss of someone they love

like green water." In Helprin's survivors, sadness (loss) and beauty (regeneration) combine in the self just as they combine in the "medium" savage beauty (shuddering trees and green water) of nature, which elicits in the survivor a hope countering despair.

Helprin's survivors in *A Dove of the East* sense a majesty in nature. In "Leaving the Church" Father Michael Trelew, dying from a heart attack, fails to have the final vision he had hoped for on his deathbed, but he does have a final mental recollection of nature's beauty: "The last thing he thought was how beautiful the summer rain in Rome" was, a hint of some sublimity in nature as comforting as the vision he had desired. The protagonist of "Katherine Comes to Yellow Sky" glimpses the same sublimity whenever she experiences the "most sober of moments" (like Leon's quiet places in "A Dove of the East" and the protagonist's quiet moments in "The Legitimacy of Medium Beauty"): "in those mountains was the source, glancing off high lighted rock faces where no man could ever go, split into rivers eastward and westward running in little fingers to every part of the land, to the oceans where it blended with the newly turned sea foam and sun." Helprin's characters find in nature a source of strength because nature hints at a source for its own existence, as if it derives from and reflects a divine origin. In "First Russian Summer," for instance, Levi's grandfather says, "God made the forest and this clean air. And even if there were a man who couldn't see that, he could see the shape of things and how astonishing they are." Usually, however, Helprin's characters do not generalize about their sense of an intimated divinity in nature. Most often they are entranced, astonished at nature's savage beauty. The regeneration of hope that they find evoked in them through nature derives from an intuitive rather than a cognitive sense of the divine source of astonishing nature. They come to feel, rather than know, that source profoundly in their encounters with nature.

The effect of nature's majesty on Helprin's survivors in *A Dove of the East* is often expressed through whatever is artistic in them, especially in musical talent. In "The Silver Bracelet," for example, Anneka, a Dutch Jewish child orphaned tragically at the age of five, has developed a passion for music. Her mother had played the viola, and music is a way for her to create beauty out of her painful memories of her mother. In fact, "it was music which made her life a life of love." Her music is a sadly beautiful act of generosity like Leon's tending the dove or Josie's caring for her children; Anneka especially loves to play for orphaned children, who imaginatively "could carve a mother or father" from the music. In order to attend a school where she will learn to perfect her talent, a school that "meant everything to Anneka," she must remove a silver bracelet her father gave her as a child, because the school requires that no student may wear jewelry. Like her music, evoking memories of her mother, Anneka's bracelet, evoking memories of her father, has been a source of deep comfort to her over the years. Against Anneka's will and to her grief, the bracelet is cut off by the headmistress. In a sense, the bracelet must be removed if Anneka is to perfect her musical talent; her sense of loss, her sense of being cut off from her parents and of being now indeed alone, must be complete if the potential for beauty in her music (derived from sadness) is to be realized.

The art produced by Helprin's survivors, like Anneka, reflects their view of nature as harshly beautiful. Like nature, art intimates some beautiful majesty, divinity, or meaning beyond the sorrowful human experiences in the material world. This capacity of art to hint at an ultimate divine reality in-

forming nature is evinced aesthetically in *A Dove of the East* through Helprin's subtle correlation of the savage beauty of nature, the human self, and art.

Reviewers of this book were quick to praise its brilliant imagery, its unusual scope and power, and its taut and lyrical prose as indications of Helprin's burgeoning literary talent. Recognition was given to his ability to transmit a sense of value through the dramatic force of his immensely readable stories. Some reviewers, however, worried that the underlying idea of the intrinsic majesty of the events narrated in these stories might be more elusive for readers than Helprin had realized. These reviewers also remarked that Helprin's intense striving for a sense of loveliness sometimes caused him to lapse into archness, to permit his language to get out of his control, and to produce a sameness of tone in the stories. Questions were also raised about whether the stories were as finished as they might be and whether Helprin's refinement of atmosphere at the apparent expense of plot and characterization detracted from the effectiveness of his work.

Helprin's second book, *Refiner's Fire: The Life and Adventures of Marshall Pearl, a Foundling* (1977), is a long episodic novel somewhat in the picaresque tradition. The story opens with Marshall Pearl dying from battle wounds received on a war front in Israel in 1973; the attending doctors have no clue to Marshall's identity and predict his sure demise. Then the novel goes into a flashback in which Marshall's mother, a refugee headed for Palestine, dies aboard ship as she gives birth to her son. The commander of the ship, Paul Levy, runs the British blockade of Palestine and with newborn Marshall is taken captive. At the age of two months Marshall is adopted by an American couple. At the age of ten he attends a summer camp in Colorado, where he falls in love with a girl named Lydia; they are separated at the end of the summer. At the age of fifteen he and his adoptive father visit Jamaica, where he joins in a battle against some Rastafarians and is seriously wounded. The following year he lives in New York with the Pascaleo family, where he falls in love with the daughter. Later he goes to Harvard, where he falls in love with an organist. He and a friend abandon Harvard and hop on a train that takes them to the Midwest, where Marshall works in a slaughterhouse for seven months. After hopping on another train, he eventually stumbles upon a biology station, where he and Nancy Baker study eagles. A subsequent episode finds him the only survivor of a shipwreck off the coast of Mexico, after which he arrives in New Orleans and is told that the ship he claims to have been on really sank years earlier. For a while he stays in South Carolina with Paul Levy.

There he discovers that Lydia, the girl he had met at summer camp when he was ten and whom he still loves, is Levy's sister. They marry, then visit Europe, where Marshall climbs the Alps. Lydia and Marshall settle in Israel and become citizens. Marshall is drafted, and with one day of his one-year term left, he is seriously wounded and lies dying in a hospital (the opening scene of the novel). In the hospital Marshall's birth father, who is also in the military, finds his son. In the final scene Marshall's eyes are flooded by sunbeams, as he rises as if in slow motion and pulls the tubes from his body: "Marshall arose and fixed his gaze on the hot rays of dawn. 'By God, I'm not down yet.'"

Ending *Refiner's Fire* with an image of transformative, regenerative dawning sunlight, Helprin recalls his use of nature imagery in *A Dove of the East*. Throughout *Refiner's Fire* light epitomizes the wondrous majesty of nature (beautiful, but not sadly or savagely beautiful as in *A Dove of the East*), as if creation were suffused with divinity. A flaming sky can look like "a fire from a purer place" than is the human realm. Marshall "had always been susceptible to the play of light and motion," as if they "were at every moment linked to an artful and all powerful God."

In *Refiner's Fire* light suggests a transcendental wholeness or pattern informing the temporal realm; in the novel light encompasses all time in a way that certain religious mystics of the past and present and certain theoreticians of the new physics today argue that all life is a manifestation of light. As Marshall explains on a starry night to Nancy Baker, an expert on eagles, "You see, we're lying here and all time is passing through us, echoes of light from the past and future as well. The whole thing." "Nothing vanishes," and thus dreams can be "remembrances of circular time, windows into a future which has once passed"; living life in the midst of circular time is like traveling "the chambers of a nautilus." When Marshall dreams that he is a soldier dying on a Civil War battlefield, he recollects "facts in his dream as though his memory of them were real." Perhaps once he was a Union soldier and has been reborn. Marshall recalls this dream of his imminent death at midpoint in *Refiner's Fire,* which is framed by an opening and closing description of him dying from wounds received on an Israeli battlefront; this design in Helprin's narrative suggests the circularity of time, conflating past (the Civil War) and future (the Israeli battle) in a dream that is at once a memory and a prediction. In *Refiner's Fire* all time, past and future, is contained in light.

While participating in a dangerous climb in order to observe eagles, Marshall relies on light to

Dust jacket for Helprin's 1977 novel, about a young man who dies of wounds suffered in the Arab-Israeli War of 1973

"save" him: "if he fell back he would be saved from the mountainous height by webs of dream-carrying light." Marshall believes that whether he should live, or die as a result of the climb, the reality of light promises a purpose or weblike design to his fate, and since light suggests that nothing vanishes, it also promises that he will in some sense continue to live in the totality of time encompassed by light and perhaps even be reborn. His awareness of this divine design or force informing life makes Marshall feel as if he were "carried on a current," by "all things tied into one flow." Whenever Marshall sees from a great height, he is reminded of this pattern intimated by nature, especially light, because from a "high view" he can "see the bold arrangement of things," that there is an Emersonian "balance to everything—symmetry, compensations."

Because nature suggests transcendental design, continuity, and perpetuity, Marshall revels in life—an explanation of why in the course of his youth he falls in love so often. The wondrous beauty of nature, particularly light, enkindles in him a recurrent hope in and affirmation of life in spite of encounters with loss, pain, and death; this fact is epitomized in the final scene of the novel, when dawning sunlight in Marshall's eyes causes him to rise from his deathbed. Marshall values intensely all sensations, not only during new and daring experiences resulting from "doing dangerous things all his life" but also during everyday living. Sleeping or waking, being hungry or sated, hearing noise or silence, seeing light or darkness—such mundane experiences are like poetic conductors; they are mystically infused and so connect us with the wondrous transcendental reality suffusing creation. The simple act of breathing, for example, is routinely taken for granted: "hold . . . your breath for as long as you can and then realize how wonderful it is just to breathe; like a dry field suddenly feeling the flood." To hold one's breath is equivalent to enduring the hardships of life, like being seriously wounded in a war; from these hardships one should not remain struck down but should rise again, to breathe again, as Marshall does in the final scene of *Refiner's Fire*.

Marshall is a Helprin survivor, someone who rises again and again in the face of the travails of life, whose internal spirit is perennially reborn. He evinces a resplendent, perpetual receptivity to the world. In a sense he is always young, and life is always new to him. He cannot remain in one place too long; as he says, "All I can do is go from place to place exhausting myself as I see what there is to see." Nevertheless, in the process of these new encounters with the wondrous force suffusing creation, his "passions had been refined in fire and in ice" and yet his "love was solid and gentle and true." Marshall's sense of the transcendent in creation has been refined by experiences of the extremes of life, and this refinement has only augmented his innocent receptivity to and appreciation of life—his love of life.

Reviewers of *Refiner's Fire* lauded Helprin's vivid imagination, his insight, and the artless grace of his style. Many critics, however, voiced strong reservations about the success of the novel. They complained of the number of exploits without a real thread of purpose or meaning, of unresolved symbolism, of weak characterization of women, and of a pervasive dreamy romanticism in the book. Several critics, who found the novel boring, suggested that this work suffered from authorial egotism, as if it were the work of uncontrolled engagement by a prodigy showing what he can do.

"Ellis Island," in Helprin's third book, *Ellis Island and Other Stories* (1981), is quite similar to *Refiner's Fire,* although a benign sense of humor is more prominent in the former. In the novel refugees come to Palestine to be reborn—"they laughed, they cried, they even kissed the ground"—and in the later no-

vella, immigrants, arriving at Ellis Island in the hope of being reborn in American freedom, cry and laugh too. The protagonist of the story is a romantic survivor, like Marshall, who possesses an exuberant will to live and who easily falls in love with women, who readily become for him symbols of life. "Palais de Justice," an account of how an old man defeats a disrespectful youth in a boat race, presents another survivor, who "had been broken and battered repeatedly—only to rise up again." Ever responsive to the "intricate and marvelously fashioned world," like Marshall, the old man "had risen each time to survive in the palace of the world by a good and just fight, by luck, by means he sometimes did not understand."

There are, as well, two nostalgic tales in *Ellis Island,* both told from the perspective of a child and both set in periods of time when an innocent receptivity to the wonder of creation was culturally more apparent in America than it is today. "Martin Bayer," set just before America's entry into World War I, recounts Martin's late-summer and life-affirming adventures as a child and his awareness of two youths "perfectly in love, innocent." Possibly reminiscent of Edith Wharton's work (but without its irony), "Martin Bayer" depicts the end of the age of innocence in America: "Even looking to the ocean's horizon, he did not sense beyond the rim the haunting battles which, at other times, were felt by all as if they were the approaching storms of the hurricane season. That day was hot and blue, with a magnificent cold wind." The other nostalgic story, "A Vermont Tale," is set "many years ago" when the narrator "was so young that each snowfall threatened to bar the door." It includes an allegorical tale within the tale that concerns the relationship of the narrator's grandparents, and in the process of being told it celebrates a time in the narrator's childhood when life seemed most wondrous, a time when "the cold outside was magical" and "the morning was so bright that it seemed like a dream."

The wonder of life, its capacity to merge magically with dream, is a feature of "The Schreuderspitze," the best story in *Ellis Island.* It is an account of Herr Wallich, a Munich photographer who loses his wife and child in a car accident. Without saying a word to anyone, he mysteriously disappears and heads for a small town where no one will notice him. In this town he plans to put himself through a "parallel ordeal" that will intensify the strain on his mind and body in a way that will permit him to overcome his despair by attaining a new balance. Behind this decision is his memory of an episode in youth camp, where it was nearly impossible to carry a bucket of water up a hill until he increased the burden and carried two buckets of water at the same time: "Though it was agony, it was a better agony than the one he had had, because he had retrieved his balance, could look ahead." The ordeal he sets for himself is the discipline of his mind and body in preparation for climbing mountains, where "he would either burst on to a new life, or . . . he would die." Death is certainly a real possibility, as the books on mountain climbing warn him, and a death wish in him is a strong contender against the possibility of his becoming a survivor. Although he rigorously trains his body, he also starves it and sometimes does not eat for days.

This attack on the body is not only symbolic of his wish to die, but it is also part of what amounts to a ritual of purification. Living in "a bare white room," fasting, and drinking "cold pure water," Wallich seeks "the diminution of his body" to prepare for the mountain summits, where "the air became purer and the light more direct." His ritual of purification, simulating death, is designed to reduce his attachment to the material world and his sense of loss in that world so that he can detect better, more purely, the transcendental reality intensely communicated through the direct light of the mountain summits.

"The mystery of light" figures prominently in a succession of dreams that Wallich has as a result of starving his body and mind. These dreams of scaling a mountain and witnessing the play of direct light on its summit indicate that his regimen has helped him nearly to transcend the boundaries of the material world: "Sometimes dreams could be so real that they competed with the world. . . . Sometimes . . . when they are real and so important, they easily tip the scale and the world buckles and dreams become real. Crossing the fragile barricades, one enters his dreams."

In these dreams of climbing mountains and witnessing direct light on their summits "above time, above the world," Wallich learns that "in central states of light he could see, he could begin to sense, things most miraculous." He realizes "that there was life after death, that the dead rose into a mischievous world of pure light, that something most mysterious lay beyond the enfolding darkness, something wonderful." His thoughts illuminated by this light, Wallich realizes, as did Marshall in *Refiner's Fire,* that time (temporal reality) is "circular and never ending," that "nothing, not one movement was lost." The containment of all time in light, its revelation of a transcendental meaning suffusing time, and its promise that he will again be united with his wife and child are epitomized for Wallich in

the ice world of the mountain summits, an *Eiswelt* like an Emersonian Over-Soul.

Because he is still in the flesh, albeit "thinned" toward death and the spirit through his ritual of fast, he can get only a glimpse—a glance at the ridge, coast, or rim—of the supranatural ideality imaged on the icy mountain summits in his real-seeming dream experiences. Where the *Eiswelt* (ice world) takes fire (that is, where light and the insight it gives are at once icily frozen and blazingly dynamic) is the edge of the mountain summit, the "sparkling ridge which looked like a great crystal spine"; here is "the high rim of things he had not seen before." Witnessing this ridge or rim of icy, yet blazing light, he kneels like an explorer "claiming a coast of the New World."

The music Wallich had listened to while training in his room had hinted at this rim or ridge of insight; the music suggested "new worlds lying just off the coast, invisible and redolent." The reader anticipates that Wallich's resolve to return to his profession, to "struggle at his craft," means that he will try to use light to make his artful photographs of nature hint, like music, at the transcendental reality (*Eiswelt*) lying just off the coast of temporal reality, at the rim of insight. Wallich is a survivor, someone who emerges from despair to reaffirm life and its manifold rich sensations because he has glimpsed in dreams and now intuitively knows of the divinity informing the astonishing beauty of nature, especially light.

Of all of Helprin's books, *Ellis Island* has enjoyed the best critical reception. Reviewers were struck by the power of imagination in these stories as well as by their rich texture and their delicate and economic style. Some applauded the gnomic and artful simplicity of the stories, though a few critics thought these narratives might communicate too obliquely and might be too unfinished, as if they were in effect watercolor sketches preliminary to a more complete work. Complaints also surfaced concerning a possible absence of a coherent vision in these stories, concerning an uncertainty of focus or tone, and concerning epiphanic moments that seem more literary than felt. Whereas Pearl K. Bell specifically refuted the underlying devotional feature Helprin has claimed for his work, other critics have emphasized Helprin's fascination with the impulse of the human spirit for transcendence, particularly as evinced in the frail but startling endurance of the human will. These latter reviews valued Helprin's ambitious reach and compassionate spirit in *Ellis Island,* a book that some critics ranked at the peak of literary achievement.

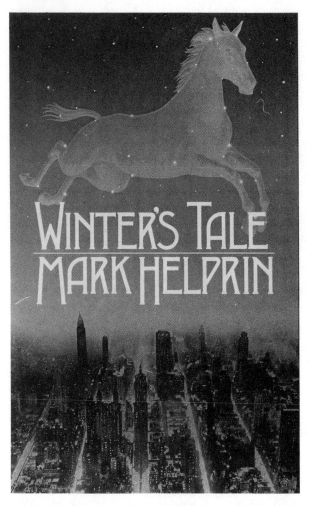

Dust jacket for Helprin's 1983 novel, about a runaway milk horse that can fly and cross time barriers

Winter's Tale (1983), Helprin's fourth book, is a somewhat eccentric, long allegorical fantasy, but from his previous stories its direction was predictable. Like "Martin Bayer," it is a highly nostalgic story focusing on the pre-World War I period as a time when American culture was particularly receptive to the wonder of life, a time when "things had been quieter, wilder, and more beautiful." Like "The Schreuderspitze," it mixes the dream world and the temporal realm, and like *Refiner's Fire,* it has a protagonist larger than life—both characteristics of romance. In fact, the epigraph of *Refiner's Fire* warned its readers to approach that novel as a romance, and *Winter's Tale* belongs to that genre, as practiced by nineteenth-century American authors, even more obviously. *Winter's Tale* reflects the tradition of romance defined by Nathaniel Hawthorne, who argued (in *The Scarlet Letter,* 1850) that romance is "a neutral territory, somewhere between the real world and fairy-land, where the Actual and the

Imaginary may meet, and each imbue itself with the nature of the other." Herman Melville remarked in *The Confidence-Man* (1857) that fiction "should present another world, and yet one to which we have a tie." Helprin shares both of these views and attempts in *Winter's Tale* to integrate the actual and the imaginary, the temporal and the dream.

The story line of *Winter's Tale* is comprised of a succession of implausible incidents, but there are subplots. Athansor, a runaway milk horse that can fly and cross the barriers of time, rescues Peter Lake, who as a result of a falling-out among thieves was about to be executed by villainous Pearly Soames. Later, after Lake falls in love with Beverly Penn (whose home he had at first tried to rob), he witnesses his lover's death and is wounded by Soames; but again Lake is rescued by Athansor, who flies into a cloud wall. Having fallen from the horse, Lake awakens nearly a hundred years later, in 1999, without his memory and without any signs of having aged. He is hired to tend the century-old machinery of a building in New York City where the *Sun* newspaper is published by Beverly's brother, Harry Penn, who eventually recognizes Lake and helps him regain his memory. As the twentieth century turns to the twenty-first century, New York City ("deep within its new dream") becomes the locus of a golden millennium, characterized by an apocalyptic winter heralding a nascent justice that will redress the wrongs of the past century and restore a sense of beauty and wonder similar to that enjoyed by the residents of Lake of Coheeries, a place of snow and ice, forever frozen in time (1899), where stillness and motion meet. Peter Lake and Athansor are killed by Soames as if they were necessary sacrifices for the emergent new city, though they still exist in the world of light. Then come (with a possible echo of Baruch Spinoza) the manifestations of "the metaphysical balance that inform all events"–"every action and every scene has its purpose"–a balance especially evident in transformed New York City in 1999–2000 as it gives expression to the beauty and wonder typical of Lake of Coheeries in 1899–1900. New York City becomes a testament to how "all the flames and sparks of justice throughout all time reach and invigorate unseen epochs," when "the reasons for everything were revealed and balances were evened."

Light in *Winter's Tale,* as in Helprin's earlier works, conveys the wonder and majesty of nature and suggests a divinity infusing life. Particularly as reflected in "splendid ice" (where motion and stillness meet, and infinity can be glimpsed), light reveals that "the universe is still and complete. Everything that ever was, is; everything that ever will be, is. . . . Though in perceiving it we imagine that it is in motion, and unfinished, it is quite finished and quite astonishingly beautiful. . . . When all is perceived in such a way as to obviate time, justice becomes apparent not as something that will be, but as something that is." So Lake of Coheeries at the turn of the nineteenth century coalesces with New York City at the turn of the twentieth century. So human artifacts (especially rainbowlike arching bridges) and natural objects fuse in Helprin's mixed metaphors, for "nature was in the beams, girders, and engines of the city . . . ; in a still life illuminated by an electric bulb as much as in a wheat-colored field in pure sunlight." So too Helprin uses the genre of romance to integrate the mundane (matter, motion, reason, and actual event) and the eternal (spirit, stillness, imagination, and dream revelation) in order to give the reader an enlightening glimpse of the essential truth of justice, balance, symmetry, design, and purpose informing life. Just as light in ice and both music and painting freeze the temporal in Helprin's narratives, "books stop time" in *Winter's Tale*. Helprin's books convey a sense of the infinite stillness and eternal coalescence of all life, the sort of encounter that permits Helprin's survivors to renew their affirmation of life, the sort of intimation that in Henry James's view only romances could convey "through the beautiful circuit and subterfuge of our thought."

The language of *Winter's Tale* often flashes with beauty and evokes a sense of wonder, but its apocalyptic vision of justice remains vague. Perhaps that vision can only be glimpsed in the book because Helprin believes that the metaphysical balance that informs creation can, as with Wallich in "The Schreuderspitze," only be glimpsed in life as when one looks at a distant rim or ridge or coast. Nevertheless, *Winter's Tale*, like *Refiner's Fire*, sprawls with vaguely related, expansive (perhaps at times authorially self-indulgent) episodes. These two long works suggest that Helprin can concentrate the force of his vision better in the short story than in the novel.

Some reviewers of *Winter's Tale* were bothered by its proliferation of episode after episode as if it were an interminable bedtime tale. Others complained about a lack of a compelling story line, essential to a successful romance, and about the failure of the grand design of the book, which struck some reviewers as confusing, fuzzy, vague, and unconvincing. As if in response, several critics thought that the highly imaginative, large-souled novel imparted a wider vision of the sort that permitted readers to see their time afresh and that urged upon them a sense of beauty that is as affirmative, restorative, and comforting as Walt Whitman's achieve-

ment. There was general agreement that in the novel Helprin takes risks—sometimes failing (as when his language becomes inflated and is made to carry excessive weight), sometimes succeeding (as when his assault on realism yields a life-affirming inspirational fantasy).

Winter's Tale remains a curious book; Benjamin De Mott confesses, for example: "I find myself nervous, to a degree I don't recall in my past as a reviewer, playing its brilliance." *Winter's Tale* does indeed intimidate, but whether it does so because its vision is really startlingly transformative or because its vision is clouded and leaves us bewildered is not clear. Nevertheless, this novel and *Refiner's Fire*, however less satisfying than his short stories, indicate that in whatever form Helprin writes, he demonstrates a literary talent that deserves appreciation, a talent to make language evoke a sense of the beauty and wonder of majestic nature (especially light), which is apparently divinely infused.

If admirers of *Winter's Tale* thought that Helprin would produce another fantasy for adults, then *A Soldier of the Great War* (1991) quickly confounded any such expectation. A realistic, sprawling novel (792 pages), *A Soldier of the Great War* takes as its canvas World War I, the event that signaled the emerging darker nature of the modern age. Helprin's ambition in this novel is not to produce simply another treatment of the futility of war and those few ennobling moments that illustrate the spasmodic flailings of modern empires. Significantly, Helprin does not portray the battlefields and geography of the western front that would be most familiar to an English-speaking reader. Instead, he sets his story in Italy, with an Italian protagonist caught up in Italy's struggles with neighboring Austria. In the novel Helprin uses the exigencies of battle and the brutality of war to offer reflections on the nature of beauty, the meaning of art, the promise of love, and the wonder of eternity. Readers familiar with Helprin's earlier work, particularly the short stories, will find many of the same themes articulated in *A Soldier of the Great War*.

In interviews following the publication of this novel Helprin told two interesting stories. The first story was that following the divided critical reception of *Winter's Tale*, Helprin's father had suggested that he produce something less fantastical and more realistic. The second story was of Helprin's encounter with an elderly Italian veteran on an Italian train platform in 1964 when Helprin was seventeen. Although the two did not exchange a word (Helprin suspects the veteran thought him a German), Helprin said that this soldier of World War I with a look that reflected "anger, pity, amusement, respect,

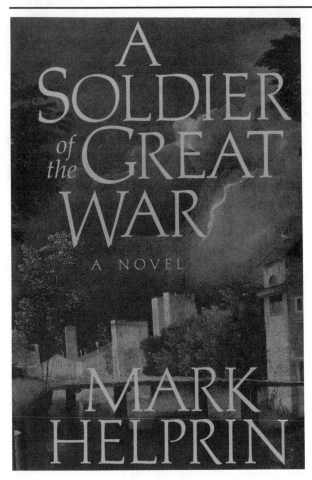

Dust jacket for Helprin's 1991 novel, about an Italian soldier in World War I

contempt, hatred . . . affection" had entrusted Helprin "with his life."

Although this is a novel of the opening decades of the twentieth century, the story begins in Rome on a hot August Sunday in 1964. Allesandro Guiliani, a retired professor, is walking to catch a motorized trolley. He is traveling up into the hills above Rome to visit his granddaughter and her family. A conversation in a bar reveals that he was, indeed, a soldier of World War I. While waiting for the trolley, he spies the proprietor's medals in a case above the bar. Allesandro remembers his own medals, which he has not looked at for many years. He does not look at them anymore. "Each one, tarnished or bright, would push him back to a time that he found both too painful and too beautiful to remember." Helprin here reveals a key paradox of *A Soldier of the Great War:* it is a novel that views the memory of war as both painful and beautiful. Helprin reveals that Allesandro was a professor of aesthetics, the study of beauty. Asked by a trolley passenger why he would study something that is all around us, he replies that it "entrances" him.

The first chapter serves as an enabling device for Allesandro to tell the story of his life. Helprin accomplishes this by presenting a petty act of injustice that makes Allesandro indignant. The trolley driver, having reached a good speed, refuses to stop for a young man running for the trolley. When the driver will not stop, Allesandro rings the bell declaring that he wants to get off. Although initially a ruse to allow the running man time to catch the trolley, the driver's further complaints cause Allesandro truly to exit the trolley. Together with the young man, a nearly illiterate factory worker, Allesandro sets off on a seventy-kilometer walk to Monte Prato. After straightening out the young man on the essential truths of life, Allesandro begins his story.

True to Helprin's vision, the tale begins in the South Tyrolean Alps, where in 1899 the nine-year-old Allesandro is taken by his father to stay in the Schlernhaus, a magnificent stone retreat. Here, as in "The Schreuderspitze" and *Refiner's Fire,* Helprin introduces the mountains as a mystical place that forms an essential background to the novel. In his adolescence Allesandro learns to climb mountains; eventually he ends up climbing and fighting tremendous battles in these same mountains. The mountains alone are not the single most thematically important element in this Helprin story. The picaresque plot of *A Soldier of the Great War* follows Allesandro's youthful adventures and philosophic education in the final years of peace before the war. His love of the beautiful and its collision with his wartime experiences provide the critical thematic conflict. Allesandro sustains his faith in the transcendent power of the beautiful by reflecting on the glories of nature not only in the mountains but also in the sky and even the birds that fly. Through this focus he attempts to overcome the horrors of war.

Allesandro's faith in the power of beauty also finds deep expression in his repeated contemplation of two paintings. Raphael's portrait of Bindo Altoviti speaks to Allesandro of eternity:

> And now that I am still I pass on to you my liveliness and my life, for you will be taken up as I once was [but] remember that it ends in perfect peace, and you will be still and content as am I, for whom centuries are not even seconds.

Even more prominent is Allesandro's profound attraction to Giorgione's *La Tempesta,* an enigmatic painting with varying interpretations. In the foreground a nude woman nurses an infant. A man stands apart from her watching. Some critics think him a shepherd, but Allesandro knows he is a soldier. Behind the people a tremendous storm rages.

For Allesandro the meaning of the painting invokes the search for family and the stability of love in the face of destruction.

A Soldier of the Great War is more than abstract speculations. It brims with life. The comic characters of Orfeo Quatta and Marshall Strassnitsky are but two examples. Orfeo, a misshapen dwarf, works for Allesandro's father as a scribe. Orfeo believes that the universe is controlled by "the gracious luminous sap that falls like the blood of the Cross from the tree in the valley of the bone-white mountains that circle the moon." Orfeo has a violent reaction when Allesandro's father purchases a typewriter for his law firm. Orfeo spends the war as a shadowy presence in the Ministry of War, where, in order to help "the gracious symmetry of the sap," he inverts and transposes all manner of orders so that "one hundred and seventy-eight sappers to Padua becomes eight hundred and seventy-one. The tenth of May becomes the fifth of November, and so on." His machinations have protected Allesandro but condemned his friends to death, and for this Allesandro cannot forgive him. Strassnitzky is a nobleman of the Austro-Hungarian empire; a pacifist, he believes that "the object of war is peace" and that his contribution is to cut out the middle part. His troops capture Allesandro, and he is recruited to write the battle history of Strassnitsky's troops; however, they are fictional battles fought against phantom armies. Allesandro composes lyrical accounts of violent battles complete with casualty lists. Any of Strassnitsky's soldiers who appear on the casualty lists are not really dead but are merely sent home to await the end of the war.

Two other scenes in the book, one deeply romantic, the other profoundly sad, distinguish the novel. In the first a wounded Allesandro is recuperating in a military hospital; a nurse sits with him, and they have long and eloquent conversations. She sits behind the immobile patient so Allesandro cannot see her. This physical proximity without vision creates a lovely and highly charged scene. Earlier in the novel Allesandro and his River Brigade are sent to Sicily to hunt deserters. After capturing many of them, Allesandro and his comrades cannot deliver them to execution, and they too desert. Captured themselves, they are imprisoned in Stella Maris, a castle-prison on the sea. As the days pass and more and more of their fellow soldiers are executed, Allesandro has several moving conversations with both prisoners and guards on the nature of death and the chance of immortality. Helprin stated in an interview at the National Humanities Center that all of his books end with a prayer. *A Soldier of the Great War* ends in just this way, as Allesandro dies while watching hunters shooting at birds:

To the sight of the swallows dying in mid air, Allesandro was finally able to add his own benediction. "Dear God, I beg of you only one thing. Let me join the ones I love. Carry me to them, unite me with them, let me see them, let me touch them," and then it all ran together, like a song.

In 1989, between the publication of *Winter's Tale* and *A Soldier of the Great War,* Helprin collaborated with Caldecott Award-winning author Chris Van Allsburg to produce *Swan Lake.* This was the first of three collaborations between Helprin and Van Allsburg. As these three children's books are thematically connected, they may be considered as a group. Helprin produced the text for the three stories, and Van Allsburg illustrated them. Helprin's intention in all three books is more than simply retelling the story made famous through the Tchaikovsky ballet. He tries to re-create the mythic dimension of the best fables to weave a tale of magic while at the same time teaching some deep truths about the nature of human life. In order for this intention to work, Helprin must write stories that will be as interesting to adults as to children. In a postmodern world inspired by the doctrine of value relativism, this is a challenging task.

Swan Lake does not begin with the traditional "once upon a time" but with the more direct "once." This is a time that has disappeared forever. The first tale tells of a young girl and an old man. They live alone in rural self-sufficiency. One day the old man tells the girl of how he once met the emperor and how he became tutor to the young prince after the death of the emperor; he also tells her of the noble Damavandian prince and his wife and how they were murdered by the regent, the evil Baron Rothbart. The little girl's mother is the daughter of the Damavandian couple, and her father is the prince. It is her destiny to descend from the safety of her mountain home to struggle with Rothbart for the throne. For adult readers Helprin offers satirical comments on espresso-fueled literary culture, income tax assessments, pompous party goers, and other modern follies. For children the message is divided between the assurance that life can be beautiful and the fact that, all too often, sadness and tragedy lurk in the beauty.

The second book, *A City in Winter* (1996), begins as the young girl journeys to the city of the evil usurper to claim the throne that is rightfully hers. This book is more comic than *Swan Lake,* with a large supporting cast of characters that owe much to Charles Dickens or to Helprin's imagination in *Winter's Tale.* The girl is protected by two palace bakery chefs and is given employment sorting yams in one of the thousand kitchens in the huge palace. Her guardian reappears and speaks of an ancient prophecy that

Dust jacket for Helprin's 1995 novel, which merges romantic fantasy and realistic reflections

foretells her ascension as queen. Although the comic tone moves the plot along at a good pace, the political allusions are a little less subtle than in the earlier book, although often entertaining. The tutor reappears to the future queen disguised as the envoy of neighboring Dolomitia-Swift; he taunts the sycophantic Duke of Tookisheim by telling him that "in Dolomitia-Swift we learned long ago that when the power of government is married with the urge to instruct, it produces the bastard of coercion." If the lesson of *Swan Lake* was the necessity of understanding the possible sadness of life, the lesson of *A City in Winter* appears to be the necessity of duty. On the last page the future queen stands before the palace door that will open to a city square filled with those who prayed for her return. She reflects that once this door is opened, it will "unleash years of war. I knew that stepping forward meant that whole families would perish, never to be remembered, and that half the kingdom would burn." Nevertheless, she opens the door since to refuse would be to embrace the worst.

The trilogy continues with *The Veil of Snows* (1997). The long war against the evil usurper has ended with his defeat and retreat into the icy and distant mountains with their mysterious Veil of Snows. The queen has married and given birth to a son. Despite the people's great relief at having been freed from the yoke of the usurper, the queen's policy of reconciliation has allowed the vulgar Tookisheim family to prosper and eventually to corrupt the new regime. The comic tone of *A City in Winter* is completely gone. *The Veil of Snows* is unremittingly somber and sad in its relation of a dream gone astray. The story is told by a "singer of tales" who was one day called before the usurper to be questioned as to the reason he still sang his tales "in the old style." Cast into prison and tortured, he is only freed when the young queen's army storms the city. He becomes a trusted confidant to the young monarch and is with her and her son when the usurper counterattacks and eventually executes her. The infant prince, strapped in a cradle on horseback, escapes when the horse bolts from the usurper's men. The singer follows the horse to the edge of the Veil of Snows; an opening appears, and horse and infant enter the snows. There they are greeted by members of the mythical Golden Horde. Twenty-five years pass; then the day arrives when the now aged singer sees an army emerging from the Veil of Snows led by the queen's husband and her son. The story ends on a hopeful note.

Critics have been as divided about Helprin's children's tales as they have been about his adult work. One reviewer called *The Veil of Snows* "poignant" and "sophisticated." Another found *A City in Winter* "overburdened by excessive writing and winking asides at an adult audience." Another reviewer thought "Helprin's original achievement," in *Swan Lake,* "is transforming the magical evanescence of the fairy tale . . . into a rational and worldly account that—by narrative suspense, wit, humor, and linguistic virtuosity—aspires to high art." Helprin the children's author does not "dumb-down" his stories, and so, just as is true of his adult works, they are difficult to grasp. Nevertheless, his challenge to the readers is interesting no matter their ages. Even readers of his adult stories will appreciate the many similar metaphors and allusions in the children's books. For example, readers of *Winter's Tale* will be intrigued by the notion of the Veil of Snows, so similar to the cloud wall in *Winter's Tale.*

Memoir from Antproof Case (1995), Helprin's fourth novel, merges the romantic fantasy of *Winter's Tale* with the realistic reflections of *A Soldier of the Great War.* "Call me Oscar Progresso" are the opening words of this novel, seemingly intended to echo the opening lines of *Moby-Dick* (1851). The narrator continues: "Or, for that matter, call me anything you want for Oscar Progresso is not my name." The narrator remains nameless throughout the novel. Like Allesandro Guiliani in *A Soldier of the Great War,* the narrator of *Memoir from Antproof Case* is also an old man looking back on his life with equal measures of sorrow and joy. As the novel begins, the narrator is sitting on a bench in a neighborhood of Rio de Janeiro writing the story of his life. The intended recipient of his story is Fumio, the illegitimate son of his wife. The title of the book refers to the antique case into which the narrator places the pages of his tale.

The novel begins in the present day, but as "Oscar" tells his story, the tale races backward and forward in time. It is constructed like a giant jigsaw puzzle in which each piece describes one aspect of the puzzle that is the narrator's fascinating life. Orphaned as a child, he has killed men, spent time in a Swiss insane asylum, flown fighters in World War II Europe, been a successful Wall Street investment banker, and been married to a woman worth billions. At the heart of the novel lie the twin obsessions of the narrator: a desire for revenge so strong that he will commit a monstrous crime and a hatred for coffee so intense that he will kill a man and divorce his beautiful wife. The aversion to coffee is at first comic, but it eventually grows darker. Helprin's narrator describes coffee as "evil because it disrupts the internal rhythm that allows a man or a woman to understand the beauty of all things." Coffee "turns your inner self into a happy sparkling clockwork, hypnotizes you with artificial joy and takes you from the sadness and deliberation that are the anchors of love." This hatred of coffee and of Brazil, a nation that exports a large amount of coffee, fills the novel. Readers might think that these anti-caffeine fulminations are a bit much, but they are essential to the plot. It is apparent that Helprin does not wish his readers to be overly sympathetic to his narrator. Unlike Allesandro Guiliani, the narrator of *Memoir from Antproof Case* is annoyingly and gratingly eccentric. His rants against coffee, against Brazil and Brazilians, and against his various enemies are sharp enough to drive many readers in search of something more congenial.

Patience is the key word. As the stories emerge from his memory and as the antproof case fills with the story of the narrator's remarkable life, Helprin moves his tale toward a conclusion that ultimately explains everything. The reasons for the desire for revenge and even the hatred of coffee are revealed. *Memoir from Antproof Case* takes as its canvas the years 1904 to 1984. Like *A Soldier of the Great War* with its tale of 1899 to 1964, Helprin paints his story on a large frame, the twentieth century, writ large. Like all of Helprin's work, *Memoir from Antproof Case* is full of the most elevated language, exotic locales, precisely described technical worlds, and perhaps most importantly, that consistent exploration of the power of love

and beauty. Like all of Helprin's novels, *Memoir from Antproof Case* concludes with a prayer:

> All this time, my heart has told me nothing but to love and protect. This message has been strong through the twists and turns, and it has never varied. To protect, and to protect, and to protect. I was born to protect the ones I love. And may God continue to give me ways to protect and to serve them, even if they are gone.

The critical response to *Memoir from Antproof Case* was generally positive and often on a level with that given to *Ellis Island.* As with the other novels, critics were at pains to point out the great risks Helprin takes with respect to both plot and style. Even while noting the occasional failure, all seemed genuinely admiring of the chances he takes. Several critics noticed that varying strands of the story only come together in the last fifty pages and wondered if all readers would have the patience to stay the course. The most significant advance *Memoir from Antproof Case* represents for Helprin's artistry might be the maturity with which he blends his previous themes of fantasy and lyrical romance with the demands of plot. *Memoir from Antproof Case* is still a picaresque journey, but now the author is more in command of his material. *Memoir from Antproof Case* is the second book of a five-book contract, and it will be interesting to see which pathways Helprin's fertile imagination now pursues.

References:
Paul Alexander, "Big Books, Tall Tales," *New York Times Magazine,* 28 April 1991, 32–36;
Pearl K. Bell, "New Jewish Voices," *Commentary,* 71 (June 1981): 62–66;
Sven Birkerts, "Pursued By a Bean," *New York Times Book Review,* 9 April 1995, p. 3;
Christopher Buckley, "A Talk with Mark Helprin: 'I May Be an Anomaly,'" *New York Times Book Review,* 25 March 1981, p. 16;
Benjamin De Mott, "A Vision of the Just City," *New York Times Book Review,* 4 September 1983, pp. 1, 21–22;
Leslie Field, "Mark Helprin and Postmodern Jewish-American Fiction of Fantasy," *Yiddish,* 7, no. 1 (1987): 57–65;
David B. Green, "An Intimate Look at a Superb Storyteller," *Vogue,* 172 (March 1982): 430–431;
Thomas Keneally, "War and Memory," *New York Times Book Review,* 140 (5 May 1991): 1–2;
James Linville, "Mark Helprin: the Art of Fiction CXXXII," *Paris Review,* 35 (Spring 1993): 160–199;
Sybil S. Steinberg, "Mark Helprin," *Publishers Weekly,* 219 (13 February 1981): 12–13, 16.

Frank Herbert

This entry was updated by Donald E. Palumbo (East Carolina University) from the entry by Robert A. Foster in DLB 8:
Twentieth-Century American Science-Fiction Writers.

BIRTH: Tacoma, Washington, 8 October 1920, to
Frank and Eileen Marie McCarthy Herbert.

EDUCATION: Attended University of Washington, 1946–1947.

MARRIAGES: March 1941 to Flora Parkinson (divorced 1945); child: Penny. 23 June 1946 to Beverly
Ann Stuart (died 7 February 1984); children: Brian
Patrick, Bruce Calvin. 1985 to Theresa Shackelford.

AWARDS AND HONORS: International Fantasy
Award for *The Dragon in the Sea,* 1956; Nebula
Award, Science Fiction Writers of America, 1965,
and Hugo Award, World Science Fiction Convention, 1966, both for *Dune;* Prix Apollo, 1978; honorary doctor of humanities, Seattle University, 1980.

DEATH: Madison, Wisconsin, 11 February 1986.

BOOKS: *The Dragon in the Sea* (Garden City, N.Y.:
Doubleday, 1956; London: Gollancz, 1960);
republished as *21st Century Sub* (New York:
Avon, 1956); republished again as *Under Pressure* (New York: Ballantine, 1974);
Dune (Philadelphia: Chilton, 1965; London: Gollancz, 1966);
The Green Brain (New York: Ace, 1966; London:
New English Library, 1973);
Destination: Void (New York: Berkley, 1966; Harmondsworth, U.K.: Penguin, 1967; revised
edition, New York: Berkley, 1978);
The Eyes of Heisenberg (New York: Berkley, 1966;
London: Sphere, 1968);
The Heaven Makers (New York: Avon, 1968; London: New English Library, 1970);
The Santaroga Barrier (New York: Berkley, 1968;
London: Rapp & Whiting, 1970);
Dune Messiah (New York: Putnam, 1969; London:
Gollancz, 1971);
Whipping Star (New York: Putnam, 1970; London:
New English Library, 1972);
The Worlds of Frank Herbert (London: New English
Library, 1970; New York: Ace, 1971);

Soul Catcher (New York: Putnam, 1972; London:
New English Library, 1973);
The God Makers (New York: Putnam, 1972; London:
New English Library, 1972);
Hellstrom's Hive (Garden City, N.Y.: Doubleday,
1973; London: New English Library, 1974);
The Book of Frank Herbert (New York: DAW, 1973;
St. Albans, U.K.: Panther, 1977);
Threshold: The Blue Angels Experience (New York: Ballantine, 1973);
The Best of Frank Herbert, edited by Angus Wells
(London: Sidgwick & Jackson, 1975);
Children of Dune (New York: Berkley, 1976; London:
Gollancz, 1976);
The Dosadi Experiment (New York: Putnam, 1977;
London: Gollancz, 1978);
The Illustrated Dune (New York: Berkley, 1978);
The Great Dune Trilogy (London: Gollancz, 1979)—includes *Dune, Dune Messiah,* and *Children of Dune;*
The Jesus Incident, by Herbert and Bill Ransom (New
York: Berkley, 1979; London: Gollancz,
1979);
The Priests of Psi and Other Stories (London: Gollancz,
1980);
*Without Me You're Nothing: The Essential Guide to Home
Computers,* by Herbert and Max Barnard (New
York: Simon & Schuster, 1980); republished as
*Without Me You're Nothing: The Home Computer
Handbook* (London: Gollancz, 1981);
Direct Descent (New York: Ace, 1980; Sevenoaks,
U.K.: New English Library, 1982);
God Emperor of Dune (New York: Putnam, 1981; London: Gollancz, 1981);
The White Plague (New York: Putnam, 1982; London: Gollancz, 1983);
The Lazarus Effect, by Herbert and Ransom (New
York: Putnam, 1983; London: Gollancz,
1983);
Heretics of Dune (New York: Putnam, 1984; London:
Gollancz, 1984);
Chapterhouse: Dune (New York: Putnam, 1985; London: Gollancz, 1985);
Eye (New York: Berkley, 1985; London: Gollancz,
1986);

Frank Herbert

Man of Two Worlds, by Herbert and Brian Herbert (New York: Putnam, 1986; London: Gollancz, 1986);

The Maker of Dune: Insights of a Master of Science Fiction, edited by Tim O'Reilly (New York: Berkley, 1987);

The Second Great Dune Trilogy (London: Gollancz, 1987)–includes *God Emperor of Dune, Heretic of Dune,* and *Chapterhouse: Dune;*

The Notebooks of Frank Herbert's Dune, edited by Brian Herbert (New York: Perigee Books, 1988);

The Ascension Factor, by Herbert and Ransom (New York: Putnam, 1988; London: Gollancz, 1988);

Songs of Muad'Dib: Poems and Songs From Frank Herbert's Dune Series and His Other Writings, edited by Brian Herbert (New York: Ace, 1992).

RECORDINGS: *Sandworms of Dune* (New York: Caedmon, 1978);

The Truths of Dune (New York: Caedmon, 1979);

The Battles of Dune (New York: Caedmon, 1979);

God Emperor of Dune (New York: Caedmon, 1982);

Heretics of Dune (New York: Caedmon, 1984).

OTHER: *New World or No World,* edited by Herbert (New York: Ace, 1970);

Nebula Awards Fifteen, edited by Herbert (New York: Harper, 1981); republished as *Nebula Winners Fifteen* (London: W. H. Allen, 1981).

Born in Tacoma, Washington, Frank Patrick Herbert is best known as the author of the Dune series. He attended the University of Washington in Seattle (1946–1947), where he later lectured (1970–1972), and worked for many years as a journalist for West Coast newspapers from San Francisco to Seattle and at a wide range of other jobs, including oyster diver and jungle survival instructor; but his experiences in the U.S. Navy during World War II and as a lay analyst have had the greatest effect on his fiction. His first science-fiction story, "Looking for Something," was published in *Startling Stories* in 1952; *The Dragon in the Sea,* his first novel, was published in 1956. The enormous success of *Dune* (1965) enabled him in 1966 to write full-time, and he ultimately published twenty-three novels (including one that is not science fiction), five collections of short stories, two nonfiction books, and two edited collections of stories. An active member of the World Without War Council, Herbert was a consultant on social and ecological problems to the Lincoln Foundation and to the governments of Vietnam and Pakistan; he also developed a six-acre ecological demonstration project in his native Washington.

Following the immense success of *Dune,* Herbert embarked on a lecture tour of college campuses in which he emphasized the relationship between the environmental concerns expressed in *Dune* and contemporary environmental issues, and in doing so, he helped spark the environmental movement in

America. In 1973 he wrote and directed *The Tillers,* a television special. In 1984 Universal Studios released a movie adaptation of *Dune* written and directed by David Lynch. Herbert was cowinner of the International Fantasy Award in 1956 for *The Dragon in the Sea,* winner of the Nebula Award in 1965 and cowinner of the Hugo Award in 1966 for *Dune,* and winner of the Prix Apollo in 1978. He received an honorary doctor of humanities degree from Seattle University in 1980. Married three times, Herbert had three children. He died of a blood clot in his lung following cancer surgery on 11 February 1986, in Madison, Wisconsin. At the time of his death he was writing a seventh volume in the Dune series with his son Brian.

Herbert's short fiction is diverse and entertaining; his novels show a unifying concern with systems and systems interactions. Physical ecology is the subject of *The Green Brain* (1966) and an important element in the Dune series as well as in the sequels to *Destination: Void* (1966), while a concern with social ecology—the dynamics of social structures and restraints, social conflicts as a means of natural selection, the nature of psychology and religion, and racial imperatives—infuses all of his novels. The most common focus of this interest in systems is an exploration of the causes, functions, and limits of human consciousness. Herbert usually views consciousness as a "systems effect," in which the whole is greater than the sum of its parts, and an understanding of this mechanism permits many of his characters to overcome social manipulation or transcend the limitations of individual memory and power. Many of his characters have formal training that enables them to control their own emotional responses and detect the subtle betrayals of emotion made by their opponents.

While some of his novels, such as *Dune* and *Dune Messiah* (1969), feature complex, brilliantly crafted plots, in others such as *Heretics of Dune* (1984) and *Chapterhouse: Dune* (1985) this complexity degenerates into baffling and nearly impenetrable complication. In many of his non-Dune novels, plot is subservient to the exploration of ideas. While *God Emperor of Dune* (1981) in particular prioritizes character, Herbert is frequently less concerned with characterization than with ideas and setting. He often employs a fragmented narrative structure, in which relatively brief episodes are introduced by quotations from invented works. Within each episode the story line progresses less by action than by observation, cogitation, and antagonistic dialogue.

This essentially static exposition is well suited to the intellectual cast of Herbert's fiction, but its dangers are serious. Often the reader is severely dis-

tanced from the action, and although Herbert frequently asserts the value of social cooperation, his books characteristically depict ruthless competition. Incessant intrigue is a convenient form in which to present intellectual adventure, and many of Herbert's characters, both protagonists and antagonists, are consummate schemers. Presumably Herbert intends to show the shortcomings of such behavior and, consequently, the flaws of social systems that demand it. However, by creating plots that depend so heavily on intrigue, he fails to provide his audience with convincing examples of social harmony. Certainly Herbert's fiction argues by negative example that one should beware of heroes, that the human tendency to follow "supermen" leads to disaster.

A writer whose fiction habitually invites the reader to think, Herbert is much more interested in posing questions than answering them. Also, as many of his novels explore the complexities of dynamical systems (such as consciousness or an ecology), which are essentially cyclical, they do not lend themselves thematically to definitive, satisfactory conclusions; Herbert's novels often quite elegantly mimic the characteristics of dynamical systems in their narrative structures while simultaneously investigating these characteristics within the narrative itself. Hence, *Dune* has five sequels (with a sixth in progress at the time of Herbert's death); *Destination: Void* has three; and *Whipping Star* (1970) has one.

Herbert's fiction argues that man must achieve a fluid balance both with his environment and within himself; failing to achieve such a balance leads either to chaos and excess or to decadence and decay. Herbert also preaches that short-sighted, simplistic solutions to complex problems must be avoided; that it is necessary to consider all alternatives before making a choice; and that the ramifications of change are beyond humanity's ability to foresee.

In *The Dragon in the Sea* Herbert minimizes his reliance on intrigue by limiting himself to an examination of psychological adaptation on a small scale. Four men of a near-future U.S. Navy take a subtug on a dangerous mission to pirate undersea oil from the Eastern Powers. The subtug represents "an enveloped world with its own special ecology," symbolically prenatal and subconscious, protected by darkness and quiet salt water from many of the dangers of the surface world. Yet, as the title suggests, the sea contains its own fearsome threats. The danger from enemy wolf packs is less threatening than two internal perils: one of the crew is a saboteur, and another, Ensign John Ramsay, through whose eyes the reader sees most of the action, is a psy-

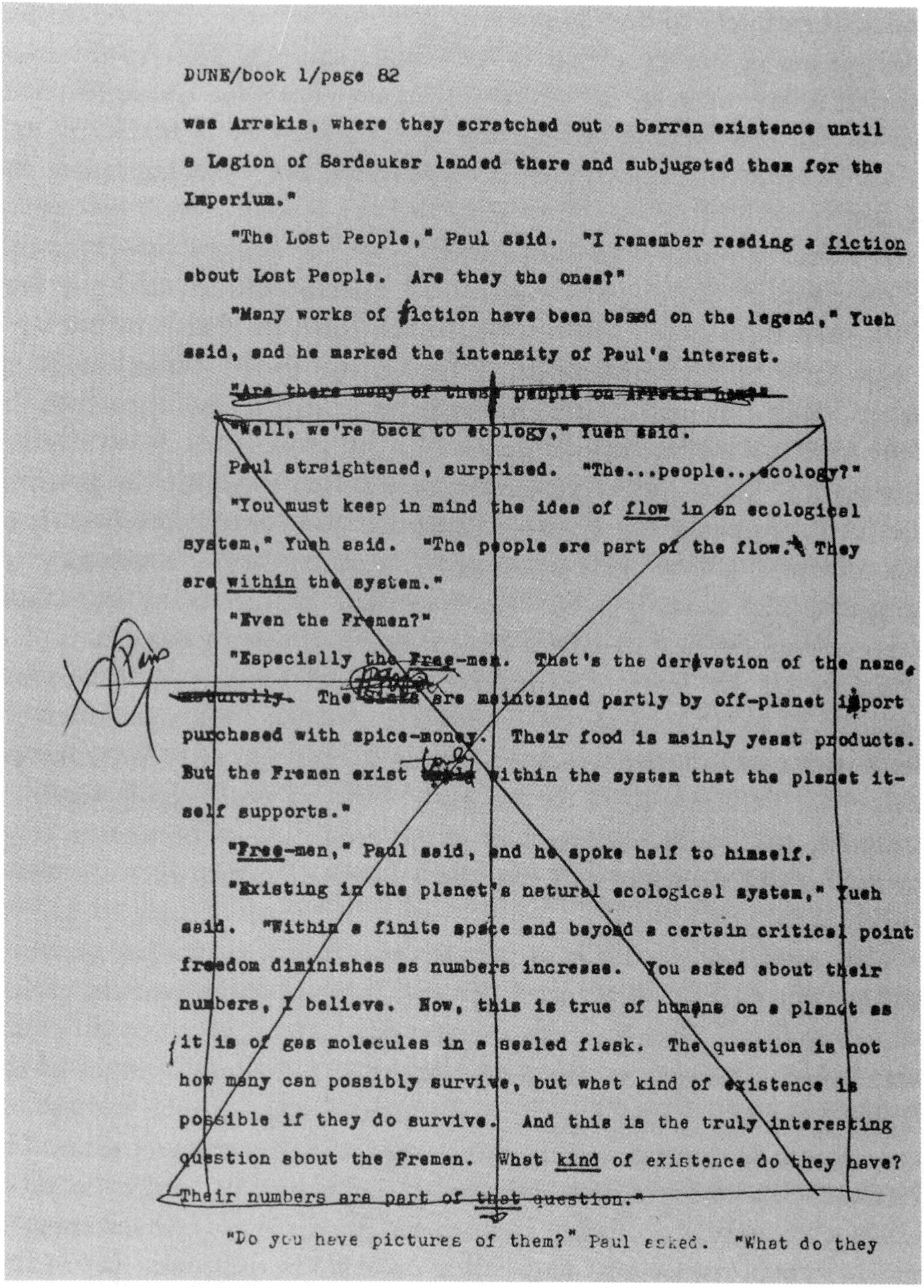

DUNE/book 1/page 82

was Arrakis, where they scratched out a barren existence until a Legion of Sardaukar landed there and subjugated them for the Imperium."

"The Lost People," Paul said. "I remember reading a _fiction_ about Lost People. Are they the ones?"

"Many works of fiction have been based on the legend," Yueh said, and he marked the intensity of Paul's interest.

~~"Are there many of these people on Arrakis here?"~~

"Well, we're back to ecology," Yueh said.

Paul straightened, surprised. "The...people...ecology?"

"You must keep in mind the idea of _flow_ in an ecological system," Yueh said. "The people are part of the flow. They are _within_ the system."

"Even the Fremen?"

"Especially the Free-men. That's the derivation of the name, ~~naturally~~. The ~~Slabs~~ are maintained partly by off-planet import purchased with spice-money. Their food is mainly yeast products. But the Fremen exist within the system that the planet it-self supports."

"_Free_-men," Paul said, and he spoke half to himself.

"Existing in the planet's natural ecological system," Yueh said. "Within a finite space and beyond a certain critical point freedom diminishes as numbers increase. You asked about their numbers, I believe. Now, this is true of humans on a planet as it is of gas molecules in a sealed flask. The question is not how many can possibly survive, but what kind of existence is possible if they do survive. And this is the truly interesting question about the Fremen. What _kind_ of existence do they have? Their numbers are part of that question."

"Do you have pictures of them?" Paul asked. "What do they

Page from the first typescript draft of Herbert's 1965 novel, Dune
(California State University, Fullerton)

chologist whose mission—to discover why subtug crews show such high rates of insanity and death in action—is in itself a threat to the crew's stability. The subtug crew responds to these pressures with adaptations that are insane when judged by outside standards. As Captain Sparrow explains, "I'm nuts in a way which fits me perfectly to my world. That makes my world nuts and me normal. Not sane. Normal. Adapted." The alternatives the subtug crew must choose between are much like that choice with which Herbert usually confronts his characters: they must adapt or die.

As in most of Herbert's earthbound novels, the ultimate insanity in *The Dragon in the Sea* is that of human society. Having dragged on for sixteen years, the vicious war with the Eastern Powers is not limited to acts of sabotage and piracy, and the surface world has become claustrophobic and paranoid. If social sanity, even in the limited sense of functional adaptation, is measured by "unbroken lines of communication," the constant bureaucratic infighting of military personnel points toward a psychotic break. Sparrow defines personal sanity as "the ability to swim . . . to understand *currents*," to which Ramsay's mentor, the sinister psychologist Dr. Oberhausen, adds the ability to "be prepared at all times to grasp a paddle"; but as the book ends, Ramsay finds himself once more a victim of political expediency.

Herbert was recognized as a major science fiction writer with *Dune*, the first novel to win both the Hugo and Nebula awards. Together with such books as Robert Heinlein's *Stranger in a Strange Land* (1961) and J. R. R. Tolkien's *Lord of the Rings* (1954-1955), *Dune* helped establish two traditions in contemporary science fiction and fantasy: the long novel and the invented-world novel, in which details of history, languages, customs, geography, and ecology (often explained in appended essays and maps) are combined with a rich complexity that engages the reader by its verisimilitude and imaginative scope. As one of the first science-fiction novels to deal with ecology, *Dune* was also influential in introducing a timely and important subject to the field. Continuously in print since its original appearance, even though it was originally rejected by twenty-two publishers, *Dune* has sold more than twelve million copies and been translated into fourteen languages. It is one of the best-selling science-fiction novels of all time and is now so firmly established in American popular culture that it has been adapted not only as a movie but also into board games, a computer game, coloring books, and a collectible card game—and has even generated *The Dune Encyclopedia* (1984).

The basic plot of *Dune* is similar to that of many of Herbert's novels: a hero with superior intelligence and special abilities struggles through complex intrigues. However, the epic scope of *Dune*, set in a traditional galactic empire, confers a special dignity on these characters and events. This civilization preserves a delicate military and economic balance between its ruling bodies, the Imperium and the Great Houses—a balance of power complicated by specialized organizations such as the Spacing Guild, which controls all interstellar traffic, and the Bene Gesserit Sisterhood, which studies politics, designs religions, furnishes consort-advisers to the nobility, and arranges noble marriages to further its secret breeding program. The goal of this program is to produce the Kwisatz Haderach, a prescient male who has full access to the genetic memories of his ancestors.

The mode of action in this galactic empire is the stuff of heroic fantasy. The ancient Butlerian jihad had outlawed the use of intelligent machines, so that a premium is placed on personal mentality, whether it be Bene Gesserit controls of mind and body, the limited prescience by which Spacing Guildsmen navigate at translight speeds, or the swift logic of a trained mentat. The Houses are free to fight among themselves, but since atomic weapons are banned and energized body shields render rapid projectile weapons useless, warfare is largely a question of tactical skill and swordplay.

The six Dune novels trace the fortunes of the Atreides family and its retainers—and, ultimately, of the Bene Gesserit Sisterhood and all humanity—over a period of nearly five thousand years. As *Dune* opens, Duke Leto has been forced to exchange his home world of Caladan, an ocean planet, for Arrakis, or Dune, a desert world that is the only source of melange, the most precious substance in the universe, an addictive spice that prolongs life and enhances psychic abilities. The gift of this valuable planet is, of course, a trap set by the Harkonnens, the Atreides' arch rivals, and soon Leto is killed, leaving his Bene Gesserit consort, Jessica, and their son, Paul, to flee into the desert, where they are taken in by the native Fremen. As Paul matures, a constant diet of melange enhances the prescient abilities for which he has been bred so that he becomes the Kwisatz Haderach and more, able to see the future as a network of probability paths that to some extent he can alter or choose between. Using the Fremen, the best warriors in the universe because of the adaptations they have made to survive their harsh environment, Paul struggles to free Arrakis from the Harkonnens and regain his birthright while avoiding the bloody, universe-spanning

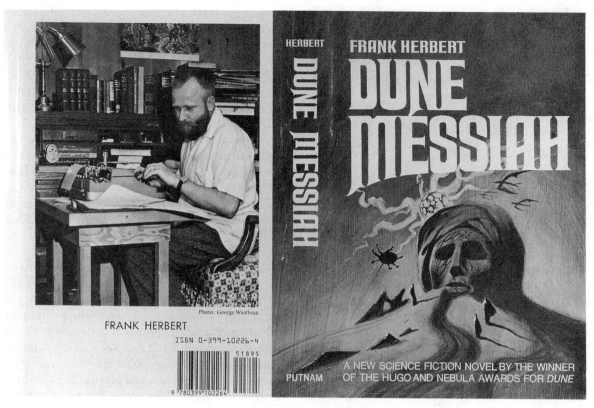

FRANK HERBERT

ISBN 0-399-10226-4

Dust jacket for the first of Herbert's five sequels to Dune

jihad—through which humanity will realize its imperative to renew itself by a crossing of "bloodlines in a great new mingling of genes"—that his visions tell him will be the all-but-inevitable consequence of his victory. This knowledge of his "terrible purpose" makes Paul regret and despise his eventual seizure of the Imperial throne, even though he has been bred and raised with fanatical single-mindedness to rule.

Some of the success of *Dune* is due to the internal conflict that springs from this ironic dilemma. Second only to his son Leto II—who is born at the climax of *Dune Messiah* and is actually the central, and most complex, figure in the Dune novels—Paul is the most fully developed of Herbert's characters. Many of the supporting characters are also well realized, especially Gurney Halleck, troubadour and swordsman; Stilgar, the epitome of traditional Fremen ways; and Baron Vladimir Harkonnen, a loathsome caricature of evil. Duncan Idaho, who is merely an important family retainer (although the greatest swordsman in history) in *Dune,* returns—in the form of a series of gholas, clones grown from dead tissue—as an increasingly crucial character in each of the five sequels. Moreover, in addition to being epic in its scope, which adds a gravity and dig-

nity to the travails of its characters, *Dune* is also mythic in its content, as Paul's adventure scrupulously corresponds to "the adventure of the hero," the "monomyth," as described by Joseph Campbell in *The Hero with a Thousand Faces* (1949). Yet the foundation of *Dune* is its setting: the planet Arrakis and its people. The ecological cycle that connects melange and the giant sandworms is one of the best examples of true scientific imagination in science fiction, and Herbert's descriptions of Dune are vivid and engrossing. The Fremen, whose culture is in essence Arabic, are impressive in their hardiness and marvelous in their adaptation to a brutal, water-poor environment and in their calm dedication to a centuries-long project to transform the desert. The Fremen thus add a human dimension to the ecology of Dune, making the mystery of the spice cycle and the harsh beauty of the planet dramatic and immediate as well as intellectually interesting. Finally, however, the unparalleled success of *Dune* is attributable to the nearly flawless integration of its intricately imagined setting, its ecological theme, its epic scope, its compelling characters, and its mythic content and structure.

While *Dune* is a science-fiction masterpiece, the five sequels are not uniformly successful. *Dune*

*Dust jacket for Herbert's 1973 novel about a human society
bred and conditioned to function like an insect society*

Messiah, a much smaller novel, lacks the scope of
Dune but compensates by being more tightly plotted
and even more densely charged with mythic or archetypal content. While also a novel of political intrigue, *Dune Messiah* is a palace melodrama as *Dune* is
an epic; yet its superbly crafted climax, in which all
the threads of the various plots and subplots converge in a single instant of intense drama and multiple revelations, is one of the most emotionally spectacular and artistically gratifying moments in the
history of science fiction. The other most notable
volume in the series is the fourth, the lengthy and
audacious *God Emperor of Dune,* which occurs more
than three thousand years after the first three novels
(which occupy a period of about twenty years, all
told) and is in large part a fascinating and highly
ironic meditation on power. While the most similar
to *Dune* of any of its sequels, *Children of Dune* does
not cohere as successfully as the first two novels in
the series, and it bogs down frequently in an overly
complicated plot. This tendency for complication
and a clutter of detail to overwhelm an already

highly complex plot is even more pronounced in
Heretics of Dune and *Chapterhouse: Dune.* Occurring
another 1,500 years after *God Emperor of Dune,* these
last two Dune novels are far too long and
windy—and suffer as well from being peopled almost
exclusively by characters who have diverged too far
from ordinary human norms to sustain the reader's
interest.

In *Dune Messiah* Paul is blinded and forced to
abdicate his throne as the result of a conspiracy that
also causes his wife, Chani, to die while giving birth
to their twins, Leto II and Ghanima. The first Duncan Idaho ghola appears in this novel as the mysterious Tleilaxu's sinister gift to Paul; he has Idaho's
body, but not his memories or personality. That the
ghola regains Idaho's persona immediately after
Chani dies is a crucial element of the conspiracy
against Paul; the Tleilaxu demonstrate their ability
to restore to a ghola its original persona as they offer
to provide Paul with a perfect ghola duplicate of
Chani in return for control of the empire, a temptation Paul resists. Both Leto II and Ghanima, like
Paul's sister Alia, are "preborn"—fully conscious of
the complete memories and personalities of their ancestors and able to foresee the future, even while in
the womb—as a result of their genetic heritage and
their mother's melange-rich diet. In *Children of Dune*
Alia marries the Idaho ghola but is eventually possessed and destroyed by the personality of Baron
Harkonnen, the maternal grandfather she kills in
Dune, who resides within her consciousness. Meanwhile, young Leto II is forced to develop his own
prescient abilities and ultimately merges symbioti-
cally with Arrakis' sandtrout (a stage in the sandworm life-cycle) while thwarting a series of assassination attempts; bonding with the sandtrout gives
Leto II invulnerability, great longevity, and inhuman speed and strength, but it also brings about his
gradual metamorphosis into a sandworm.

Thirty-five hundred years later, in *God Emperor of Dune,* Arrakis has been transformed into a
garden planet. Now the only worm left on Dune, the
monstrously transformed Leto II engineers his own
assassination at the hands of another Idaho ghola
and one of Paul's descendants, Siona, as the culmination of his millennia-spanning scheme to insure
humanity's survival by breeding it for invisibility to
prescience and then manipulating it—mainly
through imposing upon it his three thousand years
of despotic oppression—into "scattering" explo-
sively throughout the universe at his death, which
also returns the sandworms to Dune. Fifteen hundred years afterwards, in *Heretics of Dune,* Arrakis
has reverted back to desert, and Bene Gesserit
Mother Superior Taraza raises yet another Idaho

Sian Phillips, Francesca Annis, and Silvana Mangano in a scene from the 1984 movie version of Dune
(photograph by George Whitear)

ghola to be the bait in her successful plot to break finally Leto II's lingering hold on the future of humanity by luring the Honored Matres into destroying Arrakis and its worms, each of which now contains a "pearl" of Leto II's consciousness. The Honored Matres are perverse doubles of the Bene Gesserit who have returned from humanity's "Scattering" across the cosmos to conquer and enslave the Old Empire. Finally, in *Chapterhouse: Dune,* Taraza's successor, Odrade, uses both this last Idaho ghola and a clone of her father and another of Paul's descendants, Miles Teg, as instruments in her successful scheme to co-opt the Honored Matres and thus end their systematic extermination of the Bene Gesserit.

While artistically uneven, the six volumes of the Dune series provide the enormous scale on which Herbert can develop fully the ecological theme introduced in *Dune;* in this sense, the whole series is greater than the sum of its parts. Any ecology is by definition a dynamical system; and the explicit ecological theme of the Dune series is integrated with many of the other most prominent elements of the series—its plot structures, metaphors, and other motifs, and also their frequent reiteration—through mutual connections to chaos-theory concepts and structures. Chaos theory is a popularized term for dynamical systems analysis—the study of orderly patterns in turbulent, dynamical, or er-

ratic systems; and its most familiar manifestation is fractal geometry, which uses recursive equations to generate complex images characterized by the replication of similar structures on the same scale and on smaller and smaller scales, potentially ad infinitum.

Many of the characters or groups embroiled in the schemes within schemes that constitute the plot to the Dune series—Paul, Leto II, the Bene Gesserit, the Fremen, and the mentats—reveal themselves to be de facto chaos theorists in the recurring similarity of their statements or actions to chaos-theory axioms. The characteristic "pattern inside of pattern" structure of the fractal is realized in the relentlessly recurring "plans within plans within plans," "plots within plots" structure of the various characters' intrigues interacting repeatedly within each novel and in the overarching plot of the series. The fractal quality is exhibited as well in the repetition of ancillary parallel plot structures and themes in each volume of the series: the themes of metamorphosis into the other, of addiction, of secrecy and disguise, and of rebellion—as well as the interrelated themes of the journey to the underworld, tests and trials, death and rebirth, apotheosis, and revelation, all of which are subsumed into the monomyth structure, clearly manifest in *Dune,* that recurs with fascinating ironic variations and inversions in each succeeding volume of the series.

Throughout the series Herbert blends the ecological theme of *Dune* with a keen interest in religion—evident in the incorporation of Middle Eastern, Oriental, and Christian philosophies as well as in the activities of the Bene Gesserit—and with Jungian psychology, which examines the archetypal characters and incidents that comprise the monomyth. Two of the monomythic heroes in the series, Paul and Leto II as a child, are the main characters in *Dune* and *Children of Dune.* However, the monomythic hero in each remaining novel in the series is not the protagonist, but is merely an agent—and is himself a reiteration, a revenant replica: these secondary-character monomythic heroes are the first Duncan Idaho ghola, created for Paul in *Dune Messiah;* the last of the Idaho gholas created for Leto II, in *God Emperor of Dune;* the final Idaho ghola, created for the Bene Gesserit in *Heretics of Dune;* and the clone of the deceased Miles Teg, in *Chapterhouse: Dune.*

Herbert sought to capitalize on the success of *Dune* with a series of short minor novels. *The Green Brain* (1966) is an ecological novel set in Brazil. Efforts to increase human food supplies by destroying the insect population of the world have caused rapid mutations among the threatened species. Directed by a giant brain that learns how to cluster insects into simulated human forms, the insects try to warn men of the flaw in their plan. Divided by political intrigue, chiefly the attempt of the Chinese to hide the fact that their recently completed "realignment" of the insects has sterilized the soil, men do not accept the truth—that ecology requires cooperation among species—until all the main characters have been captured by the insects, killed, and restored by the green brain's advanced techniques of organ replacement.

Destination: Void (1966) tells the story of the seventh colony starship, the *Tin Egg,* sent out under Operation Consciousness. The crew of clones, carefully conditioned into selected behavior patterns and largely unaware of their manipulation by Moonbase Control, has a dual mission: to reach Tau Ceti despite deliberately planned malfunctions, and to react to the frustration of these malfunctions by becoming fully conscious. In many ways a reworking of *The Dragon in the Sea,* this book is more ambitious in its attempt to define consciousness rather than sanity. Its treatment of artificial intelligence is interesting, although the technology is unexplained, and the crew's interminable psychological conflicts, caused in large part by their prior conditioning, do not seem relevant to actual human life. True consciousness is eventually revealed to be so painful that it can be borne only against the sooth-

ing background of unconsciousness and the possibility of death, but Herbert's conclusion—with its literal deus ex machina—shifts from speculation to gimmick and deprives the reader of the opportunity to see the characters actually living with their newfound consciousness.

Each of the crew members of the *Tin Egg* represents an aspect of consciousness: Bickel, intelligence; Prudence, sensation; Timberlake, intuition; and Flattery, conscience. Also, each crew member has been feeding his mental processes into the ship computer from the beginning of the voyage; thus, it is the computer who finally forges a mechanical analogue of the human brain and becomes fully conscious continuously, as full consciousness is a heightened mental state the human crew can sustain only briefly. Finally ordered to self-destruct, the now-sentient and godlike ship chooses life instead and instantly transports itself to Tau Ceti, where it lands on a watery planet it has terraformed for human habitation and demands that its crew and cargo of hibernating colonists "decide how you will worship Me."

Destination: Void was eventually followed by three increasingly less successful sequels written in collaboration with Bill Ransom: *The Jesus Incident* (1979), *The Lazarus Effect* (1983), and *The Ascension Factor* (1988). In *The Jesus Incident,* set one thousand years after *Destination: Void,* Ship (as it is now known) has altered its demand and insists instead that the colonists merely discover how to worship. When the humans are then forced to understand their own nature for the first time—after fighting a losing battle with the planet, Pandora, and encountering its sentient alien species, Avata—Ship withdraws, leaving the colonists to themselves. Three hundred years later, in *The Lazarus Effect,* the colonists' extermination of Avata, an intelligent kelp, produces horrible ecological repercussions; but Avata is conveniently restored and retakes control of Pandora. *The Ascension Factor,* which concludes this series by returning the Pandora colonists to the void of space, was finished by Ransom after Herbert's death. In these three sequels, as in the last two volumes of the Dune series, the details get in the way of solid characterization and coherent plotting. The ecological theme in *Dune* and its preoccupation with religion are evident in these books, too, but the lavish attention to detail that makes Arrakis a fully realized setting has degenerated here into clutter.

The Eyes of Heisenberg (1966) explores genetic manipulation and immortality in a rigidly hierarchic future Earth. Salvation, when it comes, is directed by a subversive group of cyborgs, whose intentions and powers are never clearly revealed. In contrast

Herbert and his son, Brian, with whom he collaborated on the 1986 novel
Man of Two Worlds *(photograph by Theresa Shackelford)*

to this traditional pulp novel, reminiscent of A. E. van Vogt in tone and plot, *The Heaven Makers* (1968) gives a lurid twist to another old idea. Earth is the plaything of aliens, in this case a set for carefully directed dramatic productions by the Chem, whose immortality is threatened only by boredom. The illegal attraction of Earth–that Chem and humans can interbreed–proves irresistible to the aliens until Dr. Androcles Thurlow, a psychologist, convinces the Chem, who have abducted and raped his beloved Ruth, that immortality is a closed system and that the possibility of death is necessary for a meaningful, mature life.

In the tightly-written *The Santaroga Barrier* (1968), Gilbert Dasein investigates a valley in California where the inhabitants are dominated by a group-mind that controls them through Jaspers, a mildly psychedelic spore. Dasein's efforts to free himself and his fiancée, Jenny Sorge, from the group-mind raises some interesting but ultimately unresolved questions about reality, isolation, and consciousness.

Whipping Star (1970) develops a setting first used in "The Tactful Saboteur," which Herbert contributed to Groff Conklin's anthology, *Seven Trips Through Time and Space* (1968). The Bureau of Sabotage (BuSab), with its motto "In Lieu of Red Tape," is a constitutionally protected agency designed to slow the workings of a dangerously efficient government and to curb abuses of power. Jorj X. McKie, Saboteur Extraordinary, is a conventional and likable secret agent, but the real strength of the series based on his exploits lies in its many alien races, whose strange customs and abilities provide a satisfying richness of detail to fill out otherwise thin plots. In *Whipping Star* the mysterious Calebans, who control the jumpdoors that are the principal means of interstellar transportation in the ConSentiency, are withdrawing from the universe. McKie slowly learns that without the Calebans anyone who has ever used a jumpdoor will die. The last Caleban, Fannie Mae, has entered into an unbreakable contract with the sadistic Mliss Abnethe. McKie must learn Caleban thought patterns, especially the concept of "connectives," in time to find a loophole in Fannie Mae's contract before Abnethe kills her. The novel is sufficiently fast-paced and the ideas are original enough for the reader to overlook the weak explanation of connectives.

One of Herbert's short novels, *The God Makers* (1972), applies personal consciousness and social interactions directly to the concepts of peace and religion. True peace, the author states, is "an internal matter . . . a self-discipline for an individual or for an entire civilization," since externally enforced peace creates paired opposites that inevitably come into conflict. This theme is presented through the career of Lewis Orne, who works for an agency that forcibly destroys militaristic tendencies on worlds isolated from galactic civilization during the Rim Wars. The issue of peace is overshadowed by religion, for it turns out that Orne moves along a path shaped by the priests of Amel as part of the training of their acolytes in Religious Engineering. As Abbod Halmyrach of Amel explains, "All of mankind acting together represents a great psi force, an energy system. . . . Sometimes, we call this force *religion*. Sometimes, we invest it with an independent focus of action which we call God." Eventually Orne achieves godhood, frees himself from external manipulation, and gets the girl. Herbert's use of prophetic foreshadowing is pleasingly intricate and the definition of peace reasonable and instructive, but the book founders in explaining religion in terms of vaguely defined psi powers, speaking, as the Abbod puts it, "with a certain glibness of eternity, of absolutes."

Hellstrom's Hive (1973) returns to the question of what humans can learn from insect societies. A centuries-long experiment in selective breeding and social dynamics has established a society of fifty thousand people living in a Hive beneath a farm in eastern Oregon. Genetic selection and special diets have differentiated the group into insect-type castes, whose behavior is largely conditioned by chemical triggers and the greater will of the Hive. The plot of *Hellstrom's Hive* involves the efforts of a clandestine Agency to infiltrate the Hive and discover the secret of Project 40, an energy weapon with the potential to destroy the world. Nils Hellstrom, Hive leader, struggles to preserve the secret of the Hive's size and social structure until its superior inhabitants have the strength of numbers to emerge and conquer the world. As Agency and Hive battle each other with violence and political intrigue, the two sides are revealed to be equally repulsive. Neither tolerates individualism, and while the Hive places a higher priority on the lives of its members, it is just as concerned with the well-being of the truncated

lower torsos it uses as reproductive stumps. At its best, the Hive is orderly and protective, while the Agency's leaders are smarter than public officials. By the end of the book, it seems clear that whoever wins this struggle, humanity loses.

Herbert continues the theme of the irruption of a closed microsociety into an unsuspecting larger culture in *The Dosadi Experiment* (1977), another Jorj X. McKie novel. The Gowachin, the least-assimilated race of the ConSentiency, have established Gowachin and humans on Dosadi as a psychological experiment, but also to allow clandestine body transfers. However, the vicious competition for survival on Dosadi, like the Fremen adaptation to Dune's harsh environment, has produced a society whose physical and mental skills are vastly superior to those of outsiders and in which its members live by an implacable code of domination and distrust. The closest any inhabitant comes to idealism is the desire of Keila Jedrik and her followers to escape from Dosadi and avenge themselves on their unknown manipulators. McKie is sent to Dosadi as a BuSab agent under contract to the outside Gowachin. Amid a race war and under threat of planetary destruction, McKie must learn to survive on Dosadi and then determine his own role in the many-sided conflict. Although tempted by the raw power that comes with mere survival on Dosadi, in the end McKie remains true to his love of justice. He and Jedrik become lovers, escape from Dosadi, confront the originators of the Dosadi experiment, and defeat them in a trial held according to the lethal Gowachin legal code. Finally, McKie overcomes the neurotic emotional isolation that had ruined his previous fifty-five marriages, finding true love without needing anyone outside his Self.

The Dosadi Experiment is engaging adventure science fiction, with a tightly organized plot, characters who are distinguishable at least because of their racial differences, plenty of action and intrigue, and some fairly original ideas that connect well to the concern of the book with informed consent and the abuses of unrestrained power. Unfortunately, as in many of Herbert's books, the effect of this middle ground of plotting, presentation, and intended theme is undermined by flaws in the deeper matters of motivation and conception. Dosadi is an excessively complex way of hiding a body-transfer racket; it is never clear why McKie's training as a Gowachin Legum was a necessary part of the intended Dosadi cover-up, especially since McKie causes the cover-up to fail; and the implausibility of Jedrick's sudden development of the softer emotions is exceeded only by the folly of McKie's trusting her.

In *The White Plague* (1982) John Roe O'Neill, an American microbiologist vacationing in Ireland, sees his wife and children killed by an IRA bomb. Driven insane by the results of this terrorist act, O'Neill develops a contagious DNA-based disease that strikes only women in a mad effort to eradicate terrorism. The fatal disease spreads worldwide, and O'Neill ultimately returns to Ireland to see firsthand the effects of his revenge. While scientists seek a cure, political, military, and religious leaders jockey for power as usual.

In *Man of Two Worlds* (1986), written in collaboration with Brian Herbert, a militaristic Earth is about to destroy an alien race, ignorant of the fact that the very existence of Earth depends upon the imaginative powers of the aliens. Herbert has also written several dozen short stories–including "Try to Remember," "A-W-F Unlimited," "The Mary Celeste Move," and "Committee of the Whole," as well as "The Tactful Saboteur"–some nonfiction, and a novel about Native Americans titled *Soul Catcher* (1972).

With its emphasis on intrigue, consciousness, ecology, religion, supernormal mental powers, and the functional meaning of abstractions such as sanity or peace, Herbert's science fiction is primarily intellectual. While his manipulation of mentally stimulating complexities is sufficiently adroit to dazzle the reader, a closer look at many of these novels leads inevitably to a questioning of the framework that encloses this intricacy. Although those in *Dune* are conspicuous exceptions, the surface complexity of Herbert's invented societies is rarely matched by an underlying rationale for their development along these lines, and the soulless plotters who people these worlds frequently do not provide a convincingly human perspective on the action. Furthermore, the transformations of mind and body undergone by many of Herbert's characters depend on pseudosciences that are unexplained or implausible, and so the mental powers of these characters do not always provide convincing models of human consciousness.

Aside from *The Dragon in the Sea,* which succeeds in part because of its limited scope, only *Dune* and its best sequels, *Dune Messiah* and *God Emperor of Dune,* possess the successful integration of wildly diverse elements, the emotional validity, and the aura of plausibility that yield great science fiction. To some extent this limited success is no doubt the result of commercial factors; *Dune* was written over a period of time sufficiently great for its societies and intrigues to develop a coherent complexity. It is also no coincidence that the more successful of Herbert's remaining novels, such as *The God Makers* and *The*

Dosadi Experiment, are those in which the characters laugh, love, and display emotions more positive than reflexive ambition. Herbert's novels fail when all the characters act like McKie, who "has built a simulation McKie of his own who acts on the surface of the real McKie." When he takes the trouble to create characters and societies with the depth to transmit his undoubtedly sincere themes, Herbert can be an extraordinary writer. The one time he escaped completely from the commercialism of convenient artifice, he created *Dune,* an unquestioned masterpiece and the book (and series) for which he will be remembered.

Bibliography:

Daniel J. H. Levack and Mark Willard, *Dune Master: A Frank Herbert Bibliography* (Westport, Conn.: Meckler, 1988).

References:

Robert Cirasa, "An Epic Impression: Suspense and Prophetic Conventions in the Classical Epics and Frank Herbert's *Dune," Classical and Modern Literature,* 4 (Summer 1984): 195–213;

Michael R. Collings, "The Epic of *Dune:* Epic Traditions in Modern Science Fiction," in *Aspects of Fantasy: Selected Essays from the Second International Conference on the Fantastic in the Arts,* edited by William Coyle (Westport, Conn.: Greenwood Press, 1981), pp. 131–139;

Lorenzo DiTommaso, "History and Historical Effect in Frank Herbert's *Dune," Science-Fiction Studies,* 19 (November 1992): 311–325;

Ellen Feehan, "Frank Herbert and the Making of Myths: Irish History, Celtic Mythology, and IRA Ideology in *The White Plague," Science-Fiction Studies,* 19 (November 1992): 289–310;

Stephen M. Fjellman, "Prescience and Power: *God Emperor of Dune* and the Intellectuals," *Science-Fiction Studies,* 13 (March 1986): 50–63;

John L. Grigsby, "Asimov's *Foundation* Trilogy and Herbert's *Dune* Trilogy: A Vision Reversed," *Science-Fiction Studies,* 8 (July 1981): 149–155;

Grigsby, "Herbert's Reversal of Asimov's Vision Reassessed: *Foundation's Edge* and *God Emperor of Dune," Science-Fiction Studies,* 11 (July 1984): 174–180;

Jack Hand, "The Traditionalism of Women's Roles in Frank Herbert's *Dune," Extrapolation,* 26 (Spring 1983): 24–28;

C. N. Manlove, "Frank Herbert's *Dune,*" in his *Science Fiction: Ten Explorations* (London: Macmillan, 1986), pp. 79–99;

Susan McLean, "A Psychological Approach to Fantasy in the *Dune* Series," *Extrapolation,* 23 (Summer 1992): 150–158;

McLean, "A Question of Balance: Death and Immortality in Frank Herbert's *Dune* Series," in *Death and the Serpent,* edited by Carl Yoke (Westport, Conn.: Greenwood Press, 1985), pp. 145–156;

Willis E. McNelly, "Archetypal Patterns in Science Fiction." *CEA Critic,* 35 (May 1973): 15–19;

McNelly, ed., *The Dune Encyclopedia* (New York: Putnam, 1984);

Walter E. Meyers, "Problems with Herbert," *Science-Fiction Studies,* 10 (March 1983): 106–108;

David M. Miller, *Frank Herbert* (Mercer Island, Wash.: Starmont House, 1980);

Miller, "Towards a Structural Metaphysics: Religion in the Novels of Frank Herbert," in *The Transcendent Adventure: Studies of Religion in Science Fiction/Fantasy,* edited by Robert Reilly (Westport, Conn.: Greenwood Press, 1985), pp. 145–156;

Timothy O'Reilly, *Frank Herbert* (New York: Frederick Ungar, 1981);

O'Reilly, "From Concept to Fable: The Evolution of Frank Herbert's *Dune,*" in *Critical Encounters: Writers and Themes in Science Fiction,* edited by Dick Riley (New York: Frederick Ungar, 1978), pp. 41–55;

John Ower, "Idea and Imagery in Herbert's *Dune,*" *Extrapolation,* 15 (May 1974): 129–139;

Donald E. Palumbo, "'Plots Within Plots . . . Patterns Within Patterns': Chaos-Theory Concepts and Structures in Frank Herbert's *Dune* Novels," *Journal of the Fantastic in the Arts,* 8 (January 1997): 55–77;

Harold Lee Prosser, *Frank Herbert: Prophet of Dune* (San Bernardino, Cal.: Borgo Press, 1989);

Don Riggs, "Future and 'Progress' in *Foundation* and *Dune,*" in *Spectrum of the Fantastic: Selected Essays from the Sixth International Conference on the Fantastic in the Arts,* edited by Donald Palumbo (Westport, Conn.: Greenwood Press, 1988), pp. 113–117;

Astrid Schmidt-v. Muhlenfels, "The Theme of Ecology in Frank Herbert's *Dune* Novels," in *The Role of Geography in a Post-Industrial Society,* edited by Hans-W. Windhorst (Vechta: Vechtaer Druckerei und Verlag, 1987), pp. 27–34;

Leonard M. Scigaj, "'Prana' and the Presbyterian Fixation: Ecology and Technology in Frank Herbert's *Dune* Tetralogy," *Extrapolation,* 24 (Winter 1983): 340–355;

William F. Touponce, *Frank Herbert* (Boston: Twayne, 1988).

Papers:

The library of the California State University at Fullerton has a large collection of Frank Herbert's papers.

John Hersey

This entry was updated from the entries by Sam B. Girgus (University of New Mexico) in
DLB 6: American Novelists Since World War II, Second Series, *and by*
Dan R. Jones (University of Houston) in DLB 185: American
Literary Journalists, 1945–1995, First Series.

BIRTH: Tientsin, China, 17 June 1914, to Roscoe Monroe and Grace Baird Hersey.

EDUCATION: Attended Hotchkiss School; B.A., Yale University, 1936; attended Clare College, Cambridge, 1936–1937.

MARRIAGES: 27 April 1940 to Frances Ann Cannon (divorced February 1958); children: Martin, John, Ann, Baird; 2 June 1958 to Barbara Day Addams Kaufman; child: Brook.

AWARDS AND HONORS: Pulitzer Prize for *A Bell for Adano*, 1945; Anisfield-Wolf Award for *The Wall*, 1950; Daroff Memorial Fiction Award, Jewish Book Council of America, for *The Wall*, 1950; Sidney Hillman Foundation Award for *The Wall*, 1951; Howland Medal, Yale University, 1952; National Association of Independent Schools Award for *A Single Pebble*, 1957; Tuition Plan Award, 1961; Sarah Josepha Hale Award, 1963; named honorary fellow of Clare College, Cambridge University, 1967; honorary degrees include M.A., Yale University, 1947; L.H.D., New School for Social Research, 1950, and Syracuse University, 1983; LL.D., Washington and Jefferson College, 1950; D.H.L., Dropsie College, 1950; and Litt.D., Wesleyan University, 1954, Bridgeport University, 1959, Clarkson College of Technology, 1972, University of New Haven, 1975, Yale University, 1984, Monmouth College, 1985, William and Mary College, 1987, and Albertus Magnus College, 1988.

DEATH: Key West, Florida, 24 March 1993.

BOOKS: *Men on Bataan* (New York: Knopf, 1942);
Into the Valley (New York: Knopf, 1943; London: Hodder & Stoughton, 1943);
A Bell for Adano (New York: Knopf, 1944; London: Gollancz, 1945);
Hiroshima (New York: Knopf, 1946; Harmondsworth, U.K.: Penguin, 1946);
The Wall (New York: Knopf, 1950; London: Hamilton, 1950);

John Hersey (photograph by Richard De Combray)

The Marmot Drive (New York: Knopf, 1953; London: Hamilton, 1953);
A Single Pebble (New York: Knopf, 1956; London: Hamilton, 1956);
The War Lover (New York: Knopf, 1959; London: Hamilton, 1959);
The Child Buyer: A Novel in the Form of Hearings before the Standing Committee on Education, Welfare, & Public Morality of a Certain State Senate, Investigating the Conspiracy of Mr. Wissey Jones, with Others, to Purchase a Male Child (New York: Knopf, 1960; London: Hamilton, 1961);
Here to Stay (London: Hamilton, 1962; New York: Knopf, 1963);

White Lotus (New York: Knopf, 1965; London: Hamilton, 1965);

Too Far to Walk (New York: Knopf, 1966; London: Hamilton, 1966);

Under the Eye of the Storm (New York: Knopf, 1967; London: Hamilton, 1967);

The Algiers Motel Incident (New York: Knopf, 1968; London: Hamilton, 1968);

Letter to the Alumni (New York: Knopf, 1970);

The Conspiracy (New York: Knopf, 1972; London: Hamilton, 1972);

My Petition for More Space (New York: Knopf, 1974; London: Hamilton, 1975);

The President (New York: Knopf, 1975);

The Walnut Door (New York: Knopf, 1977; London: Macmillan, 1978);

Aspects of the Presidency (New Haven, Conn.: Ticknor & Fields, 1980);

The Call (New York: Knopf, 1985);

Hiroshima: A New Edition with a Final Chapter Written Forty Years after the Explosion (New York: Knopf, 1985);

Blues (New York: Knopf, 1987);

Life Sketches (New York: Knopf, 1989);

Fling and Other Stories (New York: Knopf, 1990);

Antonietta (New York: Knopf, 1991);

Key West Tales (New York: Knopf, 1994).

OTHER: *Ralph Ellison: A Collection of Critical Essays,* edited by Hersey (Englewood Cliffs, N.J.: Prentice-Hall, 1974);

The Writer's Craft, edited by Hersey (New York: Knopf, 1974).

SELECTED PERIODICAL PUBLICATIONS—UNCOLLECTED: "The Battle of the River," *Life* (23 November 1942): 99–116;

"AMGOT at Work," *Life* (23 August 1943): 29–31;

"Engineers of the Soul," *Time* (9 October 1944): 99–102;

"Dialogue on Gorki Street," *Fortune* (January 1945): 149–151;

"Kamikaze," *Life* (30 July 1945): 68–75;

"A Reporter at Large. Long Haul with Variables," *New Yorker* (8 September 1945): 44–57;

"Letter from Shanghai," *New Yorker* (9 February 1946): 82–90;

"Letter from Chunking," *New Yorker* (16 March 1946): 80–87;

"The Death of Buchan Walsh," *Atlantic Monthly* (April 1946): 80–86;

"Letter from Peiping," *New Yorker* (4 May 1946): 86–96;

"A Reporter in China. Two Weeks' Water Away," *New Yorker* (18 May 1946): 59–69; (25 May 1946): 54–69;

"The Pen," *Atlantic Monthly* (June 1946): 84–87;

"A Reporter at Large. The Communization of Crow Village," *New Yorker* (27 July 1946): 38–47;

"Red Pepper Village," *Life* (26 August 1946): 92–105;

"A Fable South of Cancer," *'47—The Magazine of the Year* (April 1947): 113–141;

"Alternatives to Apathy," *United Nations World,* 1 (May 1947): 20–21, 70–76;

"A Short Wait," *New Yorker* (14 June 1947): 27–29;

"The Novel of Contemporary History," *Atlantic Monthly* (November 1949): 80–84;

"The Mechanics of a Novel," *Yale University Library Gazette,* 27 (July 1952): 1–11;

"Test of Heart and Mind," *Life* (4 September 1964): 62–64;

"The Legend on the License," *Yale Review,* 20, no. 1 (Autumn 1980): 1–25;

"A Reporter at Large. Homecoming," *New Yorker* (10 May 1982): 49–79; (17 May 1982): 46–70; (24 May 1982): 44–66; (31 May 1982): 47–67;

"A Reporter at Large. Assymetry," *New Yorker* (7 September 1987): 36–53.

In 1950 John Hersey was considered one of the most promising young writers in the nation. His first novel, *A Bell for Adano* (1944), had won a Pulitzer Prize in 1945, while his journalistic masterpiece of 1946, *Hiroshima,* with its successful depiction of individual survivors of the atomic bombing of Japan, had an enormous emotional impact on both domestic and international audiences. His second novel, *The Wall* (1950), evoked a similar kind of emotional response from its readers. A classic description of the Holocaust, it still stands as one of the few books that has been able to relate in human terms the destruction of European Jewry by the Nazis. Hersey remained popular and prolific, publishing many works of fiction and nonfiction that deal with an enormous range of subjects and interests. However, he has been ignored by most literary scholars while others, such as Leslie Fiedler, have accused him of naively believing that problems such as racism have simple solutions. Hersey suggested that "there are several reasons why my work has not been written about more than it has. Leaving the issue of quality, or lack of it, aside for the moment, one fundamental reason, I would guess, is that I have always written against the grain, both of literary fashion and of establishment values." As early as 1949 he called his type of fiction "the novel of contemporary history," that is, "a specific genre: the

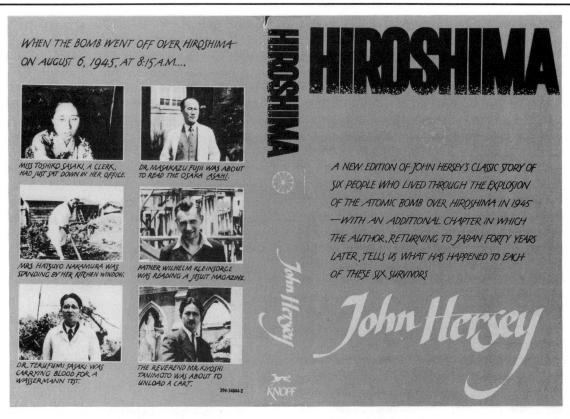

Dust jacket for the augmented edition of Hersey's 1946 book

novels which deal with contemporary events." They are, he says, part of the larger mode of the historical novel. In contrast to more avant-garde writers Hersey dedicated himself to the goal of chronicling the events and issues of his time, ranging from World War II itself, the atomic bomb, and the Holocaust to the dominant social issues of the postwar decades—such as racism, overpopulation, education, the generation gap, the attack on democratic institutions, and, more generally, the malaise of modern life.

Hersey's political ideology was related to his concept of his role as a writer. "I don't think of myself as a traditional American liberal," he wrote. "I'm not given to compromise. And I've been too skeptical of dogma to be an attached radical—attached, I mean, to any party line. So politically I'm not exactly anywhere; I work in small ways for what I believe in." Despite his claims to nonalignment, Hersey's idealistic individualism was actually in the tradition of the old-fashioned liberalism that goes back at least two centuries in American cultural history. Hersey's continuing faith in the value of education, progress, and democracy was apparent throughout all his writings. Indeed, for him the writer ought to be an educator who brings about social change. Thus, in a speech presented at Yale University and later printed in 1952 in the *Yale Univer-*

sity Library Gazette, Hersey described the motives behind *The Wall* by saying that writing is "the only hope man has of rising above his unmentionably horrible existence, his foul nest of murder, war, greed, madness and cruelty. Only the poets can persuade us to move up out of the slime into a hopeful shore, there by evolution to transform ourselves into higher and more intelligent creatures." He expressed a similar belief more than twenty years later in his introduction to *The Writer's Craft* (1974): "Art praises and nourishes life, art hates death. This is what we mean when we say we recognize power in a work of art: The life forces in us are encouraged." He continued, "True art is neither revolutionary nor reactionary. This does not mean that it is neutral. No. It is rebellious in any setting."

John Richard Hersey believed that his penchant for nonconformist views stemmed from his origins. Born on 17 June 1914 in Tientsin, China, where he spent his childhood, he expressed the suspicion "that there is something subtly alien in my work that has come from the fact that the regions of memory, for me, from which imaginative material has to come, are on the other side of the globe. Perhaps this is why my work has gone against the grain." In addition, Hersey's zealous proselytizing for faith in democracy may have derived from the

127

religious zeal of his missionary parents, Roscoe and Grace Baird Hersey. In 1925 Hersey's father contracted encephalitis, and the family returned to the United States and settled in Briarcliff Manor, New York. Hersey attended public schools there for three years. He then won a scholarship to Hotchkiss, where he supported himself by working as a waiter and by cleaning classrooms. A 1936 graduate of Yale University and an Oxford scholar, Hersey took considerable pride in the fact that he had to work to survive as a student. While at Yale, Hersey was vice-chairman and music critic on the *Yale Daily News,* earned a letter in football, and paid his way by waiting on tables, tending telephones, serving as a librarian, and working during summers as a lifeguard, an electrician's assistant, and a tutor. His first postgraduate job in the summer of 1937 was as a secretary, driver, and factotum for the novelist Sinclair Lewis.

Following his service with Lewis, he worked for several years as a journalist, including a stint from 1937 through 1944 for *Time* magazine that early on included covering events in China and Japan. During the early part of World War II, he covered the South Pacific and was cited in 1942 by the Secretary of the Navy for helping to remove wounded men from the battlefield while under fire on Guadalcanal Island. In 1943 he was a correspondent in the Mediterranean theater in the Sicilian campaign and moved on to cover Moscow in 1944. After the war, he went to work as a correspondent and editor for *Life* and *The New Yorker.* In the decades following the war, he continued active involvement in various groups concerned with educational and social issues. From 1965 to 1970 he was a master of Pierson College at Yale University and then was writer-in-residence of the American Academy in Rome from 1970 to 1971. He also taught for several years at Yale.

Hersey married Frances Ann Cannon in 1940, and the marriage ended in divorce in 1958; their children are Martin, John Jr., Ann, and Baird. Hersey and Barbara Day Addams Kaufman, whom he married in 1958, have a daughter, Brook.

From the beginning of his career Hersey sought to examine deep impulses in American culture and politics. His first book, *Men on Bataan* (1942), is a journalistic account of the fall of Bataan in April 1942. Hersey's fears about the ability of democracy to function in the midst of the war are reflected in his concern over the power, prestige, and fame of Gen. Douglas MacArthur. The book is a prelude to the journalistic style and reportorial stance Hersey refined in later works. His penchant for understatement became a defining element of his

literary journalism. He chose subjects that were deeply moral and often complex, yet his purpose in dealing with them was less to render judgment than to explore their human dimensions. In a second journalistic work dealing with the war, *Into the Valley* (1943), Hersey covered a small group of marines involved in a skirmish on Guadalcanal. Hersey's subject is not the details of a military action but the thoughts and emotions that accompany battle. *Into the Valley* received uniform praise, including a favorable comparison to Stephen Crane's *The Red Badge of Courage* (1895) and a declaration by a reviewer for *The New York Times* that Hersey was "a new Hemingway."

Hersey's fears about the internal threat to democracy represented by an ambitious and egotistic leader, as well as his faith placed in the abilities of the common man, came together in his Pulitzer Prize–winning novel, *A Bell for Adano.* When Hersey covered the Sicilian campaign in the summer of 1943, he became interested in the activities of Maj. Frank E. Toscani, the American military governor of Licata, a Sicilian seaport. Hersey's sketch of Toscani and the village appeared in the 23 August 1943 issue of *Life,* titled "AMGOT at Work" (AMGOT is the acronym for Allied Military Government Occupied Territory). Hersey expanded and fictionalized the tale and published it as *A Bell for Adano.* The novel focuses on the character of Maj. Victor Joppolo, whom the first readers of the novel saw as a heroic figure trying to bring democracy to a small Italian village. In retrospect, it is evident that there is a basic conflict in the novel between the traditional idea of democracy and the new concept of social control and political organization typified by the American military government. In dramatizing this conflict Hersey anticipated the radical attack on the liberal social programs of the 1960s.

Joppolo represents a modern version of an authentic American vernacular hero in the tradition of Mark Twain's Hank Morgan in *A Connecticut Yankee in King Arthur's Court* (1889). Joppolo is the common man raised to high places, and he believes devoutly in democracy. He tells the people of Adano that democracy means "that the men of the government are no longer the master of the people. They are the servants of the people." Like Hank Morgan he succeeds in reforming and modernizing the society over which he assumes control, emphasizing the importance of popular government, education, and honesty. His positive influence is symbolized by his providing the town with a new bell to replace the one that had been taken by the Fascists and turned into gun barrels.

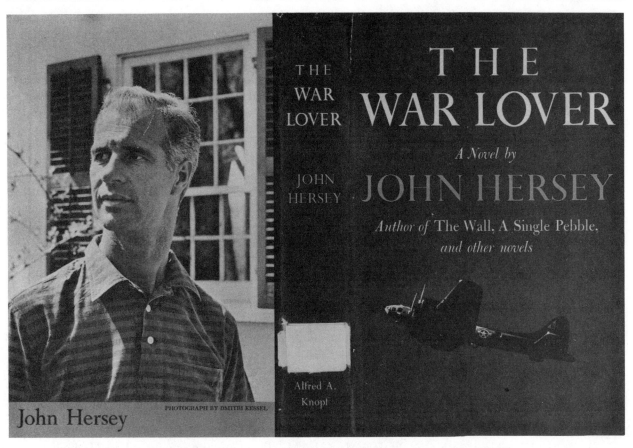

Dust jacket for Hersey's 1959 novel, which explores attitudes about war and death

However, the world Joppolo creates for his innocent followers holds unforeseen dangers related to the rise of a modern corporate and technological society. The army that Joppolo represents not only brings change and reform, it also foreshadows the modern state in its use of power. This aspect of the novel is symbolized in the character of General Marvin. Hersey finds this one figure so repulsive and dangerous that he directly addresses the reader: "But I can tell you perfectly calmly that General Marvin showed himself during the invasion to be a bad man, something worse than what our troops were trying to throw out." The major operates in conflict with Marvin and countermands one of the general's orders banning all carts from Adano, a restriction that would ruin the commerce and economic life of the town. Joppolo also stands in sharp contrast to some of the other American officers, such as navy lieutenant Crofts Livingston, who seem more like modern corporate personalities than military men.

However, the ultimate effect of Joppolo's work is to make the American occupation easier. Although eventually removed by the general, Joppolo works like a tool of the system by serving to effect Adano's transition to a modern consumer-oriented culture. He helps to make the people responsive to and dependent upon the new economic and political order. Thus, when an Italian child is killed while trying to get close to a passing military vehicle whose occupants toss candy to the children, the incident can be seen as symbolic of the relationship of the people to the new government. Following the child's death, Joppolo arranges for the children to get their presents safely just as he helped to organize the town so that it could experience the benefits of modern society. However, the price of such organization to both individuality and traditional culture clearly bothers Hersey.

Hersey's next major work, *Hiroshima,* is a modern classic partly because it incorporates so well the techniques and style of the novel within a work of journalism. Thus, in this book Hersey anticipates what later critics and writers celebrated as the new mode of the nonfiction novel, a term that Hersey disdained. When the work first appeared as the entire 31 August 1946 issue of *The New Yorker* magazine, its impact was instantaneous and unprecedented. Charles Poore of *The New York Times* noted that "Talking to people in that week, listening to the commentators on the air, reading the editorials and the columnists, you soon realized what a profound impression the story had already made." When *Hiroshima* appeared in book form, Albert Einstein ordered one thousand copies of it, and Bernard Baruch ordered five hundred. Free copies were distributed by the Book-of-the-Month Club on the grounds that nothing else in print "could be of more importance at this moment to the human race." The American Broadcasting Company had the book read on their radio stations. The interest around the nation was so great that some stations felt compelled to repeat the broadcasts, and recordings of it were made available to educational institutions. Newspapers throughout America sought rights to serialize the book; Hersey agreed but accepted no payment in return, requiring instead that the newspapers contribute to the American Red Cross. Poore summed up the reaction of most readers to the book when he wrote that "*Hiroshima* penetrated the tissue of complacency we had built up. It penetrated it all the more inexorably because it told its story not in terms of graphs and charts but in terms of ordinary human beings."

The dropping of the bomb is seen through the eyes of six survivors: Father Wilhelm Kleinsorge, a Jesuit priest; the Reverend Mr. Kiyoshi Tanimoto, minister of the Hiroshima Methodist Church; Miss Toshiko Sasaki, a young clerk in the East Asia Tin Works; Dr. Terufumi Sasaki, a young surgical resident at Hiroshima's Red Cross Hospital; Dr. Masakazu Fujii, a physician in private practice; and Mrs. Hatsuyo Nakamura, a tailor's war widow with two children. Their experiences become personal events for the reader; Hersey accomplishes this feat simply by showing rather than telling what each of the six was doing when the bomb was dropped, how they reacted to it, how they behaved afterward, and how they felt throughout their ordeals. Interior emotions and attitudes are illustrated by external action. Through his combination of journalism and novelistic character development, Hersey educated his audience about the human significance of an event so terrifying as to be nearly incomprehensible.

The basic narrative structure of the book is chronological: the account opens a few hours before the bombing and closes almost exactly one year later. The chronological scheme provides a simple, easily conceived frame for guiding the reader's perceptions. Hersey achieves a sense of authenticity by adopting an almost clinical tone in his prose. Missing from *Hiroshima* are the moral reflections of *Into the Valley* and *A Bell for Adano;* in their place are spare and meticulously documented details gleaned from close observation and careful research. Precise de-

scription becomes an instrument of comprehensibility. The six survivors Hersey chose as his subjects are decidedly unrepresentative of the general population of Hiroshima; for example, Hiroshima, with its population of 250,000, had only 150 doctors, two of whom appear in the book. Yet the very qualities that make Hersey's survivors atypical of Japanese culture also make them recognizable and even sympathetic to American readers. In addition to locating figures who adequately symbolized the reality of the atomic bomb blast, Hersey was faced with the task of translating Japanese culture into a vocabulary familiar to Western sensibilities. He does so by choosing as settings for the book institutions common to both Japanese and American cultures: churches, banks, a police station, a lower-middle-class home, hospitals, and doctors' offices. The city of Hiroshima thereby assumes a quality of everyday life that readers may associate with their own lives.

In 1985 Hersey published a fifth chapter to *Hiroshima* in which he documents the fates of the six survivors. Two–Dr. Fujii and Father Kleinsorge–have died, while the others have encountered various fortunes and misfortunes. Dr. Sasaki, the idealistic young surgeon who worked tirelessly in the days following the initial blast to care for the wounded and the dying, has become wealthy, while Mr. Tanimoto, the equally selfless Methodist minister, has met with mixed success and much disappointment in his efforts to teach the world about the horrors of the atomic bomb. The updated accounts bring the reader no closer to a comprehensive moral understanding of the bomb, and Hersey skillfully avoids using the new stories to bring narrative closure to the original text. To do so would violate his original journalistic agenda: to translate the reality of the bomb into terms salient to Western habits of mind while declining either to justify or condemn its use.

In his next work, *The Wall,* the story of the destruction by the Nazis of five hundred thousand Jews in the Warsaw ghetto, Hersey again devised a way of depicting what seemed like an unimaginable horror. He created the fictitious personal diary of the character Noach Levinson to place the story of the deterioration and destruction of Warsaw's Jews under the Nazis within an historical and cultural context. Although the diary entries cover only the period from November 1939 to May 1943, Levinson's clear memory allows him to see the connection of the present crisis to the past. Even before the advent of Nazi persecution, many of the characters had deeply ambivalent feelings about their own identities as individuals and as members of an ethnic minority. These conflicts were fed by their equally ambivalent feelings about Jewish culture and religion; but in more normal times these problems could remain submerged in the routines of everyday life. In their insecurity and defensiveness as a vulnerable minority in a crisis situation, the characters in *The Wall* discover the need for systems of belief and loyalty upon which to rest individual and group identity. In an early scene Dolek Berson, who later in the novel approaches traditional heroic proportions, resists identification with the problems and crises of his own people, telling Levinson: "This has nothing to do with me," but Levinson replies, "Yes, this has to do with you, too. And with all your mishpokhe: it concerns all your family ties."

In *The Wall,* as in *A Bell for Adano,* Hersey was deeply concerned about the ability of modern man to deal with the threat of totalitarianism. Modern man, he felt, may not only prove unable to resist the forces of totalitarianism, he may also invite them as a result of prolonged alienation and insecurity. Several characters in the novel reveal such alienation in their self-hatred and self-derision. Moreover, as individuals crumble before the Nazis, so also do families and finally the community as a whole. At the same time, Hersey refused to see such capitulation as the only alternative open to modern man. He steadfastly insisted that human individuality and responsibility may prevail. He believed man is capable of assuming moral responsibility and authority for his own actions.

Hersey's next two novels are less successful at depicting the confrontations between individuals and the dangers of modern life. Both *The Marmot Drive* (1953) and *A Single Pebble* (1956) seem somewhat abstract and allegorical. *The Marmot Drive* is Hersey's attempt to write a modern New England novel with a contemporary Hester Prynne as a heroine. Her experiences indicate that she has no usable past or tradition upon which to base a system of values and no confidence about her ability to find such guidelines in the future. Similarly, the way in which modern life cuts one off from the traditions of the past is treated in *A Single Pebble,* which concerns the journey of a young unnamed American hydraulic engineer up the Yangtze River on a Chinese junk during the 1920s. His experiences on the river cause him to rethink his own relationship as a Western technocrat to the Orient.

Hersey was far more successful in *The War Lover* (1959) in finding an adequate means to dramatize a complex set of ideas, in this case the examination of the impulse that leads some men to love war. *The War Lover* is a novel about the psychology of death as it manifests itself in the relationship between Buzz Marrow, the title character, and Charles

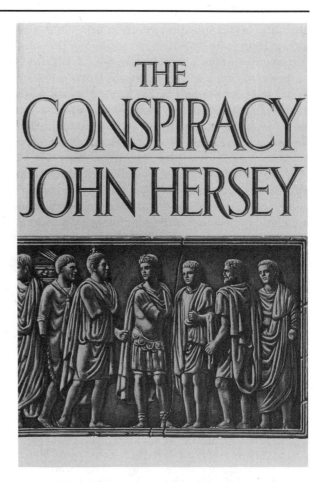

Dust jacket for Hersey's 1972 novel, in which events of Roman history serve as metaphors for modern problems

Boman, his copilot. As in other works by Hersey, the psychological enemy within concerns the author as much as the external threat. Sections called "The Raid," which deal with the hours involved in a long mission against the Germans, are interspersed with sections called "The Tour," which describe earlier missions and incidents on the ground up to the time of "The Raid." This device allows Hersey to manipulate time artfully in order to place the present in a living historical context and to offer a sophisticated psychological study of human character.

Boman and Marrow, as their names indicate, are two aspects of the same personality. Their dual controls over the plane, which is called by Marrow "The Body," further develops the suggestion that they are bone and marrow of the larger organism. At first both men seem quite different. Marrow is the dashing flying ace, while Boman is the defensive short man who has no desire to be a hero, thinking of himself as "not your typical cocky shorty. No would-be Napoleon he. No Little Corporal." However, as the novel progresses, Hersey reveals that the men are mutually dependent. Boman is too comfortable in his position of inferiority and self-denigration before Marrow. Accordingly, the counterpart to Boman's self-deprecation is Marrow's self-celebration and self-inflation. However, Marrow's seeming bravery and defiance of death really mask his enormous fear of it. At one point in the novel he castigates death as "that bastard in the sky" and says, "I'd like to kill death." Boman's defensive posture provides a needed corrective.

In order to find himself, Boman must break this cycle of interdependence; he does so through the help of Daphne, an Englishwoman who teaches him how to love by forcing him to have the courage to face his own strength and power and to deal more effectively with external threats. In contrast, Marrow, with his lack of self-knowledge, finally succumbs to his fears. In a sense Hersey is suggesting that when a democracy is at war, each participant must have the self-knowledge and the sense of purpose that can justify self-sacrifice and violence. A spokesman for this position is the character "Kid" Lynch, who says:

> Well it strikes me in this century something awful has been let loose among the so-called civilized peoples, something primitive and barbaric. I don't say the Germans have a monopoly on this . . . regression. But I figure I'm here to help put down the Nazis because right at the moment they're the most dangerous representatives of this sort of throwback we're liable to. If I can do my part in keeping this worse side of mankind in hand, I'll be satisfied, whatever happens to me.

Hersey's fear that democracy is undermined if individuals live without awareness of self and higher purpose is echoed in his next book, *The Child Buyer: A Novel in the Form of Hearings before the Standing Committee on Education, Welfare, & Public Morality of a Certain State Senate, Investigating the Conspiracy of Mr. Wissey Jones, with Others, to Purchase a Male Child* (1960). The novel dramatizes the conflict between a philosophy of education that emphasizes the need to foster individual growth and fulfillment and the demands upon educators to produce more scientists, engineers, and technicians. Presented as a transcript of hearings before a state senate committee, the novel focuses upon the educational community of Pequot, where the child buyer, Wissey Jones, wants to buy boy genius Barry Rudd in order to make him part of a technological learning network that will take full advantage of the boy's genius and develop it to its utmost. Jones works for a corporation that buys children like Barry under a defense contract and puts them through an enormously complicated but scientifically controlled dehumanizing process that ties off their emotions and senses and enables

them to develop intelligence quotients of close to 1,000. The children are then connected to computers. They spend the rest of their lives as education machines improving upon the work of the computer. When Jones is asked, near the end of the book, what end such a dehumanizing process serves, he calls it "a foolish question. He didn't even know himself. He believed it had to do with satisfying man's greatest need—to leave the earth."

In a less extreme form Jones's attitude toward education dominates the Pequot educational system. The testimony of Barry's parents, teachers, and others in the community dramatizes the inability of the educational institutions to deal with the students as individuals; instead schools tend to compartmentalize, categorize, and stereotype children. The main opponent to this inhumane philosophy is the elementary-school principal, Dr. Frederika Gozar, who attacks the educational philosophy of the state department of education because it "is based on the notion that education is a science, that the process of learning is like a process of catalysis or combustion or absorption—observable, definable, manipulable; and that Barry—volatile, mysterious, smoldering Barry—is inert experimental material." She believes that "You can't package talent, you can't put it in uniform bottles and boxes with labels," and she knows that Jones's educational philosophy is part of a larger social and political philosophy that manipulates and controls the society as a whole. Dr. Gozar realizes that the child buyer's friendly manner disguises "just one slogan: We Must All Obey." Moreover, there are many who favor his approach to education and life. Dr. Gozar's emphasis on individuality and freedom runs absolutely counter to the dominant trend. She says, "The only real defense for a democracy is improvement. Crisis and triumph over crisis. It's a failure of national vision when you regard children as weapons, and talents as materials you can mine, assay, and fabricate for profit and defense." Ultimately, however, even Dr. Gozar sells out to the child buyer, as does Barry, who decides to go with him so that he can reach the IQ level the man promises.

Written after Hersey had spent ten years as a member of and consultant to education groups on the local, state, and national levels, *The Child Buyer* excited considerable controversy. The 10 October 1960 issue of the *New Republic* magazine published extensive commentary on the questions the book raised, including articles by Margaret Halsey, B. F. Skinner, Carl F. Hansen, Robert Gorham Davis, and William Jay Smith.

Following this novel Hersey published *Here to Stay* (1962), his next venture into literary journalism. The book is a collection of nine tales of survival—from war, natural disasters, concentration camps, and other extreme situations. The complete text of *Hiroshima* is included as the last piece. The stories are collected from a variety of sources. Some are products of Hersey's World War II experiences, such as "Joe Is Home Now" and "A Short Talk with Erlanger," both of which use composite characters and situations to address the problems of returning war veterans. Other stories in the collection were included because they typify for Hersey the theme of survival. An example is "Over the Mad River," which chronicles the experiences of an elderly survivor of the floods spawned by Hurricane Diane in Connecticut in 1955. While claiming to remain faithful to the factual demands of journalism, Hersey imbues his tales with a parable-like quality consistent with the thematic character of fiction.

In 1965 *White Lotus,* a novel that received considerable critical attention because of its unusual approach to racism, appeared. The plot of *White Lotus* involves the enslavement of whites by the Chinese. The story is narrated by an American girl called White Lotus. In effect, Hersey encapsulates within the years of this white girl's adolescence and early youth the history of blacks in America. Each stage of black history from slavery through the civil rights movement is represented in Lotus's life. In so doing Hersey demonstrates an acute historical, sociological, and psychological insight into black history in America as well as a deep knowledge of the Orient of his own youth. He also demonstrates a brilliant insight into the nature of racism itself. Moreover, what makes the novel especially significant as a contribution to readers' understanding of racism is the way in which Hersey elaborates on the relationship between racism and liberalism. For the dominant yellow race of the novel, the liberal creed of China means a government of laws and justice and a culture based on serious religious principles. "Hurt no living creature" is one of the key principles of Lotus's first master, the Venerable Shen. However, the liberal philosophy of the best minds of China takes an interesting twist when directed toward enslaved whites. Since slavery and racism so strongly contradict the philosophy and attitude of the liberal culture toward human life, the culture dehumanizes the slaves and regards them as either dependent children or animals. Lotus comes to learn early that she must work to sustain this fantasy of her oppressors. Even before fully understanding the meaning of her behavior, she learns from another slave "the slaves' basic law: *No matter how frightened you are before a yellow person, no matter how angry, no matter even how*

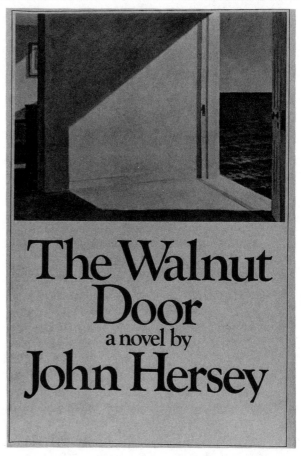

Dust jacket for Hersey's 1977 novel, about a restless craftsman trying to understand his past

happy, control your face and body; show no feeling; have a face as impassive as a figure painted on a china bowl." The effect of this attitude on the slaves is to make schizophrenia a natural psychological condition for them: "What double meanings our life had!" Lotus says. This psychological state gives the slaves a sense of "numbness," which in turn affects their attitudes toward sexuality and violence.

The novel also includes a parallel to the American civil rights movement with leaders who strongly resemble Martin Luther King Jr. and Malcolm X in style and tactics. A contrast between the slaves in the liberal society in this novel and the situation of the Jews at the end of *The Wall* dramatizes the stark differences between the way liberal and totalitarian states deal with resistors and minorities. By the end of the novel, White Lotus is startled to realize how continuing change and reform have caused her to expect fair treatment from the dominant culture. In addition, she also comes to realize how responsible she is for creating her own freedom: "I had come to realize that freedom could be felt at best only for moments: that even for the powerful, even for yellows, it was inconstant, elusive, fickle and quickly flown. . . . Freedom was not to be bestowed but grasped—and only for a moment at a time."

Freedom is to some extent a theme in *Too Far to Walk* (1966), Hersey's second novel about education in America. In writing this novel Hersey had in mind the growing number of students throughout the country in the mid 1960s who were finding themselves disenchanted with all they saw around them but who were unable to come up with satisfactory programs of action for change. Protagonist John Fist, who "had always thought of himself as a good boy," attends Sheldon College like his father before him and initially plans to follow a career and life pattern much like his father's. However, he decides that being good comes to mean little more than accommodating himself to others' expectations and demands, and he becomes alienated. At college he dreams about "fusion" and cutting across the intellectual boundaries defined by the traditional curriculum, but he finds that graduation and traditional success will require him to conform intellectually and socially. Attracted to the drug culture, Fist falls in with a devilish character named Breed who promises, "I'll give you all that you want. You'll pay for this service by turning your id over to me."

With Breed, Fist will attempt to find a new consciousness through a fusion of science and the humanities, electricity and poetry. The two sign a blood pact, and feeling an affinity for "something known as the New Morality," Fist begins a kind of Faustian adventure of experimentation with drugs. In his quest for a new freedom, Fist finds that he lost his sense of self. Thus, at the end he tells Breed that he cannot renew his contract "Because I can't go on living in a world that's on a knife-edge between hallucination and objective truth." He goes on to tell Breed: "I can't live with frenzy, visions, stupor, hangovers—and finally a tremor, a dragging foot as I walk. You sold me a bill of goods. You sold me illusions. I prefer the real world, crummy as it is." In spite of the fact that he has no firm answer to Breed's challenge of "Who's to say what's real? Do you know what's real?" Fist decides to turn away from a world that denies the existence of reality and affirms false "breakthroughs," realizing that "what you put me through was a series of flights into myself, away from other people." Instead of such a world Fist, like Hersey, prefers one involving "friction" with reality and human contact. "I've come to see," he says, "that there can't be any shortcut to those breakthroughs I yearn for. You can't imbibe them, or smoke them, or take them intravenously,

or get them by crossing your legs and breathing deeply for twenty minutes."

In a sense Hersey's next novel, *Under the Eye of the Storm* (1967), is about the graduate who never learned Fist's lessons and so must gain Fist's experience and knowledge in other ways, in this case a sailing adventure. Dr. Tom Medlar, a liver specialist, tends to see people only in terms of this organ. Not yet thirty-five, he is already sick of himself and "earnestly sick of the organ of his choice." As Tom's last name suggests, he must learn to stop meddling in others' lives and start living his own. With his wife and another couple, Tom goes out to sea and runs into a storm that frees him temporarily from the false consciousness and false sense of reality that have plagued him. Unfortunately, once the danger of the storm ends, Tom is "oppressed by a heavy sense of the discrepancies between his reading of the experiences of the storm and the versions his crew had brought away." Finally, his experiences during the storm serve only as the source for an entertaining story that Tom tells to please people.

Hersey's next two books, *The Algiers Motel Incident* (1968) and *Letter to the Alumni* (1970), are works of nonfiction on the subjects of racism and education. *The Algiers Motel Incident* is an account of the murders of three young black men during the Detroit riots of 1967. The book consists of carefully transcribed interviews with witnesses to the shooting, family members of the dead, the police and legal authorities involved in the shooting, and a host of secondary figures. There are also court transcripts, media accounts, and other official records, all linked by Hersey's narrative. *The Algiers Motel Incident* is presented as a parable of race relations and the malignant effects of prejudice, but the victims are not sufficiently ennobling, nor are the perpetrators sufficiently malicious, to reduce the tale to these terms. Ironically, it may be Hersey's integrity as a journalist that prevents *The Algiers Motel Incident* from being a more compelling story. Hersey was driven to uncover every scrap of available data in his quest for the truth behind the murders, yet the circumstances and issues of the case he revealed turned out to be too complex to fit the parable-like narrative he seems to have envisioned for the book.

In *The Conspiracy* (1972) Hersey returned to the novelistic mode to examine the problems of freedom and political corruption in modern society through the metaphoric use of Roman history. In the process he liberally alters the original accounts of Tacitus and Suetonius to tell his version of the A.D. 64 plot to kill Emperor Nero, making it clear that his inspiration for the novel comes more from recent American history than from Roman history.

The exchange of letters between the poet Lucan and the philosopher Seneca constitutes a discourse and debate on the subject of freedom. Thus, Seneca writes to Lucan: "Who is to blame for tyranny—the tyrant or the tyrannized? Who is to blame for your outbursts against me—you or I?" In the novel tyranny destroys itself through its insatiable hunger for more power, for as Seneca notes, "The aim of power is to keep power. The only real and lasting power, it should be clear is that of character, that which obliges others to follow because of admiration and love." Moreover, Seneca voices Hersey's view that the writer must express his concern for morality in public life to encourage life-enhancing impulses.

After *The Conspiracy* Hersey showed even more interest in the subject of writing. He edited *The Writer's Craft,* which includes major writers' essays on their art, and he edited a collection of essays on Ralph Ellison that includes his own introductory interview with Ellison. He also wrote two journalistic works dealing with the institution of the presidency: in *The President* (1975) he details a week he spent with President Gerald Ford, documenting the president's typical daily activities; and in *Aspects of the Presidency* (1980) he focuses on Ford and Harry S. Truman. With all of these interests, however, Hersey continued to write fiction. *My Petition for More Space* (1974) presents Hersey's dystopian vision of a world in which overpopulation, a scarcity of resources, mind control, the growth of bureaucracy, and dehumanizing administration, all define the human condition. The setting for the entire novel is a mob scene in which people are crammed together in long lines, like passengers on a rush-hour subway train, sometimes waiting for days to reach the government's "petition windows." In the society of the novel, changing a job, marrying, going to school, or moving to a new residence requires a verbal petition to an anonymous authority hidden behind opaque glass. Invariably, the petitioners are turned down, and most of them, in fact, seem so demoralized and dehumanized that approval would probably terrify them. These people do not have homes but are allotted specific amounts of space, and the narrator of the story wants to petition for more of it even though his space of seven feet by eleven feet makes him relatively well-off.

The petition lines are so crowded that people are often unable to see the faces of those in front of or behind them. There are conversations, however, and some of the people on the lines get vicarious pleasures from the close physical contact. The narrator, for example, has fantasies about the woman in front of him, encounters hostility from another man, and is bored by a grandmother who says she

appears regularly on the lines because she enjoys meeting the people on them. When he reaches the window, his petition is denied, but he decides that he probably will return to make another petition. The process of making petitions is a kind of neurotic activity that becomes an end in itself because of its capacity for providing distraction.

With his next novel, *The Walnut Door* (1977), Hersey returned once again to the subject of education. Elaine Quinlan, a Bennington graduate, and Eddie Macaboy, a former Reed College student, are both, in different ways, part of the youth culture of the late 1960s and early 1970s. Macaboy especially is obsessed with understanding his past experience in "the movement," listing his reasons for leaving college as "Disillusionment. Vietnam. Ego dilution. Deep-seated toxic reactions. 'The Movement seemed like a better education than Sociology 24.'" Macaboy soon learns that "So many of the big talkers were cowards because they'd never learned how to be afraid." The result, he feels, is the growth of a near-mystical fascination for violence and evil. Rather than continue with either politics or formal education, Macaboy moves in a different direction. Hersey portrays him as a genius who turns his newly chosen crafts of locksmithing and carpentry into an art form, and the novel becomes a study of the nature of art.

Hersey's symbol for artistic creation is a walnut door, a masterpiece of craftsmanship, that Elaine has hired Macaboy to install because someone has broken into her apartment. Ironically, Macaboy is the perpetrator of this crime. The safety Elaine craves turns into a danger in itself as she becomes his prisoner. "The company wants you to feel safe," he says sardonically to her. Accustomed to retreating within herself, Elaine finds her victimization both frightening and fascinating. She eventually grows to trust her new jailer and admits that he "had begun to make her feel supersafe." Forced by the death of his father to return to his hometown in Connecticut and confront his past, Macaboy leaves her, and her new fear is that he will not return. "For a flickering moment she wondered if Macaboy had abandoned her. Then it came to her that actually it was he, not she, who was being held captive by the walnut door." In love with him now, she feels safe and believes that an unhappy affair of a few years earlier will not be repeated. However, there is a touch of irony to the conclusion of the novel. Not being Macaboy's prisoner creates a new sense of insecurity for Elaine. Although he seems ready to move in and to establish a more permanent relationship in her apartment ("I'll have the door open," she says), the novel ends with Macaboy striving to complete his new work of art, an oak door, for another woman. He informs the new customer of his concern for "your personal safety, Mzz Creeley. Like people breaking in."

The Walnut Door integrates many of Hersey's most pervasive themes into an artistic whole illustrating his belief that a changing and dangerous world provides a continuing challenge to individual freedom. Throughout his long career Hersey believed that as a writer he could maintain such freedom through the creative act of writing about the political and moral issues that dominated modern times. He tried steadily to ameliorate the contemporary human condition by challenging and enlightening public consciousness. In *The Walnut Door* Hersey once again connects his theory of art to his liberal social philosophy. His overriding concern remained human survival with freedom and dignity.

The Call, published in 1985, remains for many critics Hersey's most accomplished novel. The story of an American missionary in China in the first half of the century, *The Call* is based on exhaustive historical research fueled by vivid and imaginative transformations of Hersey's own memories and experiences in what he referred to as his "natal land." The protagonist of the novel, David Treadup, is, like Hersey's father, a YMCA "Social Gospel" missionary. Unlike the quiet and bookish Roscoe Hersey, however, Treadup is a driven man, blinded to political and cultural realities by fierce devotion to his evangelical mission. Following the outbreak of World War II, Treadup is imprisoned in a Japanese concentration camp. Deprived of the means with which to carry out his spiritual pursuit, he submits himself to a searing self-examination that reveals the complex patterns of tyranny embedded deep within the missionary impulse. As a novel *The Call* represents Hersey's most accomplished interweaving of factual content and fictional form.

Blues, published in 1987, is a curious blend of objective fact, folklore, and observations gleaned from Hersey's twenty years of fishing for bluefish along the coast of Massachusetts. Set as a series of dialogues between a seasoned fisherman and a novice identified only as "stranger," the book is a personal exploration of the author's fascination with the sea revealed in a series of dramatic revelations opened to the stranger as he learns to fish.

Hersey's last nonfiction collection, *Life Sketches,* was published in 1989. It consists almost entirely of previously published material, much of it from early in his career. Hersey's selection is highly eclectic: profiles of John F. Kennedy and Harry S.

Truman alongside those of George Van Santvoord, the headmaster of Hotchkiss School, which Hersey attended as a boy; and Pvt. John Daniel Ramey, an illiterate World War II army recruit who learned to read and write at a special army training facility. The collection is a reminder that Hersey's journalistic talent lay in his ability to find extraordinary expressions of humanity in everyday experience, whether that experience belonged to a president or to an uneducated army private.

Hersey devoted his final years primarily to fiction. In 1990 another collection, *Fling and Other Stories,* appeared, and in 1991 he published *Antonietta,* a novel tracing the life of a violin crafted by Antonio Stradivari and named for the woman who inspired him. *Key West Tales* (1994), Hersey's final work, was delivered to his publisher six weeks before his death on 24 March 1993. These short stories consist of imaginative re-creations of life in Key West, where Hersey and his wife were part-time residents in his last years. Like some of Hersey's best literary journalism, the stories in *Key West Tales* have a fablelike quality, focusing once again on the compelling significance of everyday life. In the seamless interweaving of fact and fiction the reader finds examples of some of Hersey's most mature writing. As a collection these last stories display some of Hersey's most notable characteristics: his finely honed eye for detail, his keen sense of narrative, and his shrewd understanding of the ingredients of human character.

Interview:
Tom Spain, "PW Interviews: John Hersey," *Publishers Weekly* (10 May 1985): 232–233.

Bibliography:
Nancy Lyman Huse, *John Hersey and James Agee: A Reference Guide* (Boston: G. K. Hall, 1978).

References:
Kelsey Guilfoil, "John Hersey: Fact and Fiction," *English Journal,* 39 (September 1950): 355–360;
Nancy Lyman Huse, *The Survival Tales of John Hersey* (Troy, N.Y.: Whitston, 1983);
David Sanders, *John Hersey* (New Haven, Conn.: Yale University Press, 1967);
Sanders, *John Hersey Revisited* (Boston: Twayne, 1990);
Michael J. Yavendetti, "John Hersey and the American Conscience: The Reception of *Hiroshima,*" *Pacific Historical Review,* 43 (February 1974): 49.

S. E. Hinton

Linnea Hendrickson
University of New Mexico

BIRTH: Tulsa, Oklahoma, as Susan Eloise Hinton, 22 July 1948, to Grady P. and Lillian M. Hinton.

EDUCATION: B.S., University of Tulsa, 1970.

MARRIAGE: September 1970 to David Inhofe; child: Nicholas David.

AWARDS AND HONORS: *New York Herald Tribune* best teenage books citation, 1967, *Chicago Tribune Book World* Spring Book Festival Honor Book, 1967, *Media and Methods* Maxi Award, American Library Association (ALA) Best Young Adult Books citation, both 1975, and Massachusetts Children's Book Award, 1979, all for *The Outsiders;* ALA Best Books for Young Adults citation, 1971, *Chicago Tribune Book World* Spring Book Festival Honor book, 1971, and Massachusetts Children's Book Award, 1978, all for *That Was Then, This is Now;* ALA Best Books for Young Adults citation, 1975, *School Library Journal* Best Books of the Year citation, 1975, and Land of Enchantment Award, New Mexico Library Association, 1982, all for *Rumble Fish;* ALA Best Books for Young Adults citation, 1979, *School Library Journal* Best Books of the Year citation, 1979, New York Public Library Books for the Teen-Age citation, 1980, American Book Award nomination for children's paperback, 1981, Sue Hefly Honor Book, Louisiana Association of School Libraries, 1982, California Young Reader Medal nomination, California Reading Association, 1982, and Sue Hefly Award, 1983, all for *Tex;* Golden Archer Award, 1983; first ALA Young Adult Services Division/*School Library Journal* Author Award (later Margaret A. Edwards Award) for body of work, 1988.

BOOKS: *The Outsiders* (New York: Viking, 1967; London: Gollancz, 1970); republished together in one volume with *That Was Then, This Is Now* and *Rumble Fish* (London: Collins, 1985);
That Was Then, This Is Now (New York: Viking, 1971; London: Gollancz, 1971);

S. E. Hinton

Rumble Fish (New York: Delacorte, 1975; London: Gollancz, 1976);
Tex (New York: Delacorte, 1979; London: Gollancz, 1980);
Taming the Star Runner (New York: Delacorte, 1988; London: Gollancz, 1989);
Big David, Little David (New York: Doubleday, 1994);
The Puppy Sister (New York: Delacorte, 1995; London: Collins, 1996).

MOTION PICTURES: *Tex,* screenplay by Charles S. Haas and Tim Hunter with Hinton's assistance, Walt Disney Productions, 1982;
The Outsiders, screenplay by Kathleen K. Rowell with Hinton's assistance, Warner Brothers, 1983;

Rumble Fish, screenplay by Hinton and Francis Ford Coppola, Universal, 1983.

OTHER: "Teen-Agers Are for Real," *New York Times Book Review,* 27 August 1967, p. 26;
Autobiographical sketch, in *The Fourth Book of Junior Authors and Illustrators,* edited by Doris de Montreville and Elizabeth D. Crawford (New York: Wilson, 1978), pp. 176–177.

S. E. Hinton's young adult novels are among the best-selling books of all time and continue to be popular with adolescent readers a generation after she wrote them. Her books, especially *The Outsiders* (1967), continue to be assigned reading in middle-school and high-school English classes; yet in contrast to other well-known writers such as J. D. Salinger and Robert Cormier, there is a dearth of serious examination of her work as literature, and commentators who have looked closely have tended to be highly critical. Sometimes considered to be the book that marks the beginning of contemporary young adult literature, *The Outsiders* has also been the target of controversy and censorship. Four of Hinton's books have also been made into popular films, and critics have also strongly disagreed about the merits of these.

According to Jay Daly, whose *Presenting S. E. Hinton* (1987, 1989) is the most complete source of information on Hinton's life and work, Susan Eloise Hinton was born in Tulsa, Oklahoma, on 22 July 1948. She has one younger sister, Beverly. Her father, Grady P. Hinton, to whom she was very close, died when she was a junior in high school. His death undoubtedly influenced the writing of *The Outsiders,* for which she was presented a publisher's contract on the day of her graduation from Will Rogers High School in Tulsa.

Several facts about *The Outsiders*—that it was written by a teenager from a teenager's perspective, that it was written by a young woman in the first-person voice of a young man, and that it deals with a teenage underworld of gangs, delinquency, and violence—all added to its notoriety and popularity. Within a relatively short time the book had sold more than four million copies in the United States. The fame was difficult for Hinton, a shy, non-joining outsider herself, to handle, and she suffered writer's block, unable to write even a letter, for years afterwards. "Before it was published I thought I knew how to write. Afterwards I knew I couldn't. I was a teen-age writer, which is similar to being a teen-age werewolf, only it doesn't last as long," Hinton wrote in an autobiographical sketch for *The Fourth Book of Junior Authors and Illustrators* (1978).

She also reported that during her junior year in high school, when she was working on *The Outsiders,* she received a D in creative writing: "My revenge is to print that fact as often as possible."

In a discussion with a group of teenage readers recorded in *Top of the News* in November 1968, Hinton told the audience that her mother had not read the book until it was published and then was shocked "because she didn't know what I was doing all this time." She said, "'What are the neighbors going to say, what's the Church going to say?' But after she calmed down she decided she liked it, and then said, 'So that's why I found that switchblade in your jeans pocket!'"

After high school Hinton attended the University of Tulsa, earning a B.S. in education. There, with the help of her boyfriend, David Inhofe, whom she married after graduation, she managed to write a second novel, *That Was Then, This Is Now* (1971). "If I didn't get my two pages done, we didn't go out," she wrote in *The Fourth Book of Junior Authors and Illustrators.* After she and David were married, they went to Europe, where they lived on the southern coast of Spain for six months.

That Was Then, This Is Now, which features some of the same characters and settings as *The Outsiders,* was followed by *Rumble Fish* (1975) and *Tex* (1979). After the publication of *Tex* Hinton became involved in films. Walt Disney Productions approached her about making *Tex* into a movie, and although she had misgivings, she finally agreed as long as they let her horse, Toyota, play the lead horse. Hinton was involved in many aspects of the film, including the casting, scriptwriting, and directing, and became friends with the young stars, especially Matt Dillon.

About the same time that *Tex* was being filmed, a group of high-school students in Lone Star, California, with the help of librarian Jo Ellen Misakian, petitioned Francis Ford Coppola to make a movie of *The Outsiders.* Hinton and Coppola worked together on the film and, while consulting, spent their weekends writing a screenplay for *Rumble Fish.* The fourth film, *That Was Then, This is Now,* released in 1985 with a screenplay written by Emilio Estevez, was the only film with which Hinton was not directly involved.

There was a gap of nine years between the publication of *Tex* and *Taming the Star Runner* (1988). In the meantime Hinton's son, Nicholas David, was born in 1983. *Taming the Star Runner,* although it touches on Hinton's by-now familiar themes of alienation, change, and growing up, represents further development in Hinton's craft as a writer. In 1988 Hinton received the first Young Adult Ser-

*Dust jacket for Hinton's 1979 novel, about a troubled
fourteen-year-old in a rural setting*

vices/*School Library Journal* award (now called the
Margaret A. Edwards Award) for her lifetime contribution to the field of young adult literature.

In the 1990s Hinton published two additional
books, aimed at younger audiences. *Big David, Little
David* (1994) is a picture book based on an incident
that happened when her son entered kindergarten,
and *The Puppy Sister* (1995) is an illustrated short
novel, also based on a family incident. Both books,
but especially *The Puppy Sister,* have been well received.

It may be Hinton's fate to always be best-
known for her first book, written when she was a
teenager—a book she wrote over and over again, not
knowing, she says, what she was doing. *The Outsiders*
is cliché-ridden and melodramatic, as Hinton herself
has admitted, and despite frequent praise for its "realism," it is in many ways not realistic at all but has
characteristics of fairy tale, myth, old cowboy movies, and even of opera with its exaggeration and
heightened emotions. Yet of all her books, it is per-

haps the most memorable and the most powerful,
perhaps because it was written with the innocence
and strong emotions of youth.

Told in the voice of Ponyboy Curtis, who lives
with his older brothers Sodapop and Darry in a
tough neighborhood on the wrong side of town, the
book centers on conflicts between the Greasers, the
group to which Ponyboy belongs, and the Socs (pronounced So-shes, short for the Socials), the middle-
and upper-class kids from the other side of town.
The Greasers hang around in their jeans and leather
jackets (if they are lucky enough to have them),
smoking cigarettes, stealing hubcaps, and getting
drunk. They are angry, resentful of the Socs, who
have everything—nice clothes, nice cars—and of the
fact that the system is stacked against them. Dallas
(Dally) Winston is a little older, has been in prison,
has gotten into trouble on the streets of New York,
and is hard and cruel. Johnny Cade, perhaps the
only person Dally cares about, is neglected and
beaten by his parents and has suffered from a brutal

beating by the Socs. Cherry Valance is a Soc girl who befriends Ponyboy and Johnny but is secretly attracted to Dally.

In a fight with the Socs, Johnny saves Ponyboy from drowning, but he stabs and accidentally kills one of the Socs (Cherry's boyfriend). Dally helps Johnny and Ponyboy run away to an abandoned church in the country, where they spend their days reading *Gone With the Wind,* playing cards, smoking too many cigarettes, and eating too many bologna sandwiches. Ponyboy recites to Johnny the poem by Robert Frost titled "Nothing Gold Can Stay," a major theme of the book.

The runaway boys become heroes when they rescue children trapped in a fire at the church. Johnny is too badly injured to survive and dies a lingering death in the hospital. When Ponyboy and Dally come to tell him that the Greasers have defeated the Socs in a rumble, he tells them fighting is no use. Dally, no longer wanting to live after Johnny's death, dies violently in a shoot-out with the police. In the end, the reader is left with Johnny's message to Ponyboy to "Stay gold," that life is worth living. "Tell Dally," Johnny writes, but it is too late.

Hinton has said that one inspiration for the book was her anger at the unfairness of judging people by their appearances. In her discussion with the teenage readers in *Top of the News* Hinton says, "I used to write horse stories or cowboy stuff until one day a friend of mine was walking home from school and these 'nice' kids jumped out of a car and beat him up because they didn't like his being a greaser. This made me real mad and I just went home and started pounding out a story about this boy who was beaten up while he was walking home from the movies—the beginning of *The Outsiders.* I never had any idea of getting it published. It was just something to let off steam."

The theme of feeling like an outsider is especially strong and convincingly handled, and it is one with which teenagers readily identify. As one longtime middle-school teacher wrote in a personal letter: "*The Outsiders* was a perennial favorite—seventh and eighth graders loved it because they saw their own sense of alienation from an apparently uncaring adult world, and a longed-for comradeship with close peers. Hinton spoke to many middle-schoolers through her words, her stories, and her characters. Ponyboy was particularly appreciated by adolescent girls—they all wanted to take him home and mother him."

Each of the characters has a particular appeal. As Hinton said in her interview with William Walsh, "I'm a very strong character writer." Part of the appeal of these tough boys is their vulnerability.

They cry, they tell each other they are scared, and perhaps most important, they are like family to each other. "If it hadn't been for the gang," Ponyboy writes, "Johnny would never have known what love and affection are." Interestingly, Hinton says that one of the authors she read when she was writing *The Outsiders* was Jane Austen. "It's all in the revelation of character," Hinton told Geraldine Brennan of the *Times Educational Supplement.* Daly says that Hinton could well take as her motto F. Scott Fitzgerald's dictum, "Action is character," and heavily credits the strength of her characters for the longevity of *The Outsiders.*

There are no parents, and almost no adults, in *The Outsiders.* The parents of Darry, Sodapop, and Ponyboy have died in a car accident; Johnny's parents alternate between treating him with neglect and abuse; and Dally says his parents do not care what happens to him. The Soc who was killed, on the other hand, is portrayed as having parents who "gave in to him all the time. He kept trying to make someone say 'No' and they never did. They never did. That was what he wanted. For somebody to tell him 'No.' To have somebody lay down the law, set the limits, give him something solid to stand on. That's what we all want, really," Randy tells Ponyboy. In some ways, as Daly points out, this world without parents resembles the fantasy world of Peter Pan and the Lost Boys. In some ways it also resembles the relatively parentless world of much of children's literature, from "Hansel and Gretel" to William Golding's *Lord of the Flies* (1954).

Finally, there is the theme of change, growing up, and the difficulty of retaining one's innocence or "staying gold" in a corrupt world. As Daly points out, the only way to stay young and innocent is to die young the way Johnny and Dally do.

Critical reaction to *The Outsiders* was initially quite favorable, although some critics, such as Thomas Fleming for *The New York Times Book Review* (7 May 1967), questioned, "Can sincerity overcome clichés?" Two notable dissenters from those who praised the book are English critic David Rees, who analyzed her work in an essay in *Painted Desert, Green Shade* (1984), and Michael Malone, who published "Tough Puppies," a lengthy and mainly negative analysis of Hinton's work, in *The Nation.*

According to Rees, "It is easy to see why her work would be liked by many in their early teens, particularly boys, but it is hard to fathom the reasons why she has won critical acclaim." Among Rees's concerns with Hinton's books are their attitudes toward women; their "world of immaturity"; the endless fighting; the clichés, especially in the fight scenes; and their uncertain moral values. "The

Hinton in 1982 with Matt Dillon, who starred in the movie versions of three Hinton novels

dangerous aspect of this," says Rees, "is that immature readers will absorb the immoral and antisocial attitudes, not see them as wrong, and glorify them into something acceptable."

Malone writes, "It is difficult, if not horrifying, to think that the millions of 12-year-olds reading these 'strikingly realistic portraits of modern kids' find any more in them than the most remote connections to their own lives." Malone argues that despite the widespread praise for the books as "realistic," they are, in fact, "mythic" and more closely related to fairy tales and romances that mythologize "the tragic beauty of violent youth." Malone also questions the received opinion about Hinton's "lean Hemingway style" and "natural dialogue." He argues, "Hinton's prose can be as fervid, mawkish and ornate as any nineteenth-century romance," and he says that Ponyboy and Bryon (in *That Was Then, This Is Now*) "fling adjectives and archaic phrases ('Hence his name,' 'Heaven forbid') around like Barbara Cartland."

Malone also points out the almost obsessive attention Hinton's characters pay to their appearance, their clothing, their hair, and the color of their eyes: "A leather jacket, bloody knuckles and a sensitive soul is an irresistible combination. Pain and sadness

help, too." This criticism is ironic since one of Hinton's purposes in writing was to convey the message that people should not be judged by appearances. Malone sees Hinton's success as partly the result of successful marketing, and although it is "indisputable" that "she is able to evoke for her audience how teen-agers feel," he is not sure this ability is a good thing.

A look at the readers' comments on *The Outsiders* posted to the online bookseller Amazon.com in 1997 and 1998 turned up an amazing 146 comments, most apparently from young readers, and almost all enthusiastic about the book. A fourteen-year-old commented, "It seemed as if the book had been written for me." Another reader wrote, "I must of read it a thousand times before I finally put it down and read another book." Many respondents commented on having read the book multiple times, and many found it "by far the best book I've ever read and ever will read." Only a few readers disliked the book. This response is quite amazing for a book for teenagers written more than thirty years ago. For many young people it is the first novel they have ever read.

Hinton's second novel, *That Was Then, This Is Now*, although it covers many of the same themes as

The Outsiders, is a more tightly constructed, more disciplined book than the first. Narrated by Bryon, who lives with the golden, lionlike, and amoral Mark, his foster brother, the story is one of friendship and betrayal. Hinton says in her interview with Walsh that she "actually got Mark's personality from a cat . . . . a completely amoral little animal." Because Mark has the ability to charm and talk his way out of anything, he never gets caught. Although the world of *The Outsiders* felt like the 1950s, the world of *That Was Then, This Is Now* is that of hippies and flower-children. Although the era of the gangs is over, the violent fighting continues.

Mark and Bryon are befriended by Charlie, the local bar owner, who lets them play pool in his place to try to make money. Another major character in the book is M&M, a smart younger kid, a loner, and a protohippie, whom Mark and Bryon rescue when he is being beaten up. After Mark gets badly beaten in a fight, Bryon looks after him, and the boys talk about their friendship and old times and how things are changing, which leads Bryon to say, "that was then, this is now." Bryon falls in love with M&M's sister Cathy, and this romance begins to drive a wedge between him and Mark.

One night outside the bar, Charlie is shot to death when he tries to rescue Bryon and Mark from some thugs they have beaten at pool. About this same time, M&M runs away and joins a group of hippies, takes a psychedelic drug, and ends up on a "bad trip" from which he may never recover. When Bryon learns that Mark has been selling drugs—the same kinds of drugs that have probably damaged M&M permanently—he calls the police to come and arrest his brother and best friend. This time Mark will not escape the consequences of his behavior. The book ends, sadly, disturbingly, months later when Mark finally agrees to see Bryon, who comes to visit him in prison. Mark tells him he hates him, and Bryon concludes, "I wish I was a kid again, when I had all the answers."

The themes of *That Was Then, This Is Now* are similar to those of *The Outsiders.* Teenage boys are alone, drinking, smoking, fighting, stealing, and now also doing drugs, while their parents are absent. The division between the Socs and the Greasers has faded into the background, but there are still plenty of fights. The theme of friendship and betrayal is a dominant one, as well as the theme of growth and change. Bryon's turning on Mark and his turning away from his girlfriend, Cathy, are rather problematic events for which the reader is perhaps not adequately prepared. Hinton has said, according to Daly, that "no other book has provoked the kind of discussion of motives and per-

sonal disagreements about character that *That Was Then, This Is Now* has provoked." Daly suggests that Hinton's return to the same themes in subsequent books, and even to two of the same characters in *Tex,* indicates that she, too, may have felt at some level that she had not adequately dealt with the themes of growth and change and loss of innocence.

Malone questions the unexplained long stays of Bryon's mother in the hospital and her lack of concern about what happens to the boys, as well as the dire and dramatic pronouncement about the prognosis for M&M, while Rees praises Hinton's clear antidrug stance. The book was generally well received, although as Daly points out, many reviewers seemed not to have read the book closely or looked carefully at some of its problems but to have jumped belatedly onto the successful bandwagon of *The Outsiders.*

Rumble Fish is also a problematic book. Inspired by a photograph, which Hinton saved from a magazine, of a James Dean-like figure, Motorcycle Boy is the centerpiece of the story; however, the character the reader cares about most is Motorcycle Boy's brother, Rusty-James, the first-person narrator. Unlike Ponyboy and Bryon, Rusty-James is not a reader and a good student, so the story is told through a simpler voice than the other two books. The story is set in a frame, beginning and ending at a beach several years after the main action of the story takes place.

Rusty-James wants to be tough, good-looking, and good at everything, just like his older brother, Motorcycle Boy. Hinton has said in an interview quoted in *Something about the Author* (1990), "Rusty-James sees him one way, which is not right. . . . Motorcycle Boy's flaw is his inability to compromise, and that's why I made him colorblind. He interprets life 'in black and white,' and he has the ability to walk off and leave anything, which is what ultimately destroys him." Interestingly, Hinton adds, "Every time I get a letter from a kid who says that *Rumble Fish* is his favourite book, he's usually in the reformatory."

The story within the frame begins with a fight in which Rusty-James is badly injured. Even though he is so badly sliced with a knife that he "could see white bone gleaming through," he does not go to a hospital. Instead, his friends drag him home, pour wine on the wound, and throw the bloody sweatshirt into the corner "with the other dirty clothes." Rusty-James and Motorcycle Boy live alone with their drunken, usually absent father, who, surprisingly, was once a lawyer.

Despite his wound, Rusty-James goes to school the next day, then escapes in a flight over

Dust jacket for one of Hinton's books for younger readers

roof tops with his best friend, Steve, after being apprehended stealing some hubcaps. That night Rusty-James goes to an all-night party at a lake, and as a result the next day he is expelled from school and loses his girlfriend. To cheer him up, the boys go partying and drinking in town that night, and Motorcycle Boy tells Rusty-James how their mother abandoned them, and that he had seen her in California. Still later that night, Rusty-James is hit on the head with a tire iron and almost killed before Motorcycle Boy saves him once again. The next night, Motorcycle Boy steals some Siamese fighting fish from a pet store and is shot to death by the police.

Critical response to the book was mixed, with some reviewers seeing the book as a falling off from Hinton's earlier success and others seeing it as a stronger, more carefully structured work. Rees calls the book "tedious" and finds the characters unsympathetic, while Daly describes the book as Hinton's "most ambitious," rich and almost mythical in its imagery, and a true work of art. A reviewer for *Kirkus* (15 October 1975) called the book a "remarkably preserved specimen of rebel-without-a-cause nihilism," while Zena Sutherland in the *Bulletin of the Center for Children's Books* (December 1975) called the book "less balanced" than *The Outsiders* and characterized it as "a picture of personality disintegration. Memorable, but with no note of hope."

For many readers *Tex* is the favorite Hinton book after *The Outsiders*. Set in a rural area rather than in a city, the book tells the story of two brothers, fourteen-year-old Tex and his slightly older brother, Mason, who are left to fend for themselves by their forgetful, rodeo-riding father, Pop. When Mason sells their horses to pay the bills, Tex, who loves his horse as though it were a person, lashes out at him in anger, starting off the book with one of the bloody, violent fights that are Hinton trademarks. However, the violence in this book does not seem to overwhelm the story and the growth of the characters as it sometimes does in the earlier books. In Jamie Cole, younger sister of Tex's best friend, Hinton creates her first strong and likable female character and develops a believable relationship between Tex and Jamie.

The old Hinton theme of rich against poor emerges in the relationship between Tex and Mason and their richer friends, the Coles. Charlie Cole, a

143

student in medical school, encourages his younger brother Johnny and Tex to drink, though Mr. Cole assumes it must be Mason's fault. Another character is Lem, an old friend of Mason's, now married with a child to support, who turns to drug dealing. As in her earlier books, Hinton's stance against drugs is strong. When Tex and Mason pick up a hitchhiker who turns out to be an escaped convict and murderer, they narrowly escape with their lives. Tex feels a strange sense of connection with the man, who readers discover is Mark from *That Was Then, This is Now.* Tex's teacher, Ms. Carlson, is actually Cathy from that same book. When the news of the incident with the convict reaches him, the boys' father returns home, but he seems to be less responsible than they are. As in other Hinton stories—especially in *That Was Then, This Is Now* and *Rumble Fish*—there is a secret involving the true identity of parents that plays a crucial role in the characters' development. When Tex learns that Pop is not his real father, he runs off with the waiting Lem, accompanies him on a drug deal gone bad, and is shot in the ensuing fight.

Daly praises the mature style and conventional structure of the book and notes the strength and consistency of the characters. According to Marilyn Kaye, writing in *School Library Journal* (November 1979), "Personal discoveries emerge from the action in a natural, unpretentious, and nondidactic way as Hinton explores questions about responsibility, friendship, desire, and communication." Margery Fisher, long a Hinton supporter, also praised the book in *Growing Point* (May 1980), concluding that, "In this new book Susan Hinton has achieved that illusion of reality which any fiction writer aspires to and which few ever completely achieve." Lance Salway, in a letter to Nancy Chambers in *Signal* (May 1980), notes that, "It's odd, really, that the novel works so well when so many of the elements in the story are highly theatrical. . . . But a writer as good as Hinton can carry it off effortlessly; one believes implicitly in the characters and cares what happens to them." Other critics, however, were less completely pleased. Paxton Davis, writing in *The New York Times Book Review* (16 December 1979), felt there was "too much going on" in the book and that "*Tex* smacks, somehow, of Snoopy's 'It was a Dark and Stormy Night,' busier and more melodramatic than the real life it purports to show." Rees actually has some favorable words about *Tex,* praising the portrait of Jamie and concluding, "There is perhaps a ray of hope that S. E. Hinton will write about characters that are complex and interesting, about teenagers who do have par-

ents, and who do something other than smoke, drink, and fight."

The last of Hinton's young adult novels, *Taming the Star Runner,* shows her continued development as a writer. Written long after *Tex* and more than twenty years after *The Outsiders,* this book, like her others, concerns change, growth, and alienation. Unlike her other books, this one is written in a third-person voice, and the attention to the problems of members of an older generation, as well as to the problems of the teenage protagonist, may well reflect the perspective of a more mature Hinton.

Like most of Hinton's other heroes, Travis Harris has a violent streak. He is sent to visit his Uncle Ken after he has nearly murdered his stepfather. Although back home in the city Travis is cool, he feels totally out of place in this country town full of "hicks" and "cowboys." He gets drunk and gets into a fight in a nearby city one night, requiring Uncle Ken to rescue him and to share with him some of his own past. Travis also feels a growing attraction toward the competent Casey, Hinton's second strong female character, who teaches riding classes at his uncle's barn.

Oddly, Travis never learns to ride. Star Runner, Casey's wild, unpredictable horse—obviously a counterpart to the wild, untamed, and undisciplined aspect of Travis—seems a bit too peripheral to be the title of the book, and all the horse events could almost be part of another story. Travis's own problems are juxtaposed with those of his uncle, who is in the process of a divorce and sharing custody of his young child.

The most interesting thing about Travis is that he is not only a rebellious teen, but he is also a teenage writer. Hinton seems to have come full circle, from Ponyboy at the end of her first book writing the English paper that was to become *The Outsiders,* to the story of Travis, the teenage writing phenomenon whose story is certainly based upon her own. Like Hinton, Travis "couldn't remember when he'd first known he was going to be a writer." He even befriends "creeps" because he thinks they "might have a story." Travis's editor tells him that there are problems in his manuscript with poor spelling, with language that will keep the book from being used in schools, and with the lack of "major girl characters" and "sympathetic" adults—all criticisms that Hinton has faced. The editor also tells Travis that his book is "so full of energy, so sincere, you'll be able to get away with the melodramatics. But not twice, Travis. The critics won't be indulgent twice. You'll have to use some discipline on the next one," which is certainly a lesson Hinton learned. Even more compelling is the editor's admonition to start writing something new immediately to avoid "first-novel block." She warns Travis, "This is going to change your life." *Taming the Star Runner* ends just as Hinton's first book did, with a teenage writer sitting down with a piece of blank paper before him.

Reviews of *Taming the Star Runner* generally praised it as a more mature work. Nancy Vasilakis, writing in *Horn Book* (January/February 1989), felt that "Although the story isn't as clearly focused as some of the author's previous ones and lacks the inherent energy of its predecessors, the characterizations are stellar, and the writing demonstrates a greater level of maturity, perhaps mirroring the author's own coming of age." Patty Campbell, writing in *The New York Times Book Review* (2 April 1989), noted, "*Taming the Star Runner* is remarkable for its drive and the wry sweetness and authenticity of its voice. Gone is the golden idealism of the earlier works. . . . The autobiographical passages that give glimpses of a past painful time in her own adolescence are most interesting." Peter Hollindale, writing in *The School Librarian* (November 1989), concludes, "In her mature writing, S. E. Hinton has a wider range and a mellower, less urgent voice, but has lost none of her insight into raw life growing. *Taming the Star Runner* is a tough, eventful, gripping story and an exhilarating portrait of endangered but victorious talent."

It will be interesting to see whether Hinton will return to writing for young adults now that her son is a teenager, and if she does, how that writing will differ from her earlier work. In an interview with Geraldine Brennan in 1995, Hinton commented, "Being a parent means I can never be as objective about kids as I once was. I used to be able to say, 'I'm not a teacher, I'm not a parent, I'm not a cop—I must be on your side.'" Of *The Outsiders* she says in this same interview: "I couldn't write that book today—it's so over-the-top emotionally. But I still get letters from kids telling me they feel that way."

Interviews:

"Readers Meet Author," *Top of the News*, 25 (November 1968): 27–39;

William Walsh, "S. E. Hinton," in *From Writers to Students: The Pleasures and Pains of Writing*, edited by M. Jerry Weiss (Newark, Del.: International Reading Association, 1979), pp. 32–38;

Geraldine Brennan, "Inside the Outsider," *Times Educational Supplement*, 23 June 1995, p. 13.

References:

Jay Daly, *Presenting S. E. Hinton*, updated edition (New York: Twayne, 1989);

Geoff Fox, "S. E. Hinton," in *Twentieth-Century Children's Writers*, edited by D. L. Kirkpatrick (New York: St. Martin's Press, 1978), pp. 600–601;

Michael Malone, "Tough Puppies," *The Nation*, 242 (8 March 1986): 276–280;

David Rees, "Macho Man, American Style–S. E. Hinton," in his *Painted Desert, Green Shade: Essays on Contemporary Writers of Fiction for Children and Young Adults* (Boston: Horn Book, 1984), pp. 126–137;

John Simmons, "A Look Inside a Landmark: The Outsiders," in *Censored Books: Criticial Viewpoints*, edited by Nicholas J. Karolides, Lee Burress, and John M. Kean (Metuchen, N.J.: Scarecrow, 1993), pp. 431–441;

Steven L. Vanderstaay, "Doing Theory: Words about Words about *The Outsiders*," *English Journal*, 81 (November 1992): 57–61.

Zora Neale Hurston

This entry was updated from the entries by Lillie P. Howard (Wright State University) in DLB 51: Afro-American Writers from the Harlem Renaissance to 1940, and by Laura M. Zaidman (University of South Carolina, Sumter) in DLB 86: American Short-Story Writers, 1910–1945, First Series.

BIRTH: Eatonville, Florida, 7 January 1891, to John and Lucy Ann Potts Hurston.

EDUCATION: Attended Howard University, 1918–1924; B.A., Barnard College, 1928; graduate study at Columbia University, 1934–1935.

MARRIAGES: 19 May 1927 to Herbert Sheen (divorced 7 July 1931); 27 June 1939 to Albert Price III (divorced 9 November 1943).

AWARDS AND HONORS: Guggenheim fellowships, 1936 and 1938; honorary Litt.D., Morgan College, 1939; Anisfield-Wolf Award for *Dust Tracks on a Road,* 1942.

DEATH: Fort Pierce, Florida, 28 January 1960.

BOOKS: *Jonah's Gourd Vine* (Philadelphia & London: Lippincott, 1934; London: Duckworth, 1934);
Mules and Men (Philadelphia & London: Lippincott, 1935; London: Kegan Paul, 1936);
Their Eyes Were Watching God (Philadelphia & London: Lippincott, 1937; London: Dent, 1938);
Tell My Horse (Philadelphia: Lippincott, 1938); republished as *Voodoo Gods. An Inquiry into Native Myths and Magic in Jamaica and Haiti* (London: Dent, 1939);
Moses, Man of the Mountain (Philadelphia: Lippincott, 1939); republished as *The Man of the Mountain* (London: Dent, 1941);
Dust Tracks on a Road (Philadelphia & London: Lippincott, 1942; London & New York: Hutchinson, 1944);
Seraph on the Suwanee: A Novel (New York: Scribners, 1948);
I Love Myself When I Am Laughing . . . and Then Again When I Am Looking Mean and Impressive: A Zora Neale Hurston Reader, edited by Alice Walker (Old Westbury, N.Y.: Feminist Press, 1979);
The Sanctified Church (Berkeley: Turtle Island Foundation, 1981);

Zora Neale Hurston

Mule Bone: A Comedy of Negro Life, by Hurston and Langston Hughes, edited by George Houston Bass and Henry Louis Gates Jr. (New York: HarperPerennial, 1991).

Editions and Collections: *Spunk: The Selected Stories of Zora Neale Hurston,* edited by Bob Callahan (Berkeley, Cal.: Turtle Island Foundation, 1985);

The Complete Stories, edited by Henry Louis Gates Jr. and Sieglinde Lemke (New York: HarperCollins, 1995);

Folklore, Memoirs, and Other Writings, edited by Cheryl A. Wall (New York: Library of America, 1995);

Novels and Stories (New York: Library of America, 1995);

Sweat, edited by Wall (New Brunswick, N.J.: Rutgers University Press, 1997).

OTHER: *The First One: A Play,* in *Ebony and Topaz: A Collectanea,* edited by Charles S. Johnson (New York: National Urban League, 1927), pp. 53–57.

SELECTED PERIODICAL PUBLICATIONS–UNCOLLECTED:

POETRY

"O Night," *Stylus,* 1 (May 1921): 42;

"Poem," *Howard University Record,* 16 (February 1922): 236.

DRAMA

Color Struck, A Play in Four Scenes, in *Fire!!* 1 (November 1926): 7–15.

NONFICTION

"The Hue and Cry about Howard University," *Messenger,* 7 (September 1925): 315–319, 338;

"Cudjo's Own Story of the Last African Slaver," *Journal of Negro History,* 12 (October 1927): 648–663;

"Communication," *Journal of Negro History,* 12 (October 1927): 664–667;

"Dance Songs and Tales From the Bahamas," *Journal of American Folklore,* 43 (July–September 1930): 294–312;

"Race Cannot Become Great Until It Recognizes Its Talent," *Washington Tribune,* 29 December 1934;

"Full of Mud, Sweat and Blood," review of *God Shakes Creation* by David M. Cohn, *New York Herald Tribune Books,* 3 November 1935, p. 8;

"Stories of Conflict," review of *Uncle Tom's Children* by Richard Wright, *Saturday Review* (2 April 1938): 32;

"Negroes Without Self-Pity," *American Mercury,* 57 (November 1943): 601–603;

"The Last Slave Ship," *American Mercury,* 58 (March 1944): 351–358;

"Bible, Played by Ear in Africa," review of *How God Fix Jonah* by Lorenz Graham, *New York Herald Tribune Weekly Book Review,* 24 November 1946, p. 5;

Review of *Voodoo in New Orleans* by Robert Tallant, *Journal of American Folklore,* 60 (October–December 1947): 436–438;

"I Saw Negro Votes Peddled," *American Legion Magazine,* 49 (November 1950): 12–13, 54–57, 59–60;

"Mourner's Bench, Communist Line: Why the Negro Won't Buy Communism," *American Legion Magazine,* 50 (June 1951): 14–15, 55–60;

"A Negro Voter Sizes Up Taft," *Saturday Evening Post,* 223 (8 December 1951): 29, 50;

"Zora's Revealing Story of Ruby's First Day in Court," *Pittsburgh Courier,* 11 October 1952;

"Hoodoo and Black Magic" [weekly column], *Fort Pierce Chronicle,* 11 July 1958 – 7 August 1959;

"The Farm Laborer at Home," *Fort Pierce Chronicle,* 27 February 1959.

From the 1930s through the 1960s, Zora Neale Hurston was the most prolific and accomplished black woman writer in America. During that thirty-year period she published seven books, many short stories, magazine articles, and plays, and she gained a reputation as an outstanding folklorist and novelist. She called attention to herself because she insisted upon being herself at a time when blacks were being urged to assimilate in an effort to promote better relations between the races. Hurston, however, saw nothing wrong with being black: "I do not belong to that sobbing school of Negrohood who hold that nature somehow has given them a lowdown dirty deal." Indeed she felt there was something so special about her blackness that others could benefit just by being around her. Her works, then, may be seen as manifestos of selfhood, as affirmations of blackness and the positive aspects of black life.

Hurston wrote in her autobiography, *Dust Tracks on a Road* (1942), that she "heard tell" she was born on 7 January 1903 in Eatonville, Florida, the fifth of eight children. However, one brother gave 1891 as the year; another brother, Everette, was convinced by Hurston to set his age back seven years to cover the obvious discrepancies between what he said and what she wrote; and her brother John cited the 1903 date in a 1936 affidavit. Hurston used 1903 most often–but variously gave the year as 1900, 1901, and 1902. Hurston scholars Robert Hemenway and Alice Walker used 1901; but the 1900 census records subsequently proved she was born in 1891. Her parents, Lucy Ann Potts, a country schoolteacher, and John Hurston, a carpenter and Baptist preacher, met and married in Alabama, then moved to Eatonville, Florida, north of Orlando. Her father, a three-term mayor, helped cod-

FIRE!!

A Quarterly Devoted to the Younger Negro Artists

Premier Issue Edited by
WALLACE THURMAN

In Association With

Langston Hughes	Zora Neale Hurston
Gwendolyn Bennett	Aaron Douglas
Richard Bruce	John Davis

Table of Contents

Volume One   Number One

EDITORIAL OFFICES
314 West 138th Street, New York City

Price $1.00 per copy   Issued Quarterly

Table of contents for the single issue of the avant-garde magazine Hurston helped to found in 1926

ify the laws of this all-black community, the first to be incorporated in the United States.

Lucy Hurston died in 1904, and this fact more than any other disrupted Hurston's schooling and her life. She was passed around from relative to relative, rejected by her father and his second wife, and forced to fend for herself. At fourteen Hurston left Eatonville, working as a maid for whites but refusing to act humble or to accept sexual advances from male employers; consequently, she never stayed at one job long. Hired as a wardrobe girl with a Gilbert and Sullivan repertory company, she traveled around the South for eighteen months, always reading in hopes of completing her education. Later she enrolled in a Baltimore high school, Morgan Academy (now Morgan State University), while working as a live-in maid.

In the fall of 1918 Hurston entered Howard University, attending the college preparatory program until 1919 and taking university courses inter-mittently until 1924, paying for her expenses by working as a barbershop manicurist and as a maid for prominent blacks. At Howard she met and studied under poet Georgia Douglas Johnson and the young philosophy professor Alain Locke. She also met Herbert Sheen, who, on 19 May 1927, became her first husband. As Sheen later told Hurston's biographer, Hemenway, the marriage was doomed "to an early, amicable divorce" because Hurston's career was her first priority. In a 1953 letter to Sheen, Hurston recalls the idealistic dreams they shared in their youth, regretting nothing because she lived her life to the fullest.

Hurston had been extremely imaginative and curious as a child; these qualities inform her fiction. She records in her autobiography that as a child "I used to climb to the top of one of the huge china-berry trees which guarded our front gate and look out over the world. The most interesting thing that I saw was the horizon. . . . It grew upon me that I ought to walk out to the horizon and see what the end of the world was like." This tendency toward the picaresque colors her work. Her main characters are dreamers who long for experience and spiritual freedom and want to break with the fixity of things. Hurston's first short story, "John Redding Goes to Sea" (May 1921), was written in this picaresque tradition and was published in *Stylus,* the official magazine of the literary club at Howard University. The protagonist of "John Redding Goes to Sea" cannot "stifle that longing for the open road, rolling seas, for peoples and countries I have never seen." The story brought the young author to the attention of sociologist Charles S. Johnson, and by January 1925 Hurston was in New York City with "$1.50, no job, no friends, and a lot of hope."

She could not have arrived in New York at a more opportune time. The Harlem Renaissance, the black literary and cultural movement of the 1920s, was already under way. Countee Cullen, James Weldon Johnson, and W. E. B. Du Bois were already in New York. Other black writers from all over–Claude McKay from Jamaica, Eric Walrond from Barbados, Langston Hughes from Kansas, Wallace Thurman from Salt Lake City, Rudolph Fisher from Rhode Island, Jean Toomer and Sterling Brown from Washington, D.C.–were flocking to New York, as Hughes so aptly put it, to "express their individual dark-skinned selves." Charles Johnson was just founding *Opportunity: A Journal of Negro Life,* and he was interested in material that exemplified "New Negro" (the phrase coined by Locke) philosophy. Hurston's works celebrated blackness, and she became an enthusiastic contributor to the New Negro Renaissance literary movement.

The short story "Spunk" was published in *Opportunity* in June 1925 and in Locke's landmark publication *The New Negro* (1925). "Spunk" is a story about Spunk Banks, a "giant of a brown skinned man" who goes too far in manipulating and intimidating people. Set in a black village much like Eatonville, the story follows Banks, who "ain't skeered of nothin' on God's green footstool—nothin'." His overweening pride brings his downfall when he "struts 'round wid another man's wife" (Lena Kanty) and triggers revenge from the husband. Joe Kanty, however, is killed when he sneaks up behind Banks, for his pocket razor is no match for Spunk's army .45. Free after a brief murder trial, Spunk ironically finds he has lost his courage, for he believes he is being haunted by a big, black bobcat, Joe's ghost "done sneaked back from Hell!" The townspeople even see Joe Kanty differently; no longer thought of as the town coward, he is considered courageous for seeking revenge with only a razor. Mysteriously caught in the saw blade at the mill, Spunk suffers a grisly death; both Spunk and the townspeople credit Joe's spirit for pushing him into the saw. Hubris is punished as the once-heroic "giant" is quickly forgotten. His corpse, covered by a dingy sheet, lies on three boards on sawhorses at his wake, as the women "ate heartily . . . and wondered who would be Lena's next," and the men "whispered coarse conjectures between guzzles of whiskey."

"Spunk" illustrates Hurston's growth in the way she shows rather than tells about the characters. Her dialogue, using the rural black dialect of central Florida, reflects this increased narrative strength. In addition, Hurston seems more sure of her special expertise—the richness of Eatonville's folk beliefs. For example, the black bobcat (Joe's ghost), the three "cooling boards," and the turning of Spunk to the east as he dies all reflect this folklore.

At an awards dinner sponsored by *Opportunity,* Hurston's works won second prizes; but more important, Hurston herself was introduced to two people: novelist Fannie Hurst (*Imitation of Life,* 1933), who gave Hurston a job, and Annie Nathan Meyer, who arranged for her to receive a scholarship to Barnard College. Between 1925 and 1933 Hurston saw several of her works published, including "John Redding" and the tale "Muttsy," which appeared in *Opportunity,* and a play, *The First One,* collected in Charles Johnson's *Ebony and Topaz: A Collectanea* (1927). Hurston had made a propitious beginning, but many frustrating years passed before she published a full-length work.

"Sweat," published in the single issue of Wallace Thurman's avant-garde magazine *Fire!!* (November 1926), depicts the death of a marriage. Founded by Hurston, Hughes, and Thurman, *Fire!!* advocated writing for art's sake—contrary to writers such as Locke and Du Bois, who urged blacks to reflect a racial perspective, especially in portraying relationships with whites. Hurston succeeds in blending the vivid and intense fire of passions in this portrait of the marriage of a black couple, Delia and Sykes Jones. Set in Eatonville, the story shows how the hard work ("sweat") of Delia is counteracted by the hatred of her adulterous husband, who beats her brutally after two months of marriage, openly flaunts his extramarital affairs from the beginning, and chooses as his mistress a woman named Bertha, a big, fat "greasy Mogul . . . who couldn't kiss a sardine can . . . throwed out de back do' 'way las' yeah." Delia has slaved over whites' laundry to earn a living for fifteen years; she alone has paid for the house, and now Sykes promises to give the house to Bertha. To scare off his wife, who is terrified of snakes, he first tries taunting her with his snakelike bullwhip. When the "long, round, limp and black" whip falls across her shoulders and slithers along the floor beside her, she is so frightened that "it softened her knees and dried her mouth so that it was a full minute before she could cry out or move." When that does not work, he pens up a rattlesnake near the back door. As a final resort, Sykes tries to kill his stubborn wife by placing the deadly snake in the clothes hamper just before she is to sort the clothes. Delia escapes the poisonous fangs, but Sykes is bitten and dies. Delia refuses to warn or even help him, having understood finally how deadly his hatred of her has become; she watches him with "his horribly swollen neck and his one open eye shining with hope."

As in several of Hurston's stories, the woman is strong, proud, independent; the man does not appreciate these strengths because he feels emasculated and dependent. Sykes attempts to prove his masculinity by cruelly abusing his wife. The townspeople comment on how despicably Sykes treats Delia, saying he had "beat huh 'nough tuh kill three women let 'lone change they looks." This mistreatment is described by general-store owner Joe Clarke:

There's plenty men dat takes a wif lak dey do a joint uh sugarcane. It's round, juicy, an' sweet when dey gets it. But dey squeeze an grind, squeeze an' grind an' wring tell dey wring every drop uh pleasure dat's in 'em out. When dey's satisfied dat dey is wrung dry, dey treats 'em jes lak dey do a cane-chew. Dey throws 'em away. Dey knows whut dey is doin' while dey is at it, an' hates

Near the end of her studies at Barnard, Hurston
came to the attention of anthropologist Franz Boas,
who was then teaching at Columbia. Impressed by a
term paper Hurston had written, Boas decided to
make an anthropologist of her. Under Boas's tute-
lage, Hurston learned the value of the material she
had already incorporated into her fiction. She
learned to view the good old lies and racy, sidesplit-
ting anecdotes that were being passed around
among black folk every day in her native Eatonville
as invaluable folklore, creative material that continued the African oral tradition and reflected the ebb
and flow of a people. Encouraged by Boas and a
$1,400 fellowship from the Carter G. Woodson
Foundation, Hurston decided to collect some of this
African-American lore, to record songs, customs,
tales, superstitions, lies, jokes, dances, and games.

Unfortunately, her Southern, country subjects
balked at her "Barnard" accent, and her mission
failed. As she says in her autobiography: "When I
went about asking, in carefully-accented Barnard-
ese, 'Pardon me, do you know any folktales or folk-
songs?' the men and women who had whole treasur-
ies of material seeping through their pores looked at
me and shook their heads. No, they had never heard
of anything like that around here. Maybe it was
over in the next county. Why didn't I try over
there?" As a result, Hurston was not able to collect
enough material "to make a flea a waltzing jacket."
She did not make the attempt again until she accepted the patronage of Charlotte Osgood Mason.

Mason was a wealthy, white Park Avenue matron who supported Indian and African-American
arts and any other endeavors that she felt exemplified "primitivisms." Hurston was probably introduced to Mason by Locke, who seems to have functioned as Mason's emissary to black artists. When
Hurston met Mason in September 1927, Mason was
already the patron of Langston Hughes, Miguel Covarrubias, Louise Thompson, and Richmond
Barthé. To them and to Hurston, Mason became a
beneficent godmother and a surrogate parent, pre-
scribing and proscribing the courses of their lives.
She was impressed by Hurston's credentials, and on
1 December 1927 she drew up a formal contract that
would allow Hurston to return to the South to collect folklore. The contract promised a monthly sti-
pend of $200, a moving-picture camera, and one
Ford automobile. Hurston was "faithfully" to perform her task and "to return to Mason all of said information, data, transcripts of music, etc., which she
shall have obtained." Though this opportunity was
what Hurston needed, its accompanying restrictions
were not. Hurston felt like a child laboring under a
difficult taskmaster.

Hurston (right) with Jessie Redmon Fauset and Langston Hughes at Tuskegee Institute in 1927

theirselves fuh it but they keeps on hanging after huh
tell she's empty. Den dey hates huh fuh bein' a cane-
chew an' in de way.

Hurston reinforces this narrative action of Sykes's
horrible abuse of Delia with the traditional symbolism of the snake to represent evil in the world. Referred to as "Ol Satan" and "Ol Scratch," the snake
Sykes brings home to terrify Delia is identified with
Sykes's evil (the *s* sounds in his name hint at the
comparison), although Freudian critics may see the
snakelike whip in phallic terms as well.

"Eatonville Anthology" was published in three
installments in the *Messenger* (September–November
1926) and collected in *I Love Myself When I Am Laughing . . . and Then Again When I Am Looking Mean and Impressive: A Zora Neale Hurston Reader* (1979). This series of fourteen brief sketches, some only two paragraphs long, illustrates her artistic use of cultural experiences, fusing folklore studies with fiction. These
self-contained tales include glimpses of a woman
beggar, an incorrigible dog, a backwoods farmer,
the greatest liar in the village, and a cheating husband. They become an appropriate transition to
mark the end of her short stories of the 1920s and
the beginning of her work as folklorist.

Though between 1927 and 1931 Hurston collected substantial material from small communities in Alabama and Florida, for several years she was unable to get any of it published. With Mason's approval, she was able to feature some of it in musical revues. The bulk of it, however, remained unpublished, even after the 1931 severing of the Mason-Hurston contract (Mason continued to offer intermittent support even after the contract ended).

Hurston had gone to New York expecting to fulfill her dreams. As the correspondence between Hurston and Mason in the Alain Locke Collection at Howard University shows, however, Hurston's dreams were bitterly deferred. She was desperately trying to prove herself to Mason and to herself, and she was beginning to doubt her abilities as a writer. Feeling herself an albatross around Mason's neck, she began to consider other sources of livelihood. In one letter, she proposed opening a chicken specialty business as a way of easing the financial burden she had become to Mason.

Hurston's musical revues received good notices; however, they generated little money. Still, there was one flattering response to one of these revues, *The Great Day* (1932): "George Antheil, the French composer, paid me the compliment of saying I would be the most stolen-from Negro in the world for the next ten years at least. He said that this sort of thievery is unavoidable. Unpleasant, of course, but at the bottom a tribute to one's originality." *The Great Day*, which was first performed at the John Golden Theatre on 10 January 1932, was, like her other musical revues (staged between 1931 and 1935), Hurston's attempt to bring pure black folk culture to both Northern and Southern audiences. What she had not yet been able to publish, she was able to present on stage with authentic folk characters. Much of the basis for the script of *The Great Day* may be found in Hurston's *Mules and Men* (1935).

By 6 January 1932 Hurston was working with the Creative Literature Department of Rollins College at Winter Park, Florida, in an effort to produce a concert program of African-American art. Though she produced a successful program, her personal problems only increased. She was intermittently ill, plagued by a painful stomach ailment that was to trouble her until her death. She wrote to Mason that she had "little food, no toothpaste, no stockings, needed shoes badly, no soap." Apparently little had changed for Hurston since her penurious arrival in New York seven years earlier.

She returned to New York only to have Locke, in his role as Mason's emissary, suggest that she return south to find work. She returned to Eatonville, where the pastoral atmosphere worked wonders,

and Hurston was soon feeling "renewed like the eagle." She found time to compose a play, *Mule Bone,* with Langston Hughes, but a rift developed after Hurston tried to have the comedy staged before Hughes had completed his work on it. Meanwhile, Hurston's contact with George Antheil was paying off. In the fall of 1931 Antheil, now acting as the amanuensis of Nancy Cunard, asked Hurston to contribute some folklore essays for Cunard's *Negro: An Anthology—1931–1933* (1934). Hurston complied with six essays: "Characteristics of Negro Expression," "Conversions and Visions," "The Sermon," "Mother Catherine," "Uncle Monday," and "Spirituals and Neo-Spirituals." All six were subsequently published in the anthology.

Hurston was happy about this achievement, but she still had not published a book. She had submitted her "story book"–her cache from her folklore-collecting days–to various publishers, but none had been interested enough to print it. The "story book" did not get a serious reading until after a short story, "The Gilded Six-Bits," (published in *Story,* 1933) and her first novel, *Jonah's Gourd Vine* (1934), had appeared.

"The Gilded Six-Bits" is the best short story in the Hurston canon and it is the one most frequently anthologized. It has more depth than the other stories; its characters are more developed; and its dialect has much of the texture apparent in the novels. Like most of Hurston's works, it explores the marriage relationship and its attendant difficulties. Missie May and Joe Banks begin happily–she keeps an immaculate home and cooks his favorite food, and he works hard and lovingly throws his week's pay into the doorway to announce his homecoming. The "gilded six-bits" are the coins of the serpent who intrudes in their garden. Otis D. Slemmons, a sly woman-chaser from Chicago, sporting showy gold teeth, a five-dollar-gold-piece stickpin, and a ten-dollar-gold-piece watch charm, causes Missie May's fall from grace in Joe's eyes. Joe unexpectedly arrives early one night and catches Slemmons with Missie May; she pleads for forgiveness because she just wanted to give the gold to Joe. After three months of abstaining from any contact with his unfaithful wife, Joe relents, but he leaves Slemmons's gilded half-dollar under her pillow to show his disgust with her prostituting herself. However, with the birth of a son, who definitely resembles Joe, the proud father uses the gilded half-dollar to buy molasses candy kisses for Missie May. He then throws his week's pay of fifteen silver dollars in the doorway, and she pretends to reproach him in the exact manner as she does at the beginning of the story, as-

Hurston in Mobile, Alabama, 1927

suring the reader that the marriage has survived this test of their love.

That the temptations of Slemmons nearly destroy their happiness recalls the way big cities, with their gilded promises of easy money, lured blacks into situations that forced them to prostitute themselves and their values. Another theme is marital discord, showing how infidelity almost ruins the Banks's marriage, but renewed love, suggested by the birth of their child, saves it.

When "The Gilded Six-Bits" appeared in *Story* in August 1933, Hurston's fate was already decided. Bertram Lippincott of Lippincott publishers had read the story in manuscript and had written to inquire whether Hurston was writing a novel. She was not but said that she was; she moved from Eatonville to Sanford, Florida, and sat down to write "Big Nigger," published as *Jonah's Gourd Vine*. Hurston claims in *Dust Tracks* that the notion for *Jonah's Gourd Vine* had been in her head since 1929 but "the idea of attempting a book seemed so big, that I gazed at it in the quiet of the night, but hid it away from even myself in daylight." For one of the few times in her life, she was afraid to strike out on her own. She wanted to tell a story about "a man," but "Negroes were supposed to write about the Race Problem."

Fortunately, she wrote her story, and the novel was published the first week of May 1934. Lippincott was pleased with the novel and wrote to Carl Van Vechten, a mutual friend, that he considered the book "a really important contribution to the literature on the American Negro." The novel sold well and was even recommended by the Book-of-the-Month Club for May. Reviewers were impressed by the rich language of the novel, "its compelling beauty and deep passion." Many of the reviewers, however, missed the essence of the story.

Jonah's Gourd Vine is an impressive first novel. Set in various parts of Florida, the novel centers around John Buddy Pearson, a likable but exasperating character, modeled in part after Hurston's own father. Though a Baptist minister, John all too frequently feels the temptations of life tugging at his sleeves. He spends his Sundays in the pulpit as a holy man, but he spends Mondays through Saturdays living an adulterous life. Hurston wrote to James Weldon Johnson on 16 April 1934: "I see a preacher as a man outside of his pulpit and so far as I am concerned he should be free to follow his bent as other men. He becomes the voice of the spirit when he ascends the rostrum." The plot turns on Pearson's attempts to live this double life in a community where ministers are supposed to be above the common man and thus above reproach.

John does not understand the objections of his parishioners and refuses to live the life they prescribe for him. Through careful characterization, Hurston makes a strong case for Pearson. He is obviously the product of a philosophy which recognizes no difference between the material and spiritual realms. Larry Neal explained it best in his introduction to the 1971 reprint of the novel: what Hurston gives us in *Jonah's Gourd Vine,* says Neal, are "two distinctly different cultural attitudes toward the concept of spirituality. The one springs from a formerly enslaved communal society, non-Christian in background, where there is really no clear dichotomy between the world of spirit and the world of flesh. The other attitude is clearly more rigid, being a blend of Puritan concepts and the fire-and-brimstone imagery of the white evangelical tradition." John's problems, then, are caused by his inability to reconcile himself to the society in which he must live. The real tragedy, notes Nick Aaron Ford, is that John never really discovers "the cultural dilemma that created his frustration. His rise to religious prominence and financial ease is but a millstone around his neck. He is held back by some unseen cord which seems to be tethered to his racial heritage. Life crushes him almost to death, but he comes out of the mills with no greater insight into the deep mysteries which surround him."

Other critics have focused upon the inconsistent imagery of Jonah's gourd vine in the novel and Hurston's failure to produce a work in which the parts all work together to produce a unified whole. In spite of these problems, however, the theme of the novel is universal and handled impressively. As Hemenway remarks, "Although the sum may be less than the parts, the parts are remarkable indeed."

After *Jonah's Gourd Vine,* the "story book," called *Mules and Men,* appeared. Bertram Lippincott liked *Mules and Men* but thought it too short for publication. He wanted a $3.50 book, 180 pages more than the 65,000 words Hurston had submitted. To lengthen the book, Hurston added the "between stories conversation and business" and a condensed article on hoodoo she had written in 1931 for the *Journal of American Folklore.* The book was finally published in 1935.

As folklore, *Mules and Men* offers invaluable insight into a people and a way of life. As Boas explains in his foreword to the volume:

> To the student of cultural history the material is valuable not only by giving the Negro's reaction to every day events, to his emotional life, his humor and passions, but it throws into relief also the peculiar amalgamation of African and European tradition which is so important for understanding historically the character of American Negro life, with its strong African background in the West Indies, the importance of which diminishes with increasing distance from the south.

The last third of the book, in essence, the hoodoo article, has drawn considerable attention to Hurston. Here Hurston chronicles her many experiences with the hoodoo culture in New Orleans. In some cases she apprenticed herself to local hoodoo doctors and was able to learn several "spells" with which she later threatened her second husband, Albert Price III (a Works Progress Administration playground worker some fifteen years younger than Hurston; they were married on 27 June 1939 in Fernandina, Florida, and divorced on 9 November 1943). According to *Mules and Men* Hurston found the practice of hoodoo to be widespread, "burning with a flame in America with all the intensity of a suppressed religion."

Despite its undeniable value *Mules and Men* was unfavorably reviewed by several critics, most of them black. Sterling Brown found the picture it presented "too pastoral, with only a bit of grumbling about hard work, or a few slave anecdotes that turn the tables on old marster . . . . *Mules and Men* should

be more bitter, it would be nearer the total truth." Harold Preece, a white radical, attacked Hurston, saying, "When a Negro author describes her race with such a servile term as 'Mules and Men' critical members of the race must necessarily evaluate the author as a literary climber." Hurston certainly wanted to succeed, but whether she omitted the bitter tone of her black subjects from *Mules and Men* for this reason is by no means clear. It is probably nearer the truth to say that Hurston sought to capture the sometimes happy, affirmative side of black life, to show that the picture of blacks being "saturated with our sorrows" was a partial if not a false one.

Between novels Hurston traveled the country with her musical revues. She presented *From Sun to Sun* to audiences in Florida and *The Great Day* and *Singing Steel* to audiences in Chicago. After one of the performances in Chicago she was approached by representatives of the Julius Rosenwald Foundation who offered her a fellowship to pursue a doctorate in anthropology and folklore at Columbia University. Hurston initially accepted the fellowship but soon objected to the rigorous, partly "irrelevant" schedule she was required to follow. She bristled under the restrictions and soon left.

In the fall of 1935 she joined the WPA Federal Theater Project. While working with the Project, she was awarded a Guggenheim Fellowship to collect folklore in the West Indies. By 14 April 1936 she was in the Caribbean, collecting material for her second book of folklore, *Tell My Horse* (1938). She stopped in Haiti and Kingston, Jamaica, proposing to make an exhaustive study of *Obeah* (magic) practices. She did much more than study magic, however, for the romantic atmosphere of the islands triggered emotions that had been "dammed up in" her since she had left the United States. Back in America she had been romantically involved with a twenty-three-year-old college student who had been a member of the cast of *The Great Day.* As usual the callings of Hurston's career were stronger than those of her heart, and she had left the young man to continue to pursue what she considered her mission in life. Fortunately, she was able to transpose her emotions into literature, releasing on paper, in just seven weeks, what became her best novel, *Their Eyes Were Watching God.* Lippincott liked the story, and the book was published on 18 September 1937.

Their Eyes Were Watching God has been called "a classic of black literature, one of the best novels of the period." It is a tribute to self-assertion and black womanhood, the story of a young black woman in search of self and genuine happiness, of people rather than things, the story of a woman with her

Performers in The Great Day *(1932), one of Hurston's musical revues based on black folk culture*

eyes on the horizon. The heroine, Janie Crawford, against her better judgment, lives conventionally for much of her life. When she finds no real satisfaction in that life, she strikes out, like Huckleberry Finn, and like Hurston herself, for the territory and the possibility of a better life beyond the horizon.

Janie Crawford wants "marriage lak when you sit under a pear tree and think." The limited, non-communicative alliances that she makes, however, desecrate this image. She sees herself as a pear tree in bloom, but she is around forty years old before she finds the right "dust-bearing bee." Before that, she marries two men who represent her grandmother's and society's ideas of success. Both husbands own or acquire property, are much older than Janie, and are conventional in their thinking, the second husband even going so far as to group women with "chilluns, and chickens, and cows," all helpless beings who need a man to think and do for them. The first marriage had been arranged by the well-meaning grandmother to provide some "protection" for Janie; the second had been Janie's own doing. Janie survives these marriages by retreating into herself. She discovers that "she had an inside and an outside and how not to mix them."

Janie realizes her "pear tree" dreams with the man who becomes her third husband. Although Vergible "Tea Cake" Woods is several years

Janie's junior, he is more mature and wiser in the ways that count. Whereas Janie's other husbands had wanted to restrict Janie's participation in life, Tea Cake, a hedonist, encourages her to enjoy it to the fullest. There are no forbidden areas. The two give and take equally and, for Janie, arriving at the horizon seems imminent.

To Janie, Tea Cake is "a glance from God," the embodiment of the best life has to offer. She eagerly embraces her life with him, throwing off the shackles of womanhood and society. Though their marriage is shortened by Tea Cake's untimely death—Hurston, for reasons readers have yet to appreciate, has Janie shoot him after he is bitten by a rabid dog—Janie has lived one full life during the year and one-half of the marriage. As she tells her best friend, Phoeby: "Ah been a delegate to de big 'ssociation of life. Yessuh! De Grand Lodge, de big convention of livin' is just where Ah been dis year and a half y'all ain't seen me." As she settles down to live through her memories, she has no regrets. She has seen the light—"If yuh kin see de light at daybreak, you don't keer if you die at dusk. It's so many people never seen de light at all. Ah wuz fumblin' round and God opened de door."

The novel is a powerful affirmation of life, of physical and spiritual fulfillment. Its power is in its language, its vividly emotional, folksy, often heart-rending descriptions of the day-to-day yearnings of a woman who wanted more than a house and "respectability."

Their Eyes Were Watching God was followed by the publication of *Tell My Horse,* the book based on Hurston's findings in the West Indies. For various reasons, it did not sell well. Less interesting than *Mules and Men,* it tried unsuccessfully to analyze the politics of the West Indies. It was not really the book Hurston had wanted to write. Frightened by some of the rituals she had observed, she had felt it wiser to write a book that would be "safe and acceptable" rather than honest.

Beginning in fall 1939, Hurston worked for a time as a drama instructor at North Carolina College for Negroes at Durham. While there, she met Paul Green, who was working in the drama department at Chapel Hill. The two discussed the possibility of writing a play together, but they never got beyond the discussion stage. Hurston was nevertheless hard at work. Not only had she found time to marry Price but she had also written her third novel. *Moses, Man of the Mountain* was published in November 1939.

Moses, Man of the Mountain is an ambitious amalgam of fiction, folklore, religion, and comedy, all provocatively combined. Darwin T. Turner calls it Hurston's "most accomplished achievement in fiction"; Robert Bone says it is a "brilliant allegory" in the picaresque tradition; and Hemenway refers to it as "one of Hurston's two masterpieces of the late thirties" and "one of the more interesting minor works in American literary history."

The book is a bold, problem-ridden reworking of the Moses legend. Hurston's Israelites appear to be American blacks, and Moses is a hoodoo man. The abundant humor these changes generate frequently clashes with the solemnity of the subject. Hemenway was prompted to call the book a "noble failure." Hurston, writing to Edwin Grover, to whom she dedicated the book, admitted: "I have the feeling of disappointment about it. I don't think that I achieved all that I set out to do. I thought that in this book I would achieve my ideal, but it seems that I have not yet reached it. . . . It still doesn't say all that I want it to say." In spite of its problems, however, the novel is often compelling and deserves serious critical attention.

The winter of 1940–1941 found Hurston in New York contemplating what to write next. When her publisher suggested an autobiography, she at first balked at the idea—"it is too hard to reveal one's inner self, and still there is no use in writing that kind of book unless you do"—but soon settled in California with a rich friend, Katharine Mershon, to begin the book. From October 1941 to January 1942

she also found time to work as a story consultant at Paramount Studios. She revised the manuscript back in Florida, and *Dust Tracks on a Road* was published in late November 1942.

Unlike *Moses, Man of the Mountain,* the autobiography sold well and won the Anisfield-Wolf Award for its contribution to better race relations. Critics, however, found much to attack about the volume. Arna Bontemps concluded that "Miss Hurston deals very simply with the more serious aspects of Negro life in America—she ignores them." Others felt the book was perhaps the "best fiction she ever wrote."

Still, the book pleased many readers, for Hurston was deluged with requests for magazine articles. Soon her political views were appearing in *American Mercury, The Saturday Evening Post, Negro Digest, World Telegram,* and *Reader's Digest.* Many of these essays, because of their controversial sentiments, caused friction within the black community. In a *World Telegram* article (1 February 1943), for instance, Hurston claimed that "the Jim Crow system works." Two years later, in a December 1945 *Negro Digest* article, she was "all for the repeal of every Jim Crow law in the nation here and now." Her black readers were understandably suspicious and confused. Hurston was able to repair some of the damage with the explanation she offered through an interview with the *New York Amsterdam News:* "A writer's material is controlled by publishers who think of the Negro as picturesque. . . . There is an oversimplification of the Negro. He is either pictured by the conservatives as happy, picking his banjo, or by the so-called liberals as low, miserable, and crying. The Negro's life is neither of these. Rather, it is in-between and above and below these pictures."

When World War II began, Hurston was living in St. Augustine, Florida, teaching part-time at Florida Norman, the local black college. Later she moved to Daytona Beach where she purchased the *Wanago,* a houseboat, which allowed her to take scenic tours up and down the Halifax and Indian Rivers. She read Marjorie Kinnan Rawlings's *Cross Creek* (1942), which impressed her, and struck up a correspondence with the novelist. This relationship later helped to further Hurston's career.

Though Hurston continued to write novels, they were all rejected because they lacked the quality of her published works. No doubt the quality of these works suffered because she was "burning to write" another one, a story about "the 3000 years struggle of the Jewish Peoples for democracy and the rights of man." She eventually wrote this story under the title "Life of Herod the Great." After Hurston died, a deputy sheriff saved the four-

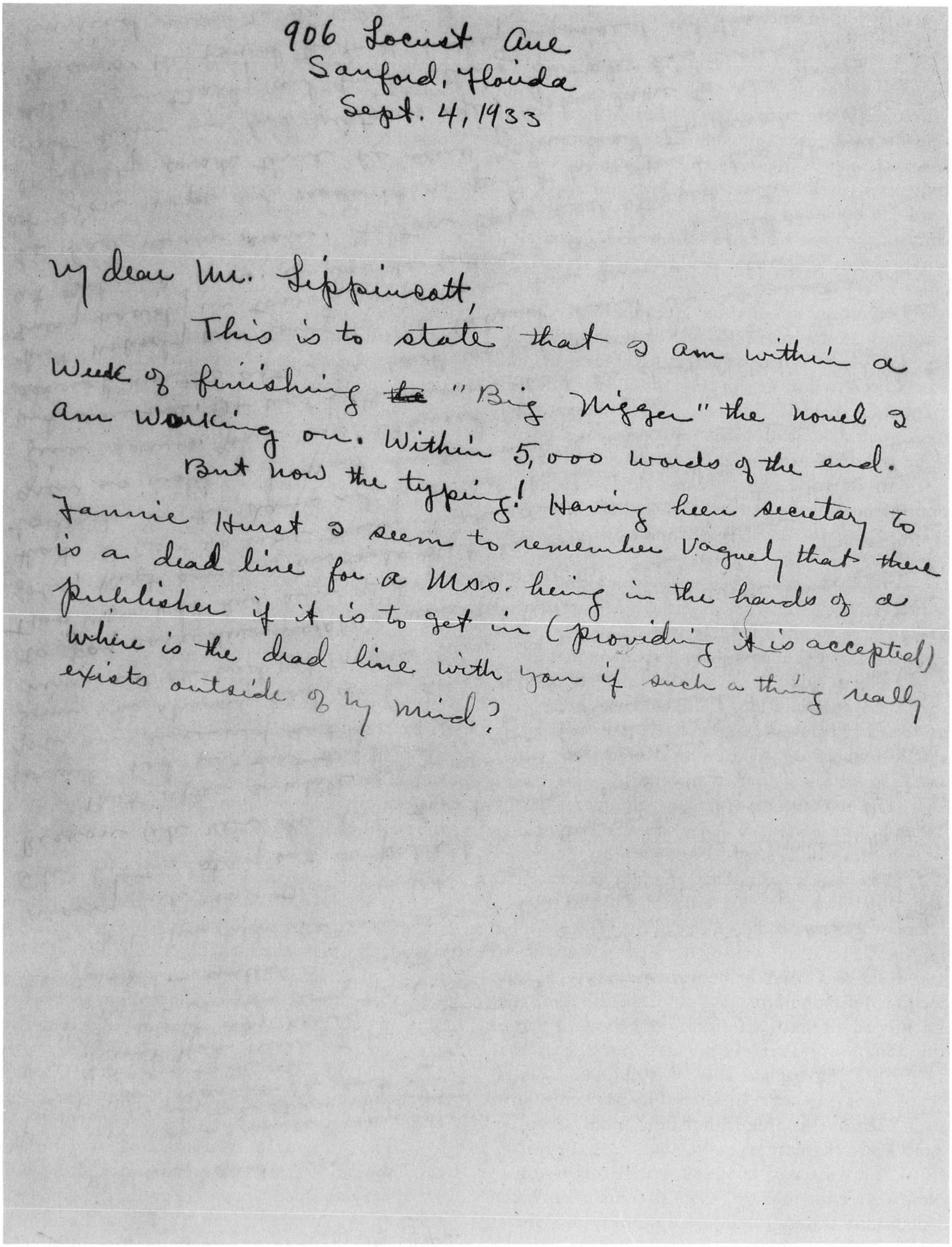

906 Locust Ave
Sanford, Florida
Sept. 4, 1933

My dear Mr. Lippincott,

This is to state that I am within a week of finishing the "Big Nigger" the novel I am working on. Within 5,000 words of the end.

But now the typing! Having been secretary to Fannie Hurst I seem to remember vaguely that there is a dead line for a Mss. being in the hands of a publisher if it is to get in (providing it is accepted) where is the dead line with you if such a thing really exists outside of my mind?

Page from the manuscript for Jonah's Gourd Vine *(1934), on the back of which Hurston drafted a letter to Bertram Lippincott (Estate of Zora Neale Hurston; Schomburg Center for Research in Black Culture, New York Public Library, Astor, Lenox and Tilden Foundations)*

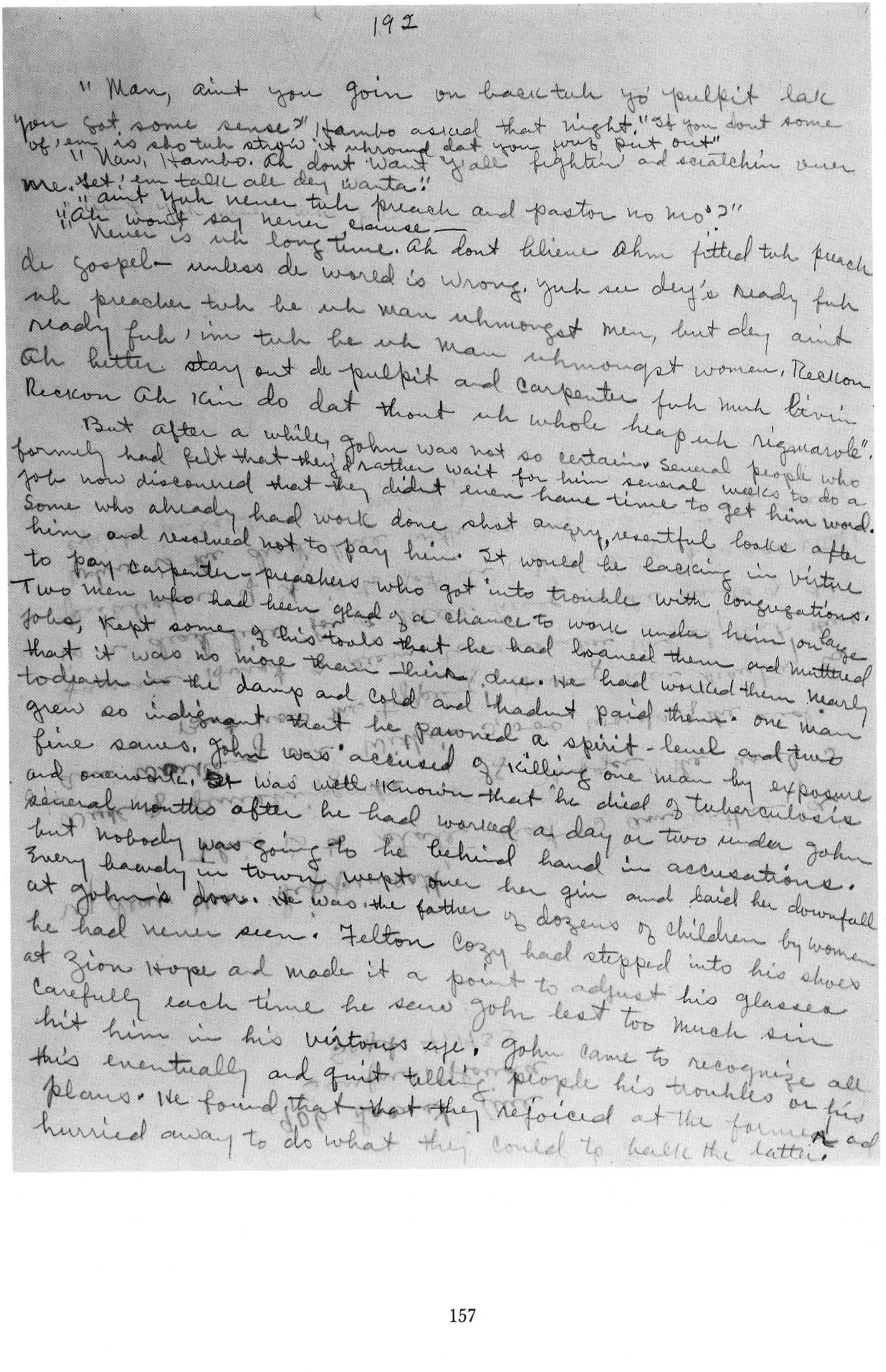

192

"Man, aint you goin on back tuh yo' pulpit lak you got some sense?" Hambo asked that night. "Ef you dont some of 'em is sho tuh strow it whroun dat you wuz put out"

"Naw, Hambo. Ah dont want y'all fightin' and scratchin' over me. Let 'em talk all dey wanta."

"Aint yuh never tuh preach and pastor no mo'?"

"Ah won't say never cause— Never is uh long time. Ah dont blieve Ahm fitted tuh preach de gospel— unless de world is wrong. Yuh see dey's ready fuh uh preacher tuh be uh man uhmongst men, but dey aint ready fuh 'im tuh be uh man uhmongst women. Reckon Ah better stay out de pulpit and carpenter fuh mah livin. Reckon Ah kin do dat thout uh whole heap uh rigmarole".

But after a while, john was not so certain. Several people who formely had felt that they'd rather wait for him several weeks to do a job now discovered that they didnt even have time to get him word. Some who already had work done shot angry, resentful looks after him and resolved not to pay him. It would be lacking in virtue to pay carpenter-preachers who got into trouble with congregations. Two men who had been glad of a chance to work under him on large jobs, kept some of his tools that he had loaned them and muttered that it was no more than their think due. He had worked them nearly to death in the damp and cold and hadnt paid them. One man grew so indignant that he pawned a spirit-level and two fine saws. John was accused of killing one man by exposure and overwork. It was well known that he died of tuberculosis several months after he had worked a day or two under john but nobody was going to be behind hand in accusations. Every bawdy in town wept over her gin and laid her downfall at john's door. He was the father of dozens of children by women he had never seen. Felton Cozy had stepped into his shoes at Zion Hope and made it a point to adjust his glasses carefully each time he saw john lest too much sin hit him in his virtuous eye. John came to recognize all this eventually and quit telling people his troubles or his plans. He found that they rejoiced at the former and hurried away to do what they could to halt the latter.

157

hundred-page Herod manuscript from being burned by a welfare-home janitor who had been instructed to destroy Hurston's personal effects. The manuscript, which is among Hurston's papers at the University of Florida Library, was badly damaged by the fire; but one surviving section was published in 1985 as an appendix to *Spunk: The Selected Stories of Zora Neale Hurston.*

Hurston's friendship with Rawlings resulted in Rawlings's publisher, Scribners, taking an interest in Hurston's work. By May 1947 Hurston had sold Scribners the option on a new novel, later called *Seraph on the Suwanee,* and had taken off for Honduras to write. The novel was published on 11 October 1948. Hurston's readers were in for a surprise: *Seraph on the Suwanee* was about white folks.

Set in various parts of Florida, *Seraph on the Suwanee* explores the psyche of Arvay Henson, a poor, neurotic white woman who feels that nothing good is ever going to happen to her because she does not deserve it. She must grow and learn to appreciate herself. The battle is an exasperatingly long one, for Arvay and for the reader, but Arvay emerges whole and with a positive sense of self. Hurston wrote to her editor that it was "very much by design" that the characters in the novel are white; she wrote to Carl Van Vechten that "I have hopes of breaking that old silly rule about Negroes not writing about white people." She had always felt that people were people, all of whom reacted in basically the same ways to the same stimuli. *Seraph on the Suwanee* was her proof of that hypothesis.

Critics have found the novel confusing and have speculated that perhaps Hurston was joining the ranks of a new group of assimilationist writers—Willard Motley, Chester Himes, and Ann Petry. Since Hurston never published another novel, it is difficult to say where her interests were tending (although the Herod manuscript seems to indicate her subject matter was undergoing a broadening treatment).

Seraph on the Suwanee sold well, and good things seemed to be developing; however, Hurston soon reached the nadir of her life. On 13 September 1948 Hurston, then living in New York, was arrested and charged with committing an immoral act with a ten-year-old, the son of a woman from whom Hurston had rented a room during the winter of 1946-1947. Though Hurston was able to prove that she had been out of the country at the time of the alleged crime, and the charges were subsequently dropped, the story was leaked to the press and sensational, humiliating news headlines followed. Hurston was devastated. She wrote to her friend Van Vechten, "I care nothing for anything anymore.... My race has

seen fit to destroy me without reason, and with the vilest tools conceived of by man so far.... All that I have ever tried to do has proved useless. All that I have believed in has failed me. I have resolved to die.... I feel hurled down a filthy privy hole." Fortunately, she did not die, though the incident took its toll. Although she continued to publish in national magazines and sold an option on another novel to Scribners, she left New York and refused to communicate with her friends.

In March 1950 she was discovered working as a maid in Rivo Alto, Florida. She claimed to be resting her mind and collecting material firsthand for a piece she intended to write about domestics; it is more probable that she needed the money.

In the winter of 1950-1951, at the invitation of friends, she moved to Belle Glade, Florida. In the spring she wrote to her literary agent that she was penniless, "just inching along like a stepped-on worm from day to day. Borrowing a little here and there." It was becoming embarrassing, she added, "having to avoid folks who have made me loans so that I could eat and sleep. The humiliation is getting to be much too much for my self-respect, to look and look at the magnificent sweep of the Everglades, birds included, and keep a smile on my face." The infrequent sale of a magazine article brought temporary relief, but over the next ten years Hurston worked at odd jobs. She lived in a one-room cabin she had purchased in Eau Gallie, while her stomach ailments and money problems made this period difficult.

In 1956 Hurston found work as a librarian at Patrick Air Force Base but was fired in 1957, ostensibly for having too much education for the job; in December 1957 she became a reporter for the *Fort Pierce Chronicle,* the local black weekly; and in 1958 she did some substitute teaching at Lincoln Park Academy, the black public school of Fort Pierce. These frequently humiliating jobs did not daunt Hurston's spirit. In 1955, in a letter to the *Orlando Sentinel,* she expressed her outrage about the 1954 Supreme Court decision on desegregation. According to Hurston it all centered around "the self-respect of my people. How much satisfaction can I get from a court order for somebody to associate with me who does not wish me near them?... It is a contradiction in terms to scream race pride and equality while at the same time spurning Negro teachers and self-association."

On 29 October 1959, after suffering a stroke, Hurston was forced to enter the Saint Lucie County Welfare Home. She died there of hypertensive heart disease on 28 January 1960 and was buried in an unmarked grave in the Garden of the Heavenly Rest, the segregated cemetery at Fort Pierce. She had died in poverty, and a collection had to be taken up to pay for her funeral. Yet Hurston had lived a rich life. She had risen from obscurity to become a member of the American Folklore Society, American Anthropological Society, American Ethnological Society, New York Academy of Sciences, and the American Association for the Advancement of Science; and she was listed in the 1937 edition of *Who's Who in America*. She had been courted by political figures and, most important, she had published an exceptional body of literature. Like Janie of *Their Eyes Were Watching God,* she had seen the "light," and no amount of dusk could dim its glow. As she wrote in 1941 while working on her autobiography:

> While I am still below the allotted span of time, and notwithstanding, I feel that I have lived. I have had the joy and pain of strong friendships. I have served and been served. I have made enemies of which I am not ashamed. I have been faithless, and then I have been faithful and steadfast until the blood ran down into my shoes. I have loved unselfishly with all the ardor of a strong heart, and I have hated with all the power of my soul. What waits for me in the future? I do not know. I can't even imagine, and I am glad for that. But already, I have touched the four corners of the horizon, for from hard searching it seems to me that tears and laughter, love and hate make up the sum of life.

Interest in Hurston had diminished long before her death. Her works had been long out of print, and the literary world was being dominated by such male giants as Richard Wright, Ralph Ellison, and James Baldwin. Fortunately, however, a few readers were beginning to discover Hurston, and in the 1970s this interest mushroomed into a coterie of Hurston followers. Comprehensive appraisal came in 1977 with Hemenway's *Zora Neale Hurston: A Literary Biography.* Acknowledging his "white man's reconstruction of the intellectual process in a black woman's mind," he offers a favorable assessment of her literary career and tries to explain her enigmatic personality. Praising her work as a celebration of black culture, he concludes that her failure to achieve recognition in her life reflects America's poor treatment of its black artists. The critical acclaim awarded Hurston's writings since the 1970s has allowed readers to discover what Alice Walker (writing in the foreword to Hemenway's biography) finds: a "sense of black people as complete, complex, undiminished human beings." She honors Hurston's genius as a black woman writer and delights in her dynamic personality: "Zora was funny, irreverent (she was the first to call the Harlem Renaissance literati the 'niggerati'), good-

looking and sexy." The University of Florida set up a Zora Neale Hurston Fellowship in Anthropology; the City of Orlando, Florida, acknowledged Hurston's accomplishments by naming a city building after her. In 1973, as a tribute to Hurston's inspiration, Walker placed a gravestone inscribed: "ZORA NEALE HURSTON / 'A GENIUS OF THE SOUTH' / 1901- - -1960 / NOVELIST, FOLKLORIST / ANTHROPOLOGIST."

Bibliographies:
Adele S. Newson, *Zora Neale Hurston: A Reference Guide* (Boston: G. K. Hall, 1987);
Rose Parkman Davis, *Zora Neale Hurston: An Annotated Bibliography and Reference Guide* (Westport, Conn.: Greenwood Press, 1997).

Biography:
Robert E. Hemenway, *Zora Neale Hurston: A Literary Biography* (Urbana: University of Illinois Press, 1977).

References:
Michael Awkward, ed., *New Essays on Their Eyes Were Watching God* (Cambridge, U.K. & New York: Cambridge University Press, 1990);
Harold Bloom, ed., *Zora Neale Hurston* (New York: Chelsea House, 1986);
Bloom, ed., *Zora Neale Hurston's Their Eyes Were Watching God* (New York: Chelsea House, 1987);
Robert Bone, *Down Home: A History of Afro-American Short Fiction From Its Beginnings to the End of the Harlem Renaissance* (New York: Putnam, 1975);
Gloria L. Cronin, ed., *Critical Essays on Zora Neale Hurston* (New York: G. K. Hall, 1998);
Arthur P. Davis, *From the Dark Tower: Afro-American Writers, 1900–1960* (Washington, D.C.: Howard University Press, 1974);
Nick Aaron Ford, *The Contemporary Negro Novel* (Boston: Meador, 1936);
Henry Louis Gates Jr. and K. A. Appiah, eds., *Zora Neale Hurston: Critical Perspectives Past and Present* (New York: Amistad, 1993);
Steve Glassman and Kathryn Lee Seidel, eds., *Zora in Florida* (Orlando: University of Central Florida Press, 1991);
Trudier Harris, *The Power of the Porch: The Storyteller's Craft in Zora Neale Hurston, Gloria Naylor, and Randall Kenan* (Athens: University of Georgia Press, 1996);
Robert E. Hemenway, "Zora Neale Hurston and the Eatonville Anthropology," in *The Harlem Renaissance Remembered,* edited by Arna Bontemps (New York: Dodd, Mead, 1972);

Karla F. C. Holloway, *The Character of the Word: The Texts of Zora Neale Hurston* (New York: Greenwood Press, 1987);

Lillie P. Howard, *Zora Neale Hurston* (Boston: Twayne, 1980);

Howard, ed., *Alice Walker and Zora Neale Hurston: The Common Bond* (Westport, Conn.: Greenwood Press, 1993);

Langston Hughes, *The Big Sea* (New York: Hill & Wang, 1963);

John Lowe, *Jump at the Sun: Zora Neale Hurston's Cosmic Comedy* (Urbana: University of Illinois Press, 1994);

Mary E. Lyons, *Sorrow's Kitchen: The Life and Folklore of Zora Neale Hurston* (New York: Scribners, 1990);

Pearlie Mae Fisher Peters, *The Assertive Woman in Zora Neale Hurston's Fiction, Folklore, and Drama* (New York: Garland, 1997);

Deborah G. Plant, *Every Tub Must Sit on Its Own Bottom: The Philosophy and Politics of Zora Neale Hurston* (Urbana: University of Illinois Press, 1995);

Eric J. Sundquist, *The Hammers of Creation: Folk Culture in Modern African-American Fiction* (Athens: University of Georgia Press, 1992);

Darwin T. Turner, *In a Minor Chord: Three Afro-American Writers and Their Search for Identity* (Carbondale: Southern Illinois University Press, 1971);

Alice Walker, "In Search of Zora Neale Hurston," *Ms.,* 3 (March 1975): 74–90;

Paul Witcover, *Zora Neale Hurston* (New York: Chelsea House, 1991).

Papers:

Major depositories of Zora Neale Hurston's manuscripts, letters, and other materials are located at various libraries: the Hurston Collection at the University of Florida Library, Gainesville; the James Weldon Johnson Memorial Collection at the Beinecke Rare Book and Manuscript Library, Yale University; the Schomburg Collection at the New York Public Library; the Alain Locke Collection, Howard University, Washington, D.C.; Fisk University, Nashville, Tennessee; and the University of South Florida.

Jamaica Kincaid

This entry was updated by Kimberly D. Blockett (University of Wisconsin–Madison) from the entry by Susan Z. Andrade (University of Pittsburgh) in DLB 157: *Twentieth-Century Caribbean and Black African Writers.*

BIRTH: St. Johns, Antigua, 25 May 1949, as Elaine Potter Richardson, to David Drew and Annie Richardson.

EDUCATION: Studied photography at the New School for Social Research in New York; attended Franconia College, New Hampshire.

MARRIAGE: 1979 to Allen Shawn; children: Annie Shawn and Harold.

AWARDS AND HONORS: Morton Dauwen Zabel Award, American Academy and Institute of Arts and Letters, for *At the Bottom of the River,* 1983; honorary degrees from Williams College and Long Island College, both in 1991, Colgate University, Amherst College, and Bard College; Lila Wallace-*Reader's Digest* Fund annual writer's award, 1992; finalist for the National Book Critics Circle Award for fiction and the OPN Faulkner Award, both for *The Autobiography of My Mother,* both 1997.

BOOKS: *At the Bottom of the River* (New York: Farrar, Straus, Giroux, 1983; London: Pan, 1984);
Annie John (New York: Farrar, Straus, Giroux, 1985; London: Picador, 1985);
Annie, Gwen, Lilly, Pam and Tulip, text by Kincaid, lithographs by Eric Fischl (New York: Whitney Museum of Modern Art, 1986; first trade edition, Knopf, in association with Whitney Museum of Modern Art, 1989);
A Small Place (New York: Farrar, Straus, Giroux, 1988; London: Virago, 1988);
Lucy (New York: Farrar, Straus, Giroux, 1990; London: Cape, 1991);
Autobiography of My Mother (New York: Farrar, Straus, Giroux, 1996);
My Brother (New York: Farrar, Straus, Giroux, 1997).

OTHER: *My Favorite Plant: Writers and Gardeners on the Plants They Love,* edited by Kincaid (New York: Farrar, Straus, Giroux, 1998).

Jamaica Kincaid (photograph © 1992 by Mariana Cook)

SELECTED PERIODICAL PUBLICATIONS–UNCOLLECTED:
FICTION
"Ovando," *Conjunctions,* no. 14 (1989): 75–83;
"The Finishing Line," *New York Times Book Review,* 2 December 1990, p. 18;
"Biography of a Dress," *Grand Street,* 11 (Spring 1992): 92–100;
"Song of Roland," *New Yorker,* 69 (12 April 1993): 94–98;
"Xuela," *New Yorker,* 70 (9 May 1994): 82–92.
NONFICTION
"Antigua Crossings: A Deep and Blue Passage on the Caribbean Sea," *Rolling Stone* (29 June 1978): 48–50;

"On Seeing England for the First Time," *Transition*, 51 (1991): 32–40;

"Out of Kenya," by Kincaid and Ellen Pall, *New York Times*, 16 September 1991, pp. A15, A19;

"Flowers of Evil: In the Garden," *New Yorker*, 68 (5 October 1992): 154–159;

"A Fire by Ice," *New Yorker*, 69 (22 February 1993): 64–67;

"Just Reading: In the Garden," *New Yorker*, 69 (29 March 1993): 51–55;

"Alien Soil: In the Garden," *New Yorker*, 69 (21 June 1993): 47–52;

"This Other Eden," *New Yorker*, 69 (28 & 30 August 1993): 69–73;

"The Season Past: In the Garden," *New Yorker*, 70 (7 March 1994): 57–61;

"Putting Myself Together," *New Yorker* (February 1995): 93–101;

"In Roseau," *New Yorker* (17 April 1995): 92–99;

"In History," *Callaloo*, 20, no. 1 (1997): 1–7.

"As I go on writing, I feel less and less interested in the approval of the First World, and I never had the approval of the world I came from, so now I don't know where I am. I've exiled myself yet again," pronounced Jamaica Kincaid in a 1990 interview with Donna Perry. Despite having produced only six slim volumes of prose–four of which include most of her already published short writings–Kincaid has already earned a reputation as a writer of distinction and is certainly one of the best known and most respected women writers from the Caribbean. There has been a virtual explosion of interest in her work in the mid 1990s, with most critical articles having been published since 1990. Kincaid's success is related to two factors that distinguish her from other contemporary writers: her rise to prominence from within the orbit of that elite American journal *The New Yorker* and her coupling of anticolonialism with an elegant modernism in much of her writing. Although the latter part of her literary education took place in the United States, it is the subject of British colonialism to which she returns again and again in her writings.

Jamaica Kincaid was born on 25 May 1949 at Holberton Hospital in St. John's, Antigua, and named Elaine Potter Richardson by her mother. Richardson was the surname of her mother, Annie, who immigrated to Antigua from Dominica and whom Kincaid names in a 1992 interview with Kay Bonetti as the person she writes for: "my great audience is this one-half Carib Indian woman living in Antigua." Kincaid's biological father, Roderick Potter, did not play a significant role in her childhood. Soon after the birth of her daughter, Annie Richard-

son married David Drew, a carpenter and cabinet-maker whom Kincaid uses as the model for her fictional fathers. She considers Drew her father and says of him that he could see a piece of furniture and copy it from sight. Annie and David Drew had three sons–Joseph in 1958, Dalma in 1959, and Devon in 1961. Kincaid dedicated her fourth book, *A Small Place* (1988), partly to her three brothers. Annie Richardson Drew taught Elaine to read when she was three and one-half years old and then sent her to a Moravian school. On her daughter's seventh birthday she gave her an Oxford dictionary.

At the same time, Annie Drew arranged for her daughter to begin apprenticing to a seamstress, and after her school day and for almost all her school years Elaine Richardson went twice a week for two hours to Miss Doreen's house. Despite her precociousness in school, there was little chance of her attending a university. She was a girl, after all, and of a poor family; only boys of her background were so singled out. Kincaid said in 1992 that she would have preferred to remain in Antigua, attend a university, and become a librarian or teacher, the professions of formidable West Indian women of her childhood experience, but had no choice other than to come to the United States: "When I first started, among the things I wanted to do was to say, 'Aren't you sorry that no greater effort was made over my education? Or over my life?'"

Soon after her seventeenth birthday in 1966 Kincaid came to Westchester County, New York, to work as an au pair. Between 1966 and 1973 she held several different jobs and studied at various institutions. She took classes at Westchester Community College, completed her high-school degree, and again became an au pair on the Upper East Side of New York City. She took classes in photography at the New School for Social Research and at Franconia College in New Hampshire before working as a receptionist with the magazine *Art Direction*. Her first publication, "When I Was Seventeen," was commissioned by *Ingenue*, a magazine that accepted her story idea of asking Gloria Steinem about what the famous feminist was like at the age of their average reader.

In 1973 Elaine Potter Richardson changed her name to Jamaica Kincaid, in part because she wanted the anonymity to write freely. She chose Jamaica because she liked its distant evocation of the Caribbean, Kincaid because it seemed to go well with Jamaica. A mutual friend introduced her to George W. Trow, who at that time wrote the popular "Talk of the Town" column for *The New Yorker* magazine, and her literary career took off. Trow began incorporating Kincaid's quotes into his column, then introduced her to William Shawn, editor of *The New Yorker*. Shawn became almost as important a figure to Kincaid's writing as was her mother; *At the Bottom of the River* (1983) and *A Small Place* are partly—and gratefully—dedicated to him. In 1976 Kincaid became a staff writer for *The New Yorker,* a position she holds to this day. Soon after, she began writing the "Talk of the Town" column herself. She said in 1992 that she wrote many "weird" and "experimental" columns at that time and that it was from them that she learned to do the stories that make up *At the Bottom of the River.* Along the way, she met and in 1979 married composer Allen Shawn, son of *The New Yorker* editor. The younger Shawn is on the faculty of Bennington College, Vermont, and he, Kincaid, and their two children, Annie (born 1985) and Harold (born 1989), live in North Bennington.

Kincaid's strong dislike of English hegemony fuels antipathy toward the entire island (as is clear from her 1991 article "On Seeing England for the First Time"), so it is ironic—yet fitting—that her literary influences are so clearly that of a colonial British subject: much of the Bible (she told Allan Vorda in 1993 that as a girl she especially enjoyed reading Genesis and Revelation), William Shakespeare, John Milton, the English Romantic poets, and nineteenth-century novelists such as Charlotte and Emily Brontë, Thomas Hardy, and Charles Dickens. She told Selwyn Cudjoe in an interview (1989), however, that reading modernist writers such as Virginia Woolf and James Joyce forever changed her approach to narrative: "And then I read [some short stories of] Alain Robbe-Grillet. . . . I cannot describe them except that they broke every rule. When I read them, the top of my head came off and I thought, 'this is really living!' And I knew that whatever I did, I would not be interested in realism."

Like many other women writers, Kincaid explores social issues within the realm of the domestic and the personal. Except for the nonfiction *A Small Place* and the nonnarrative prose of *Annie, Gwen, Lilly, Pam and Tulip* (1986), Kincaid's corpus is marked by an intense engagement with the figure of the mother. Her protagonists exhibit a poignant desire for mother love at the same time that they battle the mother figure, a dynamic that has motivated much psychoanalytic discussion. The intensely ambivalent relationship between mother and child may be read simply as a family drama centering on the young narrator's desire to assert a separate identity while fearing its concomitant separation, or it may be interpreted metaphorically as the relationship between colonizer and colonized. In this second read-

Dust jacket for Kincaid's first book, ten stories about the impact of mother love

ing the omnipotent colonizer/mother figure dominates a weaker colonized/child figure. In one of the two book-length studies of Kincaid, *Jamaica Kincaid: Where the Land Meets the Body* (1994), Moira Ferguson offers a detailed analysis of the conflation between emotion and object, the personal and political dynamic. However, Ferguson's otherwise perspicacious book exaggerates the manifest political engagement of Kincaid's work, conferring on her (and, by implication, all Caribbean people) the status of a would-be postcolonial revolutionary. This is not to deny Kincaid's stinging critique of colonialism as well as unequal gender relations in her work; however, with the exception of the powerfully polemical *A Small Place,* her writings do not express a coherent political ideology. Diane Simmons, the author of the second book-length study, *Jamaica Kincaid* (1994), observes that the mother in Kincaid's fiction inhabits "a world of conflicting cosmologies." Kincaid's mother figure, Simmons argues, presents "the daughter with an impossibly contradictory map of the world, and the daughter cannot hope to follow the mother's directions. To survive, the daughter must ignore the instructions that result from the mother's internalized contradictions; against the mother's ferocious resistance, she must seek to emulate the part of the mother that is still centered and powerful."

Kincaid's first book, *At the Bottom of the River,* is made up of ten stories or vignettes, the first seven of which had been previously published in *The New Yorker.* The vignettes are both lyrical and compelling. The lack of narrative structure, however, along with a dependence on mythopoetic imagery, make the text inaccessible to some readers. In fact, critics such as Brenda Berrian, Wendy Dutton, and Patricia Ismond suggest that *At the Bottom of the River* be read as an intertext, a companion "sister text" to the more conventionally narrated *Annie John* (1985), the later book providing a narrative frame for the more nuanced and evocative moods of the former.

Annie, Gwen, Lilly, Pam and Tulip, a separately published and relatively unknown collection of prose pieces, was originally intended to be part of *At the Bottom of the River.* Similar in theme and style, the two books are less concerned with the Caribbean than is Kincaid's other writing. While the region is not entirely absent in *At the Bottom of the River* as it is in the later *Annie, Gwen, Lilly, Pam and Tulip,* the specificity of the setting is secondary to the exploration of universal themes, principally the fall from grace, the lack of wholeness, and especially the nostalgia for the past. The brief text of *Annie, Gwen, Lilly, Pam and Tulip,* which accompanies Eric Fischel's beautiful lithographs, is composed of the "dialogues" of five female characters in a prelapsarian, sensual world, the loss of which one infers might provide artistic inspiration. In fact, looking back at *At the Bottom of the River* in her interview with Perry, Kincaid named English Romanticism as an excessive influence and characterized her work as a "very unangry, decent, civilized book" that "represents sort of this successful attempt by English people to make their version of a human being or their version of a person out of me. It amazes me now that I did that then. I would never write like that again, I don't think."

Nevertheless, "Girl," the first story of the collection, is especially noteworthy. Though on the surface it consists of a litany of rules of conduct told by a mother to her daughter, the vignette illustrates the force of maternal and social admonitions, particularly regarding sexuality; the daughter's quiet response; and, above all, the rich landscape of Caribbean culture:

Wash the white clothes on Monday and put them on the stone heap; wash the color clothes on Tuesday and put them on the clothesline to dry; don't walk barehead in the hot sun; cook pumpkin fritters in very hot sweet oil; soak your little cloths right after you take them off; . . . soak salt fish overnight before you cook it; is it true that you sing benna in Sunday school? always eat your food in such a way that it won't turn someone else's stomach; on Sundays try to walk like a lady and not like the slut you are so bent on becoming; don't sing benna in Sunday school; you mustn't speak to wharf-rat boys, not even to give directions; don't eat fruits on the street—flies will follow you; *but I don't sing benna on Sundays at all and never in Sunday school;* this is how to sew on a button; this is how to make a button-hole for the button you have just sewed on.

A bildungsroman of a working-class Antiguan girl, *Annie John* comprises eight chapter-vignettes, stories that span Annie's childhood and coming-of-age from ages ten to seventeen. The first meditates on death and explores funerals and cemeteries through the curious eyes of ten-year-old Annie. The second story-chapter, "The Circling Hand," is particularly touching and illustrates Kincaid's preoccupation with the mother/child dyad. Through a beautiful recounting of the everyday, it tells how, as a child, Annie lovingly followed her mother through her work of shopping, laundry, and cooking. The story lyrically treats the separation anxiety of daughter from mother through young Annie's anger at her mother for halting the practice of dressing her in look-alike dresses and her dismay at the prospect of venturing out into the world. The story also introduces the magical trunk, brightly colored and papered, in which Annie's mother—also named Annie John—carried her worldly goods from Dominica at age sixteen. (The younger Annie is only one year older when, at the end of the narrative, she leaves Antigua for England.) The trunk now contains little Annie's baby memorabilia and her meaningful markers of growing up, such as important clothes and report cards. Annie's anger with her omnipotent mother, who makes her study the piano and learn to sew, leads to her increasingly important relations with girls her own age, particularly Gwen and the Red Girl.

Although Gwen offers Annie a love-object replacement, it is Annie's affection for the Red Girl that most clearly indicates the process of violent overthrow of her mother as primary love object; rebelliously, Annie attempts to replace her mother with a girl of whom the elder Annie would most thoroughly disapprove. Unwashed and unkempt, the Red Girl with her unruly, flame-colored hair is symbolic of everything her mother warns against. Under the Red Girl's influence Annie becomes a tomboy, climbs trees, plays marbles, and begins to steal small amounts of money, hiding it under the house along with her marbles and stolen library books.

It is in "The Great Man in Chains" and "Somewhere, Belgium" chapters that readers see how young Annie's rebellion against colonialism, evident in her experience of colonial education, parallels the rebellion against her mother's authority. Her disdainful annotation of the picture of Columbus's fall from grace—and its discovery by her teacher—prefigures Annie's improper conversation with some boys in the street. This behavior leads to an argument:

> I looked at my mother—at her turned back this time—and she wasn't tired and old and broken at all. . . . It was I who was tired and old and broken, and as I looked at my mother, full of vigor, young and whole, I wanted to go over and put my arms around her and beg forgiveness for the thing I had just said and to explain that I didn't really mean it. But I couldn't move, and when I looked down it was as if the ground had opened up between us, making a deep and wide split. On one side of this split stood my mother, bent over my dinner cooking in a pot; on the other side stood I, in my arms carrying my schoolbooks and inside carrying the thimble that weighed worlds.

Significantly, however, after the big fight, whereupon she asks her carpenter father for a trunk and implies an impending departure to her mother, Annie becomes ill for three months. After the climactic illness she leaves for England.

Unlike the conventional bildungsroman, *Annie John* is not concerned with a sense of narrative advance into the future as much as it is with a nostalgic glance into the past. Even the final chapter, which recounts Annie's walk from her home to the jetty where she will board a ship for Barbados, then another for England, where she will take up studying to be a nurse, looks backward to memories of her childhood. Her mother's pride in little Annie's first trip to the pharmacy alone at age five stands in for the emotionalism of Annie's impending first trip away from the island at age seventeen—a trip from which she vows never to return.

"If you go to Antigua as a tourist, this is what you will see" begins Kincaid's fourth book, the nonfictional *A Small Place*. Only eighty-one pages long, this short but powerful book can best be described as an "anti-travel narrative," a riposte from the colonized to the colonizer. Responding to the hundreds of travel books written by Europeans about the Caribbean islands, Kincaid in *A Small Place* challenges the notion held by some that her work avoids politics and fails to speak meaningfully to and for black people. Its trenchant indictment of neocolonial cor-

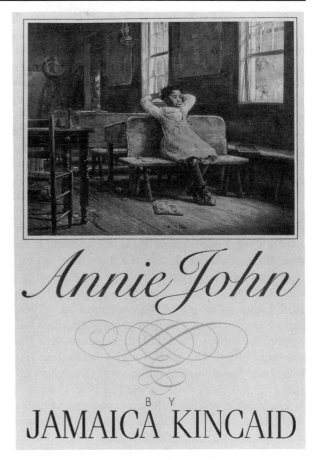

Dust jacket for Kincaid's 1985 novel, about a young girl growing up in Antigua

ruption refuses to ignore the fact that, both historically and structurally, neocolonialism is a consequence of colonialism.

Kincaid reexamines the Caribbean beauty of Antigua from the perspective of the native, exposing the poverty of the island, lack of domestic infrastructure, and other obstacles to the local quality of life. General problems associated with a nation's economic dependence on colonialism are raised, beginning with the unequal treatment for white visitors versus black natives at the airport. Not content with generalities, Kincaid points out the ironies of how the Antiguan taxi drivers' practice of driving expensive cars—filled, inappropriately, with leaded gasoline because no unleaded is available—contrasts with the humble surroundings in which they live. The circumstance can be traced directly to inexpensive loans for cars as opposed to those for houses, resulting from government ministers owning the two main car dealerships. As the narrator's eye passes over Holberton Hospital (Kincaid's own birthplace), she is moved to remark on how rich Antiguans do not use this hospital but fly to the United

States for medical treatment. Ferguson suggests it was remarks such as these that moved the Antiguan government informally to ban Kincaid from the island in 1985 when chapters of the book had begun to be published. The unofficial ban was apparently lifted in 1992.

Kincaid's polemic is not reserved exclusively for local corruption or greed. Her narrator bitterly points out that unpaid black labor provided the West with its riches. She later delivers a ferocious and elegant anti-English diatribe: "They don't seem to know that this empire business was all wrong and they should, at least, be wearing sackcloth and ashes in token penance of the wrongs committed, the irrevocableness of their bad deeds, for no natural disaster imaginable could equal the harm they did. Actual death might have been better."

In a rhetorical gesture she makes so well, Kincaid uses a small inadequacy to stand metonymically for a larger issue. Addressing the tourist directly, the narrator reminds him or her that "the contents of your lavatory," which is emptied into the ocean for lack of an adequate sewage system, just might at some time "graze gently against your ankle," thereby linking the more abstract question of the inherent ugliness of tourism with the ugliness of the material need on the part of native inhabitants for basic domestic development. An even more detailed example of Kincaid's use of metonymy to point out social problems is her extended discussion of the lack of a decent public library in Antigua, a lack she represents as shameful for a nation whose motto is "A People to Mold, A Nation to Build." She uses the fact that the library is housed in a too small, ugly room above a dry-goods store as a metaphor for the larger problems of colonial pillage and neocolonial graft and indifference plaguing contemporary Antigua.

Kincaid's *Lucy* (1990), which Ferguson calls her "first post-Antiguan novel," is set entirely outside of the Caribbean. While continuing her investigation of the elasticity of the mother/child bond in this novel, Kincaid does not use the bond as a metaphor for colonialism quite as explicitly as she does in *At the Bottom of the River* and *Annie John*. Moreover, depicting as it does a slightly older female protagonist, this novel can and does explore issues of sexuality and desire on the part of its young Afro-Caribbean protagonist. Like Kincaid's other works, it includes traces of her autobiography. Lucy Josephine Potter bears one of Kincaid's birth names as well as her birth date. Lucy's employment as an au pair to an American family also repeats some of the author's personal narrative. The tone of the novel is stronger and more bitter than that of *Annie John*.

Lucy moves from her Caribbean home to the city of New York. There she becomes the caretaker of three Euro-American children and, more important, becomes embroiled in the marriage and divorce of their parents, Lewis and Mariah, an upper-middle-class couple. (Ferguson suggests that Kincaid's refusal to give the white characters a surname functions as a literary rebuttal to the historical refusal of white slaveholders to allow their African slaves a surname.) Lucy observes and narrates the disintegration of the marriage after Lewis has an affair with Mariah's best friend. Her position as witness is underscored at this moment by her taking up photography:

> I saw Lewis standing behind Dinah, his arms around her shoulders, and he was licking her neck over and over again, and how she liked it. This was not a show, this was something real; and I thought of Mariah and all those books she had filled with photographs that began with when she and Lewis first met, in Paris in the shadow of the Eiffel Tower or in London in the shadow of Big Ben or somewhere foolish like that.... But here was a picture that no one would ever take–a picture that would not end up in one of those books, but a significant picture all the same.

As the narrative progresses, she makes friends outside the family and becomes interested in the paintings of Paul Gauguin. Instead of completing her au pair contract, she moves out with her new friend Pam, a "bad" influence; rents an apartment; and begins to explore the world of sexuality, exoticism, hallucinogenics, and hedonism of New York City in the 1960s.

The representation of the American myth of arrival in *Lucy* has provoked conflicting interpretations. In her article in *Kunapipi* (1992) Alison Donnell reads the novel as a theoretical frame that challenges Euro-American paradigms and maintains that neither West Indian "exile" nor American "arrival are complete, and, as migrant and minority, Lucy is left without belonging. America is indeed a poor shadow of her dream." Reading the journey of upwardly mobile Third World characters from colony to metropolis, Bruce Robbins in the April 1994 *Modernism/Modernity* reaches a different conclusion, suggesting that Kincaid practices a "female Naipaulism" implying a Third World subject's investment in the colonial power. Since her work is embraced by the metropolis, it could not "ultimately signify anything other than an opportunistic affirmation of the metropolis." However, accepting Robbins's reading in its entirety requires not only ignoring some of the complicated gender tensions that Lucy exhibits but also assumes that a Caribbean subject will attribute to the United States the same colonial significance it does England. Robbins's article reads Lucy as an unmediated signifier of Kincaid herself and assumes that the character will become as successful as her creator.

An important early narrative thread tying together the categories of gender, race, and culture involves Mariah and Lucy's attempts at friendship. Though full of good intentions, Mariah is often ethnocentric in her assumptions about Lucy. A notable point of contention is her ongoing attempt to convince Lucy of the beauty of daffodils because they evoke pleasant childhood memories for Mariah herself, this despite the fact that Lucy hates them and has told her of having been forced to memorize daffodil poems: "The night after I had recited the poem, I dreamt, continuously it seemed, that I was being chased down a narrow cobbled street by bunches and bunches of those same daffodils that I had vowed to forget, and when finally I fell down from exhaustion they all piled on top of me, until I was buried deep underneath them and was never seen again." Yellow imagery surrounds the two instances of conflict between the women: "She looked so beautiful standing there in the middle of the kitchen. The yellow light from the sun came in through a window and fell on the pale-yellow linoleum tiles of the floor, and on the walls of the kitchen, which were painted yet another shade of pale yellow, and Mariah, with her pale-yellow skin and yellow hair, stood still in this almost celestial light." In "Lucy and the Mark of the Colonizer" Ferguson argues convincingly that the novel includes a sustained intertextual dialogue with and response to a series of Wordsworthian daffodil poems.

While Mariah is clearly insensitive to the intellectual and cultural violence that shapes Lucy's colonial heritage, Lucy's anger toward Mariah often departs from the simple master/servant tension (recast as that between colonizer and colonized) into the mother/daughter dyad evident in *Annie John.* "The times that I loved Mariah it was because she reminded me of my mother. The times that I did not love Mariah it was because she reminded me of my mother. . . . Mariah reminded me more and more of the parts of my mother that I loved." Moreover, paralleling the subplot of Lucy's righteous colonial indignation is the less understandable fury toward her mother, with whom she refuses to communicate. (The reasons for this break on Lucy's part are never made clear; unopened letters from her mother pile up on Lucy's bureau, including the one telling her of the death of her father.) Lucy's anger toward the hapless Mariah then is not solely the passionate reaction of a young black woman to a chauvinistic white one. It fre-

Dust jacket for Kincaid's 1996 book, which continues her exploration of the mother-daughter relationship

quently also functions as a form of narrative displacement onto the motherly Mariah— who is more like the colonizer than any of Kincaid's other mother characters—of Lucy's fury toward her own mother. Perhaps this is why at the end of the narrative the protagonist so proudly proclaims herself to be a namesake of Lucifer.

In *Autobiography of My Mother* (1996) Kincaid continues her exploration of the mother/daughter relationship. Since 1991 she has also been publishing in *The New Yorker* essays stemming from the theme of gardening. Having received the Morton Davwen Zabel Award for fiction (1984), been a finalist for the prestigious Ritz Paris Hemingway Award (1985), won a Guggenheim Fellowship (1989), and succeeded in capturing the attention of critics, Kincaid at a young age has established a career that may well become of major importance as she adds to her already considerable list of accomplishments.

Most recently, that list has grown to include a nomination for the National Book Award (1998) for *My Brother,* a memoir detailing her brother's battle and eventual death from AIDS. In this book Kincaid

Dust jacket for Kincaid's 1997 book, about her brother's losing battle with AIDS

diversifies her attentions to post-colonial issues and mother-daughter relations to investigate the complexities of her feelings for her estranged sibling. Devon Drew, a closeted bisexual Rastafarian nicknamed Patches, is her youngest brother whom she hasn't seen since leaving their homeland of Antigua twenty years earlier. Her return to assist in caring for her brother necessitates a tortured recovery of her contradictory feelings of love for him and concomitant disapproval of the empty selfishness of his existence. His life (or lack thereof) becomes a symbol of the dissolution, gloom, and morbidity of the colonized culture from which Kincaid has spent years trying to separate herself. Thus, the central concern of *My Brother* is not so much how Kincaid handles her brother's impending death but, rather, how she handles the reality that he never truly lived.

As she admitted in 1990, Jamaica Kincaid in her career may have "exiled herself" and may indeed not know exactly where she fits within a conventionally delineated geography. Perhaps by not being bound to a single place or ideological perspective, she enables herself to challenge through her fic-

tion political and cultural boundaries that might otherwise confine her. Her status as a literary exile, if anything, has made her place in the world of Caribbean/postcolonial literature more secure.

Interviews:

Selwyn Cudjoe, "Jamaica Kincaid and the Modernist Project: An Interview," *Callaloo,* 12 (Spring 1989): 396–411; reprinted in *Caribbean Women Writers: Essays from the First International Conference,* edited by Cudjoe (Wellesley, Mass.: Calaloux, 1990), pp. 215–231;

Leslie Garis, "Through West Indian Eyes," *New York Times Magazine,* 7 October 1990, p. 42;

Donna Perry, "An Interview with Jamaica Kincaid," in *Reading Black, Reading Feminist: A Critical Anthology,* edited by Henry Louis Gates Jr. (New York: Meridian, 1990), pp. 492–510;

Kay Bonetti, "An Interview with Jamaica Kincaid," *Missouri Review,* 15, no. 2 (1992): 124–142;

Allan Vorda, "I Come from a Place That's Very Unreal: An Interview with Jamaica Kincaid," in *Face to Face: Interviews with Contemporary Novelists,* edited by Vorda (Houston: Rice University Press, 1993), pp. 77–105;

Moira Ferguson, "A Lot of Memory: An Interview with Jamaica Kincaid," *Kenyon Review,* 16 (Winter 1994): 163–188;

Pamela Muirhead, "An Interview with Jamaica Kincaid," *Clockwatch Review: A Journal of the Arts,* 9, no. 1–2 (1994–1995): 39–48;

Jeannine DeLombard, "My Brother's Keeper: An Interview with Jamaica Kincaid," *Lambda Book Report,* 6, no. 10 (May 1998): 14.

References:

Opal Palmer Adisa, "Island Daughter," *Women's Review of Books,* 8 (February 1991): 5–6;

Louis F. Caton, "Romantic Struggles: The Bildungsroman and Mother-Daughter Bonding in Jamaica Kincaid's *Annie John,*" *MELUS: The Journal-of-the-Society-for-the-Study-of-the-Multi-Ethnic-Literature-of-the-United-States,* 21 (Fall 1996): 125–142;

Rhonda Cobham, "Dr. Freud for Visitor?" *Women's Review of Books,* 8 (February 1991): 31–32;

Giovanna Covi, "Jamaica Kincaid and the Resistance to Canons," in *Out of the Kumbla: Caribbean Women and Literature,* edited by Carole Boyce Davies and Elaine Savory Fido (Trenton, N. J.: Africa World Press, 1990), pp. 345–354;

Covi, "Jamaica Kincaid's Political Place: A Review Essay," *Caribana,* 1 (1990): 93–103;

Alison Donnell, "Dreaming of Daffodils: Cultural Resistance in the Narratives of Theory," *Kunapipi*, 14, no. 2 (1992): 45–52;

Donnell, "When Daughters Defy: Jamaica Kincaid's Fiction," *Women*, 4 (Spring 1993): 18–26;

Wendy Dutton, "Merge and Separate: Jamaica Kincaid's Fiction," *World Literature Today*, 63 (Summer 1989): 406–410;

Moira Ferguson, *Jamaica Kincaid: Where the Land Meets the Body* (Charlottesville: University Press of Virginia, 1994);

Ferguson, "Lucy and the Mark of the Colonizer," *Modern Fiction Studies*, 29 (Summer 1993): 237–259;

Ferguson, "A Small Place: Glossing Annie John's Rebellion," in her *Colonialism and Gender Relations from Mary Wollstonecraft to Jamaica Kincaid: East Caribbean Connections* (New York: Columbia University Press, 1993), pp. 116–138;

Marianne Hirsch, "Resisting Images: Rereading Adolescence," in *Provoking Agents: Gender and Agency in Theory and Practice*, edited by Judith Kegan Gardiner (Urbana: University of Illinois Press, 1995), pp. 249–279;

Patricia Ismond, "Jamaica Kincaid: 'First They Must Be Children,'" *World Literature Written in English*, 28 (Autumn 1988): 336–341;

Louis James, "Reflections, and the Bottom of the River: The Transformation of Caribbean Experience in the Fiction of Jamaica Kincaid," *Wasafiri*, 9 (Winter 1988/1989): 15–17;

Bénédicte Ledent, "Voyages into Otherness: Cambridge and Lucy," *Kunapipi*, 14, no. 2 (1992): 53–63;

Maria Helena Lima, "Decolonizing Genre: Jamaica Kincaid and the Bildungsroman," *Genre*, 25 (Summer 1993): 1–27;

Kristen Mahlis, "Gender and Exile: Jamaica Kincaid's *Lucy*," *Modern Fiction Studies*, 44, no. 1 (1998): 164–183;

H. Adlai Murdoch, "Severing the (M)Other Connection: The Representation of Cultural Identity in Jamaica Kincaid's *Annie John*," *Callaloo*, 13 (Spring 1990): 325–340;

Murdoch, "The Novels of Jamaica Kincaid: Figures of Exile, Narratives of Dreams," *Clockwatch Review: A Journal of the Arts*, 9, nos. 1–2 (1994–1995): 141–154;

Roni Natov, "Mothers and Daughters: Jamaica Kincaid's Pre-Oedipal Narrative," *Children's Literature*, 18 (1990): 1–16;

Laura Niesen de Abruña, "Family Connections: Mother and Mother Country in the Fiction of Jean Rhys and Jamaica Kincaid," in *Motherlands: Black Women's Writing from Africa, the Caribbean and South Asia*, edited by Susheila Nasta (New Brunswick, N. J.: Rutgers University Press, 1991), pp. 257–289;

Niesen de Abruña, "Twentieth-Century Women Writers from the English-Speaking Caribbean," *Modern Fiction Studies*, 34 (Spring 1988): 85–96;

Donna Perry, "Initiation in Jamaica Kincaid's *Annie John*," in *Caribbean Women Writers: Essays from the First International Conference*, edited by Selwyn Cudjoe (Wellesley, Mass.: Calaloux, 1990), pp. 245–253;

Bruce Robbins, "Upward Mobility in the Postcolonial Era: Kincaid, Mukherjee and the Cosmopolitan Au Pair," *Modernism/Modernity*, 1 (April 1994): 133–151;

Muriel Lynn Rubin, "Adolescence and Autobiographical Fiction: Teaching *Annie John*, by Jamaica Kincaid," *Wasafiri*, 8 (Spring 1988): 11–14;

Diane Simmons, *Jamaica Kincaid* (New York: Twayne, 1994);

Simmons, "The Mother Mirror in Jamaica Kincaid's *Annie John* and Gertrude Stein's *The Good Anna*," in *The Anna Book: Searching for Anna in Literary History*, edited by Mickey Pearlman (Westport, Conn.: Greenwood Press, 1992), pp. 99–104;

Simmons, "The Rhythm of Reality in the Works of Jamaica Kincaid," *World Literature Today*, 3 (Summer 1994): 466–472;

Craig Tapping, "Children and History in the Caribbean Novel: George Lamming's *In the Castle of My Skin* and Jamaica Kincaid's *Annie John*," *Kunapipi*, 11, no. 2 (1989): 51–59;

Helen Tiffin, "Cold Hearts and (Foreign) Tongues: Recitation and the Reclamation of the Female Body in the Works of Erna Brodber and Jamaica Kincaid," *Callaloo*, 16 (Fall 1993): 909–921;

Tiffin, "Decolonization and Audience: Erna Brodber's *Myal* and Jamaica Kincaid's *A Small Place*," *Span*, 30 (April 1990): 27–38;

Helen Pyne Timothy, "Adolescent Rebellion and Gender Relations in *At the Bottom of the River* and *Annie John*," in *Caribbean Women Writers: Essays from the First International Conference*, edited by Cudjoe (Wellesley, Mass.: Calaloux, 1990), pp. 233–242;

Eleanor Ty, "Struggling with the Powerful (M)Other: Identity and Sexuality in Kogawa's *Obasan* and Kincaid's *Lucy*," *International Fiction Review*, 20, no. 2 (1993): 120–126.

Barbara Kingsolver

Gioia Woods
University of Nevada, Reno

BIRTH: Annapolis, Maryland, 8 April 1955, to Wendell Roy and Virginia Lee Henry Kingsolver.

EDUCATION: B.A. (magna cum laude), DePauw University, 1977; M.S., University of Arizona, 1981; additional graduate study.

MARRIAGES: 15 April 1985 to Joseph Hoffmann (divorced 1992); child: Camille. 30 December 1994 to Steven Hopp; child: Lily.

AWARDS AND HONORS: Feature-writing award, Arizona Press Club, 1985; Enoch Pratt Library Youth-to-Youth Books Award for *The Bean Trees,* 1988; American Library Association awards for *The Bean Trees,* 1988, and for *Homeland,* 1990; citation of accomplishment from United Nations National Council of Women of the United States, 1989; Pen/USA West Fiction Award, Edward Abbey Award for Ecofiction, and the Arizona Library Association Book of the Year award, all for *Animal Dreams,* 1991; Woodrow Wilson Foundation/Lila Wallace Fellowship, 1992; *Los Angeles Times* Fiction Prize, Mountains and Plains Booksellers Award for fiction, and Cowboy Hall of Fame Western Fiction Award, all for *Pigs in Heaven,* 1993; honorary Ph.D., DePauw University, 1995.

BOOKS: *The Bean Trees: A Novel* (New York: Harper & Row, 1988; London: Virago, 1989);
Holding the Line: Women in the Great Arizona Mine Strike of 1983 (Ithaca, N.Y.: ILR Press/New York State School of Industrial and Labor Relations, Cornell University, 1989; revised, 1996);
Homeland and Other Stories (New York: Harper & Row, 1989; London: Virago, 1990);
Animal Dreams: A Novel (New York: HarperCollins, 1990; London: Abacus, 1992);
Another America/Otra América, with Spanish translations by Rebeca Cartes (Seattle: Seal Press, 1992; expanded edition, Seattle: Seal Press, 1998);

Barbara Kingsolver (photograph by Steven Hopp)

Pigs in Heaven: A Novel (New York: HarperCollins, 1993; London: Faber & Faber, 1994);
High Tide in Tucson: Essays from Now or Never (New York: HarperCollins, 1995; London: Faber & Faber, 1996);
The Poisonwood Bible: A Novel (New York: HarperCollins, 1998; London: Faber & Faber, 1999).

OTHER: "Cabbages and Kings," in *Women Respond to the Men's Movement: A Feminist Collection,* edited by Kay Leigh Hagan (San Francisco, Cal.: HarperSanFrancisco, 1992), pp. 39–41;
"The Memory Place," in *Heart of the Land: Essays on Last Great Places,* edited by Joseph Barbato and

Lisa Weinerman (New York: Pantheon, 1994), pp. 281–289;

"Saying Adios to Ed," in *Resist Much, Obey Little: Remembering Ed Abbey,* edited by James R. Hepworth and Gregory McNamee (San Francisco: Sierra Club Books, 1996), pp. 232–233;

"Going to Japan," in *Journeys,* PEN-Faulkner Foundation (Rockville, Md.: Quill & Brush, 1996);

"Dear Mom," in *I've Always Meant to Tell You: Letters to Our Mothers,* edited by Constance Warloe (New York: Pocket Books, 1997), pp. 248–261;

"Knowing Our Place," in *Off the Beaten Path: Stories of Place,* edited by Barbato and Lisa W. Horak (New York: North Point Press, 1998), pp. 7–20.

SELECTED PERIODICAL PUBLICATIONS–
UNCOLLECTED:
FICTION
"Fault Lines," *Frontiers: A Journal of Women Studies,* 12 (Winter 1992): 182–189;

"Secret Animals," *Turnstile,* 3, no. 2 (1992): 11–22.
NONFICTION
"Tucson Residents Fight Atomic Poisoning," *The Militant,* 13 July 1979;

"World of Foes," review of *Endless Enemies: The Making of An Unfriendly World* by Jonathan Kwitny, *Progressive* (December 1984): 44–45;

"Everywoman's Answer to Octopussy: The Modern Romance," *Tucson Weekly,* 21–27 August 1985, pp. 1–5;

"What We Eat and They Don't: The Hunger Connection," *Tucson Weekly,* 9–15 October 1985, p. 2;

"Prison Poets: Dialogue from Behind the Walls," *Tucson Weekly,* 22–28 December 1986, p. 3 (44);

"A Conversation with Milosz," *Tucson Weekly,* 4–10 March 1987, p. 7;

"Albert Uplifts Anything," review of *The Floatplane Notebooks* by Clyde Edgerton, *New York Times Book Review,* 9 October 1989, p. 1;

"Some Can Whistle," review of *Some Can Whistle* by Larry McMurtry, *New York Times Book Review,* 22 October 1989, p. 1;

"Where Love Is Nurtured and Confined," review of *Me and My Baby View the Eclipse* by Lee Smith, *Los Angeles Times Book Review,* 18 February 1990, pp. 2, 9;

"Notes From Underground," review of *Where the Sun Never Shines: A History of America's Bloody Coal Industry,* by Priscilla Long, *Women's Review of Books,* 7 (June 1990): 21–22;

"Worlds in Collision," review of *Mean Spirit* by Linda Hogan, *Los Angeles Times Book Review,* 4 November 1990, p. 3;

"What Happens When Justice Turns a Blind Eye," *Newsday,* 25 October 1992;

"Between the Covers," review of *A Widow for One Year* by John Irving, *Washington Post,* 24 May 1998, sec. 10, p. 1.

Barbara Kingsolver renews the Western literary landscape by debunking the myths of individuality and self-determination. Her heroines lead meaningful lives by relying on compromise and community. Kingsolver's work reflects the real West in which she lives–a West populated by people with different values, histories, and worldviews. Her devotion to social justice and her commitment to activism shape her vision. As she writes in *High Tide in Tucson: Essays from Now or Never* (1995), "Good art is political, whether it means to be or not, insofar as it provides the chance to understand points of view alien to our own." Single mothers, Guatemalan refugees, children, even a hermit crab, are among the points of view Kingsolver presents to her readers. She has enjoyed both critical acclaim and wide readership, and has been nominated three times for the ABBY (American Booksellers Book of the Year) award by booksellers who said her books were among their favorites to sell. She is a writer of fiction, poetry, and nonfiction, but as she told interviewer Donna Perry, if she had to categorize herself by genre, she would pick storytelling.

Barbara Ellen Kingsolver grew up in rural Carlisle, Kentucky, and counts Southern writers such as Flannery O'Connor, Eudora Welty, and William Faulkner among her earliest literary influences. Born on 8 April 1955 in Annapolis, Maryland, she is the daughter of a county physician. Her youth was spent immersed in both the storytelling culture of Appalachia and the scientific culture of her father's profession. When she was in the second grade, she moved to Africa with her family, where her father worked for almost a year as a physician in the Congo. In Africa she began her lifelong habit of keeping a journal. "What I feel," Kingsolver told interviewer L. Elisabeth Beattie, "is that writing is the thing that makes my experience real to me." In 1982, twenty years after beginning her first journal, Kingsolver finally wrote there, "I am a writer." Wendell Roy and Virginia Lee Henry Kingsolver, her parents, instilled in Barbara and her siblings, Rob and Ann, a love for reading and a respect for the natural world. Biochemistry, Kingsolver insists, can be as poetic as Shakespeare. In high-school English classes, however, Kingsolver learned that lit-

Dust jacket for Kingsolver's first novel (1988), in which the characters find strength in the community they create

DePauw briefly, graduated magna cum laude in 1977, and then returned to France, where she lived until her work visa expired. During those and the following years she earned her living variously as a copy editor, typesetter, biological researcher, and translator.

When Kingsolver returned to the United States she settled in Tucson, Arizona. In 1981 she earned a master's degree in ecology and evolutionary biology from the University of Arizona. She also became active in ecological and humanitarian causes, including the Sanctuary movement to assist Central American refugees. In her early twenties Kingsolver met Joseph Hoffmann, a chemist, to whom she was married from 1985 until 1992. Together they had one child, Camille. Kingsolver sought a Ph.D. in evolutionary biology, but left academia in favor of a scientific writing position with the Office of Arid Lands Studies at the University of Arizona.

Getting paid to be a writer gave her the confidence to begin freelancing, at first for local newspapers and magazines and then for such national publications as *The Nation, The Progressive, The New York Times,* and *Smithsonian.* Through her writing Kingsolver was able to bring together her love of science and her love of the humanities. She continued her journal writing and produced "lots and lots" of poetry. In 1981, to her astonishment, she won a poetry contest sponsored by the University of Arizona and gave her first public reading. In 1983 *Virginia Quarterly Review* accepted her first "decent" fiction, a short story called "Rose-Johnny" (later collected in *Homeland and Other Stories,* 1989).

"By the early eighties," Kingsolver told Beattie, "I was starting to find my vein, pay attention to where I'd come from and listen to the voices that were really in my ear, and write things that had a little bit of emotional resonance." Major influences on her writing include her rural childhood with its exposure to storytelling, community, and social responsibility; her love and respect for the natural world; and her scientific background. Her work is deeply rooted in a sense of place, whether she is depicting rural Kentucky, the Belgian Congo, or the arid Southwest where she lives with her husband, ornithologist and musician Steven Hopp, and her daughters, Camille and Lily.

While pregnant with Camille, Kingsolver suffered from insomnia, and as a result began writing a novel. She worked exclusively at night, in the closet of her tiny one-room cottage, so as not to disturb her sleeping husband. Her doctor suggested she do something hateful such as scrubbing her bathroom tile, so as not to reward her sleeplessness—but in-

erature was about great men fighting great conflicts: man against nature, man against man, man against God. Not until 1982, when Kingsolver read *Shiloh and Other Stories,* published that year by Bobbie Ann Mason, did she realize that everyday people like the rural folk she grew up with were worthy subjects of serious literature.

Although she was a prolific writer in her youth, Kingsolver told David King Dunaway that "it never crossed my mind that I'd be a writer when I grew up because I really didn't think of writing as a profession. I didn't think of books as having been written by people like me." She did, however, consider a career as a classical pianist, a result of a youth spent virtually without television and with parents who had wide-ranging musical tastes. Kingsolver went to DePauw University in Indiana on a music scholarship, but after realizing how scarce jobs were for pianists, she switched her major to something more practical—biology.

During her junior year of college, Kingsolver left Indiana to live and work in Greece and France as an archaeologist's assistant. She returned to

stead she stayed awake crafting *The Bean Trees* (1988). Within twenty-four hours of delivering her daughter she had a book deal with Harper and Row.

Kingsolver's first novel was highly acclaimed. Jack Butler wrote for *The New York Times Book Review* (10 April 1988) that "*The Bean Trees* is as richly connected as a fine poem, but reads like realism . . . it is the Southern novel taken west." Like many stories in the Western American literary canon, *The Bean Trees* is a narrative of self-renewal brought about by a journey west. Self-named protagonist Taylor Greer leaves her Kentucky home in search of a new identity and an escape from what she sees as the inevitable future for a Pittman County girl: early pregnancy and marriage. Unlike the traditional Western hero, however, what Taylor finds is not independence, but dependence; not self-determination, but strength in community.

Kingsolver's debt in *The Bean Trees* to Doris Lessing and other women writers for whom friendship and connectedness are central narrative goals is obvious. Taylor builds a family from unlikely sources. Having been reminded by her mother of the Greer family's Cherokee heritage, her "ace in the hole," Taylor decides to explore the Cherokee nation. Stopping at a roadside cafe, she is given an unlikely gift: a Native American child who she later finds out has been sexually abused. Having no choice, Taylor drives westward with Turtle—so named because of her fierce grip.

Throughout *The Bean Trees,* Kingsolver works for both accessibility and complexity. Her imagery is obvious but rarely heavy-handed. Taylor and Turtle arrive in Arizona at sunrise on the second day of the new year. Once in Tucson, they meet Mattie, the owner of Jesus is Lord Used Tires, an auto shop that serves as a sanctuary for Central American refugees. Taylor's makeshift family grows to include her elderly neighbors, Edna and Virgie Mae; Lou Ann, a fellow single mother from Kentucky; and Esperanza and Estevan, refugees fleeing their native Guatemala. The characters, according to Karen Fitzgerald in *Ms.* (April 1988), "tug at the heart and soul. It is the growing strength of their relationships . . . that give the novel energy and appeal."

Kingsolver's characters are the working-class poor because those are the people she knows and cares about. Although her father was an educated physician, he chose to focus on healing rather than making money. As a result, many of his patients paid him with vegetables from their garden—or not at all. Kingsolver grew up among people like Taylor, who had limited opportunities beyond high

school. Being true to Taylor's voice, Kingsolver admitted to Perry, was often difficult; she found it challenging "to describe scenery that Taylor had never seen before or thoughts that Taylor maybe never thought before from that small vocabulary."

A mark of Western writers is an attentiveness to the natural world, and Kingsolver is no exception. Her favorite reading material, she declared to Beattie, is the Burpee's Seed Catalog. The predictability, the "life force," and the "living story" of the natural world is comforting to Kingsolver and to many of her characters, including Taylor and Turtle. It deeply affects the human community of *The Bean Trees.* The novel is named not only for Turtle's first word, "bean," but also for the model of community Taylor learns from the natural world. While reading to Turtle from the *Horticultural Encyclopedia,* Taylor uncovers the central metaphor of the novel:

> wisteria vines, like other legumes, often thrive in poor soil, the book said. Their secret is something called rhizobia. These are microscopic bugs that live underground in little knots on the roots. They suck nitrogen gas right out of the soil and turn it into fertilizer for the plant. "It's like this," I told Turtle. "There's a whole system for helping out the plant that you'd never guess was there." I loved this idea. "It's the same as with people. The way Edna has Virgie, and Virgie has Edna . . . and everybody has Mattie. . . . "
>
> The wisteria vines on their own would barely get by, is how I explained it to Turtle, but put them together with rhizobia and they make miracles.

As an ecologist, environmentalist, and humanist, Kingsolver constructs a world where human and nonhuman nature coexist. Behind Jesus is Lord Used Tires, for example, Mattie nurtures a "wild wonderland of flowers and vegetables and auto parts. Heads of cabbage and lettuce sprouted out of old tires. An entire rusted-out Thunderbird, minus the wheels, had nasturtiums blooming out the windows."

Kingsolver calls herself a feminist and writes "from a point of view that's unequivocally female." The majority of her characters in *The Bean Trees* and subsequent novels are women. Kingsolver's female characters perform mundane yet heroic deeds: they feed children, support friends, and restore justice, all foundational acts that sustain community.

In her next book, *Holding the Line: Women in the Great Arizona Mine Strike of 1983* (1989), Kingsolver further characterizes the ways that women create and sustain community. As a stringer for several newspapers in the early 1980s, Kingsolver covered the devastating eighteen-month strikes in three southern Arizona Phelps Dodge mining com-

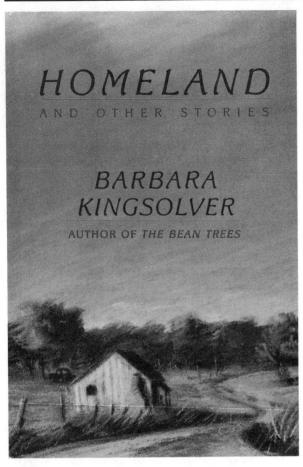

Dust jacket for Kingsolver's 1989 collection of stories that examine the significance of place and the concept of home

munities. Realizing she had hundreds of hours of taped oral history from a community rarely—if ever—documented, she decided to assemble a book.

Kingsolver had not yet written *The Bean Trees* and was a newcomer to the publishing business. She went to the library, looked through the *Literary Market Place,* and found the name of her future agent. Kingsolver revealed in her interview with Beattie what drew her attention to the listing for Frances Goldin: "She was independent. What she said about herself was, 'I do not represent any material that is sexist, racist, ageist, homophobic, or gratuitously violent.'" In 1984 Kingsolver sent Goldin a book proposal for *Holding the Line.* Because she was still working as a journalist, Kingsolver had little time to transcribe the tapes and assemble the book. After writing *The Bean Trees* during her insomnia-stricken pregnancy, Kingsolver wrote Goldin once again, asking her to take a look at that manuscript, which she thought might be a novel; Goldin agreed. In 1988, with the publication of *The Bean Trees,* Kingsolver achieved the financial security to give up freelancing and finish *Holding the Line.*

The book is both an ethnographic account of a crucial moment in labor history and a story of personal feminist transformation. In 1983 Phelps Dodge rejected a pattern settlement, provoking a confrontation with members of a dozen different miners' unions and their families. Union workers managed to shut down mining operations, but the confrontation accelerated and Phelps Dodge reopened with the help of the National Guard. A court injunction prohibited miners from striking, and wives, mothers, and daughters established an all-female picket line. Women who previously would not leave the house without their husbands' permission became vocal activists in order to save their communities. As one housewife-turned-activist reflected, "It's astonishing even to me how we women have changed. . . . I never felt like I had anything to say worth listening to. . . . It's the politicization of the community that's made everything so worthwhile."

Holding the Line thus documents what much of Kingsolver's fiction and poetry addresses: the process of recognizing the self as part of something larger. The book raises questions of economic decline, gender relationships, and corporate discrimination against Mexican Americans. Kingsolver again turns to the lives of the working class to find important material for literature. Reviews of *Holding the Line* were mixed. A 1991 critique in the *Industrial and Labor Relations Review* praises the book as a "stirring, densely documented narrative that works both as drama and social history" and recommends it for undergraduate classes focusing on labor history, women's history, or minority rights. In *The New York Times Book Review* (7 January 1990), Page Stegner, Wallace Stegner's son, faults the book for ignoring the existence of the male characters surely present during the copper strike. The narrative is compelling, he wrote, but would be more so if the women's political development were contrasted with the men's. To Perry, Kingsolver defended her narrative point of view: "I hope that people are beyond worrying that a book has to be about men to be important."

Kingsolver became closely involved with the women in the striking towns, and admits sympathy with the strikers' cause. In the preface to *Holding the Line,* she denies the possibility of objectivity, the "myth of journalism," and insists that every writer throws "his or her own shadow across the page." Hidden biases, she writes, are more dangerous than obvious ones.

The same year that *Holding the Line* appeared, Kingsolver published her first collection of short stories, *Homeland and Other Stories* (1989). Five of the stories in the collection had previously been published: two in women's magazines; two in regional magazines; and one, "Rose-Johnny," in the *Virginia Quarterly Review* and subsequently in *New Stories from the South: The Year's Best, 1988.*

Taylor Greer from *The Bean Trees* wanted to tell every story in *Homeland,* Kingsolver declared in her interview with Perry. "She had such a strong voice," Kingsolver added, "because she talks a lot like me and the people I grew up with . . . so I deliberately put her in the closet, and I moved out." This move not only anticipates *Pigs in Heaven* (1993), the sequel to *The Bean Trees,* but also allows *Homeland* to offer a variety of points of view. A middle-class male biology teacher, a working-class mom, and a Chicana striker (whose character reads like a composite of the many women Kingsolver met while researching *Holding the Line*), all narrate stories about one of the central themes in Western American literature: the tension between migration and home.

In the title story, lauded by reviewers as the strongest of the collection, Gloria St. Clair tells how she and her coal-miner father, mother, and two brothers take Great Mam, their Cherokee great-grandmother, to visit her birthplace before she dies. The family arrives in Cherokee, Tennessee, only to find it has become a tourist trap with "pictures of cartoon Indian boys urging us to buy souvenirs." Gloria begins to understand the moral complexity inherent in history: "I had a sense of something gone badly wrong, like a lie told in my past and then forgotten." Before a depressing picnic and a long drive home, Great Mam tells her great-granddaughter, "I've never been here before." The story depicts the destruction of a people's past, but manages to end hopefully by suggesting continuance of culture through story. Great Mam tells Gloria how Cherokees viewed the world before Anglo colonization, and Gloria tells her reader. "Homeland," a story Kingsolver rewrote every year for fifteen years, explicitly represents her reasons for being a writer: "I hope that story tells the burden and the joy and the responsibility of holding on to the voices that are getting lost."

Kingsolver's training in biology and fascination with the natural world are obvious in the character development and imagery throughout *Homeland.* In "Blueprints" (first published as "The Lost Language of Love" in *Mademoiselle,* May 1989), Lydia, a junior-high-school teacher who is struggling to maintain a relationship with her live-in lover, is deeply aware of her kinship with nonhuman nature: "She leaves town and walks through the hemlock forest, content to be among the mosses and bee-

tles. . . . The bugs, and the plants too, are all related to her in a complicated family tree that Lydia can describe in convincing detail." Another story, "Covered Bridges," is narrated by a middle-aged gardener and professor of botany whose wife is severely allergic to bee stings. Like many other narrators in *Homeland,* the gardener constantly muses on his relationship to place and the natural world. He questions, for example, "the fleeting certainty that I deserved the space I'd been taking up on this earth, and all the air that I breathed."

The central questions in *Homeland,* concerning how people are bound to each other and to place, anticipate Kingsolver's second novel, *Animal Dreams* (1990). Kingsolver told Beattie that she begins every novel with an important question, and writes her way toward a resolution. The question that led to the creation of *Animal Dreams,* according to Kingsolver, was,

> Why is it that some people are activists who embrace the world and its problems . . . while other people turn their back on that same world and pretend that it has no bearing on their lives? Why is it, moreover, that these two kinds of people can occur in the same family?

Animal Dreams also grows out of Kingsolver's conviction that the personal is political and that her job as a writer of fiction is, simply put, to change the world.

The characters in *Animal Dreams,* like those from Kingsolver's earlier fiction, are people who have been traditionally considered "marginal" in canonical literature. Codi and Hallie are sisters who grew up in Grace, Arizona, surrounded by a vibrant Mexican-American culture but never quite fitting in. Both sisters are deeply connected to the natural world:

> Hallie and I . . . divided the world in half, right from childhood. I was the one who went in for the instant gratification, catching bright, quick butterflies, chloroforming them in a Mason jar and pinning them onto typewritten tags with their Latin names. Hallie's tastes were quieter; she had time to watch things grow. She transplanted wildflowers and showed an aptitude for gardening. At age ten she took over the responsibility of the Burpee's catalogue.

For her part, Hallie, a pest-control hotline operator and gifted gardener, goes to Nicaragua to aid farmers. Codi unwillingly returns to Grace to take care of their father, town physician Homer Noline, who has been diagnosed with Alzheimer's disease.

The narrative develops in a nonlinear fashion, blending memories, dreams, letters, and present

Dust jacket for the 1993 sequel to The Bean Trees, *exploring the issue of white adoption of Native American children*

events. *Animal Dreams* is a complex, postmodern story that explores the relationships among memory, truth, and experience. Like Leslie Marmon Silko, Kingsolver relies on the power of stories to effect change. Events in the novel are interpreted and given importance in a variety of ways by different characters. Grace, a fictional town that resembles Clifton, one of the sites of the Phelps Dodge copper strikes that Kingsolver knew well, suffers from environmental degradation as a result of mine tailings. Orchards suffer from fruit drop; and Grace's river, as Codi discovers with her high-school science class, has a pH that "came in just a hair higher than battery acid." A familiar concern of Kingsolver's unfolds as the narrative develops: Codi begins to recognize herself as a part of the larger forces of family, community, and finally, a political universe where

atrocities in Nicaragua affect people living in Grace. Codi, with the help of a group of women who call themselves the Stitch and Bitch Club, networks to save Grace and becomes the kind of practical hero Kingsolver is known for creating.

In *Animal Dreams,* Kingsolver refuses to settle for one point of view or one dominant ideology. She interweaves contemporary and traditional Mexican American worldviews throughout the novel. Day of the Dead is celebrated by the oldest members of the Stitch and Bitch Club and the youngest child of Emelina, Codi's high-school friend and new neighbor. Kingsolver's admiration for Pueblo culture is clear in the character of Loyd, a railroad man Codi dated in high school. Loyd fosters Codi's newfound ecological awareness by introducing her to Pueblo customs.

Indeed, ecology both spiritually and intellectually informs Kingsolver's own worldview. In order to research *Animal Dreams,* Kingsolver read doctoral dissertations on kinship relations and visited a pueblo to further her knowledge of traditional Keresan cultural myths. Aspects of many native cultures, she believes, can remind Anglo-Americans of kinship with the natural world. Her training as a biologist further solidifies her sense of the interdependence of all creatures.

Animal Dreams, like *The Bean Trees* and *Pigs in Heaven,* is a deeply political novel. Kingsolver does not "inject" politics into her storytelling; she writes from what she perceives to be her place in a world of injustice. She rejects the idea that language can be separated from the political. Class, race, and gender discrimination, environmental degradation, and political inequities are realities that cannot be ignored. In an interview with Robert Epstein, Kingsolver mused that critics and other literary gatekeepers may reject her novels because they are "too political," but only one letter out of one hundred Kingsolver receives from readers complains about the political nature of her art.

Animal Dreams won many accolades: the Pen/USA West Fiction Award, the Edward Abbey Award for Ecofiction, and the Arizona Library Association Book of the Year award. Novelist Jane Smiley, reviewing *Animal Dreams* for *The New York Times Book Review* (2 September 1990), notes the complexity involved in weaving together various points of view, but ultimately praises *Animal Dreams* and its author. She writes: "Barbara Kingsolver is one of an increasing number of American novelists who are trying to rewrite the political, cultural and spiritual relationships between our country's private and public spheres."

The same can be said of Kingsolver's book of poetry, *Another America/Otra América* (1992), a conversation between North and South America. Many of the poems reflect ways in which the two continents view each other. Chilean poet Rebeca Cartes, whom Kingsolver met through joint readings and Sanctuary fund-raisers, translated Kingsolver's poems into Spanish. Each of the poems in the volume is a story; each poem critiques a social ill to which Kingsolver is exposed. The "little steam vents of the pressure cooker," as Kingsolver calls her poetry, deal with homophobia, racism, colonialism, and sexism. The poetry in this volume revolves around a favorite theme of Kingsolver's: the American cultural myth of individuality.

The book begins with a series of poems about alienation and ends with a section on political activists who have reclaimed their world. Two poems,

"This House I Cannot Leave," and "Ten Forty-Four," deal with rape. Often the American cultural attitude is that victims deserve their fate. As Kingsolver explained to Perry, in these two poems she chose to go public with a personal trauma in order to "serve people whose pain is still in the closet and who need the support of community."

While themes of conversation and conflict are evident in many of these poems, they are most fully developed in *Pigs in Heaven,* the sequel to *The Bean Trees.* The pigs in the title, as Cherokee lawyer Annawake Fourkiller tells Taylor Greer's musician boyfriend Jax, refer to a myth of six boys who refused to do their work. The pigs became the constellation known by many Westerners as the Pleiades. The message is to put community first. The myth makes concrete the American conflict that is central to the novel: the rights of the individual versus the needs of the community.

The community in question is the Cherokee Nation, and the individual is Taylor Greer. Taylor and Turtle become heroes after witnessing and saving a man who fell into a spillway at Hoover Dam. Together they appear on *The Oprah Winfrey Show.* Taylor tells Oprah's extensive audience, which includes Annawake, how she found and adopted an abandoned and sexually abused Turtle in Oklahoma. Annawake, disturbed by the events that led to the adoption of her twin, Gabriel, into a white family, and supported by the 1978 Indian Child Welfare Act, begins to investigate Taylor's story. The Indian Child Welfare Act, Annawake tells Taylor in Taylor's run-down but comfortable Tucson home, gives tribes the final say over their children's custody. Taylor asks Annawake how returning Turtle to the Cherokee tribe would be in the child's best interest. "How can you think it's good for a tribe to lose its children?" Annawake counterpoises, adding, "There's the child's best interests and the tribe's best interest, and I'm trying to think of both things."

Pigs in Heaven, like *The Bean Trees,* is punctuated by a road trip. Taylor and Turtle flee Tucson, and Taylor works a series of odd jobs before realizing the difficulty of motherhood without community support. She also comes to recognize the importance of Turtle's Cherokee heritage. The conflict between the individual and the community is resolved by a joint custody arrangement—a resolution that caused some controversy among reviewers of the novel. Some critics appreciated Kingsolver's clear vision, while others felt the author relied on a pat formula of sentimental political correctness. Nearly all agree, however, on Kingsolver's continuing commitment to the political issues familiar to many of her readers. *Pigs in Heaven* is about the difficulty of

Well, but I can also get nostalgic for the childhood of Laura
Ingalls Wilder, until it dawns on me that not once, in any of those
Little House books, does she discuss the real meaning of life without
plumbing on howling cold prairie nights. Every epoch has its ~~ups and~~ gains and
~~downs,~~ and there's no point **in** wishing my own were any different. The
lot I drew in history was to belong **to** the generation of women groomed
implicitly for wifehood, but who have ended up needing to win their
bread rather **than** bake it. I've always been happy enough to do it,
though now that I'm also ~~sole (sup porter) supporter[A01] of my child,~~ supporting a child on my own, I
occasionally wake up at night in a cold sweat on account of it; no
part of my upbringing ever prepared me to hold this ~~position~~ place at the head of the table. But it's
a blessing, I think, to my girl, who is growing up convinced that
women belong in the halls of discovery, production, and creation--
messy enterprises~~(,)~~ all. It wouldn't even occur to her to doubt it.
We've spent far more time together making kites and forts and
scientifically mounted bug collections than working on hospital
corners, and if her bed doesn't even get made, I'm the last to notice.
Sluthood has its privileges, for children too.

Housework, like the Buddha, takes many forms, depending on what
is in your heart as you approach it. I personally am inclined to
approach it the way governments treat dissent: ignore it until it
revolts. If life were a different house of cards, though, and if

Page from the typescript for one of the pieces in High Tide in Tucson: Essays from Now or Never *(1995), Kingsolver's seventh book (Collection of Barbara Kingsolver)*

single motherhood, the development of community consciousness, adoption, abuse, ethnic identity, and poverty.

Living in the Southwest, Kingsolver became aware of many cases involving the Indian Child Welfare Act. She told Perry that white adoption of Indian children had long been a form of cultural genocide, and that real cases caused her to examine the cultural codes that lead people to value individuality or community. Kingsolver began reading court transcriptions and speculating on the point of intersection between the two worldviews. Although she had previously never considered writing a sequel to *The Bean Trees,* Kingsolver admitted to Perry "that I'd set up a perfect situation in an earlier novel. Also, I realized with embarrassment that I had neglected a whole moral area when I wrote about this Native American kid being swept off the reservation. . . . It was something I hadn't thought about, and I felt I needed to make that right in another book."

Writing *Pigs in Heaven* challenged Kingsolver to mature as a novelist. Unlike *The Bean Trees,* which relies on first-person narration, or *Animal Dreams,* which alternates between first- and third-person-limited points of view, *Pigs in Heaven* is written entirely in the third-person omniscient. By making this choice, Kingsolver gives equal weight to the moral authority of both Taylor and the tribe. Responding to criticism that all her previous characters were good and all her conflicts occur off-stage (Taylor versus poverty, the Stitch and Bitch Club versus the mine company), Kingsolver forced herself to write about characters in conflict, "on the page, not off." She also created Barbie, a former waitress obsessed with the Barbie doll and given to larceny. *Pigs in Heaven,* like *Animal Dreams* and *The Bean Trees,* was an ABBY nominee. Kingsolver's third novel also won the *Los Angeles Times* Fiction Prize and the Cowboy Hall of Fame Western Fiction Award.

Following *Pigs in Heaven,* Kingsolver published *High Tide in Tucson* in 1995. She calls the collection of twenty-five essays "creative nonfiction," and likens its writing process to that of fiction. "You create characters and you have a plot," Kingsolver explained to Epstein, adding, "All of the essays are little stories that mean something. . . . You can look at the same event fifty different ways."

Thematically, *High Tide in Tucson* extends Kingsolver's interests in family, community, and the environment. In the title essay, Kingsolver observes how a hermit crab in her Tucson kitchen responds to a far-off tidal cycle. She uses the event to explore the meaning of home and mobility, and the ecological place of the human animal. The essays

are autobiographical and take as their subjects book tours; childhood; patriotism; life in the Canary Islands; Kingsolver's love of books; her critique of such writers as Henry David Thoreau, Stephen Gould, and Charles Darwin; and her stint as keyboard player in the band Rock Bottom Remainders, which also featured novelists Stephen King and Amy Tan.

Many of the essays were previously published in an eclectic array of magazines, including *Parenting, Natural History, Smithsonian Magazine, The New York Times Magazine,* and the *Lands' End* catalog. Kingsolver collected and revised the essays in order to move from behind the mask of fiction, as she told Epstein: "Everything in *High Tide in Tucson* I think I've said before . . . but this time I stepped out from behind the mask and said, 'I, Barbara Kingsolver, believe this.'" As in her fiction and poetry, her background as social activist directly influences the essays. For example, "Jabberwocky" describes Kingsolver's political point of view in art and life. While Kingsolver was protesting the Gulf War in front of the Tucson Federal Building, a man leaned out of his truck and shouted "Hey, bitch, love it or leave it!" at her. "So," Kingsolver quips, "I left."

Kingsolver's technique is recognizable in terms of the traditional essay. She uses mundane events as vehicles for deeper musings on life. In "Jabberwocky" she manipulates a stranger's insult to respond to the occasional criticism that her work is "too political," while disparaging the dominant view of the role of art in American culture:

> Real art, the story goes, does not endorse a point of view. This is utter nonsense, of course . . . and also the most thorough and invisible form of censorship I've ever encountered. . . . I spend a good deal of time defending the possibility that such things as environmental ruin, child abuse, or the hypocrisy of U.S. immigration policy are appropriate subjects for a novel.

Kingsolver has worried that perhaps some readers of her fiction miss the political messages inherent in her work. With *High Tide in Tucson* she felt she "had the chance to be more direct."

Kingsolver's commitment to activism for social justice is as apparent as her dedication to the nonhuman natural world. Her training as a scientist allows her not only to turn an informed eye toward the relationship between humans and nature but also to inspire vivid use of natural metaphors. In "Creation Stories," an essay about the sanctity of human, plant, and animal species, she writes of June in Tucson as "the season when every living thing in the desert swoons south toward some faint salt dream of the Gulf of Mexico: tasting the horizon, waiting for the summer storm."

In its first four months, *High Tide in Tucson* sold more than any of Kingsolver's previous books had during the initial months following their publication. To Kingsolver, these figures attesting to the popularity of her work validate her commitment, as a writer, to addressing political issues.

Her devotion to social justice through art continues: another novel, *The Poisonwood Bible,* appeared in the fall of 1998. In this book, zealous, uncompromising Baptist missionary Nathan Price takes his wife, Orleanna, and four daughters to the Belgian Congo in 1959, where they remain through the next three decades of stormy, violent African history. Orleanna and the four girls—teenaged Rachel, twins Leah and Adah, and five-year-old Ruth May—take turns narrating and responding to political developments in the Congo as well as the personal tragedies of the Price family.

The Poisonwood Bible garnered critical praise in advance of its release. A reviewer for *Publishers Weekly* (10 August 1998) stated that in this "risky but resoundingly successful novel," Kingsolver presents "a compelling family saga, a sobering picture of the horrors of fanatic fundamentalism and an insightful view of an exploited country crushed by the heel of colonialism and then ruthlessly manipulated by a bastion of democracy." A critic for *Kirkus Reviews* (1 September 1998) praised the "consistently absorbing narrative" as well as Kingsolver's skillful blending of the personal and the political: "Kingsolver convinces us that her characters are, first and foremost, breathing, fallible human beings and only secondarily conduits for her book's vigorously expressed and argued social and political ideas."

In 1997 Kingsolver established the Bellwether Prize for Fiction, which recognizes literature of social change. Kingsolver hopes to give American trade publishers an incentive to publish and promote the kind of fiction she most admires—fiction that exposes injustice and explores issues of social responsibility.

Interviews:

Donna Perry, "Barbara Kingsolver," in *Backtalk: Women Writers Speak Out,* edited by Perry (New Brunswick, N.J.: Rutgers University Press, 1993), pp. 145–168;

Amy Pence, "An Interview with Barbara Kingsolver," *Poets and Writers,* 21 (July 1993): 14–21;

Robert Epstein, "Barbara Kingsolver," *The Progressive,* 60 (February 1996): 33–38;

L. Elisabeth Beattie, "Barbara Kingsolver," in *Conversations with Kentucky Writers,* edited by Beattie (Lexington: University of Kentucky Press, 1996), pp. 151–171.

References:

Janet Bowdan, "Re-placing Ceremony: The Poetics of Barbara Kingsolver," *Southwestern American Literature,* 20 (Spring 1995): 13–19;

David King Dunaway, "Barbara Kingsolver," in *Writing the Southwest,* edited by Dunaway and Sara L. Spurgeon (New York: Penguin, 1995), pp. 93–107;

Bruce Fleming, "Woolf Cubs: Current Fiction," *Antioch Review,* 52 (Fall 1994): 548–565;

Maureen Ryan, "Barbara Kingsolver's Lowfat Fiction," *Journal of American Culture,* 19 (Winter 1995): 77–82;

Lisa See, "Barbara Kingsolver: Her Fiction Features Ordinary People Heroically Committed to Political Issues," *Publishers Weekly,* 237 (31 August 1990): 46–47.

Maxine Hong Kingston

This entry was updated from the entry by Pin-chia Feng
(National Chiao-Tung University, Taiwan) in
DLB 173: American Novelists Since World War II, Fifth Series.

BIRTH: Stockton, California, 27 October 1940, to Tom and Ying Lan Chew Hong.

EDUCATION: A.B., University of California, Berkeley, 1962; teaching certificate, 1965.

MARRIAGE: 23 November 1962 to Earll Kingston; child: Joseph Lawrence Chung Mei.

AWARDS AND HONORS: National Book Critics Circle General Nonfiction Award for *The Woman Warrior: Memoirs of a Girlhood Among Ghosts,* 1976; *Mademoiselle* Magazine Award, 1977; Anisfield-Wolf Race Relations Award, 1978; *The Woman Warrior* named one of the top ten nonfiction works of the decade by *Time* magazine, 1979; National Education Association writing fellow, 1980; named Living Treasure of Hawaii, 1980; *China Men* named to the American Library Association Notable Books List, 1980; National Endowment for the Arts Writers Award, 1980 and 1982; American Book Award for general nonfiction for *China Men,* 1981; Stockton (Cal.) Arts Commission Award, 1981; Guggenheim Fellowship, 1981; Hawaii Award for Literature, 1982; Hawaii Writers Award, 1983; OPN West Award in Fiction for *Tripmaster Monkey: His Fake Book,* 1989; California Governor's Art Award, 1989; Major Book Collection Award, Brandeis University National Women's Committee, 1990; American Academy and Institute of Arts and Letters, 1990; inducted into the American Academy of Arts and Sciences, 1992; Honorary degrees from Eastern Michigan University, 1988, Colby College, 1990, Brandeis University, 1991, University of Massachusetts, 1991, Starr King School for the Ministry, 1992.

BOOKS: *The Woman Warrior: Memoirs of a Girlhood Among Ghosts* (New York: Knopf, 1976; London: John Lane, 1977);
China Men (New York: Knopf, 1980);
Hawai'i One Summer: 1978 (San Francisco: Meadow Press, 1987);

Maxine Hong Kingston (photograph by Karen Huie)

Through the Black Curtain (Berkeley: Friends of the Bancroft Library, University of California, 1987);
Tripmaster Monkey: His Fake Book (New York: Knopf, 1989).

OTHER: "Cultural Mis-readings by American Reviewers," in *Asian and Western Writers in Dialogue: New Cultural Identities,* edited by Guy Amirthanayagam (London: Macmillan, 1982), pp. 55–56;
"Personal Statement," in *Approaches to Teaching Kingston's* The Woman Warrior, edited by Shirley Geok-lin Lim (New York: Modern Language Association of America, 1991), pp. 23–25.

SELECTED PERIODICAL PUBLICATIONS–
UNCOLLECTED: "Literature for a Scientific Age:
    Lorenz' King Solomon's Ring," *English Jour-
    nal,* 62 (January 1973): 30–32+;
"Duck Boy," *New York Times Magazine,* 12 June 1977,
    pp. 54–58;
"Reservations About China," *Ms.,* 7 (October
    1978): 67–68;
"San Francisco Chinatown: A View from the Other
    Side of Arnold Genthe's Camera," *American
    Heritage,* 30 (December 1978): 35–47;
"Restaurant," and "Absorption of Rock," *Iowa Re-
    view,* 12 (1981): 206–208;
"A Writer's Notebook from the Far East," *Ms.,* 11
    (January 1983): 85–86;
"An Imagined Life," *Michigan Quarterly Review,* 22
    (Fall 1983): 561–570;
"A Chinese Garland," *North American Review,* 273
    (September 1988): 38–42;
"Violence and Non-Violence in China, 1989," *Michi-
    gan Quarterly Review,* 24 (Winter 1990): 62–67;
"The Novel's Next Step," *Mother Jones,* 14 (Decem-
    ber 1989): 37–41.

One of the most outspoken contemporary feminist writers, Maxine Hong Kingston states in her autobiographical book *The Woman Warrior: Memoirs of a Girlhood Among Ghosts* (1976), "The swordswoman and I are not so dissimilar. . . . What we have in common are the words at our backs. The idioms for *revenge* are 'report a crime' and 'report to five families.' The reporting is the vengeance–not the beheading, not the gutting, but the words." With prose that both unsettles Chinese American sexism and American racism, Kingston is a "word warrior" who battles social and racial injustice. It is perhaps surprising that Kingston could not speak English until she started school. Once she had learned it, however, she started to talk stories. Decades later, this once silent and silenced woman is becoming a notable American writer.

Maxine Hong Kingston was born to Chinese immigrant parents, Tom Hong and Ying Lan Chew, in Stockton, California, on 27 October 1940. Her American name, Maxine, was after a blonde who was always lucky in gambling. Ting Ting, her Chinese name, comes from a Chinese poem about self-reliance. The eldest of the six Hong children, Kingston had two older siblings who died in China years before her mother came to the United States. Kingston recalls the early part of her school education as her "silent years" in which she had a terrible time talking. Later Maxine, who flunked kindergarten, became a straight-A student and won a scholarship to the University of California, Berkeley. In 1962 she received her bachelor's degree in English and married Earll Kingston, a Berkeley graduate and an actor. She returned to the university in 1964, earned a teaching certificate in 1965, and taught English and mathematics from 1965 to 1967 in Hayward, California. During their time at Berkeley the Kingstons were involved in the antiwar movement on campus. In 1967 they decided to leave the country because the movement was getting more and more violent, and their friends were too involved in drugs. On their way to Japan the Kingstons stopped in Hawaii, and they stayed there for seventeen years.

At first Kingston taught language arts and English as a second language in a private school. In 1977 she became a visiting professor at the University of Hawaii at Honolulu. A few days after she finished the final revisions of *China Men* (1980), a Honolulu Buddhist sect claimed Kingston as a "Living Treasure of Hawaii." Kingston herself, however, was still looking homeward, having always felt like a stranger in the islands. She and her husband moved back to California while their son, Joseph, stayed in Hawaii and became a musician. In 1992 Kingston became a member of the Academy of Arts and Sciences.

Kingston's writing relies heavily on memory and imagination. "We approach the truth with metaphors," declared Kingston in a 1983 essay, "An Imagined Life." She also told Paula Rabinowitz in a 1987 interview, "The artist's memory winnows out; it edits for what is important and significant. Memory, my own memory, shows me what is unforgettable, and helps me get to an essence that will not die, and that haunts me until I can put it into a form, which is writing." Kingston denies, however, that the use of memory in her writing is simply a form of exorcism, but she insists that it is a way to give substance to the "ghosts," or "visions," in her life. Her writing also denies classification: she is recording the biography of a people's imagination. Her first two books are Kingston's biographies of ancestors whom she has never met and records of things about which she has only heard. Imagination becomes her way to approach these characters and incidents. For instance, she imagines five ways for her father's arrival in America in *China Men*. She is proud of this imaginative feat because by inserting multiple stories into her "biographical" works she is able to transcend generic boundaries and protect the illegal aliens she is writing about at the same time. "To have a right imagination is very powerful," Kingston told Rabinowitz, "because it's a bridge between reality."

The major sources of Kingston's memory and imagination are her mother's stories and her father's silence. Kingston's father, Tom Hong, was a scholar trained in traditional Chinese classics and a teacher in New Society Village before his immigration. In the United States he washed windows until he had saved enough money to start a laundry in New York with three of his friends. Later, Hong was cheated out of his share of the partnership. He moved with his pregnant wife to Stockton and started managing an illegal gambling house for a wealthy Chinese American. A major part of his work, besides taking care of the club, was to be arrested; he was silent about his true name and invented a new name for each arrest. World War II put him out of this cycle of managing and getting arrested because the gambling house was shut down. After a period of unemployment he started his own laundry and a new life for himself and his family in America.

Brave Orchid (or Ying Lan, in Chinese), Kingston's vocal and practical mother, was a doctor who practiced Western medicine and midwifery in China. She did not join her husband in New York until 1940, fifteen years after they had parted. In America, Brave Orchid exchanged her professional status for that of a laundrywoman, cleaning maid, tomato picker, and cannery worker. Undaunted by the difficulties in her life, this "champion talker" educated her children with "talk stories," which included myth, legend, family history, and ghost tales. "Night after night my mother would talk-story until we fell asleep. I could not tell where the stories left off and the dreams began," Kingston recalls in *The Woman Warrior*. Through her talk stories, Brave Orchid extended Chinese tradition into the lives of her American children and enriched their imagination. Yet Kingston is also aware that the mother's talking stories were double-edged: "She said I would grow up a wife and slave, but she taught me the song of the woman warrior, Fa Mu Lan," Kingston recollects in *The Woman Warrior*. While Brave Orchid's storytelling was educational, it also reiterated patriarchal and misogynistic messages of traditional Chinese culture. Moreover, as in traditional Chinese education, Brave Orchid did not explain her stories. Kingston needed to interpret her mother's stories and become a storyteller herself.

Her community also played a decisive role in Kingston's writing. Comparing herself to Toni Morrison and Leslie Silko, Kingston argues that what makes their writings vivid and alive is their connection with community and tribe. Yet Kingston refuses to be "representative" of Chinese Americans. "A Stockton Chinese is not the same as a San Fran-

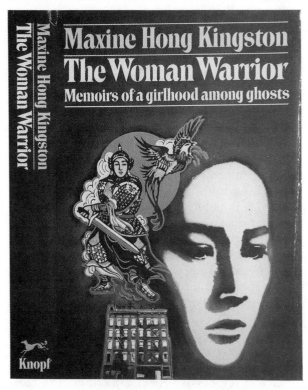

Dust jacket for Kingston's first book, based on her mother's "talk stories" about her family's life in China (courtesy of the Lilly Library, Indiana University)

cisco Chinese," Kingston stated in an interview with Arturo Islas. Unlike "the Big City" (San Francisco) and "the Second City" (Sacramento), Stockton, a city in the Central Valley of California, has a relatively small Chinese population. At most the Stockton Chinese American community is a minor subculture of Chinese America. Yet Stockton became a "literary microcosm" for Kingston, whose knowledge of China derives from its people. The language spoken in this community, a Cantonese dialect called Say Yup, supplies Kingston with distinctive sounds and rhythms. What Kingston has done in her writing is to translate the oral tradition of her community into a written one.

Moreover, the physical environment and social class in which Kingston grew up played an important role in her "education" as a writer. Kingston spent her childhood on the south side of Stockton, an area populated by mostly working-class and unemployed people of mixed races. The "Burglar Ghosts," "Hobo Ghosts," and "Wino Ghosts" that crowded young Maxine's childhood memory testify to the importance of street wisdom and survival skills. Kingston insists on the audiotape *Maxine Hong Kingston: Talking Story* (1990) that had she been born in a middle-class suburb, her struggle to be a writer would have been harder.

In contrast Kingston calls her seventeen years in Hawaii an extended vacation. Her time there provided her with the necessary distance and perspective to sort out identity problems and to finish her first two books, *The Woman Warrior* and *China Men.* Kingston was uncertain how her work would be received when she finished *The Woman Warrior.* She was ready to send this collection of fiction to other countries or keep it for posthumous publication if she failed to find a publisher. Luckily, Alfred A. Knopf gambled on this unknown writer and published Kingston's book as nonfiction. To the surprise of both publisher and writer *The Woman Warrior* became an immediate best-seller. The book won the National Book Critics Circle General Nonfiction Award in 1976 and was rated as one of the top ten nonfiction books of the decade. As late as 1989 it was still on the trade-paperback best-sellers list. Kingston's next book, *China Men,* earned her a National Book Award in 1981. Both books are widely taught in literature, women's studies, sociology, ethnic studies, and history classes.

Kingston's success, however, earned her the enmity of some Asian American critics. The most fundamental objection to *The Woman Warrior* is its generic status. Some Asian American critics question whether it is valid to call the book an autobiography when there are so many fictional elements included in her personal experience. Moreover, they fault Kingston for presenting her personal experience as "representative" of the Chinese American community. The real problem, however, seems to rest on those readers who have misconceived the text. In her 1982 essay "Cultural Mis-readings by American Reviewers" Kingston herself laments that many critics of the dominant culture have misread her and measured her against the stereotype of the exotic, inscrutable, mysterious Orient. Kingston's first two books belong to the postmodernist mixed-genre tradition. Her books are not autobiography as a specific genre but an "autobiographical form" that combines fiction and nonfiction.

One way to look at Kingston's major works is to regard them as different stories of growth. In *The Woman Warrior* the first-person narrator explores her identity formation in relation to her mother and female relatives. In *China Men* the narrator grows in her understanding of the stories of her male ancestors. Together these two books reveal the development of a Chinese American woman by uncovering the repressed stories of her family and of Chinese American history. *Tripmaster Monkey: His Fake Book* (1989), her true fiction, on the other hand, reports the artistic education of a young Chinese American bohemian, Wittman Ah Sing. Another dominant theme in each of Kingston's major books is finding a mode of articulation for her characters: the silent aunts and the narrator in *The Woman Warrior,* the reticent father and suppressed grandfathers in *China Men,* and the playwright-to-be Wittman in *Tripmaster Monkey.* Evolving along with her writing, Kingston recorded her own growing pains and her struggles to find a distinctive voice.

Kingston's main project in *The Woman Warrior* is to avenge oppression by reporting stories about the women in her family. The book opens with "No Name Woman," a story of her nameless aunt in China. This aunt became a family outcast for getting pregnant out of wedlock and finally drowned herself and her newborn baby in the family well after the villagers raided her house. Brave Orchid reveals this family secret to the young Maxine on the onset of the daughter's menstruation to caution her against sexual indiscretion. At the same time, the mother attempts to suppress this story by forbidding the daughter to repeat it. Kingston, however, purposely reports the story as an act of political resistance to Chinese patriarchy and repression in general. Furthermore she contrives different reasons for her aunt's pregnancy: the aunt could have been a victim of rape and patriarchy; she could also have been a passionate seductress and an individualist. Through active imagination, Kingston gives this aunt life and immortality in her own way.

In "At the Western Palace," the fourth section of *The Woman Warrior,* Kingston tells the story of her other silent Chinese aunt, Moon Orchid. This "thrice-told tale"–told to Kingston by her sister, who in turn heard it from her brother–is the only third-person narrative in the book, and it communicates the hazard of poor adjustment to American reality. Moon Orchid, whose name alludes to her insubstantial presence, has lived comfortably in Hong Kong on the subsidy from her husband. Through the manipulation of Brave Orchid, Moon Orchid is forced to come to America to collect her lost husband and claim her title of first wife. After she discovers her thoroughly Americanized husband, a successful doctor who has remarried to an English-speaking wife, Moon Orchid's old Chinese life based on an illusion of changeless stability is shattered. Becoming paranoid and morbidly afraid of change, Moon Orchid repeatedly claims she is being followed by foreign "ghosts." She is finally sent to a mental asylum, where she dies.

By telling Moon Orchid's story, however, the narrator creates a voice for this oppressed woman from the East. Brave Orchid diagnoses Moon Orchid's mental disorder as stemming from her misplaced spirit. By recording her aunt's disintegration,

chinamen. The Rock Springs Massacre began in a large coal mine owned by the Union Pacific; the outnumbered chinamen were shot in the back as they ran to Chinatown, which the demons burned. They shot chinamen forced out into the open; demon women and children threw the wounded back in the flames. (There was a rumor of a good white lady in Green Springs who hid China Men in the Pacific Hotel and shamed the demons away.) The hunt went on for a month before federal troops came. The count of the dead was inexact because bodies were mutilated and pieces scattered all over the Wyoming Territory. No white miners were indicted, but the government gave $150,00 in reparations to victims' families. There were many family men, then. There were families settlers; Ah Goong was running elsewhere during the Driving Out of Tacoma, Seattle, Oregon City, Albania, and Marysville. The entire chinamen population of Tacoma was packed into boxcars and sent to Portland, where they were run out of town. China Men returned to Seattle, though, and refused to sell their land and stores but fought until the army came; the demon rioters were tried and acquitted. And when the Boston police imprisoned and beat 234 chinamen, it was 1902, and Ah Goong had already reached San Francisco or China, and perhaps San Francisco again.

In Second City (Sacramento), he spent some of his railroad money at the theater. The main actor's face was painted red with thick black eyebrows and long black beard, and when he strode onto the stage, Ah Goong recognized the hero, Guan Goong; his puppet horse had red nostrils and rolling eyes. Ah Goong's heart leapt to recognize hero and horse in the wilds of America. Guan Goong murdered his enemy—crash! bang! of cymbals and drum—and left his home village—sad, sad flute music. But to the glad clamor of cymbals entered the friends—Liu Pei (pronounced the same as Running Nose) and Chang Fei. In a joyful burst of pink flowers, the three men swore the Peach Garden Oath. Each friend friend sang an aria to friendship; together they would fight side by side and live and die one for all and all for one. Ah Goong felt as warm as if he were with friends at a party. Then Guan Goong's archenemy, the sly Ts'ao Ts'ao, captured him and two of Liu Pei's wives, the Lady Kan and the Lady Mi. Though Ah Goong knew they were boy actors, he basked in the presence of Chinese ladies. They traveled to the capital, the soldiers waving horsehair whisks, signifying horses, the ladies walking between horizontal banners, signifying palanquins. All the prisoners were put in one bedroom, but Guan Goong stood all night outside the door with a lighted candle in his hand, singing an aria about faithfulness. When the capital was attacked by a common enemy, Guan Goong fought the biggest man in one-to-one combat, a twirling, jumping sword dance that strengthened the China Men who watched it. Guan Goong's two partners heard about the feats of the man with the red face and intelligent horse. The three friends were reunited and fought until Liu Pei they secured his rightful kingdom.

Ah Goong felt refreshed and inspired. He called out Bravo like the demons in the audience, who had not seen theater before. Guan

Corrected galley proof for Kingston's China Men *(from Kingston's* Through the Black Curtain, *1987)*

185

Kingston gives Moon Orchid a place in her "mother book" and appeases the aunt's spirit. She even transforms the mental hospital into a quasi-utopian community of women. For the failing Moon Orchid her stay in the mental institution paradoxically brings her needed stability and a temporary place to anchor her spirit. She also finds acceptance from her "daughters," psychiatric patients of different races, and therefore is able to talk "a new story" about perfect communication instead of her old one of persecution.

The second section of *The Woman Warrior,* "White Tigers," is an often anthologized and discussed part of the book because of its fantastic portrayal of a female avenger. This story of the swordswoman is derived from the tale of the legendary Chinese heroine Fa Mu Lan, who substitutes for her aging father in a military conscription. In Kingston's version the swordswoman studies martial arts from a pair of mysterious old couples and leads a peasant uprising against the tyrannous emperor. After she decapitates the misogynist baron who has exploited her village and ruined her childhood, the swordswoman renounces her masculine power and returns to the traditional roles of daughter-in-law, wife, and mother. In "Personal Statement" Kingston calls the story of the swordswoman "a fantasy that inspires the girls' psyches and their politics." By adopting the story of an exemplary woman who has successfully balanced her roles in the public sphere, which is almost always dominated by men, and in the private sphere of home, Kingston is imagining victory over the androcentric Chinese and Chinese American traditions.

While Kingston has been faulted by Asian American critics and sinologists for inaccurate allusions to Chinese stories, the strength of "White Tigers" comes from her rewriting of traditional legends and mythology. In "Personal Statement" Kingston explains that "myths have to change, be useful or forgotten. Like the people who carry them across the oceans, the myths become American. The myths I write are new, American." In "White Tigers," for example, Kingston creatively rewrote traditional myths and appropriates male heroic legends for her woman warrior. Through this creative mythmaking Kingston created a heroine who transgresses traditional gender boundaries. The swordswoman describes how her parents carve their names, vows, and grievances on her back. Although undeniably an act of bodily mutilation, this act represents a coveted family acknowledgment for Chinese and Chinese American women. Furthermore, Kingston's description of the script on the swordswoman's back is a deliberate combination of physical and artistic

beauty: "If an enemy should flay me, the light would shine through my skin like lace." Through this revision of the chant of Fa Mu Lan, Kingston vicariously satisfied her urgent desire for family recognition.

The mother's story, "Shaman," is situated in the middle of the book. *The Woman Warrior* not only chronicles the development of the daughter Maxine but also the mother's struggle for self-definition. "Shaman" records Brave Orchid's passage from a traditional woman to a respectable woman doctor. After the deaths of her two children born in China, Brave Orchid decides to leave her uneventful life in New Society Village to study medicine in Canton, the capital of the province. In the medical school Brave Orchid earns outstanding grades and summons the courage to challenge the "Sitting Ghost." She volunteers to spend a night in a haunted room in the dormitory, reportedly defeats the ghost as it tries to attack her, and mobilizes the whole student body to participate in her exorcising ritual. In a sense Brave Orchid's struggle with the Sitting Ghost is a symbolic battle with the limits of traditionalism. Back in her village Brave Orchid uses her intelligence to establish herself as a renowned doctor. Not unlike the fantastic swordswoman, Brave Orchid "has gone away ordinary and come back miraculous, like the ancient magicians who came down from the mountains."

Brave Orchid's American daughter must also learn to fight the "ghosts" in her life. *The Woman Warrior* is subtitled *Memoirs of a Girlhood Among Ghosts.* "Once upon a time," the narrator recalls, "the world was so thick with ghosts, I could barely breathe; I could hardly walk, limping my way around the White Ghosts and their cars." While some readers may find this use of ghosts jarring, Kingston does not use the term in any pejorative sense. Her world of ghosts is a result of her parents' refusal to acknowledge America and of the shadowy residues of the Chinese past in her childhood and young-adult life. The narrator protests, "whenever my parents said 'home,' they suspended America. They suspend America. They suspended enjoyment, but I did not want to go to China." Significantly, the reconciliation of the mother and the daughter in "Shaman" occurs after the mother finally gives up on the ancestral homeland. "We have no more China to go home to," the aged Brave Orchid laments. The daughter, now released from the "ghost" of China that was imposed on her as a child, can freely acknowledge her matrilineage: "I am really a Dragon, as she is a Dragon, both of us born in the dragon years. I am practically a first daughter of a first daughter."

This reconciliation of mother and daughter precedes "A Song for a Barbarian Reed Pipe," the last section of *The Woman Warrior,* in which Kingston recalls her struggle with a personal voice from kindergarten to the narrative present: "My silence was thickest–total–during the three years that I covered my school paintings with black paint," Kingston writes. The blackness of her paintings is not a sign of mental disturbance, as her American teachers have assumed: "I was making a stage curtain, it was the moment before the curtain parted and rose," the adult Kingston explains. Once the curtain is up, there is "sunlight underneath, mighty operas." This transformation of blackness-inarticulateness into carnivalesque drama provides an excellent metaphor for Kingston's development as a writer. Later, in *Tripmaster Monkey,* a mighty opera unfolds in Wittman's theatrical production.

The psychodrama of young Maxine's linguistic struggle is concretely enacted in an incident that takes place when she is in the sixth grade. One day young Maxine confronts and physically attacks a quiet Chinese American girl, admittedly her double, in a basement bathroom after school. Only "sobs, chokes, noises that were almost words" come out of the girl, never a comprehensible word. "If you don't talk, you can't have a personality," Maxine shouts (to herself as well as to the other girl). Maxine's sadistic cruelty signifies her own inner trauma of inarticulateness. After this underground encounter, Maxine spends eighteen months in bed "with a mysterious illness," and the quiet girl lives under the protection of her family for the rest of her life.

After years of silence the teenaged Maxine finds an angry voice in a confrontation with her mother. Before this showdown Maxine has tried unsuccessfully to confess to the two-hundred-odd offenses that she has committed in her young life, such as tormenting the silent girl and stealing from the cash register at the family laundry. "If only I could let my mother know the list," Maxine thought, "she–and the world–would become more like me, and I would never be alone again." Yet the mother puts a stop to Maxine's attempt at communication, and the pain of silence finally drives Maxine to shout out her defiance of Chinese misogynism and her desire to leave home. This triumphant voicing, however, is immediately undercut by the narrator's sorrowful reflection as an older and wiser person: "Be careful what you say. It comes true. It comes true. I had to leave home in order to see the world logically, logic the new way of seeing. I learned to think that mysteries are for explanation. I enjoy the simplicity. Concrete pours out of my mouth to cover the forests with freeways and sidewalks. Give

Cover for a Chinese translation of Kingston's China Men (1980), which proudly acknowledges the ancestral roots of Chinese Americans

me plastic, periodical tables, t.v. dinner with vegetables no more complex than peas mixed with diced carrots. Shine floodlights into dark corners: no ghost." Her ghost-free new life is based on a rootless sterility represented by the concrete and plastic culture. She has escaped the Chinese interdiction of female speech at the expense of a maternal inheritance of rich imagination. It takes years for Maxine to come to her right artistic voice.

At the end of *The Woman Warrior,* Maxine finishes her story of development with a return to her matrilineage. This reconnection is mediated through that talk story. The daughter continues the story that her mother has started–"The beginning is hers, the ending, mine"–telling about T'sai Yen, a poet who had been abducted by a nomadic tribe, had two children with the barbarian chieftain, and later was ransomed back to China. T'sai Yen brought her song, "Eighteen Stanzas for a Barbarian Reed Pipe," back, and it "translated well." For Kingston, T'sai Yen is an emblem of the artist par excellence, whose poetic power is capable of transforming a weapon, the whistling arrow, into a musical instrument. Like the transformed swordswoman in "White Tigers," T'sai Yen is a word warrior who serves as a model for the author of *The Woman War-rior*. Thus, the interpenetrating stories in *The Woman Warrior* provide a link between Kingston's past and present. The central metaphor of the book is a Chinese knot in which various strands are interwoven into a work of folk art. Kingston, as "an outlaw knot-maker," weaves the past and the present together into an intricate pattern to create her "mother book." By talking stories she successfully builds a matrilineage to counterpoint the traditional Chinese patrilineage and unmuffles a personal yet rooted voice for herself.

Published in 1980, Kingston's second book, *China Men,* is the other part of "Maxine's development." "At one time," Kingston explained, "*The Woman Warrior* and *China Men* were supposed to be one book. I had conceived of one huge book." She decided, however, to take the men's stories out of her first book because they seemed to interfere with the women's and to collect them in her "father book," a companion piece to her "mother book." Originally, Kingston wanted to call this father book "Gold Mountain Heroes." Later, however, she changed the title to *China Men* because she feared the original title might confirm a stereotypical concept that the early Chinese immigrants were merely gold diggers. Moreover, *China Men,* a literal translation of the Chinese characters for Chinese, overturns the use of the pejorative Chinamen. Hence Kingston's neologism at once embattles the historical insult of the Chinese immigrants and proudly acknowledges the ancestral roots of Chinese America.

The foremost political agenda in *China Men* is to claim America for Chinese Americans. Directly influenced by William Carlos Williams's *In the American Grain* (1925), which she calls a biography of America, Kingston purposely starts her story in 1860, where Williams stopped, and carries the American story forward. "In story after story Chinese-American people are claiming America, which goes all the way from one character saying that a Chinese explorer found this place before Leif Ericsson did to another one buying a house here. Buying that house is a way of saying that America—and not China—is his country," declared Kingston in a 1980 interview with Timothy Pfaff. In *China Men* she extends the narrator's personal story to reconstruct a family history, which in turn questions the "official" national history of America. Like the swordswoman in "White Tigers" who substitutes for her father in conscription, the narrator wages a linguistic battle to claim America for four generations of China men. In *The Woman Warrior* Maxine is weaving a strand of matrilineal line into patrilineage; in *China Men* she weaves her own sub-

jectivity into the strands of men's stories. This "ap-propriation" of the male position also presents a continuation of the word warrior's "revenge by re-port" project.

Kingston also attempts to "educate" her read-ers. She compares *China Men* to "a six-layer club sandwich or cake," interlacing six present-day sto-ries of her male relatives with vignettes of myths. She deliberately leaves it up to her readers to figure out the intertextual relationships of the myths and the modern stories. In the prologue, "On Discov-ery," Kingston revises an episode from a classical Chinese romance: while searching for the Gold Mountain, Tang Ao gets trapped in the Land of Women. He is forced by a group of Amazons to have his ears pierced, to have his feet bound, and to serve at the queen's court. In Tang Ao's story King-ston embeds a double-edged criticism of Chinese sexism and American racism. By highlighting Tang Ao's suffering in his state of effeminization, King-ston created a feminist critique of Chinese sexist practices and an allegory of the "emasculation" of the Chinese immigrants in America. By opening the book with Tang Ao's story Kingston underlines her two main goals in *China Men:* to retrieve the Chinese past and to reexamine American history.

The narrator of *China Men* identifies herself as a family historian with the self-assigned and some-times disturbing task of safekeeping family histories and memories. In a chance encounter with her newly immigrated aunt from Hong Kong, for exam-ple, the narrator first feels reluctant to listen to the aunt's horror stories of the past, but then she recalls her "duty": "I did not want to hear how she suf-fered, and then I did. I did have a duty to hear it and remember it." In "Personal Statement" Kingston talks about how women play the role of keeper and weaver of stories, whereas men tend to alienate themselves from the past: "The men have trouble keeping Chinese ways in new lands. What good are the old stories? . . . Why not be rid of the mythical, and be a free American?" Claiming an American birth-right through storytelling, however, the daughter-storyteller proves the men's desire to forget the past to be mistaken. Kingston's "rememory" of family struggles exposes a history of discrimination and paves the way for personal and communal heal-ing.

As she opens *The Woman Warrior* by retrieving the silenced discourse of a nameless aunt, Kingston prefaces the present-day stories in *China Men* with a story of her father's repressed Chinese past. "You say with the few words and the silence: No stories. No past. No China," the narrator says of her fa-ther's denial of the past. She aims specifically to counterpoint his repressive silence: "You fix yourself in the present, but I want to hear the stories about the rest of your life, the Chinese stories. . . . I'll tell you what I suppose from your silences and few words, and you can tell me that I'm mistaken. You'll just have to speak up with the real stories if I've got you wrong." In "The Father from China" the daughter-narrator proceeds to "imagine" her father's development from birth to immigration to New York. Later, Kingston admitted that she found her father's reactions satisfying because she had successfully engaged him in a literary dialogue through marginalia that he wrote in a copy of a Chinese translation of *China Men*. Tom Hong wrote his commentary on his daughter's stories in beautiful Chinese calligraphy, giving her the satisfaction of having been treated as an intellectual equal instead of as an object of abusive language in her father's misogynist curses. Moreover, she finally lured her father out of his habitual reticence and won his appreciation. Thus, the daughter succeeded in returning the repressed language to the father through her literary creation.

In "The American Father" Kingston describes the father she had known as a child in Stockton. The daughter's most painful memory in this section is perhaps the recollection of how her father became a "disheartened man" after losing his job in the gambling house. His inertia was finally broken when her sister made him so angry that he leaped from his easy chair to chase her (although this sister claims that it was the narrator who was chased). Lured into action, the father starts the family laundry business. "The American Father" ends with a description of how the father planted many trees near their house, "trees that take years to fruit," symbolizing the slow yet firm rooting of the Hong family in America.

"The Great Grandfather from the Sandlewood Mountain" and two vignettes on mortality again foreground the importance of speech. As a contract worker on a Hawaiian sugar plantation, Bak Goong (Great Grandfather) is forbidden to talk during work. As a trickster figure, the "talk addict" Bak Goong then invents ways, such as singing and coughing, to circumvent this interdiction: "The deep, long loud coughs, barking and wheezing, were almost as satisfying as shouting. He let out scold disguised as coughs." His final liberating act is to organize a shout party for his fellow Chinese workers. He mobilizes the workers to bury their homesickness and anger in a huge hole: "They had dug an ear into the world, and were telling the earth their secrets." After the party they can talk and sing at work without interference from the white overseers because the workers' unrestrained demonstration of emotion and strength has caused fear among the whites. Moreover, the new ritual of shouting attests to the fact that these Chinese workers in Hawaii are actually Americans because they help to build the land. As Bak Goong proudly exclaims, "We can make up customs because we're the founding ancestors of this place."

"The Grandfathers of the Sierra Nevada Mountains," "The Laws," and "Alaska China Men" highlight the tenacity of the Chinese Americans faced with racial discrimination in the American legal system and in daily life. The narrator places her emphasis on the collective identity of China men—her own grandfather included—in their efforts to conquer natural obstacles and to survive exclusion in America. The American railroad system is physical evidence of China men's contributions. As the narrator states, "After the Civil War, China Men banded the nation North and South, East and West, with crisscrossing steel." Thus, the granddaughter-narrator proudly calls her forefathers "the binding and building ancestors." The narrator provides a vivid description of how Bak Goong and other Chinese workers risked their lives setting off dynamite manually in baskets dangling over ravines. The group spirit of the Chinese workers is most apparent in a railroad-strike episode. After failing to gain equal treatment with white workers in negotiations with the railroad company, the Chinese railroad workers decide to stage a strike and pass on the plan inside the summer solstice cake. Their slogan for the strike is "free men, no coolies, calling for fair working conditions," and their pursuit of freedom resonates with the spirit of the American Revolution.

In the middle of *China Men* Kingston includes a catalogue of anti-Chinese exclusion laws from 1868 to 1978. This intrusion of legal documents at first seems incongruous. Yet the juxtaposition of Kingston's personal language and governmental legal language underlies the victimization of Chinese Americans by political manipulation. At the end of "The Grandfather from the Sierra Mountains" the narrator describes how Chinese workers were "driven out," even murdered, after the railroad was completed. Speaking as the daughter of those Chinese American victims, Kingston again illustrates the importance of recovering and remembering the past.

"The Making of More Americans," "The Wild Man of the Green Swamp," and "The Adventure of Lo Bun Sun" include Chinese American and sinocized European adventure stories about where and how Chinese immigrants build their homes. It also registers an ambivalence about where the "home" for Chinese Americans is. Each of the protagonists

Dust jacket for Kingston's 1989 book, in which the trickster main character claims to be "the U.S.A. incarnation of the King of the Monkeys" from Chinese myth

in the five family stories told in "The Making of More Americans," for instance, needs to decide on his home address. The ghost of Say Goong (Fourth Grandfather) lingers until his brother tells him to go back to China; cousin Mad Sao cannot continue his American life until he escorts the hungry ghost of his mother back to her home village; paranoid Uncle Bun flees America. Kau Goong (Great Maternal Uncle), on the other hand, renounces old China and his old wife and is buried in America; the Hong Kong aunt and uncle immigrate to become the newest addition to the narrator's Chinese American family.

"The Brother in Vietnam" illustrates another identity problem for Chinese Americans and clearly presents Kingston's pacifist message. Stationed in various Asian countries during the Vietnam War, he feels lost and tries to find a "center" of identity for himself. His anxiety turns into nightmares and muttering in his sleep, which wins him the title of "Champion Complainer." The brother feels ambivalent when he passes the military-security check, which serves as evidence of his Americanness: "The government was clarifying that the family was really American, not precariously American but super-American, extraordinary secure—Q Clear-

ance Americans." Yet he refuses to be trained as a language specialist for fear of being made to interrogate prisoners of wars. His refusal of linguistic exploitation by the military reinforces his kinship with his sister word warrior.

The epilogue, "On Listening," circles back to the prologue, "On Discovery." The narrator recounts a warm discussion among young Filipino Americans about the whereabouts of the real Gold Mountain. Together with "The Brother in Vietnam," this finale extends the text to the next generation of Asian Americans, as the spirit of inquiry and the ability to listen are passed on. Furthermore, Kingston illustrates how the daughter-narrator, in her attentiveness to the heteroglossic "voices" around her, blossoms into an expert storyteller.

For years Kingston was reluctant to visit China for fear that what she discovered there might invalidate everything she was thinking and writing. Her impression of China was also colored by the misogynist Chinese sayings she had heard as a child. In an 1978 essay, "Reservations about China," Kingston also criticized the practice of aborting female fetuses in Communist China. In 1980, after finishing *China Men,* Kingston finally visited China and saw for the first time the China that she had created in her imagination. As she told Rabinowitz, "I think I found that China over there because I wrote it. It was accessible to me before I saw it, because I wrote it. The power of imagination leads us to what's real. We don't imagine fairylands." The warm welcome she received from many Chinese gave Kingston a sense of homecoming, of going back to a place she had never seen but had imagined so well. Having used up her Chinese memory, she could concentrate on her American reality in her next book, *Tripmaster Monkey*.

In a 1980 essay titled "The Coming Book" Kingston envisioned writing a book that "will sound like the Twentieth Century" when read aloud. "The reader will not need a visual imagination, only ears." Nine years later, *Tripmaster Monkey* was published. In this heteroglossic novel Kingston continues her project of claiming America and further explores the mentality of Chinese American males. The male protagonist, Wittman Ah Sing, a fifth-generation Californian newly graduated from Berkeley, is a Joycean young artist and a self-appointed playwright of his tribe. Set in the 1960s, *Tripmaster Monkey* recounts Wittman's odyssey through San Francisco, Oakland, Sacramento, and Reno and his efforts to create his own "deep-roots American theater"–"A Pear Garden of the West"–that will perform a continuous play for many nights. Like Kingston's earlier books, *Tripmaster Monkey* is constructed around a web of Chinese intertexts, from the third-person narrator, identified by Kingston as Kwan Yin, the Chinese goddess of mercy, to the Chinese classical romances that serve as sources for Wittman's extended extravaganza. Nevertheless, Kingston skillfully translates these Chinese intertexts into Chinese American idioms with many allusions to Western literature, movies, and bohemian culture.

The title of the novel serves as a metaphor for the mixture of the culture of the bohemians and that of China. Wittman, experiencing drug-induced "trips" in the novel, imitates the mythical Monkey King from a Chinese classic, *Journey to the West*. The Monkey King is a rebellious and mischievous trickster figure who is capable of seventy-two transformations and who, according to legend, is responsible for the introduction of Buddhism into China from the West (India). As Wittman declares to his "would-be girlfriend" Nanci, "I am really the present-day U.S.A. incarnation of the King of the Monkeys." Like the Monkey King, Wittman wants to unsettle established institutions with his outrageous conduct. Significantly, in his one-man show Wittman raves against misleading reviews that de-

scribe his play as "East meets West" and "Exotic" by claiming that the play itself is "The Journey *In* the West." Positioning himself *in* the West, the American monkey deploys his play to embody his American "trips." In his rebuttal Wittman also speaks for Kingston, whose works have often been misread. The novel's subtitle, *His Fake Book,* again alludes to *Journey to the West,* in which the Monkey King discovers that the Heart Sutra he has sought is blank and jumps to the conclusion that the scrolls are fake. The scrolls turn out to be authentic after all, but only people with wisdom and insight can decipher them.

Another achievement of *Tripmaster Monkey* is its linguistic innovation. The novel displays an amazing verbal diversity, and as Kingston predicted, it appeals to the reader's aural sensitivity. It is also a completely American book in that Kingston constantly plays with modern American language: "I already finished writing those Chinese rhythms. So I was trying to write a book with American rhythms," Kingston told interviewer Marilyn Chin. In the Pig Woman episode, for instance, Wittman comes across a Chinese American girl, Judy Louis, on the bus to Oakland. Bored by Judy's gibberish, Wittman suddenly visualizes her as a blue boar: "He leaned back in his seat, tried forward, and she remained a blue boar. (You can make a joke about it, you know. 'Boar' and 'bore')." The fantastic metamorphosis reminds the reader of the Circe story, in which men are changed into pigs through magic. It also alludes to the Monkey King's marvelous power of transformation and to his companion, Piggy. In *Tripmaster Monkey* Kingston is a magician with words, transforming linguistic puns into imagined reality. This playfulness with language is also strongly reminiscent of James Joyce's *Ulysses* (1922), another heteroglossic novel.

Wittman's name is another deliberate linguistic game. Wittman Ah Sing is a "man of wit" aspiring to be an heir to the great American poet Walt Whitman, who "sings" about "I" so powerfully in his poetry. In an interview with Shelly Fisher Fishkin, Kingston admitted the strong influence of Whitman on *Tripmaster Monkey,* expressing admiration for the freedom and the wildness of Whitman's language, which to her sounds as though it could have come from modern 1960s slang. She even uses lines from *Leaves of Grass*–such as "Trippers and Askers"–as chapter headings in the novel. Yet her protagonist is not exactly Whitman. While trying to name his son after his favorite poet, Wittman's father, Zeppline Ah Sing, misspelled the name, demonstrating the limitation of imitation and making a

Maxine Hong Kingston in the 1980s

transformation that is necessary if Wittman is to be a unique Chinese American poet.

Ah Sing is also an American name that allows Wittman to claim his Chinese American identity. In his solo show Wittman discusses the origin of his American surname: "I'm one of the American Ah Sings. Probably there are no Ah Sings in China. You may laugh behind my family's back, that we keep the Ah and think it means something. I know it's just a sound. A vocative that goes in front of everyone's names. . . . In that Ah, you can hear we had an ancestor who left a country where the language has sounds that don't mean anything—la and ma and wa—like music." The meaningless yet musical vocative in this "new American name" signifies the Ah Sings' link to their Chinese ancestors as well as their new American identity.

In an interview with Phyllis Thompson, Kingston calls Wittman "a prankster," and "a ne'er do well." Wittman is unattractive. He is biased, egocentric, chauvinist, and has other unlikable characteristics. He snubs F.O.B.—fresh off the boat—Chinese immigrants while he himself is sensitive about being discriminated against. The feminist narrator is critical of Wittman's relationship with his "wife," Taña, commenting constantly to the reader that Wittman is going to pay for his androcentric attitude. Yet while Kingston sometimes criticizes him, at other times her treatment of him seems to be almost affec-

tionate, and she always seems to view him with interest.

Kingston's distanced, yet interested, attitude toward this male protagonist indicates a significant breakthrough. After her two successful "memoirs" written mainly from a first-person perspective, Kingston shifted to the third-person point of view for her novel to get away from the shadow of egotism. By writing about a male character, or "The Other," from a distanced perspective, Kingston told Marilyn Chin, she finally found an artistic and psychological solution to her "long struggle with pronouns." Realistically, Kingston pointed out to Fishkin, women did not have such exciting and dramatic lives in the 1960s as men did. By providing a female narrator, furthermore, Kingston dramatizes the tension between male and female perspectives: "He's very macho-spirit. The narrator is the great female, so he struggles with her and fights with her and refuses to accept reality. He has to learn to be one with the female principles of the world." At the end of *Tripmaster Monkey* the narrator allows Wittman to have the spotlight to himself and blesses him in a maternal tone: "Dear American monkey, don't be afraid. Here, let me tweak your ear, and kiss your other ear." This omniscient narrator is also reminiscent of the storyteller in Chinese folk literature and classic romances, who introduces necessary information and guides the reader. Drawing on the Chinese tradition of talk story, Kingston created her female storyteller-narrator to monitor her trickster monkey.

Wittman is a conscientious young artist-to-be struggling to find his own voice. Born backstage to members of a vaudeville troupe, Wittman "really does have show business in his blood." His artistic ambition is to be "the first bad-ass China Man bluesman of America" so that he can create a Chinese American culture that consists of something besides beauty contests and handlaundries. The most important lesson for Wittman, however, is to learn that military heroism, as represented by the heroes in the Chinese romances, is inadequate. To be a true artist Wittman needs to become a pacifist.

Kingston's own pacifism is readily apparent in *Tripmaster Monkey*. She took part in antiwar marches during her years in Berkeley and worked with a group of resisters in Hawaii to provide sanctuary to deserters. In a 1990 essay titled "Violence and Non-Violence in China, 1989," she praised the Chinese students who attempted to achieve democracy through peaceful means, and she actively supports prodemocracy Chinese student groups. In *Tripmaster Monkey* Kingston's message is unmistakably pacifist: "Our monkey, master of change, staged a fake war, which might very well be displacing some real war," the narrator says in describing the effect of Wittman's three-day play.

Wittman's carnivalesque play is a crystallization of the love of fun. He asserts that instead of digging for gold, his Chinese ancestors came to America to have a good time: "The difference between us and other pioneers, we did not come here for the gold streets. We came here to play. And we'll play again. Yes, John Chinaman means to enjoy himself all the while. . . . We played for a hundred years plays that went on for five hours a night, continuing the next night, the same long play going on for a week without repeats, like ancient languages with no breaks between words, theater for a century, then dark." Wittman's assertion undermines the stereotype of the money-thirsty Chinese and values fun over materialism. In writing *Tripmaster Monkey* Kingston was finally able to use her abundant sense of humor to the full. She commented to Arturo Islas that her readers often fail to understand the humor in her works, such as the "sitcom" in Moon Orchid's story and the trick Bak Goong plays on the white missionary women: "I guess when people come to ethnic writing," Kingston remarked, "they have such a reverence for it or are so scared that they don't want to laugh." Wittman's outrageous language and behavior, however, force the reader out of this false sense of reverence.

Moreover, Wittman's play is at once universal and culturally specific. His theater is based on the principle of expansion and inclusion: "I'm including everything that is being left out, and everybody who has no place." The content of the play, however, is distinctively Chinese American, mixing Chinese stories and American vaudeville. Bringing back the tradition of the extended theatrical performance, Wittman is able to define a community. As the narrator states, "Community is not built once-for-all; people have to imagine, practice, and re-create it." From a lonely romantic contemplating suicide at the beginning of the novel, Wittman becomes an artist able to shoulder the responsibility of re-creating his community. His play, like Kingston's writing, directly opposes American individualism and embodies the collective spirit of the Chinese American community.

In 1998 Kingston is teaching in the English department at the University of California, Berkeley, and writing a book that is tentatively titled "The Fifth Book of Peace," in which she writes about her father's death and the loss of an earlier draft for the book in the 1991 Oakland fire. She links this fire thematically to the Vietnam War, writing about the psychology of conscientious objectors during the war as it is represented by the protagonist of *Tripmaster Monkey* and about her warrior woman's heroic homecoming.

Kingston's works have enchanted and inspired many readers while enraging some others. No matter how her works are received, Kingston succeeds in her "revenge" by reporting the crimes of sexism and racism. Despite her diminutive physical stature, she deserves the title of a word warrior in every sense. Kingston's literary innovations are also significant contributions to American literature. As Kingston herself says, "I am creating part of American literature. . . ." Contemporary American literature has been enriched by the addition of the powerful words of Maxine Hong Kingston.

Interviews:

Timothy Pfaff, "Talk With Mrs. Kingston," *New York Times Book Review,* 19 June 1980, pp. 1, 25–27;

Arturo Islas, "Maxine Hong Kingston," in *Women Writers of the West Coast: Speaking Their Lives and Careers,* edited by Marilyn Yalom (Santa Barbara: Capra Press, 1983), pp. 11–19;

Phyllis Hodge Thompson, "This Is the Story I Heard: A Conversation with Maxine Hong Kingston," *Biography,* 6 (Winter 1983): 1–2;

Paula Rabinowitz, "Eccentric Memories: A Conversation with Maxine Hong Kingston," *Michigan Quarterly Review,* 26 (Winter 1987): 177–187;

Marilyn Chin, "A *MELUS* Interview: Maxine Hong Kingston," *MELUS,* 16 (Winter 1989–1990): 57–74;

Maxine Hong Kingston: Talking Story [audio tape] (NAATA, 1990);

Shelly Fisher Fishkin, "Interview with Maxine Hong Kingston," *American Literary History,* 3 (Winter 1991): 782–791;

Paul Skenazy and Tera Martin, eds., *Conversations with Maxine Hong Kingston* (Jackson: University Press of Mississippi, 1998).

References:

King-kok Cheung, *Articulated Silences: Narrative Strategies of Three Asian American Women Writers* (Ithaca, N.Y.: Cornell University Press, 1990);

Cheung, "'Don't Tell': Imposed Silences in *The Color Purple* and *The Woman Warrior*," *PMLA,* 103 (March 1988): 162–174;

Cheung, "Talk Story: Counter-Memory in Maxine Hong Kingston's *China Men*," *Tamkang Review,* 24 (Autumn 1993): 21–37;

Cheung, "The Woman Warrior versus The Chinaman Pacific: Must a Chinese American Critic Choose between Feminism and Heroism?" in

Conflict in Feminism, edited by Marianne Hirsch and Evelyn Fox Keller (New York: Routledge, 1990), pp. 60–81;

Gloria Chun, "The High Note of the Barbarian Reed Pipe: Maxine Hong Kingston," *Journal of Ethnic Studies,* 19 (Fall 1991): 85–94;

Thomas J. Ferraro, "Changing the Rituals: Courageous Daughtering and the Mystique of *The Woman Warrior,*" in *Ethnic Passages: Literary Immigrants in Twentieth-Century America* (Chicago: University of Chicago Press, 1993), pp. 154–190;

Linda Hunt, "'I Could Not Figure Out What Was My Village': Gender vs. Ethnicity in Maxine Hong Kingston's *The Woman Warrior,*" *MELUS,* 12 (Fall 1985): 5–12;

Suzanne Juhasz, "Maxine Hong Kingston: Narrative Technique and Female Identity," in *Contemporary American Women Writers,* edited by Catherine Rainwater and William J. Scheik (Lexington: University Press of Kentucky, 1985), pp. 173–189;

Elaine Kim, *Asian American Literature: An Introduction to the Writings and Their Social Context* (Philadelphia: Temple University Press, 1982);

David Leiwei Li, "*China Men:* Maxine Hong Kingston and the American Literary Canon," *American Literary History,* 2 (Fall 1990): 482–502;

Li, "The Naming of a Chinese American 'I': Cross-Cultural Sign/fications in *The Woman Warrior,*" *Criticism,* 30 (Fall 1988): 497–515;

Li, "The Production of Chinese American Literary Tradition: Displacing American Orientalist Discourse," in *Redefining the Literatures of Asian-America,* edited by Shirley Lim and Amy Ling (Philadelphia: Temple University Press, 1992), pp. 319–331;

Shirley Lim, ed., *Approaches to Teaching Kingston's* The Woman Warrior (New York: Modern Language Association of America, 1991);

Amy Ling, *Between Worlds: Women Writers of Chinese Ancestry* (New York: Pergamon Press, 1990);

Ling, "Thematic Threads in Maxine Hong Kingston's *The Woman Warrior,*" *Tamkang Review,* 14 (1983–1984): 155–164;

Patricia Linton, "What Stories the Wind Would Tell: Representation and Appropriation in Maxine Hong Kingston's *China Men,*" *MELUS,* 19 (Winter 1994): 37–48;

Margaret Miller, "Threads of Identity in Maxine Hong Kingston's *Woman Warrior,*" *Biography,* 6 (1983): 13–33;

Carol Neubauer, "Developing Ties to the Past: Photography and Other Sources of Information in Maxine Hong Kingston's *China Men,*" *MELUS,* 10 (Winter 1983): 17–36;

Leilani Nishime, "Engendering Genre: Gender and Nationalism in *China Men* and *The Woman Warrior,*" *MELUS,* 20 (Spring 1995): 67–82;

Lee Quinby, "The Subject of Memoir: *The Woman Warrior's* Technology of Idiographic Selfhood," in *De/Colonizing the Subject: The Poetics of Gender in Women's Autobiography,* edited by Sidonie Smith and Julia Watson (Minneapolis: University of Minnesota Press, 1992), pp. 297–320;

Leslie Rabine, "No Lost Paradise: Social Gender and Symbolic Gender in the Writings of Maxine Hong Kingston," *Signs,* 12 (Spring 1987): 471–492;

Roberta Rubenstein, "Bridging Two Cultures: Maxine Hong Kingston," in her *Boundaries of the Self: Gender, Culture, Fiction* (Urbana: University of Illinois Press, 1987), pp. 164–189;

Malini Johar Schueller, "Theorizing Ethnicity and Subjectivity: Maxine Hong Kingston's *Tripmaster Monkey* and Amy Tan's *The Joy Luck Club,*" *Genders,* 15 (Winter 1992): 72–85;

Linda Ching Sledge, "Maxine Hong Kingston's *China Men:* The Family Historian as Epic Poet," *MELUS,* 7 (1980): 3–22;

Mary Slowik, "When the Ghosts Speak: Oral Tradition and Written Narrative Forms in Maxine Hong Kingston's *China Men,*" *MELUS,* 19 (Spring 1994): 73–88;

Sidonie Smith, *A Poetics of Women's Autobiography: Marginality and the Fictions of Self-Representation* (Bloomington: Indiana University Press, 1987);

Alfred S. Wang, "Maxine Hong Kongston's Reclaiming of America: The Birthright of the Chinese American Male," *South Dakota Review,* 26 (Spring 1988): 18–29;

Sau-ling Cynthia Wong, "Autobiography as Guided Chinatown Tour? Maxine Hong Kingston's *The Woman Warrior* and the Chinese-American Autobiographical Controversy," in *Multicultural Autobiography: American Lives,* edited by James Robert Payne (Knoxville: University of Kentucky Press, 1992), pp. 248–275;

Wong, "Necessity and Extravagance in Maxine Hong Kingston's *The Woman Warrior:* Art and the Ethnic Experience," *MELUS,* 15 (1988): 3–26;

Wong, *Reading Asian American Literature: From Necessity to Extravagance* (Princeton, N.J.: Princeton University Press, 1993).

Papers:
A collection of Maxine Hong Kingston's papers is at the Bancroft Library, University of California, Berkeley.

Denise Levertov

This entry was updated by Christopher MacGowan (College of William and Mary) from the entry by Anne Day Dewey (Saint Louis University, Madrid, Spain) in DLB 165: American Poets Since World War II, Fourth Series.

See also the Levertov entry in *DLB 5: American Poets Since World War II, First Series.*

BIRTH: Ilford, Essex, England, 24 October 1923 to Paul Philip and Beatrice Adelaide Spooner-Jones Levertoff, came to the United States in 1948, naturalized in 1955.

EDUCATION: Privately educated; also studied ballet.

MARRIAGE: 2 December 1947 to Mitchell Goodman (divorced, 1972); child: Nikolai Gregor.

AWARDS AND HONORS: Bess Hokin Prize from *Poetry* for "With Eyes at the Back of Our Heads," 1959; Longview Award, 1961; Guggenheim Fellowship, 1962; Harriet Monroe Memorial Prize, 1964; Inez Boulton Prize, 1964; American Academy and Institute of Arts and Letters grant, 1965; Morton Dauwen Zabel Memorial Prize from *Poetry,* 1965; Lenore Marshall Poetry Prize, 1976; Elmer Holmes Bobst Award in poetry, 1983; Shelley Memorial Award from Poetry Society of America, 1984; Robert Frost medal, 1990; NEA Senior Fellowship, 1990; Lannan Award, 1993; honorary doctorates from Colby College, 1970, University of Cincinnati, 1973, Bates College, 1984, Saint Lawrence University, 1984, Bates College, 1984, Allegheny College, 1987, St. Michael's College, 1987, Massachusetts College of Art, 1989, and University of Santa Clara, 1993.

DEATH: Seattle, Washington, 20 December 1997.

BOOKS: *The Double Image* (London: Cresset Press, 1946);
Here and Now (San Francisco: City Lights Books, 1957);
5 Poems (San Francisco: White Rabbit Press, 1958);
Overland to the Islands (Highlands, N.C.: J. Williams, 1958);
With Eyes at the Back of our Heads (New York: New Directions, 1959);

Denise Levertov (photograph by Arthur Furst)

The Jacob's Ladder (New York: New Directions, 1961);
City Psalm (Berkeley, Cal.: Oyez, 1964);
O Taste and See (New York: New Directions, 1964);
Psalm Concerning the Castle (Mount Horeb, Wis.: Perishable Press, 1966);
The Sorrow Dance (New York: New Directions, 1967);
A Marigold from North Vietnam (New York: Albondocani Press & Ampersand Books, 1968);
A Tree Telling of Orpheus (Los Angeles: Black Sparrow Press, 1968);

In the Night: A Story (New York: Albondocani Press, 1968);

The Cold Spring & Other Poems (New York: New Directions, 1968);

Three Poems (Mount Horeb, Wis.: Perishable Press, 1968);

Embroideries (Los Angeles: Black Sparrow Press, 1969);

A New Year's Garland for My Students / M.I.T. 1969–1970 (Mount Horeb, Wis.: Perishable Press, 1970);

Relearning the Alphabet (New York: New Directions, 1970);

Summer Poems, 1969 (Berkeley, Cal.: Oyez, 1970);

To Stay Alive (New York: New Directions, 1971);

Footprints (New York: New Directions, 1972);

Conversation in Moscow (Cambridge, Mass.: Hovey St. Press, 1973);

The Poet in the World (New York: New Directions, 1973);

The Freeing of the Dust (New York: New Directions, 1975);

Chekhov on the West Heath (Andes, N.Y.: Woolmer/Brotherson, 1977);

Modulations for Solo Voice (San Francisco: Five Trees Press, 1977);

Life in the Forest (New York: New Directions, 1978);

Collected Earlier Poems 1940–1960 (New York: New Directions, 1979);

Light Up the Cave (New York: New Directions, 1981);

Mass for the Day of St. Thomas Didymus (Concord, N.H.: William B. Ewert, 1981);

Pig Dreams: Scenes from the Life of Sylvia: Poems (Woodstock, Vt.: Countryman Press, 1981);

Wanderer's Daysong (Port Townsend, Wash.: Copper Canyon Press, 1981);

Candles in Babylon (New York: New Directions, 1982);

Poems 1960–1967 (New York: New Directions, 1983);

Two Poems (Concord, N.H.: William B. Ewert, 1983);

El Salvador: Requiem and Invocation (Concord, N.H.: William B. Ewert, 1983);

The Menaced World (Concord, N.H.: William B. Ewert, 1984);

Oblique Prayers: New Poems with 14 Translations from Jean Joubert (New York: New Directions, 1984);

Selected Poems (Newcastle upon Tyne: Bloodaxe Books, 1986);

Poems 1968–1972 (New York: New Directions, 1987);

Breathing the Water (New York: New Directions, 1987);

Seasons of Light, by Levertov and Peter Brown (Houston: Rice University Press, 1988);

A Door in the Hive (New York: New Directions, 1989);

New and Selected Essays (New York: New Directions, 1992);

Evening Train (New York: New Directions, 1992);

Tesserae: Memories and Suppositions (New York: New Directions, 1995);

Sands of the Well (New York: New Directions, 1996);

Batterers (West Burke, Vt.: Janus, 1996);

The Stream & the Sapphire: Selected Poems on Religious Themes (New York: New Directions, 1997);

The Life around Us: Selected Poems on Nature (New York: New Directions, 1997);

This Great Unknowing: Last Poems (New York: New Directions, 1999).

OTHER: "Biographical Note," in *The New American Poetry,* edited by Donald Allen (New York: Grove, 1960), pp. 440–441;

"A Personal Approach," in *Parable, Myth, and Language,* edited by Tony Stoneburner (Cambridge, Mass.: Church Society for College Work, 1967);

Out of the War Shadow: An Anthology of Current Poetry, edited by Levertov (New York: War Resisters League, 1967);

Penguin Modern Poets 9, edited by Levertov, Kenneth Rexroth, and William Carlos Williams (Harmondsworth, U.K.: Penguin, 1967);

In Praise of Krishna: Songs from the Bengali, translated by Levertov and Edward C. Dimock (Garden City, N.Y.: Doubleday, 1967);

Rainer Maria Rilke, *Where Silence Reigns,* translated by T. G. Craig Houston, with a foreword by Levertov (New York: New Directions, 1978);

The Bloodaxe Book of Contemporary Women Poets, edited by Jeni Couzyn (Newcastle upon Tyne: Bloodaxe Books, 1984);

Beatrice Hawley, *The Collected Poems of Beatrice Hawley,* edited by Levertov (Cambridge, Mass.: Zoland Books, 1989).

TRANSLATIONS: Jules Supervielle, *Selected Writings,* translated by Levertov (New York: New Directions, 1968);

Eugene Guillevic, *Selected Poems,* translated by Levertov (New York: New Directions, 1969);

Poets of Bulgaria, edited by William Meredith, translated by Levertov and others (Greensboro, N.C.: Unicorn Press, 1985);

Alain Bosquet, *No Matter No Fact,* translated by Levertov, Sam Beckett, and Edouard Roditi (New York: New Directions, 1988);

Jean Joubert, *Black Iris: Selected Poems by Jean Joubert,* translated by Levertov (Copper Canyon, Wash.: Copper Canyon Press, 1988);

Joubert, *White Owl and Blue Mouse,* translated by Levertov (Cambridge, Mass.: Zoland Books, 1990).

In her prolific, highly regarded, sometimes controversial career, Denise Levertov has created a multidimensional body of poetry that is pervaded by her strong belief in her poetic vocation and by her ideal of personal integrity. Her meticulously crafted work involves a variety of genres—nature lyrics, love poems, poems of political protest, and Christian poetry—that converge and diverge throughout her career. In book after book she explores such themes as domesticity, romantic love, the erotic, parenting and other family relations, political change, the poet's relation to artistic tradition, and aging—nearly always with reference to contemporary issues central to women. Born in England, Levertov eventually shed the neoromanticism popular in that country during World War II and, moving to the United States in 1948, embraced the experimentation of American poetry in the 1950s. The poetic communities that she joined included the Beats, the New York School, the San Francisco Renaissance, and the Black Mountain poets, all of whom were identified by Donald Allen as "New American" poets in his influential anthology *The New American Poetry* (1960). This highly diverse community had grown from a counterculture movement that challenged the traditional meter and elevated diction of the New Critics in little magazines to become the vanguard of a major strand of postmodern American poetry that appeared by the 1960s in such magazines as Henry Rago's *Poetry.*

Closely allied during the 1950s and 1960s with the Black Mountain poets, especially Robert Duncan and Robert Creeley, Levertov was energetically involved in the contemporary discussion of poetry and poetics. Her sensual evocation of an epiphanic vision that arises from the strikingly concrete, everyday world and her poetics of "organic form" were both influential in the attempts to formulate a positive alternative to the poetic theories of the New Critics. Meanwhile, her poetry assimilated and transformed the modernist legacy of Ezra Pound, William Carlos Williams, and D. H. Lawrence. During the 1960s Levertov's work, like that of many of her contemporaries, became intensely political. Much of her controversial poetry of this period criticized American involvement in the Vietnam War and aligned her with the various movements for social reform prevalent in that decade.

The increasingly romantic style of her later poetry distanced Levertov from Creeley and Duncan and the experimental avant-garde. After her gradual conversion to Christianity in the late 1970s and early 1980s, Levertov's belief in the poet's vocation as a visionary who enriches the imaginative life of society strengthened. Many later poems are meditations on historical artifacts and biblical texts that attempt to render artistic and religious tradition as a vital presence in contemporary life. Levertov's luminous vision of nature, her unconventional love poems, her theory and practice of political poetry, and her Christian vision—as well as her attempts to weave these various strands of her work together—all represent significant contributions to postmodern poetry.

Born in England in 1923, Levertov grew up in Ilford, Essex, near London. Her immediate family included her Welsh mother, Beatrice Adelaide Spooner-Jones Levertoff, a teacher who sang, painted, and wrote; her Russian-born father, Paul Philip Levertoff, an Anglican priest and scholar who had converted from Hasidic Judaism as a student; and a musically talented sister Olga, nine years her senior, who devoted much of her adult life to political activism. (Levertov changed the spelling of her name to distinguish herself from her sister, who published a book of poetry in 1949.) An older sister, Philippa, died twelve years before Levertov was born. Levertov's intensely intellectual and artistic home life included reading aloud, attending musical performances, walking in the countryside with her older sister Olga, and being surrounded by adults who espoused various political causes (particularly protesting fascism in Spain and Germany) and who provided aid to political refugees during World War II. Levertov was educated at home, primarily by her mother, until the age of twelve, when she began ballet, piano, French, and art lessons. An avid and independent reader, she became familiar with fairy tales and also with the works of English poets such as George Herbert, John Donne, William Wordsworth, John Keats, and Alfred, Lord Tennyson. Although she studied ballet seriously and hoped as a teenager to become a dancer, Levertov entered nurses' training when she was nineteen and worked as a civilian nurse in London during World War II.

Having started writing poems at the age of five, she felt a strong sense of poetic vocation by the time she was nine or ten years old. By the age of twelve she had written to T. S. Eliot, from whom

---

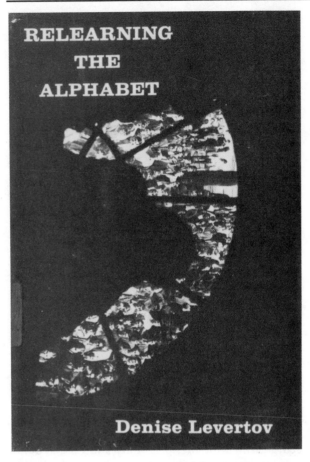

Dust jacket for the 1970 book in which Levertov attempted to find joy in "the colorful concreteness and sensuous particularity of things"

she received a response that included a critique of her poems. Herbert Read became an early friend and correspondent, occasionally offering advice and encouragement about her writing. In her late teens and early twenties, Levertov published her first poems in Charles Wrey Gardiner's *Poetry Quarterly* and in other British magazines such as *Outposts* and *Voices*. Following the acceptance of her first book of poetry, *The Double Image* (1946), she remembered entering a church "to kneel in awe because my destiny, which I had always known as a certain vague form on the far horizon, was beginning to happen."

The Double Image emulates the "new romantic" style that was prevalent during World War II in England. Poets such as those presented in Kenneth Rexroth's anthology *New British Poets* (1948) rejected the severity and experimental meters of the modernists for lush musicality in traditional meters and a melancholy beauty pervaded by a consciousness of death. Many were influenced by the poetry of Rainer Maria Rilke, whom Levertov began to read in 1946 and who remained a lifelong influence on her work. Crossing the threshold from adolescent innocence to adulthood, Levertov expressed in new romantic conventions the loss of youthful illusions. Sexual love and nature promised a worldly knowledge that is both desired and feared and that is represented by the recurrent image of a flame whose warmth and brilliance attract the moth, only to consume its fragile life. Innocence and experience yield double, contradictory knowledge. The romantic child's trust in nature's "caressing grasses" and rejuvenating power seem "tender vanity" in a harsh and disenchanting adult world. Failed communion in love brings the isolating recognition of a narcissistic projection of the self that prevents authentic communication. "Each, in the hardening crystal / a prisoner of pride, abstractedly caresses / the stranger at his side."

While *The Double Image* treats issues specific to Levertov's personal and historical circumstances during the war, she transmutes these issues to consider them in terms of the universal themes of "death," "time," "history," and "desire." Her nature imagery evokes a psychological rather than a physical landscape:

> At Durgan waves are black as cypresses,
> clear as the water of a wishing well,
> caressing the stones with smooth palms, looking
> into the pools as enigmatic eyes
> peer into mirrors, or music echoes
> out of a wood the waking dream of day,
> blind eyelids lifting to a coloured world.

The succession of contradictory images—black and clear, visual and aural, sensitive and unable to sense—dissolve the sea into an insubstantial fantasy generated by the mind in its isolation. Meditating on the eternal themes of poetry and in search of her self, Levertov finds self, the world, and even words increasingly unreal. Her poems claim a wraithlike existence. Words that for her are "valid symbols" are unable to bridge "the distance and the veil" that separate her from others. Images that tend to the gothic, such as death as an opulent bridegroom and susurrant blank verse that is rich with assonance and alliteration, intensify the theme of dreamy self-absorption. Both theme and meter remain, however, part of an inherited conception of poetry into which the poet seeks to grow and that she does not yet question.

On 2 December 1947 Levertov married Mitchell Goodman, a former soldier who had recently completed graduate work at Harvard in economics and labor relations. They moved to New York City, where their son, Nikolai, was born in 1949. With the exception of a year and one-half in Europe and two in Mexico, New York City remained their home until the late 1960s. During the eleven years that separate *The Double Image* from her next book, *Here and Now* (1957), Levertov adapted to a new culture, to motherhood, and to a new poetics, retraining herself as a poet of the post–World War II American avant-garde and assimilating the modernist legacy rejected by the neoromantic milieu in England. Although she did not publish a book during this time, she continued to write and publish poems in magazines.

Meanwhile, she met Robert Creeley in 1949, William Carlos Williams in 1951, and Robert Duncan shortly thereafter. The four formed enduring friendships fueled by an enthusiasm for and a criticism of each other's work. Levertov also joined the poetic discussions that appeared in Cid Corman's little magazine *Origin* and Creeley's *Black Mountain Review*. Contributors to these magazines were attracted by the artistic possibilities of Charles Olson's essay "Projective Verse" (1950). Olson's "composition by field," an idea based on his borrowing from field theory in physics, suggested metaphysical and formal foundations with which to replace the formal standards promulgated by the New Critics. Challenging what he termed, in reference to Keats, the "Egotistical sublime" of Western humanism, Olson advocated a poetry that rendered the artist one object among others and the poem a record of the moment-by-moment interaction of consciousness with other forces in the environment. Creeley, Duncan, and Levertov had read Pound, Williams, and Lawrence early. From these common interests and their assimilation of Olson's "composition by field," the three writers developed the shared conception of poetry and poetics for which they became known as the Black Mountain poets in the late 1950s.

Levertov's next volumes record the experiments inspired by her new environment. Although published at different times, *Here and Now* and *Overland to the Islands* (1958) are composed of poems written during the same period. Publishers Lawrence Ferlinghetti of City Lights and Jonathan Williams of Jargon Press approached Levertov at roughly the same time and chose from her stock of poems at hand, Ferlinghetti first, and Williams from the rest. The third volume, *With Eyes at the Back of Our Heads* (1959), was published by James Laughlin's New Directions, initiating Levertov's close publishing relationship with this press. *With Eyes at the Back of Our Heads* extends her new apprenticeship, as Levertov's later decision to group it with her *Collected Earlier Poems 1940–1960* (1979) indicates, but also demonstrates her assimilation of the new influences into an independent style.

The influence of Williams is primary in these experiments, although Levertov also named Wallace Stevens and Pound–particularly in his book *ABC of Reading* (1934)–as significant to her conceptions of the poet's craft and technical precision. These volumes strip away the Gothic dreamworld of *The Double Image* to explore nature, love, and art through the colloquial language of Williams's American idiom and the immediacy of sensual presence. "Tomatlan (Variations)" reveals a visual clarity, a sexual response to nature, and a counterpoint of physical description and grammatical structure characteristic of Williams:

> The green palmettos of the
> blue jungle
> shake their
> green breasts, their stiff
> green hair–
> the wind, the sea wind is come
> and touches them
> lightly, and strokes them, and
> screws them.

"The Departure" explores the energetic rhythms of American colloquial speech as Levertov perceives it:

> Have you got the moon safe?
> Please, tie those strings a little tighter.
> This loaf, push it down further
> the light is crushing it–such a baguette
> golden brown and so white inside
> you don't see every day
> nowadays.

In addition to Williams's influence, some poems assimilate the themes and vocabulary of "Projective Verse" in ways similar to the early experiments by Creeley and Duncan, structuring the poem around the interaction of elements in a particular environment and using line breaks and spacing to identify the agents that produce a particular moment. "Everything that Acts Is Actual" adopts Creeley's abstract language of the "act" to represent the relationship between two people. "A Silence" seems to revise Keats's "Ode on a Grecian Urn" by describing a vase and a broken rose in the irregular spatial dispersion and antiromantic themes typical of early Black Mountain experiments:

> Phoenix-tailed
> slateblue martins pursue
>   one another, spaced out
> in hopeless hope, circling
>   the porous clay vase, dark from
> the water in it. Silence
> surrounds the facts. A language
> still unspoken.

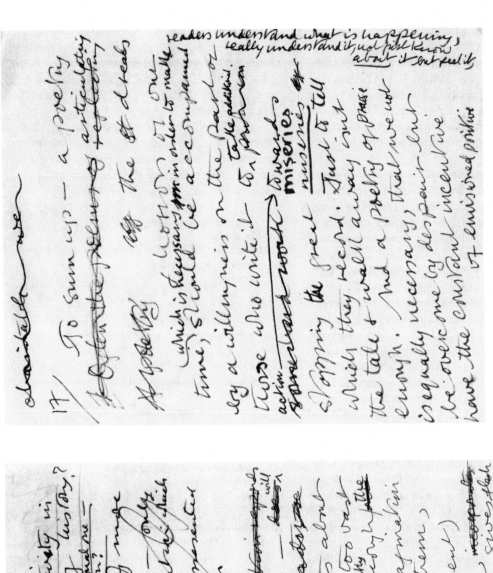

Although adopting Williams's visual precision, the lineation of the poem distinguishes the agents that compose the moment. The extra space between "one" and "another" enacts the separation between the martins, while a new line divides the clay and water. Whereas Keats's urn fuses the elements on it into a transcendence of time in the eternal moment of art, Levertov accentuates the instability and chance conjunction of a broken flower, water, and clay. The double meaning of still as "motionless" or "yet" suggests that language can merge with concrete "facts"; but it also suggests doubts about the ability of language to represent these facts accurately, an ambivalence about objectifying language that pervades contemporary poems by Creeley and Olson.

Just as she rejected romantic notions about nature, Levertov also rejects romantic notions about love and art. "The Third Dimension" apparently translates the feeling of ecstatic union with nature, a feeling associated with love, into colloquial and concrete terms: "Who'd believe me if / I said, 'They took and / split me open from / scalp to crotch, and / still I'm alive, and / walk around pleased with / the sun and all the world's bounty?" Other poems portray idiosyncratic moments in unidealized love and marriage. "I give up on / trying to answer my question, / Do I love you enough?" "Attention" and "commitment" replace the idealized love of *The Double Image*.

The appeal to a transcendent source of inspiration recedes before Levertov's evolving interest in the artist's materials and tools. "An Innocent (II): (1st version)" links the artist to a destitute man poking through garbage with "the calm intense look of a craftsman." This "prince of scavengers" who "makes / some kind of life from" an endless city of refuse shares Levertov's satisfaction in the found or overlooked object and in attention to the materials and tools that make art. "The Hands" likewise refuses escape into an ethereal beauty of music by focusing the pianist's "crablike / hands, slithering / among the keys" with "almost painful / movement." Even when Levertov describes inspiration as possession by a force more powerful than the individual, a part of her experience of creativity throughout her life, she presents her muse in concrete terms. In "The Goddess" a deity of honesty and truth expels her violently from "Lie Castle," throwing her face-down to force immediate contact with nature in the taste of mud and seeds.

The early 1960s mark Levertov's transition from her apprenticeship period to the achievement of an independent poetic vision. *The Jacob's Ladder*

(1961) and *O Taste and See* (1964) add a spiritual dimension to the vivid description she learned from Williams. At the same time, her work begins to depart from the early Black Mountain emphasis on the idiosyncratic to discover moments of epiphanic beauty or coherence in everyday experience. Sensual images become a "Jacob's ladder" that extends from earth to heaven and permits commerce between the two regions. The sensual world both enables perception of a spirit beyond material fact and becomes the medium through which the poet represents her own spiritual experience. This spirit life does not cohere into a specific cosmology; Levertov seeks rather to represent the particular vitality of each being. The last two stanzas of "Six Variations," for example, contrast the animating power of light with that of human consciousness.

v
The quick of the sun that gilds
broken pebbles in sidewalk cement
and the iridescent
spit, that defiles and adorns!
Gold light in blind love does not distinguish
one surface from another
. . . .

vi
Lap up the vowels
of sorrow,
transparent, cold
water-darkness welling
up from the white sand.
. . . .
Through the hollow globe, a ring
of frayed rusty scrapiron,
is it the sea that shines?
It is a road at the world's edge?

Light, capable of "blind love," reveals the "quick" beauty and life of the concrete. In contrast, the human awareness of loss or absence discovers the limits of sensual being. The contrasting short *i* and long *o* sounds reinforce the sharpness of the visible world and the flowing, inchoate quality of desire. While Levertov does not abandon the colloquial, this more crafted music becomes an important technique through which she communicates the coherence and beauty that she finds in the everyday world.

This intensified musicality is one element in an increasingly literary emphasis in Levertov's work of the early 1960s, an emphasis that she shared with Creeley and Duncan during this period. Through her deepening friendship with Duncan and their mutual admiration for the then nearly forgotten poet H. D. (Hilda Doolittle), Levertov began to see

Cover for Levertov's 1972 book, which expresses her strong anti–Vietnam War sentiment

poetic tradition as a resource that sustains the life of the imagination by providing examples of a richer vision that enhances ordinary perception. In the 1962 essay "H. D.: An Appreciation" Levertov writes that she admires in H. D.'s writing "the play of sound," "the interplay of psychic and material life," and "The interpenetration of past and present, of mundane reality and intangible reality," a description that fits her own poetic concerns. Mythological figures such as Ishtar, angels, elves, and literary epigraphs and dedications, as well as natural objects, inspire the poems. Daily events are framed as rituals evoking the divine presence in the ordinary fact. Through her exploration of tradition, Levertov began to rediscover her European roots. Joan Hallisey has traced the influence of Martin Buber's *Tales of the Hasidim* (1948) in the mystical appreciation of the immediate and everyday world in *O Taste and See*. Boris Pasternak and Henrik Ibsen join Williams and Pound as literary ancestors. Although Levertov developed its significance in different contexts throughout her life, her epiphanic experience

of the everyday world in its immediate and concrete particularity forms the core of her mature poetic vision.

The early 1960s brought increased recognition to the poets of the New American poetry, who gained wider exposure in poetry readings; in the proliferation of little magazines such as *Evergreen, Kulchur,* and *Floating Bear;* and in the publication of their work in mainstream magazines such as *Poetry* during Henry Rago's editorship. During this time Levertov began her professional career as a poet, supporting herself by readings, writing, and teaching. In addition to giving more-frequent readings, she served as poetry advisor to Norton Publishing Company and as the poetry editor for *The Nation* in the 1960s. During this decade she also held part- and full-time teaching positions at Drew University; the City College of New York; Vassar College; University of California, Berkeley; and the Massachusetts Institute of Technology. She taught at Tufts University in the 1970s and at Brandeis University and Stanford University in the 1980s.

Although appreciating the work of poets as diverse as Allen Ginsberg, Gary Snyder, and Adrienne Rich, Levertov felt her closest affinity with Creeley and Duncan. Their commitment to poetry as a means to intensify and purify ordinary language became the hallmark of Black Mountain poetry in the 1960s. Within the discussion of poetry among the New American poets, this emphasis distanced them from what Levertov termed the "confessional" tendency of the Beats to publicize the private realm and to employ the chatty or ironic tone of New York poets such as Frank O'Hara and John Ashbery. The emphasis also drew critical fire. In his magazine *The Sixties,* Robert Bly attacked Duncan's and Levertov's literary allusions as an artificial and inauthentic inducement of vision.

During the 1960s Levertov formulated and refined a theory of poetry that underlay her luminous epiphanies from the concrete realities of the world, epiphanies that remained at the core of her poetics. Her 1965 essay "Some Notes on Organic Form" was one of many poetic theories developed at this time as Levertov and her contemporaries sought to explain their departures from traditional forms. Seeking to refute the equation of free verse with arbitrary meter, Levertov's essay defines "organic" form as fidelity to a form that is inherent in a thing or in an interplay among several things–"inscape"–or in an experience–"instress." *Inscape* and *instress* are terms borrowed from Gerard Manley Hopkins, and Levertov's use of the word *organic* indicates her indebtedness to the works of Samuel Taylor Coleridge and Ralph Waldo Emerson.

For Levertov, poems emerge from "an intuition of order, a form beyond forms, in which forms partake, and of which man's creative works are analogies, resemblances, natural allegories." Although her emphasis on the interplay among things and the process of experience derives from Williams and from a Black Mountain emphasis on the process of perception, her Wordsworthian conception of a single form unifying human and natural life departs from both. Levertov thus modified Creeley's process-oriented statement that "form is never more than the extension of content" with the assertion that "Form is never more than a revelation of content." This conception of form remained the basis of her critical and theoretical writings. Later essays such as "On the Function of the Line" (1979) describe poetic form as a visual and musical "score" or performance guide through which the reader may grasp the poet's experience. Her essay "On the Need for New Terms" (1986) replaces the overused organic with exploratory and reiterates Levertov's "passion . . . for the vertebrate and cohesive in all art."

In the 1960s the events of the war in Vietnam introduced one of the major contexts in which Levertov developed the significance of her poetic epiphanies—the political—when, like many of her contemporaries, she found both her life and her poetry politicized by American engagement in the war in Southeast Asia. Involved in the mid 1960s in RESIST, a movement to encourage draft resisters, she grew increasingly active politically, attending peace rallies, organizing readings and other protest events, participating in 1969 in the People's Park in Berkeley (a grass-roots effort to create a park on abandoned university land), and visiting North Vietnam with Muriel Rukeyser and Jane Hart in 1972. The years of the late 1960s brought both personal and political crises as Levertov struggled with tensions in her marriage, depression, and the strain of her continuous involvement in political activism. This time of crisis triggered an effort by Levertov to rethink her poetic vision—the progress and growing pains of which are recorded in her remarkably prolific output of the next few years: *The Sorrow Dance* (1967), *Relearning the Alphabet* (1970), *To Stay Alive* (1971), and *Footprints* (1972).

The first and last sections of *The Sorrow Dance*, "Abel's Bride" and "Life at War," locate Levertov's poetic crisis in the inadequacy of her poetics of the luminous concrete to express suffering. "A Lamentation" opens with the question: "Grief, have I denied thee?" and describes Levertov's childhood theatrical performance as "Summer" as a betrayal of

her "autumn birthright." Celebrating the fullness of the presence of nature now seems insufficient, "[h]ypocrisies / of seemly hope . . . if the day / is no day for miracles." While "Abel's Bride" presents Levertov's sorrow as a vaguely defined woman's sorrow, "Life at War" describes the horror of war as a crippling intrusion into her search for beauty, "the imagination / filmed over with the grey filth of it." Levertov's early war poems extend rather than depart from her poetics of presence, using vivid representation to make the brutality of the war immediate to her readers and to render human the impersonal statistics of the media and demonized "enemy."

Relearning the Alphabet achieves a shaky resolution of Levertov's crisis of vision. Although discovering renewed joy in the colorful concreteness and sensuous particularity of things, the poet remains conscious of the limitations of this vision. "Reduced to an eye / I forget what / I / was." While looking occasionally to her poetics of the 1940s to recover her subjective voice, she finds as yet no access to her inmost self. In her long poem "A Tree Telling of Orpheus" she dramatizes the transformation of nature into words not as escape into the impersonal life of things but as an agonized awakening into human consciousness:

> He told of the dreams of man, wars, passions, griefs,
>   and I, a tree, understood words—ah, it seemed
> my thick bark would split like a sapling's that
>   grew too fast[.]

Levertov's search for a language of self seems most successful when she returns to the interpersonal source of her poetic vision that was prominent in her exploration of love in *The Double Image* but developed only intermittently throughout the 1950s and 1960s. Commemorating her sister's death in 1964, the "Olga Poems" of *The Sorrow Dance* powerfully render her passionate, tormented sister. As Levertov is alternately "the little sister / beady-eyed in the bed. . . . My head / a camera," watching her sister, Olga "kneeling / to undress, / scorching luxuriously, raking / her nails over olive sides," and then the adult analyzing her sister's frustrated idealism, the "rage for order" / that "disordered her pilgrimage," the sister becomes a presence whom Levertov creates from a wealth of memory and cultural allusion that is focused by deep personal emotion. In the same way, Levertov's renewed joy in daily existence in *Relearning the Alphabet* is awakened through renewed love in her marriage, as her relation to nature becomes grounded in human community. The cycle *A New Year's Garland for My Students / M.I.T.: 1969–1970* (1970) continues a playful exploration and an

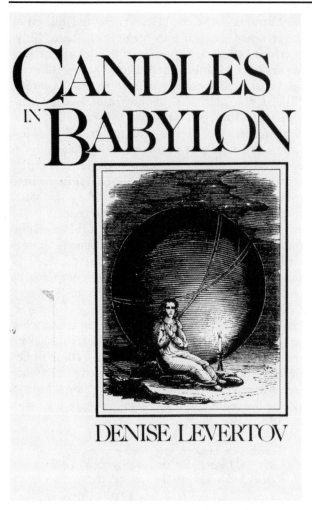

*Cover for Levertov's 1982 book, which includes poems that reveal
her integration of Christian faith and political activism*

expansion of imagery and poetic conceit that emphasizes the relationships between people rather than things.

Levertov's exploration of Olga's personality—passionate, manipulative and even demonic in her political frustration as an adult—begins the poet's effort to define the relation between an ideal vision and political activism. Much of Levertov's political vision hinges on the opposition of peace to war, nature to technology, and communism to imperialist capitalism, in a sort of political dualism that typified many political reform movements in the 1960s. Her most controversial volume, *To Stay Alive,* composed almost entirely of the long poem "Staying Alive," places her short lyric visions in a long documentary diary of her political experiences from late 1967 to 1970, including such events as de Courcy Squire's hunger strike, political rallies, waiting for her husband's trial for aiding draft resisters, the People's Park protests, and her travels in Europe.

Embedded in a collage of verbatim newscasts, revolutionary slogans, conversations, diary entries, letters from others, and memories, Levertov's lyric passages become a part of the society from which poetic vision springs and to which it, in turn, speaks. "Staying Alive" seeks to give substance to the protesters' ideal of peace abroad and social revolution at home, the same ideal to which Levertov committed herself. The poem's concrete instances of communal harmony, poetic images of harmony in nature, of childhood memory, and of poetic tradition all contribute to an explication of the popular slogan "Revolution or death." Levertov presents the meaning of the slogan as one defined by a democratic consensus that provides for the interplay between the individual and collective, an interplay that governs both her poetry and the group's language. Her preface to *To Stay Alive* locates her poetics not in extraordinary vision but in the typicalness of her experience as a citizen of her era. So completely does she fuse personal and political history that the poem is at once a record of her changing self-conception as a political activist and a vivid history of the protest movement.

The poems Levertov wrote about the Vietnam War received mixed reviews. Dorothy M. Nielson and Paul Lacey praised their discovery of forms and their use of language as being fully appropriate to the political issues they explored, and Hayden Garruth hailed Levertov's political and antiwar poems as work that approached the status of an epic. Other poets and critics, however, attacked Levertov's poetry about the Vietnam War as crude and unpoetic. In the judgment of Duncan, Levertov accepted too readily the problematic language of public debate and thus denied the poet's responsibility to stretch language and the imagination to their full potential; she did this by employing disclaimers such as that concerning her use of revolution as "The wrong word / . . . / But it's the only / word we have." Other critics faulted the documentary emphasis in the poetry. Charles Altieri criticized Levertov's "aesthetics of presence," with its focus on the concrete image, as being inadequate to represent the complex political and ethical issues and their contexts. While "Staying Alive" lacks the intensive phonetic and verbal play of Levertov's short lyrics, this long poem attempts to root the value of poetic language in its audience (as represented in the poem) rather than in its formal autonomy.

Levertov herself reconsidered the politics of her poetics, questioning her love for "surfaces that are their own / interior life" and questioning, too, the life of poetry among its readers and its audience. She records that Chuck Matthew read "A Man," a poem from *The Sorrow Dance* that is about the personal wisdom gained from experience, at a rally. In the charged context it acquired an overtly political tone. In "Staying Alive" Levertov's image of social harmony as a communion chalice is stripped of its inspirational power by the anger of the revolutionaries "shattering / the patient wineglasses / set out by private history's ignorant / quiet hands." New, seemingly inchoate images gain substance when embraced by the crowd, however. Like "islands" in muddy "floodwaters," they lead her to suggest that "Maybe what seems / evanescent is solid." While such an explanation may not justify Levertov's poetic choices, unresolved images like that of water—alternately the all-embracing sea as unity, crystalline ice as a sign of natural order, and a torrential stream as a metaphor for history—dramatize the absence of a poetic coherence and a fixed truth in the historical process.

The end of "Staying Alive" conveys Levertov's exhaustion from her sustained political activity and the painful loss of self that resulted from her commitment to a group effort. While she remained active in peace rallies and antinuclear protests and she continued to write political poetry, she began at this time to focus more and more on the individual, rather than the group, as the source of political change. Levertov's intensive involvement in public politics and the changes in her poetic practices alienated her from Duncan, and she and Creeley also drifted apart, ending the close friendships and shared poetic concerns that earlier identified the three as Black Mountain poets. An angry exchange of letters between Levertov and Duncan after the publication of her book *To Stay Alive* demonstrated their diverging poetics and foreshadowed the different strains of political poetry that emerged in the 1970s and 1980s. Whereas Levertov moved toward a romantic voice and a commonly understood language as the vehicles of protest poetry, Creeley and Duncan continued to maintain that political critiques and poetic originality emerged only from experimental poetry that challenged the norms of syntax and poetic form.

Levertov's participation in an international struggle for peace and her increasingly international reputation in the late 1960s widened her interest in and contact with an international community of poets and revolutionaries. Her increased engagement in an international poetic tradition led, among other things, to several experiments in translation. In 1967 she collaborated with Edward C. Dimock in the translation of Bengali love songs. She also published translations of Jules Supervielle, Eugene Guil-

levic, Jean Joubert, Alain Bosquet, and a collection of Bulgarian poets. Although a fairly literal translator, Levertov sometimes altered the original texts to accentuate her own poetic preferences. Whereas Joubert, for example, frequently uses long, flowing lines to establish a rhythmic momentum independent of meaning, Levertov breaks some lines to achieve the scoring of concrete detail and the visual clarity that is characteristic of her own poems. Levertov's contact with an international community also reinvigorated her engagement of European literary traditions, her reading of which increasingly lent her visions authority and provided examples for experimentation.

Retreating from the attempt to embed poetic language in political language, Levertov's next two volumes, *Footprints* (1972) and *The Freeing of the Dust* (1975), accentuate the distance between her poetic and political visions. Lacking the social context that was provided in *To Stay Alive,* the glowing moments of *Footprints* seem spare and isolated. Many poems are sequences of brief, unconnected images, as in "Brass Tacks":

i

The old wooden house a soft
almost-blue faded green
embowered in southern autumn's
nearly-yellow green leaves,
the air damp after a night of rain.

ii

The black girl sitting alone in the back row
smiled at me.

While "Brass Tacks" presents such images as consoling essentials of experience, Levertov pares them to independent glowing presences rather than weaving them into a larger scheme in the poem. Many of the political poems are structured by the stark opposition between the images of beauty that strengthen her and the horror of war, presenting a simultaneity of opposites that remains a recurrent theme in her writing.

Near Saigon,
in a tiger-cage, a woman
tries to straighten her
*   cramped spine*
and cannot.

Unclenched fist
cinnamon warmth of winter light,
revelation, communion.

While the book introduces Levertov's ecological concerns into her representation of natural beauty, it also turns to the private realm to speak of childhood memories and Levertov's divorce from her husband. Although these poems explore the imaginative vision for its own sake, they frequently make the speaker's position explicit. The opening series of poems on views from an airplane, for example, expresses a consciousness of the technologies that frame vision and that are less prominent in Levertov's earlier work.

If this poetry records a growing distance between the personal and political dimensions of her life, Levertov's theoretical writings of the mid 1970s seek to reunite them in a refined conception of political poetry. Motivated by her desire to defend the possibility of political poetry, both traditional and contemporary, against its critics, she rethought the relation between the personal and political. In her 1975 essay "On the Edge of Darkness: What is Political Poetry?" she asserts the compatibility of lyricism and political message, arguing that the personal testimony of a lyric voice is the most powerful tool of political advocacy. She writes that the goal of politically committed writers should be "such osmosis of personal and public, of assertion and song, that no one would be able to divide our poems into categories." Levertov's subsequent political poetry locates the source of change in the development of individual vision, in developing the role of the imagination in constructing a community where individual and collective growth coincide.

Like *The Freeing of the Dust, Life in the Forest* (1978) develops deeply personal subjects, including the death of Levertov's mother in 1977 and Levertov's growth in the love relationships that followed her divorce. She attempts, however, to give these themes a significance that transcends their personal dimension. The introductory note to the book describes her desire to emulate the antifascist Italian poet Cesare Pavese, whose poems about his local Piedmont area and its people in *Lavorare Stanca* (*Hard Labor,* 1943) reveal his character through his bond to the land and community. Following Pavese's model, Levertov seeks to use landscape and portrait to "avoid overuse of the autobiographical, the dominant first-person singular of so much of the American poetry—good and bad—of recent years." Levertov's poems about her mother's death portray her mother's character by describing such works as her garden. The poems suggest an acceptance of the finality of death and change, evoking the Mexican landscape as it reclaims the garden as wilderness. The different selves that emerge in two cycles of love poems also explore the relationship between character and natural and social environment. The playful, self-mocking "Modulations for Solo Voice" dissects the various traditional and nontraditional stances Levertov adopts as she attempts to find communion in a new love relationship. Titles such as "The Phonecall," "Psyche in Somerville," and "A Woman Pacing Her Room, Rereading a Letter, Returning Again and Again to Her Mirror" expose the destructive cultural forms that importantly mediate interpersonal relations.

"Metamorphic Journal," however, describes the growth of self that may be gained from the experience of love, in the lovers' mutual reflection. In this sequence the images of trees, rivers, and flame, through which Levertov attempts to grasp the lovers and their relationship, develop a cosmology that invests the lovers' whole environment with meaning. For Levertov the imagination originates in the agency through which people make sense of their world and their interpersonal relations. On the other hand, certain images convey an uncertainty about this process of growth through mutual reflection. The image of water as a mirror suggests narcissism, and a final image of the imagination's creations as fire-cast shadows on a cave wall alludes to Plato's illusory knowledge of mere opinion. Still, the poem begins to envision the more fruitful relationships between individuals that emerge in Levertov's mature politics of the personal.

Levertov's next volume, *Candles in Babylon* (1982), integrates more closely the subjects of nature, politics, and love, each of which had been for the most part developed separately since the early 1970s. The five sections of the book establish a new significance to Levertov's romantic identification with nature. While some poems abjure a romantic innocence of perception, considered inappropriate given both her own aging and experience and the horrors of contemporary history, nature comes to play a new role in Levertov's poetic portrayal of her contemporary social context. The second section of the book, "Pig Dreams," is a playful Wordsworthian Prelude of the pet pig, Sylvia. Here Levertov traces the growth of Sylvia's specifically porcine "culture" and religious reverence for nature to her natural needs and pleasures and her friendships with other farm animals. Sylvia's empathetic extension into their lives produces the interplay of similarity and difference through which she comes to know herself and her place in the farm community.

While Sylvia's Vermont farm represents an idyll of harmonious, intimate community, Levertov uses this ideal to criticize the alienating "Babylon" of mass culture in which she finds herself. Images of this culture, presented as a dark movie theater that isolates individuals while holding them in passive thrall to its visions of technological power and Cold War ideology, convey a social environment that prevents the individual from growth and authentic engagement in the world. In the rest of *Candles in Babylon,* the poems seem to explore the means by which imaginative vision can take root in a world that is politically alienating. The characteristic of empathy, embodied in the flexible octopus for whom "any shelter it can find is home," becomes a means to social and political connectedness. Identifying with the "steadfast ranks" of mountains or the "alertness of red rooftiles," the octopus not only anchors its own existence in the world by rendering the alien familiar but also provides an example for others to do the same. Increasingly, Levertov's poems on nature and art suggest ways in which individuals may "domesticate" seemingly alien aspects of their environment and reconstruct social institutions on the basis of genuine and intimate personal relations. For the poet, empathetic reflection is a virtue that both increases one's sensitivity toward fellow beings and also enriches the individual through his or her act of imagining the lives of others.

The final section of *Candles in Babylon* introduces Levertov's Christian beliefs as another major context in which she develops the varied meanings of her concrete epiphanies. As a logical outgrowth of the political ideal presented in the book, a belief in the Christian God who is presented in a "Mass for the Day of St. Thomas Didymus" becomes the basis for a potential social harmony that recognizes the metaphysical unity of all beings as creatures of a benevolent deity. Represented as the weak, newborn lamb of Christ, Levertov's Christian God is also a fragile vision of innocence and goodness whose very existence depends on its protection by all. As an element of the collective imagination, Christianity thus provides what Albert Gelpi has called "the transcendent third term that bridges the rupture between individual epiphany and public calamity" in Levertov's poetry.

In her treatment of gender issues, Levertov states quite clearly that as a poet she is not a feminist. Her 1982 essay "Genre and Gender v. Serving an Art" treats gender as one aspect of the specific and immediate situations from which the poet develops meanings that "will transcend gender." Denying the existence of a poetics that is specific to women, she writes, "I don't believe I have ever made an aesthetic decision based on my gender." Although she frequently portrays women's experiences and writes explicitly in a woman's voice, many of her poetic choices may be attributed to other interests. Her frank exploration of sexuality, for instance, is typical of many poets of the 1950s and 1960s, and she shares her emphasis on themes of domesticity with Creeley and Duncan. Linda A. Kinnahan argues persuasively that Levertov's attention to the specifics of women's lives develops a legacy of Williams's attention to the local and the sexual aspects of experience, a legacy that provided an enabling model for contemporary women poets to write as women.

Levertov's love poems reflect a variety of concerns that develop throughout her writing–from her early love lyrics, written in the dreamy unreality of her neoromanticism, to her frankly erotic poems and her poems on marriage, replete with the antiromantic sensual immediacy of the 1950s and 1960s. Likewise, her poems about the personal growth that is achieved through the transformations of love illustrate her interest in the interpersonal realm as an integral part of her political vision in the 1970s and 1980s. Her most recent love lyrics examine the conflicts between sexual and romantic love and the process of physical aging. Frequently writing directly from her particular sexual and socio-economic situation, Levertov, nevertheless, also adopts other women's voices–such as those of Ishtar, Rose White and Rose Red, and the much traveled, wine-drinking old soothsayer–not to critique them as models of a particular kind of femininity but rather, as she does with other cultural themes, to reveal them as familiar cultural influences that live in and shape her imagination.

Because she writes as a daughter, lover, wife, mother, and sister, Levertov's poetry explores various aspects of women's sexuality, their domestic culture, their poetic identity, and their roles in the cultural imagination of myth and fairy tale. Then, too, her relation to Olson's phallic theory of "projective" verse and the "objectifying" poetics that undergird the Black Mountain poetics is significant for her poetic development. Perhaps unconsciously, her *Collected Earlier Poems 1940–1960* presents the transition to the Black Mountain style as a shift from women portrayed as subject to women seen as object. "Who He Was," the last of the poems strongly grounded in iambic pentameter, describes a woman feeling the movements of her unborn child and wondering who the child will become. In contrast, the next two poems, which adopt the shorter lines and less regular meter of her American environment, describe the woman from the outside. "Kresch's Studio" describes the artist's model "in taut repose, intent / under violent light that pulls / the weight of breasts to answer the long / shadow of thighs, / confronts angles with receding / planes." "A Woman" attempts to understand a woman's unsettled emotions in her "remote," glittering green eyes but finds no key in this specific physical detail.

In *With Eyes at the Back of Our Heads,* "A Ring of Changes," a poem written to reconcile an argument between husband and wife, dramatizes an early version of Levertov's interpersonal poetics as a feminine transgression. While the man sits alone like the creator God of Genesis "forming darkness into words," the woman wishes to shed her angry pride, "to dig shame up, a buried bone / and tie it to my breast— / (would it change, in time, / to an ornament?)." Although this beginning generates a poem of reconciliation, the resemblance of the bone to Hester Prynne's embroidered *A* in *The Scarlet Letter* (1850) explains an ambivalence about the interpersonal, rather than the autonomous source of poetic vision, in terms of gender. Levertov's vision of interpersonal relationships develops fully only when she engages her love for the impersonal life of things, learned from Williams, in a social context, whether that context be interpersonal or publicly political.

Levertov's images of women challenge conventional conceptions of women's creativity. Deborah Pope and Sandra Gilbert have studied the tension between two women, one wholesome, charitable, and domestic, the other artistic, glamorous, and non-nurturing. Poems such as "In Mind" and "The Earthwoman and the Waterwoman" dramatize the tension between the housewife or mother on the one hand and the artist on the other, with biological and artistic creativity frequently presented as mutually exclusive options for the female artist. In contrast, Kinnahan and Susan Stanford Friedman have explored Levertov's construction of a matrilinear tradition of poetic vision that was inherited from her mother and that seems to reconcile this tension.

Levertov's political vision tends to be colored by the political romanticism of the 1960s and the feminist critiques of patriarchy that present a female-dominated culture as a positive alternative to a violently destructive male-dominated public world. Levertov's political ideals, grounded in a domesticity and harmony with nature traditionally associated with women, contrast with the public world of technology, rationality, and politics associated with men. While rarely involved in detailed critiques of the social institutions that shape gender roles in society, Levertov nevertheless explores the powerful ways in which institutions shape the cultural imaginations of both men and women.

Levertov in *Oblique Prayers: New Poems with 14 Translations from Jean Toubert* (1984) uses brief images and short lines to praise the wisdom to be gained from the fragmentary fact: "half a loaf / re-

veals / the inner wheat: / leavened / transubstantiation." Levertov focuses on the individuality of particular beings, attempting to approach God by grasping the particular "divinity," or spirit, of a tree, river, flower, and even herself, in "Of God and of the Gods." This intensive focus on the individual creature in its reality stems both from a reverence for all nature as divine creation and from a heightened consciousness of the changing meaning of experiences:

Felt life
grows in one's mind:
each semblance

forms and
reforms cloudy
links with
the next

and the next.

Increasingly tolerant of contradictions, Levertov represents her life as composed of patterns or threads of a fabric whose order she herself cannot grasp. In contrast to the weak lamb of "Mass for the Day of St. Thomas Didymus," the God of *Oblique Prayers* is a remote weaver whose purpose the individual cannot fathom: "our eyes, / our lives, too close to the canvas, / enmeshed within / the turning dance, / to see it [perfection]."

Levertov's ecological concerns find expression in poems in which she delves into the actual relationship between human and other natural beings. The sequence "Gathered at the River" employs techniques that recur in Levertov's later nature poetry. Personifying trees as fearful of their extermination by a nuclear holocaust, the poem extends Levertov's interpersonal poetics to include the non-human beings in nature. Levertov frequently uses images of a family or a single organism to signify the interdependence of human and natural life in the single ecosystem of the earth; she also evaluates human actions in terms of their impact on the earth and its inhabitants, and she seeks to awaken a sensitivity to and respect for the creatures and the patterns of life that are seemingly independent of human interest, yet worthy of equal respect.

Oblique Prayers thus blends the Christian and ecological visions that enlarge the field of the poet's earlier poetic concerns. In her 1991 essay, "Some Affinities of Content," Levertov describes the reading she prefers at this time to be "a certain kind of poem about the world of nature written predominantly by poets of the Pacific Northwest, and poems of various provenance that were concerned more or less with matters of religious faith," primarily although not exclusively in a Christian or Jewish context. Among the latter she includes Ben Sáenz, Lucille Clifton, and Czeslaw Milosz, in whose work spiritual longing includes "the quest for or the encounter with God." The "affinities" between these two groups lie for Levertov in their sense of life "on pilgrimage," "in search of significance underneath and beyond the succession of temporal events." In her later poetry Nature and God are the subjects that provide frameworks for a moral and spiritual understanding, one that surpasses the restrictive, human-centered views offered by technology and political history.

Breathing the Water (1987) and A Door in the Hive (1989) retain the focus on the concrete world exemplified in Oblique Prayers, but these books introduce the stronger mystical vision that informs much of Levertov's later poetry. Grounded in the visionary traditions of Rilke's conception of poets as "bees of the invisible," creatures that distill pollen into honey, and also in a Christian reverence for each object as a miraculous creation capable of providing knowledge of God, this heightened vision focuses increasingly on those moments of perception when physical matter is somehow transformed into a spiritual essence. As Levertov's poetic vision deepens, she moves from a pure meditation on the natural object to the creation of artistic moments or patterns that serve as the "doorkey" or "embrasure" to a fuller and larger vision. In "Athanor," for example, a dog-food bag gilded by light becomes a "fleeting conjugation / of wood and light, embrace that leaves wood / dizzying and insubstantial." In "From the Image-Flow—Death of Chausson, 1899" the poet imagines the death of the composer as a synesthesia of a mauve stream of music and green leaves, culminating in silence.

For Levertov, the composed rather than the found poetic object becomes central in stimulating the imagination. Occasionally poems in these volumes express an uncertainty about what seems to be Levertov's new relation to nature, with the speaker dramatized in "The Spy" as a spy and in "Captive Flower" as a jailer. Two sections titled "Spinoffs" establish the quasi-generic character of the spinoff as "a verbal construct which neither describes nor comments but moves off at a tangent to, or parallel with, its inspiration."

While Levertov's Rilkean visions delight in description and imaginative vision for their own sake, her poems on Christian themes frequently contemplate the relation of the poetic illumination to personal life, history, and cosmology. In Breathing

Dust jacket for Levertov's 1997 book of poems that she says "trace my own slow movement from agnosticism to Christian faith"

the Water the sequence "The Showings: Lady Julian of Norwich, 1342–1416" explores the mystic's visions elicited by the everyday world by employing rich biographical and historical detail, such as the child's wonder at a newly laid egg or a hazelnut, even in the "dark times" of war and plague in the late Middle Ages. Levertov emphasizes Julian's desire to experience the crucifixion of the flesh as a compassionate act of empathy with all human suffering. Julian's clinging to joy amid such suffering, "like an acrobat, by your teeth, fiercely," represents a faith that is foreign yet admirable to Levertov. In direct address, Levertov conjures Julian as a model of a faith alien to the modern mind yet empowering in the struggle toward goodness—after deeds, quoting Julian, "so evil / . . . / it seems to us / impossible any good / can come of them."

Levertov's "El Salvador: Requiem and Invocation," a libretto written for the composer Newell Hendricks and included in A Door in the Hive, seeks a Julian-like way to heal suffering. Taking as its occasion the murder of Archbishop Romero, three Mary Knoll sisters, and a lay volunteer in El Salvador, the "Requiem" attempts to render those murdered or silenced by the oppressive regime as a sustaining source of resistance. The poem returns to the collage style of *To Stay Alive,* using the language of torturers, Mayan prayers, and the words of the martyrs to represent the political struggle. Levertov contrasts an idealized precolonial Mayan culture, in which labor and prayer, human and natural life were in harmony, with a Western, money-driven economy of scientific "progress." While denying the possibility of a return to the earlier Mayan life, she presents the Christian vision of community held by those murdered, a community based on mutual respect and "listening," as a foundation for dignity and hope in society. A requiem rather than a documentary, the poem moves from pain and despair to search out a way from violence toward healing, finding in its commemoration of the dead "the knowledge / that grows in power / out of the seeds of their martyrdom."

Later, in *A Door in the Hive,* Levertov portrays the power of Christian belief as it is manifested in an individual life. In this collection poems on the Christian themes of the Annunciation, the Nativity, and the Harrowing of Hell not only continue the rich illumination of Christian texts with humble, everyday detail that was begun in "The Showings" but also, just as her Rilkean visions do, seek to reveal the points at which divinity may become incarnate in the individual being. "Annunciation," for example, evokes the possibility of a divine incarnation that is imminent in the everyday world. "Aren't there annunciations / of one sort or another / in most lives?" Emphasizing the "compassion," "intelligence," and "courage" with which the Virgin Mary embraces her role as the mother of Jesus, Levertov seeks to translate a tradition of miracles into material and psychological circumstances more acceptable to the modern mind.

Even as Levertov affirms the activity of spirit in the daily life of the individual and society, *A Door in the Hive* betrays the uneasy relationship that exists between heightened vision and actual history. "Flickering Mind" explores the tension between the individual's desire to contemplate God's presence in all being and the individual mind's earthbound tendency to "wander." Although Levertov has said that she intends no particular relation between the two poems, a poem ending one section praises a blind man who is living at the edge of a cliff for breathing "face to face with desire," while the first poem of the next section suggests the limitations of such a private vision. "Distanced" is a poem that contrasts the witnessing of life from afar with the actuality of immediate experience by presenting an image of shepherds in the mountains who "marvel" and "sorrow"

at the sack of a city below them. They feel the "pity and dread" of tragic drama but perceive the people fleeing the city as a "river" without faces or blood. "Where Is the Angel?" seeks an angry wrestling by which to break the gentle September beauty, which, like glass, separates Levertov from the turbulence of history: "History / mouths, volume turned off." Questioning the value of her beautiful images, the poet feels isolated from the wounding engagement in history that mars such perfection, "so curses and blessing flow storming out / and the glass shatters, and the iron sunders."

Levertov's *Evening Train* (1992) records the experience of settling in her new home in Seattle, her dialogue with representations of nature created by poets of the Pacific Northwest, her struggle as an aging woman to understand the difficult meanings of love, and her response to the Persian Gulf War that pitted the United States against Iraq in 1991. In one poem, still conscious of mystery and delighted by descriptions, she nevertheless finds herself enjoying "the leisure of mind / to lean on the fence and simply look" and is thereby reluctant to synthesize or assign meaning–whether to the neighboring mountain, a photo of a friend, or barnyard doves and chickens. In another poem, torn between the "two magnets" of nature and art, "Rock Simple or Rock Wrought," and "tools of Geology or tools of Art," she initiates a dialogue that contrasts the American tradition of immersion in nature and her European love of ancient cultural traditions. As in her earlier writing, some of Levertov's best poems emerge when she weaves the different strands of her writing into the evolving situations of personal experience. The longer line in many of these poems, the line she used in her earlier works inspired by Pavese, serves as a formal signal of her thematic return to Pavese's integration of person and place.

While the first section of the book, "Lake Mountain Moon," finds the pulse of the poet's new environment, both in its natural and its man-made dimensions, subsequent sections interpret human creations through metaphors of the mist, the ancient rock, and the shadow of this landscape. "Stele," a response to a stone funerary relief, also describes the moments between a man and woman parting in terms of the "land of shadow" and "road of cloud" each is about to inhabit. In a later sequence the speaker reprimands herself for falling in love just when she had decided that she was too old for its demands; then she turns to her landscape for its "stoic" wisdom. "Shameless heart! Did you not vow to learn / stillness from the heron, / quiet from the mists of fall, / and from the mountain–what was it? / Pride? Remoteness?" "Witnessing from Afar" addresses the problem of identifying with or speaking for victims who are far away by focusing on the nearer effects of war and ecological disasters at home. Whether in the swimmers' denial that a lake is seriously polluted, in the dehumanization of the language of high-technology war and video games, or even in the substitution of *may* for *might* in contemporary speech, the poet recognizes and deplores the tendency to deny the real and final effects of human actions, and, thus, of responsibility for those actions. Whether her subject is the burial of Iraqi soldiers while they are still alive, a neighboring heron, or the stone of a medieval cathedral, Levertov, as she does in her earlier work, makes whatever is vitally important to her vivid and compelling.

In the five years after *Evening Train* Levertov published one new collection of poems, *Sands of the Well* (1996). She also published *Tesserae: Memories and Suppositions* (1995), a series of prose autobiographical sketches largely concerned with the first twenty-five years of her life, before she settled in the United States. She also arranged two small volumes of previously published poems, *The Life Around Us* and *The Stream & the Sapphire* (both 1997). The two collections center on two of the major strands of her late poetry and are subtitled respectively "Selected Poems on Nature" and "Selected Poems on Religious Themes." In a short preface to each book, Levertov notes that in her nature poems she is driven to write, as well as poems of celebration, poems of "lament . . . anger, and . . . the expression of dread." Among the poems on religious themes, she notes in the other preface, are poems that "trace my own slow movement from agnosticism to Christian faith." A book of forty poems titled *This Great Unknowing: Last Poems* will appear in 1999.

The final section of *Sands of the Well* is an affirmation of that faith, couched in terms of awe and wonder and acknowledging her own need for the power of miracle to have "its ground / its roots / in bone and blood." The book opens with the poet facing uncertainty, change, and encroaching death (Levertov's illness had been diagnosed some time before). The book then moves into poems of the same quiet but passionate observation of details—a cobweb, a heron, an evening bus—that had characterized *Evening Train,* and these are set, again as in the earlier volume, against the ever changing but always present mountain. A few poems concern memories of her mother's early life; others view her own life, from the perspective of a life lived fully and intensely as lover, activist, and writer. The book then sets these themes alongside its closing poems of personal faith.

Through her many writings and her abounding creativity, Levertov's ability to create luminous representations of the material world in its sensuous existence remains her greatest talent and the distinguishing feature of her mature poetic vision. By poetry that finds epiphanies in the concrete world of experience, and by her theory of "organic form," which emerges from a grounding of form in the object and an appreciation for the poetic possibilities of colloquial language, Levertov is linked both to William Carlos Williams and to the Black Mountain poets; but the increasingly romantic direction in which she developed her poetics kept her from continuing the avant-garde's challenge to linguistic conventions, thereby significantly distancing her from one major legacy of the Black Mountain poets. Especially in her later work, Levertov aspired to translate the high calling and visionary power of the romantic and modernist poet into forms and terms comprehensible to a scientifically skeptical mass culture.

This effort sharply distinguishes her from such contemporaries as the Language poets—Charles Bernstein and Susan Howe, for example—who believe that genuine creativity requires a radical formal experimentation that challenges the traditional lyric forms and voice. Levertov's focus on the individual imagination as the source of political change further contrasts with these poets' desire to expose and disrupt the power of linguistic conventions, a disruption they assume will ultimately undermine other institutions they oppose. For critic Cary Nelson, the confidence that Levertov places in the power of individuals seems naive; for others, such as Albert Gelpi, her focus on the individual's potential to effect change, and her distinctively articulate personal voice, are sources of power and beauty.

Levertov's writing is perhaps most successful when she focuses the rays of its different subjects and styles through the lens of her personal, lived experience, sensitively revealing in her scrupulously crafted poems the vital relationship between the individual self and the world. Meanwhile, her ongoing efforts to fathom and express the problematic intersections between the public and private realms of society, between a Christian cosmology and the world of strictly scientific fact, and between literary tradition and the darknesses of contemporary history have helped build important new bridges across the difficult cultural landscape of contemporary poetry.

Denise Levertov died at the age of seventy-four in Seattle, Washington, on 20 December 1997 of complications from lymphoma. Earlier that year, her former husband, Mitchell Goodman, the subject of many of her earlier love poems before their divorce in the 1970s and companion to many of her earlier political activities, also died, and only a few weeks before Levertov's death James Laughlin, founder of New Directions and Levertov's friend and publisher for more than thirty-five years, died. According to friends, Levertov died before being able to put to paper a poem she had composed for his memorial service.

Levertov had given permission before her death for the publication of her correspondence with William Carlos Williams, a poet who was a major influence on her in the 1950s and whose work she commented on in various poems and essays throughout her career. The letters amount to a narrative on Levertov's adopting, sometimes somewhat self-consciously, she later admitted, the directness and less formal diction of her adopted country. *The Letters of Denise Levertov and William Carlos Williams* (1998) cover Levertov's first years in New York City as well as her two years in Mexico. In them she moves from being a worshipful disciple of the older poet to having the confidence of an equal in exchanges about their work and that of their contemporaries.

Levertov's poetry in her final decade of writing embraced her English and wider European heritage much more fully than earlier, although the extent to which she had come to be viewed, at least in England, as an American poet was revealed in the difference between the warm praise of her life and work in an obituary in *The New York Times* and an error-filled and patronizing notice in the *Times* (London), which opened with the assertion that her "reputation stands far higher in the cliquish world of poetry in North America than in her native Britain." Throughout her career Levertov was no stranger to literary and political battles, but she might well have been disappointed at such language of division, given her own multicultural roots and the emphasis in her work on uniting cultures and races through an awareness of their common spiritual heritage and their common responsibility to a shared planet.

Letters:

The Letters of Denise Levertov and William Carlos Williams, edited by Christopher MacGowan (New York: New Directions, 1998).

Interviews:

David Ossman, "An Interview with Denise Levertov," in his *The Sullen Art* (New York: Corinth Books, 1963), pp. 73–76;

Walter Sutton, "A Conversation with Denise Levertov," *Minnesota Review,* 5 (October–December, 1965): 322–328;

E. G. Burrows, "An Interview with Denise Levertov," *Michigan Quarterly Review,* 7 (1968): 239–242;

Ian Reid, "'Everyman's Land': Ian Reid Interviews Denise Levertov," *Southern Review: Literary and Interdisciplinary Essays, South Australia,* 5 (1972): 231–236;

William Heyen and Anthony Piccione, "A Conversation with Denise Levertov," *Ironwood,* 4 (1973): 21–34;

William Packard, ed., "Craft Interview with Denise Levertov," *New York Quarterly,* 7 (1974): 79–100;

John K. Atchity, "Denise Levertov: An Interview," *San Francisco Review of Books,* no. 4 (March 1979): 5–8;

Sybil Estess, "An Interview with Denise Levertov and a Biographical Note," in *American Poetry Observed: Poets and Their Work,* edited by Joseph David Bellamy (Chicago: University of Illinois Press, 1984), pp. 155–167;

Lorrie Smith, "An Interview with Denise Levertov," *Michigan Quarterly Review,* 24 (1985): 596–604;

Conversations with Denise Levertov, edited by Jewel Spears Brooker (Jackson: University Press of Mississippi, 1998);

Nicholas O'Connell, "A Poet's Valediction," *Poets & Writers,* 26 (May/June 1998): 20–25.

Bibliographies:

Robert A. Wilson, *A Bibliography of Denise Levertov* (New York: Phoenix Book Shop, 1972);

Liana Sakelliou-Schultz, *Denise Levertov: An Annotated Primary and Secondary Bibliography* (New York: Garland Publishing, 1988).

References:

Charles Altieri, "Denise Levertov and the Limits of the Aesthetics of Presence," in *Denise Levertov: Selected Criticism,* edited by Albert Gelpi (Ann Arbor: University of Michigan Press, 1993), pp. 126–147;

Robert Bly [Crunk], "The Work of Denise Levertov," *Sixties,* 9 (Spring 1967): 48–65;

Susan Stanford Friedman, "Creativity and the Childbirth Metaphor: Gender Difference in Literary Discourse," *Feminist Studies,* 13, no. 1 (1975): 328–341;

Albert Gelpi, ed., *Denise Levertov: Selected Criticism* (Ann Arbor: University of Michigan Press, 1993);

Joan Hallisey, "Denise Levertov's 'Illustrious Ancestors': The Hassidic Influence," in *Denise Levertov: Selected Criticism,* edited by Gelpi (Ann Arbor: University of Michigan Press, 1993), pp. 260–267;

Linda A. Kinnahan, "Denise Levertov: The Daughter's Voice," in her *Poetics of the Feminine: Authority and Literary Tradition in William Carlos Williams, Mina Loy, Denise Levertov, and Kathleen Fraser* (Cambridge: Cambridge University Press, 1994), pp. 125–182;

John Lowney, "'Pure Products': Imitation, Affiliation, and the Politics of Female Creativity in Denise Levertov's Poetry," in *The American Avant-Garde Tradition: William Carlos Williams, Postmodern Poetry, and the Politics of Cultural Memory* (Lewisburg, Pa.: Bucknell University Press, 1997), pp. 74–100;

Harry Marten, *Understanding Denise Levertov* (Columbia: University of South Carolina Press, 1988);

James F. Mersmann, "Denise Levertov: Piercing In," in his *Out of the Vietnam Vortex: A Study of Poets and Poetry against the War* (Lawrence: University Press of Kansas, 1974), pp. 77–106;

Peter Middleton, *Revelation and Revolution in the Poetry of Denise Levertov* (London: Binnacle Press, 1981);

Dorothy M. Nielson, "Prosopopoeia and the Ethics of Ecological Advocacy in the Poetry of Denise Levertov and Gary Snyder," *Contemporary Literature,* 34 (Winter 1993): 691–713;

Deborah Pope, "Homespun and Crazy Feathers: The Split-Self in the Poems of Denise Levertov," in *Critical Essays on Denise Levertov,* edited by Linda Welshimer Wagner (Boston: G. K. Hall, 1991), pp. 73–97;

Audrey Rodgers, *Denise Levertov: The Poetry of Engagement* (Rutherford, N.J.: Fairleigh Dickinson University Press, 1993);

Leonard Schwartz, "Guillevic/Levertov: The Poetics of Matter," *Twentieth Century Literature,* 38 (Fall 1992): 290–298;

Nancy Sisko, "To Stay Alive: Levertov's Search for a Revolutionary Poetry," *Sagetrieb,* 5 (Fall 1986): 47–61;

Linda Wagner, *Denise Levertov* (New York: Twayne, 1967);

Wagner, ed., *Critical Essays on Denise Levertov* (Boston: G. K. Hall, 1991);

Wagner, ed., *Denise Levertov: In Her Own Province* (New York: New Directions, 1979);

Edward Zlotowski, "Levertov and Rilke: A Sense of Aesthetic Ethics," *Twentieth Century Literature,* 38 (Fall 1992): 324–342.

Papers:
The Denise Levertov papers are housed in Special Collections, Green Library, Stanford University. Significant Levertov correspondence and manuscripts are also included in the Creeley papers at Stanford University, the Duncan papers in the Poetry/Rare Books Collection of the Lockwood Library at the State University of New York at Buffalo, and the Williams papers at the Beinecke Library of Yale University.

Robert Lowell

This entry was updated from the entry by Ashley Brown (University of South Carolina)
in DLB 169: American Poets Since World War II, Fifth Series.

BIRTH: Boston, Massachusetts, 1 March 1917, to Robert Traill Spence and Charlotte Winslow Lowell.

EDUCATION: Attended St. Mark's School; attended Harvard University, 1935–1937; A.B. (summa cum laude), Kenyon College, 1940; additional study at Louisiana State University, 1940–1941.

MARRIAGES: 2 April 1940 to Jean Stafford (divorced June 1948). 28 July 1949 to Elizabeth Hardwick (divorced 1972); child: Harriet Winslow. 1972 to Lady Caroline Blackwood; child: Robert Sheridan.

AWARDS AND HONORS: National Institute of Arts and Letters Award, 1947; Guggenheim Fellowship, 1947; Pulitzer Prize for *Lord Weary's Castle*, 1947; Harriet Monroe Poetry Award, University of Chicago, 1952; Guinness Poetry Award (Ireland, shared with W. H. Auden, Edith Sitwell, and Edwin Muir) for "Skunk Hour," 1959; National Book Award for *Life Studies*, 1960; Boston Arts Festival Poet, 1960; Harriet Monroe Memorial Prize, Poetry, 1961; Bollingen Prize in Poetry for translation, Yale University Library, for *Imitations*, 1962; Levinson Prize, Poetry, 1963; Golden Rose Trophy, New England Poetry Club, 1964; Obie Award for best new play for *The Old Glory, Village Voice*, 1965; Sarah Josepha Hale Award, Friends of the Richards Library, 1966; National Council on the Arts grant to produce *Prometheus Bound*, 1967; Copernicus Award, Academy of American Poets, 1974; Pulitzer Prize for *The Dolphin*, 1974; National Medal for Literature, National Academy and Institute of Arts and Letters, 1977; National Book Critics Circle Award for *Day by Day*, 1978, and posthumous nomination (in criticism) for *Collected Prose*, 1987; LittD., Williams College, 1965, and Yale University, 1968; and honorary degree, Columbia University, 1969.

DEATH: New York, New York, 12 September 1977.

BOOKS: *Land of Unlikeness* (Cummington, Mass.: Cummington Press, 1944);

Robert Lowell

Lord Weary's Castle (New York: Harcourt, Brace, 1946);

Poems 1938–1949 (London: Faber & Faber, 1950);

The Mills of the Kavanaughs (New York: Harcourt, Brace, 1951);

Life Studies (New York: Farrar, Straus & Cudahy, 1959);

Imitations (New York: Farrar, Straus & Giroux, 1961; London: Faber & Faber, 1962);

For the Union Dead (New York: Farrar, Straus & Giroux, 1964; London: Faber & Faber, 1965);

The Old Glory (New York: Farrar, Straus & Giroux, 1965; London: Faber & Faber, 1966; revised edition, New York: Farrar, Straus & Giroux, 1968);

Near the Ocean (New York: Farrar, Straus & Giroux, 1967; London: Faber & Faber, 1967);

The Voyage & Other Versions of Poems by Baudelaire (London: Faber & Faber, 1968; New York: Farrar, Straus & Giroux, 1969);

Notebook 1967-68 (New York: Farrar, Straus & Giroux, 1969); revised and republished as *Notebook* (New York: Farrar, Straus & Giroux, 1970; London: Faber & Faber, 1970);

The Dolphin (New York: Farrar, Straus & Giroux, 1973; London: Faber & Faber, 1973);

For Lizzie and Harriet (New York: Farrar, Straus & Giroux, 1973; London: Faber & Faber, 1973);

History (New York: Farrar, Straus & Giroux, 1973; London: Faber & Faber, 1973);

Selected Poems (New York: Farrar, Straus & Giroux, 1976);

Day by Day (New York: Farrar, Straus & Giroux, 1977);

Collected Prose, edited by Robert Giroux (New York: Farrar, Straus & Giroux, 1987).

TRANSLATIONS: Jean Baptiste Racine, *Phaedra,* in *Phaedra and Figaro* (New York: Farrar, Straus & Giroux, 1961; London: Faber & Faber, 1963);

Aeschylus, *Prometheus Bound* (New York: Farrar, Straus & Giroux, 1969; London: Faber & Faber, 1970);

Aeschylus, *The Oresteia* (New York: Farrar, Straus & Giroux, 1979).

For some readers and critics Robert Lowell stood at the center of his literary generation, and by the mid 1960s one admirer, Irvin Ehrenpreis, was referring to "The Age of Lowell." One can see why. Lowell was associated with nearly all the important American poets of the first half of the twentieth century, and long before the end of his life he seemed to be their heir. His appeal was not only literary. He involved himself to an unusual degree with the public events of his time, just as he brought his private life into public view by way of his poems. He was at once the poet of the American empire—sometimes resembling Virgil, sometimes Juvenal, sometimes Horace—and the alleged father of "confessional poetry." He wrote a great deal during his last decade, from 1967 to 1977, but so far few readers have assimilated his late work. His great poems, or at least the familiar ones, all come before 1967. In the near future there will doubtless be textual criticism of Lowell's poetry; few poets have revised so rapidly and extensively. A vari-

orum Lowell may or may not make these things easier for readers.

Robert Traill Spence Lowell was born in Boston on 1 March 1917. His family, long distinguished in that city, included other literary persons: his Lowell grandfather (for whom he was named), James Russell Lowell, and Amy Lowell. For two years he attended St. Mark's School in Massachusetts (of which his grandfather had once been headmaster). On the faculty was Richard Eberhart, a young American poet about whom Lowell said many years later, "There was someone there whom I admired who was engaged in writing poetry."

He went to Harvard, like all Lowells before him, but he left after two years. Although he was already acquainted with Robert Frost, Lowell sought his instruction in poetry elsewhere. About this time, in 1937, he met the English novelist Ford Madox Ford, who was about to travel to Tennessee to visit Allen Tate and his wife, the novelist Caroline Gordon; Ford evidently invited the young man to accompany him. Thus, Lowell was brought into the presence of a distinguished Southern poet who was to have a considerable influence on his work. He pitched a tent in the Tates' front yard and spent the summer there, writing poetry in an almost obsessive way. In the fall of that year he went to Kenyon College in Ohio to study with John Crowe Ransom (Tate's first master); he remained there until 1940, when he graduated summa cum laude with a degree in classics. Among the close friends he made were Randall Jarrell, the poet, and Peter Taylor, the short-story writer. At the same time, in 1940, he became a Roman Catholic and married a young novelist, Jean Stafford. (Stafford, who died in 1979, was the author of three novels and several collections of stories; she occasionally figures in Lowell's poetry.) To round out his education with the Southern literati, Lowell studied for a year at Louisiana State University with Cleanth Brooks and Robert Penn Warren.

Lowell worked for a time in New York City with the Catholic publishing house of Sheed and Ward, but he and Stafford spent 1942-1943 in the mountains of Tennessee, where they shared a house with the Tates. It was here that many of the poems in his first book were written. Then, in the middle of World War II, Lowell was jailed as a conscientious objector to the Allied bombing of German civilians. (This interlude in his life is the basis of a poem called "Memories of West Street and Lepke" in *Life Studies,* published in 1959.) In 1944

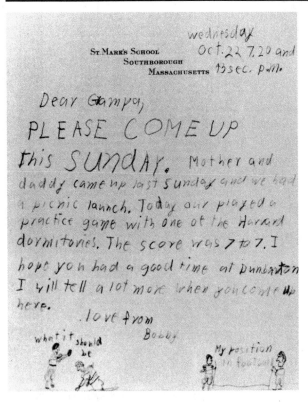

*Letter from Lowell to his grandfather Arthur Winslow, 1930
(Houghton Library, Harvard University)*

his first book, *Land of Unlikeness,* was published in a small edition by the Cummington Press in Massachusetts; it was introduced by Tate.

Tate's introduction is a brilliant account of Lowell's poetry at that time, and in two sentences he foretold the course of Lowell's career:

> On the one hand, the Christian symbolism is intellectualized and frequently given a savage satirical direction; it points to the disappearance of the Christian experience from the modern world, and stands, perhaps, for the poet's own effort to recover it. On the other hand, certain shorter poems, like "A Suicidal Nightmare" and "Death from Cancer," are richer in immediate experience than the explicitly religious poems; they are more dramatic, the references being personal and historical and the symbolism less willed and explicit.

An example of the former kind of poetry that Tate mentions is the opening stanza of "On the Eve of the Feast of the Immaculate Conception":

> Mother of God, whose burly love
> Turns swords to plowshares, come, improve
>   On the big wars
> And make this holiday with Mars
> Your Feast Day, while Bellona's bluff
> Courage or call it what you please
>   Plays blindman's bluff
>   Through virtue's knees.

The ironic contrast between the Mother of God and the Roman god of war is boldly stated as a metaphysical conceit; the sarcasm is only too evident. This passage comes close to being the norm for *Land of Unlikeness.* The strength of feeling never relents. Both private and public aspects of Lowell's life at this time account for the tone of the poetry: his defiance of his parents in different ways, one of them being his conversion to Catholicism; and the wartime events that he saw as more complicated than most people would. (Early in the war, however, he attempted to enlist in the navy.) The terms of this kind of poetry are large, almost cosmic, and they sometimes lead to the excesses of metaphor that one associates with the decline of the metaphysical style in the seventeenth century. Most of these poems have never been reprinted, at least not in their original form.

The other kind of poetry that Tate describes is just beginning to emerge in this first book; it can be seen at its best in the sequence on Lowell's grandfather Arthur Winslow. The "personal and historical" references are very specific, and one can easily say in retrospect that Lowell's particularity is one of his strong points as a poet. This sequence was reprinted in his famous second book, *Lord Weary's Castle* (1946), where the particularity is even more evident. In the early version, for instance, he speaks of "The craft that netted a million dollars, late / Mining in California's golden bays / Then lost it all in Boston real estate." In the revised version in *Lord Weary's Castle* the poeticism of "Mining in California's golden bays" becomes "Hosing out gold in Colorado's waste," which is probably more accurate as family history and certainly more precise in physical details. The precision is there even when Lowell is imagining a situation. In "Exile's Return," the first poem in *Lord Weary's Castle,* he describes a scene that is evidently wartime Germany; it looks authentic. What the poet has in fact done is to lift details from Thomas Mann's story "Tonio Kröger" (1903) and rearrange them, heighten them, for maximum effect. Lowell very early became a master at making poetry out of prose; his eye for the precise detail is unusually keen.

At this stage in his career he resembled at least one classic American writer, Nathaniel Hawthorne, in that he seemed to do his best work when he turned his attention to the history of his own people. And for a young writer in the mid twentieth century, there was an accumulated literary history such as did not exist when Hawthorne started. Hawthorne himself is part of this history; so is Jonathan Edwards, and two of the finest poems in *Lord Weary's Castle* ("Mr. Edwards and the Spider" and "After

216

the Surprising Conversions") are transmuted from well-known passages in Edwards's highly charged prose. One intensely satiric poem, the sonnet called "Concord," was carried over from *Land of Unlikeness* to *Lord Weary's Castle,* but with drastic changes. In the earlier version Ralph Waldo Emerson is the special focus of criticism: "Concord, where the Emersons / Washed out the blood-clots on my Master's robe." Two years later this passage becomes, less severely,

> Concord where Thoreau
> Named all the birds without a gun to probe
> Through darkness to the painted man and bow:
> The death-dance of King Philip and his scream
> Whose echo girdled this imperfect globe.

Here Emerson is not directly named; nor does his disciple Thoreau come in for the same criticism. The last line, which is carried over almost intact, is itself an "echo" of Emerson's most famous line in "The Concord Hymn."

It was Herman Melville, however, who most deeply engaged Lowell's imagination in those days. "The Quaker Graveyard in Nantucket," a magnificent baroque elegy in seven parts, would have been impossible without *Moby-Dick* (1851). (Lowell's poem was originally called "To Herman Melville.") It no doubt owes much to the John Milton of "Lycidas" (1637), and indeed this is appropriate because Lowell's poem is about the death of his cousin Warren Winslow, a naval officer who drowned in the North Atlantic during the war. The rhetoric is closer to Melville's, as in this passage:

> The winds' wings beat upon the stones,
> Cousin, and scream for you and the claws rush
> At the sea's throat and wring it in the slush
> Of this old Quaker graveyard where the bones
> Cry out in the long night for the hurt beast
> Bobbing by Ahab's whaleboats in the East.

Melville remained an important point of reference in Lowell's mind if not in his poetry, which became less baroque. Near the end of his life he put *Moby-Dick* beside the great epics of earlier literary periods. In an unfinished essay called "New England and Further," part of which was posthumously published in 1979, he wrote:

> Often magnificent rhythms and a larger vocabulary make it equal to the great metrical poems. . . . It is our best book. It tells us not to break our necks on a brickwall. Yet what sticks in the mind is the Homeric prowess of the extinct whaleman, gone before his prey.

The kinesthetic quality of the passage quoted from "The Quaker Graveyard" is fairly typical of early Lowell. Here and there, as in the sixth section of the poem ("Our Lady of Walsingham"), a quiet moment occurs; but generally the rhetoric surges in response to a deeply felt subject.

Lord Weary's Castle received the Pulitzer Prize in 1947. By that time it had been reviewed at length; one review in particular, Randall Jarrell's in the *Nation* (18 January 1947), became famous in its own right as an example of a poet-critic generously recognizing the arrival of a young master. Indeed his description of Lowell's central theme—the "wintry, Calvinist, capitalist world" against which the poet set himself—was the basis for much subsequent commentary.

Lowell's poetry continued to move in the direction that Tate had predicted it would: the poems became more dramatic as they depended less on the "willed" Christian symbolism. The characteristic poems of the next few years were in fact dramatic monologues. Seven of them made up *The Mills of the Kavanaughs* (1951). The title poem, which is Lowell's longest single work (608 lines, arranged in 38 rhymed stanzas), has never been well received even by his most sympathetic critics. Its narrative does not move; its large symbolism is forced. The heroine, a widow lamenting her husband, identifies herself with Persephone, whose statue stands on the grounds of her husband's house in Maine. There is no real action. On the other hand, two of the shorter poems, running to three or four pages, are highly successful: "Mother Marie Therese" and "Falling Asleep over the Aeneid." They are written in heroic couplets and may owe something to Robert Browning and Yvor Winters, but they sound like Lowell, with their vigorous runover lines and emphatic rhythms. "Mother Marie Therese" is also a poem of lament, in this case for a nun who drowned in 1912 (Lowell may have been thinking of Gerard Manley Hopkins's 1875 poem "The Wreck of the Deutschland"); the speaker is herself a Canadian nun "stationed in New Brunswick." The poem is wonderfully conversational at times, but it gathers up to a pitch of feeling at the end, when the poet somewhat boldly rounds it out with three couplets using the same rhyme.

"Falling Asleep over the Aeneid" is a masterpiece; Robert Fitzgerald called it "that marvel of dream work as historical imagination." The speaker, an old man in Concord reading Virgil on Sunday morning, is immediately brought before the reader:

Randall Jarrell, Lowell, and Peter Taylor in Greensboro, North Carolina, 1948

The sun is blue and scarlet on my page,
And *yuck-a, yuck-a, yuck-a, yuck-a,* rage
The yellowhammers mating. Yellow fire
Blankets the captives dancing on their pyre,
And the scorched lictor screams and drops his rod.

Lowell had perhaps learned something about composition from Wallace Stevens's "Sunday Morning," where bird and fruit and sun, introduced in the opening lines, are carried through the poem in a series of transfigurations. Here the flame colors of the bright morning sun are intensified by the yellow wings of the birds that the old man only hears, but then the colors are absorbed by the fire that leaps from the page, as it were, with the lictor's scream. (The funeral of the heroic young Pallas in the *Aeneid* is the episode that takes over the old man's dream.) Fire and bird move through the poem in many ingenious ways, and they prepare for the end, where the dreamer recalls his uncle, a young Union officer in the Civil War, "Blue-capped and bird-like," at his funeral. Thus, two eras of history are brought into relationship.

When *The Mills of the Kavanaughs* was published in 1951, Lowell was living in Italy. His marriage with Jean Stafford had ended in 1948; in the following year he married Elizabeth Hardwick, a novelist from Kentucky. The Lowells lived at different places in Europe, but Italy seemed to have the great-

est attraction for them, as it did for many American poets during the 1950s. (Eventually, after his death, some of his Italian friends, including his translator, brought out an impressive volume of tributes.) He was also becoming known in London, and as early as 1950 Faber and Faber, the publishing house of which T. S. Eliot was a director, began to publish his work. In time Lowell's reputation in London was possibly even larger than it was in the United States. After the death of his mother in 1954 in Italy, he returned with his wife to live in a house on Marlborough Street in Boston. He had left the Catholic Church. Perhaps for the moment there was nothing urgent to write about, and the few poems that he composed during this period were usually elegies for literary friends such as Ford Madox Ford and the philosopher George Santayana, whom he had visited in Rome.

The great change that came over his poetry in the late 1950s is now well known. In 1957 he was writing his autobiography in prose, and this became the actual source for a group of highly personal poems that, to some early readers, were only chopped-up prose fragments. The first of the new poems, and probably the most famous, is "Skunk Hour," which was started in August 1957. It is modeled on Elizabeth Bishop's "The Armadillo," according to Lowell's own account. (Bishop's poem, which is set in Brazil, is dedicated to Lowell.) Her versification and open texture suggested an "easier" mode of poetry. In each case a single animal emerges at the end of the poem in a kind of affirmation. According to Lowell (whose account of the composition of the poem is found in *The Contemporary Poet as Artist and Critic,* 1964), he worked backward. The poem became intensely personal in a way that Bishop's is not. Finally he wrote the four opening stanzas (half the poem) as a social setting: a declining Maine seaside town. The characteristic pronoun here is *our,* but the sense of community is precarious. The heart of the poem is the pair of stanzas that comes between the social setting and the image of the skunk and her kittens who take over the deserted town at the end:

> One dark night
> my Tudor Ford climbed the hill's skull;
> I watched for love-cars. Lights turned down,
> they lay together hull to hull,
> where the graveyard shelves on the town. . . .
> My mind's not right.
>
> A car radio bleats,
> "Love, O careless Love. . . ." I hear
> my ill-spirit sob in each blood cell,
> as if my hand were at its throat. . . .
> I myself am hell;
> nobody's here—[.]

This passage is quintessential Lowell. Intensely private though it is (to a certain kind of reader it comes close to being a psychiatric case history), it has its public dimension. As some readers have noted, it is a version of the "dark night of the soul" of San Juan de la Cruz, although without the sense of a spiritual progression that the great Spanish mystic followed. "I myself am hell" is borrowed from *Paradise Lost*—a line spoken by Satan, spying on Adam and Eve. Between these two noble literary sources Lowell drops a phrase from a rather banal song that is being half-heard by millions, but it attains a certain pathos in this context. The speaker verges, perhaps, on a self-pity that could be disastrous for the poem ("the hill's skull" suggests Golgotha), but there is also a laconic detachment that comes out in "I myself am hell," which stands in a line by itself, like "My mind's not right" in the preceding stanza. Most readers cannot avoid knowing what Lowell brings into so many of these poems: his recurrent mental illness. Robert Fitzgerald, who knew him well, has stated this firmly but sympathetically: "behind those poems and henceforth all his work is his breakdown of 1949 and the necessity he now felt of governing his greatness with his illness in mind. Manic attacks now and again would put him in the hospital, overborne by the fever that one had felt to be just beyond some of his poems from the beginning."

"Skunk Hour," although first in order of composition, comes last in the group of fifteen poems that Lowell calls "Life Studies." It is led up to gradually by poems about an uncle, his great-aunt Sarah, his Winslow grandparents, his father, and his mother; the family relationships intensify painfully. There are beautiful idyllic moments; thinking of his grandparents, he says:

> Then the dry road dust rises to whiten
> the fatigued elm leaves—
> the nineteenth century, tired of children, is gone.
> They've all gone into a world of light; the farm's my own.

As the reader moves closer to the present, the tone is clipped and sardonic:

> Father's death was abrupt and unprotesting.
> His vision was still twenty-twenty.
> After a morning of anxious, repetitive smiling,
> his last words to Mother were:
> "I feel awful."

The poet's father is the central figure in a prose memoir, "91 Revere Street," which forms the centerpiece of *Life Studies.* Rather curiously, it does not immediately precede the group of family poems. Intervening are four poems on literary figures (Ford, Santayana, the poets Delmore Schwartz and Hart Crane) whom Lowell admired. Ninety-one Revere Street was the address of the house where the Lowells lived for a few years in the 1920s; here the psychological battle between husband and wife was fought out. Lowell's mother, neurotic but obviously strong in her own way, won; she forced her husband to retire from the navy. He moved into the business world with a marked lack of success, and the poem called "Commander Lowell" presents his declining years without comment; he is almost a figure of comedy. He died in 1950. While he was alive, Lowell wrote and published in *Lord Weary's Castle* a poem called "Rebellion," which suggests a more painful relationship between father and son. Once, during his Harvard days, he knocked his father down in a quarrel over a girl. Lowell returns to this incident in a short sequence of poems, "Charles River," in *Notebook 1967–68* (1969).

His mother is never really described, although her presence is strongly felt in various places. She is, finally, an object; one can only speculate on the feelings that lie behind this passage:

NEW POEMS BY

ROBERT LOWELL

FOR THE UNION DEAD

Francis Parker

Cover for Lowell's 1964 collection. The title poem commemorates Col. Robert Shaw and his African American troops, who were killed in the Civil War.

When I embarked from Italy with my Mother's body,
the whole shoreline of the *Golfo di Genova*
was breaking into fiery flower.
The crazy yellow and azure sea-sleds
blasting like jack-hammers across
the *spumante*-bubbling wake of our liner,
recalled the clashing colors of my Ford.
Mother travelled first-class in the hold;
her *Risorgimento* black and gold casket
was like Napoleon's at the *Invalides.*

The "Life Studies" sequence composes a kind of fragmentary novel in verse, not unlike James Joyce's *A Portrait of the Artist as a Young Man* (1916). Since Lowell was an influential teacher by now (he held temporary posts at several American universities), many younger writers who were at one time his students—such as W. D. Snodgrass and Anne Sexton—were associated with him as "confessional" poets. Yet this association appears to have been somewhat exaggerated. Snodgrass's *Heart's Needle* (1959) was written before *Life Studies,* and the an-

guished revelations of Anne Sexton and Sylvia Plath are poetry of a rather different kind from Lowell's. Their work, for the most part, lacks his wit and detachment and public dimension.

Life Studies has been considered a landmark in contemporary poetry by many critics; its importance was almost immediately recognized, and in 1960 Lowell received the National Book Award. About this time he moved to New York City with his wife Elizabeth Hardwick and daughter, Harriet. Thus began a decade during which he was involved in public affairs, or at least public artistic projects, including the theater. Early in the decade he read a new poem, "For the Union Dead," at an arts festival on the Boston Common. It is a more accessible piece than most of *Life Studies* or certainly *Lord Weary's Castle,* even for those readers (or auditors) uninstructed in Boston history and the aftermath of the Civil War. The open texture of *Life Studies* has now been extended to the modern scene and the history that has led up to it. Although "For the Union Dead" starts out as a private meditation, it soon moves to Boston Common itself:

Parking spaces luxuriate like civic
sandpiles in the heart of Boston.
A girdle of orange, Puritan-pumpkin colored girders
braces the tingling Statehouse,
shaking over the excavations, as it faces Colonel Shaw
and his bell-cheeked Negro infantry
On St. Gaudens' shaking Civil War relief,
propped by a plank splint against the garage's earthquake.

This passage takes the reader to the central historic situation. Col. Robert Shaw of Boston, who commanded a regiment of black troops, was killed in July 1863 in an assault on Fort Wagner, South Carolina. Although Lowell presents him as an example of idealism and youthful beauty, he was scorned by his father; he was buried in a ditch, where his "body was thrown / and lost with his 'niggers.'" Lowell juxtaposes the events of three generations: Shaw's actual death and anonymous burial; the dedication of the memorial to him and the Union dead in the 1890s; and the present moment, when ideals, it is suggested, have eroded along with much else:

The ditch is nearer.
There are no statues for the last war here;
on Boyleston Street, a commercial photograph
shows Hiroshima boiling
over a Mosler Safe, the "Rock of Ages"
that survived the blast. Space is nearer.
When I crouch to my television set,
the drained faces of Negro school-children rise
like balloons.

Future readers may require footnotes to identify a few of the details from the 1960s—the civil rights struggle, the advertising slogans of the period, even the design of American automobiles. Lowell's sense of particularity is brilliant; the details could hardly be better chosen. Here the reader is close to the pop art of the 1960s, with its jaunty arrangements of familiar objects, its air of being both inside and detached from popular culture. The poem, however, is beautifully composed. The motif of the fish, introduced in the opening stanzas with the old South Boston Aquarium, is sarcastically alluded to midway ("Their monument sticks like a fishbone / in the city's throat"), and then it rounds out the poem:

The Aquarium is gone. Everywhere,
giant finned cars nose forward like fish;
a savage servility
slides by on grease.

"For the Union Dead" gave the title to Lowell's next book, which came out in 1964. This collection is miscellaneous in character. It includes personal vignettes, poems derived from the prose of friends such as Elizabeth Bishop and Mary McCarthy, recastings of older poems by Lowell himself, and even commissioned poems. "Hawthorne" was written to commemorate the centenary edition of that author's works published by the Ohio State University Press. This and its companion piece, "Jonathan Edwards in Western Massachusetts," as Lowell says, are based on prose passages by their subjects. These poems are highly interesting to Lowell's public, of course, because they return to New England writers who have always meant a great deal to him. His attitude toward them is now more relaxed, as is the mode of the verse.

One sequence in this collection is almost entirely concerned with the public world: "July in Washington," "Buenos Aires," and "Dropping South: Brazil." They suggest a quasi-political attitude that would soon become very explicit in Lowell's work. He chose the first one, in fact, when he was asked to submit a favorite poem from his own work, along with a work he admired from the past, to an anthology, *Preferences* (1974), edited by Richard Howard. Lowell paired "July in Washington" with Melville's "The House-Top," a poem about the draft riots in New York City in July 1863. Howard in a brief commentary mentions the "seditious tropical summers of America's cities" that are often a background to political stresses if not disasters. Lowell's poem this time is built up on the motif of the circle. The actual plan of Washington makes this credible, but the opening couplet involves more: "The stiff spokes of

this wheel / touch the sore spots of the earth." Then the poem on Buenos Aires has its focus in a graveyard of Republican martyrs during a chilly Argentine winter. In the poem on Brazil, although it is written mainly from the point of view of a tourist on Copacabana Beach, Lowell reflects that "inland, people starved, and struck, and died— / unhappy Americas, ah *tristes tropiques!*"

In 1969 Lowell remarked in an interview with the Caribbean novelist V. S. Naipaul, "America with a capital *A* I find a very hard thing to realise. It's beyond any country, it's an empire. I feel very bitter about it, but pious, and baffled by it." This summary of his feelings has a certain ambiguity about it. He had long been concerned about the outcome of American history, like an earlier Bostonian, Henry Adams, and his feeling that it was being betrayed ran very strong. In 1965 he was invited by President Lyndon Johnson, as one of a small group of distinguished American artists, to attend the White House Festival of the Arts. He turned down the invitation in a public statement of protest against American involvement in the Vietnam War: "We are in danger of imperceptibly becoming an explosive and suddenly chauvinistic nation, and we may even be drifting on our way to the last nuclear ruin." Then in October 1967 he participated with several other literary figures in the famous "march" on the Pentagon, which ended with mixed results but was highly publicized. Lowell himself wrote two poems about it for *Notebook,* but a more famous and extensive account of this incident, in which he has a prominent part, is found in Norman Mailer's *The Armies of the Night* (1968).

Lowell was becoming known in other ways. Like many other modern poets, he was attracted by the theater. In 1961 he was asked to translate Jean Baptiste Racine's *Phèdre;* he did this in heroic couplets, the nearest English equivalent to the French alexandrines. Critical opinion has been mixed about the result, and perhaps it should be regarded as an "imitation" of Racine. (In 1961, the same year as his *Phaedra,* Lowell brought out his controversial book called *Imitations,* which consists of versions of poetry from several languages.) This was the first of the theater projects that Lowell started, and *Phaedra* was seriously considered by two Broadway producers in 1962. Another venture was his collaboration with Leonard Bernstein on a symphony, *Kaddish;* before it broke off, Lowell wrote three poems, remarkably formal, even stately, for a musical setting. (They were published for the first time in *Ploughshares* in 1979.) In 1965 Lincoln Center commissioned an acting version of Aeschylus's *Oresteia;* this was mostly finished but never produced; eventually it was pub-

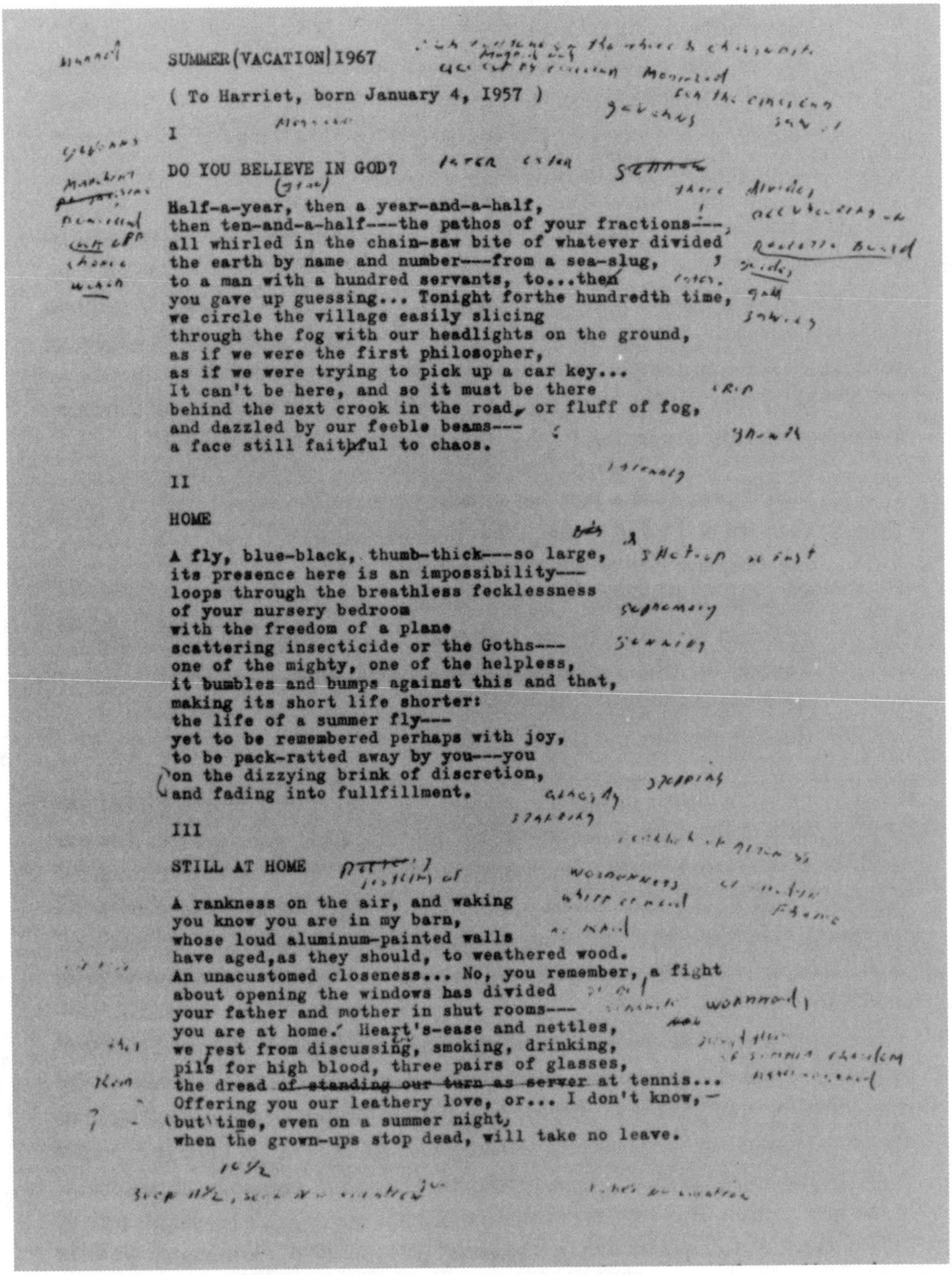

SUMMER (VACATION) 1967

(To Harriet, born January 4, 1957)

I

DO YOU BELIEVE IN GOD?

Half-a-year, then a year-and-a-half,
then ten-and-a-half----the pathos of your fractions---,
all whirled in the chain-saw bite of whatever divided
the earth by name and number----from a sea-slug,
to a man with a hundred servants, to...then
you gave up guessing... Tonight forthe hundredth time,
we circle the village easily slicing
through the fog with our headlights on the ground,
as if we were the first philosopher,
as if we were trying to pick up a car key...
It can't be here, and so it must be there
behind the next crook in the road, or fluff of fog,
and dazzled by our feeble beams---
a face still faithful to chaos.

II

HOME

A fly, blue-black, thumb-thick----so large,
its presence here is an impossibility---
loops through the breathless fecklessness
of your nursery bedroom
with the freedom of a plane
scattering insecticide or the Goths---
one of the mighty, one of the helpless,
it bumbles and bumps against this and that,
making its short life shorter:
the life of a summer fly---
yet to be remembered perhaps with joy,
to be pack-ratted away by you---you
on the dizzying brink of discretion,
and fading into fullfillment.

III

STILL AT HOME

A rankness on the air, and waking
you know you are in my barn,
whose loud aluminum-painted walls
have aged, as they should, to weathered wood.
An unacustomed closeness... No, you remember, a fight
about opening the windows has divided
your father and mother in shut rooms---
you are at home. Heart's-ease and nettles,
we rest from discussing, smoking, drinking,
pils for high blood, three pairs of glasses,
the dread of standing our turn as server at tennis...
Offering you our leathery love, or... I don't know, —
(but time, even on a summer night,
when the grown-ups stop dead, will take no leave.

Typescript for the opening poem of Lowell's 1973 book For Lizzie and Harriet *(Houghton Library, Harvard University)*

lished in 1979. Lowell's prose version of Aeschylus's *Prometheus Bound* was actually produced at the Yale Drama School with an international cast two years before it was published in 1969.

By far his most successful work for the theater was the group of short plays called *The Old Glory* (1965). There was at least one good reason for this success. Originally intending to write an opera libretto based on Melville's "Benito Cereno" (1856), Lowell instead quickly wrote a play. Then he added two plays from stories by Hawthorne, "Endicott and the Red Cross" and "My Kinsman, Major Molineux." Taken together (with "Benito Cereno" presented last), they compose a trilogy on the emergence of the United States out of its colonial past. According to Lowell in a late interview in London, the title, *The Old Glory,* has two meanings: "it refers both to the flag and also to the glory with which the Republic of America started." Thus, his lifelong engagement with Hawthorne and Melville—his major American sources, one might say—paid off handsomely again. The original production of the play in New York, a considerable critical success, received many prizes.

In 1967 Lowell brought out *Near the Ocean,* a handsome book (illustrated by the famous Australian painter Sidney Nolan) that included his most formal poetry since *The Mills of the Kavanaughs.* The earlier book was mostly written in heroic couplets; part of this one is written in tetrameter couplets, the poetic form of which the seventeenth-century poet Andrew Marvell was the master in English verse. Lowell's versification is not as strict as Marvell's, but almost playfully he runs his couplets through sentences of eight lines, the length of a stanza. The tone is playful, too, as the reader moves in and out of a charming domestic scene (a house Lowell inherited in Maine) in the manner of Marvell's "Upon Appleton House," which may well be the general model; he uses the same eight-line stanza. Lowell, like his great predecessor, touches on some serious issues. The opening lines of the first poem in the sequence, "Waking Early Sunday Morning" (now rather famous among Lowell's readers), make that clear:

> O to break loose, like the chinook
> salmon, jumping and falling back,
> nosing up to the impossible
> stone and bone-crushing waterfall—
> raw-jawed, weak-fleshed there, stopped by ten
> steps of the roaring ladder, and then
> to clear the top on the last try,
> alive enough to spawn and die.

It is part of the attractiveness of these poems that they can advance so quickly to matters of church and state and society and absorb them into their easy rhythms:

> O to break loose. All life's grandeur
> is something with a girl in summer . . .
> elated as the President
> girdled by his establishment
> this Sunday morning, free to chaff
> his own thoughts with his bear-cuffed staff,
> swimming nude, unbuttoned, sick
> of his ghost-written rhetoric!

The "President" is Lyndon Johnson; the occasion is the summer of 1965. Lowell has recently turned down the invitation to the White House Festival of the Arts, and this witty passage does indeed stand in contrast to the now-forgotten speeches by the official hack writers. Lowell can be forceful about some things; in Central Park, almost at the door of his apartment house, he finds fear and poverty lurking amid the flowering shrubs; public sexual activity in the park is perhaps a correlative to these grimmer aspects of the contemporary scene. Lowell had a divided mind about the five poems in this group. While he retained the poems in this "Near the Ocean" group in his *Selected Poems* (1976), he cut four of them down, so drastically in some cases that they hardly resemble the originals. Such was his restless way with his own work.

The second half of *Near the Ocean* consists of translations, or "imitations"—the precise term is not easy to establish here. The poets whom he uses are mainly Horace, Juvenal, and Dante (*Inferno,* 15). Of these distinguished works, the longest is Juvenal's Satire 10, "The Vanity of Human Wishes," occupying forty of Lowell's pages. Since we already have Samuel Johnson's famous "imitation" of this poem, we might remark that Lowell's version is closer to Juvenal than Johnson's. Lowell's is done in blank verse. (Juvenal used no rhymes.) And the effect of the Lowell version is to suggest, somehow, a comparison between Juvenal's Rome and the American empire of the 1960s. Although the tone of this great work is truly Juvenalian in Lowell's hands, it has a thematic connection with the "Horatian" poems in the first part of the book. (Marvell, the general model there, is perhaps the most Horatian of English poets.)

No sooner had *Near the Ocean* been published and *Prometheus Bound* been produced at Yale in 1967 (the latter work, the most extravagant thing that Lowell ever wrote, is also an indirect commentary on the 1960s), than Lowell started on a large venture of another sort—*Notebook 1967-68.* Lowell's

ROBERT LOWELL

HISTORY

FARRAR, STRAUS AND GIROUX
NEW YORK

Title page for Lowell's 1973 book, a collection of chronologically arranged sonnets about literary and historical figures

friend John Berryman had already begun his ambitious and much-praised *Dream Songs* (the first part, published in 1964, won the Pulitzer Prize), and now the small audience for contemporary poetry watched two important writers—both published by Farrar, Straus and Giroux—quickly building up large sequences of short poems. In each case the overall form was the diary. Berryman used an original six-line rhymed stanza throughout; Lowell committed himself to the unrhymed sonnet. The resemblances and differences between the two are fascinating to study. Berryman, who killed himself early in 1972, probably had no intention of rearranging the plan of his work, but Lowell's soon took some unexpected turns.

Notebook 1967-68 is a kind of diary, but the form is cyclic: Lowell prints a list of dates for 1967-1968 at the back of the book to remind the reader of the disasters of the year, beginning and ending with the Vietnam War and including the assassinations and major political upheavals. Even

though public events seem to get out of control and affect everyone's destiny, there are moments of reminiscence and private satisfaction (Jarrell and Taylor at college in the 1930s, or Elizabeth Schwarzkopf singing in New York). There are also many characters out of history, European and American. Although the poems are arranged in groups, some of them are not closely connected: for instance "Names," which merely brings together the figures of Sir Thomas More, Napoleon, and others. As Lowell himself says, the pattern is "jagged" and created largely by association. At the end a small group dedicated to his wife Elizabeth Hardwick is somewhat inconclusive. In the following year Lowell issued a revised and expanded edition. Some of the material here is more private than ever; it is even drawn from people's letters and conversations.

In 1973 Lowell brought out three books simultaneously: *For Lizzie and Harriet, The Dolphin,* and *History,* all written in unrhymed sonnets. In these volumes he has broken up the expanding *Notebook* project (undated in the revised, 1970 edition) into public and private sectors. *For Lizzie and Harriet* deals with Elizabeth Hardwick and their daughter; many of the poems were scattered through the two editions of *Notebook.* The poems in *The Dolphin,* however, are mostly new; they are concerned with his third wife, Lady Caroline Blackwood, whom he married in 1972; their son, Sheridan; and his life in England. There are obvious personal reasons, then, for separating the phases of a complicated existence.

History, the longest of the three books, includes most of the "public" poems from *Notebook,* sometimes reworked, with about eighty new poems. Many of these are about prominent literary figures, from Juvenal to Berryman, but there are a fair number about men of power as different as Maximilien-François Robespierre, Che Guevara, and Martin Luther King Jr. The arrangement is now linear or chronological, and almost every period of Western history is touched on. Lowell was always deeply interested in history; he knew the great historians better than most people. Here, then, is his personal vision of history, fragmentary though it appears. History is, in its way, a kind of epic; and Lowell would probably have agreed with Ezra Pound that an epic is simply a poem about history. It is Pound, finally, whom Lowell most resembles among the modern poets. Lowell met him as early as 1948, when he was the consultant in poetry at the Library of Congress. (Pound was kept in St. Elizabeth's Hospital in Washington from 1945 to 1958.) He admired Pound, often saw him in Washington and sometimes later in Italy, and kept his portrait above the desk in his study. By the time of

History the scale and variety of Lowell's work had begun to resemble Pound's: the extensive translations and "imitations," the restless quest for new models, the ventures into personal epic. There is also an unevenness that is undeniable, in *History* as in the *Cantos* (1925-1960), and in Lowell's case the commitment to the unrhymed sonnet may have been a limitation of a kind. Everything has to be put in the same mold. The *Cantos,* at least the early ones, often have a sustained yet varied rhythmic interest that Lowell hardly approaches. Had he lived, Lowell would probably have done something more with *History,* which includes much of a lifetime's experience.

There are further rearrangements in *Selected Poems,* a kind of interim volume. In a sense Lowell agreed with the general estimate of his work by including almost everything from *Life Studies* except the prose centerpiece. Like Pound's *Hugh Selwyn Mauberley* (1920), it seems to be something that all readers endorse. At this point Lowell was writing the poems that would make up his last book—the last book published in his lifetime, *Day by Day,* which appeared shortly before his death in September 1977. These late poems continue what he called his "verse autobiography," but often in a somewhat muted way. He no longer uses the elaborate narrative structure of some of the earlier poetry, or even the unrhymed sonnets of the *Notebook* period. His new marriage brings some happiness, especially with his infant son, but there are tensions and breakdowns, usually brought into his poems in this hesitant and oblique manner:

> To each the rotting natural to his age.
> Dividing the minute we cannot prolong,
> I stand swaying at the end of the party
> a half-filled glass in each hand—
> I too swayed
> by the hard infatuate wind of love
> they cannot hear.

This book unexpectedly marked the end of Lowell's career. He died in a taxi that was taking him from New York City's Kennedy Airport to the apartment on West Sixty-Seventh Street where he intended to join Elizabeth Hardwick. His marriage to Lady Caroline Blackwood had evidently failed, and he wanted to resume his life in New York. His reputation in England had been extraordinary. At one point he was seriously considered for the position of professor of poetry at Oxford, an elected post that had recently been held by W. H. Auden. He was never, however, an expatriate in the manner of Henry James and Eliot. His cultural base was in America and especially Boston.

One is reminded of his American antecedents and connections by his major posthumous work, *Collected Prose,* edited in 1987 by the distinguished publisher Robert Giroux, who had been Lowell's editor for many years. This book, coming out a decade after the poet's death, traces his associations with many great poets of the past, beginning with Homer. An essay on the *Iliad,* written when he was only eighteen, already demonstrates his admiration for epic form and magnitude. Perhaps his own tendency toward epic, which was apparent in his poetry long before *History,* was based on his early response to Homer. Few poets in the last part of the twentieth century have had this sense of grandeur; most would probably agree with Lowell's friend Elizabeth Bishop, who once said, "I'm not interested in big-scale work as such. Something needn't be large to be good."

The first section of *Collected Prose* consists of eighteen brief essays, more tributes than formal criticism, concerned with the literary figures who had some part in Lowell's career. They include Ford, Ransom, William Carlos Williams, Eliot, Tate, Warren, Bishop, and Jarrell. (Others—such as Frost, Stevens, and Auden—are simply the subject of Lowell's admiration.) Lowell's poetry might never have evolved in the way that it did without the examples of these figures, some of whom became close friends. The tributes that Giroux assembled are thus part of a literary biography. Lowell picked up from Jarrell the practice of listing his favorite (presumably the finest) poems by the writers whose work he was reviewing. This section of *Collected Prose* is thus an index to Lowell's taste, which was remarkable. Most of his judgments stand very well a generation later.

The heart of *Collected Prose* is a group of essays, two of them unfinished, which take up Lowell's profound interest in the literary tradition of New England. The longest, "New England and Further," is a survey of authors from Cotton Mather to Frost, Stevens, and Eliot. According to Giroux's editorial note, it was written in Maine during two periods, the late 1960s and the final months of Lowell's life in 1977. What is remarkable is that he wrote without access to his library. One assumes that he had lived with some of these writers so long that he could almost quote their works at times. This is not the product of a specialist in American literature but a poet's personal reactions to and reminiscences of a literary tradition. There is nothing systematic about it, and many of Lowell's formulations are hardly more than brilliant epigrams. For example, he says of Emily Dickinson: "Her divine waywardness, whose success is impossible to approve or condemn,

Lowell in Cambridge, Massachusetts, April 1977 (photograph © 1990 by Judith Aronson)

separates her from the perfection of Marianne Moore and Elizabeth Bishop." Lowell gives this bit of reminiscence by way of introduction to Frost: "A lifetime ago, a morality ago, my mother warned me off the moderns, Eliot and Tate, and, as a curative, misquoted Robert Frost, thought to be understandable to everyone, including herself, to be healthy, wise, and no nihilist to the middle class. My personal and critical love of Frost survived this recommendation of everything I hated." Then he describes Frost as "*the* American formalist"; along the way he mentions Paul Valéry, William Butler Yeats, Sir Walter Ralegh, Ben Jonson, and other poets to make his point. Reading Lowell's criticism is a liberating experience.

In "New England and Further" Melville's poetry rates only a page or so of commentary. The following essay, "Epics," takes up *Moby-Dick:* "It's our epic, a New England epic." Lowell in fact puts Melville in a line of descent from Homer, Virgil, Dante, and Milton. Clearly Melville meant more to him than any other American writer, and from time to time, as in "The Quaker Graveyard in Nantucket"

and the play that he made from "Benito Cereno," Melville was actually his model. What he seemed to admire most was the "magnificent rhythms" and large vocabulary of *Moby-Dick.* Giroux thinks that this essay was intended as the conclusion to "New England and Further." At any rate, it almost seemed to circle back to Lowell's youthful essay on the *Iliad,* which in retrospect points toward so much in his career.

The remaining section of *Collected Prose* consists of Lowell's commentaries on his own work. In this age of the tape recorder and the published interview, the two longest pieces are the interviews with Frederick Seidel (Boston, 1961) and Ian Hamilton (England, 1971). Seidel and Hamilton were unusually well informed about Lowell and knew how to ask the right questions. The resulting conversation pieces remain valuable for the interested student. Hamilton, a British poet and critic, later wrote the first biography of Lowell, published in 1982, only five years after the poet's death. Lowell's heirs and many friends for the most part cooperated with the biographer; the result was a highly detailed and candid account of a life that was often painful to those close to the poet. His recurrent mental illness, already apparent by the late 1940s, was self-destructive at times, but an outsider can only marvel at Lowell's strength of mind that pulled him out of his crises and allowed him to function so effectively as a creative personality.

Lowell's reputation more than twenty years after his death is still high, but two generations of younger poets are more likely to look to Elizabeth Bishop as the finest poet of a group now mostly departed. Some of Lowell's work, such as the translations from Aeschylus, "The Mills of the Kavanaughs," and the hundreds of pages of poems in *History,* are never mentioned now. The best poems, early and late, are still impressive. A biography by Paul Mariani, *Lost Puritan: A Life of Robert Lowell* (1994), has drawn attention to Lowell's work again, and Frank Bidart, Lowell's literary executor, plans to publish his edition of *Collected Poems,* something that is needed for a full assessment of a remarkable career.

Interviews:

"Et in America ego–The American poet Robert Lowell Talks to the Novelist V. S. Naipaul about Art, Power, and the Dramatisation of the Self," *Listener,* 4 (September 1969): 302–304;

Jeffrey Meyers, ed., *Robert Lowell, Interviews and Memoirs* (Ann Arbor: University of Michigan Press, 1988).

Bibliography:

Patrick K. Miehe, *The Robert Lowell Papers at the Houghton Library, Harvard University: A Guide to the Collection* (New York: Greenwood Press, 1990).

Biographies:

Ian Hamilton, *Robert Lowell: A Biography* (New York: Random House, 1982);

Paul Mariani, *Lost Puritan: A Life of Robert Lowell* (New York: Norton, 1994);

Richard Tillinghast, *Robert Lowell's Life and Work: Damaged Grandeur* (Ann Arbor: University of Michigan, 1995).

References:

Rolando Anzilotti, ed., *Robert Lowell: A Tribute* (Pisa: Nistri-Lischi Editori, 1979);

Steven Gould Axelrod and Helen Deese, eds., *Robert Lowell: Essays on the Poetry* (Cambridge & New York: Cambridge University Press, 1986);

Axelrod, *Robert Lowell: Life and Art* (Princeton, N.J.: Princeton University Press, 1978);

Harold Bloom, ed., *Robert Lowell* (New York: Chelsea House, 1987);

Philip Cooper, *The Autobiographical Myth of Robert Lowell* (Chapel Hill: University of North Carolina Press, 1970);

John Crick, *Robert Lowell* (Edinburgh: Oliver & Boyd, 1974);

William Doreski, *The Years of Our Friendship: Robert Lowell and Allen Tate* (Jackson: University Press of Mississippi, 1990);

Richard J. Fein, *Robert Lowell* (New York: Twayne, 1970);

Robert Fitzgerald, "The Things of the Eye," *Poetry,* 132 (May 1978): 107–111;

Henry Hart, *Robert Lowell and the Sublime* (Syracuse, N.Y.: Syracuse University Press, 1995);

Philip Hobsbaum, *A Reader's Guide to Robert Lowell* (New York: Thames and Hudson, 1988);

Michael Lond and Robert Boyers, eds., *Robert Lowell: A Portrait of the Artist in His Time* (New York: David Lewis, 1970);

Norman Mailer, *The Armies of the Night* (New York: New American Library, 1968);

Jerome Mazzaro, *The Poetic Themes of Robert Lowell* (Ann Arbor: University of Michigan Press, 1965);

Jeffrey Meyers, *Manic Power: Robert Lowell and His Circle* (London & New York: Macmillan, 1987);

Thomas Parkinson, ed., *Robert Lowell: A Collection of Critical Essays* (Englewood Cliffs, N.J.: Prentice-Hall, 1968);

Marjorie Perloff, *The Poetic Art of Robert Lowell* (Ithaca, N.Y.: Cornell University Press, 1973);

Norma Procopiow, *Robert Lowell, the Poet and His Critics* (Chicago: American Library Association, 1984);

Mark Rudman, *Robert Lowell, an Introduction to the Poetry* (New York: Columbia University Press, 1983);

Salmagundi, special Lowell issue, 1, no. 4 (1966–1967);

Sarah Payne Stuart, *My First Cousin Once Removed: Money, Madness, and the Family of Robert Lowell* (New York: Harper Collins, 1998);

Peter Taylor, "Robert Trail [*sic*] Spence Lowell," *Ploughshares,* 5, no. 2 (1979): 74–81;

Alan Williamson, *Pity the Monsters: The Political Vision of Robert Lowell* (New Haven: Yale University Press, 1974);

Stephen Yenser, *Circle to Circle: The Poetry of Robert Lowell* (Berkeley: University of California Press, 1975).

Papers:

The principal collection of Robert Lowell's papers is held by the Houghton Library, Harvard University.

Archibald MacLeish

*This entry was updated from the entries by James L. McWilliams III (University of Texas at Austin)
in* DLB 7: Twentieth-Century American Dramatists, *and by Victor H. Jones
(Indiana State University) in* DLB 45: American Poets, 1880–1945, First Series.

See also the MacLeish entries in *DLB 4: American Writers in Paris, 1920–1939* and *DLB Yearbook 1982.*

BIRTH: Glencoe, Illinois, 7 May 1892, to Andrew and Martha Hillard MacLeish.

EDUCATION: Attended Hotchkiss School; A.B., Yale University, 1915; LL.B., Harvard University, 1919.

MARRIAGE: 21 June 1916 to Ada Hitchcock; children: Kenneth, Brewster Hitchcock, Mary Hillard, William Hitchcock.

AWARDS AND HONORS: John Reed Memorial Prize, 1929; Shelley Memorial Award for Poetry, 1932; Pulitzer Prize in poetry for *Conquistador,* 1933; Golden Rose Trophy of New England Poetry Club, 1934; Levinson Prize for group of poems published in *Poetry,* 1941; Bollingen Prize in Poetry from Yale University Library, 1952, Pulitzer Prize in poetry, 1953, and National Book Award in poetry, 1953, all for *Collected Poems, 1917–1952;* Boston Arts Festival poetry award, 1956; Sarah Josepha Hale Award, 1958; Chicago Poetry Day Poet, 1958; Antoinette Perry ("Tony") Award in drama, 1959, and Pulitzer Prize in drama, 1959, for *J. B.: A Play in Verse;* Academy Award ("Oscar") for best screenplay, Academy of Motion Picture Arts and Sciences, 1966, for *The Eleanor Roosevelt Story;* Presidential Medal of Freedom, 1977; National Medal for Literature, 1978; Gold Medal for Poetry, American Academy of Arts and Letters, 1979; honorary degrees include M.A. from Tufts University, 1932; Litt.D. from Colby College, 1938, Wesleyan University, 1938, Yale University, 1939, University of Pennsylvania, 1941, University of Illinois, 1946, Washington University, 1948, Rockford College, 1953, Columbia University, 1954, Harvard University, 1955, University of Pittsburgh, 1959, Princeton University, 1965, University of Massachusetts, 1969, and Hampshire College, 1970; L.H.D. from Dartmouth University, 1940, and Williams College, 1942; D.C.L. from Union College, 1941, and University

of Puerto Rico, 1953; LL.D. from Johns Hopkins University, 1941, University of California, 1943, Queen's University at Kingston, 1948, Carleton College, 1956, and Amherst College, 1963.

DEATH: Boston, Massachusetts, 20 April 1982.

BOOKS: *Class Poem 1915* (New Haven: Yale University, 1915);
Songs for a Summer's Day (New Haven: Yale University Press, 1915);
Tower of Ivory (New Haven: Yale University Press, 1917; London: Milford, 1917);
The Happy Marriage and Other Poems (Boston & New York: Houghton Mifflin, 1924);
The Pot of Earth (Boston & New York: Houghton Mifflin, 1925);
Nobodaddy (Cambridge, Mass.: Dunster House, 1926; London: Jackson, 1926);
Streets in the Moon (Boston & New York: Houghton Mifflin, 1928);
The Hamlet of A. MacLeish (Boston & New York: Houghton Mifflin, 1928);
Einstein (Paris: Black Sun Press, 1929);
New Found Land: Fourteen Poems (Paris: Black Sun Press, 1930; Boston & New York: Houghton Mifflin, 1930);
Housing America, anonymous (New York: Harcourt, Brace, 1932);
Conquistador (Boston & New York: Houghton Mifflin, 1932; London: Gollancz, 1933);
Poems, 1924–1933 (Boston & New York: Houghton Mifflin, 1933); abridged as *Poems* (London: Boriswood, 1935);
Frescoes for Mr. Rockefeller's City (New York: John Day, 1933);
Panic: A Play in Verse (Boston & New York: Houghton Mifflin, 1935; London: Boriswood, 1936);
Jews in America, anonymous (New York: Random House, 1936);
Public Speech: Poems by Archibald MacLeish (New York: Farrar & Rinehart, 1936; London: Boriswood, 1936);

Archibald MacLeish

The Fall of the City (London: Boriswood, 1937; New York & Toronto: Farrar & Rinehart, 1937);

Land of the Free (New York: Harcourt, Brace, 1938; London: Boriswood, 1938);

Air Raid (New York: Harcourt, Brace, 1938; London: John Lane/Bodley Head, 1939);

America Was Promises (New York: Duell, Sloan & Pearce, 1939; London: John Lane/Bodley Head, 1940);

The Irresponsibles: A Declaration (New York: Duell, Sloan & Pearce, 1940);

The Next Harvard, as Seen by Archibald MacLeish (Cambridge, Mass.: Harvard University Press, 1941);

A Time to Speak: The Selected Prose of Archibald MacLeish (Boston: Houghton Mifflin, 1941; London: Allen & Unwin, 1941);

The American Cause (New York: Duell, Sloan & Pearce, 1941);

American Opinion and the War: The Rede Lecture (Cambridge: Cambridge University Press, 1942; Cambridge: Cambridge University Press / New York: Macmillan, 1942);

A Time to Act: Selected Addresses (Boston: Houghton Mifflin, 1943; London: Allen & Unwin, 1945);

The American Story: Ten Broadcasts by Archibald MacLeish (New York: Duell, Sloan & Pearce, 1944)—includes *The Admiral, The Names for the Rivers, The American Name, The Discovered, The American Gods, The Many Dead, Ripe Strawberries and Gooseberries and Sweet Single Roses, Between the Silence and the Surf, Nat Bacon's Bones,* and *Socorro, When Your Sons Forget;*

Actfive and Other Poems (New York: Random House, 1948; London: John Lane/Bodley Head, 1950);

Poetry and Opinion: The Pisan Cantos of Ezra Pound (Urbana: University of Illinois Press, 1950);

Freedom Is the Right to Choose: An Inquiry into the Battle for the American Future (Boston: Beacon Press, 1951; London: John Lane/Bodley Head, 1952);

Collected Poems, 1917–1952 (Boston: Houghton Mifflin, 1952);

The Trojan Horse (Boston: Houghton Mifflin, 1952);

This Music Crept by Me Upon the Waters (Cambridge, Mass.: Harvard University Press, 1953);

Songs for Eve (Boston: Houghton Mifflin, 1954);

Art Education and the Creative Process (New York: Museum of Modern Art, 1954);

J.B.: A Play in Verse (Boston: Houghton Mifflin, 1958; London: Secker & Warburg, 1959);

Poetry and Journalism (Minneapolis: Minnesota Pamphlets, 1958);

Poetry and Experience (Boston: Houghton Mifflin, 1961; London: John Lane/Bodley Head, 1961);

Three Short Plays (New York: Dramatists Play Service, 1961)—includes *The Secret of Freedom, Air Raid,* and *The Fall of the City;*

The Collected Poems of Archibald MacLeish (Boston: Houghton Mifflin, 1963);

The Dialogues of Archibald MacLeish and Mark Van Doren, edited by Warren V. Bush (New York: Dutton, 1964);

The Eleanor Roosevelt Story (Boston: Houghton Mifflin, 1965);

An Evening's Journey to Conway, Massachusetts (Northampton, Mass.: Gehenna Press, 1967);

Herakles: A Play in Verse (Boston: Houghton Mifflin, 1967);

A Continuing Journey (Boston: Houghton Mifflin, 1968);

The Wild Old Wicked Man and Other Poems (Boston: Houghton Mifflin, 1968; London: W. H. Allen, 1969);

Scratch (Boston: Houghton Mifflin, 1971);

Champion of a Cause: Essays and Addresses on Librarianship, edited by Eva M. Goldschmidt (Chicago: American Library Association, 1971);

The Human Season: Selected Poems 1926–1972 (Boston: Houghton Mifflin, 1972);

The Great American Fourth of July Parade: A Verse Play for Radio (Pittsburgh: University of Pittsburgh Press, 1975);

New and Collected Poems, 1917–1976 (Boston: Houghton Mifflin, 1976);

Riders on the Earth: Essays and Recollections (Boston: Houghton Mifflin, 1978);

Six Plays (Boston: Houghton Mifflin, 1980)—includes *Nobodaddy, Panic, The Fall of the City, Air Raid, The Trojan Horse,* and *This Music Crept by Me Upon the Waters;*

Collected Poems, 1917–1982 (Boston: Houghton Mifflin, 1985).

PLAY PRODUCTIONS: *Union Pacific: A Ballet,* libretto by MacLeish, music by Nicholas Nabokoff, and choreography by Leonide Massine, New York, St. James Theatre, 25 April 1934;

Panic: A Play in Verse, New York, Imperial Theater, 14 March 1935;

The Trojan Horse: A Play, London, BBC Radio, 1952; Cambridge, Mass., Poets' Theatre, 23 October 1953;

This Music Crept by Me Upon the Waters, London, BBC Radio, 1953; Cambridge, Mass., Poets' Theatre, 23 October 1953;

J.B.: A Play in Verse, New Haven, Yale University Theatre, 22 April 1958; New York, ANTA Theatre, 11 December 1958;

The American Bell, music by David Amram, Philadelphia, Independence Hall, 1962;

Herakles: A Play in Verse, Ann Arbor, Lydia Mendelssohn Theatre, University of Michigan, 27 October 1965;

The Play of Herod, prose narration by MacLeish, New York, Church of St. Mary the Virgin, 27 December 1968;

Scratch, New York, St. James Theatre, 6 May 1971.

MOTION PICTURES: *The Spanish Earth,* by Ernest Hemingway with additional material by MacLeish and Lillian Hellman, Contemporary Historians, 1937;

Grandma Moses, Falcon Films, 1950;

The Eleanor Roosevelt Story, Allied Artists/American International, 1965.

TELEVISION: *The Secret of Freedom,* NBC, 1960;

An Evening's Journey to Conway, Massachusetts, WNET, 3 November 1967.

RADIO: *The Fall of the City: A Verse Play for Radio,* CBS, 11 April 1937;

Air Raid: A Verse Play for Radio, CBS, 27 October 1938;

America Was Promises, music by Nicholas Nabokoff, CBS, 5 April 1940;

The States Talking, CBS, 1941;

The American Story: Ten Broadcasts by Archibald MacLeish, NBC, February–April 1944;

The Son of Man, music by Johann Sebastian Bach, CBS, 1947;

The Great American Fourth of July Parade: A Verse Play for Radio, Pittsburgh, Carnegie Music Hall, 18 April 1975.

OTHER: Felix Frankfurter, *Law and Politics: Occasional Papers of Felix Frankfurter,* edited by MacLeish and E. E. Prichard Jr. (New York: Harcourt, Brace, 1939).

"Ars Poetica" and Archibald MacLeish are inextricably bound for most readers of modern American poetry, but neither this poem nor "The End of the World" (both first collected in *Streets in the Moon,* 1928) nor MacLeish's other heavily anthologized poems, such as "You, Andrew Marvell" (*New Found Land,* 1930), begin to capture the range and variety of his work. In addition to these and other excellent lyric poems, he wrote an epic (*Conquistador,* 1932), several effective satires, and no fewer than ten verse plays for radio and stage. He was also a lawyer, an editor, a Librarian of Congress, an assistant secretary of state, one of the founders of UNESCO, a teacher, and a literary critic. Through nearly all of the phases of his career, MacLeish urged understanding (awareness) and love as necessary to the human revolution (the beginning of which he associated with the American Revolution) for which he so consistently and persuasively spoke. MacLeish should be remembered for this humane voice through the several decades of the twentieth century in which there appeared to be little to be optimistic about; he should also be remembered for his virtuosity in lyric poetry and verse plays and for his contribution to the development of the modern verse play for stage and radio.

Archibald MacLeish was born in Glencoe, Illinois, "in a wooden chateau" overlooking Lake Michigan, the son of Andrew MacLeish and his third wife, Martha Hillard MacLeish. Andrew was a Glasgow Scot, Martha a Connecticut Yankee. The young MacLeish attended public schools in Glencoe and the Hotchkiss School in Lakeville, Connecticut (1907–1911), a preparatory school he hated but which prepared him for Yale. At Yale he wrote poetry and short stories for the *Yale Literary Magazine,* joined the swimming team, and played center on the freshman football team. MacLeish later remembered the Harvard coach called him the "dirtiest little sonofabitch of a center to visit Cambridge, Massachusetts." The poet wittily noted that he really did not deserve the "honor" because he was not all that little. He completed his degree in 1915 and was elected to the Phi Beta Kappa Society, but he said his education did not really begin until he entered Harvard Law School in 1915. At Harvard he began to study that profession whose business it is "to make sense of the confusion of what we call human life." Eventually, he would turn from law to poetry because the business of poetry was likewise to

MacLeish and his wife, Ada, circa 1918

"make sense of our lives. To create an understanding of our lives. To compose an order which the bewildered, angry heart can recognize. To imagine man."

Before MacLeish earned his law degree, he married Ada Hitchcock of Farmington, Connecticut, on 21 June 1916. A gifted singer, Ada MacLeish supported the young poet's desire to master his craft. Their marriage lasted until his death. In 1917 MacLeish entered the U.S. Army in World War I as an ambulance driver, "so as to do the right thing and not be hurt. In France got shifted to the Field Artillery out of shame." He advanced to the rank of captain by the end of the war. The poet's younger brother, Kenneth, was a Navy flyer; he was shot down and killed in 1918. MacLeish never forgot this death and wrote several poems about it.

Tower of Ivory (1917), MacLeish's first full-length volume of poetry, was seen through publication by Lawrence Mason (a Yale English instructor) while MacLeish was in the army. The poems in the volume are technically good but are conventional in form, the poetry of a young man. "Our Lady of Troy," however, merits comment. This blank-verse play, in which Faustus evokes Helen of Troy for the students at the inn in Rimlich, is important for Faustus's notion that "There's nought to fear from Heaven through to Hell; / Nothing that mind can't solve. Mind is the king." Later Faustus says that he, like Eve, has digressed somewhat from Eden: "Man must ever set his face / Toward the sunset, make his pilgrimage / Into the West. There is no pause for dream / With all the shining kingdom of the mind, / All truth, all science, all the stars to reap / And time forever clattering at heel / Like bone the children tie to yelping curs. / So then, our true mathesis, next and next!"

In this brief play MacLeish first introduces the idea of man searching, fearing nothing, trying to shape his life through his own efforts. He has departed from the Garden of Eden and must forever move westward. The reference to Eve may be ironic, but eventually MacLeish employed the Eve-like woman to accompany the searcher and to keep him in touch with the natural world. This play and MacLeish's other plays exhibit in one way or another most of the themes that MacLeish dealt with in his lyric poetry.

Seven years passed before MacLeish published another volume of poetry. After World War I, he returned to Harvard and, leading his class in his senior year, took his LL.B. degree in 1919. For the next two years he was a successful trial lawyer in the firm of Choate, Hall, and Stewart of Boston. By the winter of 1923, however, MacLeish was no longer content to be a weekday lawyer and weekend poet. On the same day he was elected to partnership in the firm, he resigned the practice of law and made plans to take his wife and two children to Paris on what little resources they had. MacLeish dated the beginning of his adult life from this moment.

In France he lived, studied, and perfected his craft among the greatest literary figures of the era—including Ernest Hemingway, James Joyce, F. Scott Fitzgerald, and Ezra Pound. At the same time he also came into contact with T. S. Eliot, E. E. Cummings, and William Butler Yeats. Particularly influential were Eliot and Pound, who introduced MacLeish to the innovative work of nineteenth-century French poets such as Arthur Rimbaud and great Oriental poets such as Tu Fu and Li Po. Eliot also alerted MacLeish to the potential of drama as a means of poetic expression, especially when making use of legend, folklore, and mythology. MacLeish had to reschool himself to learn the craft of poetry, just as his friends (Hemingway, Fitzgerald, and John Dos Passos) were working to learn the craft of fiction.

Early products from the beginning of his "adult life" were *The Happy Marriage and Other Poems* (1924) and *The Pot of Earth* (1925). *The Happy Mar-riage* is a book of traditional poetry, including, among several lyrics, a sonnet cycle that Harriet Monroe admired. In *Poetry* (April 1926) she marveled at the young poet's virtuosity with the "sonnet instrument, playing it to soft violin-like cadences." *The Pot of Earth,* written under the influence of Eliot, is about the death and renewal in a wasteland where life inexplicably and mysteriously goes on.

In 1926 MacLeish published *Nobodaddy,* another play in blank verse. The title comes from William Blake, who joined "nobody" and "daddy" to create a derisory name for the grim God of prohibitions often associated with the Old Testament. The play depicts Adam and Eve emerging from the sleep of Eden, a state or condition in which they had lived in ignorant and unconscious harmony with their surroundings and in obedience to the will of God. When Adam chooses to know, he chooses consciousness and so separation from God and from Eve as well. This choice requires that he make his way in the desert with Eve by his side. In the second act the conflict continues, with Cain representing the forces of consciousness and Abel of unconsciousness. Abel would return to the garden, to sleep, to total reliance on the will of God. When Cain kills Abel, he chooses the desert, where he will have to imagine his world and work to bring it into being. The play, then, is a twentieth-century interpretation of the Cain-Abel myth, in which the Adam/Cain figure rejects God's inexplicable and arbitrary ways and chooses the world. This figure (Adam/Cain) is capable of knowing himself (of knowing his separateness from others and from the garden) and can know both good and evil. He would not return to the garden if he could.

The reviews of *Nobodaddy* were mixed. R. P. Blackmur, for instance, saw the conflict between Cain and Abel (reason and nature) as powerful and effective but argued that MacLeish did not handle Eve effectively, that she should have been able to understand her creations and so to have reconciled the opposites they imply.

If *Nobodaddy* states an important theme in MacLeish's work, *Streets in the Moon,* published in 1928, is his first truly important collection of poetry. In the fifty-two poems in the volume MacLeish's technique has changed. He could still write in traditional rhymed verse forms, as sonnets such as "Chiaro-scuro" and "Conversation Balnweáire" and as the seemingly simple iambic tetrameter quatrains of "*L'an trentiesme de mon eage*" show. Yet he was developing his own style of poetry, too, lines such as those in "Ancestral," which experiments with sonnet form. The lines only suggest rhymes and illustrate what John Ciardi called MacLeish's "chop line," seen in this excerpt, where the speaker recalls falling asleep beneath the stars:

Gathering darkness:
                    I was small.
                              I lay
Beside my mother on the grass, and sleep
Came—

MacLeish had reschooled himself well; he had learned to render experience (Pound's term), rather than to describe it. "Reading Opposite the Lamp," for instance, renders the physical movements of the eye in reading as well as the understanding of the experience that is the purpose of reading poetry in the first place.

Streets in the Moon is much more than testimony to MacLeish's changed technique. Most of the speakers or characters in the poems are related to the Adam/Cain figure. Each is forced to make his way in the world without any apparent help from God. Thus the characters speak to the human situation of those residing in a wasteland. The light for the speakers is only dim moonlight, but it is there. To some of them the light reveals only death, as in "No Lamp Has Ever Shown Us Where to Look" and "Interrogate the Stones"; to others it reveals nothingness, as in "The End of the World." For all, the way is difficult to read, as in *"Le seul malheur est que je ne sais pas lire"*; for many there is a sense of having lost something, as in "Ancestral." Some of the poems ("Selene Afterwards") reveal the isolation so many people in the twentieth century have felt. The attitudes of the speakers toward their situation in the "desert" vary, but irony (more or less grim) in poems such as "Some Aspects of Immortality," "The End of the World," and "Man" is common. Many of the poems in the second part of the book, "Several Shadows of a Skull," speak to man's awareness of and behavior in the face of his certain death. Noteworthy is "Einstein" (also published separately in 1929), a long blank-verse poem in which the central character refuses to stop his search for understanding in the face of his inability to understand. Always flung back at him is "himself to answer him." That is to say, he is the answer to his own fate.

MacLeish's Einstein, like his Faustus, Adam, and Cain, seeks answers to his questions. Such seeking exists in MacLeish's work in many variations, one important variation being through poetry (art), as in "Ars Poetica." A poem, as "Ars Poetica" makes clear, captures a human experience of grief, or love, or loneliness, or memory. Thus a poem becomes a way of knowing, of seeing, albeit through the senses, the emotions, and the imagination. Mac-

MacLeish in the 1930s, at the time he wrote for Fortune

Leish often said that the function of a poem is to trap "Heaven and Earth in the cage of form."

If it was true, as MacLeish thought, that an era had ended after World War I and that a new era (the "wasteland" era) had begun, there were still moments when nature seemed to provide comfort. MacLeish tries to capture this feeling in "Memorial Rain," the end of which permits the reader to forget from time to time the bad that is apparent by choosing consciousness and holding dear the good—beauty, courage, and love.

Generally speaking, MacLeish did not dwell too long on the lost paradise. He accepted the new era and, confident that man controlled his own destiny, saw promise in America, that continent in the West where the desert might be conquered. MacLeish as teacher, politician, and poet spent the remainder of his life trying to help man realize the promise of America, that promise having begun, in his mind, with the American Revolution.

In 1928 MacLeish returned to America, settling on Uphill Farm in Conway, Massachusetts. MacLeish told Bill Moyers that he and his wife loved the house for its beauty and simplicity. It had been "improved," MacLeish noted, but he and his wife restored it by removing the improvements. As they moved in, he was also unsuccessfully trying to get Houghton Mifflin to change the way *The Hamlet of A. MacLeish* (1928) appeared on the printed page. This poem, an interior monologue after the manner of Eliot's "The Love Song of J. Alfred Prufrock" (1915), is MacLeish's version of the Hamlet story. The speaker, identified as "MacLeish," ruminates on the difficulty of accepting the pain and suffering in his life, and while he knows that he must accept these conditions of life, he ends by echoing Hamlet: *"Thou wouldst not think / How ill all's here about my heart!"*

MacLeish's first collection of poetry published after his return home was *New Found Land: Fourteen Poems* (1930, published earlier the same year in Paris), the title being descriptive of MacLeish's belief about the promise of America. The speakers in the poems are initially torn between the values of Europe and those of America, but ultimately they choose the latter. In making this choice, already anticipated in *Streets in the Moon,* MacLeish wished to help shape the land of his birth, acknowledging human mortality but putting it in perspective through the joy he finds in life—in friends, in loved ones, in the beauty of the natural world, and in the recollection of people who settled the continent. In "Salute" he praises the sun, "symbol of the West," as Grover Smith put it, instead of the moon. In the light of the sun man can see more clearly that he is mortal, and this knowledge may help him to choose his life more consciously, should he be willing to accept the responsibility of consciousness. In "Tourist Death" the speaker sees that life is more than death; it "is a haft that has fitted the palms of many, / Dark as the helved oak, with sweat bitter, / Browned numerous hands: Death is the rest of it." In the new found land, then, a man can make his life. This new found land, MacLeish wrote in "American Letter," is "Neither a place . . . nor a blood name." It is "West and the wind blowing." It is a shining idea in men's minds, and much as the speaker yearns for the lost world (the world of the garden), MacLeish knows there is no turning back for Americans. They must accept their land and the people on it:

> Here we must eat our salt or our bones starve.
> Here we must live or live only as shadows.
> This is our race, we that have none, that have had
> Neither the old walls nor the voices around us,
> This is our land, this our ancient ground—

Appropriately enough the collection ends with a celebration of American life in New York City in ". . . . . & Forty-Second Street."

Before MacLeish took permanent root in Conway, he wrote *Conquistador,* published in 1932, another poem of discovery. The poem was generated by MacLeish's reading of Bernál Diaz del Castillo's *True History of the Conquest of New Spain* (1632) and of his having followed the route of the conquistadors himself in Mexico during February of 1929. The epigraph to the poem, from canto twenty-five of Dante's *Inferno,* explains the nature of Bernál's discovery in New Spain; it is a discovery made by the senses of the common man, whom Bernál represents. The epigraph is also important because it is written in the terza-rima form, a variation of which MacLeish uses in the epic itself. That the speaker in the poem is a common soldier is also important because MacLeish had become interested in the fate of the individual without a race or without, really, a country or language; in short, the typical American. This man, like Bernál, is tied to the natural world through his senses, his emotions, his imagination. The beginning of the seventh book shows Bernál's connections with his world:

> *To the place called the Red Land. . . .*
>   and between the
> Fields valleys of great depth: and went down and
> Marched in the valleys:
>   and the pools were green a
> Copper water: and stank: the earth powder:
> No stalk of leaf in all those valleys:
> We alone there and the whispering ground.
>
> The great heat of the sun on us: neither shadow:
> Neither shade of the cracked rock in that cañon;
> The tree of the sun on our necks: the burning saddle:
>
> So we came to strath's end: lanterns:
> Cricked walls: heaped plaster: smell of the
> Old men: of the straw: the dogs scattering.

Bernál's world contained few abstractions. The reader's senses of sight, touch, hearing, and smell are all appealed to in this passage. Bernál learns through these senses, the way MacLeish seems to suggest most people learn.

This passage also demonstrates MacLeish's modified terza rima, which relies primarily on assonance near or at the end of the line rather than end rhymes for linkage: for example, "between the" in the first line links to "green a" in the third; "down" in the second links to "powder" in the fourth and "ground" in the sixth. This subtle pattern is carried through the fifteen books of the poem, unifying the lines of the stanzas in the ear (often unconsciously) of the reader and testifying to MacLeish's technical virtuosity. The assonance MacLeish employs in *Conquistador* is a common feature in much of his poetry, although he employs end-rhymed lines and free verse as well.

MacLeish was awarded his first Pulitzer Prize for *Conquistador,* and Monroe's positive response in *Poetry* (July 1932) to his efforts with the form and with the epic theme might be taken as representative. She said that MacLeish had written in a subtly "adroit terza-rima of assonances" that "ambush and conquer" the reader with their "half-tones and strangely varied harmonies." There were dissenters, of course. Blackmur, writing in *American Mercury* (April 1934) found it and *The Hamlet of A. MacLeish* "unintegrated, fragmentary, disjunctive . . . failing of the purpose they manifest so well in detail."

Back in the United States permanently, MacLeish accepted a position on the editorial staff of *Fortune* magazine, a job he held from 1928 to 1938. MacLeish wrote about present, past, and future life in the United States, revealing some of his preoccupations: Diego Rivera murals, Rockefeller Theatre, Franklin D. Roosevelt, the secretary of state, the Securities Act, skyscrapers, Social Security, South America, Soviet art, and taxation. Given MacLeish's interests in American life in the modern world and given his belief that the "end and purpose" of the poet is "to serve the time; to write, whatever comes of it," as a child of his age, it is little wonder that the voice in his poetry became more and more public and more and more American. In *Frescoes for Mr. Rockefeller's City* (1933) MacLeish's public voice, larded with irony, begins to emerge.

MacLeish's frescoes begin with the beauty of the land itself in "Landscape as a Nude," where the natural beauty of America is contrasted with the cultivated beauty of England and Italy; it is a western beauty. "Wildwest" pictures those who first loved the land, the American Indians. Certainly Crazy Horse fought for his land, asserts the speaker; it was his land, and when he "was there by the Black Hills / His heart would be big with the love he had for that country / And all the game he had seen and the mares he had ridden / And how it went out from you wide and clean in the sunlight." In "Burying Ground by the Ties" MacLeish honors the builders of modern America, the common man from all parts of the world. In "The Empire Builders," however, MacLeish harshly charges Josiah Perham, Jay Cooke, J. P. Morgan, William Averell Harriman, Cornelius Vanderbilt, Andrew Mellon, and Bruce Barton with betraying the promise of the land. At the end of an imagined tour of frescoes portraying the achievements of the empire builders, the tour guide concludes:

You have just beheld the Makers making America:
They screwed her scrawny and gaunt with their seven year panics:
They bought her back on their mortgages old-whore-cheap:
They fattened their bonds at her breasts till the thin blood ran from them:
Men have forgotten how full clear and deep
The Yellowstone moved on the gravel and grass grew
When the land lay waiting for her westward people!

MacLeish's frescoes provided the reader with images of the promises that had been lost and of the current dangers. Chief among these dangers were the unbridled economic greed of the empire builders and communism, which he attacks in "Background with Revolutionaries." Both capitalists and communists abandoned the pursuit of the human revolution in this country, the first unaware of or indifferent to the natural world, the second fearful of it. Both take refuge behind inhumane and fatalistic abstractions ("laissez faire" economics and "dialectical materialism") which free them from the burden of responsibility for themselves and for their fellowmen.

There may have been another danger, too, this one for the artist: in "Oil Painting of the Artist as the Artist," MacLeish attacked the "plump Mr. Pl'f" who had washed his hands of America, "an émigré from his own time." The target of this satire is in part expatriates. MacLeish observed that such writers as Fitzgerald, Hemingway, Dos Passos, Pound, Cummings, and Eliot were not among them. In fact, he said that in his six years in Paris he never met an expatriate. The "lost generation" was not lost, he said; "the world out of which that generation came was lost. And it was not a generation of expatriates who found themselves in Paris in those years but a generation whose *patria,* wherever it may once have been, was no longer waiting for them anywhere." These so-called expatriates, then, were among those who first realized and captured in their work the lost age in which they lived. Each of them, as has often been noted, saw different solutions to the same basic problem, MacLeish's solutions being the application of consciousness and love to human efforts to continue the revolution of man. Expatriates, the Mr. Pl'fs in the world of art, found that "The dead are excellent hosts" and so rejected the present and the possibilities of the people in their native land.

Frescoes for Mr. Rockefeller's City was the first of MacLeish's volumes of poetry to be heavily attacked on political grounds. Michael Gold, writing for the *New Republic* (25 July 1933), took particular exception to "Background with Revolutionaries," the last of six poems in the collection; he charged MacLeish with holding Marxists, Jews, and socialist

Title page for MacLeish's 1932 poem, for which he received a Pulitzer Prize

intellectuals in contempt and called the poet an "unconscious fascist." At the other extreme of critical response was Theodore Morrison's view in the January 1934 *Atlantic* that the collection was nationalistic, patriotic verse that ought to be savored.

MacLeish's first contact with the professional stage came in 1934 when he wrote the libretto for *Union Pacific,* a ballet based on the construction of the first transcontinental railroad and the golden spike ceremony marking its completion on 10 May 1869, at Promontory Point, Utah. Scored by Nicholas Nabokoff, choreographed by Leonide Massine, and produced by the Monte Carlo Ballet Russe, *Union Pacific* opened at the Saint James Theatre on 25 April 1934 with assistance from the Federal Theatre Project and toured widely in the United States and Europe.

MacLeish's next book was another verse play—*Panic* (1935). Always interested in verse form, MacLeish tried in this play to use a rhythm that captured American English as opposed to British English. In his preface to the first version of the play, MacLeish explained that American speech, to his ear, was in falling rather than rising rhythms and that it was more sharply accented than British English. For this reason, blank verse was unsuitable for American verse drama. The best solution, he thought, was "in the direction of a prosody frankly built upon accents without regard for syllabic interval." For the principal speakers, he wrote in a five-stress line without regard for the number of syllables in the line; for the minor characters, he chose a three-stress line, also without regard for the number of syllables. Both lines are in essentially falling rhythms and in both lines the stresses fall on the words "suggested by the sense."

The play had a three-day run at the Imperial Theater in New York, directed by Jimmy Light and starring Orson Welles. About the Great Depression, then in "its sixth unendurable year," the play involves the bankruptcy and suicide of McGafferty, one of the leading and wealthiest industrialists and bankers in the nation. McGafferty fails not through historical necessity—the charge of the Communists—but through a loss of vision, courage, and love. McGafferty, speaking about the suicide of his colleague Shelton, might well have been speaking about himself. Shelton had believed in the capacity of the American to build his republic, to "shape his world":

Now there was no future: only fate.
(*pause*)
Our fathers forged their destiny themselves like
men . . .
            We take it, spoon-fed, from the prophets,
priests, who know the age of man is done,
the age of faceless masses is beginning . . .
(*pause*)
Necessity has murdered time. . . .

Preoccupied with the abstractions of economic theory, McGafferty has also lost his capacity to love. Ione, his mistress, tries to help him recover his feeling for life but knows that she has failed: "You're gone and when I call to you it's someone / else turns back to speak. (*silence*) I do not / *know* you. . . . "

By far the most interesting response to *Panic* came from the exchange between the poet and the "editors of *The New Masses* and some of their Marxist friends." MacLeish met with these critics after the third performance, their debate taking place on stage. His critics believed in historical determinism; he did not. They, MacLeish said in a new preface to *Panic* in *Six Plays* (1980), "believed that history was made by immutable laws divulged by suitable oracles while the author continued to put his trust in the

Jeffersonian doctrine that History is made by men. And this difference . . . affected their respective views of the Great Depression." For them "the Great Depression proved the truth of historical determinism: the Pytho of London had foretold the inevitable collapse of capitalism and here it was collapsing, taking self-government and the private activities of human beings with it." For MacLeish the Great Depression was caused by "human stupidity and cowardice and greed," and he quoted "Roosevelt's observation that we had nothing to fear but fear itself, meaning that men, as they had caused the Depression, could put an end to it themselves if they could find the courage."

MacLeish's desire to capture his era in the cage of form and to help shape his times sometimes went beyond poetry to something approaching political rhetoric, as he himself recognized. Some of his poems, he told Mark Van Doren, "were filled with political passion either berating the Marxists or berating their opposites. . . . Something, something went wrong there." Although MacLeish does not mention any specific poems that suffer in this way, he may well have had in mind some of the poems from *Public Speech* (1936). "Speech to Those Who Say Comrade" attacks Marxists, for instance, pointing out that shared experience rather than words makes brotherhood; "Speech to the Detractors" attacks those who detract from the pursuit and love of excellence, "Whether of earth or art, / Whether the hare's leap or the heart's recklessness." "Speech to a Crowd" chides those who do not use their eyes to see (understand) their reality and indicates that in worshiping too long the murdered gods (the past) they have missed their chances. Leave the dead (those who do not understand the possibilities of life) to lament their fate and "Laugh at them!," he advises: "But we who work have end of work together. / Tell yourselves the earth is yours to take! / Waiting for messages out of the dark you are poor. / The world was always yours: you would not take it."

In "The German Girls! The German Girls!" the speaker addresses the German girls who, having been betrayed by romantic and militaristic notions about reality, are brought to their senses by a questioning voice, an inner voice. Theirs, finally, is the responsibility for having been deceived. They are the ones who acceded to the wishes of the men, who gave themselves to the "mounted men." Unconsciously the girls know one of the worst of all paradoxes: "Only by a woman's tenderness can come / The midnight volley and the prison drumbeat." The Eve figure has a responsibility in the fate of man, too.

In "Pole Star," the first poem in *Public Speech,* the pole star symbolizes love that may still guide when liberty, pride, and hope (other guides) have

vanished. "Love's star will not" vanish; "Love is that waking light / That leads now when all others darken." This guide, however, is also difficult to see and easily missed. In fact, this guide is the one most missing for all the characters depicted in *Public Speech*. It is missed largely through commitments to abstractions or to the past.

About half of the poems in the volume are love lyrics (private speech); the most notable of these are the ten poems comprising "The Woman on the Stair." This sequence is about the betrayal of love, the isolation that follows, and the difficulty that the young man in particular has in forgetting what has happened. In the last poem, "The Release," the young man manages to remember his beloved as she was when they were in love. In that memory she is still perfect.

In 1937 MacLeish wrote *The Fall of the City,* his first verse play for radio. With Welles playing the role of a radio announcer reporting on and interpreting the actions and words of other characters, the play dramatizes the thoughts and actions of the citizens of the free city of Tenochtitlàn prior to the conquest. Before the historical fall of the city, a dead woman allegedly "appeared at noon at the tomb's door to prophesy: 'The city of masterless men will take a master.'" In the play MacLeish uses this legend near the opening:

> The city of masterless men
> Will take a master.
> There will be shouting then:
> Blood after!

Members of the crowd and the announcer try to interpret the meaning of her words but fail. A messenger arrives, warning that the conqueror has landed and is marching toward the city:

> beware of him!
> All doors are dangers.
> The warders of wealth
> Will admit him by stealth.
> The lovers of man
> Will invite him as friend.
> The drinkers of blood
> Will drum him in suddenly.
> Hope will unlatch to him:
> Hopelessness open.

The conqueror has wide appeal, reminiscent of the appeal of Lenin, Adolf Hitler, and Benito Mussolini, leaders MacLeish surely had in mind, for he charged them with betraying the revolution of man. The Orator speaks, telling the people not to fear and to resist tyranny by refusing to take up weapons. To live by arms is to invite death by arms:

MacLeish with Orson Welles and William Robson, preparing to broadcast MacLeish's radio drama Air Raid, *27 October 1938 (The New York Public Library at Lincoln Center, Astor, Lenox and Tilden Foundations)*

"Force is a greater enemy than this conqueror— / A treacherous weapon."

The argument of the pacifistic Orator seems to prevail and the Announcer, functioning like a Greek chorus, approves the Orator's words:

> Men forget these truths in passion:
> They oppose the oppressors with blind blows:
> They make of their towns tombs: of the roofs burials:
> They build memorial ruins to liberty:
> But liberty is not built from ruins:
> Only in peace is the work excellent. . . .

A second messenger interrupts the celebration following the Orator's words with the news that the conqueror has arrived. Duty-bound to warn the people, the Messenger explains the conqueror's motives—fame, ambition, glory—and his technique: "He brings his own enemy," a scapegoat whom he sets up at every opportunity and characterizes as bloody and vicious. He then attacks the scapegoat, "knocking him down / In every town square / Till hair's on his blade / and blood's all about." The second messenger seems to prevail, but the Priests appear and urge the people to abandon the world and to place all trust in the gods, a position not unlike Abel's in *Nobodaddy*. The crowd wavers in its support of the messenger and turns to the gods. A General reminds the people of what they all should have known, that

> Freedom's the rarest bird!
> You risk your neck to snare it—
> It's gone while your eyeballs stare!

The General appeals to their love for family and freedom and urges them to resist the tyrant lest their children crawl for their failure to fight. The people, however, are too fearful; they see their city, what they had built with their own lives, as doomed:

> Let the conqueror have it! It is his!
> The age is his! It's his century!
>
> Our institutions are obsolete.
> He marches a mile while we sit in meeting.
> . . . .
> The age demands a made-up mind.
> The conqueror's mind is decided on everything.

The people succumb, bowing to the conqueror as soon as he appears; but the Announcer, standing

238

to report the events, sees the conqueror raise his visor and whispers that "The helmet is hollow!" The cowering people do not see; they "invent their oppressors: they wish to believe in them / They wish to be free of their freedom: released from their liberty:— / The long labor of liberty ended!" The play concludes with the Citizens saying, in joy: "The city of masterless men has found a master / The city has fallen! / The city has fallen!" The Announcer adds in "*flat*" voice his agreement: "The city has fallen," and the play ends.

In *The Fall of the City* MacLeish again showed himself a child of his era by attempting to dramatize a major trend of thought that he fears; he tried to help shape the era by pointing out its faults and implicitly urging their correction. He did not want Americans to give up the freedom to govern themselves as he thought the Europeans (especially the Germans) were then doing.

Most critics commended MacLeish's efforts, both for the opposition of the play to blind acceptance and for the poet's attempt to use a verse form that would appeal to a mass audience. Malcolm Cowley, writing in the *New Republic* (26 May 1937), thought the emptiness of the conqueror effective and said that it reminded him of Hitler and Mussolini. Only one critic, Randall Jarrell, censured the play severely; he believed it was an oversimplified, false interpretation of reality that was filled with "useless sensationalism and exoticism" and that it was "internally inconsistent."

Air Raid (1938) has its origin in MacLeish's response to Pablo Picasso's *Guernica* (1937). Like *Fall of the City, Air Raid* is a verse play for radio. It features an announcer describing what he sees and hears as the people (mostly women) go about their lives, ignoring the threat of the air raid. They do not understand at first that modern war has arrived, that they will be attacked as though they were soldiers, that the conqueror's army has been modernized, and that it arrives over the city in dive bombers. MacLeish captures the horror of their growing realization.

Air Raid received less comment than *Fall of the City,* most of it, however, being favorable: John Brooks Wheelwright thought it MacLeish's best effort to that time. Signi Lenea Falk later commented on MacLeish's effective handling of the contrast between life in the small Spanish town and the devastation of the air raid and noted that the announcer's objectivity was a comment on the callousness of modern times toward suffering.

In 1938 MacLeish left his editorial post at *Fortune* to become curator of the Nieman Foundation of Journalism at Harvard, and the next year he became

Librarian of Congress, a post he held until 1944. In addition to this service MacLeish was director of the U.S. Office of Facts and Figures (1941–1942), assistant director of the U.S. Office of War Information (1942–1943), and assistant secretary of state (1944–1945). He wrote many essays during these years, his voice powerful and eloquent in its support of the human revolution and fervent and effective in its opposition to political indifference and totalitarianism.

America Was Promises (1939) reflects MacLeish's abiding love of the land and of the promise the American continent holds for its inhabitants. Like so many of his poems, this one presents a speaker who reminds Americans of what they have lost or are in danger of losing. "America was promises to whom?" the speaker asks; then he answers that Thomas Jefferson, John Adams, and Thomas Paine knew. The answer is: "the promises are theirs who take them! / Believe unless we take them for ourselves / Others will take them for the use of others!"

The title of "Colloquy of the States" (first published in the October 1929 issue of *Atlantic Monthly*), accurately describes the action presented—voices of the various states of the union commenting on alleged impurities in Americans because they, unlike those living near the Rhine (the Germans, of course, and Hitler's notion of Aryan supremacy), are of mixed blood or mixed nationalities. The voices refute the argument of Hitler, pointing out that his argument is the sort that Americans, choosing freedom, abandoned at the beginning of the American Revolution. Hitler's argument is atavistic, relieving the individual of responsibility for himself.

After the war MacLeish served his country and the world in helping to found UNESCO, participating in this endeavor throughout 1945 and 1946. His only artistic output between 1939 and 1947, besides *America Was Promises* and volumes of political prose, came in the form of radio broadcasts such as *The States Talking* (1941) and *The American Story* (1944). Patriotic and highly successful, *The American Story* was actually ten separate broadcasts dramatizing the birth and rise of America from the time of Christopher Columbus to the time of George Washington. MacLeish's only religious radio play, *The Son of Man,* was broadcast by CBS in 1947.

Another collection of his poetry did not appear until 1948, with the publication of *Actfive and Other Poems.* "Actfive" is a dramatic poem in three parts. Part one opens with "*the King unthroned, the God / Departed with his leopards serpents / Fish, and on the forestage Man / Murdered.*" The question asked is, who will be the "hero in the piece?" MacLeish imagines the aftermath of a totally destructive war and wonders

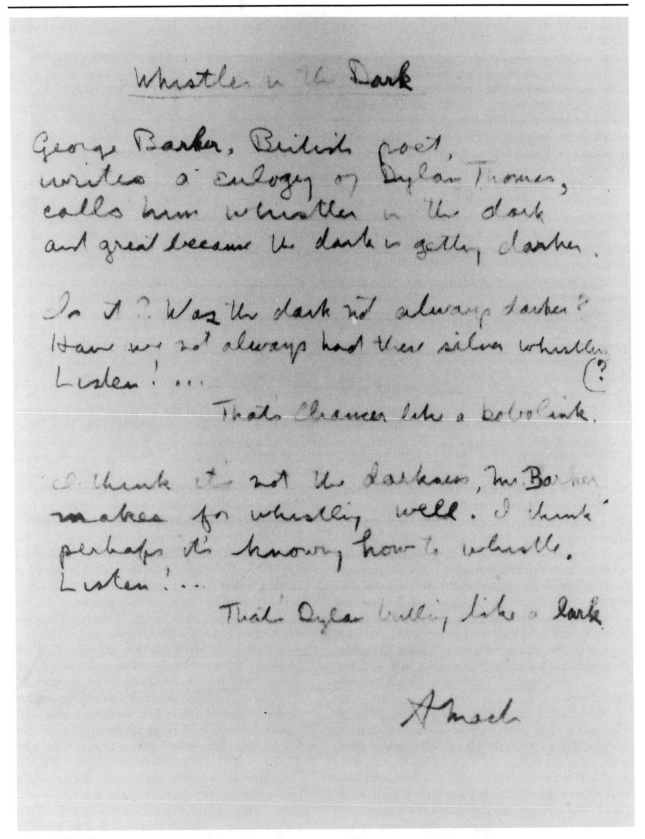

Page from MacLeish's notebooks (Estate of Archibald MacLeish)

what has happened to humanity. Part two is a masque of mummers who trace various heroes through history up to "The Crowd" as hero. The third part of the poem announces that "Every age must have its hero: / Even the faint age of fear— / Even here, in this belated place / Deserted by the God, wherein the King / Abandons, and the shape of Man / Lies murdered in his deeds of grace." In the end, however,

> The heart persists. The love survives.
> The nameless flesh and bone accepts
> Some duty to be beautiful and brave
> Owed neither to the world nor to the grave
> Nor to the stone God nor the exiled King
> Nor Man, the murdered dream, nor anything
> But only to the flesh and bone.

As in *Nobodaddy* the central character, knowing good and evil, continues; he endures and he loves, without a god, without a king. Man will keep trying because the heart (love of life itself) persists.

Hayden Carruth, writing for *Poetry* (February 1949), judged this collection too public and propagandistic. Among later critics, Falk thought it revealed "MacLeish's belief that a country reflects the image it worships," while for Grover Smith it clarified what MacLeish had been trying to say in his poetry.

While MacLeish was Boylston Professor of Rhetoric and Poetry at Harvard (1949–1962), he became interested in the cause of Ezra Pound, and in 1950 he delivered *Poetry and Opinion: The Pisan Cantos of Ezra Pound* as a lecture at the University of Illinois. This work supported the right of poets, including Pound, to present the world as they see it, without fear of critics who object to the poets' work on any grounds other than those of the art itself. MacLeish was instrumental in getting Pound released from St. Elizabeths Hospital in Washington, D.C., where he had been placed in 1948 because he was judged mentally deranged and thus unable to stand trial for his treasonous statements in support of Mussolini during World War II. MacLeish's willingness to defend Pound's poetry is important, for in the United States McCarthyism was on the rise. McCarthyism took advantage of the Americans' desire for security, for an end to both World War II and the Cold War which followed. If gaining that security meant the loss of individual freedom of expression, however, MacLeish was opposed, and the threat of McCarthyism surely meant such a loss to the poet. In fact, MacLeish had McCarthyism in mind when he wrote *The Trojan Horse* (1952).

With *The Trojan Horse*, MacLeish again sought to warn Americans of the dangers in their world.

The action of this verse play for radio begins when the Trojans find the wooden horse left outside the walls of Troy, the Greeks having apparently departed. The basic conflict in the play is between those who wish to tear down the walls to bring the horse (a material sign from the gods, they argue) into the city and those who wish the walls to stand, thinking that the signs from the gods are internal and heart-felt, not material. Their god is something to be loved, not feared; and, they argue, this love—freely given by the Trojans—is what caused the citizens to defend Helen and Paris's right to choose each other in the first place.

Laocoön, opposing the idol-worshiping faction, recommends shoving the wooden horse over the cliff and into the sea. Although the people hear Laocoön's words, they do not understand them, just as they do not understand the prophetic question of Cassandra: "Who rides the horse that has no rider?" When Laocoön and his sons are killed offstage by the serpents, the case against his argument is even stronger. When Helen approaches the horse and calls to the Greeks hidden inside, they do not answer, but she senses that they are there and flees. The people do not understand, still, and they breach their own walls. At the end of the play, Cassandra weeps, prophetically seeing the burning and sacking of the city.

MacLeish's concern is clear enough: there was a danger in the United States that people would accept the hypocrisy of McCarthyism, unwittingly participate in the destruction of the principles the republic was built on, and so destroy their own nation. In *The Trojan Horse* the causes of the people's failure are again lack of awareness of the truth and the loss of faith in the principles of the human revolution. More than anything else, MacLeish wanted Americans to pursue and to perpetuate the revolution, begun in this country but having its roots in the Adam/Cain choice to leave the garden.

Collected Poems, 1917–1952 (1952) added some forty-one new poems to MacLeish's lyric output. Although he was still writing some public poetry, MacLeish's voice in most of the new poems is less public than in any volume since *Frescoes for Mr. Rockefeller's City*. Most public of the poems is "At the Lincoln Memorial," a poem that asks the reader to reflect on Lincoln's struggle to save the union and "To renew / That promise and that hope" with which the nation began but which are in jeopardy. The theme of the westward journey away from paradise is developed in the poet's favorite terza-rima form in "Calypso's Island," where the speaker chooses the real world and his Penelope over the paradise and the enchantress. He would leave the garden, longing "for the

*Title page for MacLeish's 1958 verse play, a modern retelling
of the story of Job*

cold, salt, / Restless, contending sea and for the island / Where the grass dies and the seasons alter: / Where that one wears the sunlight for a while."

Several poems in the new group speak to MacLeish's efforts as poet. In "A Man's Work" MacLeish laconically notes that the wild apple tree and the wild oak tree thrive in the world, while his tree, the cedar, is "silent with its fruit to bear." "Hypocrite Auteur," recalling Eliot's "hypocrite lecteur" in *The Waste Land* (1922), shows again the function of the poet—to capture his era. "An age becomes an age, all else beside," says the poem, "When sensuous poets in their pride invent / Emblems for the soul's consent / That speak the meanings man will never know / But man-imagined images can show: / It perishes when those images, though seen, / No longer mean." The poet, the artist, deserted by the world, provides man with metaphors that will help him understand what his still-not-understood senses tell him, that life—heroic life—is still possible.

Taken together, all the new poems in *Collected Poems, 1917–1952* are admirable efforts, and MacLeish was awarded his second Pulitzer Prize for the book. The publication of this book, his first collec-

tion of poetry since 1933, also provided the critics with an opportunity to assess his work in toto. Almost all of them found weaknesses, but many of them concluded that MacLeish had made in one way or another a significant mark in American literature. Kimon Friar, writing in the *New Republic* (15 December 1952), called MacLeish a poet of action, who attempted "to unite the inner and outer man." Writing later, Falk thought the new poems showed that MacLeish, despite his political involvement, still had his lyric gift.

MacLeish indeed had not lost his lyric gift, for his next work, *This Music Crept by Me Upon the Waters* (1953), a verse play for radio, is more lyrical than dramatic. Most readers find it too chatty. Frequently compared to Eliot's *The Cocktail Party* (published in 1950), *This Music Crept by Me Upon the Waters* is a melodious mood play of ambiguous meaning. With its ten characters and contemporary, Caribbean island setting, the play delves into different attitudes toward happiness and paradise. In the end every chance for happiness is either missed or squandered. Though there is little consensus on the matter, a plurality of critics saw the play as a slap on the wrists of Americans who have paradise within their grasps but, for whatever reason, let it slip away.

Perhaps the loveliest of MacLeish's post-World War II work is the collection of twenty-eight poems called *Songs for Eve* (1954), in which the poems recall the idea behind *Nobodaddy*. In the first poem, "What Eve Sang," Eve is conscious of her self, of knowing. Although "Space-time / Is all there is of space and time," there is more than mere existence in space and time. There is also a song of "rhyme / For all of space and all of time." That rhyme is the song of her awareness of human existence and its passing, the knowledge sought by Adam and Eve. Before their awakening they were unconscious of their existence and so merely living in space and time. For all the sorrows of a life of knowledge, Eve is glad to have left the green tree (the garden) and accepted the dry tree (the wasteland where death is certain but known). In the world of the green tree, "Waking is forbidden," and for this reason Eve says she is thankful for the Fall:

The Fall! she said—
From earth to God!
Give thanks, she said for branch and bole,
For Eve who found the grace to fall
From Adam, browsing animal,
Into the soaring of the soul!

Eve accepts her destiny—the "Dry tree, / Man's tree, / Eternity." It is the tree of her sons, and because of it, man can order and create, make his own world. Ironically, then, his knowledge of his mortality permits him to transcend it through his creations.

Four years after *Songs for Eve* MacLeish published *J.B.* (1958), the verse play for which he is best known and for which he was awarded his third Pulitzer Prize. The play generated controversy, especially among those who accused MacLeish of advocating mere sex as a cure for the devastation depicted in the play. Such a reading, MacLeish told a group of student actors at Greenfield Community College in Massachusetts (15 October 1974), was fatuous. He went on to explain to the young actors that the play was not a conflict between God and man but between justice and love. This theme is twice repeated by Nickles near the opening of the play when he recalls Job's song:

> "If God is God he is not good,
> If God is good he is not God;
> Take the even, take the odd,
> I would not sleep here if I could
> Except for the little green leaves in the wood
> And the Wind on the water."

This love for life, expressed in the last two lines of the song, is what J.B. loses in the course of the action of the play; it is up to his Eve-like wife, Sarah, to help him regain that love. The function of Sarah is different from the function of Job's wife in the Biblical version and constitutes MacLeish's major addition to the story.

The play, MacLeish said, was generated by his haunting recollection of a woman who had been bombed out three times during the London bombings. Where was justice? The play at last took form only when MacLeish conceived of Zuss and Nickles, the two circus workers who play God and Satan, for it was MacLeish's conception of their watching the performance of their "play" that gave him the perspective he needed to complete the work.

The action of the play is distributed over a prologue and eleven scenes. In the prologue, Nickles and Zuss, two has-been and slightly resentful actors who see little justice in their situation, decide to put the story of Job on the stage, Zuss wearing the mask of God (whose eyes are closed, thus reminiscent of the seemingly indifferent or withdrawn God in some of MacLeish's earlier poetry) and Nickles wearing the mask of Satan (cynically aware, his eyes open and "wrinkled with laughter" but his mouth "drawn down in agonized disgust"). The action of the updated Job story then begins. J.B. is a vigorous, prosperous, life-loving New Englander who believes in a just and merciful God who gives freely his gifts

to all who will accept them. Sarah, J.B.'s wife, is less certain. Although she holds that God is just—He both rewards and punishes—she thinks that man must earn his rewards and that J.B. is prosperous because he has earned the right to trust to his luck rather than because of God's grace. Sarah's argument for justice is more like Eve's or Cain's; J.B.'s view is more trusting, like Abel's. In any case, J.B. sees Sarah's view as nonsense:

> We get the world for nothing, don't we?
> It's given to us, gift on gift:
> Sun on the floor, airs in the curtain.

During the next ten scenes, J.B. loses sight of the meaning of his words because everything is taken away from him—his wealth, his home, his five children, and even his wife. Coming to comfort J.B. are the worldly communist, the psychologist, and the priest. The communist assures him that his only wrong was being in the "Wrong class" in the "wrong century— / You pay for your luck with your licks, that's all." The psychologist tells him that he is not guilty but is a victim of guilt, or that if he is guilty, the guilt is deep, inevitable, and not yet known. J.B. rejects this argument because it, like the argument of the communist, refuses to recognize human responsibility. J.B. rejects the priest's argument that he is sinful because he is a man; this argument implicates God in man's sin, and J.B. refuses to accept God's involvement. Still, J.B. refuses to repent of a sin of which he is unaware and contends with God (the Distant Voice in the play). Job repents of his contentiousness, at last, and accepts God's authority. As Nickles had predicted, God wins, returning to J.B. all that had been taken from him. MacLeish's point is not that J.B. gets everything back but that he takes it back, accepts it, because even though he cannot understand God's justice he is still able to love life in the world. If justice cannot be seen and so depended upon as a guide for action, love can (as in "Pole Star"), which is the meaning of Sarah's words at the curtain:

> Blow on the coal of the heart.
> The candles in churches are out.
> The lights have gone out in the sky.
> Blow on the coal of the heart
> And we'll see by and by. . . .

J.B. helps her, *"lifting and straightening the chairs,"* as she continues: "We'll see where we are. / The wit won't burn and the wet soul smoulders. / Blow on the coal of the heart and we'll know . . . / We'll know. . . ."

Some of the negative criticism quarreled with MacLeish's conception of J.B., thinking of him, in Ciardi's words, as a "shallow, self-righteous fathead." In *The New Yorker* (20 December 1958) Kenneth Tynan said the play was written in "bumpy alliterative verse" and called it medieval in "narrative technique." There was positive criticism, too. Eleanor Sickles argued that *J.B.* reflected Mac-Leish's lasting interest in the Fall, which began in *Nobodaddy*. She saw J.B. as a tragic hero whose flaw was a "smug arrogant assumption that 'the God of Galaxies' is a special friend and patron of his," and, she explained, J.B. was brought to perceive the "cosmic power and mystery beyond reach of man's thought," and he thus accepted his separation from paradise and "the mystery of the green tree." All critics concurred on one point: *J.B.* was a genuine rarity—a commercially successful religious verse play in an age of secular prose.

Ciardi, for all his criticism of character, thought that MacLeish might be a great dramatist because he forged "a true poetic stage line for our time," the line showing range, poetic identity. Mac-Leish himself had something to say about the verse. It is, he told the young players at Greenfield, rhythmical, not metrical, based on a four-stress line. There were two ways in which it might be misread—one was to read it as though it were being recited, the other as though it were not verse. As with the verse in *Panic,* the line itself is crucial, the stresses falling where the sense would naturally place them.

After his retirement from Harvard in 1962, MacLeish became Simpson Lecturer at Amherst (1963–1967), writing *Herakles: A Play in Verse* (1967) during this time. Like *Nobodaddy* and *J.B.* as well as *The Trojan Horse, Herakles* updates a myth that speaks to the modern era. Professor Hoadley has gone to Greece, having just received a prize in Stockholm for his scientific achievements. He and his fellow scientists have made the world safe for man, but in the process they have unwittingly forgotten their own loved ones and the simple joys of their lives. Modern man as scientist, then, is like Herakles, who, having completed the twelve humbling tasks and now ready for the promise of the gods, turns to them and gets no answer. Like the other MacLeish heroes, he seeks his own answers and refuses to accept the gods' refusal to answer him. His wife, like Sarah in *J.B.,* tries to comfort him for the madness (and the death of his children) that has come to him. He will not yet accept her efforts, however, and the story ends with Herakles pursuing as he has always pursued. Herakles is like J.B. in that he desires to know, and not for selfish

motives, but he is unlike J.B. in that he refuses to accept his limitations. In this respect he is more like Adam or Cain or Peter. The play received as much positive criticism as any of MacLeish's work since *Streets in the Moon.* Richard Eberhart called it "a splendid new creation in American verse drama, splendid, swift, passionate, just." The play has "something to say," said John Wain in the *New Republic* (22 July 1967), "and succeeds in saying it."

The Wild Old Wicked Man and Other Poems (1968) shows MacLeish at his lyric best. The title poem depicts the old man as too old to love, yet still loving: "Too old for love and still to love . . . / For what," he asks, answering himself with more questions: "For one more flattering proof / the flesh lives and the beast is strong?" There is for this aging Adam no end to the search. Other poems on this theme are "The Tyrant of Syracuse," "Hotel Breakfast" (a beautiful little love lyric), and "Survivor." For Grover Smith, the collection shows "Adam victorious, fallen upwards into a stasis of art and beauty."

During the upheaval of the late 1960s, Mac-Leish witnessed a battle between law and order on the one hand and individual liberty on the other that threatened to destroy the Union. In response he wrote *Scratch* (1971), his only prose play. Suggested by "The Devil and Daniel Webster" (1937), a short story by Stephen Vincent Benét, *Scratch* employs the legend of the famed Yankee orator as a plea for liberty and union. MacLeish also felt the play was an appropriate fable for an age of affluence when men sold their souls and individual freedom in return for creature comforts on the installment plan. *Scratch* premiered at the Saint James Theatre on 6 May 1971, but closed after a run of only four performances. The critics did not find much to like in this play.

The first twenty-seven poems of *New and Collected Poems, 1917–1976* (1976) continue the themes of *The Wild Old Wicked Man and Other Poems.* This collection is dedicated to MacLeish's wife and includes several autobiographical poems—including "The Old Gray Couple (1)" and "The Old Gray Couple (2)," which show in turn how everything that the couple know, they know together, except for their certain deaths, which each faces separately in the night; the second poem notes that "love, like light, grows dearer toward the dark." Other autobiographical poems in the collection hark back to the poet's years in the army and to the death of his brother Kenneth. "Family Portrait" captures the speaker's feeling of guilt as he thinks about his brother's death. "Pablo Casals" and "A Good Man in a Bad Time" praise excellence, the first in music, the second in politics. "Night Watch in the City of

Boston" contrasts Rome, the city of God, with Boston, the city of Man and "Mother of the Great Republic," and expresses the hope that even in the darkness of the present, the Republic stands. MacLeish's public voice reemerges.

The patriotic theme of "Night Watch in the City of Boston" and the public voice in which the poem is couched also are apparent in *The Great American Fourth of July Parade* (1975), MacLeish's last verse play for radio. In the play Adams and Jefferson are resurrected on the occasion of the American bicentennial celebration to counteract the hypocrisy of the political orator who asserts that "THE U.S.A. IS NUMBER ONE!" and the cynicism of the Sweet Young Thing who says "shit" in response to her schoolmarm's patriotic and sentimental response to the memory of Jefferson and Adams. Jefferson recalls his letter turning down the invitation to attend the fiftieth anniversary of the Republic. About the Declaration and the revolution it spawned, he wrote, "May it be to the world . . . / what I believe it will be: to some parts sooner, to others later, but / finally to all. . . . " Jefferson's argument prevails.

MacLeish's life, even during his retirement, was active. Typically, he told Bill Moyers, he would rise early in the morning and write until about noon; he would dine then and work with his hands in the afternoon. Such manual labor, he said, helped him to think, usually unconsciously. The evenings were often capped by conversations with guests or with reading. He was to have been honored by a symposium at Greenfield Community College in Greenfield, Massachusetts, on the occasion of his ninetieth birthday. MacLeish himself had chosen the participants for the symposium. The poet-playwright died on 20 April 1982, some three weeks before the symposium on 7 and 8 May 1982.

From the beginning of his career MacLeish was interested in the potential of man to create a society in which he could live justly and happily. To live in this way, he believed, required awareness and love, neither characteristic by itself being quite enough; but love, the way of Jesus, as MacLeish put it to Moyers, was a way that was clearly obtainable even if justice was not.

MacLeish's poetry and verse plays will probably suffer when compared to the work of other poets from his era. Still, his work shows a consistent concern for the craft of lyric and epic poetry as well as verse drama (to which he made important contributions). His effort to develop a wider audience for poetry by adopting a more public voice should also be acknowledged. MacLeish seemed to ask, in a world increasingly hostile to the poem, how can the poet help shape his society? His answer was to attach himself to the world in the ways that most men do—through the senses and the emotions. In some of his work MacLeish was unable to realize his intentions. In most, he did. In a few he managed to "capture Heaven and Earth in the cage of form." Never content simply to mirror his age, MacLeish strove always to fulfill his own stringent demand: "Poets, deserted by the world before, / Turn 'round into the actual air: / Invent the age! Invent the metaphor!" Thus, as poet and playwright, MacLeish toiled to unearth the metaphors that would provide a sense of direction to American life through some of the most turbulent decades of the twentieth century.

Letters:

Letters of Archibald MacLeish, edited by R. H. Winnick (Boston: Houghton Mifflin, 1983).

Interviews:

Benjamin DeMott, "The Most Compelling Acts of Love to Touch My Life," *Today's Health,* 51 (February 1973): 39–40, 60–62, 64;

Bill Moyers, "A Conversation with Archibald MacLeish," *Bill Moyers Journal,* PBS television, 7 March 1976;

Richard Meryman, "Archibald MacLeish: The Enlarged Life," *Yankee,* 45 (January 1981): 72–77, 116–118;

Robert Cowley, "America Was Promises: An Interview with Archibald MacLeish," *American Heritage,* 33 (August–September 1982): 22–32;

Bernard A. Drabeck and Helen E. Ellis, eds., *Archibald MacLeish: Reflections* (Amherst: University of Massachusetts Press, 1986).

Bibliographies:

Arthur Mizener, *Catalogue of the First Editions of Archibald MacLeish* (New Haven: Yale University Press, 1938);

Edward J. Mullaly, *Archibald MacLeish: A Checklist* (Kent, Ohio: Kent State University Press, 1973);

Margaret E. C. Howland, *Descriptive Catalog of the Archibald MacLeish Collection at Greenfield Community College* (Greenfield, Mass.: The College, 1991–1993);

Helen E. Ellis and Bernard A. Drabeck with Howland, *Archibald MacLeish: A Selectively Annotated Bibliography* (Lanham, Md.: Scarecrow Press, 1995).

Biography:

Scott Donaldson in collaboration with R. H. Winnick, *Archibald MacLeish: An American Life* (Boston: Houghton Mifflin, 1992).

References:

David Barber, "In Search of an 'Image of Mankind': The Public Poetry and Prose of Archibald Mac-Leish," *American Studies,* 29 (Fall 1988): 31–56;

Barber, "It's All in the Name: The *Einstein* of Archibald MacLeish," *American Poetry,* 8 (Fall 1990): 57–69;

Nancy L. Benco, "Archibald MacLeish: The Poet Librarian," *Quarterly Journal of the Library of Congress,* 33 (1976): 233–249;

R. P. Blackmur, "A Modern Poet in Eden," *Poetry,* 28 (September 1926): 339–342;

John Ciardi, "Birth of a Classic," *Saturday Review,* 41 (8 March 1958): 11–12, 48;

Ciardi, "J.B. Revisited," *Saturday Review,* 43 (30 January 1960): 39, 55;

Ciardi, "The Poetry of Archibald MacLeish," *Atlantic,* 191 (May 1953): 67–68;

Bernard A. Drabeck, Helen E. Ellis, and Seymour Rudin, eds., *The Proceedings of the Archibald MacLeish Symposium, May 7–8, 1982* (Lanham, Md.: University Press of America, 1988);

Richard Eberhart, "Archibald MacLeish's Herakles," *Virginia Quarterly Review,* 143 (Summer 1967): 499–503;

Signi Lenea Falk, *Archibald MacLeish* (New York: Twayne, 1965);

Donald Hall, "Archibald MacLeish: On Being a Poet in the Theater," *Horizon,* 2 (January 1960): 48–56;

Randall Jarrell, "Fall of the City," *Sewanee Review,* 51 (April 1943): 267–280;

Massachusetts Review, special MacLeish issue, 23 (Winter 1982);

John Timberman Newcomb, "Archibald MacLeish and the Poetics of Public Speech: A Critique of High Modernism," *Journal of the Midwest Modern Language Association,* 23 (Spring 1990): 9–26;

Eleanor Sickles, "Archibald MacLeish and American Democracy," *American Literature,* 15 (November 1943): 223–237;

Sickles, "MacLeish and the Fortunate Fall," *American Literature,* 35 (May 1963): 205–217;

Grover Smith, *Archibald MacLeish* (Minneapolis: University of Minnesota Press, 1971);

John Brooks Wheelwright, "Toward the Recovery of Speech," *Poetry,* 54 (June 1939): 164–167;

Morton Zabel, "The Poet of Capitol Hill," *Partisan Review,* 8 (January 1941): 2–19; 8 (March 1941): 128–145.

Papers:

Archibald MacLeish's papers, memorabilia, tapes, interviews, and manuscripts are collected in the following locations: Greenfield Community College, Greenfield, Massachusetts; the Library of Congress; Houghton Library at Harvard; and the Beinecke Library at Yale.

Bobbie Ann Mason

This entry was updated by John D. Kalb (Salisbury State University)
from his entry in DLB 173: American Novelists Since World War II, Fifth Series.

See also the Mason entry in *DLB Yearbook 1987*.

BIRTH: Mayfield, Kentucky, 1 May 1940, to Wilburn Arnett and Christianna Lee Mason.

EDUCATION: B.A., University of Kentucky, 1962; M.A., State University of New York at Binghamton, 1966; Ph.D., University of Connecticut, 1972.

MARRIAGE: 12 April 1969, to Roger B. Rawlings.

AWARDS AND HONORS: National Book Critics Circle Award nomination, American Book Award nomination, PEN/Faulkner Award for fiction nomination, and Ernest Hemingway Foundation Award for best first fiction, all for *Shiloh and Other Stories,* all 1983; National Endowment for the Arts Fellowship, 1983; Pennsylvania Arts Council grant, 1983; Guggenheim Fellowship, 1984; American Academy and Institute of Arts and Letters award, 1984; National Book Critics Circle Award nomination and Southern Book Award, both for *Feather Crowns,* both 1994.

BOOKS: *Nabokov's Garden: A Guide to Ada* (Ann Arbor, Mich.: Ardis, 1974);
The Girl Sleuth: A Feminist Guide to the Bobbsey Twins, Nancy Drew, and Their Sisters (Old Westbury, N.Y.: Feminist Press, 1975);
Shiloh and Other Stories (New York: Harper & Row, 1982; London: Chatto & Windus, 1982);
In Country (New York: Harper & Row, 1985; London: Chatto & Windus, 1986);
Spence + Lila (New York: Harper & Row, 1988; London: Chatto & Windus, 1989);
Love Life: Stories (New York: Harper & Row, 1989; London: Chatto & Windus, 1989);
Feather Crowns (New York: HarperCollins, 1993; London: Chatto & Windus, 1993);
Midnight Magic: Selected Stories of Bobbie Ann Mason (Hopewell, N.J.: Ecco, 1998).

Bobbie Ann Mason grew "so sick of reading about the alienated hero of superior sensibility"

Bobbie Ann Mason (photograph by Thomas Victor)

who so frequently dominates twentieth-century American literature that she decided to write fiction about the antithesis. Her characters are ordinary, working-class denizens of rural western Kentucky, often living in Hopewell, her fictional version of her own hometown, Mayfield, or in some unnamed town equally distant from Paducah (which is at least sizable enough to warrant a shopping mall) and nearly a world away from the cities of Louisville and Lexington or St. Louis, Missouri. Her plainspoken characters are presented in a direct and unadorned style, which frequently earns her the label of minimalist, "dirty" realist, or—as she recalls John Barth's description—"blue-collar hyper-realist super-minimalist," or "something like that." Mason says her style "comes out of a way of hearing people talk." Typically her characters have arrived at transitional points or impediments in their lives, and while language may fail them in their efforts to articulate their needs and surmount their obstacles, they often find common bonds through popular culture (music, movies, and television) and commerce (brand-name products and shopping malls), which invade their formerly remote region. Mason is among the first to use seriously the so-called low art of popular culture as an important underpinning to her literature and the lives of her characters. While she portrays the encroaching impact of urban America on her rural occupants—Wal-Mart replaces the country store, fast food substitutes for traditional home cooking—she usually does so not as a criticism but as a means of providing an accurate and realistic depiction of the people within their changing environments. Her inclusion of these popular elements enhances the sense of meeting real people engaged in their everyday lives.

Bobbie Ann Mason was born on 1 May 1940 in Mayfield, Kentucky, the first of Wilburn Arnett and Christianna Lee Mason's four children, three daughters and one son. The family farm was located just far enough outside Mayfield that she attended a rural elementary school, which she says had "terrible teachers and poor students" and left her wanting to attend the more urban Mayfield schools. She did attend Mayfield High School, and in 1960 she wrote for the local newspaper, the *Mayfield Messenger*. In 1962 she earned her B.A. degree from the University of Kentucky. Following her graduation, she moved to New York City, taking a job as a writer with Ideal Publishing Company, publisher of fan magazines such as *Movie Stars, Movie Life*, and *T.V. Star Parade*. After about a year in New York she returned to school, receiving an M.A. degree from the State University of New York at Binghamton in 1966 and a Ph.D. in English from the University of Connecticut in 1972. She married writer Roger B. Rawlings on 12 April 1969.

Mason's first published book was her doctoral dissertation, *Nabokov's Garden: A Guide to Ada* (1974), which was followed by another nonfiction work, this time one that paid homage to her childhood heroines, *The Girl Sleuth: A Feminist Guide to the Bobbsey Twins, Nancy Drew, and Their Sisters* (1975). Meanwhile, she taught journalism part-time at Mansfield State College in Mansfield, Pennsylvania, from 1972 to 1979 and began crafting short stories. This return to fiction writing had followed a long, meandering path.

Mason had first tried her hand at writing fiction when she was a child, but "along the way I was stymied quite a lot." She told Lila Havens that she took two creative-writing courses in college and "was committed to writing then, but I didn't get enough encouragement" to continue. She hoped that graduate school would help her learn how to write, but she found the study of literature a distraction from writing fiction. Although she conceded in the same interview that graduate school had some benefits "because I hadn't ever read very much," Mason also complained to Havens that no one told her that graduate school "was a training ground for critics." She told Albert E. Wilhelm, "I'm always embarrassed by references to this Ph.D. because I don't relate back to that and I didn't carry forward any particular knowledge about literature that I studied." Since her childhood was shaped by "isolation and a desire to get out of this isolation," she identifies Nancy Drew and the Bobbsey Twins as her most powerful and lasting "literary" influences: "Those books contain very innocent dreams of quests for clarity, solving a mystery, and wanting to go somewhere, do something, and be somebody. The Bobbsey Twins got to go on a vacation in every single book." When it came to writing on her own, Mason "had to learn how to write from scratch: no amount of studying literature prepared me for knowing how a story is coaxed out of the imagination." Not until she was in her late thirties did she find the encouragement she needed to become a full-time writer, when she, in her words, "boldly and arrogantly sent my second finished story to *The New Yorker*."

Although this story and eighteen others that followed it were rejected by *The New Yorker*, the second rejection began a correspondence between Mason and editor Roger Angell. "Roger was the first person in the world who ever said to me, 'You're a writer, you have talent'"—encouragement enough to keep her writing and submitting until her twentieth submission, the short story "Offerings," was accepted and published in the 18 February 1980 issue. After the publication of two more stories in *The New Yorker*, the magazine made a first-reading agreement with her—the beginning of a long-standing relationship with *The New Yorker* that continues. She not only provides short stories but also frequently contributes to "Talk of the Town" and "Shouts and Murmurs." "Offerings" and fifteen other short stories—works that first appeared in *The New Yorker, The Atlantic Monthly, Redbook,* and other publications—are collected in her first book of fiction, *Shiloh and Other Stories* (1982), which was nominated for a National Book Critics Circle Award, an American

Book Award, and a PEN/Faulkner Award and earned her the 1983 Ernest Hemingway Foundation Award for best first fiction. She has also had stories selected for *Best American Short Stories* (1981 and 1983) and The Pushcart Prize (1983 and 1996).

All the stories in *Shiloh and Other Stories* feature men and women who have reached some sort of impasse or transitional point in their lives and are searching for catalysts to move them forward, if only just a bit. Most are written in the present tense and arrive at open-ended conclusions. For instance, in "Shiloh" truck driver Leroy Moffitt, at home with his wife, Norma Jean, for the past three months because he has badly injured a leg in an accident, "is not sure what to do next," although he is fairly certain he will not return to making long hauls. When Leroy and Norma Jean married at eighteen, she was pregnant with a child who died in infancy of sudden infant death syndrome. Placed in close quarters for the first time since their marriage sixteen or so years earlier, they begin to notice things about one another that were previously easy to overlook.

After Leroy dabbles with craft kits, he toys with the notion of selling his rig and building a log house, "a real home" for Norma Jean, who wants no part of living in a log cabin. As they sit at the kitchen table, both preoccupied with their singular pursuits—Norma Jean working on an essay for her adult-education class, Leroy working on his building plans with Lincoln logs—"Leroy has the hopeful thought that they are sharing something," but he then realizes his wife is "miles away." Even though he knows their marriage is ending, they take a last trip together to the Civil War battleground at Shiloh, the site of Leroy's mother-in-law's honeymoon and a place she has been pestering them to visit. This trip to Shiloh becomes the setting for the final stage of Leroy and Norma Jean's marriage, not the renewal of their relationship as Leroy might have hoped. Norma Jean finally explains to Leroy that their marriage is over, and he realizes that his dream of building the log house was an empty notion: while he has been trying to repair the dwelling of his marriage, his wife has moved on to other possibilities.

Mason has identified "Residents and Transients," the ninth story in the collection, as the thematic center of *Shiloh and Other Stories:* "there are some people who would just never leave home, because that's where they're meant to be; and others are, well, born to run." Mary, the narrator of "Residents and Transients," had come back to rural Kentucky three years before the story opens, following an eight-year absence "pursuing higher learning." After she and her husband, Stephen, settle in the

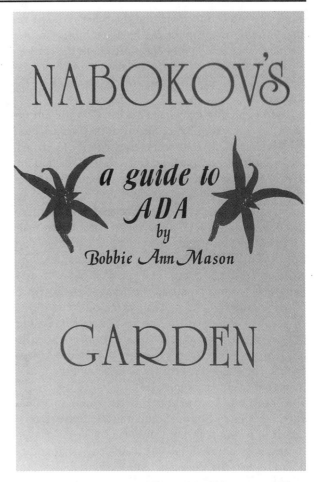

Dust jacket for Mason's first book (1974), based on her dissertation at the University of Connecticut

farmhouse that her parents have left to move to Florida, she wonders "why I ever went away." When Stephen's job takes him to Louisville, where he is house hunting, Mary begins an affair with her dentist, Larry. The attachment to Larry is most likely superficial and not long-lasting—after all, he finds her every utterance amusing, even the serious ones. Of more importance is her renewed love affair with her parents' farmhouse and cornfields, which came with a family of barn cats that has gradually moved into the house. The issue of residents and transients arises as she explains to Larry that she has been "reading up on cats," which, in the wild, fit into these two broad categories. While scientists first believed that the residents, those who establish home territories, were superior to transients, "the bums, the losers" who were "on the move," new research suggests "that the transients are the superior ones after all, with the greatest curiosity and most intelligence." At the end of the story Mary is as undecided about moving as the scientists are about these cats. As she looks into the odd eyes of a cat named Brenda—one green and the other red—she realizes she is "waiting for the light to change" to determine whether to go or stay. Although the choices Mason's characters frequently face seem easy to define, their possibilities are often narrowly constricted.

In depicting transients Mason uses the phrase "born to run" from Bruce Springsteen's song of that title—a borrowing that seems particularly appropriate in light of her abundant use of popular music, television, brand-name products, and other artifacts of popular culture in most of her writing. The characters in her stories listen to rock and Top 40 radio stations, watch *WKRP in Cincinnati* and Johnny Carson, get their information from *The Today Show* and *Donahue,* drink Coke and Dr. Pepper, eat at McDonald's and Burger King, and work at Kroger and Kmart. It is not surprising then, that Springsteen's "Born in the U.S.A." is the source of the two-line epigraph to Mason's first published novel, *In Country* (1985), a work set in 1984 that explores the still-lingering impact of the Vietnam War on the American psyche: "I'm ten years burning down the road / Nowhere to run ain't got nowhere to go."

Mason did not set out to write about Vietnam. She told Wendy Smith, "I had almost all the characters in my mind, doing things and going through scenes, long before I had any knowledge that any of it had to do with Vietnam," but "I think it came out of my unconscious the same way it's coming out of America's unconscious." A story that Mason says was initially "inspired by some kids I saw on the street corner selling flowers" grew into a potent portrayal of the long-term effects of Vietnam on Samantha Hughes, a recent high-school graduate who never knew her father, Dwayne, because he was killed in the war; on Samantha's mother's brother Emmett Smith, who enlisted following the death of his brother-in-law; and on Emmett's veteran buddies who, like him, still have trouble readjusting to everyday life. Moreover, Mason looks deeply into the broad impact of the Vietnam War on the American psychological landscape as a whole.

In the summer of 1984, nearly ten years since the fall of Saigon, Samantha, Emmett, and his friends—denizens of the ironically named Kentucky town of Hopewell—have yet to come to grips with the Vietnam experience. Protagonist Samantha Hughes, known as "Sam," whose consciousness drives the narrative of *In Country,* suffers the same naive innocence about Vietnam that grips much of America. Not certain what Vietnam was all about, only that her father died there, she begins a quest for her father, for some notion of his identity and the ways in which his life filters into her own. As an inquisitive seventeen-year-old, Sam offers an adolescent point of view, sometimes to the point of irritating the reader with her childish notions, other times offering more mature judgments about the behavior of others. For instance, when she tries an affair with Tom, one of the local veterans and a potential conduit to the past that eludes her, their attempt at sex ends abruptly when Tom is unable to maintain an erection. He points out that his impotence is a physical symptom of his psychological problems, that he loses the struggle of "mind over matter," in which his mind "takes me where I don't want to go." When he half-jokingly suggests that what he needs is a $10,000 penile implant, she quickly surmises that indeed that is what he needs, and perhaps—overgeneralizing as a child would—that Emmett's problem with his sometime girlfriend Anita would be similarly and as easily solved. This childish generalization smacks of an American search for simple solutions to complex problems.

On the other hand, Sam gains a mature insight into the way in which Emmett's focus on birds—in search of the elusive white egret, his only beautiful memory of Vietnam—is a means of maintaining his sanity: "If he concentrated on something fascinating and thrilling, like birds soaring, the pain of his memories wouldn't come through." Yet such maturity is rare in this young woman, who has spitefully stayed behind in Hopewell, ostensibly to look after her troubled uncle, rather than join her mother, Irene, in Lexington. Irene has recently married Larry Joiner—whom Sam has unaffectionately nicknamed "Lorenzo Jones"—and they have a baby of their own, Heather, who seems to have added to Sam's feelings of displacement. Her jealousy at no longer being the sole beneficiary of her mother's love turns to spiteful anger at her mother's inability to help in the quest for her father. Irene and Dwayne had been married for only a month before he shipped out, and she can barely remember him.

Elements of popular culture—as ubiquitous in this novel as they are in Mason's short stories—provide a means through which Sam makes her efforts to integrate herself with the past and with the people in her present, using songs contemporary to the summer of 1984—such as "Born in the U.S.A.," which Mason has called "an anthem for Vietnam vets"—as a cultural connection to the war and its disillusioned survivors. Sam's interest in the so-called classic rock of her parents' generation, the music coincident to the war years themselves, serves as a pathway to the past. For much of the narrative she searches the radio airwaves and record stores for a newly released Beatles song, "Leave My Kitten Alone," a sound bite from the past: "She had to find

Bobbie Ann Mason's first published book of fiction, *Shiloh and Other Stories*, won the PEN/Hemingway Award and was a finalist for the National Book Critics Circle Award, the American Book Award, and the PEN/Faulkner Award. A native of Kentucky, Bobbie Ann Mason lives in rural Pennsylvania.

ISBN 0-06-015469-1

IN COUNTRY

BOBBIE ANN MASON

A NOVEL

BOBBIE ANN MASON

Author of Shiloh and Other Stories

Harper & Row

Dust jacket for Mason's first novel, which explores the effects of the Vietnam War ten years after its end

that record. . . . It was a fresh message from the past, something to go on." She hopes that by sharing this discovery with her mother she will negotiate the differences that separate them. When her mother visits Hopewell, Sam hopes Irene will respond positively to the Kinks album she plays or to the musicians on MTV, but Irene is preoccupied with the present task of tending to her second daughter, Heather. Her mother's seeming disaffection with these cultural artifacts and the realization that her father did not live to hear the Beatles's 1967 album *Sergeant Pepper's Lonely Hearts Club Band* come as immense disappointments to Sam.

Likewise, Emmett is preoccupied with his daily struggle with the memories and losses of his experiences as a soldier in Vietnam. He suffers from sudden throbbing headaches and a spreading case of chloracne, both ostensibly symptoms of his exposure to Agent Orange. While her depictions of her characters illustrate Mason's understanding of the American people's selective amnesia when it comes to the Vietnam War, her portrayals of Agent Orange victims—Buddy Mangrum's intestinal and liver problems and his daughter's birth defects are directly attributable to his exposure to this chemi-

cal—and their treatment by the Veterans Administration (VA) indicate a serious indictment of the American government for its failures to deal appropriately with the veterans of this unpopular war. (Emmett's doctor prescribes Tylenol for the headaches and a restrictive diet appropriate for ordinary adolescent acne.) While some veterans, as Sam realizes, "adjusted perfectly well," others need help with their physical, mental, and emotional problems, and the VA, Mason says, has been ineffectual at best.

Emmett has never readjusted to civilian life. He is unemployed and aimless until he becomes "obsessed" with finding the source of a leak in the basement. His efforts at "Fixing a Hole" (as a song on the Beatles's *Sergeant Pepper* album would have it) keep his mind from wandering and provide a means of concentrating on something outside himself while focusing on what desperately needs repair within. His efforts expose a crack running the length of the foundation of his house, symbolic of the fissures the war has caused in his own personal psyche and that of the nation as a whole. While he jokes, "My basement's flooded and my foundation's weak. . . . And my house may fall down," his excavation focuses on repairing the real damage to his mental and emo-

251

tional house and healing the figurative "tipped heart" from which he suffers. As he later reveals to Sam, "I'm damaged. It's like something in the center of my heart is gone and I can't get it back. . . . I work on staying together, one day at a time. . . . It takes all my energy." Once he has exposed the foundation, discovered the crack, and felt for dry rot, he realizes that this project, like the process of his self-repair, is only beginning. Despite all his efforts at focusing his attention on foundations or birds, by the time he makes his second plan–a trip to the Vietnam Veterans Memorial in Washington, D.C.–he still "can barely get to the point where I can be a self to get out of."

The trip with Sam and Mamaw (her Grandmother Hughes) to the memorial, which frames the narrative as parts 1 and 3 of the novel, suggests that Emmett is able to continue his newly begun process of self-repair. In the final scene, when he discovers the names of his fallen comrades on the wall, "slowly his face bursts into a smile like flames."

Sam's final state is more ambiguous than Emmett's. Some critics have seen her venturing to Cawood's Pond and pretending to be a soldier "humping the boonies" as demonstrating her maturity and growth. While Sam's relentless search for her father entails a search for the "truth" of the war in Vietnam, she, like many Americans, looks for the easy answers. Emmett and Sam share an infatuation with the popular television series *M*A*S*H,* a program set during the Korean conflict but in its contemporaneity a cultural artifact of the Vietnam War years. Years earlier, when Sam first saw the episode in which the character Colonel Blake is killed, "his death was more real to her than the death of her own father." Now offered nightly in seemingly perpetual syndication, the program frequently portrays simplistic solutions to complex problems. When she was younger, Emmett's stories about Vietnam–before Irene got him to stop telling them–gave Sam the notion of "a pleasant countryside, something like Florida, with beaches and palm trees and watery fields of rice and green mountains." In order to discover her father's experiences, Sam needs to dispense with these postcard and television images.

Early in the book, when Emmett has an "episode" at Cawood's Pond, a "momentary freak-out," or flashback to the war, Sam thinks he needs to talk as the characters on *M*A*S*H* would talk to the psychiatrist Dr. Freeman, even though she realizes "that on TV, people always had the words to express their feelings, while in real life hardly anyone ever did." In her more mature moments she recognizes that "sometimes, things were too simple" on *M*A*S*H* and "how naive the words were" to the

Beatles's "All You Need Is Love." Yet her final excursion to Cawood's Pond stems from adolescent pique. She acquires Dwayne's war journal from her grandparents and, oddly yet appropriately, goes to the mall to read it. Within these pages she discovers the soldier-father who has so eluded her. Unlike the letters he wrote to Irene, which cover up and divert attention from the brutality of his environment, Dwayne's journals record the horror and the killing with precision. "Her father hadn't said how he felt about killing the V.C. He just reported it, as though it were something he had to do sooner or later, like taking a test in school." Horrified that her father and Emmett had participated in such activity, she feels that "everything seemed suddenly so real it enveloped her, like something rotten she had fallen into, like a skunk smell." When she arrives home dreading the sight of Emmett, she is furious to find he has gone and has flea-bombed the house. Leaving Emmett the diary and a note asking, "Is that what it was like over there? If it was, then you can just forget about me," she runs away from home and the truth.

While spending a night at Cawood's Pond, she fantasizes that she is "in country," but when Emmett finds her the next morning, he points out the futility of her efforts: "You think you can go through what we went through out in the jungle, but you can't. This place is scary, and things can happen to you, but it's not the same as having snipers and mortar fire and shells and people shooting at you from behind bushes." Her childishly dramatic note and her make-believe "humping the boonies" underscore her immaturity when it comes to dealing with the Vietnam War and veterans. Despite Emmett's warning, Sam–like the nation as a whole–persists in searching for easy solutions. When she and Emmett have an emotional confrontation, she thinks he is "going to come out with some suppressed memories of events as dramatic as the one that caused Hawkeye to crack up in the final episode of *M*A*S*H.*" While Emmett does have a bit of a cathartic episode when he finds her at the pond and he does arrive at the resolve to travel to the Vietnam Veterans Memorial, the process of his healing is only beginning. Similarly, Sam is only beginning to move from adolescence into womanhood. Even on the trip to Washington, she persists in fantasizing about Tom and about Bruce Springsteen pulling her onto the stage for some "Dancing in the Dark." Yet she has decided to join her mother in Lexington, where she will attend the University of Kentucky, instead of staying in Hopewell and enrolling at nearby Murray State, as she had planned earlier. Meanwhile, Emmett will take over Sam's job at the Burger Boy

Dust jacket for Mason's 1988 novel, dealing with a middle-aged couple who face the wife's impending death

and attend to those repairs to the house in Hopewell. In a text underscored by popular music, television programs, movies, videos, brand names, and shopping malls, Mason rejects the easy, readily available sort of "solutions" offered by popular culture, instead leaving the conclusion of *In Country* appropriately open-ended.

Mason's second novel, *Spence + Lila* (1988), portrays a family in crisis as the aging matriarch, Lila, is in the hospital in Paducah for breast-cancer surgery. The novel is a masterful depiction of the bonds of love between a couple in their sixties as they face their dilemma without the words to express either their fears or their devotion to one another. The novel also looks beyond the changes in this couple's relationship over their many years together to the alterations to their farm and a once-isolated rural South brought about by the invasion of popular culture and the media, the development of shopping malls and connective highways, and the growing economic impossibility of making a living on a small family farm.

Inspired in part by Mason's mother's mastectomy, *Spence + Lila* is dedicated to her parents, siblings, and husband. The title presents the names of Spence and Lila as though they were carved by two young lovers on a tree or a school desk, or as they might appear in a family tree. The novel portrays this couple as facing the real possibility that one may soon be "minus" the other and much less than the "sum" they have become together. The novel is told in present tense by a third-person, limited-omniscient narrator, with the perspective of the chapters alternating between Spence and Lila. (This alternation of controlling consciousness follows a consistent pattern for the first half of the novel, while in the latter portion two or three consecutive chapters may be from one or the other character's purview.) Mason's younger sister LaNelle illustrated *Spence + Lila*.

Separated for the first time since World War II, the protagonists worry about one another; yet they manage to face their present circumstances with humor and grace despite their justifiable trepidations. After more than forty years of marriage, Spence and Lila Culpepper are both somewhat surprised to be as old as their chronological years indicate, with three adult children—Nancy, Cathy (or "Cat"), and Lee—caught in the challenges and adversities of their own lives. Nancy Culpepper Cleveland and her family made earlier appearances in two of the stories in *Shiloh and Other Stories:* "Nancy Culpepper" and "Lying Doggo." In the former the transient Nancy returns home to her parents' western Kentucky farm to help them move her grandmother into a nursing home; in the latter, one of Mason's rare stories set outside Kentucky (in rural Pennsylvania), Nancy, husband Jack, and son Robert struggle with the necessity of having their aging dog, Grover Cleveland, put to sleep. (The character of Nancy Culpepper is the closest Mason, who has no children, comes to self-portraiture in her fiction.)

Once again Mason's protagonists are rural folk of western Kentucky, who in this case experience culture shock in the modern hospital in Paducah and share a skepticism about language as a means of communicating one's feelings. Spence thinks, "He could say to Lila, 'It's all right. Your breast isn't your life. You can live without it, and I'll accept that.' . . . Words are so inadequate. Phony. Nobody he knows says things like that anyway." Like Sam, he realizes these sorts of words are said by characters who have scriptwriters, not real human beings: "Real love requires something else, something deeper. And sometimes a feeling just goes without saying." *Spence + Lila* is a novel about real love—not saccharine-sweet sentimentality, but the well-aged version of love between two people who have shared a long, sometimes difficult and trying, life together. "Everything he does is for her, even when he goes his own way and she is powerless to stop him," even when he teases her, knowing teasing "rattles her, but it would be out of character for him to behave any other way, and she would respect him less." Uncomfortable as his visits make him, Spence comes every day to see Lila in the hospital. His feeling of impotence, his inability to help Lila, frustrates him. When he suspects that she will need cobalt treatments following her surgery and fears the outcome because he knows of others, such as Lila's friend Reba, who died shortly after beginning such treatments, he realizes he would be unable to object to such a prescription for Lila's health: "There are no significant choices most of the time. You always have to do what has to be done. It's like milking cows. When their bags are full, they have to be milked." Mason expertly conveys the sense that Spence and Lila no longer control their circumstances once they remove themselves from the family farm and enter the domain of doctors and medical science.

Their grown daughters Cat and Nancy are not so easily cowed by the experts. They ask questions of the doctors and challenge their assumptions, something neither parent can do successfully or forcefully enough. When Nancy asks about lumpectomy versus mastectomy, "Lila sees Spence cringe. Nancy has always asked questions and done things differently, just to be contrary." (Yet Spence later admits his pride in his contrary daughter.) When the doctor turns to Lila for questions, she admits, "All the big words make me bumfuzzled. I guess you know your stuff." When the doctor informs Lila that they had indeed removed her breast and told her she "can live without a breast," Lila thinks she may have replied, while still under the influence of the anesthesia, "It would be like living without balls. . . . You'd find that surprising too, but you could probably get along without them." She is embarrassed by the thought that she might have said such a thing, but she is also "surprised Nancy hasn't said the same thing to the doctor's face."

Lila worries about Spence and how he will manage without her. Because they are human beings, all the characters are equally concerned about their own self-interests as well. Lila considers, "If Spence went first . . . She would be afraid to stay on the farm alone, with all the crime spreading out from town into the country these days." She also thinks about the difficulty of finding the words to convey feelings: "Growing into old age toward death is like shifting gears in a car; now she's going into high gear, plowing out into one of those interstates, racing into the future, where all her complicated thoughts that she has never been able to express will be clear and understandable. Her mind cannot grasp these thoughts exactly, but there is something important about movement that she wants to tell."

Moving beyond the changes in the lives of two aging individuals, Mason also considers changes in the rural environment. Their son, Lee, who is always trying to convince Spence to sell some of their land for development, chose not to learn farming and instead "has to work even harder at his factory job." "It makes Spence sick" that Lee "owes almost four hundred dollars a month for a squatty little brick house on a hundred-foot lot in town with no trees." Spence loves his farm: "This is all there is in the world—it contains everything there is to know or possess, yet everywhere people are knocking their brains out trying to find something different, something better." He also realizes, however, that "nowadays" there "wouldn't be a living" in farming a place the size of his because "a young couple would have to borrow too much to start out."

More important to Spence are the changes of attitudes and values in the modern world that has intruded in his isolated haven. While he seems for the most part to take the changes in stride, when he goes to Wal-Mart, he finds "All the coffee makers and video games and electric ice-cream parlors" he sees there "depressing. People are buying so much junk, thinking it will make them happy. And then when they can't even make a path across the floor through their possessions, they have a yard sale." And without anyplace for folks to go, they "either get drunk or go crazy." Spence "can't imagine what the world is coming to" with the increase in armed robberies and break-ins in his once safe environment. Similarly, Lila thinks that "The world has changed so much: cars, airplanes, television," in the years since she and Spence were wed, and although she "tries to go along with anything new. . . . It still hurts her to see liquor kept in a house where there are children, to see farmers out spreading manure on their fields on Sundays, to see young people fall away from the church." She undoubtedly shares Spence's distaste for television evangelists and would be as shocked as he if she knew that one of their neighbors grows marijuana plants among his corn, although Spence can understand the economic necessity of this lucrative cash crop. Likewise, she also would concur with Spence's notion that their farm "is the main thing there is—just the way things grow and die, the way the sun comes up and goes down each day. These are the facts of life."

In one of the most humorous scenes in the novel the family plays catch with a prosthetic breast after Lila exclaims, "I ain't spending a hundred and fifty dollars for a falsie." As is typically the case with Mason's humor, there is a serious undertone to this playful scene. The woman who brought the prosthesis also offers a packet of "letters to daughters and sons and husbands" to convey a mastectomy patient's feelings "at this delicate time when you need emotional support." These form letters are another example of simplistic scriptwriting that cannot accurately convey Lila's true feelings. Before leaving the hospital Lila manages to thank her daughters in her own words—"I was always used to doing for y'all, and I never expected you to do for me this way"—but the response she desires from her children is "not words. . . . Holding her child is enough, and Nancy is clinging to her."

By the end of the novel Lila has lost her breast, endured a second operation on her neck to remove the arterial plaque that has caused a series of "tiny strokes," and returned to the "place" they love so

Dust jacket for Mason's 1989 collection of stories, in which potentially sad or happy moments suddenly come into focus

well. Although she will still need to undergo chemotherapy for cancer, which has spread into her lymph nodes, and the prognosis is less than certain, her escape from the hospital and return to their home offer their own therapy. Standing in her garden, Lila responds with laughter to Spence's sexually suggestive comment that he has "a cucumber that needs pickling."

The novel ends with a description of Lila's laughter: "The way she laughs is the moment he has been waiting for. . . . Her cough catches her finally and slows her down, but her face is dancing like pond water in the rain, all unsettled and stirring with aroused possibility." Mason ends the story of this couple ambiguously with the return to the family farm and the idyllic garden, this place where the "facts of life" are part of the fabric of their interwoven everyday lives and their love for each other has been indelibly etched.

The various ways in which people handle love (or lack of it) serve as the central issue in Mason's second collection of short fiction, *Love Life: Stories* (1989). This volume comprises fifteen stories that originally appeared in various magazines, including *The New Yorker, The Atlantic Monthly, Mother Jones,* and *Harper's.* In this volume about half the stories are in the present and half in the past, unlike *Shiloh and Other Stories,* in which all but three stories are narrated in the present tense. In her interview with Bonnie Lyons and Bill Oliver, Mason explained another difference between the two collections: "I think the characters' world changed a good bit between the two. I think life was changing so fast that they got more sophisticated, . . . and I'd like to think that the stories have gotten more complex." Perhaps the alternating narratives for two of the stories are examples of the increased complexity to which Mason refers.

As in *Spence + Lila,* the third-person, present-tense narration of the title story alternates between two perspectives. "Love Life" is narrated from the viewpoints of Opal, a retired Hopewell High School teacher and avid MTV viewer, and her niece Jenny, who has returned to Hopewell from Denver, Colorado. One perceived distinction between Opal and Jenny–beyond their age discrepancy–concerns their love lives: "Opal is not wholly without experience," for there have been men in her life, "though nothing like the casual affairs" in which she supposes Jenny has engaged. Yet Opal and Jenny are similar in their reticence to reveal much of themselves to others. "People confide in Jenny, but Jenny doesn't always tell things back," and Opal is startled by Jenny's tendency to ask personal questions. "Jenny wants to know about her aunt's past love life, but Opal won't reveal her secrets." When Jenny finally begins to explain that she shed tears over the family burial quilt because it reminded her of a former boyfriend who had died, Opal first fears she'll "be required to tell something comparable of her own." (Yet Jenny finds the quilt beautiful and takes it to her apartment, while Opal says it is "ugly as homemade sin" and is relieved to be rid of it.) Jenny's fascination with other people's lives and loves is her way of not dwelling on her own failures–just as her studied observation of other people's physical handicaps betrays, yet keeps her from focusing on, her own emotional damage. Despite both their fears, Opal is able to comfort Jenny as she reveals her confused emotional state after the death of her former lover, the reason her restlessness brought her back to Hopewell. Opal advises her, "Don't look back, hon"–advice that might apply to most of the protagonists in these stories, as they struggle to understand their own love lives, to recover from lost loves, or to learn to love their own lives.

The narrative technique of "Marita" is less successful. The story alternates between the first-person-present narration of the pregnant title character, who cannot tell her mother what happened at college because "I don't know who he was–it was

one of two interchangeable guys, guys I don't know or care to know," and the third-person-past perspective of Marita's mother, Sue Ellen, who figures out Marita's problem and offers the solution of an abortion. The shift in tense and person between these alternating perspectives seems merely complexity for the sake of complexity.

As in Mason's earlier fiction, popular culture lays the groundwork for the stories in *Love Life,* as characters watch reruns of television shows such as *Hogan's Heroes* and *Mary Tyler Moore* (in "Airwaves"), stay up late for *Nightline* and David Letterman (in "Marita"), wake to Rock 95 (in "Airwaves"), listen to radio psychics (in "Sorghum"), and measure their experiences by the topics Phil Donahue covers on his programs (in "Hunktown" and "Airwaves"). Among the best stories in this collection is "Piano Fingers," in which Dean, who is twenty-six years old and feels "suspended somewhere between childhood and old age," is about to lose his job at the downtown drugstore because his boss is going to sell the business. He is also troubled by his marriage, not because there is any lack of love between him and his wife, Nancy, but because everyday "stuff gets in the way." Dean thinks he could write better programs than the "garbage on TV" and often imagines himself as amateur detective Ballinger, "an ordinary guy" who "always manages to turn up the key piece of evidence the authorities have missed." Ever hopeful, Dean buys his daughter Jennifer a practice keyboard he can ill afford because Jennifer's teacher said she has "piano fingers."

One day while sitting in the car, waiting for Jennifer's lesson to end, "The sound of wet leaves against the car on a late-autumn day makes him feel nostalgia for something, he can't remember what," and he realizes something that perhaps describes what most of the stories in *Love Life* are about: "there are such moments, such sensations, that are maybe not memory but just things happening now, things that come into focus suddenly and can be either happy or sad." These potentially happy or sad sudden moments form the crux of much of Mason's writing, and most of her characters face possibilities such as Dean does when he studies the reflection of downtown lights on a bank window: "Some of the lights in the window are reflections of reflections, like a kaleidoscope of possibilities for his life. His trouble, he realizes, is that there are too many choices," and to settle on just one "would mean missing out on almost everything." As Mason told Wilhelm, "the way the South is changing is very dynamic and full of complexity. There's a certain energy there that I don't notice in other parts of the country. It comes out of an innocent hope of possi-

Bobbie Ann Mason, Talk of the Town

ASBURY PARK, ~~1989~~

Three ladies of our acquaintance motored recently across Maryland and

Pennsylvania to the New Jersey shore. The ladies, in summer dresses and ~~Dr.~~

~~Scholl's~~ sandals, drove down the Garden State Parkway, a pleasant, tree-lined

drive, to Exit ~~117,~~ 105 and down Route 71 through Asbury Park, Ocean Grove, (Belmar,

Avon-by-the Sea) and other attractive towns, stopping at a quaint hotel in

Spring Lake. The ladies noted how clean and nice the New Jersey shore was.

"This is much more tasteful than Ocean City, Maryland," they said.

They were on a pilgrimage. One of the ladies had left her husband *for the weekend* once

and flown to Houston ~~just~~ to see a Bruce Springsteen concert. Another one had

fainted ~~once~~ at a "Born in the U.S.A." stadium concert in Washington, D.C. And

the third ~~one~~ had stood in line all night for Springsteen tickets once, despite

chicken pox.

"We're really in New Jersey!" cried the one who had been to Houston. "He

has probably been on this highway. His car has no doubt stopped at this stop

light!"

A guy behind them was combing his hair in the mirror of his beat-up old

Chevy. It looked like him, but it wasn't ~~him.~~

Asbury Park's boardwalk is crumbling, the old Victorian-Art Deco-Colonial

splendor, *and* ~~in ruin,~~ some of the shops boarded up. The casino is still alive*ly*,

though, its brick building boldly framed by a line~~up~~ *chorus* of green tarnished-copper

sea monsters (winged horses with flippers and mermaid tails). After visiting

Olympic Bob's Palace ~~of Fun~~ (claustrophobic indoor rides with loud noises and

flashing lights) the ladies sauntered down the boardwalk in the bright sun. They saw

Sandy's Arcade, the convention hall, Ho-Jo's by-the-sea, the nut shops, the

Page of a typescript for a 1989 "Talk of the Town" contribution by Mason for The New Yorker *(Collection of Bobbie Ann Mason)*

bility. My characters have more opportunities in their lives than their parents did." While the myriad possibilities can make resolving their life and love struggles difficult for her characters, most of Mason's stories, as she told Lyons and Oliver, "tend to end at a moment of illumination." "Piano Fingers" ends with one of Mason's typically hopeful illuminating images: as Dean and his daughter sit in the car, snow begins to fall, landing on his windshield in "big beautiful splotches—no two alike."

A reluctant transient herself, Mason visited Kentucky regularly, about twice a year, and always thought about returning there to live. Shortly before the death of her father in 1990, she moved to Lexington for an extended stay and dedicated her next novel, *Feather Crowns* (1993), to the memory of her father. In this work she abandoned the dynamic present moment of her hometown, writing instead an historical novel set primarily at the turn of the century. (The earliest time period in any of her previous fiction was the mid twentieth century in "Detroit Skyline, 1949," collected in *Shiloh and Other Stories*.) Despite its historical setting, *Feather Crowns*, winner of the Southern Book Award, a finalist for the National Book Critics Circle Award, and the recipient of an enormously positive critical response, treats a phenomenon that continues to exist in the present: the protagonist, Christianna Wilburn Wheeler, comes under the scrutiny of the media of her day, becoming a national celebrity, the equivalent of a present-day pop-culture icon.

During their courtship James Reid Wheeler has told Christianna Wilburn (Mason chose her mother's and father's first names for her heroine), how "he burned" to return to his "daddy's place, where I was raised" once his Uncle Wad "turns loose that section of land I'm supposed to have," where he could "have fields of dark tobaccer and a fruit orchard and a herd of cattle and a stable full of horses, as well as pigs and hens and geese." After their marriage in 1890 and the birth of their third child a few years later, they have moved to this family farm in Hopewell, Kentucky, 150 miles from Christie's home in Dundee. James's description has made the Wheeler farm sound like paradise, but being crammed into the Wheeler homestead with the sizable Wheeler clan for their first year in Hopewell is anything but idyllic: James, Christie, and their three children—Clint, Jewell, and Nannie—are "bunched into one of five small upstairs bedrooms" in a house that is already filled with "Wad and Amanda and their two girls, Lena and Little Bunch; and Wad's sister Alma and her husband, Thomas Hunt, with their five children; as well as Boone,

Wad and Alma's sickly brother, and Mammy Dove, their mother."

Christie manages to forge an alliance with Amanda (or Mandy), Wad's young second wife, who early on tells Christie, "We've got to stick together or these Wheelers will be the death of us." Forced to work in the tobacco fields, Christie grows to hate "the dark-leaf tobacco James loved so much." With the plummeting price of tobacco and their more than $1,000 debt to Wad for their land, Christie and James can ill afford another pregnancy.

In February 1900, when she delivers previously unheard-of quintuplets, Christie and her babies quickly become media darlings. The mayor of Hopewell names her Mother of the Year; the story is picked up by a St. Louis paper and eventually newspapers nationwide; companies offer the family free merchandise so they can identify themselves in their advertisements as the equivalent of "official sponsors" of the Hopewell Quintuplets; and the railroad adds a stop near the Wheelers' farm so that curious onlookers can come right into Christie's living room to see the natural wonders for themselves. Perhaps the public interprets the birth of the quintuplets as the "cataclysmic upheaval of the earth" that a "noted prognosticator" predicted for the new year of the new millennium, an earthquake to rival the earthquakes of 1811 and 1812 (which had severely altered the western Tennessee landscape).

Mason portrays Christie as a woman on the cusp of the modern age. On the one hand she is frequently influenced by the superstitions and the conventions of her time, while on the other she is a singularly modern woman trapped within those conventions. For instance, Christie enjoys sex, the "unspeakable" pleasures her mother would call "the wifely duty" but that she and James euphemistically refer to as "plowing." Yet, when—despite her exhaustive efforts—she helplessly watches as one by one the five babies who were a result of their parents' "lusty and reckless indulgence" die within a month of their birth, she assumes she is being punished for her sins. Foreshadowing the deaths of the babies, Mason juxtaposes a description of the hungry lust that resulted in the babies' conception with a scene in which elder son Clint tells his brother about the predicted earthquake: "The ground will open into a big ditch and swaller us up." When some of the feathers from the deceased babies' bed are discovered to be in the "bird nest shape" of two feather crowns, Amanda says the appearance of these crowns means "the babies are in Heaven." Christie tries to take comfort in this sign, but she knows that such crowns are traditionally predictors of death. The modern woman in her would like to

*Dust jacket for Mason's 1993 novel, about the media frenzy surrounding the birth of
quintuplets to a Kentucky farm couple at the turn of the century*

believe that they are merely coincidental and not particularly meaningful.

The quintuplets' deaths are even more horrible because the 1900 version of the media spotlight is focused unmercifully on Christianna and her family. Driven by a misguided notion of obtaining some revenge on the curious, she agrees to accompany the preserved bodies of her infants on what the Hopewell Chronicle calls "an educational series of lectures and diversions, for the purpose of educating the generally curious and concerned public about the Hopewell Quintuplets and the miraculous event that ended so unfortunately for the Wheelers," but the tour degenerates into a carnival sideshow attraction. Christie's nineteenth-century sentiments would

seem to preclude leaving her three children behind and taking a ten-week-long, arduous journey with the preserved bodies of her infants in one glass case and the feather crowns in another.

Amanda, who desires to escape the Wheelers and see the world, is envious when Christie gets the opportunity to travel. Her attraction to Alma's husband, Thomas Hunt, comes primarily from his stories about his excursions as a traveling salesman, which serve as a means through which she can at least vicariously "escape" the confines of the Wheeler household and dream of adventures far removed from her crude tyrant husband, Wad. She eventually has a brief sexual dalliance with Thomas and finds her final escape through suicide.

Ostensibly, Christie and James decide to make the trip for economic reasons–one hundred dollars a week for ten weeks will make short work of their debt to Wad–and because Christie "wasn't ready to let go of her babies. If the world killed her babies and wanted to see them dead to draw some lessons from them, then she would show people more than they bargained for. She'd show them with spite burning in her eyes." Her "urgent purpose" is "to get revenge . . . on people she didn't even know." Yet the modern woman in Christie also feels "a rumble of expectation" in going "to new places," not only to relieve her grief but also to encounter the teeming world that awaits her. This journey, however, exploits the grief of Christie and James, whose trauma is further compounded by the culture shock they experience. The trip nearly destroys the fragile relationship between James and Christie, but they somehow manage to rediscover "the dance they had begun long ago."

While she creates wonderful characters in *Feather Crowns*–particularly the troubled Christie and the Wheeler clan–and successfully delineates the exploitative nature of the family, the general populace, science, and industry, Mason's third, longest, and most ambitious novel is somewhat unsatisfying. Perhaps the focus on the "moment" of the first year of the millennium as it filters into a family's tragedy was insufficient to give a full sense of Christie's life. The novel ends with two coda sections: Christie's 1937 visit to the Dionne quintuplets and a "transcription" of a message to her granddaughter Missy that Christie recorded in 1963, on her ninetieth birthday. The final first-person section is particularly troublesome. While Christie sometimes uses diction appropriate to her region and level of education–in statements such as "I was always busy a-doing something and trying to find out something that nobody else would think to fool with"–she also voices insights in words more appropriate to Mason's third-person narrator, as when Christie says, "I wanted the free and unattached generousness of stranger meeting stranger, where nothing familiar can cast a shadow of obligation on you, or a mirror reflection." This incongruous narrative seems more a device to reach the end of the novel than the sort of satisfying conclusion the novel deserves. While Christie says "I have had quite a life," Mason's novel provides only a defining moment in that life, not the string of moments that give breadth and depth to a life.

In her fiction Mason has captured the influence of American popular culture on her once remote region and studied the troublesome impasses and transitional points in the lives of her memorable

working-class, plain-speaking characters. Despite the trial that life in the twentieth century brings to these ordinary people, they manage to find hope and possibility rather than despair. *Midnight Magic: Selected Stories of Bobbie Ann Mason* (1998), unfortunately, offers the readers of Mason's fiction no new material. Instead, Mason merely picked out seventeen stories from the *Shiloh* and *Love Life* story collections and added a brief introduction to these 1980s offerings in which she muses that "The mystery of writing is much like driving into the darkness in the middle of the night." While this collection may help acquaint new readers and reacquaint others with some of Mason's favorite stories, it would be much more gratifying were she to find new characters on whom–in terms of her metaphor–to shine her "headlights" in order "to illuminate them and their ways of doing and loving and being."

Interviews:

Wendy Smith, "PW Interviews Bobbie Ann Mason," *Publishers Weekly,* 228 (30 August 1985): 424–425;

Lila Havens, "Residents and Transients: An Interview with Bobbie Ann Mason," *Crazy Horse,* 29 (Fall 1985): 87–104;

Enid Shomer, "An Interview with Bobbie Ann Mason," *Black Warrior Review,* 12 (Spring 1986): 87–102;

Michal Smith, "Bobbie Ann Mason: Artist and Rebel," *Kentucky Review,* 8 (Autumn 1988): 56–63;

Albert E. Wilhelm, "An Interview with Bobbie Ann Mason," *Southern Quarterly,* 26 (Winter 1988): 27–38;

David Y. Todd, "A Conversation with Bobbie Ann Mason," *Boulevard,* 4–5 (Spring 1990): 132–45;

Bonnie Lyons and Bill Oliver, "An Interview with Bobbie Ann Mason," *Contemporary Literature,* 32 (Winter 1991): 449–470;

Dorothy Combs Hill, "An Interview with Bobbie Ann Mason," *Southern Quarterly,* 31 (Fall 1992): 85–118.

References:

Edwin T. Arnold, "Falling Apart and Staying Together: Bobbie Ann Mason and Leon Driskell Explore the State of the Modern Family," *Appalachian Journal,* 12 (Winter 1985): 135–141;

Linda Adams Barnes, "The Freak Endures: The Southern Grotesque from Flannery O'Connor to Bobbie Ann Mason," in *Since Flannery O'Connor: Essays on the Contemporary American Short Story,* edited by Loren Logsdon and Charles W. Mayer (Macomb: Western Illinois University, 1987), pp. 133–141;

Ellen A. Blais, "Gender Issues in Bobbie Ann Mason's *In Country*," *South Atlantic Review,* 56 (May 1991): 107–118;

Hal Blythe and Charlie Sweet, "The Ambiguous Grail Quest in 'Shiloh,'" *Studies in Short Fiction,* 32 (Spring 1995): 223–226;

David Booth, "Sam's Quest, Emmett's Wound: Grail Motifs in Bobbie Ann Mason's Portrait of America After Vietnam," *Southern Literary Journal,* 23 (Spring 1991): 98–109;

Robert H. Brinkmeyer Jr., "Finding One's History: Bobbie Ann Mason and Contemporary Southern Literature," *Southern Literary Journal,* 19 (Spring 1987): 20–33;

Brinkmeyer, "Never Stop Rocking: Bobbie Ann Mason and Rock-and-Roll," *Mississippi Quarterly,* 42 (Winter 1988–1989): 5–17;

Tina Bucher, "Changing Roles and Finding Stability: Women in Bobbie Ann Mason's *Shiloh and Other Stories,*" *Border States,* 8 (1991): 50–55;

Sandra Bonilla Durham, "Women and War: Bobbie Ann Mason's *In Country,*" *Southern Literary Journal,* 22 (Spring 1990): 45–52;

June Dwyer, "New Roles, New History and New Patriotism: Bobbie Ann Mason's *In Country,*" *Modern Language Studies,* 22 (Spring 1992): 72–78;

Richard Giannone, "Bobbie Ann Mason and the Recovery of Mystery," *Studies in Short Fiction,* 27 (Fall 1990): 553–566;

Owen W. Gilman Jr., "In Which Country," in his *Vietnam and the Southern Imagination* (Jackson: University Press of Mississippi, 1992), pp. 45–60;

Judith Hatchett, "Making Life Mean: Bobbie Ann Mason's *Feather Crowns,*" *Kentucky Philological Review,* 9 (1994): 12–15;

Barbara Henning, "Minimalism and the American Dream: 'Shiloh' by Bobbie Ann Mason and 'Preservation' by Raymond Carver," *Modern Fiction Studies,* 35 (Winter 1989): 689–698;

Darlene Reimers Hill, "'Use to, the Menfolks Would Eat First': Food and Food Rituals in the Fiction of Bobbie Ann Mason," *Southern Quarterly,* 30 (Winter–Spring 1992): 81–89;

Katherine Kinney, "'Humping the Boonies': Sex, Combat, and the Female in Bobbie Ann Mason's *In Country,*" in *Fourteen Landing Zones: Approaches to Vietnam War Literature,* edited by Philip K. Jason (Iowa City: University of Iowa Press, 1991), pp. 38–48;

Yonka Krasteva, "The South and the West in Bobbie Ann Mason's *In Country,*" *Southern Literary Journal,* 26 (Spring 1994): 77–90;

G. O. Morphew, "Downhome Feminists in *Shiloh and Other Stories,*" *Southern Literary Journal,* 21 (Spring 1989): 41–49;

Harriet Pollack, "From *Shiloh* to *In Country* to *Feather Crowns*: Bobbie Ann Mason, Women's History, and Southern Fiction," *Southern Literary Journal,* 28 (Spring 1996): 95–116;

Barbara T. Ryan, "Decentered Authority in Bobbie Ann Mason's *In Country,*" *Critique,* 31 (Spring 1990): 199–212;

Matthew C. Stewart, "Realism, Verisimilitude, and the Depiction of Vietnam Veterans in *In Country,*" in *Fourteen Landing Zones: Approaches to Vietnam War Literature,* pp. 166–179;

Leslie White, "The Function of Popular Culture in Bobbie Ann Mason's *Shiloh and Other Stories* and *In Country,*" *Southern Quarterly,* 26 (Summer 1988): 69–79;

Albert E. Wilhelm, "Bobbie Ann Mason: Searching for Home," in *Southern Writers at Century's End,* edited by Jeffrey J. Folks and James A. Perkins (Lexington: University Press of Kentucky, 1997), pp. 151–163;

Wilhelm, "Making Over or Making Off: The Problem of Identity in Bobbie Ann Mason's Short Fiction," *Southern Literary Journal,* 18 (Spring 1986): 76–82;

Wilhelm, "Private Rituals: Coping with Change in the Fiction of Bobbie Ann Mason," *Midwest Quarterly,* 28 (Winter 1987): 271–282;

Marjorie Winther, "*M*A*S*H,* Malls and Meaning: Popular and Corporate Culture in *In Country,*" *Literature Interpretation Theory,* 4 (1993): 195–201.

Margaret Mitchell

This entry was updated by David O'Connell (Georgia State University)
from the entry by Earl F. Bargainnier (Wesleyan College) in
DLB 9: American Novelists, 1910–1945.

BIRTH: Atlanta, Georgia, 8 November 1900, to Eugene Muse and Maybelle Stephens Mitchell.

EDUCATION: Attended Smith College, 1918–1919.

MARRIAGES: 2 September 1922 to Berrien Kinnard Upshaw, (divorced 16 October 1924); 4 July 1925 to John Robert Marsh.

AWARDS AND HONORS: Pulitzer Prize and National Book Award for most distinguished novel, American Booksellers Association, both 1937, and Carl M. Bohnenberger Memorial Medal, 1938, all for *Gone With the Wind;* honorary M.A., Smith College, 1939; named honorary citizen of Vimoutiers, France, for helping the city obtain American aid after World War II, 1949; featured on a one-cent U.S. postage stamp, 1986; film version of *Gone With the Wind* featured as part of a stamp series on 1939 films, 1989; inducted into Georgia Women of Achievement, 1994.

DEATH: Atlanta, Georgia, 16 August 1949.

BOOKS: *Gone With the Wind* (New York & London: Macmillan, 1936);
Lost Laysen, edited by Debra Freer (New York: Scribners, 1996; London: Orion, 1996).

Margaret Munnerlyn Mitchell was born in Atlanta, Georgia, where she lived her entire life. The daughter of Eugene Mitchell, an attorney and president of the Atlanta Historical Society, she grew up surrounded by talk of the city and its central event: the fall to General Sherman's forces in 1864, which she was to re-create in *Gone With the Wind* (1936). She attended Smith College for one year, but the death of her mother required her to return home to manage the household of her father and older brother. Known as Peggy to her friends, she used the nickname when she began to write for the *Atlanta Journal* in 1922. In her four years as a newspaperwoman, she wrote 129 signed articles for the

Margaret Mitchell

Sunday *Journal Magazine,* as well as many unsigned ones. These articles ranged from interviews with murderers, heiresses, and Rudolph Valentino to a series on Georgia's Confederate generals.

An unsuccessful marriage to Berrien Kinnard Upshaw in 1922 ended in divorce, and in 1925 she married John Robert Marsh, who had been best man at her first wedding. Marsh was employed by the Georgia Power Company, eventually becoming its director of advertising. Their marriage was totally happy, even though they shocked Atlanta society in the 1920s by having two cards on the door of their apartment: Mr. John R. Marsh and Miss Margaret M. Mitchell. A year after their marriage, she was forced to resign her position with the *Atlanta Journal* as a result of an ankle injury. With the encouragement of her husband, she began to write a novel.

For ten years she worked on that novel, though most of it was completed by 1929. Writing the last chapter first, she wrote sections out of sequence, as she desired. These various sections, some typed in completed form and others in messy manuscript, piled up around the apartment. Though friends knew that Mitchell was writing something, she said little about it. Then in the spring of 1935 Harold S. Latham, editor for Macmillan, began a tour of the United States in search of publishable manuscripts. His first stop was Atlanta, where he was told of Mitchell's manuscript. At first, she denied having written anything. Her later explanation was "I just couldn't believe that a Northern publisher would accept a novel about the War Between the States from the Southern point of view." Just before Latham was to leave the city, she brought him the five-foot pile of typescript. By July, Macmillan had decided to publish the novel, then titled "Tomorrow Is Another Day," with a heroine then named Pansy.

With the acceptance, events in the phenomenon that was to be *Gone With the Wind*–the final title was taken from Ernest Dowson's 1896 poem "Cynara"–began to occur. First, Mitchell spent six months rechecking the historical facts of the novel. On several occasions she stated that she took greater pride in its accurate dates, places, dialects, and architectural details than in its plot or style, and she dreaded having an historical error found. Meanwhile, Macmillan was spending an inordinate amount on advertising for a novel by an unknown writer. Originally intended for publication on 31 May 1936, the novel did not appear until 30 June, because the Book-of-the-Month Club chose it as the July selection. Most of the reviews ranged from favorable to enthusiastic, with the exception of those in the "left-wing" press, which condemned it as a glorification of racism. In any case, the book broke all publication records: 50,000 copies sold in one day, a million sold in six months, two million in a year. The entire nation seemed entranced with the gigantic novel (1,037 pages and 460,000 words), much to the bewilderment of Mitchell: "it is basically just a simple yarn of fairly simple people. There's no fine writing, there are no grandiose thoughts, there are no hidden meanings, no symbolism, nothing sensational." Nevertheless, it won both the Pulitzer Prize and the National Book Award in 1937.

In spite of the furor Mitchell remained quite humble about the novel. She considered herself an amateur and repeatedly made such statements as "I'm not a stylist, God knows, and I couldn't be if I tried." She was also distressed by the invasion of her and her husband's privacy. Requests for autographs, interviews, and speeches were politely but

firmly refused. There were times that she seemed to wish the novel out of existence. When on 30 July 1936 she signed a contract with David O. Selznick granting him the film rights for $50,000–the highest fee Hollywood had ever paid to that date for a novel–she demanded a clause absolving her of any part in the filming. For more than three years she steadily resisted efforts to involve her in the making of the motion picture, and though she was successful, she was not to be free of the novel. She had to become an international businesswoman, dealing with copyrights, translations, and piracies until her death. Her and her husband's extended periods of ill health also contributed to the fact that she was to write no more–except for her many and engaging letters.

In his review for the *New Republic,* Malcolm Cowley described *Gone With the Wind* as "an encyclopedia of the plantation legend," and he was echoed by others. Mitchell always denied such charges: "I've always been slightly amused by the New York critics who referred to GWTW as a 'moonlight and magnolia romance.' My God, they never read the gentle Confederate novel of the Nineties, or they would know better." Instead of cavaliers and belles, she wrote of the north Georgia yeoman gentry; instead of white columned mansions on huge plantations, she wrote of rambling houses on red-clay farms. The historical events are presented through two families, the O'Haras of Tara and the Wilkeses of Twelve Oaks, surrounded by their slaves, acquaintances, friends, and relatives. The four central characters are Scarlett O'Hara; the two men in her life, Rhett Butler and Ashley Wilkes; and Melanie Hamilton, who marries Ashley. In these four characters Mitchell broke the mold of the plantation belle and young cavalier, which had lasted since the 1880s, by splitting the stereotypical features. Melanie is given the fragility, grace, and chasteness associated with the belle, while Scarlett is given the coquetry and energy. Ashley is given the chivalry, sense of honor, spiritual nature, and self-sacrifice of the cavalier, but Rhett has all of the dash, charm, and vigor of the type. The result is that Scarlett and Rhett dominate the novel, while Melanie and Ashley seem anemic by comparison. Also, Scarlett and Rhett are "outlaws" to the myth of the Old South, for though they accept the comforts of their social system, they accept its rules and regulations only so long as these do not interfere with their freedom of action. The experiences of these four characters during and after the Civil War are directly related to this characterization. Melanie and Ashley represent the principles of the old society; she dies and he is broken in spirit. The pragmatic Rhett leaves for

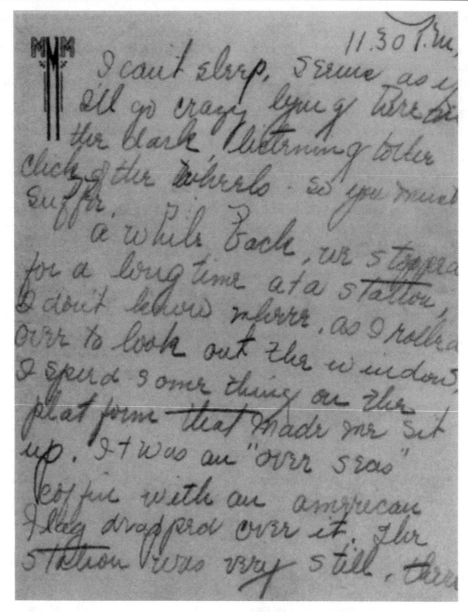

Page from an August 1920 letter from Mitchell to Henry Love Angel (Road to Tara Museum, Atlanta, Georgia)

Charleston at the end to come to terms with the world as it is, and Scarlett survives.

Mitchell defined the theme of *Gone With the Wind* as simply "survival." The Civil War decimated the economy of Georgia, and Scarlett's determination never to be hungry again, whatever the cost, and her final decision to return to Tara, which she realizes is the natural sustainer of her and hers, exemplify Mitchell's aim. Melanie may die, Ashley may be a lost soul, Rhett may leave, but Scarlett and Tara endure. In presenting this theme Mitchell offers her readers a plethora of other attractive elements. The novel is nostalgic, regionally patriotic, romantic, filled with stirring events, and crammed with information about antebellum, bellum, and postbellum Georgia: its physical characteristics, customs, beliefs, and manners. All of these elements, along with the vivid characterizations of Scarlett and Rhett and the narrative sweep, combine to provide an epic account of the fall of a traditional society and the way its inhabitants cope. They have created an alluring, perhaps the dominant, image of the entire South for millions of readers.

The success of *Gone With the Wind* has been long lasting. As of 1998, it is generally recognized as the best-selling book of all time, after the Bible, with some twenty-three million copies sold worldwide. It is also the longest novel transferred to Braille: thirty

Mitchell in 1921

volumes. The 1939 film version of the novel has remained a classic in that genre and continues to be released for new audiences. Its first presentation on television on 7 November 1976 was at the time "the highest rated television program ever presented on a single network." According to figures released in 1996, 197.5 million people had gone to a theater to see *Gone With the Wind*. The rerelease in 1998 of a new digitally enhanced print of the original swelled these figures even more. Mitchell's estate authorized the 1991 sequel, *Scarlett*. Written by Alexandra Ripley (and later turned into a successful television movie), it sold millions of copies but lacked the storytelling power of the original. In spite of its enormous popularity and amazing ability to capture the imaginations of millions of readers, *Gone With the Wind* has only recently begun to receive the serious study that it deserves as a work of literature.

Recent studies have revealed more about Mitchell's personal and private life during the 1920s while she was writing her novel than was known earlier. Pivotal to these reassessments is that Mitchell drew upon family lore much more than had previously been thought. When asked, in 1936 and

in later years, if the characters of *Gone With the Wind* bore any resemblance to anyone she had ever known, she always shrugged off the question by stating that they were composites that bore no relationship to anyone in particular. More recent information, however, reveals that the Irish/American identity given to Scarlett O'Hara and her family, as well as to their family plantation, Tara, is derived from the family stories told by Mitchell's mother and her maternal great-aunts. Mitchell's great-grandfather Philip Fitzgerald is the model for Gerald O'Hara, while his daughter, Annie Fitzgerald Stephens (Mitchell's grandmother), inspired the legendary Scarlett O'Hara.

Recent analyses also show that Mitchell's book does not set out to defend slavery, but rather to portray a family of whites who tried to treat their slaves as humanly as possible. It is important to recall that when Scarlett returns to Tara after the burning of Atlanta in November 1864, the one hundred field hands of Tara have all run away. Their freedom is not an issue in the novel. What Mitchell does explore, however, are the deep bonds of affection that grow up between Scarlett and members of her extended family on the one hand, and five key black characters on the other: Mammy, Pork, Dilcey, Prissy, and Uncle Peter. Mitchell's point is that despite the law of the land as it existed in the South at that time, a law which stated that black folks were simply property, such bonds could be developed in certain circumstances.

The study of Mitchell's life and her novel have received an added boost in recent years through the creation of the Margaret Mitchell House in Atlanta. This museum and cultural center is located in midtown Atlanta in the building where Mitchell lived while she was writing the novel in the late 1920s. One of the interesting facts to come to light in conjunction with the creation of the Margaret Mitchell House is that Mitchell spent a large sum of money to pay for the medical education of young black graduates of Morehouse College, the famous black school in Atlanta. When Mitchell learned that her maid and laundress, Carrie Holbrooks, who was dying of cancer in 1946, could not be received at any of the white hospitals in Atlanta because of her race, she was upset. Determined to do something about the poor medical care afforded to blacks, Mitchell contacted Dr. Benjamin Mays, the president of Morehouse College at that time, with the idea of funding a scholarship program for the education of black doctors. Some twenty-five young black men eventually received their medical training in this way, without knowing—until recently—that Mitchell had paid for their professional education and training.

After Mitchell's death, her husband and her brother, Stephens Mitchell, destroyed most of her manuscripts and personal papers at her request. However, in April 1995 a new text was discovered: the tale of *Lost Laysen* (1996), which Mitchell had written between 10 July and 6 August 1916. The story behind *Lost Laysen* is more romantic than the tale itself. Mitchell wrote the novella in two composition notebooks, which she gave to Henry Love Angel, one of her suitors, who had wanted to marry her. Angel preserved the notebooks, along with letters from Mitchell and photographs, but took the story of his relationship with Mitchell to his grave in 1945; fifty years later his son brought the materials to light, and the text was published in 1996.

Lost Laysen, set in the South Pacific, is the melodramatic tale of beautiful and independent Courtenay Ross; Billy Duncan, the rough-hewn sailor who falls in love with her immediately but knows he is not of her class; and Douglas Steele, her gentleman suitor. When Courtenay is accosted by the "archfiend" Juan Mardo, both Steele and Duncan seek revenge, and there is a cataclysmic ending involving a volcanic eruption and the destruction of the island, Laysen. The published text includes a biographical introduction with many photographs and selections from Mitchell's letters to Angel. As Ruth Coughlin pointed out in *The New York Times Book Review* (23 June 1996), "The archival material is the clear winner here. As for the text–frankly, Scarlett, you won't give a damn."

On 11 August 1949, while on her way to a film with her husband, Mitchell was struck by an automobile. Never regaining consciousness, she died on 16 August. The legacy of this tiny woman from Atlanta rests in her immense novel, which for more than sixty years has been, whatever its faults, a principal image-maker of the South and a cultural phenomenon of the nation.

Letters:

Margaret Mitchell's Gone With the Wind Letters, 1936–1949, edited by Richard Harwell (New York: Macmillan, 1976);

A Dynamo Going to Waste: Letters to Allen Edee, 1919–1921, edited by Jane Bonner Peacock (Atlanta: Peachtree, 1985).

Biographies:

Anne Edwards, *Road to Tara: The Life of Margaret Mitchell* (New Haven: Ticknor & Fields, 1983);

Darden Asbury Pyron, *Southern Daughter: The Life of Margaret Mitchell* (New York: Oxford University Press, 1991);

Marianne Walker, *Margaret Mitchell and John Marsh: The Love Story Behind Gone With the Wind* (Atlanta: Peachtree, 1993).

References:

Herb Bridges, *"Frankly My Dear–": Gone With the Wind Memorabilia* (Macon, Ga.: Mercer University Press, 1986);

Bridges, *Gone With the Wind: The Definitive Illustrated History of the Book, the Movie, and the Legend* (New York: Simon & Schuster, 1989);

Robert Y. Drake Jr., "Tara Twenty Years After," *Georgia Review,* 12 (1958): 142–150;

Finis Farr, *Margaret Mitchell of Atlanta: The Author of "Gone With the Wind"* (New York: Morrow, 1965);

Dawson Gaillard, "*Gone With the Wind* as Bildungsroman or Why Did Rhett Butler Really Leave Scarlett O'Hara," *Georgia Review,* 28 (1974): 9–18;

Blanche H. Gelfant, "*Gone With the Wind* and the Impossibilities of Fiction," *Southern Literary Journal,* 13 (1980): 3–31;

Ira Joe Johnson and William G. Pickens, *Benjamin E. Mays and Margaret Mitchell: A Unique Legacy in Medicine* (Winter Park, Fla.: Four-G Publishers, 1996);

David O'Connell, *The Irish Roots of Margaret Mitchell's Gone With the Wind* (Decatur, Ga.: Claves & Petry, 1996);

William Pratt, *Scarlett Fever* (New York: Macmillan, 1977);

Helen Taylor, *Scarlett's Women: Gone With the Wind and its Female Fans* (New Brunswick, N.J.: Rutgers University Press, 1989).

Papers:

The two largest collections of Margaret Mitchell's correspondence, editions, and other materials are held by the University of Georgia, Athens, and the Atlanta Public Library.

N. Scott Momaday

This entry was updated by Matthias Schubnell (University of the Incarnate Word) from his entry in DLB 175: Native American Writers of the United States.

See also the Momaday entry in *DLB 143: American Novelists Since World War II, Third Series.*

BIRTH: Lawton, Oklahoma, 27 February 1934, to Alfred Morris and Mayme Natachee Scott Momaday.

EDUCATION: Attended Augusta Military Academy; A.B., University of New Mexico, 1958; M.A., Stanford University, 1960, Ph.D., Stanford University, 1963.

MARRIAGES: 5 September 1959 to Gaye Mangold (divorced); children: Cael, Jill, Brit; 21 July 1978 to Regina Heitzer (divorced); child: Lore (daughter).

AWARDS AND HONORS: Academy of American Poets prize for "The Bear," 1962; Guggenheim Fellowship, 1966–1967; Pulitzer Prize for fiction for *House Made of Dawn,* 1969; National Institute of Arts and Letters grant, 1970; shared Western Heritage Award with David Muench for *Colorado: Summer, Fall, Winter, Spring,* 1974; Premio Letterario Internazionale Mondelo, Italy, 1979.

BOOKS: *The Journey of Tai-me* (Santa Barbara, Cal.: Privately printed, 1967);
House Made of Dawn (New York: Harper & Row, 1968; London: Gollancz, 1969);
The Way to Rainy Mountain (Albuquerque: University of New Mexico Press, 1969);
Colorado: Summer, Fall, Winter, Spring, with photographs by David Muench (New York: Rand McNally, 1973);
Angle of Geese and Other Poems (Boston: Godine, 1974);
The Colors of Night (San Francisco: Arion, 1976);
The Gourd Dancer (New York & London: Harper & Row, 1976);
The Names: A Memoir (New York: Harper & Row, 1976);
The Ancient Child (New York: Doubleday, 1989);
In the Presence of the Sun: A Gathering of Shields (Santa Fe, N. Mex.: Rydal, 1992);

N. Scott Momaday (photograph © by Nancy Crampton)

In the Presence of the Sun: Stories and Poems, 1961–1991 (New York: St. Martin's Press, 1992);
Circle of Wonder: A Native American Christmas Story (Santa Fe, N. Mex.: Clear Light, 1994);
The Man Made of Words: Essays, Stories, Passages (New York: St. Martin's Press, 1997).
Editions: *The Way to Rainy Mountain* (Albuquerque: University of New Mexico Press, 1976);
The Gourd Dancer (Tucson: University of Arizona Press, 1976);
The Names: A Memoir (Tucson: University of Arizona Press, 1976);
The House Made of Dawn (Tucson: University of Arizona Press, 1996);

The Names (Tucson: University of Arizona Press, 1996);

The Way to Rainy Mountain (Tucson: University of Arizona Press, 1996).

PLAY PRODUCTION: *The Indolent Boys,* Syracuse, New York, Syracuse Stage, 8 February 1994.

OTHER: *The Complete Poems of Frederick Goddard Tuckerman,* edited by Momaday (New York: Oxford University Press, 1965);

"The Man Made of Words," in *Indian Voice: The First Convocation of American Indian Scholars,* edited by Rupert Costo (San Francisco: Indian Historian Press, 1970), pp. 49–84; reprinted in *Literature of the American Indian,* edited by Abraham Chapman (New York: New American Library, 1975), pp. 96–110; reprinted in *The Remembered Earth,* edited by Geary Hobson (Albuquerque: University of New Mexico Press, 1981), pp. 162–173;

"I Am Alive," in *The World of the American Indian,* edited by Jules B. Billard (Washington, D.C.: National Geographic Society, 1975), pp. 11–26;

"Native American Attitudes toward the Environment," in *Seeing With a Native Eye,* edited by Walter Holden Capps (New York: Harper & Row, 1976), pp. 79–85;

"Landscape with Words in the Foreground," in *Old Southwest, New Southwest: Essays on a Region and Its Literature,* edited by Judy Nolte Lensink (Tucson: Tucson Public Library, 1987), pp. 1–5.

SELECTED PERIODICAL PUBLICATIONS–UNCOLLECTED: "Eve My Mother, No," *Sequoia,* 5 (Autumn 1959): 37;

"Los Alamos," *New Mexico Quarterly,* 29 (Fall 1959): 306;

"The Well," *Ramparts,* 2 (May 1963): 41–43;

"Learning from the Indian," *Viva: Northern New Mexico's Sunday Magazine* (9 July 1972): 2;

"Figments of Sancho Panza's Imagination," *Viva: Northern New Mexico's Sunday Magazine* (31 December 1972): 2;

"Finding a Need for Nature," *Viva: Northern New Mexico's Sunday Magazine* (13 May 1973): 2;

"A Vision beyond Time and Place," *Life* (July 1976): 67.

When N. Scott Momaday received the 1969 Pulitzer Prize for fiction for his first novel, *House Made of Dawn* (1968), the literary community recognized the arrival of a major contemporary Native American writer; the event marked the beginning of what Kenneth Lincoln would later describe as the Native American Renaissance. Since then Momaday has told his story and the stories of his people, the Kiowa, in such works as *The Way to Rainy Mountain* (1969), *The Gourd Dancer* (1976), *The Names: A Memoir* (1976), *The Ancient Child* (1989), and *In the Presence of the Sun: A Gathering of Shields* (1992). By drawing attention to the high quality and cultural richness of Native American writing, his success has prepared the way for a generation of indigenous writers whose works expand and enrich the canon of American literature. Many Native American writers, among them the Acoma poet Simon Ortiz and the Laguna poet and critic Paula Gunn Allen, have acknowledged their literary debt to Momaday, and Momaday's use of mythic subtexts in *House Made of Dawn* may have influenced Leslie Marmon Silko and Louise Erdrich, who used and developed this technique in *Ceremony* (1977) and *Tracks* (1988), respectively. Silko's memoir, *Storyteller* (1981), also bears some similarities to Momaday's *The Names*. In a more general sense, Momaday's work is important because it is grounded in aboriginal oral traditions, sacred landscapes, and ancient ritual. It speaks to the reader in ancestral voices, simultaneously remote and immediate, and it is informed with the rhythms of magic formulas and the mysterious power of images originating in prehistoric petroglyphs and ancient cave paintings.

Momaday's work, however, reflects the multiple cultural contexts and traditions into which he was born or that he explored later as a student of literature and painting. It thus poses particular challenges, for Momaday writes out of the tension between these ethnic worlds, assimilating and synthesizing a wide variety of elements from Native American, European American, and European oral, literary, and artistic traditions. Only against this complex background does the full significance of Momaday's contribution to American letters become apparent. Thus, it is imperative that the critic transcend any narrow notion of Momaday's identity as a modern Kiowa and approach him as a sophisticated, multicultural writer.

This critical principle applies equally to Momaday's paintings and drawings, for besides being a major literary figure he has received recognition as an artist. As the son of a well-known painter, Momaday was exposed to the visual arts as a child; but it was not until 1974, when he took art classes from Leonard Baskin, that he began to pursue this talent seriously. Since then, his drawings and paintings have become an integral part of his creative work. Visual and literary expression merge in some of Momaday's earliest paintings of Kiowa shields, on whose images calligraphic poems are superimposed, and *The Names* includes many drawings by the author. Momaday's latest works reflect his growing integration of art and literary expression: his watercolor portrait of a bear on the dust jacket of *The Ancient Child* represents the unifying symbol of the novel, while the work itself offers Momaday's definition of a Native American version of Expressionism; his suite of sixteen shield drawings and sixteen stories in *In the Presence of the Sun: A Gathering of Shields* and the extensively illustrated *In the Presence of the Sun: Stories and Poems, 1961–1991* also testify to Momaday's remarkable dual talent. In the latter work Momaday acknowledges Emil Nolde, Francis Bacon, Pablo Picasso, and George Baselitz as major influences on his art. In 1993 a twenty-year retrospective exhibition of Momaday's work at the Wheelwright Museum in Santa Fe acknowledged his stature as a significant contemporary Indian artist.

Navarro Scott Mammedaty was born in Lawton, Oklahoma, on 27 February 1934 to Alfred Morris Mammedaty, a full-blooded Kiowa, and Mayme Natachee Scott Mammedaty, who is of Scottish, French, and Cherokee descent. Later his father changed the spelling of the family name to Momaday. When Scott was six months old, Pohd-lohk, a Kiowa elder, named him Tsoai-talee (Rock Tree Boy), thus linking the child to one of the ancient stories in Kiowa mythology: to account for the origin of Devils Tower, the strange landmark in what is now northeastern Wyoming that they had come upon on their journey south from the Yellowstone area, the Kiowa created a story about a boy who was transformed into a bear and chased his seven sisters up a tree; the tree became Devils Tower and the sisters became the Big Dipper. To reinforce this mythic connection, his parents took him to Devils Tower. The myth has become so much a part of Momaday's identity that his writings gravitate to it again and again; it provides the unifying subtext for *The Ancient Child.*

When Momaday was two, his parents left Kiowa country for a series of teaching positions: on the Navajo reservation at Shiprock, New Mexico; at Tuba City and Chinle, Arizona; and, in 1946, at a two-teacher day school at Jemez Pueblo, New Mexico. As a Kiowa among Navajo and Pueblo people who was also being guided by his parents toward success in the larger society beyond Jemez, Momaday inhabited a complex world of intersecting cultures. The need to accommodate himself to these circumstances prepared him for the perceptive treatment of encounters with various cultures that characterizes his literary work.

Momaday's parents, Al and Natachee Momaday, 1933 (photograph courtesy of N. Scott Momaday)

Momaday's formal education took place at the Franciscan Mission School in Jemez; the Indian School in Santa Fe; high schools in Bernalillo, New Mexico; and the Augusta Military Academy in Fort Defiance, Virginia. In 1952 he entered the University of New Mexico at Albuquerque as a political science major with minors in English and speech. He spent 1956–1957 in the law program at the University of Virginia, where he met William Faulkner; the encounter helped to shape Momaday's early prose and is most clearly reflected in the evocation of Faulkner's story "The Bear" (1942) in Momaday's poem of that title (collected in *Angle of Geese and Other Poems,* 1974). Returning to the University of New Mexico, Momaday graduated in 1958 and took a teaching position on the Jicarilla Apache reservation at Dulce, New Mexico. There he met and, on 5 September 1959, married Gaye Mangold. They had three daughters: Cael, Jill, and Brit.

Content with his new career, Momaday had no plans for further academic training; but in 1959, on the urging of a friend, he applied for and received a Wallace Stegner Creative Writing Fellowship to Stanford University. There the poet and critic Yvor Winters became his mentor, his friend, and the single most important influence on his early career. Winters persuaded Momaday to pursue a doctorate in American literature and proposed and supervised his thesis, an edition of the works of the nineteenth-century poet Frederick Goddard Tuckerman that was published by Oxford University Press in 1965. In a letter to the editor published in the 23 February 1967 issue of *The Reporter* Winters predicted Momaday's impending literary acclaim. He also critiqued the drafts of *House Made of Dawn,* which, to him, provided further evidence of Momaday's immense talent. Winters's untimely death in 1968, a year before Momaday's Pulitzer award, prevented him from seeing his pronouncements on his student's literary potential validated.

After receiving his Ph.D. in 1963 Momaday taught at the University of California, Santa Barbara. The origin of *House Made of Dawn* can be traced to the early 1960s, when Momaday was working on his doctorate at Stanford. Having initially conceived the work as a cycle of poems, Momaday had turned to prose and, in 1963, had published a short story, "The Well," that anticipates the themes of culture clash, witchcraft, and identity conflict that he develops in depth in the novel. While the story is set on the Jicarilla Apache reservation, where he had taught in 1958, as the settings for *House Made of Dawn* Momaday chose Jemez, which is called Walatowa in the novel, and—as the urban counterpoint to the Pueblo world—Los Angeles.

Abel, the protagonist of *House Made of Dawn,* is a composite of individuals Momaday knew in Jemez: young men whose inability to cope with conflicting cultural patterns led them into alcoholism, violence, and death and veterans who failed to reintegrate themselves into their tribal community after fighting in World War II. Abel's troubles, however, are not caused by his exposure to the world beyond the Indian village; his war experiences and the alien milieu of the modern American city only deepen an identity crisis that already troubles Abel as a young man. Isolated within the tribe—his father was an outsider who left the family—and further set apart by the deaths of his mother and brother, Abel grows up with his grandfather, Francisco, who tries, with little success, to teach him the old ways. Abel's killing of an eagle he has captured shows his ignorance of the traditional hunting code. His distance from his people's ceremonial life results in a generational conflict with Francisco: "You ought to do this and that, his grandfather said. But the old man had not understood, would not understand, only wept, and Abel left him alone. It was time to go, and the old man was away in the fields."

Abel's quest for identity leads him first into World War II and then back to his village, where he tries to attune himself to the land and his people's traditions. Failing to resolve his inner conflict by ceremonial means, he seeks solace in a sexual encounter with Angela St. John, who initially exploits Abel but will later become instrumental in his healing process; finally, he kills a mysterious albino whom he identifies as a witch. In disposing of the "evil spirit" Abel, for the first time, acts in accordance with tribal law, signaling his return to his tribe. He is convicted of murder, however, and sent to jail, a world in which he is ill equipped to survive.

The remainder of the novel traces Abel's struggle to escape the conflicting cultural forces that threaten to tear him apart after his release from eight years in prison and his relocation to Los Angeles. The disjointed structure of the work, particularly in the chapter "The Priest of the Sun," owes much to Faulkner's narrative technique and reflects the protagonist's confusion, gradual disintegration, and near death. Yet it also holds the seed of Abel's restoration to his homeland and its ancient ceremonies. Abel's vision of the runners after evil, following his nearly fatal beating by an evil policeman, "Culebra" Martinez, reveals to him the possibility of dealing with witchcraft ceremonially rather than through violence. This experience lays the foundation for Abel's renewed faith in his own culture. His friend Ben Benally's Navajo night chant, from which the novel takes its title, helps to restore Abel's psychic balance by centering him in "the house made of dawn"—the Navajo universe—and by pleading for the restoration of his mind, body, and voice. Ben and another character, the Reverend John Big Bluff Tosamah, are foils for Abel. Ben tries to live the American Dream and constantly talks about it, but his imagination is still centered in the Indian world. Tosamah, an urban Indian, lacks any understanding of or sympathy for Abel. Tosamah is important in the novel for articulating, in his sermon on the Gospel of John, the contrast between the written word and the oral tradition.

Abel's visit with Angela as he recovers in Los Angeles also helps his healing process. Their seemingly frivolous affair turns out to have had a profound effect on Angela, engendering love for her previously unwanted child, which she now regards not as her husband's but as Abel's, and leading her to an insight into Abel's tribal heritage. While much in the novel suggests that the bridging of cultures is impossible—the difficulty that the two Catholic priests have in understanding their Pueblo flock is an example—the conclusion of Abel's and Angela's relationship offers hope for cultural synthesis.

Abel's final encounter with the dying Francisco further prepares him for his reintegration into his culture. Francisco's last utterances—fragmented lessons on the importance of the land, the solar calendar, and hunting ceremonies (Francisco's account of his successful bear hunt contrasts directly with Abel's failure to act appropriately on his eagle hunt)—prompt Abel to prepare Francisco's body for burial in the traditional manner. Abel's subsequent joining of the race of the dawn runners confirms the restoration of his body, and his singing of "House Made of Dawn" as he runs affirms that he has left inarticulateness and alienation behind and is running toward a new day for both himself and his tribe.

Not all critics have interpreted the conclusion of the novel so positively; Charles Larson, for example, views the ending as a run toward death. This reading, however, fails to acknowledge not only the dawn imagery that permeates the novel but also the significance of the healing ceremony and the mythic subtexts that Susan Scarberry-García explains in her *Landmarks of Healing: A Study of* House Made of Dawn (1990).

House Made of Dawn dramatizes the difficulties Native Americans face in reconciling the conflicting demands of different cultures; Momaday's next work delineates his own construction of a contemporary Kiowa identity. Its blending of myth, history, and personal experience makes *The Way to Rainy Mountain*—published in 1969, the year he became associate professor of English and comparative literature at the Berkeley campus of the University of California—perhaps Momaday's most original contribution to American literature. In his essay "The Man Made of Words" (1970) Momaday asserts that "we are what we imagine. Our very existence consists in our imagination of ourselves." In his early thirties Momaday began to wonder about his place in the history of the Kiowa; the result was a deeply personal, spiritual, and artistic groping for connections to a tribal world that, as Momaday soon discovered, remained only in fragments. His viewing of the Kiowa's sacred Sun Dance doll, the Tai-me, in 1963 and his subsequent journey to Rainy Mountain Cemetery, near Mountain View, Oklahoma, where many of his ancestors are buried, were the first critical stages on his journey into his tribal past. The first encounter afforded Momaday a deeply religious experience of lasting consequence; his presence among his dead ancestors resulted in a sense both of continuity and of disconnection that is captured in the concluding poem of the book, "Rainy Mountain Cemetery." While the poem portrays the geographical end of the Kiowa's migration, it also conveys the state of mind that led Momaday to embark on his own actual and imaginative retracing of their journey.

Momaday as a child (photograph courtesy of N. Scott Momaday)

A problem Momaday faced in delving into the oral tradition of his people was that he could not speak Kiowa. His father helped him to collect and translate the material from Kiowa storytellers that was privately printed in 1967 in an edition of one hundred copies as *The Journey of Tai-me*. As he reworked this collection, he added two framing poems—"Headwaters," dealing with the emergence of the Kiowa through the hollow log, and "Rainy Mountain Cemetery," about the final destination of his ancestors—a prologue, an introductory essay, and an epilogue. The prologue and introductory essay include, as Winters put it in his letter to the editor of *The Reporter,* where the introductory essay first appeared on 26 January 1967, "the history of a people (the Kiowas) and the pathos of their combined grandeur and triviality; the biography of a Kiowa (Aho), in which the history is summed up; a commentary on both by the grandson and author." The prologue and the introductory essay reveal Momaday's connection to his past through Aho and provide an historical framework that helps the reader to place the twenty-four triads that make up the three sections of the book: "The Setting Out," "The Going On," and "The Closing In." Each triad consists of a mythical, an historical or anthropological, and a personal rendering of Kiowa experience and documents a moment in the rise and fall of Kiowa culture as it moved from the Yellowstone area to the Great Plains, Oklahoma, and the Staked Plains of Texas, with occasional expeditions as far as Mexico. The journey lasted from the late 1600s to 1887, when the last Sun Dance was held on the Washita River. In *The Way to Rainy Mountain* the landscape is both the common denominator of the Kiowa's evolution as a tribe and a formative influence on their perception of the world and of themselves as a people. Momaday's emphasis on the sacredness of a "remembered earth" is an early expression of the concern for nature and sacred places that places him in the forefront of contemporary environmental thinkers.

"The Setting Out" emphasizes the mystery of creation and the vulnerability of the Kiowa as they struggled to establish themselves as a community. While many triads center on the theme of separation, others teach the sacredness of language as the principal means of dealing with reality. Some triads relate the adventure of the mythical Hero Twins and convey the emerging veneration of the Sun as a deity. The arrival of the Tai-me religion, which came later, is the focus of a separate triad. While this first section of the book describes the gradual physical and spiritual consolidation of the Kiowa people, "The Going On" portrays them in firm control of their environment and their destiny. Through their mastery of word magic they direct natural and supernatural forces; expert horsemen, they excel as hunters, warriors, and explorers; and their tribal laws assure communal harmony by severely sanctioning antisocial behavior. "The Closing In" traces the demise of the Kiowa through disease, military defeat, and the loss of their horses, courage, and moral values. The falling of the Tai-me bundle from its ceremonial stand signals an impending spiritual crisis, just as the falling of the stars in 1833, described in the epilogue, had heralded the collapse of the Kiowa world.

The tone of *The Way to Rainy Mountain* is formal, often grave. It relates the journey of a people with pathos and respect, yet without regret or bitterness for the horrors that accompanied the final stage of traditional Kiowa culture. Far from dwelling on the losses, the work celebrates the continuity of the tribal spirit as it prevails in the imagination and artistic expression of a contemporary heir to a proud tradition.

The Way to Rainy Mountain has been widely anthologized and may well be the principal work for which Momaday will be remembered. The publication in 1988 of the seventeen essays in *Approaches to Teaching Momaday's* The Way to Rainy Mountain, edited by Kenneth M. Roemer, in the Modern Language Association's prestigious Approaches to World Literature series, has ensured the presence of the work in the American classroom, where it serves not only as a nontraditional expression of American cultural history but also as a model for students in articulating their own personal histories.

Momaday returned to Stanford as a professor of English in 1973. He wrote a column for *Viva: Northern New Mexico's Sunday Magazine* from April 1972 to December 1973; he also wrote many articles dealing with environmental issues from an Indian perspective, including "An American Land Ethic" (1970), "Learning from the Indian" (1972), "Finding a Need for Nature" (1973), "I Am Alive" (1975), "Native American Attitudes toward the Environment" (1976), and "A Vision beyond Time and Place" (1976). "A First American Views His Land" (1976) appeared in the U.S. bicentennial issue of *National Geographic Magazine*. Momaday also communicates his native perception of the natural world in two poems from this period, "The Delight Song of Tsoai-talee" and "New World."

Colorado: Summer, Fall, Winter, Spring (1973), Momaday's most sustained piece of nature writing, follows logically from his precise descriptions of nature and evocations of the spiritual and mythic significance of the Southwestern landscape in *House Made of Dawn* and *The Way to Rainy Mountain*. In the novel Momaday emphasizes that Abel's reawakening to the rhythms of his ancestral land is a prerequisite for the restoration of his physical and psychic health, and one of the most frequently quoted passages from *The Way to Rainy Mountain* anticipates Momaday's concern for an appropriate relationship of humanity to the earth:

> Once in his life man ought to concentrate his mind upon the remembered earth, I believe. He ought to give himself up to a particular landscape in his experience, to look at it from as many angles as he can, to wonder about it, to dwell upon it. He ought to imagine that he touches it with his hands at every season and listens to the sounds that are made upon it. He ought to imagine the creatures there and all the faintest motions of the wind. He ought to recollect the glare of the noon and all the colors of the dawn and dusk.

His 1970 essay "The Man Made of Words" addresses the destructive influence of technology and modernity in eroding one's sense of place: "We have suffered a kind of psychic dislocation of ourselves in time and space. . . . I doubt that any of us knows where he is in relation to the stars and the solstices. Our sense of natural order has become dull and unreliable." Momaday then shows how people can overcome their detachment from the land by sharpening their vision of nature and formulating a new land ethic.

Colorado, a collaboration with the photographer David Muench, follows in the tradition of Mary Austin and Ansel Adams's *Taos Pueblo* (1930), which sought to evoke a specific place through the juxtaposition of images and words. Momaday paints and sketches the changing landscape of the Rocky Mountains through the seasonal cycle with a subtle verbal palette, anticipating his branching out into the visual arts the following year. His surfaces are alive with textures and hues, colors and shadows; yet Momaday is not content with capturing the surface of nature. His vignettes conjure up the geologic processes at work below the ground and delineate the minute and incremental changes in the Colorado landscape. This evocation of geologic time not only puts into perspective the human presence in the land but also instills a sense of awe at nature's creative energy at work across the ages.

Perhaps the most memorable passages in *Colorado* are those in which Momaday reminds the reader that the earth is alive and vital and that human beings ought to incorporate this vitality into their lives. When he is infused by the "keen sense of the original earth, of its deep, definitive life," or when the impulse of life emanating from a glorious landscape takes hold of him, Momaday's mysticism is reminiscent of Loren Eiseley's. When he finds his participation "in the irresistible continuum of life" confirmed in the bristlecone trees, "the thorns of the ancient earth," he contemplates his own immortality within the cosmic design. Momaday's nature writings call for a greater spiritual and emotional involvement in the physical world. They seek to break down the anthropocentric, detached view of nature and restore the wonder, enchantment, and sense of the sacred that have been lost as nature has become the domain of science and technology.

In 1974 Momaday taught for a year at the University of Moscow. His poetry first appeared in book form that year in a handsomely published chapbook, *Angle of Geese and Other Poems,* and then in 1976 in *The Gourd Dancer.* All the poems from *Angle of Geese* are republished in *The Gourd Dancer,* along with two dozen additional pieces. These small collections represent almost twenty years of poetic expression, suggesting that Momaday heeded the advice he received from Winters in a letter dated 15 July 1964: "any poet with a critical conscience will publish a small body of work."

Cover for the paperback edition of Momaday's 1969 book, about the final migration of the Kiowa tribe

Momaday had begun his career as a poet, and his first published works were two poems that appeared in 1959: "Eve My Mother, No" in *Sequoia* and "Los Alamos" in the *New Mexico Quarterly.* Winters's influence is reflected in Momaday's syllabic, postsymbolist poetry: Winters urged his students to organize poetic lines by the number of syllables, regardless of how they went together metrically, and to avoid the obscurity of symbolist poetry by first conceptualizing an abstract idea within a rational framework and then conveying the idea through a cluster of sharp sensory details. Typical of this method among Momaday's earlier poems are "Angle of Geese," "Comparatives," "New World," "Buteo Regalis," and "The Bear," for which he received the 1962 Academy of American Poets prize. Many of his other poems, however, might be called prose poetry; among these are "The Stalker," "The Colors of Night" sequence, and "The Fear of Botalee," all of which are reminiscent of the pieces in *The Way to Rainy Mountain.* Still others, including "Plainview: 2" and "The Delight Song of Tsoai-talee," imitate the traditional poetic forms of Native American prayers and chants.

Among the themes Momaday examines in *The Gourd Dancer* is the spirit of the wilderness in "The Bear," a poetic reexpression of Ike McCaslin's encounter with Old Ben in Faulkner's short story. The mystery of death is probed in "Angle of Geese," which contrasts human death with a death in nature; in "Comparatives," which views death against the backdrop of geological time; and in "Before an Old Painting of the Crucifixion," which resembles Wallace Stevens's "Sunday Morning" (1915) in its questioning of Christ's resurrection. "The Gourd Dancer" is a moving tribute to Mammedaty, Momaday's grandfather. "Earth and I Gave You Turquoise," "New World," "Carriers of the Dream Wheel," "The Eagle Feathered Fan," and "The Delight Song of Tsoai-talee" celebrate the natural beauty of America and the spiritual power of its indigenous people.

Among the poems dealing with significant figures and places in Momaday's experience is "Forms of the Earth at Abiqui," a tribute to his friendship with Georgia O'Keeffe and to their mutual regard for the New Mexican landscape. "Krasno-presnenskaya Station" and "Abstract: Old Woman in a Room" reflects his 1974 visit to Moscow. In "Long Shadows at Dulce" he recalls the change from fall to winter on the Jicarilla Apache reservation, and "To a Child Running with Outstretched Arms in Canyon de Chelly" may be a flashback to his own childhood. The poems in *The Gourd Dancer* are testimony to Momaday's precision and depth of vision, his poetic control, and his ability to fuse philosophical themes and vibrant images.

Momaday's other major publication of 1976, *The Names: A Memoir,* is best described as an extension of *The Way to Rainy Mountain:* while the earlier work conveys the mythic and historical precedents to Momaday's personal experiences in story fragments within an associative structure, *The Names* is a chronological account of his childhood and adolescence. Mick McAllister described the book in *Southern Review* (1978) as "a portrait of the artist as a young Indian." As in *House Made of Dawn,* Momaday employs modern narrative techniques ranging from the long, unpunctuated stream-of-consciousness passage in part 3 to the presentation of individual scenes from multiple narrative perspectives. Writing in a middle ground between fiction and history, Momaday imagines conversations with ancestors and Kiowa elders he never actually met. The book is enriched with photographs and drawings by the author; dialogue fragments and vignettes evoking the landscapes of Kentucky, Oklahoma, and New

Mexico; poems; and a short story. The structure of the book is designed to adapt the Western literary genre of autobiography to his purpose of describing his emerging tribal self, thus accommodating the dual aspects of his personal and communal identities. Momaday achieves this end by prefacing his own story in part 1, which comprises a quarter of the memoir, with accounts of his racial and familial past, extending back four generations into his Kiowa, French, Cherokee, and Scottish ancestry. By framing the four parts of the memoir (4 is a sacred number for many Native American tribes) with a prologue and an epilogue, he also reconciles the Western idea of linear, chronological time with the Native American concept of cyclical, mythic time.

The four parts follow, chronologically and geographically, Momaday's childhood and adolescence from his birth in Oklahoma to his late teens in New Mexico. The prologue conjures up the moment of tribal origin, relating the Kiowa's emergence from a hollow log into the world; the epilogue describes Momaday's personal encounter with a hollow log as he retraces the Kiowa migration route. This passage illustrates the author's imaginative participation in the daily lives of his ancestors as he makes his way back to the tribe's place of origin. His linear journey through personal and historical time and geography intersects with the mythic world of the Kiowa.

Apart from the autobiographical information *The Names* provides, the main interest of the work lies in the way it illustrates Momaday's contention in "The Man Made of Words" that one creates oneself through an act of the imagination. His own Kiowa name is of particular significance in this context, for the act of naming is equivalent to the act of creation: the text opens with the assertion, "My name is Tsoai-talee, I am, therefore, Tsoai-talee; therefore I am." Momaday further elaborates this idea, which is the philosophical underpinning of the whole work: "The storyteller Pohd-lohk gave me the name Tsoai-talee. He believed that a man's life proceeds from his name, in the way that a river proceeds from its source." Names, language, stories, and myths, Momaday argues, engender a sense of personal identity through a necessary and continuing process of the imagination.

To underscore the centrality of this concept, Momaday concludes part 4 on the same note as that on which he opened the book. In a highly symbolic scene he relates his fall from innocence to experience as he loses his footing while descending the red mesa near Jemez on the day before his departure to the military academy in Virginia. With the benefit of hindsight, the mature Momaday articulates the significance of this event: "I should never again see the world as I saw it on the other side of that moment, in the bright reflection of time lost. There are such reflections, and for some of them I have the names." The fall symbolically marks the transition from history into myth—the beginning of Momaday's mythopoetic journey between his present and the Kiowa's tribal past. Having been cast off from the rock of youth, Momaday enters the world at large. He carries with him the names that hold the essence of his ancestors and the seeds of stories, providing him with the framework and the material for telling his own story. After all, Momaday explains, "life . . . is simply the construction of an idea of having existence, place in the scheme of things." This definition equally applies to Momaday's idea of art, for his writings simply express the continuing story of his place in the collective stories of his people.

On 21 July 1978 Momaday married Regina Heitzer, whom he had met while he was a visiting professor at the University of Regensburg in Germany; they have a daughter, Lore. In 1981 Momaday moved to the University of Arizona in Tucson, where he is Regents Professor of English.

In the thirteen years between *The Names* and *The Ancient Child* Momaday's published output was minimal. Literary critics, however, were busy analyzing his previous writings, producing a quickly growing body of scholarship that included the first book-length studies devoted exclusively or in part to his work. Three chapters in Alan R. Velie's *Four American Indian Literary Masters* (1982) focus on Momaday, and Lincoln's *Native American Renaissance* (1983) dedicates one chapter to a discussion of Black Elk and Momaday as "word senders." In 1985 Matthias Schubnell's critical biography, *N. Scott Momaday: The Cultural and Literary Background,* placed Momaday in the larger cultural and intellectual context that has shaped his work. Roemer's *Approaches to Teaching Momaday's* The Way to Rainy Mountain reinforced Momaday's reputation as not only the leading Native American writer of his generation but also as a major literary figure in America.

The Ancient Child was greeted with mixed reviews; most critics, however, agreed that it was a novel of extraordinary complexity. The similarities between *The Ancient Child* and *House Made of Dawn* are obvious: the protagonists embark on journeys to recover their tribal sense of self, guided by initiation helpers who lead them to a new understanding of names, myths, and rituals; both awaken to the spiritual significance of their ancestral land and restore their voices in the context of an oral culture. In *The Ancient Child* this process of healing and self-discovery is facilitated through art, specifically

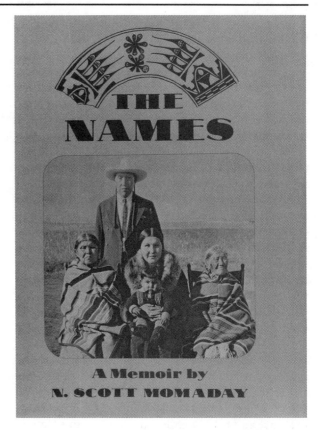

Dust jacket for Momaday's 1976 account of his childhood and adolescence

painting. The novel probes the sources of human creativity in what may best be described as a Kiowa version of Expressionism.

No other work by Momaday demands as broad a cultural and literary approach as *The Ancient Child*. One can appreciate *House Made of Dawn* without reference to Faulkner or D. H. Lawrence, and *The Names* works without an awareness of Isak Dinesen's influence; but Momaday's references to George Bizet, Jacques Brel, Katsushika Hokusai, Franz Kafka, and particularly to Emil Nolde and his painting *Wanderer among the Stars* demand that these leads be followed to do the novel justice. This is a task that awaits critical attention.

The novel traces the respective transformations of Locke "Loki" Setman, a successful but disingenuous Kiowa painter, and Grey, a young woman of Navajo and Kiowa descent. Set, as he is called, has sold out his art for commercial success. Approaching midlife, he recognizes that he is about to lose his soul. A mysterious telegram that calls him back to his native Oklahoma to visit an old woman named Kopemah, who is on her deathbed, sets in motion a series of events that lead him to reclaim his lost tribal identity. Under the guidance of Grey, Set confronts "the ancient child" within him and accepts his destiny as the modern incarnation of the bear whose origin is told in the ancient Kiowa myth about Devils Tower.

In her encounter with Set, Grey, too, undergoes a transformation: she evolves from an immature, narcissistic girl with a fantasy crush on Billy the Kid to a medicine woman who carries out the traditional responsibilities associated with this role. While Momaday's treatment of Billy the Kid expands the mythic dimension of the novel by bringing to life the exploits of this semilegendary figure of the American frontier, it tends to get in the way of the main plot. Another problem is that Grey's relinquishing of her imaginary allegiance to Billy implies that to be true to her Indian identity she must leave behind the immature myths of the American West. In a novel that affirms the universality of myth this is a troubling feature, and it contradicts the author's own experience of reconciling myths of various cultural origins.

An illustration of Momaday's virtuosity in synthesizing multiple cultural, philosophical, mythical, and literary borrowings is his choice of the protagonist's name. Combining Kiowa culture, John Locke's philosophy, Latin etymology, Norse mythology, and a 1926 children's book about Navajo and Pueblo life in the Southwest by Grace Moon, the name signifies the protagonist's inner divisions and provides a chart of his quest for vision and transformation. The significance of one's name in Indian cultures is far-reaching: it reflects the individual's essence, changes, accomplishments, and, as Momaday explains in "Figments of Sancho Panza's Imagination" (1972), his or her origin and destiny: "The name was that of the seed, from which the man issued into the world as well as that of the memory into which the man dissolves." Set's first name, the name of his mother, reflects his biological and cultural ties to the modern, Western world that has obliterated his tribal consciousness. For the seventeenth-century empiricist philosopher Locke, the mind at birth is a tabula rasa, a blank slate on which ideas are inscribed by experience; he vehemently attacks the Rationalist notion of innate ideas. This position precludes any concept of a racial or tribal memory.

When Set first visits Oklahoma, his modern, empirical consciousness initially denies and then evades the intuitive pull to his tribal homeland, the geographical center of the bear myth to which he is tied by his last name, which (according to James Mooney's *Calendar History of the Kiowa Indians*, 1898) means "Bear Man" or "Bear Above." Set's task is to reconnect himself through visions and dreams to his tribal collective memory, thereby to encounter the ancient child and affirm his "bearness." Thus, his first and last names mark the boundaries of the field of tension between his modern, empirical mindset and his primal, tribal mentality.

Set's nickname, Loki, offers other clues to the situation in which he finds himself. *Loci* is Latin for "of place" or "belonging to a place," and in the context of Set's repressed tribal allegiance it becomes apparent that he must surrender to the genius loci, the spirit of his tribal homeland, before he can escape his limiting modern mentality and find his true personal and artistic identity. His journey culminates in his visit to Tsoai, or Devils Tower, the geographic embodiment of the myth about the seven sisters and their brother who were transformed into the Big Dipper and the Bear. To become the Bear Man, the embodiment of the powerful bear medicine, Set must venture to the place of the mythic origin of his name.

On his first arrival in Oklahoma, Set senses that he is approaching a personal revelation:

> The bare ground of the path was saturated with softest sanguine light. He could not remember having seen earth of that color; it was red: earlier a flat brick red, now deeper, like that particular conte crayon that is red and brown, like old blood, at the same time—or catlinite, the color of his father's name.

His intuitive acknowledgment that he is nearing the place where his native earth, bloodline, and bear identity converge foreshadows the process of awakening he is about to experience under the influence of the spirit of place. At the close of the novel Set reenacts the bear-transformation myth in the shadow of Devils Tower: "Shapes and shadows shifted upon the great green igneous columns, upon the huge granite planes, across the long black vertical fissures." Momaday thus not only unifies the titles of the four books of the novel—"Planes," "Lines," "Shapes," and "Shadows"—into a sketch of Tsoai, but he also indicates that Set has finally placed the fragments of his Kiowa identity into a cohesive whole, that his self has merged with the mythic place that held his destiny.

While Kiowa mythology is the guiding force in Set's quest for identity, Momaday ties his story into a larger mythic context that suggests the universal power of myth to shape human lives. Loki is one of the major figures in Nordic mythology, a trickster god. His name is associated with Ansuz, the third of twenty-five Viking runes and one of the thirteen runes in the cycle of initiation. Ralph Blum notes in *The Book of Runes* (1993) that Ansuz represents "Signals, the Messenger Rune, The God Loki," and he points out that it heralds a new stage in life, initiated by sacred knowledge and unexpected new connections that emerge as unconscious motives become integrated with conscious intentions. The strength that results from this exploration of life's foundation empowers the individual to support his family and community. In this context the relevance of Set's nickname becomes readily apparent: sacred knowledge, initiation, new connections, and pathways leading to new stages in life link him to Kopemah, Grey, and the bear medicine bundle; the unconscious is the individual's basis of selfhood and the origin of the visions Set transforms into painted canvases; and the final acquisition of community manifests itself in Set's foundation of a family with Grey and his return to his tribe's mythic world. The nickname Loki, then, stands for the formative process Set undergoes once he has fallen under the influence of Grey and the spirit of his tribal homeland.

There is yet another revealing context for the nickname of Momaday's protagonist: Moon's 1926 juvenile novel *Chi-weé and Loki in the Desert*. Moon's text chronicles the adventures of a Pueblo boy and a Navajo girl, ranging from horse racing and hunting to being kidnapped in the desert; pertinent to Momaday's novel is an episode in which Loki, after killing a rabbit, gets his foot caught under a large rock. As the boy ponders his fate of dying alone in the desert, he hears something: "Nearer and nearer came the sound, and I felt very sure now what it was, and in a very little I could see him coming through the sage–it was a bear–a great one!" Like Set in his dream encounter with the bear in Momaday's novel, Loki tries to speak out, but he cannot. Both remain speechless as the bears confront them, but eventually they are liberated by the bears–literally so in Moon's book, as the bear lifts the rock to get at the rabbit. Set's liberation is figurative, for the confrontation with the bear finally restores him to his aboriginal identity and strips from him the false modern sense of self that had held him captive.

Analyzing the name of his protagonist brings to light not only Momaday's economy as a writer–the central issues of the novel are compressed in a single name–but also his interest in broadening the cultural context of his work. Momaday's writings hold many delightful surprises for those who approach him not simply as a Native American or Kiowa writer but as a borrower and synthesizer of all of the cultural resources at his disposal.

Momaday's reference to the German Expressionist painter Nolde serves as another example of his artistic inclusiveness and points to a significant

Momaday's 1987 self-portrait as a bear, linking himself to a Kiowa myth about the origin of the strange rock formation known as Devils Tower (courtesy of N. Scott Momaday)

subtext in the novel. Set's lover Lola Bourne's likening of Set's painting *Night Window Man* to Nolde's *Wanderer among the Stars* introduces an intricate web of connections between Set's groping for his inner self through his painting and Nolde's Expressionist theory. Moreover, as Set distances himself from the dictates of the art market, he begins to share the Expressionist belief that art must take its origin in a particular geographic location whose influence is channeled through the artist's unconscious. Other tenets of Expressionist art expounded in the novel include the use of myths and tribal expression as models for modern painting, the spontaneous expression of a subjective vision of reality through a vocabulary of colors, and the yearning to retrieve a childlike, uncorrupted view of the world.

Thus, in his search for a primal, mythic mentality through which he may retrieve his true identity and reinvigorate his artistic power, Set follows many Expressionist artists, Nolde among them, who turned away from modern civilization to restore the power of myths and affirm the role of place and the unconscious in the genesis of artistic expression.

The same creative forces gave rise to Momaday's next work, *In the Presence of the Sun: A Gathering*

Momaday at the base of Devils Tower (photograph by Kevin Woster)

of Shields. This collection of sixteen drawings of shields and sixteen accompanying stories was published in 1992 in a limited edition of 140 copies, 26 of which were hand colored, by Rydal Press of Santa Fe. This edition was followed by a separate edition, limited to forty-eight copies, of the drawings alone. While the full visual effect and the exceptional bookmaker's craft of the Rydal Press edition are lacking in the St. Martin's Press trade edition, *In the Presence of the Sun: Stories and Poems, 1961–1991*– also published in 1992–the magic of the text is not.

In his introduction to *In the Presence of the Sun: A Gathering of Shields,* "A Word on the Plains Shields," Momaday describes the shields as artifacts, weapons, objects of beauty, and symbols of the bearer's essence. The vision that leads to the design and construction of the shield is sacred and providential. The story on each shield is taken from the oral tradition, and the power of the text is reinforced by its structure, which revolves around the magic number 4. To purify the spirit through the encounter with the shields, Momaday recommends that "the stories ought to be told in the early morning or late afternoon, when the sun is close to the horizon, and always in the presence of the sun."

Reminiscent of Momaday's best writing in *The Way to Rainy Mountain,* each story captures some

quintessential moment in the shield bearer's life and relates how the shield shapes his destiny. Some stories tell of triumph through the strength, courage, and perseverance that emanated from the vision, while others relate decline and loss. Some of the shields symbolize the tie to the land, others the bond between generations, while yet others affirm the communion between mortals and supernatural powers. *In the Presence of the Sun: A Gathering of Shields* functions in much the same way as the secular, pictorial calendar histories of the Kiowa, which aimed to preserve memorable personages and events in the collective tribal mind; but Momaday's intent is to bring the reader into the presence of the sacred.

In addition to reprinting the text and the shield drawings, the trade edition, *In the Presence of the Sun: Stories and Poems, 1961–1991,* includes fifty-four paintings and drawings in a variety of media, twenty-nine poems of the original forty-three in *The Gourd Dancer,* the poems and stories about Billy the Kid that were interspersed in *The Ancient Child,* and twenty-seven new poems. The Billy the Kid material explores the split in this figure's personality between the sensitive, considerate, polite young man loved by women of all ages and the sharklike instinctual death force capable of the cold-blooded murders on which his legendary reputation rests. Of the new poems, "The Great Fillmore Street Buffalo Drive," a moving evocation of an urban Indian's vision of the Kiowa's glory days, stands out, as do "December 29, 1890–Wounded Knee Creek" and "Fort Sill–Set-angia," which preserve, in Momaday's precise diction and haunting images, the memory of Indians dying. The final poem, "At Risk," is a major addition to Momaday's poetic canon. Its persona's descent into the remote past not only provides a poetic commentary on the novel *The Ancient Child* but also reveals Momaday's artistic struggle as he traverses existential crises and the realms of ancient myths and ritual in search of authentic expression. It delineates the risk the writer must accept as he or she, like a shaman or medicine woman, conjures up the irresistible power of words to shape reality.

In 1994 Momaday published *Circle of Wonder: A Native American Christmas Story,* set in Jemez Pueblo, Momaday's childhood home, which first appeared in *The Names: A Memoir.* Momaday's latest work, published in 1997, is a collection titled *The Man Made of Words: Essays, Stories, Passages,* that brings together material written and published over a period of three decades. It is essential reading for anyone seeking an introduction to Momaday's central concerns: the art of storytelling, the history of Indian-white relations, the idea of the sacred, the Native

American land ethic, and the myth of the American West, to name a few. These essays provide excellent background material for the study of Momaday's fiction and poetry, show his penchant for travel writing–he conjures up the spirit of place no matter whether he writes about New Mexico, Russia, Bavaria, or Spain–and affirm his commitment to preserving natural sites not only on ecological but also on spiritual grounds. "An American Land Ethic," "Sacred Places," "Revisiting Sacred Ground," and "I Wonder What Will Happen To the Land" represent some of his most explicit statements on environmental ethics and provide a key to reading Momaday's work in the context of American nature writing.

N. Scott Momaday is steeped in both Native and European-American traditions, and his synthesis of these sources is a hallmark of his work. In drawing on the most ancient and sacred traditions of his and other Native people, who have called America home for at least thirty thousand years, he has actualized what William Carlos Williams, in *In the American Grain* (1925), identified as the crucial step toward creating truly American art: descending into the American earth, touching its aboriginal spirit, and allowing it to inform one's artistic creation. He conceives his writings and paintings with the spirit of a cave painter, a maker of masks, a shaman, an ancient storyteller, a night chanter, and a shield maker. As he puts it in "The Native Voice," the opening chapter of the *Columbia Literary History of the United States* (1988), the American Indian oral tradition "is so deeply rooted in the landscape of the New World that it cannot be denied. And it is so distinguished an expression that we cannot afford to lose it." As one listens to Momaday's native voice, one's sense of American literature is enlarged and newly defined.

Interviews:

Charles L. Woodward, *Ancestral Voice: Conversations with N. Scott Momaday* (Lincoln: University of Nebraska Press, 1989);

Daniele Fiorentino, "The American Indian Writer as Cultural Broker: An Interview with N. Scott Momaday," *American Studies in Indian Literatures,* 8 (Winter 1996): 61–72;

Matthias Schubnell, ed., *Conversations with N. Scott Momaday* (Jackson: University Press of Mississippi, 1997).

Biographies:

Martha Scott Trimble, *N. Scott Momaday,* Boise State Western Writers Series, no. 9 (Boise: Boise State University Press, 1973);

Matthias Schubnell, *N. Scott Momaday: The Cultural and Literary Background* (Norman: University of Oklahoma Press, 1985).

References:

Peter G. Beidler, "Animals and Human Development in the Contemporary American Indian Novel," *Western American Literature,* 14 (Summer 1979): 133–148;

Randall C. Davis, "'Something Other and Irresistible and Wild': Bear in the Work of N. Scott Momaday," *JAISA: The Journal of the Association for the Interdisciplinary Study of the Arts,* 1, no. 2 (1996): 79–87;

Roger Dickinson-Brown, "The Art and Importance of N. Scott Momaday," *Southern Review,* new series 14 (January 1978): 30–45;

Kathleen Donovan, "'A Menace Among the Words': Women in the Novels of N. Scott Momaday," *Studies in American Indian Literatures,* 6 (Winter 1994): 51–76;

Lawrence J. Evers, "Words and Place: A Reading of *House Made of Dawn,*" in *Critical Essays on American Indian Literature,* edited by Andrew Wiget (Boston: G. K. Hall, 1985), pp. 211–227;

Philip Heldrich, "Constructing the Self Through Language and Vision in N. Scott Momaday's *The Ancient Child,*" *Southwestern American Literature,* 22, no. 2 (1997): 11–19;

Marion Willard Hilton, "On a Trail of Pollen: Momaday's *House Made of Dawn,*" *Critique,* 14, no. 2 (1972): 60–69;

Bernard Hirsch, "Self-Hatred and Spiritual Corruption in *House Made of Dawn,*" *Western American Literature,* 17 (Winter 1983): 307–320;

Linda Hogan, "Who Puts Together," *Denver Quarterly,* 14, no. 4 (1980): 103–111;

Larry Landrum, "The Shattered Modernism of Momaday's *House Made of Dawn,*" *Modern Fiction Studies,* 42, no. 4 (1996): 763–786;

Charles Larson, *American Indian Fiction* (Albuquerque: University of New Mexico Press, 1978), pp. 78–96;

Kenneth Lincoln, *Native American Renaissance* (Berkeley: University of California Press, 1983), pp. 95–121;

Lincoln, "Tai-Me to Rainy Mountain: The Making of American Indian Literature," *American Indian Quarterly,* 10 (Spring 1986): 101–117;

Harold S. McAllister, "Be a Man, Be a Woman: Androgyny in *House Made of Dawn,*" *American Indian Quarterly,* 2 (Spring 1975): 14–22;

McAllister, "Incarnate Grace and the Paths of Salvation in *House Made of Dawn*," *South Dakota Review,* 12, no. 4 (1974): 115–125;

Mick McAllister, "The Topology of Remembrance in *The Way to Rainy Mountain*," *Denver Quarterly,* 12, no. 4 (1980): 19–31;

Carol Oleson, "The Remembered Earth: Momaday's *House Made of Dawn*," *South Dakota Review,* 11, no. 1 (1973): 59–78;

Louis Owens, *Other Destinies: Reading the American Indian Novel* (Norman: University of Oklahoma Press, 1992), pp. 90–127;

Paintbrush: A Journal of Contemporary Multicultural Literature, special issue, "The World of N. Scott Momaday," edited by Richard F. Fleck, 21 (Autumn 1994);

Catherine Rainwater, "Planes, Lines, Shapes, and Shadows: N. Scott Momaday's Iconographical Imagination," *Texas Studies in Literature and Language,* 37 (Winter 1995): 376–393;

Kenneth M. Roemer, "Ancient Children At Play—Lyric, Petroglyphic, and Ceremonial," in *Critical Perspectives on Native American Fiction,* edited by Fleck (Washington, D.C.: Three Continents, 1993), pp. 99–113;

Roemer, "Survey Courses, Indian Literature, and *The Way to Rainy Mountain*," *College English,* 37 (February 1976): 619–624;

Roemer, ed., *Approaches to Teaching Momaday's* The Way to Rainy Mountain (New York: Modern Language Association, 1988);

Susan Scarberry-García, *Landmarks of Healing: A Study of* House Made of Dawn (Albuquerque: University of New Mexico Press, 1990);

Matthias Schubnell, "Locke Setman, Emil Nolde and the Search for Expression in N. Scott Momaday's *The Ancient Child*," *American Indian Quarterly,* 18 (Fall 1994): 468–480;

Schubnell, "N. Scott Momaday," in *American Nature Writers,* volume 2, edited by John Elder (New York: Scribners, 1996), pp. 639–649;

Alan R. Velie, "*House Made of Dawn:* Nobody's Protest Novel," in his *Four American Indian Literary Masters* (Norman: University of Oklahoma Press, 1982), pp. 51–64;

Velie, "The Return of the Native: The Renaissance of Tribal Religions as Reflected in the Fiction of N. Scott Momaday," *Religion and Literature,* 26 (Spring 1994): 135–145.

Tim O'Brien

*This entry was updated by Thomas Myers (Saint Norbert College)
from his entry in* DLB 152: American Novelists
Since World War II, Fourth Series.

See also the O'Brien entry in *DLB Yearbook 1980*
and *DS 9: American Writers of the Vietnam War: W. D.
Ehrhart, Larry Heinemann, Tim O'Brien, Walter McDonald, John M. Del Vecchio.*

BIRTH: Austin, Minnesota, 1 October 1946, born
William Timothy O'Brien to William Timothy and
Ava E. Schultz O'Brien.

EDUCATION: B.A. (summa cum laude), Macalester College, 1968; graduate study at Harvard University.

MARRIAGE: 1973 to Ann Elizabeth Weller (divorced 1995).

AWARDS AND HONORS: O. Henry Memorial
Awards for chapters of *Going After Cacciato,* 1976 and
1978; National Book Award, for *Going After Cacciato,*
1979; Guggenheim Foundation fellowship, 1981;
Vietnam Veterans of America award, 1987; Heartland Prize, *Chicago Tribune* for *The Things They Carried,* 1990; Prix du Meilleur Livre Étranger for *The
Things They Carried,* 1992; James Fenimore Cooper
Prize for best novel based on a historical theme for
In the Lake of the Woods, 1995; also received awards
from the National Endowment for the Arts, the
Massachusetts Arts and Humanities Foundation,
and the Bread Loaf Writers' Conference.

BOOKS: *If I Die in a Combat Zone, Box Me Up and Ship
Me Home* (New York: Delacorte/Seymour Law-
rence, 1973; London: Calder & Boyars, 1973;
revised edition, New York: Delacorte/Sey-
mour Lawrence, 1979);
Northern Lights (New York: Delacorte/Seymour Law-
rence, 1975; London: Calder & Boyars, 1976);
Going After Cacciato (New York: Delacorte/Seymour
Lawrence, 1978; London: Cape, 1978);
The Nuclear Age (New York: Knopf, 1985; London:
Collins, 1986);
The Things They Carried (Boston: Houghton Mifflin/
Seymour Lawrence, 1990; London: Collins,
1990);

Tim O'Brien (photograph © by Jerry Bauer)

In the Lake of the Woods (Boston: Houghton Mifflin/
Seymour Lawrence, 1994; London: Flamingo,
1995);
Tomcat in Love (New York: Broadway Books, 1998).

SELECTED PERIODICAL PUBLICATIONS–
UNCOLLECTED: "Claudia Mae's Wedding
Day," *Redbook,* 141 (October 1973): 102–103;
"Where Have You Gone, Charming Billy?" *Red-
book,* 145 (May 1975): 81, 127–132;
"Landing Zone Bravo," *Denver Quarterly,* 4 (August
1975): 72–77;
"Speaking of Courage," *Massachusetts Review,* 17
(Summer 1976): 243–253;

"The Way It Mostly Was," *Shenandoah,* 27 (Winter 1976): 35–45;

"Keeping Watch by Night," *Redbook,* 148 (December 1976): 65–67;

"The Fisherman," *Esquire,* 88 (October 1977): 92, 130, 134;

"Calling Home," *Redbook,* 150 (December 1977): 75–76;

"The Nuclear Age," *Atlantic,* 243 (June 1979): 58–67;

"Civil Defense," *Esquire,* 94 (August 1980): 82–88;

"Underground Tests," *Esquire,* 104 (November 1985): 252–254, 256, 258–259;

"Enemies and Friends," *Harper's,* 280 (March 1990): 30–31;

"Field Trip," *McCall's,* 117 (August 1990): 78–79;

"The People We Marry," *Atlantic,* 269 (January 1992): 90–98;

"Loon Point," *Esquire,* 119 (January 1993): 90–94;

"How Unhappy They Were," *Esquire,* 122 (October 1994): 136–138;

"The Vietnam in Me," *New York Times Magazine,* 144 (2 October 1994): 48–57;

"Faith," *New Yorker,* 71 (12 February 1996): 62–67;

"Class of '68," *Esquire,* 129 (March 1998): 160.

Tim O'Brien, a contemporary American novelist and short-story writer of immense imaginative power and range, freely admits that the Vietnam War was the dark, jarring experience that made him a writer. In a 1993 interview (unpublished) he described the war as the "Lone Ranger watershed event of my life," and the time before his induction into the United States Army as "a horrid, confused, traumatic period–the trauma of trying to decide whether or not to go to Canada." O'Brien went to Vietnam and served there in the Fifth Battalion, Forty-Sixth Infantry–the U.S. Army's Americal Division–from January 1969 to March 1970, patrolling the deadly Batangan Peninsula and the tragic villages of My Lai after the massacre there in March 1968. Unlike many of his peers, O'Brien returned to America sound of mind and body if not of spirit. He wrote of his war experience in a spare, poetically allusive, and classically toned personal memoir, *If I Die in a Combat Zone, Box Me Up and Ship Me Home* (1973). His subsequent stories and novels, including the National Book Award-winning *Going After Cacciato* (1978), have all featured the Vietnam War as either a real or a ghostly presence. O'Brien examines the wrenching transformation of sense and sensibility in fictions that are evocative, challenging meetings of imagination and memory, of the created and the re-created, of the impossible and the possible.

Critics have often placed O'Brien within the somewhat limited category of "war writer." Milton J. Bates, assessing O'Brien's ongoing obsession with the myth of courage, places him "in the tradition of our great war novelists–Crane, Hemingway, Jones, Mailer, and Vonnegut." In Philip D. Beidler's *Re-Writing America,* Philip Caputo, himself a Pulitzer Prize-winning Vietnam writer whose memoir *A Rumor of War* reveals strong affinities with O'Brien's, finds his peer standing "solidly within the tradition of midwestern soldier-poets. Indeed, it is Ernest Hemingway that a reader hears most often in much of O'Brien's work–the spare, rhythmic repetition of key words and phrases; the hard, disciplined control of idea and emotion in sentences and paragraphs that are models of the stoic understatement; the darkly ironic gestures; and the classical imperatives of courage and cowardice, transgression and expiation, of Hemingway's best stories and novels.

Such comparisons, if containing more than an ounce of truth, are finally too easy and too constraining for a writer of O'Brien's thematic preoccupations and stylistic innovations. What a reader finds in his work, from the classical, meditative early memoir to the postmodern, darkly comic *Tomcat in Love* (1998), is the remarkable education and evolution of a writer whose fundamental themes, "discipline, honesty, integrity, understanding, acceptance, endurance," as Beidler notes, grant his work larger, even universal, significance. O'Brien certainly belongs to the small platoon of great American war writers that has walked through native mythic terrain, a literary outfit begun by James Fenimore Cooper, but in ambition and achievement he also demands induction into the larger unit of artists who are simply called important American writers. Like Mark Twain's Huckleberry Finn, O'Brien is a natural storyteller who can spin a tale with the best of them. Like Herman Melville's Ishmael, he is also a figure who would cast off from safe harbors and dive deeply into the primal American soul and psyche. If his diving is toward hot landing zones rather than the Leviathan, his frequent revisitations to the Vietnam War do not limit his thematic and symbolic reach. About the heart of his fiction the author in 1984 asserted, "My concerns have to do with the abstractions: What's courage and how do you get it? What's justice and how do you achieve it? How does one do right in an evil situation?" O'Brien has resisted the designation "war writer"; while admitting it was his Vietnam experience that demanded he become a writer, he calls the term "meaningless." The author of some of the most striking narratives of warfare, both real and imagined, in the entire corpus of American literature,

Dust jacket for O'Brien's first book (1973), a memoir of his war experiences in Vietnam

O'Brien argues finally that "War stories aren't about war—they are about the human heart at war."

Beyond his war, any war, he recurrently explores a few specific subjects and themes: the continual interplay of fact and imagination in fiction and in life; the compulsive, absurd, noble quest for human truth; the difficulty in defining and obtaining the elusive quality of courage; and the ongoing human need for the fragile, made-up, explanatory device called story. Indeed, O'Brien's prime theme finally is not that war maims and destroys—an obvious truism—but that storytelling explains, connects, and ultimately saves the teller and the listener. As O'Brien asserts in *The Things They Carried* (1990), "The thing about a story is that you dream it as you tell it, hoping that others might dream along with you, and in this way memory and imagination and language combine to make spirits in the head."

O'Brien's ability to dream his stories and novels and to make his readers dream them, too, has made him a major voice in American fiction since the early 1970s and has garnered him substantial recognition. In addition to the National Book Award, O'Brien has received France's prestigious Prix du Meilleur Livre Étranger, the *Chicago Tribune* Heartland Prize, and the James Fenimore Cooper Prize from the Society of American Historians; has won *Esquire,* O. Henry, and Pushcart prizes for his short fiction; has been the recipient of awards from the National Endowment for the Arts, the Guggen-

heim Foundation, and the Massachusetts Arts and Humanities Foundation; and has seen his works translated into several foreign languages. Much more than a chronicler in fiction of a single, problematic war, O'Brien is now valued by critics and readers as a true American historian of the most valuable kind: the artist of the hidden recesses of the human heart and soul.

O'Brien does not deny the natural placement of his work within the larger corpus of war writing; indeed, considering his own writing in that context, he revealed in 1992 that "when I read the best things by Crane or Tolstoy, I feel a sense of confirmation." He faces, however, the ongoing paradox of the important literary artist, asserting that "a good writer must write beyond his moment, but he does have to be rooted to a lived-in world—like Conrad, Shakespeare, and Homer." If there does exist an American Joseph Conrad or a Homer of the Vietnam War, an artist who has melded that particular trauma with universal themes, that figure would seem to be Tim O'Brien, a writer who again and again has voyaged out into dangerous historical and imaginative waters only to return home with tales worth telling, American encounters with new cultural deceptions, with fresh hearts of darkness.

O'Brien's evolution as a storyteller seems the familiar stuff of the midwestern poet-novelist. Born on 1 October 1946 in Austin, Minnesota, he grew, as he relates in *If I Die in a Combat Zone,* "out of one war and into another. . . . My bawling came with the first throaty note of a new army in spawning." He matured in another Minnesota town, Worthington, where his father, William Timothy O'Brien, sold life insurance and his mother, Ava, raised him, his brother, Greg, and his sister, Kathy. His family life included a house full of books; as a boy O'Brien was a voracious reader who also tried his best to play little league baseball and to grow into the sturdy young man his environment demanded. He attended Worthington Senior High School and Macalester College in St. Paul, where he graduated summa cum laude in 1968, having earned a degree in political science. Despite having lived in the Boston area since 1970, when he entered the Ph.D. program in government at Harvard, O'Brien continued to see himself as a Midwesterner. His decision to remain in the East after his early writing success, however, does reveal something about his ambivalent connection to the America of his boyhood. His early works, especially *If I Die in a Combat Zone* and his first novel, *Northern Lights* (1975), include many passages that evoke the stolid provincialism that has recommended to many a young writer a permanent artistic and emotional exodus. Of his boyhood O'Brien said in 1992, "Writers are connected. I'm connected to my past, but we're connected to bad things, too. There were things about the Midwest that I liked. But my dominant recollection . . . is one of a kind of seething rage. Even as a kid I felt that way. Small town gossip and the values of those places."

In August 1968 after graduation from Macalester, O'Brien was drafted into the army, an event that produced a major emotional crisis for him. Finding the conflict morally reprehensible and emotionally unacceptable, he considered Canada or jail but finally did not choose flight or incarceration over Vietnam. He admits the prospect of losing friends and family and the censure of his culture overcame his personal objections, and he found himself dragged inexorably toward war. As he records in his memoir, "in the end, it was less reason and more gravity that was the final influence."

His decision to accept induction into the armed forces might be seen as an American literary *felix culpa* (fortunate fault), for the war was the event that made him a writer. His service in Vietnam as an infantryman with the Americal Division presented him with jarring, traumatic material, but it also made writing a need rather than a choice. Seeing the many physical and emotional atrocities; watching friends destroyed or maimed in meaningless search-and-destroy missions and village searches; battling the fear, boredom, and deadliness of America's

longest war, one to which he had pronounced moral objections—all of this and more supplied O'Brien with the two great themes that have powered all of his novels and short fiction: the ongoing quest to acquire or simply to define courage and the desperate need to attain redemption after sin. Careful to avoid cliché, O'Brien rejects the pat line "It was horrible but it makes a man out of you," finding in such sentiment "a certain B-movie quality."

Before Vietnam, O'Brien's commitment to the life of the writer was desultory at best. He wrote his first story at the age of nine, a piece called "Timmy of the Little League." He credits "Miss Wiek, my junior high school English teacher," as a great writing influence but describes his overall commitment to his craft in high school and college as "a flickering rather than a burning desire." As a college student he wrote a novel set in Czechoslovakia, a "love story set within the political changes there" that remained, he is thankful, unpublished. In another familiar pattern of American fiction writers, O'Brien also served a literary novitiate as a journalist. Before Vietnam he worked as a sports reporter for the *Worthington Daily Globe;* between May 1973 and August 1974, while he was in the Ph.D. program at Harvard, he served two summers as a reporter for the *Washington Post,* learning the "discipline of the newspaper story, the importance of correct grammar and active verbs." Again, comparisons to the biographies of Crane and Hemingway are inevitable—the correspondent as storyteller who hones his spare, athletic prose with the tools of the working newspaperman. Although his lean, understated prose clearly puts him within the long tradition of the American journalist-fabulist, O'Brien has consistently forged his own imaginative and stylistic pathways through the rich terrain of the story and the novel.

O'Brien admits his debt as a writer to the modern pantheon of American writers that includes F. Scott Fitzgerald, William Faulkner, and Hemingway, but he also credits the influence of "a lot of nameless books." Critics have made much of O'Brien's intricate interplay of imagination, memory, and experience in his novels, his cutting back and forth through time, and as influences he points not only to Faulkner but also to James Joyce and Homer as masters of "nonlinear time, the experience of one's life as jumps and starts." He feels a strong kinship to such contemporary American writers as Robert Stone, Tom McGuane, and Philip Caputo because of the types of stories they tell and the chances they take: "A lot of fiction doesn't aspire high enough," says O'Brien of the contemporary scene. He admires fiction written without compromise, what he

Dust jacket for O'Brien's 1978 novel, which received a National Book Award

calls "all or nothing tales," and in the work of Stone and the others he finds strong analogues to his own artistic values and concerns. The writer O'Brien has mentioned most often, however, is neither American nor contemporary. As a writer who features themes of innocence and experience, transgression and expiation, O'Brien asserted, "I also have a lot in common with Conrad in many ways, especially when I think of *Lord Jim.* Good stories somehow have to do with the awakening into a new world, something new and true, where someone is jolted out of a kind of complacency and forced to confront a new set of circumstances or a new self" (*Missouri Review,* 1991). O'Brien is particularly attracted to fictions that feature heroes who sin or fail and then must make amends, figures who must live with memories that hurt and shame but that finally compel the bearer to evolve, to find forgiveness. He says, simply, "We write about the mistakes we make in our lives—we have to write about them."

After his return from Vietnam, O'Brien was at Harvard from 1970 to 1976 taking classes, passing his orals, making ends meet as a teaching assistant and a reporter, thinking about his dissertation, but mostly becoming a distinctive new voice in American letters. During his time at Harvard he published two books, the first of which was his memoir. O'Brien's achievement in *If I Die in a Combat Zone* was twofold. First, he established his literary voice by creating a striking personal meditation whose somber,

classical tones and poetic effects immediately prompted critics such as Beidler to place his work "in the central tradition of American spiritual autobiography . . . the tradition of Edwards and Woolman, of Franklin and Thoreau and Henry Adams." In a more local historical way, however, *If I Die in a Combat Zone* was one of the key texts of the 1970s that placed Vietnam back within American historical memory just as cultural exhaustion and collective amnesia had become national conditions. Like Philip Caputo's *A Rumor of War* (1977) and Michael Herr's *Dispatches* (1977), personal historical-artistic statements that would follow O'Brien's lead, in the memoir O'Brien offers a version of himself who is both a participant telling one man's story and a symbolic emissary of his culture who exchanges traditional and pop culture myth for the hard-earned knowledge of personal transgression and historical experience. O'Brien succeeds in joining the newly historical with the long-standing mythic, the particular with the general, and the local with the universal in the memoir. Noting the striking, classical voice of the book, Annie Gottlieb invoked the phraseology of Aristotle in her 1 July 1973 review in *The New York Times,* assessing O'Brien's first work as "a beautiful, painful book, arousing pity and fear for the daily realities of a modern disaster."

Early in the book O'Brien defines the memoir as both product and process with some key inquiries: "Do dreams offer lessons? Do nightmares have themes? . . . Can the foot soldier teach anything important about war, merely from having been there? I think not. He can tell war stories." O'Brien describes his own memoir not as autobiography but as a work of literary imagination. A poetic-philosophical sensibility controls the account of a young infantryman's passage through a year at war, always seeking the proper cultural touchstones for its experience and education: in the course of O'Brien's painful education at the firebases, in the jungle, and at the villages of My Lai is the desperate attempt to find reliable cultural explanations of the most jarring lessons of new history. There is also the necessary quest for models of proper behavior, a list that grows shorter as O'Brien finds various aspects of popular and classical myth inapplicable to his condition. The most concentrated part of the search is for an adequate definition of courage, the theme that is central to all of O'Brien's work. Despite the comparisons made by his critics, O'Brien asserted early in his career that his conclusions could not be a mere restatement of Hemingway. Considering the phrase most often attached to his predecessor, O'Brien reveals in the memoir that "grace under pressure isn't sufficient. It's too easy to affect grace, and it's too hard to see through it. . . . Grace under pressure means you can confront things gracefully or squeeze out of them gracefully. But to make those two things equal with the easy word 'grace' is wrong. Grace under pressure is not courage."

The great cultural irony of *If I Die in a Combat Zone* is that to find a proper standard of courage within a fragmented, postmodern war, one whose prime features are chaos and unreadability. O'Brien must swim back against the current of history to a time well before Hemingway and the modernist sensibility. To be hard-boiled and taciturn in the face of the kind of cultural tragedy Vietnam was for O'Brien was not enough. He returned in the memoir to older, dust-covered definitions of courage and virtue. Vietnam seemed to shatter many classical imperatives, and many World War I literary artists "Ezra Pound, Wilfred Owen, Siegfried Sassoon and others" would nod in agreement with O'Brien when he asserts, "Horace's old do-or-die aphorism— '*Dulce et decorum est pro patria mori*'—was just an epitaph for the insane." O'Brien, to be able to write about his war not only in his classical memoir but also in the more daring fictions to come, seeks and finds a standard with the help of another ancient thinker. He finds his man not in Shane, the mythic hero of the American West, not in Hemingway's Frederic Henry, but in a Greek philosopher.

Responding to the Socratic dialogue called *Laches,* O'Brien concludes, "Proper courage is wise courage. It's acting wisely, acting wisely when fear would have a man act otherwise. It is the endurance of the soul in spite of fear—wisely." Although he finds in Plato a meaningful four-part definition of virtue—courage, temperance, justice, wisdom—and an acceptable definition of courage as "wise endurance," he also discovers Vietnam to be nearly void of those necessary qualities. Instead of Socrates, he finds morally myopic chaplains; foolhardy, vicious, or cowardly commanding officers; increasingly brutal and brutalized peers. After one of many losses of personal and collective discipline in the field, he can only write that "it was good to walk from Pinkville and to see fire behind Alpha Company, just as pure hate is good" and can only nod in tragic agreement when his best friend in another area of Vietnam tells him in a letter that "what I see is evil."

If I Die in a Combat Zone is a remarkable first work, a moving attempt by one literary "grunt" to reconcile ancient virtue with contemporary evil, but it was only the first chapter in O'Brien's ongoing quest to explore the ramifications of "wise endurance" in a contemporary landscape seemingly sandblasted of such noble imperatives. That critics see the memoir as a "real" story distinct from his subsequent fiction is to O'Brien a false distinction. Some of the characters in the memoir are real but others are invented; he describes the book as "eighty-five percent a work of the imagination." What he did discover in writing the memoir was the difference between facts and the truth, and it is the latter quality that O'Brien would pursue down innovative fictional pathways. Of that elusive prize in *If I Die in a Combat Zone* he said in 1984, "Truth doesn't reside in the surface of events. Truth resides in those deeper moments of punctuation, when things explode. So you compress the boredom down, hinting at it but always going for drama—because the essence of the experience was dramatic. You tell lies to get to the truth."

The next dramatic "lie" that O'Brien would tell came in 1975 with his first novel, a long, darkly poetic, sometimes parodic story of two brothers and their ongoing quest for proper courage and personal virtue. The setting of *Northern Lights* is Sawmill Landing, a hard, cold Minnesota town where Pehr Lindstrom Peri, minister of Damascus Lutheran Church, tries to raise his two sons, Paul and Harvey Perry, to endure stoically whatever life may throw at them. Harvey, the athletic, physically courageous brother, goes to Vietnam and returns, like Hemingway's Jake Barnes, with a wound from the war. Paul, the softer, more passive sensibility, works inef-

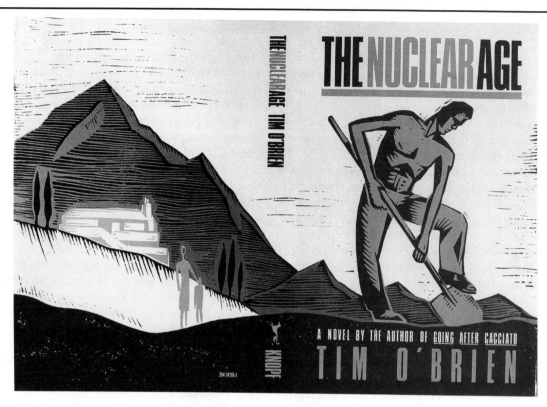

Dust jacket for O'Brien's 1985 novel, which explores the effects of living under the threat of atomic warfare

fectually as a county farm agent and nestles in the sheltering arms of his wife, a maternal-sexual presence with the symbolic name of Grace. Harvey returns from Vietnam as damaged goods both physically and psychically, and the brothers collide, antagonize, and test each other: in response to the father's apocalyptic obsessions (foreshadowing O'Brien's 1985 novel, *The Nuclear Age,* he is intent on building a bomb shelter); in a not-quite-defined rivalry for the affections of a beautiful, wild young woman named Addie; in opposition or adherence to untested cultural definitions or standards of courage, self-sufficiency, and manhood.

The novel includes some elements that O'Brien does not entirely harmonize. Part of the book is a long parody of Hemingway that some early critics took too seriously. Roger Sale in the 13 November 1975 *New York Review of Books* concluded that "*Northern Lights* is too literary much of the time, but fine when it is not" and, taking the parody to be serious imitation, asked, "Is it possible to read *The Sun Also Rises* too often? . . . O'Brien has read it too often, let it sink into him too deeply." Other reviewers also found the book too long, too self-conscious, and too artificially literary. Of the long parodic sequence O'Brien said, "I tried to make fun of Hemingway. I respect Hemingway's work, and some of it I love. But sometimes I find myself being irritated

by a kind of macho simplicity and by the way women are treated almost as little pawns to be moved around from place to place. That's not always true of his women, but often it is true, I think" (*Missouri Review,* 1991).

The climax of *Northern Lights* is an arduous ski trip the two brothers undertake together that a killer blizzard turns into a physical and emotional struggle for survival. Paul saves himself and his brother and begins to reconcile his feminine side that his father tried to expunge with traditional male definitions of heroism. In its deft exploration of gender in relation to identity, strength, endurance, and courage, the novel is an interesting one. Critics of O'Brien's work have sometimes complained that he fails to create three-dimensional female characters, but *Northern Lights* is an early attempt to isolate and explore both the male and the female in every human being, fictional or real. Of men and women, O'Brien said, "We're different, yes, but we're not that different. We all experience anger. We experience lust. We experience terror. We experience curiosity and fascination for that which repels us. All of us" (*Missouri Review,* 1991).

Although the original reviews of the novel were lukewarm at best, recent opinion has reversed this judgment somewhat. In perhaps the best specific reading of the novel, Bates concludes that "in its juxtaposition of masculine and feminine, woods and pond, apocalypse and salvation, endurance and love, it nevertheless has that 'mythic quality' O'Brien considers essential to a good story." Seeing the book over greater distance and within the context of O'Brien's evolving literary career, Beidler in 1991 assessed the novel sixteen years after its publication, finding in it "the stirrings of a stylistic experimentation of uncommon power and originality."

In retrospect, O'Brien calls *Northern Lights* "my training novel, my *Torrents of Spring*" and claims he would like to revise it, to cut it by eighty or ninety pages. At the time of its publication, critical reaction certainly gave no indication that within four years O'Brien would be the recipient of the National Book Award. Leaving Harvard with his degree unfinished, he was now committed full-time to his craft. "Instead of writing my dissertation," he says, "I was writing what I needed to write." Had he not become a writer, O'Brien feels he might have become a foreign service officer or an employee of the State Department, perhaps a government functionary of the type Melville or Conrad would have employed for dramatic, ironic effect. Without his Ph.D. and with his literary apprenticeship behind, O'Brien set to work on the novel that would show the true flowering of the "uncommon power and originality" Beidler and many other commentators would soon describe at length and with great enthusiasm.

O'Brien left Harvard but remained in the Boston area. With his academic ties cut, he devoted his full energies to a novel that would take many readers and critics off guard. Part reality, part memory, part fantasy or dream, *Going After Cacciato* (1978) established O'Brien as an important American writer whose subject happened to be the Vietnam War. To this day O'Brien insists it is not a war novel at all, but he also understands why the novel confused readers entering its stylistic terrain with specific if limited expectations. Playing the reader's role, O'Brien in 1984 commented, "if I were to pick up my own book and read it, my feeling would be that I wasn't really reading a war novel; I would perhaps feel that a trick had been played on me. . . . It's quirky. It goes somewhere else; it goes away from the war. It starts there and goes to Paris. A peace novel, in a sense."

What O'Brien offered his readers in 1978 was a novel that seemed a strange blend of the real and the fantastic, the remembered and the imagined, an elaborate literary game that was deadly serious about its subjects, a text in which time and space were arranged at odd angles, in nonlinear arrangements. The book is ostensibly the travel tale of a young foot soldier named Cacciato (Italian for "the

hunter"), "dumb as a bullet," who decides one day to walk 8,600 miles to Paris, but the real central character, the controlling narrative voice, is Spec Four Paul Berlin, who with his overaged, disaffected lieutenant and the rest of the Third Squad, must track down the young deserter and bring him back to the war. The book begins with a somber, spare evocation of the tragic realities of the Vietnam War; O'Brien offers the reader a litany of the dead that quickly finds its opposite number in the celebration of the power of imagination to deal with the terrible facts of Vietnam. One of the lessons O'Brien offers in *If I Die in a Combat Zone* is that "soldiers are dreamers," the same epigraph from Sassoon that precedes the first chapter of *Going After Cacciato*. It is a well-chosen assertion, for what the reader discerns slowly is that this war novel is really an instruction manual on how to survive traumatic history through the power of imagination, through the need to tell a war story that is much more than a war story. Said O'Brien in 1984, "The very themes of the book are imagination and memory. In that sense it's about how one goes about writing fiction, the fictional process."

The novel is actually an elaborate frame tale, one in which the geometry often seems akin to the eye-fooling perspective of an M. C. Escher drawing. Author O'Brien creates the story of "author" Paul Berlin, a soldier afflicted with a major case of "fear biles," who while on guard duty one night by the South China Sea tells a story, an apparently fantastic tale about his and the Third Squad's journey to Paris in pursuit of Cacciato. In his observation post, the present time of the novel, Berlin writes a novel of a certain kind, one that is an elaborate interpenetration of memory and imagination, hope and loss. The tripartite structure of the novel is at first puzzling, but a reader soon learns that memory and imagination, the real and the possible, affect the quality and nature of each other as Paul writes in the guard tower. The tragic realities and the unacceptable history of the Vietnam War affect the parameters and features of what Paul Berlin is able to conjure in his imagination, but O'Brien makes it clear how the power of dreams also creates the real world.

Many early critics concentrated on the seemingly fantastic elements of the story without taking full account of the overall architecture and made comparisons based on that focus. Speaking for many, Richard Freedman in *The New York Times Book Review* (12 February 1978) asserted that "clearly we are dealing here with what the new South American novelists would call 'magical realism.'" There is, however, a large difference between

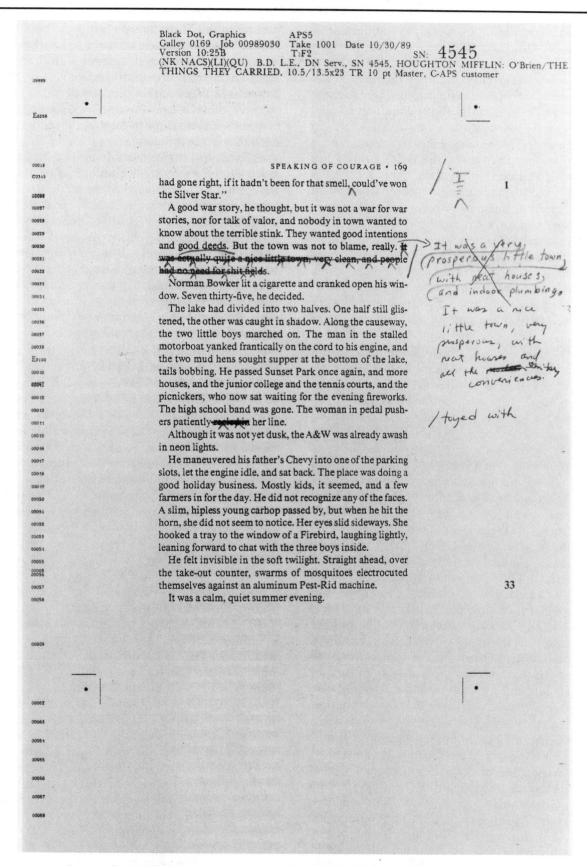

Page proof, with O'Brien's corrections, for The Things They Carried *(Collection of Tim O'Brien)*

O'Brien's novel and a work such as Gabriel García Marquez's *One Hundred Years of Solitude* (English translation, 1970), a novel in which supernatural and fantastic occurrences coexist in the same textual time and space with realistic happenings. Early in *Going After Cacciato,* Paul Berlin and the Third Squad fall magically through a hole into an elaborate underground tunnel complex, a moment that may convince a reader that he or she is following Alice through a Vietnam wonderland. O'Brien carefully juxtaposes that apparently fantastic occurrence with Berlin's terrible memory of the destruction of a village called Hoi An. He remembers his and the Third Squad's desire for revenge, the words "Kill it" coming from his lips. He remembers finally that "the village was a hole," a dark remnant of the war within his consciousness that Berlin "writes" anew as the tunnel sequence where imagination attempts to mediate and bargain with the unacceptable history of the war.

O'Brien rejects the "magical realism" tag for the novel, asserting that *Going After Cacciato* is truly about "the reality of our dreams, our daydreams in particular, the work of our imagination. There's nothing unreal or surreal about it." He is particularly amused by the suggestion that he was consciously or unconsciously airlifting the fictional technique and style of García Marquez to the jungles and mountains of Vietnam; of *One Hundred Years of Solitude* he said in 1984, "I just hated it. My wife read it and loved it, but I got through about three pages. . . . I remember the paragraphs were extraordinarily long, and I didn't like wending my way through long paragraphs." By wending their way through O'Brien's memory-dreamscape in *Going After Cacciato,* however, readers encounter O'Brien's familiar themes reconstituted and restated: the need to find personal courage in the face of overwhelming fear; the imperative to find a moral center within historical circumstances that consistently blunt such pretensions; the necessity of dreams, imagination, and stories as the protective flak jacket for everyone, whether in real combat zones or not.

The true battle in *Going After Cacciato* is not so much between memory and imagination as it is between the desire for freedom and safety and the terrible constraints of duty. Throughout the book O'Brien makes a dazzling display of both his and Paul Berlin's imaginations. Both write well—and creatively. At one juncture Cacciato rescues the Third Squad from a Tehran prison using a 1964 Chevy Impala as a getaway car, but there are also drags and obstacles on the imagination throughout the narrative, and for a good thematic reason. The climax of the debate between duty and freedom occurs when the Third Squad reaches Paris and Paul Berlin, the spokesperson for duty, and Sarkin Aung Wan, a mysterious female refugee who champions freedom, have their own dreamlike version of the Paris Peace Talks. Sarkin counsels Berlin to remain in Paris to make a separate peace, asserting, "For just as happiness is more than the absence of sadness, so is peace infinitely more than the absence of war. Even the refugee must do more than flee. He must arrive." From the beginning of the novel onward, Paul Berlin has been a fine creative writer of his own impulse toward freedom, asserting of his imaginative escape to Paris that "it could be done." At the end of the novel, however, his is a different voice, one that has tested through the power of story the limits of that narrative. Facing the attractive, powerful argument of Sarkin, he finally admits, "Even in imagination we must be true to our obligations, for, even in imagination, obligation cannot be outrun. Imagination, like reality, has its limits."

Imagination is not vanquished, however, and O'Brien makes it clear that all of the other members of the Third Squad will have to write their own personal "Goings After Cacciato." What both Paul Berlin and Tim O'Brien achieve in the novel is finally anything but fantastic: it is the real negotiation, the ongoing everyday dialectic, between dream and fact, the real and the possible, that constitutes reality. Is Paul Berlin, as he pursues proper notions of duty and courage, Tim O'Brien himself? O'Brien in 1984 said, "he's more of a dreamer than I was, I think. He spends much more of his time in dream. . . . He's more frightened than I was—and I was very, very frightened." There are clear similarities, however, among the "Tim O'Brien" he creates in his memoir, Paul Perry from his first novel, and Paul Berlin in *Going After Cacciato.* All search seriously for a standard of courage that is not just intellectually and emotionally sound but historically applicable and livable. All achieve only partial, contingent, or qualified success in that quest. In *Going After Cacciato* both "writers" achieve clear victories on a certain level. Of the relationship of Tim O'Brien's storytelling to Paul Berlin's in the observation post by the South China Sea, perhaps Eric James Schroeder says it best: "O'Brien's own 'inner peace' is ultimately achieved in the writing of *Cacciato.* Paul Berlin's activity in the tower becomes a metaphor for O'Brien's own creative act." It is appropriate that at the end of the novel a new story is just beginning, this time by the commanding officer of the Third Squad, who, thinking of the impossibility of Cacciato's proposed walk to Paris, suggests, "And who knows? He might make it. He might do all right. . . . Miserable odds, but–."

After the early critical reception to *Northern Lights* in 1975, many critics might have suggested there were also miserable odds against O'Brien's winning a National Book Award, at least so soon. With *Going After Cacciato* he demonstrated that this, too, could be done, that events of the imagination could produce miracles both inside and outside the text. In his review Freedman suggested that "to call *Going After Cacciato* a novel about war is like calling *Moby-Dick* a novel about whales." Freedman soon found a large regiment of critics and readers that would nod to that assertion, but the novel produced for O'Brien another artistic irony. By producing the first novel of the Vietnam War that critics were calling an instant American classic comparable to the best of Crane or Hemingway, O'Brien wedded himself more solidly than ever to the term *war writer*. Three books into his career, he was being called by more and more critics America's best war writer on America's worst war.

It would be seven years before O'Brien would offer his critics and readers a new novel, this time one set on the American home front of nuclear paranoia, radical politics, and revolutionary terrorism. *The Nuclear Age* (1985) is in many ways O'Brien's most culturally ambitious work—a sprawling, darkly funny historical saga of what it meant to grow up with the persistent threat of the atomic flash—to reach intellectual and emotional maturity during the life and death of the antiwar movement, to see America's collective nervous breakdown of the 1960s and 1970s give way to the uneasy ennui and exhaustion of the 1980s. Some similarities exist between *The Nuclear Age* and *Going After Cacciato* in the way O'Brien handles time and history. Again there is a frightened protagonist, William Cowling, who is digging a hole to protect his poetic flight-attendant wife, Bobbi, his precocious daughter, Melinda, and himself from what he feels is imminent nuclear apocalypse. Like Paul Berlin in the observation post, William looks backward from the present time of the novel, 1995 in Montana, through turbulent American history and through his own comic-tragic evolution. If the immediate threats of history are less imminent to William Cowling than to Paul Berlin, they are also larger, for the hero of *The Nuclear Age* trembles not just for himself and his immediate peers but for mankind. Fear for the squad has been replaced by the nightmare of species suicide. In Vietnam, Paul Berlin surveys the damage from the elevated perspective of the tower and his creative imagination; at the end of the millennium in a chaotic American free-fire zone, William Cowling can only burrow deep below ground and wait for the end.

"Am I crazy?" William Cowling asks on the first page of the novel, and the reader must compare

Dust jacket for O'Brien's 1994 novel, about a politician whose past wartime activities destroy his career and marriage

at all times contemporary historical hopes and fears to the "quality of obsession" that the hero personifies. O'Brien takes his protagonist from his boyhood fear of Soviet first strikes in 1958—the young William attempts to build a bomb shelter from lead pencils in the family basement—to his final moments of sanity/insanity as he contemplates destroying himself and his family in 1995 in order to save them. Between those two fearful, obsessive moments, O'Brien offers the reader his hero's travelogue through the 1960s and 1970s, a comic-symbolic trek that features his involvement with a group of campus radicals who move from mild civil disobedience to violent revolutionary action. If Paul Berlin makes a poor foot soldier in Vietnam, William Cowling is a sorry terrorist, a disaffected figure who cannot buy into deathly tactics on the home front any more than O'Brien's protagonists can in the jungles and villages of Vietnam.

O'Brien's treatment of the New Left in *The Nuclear Age* is satiric, and the characters are often deliberate caricatures. With a homemade sign that says

"THE BOMBS ARE REAL," Cowling becomes a one-student protest at Peverson State College–"Pevee State"–but he soon finds himself a member of "The Committee," a group of self-designated revolutionaries that includes a politicized former cheerleader, an activist linebacker, and an overweight young woman who combines leftist politics with the compulsive consumption of junk food. As the group drifts more and more toward irrevocable violence, William becomes less certain of his commitment, more fearful and alienated. The committee eventually is trained for destructive imperatives in Cuba and participates in bombings, thefts of military weapons, and, finally, the absurd procurement of Cowling's worst nightmare, a live nuclear warhead, the ultimate tool for true apocalyptic terrorism. As his peers move toward inevitable meltdown and personal Armageddon, Cowling burrows deeper into his psychic hole. When revolutionary civil disobedience–years of what he calls "Kentucky Fried Terror"–finally kills all of his friends from the 1960s and 1970s, Cowling retreats more deeply, making his wife and daughter prisoners of contemporary history, concluding of his age, "The world has been sanitized. Passion is a metaphor. All we can do is dig."

What becomes clear in the novel is O'Brien's own ambivalence to the leftist politics, the civil disobedience, and the cultural upheaval of America in the 1960s and 1970s. Looking backward, his protagonist asks, "What *happened?* Was it entropy? Genetic decay? Even the villains are gone. . . . And who among us would become a martyr, and for what?" He describes the period as a time of great energy, but energy of a kind that is more pyrotechnic than useful or constructive–lots of flash and dazzle, questionable substance. The radicals in the novel are brave, driven, dedicated to their own manic mission, but depicted as more tragic than heroic. Indeed, there is a decidedly entropic feel to the book as O'Brien's own uncertainty toward his characters and their politics plays itself out in increasingly doomed enterprises.

It is tempting perhaps to read William Cowling as an imaginative variant of O'Brien himself, the domestic alternative to the young foot soldier who did go to Vietnam. Would he have been a different type of warrior, one fighting to stop a war rather than serve it? O'Brien uses a line from William Butler Yeats recurrently in the book–*"We had fed the heart of fantasies, the heart's grown brutal from the fare."* Part of the enjoyment and the frustration of reading *The Nuclear Age* comes from the unresolved tensions that permeate the text, for O'Brien treats the social activism in the novel both satirically and respect-

fully. He both fears and admires the "quality of obsession" he creates and, to his credit, does walk a fine, dangerous, fragile line between love and death, between affirmation and apocalypse.

At the end of the novel O'Brien offers an important debate. If Sarkin Aung Wan and Paul Berlin in *Going After Cacciato* enter into important negotiations involving freedom and duty, the final exchange in *The Nuclear Age* is potentially more crucial, even terminal. At the climax the hole beckons to the hero, *"I am, in modesty, Neverness. I am the be-all and end-all. I am you, of course. I am your inside-out–your Ace in the Hole."* The voice of the end–the end of fear, the end of uncertainty, the end of anxiety–the hole offers peace as nothingness. Cowling, however, a twitch of the finger from his loved ones' and his own personal apocalypse, chooses death's opposite, with all of the ongoing dangers that that choice entails. Asserts Cowling finally, "I will hold to a steadfast orthodoxy, confident to the end that E will somehow not quite equal mc^2, that it's a cunning metaphor, that the terminal equation will somehow not quite balance." This is a mature and sane response to questions raised in all of his works, but the answer is also complex and demanding: to live with fear, one must posit hope; to counter the certainty of death, one must traffic in the absurd, terrible substance called love.

When *The Nuclear Age* appeared, critical reaction was harsh; as if by leaving the literal combat zone of Vietnam behind, O'Brien had cut himself off from the wellspring of his imaginative power. Many critics were not willing to grant him true creative vision in the wider historical field of fire he chose to inhabit. Reviewers praised certain aspects of the book, but many felt it failed as a whole, primarily because O'Brien was not writing about what he knew best. David Montrose, for instance, praised "the lean clarity of O'Brien's prose" in *The Times Literary Supplement* of 28 March 1986; he also created a bandwagon of complaints other critics would climb aboard–"The principal flaw is O'Brien's inability to create believable urban guerrillas: Cowling's antiwar brothers and sisters come across as tepid cartoons."

O'Brien, however, says that many aspects of the novel are deliberately "cartoonlike, wildly exaggerated" and that those anticipating or demanding traditional realism are missing both the essence and the more subtle features of the novel. He wrote the novel as "a funny, comedic work," but he also describes it as "a meticulously structured book–a patterned book in which the lines increase on a mathematical scale." He likens *The Nuclear Age* to some of the novels of Jim Harrison and Tom McGuane, writers whose tough prose conceals a fragility, "a sense of the collapse all around us." Despite the panning by several critics, O'Brien calls *The Nuclear Age* "my strongest book by far," adding wryly that his reaction is certainly "what Melville would say about *Pierre*."

O'Brien admits to taking secret pleasure in the hidden structure of his apocalyptic comedy, and he also is interested in seeing how *The Nuclear Age* will meet the test of time. While enduring the confusion and disappointment the novel produced, O'Brien was already journeying back to the Vietnam killing ground of *If I Die in a Combat Zone* and *Going After Cacciato*, the imaginative territory of his greatest literary successes. Throughout his career O'Brien has published many stories or excerpts from his fiction that have become chapters or parts of the larger works; many of the best pieces originally appeared in *Esquire*. In 1981 that magazine published "The Ghost Soldiers," a striking Vietnam tale of revenge and expiation that also garnered an O. Henry Award. Some of his most demanding, innovative, and critically praised stories appeared in the same magazine after the publication of *The Nuclear Age*: "The Things They Carried" in 1986, "How to Tell a True War Story" in 1987, "Sweetheart of the Song Tra Bong" and "The Lives of the Dead" in 1989. Although these individual tales were clearly some of O'Brien's finest short pieces, critics and readers were not fully prepared for what their effect would be in combination with other new stories. O'Brien was about to publish a work that would not only break new personal ground for him as a writer but also would test the ability of his critics to adhere to familiar generic distinctions.

In the chapter of *The Things They Carried* (1990) titled "Spin," a narrator and central character named Tim O'Brien, "forty-three years old, and a writer now," offers a key assessment of the value of the "real" Tim O'Brien's challenging new work, of all great literary art: "Stories are for joining the past to the future. . . . Stories are for eternity, when memory is erased, when there is nothing to remember except the story." Creating a version of himself that is both real and imaginary, offering a group of stories that seem to be simultaneously a novel, a story collection, a literary autobiography, a personal confession of transgression and forgiveness, and a meditation on the art of fiction, *The Things They Carried* would be perceived as the most innovative and challenging book he had written to date. All of his established subjects and themes are here: the search for a workable definition of courage; the need to transmute terrible memory into a livable present; the responsibility of the living to the dead to keep them

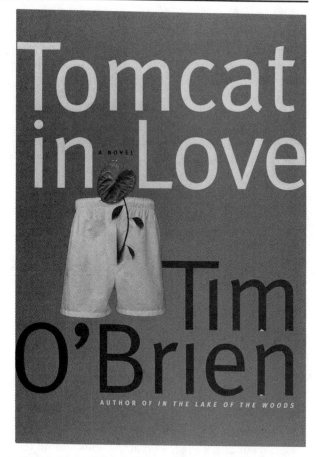

Dust jacket for O'Brien's 1998 tragicomedy, about a womanizing professor seeking revenge against his former wife

alive somehow; the wonderful, terrible nature of storytelling itself. Is the work a novel or a collection of stories? The answer would seem to be a simple—and ironic—yes. Characters appear and reappear in the different chapters, sometimes complementing, sometimes contradicting their own words and actions or those of other characters. Some of the stories are realistic and dramatic, some metafictional and philosophical, and all are spare, economical, ironic—live literary rounds that are both beautiful and brutal, terrible and true.

The most challenging feature of the book is the controlling narrator, the character named Tim O'Brien who both is and is not the "real" one. Many of Melville's commentators have noted how in *Moby-Dick*, Ishmael at times seems merely the author himself, ruminating over and glossing his own creations and his own pretensions. Likewise in *The Things They Carried*, there is not only a pronounced metafictional feel—the implicit argument for the utter interchangeability and fluidity of life and art—but also the perception by the reader that finally any attempt to separate the author from the narrator-hero is a fool's errand. The work is the most serious literary game O'Brien had yet played, and throughout the strangely connected and affiliated chapters, which are also discrete tales, he preserves a weighty contradiction: that it is possible to revel in the glories of sheer imagination—storytelling in its purest, most shameless form—while revealing the most terrible truths about human beings.

Many critics were not certain how to appraise the book. In the 11 March 1990 *The New York Times Book Review,* Robert R. Harris wrote, "This is a collection of interrelated stories. . . . The publisher calls the book 'a work of fiction,' but in no real sense can it be considered a novel. No matter. The stories cohere . . . he not only crystallizes the Vietnam experience for us, he exposes the nature of all war stories." Harris's arguments for coherence and universality do much to capture the unusual effects of *The Things They Carried,* for, in a radically different way from his earlier combat-zone narratives, the work depicts Vietnam as both "this war" and "any war"; O'Brien also achieves an organic unity among the tales that preserves their individual integrity while simultaneously displaying their interrelatedness. O'Brien confesses that the book is "all invented," that despite the presence of a version of himself as the narrative glue, the work is actually in the "form of the memoir as a way of telling a made-up story." The last comment suggests that the book should feel like *If I Die in a Combat Zone* at certain junctures, like *Going After Cacciato* at others. It does, but it also includes an affable quirkiness, a feeling that belies the often dark events within its pages and makes the work a new point of departure for O'Brien even at the moments it appears to be a return to old fictional landscapes.

In the 2 April 1990 *Newsweek* Peter Prescott said of the book, "Wars seldom produce good short stories, but two or three of these seem as good as any short stories written about war." Some readers would contend that that number should be enlarged. The first chapter bears the title of the book; it also bears the weight of the entire experience of the soldier in Vietnam, condensed and concentrated as a remarkable physical, emotional, and spiritual inventory. Some of what the men carry is visible, quantifiable, but the most important things are not. Creating one character who recurs in the early chapters, O'Brien writes, "As a first lieutenant and platoon leader, Jimmy Cross carried a compass, maps, code books, binoculars, and a .45-caliber pistol that weighed 2.9 pounds fully loaded. He carried a strobe light and the responsibility for the lives of his men." Because the psychological and spiritual inventories are offered matter-of-factly, without judgment, they gain significance and power. As O'Brien

summarizes, "They carried all they could bear, and then some, including a silent awe for the terrible power of the things they carried."

Many of the characters gain form and feature as they appear and reappear in several stories. The chief carrier of evil in the text, for example, is a soldier named Azar: in "Spin" he straps a mine to another soldier's puppy and blows it to pieces, exclaiming to his disgusted peers, "What's everybody so upset about? . . . I mean, Christ, I'm just a *boy.*" In "The Man I Killed" Azar examines the enemy soldier the fictional, traumatized Tim O'Brien has just killed and observes, "On the dead test, this particular individual gets A-plus." In "The Ghost Soldiers" Azar's brutality finally pushes the fictional Tim O'Brien and another soldier to contemplate killing him. As Azar gains definition and significance from story to story, so do evil, frustration, and loss.

Adjacent tales often do much more than enhance character. In "Speaking of Courage" Norman Bowker is the central figure in a painful coming-home story about the loss of a friend and O'Brien's prime theme, the failure to be courageous. In the next tale, "Notes," O'Brien creates a version of himself giving the history of the preceding story that is revealed as "a suggestion of Norman Bowker, who three years later hanged himself in the locker room of a YMCA in his hometown in central Iowa." The following story, "In the Field," however, complicates whatever conclusions the reader may have drawn, offering Bowker again at the scene of his friend's death, this time remarking of the loss, "Nobody's fault . . . Everybody's." Such accumulation of possibility is more than perverse gamesmanship on O'Brien's part, and in "How to Tell a True War Story," the key chapter in regard to his philosophy of storytelling, he argues strongly for a clear understanding of the difference between fact and truth. He states early in the chapter that "in any war story, but especially a true one, it's difficult to separate what happened from what seemed to happen"; he also contends that, for even the best of writers, a true war story sometimes "is just beyond telling." The effect of O'Brien's meditation is to bring the veracity of all of his stories into question at the very moment it makes such worries irrelevant. Is this puzzling, enchanting book finally memoir or fable? Again the answer is an emphatic yes. How can a reader know if a story is true? For O'Brien and his characters it comes down to a basic experience: "It comes down to gut instinct. A true war story, if truly told, makes the stomach believe." As storyteller, O'Brien in *The Things They Carried* discards once and for all concern with strict adherence to fact. As he has revealed in a 1991 interview in the *Missouri Re-*

view, "Ninety percent or more of the material is invented, and I invented ninety percent of a new Tim O'Brien, maybe even more than that." More than ever, he is telling lies to get to the truth.

The "new" O'Brien is a wonderful teller of tales. Some of the stories remain in the imagination like strange inscriptions of terrible import. In "Sweetheart of the Song Tra Bong" O'Brien offers the American "girl next door" as an updated version of Conrad's Kurtz. When a soldier brings his girlfriend to Vietnam, she becomes involved in special duties with the Green Berets but soon becomes too attuned to the call of the wild even for them. At the end of the story O'Brien describes her as having "crossed to the other side. She was part of the land. She was wearing her culottes, her pink sweater, and a necklace of human tongues. She was dangerous. She was ready for the kill." The frequent descent into pure evil, however, is met in *The Things They Carried* by equally powerful salvational gestures. In the final chapter, a story called "The Lives of the Dead," the fictional Tim O'Brien—or is it the real one?—asserts simply, "But this too is true: stories can save us." Contemplating lost friends, fictional and real, living and dead, O'Brien lets the reader know that the person truly saved in the leap of faith called storytelling is most often the teller. *The Things They Carried* is yet another group of war stories by yet another war writer. O'Brien transcends those categories to demonstrate once more that story is not an option but a need. As "The Lives of the Dead" and the book itself come to an end, the narrative loops back to its first word, to the beginning of the writer's own creative consciousness. Like a Vietnam version of Joyce's Stephen Dedalus, O'Brien concludes, "I'll never die. I'm skimming across the surface of my own history, moving fast, riding the melt beneath the blades, doing loops and spins, and when I take a high leap into the dark and come down thirty years later, I realize it is as Tim trying to save Timmy's life with a story."

If *The Things They Carried* proved O'Brien to be a stylistic risk taker and innovator with his own well-established themes, his next book revealed that he was becoming an even more daring and compelling magician of postmodern fictional strategies. *In the Lake of the Woods* (1994) is a remarkable novel for a writer who has already delivered so many surprises in his writing, for in the newest book O'Brien offers a depiction of human mystery, secret sin, and the dark, tragic effects of contemporary American history that again rubs away the artificial line between the literary and historical imagination but does so in new, unexpected ways.

One main character is again a Vietnam veteran, John Wade, who has been a rising Minnesota politician but whose senatorial campaign and personal life have been derailed by disclosures of his participation with Lt. William Calley and his men in the My Lai massacre. A practitioner of magic since boyhood who gives himself the nickname "Sorcerer" in Vietnam, Wade attempts to cover up his participation in the evil of the My Lai episode, but *In the Lake of the Woods,* while exploring a contemporary Conradian scenario in Vietnam, is most truly about men and women: love, marriage, and the terrible, inevitable secrets husbands and wives keep from each other. Within a fictional landscape teeming with real historical personage, event, and voice—O'Brien's strategies often remind one of John Dos Passos's daring blends and collages of art and history in the *U.S.A.* trilogy—is a daring postmodern detective novel, a larger, even universal, exploration of what, says O'Brien, "deceit can do to the human heart."

In the Lake of the Woods is a striking achievement for many reasons. Another protagonist in the novel is Wade's wife, Kathy, whose sudden, strange disappearance is the story line that bears the weight of O'Brien's significant psychological and spiritual meditations on the nature of love and the difficulty, even the impossibility, of truly knowing another human being. John and Kathy Wade are both American secret sharers, and O'Brien combines in a truly masterful way the specifically historical, the daringly creative, and the richly universal threads of his intricate web of epistemological inquiry and emotional exploration. O'Brien serves as narrator and commentator in a set of intriguing author's notes, an American version of Conrad's Marlow, as he responds to the male and female hearts of darkness of John and Kathy Wade. A reader hears in the novel odd, compelling echoes of other great writers and texts—from Nathaniel Hawthorne's obsession with secret sin to Thomas Pynchon's concerns with postmodern cabal, conspiracy, and the problem of reading in a darkened American cultural landscape—but O'Brien's own originality is never diminished. While participating in the search for the missing Kathy Wade and learning more about the hidden recesses of her tormented husband and her own buried secrets, the reader also rewalks the dead land of national ethical and moral imperatives that extends from My Lai through the 1990s and moves back in time to other violent impulses and dark moments in American history: the massacres of Native Americans at Sand Creek and Wounded Knee; the brutal, vengeful British military action at Lexington and Concord.

Within the highly charged energy field of fiction and historical elements comprising *In the Lake of the Woods* lies a story that remains compelling to all readers: the portrayal of well-intentioned hearts coming to terms with their own capacities for weakness, for deceit, for failure, and, sometimes, for real evil. In one of the important author's notes that gloss and complicate the motives of his protagonists, O'Brien makes the key revelation, a confession that speaks finally not just of *In the Lake of the Woods* but of his entire corpus of work: "What drives me on, I realize, is a craving to force entry into another heart, to trick the tumblers of natural law, to perform miracles of knowing. It's human nature. We are fascinated, all of us, by the implacable otherness of others." Despite *Time* magazine's selection of the work as the best American novel of 1994, O'Brien felt he had perhaps come to the end of something. In an interview he said, "I don't know if I'll ever do another novel. . . . With *In the Lake of the Woods,* I feel like I've completed the things I have to say about myself and the world I've lived in. And I've also completed a kind of search. I can't see anywhere else to go beyond where John Wade is . . . I'm just gonna head north. See what happens."

In reality O'Brien headed far east, back to Vietnam for the first time since the war and published a dark, powerful account in *The New York Times* of a period of artistic doubts and ruined relationships; he admits he considered at the time ending more than just his literary career. In the 1994 feature, O'Brien recounts both returning to the haunted villages of My Lai and losing the woman he loved, experiencing once again the prime, hard-earned lesson of his own characters, asserting that "intimacy with death carried with it a new intimacy with life." Passing through his own dark night of the soul, he confesses, "Last night suicide was on my mind. Not whether, but how. Tonight it will be on my mind again. Now it's 4 A.M., June the 5th. The sleeping pills have not worked. I sit in my underwear at the unblinking fool of a computer and try to wrap words around a few horrid truths."

From *If I Die in a Combat Zone* onward, O'Brien has always mixed comic and tragic modes in dazzling ways, but the writer emerged from his encounters of the mid 1990s with doubt and despair in Vietnam and America with perhaps his most unexpected work to date. The "unblinking fool" of *Tomcat in Love* (1998) is one Thomas H. Chippering, professor of linguistics at the University of Minnesota, a six-foot, six-inch womanizing, self-absorbed literary hero who suffers from post-traumatic stress and doubt on physical, emotional, and spiritual battlefields. Both endearing and reprehensible, romanti-

cally determined and existentially spent, Chippering draws the reader into a truly jarring postmodern tragicomedy, one fraught with both sexual vengeance and narrative peril and energized by some of O'Brien's most daring combinations of romantic and contemplative gestures and strategies. The book includes paradoxically some of O'Brien's funniest and saddest prose, enfolding complex truths of love and loss, transgression and expiation, dark delusion and salvational epiphany.

Audacious in plot, tone, characterization, and metafictional feature, *Tomcat in Love* offers a first-person narrator who tells his tale to an imagined female reader, one whose lover has made of her the same cuckolded victim Chippering imagines himself to be. The hero's Vietnam experience is a meaningful back-story of both comically absurd and frighteningly real dimensions, but Chippering's most important missions occur not during the war but after. They are not political-military operations but romantic-sexual sorties of the most disturbing kind; they take place not in the Mekong Delta or the Batangan Peninsula but in the alienating American placidity of Tampa, Florida, and the snowbound midwestern monotony of Owago, Minnesota, a fictional variant of O'Brien's hometown of Worthington on which the author unleashes his satirical big guns. Again and again in his stories and novels, O'Brien has dramatized that the pursuit of real and imagined enemies invariably takes human beings into the deepest recesses of their own hearts and souls, and that their capacities for malice and retribution, for love and peace, are equally prodigious and absurdly dependent. The enemies of the hero in *Tomcat in Love* are neither the Viet Cong nor the North Vietnamese army but rather Chippering's unfaithful wife, Lorna Sue, her new Tampa tycoon husband, and her obsessively protective brother. The historical sweep of the novel is 1952 to the present, Vietnam and the United States, but the true emotional and intellectual topography of the book is within Chippering's shattered psyche as he attempts to wreak vengeance in Florida and Minnesota, a frighteningly funny operation that takes him to the brink of his own destruction.

Is Thomas Chippering, O'Brien's reconstituted hero in *Tomcat in Love,* a figure who engenders gentle sympathy, grudging understanding, or passionate castigation by readers, male and female? He seeks and revels within flirtation and dalliance—some real, much imagined—at every turn; indeed, he constantly requires female admiration like a terminally ill patient needs an intravenous drug. Chippering is the central aesthetic risk in a novel rife with such gambles; critic John Mort notes that

-3-

"Very nice," said the dealer, who was twenty-two or

twenty-three, slim-hipped, with braided black hair and black

eyes and brown skin. She chopped down the cards and

shuffled, chatting with Amy about weddings and honeymoons.

"I get married in October," the girl said, "except I'm

stuck in this two-bit shit hole. No ~~lie~~ joke, with my luck I'll end up --no joke--

honeymooning in my fiance's ~~trailer~~ Winnebago." She laughed snorted. "As if

I don't already know every square inch."

The dealer's ~~cheap~~ engagement ring ~~twinkled~~ glittered like looked cheap and gaudy against the

green felt. Amy tipped her twenty-five dollars.

"what about you?" "~~Big~~ So you had yourself a wedding?" the girl said. "Big wedding?"

"Pretty big," ~~Amy~~ Amy said.

"What was ~~your~~ the music?" . I'll bet it was.

"Music?"   Lucky sh'ts

"At the wedding."   ~~WASPS~~ like you, no
                                               ~~offense but~~ i'll bet
"Oh, that. ~~Who knows~~ Rogers and Hammerstein. Who knows?" Amy cut the cards.   it was one huge,
                                               gorgeous-ass wedding.
"You should walk," said the dealer, "while the   The dealer square the
                                               cards. and held the
walking's profitable."   out ~~for~~. ..you wore white-"
                                               "Blue," said Amy. white
"Six thousand again," said Bobby.

"She might be right," said Amy.

"She might be."

They were dealt a six and a ten. Amy stayed; the

pretty young dealer broke on a fifteen.   (Stet)

"Just my rotten pissy luck," the girl ~~said~~ muttered.

Amy tipped her fifty dollars. A crowd had gathered,

Page from a draft for O'Brien's short story "The Streak" (Collection of Tim O'Brien)

"Tom's a bedlam, and, like Portnoy, ends up in the care of a psychiatrist. He's the classic lying narrator, a likable sociopath." Chippering also fosters echoes of other protagonists: Joseph Heller's war-doomed, lovestruck Yossarian; Henry Fielding's bawdy picaresque hero, Tom Jones; and Nabokov's word-drenched, womanizing Humbert Humbert. The final chapters of the novel, however, offer shattering, necessary illuminations to both Chippering and the reader; as Mort contends, "his story is simple: love is hard to find, hardest of all when you desperately need to find it."

Such complex simplicity has always been the author's game. What does O'Brien say of a novel that is perhaps his most different, surprising exploration of the human heart in conflict with itself? To describe his latest creation, he looks all the way back to *If I Die in a Combat Zone:* "Though I am known as a 'Vietnam writer'–whatever that may be–I have always pegged myself more as a 'love writer,' and in that regard *Tomcat in Love* is no departure at all. I am still circling, after nearly thirty years, the same old obsession: how far we go to win love, to keep love, to love ourselves." If the novel is truly an artistic advance by O'Brien, that movement surely lies in how the comic audacity of the novel coexists preposterously with its tender truths, its self-absorbed obsessions, its courageous confessions. A hilarious, disgruntled, confused reply by its hero to postmodern, empowered American womanhood, a serious meditation on the shattering effect of lost love and the redemptory power of newfound love, *Tomcat in Love* takes precarious narrative high ground. Late in the novel, Thomas Chippering says to the reader, "Each of us, I suppose, needs his illusions. Life after death. A maker of planets. A woman to love, a man to hate. Something sacred." O'Brien understands the suicide mission of attempting to understand fully true love, but, exploring ever more deeply its four corners of mind, body, soul, and heart, he also testifies that he will have no commerce with narrative cowardice, make no false truce with emotional reality.

It has been a long, storied journey already for O'Brien: from the nine-year-old who wrote "Timmy of the Little League" to the mature, contemplative, innovative Tim O'Brien of *Tomcat in Love.* Readers and critics will wait eagerly to see what the war writer will create next, what new "miracles of knowing" he will achieve in his fictions. Living and working today in Cambridge, Massachusetts, he continues to play the role of the transplanted Midwesterner, living a full-time writer's life that he feels to most people would appear "extremely boring." His work habits are disciplined and his outside diver-

sions few and simple. He works from early morning to dinnertime, including weekends and holidays; his hobbies include golf and reading at night. Asked why he keeps his existence so basic and streamlined, he says, sounding like one of his own heroes, "the life of the imagination is enough."

What may lie ahead for Tim O'Brien? Many readers will hope that he will continue the artistic journey he began more than two decades ago: that he will offer his readers future stories and novels, "true or untrue," that will energize memory and imagination, conscience and fancy. O'Brien certainly knows the personal value of the well-told tale–"Good stories can be true or untrue," he said in 1992. "It doesn't really matter too much, provided that the story does to the spirit what stories should do, which is to entertain, but entertain in the highest way, entertain your brain and your stomach, and your heart, and your erotic zones, and make you laugh." One thing is certain: whatever he writes in the future will be aimed at both head and heart, at both body and soul. Surely readers and critics will hope that a certain paradox will remain strangely valid–that his truth-filled lies will continue to make the stomach believe.

Interviews:
Larry McCaffery, "Interview with Tim O'Brien," *Chicago Review,* 33 (1982): 129–149;

Thomas LeClair and McCaffery, *Anything Can Happen: Interviews with Contemporary American Novelists* (Urbana: University of Illinois Press, 1983), pp. 262–278;

Eric James Schroeder, "Two Interviews: Talks with Tim O'Brien and Robert Stone," *Modern Fiction Studies,* 30 (Spring 1984): 135–164;

Martin Naparsteck, "An Interview with Tim O'Brien," *Contemporary Literature,* 32 (Spring 1991): i–ii;

Steven Kaplan, "An Interview with Tim O'Brien," *Missouri Review,* 14 (1991): 93–108;

"*Artful Dodge* Interviews Tim O'Brien," *Artful Dodge,* 22–23 (1992): 74–90;

John Mort, "The *Booklist* Interview: Tim O'Brien," *Booklist,* 90 (August 1994): 1990–1991.

Bibliography:
Catherine Calloway, "Tim O'Brien (1946–): A Primary and Secondary Checklist," *Bulletin of Bibliography,* 50 (September 1993): 223–229.

References:
Milton J. Bates, "Tim O'Brien's Myth of Courage," *Modern Fiction Studies,* 33 (Summer 1987): 263–279;

Philip D. Beidler, *American Literature and the Experience of Vietnam* (Athens: University of Georgia Press, 1982);

Beidler, *Re-Writing America: Vietnam Authors in Their Generation* (Athens: University of Georgia Press, 1991);

Maria S. Bonn, "Can Stories Save Us?: Tim O'Brien and the Efficacy of the Text," *Critique,* 36 (Fall 1994): 2–15;

Bonn, "A Different World: The Vietnam Veteran Novel Comes Home," in *Fourteen Landing Zones: Approaches to Vietnam War Literature,* edited by Philip K. Jason (Iowa City: University of Iowa Press, 1992), pp. 1–14;

Thomas G. Bowie Jr., "Reconciling Vietnam: Tim O'Brien's Narrative Journey," in *The United States and Vietnam from War to Peace,* edited by Richard M. Slabey (Jefferson, N.C.: McFarland, 1996), pp. 184–197;

Catherine Calloway, "'How to Tell a True War Story': Metafiction in *The Things They Carried,*" *Critique,* 36 (Summer 1995): 249–257;

Calloway, "Pluralities of Vision: *Going After Cacciato* and Tim O'Brien's Short Fiction," in *America Rediscovered: Critical Essays on Literature and Film of the Vietnam War,* edited by Owen W. Gilman Jr. and Lorrie Smith (New York: Garland, 1990), pp. 213–224;

G. Thomas Couser, "*Going After Cacciato:* The Romance and the Real War," *Journal of Narrative Technique,* 13 (Winter 1983): 1–10;

Toby Herzog, "*Going After Cacciato:* The Soldier-Author-Character Seeking Control," *Critique,* 24 (Winter 1983): 88–96;

Dale W. Jones, "The Vietnam of Michael Herr and Tim O'Brien: Tales of Disintegration and Integration," *Canadian Review of American Studies,* 13 (Winter 1982): 309–320;

Steven Kaplan, *Understanding Tim O'Brien* (Columbia: University of South Carolina Press, 1995);

Kaplan, "The Undying Uncertainty of the Narrator in Tim O'Brien's *The Things They Carried,*" *Critique,* 35 (Fall 1993): 43–52;

Katherine Kinney, "American Exceptionalism and Empire in Tim O'Brien's *Going After Cacciato,*" *American Literary History,* 7 (Winter 1995): 633–653;

Don Lee, "About Tim O'Brien," *Ploughshares,* 21 (Winter 1995–1996): 196–202;

John G. Leland, "Writing About Vietnam," *College English,* 43 (November 1981): 739–740;

Timothy J. Lomperis, *"Reading the Wind": The Literature of the Vietnam War* (Durham, N.C.: Duke University Press, 1987);

Gene Lyons, "Pieces of a Vietnam War Story," *Nation,* 224 (29 January 1977): 120–122;

Dean McWilliams, "Time in Tim O'Brien's *Going After Cacciato,*" *Critique,* 29 (Summer 1988): 245–255;

Thomas Myers, *Walking Point: American Narratives of Vietnam* (New York: Oxford University Press, 1988);

Edward F. Palm, "Falling In and Out: Military Idiom as Metaphoric Motif in *Going After Cacciato,*" *Notes on Contemporary Literature,* 22 (November 1992): 8;

Michael W. Raymond, "Imagined Responses to Vietnam: Tim O'Brien's *Going After Cacciato,*" *Critique,* 24 (Winter 1983): 97–104;

Arthur M. Saltzman, "The Betrayal of the Imagination: Paul Brodeur's *The Stunt Man* and Tim O'Brien's *Going After Cacciato,*" *Critique,* 22, no. 1 (1980): 32–38;

Eric James Schroeder, "The Past and the Possible: Tim O'Brien's Dialectic of Memory and Imagination," in *Search and Clear: Critical Responses to Selected Literature and Films of the Vietnam War,* edited by William J. Searle (Bowling Green, Ohio: Bowling Green State University Press, 1988), pp. 116–134;

Robert M. Slabey, "*Going After Cacciato:* Tim O'Brien's 'Separate Peace,'" in *America Rediscovered: Critical Essays on Literature and Film of the Vietnam War* (New York: Garland, 1990), pp. 205–212;

Lorrie N. Smith, "'The Things Men Do': The Gendered Subtext in Tim O'Brien's *Esquire* Stories," *Critique,* 36 (Fall 1994): 16–40;

Gregory Stephenson, "Struggle and Flight: Tim O'Brien's *Going After Cacciato,*" *Notes on Contemporary Literature,* 14 (September 1984): 5–6;

Mark Taylor, "Tim O'Brien's War," *Centennial Review,* 39 (Spring 1995): 213–230;

"Tim O'Brien," *Current Biography,* 56 (August 1995): 52–55;

Dennis Vannatta, "Theme and Structure in Tim O'Brien's *Going After Cacciato,*" *Modern Fiction Studies,* 28 (Summer 1982): 242–246;

Bruce Weber, "A Novelist Wrestles with Love and War," *New York Times,* 2 September 1998, B1+;

Albert E. Wilhelm, "Ballad Allusions in 'Where Have You Gone, Charming Billy?,'" *Studies in Short Fiction,* 28 (Spring 1991): 218–222;

Daniel L. Zins, "Imagining the Real: The Fiction of Tim O'Brien," *Hollins Critic,* 23 (June 1986): 1–12.

Tillie Olsen

This entry was updated by Agnes Toloczko Cardoni (King's College, Wilkes-Barre)
from the entries by Marleen Barr (Virginia Polytechnic Institute and State University)
in DLB 28: Twentieth-Century American-Jewish Fiction Writers, and by
Carolyn and Ernest Rhodes (Old Dominion University) in DLB Yearbook 1980.

BIRTH: Omaha, Nebraska, 14 January 1913?, to Samuel and Ida Beber Lerner.

EDUCATION: Stanford University creative writing fellowship, 1956-1957.

MARRIAGE: 1936 to Jack Olsen; children: Karla Olsen Lutz, Julie Olsen Edwards, Katherine Jo, Laurie.

AWARDS AND HONORS: Ford Foundation grant in literature, 1959; O. Henry Award for best American short story for "Tell Me a Riddle," 1961; fellowship, Radcliffe Institute for Independent Study, 1962-1964; National Endowment for the Arts grant, 1968; Guggenheim Fellowship, 1975-1976; award in literature, American Academy and National Institute of Arts and Letters, 1975; Ministry to Women Award, Unitarian Women's Federation, 1980; British Post Office and B. P. W. award, 1980; Tillie Olsen Day designated in San Francisco, 1981; Bunting Institute fellowship, Radcliffe College, 1985; Rea Award, 1994; honorary degrees include Doctor of Arts and Letters, University of Nebraska, 1979, and Hobart and William Smith College, 1984; L.H.D., Clark University, 1985; Litt.D., Knox College, 1982, Albright College, 1986, Wooster College, 1991, Mills College, 1995, and Amherst College, 1998.

Tillie Olsen

BOOKS: *Tell Me a Riddle* (Philadelphia: Lippincott, 1961; London: Faber & Faber, 1964);
Yonnondio: From the Thirties (New York: Delacorte, 1974; London: Faber, 1974);
Silences (New York: Delacorte/Seymour Lawrence, 1978; London: Faber, 1978).

OTHER: "A Biographical Interpretation," in *Life in the Iron Mills; or, The Korl Woman,* by Rebecca Harding Davis (Old Westbury, N.Y.: Feminist Press, 1972); book revised and expanded as *Life in the Iron Mills, and Other Stories,* by Davis, edited by Olsen (Old Westbury, N.Y: Feminist Press, 1985);
Mother to Daughter, Daughter to Mother, Mothers on Mothering: A Daybook and Reader, edited by Olsen (Old Westbury, N.Y: Feminist Press, 1984)—includes "Dream Vision," by Olsen, pp. 261-264;
Claudia Tate, ed., *Black Women Writers at Work,* foreward by Olsen (New York: Continuum, 1986);
Edith Konecky, *Allegra Maud Goldman,* introduction by Olsen (New York: Feminist Press, 1987);

"Mother and Daughters," by Olsen and Julie Olsen Edwards, in *Mothers and Daughters: That Special Quality: An Exploration in Photographs,* by Edwards and Estelle Jussim (New York: Aperture, 1987);

"Personal Statement," in *First Drafts, Last Drafts: Forty Years of the Creative Writing Program at Stanford University,* edited by William McPheron and Armor Towles (Stanford, Cal.: Stanford University Libraries, 1989);

"Not You I Weep For," in *First Words: Earliest Writings From Favorite Contemporary Authors,* edited by Paul Mandelbaum (Chapel Hill, N.C.: Algonquin Books, 1993);

Alexander Saxton, *Bright Web in the Darkness,* afterword by Olsen (Berkeley: University of California Press, 1997).

SELECTED PERIODICAL PUBLICATIONS–

UNCOLLECTED: "I Want You Women Up North to Know," *Partisan,* 1 (March 1934): 4;

"There is a Lesson," *Partisan,* 1 (April–May 1934): 4;

"Thousand-Dollar Vagrant," *New Republic,* 80 (August 1934): 67–69;

"The Strike," *Partisan Review,* 1 (September–October 1934): 3–9;

"Requa," *Iowa Review,* 1 (Summer 1970): 54–74;

"The Thirties: A Vision of Fear and Hope," *Newsweek* (3 January 1994): 26–27.

Tillie Olsen is a feminist and working-class author who began writing in the 1930s. Robert Coles commented in *The Nation,* "Everything Tillie Olsen has written has become almost immediately a classic." Though she is most famous for her short-story collection *Tell Me a Riddle* (1961), Olsen is also recognized as a teacher and an activist. She has taught or been writer in residence at several universities, including Amherst College, Stanford University, M.I.T., and Kenyon College. She has been the recipient of several honorary degrees as well as many other awards. On 1 March 1998 she was honored at Cabrillo College, Aptos, California, for her short stories and essays depicting the lives of working-class people with "respect, profound understanding and deep love."

In addition to her attention to working-class people, Olsen explores the literary tragedy of silenced writers, creative spirits killed by such potent poisons as class and gender. She reminds readers that, because they had to work and serve as the "essential angels" of their household, some of William Shakespeare's sisters failed to write. As she explains in *Silences* (1978), Olsen's own responsibilities came close to thwarting her artistic pursuits: "As for myself, who did not publish a book until I was fifty, who raised children without household help . . . who worked outside the house on everyday jobs as well . . . who could not kill the essential angel (there was no one else to do her work) . . . [I was] as distant from the world of literature most of my life as literature is distant (in content too) from my world." There is a mirroring, reciprocal relationship between the facts of Olsen's life and the major concerns of her work. Her fiction bridges the distance between her own world and the world of literature. Her personal remarks in a talk at Radcliffe in 1963 (later included in *Silences*) describe instances when words die, the tragedy of a writer who is often silenced:

> The habits of a lifetime when everything else had to come before writing are not easily broken, even when circumstances now often make it possible for writing to be first; habits of years–response to others, distractibility, responsibility for daily matters–stay with you, mark you, become you. The cost of "discontinuity" . . . is such a weight of things unsaid, an accumulation of material so great, that everything starts up something else in me; what should take weeks takes me sometimes months to write; what should take months, takes years.
>
> I speak of myself to bring here the sense of those others to whom this is in the process of happening (unnecessarily happening, for it need not, must not continue to be) and to remind us of those (I so nearly was one) who never come to writing at all.

So close herself to being unable to write, Olsen speaks for those who do not have the wherewithal to produce art and for those whose art has not received the attention it deserves. She has articulated the suffering of humanity; participated in the public political sphere; reclaimed women's "lost" texts; examined the relationship between creativity, sex, and class; and successfully combated silence. Although Olsen's output is small, her work is important because it gives a voice to people who are routinely not heard. Her characters speak with the authentic cadences of ordinary people. Here, for example, is the voice of Whitey in "Hey Sailor, What Ship?" (first published in *New Campus Writing,* 1957): "Wha's it so quiet for? Hey, hit the tune box. . . . Wha time's it anyway? Gotta. . . . "

Tillie Lerner Olsen was born on 14 January 1912 or 1913, the second of Samuel and Ida Lerner's seven children. The Lerners were Jewish immigrants who had fled Russia after the 1905 rebellion. While Olsen was growing up, she lived in an environment where economic pressure was juxtaposed with political commitment: Samuel Lerner, who labored as a farmer, packinghouse worker,

Page from Olsen's notebook for her 1961 story collection, Tell Me a Riddle. *The size of the original page is approximately three inches by five inches (Collection of Tillie Olsen).*

painter, and paper hanger, also became state secretary of the Nebraska Socialist Party. Like her father, Olsen of necessity held many jobs, but these did not stop her from being politically active. After the need for employment forced her to leave high school before graduating, she worked as a trimmer in a slaughterhouse, a power-press operator, a hash slinger, a mayonnaise-jar capper in a food processing plant, and a checker in a warehouse. Olsen carried on the family tradition of trying to better people's lives by joining the Young Communist League when she was eighteen. She was arrested in Kansas City for trying to organize packinghouse workers. While in jail, where she did not have adequate medical care, she became ill with pleurisy, which almost developed into tuberculosis. By 1933 Olsen had moved from the Midwest to California; San Fran-

cisco became her permanent home. She continued her political activities as a participant in the San Francisco Longshoremen's Strike of 1934. She worked in support of the union and, once again, spent time in jail. In 1936 she married Jack Olsen, a printer and union man. She had four daughters and worked to support them by holding such jobs as waitress, shaker in a laundry, secretary, transcriber in a dairy-equipment company, and Kelly Girl.

Olsen had also begun to write during those years. A short story, "The Iron Throat" (which later became part of her 1974 novel, *Yonnondio: From the Thirties*), and an article, "The Strike," had appeared in the *Partisan Review* in 1934, and the *New Republic* published her autobiographical essay, "Thousand-Dollar Vagrant," the same year. But the demands of work and family meant that her literary aspirations were put on hold for more than two decades.

When she won a Stanford University creative writing fellowship for eight months in 1956–1957, just a year after enrolling in a San Francisco State University creative writing course, Olsen was given the economic freedom that enabled her to create Whitey and other characters. Instead of having to work outside her home, Olsen wrote "I Stand Here Ironing," "Baptism" (published as "O Yes" in *Tell Me a Riddle*), and "Hey Sailor, What Ship?"; she also began "Tell Me a Riddle." In 1957 she had to return to regular employment, putting her writing on hold again until 1959, when a Ford Foundation grant enabled her to complete "Tell Me a Riddle" and to have it published in the collection that bears its name. "Tell Me a Riddle" won the O. Henry Award for the best short story of 1961.

David and Eva, the protagonists of "Tell Me a Riddle," are a Jewish immigrant couple who have struggled to survive—and struggled with each other—throughout their forty-seven-year marriage. Although both of them worked hard, the story stresses that Eva's lot is worse than that of her husband. While David at least found pleasure in the company of friends at his lodge, Eva did not have access to the company of the authors she enjoyed: "She thought . . . of that young wife, who in the deep night hours while she nursed the current baby, and perhaps held another in her lap, would try to stay awake for the only time there was to read. She would feel again the weather on the outside of his cheek when, coming late from a meeting, he would find her so, and stimulated and ardent, sniffing her skin, coax: 'put the book away, don't read, don't read.'"

Eva has found life difficult in America. Busy by day with children and household chores, she has had time for little else. David is incapable of understanding her need for silence and order in their own home once the children are grown and gone. After Eva falls ill, David takes her on a round of family visits to see the children and grandchildren. There are "grandboys" who "do not know what to say" when David and Eva visit. There is also a newborn grandchild whom Eva refuses to cuddle: "A new baby. How many warm, seductive babies. She holds him stiffly, *away* from her, so that he wails. A long shudder begins, and the sweat beads on his forehead."

When Eva can no longer travel, some of the children come to her. Clara, the eldest, and Lenny both harbor unvoiced bitterness toward their mother, whom they think of as remote and emotionally unavailable. Later, when "Hannah's Phil" gives

the diagnosis, "cancer everywhere," David follows Phil's advice and takes Eva to the ocean near San Francisco.

Here granddaughter Jeannie nurses Eva through her terminal illness. She brings comfort to her grandmother, spending time listening to Eva's ramblings about her days in Russia during the Revolution or about books she has read, filling the room with words: "she who in her life had spoken but seldom and then only when necessary . . . now in dying spoke incessantly." Jeannie shares a visit from a Samoan friend and tells stories of Mexican families she had served as a visiting nurse; she tends to Eva's bodily and emotional needs. She even teaches David how to accept the role he is assigned: to witness Eva's struggle and to listen as she recites from books, as she sings songs from the old country, and as she makes no mention of him or their children.

Toward the end of Eva's life, Jeannie sketches her grandmother on the hospital bed, depicting her grandfather alongside on the double bed, "and their hands, his and hers, clasped, feeding each other. And as if he had been instructed he went to his bed, lay down, holding the sketch . . . and with his free hand took hers back into his." On Eva's last day Jeannie comforts David: "Grandaddy, Grandaddy, don't cry. She is not there. On the last day, she said she would go back to when she first heard music . . . Leave her there, Grandaddy . . . Come back and help her poor body to die." Life and death have been hard for Eva, but Jeannie has helped her attain some final measure of dignity, in both spirit and body.

"I Stand Here Ironing," the first story in *Tell Me a Riddle,* begins with the voice of a mother: "I stand here ironing, and what you asked me moves tormented back and forth with the iron." This sentence typifies Olsen's fiction: a mother/worker, an ordinary person, is given an opportunity to speak, is invited to tell her story. This particular mother, like many mothers, is concerned that she did not raise her daughter properly. The necessity of earning a living prevented her from spending sufficient time with her child, Emily: "Her father left me before she was a year old. I had to work her first six years when there was work, or I sent her home and to his relatives. There were years when she had care she hated." Lack of money kept Emily's "child cry"— "That time of motherhood . . . when the ear is not one's own but must always be racked and listened for the child cry, the child call"—from reaching the attentive ear of her mother.

The story focuses upon the waste of artistic, as well as maternal, creativity. Emily, who is not pretty, not popular, and not studious, does excel in

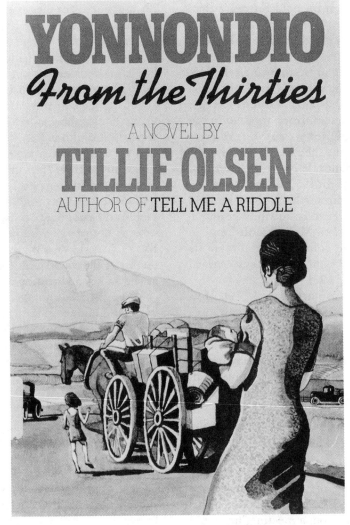

Dust jacket for Olsen's 1974 novel, which depicts the harsh living conditions of the working class

one area: audiences respond to her enthusiastically when she performs as a clown. Yet because there is not enough money, her talent becomes "eddied inside, clogged and clotted": "You ought to do something about her with a gift like that—but without money, or knowing how, what does one do?"

The mother wishes her daughter to know that even though a lack of money has hampered Emily's personal and creative development, "there is still enough left to live by." Emily is an individual, "more than this dress on the ironing board, helpless before the iron"; she is more than a member of a certain economic class who can be helplessly molded and shaped by her social position. Even though Emily, like Olsen, receives neither her mother's full attention nor the funds to pursue her talent, she (again like Olsen) can escape from being completely controlled by her disadvantages.

"Hey Sailor, What Ship?" the story that follows "I Stand Here Ironing" in *Tell Me a Riddle,* also discusses the waste of human potential. Whitey, the protagonist, is a sailor who has never developed close familial relationships. The family of his friend Lennie, whose life he once saved, provides "the only house in the world he can come into and be around people without having to pay." Yet because Whitey is different, because a sailor's language is not appropriately spoken in a respectable home, he pays the price of exclusion. Jeannie, the daughter of this family (who also appears in "Tell Me a Riddle" and in "O Yes"), articulates her concern: "I've got some friends coming over. . . . Whitey, please, they're not used to your kind of language." Whitey is thus another of Olsen's characters who is silenced because of his social position. The sailor who carries a card that reads "When in Managua it's Marie's for

304

Hospitality" does not find hospitality in his friend's home.

Instead Whitey will have to pay for all the hospitality he receives. Money cannot buy him a place in Lennie's family or permanent rights to feel a child's warmth: "this helpless warmth against him, this feel of a child—lost country to him and unattainable." Although he has the money to buy women and to buy gifts for Lennie's family, he does not have access to the love of a woman and to the gift of familial love. He is aware that his relationships are empty: "Shove it, Lennie. So you're a chunk of my life. So?" When he leaves Lennie's house and looks down at similar houses in San Francisco, he knows that he will be forever barred from the relationships that are lived out in those buildings: "he can see the city below him, wave after wave, and there at the crest, the tiny house he has left, its eyes unshaded." Lennie and his wife, Helen, have asked repeatedly, "What's going to happen to you, Whitey?" As Elaine Neil Orr suggests, "Whitey is clearly descending to the depths," where there is little hope for him. The story leaves the reader to supply the answer to Lennie and Helen's question.

"O Yes," the third story in Tell Me a Riddle, also focuses upon a terminated relationship, exploring why the friendship between Carol, a white girl, and Parialee, a black girl, is destroyed by economic and social pressures. Young Carol enters the black world and hears the words that give the story its title: "Any day now I'll reach that land of freedom, Yes, O Yes." When Carol questions the intensity of these words, her mother thinks, "emotion . . . a characteristic of the religion of all oppressed peoples." The girls' friendship is strained as society encourages them to assume the roles of the oppressed and the oppressor. Blacks and whites inhabit separate worlds; the differences in their environments are illustrated by the fact that Carol faints while she is in the black church.

The girls are exposed to different social expectations. Parialee is immersed in black life, "collecting" experiences "Like her own crowd. Like jivetalk and rhythmandblues. Like teachers who treat her like a dummy and white kids who treat her like dirt." Carol learns "how they sort," the appropriate mode of dress and behavior for a proper white girl. The economic and social reasons for the rift between them cannot be separated. While Carol enjoys herself after school, Parialee must return home to compensate for the absence of her working mother, Alva: "Carol is off to a club or skating or library or someone's house, and Parry can stay for kickball only on rare afternoons when she does not

have to hurry home where Lucy, Bubbie, and the cousins wait to be cared for, now that Alva works the four to twelve thirty shift." It is clear that the girls' friendship is wrenched apart because "Parry's colored and Carrie's white." Here, again, Olsen describes how economic need and the demands of a large family stifle an individual's personal development.

The story ends with a note of hope, however. Upon discovering the existence of evil, instead of complacently accepting this knowledge Carol questions her mother: "Oh why is it like it is and why do I have to care?" Like the mother in "I Stand Here Ironing," Carol's mother remains silent. Only the reader hears her thoughts: "Caring asks doing. It is a long baptism into the seas of humankind, my daughter. Better immersion than to live untouched." Despite the challenges of race and class, the rewards of human connection and relationship outweigh the pains of immersion.

After the publication of Tell Me a Riddle, Olsen received fellowships from the Radcliffe Institute (1962-1964) and the National Endowment for the Arts (1968). Between 1969 and 1972 she taught at three universities: Amherst, the University of Massachusetts (Boston), and Stanford. While she was writer in residence at M.I.T. (1973), she received a grant from the MacDowell Colony. Olsen then returned to the University of Massachusetts (1973-1974) as a distinguished visiting professor.

The support of the MacDowell Colony allowed her to publish the novel Yonnondio, which she had begun working on when she was nineteen but which she had to set aside to make a living. "A Note About This Book" explains that the novel has "ceased to be solely the work of that long ago young writer and, in arduous partnership, became the older one's as well." Hence Yonnondio, which derives its title and epigraph from Walt Whitman's "Yonnondio"—a lament for the Native American tribe whose "wailing word is borne through the air for a moment, / Then blank and gone and still, and utterly lost"—is a once-silenced text that has been reclaimed.

Yonnondio, which endeavors to keep the word of the American working class from being utterly lost, resembles the work of another nearly silenced writer: Rebecca Harding Davis, whose writing was rediscovered by Olsen. Davis, the author of Life in the Iron Mills (Atlantic Monthly, 1861), a text that also speaks for the working class, has been Olsen's model since she was a teenager. Olsen suggested that the Feminist Press republish Life in the Iron Mills, and she wrote the introduction to the 1972 edition for that press, later editing an expanded 1985 edition. (In 1973 the Feminist Press also republished Agnes Smedley's *Daughter of Earth* [1929] and Charlotte Perkins Gilman's *The Yellow Wallpaper* [1899] at Olsen's suggestion.) Both *Life in the Iron Mills* and *Yonnondio* are, in Olsen's words, "fiction which incorporates social and economic problems directly, *and in terms of their effects upon human beings,*" books that prove "Literature can be made out of the lives of despised people." Hence, *Yonnondio,* like *Tell Me a Riddle,* directly addresses the problems of these "despised people": large families, temporary residences, lack of educational opportunities, lack of resources to nurture creativity.

In *Yonnondio* the descriptions of the working person's lot are more graphic than those found in *Tell Me a Riddle.* One example is an accident involving some meat-packing industry workers who are in the path of emissions from a broken steam pipe: "Peg and Andra and Phelomena and Cleola directly underneath fall and writhe in their crinkling skins, their sudden juices. Lena, pregnant, faints. . . . Ella, already at the work of calming, of rescue, thinks through her own pain: steamed boiled broiled cooked *scalded.*" These "ordinary" victims with romantic-sounding names are not at the center of this novel, however; its focus is quite difficult to pinpoint. The text is at once a call for political action, the story of the Holbrook family's futile life, the story of young Mazie Holbrook's development, and a statement about the suffering of the working class.

These elements coalesce when *Yonnondio* is viewed as more than a working-class novel; it is a feminist working-class novel. The scalded workers are all women; Mazie is the only young Holbrook who emerges as a distinct individual; and despite all the problems of Jim Holbrook, his wife Anna is the one who receives most of the reader's sympathy. In its depiction of the lives of the working class, *Yonnondio* stresses that certain members of this class must cope with the worst conditions: poor women, those who are silenced even on the rare occasions when men of their class are allowed to speak. The novel directly states that women are left the most unpleasant jobs: "Breathing with open mouth, the young girls and women in casings, where men will not work. Year-round breathing with open mouth, learning to pant shallow to endure the excrement reek of offal, the smothering stench from the blood house below." However, instead of concentrating upon the horrible experiences of women factory workers, the novel describes the problems of one woman whose life revolves around the domestic sphere. Mazie's conversation with her mother implies that women unfairly assume the burden of domestic responsibility:

Dust jacket for Olsen's 1978 nonfiction collection, in which she explains how circumstances such as class and gender can hamper literary work

> "Why is it always me that has to help? How come Will [her brother] gets to play?"
> "Will's a boy."
> "Why couldn't *I* get borned a boy?"

This conversation occurs at the end of the novel, after Mazie has grown up watching her mother's biological and social victimization. Anna cannot make enough money; she also cannot stop making too many babies.

In addition to speaking about man's inhumanity to workingmen, *Yonnondio* also refuses to be silent about workingmen's inhumanity to their wives. Jim Holbrook uses his family—and especially his wife—as scapegoats upon which to vent his emotions: "For several weeks Jim Holbrook had been in an evil mood. The whole household walked in terror. He had nothing but heavy blows for the children, and he struck Anna too often to remember." Anna has no such outlet. Nor can she relieve her frustrations verbally. Jim complains about the quality of her work: "Any time I want sewage to eat I can get it on the job." Anna complains to no one.

He does not welcome her words: "Goddam woman—what's the matter with her anyhow? Don't even have a wife that's a wife anymore—just let her say one word to me and I'll bash her head in." When she does voice an objection, her words are unheard.

Anna becomes dangerously ill as a result of miscarriage. In addition to her poverty, Jim is a major cause of Anna's suffering. He holds one terrible job at a time. She holds three simultaneously: wife of an insensitive husband, mother to children whose lives will ultimately be as hopeless as her own, and part-time laundress. Like Eva in "Tell Me a Riddle," Anna is defeated because she satisfies others at her own expense: "She fed and clothed the children, scrubbed, gave herself to Jim, clenching her fists against a pain she had no strength to feel." What Jim describes as "a woman's goddam life" is much worse than his own.

Hopelessness pervades the novel. Jim makes no progress even though he strives to give his family a better life. When readers first encounter him, he is employed as a miner; at the end of the novel, although he has held many jobs, he again works in a mine. Anna suffers from satisfying the demands of her large family, and when she satisfies her husband's demands, her family grows larger. Because they will not receive an adequate "edjication," the Holbrook children will eventually relive their parents' problems. This probability might explain why, with the exception of Mazie, the children are not given individual characteristics. Since it is virtually impossible for them to escape filling a predetermined social niche, they are robbed of their individuality. Regardless of how many times their family moves, or how many jobs their father holds, a better life is beyond their reach.

Five-year-old Will Holbrook already understands the implications of this statement: "Five years. I'm wearin your [Mazie's] old coat, a girl's coat. For why?" Although Will may spend his life questioning his poverty, he may never find the answer of how to escape its generational cycle. Young Will, who must wear a girl's coat, is the son of a man who cannot afford to buy the proper attire for his job. Regardless of their labor, the Holbrooks are excluded from the good life, despised.

Mazie thinks about this exclusion while she and members of her family traverse the lawns of the rich in search of dandelions for their table: "A vague shame, a weedy sense of not belonging, of something being wrong about them, stirred un-

easy through Mazie." The Holbrook family has grown haphazardly, and it must take root where it can: "when the seed strikes stone; the soil will not sustain; the spring is false; the time is drought or blight or infestation; the frost comes premature," Olsen writes in *Silences*.

It is not surprising that Olsen was thinking about writers—especially women writers—when she wrote those words. In addition to creating memorable female characters such as Anna and Eva, Olsen is an important feminist educator. Her courses, which have titles such as "Literature of the Working Class and the Human Struggle for Freedom" and "Women in Fact and Fiction," have introduced male and female students to long-forgotten works by women. After it was published in the *Women's Studies Newsletter,* the reading list she developed was used widely in women's studies courses. Her articles, such as "Silences: When Writers Don't Write" (*Harper's,* October 1965) and "Women Who Are Writers In Our Century: One Out of Twelve" (*College English,* October 1972), have been included in many women's studies courses throughout the United States. These two essays are republished in *Silences* (1978), a collection of Olsen's work that "is concerned with the relationship of circumstances—including class color sex; the times, climate into which one is born—to the creation of literature." Appropriately, *Silences,* the work of an influential college professor who never had a formal college education, "is not an orthodoxly written work of academic scholarship." Like her fiction, Olsen's nonfiction "came slow, hard won."

Since "Silences" begins by mentioning the silences of great men—"Thomas Hardy, Melville, Rimbaud, Gerard Manly Hopkins"—it illustrates that the articulation of feminist discourse is slow and hard won. In the essay women are only one of the four categories of "mute inglorious Miltons": "those whose waking hours are all struggle for existence; the barely educated; the illiterate; women." Olsen insists upon including men: "we are in a time of more and more hidden and foreground silences, women *and* men." When ideas in "Silences" were first made public as Olsen's oral presentation at the Radcliffe Institute (1963), the members of the Institute's weekly colloquium heard her say that both class and gender are responsible for eradicating creativity. The essay names and defines the circumstances that retard the work of women writers. The following explanation is offered by Olsen, a member of the working class and a mother: "But women are traditionally trained to place others' needs first, to feel these needs as their own . . . their sphere, their satisfaction to be in making it possible for others to use their abilities. . . . Motherhood means being instantly interruptable, responsive, responsible. It is distraction, not meditation, that becomes habitual; interruption, not continuity." The reason "Silences" is a feminist essay is analogous to the reason *Yonnondio* is a feminist novel. *Yonnondio,* a working-class text, includes the viewpoint of women; "Silences," the subtitle of which includes the generic term *writers,* includes a discussion of writers who are women.

Although the silences of women are discussed separately in Olsen's essay about human silences, the piece seems finally to reject categories. She mentions Rebecca Harding Davis together with luminaries, and a discussion of her personal silences appears with a consideration of those of famous male writers. When "Silences" gives a voice to women, it refuses to silence men.

Not so for "One Out of Twelve: Writers Who Are Women In Our Century"; published seven years after "Silences," it is the more vehemently feminist of the two pieces. Its subject is "the lives and work of writers, women, in our century." It literally lists the social and critical attitudes that devalue the work of women writers. Olsen encourages female professors to correct a curriculum that fosters such devaluation: "Teach women's lives through the lives of the women who wrote the books, as well as through the books themselves; and through autobiography, biography, journals, letters." Her personal remarks, which are included so that others will learn from her experience, are quite congruent with the didactic tone of the essay: "I speak of myself to bring here the sense of those others to whom this [discontinuity] is in the process of happening . . . and to remind us of those . . . who never come to writing at all." Strong words conclude her personal remarks: "We who write are survivors."

The term "survivors" brings class to mind, as does Olsen's discussion of Virginia Woolf's "angel in the house." Olsen defines another angel who is not a part of privileged women writers' lives: *"the essential angel"* who "must assume the physical responsibilities for daily living, for the maintenance of life." Olsen's essay reminds readers that not all women writers have servants; it speaks for the lower-class woman writer, as her fiction speaks for the woman worker.

The two opening essays of *Silences,* like all of Olsen's written work, state that no one should be barred from experiencing "the whole of *human life.*" Women—and all people who do not belong to the privileged class—should not be confined to a sphere where their full, human creative potential is denied. Olsen's feminism is an integral part of her humanism.

While discussing Davis in *Silences,* Olsen states, "What Virginia Woolf wrote of Elizabeth Barrett Browning characterizes Rebecca as well: 'a true daughter of her age: passionate interest in social questions, conflict as artist and woman, longing for knowledge and freedom.'" Olsen might well have added that these words also describe her own life and work.

References:

Agnes Toloczko Cardoni, *Women's Ethical Coming-of-Age: Adolescent Female Characters in the Prose Fiction of Tillie Olsen* (Lanham, Md.: University Press of America, 1998);

Constance Coiner, *Better Red: The Writing and Resistance of Tillie Olsen and Meridel Le Sueur* (New York: Oxford University Press, 1995);

Mara Faulkner, *Protest and Possibility in the Writing of Tillie Olsen* (Charlottesville: University Press of Virginia, 1993);

Joanne S. Frye, *Tillie Olsen: A Study of the Short Fiction* (New York: Twayne / London: Prentice-Hall International, 1995);

Elaine Hedges and Shelly Fisher Fishkin, eds., *Listening to 'Silences': New Feminist Essays* (New York: Oxford University Press, 1994);

Abigail Martin, *Tillie Olsen* (Boise, Idaho: Boise State University, 1984);

Kay Hoyle Nelson and Nancy Huse, eds., *The Critical Response to Tillie Olsen* (Westport, Conn.: Greenwood Press, 1994);

Elaine Neil Orr, *Tillie Olsen and a Feminist Spiritual Vision* (Jackson: University Press of Mississippi, 1987);

Mickey Pearlman and Abby H. P. Werlock, *Tillie Olsen* (Boston: Twayne, 1991);

Nora Ruth Roberts, *Three Radical Women Writers: Class and Gender in Meridel Le Sueur, Tillie Olsen, and Josephine Herbst* (New York: Garland, 1996);

Deborah Rosenfelt, "From the Thirties: Tillie Olsen and the Radical Tradition," *Feminist Studies,* 7 (Fall 1981): 371–406.

Papers:

An archive of Tillie Olsen's papers is housed in the Department of Special Collections, Green Library, Stanford University, Stanford, California. Portions of the manuscript of *Yonnondio* are in the Berg Collection of English and American Literature in the New York Public Library.

Katherine Anne Porter

This entry was updated by Ruth M. Alvarez (University of Maryland) from the entry by Joan Givner (University of Regina) in DLB 102: American Short-Story Writers, 1910–1945, *Second Series.*

See also the Porter entries in *DLB 4: American Writers in Paris, 1920–1939; DLB 9: American Novelists, 1910–1945; DLB Yearbook: 1980;* and *DS 12: Southern Women Writers: Flannery O'Connor, Katherine Anne Porter, Eudora Welty.*

BIRTH: Indian Creek, Texas, 15 May 1890, born Callie Russell Porter to Harrison Boone and Mary Alice Jones Porter.

EDUCATION: Attended private school: Thomas School, San Antonio, Texas.

MARRIAGE: 20 June 1906 to John Henry Koontz (divorced, 1915); married 11 March 1933 to Eugene Dove Pressly (divorced, 1938); married 19 April 1938 to Albert Russel Erskine Jr. (divorced, 1942).

AWARDS AND HONORS: Guggenheim fellowships, 1931, 1938; first annual gold medal, Society of the Libraries of New York University, for *Pale Horse, Pale Rider,* 1940; Library of Congress fellowship in regional American literature, 1944; chosen one of six representatives of American literature at International Expositions of the Arts in Paris, 1952; Ford Foundation grant, 1959–1961; State Department grants for international exchange of persons to Mexico, 1960, 1964; first prize, O. Henry Memorial Award, for "Holiday," 1962; Emerson-Thoreau Bronze Medal for Literature, American Academy of Arts and Sciences, 1962; Pulitzer Prize and National Book Award, both 1966, for *The Collected Stories of Katherine Anne Porter;* gold medal, National Institute of Arts and Letters, 1967; creative arts award, Brandeis University, 1972; honorary degrees include D.Litt. from the Women's College of the University of North Carolina, 1949, Smith College, 1958, and Wheaton College, 1958; D.H.L. from University of Michigan, 1954, and University of Maryland, 1966; and D.F.A. from LaSalle College, 1962.

DEATH: Silver Springs, Maryland, 18 September 1980.

Katherine Anne Porter, 1954 (photograph by Eck Stanger; Papers of Katherine Anne Porter, Special Collections, University of Maryland Libraries)

BOOKS: *My Chinese Marriage,* ghostwritten for Mae Watkins Franking (New York: Duffield, 1921);
Outline of Mexican Popular Arts and Crafts (Los Angeles: Young & McCallister, 1922);
Flowering Judas (New York: Harcourt, Brace, 1930); enlarged as *Flowering Judas and Other Stories* (New York: Harcourt, Brace, 1935; London: Cape, 1936);
Hacienda (New York: Harrison of Paris, 1934);
Noon Wine (Detroit: Schuman's, 1937);
Pale Horse, Pale Rider: Three Short Novels (New York: Harcourt, Brace, 1939); republished as *Pale*

Horse, Pale Rider and Other Stories (London: Cape, 1939);

Selected Short Stories (New York: Editions for the Armed Forces, 1941);

The Leaning Tower and Other Stories (New York: Harcourt, Brace, 1944; London: Cape, 1945);

The Days Before (New York: Harcourt, Brace, 1952; London: Secker & Warburg, 1953);

A Defense of Circe (New York: Harcourt, Brace, 1955);

The Old Order: Stories of the South from Flowering Judas; Pale Horse, Pale Rider; and The Leaning Tower (New York: Harcourt, Brace, 1955);

A Christmas Story (limited edition, New York: Mademoiselle, 1955; trade edition, New York: Seymour Lawrence, 1967);

Ship of Fools (Boston & Toronto: Atlantic Monthly/ Little, Brown, 1962; London: Secker & Warburg, 1962);

The Collected Stories of Katherine Anne Porter (London: Cape, 1964; New York: Harcourt, Brace, 1965; enlarged edition, London: Cape, 1967);

The Collected Essays and Occasional Writings of Katherine Anne Porter (New York: Delacorte, 1970);

The Never-Ending Wrong (Boston: Little, Brown, 1977; London: Secker & Warburg, 1977);

"This Strange Ole World" and Other Book Reviews, edited by Darlene Harbour Unrue (Athens & London: University of Georgia Press, 1991);

Uncollected Early Prose of Katherine Anne Porter, edited by Ruth M. Alvarez and Thomas F. Walsh (Austin: University of Texas Press, 1993);

Katherine Anne Porter's Poetry, edited, with an introduction, by Darlene Harbour Unrue (Columbia: University of South Carolina Press, 1996).

OTHER: *What Price Marriage?* edited as Hamblen Sears (New York: J. H. Sears, 1927).

TRANSLATIONS: *Katherine Anne Porter's French Song-Book* (Paris: Harrison of Paris, 1933);

Jose Joaquin Fernandez de Lizárdi, *The Itching Parrot,* translated, with an introduction, by Porter (Garden City, N.Y.: Doubleday, Doran, 1942).

Katherine Anne Porter's literary reputation rests on the twenty-seven stories in her *Collected Stories* (1964) rather than on the best-selling novel *Ship of Fools* (1962), on which she worked intermittently for thirty years. She was one of the most brilliant practitioners of the art of the short story, and because of her style (personal as well as literary), she was an important influence on the generation of

writers that followed her, including William Humphrey, William Goyen, Tillie Olsen, Carson McCullers, Flannery O'Connor, and Eudora Welty. During her lifetime, Porter's work won praise for its style and was the focus of close readings.

Two years after her death, *Katherine Anne Porter: A Life* (1982; republished with a new preface in 1991), the first full-length scholarly biography, appeared. Coincidentally, the growing volume and sophistication of feminist criticism was providing new insights into women writers and their works. New interpretations of the art and life of Katherine Anne Porter developed as a result of this pioneering scholarship.

Born Callie Russell Porter in a small log house on a farm in the central Texas community of Indian Creek, she was the fourth of five children of Mary Alice Jones Porter and Harrison Boone Porter. Her mother died before she was two, and the four surviving children (Porter, two sisters, and a brother) were raised by their paternal grandmother, Catherine Anne Porter, in Kyle, Texas. This household, dominated by a strong-willed woman, shaped her attitude toward gender roles and greatly influenced her aspirations, unusual in a woman of her time, for a career.

Notable among Porter's childhood experiences was the beginning of a lifelong friendship with a neighborhood child whom she perceived as an alter ego. The same age as Porter and, like her, one of four children, Erna Schlemmer belonged to an industrious family of German immigrants. From this early association Porter developed the interest in Germans that recurs in her stories and in her novel. The Schlemmers were remarkable in the small town for their cultural interests and for their trips to Germany. Porter recorded memories of the family in her story "The Leaning Tower" (*Southern Review,* 1941; collected in *The Leaning Tower and Other Stories,* 1944).

The death of Porter's grandmother in 1901 left the family emotionally and financially adrift. During a period of dislocation after the grandmother's death, her father left Porter with some cousins while he tried to resettle the family in San Antonio. These cousins (the Thompsons), their dairy farm, and their hired man provided rich material, which Porter used more than thirty years later for the story *Noon Wine* (*Story,* June 1937; published separately later that year).

In San Antonio, Porter experienced the last formal education she would receive. She and her older sister, Annie Gay (called Gay), attended the Thomas School, an excellent private girls' school (non-sectarian Christian). Equipped with the training she had there, Porter and her sister subsequently taught elocution, singing, and dramatic arts in a rented room in Victoria, Texas, where the family had moved from San Antonio.

A month after her sixteenth birthday, Porter married John Henry Koontz on 20 June 1906. Her twenty-one-year-old husband worked as a railway clerk in Louisiana and was a member of a prominent ranching family in the town of Inez, not far from Victoria. The Koontzes were of German-Swiss descent and Catholic, and Porter (who had adopted the name Katherine Russell) was attracted to the rituals of their church. She converted to Catholicism when she was twenty. Her experiences at this time in two heavily patriarchal institutions—the Koontz family and the Catholic church—were later to inform the story "Holiday" (*Atlantic Monthly*, December 1960; also in *Collected Stories*), which describes the sojourn of a young woman amid a German farming family in rural Texas.

In spite of Porter's conversion to her husband's faith, the marriage had been troubled from the beginning. She longed for a child and for an outlet for her artistic aspirations. When John Henry Koontz found work as a traveling salesman for a wholesale grocery firm, the couple moved to Houston in 1908. Around 1912 they moved to Corpus Christi, where Porter was eventually reunited with her old friend Erna Schlemmer, now Mrs. Glover Johns. Once again Erna's life provided a dramatic contrast with Porter's. Erna's husband was a successful businessman, and she was a contented wife and mother. Erna was shocked when Porter decided to leave her husband and try for a career as a movie actress. To this end, Porter left Koontz in the spring of 1914 for Chicago, where there were several large movie studios. The nine-year marriage ended in divorce in June 1915, and Porter at that time assumed the name Katherine Anne Porter.

Dissatisfied with movie work in the fall of 1914, she went to Gibsland, Louisiana, to help Gay, who had been deserted by her husband and was undergoing a difficult pregnancy. In order to help support her sister, her niece Mary Alice, and the expected child, Porter made herself a costume and performed a song-and-dance routine on the Lyceum circuit in small towns in Louisiana. Eventually Gay regained her health; her husband returned; and Porter set out once more hoping to start a new life, this time in Dallas. She was there only a short time before she contracted tuberculosis.

Porter had thought often about the experience of death and rebirth, being preconditioned to the experience of being "born again" at the revivalist

Porter (left) with her paternal grandmother, Catherine Anne Porter, and her sister, Mary Alice, circa 1893–1894 (Papers of Katherine Anne Porter, Special Collections, University of Maryland Libraries)

meetings of her childhood. She told interviewer Barbara Thompson in 1963, "I knew what death was, and had almost experienced it. I had what the Christians call the 'beatific vision,' and the Greeks called the 'happy day,' the happy vision just before death. Now if you have had that, and survived it, come back from it, you are no longer like other people." In her fictional and autobiographical accounts she indicates that this experience happened during the plague of influenza that swept the United States at the end of World War I. She did nearly die of influenza in Denver in October 1918. Her family had already made arrangements for her burial, and the newspaper had prepared her obituary, when a shot of strychnine administered by an intern brought her back to life. That incident, however, was brief. In fact, her long bout with tuberculosis and her various hospitalizations were the turning points in her life.

When she first fell ill in 1915, since she had no means of support, she was sent to a grim "pesthouse" for the indigent in Dallas. Then in spring 1916 her brother managed to find the money to send her to Carlsbad Sanatorium near San Angelo in west Texas, a pleasant hospital sometimes described as having the atmosphere of a college campus. It was here that the fear of death, the long period of inactivity, the time for reflection, and the close camaraderie of a group of intelligent and interesting young women caused her to reassess her life and redefine her goals. Among her fellow patients was Kitty Barry Crawford, one of the first women journalists in Texas and a committed career woman. Through this friendship Porter learned of Kitty's old school friend, Jane Anderson, a journalist and fiction writer who sent letters from England of her life there and her friendship with Joseph Conrad.

When she left her husband, Porter had aspired to the most likely career for a woman of beauty and grace—that of a stage performer. After Carlsbad, however, she no longer thought of the performing arts as the only outlet for female expression; she thought of writing. Crawford and her husband ran the *Fort Worth Critic,* a newspaper. In September 1917 Porter began to work on the paper. In spring 1918, when Crawford's slow recovery made the move to a more healthful climate necessary, Porter accompanied her to Denver and shared a house with Crawford and her daughter after Anderson, recently returned from Europe, moved out. In September 1918 Porter began work on the *Rocky Mountain News.* There she did the work usually assigned to female reporters, covering the social events and the entertainment news. Yet the paper was a prestigious one, her position a step up from the *Fort Worth Critic,* and soon she had the title of dramatic editor.

Anderson had not proved an encouraging mentor to Porter. Rather she looked down on her as provincial, inexperienced, and uneducated. Yet Anderson's experiences and her published stories gave Porter an idea of what she wanted to do next. Also, she met the musicologist Deems Taylor, who had come to Denver for a summer music festival. He advised her to go to New York, and, with Denver colleague Eva Chappell, she moved there in October 1919.

In New York she did publicity work for a movie company and produced the first of her fiction to reach publication, four "retold" stories. The first three—"The Shattered Star," "The Faithful Princess," and "The Magic Ear Ring"—were published in *Everyland,* a children's magazine, January through March 1920 (republished in *Uncollected Early Prose* in 1993). Through Berta and Elmer Hader, illustrators for the magazine, Porter contracted to write these stories derived from various myths and legends. The fourth "retold" story, "The Adventures of Hadji: A Tale of the Turkish Coffee-House," appeared in *Asia* (August 1920; republished in *Uncol-*

lected Early Prose), where *My Chinese Marriage,* a book she agreed to ghostwrite, was originally published between June and September 1921. This work is the story of a Michigan woman who had married a Chinese student and lived briefly as his wife in China. The most important influence on the future direction of her career, however, was her meeting with an interesting group of young Mexican artists and revolutionaries—among them Adolfo Best-Maugard. Inspired by their accounts of Mexico, armed with introductory letters to their friends and with contracts for some journalistic work to provide her support, Porter in late 1920 headed south by train and arrived in Mexico City in time to witness Alvaro Obregón's inauguration as president.

By this time her writing ambitions had formed clearly in her mind. She had vowed in a letter to her sister when she headed for New York that she intended one day to write as well as anyone in the United States. Eventually she made good that vow, but it was another ten years before she won recognition. As she entered her third decade, she was only too conscious of her lack of qualifications for her chosen career. When she compared herself with Crawford, Anderson, and the talented women she met in New York—such as Ernestine Evans, Genevieve Taggard, Bessie Beatty, and Rose Wilder Lane—she could not help being conscious of her educational deficiencies. She had left school when she was fourteen and had never traveled abroad or learned a second language. The excursion to Mexico promised to make up some of her deficiencies in education and at the same time provide the wider range of experience that would prove the proper stuff of fiction.

Her first six months in Mexico City during a time of political turmoil could hardly have been more eventful. Her friends included foreigners such as Joseph Retinger; social activists such as Robert and Thorberg Haberman; Mexican political figures such as Manuel Gamio, Luis Morones, and Felipe Carrillo Puerto; and artists such as Best-Maugard, Xavier Guerrero, and Roberto Montenegro. Through her friends she was drawn into political intrigue and eventually fled the country in autumn 1921. She found a haven once again with Crawford in Fort Worth.

Ever restless, she left in early 1921, packing up her drafts of stories and returning to Greenwich Village. Several months later she was invited back to Mexico to write the catalogue for a proposed traveling exhibition of Mexican folk art (which was published in 1922). She departed in April 1922 for ten weeks in Mexico.

Porter (seated, far left) with friends in Kyle, Texas, circa 1902; on Porter's left is her childhood friend Erma Schlemmer (Papers of Katherine Anne Porter, Special Collections, University of Maryland Libraries)

On her return to New York, Porter made unsuccessful attempts to market the work of Diego Rivera and Miguel Covarrubias in New York and resumed her freelance writing career. The exhibit for which she had written the catalogue opened in Los Angeles in November 1922 for a two-week run, its tardy arrival from Mexico having occasioned the loss of exhibit space at the Los Angeles Museum. At this time she completed "María Concepción," which was published in *Century* in December 1922 and collected in *Flowering Judas* in 1930.

Nothing betrays so dearly Porter's lack of ease with her role as professional writer as her need to fantasize about her own creative process. Once her work was published, the problem disappeared because she could slip into the role of performer. In that guise she loved reading her stories on platforms and stages across the country (preferably under a single spotlight), elegantly coiffed and gowned, sometimes with a corsage (by her own account as big as a cabbage), and sometimes (according to Flannery O'Connor in a 14 April 1958 letter to Cecil Dawkins) with long evening gloves that impeded her turning of the pages. The actual writing, however, presented difficulties. Typically, she described herself as going into self-imposed confinement with her muse. She loved telling the stories of these retreats—adumbrating the items in her spare but nutritious diet—as if speaking of pregnancies. She said "María Concepción" had a gestation period of seventeen days and seventeen nights in a rooming house in Washington Square.

This story, which she designated as her first, was told to her by an archaeologist friend in Mexico City, and it resembles the fiction she had already published in its depiction of a strong woman character who triumphs over her weak husband, takes control of her own life, and sets her world in order. Her second story, "The Martyr," was based on her observations of Diego Rivera. It also appeared in *Century* magazine (July 1923; also in *Collected Stories*), as did one of her essays about Mexico. In June 1923 Porter returned to Mexico to gather materials for a special issue of *Survey Graphic* (published in April 1924). During this visit of several months, she observed firsthand the creation of large-scale public art on the walls of public buildings and developed a closer association with Rivera. Porter's interest in and work on Mexico continued until 1930, when she returned for her last protracted stay in the country. However, she began to turn more directly toward her own experience and background for material for her fiction between 1923 and 1930. During this period she lived primarily in New York City, but she also spent significant periods in Connecticut and Massachusetts.

Porter continued to gain strength as a short-story writer. Of the stories written during the mid 1920s, "Holiday" is paradigmatic. She wrote Genevieve Taggard on 14 November 1924 that she had finished the story in a bath of sweat. That verdict was overly optimistic for, in fact, she could not decide on the ending. She set the story aside, finishing and publishing it only in 1960–a long struggle even for a writer noted for procrastination and for the inability to complete works in progress. In her envoi to *Collected Stories* she diagnosed her problem accurately. She wrote that the story reflected "one of my prolonged struggles, not with questions of form or style, but my own moral and emotional collision with a human situation I was too young to cope with at the time it occurred."

The story, written in the first person, describes the brief stay of the nameless narrator in the home of some Germans in rural Texas. The young woman by choice takes an attic room, where she hopes to write letters and read nineteenth-century romantic novels left by a previous guest. The Muller family's nationality indicates Porter's usual association of the German and the patriarchal. The family could hardly be more patriarchal in its structure–the men and children sit at different sides of the table, the women standing behind the men to serve them. The narrator's anomalous position at the table points to the theme of the story: the exploration of the place in a patriarchal community of the woman who does not fill the traditional roles of wife and mother. At the climax of the story the narrator is left behind by the family as they attend the burial of the mother, who has died suddenly and unexpectedly. Also left behind is the crippled, uncoordinated, mute servant girl Ottilie. The narrator, hearing Ottilie howling like a member of a subhuman species, learns that she is actually a daughter of the family, grieving for her mother. The two have a brief outing together and share a moment of camaraderie in the spring sunshine. In the outcast, speechless girl, the narrator recognizes briefly an image of herself, an alter ego. If the resolution of the story eluded Porter, it was because she never managed to resolve her own ambivalent feelings toward patriar-

chal society. She never managed to belong, but she never reconciled herself to not belonging, and the idea of being an outcast (bringing back memories of her childhood) frightened her. In "Holiday" her feelings about aligning herself with women find expression in the narrator's brief outing with the grotesque figure of Ottilie. At one point, as she tries to grasp the servant girl, the narrator's "fingers slipped between her clothes and bare flesh." The narrator crosses "the shallow ditch where the small road divided from the main travelled one," but such deviations and by-ways are not for her, and she quickly returns to the main thoroughfare.

"The Cracked Looking Glass," also begun in the mid 1920s, was successfully finished and published in May 1932 (in *Scribner's Magazine;* collected in *Flowering Judas and Other Stories,* 1935). Its theme is a variation of that of "Holiday," in that it describes the adventures of an anomalous woman. Nominally, Rosaleen is a dutiful daughter of the patriarchy, a married woman. Actually, she is frustrated in her role as wife because of her husband's age and impotence; she was cut off from the role of mother with the early death of her only child. She is caught in the double bind of being married to an ineffective man and at the same time prevented from using her own energies. Nevertheless, Rosaleen tries to find expression for her creative energy in nontraditional ways. She forms liaisons with young men, and, through her storytelling, she mesmerizes anyone who will listen. When her frustrations become unbearable, she takes a holiday from her married life on the pretext of a reunion with her sister. Unfortunately, a chance encounter with a young man turns nasty, and fearing disgrace, she returns thankfully to the safety of the domestic hearth and to the fragmented image of herself that she finds in her cracked mirror. The dream she has had at the beginning of the story, that of a prowling cat who ends up in a trap, has proved prophetic.

While the resolutions to these two stories evaded Porter and delayed their publication, other works were brought to completion. "Virgin Violeta," the last of the early Mexican stories, published in *Century* in December 1924 (also in *Collected Stories*), is based on Porter's shocked reaction to the Nicaraguan poet Saloman de la Selva's account of the seduction of a young girl. In the story, young Violeta watches the mannered courting gestures of her older sister and her male cousin, Carlos. These take place under the half-alert eyes of the girls' mother and under a framed picture of the Virgin and St. Ignatius Loyola. Violeta, spontaneous and natural like a wild creature, resists being "framed." She leaves herself open to the illicit sexual advances of the cousin, and the story ends with her terror, her hysteria, and, finally, her reduction to the status of a child protected by her parents. Her fright is caused not only by what she unleashed in Carlos but also in herself: "He was loathsome. She saw herself before him, almost as if his face were a mirror. Her mouth was too large; her face was simply a moon; her hair was ugly in the tight convent braids."

In another successfully completed story, "Magic" (*transition*, Summer 1928; also in *Flowering Judas*), a woman is "framed," her image reflected in a mirror as her storytelling maid brushes her hair. The woman is riveted by a story of the violent abuse of a prostitute in a New Orleans brothel. The prostitute runs away, but as in so many of Porter's stories of escape from the degrading or menial life of patriarchal institutions, her flight turns out to be only a brief "holiday." She is brought back by a magic spell, is welcomed by the madam and the male clients, and settles down in what she now recognizes as her home. What connection the respectable listener makes between her own life and her maid's story can only be guessed, as she stares at her reflection and sniffs her perfume.

During this period of residence in New England and New York, Porter made many literary friends who influenced her work in various ways. Some were women, such as Ernestine Evans, Genevieve Taggard, Elinor Wylie, and, most important, Josephine Herbst, who became a friend of longstanding. There were also suitors and lovers. Sumner Williams, a Harvard-educated bachelor, urged marriage. A Chilean lover, Francisco Aguilera, echoing Shelley's poem "From Ariel to Miranda," gave her the name "Miranda," which she later used for the name of her fictional representative. She often said that her story "Rope" (*The Second American Caravan*, 1928; also in *Flowering Judas*)—a vivid account of marital discord—was based on the quarrels of friends and their husbands, but it seems more likely that it was based on her own relationship with Ernest Stock, with whom Porter lived in Connecticut during the spring and summer of 1926.

She also met at this time a group of sophisticated Southerners who became lifelong friends: Allen Tate, Caroline Gordon, Andrew Lytle, and Robert Penn Warren. Some of them were working on biographies, and following their example, Porter decided to try her hand at the genre. Her choice of subject—the New England theologian Cotton Mather—seems at first glance a surprising departure from her usual themes, but in fact she had always been interested in witchcraft, witches, and religious fanaticism. It was Mather's role in the Salem witch trials that drew her to him, and in order to do

Porter in 1923, when she was living on Gay Street in Greenwich Village

the research at the Essex Institute she spent several months in late 1927 and early 1928 in Salem. Earlier, in the summer of 1927, she journeyed into Boston to join many of her friends who were involved in the protest movement surrounding the executions of Nicola Sacco and Bartolomeo Vanzetti.

Her time in Salem did not lead to the completion of her biography, but it did have another unexpected result. The dark atmosphere of the town contrasted with warm memories of her childhood in rural Texas. Setting aside the biography, she wrote "The Fig Tree," based on recollections of the strong matriarchal figures of her paternal line. This was an important turning point because it signaled her discovery of the rich lode of material to be found in her Texas roots, and it provided the subject matter and setting of the best of her subsequent stories. In retrospect it seems clear that Porter's art was moving steadily and surely toward maturity. Yet as she approached forty, struggling with the (for her) impossible Cotton Mather project and publishing at most two stories a year, she felt that she was making little progress. In addition her personal life was often tormented. The series of lovers at once reflected and reinforced her own uncertainties about herself. They were all different, each one assigning to her a different, unsatisfactory role, each one doomed to fail. Sumner Williams had wanted to make her his wife, to support and protect her in a traditional marriage, but she knew that wouldn't work; Aguilera, serenading her as Miranda, saw her as a beautiful work of art and muse but had no intention of marrying her; Ernest Stock was handsome but ineffectual; the Mexican wax caricaturist Luis Hidalgo was moody and culturally incompatible; Matthew Josephson, happy with his own wife and children, wanted her for his mistress while he acted as her literary mentor. This last relationship disappointed her and pushed her toward the breakdown in health she suffered in 1928.

Some of the anguish of that relationship and the discomfort with herself is expressed in one of her best stories, "Theft" (*Gyroscope,* November 1929; also in *Flowering Judas and Other Stories*), in which a nameless woman comes to see that her own passivity and failure to assert herself sours all her relationships and encourages unscrupulous people to exploit her. The final revelation of the story is that the woman not only is causing her own losses but also is responsible for the moral decline of those around her.

Porter also had many loyal friends who frequently offered to help her. Herbst once complained that she herself was perceived as a strong, self-sufficient woman and that no one felt protective toward her as they did toward the apparently vulnerable and charming Porter. Herbst's comment is well illustrated by the events of 1928, when, in the wake of Porter's ill health, her New York friends rallied to send her to Bermuda to rest, recover, and work on the biography of Mather.

The five months Porter spent in Bermuda were some of the most productive of her life, but not in the way she or her friends anticipated. The biography was not finished, but instead many of her future successful stories began to take shape. Unexpectedly she found in her new surroundings an atmosphere conducive to the development of her Texas stories. In the stories she told to her friends, she presented her early life as one of Southern gentility. In Bermuda, renting the gracious home of an affluent local family, she found the physical details of the ancestral home for which she longed. There "Old Mortality" (in *Pale Horse, Pale Rider,* 1939) and the stories of "The Old Order" sequence (in *The Leaning Tower*) began to form in her mind.

Years later she acknowledged the five months in Bermuda as a period of great creativity, whose momentum led to contracts with Harcourt, Brace for a collection of previously published short stories and for a novel set in Mexico. The collection of short stories *Flowering Judas* takes its title from the story of the same name, begun by Porter in New York before her Bermuda sojourn. First published in *Hound and Horn* in Spring 1930, "Flowering Judas" drew on Porter's experiences and observations in Mexico in 1920–1921. One was her experience with a fat revolutionary whose unwelcome attentions had made one of Porter's friends, Mary Doherty, ask Porter to act as chaperone while he serenaded her on his guitar. The other was a story Porter sometimes attributed to Doherty about a young revolutionary in prison who had persuaded her to let him have more than the usual harmless number of sleeping pills she normally carried to him in jail. When Doherty returned the next day, she discovered that the young man had killed himself. She purportedly told Porter about a terrible dream she had in which the young man appeared and accused her of killing him.

Porter named the obese revolutionary Braggioni and made him, like all her villains, a complete caricature. He looms in the story like a huge purple-and-yellow Easter egg. With a cat's eyes and a pig's paunch, he is the hideous embodiment of the seven deadly sins. In contrast to Braggioni is the young, innocent prisoner, Eugenio. Yet the focus is on neither of these characters but on the supposedly innocent girl, Laura. Like the protagonist of "Theft" she turns out, through her passivity, to be responsible for the abuses that go on around her. She promotes Braggioni's wickedness by not resisting him and is, therefore, guilty for causing his moral decline and his neglect of his wife as well as for causing the death of Eugenio. The implication is that if Braggioni is a self-serving, self-indulgent villain, he has not always been so. Once he was a young idealist in both politics and love. It is Laura, the main character, and those like her who caused him to change from idealist to opportunist. In turn, the story explores Laura's own indifference and alienation. They are caused by her own sense of uncertainty about herself, her loss of the religious faith of her childhood, and her anomalous position as an independent woman living outside the family structure.

Porter's strength was not in showing growth and change in her characters, and in any event such a method was more appropriate to the novel than the short story. Instead, it was in a spontaneous discovery she made of a method of suggesting all the ramifications of the situation. As the story was nearing completion, a pattern of symbolism appeared to her, not imposed upon the story but implicit in it, an extended use of the symbolic naturalism she had

August 28, 1931

Caroline darling:

It simply was not possible to write until now. And here we are six days out, already striking across from the Caribbean Islands to the Canaries: fifteen days, they tell me, from yesterday. Five days before, and probably ten to fourteen more from the Canaries to Gijon, to Southampton, to Bremen.. Then by train to Paris, and so on down to Nice. We will have spent about five weeks on this boat before we are finished.. A combination freighter and passenger ship, very steady, very broadbottomed and German in her style, doing sixteen knots an hour and keeping a level keel.

I thought of all possible ways to get by to see you, then go on and sail from New York and have it over, a week's voyage, without simply spending the whole first quarter of my allowance, and there was NO way. I wished to see my father too, and had great plans to fly over to Brownsville. But the money began to melt so alarmingly, I could do nothing but take the first boat and go on...

There is so much to say, but time to say it, too, at last. My bad luck overtake me if ever again I go through the hell of house wrecking which attends my every change of scene. I'm going to live in rooms, or a room, in inns, pensions, hotels: I don't know what, but never again shall I collect the odds and ends of a household until I have a roof of my own to cover them.

The cats were found good homes, the dog was disposed of to some one who wanted him, the baby turkeys and their mama went to Teodora, and the sticks of furniture were peddled here and there at five cents on the dollar, all this in the uproar of getting necessary papers together, write a last minute review; Lord, why tire you out with the list of things which make such a scramble at the last second? You know all about getting off to Europe as we seem to do it.

First page of a letter from Porter to Caroline Gordon, written during the voyage that provided the genesis for Ship of Fools *(Princeton University Library)*

used in "Theft." As she told interviewer Barbara Thompson in 1963, she remembered the Judas tree in the little Mexican patio where Mary Doherty lived, and it suggested to her the betrayal of Jesus by Judas Iscariot. The tree suggested lines in T. S. Eliot's poem "Gerontion" (1920), a description of spiritual aridity and betrayal:

> . . . In the juvescence of the year
> Came Christ the tiger
>
> In depraved May, dogwood and chestnut, flowering judas,
> To be eaten, to be divided, to be drunk
> Among whispers. . . .

She also thought of the epigraph Eliot used for his poem, from William Shakespeare's *Measure for Meas-* *ure,* a play also closely related to her theme: "Thou hast nor youth nor age / But as it were an after dinner sleep / Dreaming of both."

Above all, she thought about the source of Eliot's description of the dogwood and flowering judas in Henry Adams's account of the eastern springtime. It had been a little more than a year since she read and discussed Adams's autobiography, *The Education of Henry Adams* (written in 1905; commercially published in 1918), with Josephson, and she remembered "The Dynamo and the Virgin," in which Adams compares his feelings on seeing the forty-foot dynamo with those of an early Christian contemplating the cross. The chapter suddenly seemed highly relevant to Laura's sense of being

317

stranded between the lost religion of her childhood and her inadequate faith in machines. With her title Porter brought Eliot's and Adams's works to bear on her theme, and the rich superstructure of symbolism lifted the story onto a new plane and marked a great step forward in her art.

The story appeared in the spring of 1930 as Porter returned to Mexico for her longest period of residence in that country (April 1930 to August 1931). Soon after she arrived in Mexico, she met Eugene Dove Pressly, a young man fourteen years her junior, who became her companion for the next few years and her third or fourth husband in 1933. (Apparently, Porter married at least once, and perhaps twice, in Texas shortly after her divorce from John Henry Koontz in June 1915.)

Pressly, who worked as a secretary for the Crane Foundation in Mexico City, was an attractive man who had a surly, withdrawn personality. Most of Porter's old friends disliked him, interpreting his silence (perhaps correctly) as hostility. All agreed that he lacked the stature of Porter, who was already beginning to be highly regarded by other American contemporary literary figures. Always ready to mock her own garrulousness, Porter said that he had no need to talk because she talked so much. No doubt his subdued nature was largely responsible for the relative success of this relationship, which lasted longer than any other in her life. If he seemed to outsiders dull and ineffective beside his forceful partner, that situation was one which, to her, was a familiar repetition of her childhood home. Pressly provided the traditional heterosexual relationship she needed and at the same time allowed her a certain amount of autonomy within that relationship.

Since the union with Pressly encouraged the side of her that yearned for a traditional domestic life, in March 1931 she threw herself into that life. With Pressly and Mary Doherty she rented a large house in Mixcoac, spent much time acquiring furniture and tending the garden, collected a menagerie of small animals, entertained a great deal, and had a stream of house guests, including Hart Crane, Peggy Cowley, and other Americans. Not surprisingly, she made little progress on the Mexican novel, which was destined like the Cotton Mather project never to be finished.

The time in Mexico did, however, yield one important work. In December 1930 she had met the Russian film director Sergei Eisenstein, who was making *Que Viva Mexico* (unfinished but later edited and released as *Thunder Over Mexico*, 1933). She was invited to spend a few days in July 1931 at Hacienda Tetlapayac in the state of Hidalgo, one of the loca-

tions on which the film was shot. The three-day visit provided the materials for "Hacienda," a nonfiction version of which was published in the October 1932 issue of *Virginia Quarterly Review* before its separate publication as a work of fiction in 1934. The long story is a roman à clef that provides a vivid portrait of Eisenstein, his entourage, and various Mexican actors and assistants, including Adolfo Best-Maugard. It also expresses Porter's own feelings about Mexico as she prepared to leave it for the last time. Thoroughly disillusioned with the political and social atmosphere, she returned subsequently only for brief visits as an invited guest, and then only decades later. Of course Porter's restlessness and desire to move was only partly related to the country itself. Her unresolved personal conflicts made her prey to dissatisfaction with all locations and, feeling alienated everywhere, she always hoped that she might feel at home in some other, distant, future place. In August 1931 her desire to move was encouraged by the Guggenheim Foundation, which had awarded her a fellowship. She decided to go, as she had long wished, to Europe.

For the journey to Europe with Pressly, Porter chose the cheapest means of travel she could find, the S.S. *Werra*, which she called a tramp steamer disguised as a passenger ship. The *Werra* left from Veracruz and called along the way at various ports, including Havana and Tenerife. The passengers were of all nationalities, including Germans returning thankfully to their homeland after long periods of "exile" in Mexico. Since she was not married to Pressly, Porter was assigned to a cabin with two other women, and, gregarious by temperament, she got to know many of the passengers. She took detailed notes on the journey and immediately saw in it the possibility for a story, which she tentatively called "Promised Land." It eventually grew into *Ship of Fools*.

She said later that when she set out on her first trip to Europe, her destination was France and that she landed in Germany only because she chose a German ship bound for Bremen as the cheapest available transportation. Yet the interest in that country sparked by her association with German families in Texas (she did, in fact, tell Erna Schlemmer that she went to Germany on her account) drew her to the country and kept her in Berlin for four months after arrival.

She was, as usual, feeling frustrated because so few of her planned fictions were ever finished. Most of her friends published far more than she did, and she began to despair of ever accomplishing what she knew she was capable of. Once in Berlin, she tried to cut down on the distractions and live in isolation and write. Pressly went off to Spain, where his knowledge of the language qualified him for a secretarial job at the American Embassy. Porter remained behind in a pension. Pressly's absence did not, of course, guarantee for Porter a cloistered productive time. Almost immediately she made contact with the American community and was being escorted around Berlin by Herbert Klein, a young journalist, and attending soirees at the home of Sigrid Schultz, the head of the *Chicago Tribune* bureau. At one of the dinner parties in Berlin she attracted the attention of Hermann Goering and was escorted by him (accompanied by his bodyguard) on at least one outing to a nightclub. Once again, her active life and lively, gregarious personality were exposing her to experiences that provided the material for fiction, if she could only find the time and concentration. In one sense she was working on future fiction, because in Berlin, as on the S.S. *Werra,* she kept detailed accounts of everything that happened. Not only did she write up her impressions for future use, but her loneliness and sense of isolation also made her a copious letter writer. Her letters to such friends as Malcolm Cowley and Caroline Gordon and her daily outpourings to Pressly were almost as long as stories. Without realizing what she was doing, she was writing draft after draft of "The Leaning Tower," sharpening and refining her observations and expressions in preparation for the time when she would write the final version.

In the early months of 1932 she decided to go to Spain and marry Pressly. A stopover in Paris caused her to change her mind, and after a short visit with Pressly in Madrid she returned to Paris. She valued the stability of Pressly's devotion but said she had fallen in love with Paris, and the city was his only rival. However, when he received a lifetime appointment in the American foreign service that took him to Basel, Switzerland, Porter joined him there in June 1932. One of the most important results of her months in Basel was that the place sparked memories of her early years in Texas, just as her time in Salem, Massachusetts, had done years before. She wrote the first draft of "Noon Wine," the story that, more than any other, captures the atmosphere of her native state. The work describes the effect on a failing dairy farm of a mysterious stranger from another region—a hired man—who proves to be the salvation of the little farm. The harmony caused by his presence is abruptly shattered when an unscrupulous character comes from the North, announcing that the hired man is an escaped criminal and seeking to return him to prison. In a moment of rage the owner of the

Eugene Dove Pressly, whom Porter married on 11 March 1933 (photograph by Porter; Papers of Katherine Anne Porter, Special Collections, University of Maryland Libraries)

farm kills the bounty hunter and, finally, after many vain efforts to convince his neighbors that he is not a murderer, kills himself. The title of the story suggests the rough wine of a southern region, well expressing Porter's consciousness that she was mythologizing and capturing the essence of her own region. In an essay, "Noon Wine: The Sources" (*Yale Review,* September 1956), she accurately describes the effect of her European travels on her own understanding of Texas: "My time in Mexico and Europe served me in a way I had not dreamed of, even, besides its own charm and goodness: it gave me back my past and my own house and my own people—the native land of the heart."

The story, begun in Basel, was not finished there because once again she moved. The reason this time was that Pressly was posted to the American Embassy in Paris, where both of them longed to live. When they were settled exactly where they wished to be and with a steady income, there seemed no reason not to marry. On 11 March 1933 Porter married Pressly in a small ceremony attended by Ford Madox Ford and his companion Janet Biala.

The next three years and ten months, during which she was Mrs. Eugene Pressly, living first in a small apartment overlooking a convent on the boulevard Montparnasse and later in a pleasant studio apartment on rue Notre Dame des Champs, were perhaps the happiest of her life. Since Pressly was away all day, she had time to work. She developed a pleasant group of friends, and the café society of Paris curbed to some extent her hospitality and prevented another lapse into domesticity on a large scale. She met Matthew Josephson again, as well as her old friend Josephine Herbst, and further developed relationships with friends who were to be lifelong supporters—Glenway Wescott, Barbara Harrison (who later married Wescott's brother Lloyd), and Monroe Wheeler.

Porter often wondered why Paris should have cast such a spell on her and caused such a flowering of her art. She said she did not love the cold drizzling gray city for all the obvious reasons—the American bar life, the pretty clothes, the people, the theaters, the art shows, and the music. Perhaps the best account of the coming together of external circumstances with her internal development, producing her full maturity as a writer, is given in her 29 April 1945 letter to Herbst:

> I didn't begin to feel contemporary, or as if I had come into my proper time of life until just a few years ago. I think after I went to Europe—Europe was the place for me, somehow, Paris the city, France the country. From there, I got a perspective and somehow without struggle my point of view fell into clear focus, right for me, at any rate; and what other rightness is there for the individual.

Perhaps the crucial factor was the geographical and cultural distance of Paris from Texas. No place could have been more antithetical to Texas than Paris, and it gave her a new perspective on her early years. She was able to contemplate her childhood in an atmosphere that revived no painful memories of poverty, death, and strict fundamentalist morality. In Paris she researched her family's roots because, she said, she did not want to feel like an exile. Yet for all the so-called research, the family past she reconstructed was based more on her imagination than on historical records, and the result was not factual but fictional. In a speech she gave at the urging of Sylvia Beach to the American Women's Club in Paris in November 1935, she spoke of a novel-in-progress about her family, the first section of which was called "Legend and Memory." In April 1934 Porter had sent Donald Brace a manuscript with this title. It included six stories, all of which

eventually appeared with "The Fig Tree" under the rubric "The Old Order" in Porter's *Collected Stories*.

During Porter's nearly four years in Paris, while many works were started only to be abandoned, others did actually come to fruition, were sent out, and published. Porter had always relied on the assistance of friends in placing her work. Herbst and Josephson had been instrumental in placing two early stories in *transition*. Now, once again, friends helped to usher her work into print. Barbara Harrison and Monroe Wheeler ran a small press called Harrison of Paris, which published fine editions. They brought out *Katherine Anne Porter's French Song-Book* in 1933 and *Hacienda* in 1934. Adding to her sense of accomplishment, Harcourt, Brace in 1935 republished the *Flowering Judas* collection, adding "Theft" and "That Tree" along with two new stories: "The Cracked Looking-Glass" and "Hacienda." Other friends back in the United States were now associated with important literary magazines—Allen Tate with the *Virginia Quarterly Review* and Robert Penn Warren with the *Southern Review*. Tate and Warren published the stories in the "Legend and Memory" manuscript in those publications when Harcourt, Brace was not able to place them elsewhere.

Two of those stories, both published in 1935, are remarkable treatments of a subject that had appeared in "Virgin Violeta"—sexual terror. The difference is that, whereas in the early version of the theme she had distanced herself from her subject, she now moved courageously into her own autobiographical experience. In "The Grave" (*Virginia Quarterly Review*, April 1935; also in *The Leaning Tower*), through her fictional representative Miranda Gay, Porter describes an incident that had happened about the time her grandmother died in 1901. Porter was accompanying her brother on a rabbit-shooting expedition when he shot and eviscerated a female rabbit carrying young. In the story Miranda is just experiencing the first stirrings of her female destiny. She is growing tired of being a tomboy and yearns for the trappings of femininity: pretty clothes, jewelry, and perfumes. The knowledge thrust upon her so crudely and abruptly when her brother lays open the womb of the dead rabbit is a shock. Yet this knowledge of the other, more dangerous, side of female destiny seems something she has really known all along (Miranda's mother, like Porter's own, had died as a result of childbearing).

The rabbit incident is powerful enough to stand alone as a complete story, but Porter adds another dimension by placing it in the context of Miranda's whole life, showing that the effects of this small event are neither trivial nor transient and that the past is not easily sloughed off. She tells of Miranda years later walking through the marketplace of a strange city in a strange country; a Mexican-Indian vendor shows her a tray of dyed sugar sweets. Suddenly the sights and sounds converge to bring back to her mind, from where it has long lain buried, the memory of her brother and the rabbit. The memory horrifies her, reinforcing the frightening nature of the incident and showing the capacity of past experiences to lie dormant and make an unexpected ambush.

The story is one of Porter's finest and most popular, frequently anthologized and endlessly explicated. Students of her work have commented on the grave image, which links the episodes and underscores the connection of life and love and death. They have continued to explore the suggestion of such objects as the coffin screw, shaped like the dove of Venus (symbol of earthly love), and the womb-grave of the dead rabbit. Like "Flowering Judas," this story is one of the great achievements of her art as a short-story writer.

"The Circus" (*Southern Review,* July 1935; also in *The Leaning Tower*) is an almost equally powerful treatment of the same theme. Here Miranda has her first experience of a family excursion. She is taken to the circus in the company of her older cousin who is also named Miranda Gay, the family beauty, and young Miranda wishes to be "exactly like her" when she grows up. She is still a child, however, and does not understand why little boys stand under the bleachers looking under the skirts of the women and grinning without friendliness. The sinister grins of the boys are replicated by one of the circus clowns, who dangles apparently out of control from the high wire. His head turns from side to side like a seal, and he blows "sneering kisses from his cruel mouth." At the sight of the man's face, Miranda is overwhelmed with fear and is carried out, screaming hysterically. As in "The Grave," the terror of the moment comes back to haunt her as a nightmare. Thus, Porter was able to bear witness unflinchingly to her own deepest inner terrors.

Having through time, geographical distance, and fictional shaping reassembled her own past and achieved success as a writer, it was perhaps natural that she should wish to reinforce her newly achieved sense of wholeness by returning to her family and to the scenes of her childhood. To this end, she left Pressly in Paris in February 1936 and made the trip to the United States. In New York she visited the friends recently returned from Paris who had already become important to her—Monroe Wheeler, Glenway Wescott, and Barbara Harrison, who had just married Glenway's brother. The most important part

Dust jacket for Porter's 1939 collection of novellas based on events in her life before 1920

of her trip, however, was her visit to Houston, where her sisters and brother now lived. Greeted as a returning celebrity, she made acquaintance with the next generation of the family—her sister Gay's daughter, Ann, and her brother's son, Paul. For the rest of Porter's life and in spite of temporary quarrels, Ann and Paul became her protégés and surrogate children. With her father and sisters, Porter made the pilgrimage back to Indian Creek, where she was born and where her mother was buried. It was an important scene of reconciliation with her past, and she celebrated it in a poem, "Anniversary in a Country Cemetery," recalled it often, and ever afterward thought of Indian Creek as her home.

She had hoped that her teenage niece, Ann, who was interested in ballet, would join her in Paris, but when Porter returned, her situation there began to deteriorate. Sometimes she later explained her quick return to the United States as being due to the European political situation. In fact, her relationship with Pressly was coming to an end; her creativity was at its peak; and once again she needed a change of surroundings.

In October 1936 Porter and Pressly left Paris and, on arrival in New York, went their separate ways. Porter went into a period of seclusion in an inn in Pennsylvania, choosing that location in part because it was near to Erwinna, the home of Herbst.

Porter's difficulties with the final drafts of stories that were almost complete in her mind had various causes. She was always prey to distractions and to affairs of the heart; she had developed in her best stories the techniques of probing painfully repressed experiences, and this process, as she aptly expressed it herself, was as painful as tapping spinal fluid. There was another compelling reason for her difficulty in completing projects. This was her difficulty in reconciling herself to the activity of being a professional writer, not associated in her mind with femininity. This difficulty was shared by many of her writer friends and literary admirers, who, captivated by her delicacy and beauty, related to her as suitors rather than as fellow professionals. Wescott, for instance, described her fancifully as looking like Marie Antoinette Porter playing her typewriter as if it were a spinet. The poet-priest Raymond Roseliep wrote many poems praising her beauty, depicting her in her library with volumes of Cotton Mather, Laurence Sterne, and Voltaire, resting her hand beside them "moonflower pale / light as a mussel shell." The descriptions are charming, but they were highly destructive as she waged her own constant struggle between being an artist and being a desirable woman.

She could best cope with the tensions generated by that struggle by going into seclusion. Of the many retreats she made during her life, none was more productive than the period she spent in the Water Wheel Tavern in Doylestown, Pennsylvania. There she finished the two "short novels" "Noon Wine" and "Old Mortality" and was well into a third—"Pale Horse, Pale Rider"—before returning to Pressly in New York in late December 1936.

In the early months of 1937 there was a brief attempt to patch up the marriage, painfully complicated by his reluctance to admit that the relationship was over and by her desire to be free. On 31 March 1937 he finally left New York for a three-month job in Venezuela. Porter left New York in June, traveling to Texas for her father's eightieth birthday. In July she made the first of many annual appearances at the Olivet College writers' conference in Michigan. She spent the month of August at Benfolly, the home of Caroline Gordon and Allan Tate in Tennessee. She was not the only writer visiting the hospitable Tates; Robert Lowell, eager to learn from Tate, had set up a tent in the garden, and Albert Erskine, the business editor of the *Southern Review,* was also a guest. Erskine had fallen in love with Porter's stories that had been published in the review, and now the young man fell in love with their glamorous silver-haired author. When the two sat up talking long into the night, Tate lay awake listening to them, incredulous that, despite the twenty-year age gap between them, they should be lovers.

In September, Porter settled in an apartment in New Orleans, and Erskine made regular weekend visits from Baton Rouge (he was a graduate student at Louisiana State University) to be with her. During those weeks, she tried to maintain the momentum in her writing that she had established in the previous fall. Inevitably, the excitement of the affair slowed down the progress of her fiction, and perhaps for that reason, when she visited her family for Christmas, she decided to remain in Houston for the next few months. She told Erskine she had developed bronchial troubles and had to stay near her family doctor, but her health seems to have been the excuse rather than the reason for her decision to find an apartment in Houston.

She had managed to finish "Pale Horse, Pale Rider" in late December 1937 prior to leaving for Houston. This "short novel" in *Pale Horse, Pale Rider* (first published in *Southern Review,* 1938) was based on her experiences twenty years earlier when she nearly died of influenza in Denver. The details of her life and work in the story, when compared with the columns she wrote in the *Rocky Mountain News,* are so accurate that she may have been working from a draft written close to the time of the actual events. Yet when she created the character of Adam, Miranda Gay's love interest, she drew on Erskine and Pressly. The story became Porter's portrait of the artist as a young woman, the story of an aspiring writer struggling to survive the many forces threatening her existence. Miranda is sickened by the anti-German propaganda, the trumped-up patriotism, and the exploitation and materialism of the patriarchal figures in authority, in the military, and on the paper for which she works. Her lover dies, and she almost dies, but ultimately she emerges, alive but much changed by her experiences. With that ambitious story successfully completed, Porter again took up "Promised Land," the story based on the journey she had made in 1931 from Vera Cruz to Bremerhaven, Germany.

In Houston she exchanged daily letters with Erskine. Many of these dealt with his urging her to marry him and with her resistance. Finally she gave in and decided that what he wished was what she also wished. Her divorce from Pressly was finalized on 9 April 1938; on 16 April, Erskine came to Houston to drive her back to Louisiana. She carefully prevented his meeting her family and went with him to Baton Rouge, where the two were married, with Robert Penn Warren acting as best man, on 19 April.

The marriage was doomed almost from the moment the vows were taken. In the first place, Erskine, who was in his mid twenties, learned only during the actual wedding ceremony that Porter was approaching fifty. His shock deeply humiliated Porter. In addition, he turned out to be much more assertive than the taciturn Pressly. He resented his wife's attendance at conferences and the time she spent on her work. Apart from his objections to her activities, he was the constant distraction that any partner would have been for her. She once more played the role of housewife, making a home, cooking on a grand scale, entertaining, and socializing. In her 1938 Christmas letter to Erna Schlemmer Johns she wrote almost boastfully of her marital happiness, clearly sensing that it was this aspect of her life rather than her literary achievements that represented status in Erna's eyes. Her letter could not have been more false, because the truth of her situation during the next few years was that personal unhappiness and literary success went hand in hand. In 1939 she published *Pale Horse, Pale Rider,* a collection of three of her best pieces of fiction. She characterized these three as "short novels." They included the title work, "Noon Wine," and "Old Mortality." She was the heroine of the hour, and when she returned to the conference at Olivet College after its publication, the audience applauded spontaneously when she entered the room.

On the literary horizon there was only one cloud. The Texas Institute of Letters, the chief literary body in her native state, had just established a prestigious award. When she was told that she was certain to win, she was jubilant at the thought of gaining honor in her own state, and the medal promised to put the final touch on her reconciliation with her roots. The medal, however, went instead to J. Frank Dobie for his book *Apache Gold and Yacqui Silver* (1939), the decision being justified by the "indigenous nature of his subject matter" and his long residence in Texas. Porter was outraged, and all the recent goodwill toward her native state collapsed in an instant. Over the years the attempted rapprochement between Porter and Texas was repeated. She thought that the University of Texas was going to name a library for her; she planned to return to live where she had grown up, on the outskirts of Austin. The University of Texas thought that she would give her papers to its library. Nothing ever came of these plans. Porter yearned always to be accepted as the first and most distinguished Texas writer–which she was–but that honor and all

Porter with her third husband, Albert Erskine, whom she married on 19 April 1938

the attendant honors went instead to Dobie. It was he who had a room set up in his honor, a literary fellowship named for him, and eventually a university chair named for him. Although writers such as William Humphrey and William Goyen have acknowledged that they were inspired by Porter, the apparently virile image of Dobie as literary forebear seems to have been more acceptable to Texans.

The end of her fifth decade should have been the happiest time of Porter's life because she was at the peak of success, but disappointments came crowding in. She and Erskine decided to separate in spring 1940, and she traveled north to Yaddo, the artist's colony in upstate New York. Once again her recent achievements caused her to be received almost with reverence, and the unofficial title "Queen of Yaddo" was given to her. She mourned the fall of France, her failed marriage, and the conclusion that she would never be a wife. She despaired over her homelessness (reinforced by her estrangement from Texas), worried about her state of financial insolvency, and tried to write.

As she listened to the radio accounts of events in Europe, her thoughts turned to her months in

Berlin in 1931, and it was the story of that time, "The Leaning Tower," that claimed her attention. She saw that, from her present perspective, she could finish it. By doing so she hoped to solve several of her problems. She would feel that she had rallied her creative energies once more, and she hoped she could sell the story for a good price. There was also another factor. She had been worrying a great deal about what the artist should do in time of war and, with her strong moral sense, had wondered if her own kind of writing, based on her own personal inner life, was not somehow irrelevant in a time of global disaster. The Berlin story was not narrowly personal, and since it dealt with the menace of the Nazi party, she felt that it was a contribution to the war effort.

In her final version she drew on experiences of a widely disparate kind. For the first and only time she made her fictional representative male, a choice that possibly reflects her identification with Pressly during the Berlin period. For protagonist Charles Upton's childhood friend Kuno Hillentafel, whose German background and German holidays had first stimulated his interest in Germany, she drew on her own memories of Erna Schlemmer:

> He and Kuno did not remember when they had not known each other. Their first recollection was of standing next to each other in a row of children like themselves, singing, or some such nonsense–it must have been kindergarten. . . .

> Mr. Hillentafel took his family back to Germany for a few months every two years, and Kuno's postcards, with their foreign stamps, coming from far-off places like Bremen and Wiesbaden and Mannheim and Heidelberg and Berlin, had brought the great world across the sea, the blue silent deep world of Europe, straight to Charles' door.

In depicting the boarders of Rosa Reichl's pension, where she had stayed in Berlin, Porter did not change the names but modified the characters, often grafting onto them traits of people she had known elsewhere. Rosa, whom she had really liked, she turned into an unpleasant character. She suppressed Rosa's anti-Semitism but heightened other offensive characteristics, making the landlady barely able to mask her hatred for the American Upton, whose rich country she believed responsible for the poverty of her own.

Herr Bussen, a young Dalmatian student, is the closest to the original of her characters, and she used a melancholy conversation she had with him in the hall about Rosa's insults to him and another male boarder. For the military boarder she had not

actually seen, she used the character of Hermann Goering, but she suppressed what Goering had told her about Jews, that they were the ruin of Germany and that, once the Hitler regime was established, there would not be a Jew left in Germany with any political or cultural or economic power. She did, however, use Goering's Nietzschean views.

For the Polish boarder, Tadeusz Mey, she used the appearance, mannerisms, and even whole speeches of Joseph Retinger that she had recorded twenty years earlier in Mexico City. She even gave her character the family name of Retinger's guardian, Zamoyski (spelled differently). When Mey is introduced, he says: "Tadeusz Mey. Polish in spite of the misleading name. Indiscreet grandmother married an Austrian. The rest of my family have names like Zamoisky, lucky devils." And her notes for the story show that she used the memories of another Pole, Janice Tworkov Biala, the companion of Ford Madox Ford: "The Polish Jews also believe that a Jew must not pass a Catholic Church at midnight, for at that moment the souls of all members of the congregation who have died that year will rush out in the shape of swine and drown him (told to me by Biala, Polish Jewish painter as told from her grandmother)."

In this story she uses again the symbolic method that had proven so effective in "Flowering Judas." Here the symbolic structure developed from a cheap souvenir of the Leaning Tower of Pisa, which Pressly had crumpled in his hand as they looked at pensions in Berlin.

On its simplest level it is a tawdry tourist souvenir, as fragile and insubstantial as the dreams of the characters. The original, built in the fourteenth century as a bell tower, is an ornate and impressive structure in sturdy white marble. Yet a weakness in the foundations caused it to settle and lean, so that it cannot be used as a bell tower and must receive injections of cement to prevent its collapse. Thus it suggests the Germany that Porter saw, so apparently solid and substantial, and yet undermined by a basic flaw in its foundations.

The Leaning Tower of Pisa, furthermore, has sinister overtones from its association with Canto XXXIII of *The Inferno,* in which Dante meets the traitors to their own country. Dante's central figure here is Ugolino of Pisa, who conspired with an enemy party of that city to defeat a rival faction within his own Guelph party. His treachery merely served to weaken his own party, so that he found himself at the mercy of the very enemy with whom he had conspired. He was imprisoned with his children and grandchildren in a tower (not the Leaning Tower, although Dante's story is closely connected with

Pisa through Ugolino's imprecation against that city); the keys were thrown away; and he was forced to watch his children and grandchildren die of hunger before he himself starved to death. Although critics disagree about the meaning of Ugolino's statement that, after the deaths of his children, hunger had more power than grief, a frequent conclusion has been that Ugolino resorted to cannibalism. Even if the historical facts behind Dante's story do not entirely justify this interpretation, the fact that Ugolino in hell is feeding upon the skull of his enemy suggests that Dante saw such activity as the appropriate fate for those who hope to advance themselves by destroying their own kind and kin.

The account of the chance-gathered occupants of Rosa Reichl's pension, all wanderers or defectors from their native lands, is full of images from the Ugolino story. The claustrophobic atmosphere of the house in which they are all shut up, waiting for disaster and with no means of escape (only for Upton is a ship coming from America), is conveyed in images of imprisonment, starvation, cannibalism, death, and hell.

The Leaning Tower of Pisa has always been associated with Galileo because of his birth in that city, and according to legend he once dropped weights from the tower to test his theory of the velocity of falling bodies. Since the life story of Galileo evokes and dramatizes the dilemma of the clear-sighted man in a misguided society, it is relevant to the predicament of the man of vision in Nazi Germany. When Porter was asked about the responsibility of writers in time of war, she replied, "The responsibility of the artist toward society is the plain and simple responsibility of any other human being, for I refuse to separate the artist from the human race: his prime responsibility 'when and if war comes' is not to go mad" ("Three Statements about Writing," in *The Collected Essays and Occasional Writings of Katherine Anne Porter,* 1970).

A more detailed answer to the question is found in "The Leaning Tower." While one cynical artist retreats into the romantic music of Frédéric Chopin, Upton does not see his art as a refuge or a retreat. He sees clearly what is going on around him, does not deceive himself, and records the ghastly caricatures of human beings that he sees.

It seems possible that if Porter had settled down quietly at Yaddo and kept on working, the flow of creativity that produced this fine story might have been sustained. Instead of doing so, however, she found another major distraction. She decided to solve her problem of homelessness by buying a house in the Saratoga Springs area.

Porter in 1947 (photograph by George Platt Lynes)

Not only did the purchasing of the house, the arranging for renovations, and the choosing of furniture prove to be a major distraction, but it also plunged her into financial difficulties. First of all, the projected sale of "The Leaning Tower" for a large sum of money to *Harper's Bazaar* had fallen through. She had sent in the story, and, as she wrote in a 21 January 1941 letter to Glenway Wescott, it had been returned to her "most expertly disemboweled" by one of the editors. Porter realized that the story was quite long, but she had understood it was to run in two installments. Furious, Porter demanded that the story be returned rather than have it appear in a shortened form. She then sold it to the *Southern Review* for a mere three hundred dollars. Then, in an effort to raise money for her house, she signed several contracts for works that she could not possibly finish on time. These included a novel then called "No Safe Harbor," which was to be an extended version of "Promised Land," based on her journey to Germany ten years earlier. The contracts and deadlines, as they always did, set up a sense of panic, which in turn led to creative paralysis.

She was fifty years old, lonely, unhappy, financially insolvent, and, after she moved into her house, geographically isolated. Most discouraging of all was her sense that her creative powers were failing, and the cap sheaf of her misery was that in spring 1942 she had to undertake alone the dreary journey to Reno, Nevada, to get the quick divorce

Erskine was now urging on her because he wanted to remarry. Perhaps her desperation alone can account for what took place during her period of residence in Reno.

Porter shared with many writers of her generation the anti-Semitism rife in America before World War II. To that she added her own deeply ambivalent feelings toward African Americans. She publicly opposed integration in 1958, and she privately jotted slurs against blacks and Jews in her papers and books. Her doing so conflicts with virtually all of her public positions and with the personal relationships she developed with individuals, both Jewish and African American. It also conflicts with the high moral tone she adopted toward Nazi Germany and with the political acumen she claimed as a result of her firsthand experience of events in Mexico and in Germany. Like her attitudes toward feminism, her attitudes toward politics were ambivalent and confused. When she was interviewed by FBI agents on the subject of Josephine Herbst in Reno, she recounted Herbst's radical activities to the authorities. Herbst knew that someone had informed against her but never guessed the identity of the informant, and the friendship between the two women continued.

At this time Porter's publishers optimistically expected the novel. Instead, they were besieged by constant requests for money—further advances on works-in-progress, pleas for new contracts, and instructions to sell parts of unfinished works to well-paying magazines. In 1944, therefore, Harcourt, Brace published her third and last volume of previously uncollected stories—*The Leaning Tower and Other Stories*. Only two of the stories had been finished in the last eight years, and most of the volume consisted of stories written and published during her years in Paris. The book was deservedly praised, but Porter's most productive period of creativity was over.

She continued to work at her writing, occasionally publishing stories and essays, working intermittently on the novel, in which the interest of publishers and readers never abated. Her own life, moreover, continued to be as eventful as ever. In January 1944 she moved to Washington, D.C., where Tate, who held the first Chair of Poetry at the Library of Congress, recommended that she be asked to fill out John Peale Bishop's uncompleted term as Fellow of Regional Literature. After that, she went to Hollywood and worked for about two years as a scriptwriter. Her success with a summer class at Stanford University in 1947 led to the first of several teaching stints at universities: Stanford University (1948-1949); University of Michigan

(1953-1954); University of Liege (Fulbright Fellow, 1954); University of Virginia (1958); and Washington and Lee University (1959). Porter supplemented her income by giving readings and lectures and by appearing on radio and television. When not in residence at one of the academic institutions above, she lived for extended periods in three places: New York City (1949-1953); Southbury, Connecticut (1955-1958); and Washington, D.C. (1959-1962).

Ship of Fools was published on 1 April 1962. Not surprisingly for a work that had been so long anticipated, it achieved instant best-sellerdom. In addition, the movie rights were sold soon after publication, and the film, directed by Stanley Kramer, had a brilliant cast that included Vivien Leigh, Simone Signoret, Lee Marvin, Jose Ferrer, Jose Greco, and Oskar Werner. As a result, Porter achieved in her mid seventies the financial security that had eluded her for most of her life. Henceforth, as long as her strength lasted, she was able to travel and to live comfortably. Furthermore, she could boast that she had earned it all herself.

After the immediate excitement had subsided, more-sober critical judgments were made. It was generally agreed that her reputation would rest not on the novel—which upon reflection appeared to have some major flaws—but on her short stories. This consensus was evident when the *Collected Stories*, published in 1964, won both a National Book Award and a Pulitzer Prize.

When in 1940, at the time of the fall of France, she had written an introduction to the Modern Library edition of *Flowering Judas and Other Stories*, Porter said that her aim in all her work had been "to understand the logic of this majestic and terrible failure of the life of man in the Western World." *Ship of Fools* was clearly her final and most ambitious attempt to achieve her aim. As on her own journey, her fictional ship was headed toward a Germany in which Hitler was just beginning his rise to power. The ship *Vera* was presented as a microcosm of Europe in 1931, written with the immediacy of observations made at the time and finished decades later with the benefit of hindsight. She summed up her theme in a September 1961 talk she gave to students at the University of Wichita in Kansas (in *Katherine Anne Porter: Conversations*, 1987):

I had seen these criminals—these clowns—like Hitler, and was stricken by an idea: if people like this could take over the world! Of course there were all the good people who didn't believe in the clowns, but they still let the clowns commit the crimes good worthy people would commit if only they had the nerve. How else to account for the collusion in evil that enables a creature like

Porter holding the key to the Katherine Anne Porter Room of the University of Maryland library, presented to her by University of Maryland president Wilson Elkins (to her right) on 15 May 1968 (photograph by Bill Clark; Papers of Katherine Anne Porter, Special Collections, University of Maryland Libraries)

Mussolini, or Hitler, or Huey Long, or McCarthy . . . to get hold of things?

The tragedy of our times is not an accident but a total consent.

It was an assessment of a situation she may not have fully understood. Oddly enough, the movie version of the novel, by making one small change, illustrated how dangerously near to melodrama her vision was. The film transformation of Herr Rieber, her caricature of a Jew, into a benign character made the good/evil conflict apparent. An anonymous reviewer in the *The Times Literary Supplement* (2 November 1962) expressed well the final verdict on the novel: "One cannot help wondering whether she *knows* enough—of German history, of the sources of modern anti-Semitism, of European middle-class speech and values—or whether that knowledge has penetrated the exquisite, but very special range of her feelings."

For all that, *Ship of Fools* presented the culmination of the theme that had run through her work as a powerful undertow since the beginning—the plight of women trying to live and express themselves in a patriarchal society. She had written in "Holiday," the story that had for so long resisted resolution, "I felt divided into many fragments, having left or lost a part of myself in every place I had travelled, in every life mine had touched, above all, in every death of someone near to me that had carried into the grave some part of my living cells."

If Porter was not equipped for the ambitious scope of the theme she articulated in many interviews, she was more sure than ever before in her treatment of the powerful concern that had always informed her work—the destiny of the woman who refuses to be confined by the limited roles allotted to her under patriarchy. Her German boat under a German captain, assisted by a German doctor, becomes in her hands, once again, a representative patriarchal institution. When she traveled to Germany in 1931, she was struggling with the work of Virginia Woolf, and *Ship of Fools,* like *The Voyage Out* (1915), includes all the possible female roles. There are wives and widows, prostitutes, virgins, and a

327

Porter on the balcony of her College Park, Maryland, apartment in 1975 (photograph by Paul Porter)

bride. Yet three characters seem closely related as Porter's own fictional representatives, a fact noted by critic Daniel Curley, who found three Mirandas in *Ship of Fools,* and by Stanley Kramer. These characters are the young artist Jenny Brown, the middle-aged divorcée Mary Treadwell, and the aristocratic political activist La Condesa, now in her advanced years and still a brave soul in spite of her drug addiction and predilection for young men.

At first glance the ending of the novel might seem to be as unresolved as the endings of "Holiday" and "The Cracked Looking Glass." The joy that many of the characters feel at the end of the voyage, when they see their fatherland, is undercut by the knowledge of the political morass into which they are headed. At the same time, the three women characters closely associated with Porter's point of view make strong gestures of independence and defiance. They are not drawn back into traps, domestic or otherwise, as were so many of the characters in the earlier stories—such as Violeta, Rosaleen, the narrator in "Holiday," and the prostitute in "Magic." La Condesa refuses the conciliatory gestures of Dr. Schumann and leaves him to face the knowledge of his shameful exploitation of her. Mary Treadwell strikes back at the drunken oaf who insults her and all women. It is true that she is lonely as she sails away from the *Vera,* but she is also

self-sufficient and knows where she is headed. Above all, Jenny Brown, locked in a destructive relationship with her lover, determines that "this business" is not going to throw her off track as an artist. She realizes that there is going to be something more important in her life than David Scott or any other man.

Porter had eighteen more years in which to enjoy the material rewards of her novel, to celebrate the collections of her stories and essays, and even to produce a new work. *The Never-Ending Wrong* (1977), an account of her participation in the Sacco-Vanzetti protests, was published three years before her death, to coincide with the fiftieth anniversary of the execution.

Perhaps the most important development of her last years for students of her work was her donation of her papers and her personal library to the University of Maryland. Over the years Porter had toyed with the idea of giving her papers to various institutions, including the University of Texas at Austin and the Library of Congress. However, in December 1966 she announced her bequest to the University of Maryland would include not only her papers and books but also significant items of memorabilia from her home. Porter's high regard for University of Maryland President Wilson Elkins and his wife, fellow Texas natives, and the close proximity of the university to her home in Washington, D.C., were factors that led to the decision. The university opened the Katherine Anne Porter Room in McKeldin Library on 15 May 1968, Porter's seventy-eighth birthday. Until her health declined in the mid 1970s, Porter often visited the Porter Room, reviewing her papers and books, and participated in campus life.

The geographical separation of her literary and physical remains was indicative of a lifelong ambivalence on many subjects, most of all her relationship with her native state. After her death, her ashes were, at her request, taken back to Texas, to the cemetery in Indian Creek where her mother was buried.

Posthumous publications of Porter's work include correspondence, book reviews, fiction, nonfiction, and poetry. Isabel Bayley, Porter's literary trustee, edited *Letters of Katherine Anne Porter,* which was published on the one-hundredth anniversary of her birth. In 1991 Darlene Harbour Unrue brought together Porter's previously uncollected book reviews in *"This Strange, Old World" and Other Book Reviews. The Uncollected Early Prose of Katherine Anne Porter* (1993), edited by Ruth M. Alvarez and Thomas Walsh, includes fiction and nonfiction, both unpublished and previously published, written between 1920 and 1932. *Katherine Anne Porter's Poetry,* edited, with an introduction, by Darlene Harbour Unrue, appeared in 1996.

Letters:

Letters of Katherine Anne Porter, selected and edited, with an introduction by Isabel Bayley (New York: Atlantic Monthly, 1990).

Interviews:

Barbara Thompson, "The Art of Fiction XXIX–Katherine Anne Porter: An Interview," *Paris Review,* no. 29 (Winter–Spring 1963): 87–114;

Enrique Hank Lopez, *Conversations with Katherine Anne Porter: Refugee from Indian Creek* (Boston: Little, Brown, 1981);

Joan Givner, ed., *Katherine Anne Porter: Conversations* (Jackson & London: University Press of Mississippi, 1987).

Bibliographies:

William A. Sylvester, "A Selected and Critical Bibliography of the Uncollected Works of Katherine Anne Porter," *Bulletin of Bibliography,* 19 (January–April 1947): 36;

Edward Schwartz, "Katherine Anne Porter: A Critical Bibliography," *Bulletin of the New York Public Library,* 57 (May 1953): 211–247;

Louise Waldrip and Shirley Ann Bauer, *A Bibliography of the Works of Katherine Anne Porter and A Bibliography of the Criticism of the Works of Katherine Anne Porter* (Metuchen, N.J.: Scarecrow Press, 1969);

George Bixby, "Katherine Anne Porter: A Bibliographical Checklist," *American Book Collector,* new series, 1 (November–December 1980): 19–33;

Joan Givner, Jane DeMouy, and Ruth M. Alvarez, "Katherine Anne Porter," in *American Women Writers,* edited by Maurice Duke, Jackson R. Bryer, and M. Thomas Inge (Westport, Conn.: Greenwood Press, 1983);

Kathryn Hilt and Ruth M. Alvarez, *Katherine Anne Porter: An Annotated Bibliography* (New York: Garland, 1990).

Biography:

Joan Givner, *Katherine Anne Porter: A Life* (New York: Simon & Schuster, 1982; London: Cape, 1983; revised edition, Athens: University of Georgia Press, 1991).

References:

Charles A. Allen, "Katherine Anne Porter: Psychology as Art," *Southwest Review,* 41 (Summer 1956): 223–230;

Allen, "The Nouvelles of Katherine Anne Porter," *University of Kansas City Review,* 29 (December 1962): 87–93;

Thomas Austenfeld, "Katherine Anne Porter Abroad: The Politics of Emotion," *Literatur in Wissenschaff und Unterricht,* 27 (1994): 27–33;

Harold Bloom, ed., *Katherine Anne Porter: Modern Critical Views Series* (New York, New Haven & Philadelphia: Chelsea House, 1986);

Will Brantley, *Feminine Sense in Southern Memoir: Smith, Glasgow, Welty, Hellman, Porter, and Hurston* (Jackson: University Press of Mississippi, 1993);

Robert H. Brinkmeyer Jr., *Katherine Anne Porter's Artistic Development: Primitivism, Traditionalism, and Totalitarianism* (Baton Rouge: Louisiana State University Press, 1993);

Virginia Spencer Carr, ed., *"Flowering Judas": Katherine Anne Porter* (New Brunswick, N.J.: Rutgers University Press, 1993);

George Cheatham, "Death and Repetition in Porter's Miranda Stories," *American Literature,* 61 (December 1989): 610–624;

George Core, "The Best Residuum of Truth," *Georgia Review,* 20 (Fall 1966): 278–291;

Daniel Curley, "Katherine Anne Porter: The Larger Plan," *Kenyon Review,* 25 (Autumn 1963): 671–695;

Jane DeMouy, *Katherine Anne Porter's Women: The Eye of Her Fiction* (Austin: University of Texas Press, 1983);

Winfred S. Emmons, *Katherine Anne Porter: The Regional Stories* (Austin: Steck-Vaughn, 1967);

Joan Givner, "The Genesis of *Ship of Fools,*" *Southern Literary Journal,* 10 (Fall 1977): 14–30;

Givner, "Her Great Art, Her Sober Craft: Katherine Anne Porter's Creative Process," *Southwest Review,* 62 (Summer 1977): 217–230;

Givner, "Katherine Anne Porter and the Art of Caricature," *Genre,* 5 (March 1972): 51–61;

Givner, "Katherine Anne Porter, Eudora Welty and *Ethan Brand,*" *International Fiction Review,* 1 (January 1974): 32–38;

Givner, "Katherine Anne Porter: Journalist," *Southwest Review,* 64 (Autumn 1979): 309–321;

Givner, "The Plantation of This Isle: Katherine Anne Porter's Bermuda Base," *Southwest Review,* 63 (Autumn 1978): 339–351;

Givner, "Porter's Subsidiary Art," *Southwest Review,* 59 (Summer 1974): 265–276;

Givner, "A Re-reading of Katherine Anne Porter's 'Theft,'" *Studies in Short Fiction,* 6 (Summer 1969): 463–465;

Givner, "Two Leaning Towers: Viewpoints by Katherine Anne Porter and Virginia Woolf in 1940," *Virginia Woolf Quarterly,* 3 (June 1977): 85–90;

Caroline Gordon, "Katherine Anne Porter and the ICM," *Harper's,* 229 (November 1964): 146–148;

Lodwick Hartley, "Katherine Anne Porter," *Sewanee Review,* 48 (April 1940): 206–216;

Hartley, "The Lady and the Temple," *College English,* 14 (April 1953): 386–391;

Hartley and George Core, eds., *Katherine Anne Porter: A Critical Symposium* (Athens: University of Georgia Press, 1969);

Willene Hendrick and George Hendrick, *Katherine Anne Porter,* revised edition (Boston: Twayne, 1988);

James William Johnson, "Another Look at Katherine Anne Porter," *Virginia Quarterly Review,* 36 (Autumn 1960): 598–613;

S. Joselyn, "Animal Imagery in Katherine Anne Porter's Fiction," in *Myth and Symbol,* edited by Bernice Slote (Lincoln: University of Nebraska Press, 1963), pp. 101–115;

David Laskin, *A Common Life: Four Generations of American Literary Friendship and Influence* (New York: Simon & Schuster, 1994): 189–281;

Helen Fiddyment Levy, *Fiction of the Home Place: Jewett, Cather, Glasgow, Porter, Welty, and Naylor* (Jackson: University Press of Mississippi, 1992);

M. M. Liberman, *Katherine Anne Porter's Fiction* (Detroit: Wayne State University Press, 1971);

Clinton Machann and William Bedford Clark, eds., *Katherine Anne Porter and Texas: An Uneasy Relationship* (College Station: Texas A & M University Press, 1990);

Debra A. Moddelmog, "Concepts of Justice in the Work of Katherine Anne Porter," *Mosaic,* 26 (1993): 37–52;

Harry John Mooney Jr., *The Fiction and Criticism of Katherine Anne Porter* (Pittsburgh: University of Pittsburgh Press, 1957; revised, 1962);

William L. Nance, *Katherine Anne Porter and the Art of Rejection* (Chapel Hill: University of North Carolina Press, 1964);

Robert L. Perry, "Porter's 'Hacienda' and the Theme of Change," *Midwest Quarterly,* 6 (Summer 1965): 403–415;

Leonard Prager, "Getting and Spending: Porter's 'Theft,'" *Perspective,* 11 (Winter 1960): 230–234;

Marjorie Ryan, "*Dubliners* and the Stories of Katherine Anne Porter," *American Literature,* 31 (January 1960): 464–473;

Edward Greenfield Schwartz, "The Fictions of Memory," *Southwest Review,* 45 (Summer 1960): 204–215;

Schwartz, "The Way of Dissent: Katherine Anne Porter's Critical Position," *Western Humanities Review,* 8 (Spring 1954): 119–130;

William Bysshe Stein, "'Theft': Porter's Politics of Modern Love," *Perspective,* 11 (Winter 1960): 223–228;

Janis P. Stout, *Katherine Anne Porter: A Sense of the Times* (Charlottesville: University Press of Virginia, 1995);

Stout, "Katherine Anne Porter's 'Reflections of Willa Cather': A Duplicitous Homage," *American Literature,* 66 (1994): 719–735.

Stout, *Strategies of Reticence: Silence and Meaning in the Works of Jane Austen, Willa Cather, Katherine Anne Porter, and Joan Didion* (Charlottesville: University Press of Virginia, 1990);

James T. F. Tanner, *The Texas Legacy of Katherine Anne Porter* (Denton: University of North Texas Press, 1990);

Mary E. Titus, "The 'Booby Trap' of Love: Artist and Sadist in Katherine Anne Porter's Mexico

Fiction," *Journal of Modern Literature,* 16 (1990): 617–634;

Titus, "Katherine Anne Porter's Miranda: The Agrarian Myth and Southern Womanhood," in *Redefining Autobiography in Twentieth-Century Women's Fiction: An Essay Collection,* edited by Janice Morgan and Colette T. Hall (New York: Garland, 1991);

Titus, "'A Little Stolen Holiday': Katherine Anne Porter's Narrative of the Woman Artist," *Women's Studies,* 25 (1995): 73–93;

Titus, "'Mingled Sweetness and Corruption': Katherine Anne Porter's 'The Fig Tree' and 'The Grave,'" *South Atlantic Review,* 53 (May 1988), 111–125;

Darlene Harbour Unrue, ed., *Critical Essays on Katherine Anne Porter* (New York: G. K. Hall, 1997);

Unrue, "Katherine Anne Porter and Henry James: A Study in Influence," *Southern Quarterly,* 31 (1993): 17–28;

Unrue, "Katherine Anne Porter and *The Southern Review,*" in *"To Love So Well the World": A Festschrift in Honor of Robert Penn Warren,* edited by Dennis L. Weeks (New York: Peter Lang, 1992);

Unrue, *Truth and Vision in Katherine Anne Porter's Fiction* (Athens: University of Georgia Press, 1985);

Thomas F. Walsh, "Deep Similarities in 'Noon Wine,'" *Mosaic,* 9 (Fall 1975): 83–91;

Walsh, "The Dream Self in 'Pale Horse, Pale Rider,'" *Wascana Review,* 2 (Fall 1979): 61–79; reprinted in *Katherine Anne Porter,* edited by Harold Bloom;

Walsh, "Identifying a Sketch by Katherine Anne Porter," *Journal of Modern Literature,* 7 (September 1979): 555–561;

Walsh, *Katherine Anne Porter and Mexico: The Illusion of Eden* (Austin: University of Texas Press, 1992);

Walsh, "The Making of 'Flowering Judas,'" *Journal of Modern Literature,* 12 (March 1985): 109–130;

Walsh, "Xochitl: Katherine Anne Porter's Changing Goddess," *American Literature,* 52 (May 1980): 183–193;

Robert Penn Warren, ed., *Introduction to Katherine Anne Porter: A Collection of Critical Essays* (Englewood Cliffs, N.J.: Prentice-Hall, 1979);

Warren, "Katherine Anne Porter (Irony with a Center)," *Kenyon Review,* 4 (Winter 1942): 29–42;

Eudora Welty, "My Introduction to Katherine Anne Porter," *Georgia Review,* 44 (1990): 13–27;

Glenway Wescott, "Katherine Anne Porter Personally," in his *Images of Truth* (New York: Harper & Row, 1962), pp. 25–58;

Ray B. West Jr., *Katherine Anne Porter* (Minneapolis: University of Minnesota Press, 1963);

West, "Katherine Anne Porter: Symbol and Theme in 'Flowering Judas,'" *Accent,* 7 (Spring 1947): 182–187;

Joseph Wiesenfarth, "Illusion and Allusion: Reflections in 'The Cracked Looking-Glass,'" *Four Quarters,* 12 (1962): 30–37;

Wiesenfarth, "Internal Opposition in Porter's 'Granny Weatherall,'" *Critique,* 11, no. 2 (1969): 47–55;

Wiesenfarth, "Negatives of Hope: A Reading of Katherine Anne Porter," *Renascence,* 25 (Winter 1973): 85–94;

Wiesenfarth, "The Structure of Katherine Anne Porter's 'Theft,'" *Cithara,* 10 (May 1971): 64–71;

Edmund Wilson, "Katherine Anne Porter," *New Yorker,* 20 (30 September 1944): 64–66; republished in his *Classics and Commercials: A Literary Chronicle of the Forties* (New York: Farrar, Straus, 1950), pp. 219–223.

Papers:

The University of Maryland Libraries are the chief repositories of Porter material, including most of her manuscripts, papers, correspondence, personal library, books, phonograph records, photographs, furniture, and assorted memorabilia. Other libraries have small collections of Porter material. After the University of Maryland, the Beinecke Rare Book and Manuscript Library of Yale University is the largest repository of Porter material. It holds, for example, her important correspondence with George Platt Lynes, Robert Penn Warren, Matthew Josephson, and Josephine Herbst.

Ayn Rand

Laurence Miller
Western Washington University

BIRTH: St. Petersburg, Russia, as Alice (Alysia) Rosenbaum, 2 February 1905, to Franz and Anna Rosenbaum; immigrated to the United States, 1926; naturalized U.S. citizen, 1931.

EDUCATION: Bachelor's degree, University of Petrograd, 1924.

MARRIAGE: 15 April 1929 to Charles Francis "Frank" O'Connor (died 1979).

AWARD: Honorary Doctor of Humane Letters, Lewis and Clark College, 1963.

DEATH: New York, New York, 6 March 1982.

BOOKS: *We the Living* (New York: Macmillan, 1936; London: Cassell, 1936; revised edition, New York: Random House, 1959);
Night of January 16th: A Comedy-Drama in Three Acts, edited by Nathaniel Edward Reeid (New York: Longmans, Green, 1936; revised edition, New York: World, 1968);
Anthem (London: Cassell, 1938; Los Angeles: Pamphleteers, 1946);
The Fountainhead (Indianapolis: Bobbs-Merrill, 1943; London: Cassell, 1947);
Atlas Shrugged (New York: Random House, 1957);
For the New Intellectual: The Philosophy of Ayn Rand (New York: Random House, 1961);
The Virtue of Selfishness, a New Concept of Egoism, with articles by Nathaniel Branden (New York: New American Library, 1964);
Capitalism, the Unknown Ideal, with articles by Branden, Alan Greenspan, and Robert Hessen (New York: New American Library, 1966);
Introduction to Objectivist Epistemology (New York: Objectivist, 1967);
The Romantic Manifesto: A Philosophy of Literature (New York: World, 1969; revised, New York: World, 1975);
The New Left: The Anti-Industrial Revolution (New York: New American Library, 1971); republished with additional material as *Return of the Primitive: The Anti-Industrial Revolution,* edited by Peter Schwartz (New York: Meridian, 1999);
Philosophy, Who Needs It (Indianapolis: Bobbs-Merrill, 1982);
The Early Ayn Rand: A Selection from Her Unpublished Fiction, edited by Leonard Peikoff (New York: New American Library, 1984);
The Voice of Reason: Essays in Objectivist Thought, edited by Peikoff (New York: New American Library, 1989);
The Ayn Rand Column: A Collection of Her Weekly Newspaper Articles, Written for the Los Angeles Times; with Additional, Little-Known Essays, edited by Schwartz (Oceanside, Cal.: Second Renaissance Books, 1991); revised as *The Ayn Rand Column: Written for the Los Angeles Times* (New Milford, Conn.: Second Renaissance Books, 1998);
Ayn Rand's Marginalia: Her Critical Comments on the Writings of Over 20 Authors, edited by Robert Mayhew (New Milford, Conn.: Second Renaissance Books, 1995);
Journals of Ayn Rand, edited by David Harriman (New York: Dutton, 1997);
The Ayn Rand Reader, edited by Peikoff and Gary Hull (New York: Plume, 1999).

PLAY PRODUCTIONS: *Penthouse Legend,* produced as *Woman on Trial,* Hollywood, Hollywood Playhouse, October 1934; produced as *Night of January 16th,* New York, 1935;
The Unconquered, New York, Biltmore Theatre, 14 February 1940.

MOTION PICTURES: *Love Letters,* Paramount Pictures, 1945;
You Came Along, Paramount Pictures, 1945;
The Fountainhead, Warner Brothers, 1949.

OTHER: *The Objectivist Newsletter,* volumes 1–4, edited by Rand and Nathaniel Branden, 1962–1965; republished in one volume (New York: Objectivist, 1967);

Ayn Rand in a publicity photo for the 1949 movie version of
The Fountainhead

The Objectivist, volumes 5–10, edited by Rand and Branden, 1966–1971; republished in one volume (Palo Alto, Cal.: Palo Alto Book Service, 1982);

The Ayn Rand Letter, volumes 1–4, edited by Rand, 1971–1976; republished in one volume (Palo Alto, Cal.: Palo Alto Book Service, 1979).

Ayn Rand's novels *The Fountainhead* (1943) and *Atlas Shrugged* (1957) develop her philosophy of objectivism, which challenged conventional values by emphasizing laissez-faire capitalism, individualism, and opposition to altruism. After her novels, Rand promoted objectivism in several works of nonfiction and three periodicals during the 1960s and 1970s. Though it developed into a movement, objectivism was eventually undermined by personal conflicts between Rand and other followers. Still, in the time since her death in 1982, her books continue to sell and have adherents.

Ayn Rand was born Alice (Alysia) Rosenbaum on 2 February 1905, in St. Petersburg, Russia. Her father, Franz Rosenbaum, was a faculty member in the chemistry department at the local university. Rand's mother, Anna Rosenbaum, cared for the house and entertained frequently. Rand, who felt that her father was indifferent to her and was contemptuous of her mother's preoccupation with socializing, was a precocious and highly intelligent child who eschewed friendships in favor of intellectual endeavors and the world of ideas. She attended the University of Petrograd from 1918 to 1924 and graduated with highest honors in history.

Rand read widely and avidly in her early years, and several key events between childhood and college influenced her writing. A child who knew by the age of eight that she wanted to be a writer, she was most influenced by the writings of Maurice Champagne, Victor Hugo, and Friedrich Nietzsche. Rand read Champagne's adventure story, "The Mystical Valley," in a French magazine in 1914; for her, its protagonist, Cyrus, a totally self-confident man of action, intelligence, and courage, became an ideal of manhood. In fact, Cyrus became the basis for all the fictional heroes and heroines she later created.

She gained a sense of what a novel should be from Hugo—the creation of heroic, larger-than-life characters; complex and ingenious plots unfolding on a grand and unexpected scale that still managed to incorporate themes, ideas, and action. Although Rand disagreed with much of what Nietzsche believed, she viewed him as a spiritual ally who had a similar view of man that emphasized the heroic, defended individualism, and despised altruism. Like Rand, Nietzsche believed that an individual man's purpose should be directed toward his own personal happiness.

Rand's development was further influenced by dramatic events in Russia. Believing that people should be free to determine their own actions and goals, she vigorously opposed government authority. For her, Communism meant living for the State. Rand and her family suffered severe deprivations at the hands of the Communists, and Rand remained a lifelong staunch anti-Communist. Still following Nietzsche, she was also a lifelong atheist, believing that the concept of God was rationally indefensible and degrading to man because it focused on mysticism rather than reason.

Rand's intellectual and philosophical foundation was thus firmly in place when relatives who had previously immigrated to New York City provided for her to immigrate to America in 1926. Along the way she changed her first name to Ayn, after a Finnish writer, and her last name to Rand, after her Remington-Rand typewriter. She spent her early years in America in the movie industry, working in the prop and costume departments and also as an extra in movies. She married another extra, Charles Francis "Frank" O'Connor, in 1929 and became an American citizen in 1931. Most important, from the viewpoint of her later career, she spent these initial years cultivating and honing her writing skills, learning English, and writing several unpublished short stories and screenplays.

Rand's career as a novelist began with her first published book, *We the Living* (1936). The novel took three years to complete, largely because her work in the movie industry placed heavy demands on her time. Moreover, while learning to write in a new language, she continued to be a perfectionist, demanding clarity and precision in her writing. Nevertheless, the book was rejected by several publishers. A play Rand wrote in 1933 called *Penthouse Legend* was produced on Broadway in 1935 (and pub-

lished in 1936) as *Night of January 16th*. However, the play, more an entertainment than a reflection of her beliefs and philosophy, did not truly represent her emergence as a significant writer. It did at least help her to become known in East Coast cultural circles.

More importantly, Macmillan published *We the Living* in April 1936. The Russian setting of the novel reflects Rand's earlier experiences under Communism. Its plot focuses on a young female protagonist, Kira Argounova, in totalitarian Russia who becomes the mistress of a Communist, Andrei Taganov, in order to save the life of the man she loves, Leo Kovalensky. The interplay of these three characters against a background of villainous and statist Communism allowed Rand to introduce her essential philosophy. The story ends as Andrei finds out about Kira and Leo, realizes the evils of Communism, and kills himself. Leo, broken in spirit and without hope in a Communist society, leaves Kira, who attempts to depart Russia but is shot at the border.

Rand was pleased with the structure and plot of the book. Valorizing the sanctity of human life rather than the supremacy of the state, the novel emphasizes that the state, though able to destroy a person, cannot destroy the individual spirit. However, Rand became dissatisfied with parts of the book, believing them to be overwritten. She thought that her writing was too romantic and lush and Kira too openly emotional. Rand realized that in order to obtain the strongest emotional response from her readers, she needed to be more subtle and less explicit in her writing. In her later novels emotions were minimized or subordinated to intellect, and reason was implicitly and indirectly expressed through actions. For Rand, reason was man's only means of perceiving reality and his only guide to action; feelings, she asserted, revealed nothing about facts and did not facilitate cognition.

Though Rand was commended for her narrative and dramatic skills, *We the Living* was reviewed negatively. In a time when Communism was viewed by many influential intellectuals as a noble ideal, the anti-Communist tone and argument of the book were especially criticized. Initial sales of the novel were slow, but picked up dramatically within a year because of favorable publicity. Unfortunately, by that time, Macmillan had already destroyed the type and the novel was out of print.

In 1935 Rand, now a mature and gifted writer, began work on *The Fountainhead,* a novel with which she would be pleased and which would make her famous. While *The Fountainhead* was considerably more complicated in theme, plot, and character than

Rand and several of her friends at the wedding of Nathaniel Branden's sister; Nathaniel and Barbara Branden are third and fourth from left, and Frank O'Connor and Rand are second and third from right

We the Living, Rand was in command throughout stylistically and intellectually, and she clearly and persuasively presented complex ideas. The book is idiosyncratic, quite remarkable in its literary style and plot, the complexity and interest of its several memorable characters, the interweaving of her philosophy within the framework of fiction, and its epic scope and grandeur.

Through overt philosophizing, *The Fountainhead* expresses Rand's concept of the ideal man. Her characters reflect her philosophical principles, which in turn direct her characters' behavior. The novel recalls certain nineteenth-century novels that provided what George Eliot called a "complete theory of life and manual of divinity, in a love story." Rand referred to her style "of writing in essentials and in terms of universal values" as "Romantic Realism." Writing *The Fountainhead* did not proceed uninterrupted in large part because financial exigencies forced Rand to divert her attention to other, more short-term projects. Two plays, "Ideal" (1934) and "Think Twice" (1939), went unproduced. A play version of *We the Living,* titled *The Unconquered,* was produced in 1940 but closed after only five performances.

The Fountainhead is an idiosyncratic vision of egoism, good and evil, individualism and the human spirit, dramatized in fiction. In this novel, life is de-

picted not as it is, but as it could be and should be. Thematically, the book concerns the struggle of individualism versus collectivism, with Rand's fundamental premise being that one's existence and well-being depend on actions that promote survival. The book again emphasizes that reason, guided by an appropriate code of values and morality, makes possible truly meaningful action. Moreover, such reason is possible only for the heroic individualist, who is entirely independent, self-sufficient, and productive. His convictions, values, and goals are the product of a clear intelligence and a rational mind and come entirely from within himself. He exerts man's fundamental right to enlightened self-interest, the virtue of selfishness. One must, the novel argues, live for the self without placing others above the self. The collectivist, in contrast, is controlled and shaped by other men, a soulless second-hander lacking inner direction. He is an altruist, placing the welfare of others above his own. Thus altruism subverts productivity and creativity. The novel insists that, in the end, good will triumph because only good can build and create. Evil is impotent and self-creating because it can only destroy.

The Fountainhead chronicles the struggles of architect Howard Roark, who exemplifies Rand's ideal man. Rand chose architecture for the subject because she viewed the skyscraper as the perfect symbol of man's greatest achievements. Roark's struggle and ultimate triumph over an evil society is made interesting and memorable by his conflicts with a colorful cast of imperfect people. The heroine, Dominique Francon ("Myself in a bad mood," Rand observed), is an emotionally withdrawn and self-destructive idealist. Gail Wynand, the newspaper publisher, has the potential to become heroic like Roark, but destroys himself by seeking power and yielding to the collective masses. Peter Keating, also an architect, is the opposite of Roark. He is the ultimate second-hander whose life is a series of practical compromises, a man devoid of independent action. Finally, Ellsworth Toohey, the architectural critic who insidiously and deliberately attacks and tries to destroy all that Howard Roark personifies, represents the quintessentially evil man.

Prior to *The Fountainhead,* Rand had published another enduring work of fiction, the novella *Anthem* (1938). Told as a sequence of flashbacks, it is an interesting blend of science fiction and fantasy with an uncharacteristically lyrical style. In fact, Barbara Branden, in her biography, *The Passion of Ayn Rand* (1986), compared *Anthem* to a prose poem. *Anthem* is entirely consistent with Rand's philosophy. In a totally collectivized world the words "I" and "He/She" have been replaced by "We" and "They." All past achievements in art, industry, and science have disappeared from life and from memory. The hero, determined to acquire knowledge, rediscovers the electric light. Subsequently, he and his woman friend are forced to flee into an uncharted wilderness, where they rediscover the meaning of the words "I" and "We" and formulate plans to establish a new society.

Rand initially failed to find an American publisher for *Anthem;* Barbara Branden suggested that, as with *We The Living,* it was too political and antisocialist. Rand did, however, succeed in getting the novel published in England; it was not published in America until 1946. Initial attempts to publish *The Fountainhead* paralleled the same bleak experience of *We The Living,* and Rand worried it would suffer the same fate. Twelve publishers rejected it as being commercially unsuitable because it was too politically and philosophically controversial, too intellectual, too improbable a story, too long, poorly written, and dull, and employed an unsympathetic hero. Finally, an editor at Bobbs-Merrill, Archie Ogden, was favorably impressed and recommended that the book be published. In one of those legendary stories in book publishing, the front office rejected Ogden's recommendation. In true Randian heroic fashion Ogden replied, "If this is not the book for you, then I am not the editor for you." The reply was, "Far be it from me to dampen such enthusiasm. Sign the contract. But the book better be good." Thus in May 1943 *The Fountainhead* was published.

The debut of the book was anything but auspicious. Advertising and early reviews misrepresented the book as being about architecture and slum dwellers. Many major publications did not review it, and many of the reviews that did appear were negative. The most notable exception was *The New York Times Book Review* (16 May 1943), in which Lorine Pruette praised the power, brilliance, beauty and thought-provoking quality of Rand's writing and correctly recognized that the central concern in *The Fountainhead* was individualism.

When initial sales of *The Fountainhead* were slow, Rand worried that the book would go the same way as *We The Living;* but as the book began to find its audience, a second printing appeared, and sales accelerated dramatically. The paperback edition was published in 1952, and a decade later more than one million copies were in print. The novel struck an undeniable chord in many readers. Rand received enormous amounts of mail telling how the book had changed individual lives and motivated people to work for a new vision. Nathaniel Branden, later Rand's protégé and intellectual heir, was fourteen when he read the book, and later recalled "the sense of a door opening, intellectually, spiritually, psychologically—a passageway into another dimension, like a summons from the future."

Rand wrote the screenplay for the 1949 movie version of *The Fountainhead,* which starred Gary Cooper and Patricia Neal. The reception of *The Fountainhead* gave Rand financial independence and allowed her, for the first time, to devote herself full-time to writing. Her new celebrity provided her considerable exposure; for instance, in 1947 she appeared before the House Un-American Activities Committee, as a friendly witness, to express her concern about the influence of Communism in American movies. (Rand had written a pamphlet that year, *Screen Guide for Americans,* for an anti-Communist organization, in which she discussed these concerns.) She insisted, however, that she would testify only on ideological issues. Rand called the hearings a disgusting spectacle, and in later years expressed ambivalent feelings about her appearance.

In October 1957 Rand published *Atlas Shrugged,* which took more than a decade to write. It is 1,168 pages long, features a sixty-page speech, and represents the maturation of Rand's evolving philosophy. The focus shifts from architecture to the railroad, the central industry that touched all other industries and was the circulatory system that kept America alive. *Atlas Shrugged* is a mystery ("Who is John Galt?") and an action tale written on a grand scale, combining, Rand said, "metaphysics, morality, economics, politics and sex." This time, Atlas represented Rand's ideal man—a man of the mind supporting the world on his shoulders and making civilization possible. When Atlas is manipulated and subjugated by an increasingly collectivist society, he rebels and society collapses.

The incarnation of Atlas and the apotheosis of human potential, John Galt instigates and leads the revolt featured in the novel. Practicing unbreached rationality—the commitment to fully use his mind and to respect facts, reality, and logic—Galt epitomizes intelligence, serenity and joy in living, productivity, self-esteem, courage, and a profound contempt of evil. Galt is complemented by a cast of memorable characters. Dagny Taggart is Rand's conception of the ideal woman, a female version of Howard Roark ("Myself, with any possible flaws eliminated," Rand stated). Hank Rearden, according to Rand, is "the American businessman at his best, self-made, inventive, resourceful, unselfpitying—and much too innocent for his own good." Francisco d'Anconia, who is on the same level as Galt, his best friend and comrade-in-arms, willfully destroys his multibillion-dollar industry in support of Galt's principles. James Taggart is Dagny's brother and her philosophical antithesis. Rand described Lillian Rearden, Hank's wife, as "the archetype of the humanitarian liberal pseudointellectual who despises and hates the industrialist."

Atlas Shrugged, while further developing themes introduced in *The Fountainhead,* presents important new aspects of Rand's still-evolving philosophy of objectivism. In the later novel, she differentiates between errors of knowledge and breaches of morality. Even though Dagny Taggart and Hank Rearden commit errors of knowledge by not immediately joining the strike, they are still depicted as honorable and good people. Implicit in the novel is the idea that evil results only from breaches of morality; and a related concept, "sanction of the victim," concerns honorable and able people allowing evil to occur. Rand argues that, by being altruistic and conceding moral superiority to their oppressors, such people permit their virtues to be used unjustly against them. Against such sanction of the victim, John Galt organizes the strike of the mind. Finally, *Atlas Shrugged* rejects the dichotomy of body and mind (soul), which Rand believed led to the denigration of activities as diverse as sex and industrial production as mindless, physical, nonspiritual activity. Rather, the novel insists that mind and body are

one, and all of these activities flow naturally from a free mind.

Rand believed that capitalism is the only moral economic system because it is based on the inviolability of human rights, and *Atlas Shrugged* is a paean to unfettered laissez-faire capitalism. The novel argues that capitalism symbolizes the importance of work and gives man the right to his own mind and to his happiness. Industrial achievement and innovation are synonymous with intelligence, courage, and integrity, while altruism, the belief that man's first duty is to sacrifice his individual right to exist in the interest of the common good, is incompatible with capitalism.

In a capitalist economy run by ideal people of the highest moral integrity, the well-being of all citizens is maximized. To achieve such a state, in the words of John Galt,

> man must hold these things as the supreme and ruling values of his life: Reason—Purpose—Self-esteem. Reason, as his only tool of knowledge—Purpose, as his choice of the happiness which that tool must proceed to achieve—Self-esteem, as his inviolate certainty that his mind is competent to think and his person is worthy of happiness, which means worthy of living.

Atlas Shrugged was Rand's last work of fiction. In the novel, she had presented her philosophy to her satisfaction and felt there was nothing more to say. The reviews echoed those of her earlier works, and in fact were even worse. Although there were several good reviews, most of the big-city, major-market reviewers savaged the book, charging it with being drab, cumbersome, lumbering, and terribly written. Further, the novel was accused of being pro-Nazi, immoral, anti-religious, undemocratic, hateful, and destructive. When initial sales of *Atlas Shrugged* were less than expected, Random House feared the book would fail. Once again, however, after the book reached its audience, sales increased dramatically and the novel eventually became a runaway success in both hardback and paperback.

Readers who consider *Atlas Shrugged* a masterpiece point to Rand's first-rate narrative skill and mastery of plot construction; her proficiency at suspense; the fast pace of action; and the melodramatic, spectacular scene. In addition, they praise her attention to detail; her mastery and control in organizing complex themes and ideas; the elaborate structure of the text; and its compelling power and drama. *Atlas Shrugged* has come to be viewed as a provocative, stimulating, and revolutionary book of ideas.

Nevertheless, *Atlas Shrugged* often reads like an overstated, pedantic, and dry primer of objectivism. The interactions between characters are, at times,

April 4, 1938   (1)

Summary of last part

Roark blows up housing project.

His arrest. Fury of public indignation. Strike against Ford building.

Wynand's crusade & failure. He turns against Roark. Wynand's tragedy.

Dominique - Roark. Her confession of love. He agrees to escape.
Their night together at her country house.

First day of trial, Roark absent. That night - drive to airport.

Fire on Ford building. Roark - arrest.

Wynand's return from Washington. He learns the truth.

Wynand - Dominique. Her confession. Wynand gives "cork handle" to Toohey.

Next morning. Wynand's statement in the papers. His scene with Dominique.

The trial. Rise of Wynand papers during trial.

The verdict - "not guilty". Roark at Ford building, plan to re-build housing project.

Dominique leaves for Europe. Wynand's divorce.

Wynand's decision about his building. Roark - Wynand.

Dominique's return from Europe. Dominique at the Wynand building.
Her ride in the elevator.

Manuscript page of notes Rand made for her 1943 novel, The Fountainhead *(Ayn Rand Institute, Marina del Rey, California)*

didactic and lacking in feeling, emotion, and spontaneity. In particular, John Galt comes across as a mysterious, symbolic abstraction rather than a flesh-and-blood human being. It should be pointed out that Rand intended Galt to be godlike, and as she stated, "One does not approach a god too closely—one does not get too intimate with him—one maintains a respectful distance from his inner life." The characters (as Rand herself could be) often seem overly harsh, contemptuous, judgmental, and unforgiving of individuals to whom they are philosophically opposed.

The favorite Rand characters of many readers are Hank Rearden and Kira Argounova, precisely because they come across as being the most emotional and human of her creations. Rand has been criticized for disparaging and minimizing emotions. Nathaniel Branden observed, for instance, that the characters in *Atlas Shrugged* are unable to listen to their feelings, reflect on them, and gain insights that could modify thinking. Rand repeatedly admitted she knew nothing about psychology, and had she known more about it, she might have given emotions a more central and trusted place in her philosophy.

Some readers have detected sadomasochistic undertones and sexual violence in her work and see such concerns as reflecting Rand's lifelong hero-worship and belief in the physical and sexual dominance of men. Indeed, Rand stated that "Dagny is a man worshiper, as any heroine of mine would have to be. Man is the ultimate." The most famous instance of sexual violence in her fiction is the so-called "rape" scene in *The Fountainhead*. After considerable verbal foreplay, Howard Roark has what some critics have interpreted as forced sex with Dominique Francon. The feminist Susan Brownmiller, in her 1975 work *Against Our Will: Men, Women and Rape*, decried this scene as the central shame of modern fiction and accused Rand of being a traitor to her own gender. Rand countered that no rape occurred and that any such act would be disgusting and unthinkable to any of her heroes. Of what happened to Dominique, said Rand, "If that was rape—it was rape by engraved invitation."

Still others, while praising Rand's comprehensive, systematic, closely reasoned and rigorously logical philosophy, dispute the validity of some of the fundamental premises of that philosophy. Hiram Haydn, Rand's editor in chief at Random House, considered her philosophy to be "one kind of arid intellectual triumph, a tour de force that commanded admiration," but believed that its social and political consequences were troubling.

In 1959 a revised edition of *We the Living* was published. The most controversial of the revisions, because Rand did not mention it in her introduc-

tion, was her excision of a passage, reminiscent of Nietzsche, in which Kira justifies the use of force in the name of right and debates the propriety of bloodshed under certain circumstances. Eventually, Rand rejected the use of force as a means to an end and argued that it was justified only in response to force initiated by someone else.

After publication of *Atlas Shrugged* Rand wrote only nonfiction essays about objectivism, a philosophy that stimulated considerable interest. She received many requests to provide more information concerning it. With Rand's full support, Nathaniel Branden (born Nathan Blumenthal) founded the Nathaniel Branden Lectures (later called the Nathaniel Branden Institute or NBI) in 1958. These lectures on specific aspects of objectivism were given by members of Rand's inner circle of friends and associates (the "Collective" or "The Class of '43"). Rand answered questions following the lectures. A four-page monthly newsletter, *The Objectivist Newsletter*, edited by Rand and Branden, was started in 1962 and by 1966 had grown into a small monthly magazine, *The Objectivist*. In addition, Rand wrote pamphlets and articles that analyzed various issues and subjects from an objectivist viewpoint. By the 1960s, the increasing success of NBI and Rand's popularity had attracted many followers, and objectivism was now a genuine movement.

Rand published eight more books after her last novel. *Night of January 16th* was republished in 1968 with an introduction by Rand, while the other seven books, ranging over a variety of subjects from an objectivist perspective, were largely collections of her previously published essays with new introductions by her, though some of the books included new material. The titles of these collections of nonfiction are *For the New Intellectual: The Philosophy of Ayn Rand* (1961); *The Virtue of Selfishness, a New Concept of Egoism* (1964); *Capitalism, the Unknown Ideal* (1966); *Introduction to Objectivist Epistemology* (1967); *The Romantic Manifesto: A Philosophy of Literature* (1969); *The New Left: The Anti-Industrial Revolution* (1971); and *Philosophy, Who Needs It* (1982).

Despite Rand's success and fame, her life after the publication of *Atlas Shrugged* was unhappy and difficult. Her husband's health deteriorated because of a progressive dementia, and he died in 1979. Rand also suffered serious health problems that drained her energy and made it difficult for her to write. She severed ties with many of her best friends because of her intolerance for their presumed deviation from objectivist principles or because they failed to meet unreasonable demands she made of them. Rand's primary goal was to foster the accep-

Rand and her husband, Frank O'Connor, in New York, 1947

tance of objectivism and to change America, but her affair with Nathaniel Branden destroyed this goal.

According to Branden, Rand saw in him the character traits she celebrated in her writing. The affair ("It's a rational universe: this *had* to happen," Rand said) was conducted with the full knowledge but less than wholehearted approval of their respective spouses. It began in June 1954 and was intended to be only platonic. Not wanting to look foolish by being involved with a much younger man, Rand originally envisioned the relationship as lasting only a year or two. Nevertheless, four months after it began, the relationship became sexual, and it continued until 1958.

In 1958, after *Atlas Shrugged* was published, Rand suffered severe depression caused by a combination of factors: a letdown from the exhilaration and drive of writing the book; the vitriolic criticism directed against her; the misrepresentation of her ideas; and the lack of support from anyone of intellectual substance whom she admired. She became increasingly isolated, withdrawn and bitter at what she felt to be the mediocrity of the world. Unable to write, she put her relationship with Branden on hold.

With the passage of time, the mushrooming popularity of objectivism, and the success of NBI, Rand's spirits slowly revived. In 1964, now nearly

sixty, she tried to rekindle the relationship with the thirty-five-year-old Branden, unaware that in the interim Branden had become intimately involved with a married NBI student. Not until four years later did Branden tell Rand about this relationship.

A stunned, humiliated, and angry Rand sought retribution and removed Branden from any role in NBI and *The Objectivist*. His name on the dedication page of *Atlas Shrugged* and Rand's concluding acknowledgment of him were omitted in later editions. Ultimately Rand severed all direct communication with Branden and tried unsuccessfully to prevent a book he had written (*The Psychology of Self-Esteem,* 1969) from being published. In the May 1968 issue of *The Objectivist* (published in October), she wrote a six-page article informing her readers of the break and giving reasons for it, although she never revealed their affair or accepted any responsibility for what had happened. Instead, the article was a litany of accusations concerning Branden's personal and professional conduct, some of them half-truthful and others outright lies. The article created divided loyalties and disillusionment, basically ending objectivism as an organized movement. Rand severed her ties with NBI in September 1968, effectively killing it. *The Objectivist* was replaced in 1971 with *The Ayn Rand Letter,* irregularly published until 1976 for a dwindling audience. Rand spent her remaining years caring for her increasingly ill husband, writing relatively little, making some public appearances, working on a television miniseries of *Atlas Shrugged* that was never produced, and becoming increasingly bitter and disenchanted with the direction in which the world was moving. Her health slowly deteriorated from the postoperative effects of surgery, first for lung cancer and later for gallstones, and she died on 6 March 1982.

Rand has been accused by her critics of being a hypocrite and proof positive of the invalidity of her philosophy, with particular attention directed at her lack of insight into and control of her own motivations and emotions. (Rand had claimed that "I've never had an emotion I couldn't identify or an emotion that clashed with reason.") However, her supporters argue that she transcended her personal limitations and imperfections to effectively convey a vision of humankind at its best and most heroic. What is important is her continuing popularity. Her books annually sell three hundred thousand to five hundred thousand copies; and in 1991, the Library of Congress reported that *Atlas Shrugged* was surpassed only by the Bible as the book considered to be the most influential in the lives of its readers. Study groups and conventions concerning her work continue to be held. An article in *The Economist* (25 December 1993 – 7 January 1994) ranked Rand favorably with other important figures in influence, originality, intellectual coherence and devotion of followers.

Working outside academia, Rand developed a philosophy that offers an accessible, plausible, and compelling view of life. Inevitably, it does raise legitimate points of disagreement. Nathaniel Branden, for example, wished that more attention had been paid to feelings, kindness and compassion, rather than an "intellectualized" kind of benevolence. Instead, Rand's form of idealism stressed independence, honesty, justice, and self-responsibility. Thus, readers were provided a philosophy that could help them to grow and to direct their lives in a moral way that would maximize their productivity and happiness.

Rand emerges as a distinctive combination of novelist and philosopher who successfully integrated a serious message into the mode of popular fiction. With her complex persona of an enormously determined, single-minded, and flawed figure, she is ensured a place as one of this century's most controversial, colorful, and influential writers.

Letters:
Letters of Ayn Rand, edited by Michael S. Berliner (New York: Dutton, 1995).

Interview:
Alvin Toffler, "A Playboy Interview: Ayn Rand," *Playboy,* 11 (March 1964): 35–64.

Bibliography:
Vincent L. Perrin, *Ayn Rand–First Descriptive Bibliography* (Rockville, Md.: Quill & Brush, 1990).

Biographies:
Barbara Branden, *The Passion of Ayn Rand: A Biography* (Garden City, N.Y.: Doubleday, 1986);
Nathaniel Branden, *Judgment Day: My Years with Ayn Rand* (Boston: Houghton Mifflin, 1989).

References:
James Thomas Baker, *Ayn Rand* (Boston: Twayne, 1987);
Harry Binswanger, ed., *The Ayn Rand Lexicon: Objectivism from A to Z* (New York: New American Library, 1986);
Nathaniel Branden and Barbara Branden, *Who is Ayn Rand?* (New York: Random House, 1962);
Douglas J. Den Uyl and Douglas B. Rasmussen, eds., *The Philosophic Thought of Ayn Rand* (Urbana: University of Illinois Press, 1984);
Peter F. Erickson, *The Stance of Atlas: An Examination of the Philosophy of Ayn Rand* (Portland, Ore.: Herakles Press, 1997);
Mimi Reisel Gladstein, *The Ayn Rand Companion* (Westport, Conn.: Greenwood Press, 1984);
Gladstein and Chris Matthew Sciabarra, eds., *Feminist Interpretations of Ayn Rand* (University Park: Pennsylvania State University Press, 1999);
Ronald E. Merrill, *The Ideas of Ayn Rand* (La Salle, Ill.: Open Court, 1991);
William F. O'Neill, *With Charity Toward None: An Analysis of Ayn Rand's Philosophy* (New York: Philosophical Library, 1971);
Leonard Peikoff, *Objectivism: The Philosophy of Ayn Rand* (New York: Dutton, 1991);
Claudia Roth Pierpont, "Twilight of the Goddess," *New Yorker,* 71 (24 July 1995): 70–81;
Chris Matthew Sciabarra, *Ayn Rand: The Russian Radical* (University Park: Pennsylvania State University Press, 1995).

Papers:
A collection of Ayn Rand's papers, including drafts, galleys, and proofs of her novels, is housed at the Library of Congress; archives that include her journals are housed at the Ayn Rand Institute, Marina del Rey, California.

John Crowe Ransom

*This entry was updated from the entry by Thomas Daniel Young (Vanderbilt University)
in* DLB 45: American Poets, 1880–1945, First Series.

BIRTH: Pulaski, Tennessee, 30 April 1888, to John
James and Ella Crowe Ransom.

EDUCATION: A.B., Vanderbilt University, 1909;
B.A. in Litterae Humaniores, Christ Church College,
Oxford, 1913; attended University of Grenoble,
briefly, after World War I.

MARRIAGE: 22 December 1920 to Robb Reavill;
children: Helen, David Reavill, John James.

AWARDS AND HONORS: Rhodes Scholar, Oxford
University; Guggenheim Fellowship, 1931; Bollingen
Prize in Poetry, 1951; Russell Loines in Literature,
National Academy of Arts and Letters, 1951; honored
at Chicago Poetry Day, 1957; Brandeis University
Creative Arts Award, 1958–1959; Academy of Ameri-
can Poets Fellowship, 1962; National Book Award for
Selected Poems, 1964; National Endowment for the Arts
Grant, 1967; Emerson-Thoreau Medal, American
Academy of Arts and Sciences, 1968; and Gold
Medal, National Institute of Arts and Letters, 1973.

DEATH: Gambier, Ohio, 3 July 1974.

BOOKS: *Poems About God* (New York: Holt, 1919);
Chills and Fever (New York: Knopf, 1924);
Grace After Meat (London: Leonard & Virginia
    Woolf at the Hogarth Press, 1924);
Two Gentlemen in Bonds (New York: Knopf, 1927);
*God Without Thunder: An Unorthodox Defense of Ortho-
    doxy* (New York: Harcourt, Brace, 1930; Lon-
    don: Gerald Howe, 1931);
The World's Body (New York & London: Scribners,
    1938);
The New Criticism (Norfolk, Conn.: New Directions,
    1941);
Poetics (Norfolk, Conn.: New Directions, 1942);
A College Primer of Writing (New York: Holt, 1943);
Selected Poems (New York: Knopf, 1945; London:
    Eyre & Spottiswoode, 1947; revised and en-
    larged edition, New York: Knopf, 1963; re-
    vised and enlarged again, New York: Knopf,
    1969; London: Eyre & Spottiswoode, 1970);
Poems and Essays (New York: Vintage, 1955);

John Crowe Ransom

Beating the Bushes: Selected Essays 1941–1970 (Norfolk, Conn.: New Directions, 1972).

OTHER: "Statement of Principles" and "Reconstructed but Unregenerated," in *I'll Take My
Stand: The South and the Agrarian Tradition, by
Twelve Southerners* (New York: Harper, 1930),
pp. ix–xxi, 1–27.

John Crowe Ransom was one of the most ver-
satile and significant men of letters of his genera-

tion. As poet Isabel Gambel MacCafrey has written, "he provided a small but accurate mirror of the modern sensibility. . . . He has been celebrated rightly, as the poet of perilous equilibrium, of dichotomies and ironies, of tension and paradox." Some critics, nevertheless, think his contributions as critic, editor, and teacher were of even greater importance to modern American letters than his poetry. He was, many believe, the most original theoretical literary critic produced in America in the twentieth century. He not only elaborated exciting and perceptive theories of the nature and function of poetry, but he also provided invaluable demonstrations of how poetry is to be read if it is to function as a legitimate means of cognition, if it is to furnish "the kind of knowledge by which we must know what we have arranged we cannot know otherwise." Others point out that Ransom was a teacher of great dedication and skill. To list the important poets and critics who studied with him is to name some of the best-known authors of the twentieth century: Allen Tate, Robert Penn Warren, Donald Davidson, Andrew Lytle, Cleanth Brooks, Randall Jarrell, Peter Taylor, Robert Lowell, George Lanning, Robie Macauley, Ted Borgardus, Anthony Hecht, James Wright, and Eric Bentley. For more than two decades he was editor of the *Kenyon Review,* one of the most influential and distinguished literary journals of the country.

For his poetry he won many awards, including a Guggenheim Fellowship (1931), the Bollingen Prize in Poetry (1951), the Russell Loines Award in Literature of the National Academy of Arts and Letters (1951), Academy of American Poets Fellowship (1962), and a National Book Award for *Selected Poems* (1964).

Born in Pulaski, Tennessee, the son of John James Ransom, an erudite Methodist minister, and Ella Crowe Ransom, a former music and French teacher, John Crowe Ransom grew up in the several villages and small towns in middle Tennessee, where his father preached. Between Ransom's third and eleventh years, his father served four churches: Spring Hill, Franklin, Springfield, and North High Street in Nashville. Because the Methodist Conference came in October of each year, the education of the minister's children was often difficult. Each year when school opened in September, Ransom recalled many years later, the elder Ransom would say, "John, there's no need to enter school because we might move." Ransom, his brother, and two sisters, therefore, were taught at home by their parents. When the Reverend Dr. Ransom was moved to Nashville, however, he enrolled the children in public school. Although John had never been to school

before and was only ten years old, after much shifting from grade to grade, he was finally placed in the eighth grade. At the end of the year the principal and several of the teachers convinced Dr. Ransom that his precocious young son should be enrolled in one of the several good preparatory schools in the area, institutions which were preparing their students for the demanding classically oriented curriculum of Vanderbilt University. Young John enrolled in the Bowen School, at 15th Avenue and Broadway, only six blocks from the university. On Thursday, Friday, and Saturday, 14–16 May 1903, only a week before he was to be graduated, he took the demanding entrance examination for Vanderbilt and made the highest score on all five of the examinations he took: English, American history, mathematics, Latin, and Greek. On the basis of his performance on the examinations, he was admitted, although he was a full year below the official minimum age for admission.

After two years at the university, he had to withdraw for financial reasons and taught in secondary schools, one year in Mississippi and one in Tennessee, before returning in 1907 to graduate Phi Beta Kappa and number one in the class of 1909. He returned to teaching in a private academy for a year before enrolling in Christ Church College, Oxford, as a Rhodes Scholar. In 1913 he earned a B.A. in Litterae Humaniores ("The Greats")–Greek and Latin history, literature, and philosophy, all read in the original languages. From Oxford he went to teach Latin and Greek at the Hotchkiss School in Lakeville, Connecticut, but after one year he returned to teach at Vanderbilt. He took the job because his parents, who lived in Nashville, strongly encouraged their son, whom they had seen only twice in four years, to accept the instructorship offered him by Edwin Mims, head of the English department.

The year following his return to Nashville he joined a group of students, faculty members, and members of the community who were meeting at the apartment of Sidney Mttron Hirsch–a Jewish mystic and etymologist, who lived only two blocks from the campus–to discuss religion and philosophy. At that time the group also included Donald Davidson, Alec B. Stevenson, Walter Clyde Curry, and Stanley Johnson. About a year later Donald Davidson was surprised when Ransom announced that he had written a poem and wanted to read it to him. The poem, titled "Sunset," was written in free verse, the only poem Ransom would ever publish in that form. (In *The World's Body* [1938], his first book of criticism, he explains the reasons for his preference for meter: "When a poet confronts an object, he is tempted to react immediately, but art restrains the

Robb Reavill, at the time of her marriage to Ransom, 1920

natural man. It puts the object out of his reach; or more accurately, removes him where he cannot hurt the object, nor disrespect it by taking his practical attitude towards it." Ransom argued that all aspects of literary form, especially the meter, restrain the poet and prevent him from assaulting the "precious object," the subject of the poem, directly and trying to use it.) Ransom continued to write verse, and when he had completed five or six poems, he sent them to Christopher Morley, with whom he had been at Oxford, and asked if he could place them in an Eastern journal. Upon Morley's recommendation poems were taken by the *Independent, Contemporary Verse,* and the *Liberator.* Morley also published some of the poems Ransom had sent him in his column in the Philadelphia *Evening Public Ledger.*

Ransom also showed these and several other poems to Davidson in the summer of 1917 while they were both serving as cadets at the First Officers Training Camp at Fort Oglethorpe, Georgia. Ransom gave Davidson carbon copies of the poems, and Davidson carried them with him when he went overseas. "When I read those poems in France, by candlelight in some peasant's home in the Côte d'Or or Yvonne, or some ruined village near the Western Front," Davidson wrote in *Southern Writers in the Modern World* (1958), "they still blurred my exploring, eager eyes, even though at that distance I could more gratefully recognize in them the Tennessee country I had left."

Ransom had completed enough poems for a book before he went overseas in August 1917, but while he was on active duty in France, he carefully revised them before sending them to Morley with the request that he try to place them with a New York publisher. After several abortive attempts, Morley was able to get Henry Holt to agree to publish them. The volume appeared as *Poems About God* (1919), by Lieutenant John C. Ransom, while its author was still in Europe. For a first book of poems by an unknown poet who does not mention the war, except in his preface, the book was widely and generally favorably reviewed, although most of the reviewers missed the general thrust of the book—a young man expressing his amazement, his wonder and awe, and his concern, for the ways in which God makes himself manifest in the world. Several reviewers even found the poet's use of God sacrilegious. The reviewer for *Poetry* found the poems "brittle," but liked the deliberate childlike method of presentation. The reviewer for the *Nation* doubted the poet's "sincerity," saying it seemed "more strained than real." Charles W. Stork compared Ransom favorably with Conrad Aiken and Witter Bynner, writing that Ransom was a "voracious realist," had an "antisocial bent," and found the "religion of uneducated folk . . . ridiculous."

Both Stork and the reviewer for the *Nation* correctly found influences of Hardy and Frost, but none, it would seem, was quite as wide of the mark as Louis Untermeyer, who wrote in his review for the *Dial,* "The lines run from the surprisingly powerful to the incredibly banal." He ended his short notice by placing Ransom among the young poets reacting against "purely decorative literature by establishing some previously neglected attitudes toward a free but earth planted naturalism." The members of this school, Untermeyer added, "insist upon a return . . . to brutality." This review, Ransom wrote Robert Graves, who was beginning the correspondence that would result in Graves's bringing out a British edition of Ransom's poetry, gave him most concern because it was so far from what he was attempting to do and "Untermeyer has established in some circles a reputation as the foremost critic of modern literature."

The reader of Ransom's mature verse may well understand the poet's reason for wishing to suppress *Poems About God.* As Ransom declares in the preface: "Most of these poems about God were complete a year ago, that is at about the time when the great upheaval going on in God's world engulfed our country too. Since then I have added a little only, and my experience has led me so wide that I can actually look back upon these antebellum accomplishments with the eye of the impartial spectator. . . . In this reviewing act I find myself thinking sometimes that the case about God may not be quite so desperate as the young poet chooses to believe. But it is not for that reason that I shall ever think of suppressing a single one of his poems." Ransom's disaffection with this early verse was not because of the subjects treated or the attitudes expressed, but because of the manner in which these subjects and attitudes are presented. The poems put too much emphasis on what Ransom would later call their "structure," their logical argument and paraphrasable content, and not enough upon their "rich but irrelevant local texture"–figurative language, the metaphor, allusiveness, connotation. Wit and irony, the play of literary and archaic language against modern idiom and colloquial usage is not obvious enough in the tone of the poems. Too many answers are given, and too few problems are left unsolved, so the poems are almost completely devoid of ambiguity, dichotomy, and paradox.

The early poems, like their successors, however, are fables, anecdotes, or simple narratives concerned with the inevitable decay of youthful vigor and energy, with man's dual nature and the disparity between what he should reasonably receive from life and what he usually will get. Their obsessive theme is that of the mature poetry: mutability, decay, and death. If the world is not controlled by a malignant sovereign, at least it is under the unseeing, and apparently uncaring, eye of an indifferent one. The poems are obviously set in middle Tennessee in which Ransom grew up, and the speaker is Ransom himself. Never again would Ransom write poetry with such an unmistakable autobiographical bias. Even more vexing to the poet than this obvious lack of aesthetic distance–he would later remedy this defect through the use of a fictive persona and the development of the texture of the poem–are the many instances of amateur craftsmanship: the flat and conventional diction, the sentimental tone, the awkward and ineffective use of meter, the obvious and heavy-handed irony.

Like many of the characters in Ransom's verse, however, many of these earlier characters are overcome with grief because they cannot accept the nature of the world in which they have to live. In "The Cloak Model" a stranger calls the young protagonist aside to observe a store-window mannequin and to contemplate the following proposition:

Ransom with his daughter, Helen, and his son, Reavill, 1924

"I wish the moralist would thresh
(Indeed the thing is very droll)
God's oldest joke, forever fresh:
The fact that in the finest flesh
There isn't any soul."

In "Grace" the young protagonist is deeply puzzled by the manner in which God has allowed the hired man to die–ignobly in his own vomit:

But this was a thing that I had said,
I was so forward and untamed:
"I will not worship wickedness
Though it be God's–I am ashamed!
For all his mercies God be thanked
But for his tyrannies be blamed!
He shall not have any love alone,
With loathing too his name is named."

The conflict between body and soul is clearly pointed out in "Morning":

Three hours each day we souls,
Who might be angels but are fastened down
With bodies, most infuriating freight,
Sit fattening these frames and skeletons
With filthy food, which they must cast away,
Before they feed again.

The theme of the passing of youthful energy and beauty, a theme which Ransom found almost excessively attractive throughout his career, is presented, too explicitly he would later think, in "Under the Locusts":

Dick's a sturdy little lad
Yonder throwing stones;
Agues and rheumatic pains
Will fiddle on his bones
. . . .
Jenny and Will go arm and arm.
He's a lucky fellow;
Jenny's cheeks are pink as rose,
Her mother's cheeks are yellow.

The protagonist of "The School" is surely Ransom the country boy from Tennessee who has studied at Vanderbilt and Oxford:

Equipped with Grecian thoughts, how could I live
Among my father's folk? My father's house
Was narrow and his fields were nauseous.
I kicked his clods for being common dirt,
Worthy a world which never could be Greek;
Cursed the paternity that planted me
One green leaf in a wilderness of autumn;
And wept, as fitting a fruitful spirit
Sealed in a yellow tomb.

While Ransom was serving in the army in France, he seriously considered moving to New York and attempting to make his way in publishing and freelance journalism—in a manner similar to that in which Malcolm Cowley, among others, earned his living while he was learning his trade—and he even asked Morley to help him find a place with a publishing company. When he arrived in New York, however, he found such positions were scarce and paid little. He left for Nashville, planning to visit briefly with his parents, whom he had not seen for two years, before returning to New York and continuing his search for a satisfactory position. His parents, who had aged noticeably during Ransom's absence, were obviously disappointed that their son intended to leave again so soon. When Edwin Mims offered to promote him to assistant professor and raise his salary to $1,700 a year, Ransom decided to stay at Vanderbilt for one year before returning to New York. He remained not for

one year but for almost twenty before leaving not for New York but for Kenyon College.

Early in January 1920 Elizabeth Kirkland, daughter of the chancellor at Vanderbilt, invited three of her friends from Wellesley College to visit her for ten days in Nashville, and Kirkland's mother notified four young bachelors on campus that they were to entertain the girls during their visit. One of the visitors was Robb Reavill of Colorado and one of the bachelors was Ransom. These two married after a brief acquaintance and had three children: Helen Ransom Forman, David Reavill, and John James (Jack). The union was broken only by Ransom's death more than fifty years later.

During the years after Ransom's return to Vanderbilt, he had resumed attending the meetings of the Fugitives in the home of James M. Frank, Sidney Hirsch's brother-in-law. The nature of the meetings soon changed. After his first book of poetry was published, although he was already dissatisfied with some of this early verse, he was definitely committed to poetry. He quickly assumed leadership of the group, and the discussions shifted from philology, philosophy, and religion to the details of the form and structures of poetry.

At each meeting one or more poets brought poems they had written and read them aloud, as the other members followed the reading closely on a copy provided each of them by the poet. After the reading a discussion began, and as Donald Davidson wrote, "it was likely to be ruthless in its exposure of any technical weakness as to rhyme, meter, imagery, metaphor, and was often minute in analysis of detail."

In March 1922, after a little more than a year of the kind of meetings described above, Hirsch suggested that the group had written enough poetry of high quality to publish a magazine. Thus the *Fugitive,* a journal of verse and brief critical commentary, was born, and between June 1922 and December 1925 nineteen issues were published. This little magazine brought the "high modernism" of T. S. Eliot and Ezra Pound to Southern poetry and, as William Pratt has written, its contributors "have shown greater perseverance" in directing the course of modern poetry than any other group in America.

The split between society and the past is again presented in "Ego," the first poem in the first volume of the *Fugitive:*

You have heard something muttered in my scorn:
"A little learning addeleth this man's wit,
He crieth on our dogmas Counterfeit!

Philip Blair Rice, Ransom, and Norman Johnson at the founding of the Kenyon Review, *1939
(Kenyon College Archives)*

And no man's bubble 'scapeth his sharp thorn;

"Nor he respecteth duly our tall steeple,
But in his pride turning from book to book
Heareth our voice and hardly offereth look,
Nor liveth neighborly with these the people."

With reason, friends, I am complained upon,
Who am a headstrong man, sentenced from birth
To love unusual gods beyond all earth
And the easy gospels bruited hither and yon.

So the poet calls upon his "seven of friends" (Davidson, Curry, Frank, Hirsch, Johnson, Stevenson, and Tate) to "acquit" him of "that stain of pride" and to answer "whether / I am so proud a Fool, and godless beside." When one recalls that a basic critical principle of Ransom's was that a poem should remain "almost anonymous," he can understand why these poems were not reprinted for nearly fifty years. Davidson was surprised that Ransom wanted to suppress the poems that he had pored over in France. A new member of the group, however, Tate was pleased that Ransom was dissatisfied with his early verse. He was delighted with the kind of poems Ransom was then bringing to the meetings. He expressed his reactions to his first Fugitive meetings in *Memoirs and Opinions* (1975):

> John Ransom always appeared at the Fugitive meetings with a poem (some of us didn't), and when his turn came he read it in a dry tone of understatement. I can only describe his manner in those days as irony which

was both brisk and bland. Before we began to think of a magazine (the *Fugitive* was not begun until April 1922), John had written a poem which foreshadowed the style for which he became famous. . . . I marvelled at it because it seemed to me that overnight he had left behind him the style of his first book and, without confusion, had mastered a new style.

The poet had found his distinctive voice, and no longer was there the confusion of the earlier poems. The poem to which Tate referred is "Necrological," in which, for the first time, Ransom employed the vocabulary, syntax, imagery, rhythm, and persona that would be characteristic of all his future verse. The poem, Ransom said many years later, was suggested by the career of Charles the Bold of Burgundy, who was slain in battle and his body left on the battlefield to be devoured by the wolves. The morning following the battle a young friar says "his paternosters," scourges "his limbs" and goes out upon the battlefield, and what he sees and experiences there brings him face to face for the first time with some of the mysteries of human existence:

> Day lightened the place where the battle had been won.
> The people were dead—it is easy he thought to die—
> These dead remained, but the living were all gone,
> Gone with the wailing trumpet of victory.

As the friar wanders among the pillage, he ponders a troublesome question, "With much riddling his head became unruly." Can one understand, justify, reconcile the suffering and death that have occurred on this field with the concept of a personal, loving God? Is there logical cause for human strife and suffering, for sacrifice and love, for devotion to a cause, however sacred, if the winner of this day's engagement goes only to meet death in another, the next day or the day after?

> The lords of chivalry lay prone and shattered
> The gentle and the bodyguard of yeoman
> Bartholomew's stroke went home—but little it mattered,
> Bartholomew went to be stricken of other foemen.

The young friar, devout and learned in theology, finds keeping his faith in the face of this, his first encounter with the real world, difficult indeed.

As he walks through the battlefield, he notes "the dead wore no raiment against the air / Bartholomew's men had spoiled them where they fell." Some of the bodies "were whitely bare," "some gory and fabulous" where they had been pierced by the sword and then eaten by the "grey wolf." It is easy to die, the friar concludes. Then, as the friar wanders under "the blue ogive of the firmament," he notes three particularized scenes, three tableaux, that seem to bring together his scattered reflections: one is a dead warrior whose "leman, who with her flame had warmed his tent, / For him enduring all men's pleasantries," had died clutching his knees. The second is a white stallion which had thrown its rider and "spilled there his little brain" and the "groin of the knight was spilled by a stone." The third is a knife with a "crooked blade," an instrument made especially for slaughter. The friar pulls it from the "belly of a lugubrious wight"; he feels its sharp edge and notes it was "cunningly made." At this point the poet interposes a comment: "But strange apparatus was it for a Carmelite." Then in a concluding stanza Ransom attempts to demonstrate his theory that a poem can reveal a quality of knowledge that one can get nowhere else. He endeavors to reconstitute the friar's experience so that the reader may share it with him and may learn what he has learned:

> Then he sat upon a hill and bowed his head
> As under a riddle, and in a deep surmise
> So still that he likened himself unto those dead
> Whom the kites of Heaven solicited with sweet cries.

This poem, like so many of Ransom's other poems, ends inconclusively or at best ambiguously. The reason is that Ransom's poetry often asks the difficult questions, those for which there is no easy answer. The ending of "Necrological" seems vague because the friar cannot assimilate all he has experi- enced. He has surely learned how little value one human being places on the life of another, how precarious human life is. He has learned, too, of how unpredictable the world is. A stallion dies because he is hit in the head; it is a knight who is felled by a stroke in the groin. Most of all he has learned of human love when he sees the leman who has endured "all men's pleasantries" and even given up her life so that she might be near the one she loves. The friar is so deeply engrossed in thought that he is like the dead bodies of the knights in whom only the vultures seem interested. The friar learns that the human body, to which he has given little consideration before, is more than a mere depository for the soul and that there is a kind of love quite different from the adoration he feels for his blessed lord. He knows he has broadened the range of his experience. He is on the verge of understanding that the monistic system of his church cannot explain the inexhaustible ambiguities and paradoxes of the world outside his monastery. He is, as Robert Buffington has pointed out, a monist on the point of becoming a dualist.

During 1923 Ransom published twenty-three poems written in what Tate has called his "mature manner," including some of his best: "Bells for John Whiteside's Daughter," "Philomela," "Conrad at Twilight," "Blackberry Winter," "Emily Hardcastle, Spinster," "Here Lies a Lady," "Captain Carpenter," "Spectral Lovers," and "Vaunting Oak." As he wrote Robert Graves, who had written him a letter praising *Poems About God* shortly after its appearance, he was devoting every moment he could steal from his academic duties to poetry. Also, he often felt "hampered and tortured" as he searched for a form to carry his themes. He had tried, he wrote, "the modern irregular forms effected over here by some clever people," but he was convinced they would not function for him. He was concerned, too, that his verse would make him unpopular because, if he were honest to his art, he would create the impression that he was "a rebel and a poor admirer of our beloved world." What Ransom was reporting, of course, was that he was attempting in his poetry to re-create a view of reality that depicted a broad disparity between the real world and the fantasy world of the idealists. He was trying to avoid what he later called Platonic or bogus poetry—that is, poetry in which images are used merely to illustrate ideas. With the greatest accuracy and precision possible, he wanted to point up the inexhaustible ambiguities, the tensions, the paradoxes, and the ironies that make up the world in which man must live.

Ransom informed Graves of his dissatisfaction with *Poems About God,* finding them now, he wrote, "very juvenile in spots." In the same letter he enclosed some of his more recent poems, including "Philomela," so that Graves could see the "sort of things that interests me now." Graves offered to try to find Ransom a British publisher and asked if he would allow any of the poems to appear in periodicals before the book was published. Ransom responded immediately: "You have my permission to use anything of mine anywhere and at any time. And to retitle anything, or to edit as you please." As soon as Ransom had accumulated a sufficient number of poems for a volume, he sent them to Graves, under the working title of "Philomela." The manuscript which Holt had just refused included forty-six poems of which about half were revised versions of poems from *Poems About God* and about half had been written since that volume appeared. The poems were arranged, he wrote Graves, in the order in which they were written, and he hoped they would be published in this sequence because he thought it would show a "regular progress in technique." Graves liked the new poems—and Ransom's revisions of the old ones—but the title displeased him. He suggested that the book be called *Grace After Meat,* a title to which Ransom objected because it emphasized "Grace," a poem he now found "too raw" and "an artistic offense." "I would rather pass for an artist," he wrote Graves, "than exhibit my history." If Graves did not like "Philomela," he suggested as possible titles: "Vaunting Oak," "Under the Locusts," or "Mortal Oak."

At about the time Ransom sent this manuscript to Graves, he sent Morley *Chills and Fever,* informing him that Holt had refused "Philomela" and requesting him to see if any other New York publisher would be interested in a volume of "all new poems." Just before Graves, with the help of T. S. Eliot, had convinced the Hogarth Press to bring out *Grace After Meat,* Morley wrote Ransom that Alfred A. Knopf was delighted to get *Chills and Fever.* On 4 July 1924 Ransom finished reading proofs for *Chills and Fever* and wrote Graves:

> I liked the looks of the book, in fact felt weakly tender over it. . . . Then I thought of what the public would think; or rather, how they wouldn't be able to think anything; it would be for them a hopelessly hard nut to crack. For odd as it may seem to you, I can assure you that my simple strains will not find in Nashville, not even among fond relatives, nor well wishers, more frequent than I deserve, more than two persons who will guess what I am after (I make loyal exception to my Fugitive brethren of course); and in the whole United States I should imagine there are not fifty who *could* read it with sympathy and not even ten who *will*.

Chills and Fever appeared in New York in August 1924 and *Grace After Meat* in London three months later. Both of the books were well received by the critics, most of whom recognized them as important volumes by a gifted poet. The reviews were not brief notices, as those of *Poems About God* had been, but serious assessments of the poet's intentions and accomplishments. The poets to whom Ransom was compared this time were not Frost and Hardy, but T. S. Eliot and Ezra Pound. Writing for the *Yale Review,* Louis Untermeyer called Ransom "an imaginative poet, a technician of brilliance, a storyteller of power, whose flavor is as individual as that of any American writing today." *Chills and Fever,* he concluded, "seems the best volume of American verse which has lately come to this reviewer's table. No book of the year—and not many of the last decade—has revealed a finer craftsman, a more sensitive musician, a richer personality. In short—if I may be allowed the uncommon extravagance of the capital—a Poet." The most perceptive statement, perhaps, came from John McClure, associate editor of the New Orleans *Double-Dealer,* an influential little magazine in which the work of many soon-to-be important young writers first appeared. "Mr. Ransom," he wrote in the *Times-Picayune,* "has developed the intellectually expressive cadence to a point probably not excelled by any American—not even by Eliot, Pound, or Stevens, and certainly not by Frost."

Since *Grace After Meat* was published only a few months after *Chills and Fever* and since all of the poems in *Grace After Meat* had already appeared in one or the other of Ransom's two previously published books, it was not widely reviewed. It did provoke, however, what Ransom regarded as "the most philosophic statement of my position that I have seen, though not the most favorable." This "statement" was included in Edwin Muir's review in the *Saturday Review of Literature.* Muir found *Grace After Meat* the second most important literary event in recent weeks, the most important being the publication of Edith Sitwell's *Troy Park.* Looking among his British contemporaries to find the poet Ransom most resembled, Muir wrote, he thought immediately of Robert Graves: "Their ways of apprehending life and handling experience, their preoccupation at the same time with quite ordinary facts and metaphysical problems, their serious attempts to come to terms with themselves and their surroundings, their assumption of intellectual detachment as a means to this." At the same time Muir was persuaded that Ransom was "bolder both in thought and technique" than Graves, as well as more intellectual. Muir insisted that Ransom had what Graves

Allen Tate and Ransom, 1949 (Kenyon College Archives)

most important poets of the era. The review that Ransom said had given him the "most honor and inward examination" that he had ever "secured from any source" was written by Tate and appeared in the *Nation* for 30 March 1927. "The fourth volume of Ransom's poetry," Tate began, "is not the equal in brilliant variety of technical effects or in range of subject matter of *Chills and Fever*" (1924); nevertheless, it was "the qualitative equal of anything else he has ever done," and it "precipitates the particular essence" which is Ransom's:

> Mr. Ransom is the last pure manifestation of the culture of the eighteenth-century South; the moral issues which emerge transfigured in his poetry are the moral issues of his section, class, culture, referred to their simple fundamental properties. . . .
>
> Two of Mr. Ransom's qualities in especial connect him with the culture which in its prime registered its genius in politics and law; rationalism and the code of noblesse oblige. These qualities, informing every poem, dictate the direction of his artistic vision. . . . Rationalism . . . stiffens his poetry with an irony and lucidity, and a subtlety, which elevate it with a unique distinction in the present American scene. . . . Mr. Ransom can render a beautiful commentary upon his tragic personal vision because he accepts the code within which the characters struggle. . . . In every poem he is either the satirist or the ironist; and as a fine minor artist he has always the same thing to say, in new and unpredictable images.

did not, a "heraldic quality . . . the ability to translate experience into something which is half myth, half philosophic fable, and in doing that to chill and clarify it." For Muir, however, the basic weakness of the poetry was its cold intellectualism; it thereby missed greatness because the truly "great poet gains freedom from his sufferings by realizing them completely in a living act of the imagination." Ransom's kind of poetry, Muir concluded, had not been written so well since the seventeenth century, and this fact made him "one of the most interesting poets of our time."

Ransom's last book of original verse, *Two Gentlemen in Bonds,* was published by Knopf in January 1927. This volume, not all of which is of the unmatched brilliance of *Chills and Fever,* includes some of Ransom's most enduring poetry: "Antique Harvesters," "Blue Girls," "Dead Boy," "The Equilibrists," "Janet Waking," "Man Without Sense of Direction," "Survey of Literature," "Piazzi Piece," "Our Two Worthies," and "Vision by Sweetwater." This book was greeted by almost all the better-known critics as a major achievement of one of the

Almost the whole of Ransom's poetic career falls within an eleven-year period, from 1916 to 1927. He published fewer than 160 poems, and his first *Selected Poems* (1945) includes only five poems written after 1927. The enlarged edition of *Selected Poems* (1963) includes some new stanzas and many revised lines but no new poems. The last *Selected Poems* (1969) includes eighty poems, including twelve sonnets from *Two Gentlemen in Bonds* along with a revised version of each. Although Ransom wrote poetry for only a brief period and his output during these years was far from prolific, within the restrictions he placed upon himself both in theme and genre his contributions are considerable. Although he wrote only one entirely new poem after 1939, he was, as he expressed it, always "tinkering" with the old ones. William Pratt has noted fourteen different versions of "Tom, Tom the Piper's Son," written between 1924 and 1969. Fortunately, as Robert Buffington and others have pointed out, Ransom changed his best poems little.

Although in his prose essays Ransom would never admit that he knew exactly what Eliot meant by the "dissociation of sensibility"–he used what he called his "structure-texture formulation" to identify the unique nature of poetic discourse–several critics have pointed out that Eliot's phrase can be prof-itably used to denote a persistent theme in Ransom's poetry. In one of the first serious attempts to assess Ransom's poetic achievement, Robert Penn Warren pointed out: "To an astonishing degree, in far more than a majority of the cases, the hero or heroine of the poem is a sufferer from that complaint of 'dissociation of sensibility.' The poem itself is a commentary on the situation, its irony deriving from the fact that these otherwise admirable people 'cannot fathom or per-form their nature.'" Many later critics have agreed with and elaborated on Warren's thesis. In *Modern Poetry and the Tradition* (1939), Cleanth Brooks suggested that "a divided sensibility" is one of Ransom's major concerns. Like other modern critics, F. O. Matthiessen attempted to explain the schism by pointing out that the modern sensibility is "torn between reason and imagination, between science and faith."

In "Necrological" the young friar is rendered in-capable of action by the impact upon his sensibility of the difference between the adoration he feels for his lord and the physical love shared by the knight and his leman. Another of Ransom's characters who can-not perceive the duality of his nature is the protagonist of "Man Without Sense of Direction." Although it would seem that this man should be living a full and satisfying life, something is not quite right. Despite his "noblest mind and powerful leg," he is far from satis-fied, and although he is aware that his life is incom-plete, he is not fully aware of what is lacking. As War-ren pointed out, he can neither "fathom nor perform his nature." His impotence and ignorance make poign-ant demands on our sympathy:

> And he writhes like an antique man of bronze
> That is beaten by furies visible,
> Yet he is punished not knowing his sins
> And for his innocence walks in hell.

His incompleteness is expressed in physical terms. He has a "small passion," which he "feigns large," and he is "flushed" with passion as he emerges from his wife's bedroom. Almost immediately, however, his lips are cold, and he is "cold as dead." That this man is incapable of genuine human love is obvious; even more pa-thetic is the alarming fact that not only is his plight hopeless but that he is not really aware of the sad state he is in:

> But let his cold lips be her omen,
> She shall not kiss that harried one
> To peace, as men are served by women
> Who comfort them in darkness and in sun.

This fragmented and incomplete state of man is the basic thematic concern of some of Ransom's best-known poems. In "Winter Remembered" the man is separated from his loved one for no recorded reason–though it is revealed that he has a wound, presumably a spiritual one–and he is deeply af-fected by the separation. The inability to experience love, or as Ransom expresses it, the "cry of Ab-sence, Absence in the heart" sends him out of the warm house into the icy weather. Metaphorically, Ransom is demonstrating the man's lack of love, and his miserable state is delineated in one of the most evocative images in Ransom's poetry:

> Dear love, these fingers that had known your touch
> And tied our forces first together
> Were ten poor idiot fingers not worth much,
> Ten frozen parsnips hanging in the weather.

Ransom once suggested, as F. Scott Fitzgerald noted, that modern man must hold in his mind si-multaneously two contradictory ideas. He is forever confronted by questions that demand answers but for which he has none. This situation is presented in "The Equilibrists," in which two lovers are caught between two equally strong but opposing forces. As the title suggests, they can be likened to the juggler who has to keep two balls in the air simultaneously or the performer who walks the tight wire high in the air and must retain his poise and balance, for to fall off on either side would be disastrous. The lov-ers are in a "torture of equilibrium" for "They burned with fierce heat to come near, / But honor beat them back and kept them clear." The "two painful stars" cannot defy the natural laws but must keep their orbit lest they explode; the two lovers must follow the basic principle behind their human-ity even though doing so ruins their opportunity to be lovers. They can neither consummate their pas-sion nor free themselves of compelling desire. Even the woman's mouth, a "quaint orifice," delivers con-tradictory messages. From it comes heat when the lovers kiss, but this passion loses its force in the light of the "cold words [that] came down spiral from the head." Passion and reason both come from their ba-sic nature; yet, passion tells them to become lovers, reason to remain innocent and pure. The eyes say: "Never mind the cruel words," but "what they said, the doves came straightway flying / And unsaid: Honor, Honor, they kept crying." Ransom is obvi-ously providing a foundation for his own dualism. How much easier it would be if this were a hedonis-tic world so that each lover could enjoy the other's body unmolested; or if it were a pure, idealistic world so that they could live without passion or de-sire. It is, however, neither and both. Although the persona sympathizes with the plight of the lovers,

Painted Head

By dark severance the apparition head
Smiles from the air a capital on no
Column on a Platonic perhaps head
On a canvas sky depending from nothing;

Stirs up an old illusion of grandeur
By tickling the instinct of heads to be
Absolute and to try decapitation
And to play truant from the body bush;

But too happy and beautiful for those sorts
Of head (homekeeping heads are happiest)
Discovers maybe thirty unwidowed years
Of not dishonoring the faithful stem;

Is nameless and has authored for the evil
Historian headhunters neither book
Nor state and is therefore distinct from tart
Heads with crowns and guilty gallery heads;

So that the extravagant device of art
Unhousing by abstraction this once head
Was capital irony by a loving hand
That knew the no treason of a head like this;

Makes repentance in an unlovely head
For having vinegarly traduced the flesh
Till, the heart flesh recusing, the hard egg
Is shrunken to its own deathless surface;

Calls up this image? The body bears the head
(So hardly one they, terribly are two)
Feeds and obeys and unto pleads what end?
Not to the glory of tyrant head but to

The estate of body; beauty is of body;
The flesh contouring shallowly on a head
Is a rock-garden needing body's love
And best bodiness to colorify

The big blue birds sitting and sea-shell flats
And caves, and on the iron acropolis
To spread the hyacinthine hair and rear
The olive garden for the nightingales.

John Crowe Ransom

Manuscript for a Ransom poem (from D. David Long and Michael R. Burr, eds., John Crowe Ransom: A Tribute from the Community of Letters, *1964)*

with their passion demanding fulfillment, he also understands the necessity of the moral restrictions that prohibit the consummation of their desire. (In his essay "Forms and Citizens" Ransom argued that restraining this natural impulse turns what man may feel for any woman into a more complicated emotion that he has for only one woman. The woman becomes, he says elsewhere, a "precious object," and lust matures into love.)

Although the conflict between the two lovers demands resolution, it remains unresolved. The lovers remain suspended in the terrible void that develops between them, completely at the mercy of the conflicting forces that destroy a unified approach to life, and the polarities will never be terminated. They will remain in this "torture of equilibrium" throughout eternity.

> For spin your period out, and draw your breath,
> A kinder saeculum begins with Death,
> Would you ascend to Heaven and bodiless dwell?
> Or take your bodies honorless to Hell?
>
> In Heaven you have heard no marriage is,
> No white flesh tinder to your lecheries,
> Your male and female tissue sweetly shaped
> Sublimed away, and furious blood escaped.
>
> Great lovers lie in Hell, the stubborn ones
> Infatuate of the flesh upon the bones;
> Stuprate, they rend each other when they kiss,
> The pieces kiss again, no end to this.

Given the nature of the world and expectations of the one to come, Ransom underscores the plight of his doomed lovers by composing an epitaph "to memorize their doom":

> *Equilibrists lie here; stranger, tread light;*
> *Close, but untouching in each other's sight;*
> *Mouldered the lips and ashy the tall skull.*
> *Let them be perilous and beautiful.*

Conversing with Cleanth Brooks and Robert Penn Warren in *Understanding Poetry,* Ransom remarked: "Death is the greatest subject of poetry, the most serious, . . . there's no recourse from death except that we learn to face it, to get on speaking terms with it." One is not surprised to find, therefore, that fully a third of Ransom's mature verse is concerned with mortality: the inevitable decay of feminine beauty, the fleetingness of youthful energy, and the awful certainty of death. Many of that small handful of poems which Randall Jarrell certified as "perfectly realized and occasionally almost perfect" treat this theme, including "Bells for John Whiteside's

Daughter," Ransom's most-often anthologized poem:

> There was such speed in her little body,
> And such lightness in her footfall,
> It is no wonder that her brown study
> Astonishes us all.
> . . . .
> But now go the bells, and we are ready,
> In one house we are sternly stopped
> To say we are vexed at her brown study,
> Lying so primly propped.

In its movement from "Astonished" to "vexed" the poem delineates exactly how an adult, perhaps a neighbor, is affected by the death of a young girl. Apparently he does not know her well; her only direct effect upon him has been that of a slight nuisance as the noise of her childhood games in the orchard below has disturbed his adult contemplation. Her energy and vitality seem endless. She is never still; therefore his first reaction when he sees her "brown study"—a lifelike little body lying so still and apparently so meditative—is astonishment. He is surprised that she is so different from the way he remembers her. The thought of a moment, however—rendered by almost three-fifths of the poem presented without any full stops—causes his reflection to move from this individual girl to what she represents. The quality of the icons, to use a critical term of Ransom's, which contribute the rich texture to the poem, clearly reveal the metaphysical nature of the brief reflection—"orchard trees," "arms against her shadow," "lazy geese . . . / Dripping their snow on the green grass," crying "in goose, Alas, / for the tireless heart." Taken together the elements of this meditation portray the human predicament.

After his first reaction of surprise and astonishment, he has now placed the unexpected death of the little girl in another perspective. His astonishment has turned to "vexation." He is outraged at this apparently useless and senseless destruction of youthful vitality. He can only surmise that this death is merely another example of the inscrutability, of the paradoxical and ambiguous nature, of the world in which he must live. There is no way he can make this experience compatible with the view of a meaningful universe controlled by an omnipotent and meaningful God.

The irony of the poem depends upon the contrast of the stock response to death with that which is expressed. The poet employs the same technique in "Dead Boy," which reports several reactions to the death of the little cousin: the simple objective statement "The little cousin is dead" is undercut by the description of his death as "foul subtraction"; the boy, a member of an ancient Virginia family is mourned by

JOHN CROWE RANSOM
Beating
the Bushes

Selected Essays 1941-1970

Dust jacket for Ransom's 1972 collection of essays, which includes some of the writings on literary criticism that he published in the Kenyon Review

many relatives and by the narrator, who belongs to the "world of outer dark." Neither he nor the relatives, but obviously for different reasons, "like the transaction." The death of the boy can hardly be expressed by the vague and scientific word "abstraction," for, although he was a "sword beneath his mother's heart" and although to no one but the mother perhaps was he ever lovable, "never / Woman bewept her babe as this is weeping." Then there are the ritualistic and ceremonial expressions of the elder statesman, who "have strode by the box of death" and the official statement of the minister who proclaims: "The first-fruits . . . the Lord has taken." The final statement comes from the "noble house" which suffers a "deep dynastic wound." Although the boy is "a pig with a pasty face," he has been taken "by foul subtraction," a "green bough from Virginia aged tree," and the narrator sees in him "the fore-bears' antique lineaments." With the death of the little boy passes the expectations for the continuation of the family. The narrator's grief is

less personal than the mother's, but he sees in the little boy's death "a deep dynastic wound," a basic description of the elemental process of life.

"Janet Waking" illustrates what Graham Hough has called Ransom's ability to put "massive . . . facts in small or delicate settings." Through the death of her pet hen, a young girl confronts for the first time the most painful and pervasive fact of human existence. Again, Ransom controls his tone by the use of point of view; the simple facts of the poem are presented from the alternating perspectives of a child and an adult. After Janet has slept "Beautifully" until it is "deeply morning," her first thought on waking is of her "dainty-feathered hen." She wonders "how it had kept." Pausing just long enough to kiss her mother and father, she rushes out to the chicken's house, but "Her Chucky had died." Then the perspective shifts from that of the child to that of the adult, and the differing attitudes expressed in this dual point of view produce a tone that is a masterful blending of pathos and humor. Again the poet avoids the soggy sentimentalism that the subject, the death of a pet, seems to demand:

It was a transmogrifying bee
Came droning down on Chucky's old bald head
And sat and put the poison. It scarcely bled.
But how exceedingly
And purply did the knot
Swell with the venom and communicate
Its rigor! Now the poor comb stood up straight
But Chucky did not.

Janet implores her chicken to rise and walk upon the grass as it always has, but it cannot because it has been "Translated far beyond the daughters of men." (Janet does not understand that her hen has been visited by a "transmogrifying bee"—one that has altered the hen's metaphysical state.) Janet insists that her father awaken her chicken and will not believe him when he says he cannot because she "will not be instructed in how deep was the forgetful kingdom of death." Janet is too young, too full of life, to understand her most significant human trait—the inevitability of death.

Few modern poets have succeeded, as Ransom has, in making his readers aware of the ravages of time, of the shortness of human life, and of the inevitable decay of feminine beauty and vigor. Two of his best-known poems on the subject of change are "Blue Girls" and "Vision by Sweetwater." The vastly dissimilar ways in which this theme is developed in these poems demonstrate both the poet's technical skills and his ability to place his personal stamp on materials far from original. He takes the traditional carpe diem motif and makes it his own. In "Blue Girls" a group of young girls, students in a fashionable boarding school, are shown parading their beauty, apparently unaware of how time will affect them. The narrator observes them and muses that they should "practice" their beauty and think no more of the future than blue birds that go "chattering on the air." They must not listen to their teacher because their adult rational understanding of how time affects physical beauty might destroy the girls' unselfconscious enjoyment of the moment. The narrator could but does not explain this basic law of life, for if he shared with the girls what he has learned from experience, he might disturb one of the basic patterns of life. The time to practice beauty instinctively is in youth. If one becomes self-conscious and begins to reflect upon experience, to rationalize all of his expectations, he will exaggerate the conflict between abstract thought and natural action. The persona is aware that the girls are silly and vain and in their innocence unawakened, but given the nature of the world and the fragility of their natural beauty, he cannot advise them to give up their unreflective approach. To think too much about experience is to preclude the possibility of living a complete and satisfying life. In "Vision by Sweetwater" the horror of youthful beauty and energy being inevitably destroyed by the passing of time brings a scream "From one of the white throats which it hid among."

Some of the poems written between 1924 and 1927, particularly "Old Mansion" and "Antique Harvesters," reveal the growing economic and political concerns that led Ransom into the Agrarian movement. These poems, however, like so much of Ransom's other verse, are concerned with mutability. Social and political institutions are subject to change, as are their human creators. In "Old Mansion" the poet urges that ideals be preserved even when the institutions which embody them pass away. Although the culture of the Old South is doomed, as all things fall victims to time and change, one needs to participate in the traditions of that culture; for only in a sensitive awareness of the past can one perceive a sense of stability and permanence in the flux of an ever-changing world. In the description of the old mansion one can see the traditional virtues to which the poet refers:

Stability was the virtue of its rectangle
Whose line was seen in part and guessed in part
Through trees. Decay was the tone of old brick and shingle.
Green shutters dragging frightened the watchful heart.

To assert: Your mansion, long and richly inhabited,
Its porches and bowers suiting the children of men,

Will not forever be thus, O man, exhibited,
And one had best hurry to enter it if one can.

In his use of wit and irony, in the tension and paradox characteristic of his best verse, Ransom is distinctively a modern poet. His attitudes and the poetic forms he employs, however, reflect his interest in the traditional. "Antique Harvesters" opens in autumn, the time of harvest, and the spokesman calls his friends and neighbors together to bring in the bounties that nature has provided. On the surface it seems a modest production: "A meager hill of kernels, a runnel of juice," a few "spindling ears"; "Declension looks from our land, it is old." The young men in the party are disappointed because the yield is so meager. Although the old endure and "shall be older," the young want no "sable" memories; they see only the "spindling ears." They want material values, a bountiful yield of that which can be used; they do not know that "One spot has special yield," that it is a precious object, because it has worth beyond its utilitarian value; it is particularly fertile because it was drenched in heroes' blood.

In *The World's Body* Ransom argued that religion exists for its ritual rather than for its dogma. Ritual combines the attitudes, customs, habits, and rites through which man restrains the more basic side of his nature. The harvest of which the persona speaks is a ritual and from the "ample chambers" of the old men's hearts comes another echo suggested by an activity that is traditionally ritualistic. This activity is fox hunting:

Here come the hunters, keepers of a rite;
The horn, the hounds, the lank mares coursing by
Straddled with the archetypes of chivalry;
And the fox, lively ritualist, in flight
Offering his unearthly ghost to quarry;
And the fields themselves to harry.

The persona calls upon the young men to resume the harvest and reap the real yield that the section has produced. They should get to know their "famous Lady's image"; it is revealed now, though perhaps not in its full splendor, and soon it will disappear, as everything must into nothingness.

This poem, which Ransom often called his Southern poem, suggests some of the thought that went into *I'll Take My Stand: The South and the Agrarian Tradition, by Twelve Southerners* (1930), written by Ransom and eleven other Southerners: Donald Davidson, Allen Tate, Robert Penn Warren, Frank Owsley, Lyle Lanier, John Gould Fletcher, H. B. Kline, Stark Young, Andrew Nelson Lytle, H. C. Nixon, and John Donald Wade. This book, to which Ransom contributed the introduction ("A

Statement of Principles") and the lead essay ("Reconstructed but Unregenerate"), argues that modern man must be aware of the evils inherent in a social order dominated by uncontrolled materialism.

Any final estimate of Ransom's achievement must begin with his poetry. Given the severe limits he placed upon his efforts in this genre, the quality of his contribution is remarkable. In a small handful of poems, all of which can be printed in a hundred pages, he accurately mirrored the modern sensibility. He produced a dozen or so poems that are almost perfect and that reflect the virtues of modern poetry at its best, combining delicacy with strength, elegance with earthiness. Not only is he, as Allen Tate has proclaimed, one of the "best elegiac poets in the language," few poets of his generation have been able to represent with greater accuracy and precision the inexhaustible ambiguities, the paradoxes and tensions, the dichotomies and ironies that make up the life of modern man.

Letters:

Selected Letters of John Crowe Ransom, edited by Thomas Daniel Young and George Core (Baton Rouge & London: Louisiana State University Press, 1985).

Bibliography:

Thomas Daniel Young, *John Crowe Ransom: An Annotated Bibliography* (New York & London: Garland, 1982).

Biography:

Thomas Daniel Young, *Gentleman in a Dustcoat: A Biography of John Crowe Ransom* (Baton Rouge: Louisiana State University Press, 1976).

References:

Cleanth Brooks, *Modern Poetry and the Tradition* (Chapel Hill: University of North Carolina Press, 1939);

Robert Buffington, *The Equilibrist: A Study of John Crowe Ransom's Poems, 1916–1963* (Nashville: Vanderbilt University Press, 1967);

Mark Jancovich, *The Cultural Politics of the New Criticism* (Cambridge & New York: Cambridge University Press, 1993);

Karl F. Knight, *The Poetry of John Crowe Ransom: A Study of Diction, Metaphor and Symbol* (The Hague: Mouton, 1965);

Mark G. Malvasi, *The Unregenerate South: The Agrarian Thought of John Crowe Ransom, Allen Tate, and Donald Davidson* (Baton Rouge: Louisiana State University Press, 1997);

Thornton H. Parsons, *John Crowe Ransom* (New York: Twayne, 1969);

Kieran Quinlan, *John Crowe Ransom's Secular Faith* (Baton Rouge: Louisiana State University Press, 1989);

Louis D. Rubin Jr., *The Wary Fugitives: Four Poets and the South* (Baton Rouge: Louisiana State University Press, 1978);

Miller Williams, *The Poetry of John Crowe Ransom* (New Brunswick: Rutgers University Press, 1972);

Thomas Daniel Young, ed., *John Crowe Ransom: Critical Essays and a Bibliography* (Baton Rouge: Louisiana State University Press, 1968).

Papers:

The libraries at Vanderbilt University, Kenyon College, Princeton University, Yale University, Indiana University, Stanford University, and Washington University have collections of John Crowe Ransom's papers.

Marjorie Kinnan Rawlings

This entry was updated by Rodger L. Tarr (Illinois State University) from the entries by Samuel I. Bellman (California State Polytechnic University, Pomona) in DLB 9: American Novelists, 1910–1945, and by Reese Danley Kilgo (University of Alabama, Huntsville) in DLB 22: American Writers for Children, 1900–1960.

See also the Rawlings entry in *DLB 102: American Short-Story Writers, 1910–1945, Second Series.*

BIRTH: Washington, D.C., 8 August 1896, to Arthur Frank and Ida May Traphagen Kinnan.

EDUCATION: A.B., University of Wisconsin, 1918.

MARRIAGES: May 1919 to Charles A. Rawlings Jr. (divorced 1933); 27 October 1941 to Norton Sanford Baskin.

AWARDS AND HONORS: second place, *McCall's* Child Authorship Contest, for short story, 1912; second place, Scribner Prize Contest, for novella *Jacob's Ladder,* 1931; O. Henry Memorial awards for short story "Gal Young Un," 1933, and for short story "Black Secret," 1946; elected to National Academy of Arts and Letters, 1938; Pulitzer Prize for fiction for *The Yearling,* 1939; Newbery Medal Honor Book for *The Secret River,* 1956; Lewis Carroll Shelf Award for *The Yearling,* 1963; honorary degrees include LL.D., Rollins College, 1939, and L.H.D., University of Florida, 1941.

DEATH: St. Augustine, Florida, 14 December 1953.

BOOKS: *South Moon Under* (New York & London: Scribners, 1933; London: Faber & Faber, 1933);
Golden Apples (New York: Scribners, 1935; London: Heinemann, 1939);
The Yearling (New York: Scribners, 1938; London & Toronto: Heinemann, 1938);
When the Whippoorwill— (New York: Scribners, 1940; London & Toronto: Heinemann, 1940);
Cross Creek (New York: Scribners, 1942; London & Toronto: Heinemann, 1943);
Cross Creek Cookery (New York: Scribners, 1942); republished as *The Marjorie Kinnan Rawlings Cook-*

Marjorie Kinnan Rawlings

book: Cross Creek Cookery (London: Hammond, Hammond, 1960);
Jacob's Ladder (Coral Gables, Fla.: University of Miami Press, 1950);
The Sojourner (New York: Scribners, 1953; London: Heinemann, 1953);
The Secret River (New York: Scribners, 1955);
The Marjorie Rawlings Reader, edited by Julia Scribner Bigham (New York: Scribners, 1956);

357

Short Stories by Marjorie Kinnan Rawlings, edited by
   Rodger L. Tarr (Gainesville: University Press
   of Florida, 1994);
Poems by Marjorie Kinnan Rawlings: Songs of a Housewife,
   edited by Tarr (Gainesville: University Press
   of Florida, 1997).

SELECTED PERIODICAL PUBLICATIONS–
UNCOLLECTED:
FICTION
Mountain Prelude [novel], *Saturday Evening Post* (26
   April 1947): 15-17, 67-68, 70-72, 74; (3
   May): 36-37, 132, 134, 137, 139-140, 142; (10
   May): 38-39, 140, 142, 144-147; (17 May):
   40-41, 153, 155-156, 158-159, 161; (24 May):
   36-37, 83, 86, 90, 92, 95, 97; (31 May): 40,
   45-46, 48, 50.
NONFICTION
"I Sing While I Cook," *Vogue,* 93 (15 February
   1939): 5-7;
"Regional Literature of the South," *College English,* 1
   (February 1940): 381-389;
"Trees for Tomorrow," *Collier's,* 117 (8 May 1943):
   14-15, 24-25;
"Florida: A Land of Contrasts," *Transatlantic,* 14
   (October 1944): 12-17;
"Florida: An Affectionate Tribute," *Congressional Re-
   cord (U.S.),* 2 March 1945, pp. 1692-1693;
Autobiographical sketches, *Los Angeles Times,* 26
   April 1953, p. 1; 3 May, p. 6; 10 May, p. 6; 17
   May, p. 7; 24 May, p. 6.

Marjorie Kinnan Rawlings is known primarily
for her Pulitzer Prize-winning novel *The Yearling*
(1938). Most of her fiction and nonfiction deals with
poor, backcountry Floridians (called "crackers") and
with man's need to be in harmony with his natural environment. Her life in the Florida woods, which furnished her with much of the material that she wrote
about so sympathetically, represented a reaction
against the urban life she violently detested.

   Born on 8 August 1896 and raised in Washington, D.C., Marjorie Kinnan, as early as the age of six,
expressed an interest in writing, and for the next
decade or so contributed to the children's pages of *The
Washington Post.* At fifteen she won a prize for her
story, "The Reincarnation of Miss Hetty," which she
had entered in *McCall's* Child Authorship Contest.
Her father, to whom she had been very close, died in
1913, and the following year she moved with her
mother and brother to Madison, Wisconsin, where
she enrolled in the University of Wisconsin. Here,
while working toward her bachelor of arts degree
(which she received in 1918), she was active in several
campus organizations, including the dramatic society,

and was elected to Phi Beta Kappa. Following
graduation she was a publicist for the YWCA in
New York City, and in 1919 she married writer and
boating enthusiast Charles A. Rawlings Jr. The couple moved to Rochester, New York, where Marjorie
Rawlings did advertising and newspaper writing
and tried unsuccessfully to find a publisher for her
fiction. Between 1926 and 1928 she wrote nearly
five hundred witty, satirical newspaper poems under the header "Songs of a Housewife" for the *Rochester Times-Union,* as well as a novel, as yet unpublished, titled "Blood of My Blood," which she called
"Poor Jane Austen."

   In 1928 the couple bought a seventy-two-acre orange grove at Cross Creek, near Hawthorne, Florida.
Here she found the environmental harmony she had
wanted and again attempted to write for commercial
publication. Before long her stories about life in the
scrub and hammock country of northern Florida were
being published and attracting an audience, not the
least of whom was the celebrated editor Maxwell E.
Perkins of Scribners. One reason was the authentic
"feel" of her writing. So sympathetic did Rawlings
find this sparsely settled, semi-wilderness area that on
more than one occasion she lived with a cracker family for a time in order to garner materials and atmosphere for her writings. The novella *Jacob's Ladder* (first
published in *Scribner's Magazine,* April 1931) and "Gal
Young Un" (1932) won story prizes, and her first
novel, *South Moon Under* (1933), which came out the
year of her divorce from Charles Rawlings, was a
Book-of-the-Month Club selection. Content to remain
alone in her cottage at Cross Creek after the divorce,
Rawlings wrote steadily. Another novel, *Golden Apples,*
appeared in 1935, followed by *The Yearling* in 1938.

   After the enormous popular success of *The Yearling* she published a collection of short stories, *When the
Whippoorwill–* (1940). The next year she married Norton Sanford Baskin, a Florida hotel and restaurant operator. In 1942 she produced her autobiography, *Cross
Creek,* and an accompanying short, chatty cookbook,
Cross Creek Cookery. A libel suit brought against her by a
neighbor who had felt maligned by a descriptive passage in *Cross Creek* marred Rawlings's life somewhat in
the mid 1940s; Rawlings ultimately lost the suit and
had to pay nominal damages for "invasion of privacy."

   Following World War II Rawlings continued to
maintain her home at Cross Creek, although she frequently resided in St. Augustine and then in Crescent
Beach to be near the work of her husband. In 1947 she
spent the summer in Van Hornesville, New York, and
liked the area so well that she bought an old farmhouse for use as a summer home. Here, living alone,
she would spend part of each year until the end of her

The Yearling

A column of smoke rose from the cabin chimney, thin and straight

straight as a cat-tail. The smoke was blue where it left the red of the

clay. Then it trailed into the blue of the April skyx and,

strangely, was no longer blue but gray.

The boy Jody watched it, speculating. The fire on the kitchen hearth

was dying away. His mother was finishing hanging up the pots and pans

after the noon dinner. The day was Friday. She would sweep the floor with

a broom of ti-ti and then, if he were lucky, she would scrub it with the

corn-shucks scrub, and never miss him until he had reached the Creek. He

stood a minute, balancing the hoe on his shoulder.

                    unweeded
          The clearing itself was pleasant if the/rows of young shafts

of corn were not before him. The wild bees had found the chinaberry tree

by the front gate. They burrowed into the fragile lavender blooms as

greedily as though there were no other flowers in the scrub; as though

they had forgotten the yellow jessamine of March; the sweet bay and the

magnolias ahead of them in May. It occurred to him that he might follow
                                                              might
the swift line of flight of the black and gold bodies, and so find a bee-
     full of amber honey.
tree./ The winter's cane syrup was gone, and the jellies. His
                                          most of
   Finding a bee-tree was nobler work than hoeing, and the

corn could wait another day, afternoons filled with such a balmy

stirring were not to be taken lightly. He forgot that the honey-comb would

Page from the revised typescript for Rawlings's 1938 novel about a boy and his pet deer (University of Florida Library)

CROSS CREEK

By

Marjorie Kinnan Rawlings

Decorations by
EDWARD SHENTON

New York
CHARLES SCRIBNER'S SONS
1942

Title page for Rawlings's memoir recounting her life in Florida

life. *The Sojourner,* her last novel and possibly one of her most important works, appeared in 1953. At the end of that year, Rawlings became ill at Crescent Beach and died at a St. Augustine hospital on 14 December. She was fifty-seven. Her burial was at Antioch Cemetery, near Cross Creek.

South Moon Under is a deceptively quiet idyll of the Ocala Scrub region, the story of a cracker boy named Lant who lives alone with his mother under arduous conditions. In order to support the two of them Lant eventually becomes a moonshiner, and when a treacherous cousin informs on him to the Prohibition agents, Lant kills him. In specific language and theme *South Moon Under* prefigures *The Yearling.* As in the later novel, cracker life is convincingly depicted, and the book also incorporates folklore dealing with the moon and its phases. The novel was both a popular and a critical success. In addition to its selection by the Book-of-the-Month Club, it was a finalist in the Pulitzer Prize competition.

Golden Apples also deals with life in the Florida hammock country near the Ocala Scrub, this time late in the nineteenth century. A scapegrace Englishman

named Tordell is banished to an ancestral orange-grove estate in that region. There he seduces and impregnates a poor cracker girl named Allie. Later, after having been mistreated by the cruel, unfeeling Tordell, Allie dies in childbirth, leaving only her brother to mourn her passing. Several other characters also feel betrayed by love after giving themselves to the unworthy objects of their affections. The characters in the book are generally unrealistically drawn; the plot is weak; and reviewers clearly indicated their disappointment, even though Perkins thought the book was one of her best. Rawlings called *Golden Apples* "interesting trash," although such harsh judgments of her own work were typical. Nevertheless, with its theme of love as a betrayer, it broadens the reader's understanding of what Rawlings felt about human society in contrast to the healing effect of the Florida woods.

The Yearling was a tremendous popular success from the time of its publication in April 1938. It became a best-seller, a Book-of-the-Month Club selection, and winner of the Pulitzer Prize for fiction in 1939; a popular film version appeared in 1946; and it has been translated into thirteen languages. It has maintained a secure place on library shelves and in children's hearts, because it has the timeless appeal of a great literary work: unforgettable, well-developed characters, made "real" by their humanity; vivid setting, a place and time so well drawn as to make the north Florida scrub country of the late nineteenth century familiar to millions; plot and theme intricately related to create a universal experience.

The Yearling was a novel that Perkins had suggested that Rawlings write. A simple tale of a year in the life of twelve-year-old Jody Baxter, who lives on a hammock in the Florida scrub sometime shortly after the Civil War, it is a story of relationships—primarily those of Jody with his father and his pet deer. Its theme is that of growing up, of a child's leaving the security and innocence of childhood and having to realize and accept the responsibility and pain that being an adult means in any society. The world of the Baxters is a simple and elemental one, and the life struggle is that of survival, a continuing battle against a black bear named Ol' Slewfoot and against death.

Jody's father, Penny Baxter, sums up his philosophy and view of life for his son:

Ever' man wants life to be a fine thing, and a easy. 'Tis fine, boy, powerful fine, but 'tain't easy. Life knocks a man down and he gits up and it knocks him down again. I've been uneasy all my life. . . . I wanted to spare you, long as I could. I wanted you to frolic with your yearlin'. I knowed the lonesomeness he eased for you. But ever' man's lonesome. What's he to do then? What's he to do when he gits knocked down? Why, take it for his share, and go on.

With unspeakable effort Jock dragged him to clear ground as the fire enveloped the cockpit.

Mountain Prelude *By MARJORIE KINNAN RAWLINGS*

THE SKY HAD ROBBED HELEN JACKSON OF EVERYTHING SHE LOVED. COULD THE EARTH EVER GIVE HER PEACE

AGAIN, ANY REASON FOR LIVING? BEGINNING A POWERFUL, POIGNANT NOVEL BY THE AUTHOR OF THE YEARLING.

THE white window curtains blew straight out into the room. An elm tree outside, pale green with spring, fought the strong March wind with slender boughs, lashed and tumbled, then gave up the struggle and leaned easily with the pressure, like an eagle soaring. The room was a boy's room. It was the room of a boy entirely mad with the very thought of airplanes. The walls were covered with colored prints of planes, with drawings and photographs of planes; and hanging from the ceiling, models of planes swung back and forth in the swift-flowing air. Photographs of a man in Air Force uniform, alone, in group pictures or standing by a B-17, air trophies here and there, a plane propeller, compass and calipers, indicated that the occupant of the room had learned his love of flight from one with war experience.

The occupant was certain, at the moment, that he was actually his father, Maj. Hank Jackson. He sat tensely in the pilot's seat of a toy airplane in the center of the large room. It was more than a toy, a full six feet in length, complete in its detail to the lifelike instrument panel. The "major" would have denied it, but he was twelve years old. His copilot or passenger—for sometimes he was one and then again the other—was a large collie dog, who sat gravely behind him, waiting for the take-off. Yesterday the dog had been Colonel Scott, the copilot. Today he was General Eisenhower, being flown on a most secret mission. To have him answer a question, however, it was necessary to address him by his true, everyday name, which was simply Jock.

The major revved his four motors. "R-r-r-r-r-r!" he rumbled.

He adjusted his earphones and spoke in a low voice into the mouthpiece on his flat chest.

"Jackson away," he murmured. "Jackson away." He turned sideways and held the mouthpiece to Jock's nose. "Eisenhower away," he said firmly. "Keep it secret." He poked Eisenhower in the ribs, and the general obliged with a short snappy bark to the control tower.

The major frowned. "Darn," he said to the general. "I'm sure I know what to do next, but I'd better look."

He leafed open a book, Flight Instructions for the Beginner. The general rested his head on the major's shoulder, and the major patted it absently. "Oh, sure. I had it right. Here we go, Ike!"

The great ship was roaring down the runway. The major pulled back on the control stick. For

15

First page of the 26 April–31 May 1947 serialization of the novel Rawlings developed from her 1936 story "A Mother in Mannville"

The Yearling is a long book, consisting of thirty-three chapters, more than four hundred pages. Each chapter is a small idyll in itself, an episode in the daily life of the Baxters as they farm and fish and hunt for their living, as they visit their neighbors or go to "the Christmas doin's" in the riverport village of Volusia. The story is told entirely from the viewpoint of Jody. It is meticulously accurate in its description of frontier life in the Florida scrub, a life which, Rawlings learned, had remained almost the same between the time of her book's setting and when she came there some five decades later.

Jody Baxter is a solitary child whose nearest playmate is Fodderwing, a young crippled son of the nearest neighbors, the Forresters. Fodderwing's death is one of life's first blows to Jody in this last year of his childhood; his loneliness becomes more intense, eased only by the adoption of Flag, the fawn, as his first and only pet. Ma Baxter is a sour and somewhat embittered woman, scarred by the hard life and loss of all her earlier-born children. Jody's deepest loves are his father and Flag; the killing of Flag, who cannot be kept from eating the corn crop that is the mainstay of the Baxters' food supply, is Jody's final crossing from childhood to adulthood. The title of the book refers both to Jody and the deer; in the animal world, a yearling is one who is just entering maturity.

At the end of the book, Penny Baxter, who is sick in bed and cannot do the task himself, has to order Jody to shoot the deer. Jody cannot do it, but has to finish the job when Ma Baxter shoots and only wounds the animal. He then runs away, bereft and desperate in his grief, but has to return home, to face life as it is, and to assume adult responsibilities. Becoming an adult is a natural part of life, but leaving childhood behind, like leaving anything, is sad. The last paragraphs of the book sum up and echo this universal emotion as Jody experiences it:

> He found himself listening for something. It was the sound of the yearling for which he listened, running around the house or stirring on his moss pallet in the corner of the bedroom. He would never hear him again. He wondered if his mother had thrown dirt over Flag's carcass, or if the buzzards had cleaned it. Flag—He did not believe he should ever again love anything, man or woman or his own child, as he had loved the yearling. He would be lonely all his life. But a man took it for his share and went on.
>
> In the beginning of his sleep, he cried out, "Flag!"
>
> It was not his own voice that called. It was a boy's voice. Somewhere beyond the sinkhole, past the magnolia, under the live oaks, a boy and a yearling ran side by side and were gone forever.

Cross Creek and its accompanying *Cross Creek Cookery* reveal another side to Rawlings: that of the pastoral philosopher who cherishes solitude but loves to cook for company. *Cross Creek,* with its reflective observations on such things as life in the woods, solitude, visitors, and "brute neighbors," bears respectful comparison with Henry David Thoreau's *Walden* (1854). Much of the author's own Florida experience is candidly presented here; one of the best chapters in the book is her hauntingly beautiful account of a precarious boat trip on the Saint Johns River, "Hyacinth Drift" (first published in *Scribner's Magazine,* September 1933). Though *Cross Creek* is less well known than *The Yearling,* it was offered as a Book-of-the-Month Club selection and has remained popular. The descriptions of persons and places in *Cross Creek* are exceptionally good; Rawlings reveals herself, her philosophy of life, and her mystical feeling for the land and nature. The last essay in the book, "Who Owns Cross Creek?" shows her feeling for the land:

> Who owns Cross Creek? The red-birds, I think, more than I for they will have their nests even in the face of delinquent mortgages. And after I am dead, who am childless, the human ownership of grove and field and hammock is hypothetical. But a long line of red-birds and whippoorwills and bluejays and ground doves will descend from the present owners of nests in the orange trees, and their claim will be less subject to dispute than that of any human heirs. Houses are individual and can be owned, like nests, and fought for. But what of the land? It seems to me that the earth may be borrowed but not bought. It may be used, but not owned. It gives itself in response to love and tending, offers its seasonal flowering and fruiting. But we are tenants and not possessors, lovers and not masters. Cross Creek belongs to the wind and the rain, to the sun and the seasons, to the cosmic secrecy of seed, and beyond all, to time.

Because of Rawlings's depiction, Cross Creek now belongs to the world.

When the Whippoorwill— is a story collection dealing principally with cracker life. Three of its best stories are "Gal Young Un" (which won the O. Henry Memorial Award in 1932), *Jacob's Ladder* (winner of second place in the 1931 Scribner Prize Contest), and a 1939 *Saturday Evening Post* tale, "Cocks Must Crow." The first two are about the hardships and dilemmas of poor, unknowing crackers. In "Gal Young Un" a rake-hell bootlegger seduces a lonely woman of sustenance, whom he marries, as well as a young woman whom he lives with openly. This curiously feminist tale hinges on the retribution the wife exacts on the husband and the compassion she displays toward the young waif. *Jacob's Ladder* is about a nearly destitute couple dogged by misfortune yet determined to survive against all odds. The masterfully written "Cocks Must

Crow," a rousing tale of a married couple's struggle over the husband's masculine attraction to cockfighting, includes some of the author's most memorable lines of dialogue. Nevertheless, the most celebrated story to appear in *When the Whippoorwill-* is "A Mother in Mannville," Rawlings's autobiographical story of a young North Carolina orphan whom she befriended and almost adopted. The story was later adapted for the film *The Sun Comes Up* (1948), starring Jeanette MacDonald and Lassie. Despite these strengths, *When the Whippoorwill-* did not receive the response it deserved.

The Sojourner, Rawlings's last novel, preserves the rural atmosphere of her other work but is set in upstate New York. The pedestrian style and weak character depiction of the book are in striking contrast to its high seriousness and the intensely personal philosophy the author projects. *The Sojourner* is really a fitting envoi in many ways for Rawlings's life and work. This hypersensitive, introverted, and essentially solitary woman produced a remarkable story of two long-separated brothers and the essential rootlessness and loneliness of man. Several reviewers and commentators disparaged the novel, and Julia Scribner Bigham made no mention of it at all in her *Marjorie Rawlings Reader* (1956); however, *The Sojourner* was a Literary Guild selection and went through several editions in the United States and in England, where it was also a book-club choice.

The posthumous publication of a small book written especially for young children, *The Secret River* (1955), completed the literary contributions of Rawlings. Illustrated by Leonard Weisgard, it is a pleasant little story—almost a fragment—about a little girl, Calpurnia, who finds a beautiful river teeming with fish and brings back enough to save her father's fish market from hard times, but can never go back to that lovely enchanted land again. The characters are not developed enough for racial or ethnic identification; from the illustrations Calpurnia might be a little black or Indian child, and from the setting she could be a cracker, although the dialect she speaks is neither black nor cracker. Even this small book, though, displays the natural setting that Rawlings portrayed so well and the theme of the brevity and enchantment of childhood.

Rawlings remains a significant figure in twentieth-century American literature, primarily for *South Moon Under, The Yearling, Cross Creek,* and *The Sojourner:* forceful accounts of a lonely protagonist fighting on dauntlessly in the face of debilitating disillusionment and personal loss. Although considered a regional writer by some critics because much of her work deals with the Florida scrub and hammock country, Rawlings rejected such a label, being concerned (as she made clear) with larger meanings rather than quaint speech and behavior patterns. Most of her books remain in print, and if she does not gain the critical respect her best work merits, it seems certain that she will continue to retain a sizable popular following, evidenced by the growing membership in the Rawlings Society and by the fact that the *Journal of Florida Literature* and the *Rawlings Newsletter* are both devoted to her life and writings.

Letters:
Selected Letters of Marjorie Kinnan Rawlings, edited by Gordon E. Bigelow and Laura V. Monti (Gainesville: University of Florida Press, 1983);

Max and Marjorie: The Letters Between Maxwell E. Perkins and Marjorie Kinnan Rawlings, edited by Rodger L. Tarr (Gainesville: University Press of Florida, 1999).

Bibliography:
Rodger L. Tarr, *Marjorie Kinnan Rawlings: A Descriptive Bibliography* (Pittsburgh: University of Pittsburgh Press, 1996).

Biography:
Elizabeth Silverthorne, *Marjorie Kinnan Rawlings: Sojourner at Cross Creek* (Woodstock, N.Y.: Overlook, 1988).

References:
Patricia Nassif Acton, *Invasion of Privacy: The* Cross Creek *Trial of Marjorie Kinnan Rawlings* (Gainesville: University of Florida Press, 1988);

Samuel I. Bellman, *Marjorie Kinnan Rawlings* (New York: Twayne, 1974);

Gordon E. Bigelow, *Frontier Eden: The Literary Career of Marjorie Kinnan Rawlings* (Gainesville: University of Florida Press, 1966);

Julia Scribner Bigham, Introduction to *The Marjorie Rawlings Reader* (New York: Scribners, 1956), pp. ix–xix;

Idella Parker and Mary Keating, *Idella: Marjorie Rawlings' "Perfect Maid"* (Gainesville: University Press of Florida, 1992);

Carol Anita Tarr and Rodger L. Tarr, introduction to *Cross Creek,* by Rawlings (Jacksonville, Fla.: South Moon Books, 1992).

Papers:
The University of Florida and Princeton University have large collections of Marjorie Kinnan Rawlings's papers, letters, and manuscripts.

Adrienne Rich

This entry was updated by Sylvia Henneberg (Morehead State University) from the entries by Anne Newman (University of North Carolina, Charlotte) in DLB 5: American Poets Since World War II, First Series, and by Elizabeth Meese (University of Alabama) in DLB 67: Modern American Critics Since 1955.

BIRTH: Baltimore, Maryland, 16 May 1929, to Arnold Rice and Helen Elizabeth Jones Rich.

EDUCATION: A.B. (cum laude), Radcliffe College, 1951.

MARRIAGE: 26 June 1953 to Alfred Haskell Conrad (died 1970); children: David, Paul, Jacob.

AWARDS AND HONORS: Yale Series of Younger Poets prize for *A Change of World,* 1951; Guggenheim Fellowships, 1952 and 1961; Ridgely Torrence Memorial Award, Poetry Society of America, 1955; National Institute of Arts and Letters Award, 1960; Phi Beta Kappa Poet, College of William and Mary, 1960, Swarthmore College, 1965, and Harvard University, 1966; National Institute of Arts and Letters Award for poetry, 1961; Amy Lowell Fellowship, 1962; Bollingen Foundation Fellowship for translation of Dutch poetry, 1962; National Translation Center grant, 1968; Eunice Tietjens Memorial Prize, *Poetry* magazine, 1968; National Endowment for the Arts Grant, 1970; Shelley Memorial Award, Poetry Society of America, 1971; Ingram-Merrill Foundation grant, 1973–1974; National Book Award for *Diving into the Wreck: Poems 1971–1972,* 1974; National Book Critics Circle Award for Poetry nomination for *The Dream of a Common Language: Poems 1974–1977,* 1978; Fund for Human Dignity Award, National Gay Task Force, 1981; Ruth Lilly Poetry Prize, Modern Poetry Association and American Council for the Arts, 1986; Brandeis University Creative Arts Medal in Poetry, 1987; National Poetry Association Award for Distinguished Service to the Art of Poetry, 1989; Elmer Holmes Bobst Award in Arts and Letters, New York University Library, 1989; Bay Area Book Reviewers Award in Poetry for *Time's Power: Poems 1985–1988,* 1990; *The Common Wealth* Award in Literature, 1991; Robert Frost Silver Medal for Lifetime Achievement in Poetry, Poetry Society of America, 1992; William Whitehead Award of the Gay and Lesbian Publishing Triangle for Lifetime Achievement in Letters, 1992; Lambda Book Award in Lesbian Poetry for

Adrienne Rich

An Atlas of the Difficult World: Poems 1988–1991, 1992, and for *Dark Fields of the Republic: Poems 1991–1995,* 1996; Lenore Marshall/*Nation: Poems* and *Los Angeles Times* Book Award in poetry, 1992, and The Poets' Prize, 1993, all for *An Atlas of the Difficult World: Poems 1988–1991;* John D. and Catherine T. MacArthur Foundation Fellowship, 1994; Dorothea Tanning Prize, Academy of American Poets, 1996; honorary doctorates from Wheaton College, 1967; Smith College, 1979; Brandeis University, 1987; College of Wooster, Ohio, 1987; Harvard University, 1990; City College of New York, 1990; and Swarthmore College, 1992.

BOOKS: *Ariadne, A Play in Three Acts and Poems* (Baltimore: Privately printed by J. H. Furst, 1939);
Not I, But Death, A Play in One Act (Baltimore: Privately printed by J. H. Furst, 1941);

A Change of World (New Haven: Yale University Press, 1951);

The Diamond Cutters and Other Poems (New York: Harper, 1955);

Snapshots of a Daughter-in-Law: Poems 1954–1962 (New York & Evanston: Harper & Row, 1963; New York: Norton, 1967; London: Chatto & Windus/Hogarth Press, 1970);

Necessities of Life: Poems 1962–1965 (New York: Norton, 1966);

Selected Poems (London: Chatto & Windus/Hogarth Press, 1967);

Leaflets: Poems 1965–1968 (New York: Norton, 1969; London: Chatto & Windus/Hogarth Press, 1972);

The Will to Change: Poems 1968–1970 (New York: Norton, 1971; London: Chatto & Windus, 1972);

Diving into the Wreck: Poems 1971–1972 (New York: Norton, 1973);

Poems: Selected and New, 1950–1974 (New York: Norton, 1975);

Of Woman Born: Motherhood as Experience and Institution (New York: Norton, 1976; London: Virago, 1977); republished with a new introduction by Rich (New York: Norton, 1986);

Twenty-One Love Poems (Emeryville, Cal.: Effie's Press, 1976);

The Dream of a Common Language: Poems 1974–1977 (New York: Norton, 1978);

On Lies, Secrets, and Silence: Selected Prose 1966–1978 (New York: Norton, 1979);

A Wild Patience Has Taken Me This Far: Poems 1978–1981 (New York: Norton, 1981);

Sources (Woodside, Cal.: Heyeck Press, 1983);

The Fact of a Doorframe: Poems Selected and New 1950–1984 (New York: Norton, 1984);

Your Native Land, Your Life: Poems (New York: Norton, 1986);

Blood, Bread, and Poetry: Selected Prose 1979–1985 (New York: Norton, 1986);

Time's Power: Poems 1985–1988 (New York: Norton, 1989);

An Atlas of the Difficult World: Poems 1988–1991 (New York: Norton, 1991);

What Is Found There: Notebooks on Poetry and Politics (New York: Norton, 1993);

Collected Early Poems 1950–1970 (New York: Norton, 1993);

Adrienne Rich's Poetry and Prose, selected and edited by Barbara Charlesworth Gelpi and Albert Gelpi, Norton Critical Edition (New York: Norton, 1993);

Dark Fields of the Republic: Poems 1991–1995 (New York: Norton, 1995);

Midnight Salvage: Poems 1995–1998 (New York: Norton, 1999).

OTHER: *The Best American Poetry,* edited, with an introduction, by Rich (New York: Scribners, 1996).

SELECTED PERIODICAL PUBLICATIONS–UNCOLLECTED: "Poetry, Personality, and Wholeness: A Response to Galway Kinnell," *Field: Contemporary Poetry and Poetics,* 7 (Fall 1972): 11–18;

"Feminism and Fascism: An Exchange," by Adrienne Rich and Susan Sontag, *New York Review of Books,* 22 (20 March 1975): 31–32;

"An Interview with Audre Lorde," *Signs: Journal of Women in Culture and Society,* 6 (Summer 1981): 713–736; other portions of this interview in *Woman Poet: Women–in–Literature,* 2 (Summer 1981): 18–21;

"Poetry for Daily Use," *Ms.,* 2 (September 1991): 70–75;

"Notes for a Magazine: What Does Separatism Mean?" *Sinister Wisdom,* 18 (Fall 1981): 83–91;

Introduction to *A Muriel Rukeyser Reader,* edited by Jan Heller Levi (New York: Norton, 1994), pp. xi–xv;

"Arts of the Possible," *Massachusetts Review,* 38 (Autumn 1997): 319–337; 38 (Winter 1997–1998): 595–598.

Adrienne Rich is one of the foremost poets and feminists of modern times. Her work spans more than forty years of her adult life, beginning in 1951 when she won the Yale Series of Younger Poets prize for *A Change of World* (1951). Ever since, Rich's work, both her poetry and her prose, has reflected a deep commitment to changing existing power relations in the world. Her sense of urgency for change has led her to see her writing as "the graph of a process still going on" and "a continuing exploration," as she states in her foreword to *Poems: Selected and New, 1950–1974* (1975). In *Blood, Bread, and Poetry: Selected Prose 1979–1985* (1986) she further informs her readers that from 1956 on, she dated her poems because

I was finished with the idea of a poem as a single, encapsulated event, a work of art complete in itself; I knew my life was changing, my work was changing, and I needed to indicate to readers my sense of being engaged in a long, continuing process.

Much of her achievement resides in her willingness to resist stasis and her ability to revise her positions and poetics in response to the changes she desires and witnesses in her life and surroundings. Merging public and private life as well as politics and poetry, she has explored the figuration of the (often but not always female) individual in various positions along a continuum of possibilities: dutiful daughter, heterosexual lover, wife, widow, daughter-in-law, granddaughter, mother, lesbian lover, Jew, U.S. citizen, Holocaust victim, revolutionary, soldier in war, child, and adult. Allowing her prose and poetry to inform each other, Rich has created multiple levels of awareness for herself and her readers and has, over time, moved toward a greater understanding of the plurality of her own background, of women in general, and finally of the human race. While her early volumes construct the poet as a male speaker and her mid-career works center on her female gender and lesbian sexuality, her most recent books cast her as a Whitmanian figure whose purpose is to encompass the entire "difficult world" with all its diversity in gender, sexuality, age, race, ethnicity, and nationality.

Born in Baltimore, Maryland, on 16 May 1929, Adrienne Cecile Rich is the elder of two daughters. She was educated at home until the fourth grade and gained early encouragement for her artistic and intellectual work from her father, Arnold Rice Rich, a pathologist working as a professor and researcher at Johns Hopkins Medical School at the time of her birth, and her mother, Helen Elizabeth Jones Rich, a piano player and composer who sacrificed a career in music in order to assume the duties of a housewife and mother.

Two pieces of juvenilia (a three-act play and poems privately printed when she was ten; a one-act play privately printed when she was twelve) are indications of the early support for Rich's interest in writing. She graduated with honors from Radcliffe College in 1951, the same year her first collection of poetry was published. In 1953, after traveling to Europe on her first Guggenheim Fellowship, she married Alfred H. Conrad, an economist teaching at Harvard University. Their three sons—David, Paul, and Jacob—were born in 1955, 1957, and 1959. Preoccupied with her role as wife and mother, Rich underwent a long hiatus in her writing, finding it impossible to reconcile what she terms "the energy of creation" and "the energy of relation." The experience of motherhood was to radicalize her, as she notes in *Of Woman Born: Motherhood as Experience and Institution* (1976). In 1961 a second Guggenheim Fellowship allowed her to travel to the Netherlands, where she began work on translations of Dutch poetry.

The family moved from Cambridge to New York City in 1966 when Rich's husband started teaching at the City College of New York. Rich began her own teaching career, which has included positions at Swarthmore College, Columbia University, Brandeis University, City College of New York, Bryn Mawr College, Rutgers University, Cornell University, Scripps College, San Jose State University, and Stanford University. Teaching at the City College of New York in the Open Admissions and SEEK (Search for Elevation, Education, and Knowledge) programs in the 1960s proved particularly enriching for her as she was brought into contact with African-American writers June Jordan and Audre Lorde, her colleagues at CCNY.

Within a two-year span Rich faced her father's death in 1968 and her husband's suicide in 1970. In 1976 she came out as a lesbian, publishing much of her poetry in such feminist journals as *Amazon Quarterly, Heresies,* and *13th Moon.* She began a lifelong relationship with the writer Michelle Cliff, with whom she left New York to move to Montague, Massachusetts, and with whom she edited the lesbian-feminist journal *Sinister Wisdom* from 1981 to 1983. The progression of her rheumatoid arthritis—a condition that had manifested itself as early as 1952—was one of the factors that brought Rich to the milder climate of the West Coast in 1984. She continues to reside in California.

Rich's first volume of poetry, *A Change of World,* published when she was only twenty-one, includes highly formalistic poems that fashion an objective, intensely individualized, detached, and apparently gender-neutral voice. In his introduction to the collection, W. H. Auden praised poems that "speak quietly but do not mumble, respect their elders but are not cowed by them, and do not tell fibs." During this time, as Rich recalls in her influential essay "When We Dead Awaken: Writing as Re-Vision" (1971), she was used to writing for "The Man," first her father, then male writers and teachers. Commenting upon her early poetry, she states: "I know that my style was formed first by male poets: . . . Frost, Dylan Thomas, Donne, Auden, MacNeice, Stevens, Yeats. What I learned chiefly from them was craft." In these poems she spoke through personae or used other distancing techniques, following the prevalent poetic ideal of objectivity that was intended to express the universal through restraint of personal emotion. Her major themes, too, were among the most often employed of the time: the poems in *A Change of World* concern sterility and loss in modern life. Art itself, isolated and pure, is seen as the primary source of fulfillment and protection in a world of threatening change. Several poems directly concern the effort to confine and control emotion through aesthetic form. "At a Bach

Concert," for example, reveals Rich's concept of poetry at this period of her life, as she defines it through an analogy to music: "A too-compassionate art is half an art. / Only such proud restraining purity / Restores the else-betrayed, too-human heart."

Two other poems that deal with defense against inner turmoil are portraits of women engaged in handiwork. Even this early in her work, Rich extends the meaning of such traditional activity beyond its usual implication of passive, patient acceptance. In "Mathilde in Normandy" the woman waits for men who are away at war:

> Say what you will, anxiety there too
> Played havoc with the skein, and the knots came
> When fingers' occupation and mind's attention
> Grew too divergent[.]

Here the pattern has been distorted by violent activities that divert the mind.

The portrait of the woman in "Aunt Jennifer's Tigers" is presented with economy through the tension of opposing images. The condition of Aunt Jennifer herself,

> Aunt Jennifer's fingers fluttering through her wool
> Find even the ivory needle hard to pull.
> The massive weight of Uncle's wedding band
> Sits heavily upon Aunt Jennifer's hand.

is poised against her choice of subject for the tapestry: "The tigers in the panel that she made / Will go on prancing, proud and unafraid." Rich's further comments on this poem give insights into both the form and intention of much of her earlier poetry:

> It was important to me that Aunt Jennifer was a person as distinct from myself as possible—distanced by the formalism of the poem, by its objective, observant tone. . . . In those years formalism was part of the strategy—like asbestos gloves, it allowed me to handle materials I couldn't pick up bare-handed.

Thus, her first collection, which has been justly praised for its fine craftsmanship, has many echoes of her masters and muted notes of her personal voice.

Rich's second volume, *The Diamond Cutters and Other Poems* (1955), continues in much the same tone and style; again the major theme is the need for caution and control in art and life. The title poem proposes the diamond cutters' techniques of cutting and polishing the gem as a model for work: "Be serious, because / The stone may have contempt / For too-familiar hands," and "Respect the adversary, / Meet it with tools refined, / And thereby set your

Dust jacket for Rich's 1971 collection, in which she adapted cinematic techniques for her poems

price." The form of the poem, like the art it defines, is delicate and controlled.

Some of the poems in this collection, written while Rich was traveling in England and Europe in 1952–1953, are about famous places. These, and even less exotic spots, are viewed through the detachment of the tourist, though the particular scene may act as backdrop for a subdued expression of pain in a fallen world. "A Walk by the Charles" is a good example of this type of poem, in which the visual and musical renditions of landscape combine with philosophical contemplation.

The language of the poems is often dependent upon literary allusion and authority, and the style is dependent upon her mentors. For example, in two monologues she skillfully maintains the conversational tone within the iambic pentameter form, but the Frostian manner is so marked that it becomes distracting. In these poems she reveals the marriage relationship as the center of the problem: the woman speaking in "The Perennial Answer" responds to her frustration with a destructive, neurotic energy; the woman in "Autumn Equinox" responds with quiet acceptance of her diminished expectations of life.

The Diamond Cutters has been recognized for strengths similar to those of Rich's first volume; but mixed with the strong praise were hints of disappointment—questioning whether she was growing as a poet or settling into, and for, an achieved style with too much facility and overdependence on models. Rich's own reaction supports this doubt: "By the time that book came out I was already dissatisfied with those poems, which seemed to me mere exercises for poems I hadn't written." That she refused to continue writing in a form she had outgrown is clearly demonstrated in her next book.

During the eight years between the publications of *The Diamond Cutters* and *Snapshots of a Daughter-in-Law: Poems 1954–1962* (1963), Rich had heavy responsibilities as a wife and the mother of three young sons. Looking back at her feelings during that period of her life, she says:

> I was writing very little, partly from fatigue, that female fatigue of suppressed anger and loss of contact with my own being; partly from the discontinuity of female life with its attention to small chores, errands, work that others constantly undo, small children's constant needs. . . . I felt . . . guilt toward the people closest to me, and guilt toward my own being.

The sense of frustration, guilt, and suppressed anger is a major theme of *Snapshots of a Daughter-in-Law*.

Some of the poems, such as "The Knight," are traditional in structure, close to the style of her first books. "The Knight" is an effective poem, but Rich is still distancing her personal voice, identifying with the masculine side (which she feels society has defined as the creative aspect of the individual). Nevertheless, the poem does express the conflict between her burden of enervating responsibilities and her creative side, as well as the need to free herself from poetic conventions:

> Who will unhorse this rider
> and free him from between
> the walls of iron, the emblems
> crushing his chest with their weight?

Poems later in the book show that Rich has broken out of her armor. The change reflects, to a degree, the trend in American poetry in the mid twentieth century to move away from meter, set stanzas, and rhyme to a more open form, consistent with the move away from objectivity to speaking in the more personal voice. Rich's breakthrough in poetry, however, is also closely connected with the growing consciousness of herself as artist and woman. As she says:

> In the late fifties I was able to write, for the first time, directly about experiencing myself as a woman. . . . Until then I had tried very hard not to identify myself as a female poet. Over two years I wrote a ten-part poem called "Snapshots of a Daughter-in-Law" (1958–1960), in a longer looser mode than I'd ever trusted myself with before. It was an extraordinary relief to write that poem.

In this poem, which was "jotted in fragments during children's naps, brief hours in a library, or at 3:00 A.M. after rising with a wakeful child," and many later ones in the volume, she clearly begins to deal more directly with experience. Her form is modulated to portray the dynamics of the inner world; the "instrument" of form has shifted from that of the diamond cutter who produces beautifully polished, set pieces to that of the photographer who tries to catch the unposed portrait. In "Snapshots of a Daughter-in-Law" form and rhythm tend to reproduce the thought patterns of the woman, although, as Rich has said, she was not yet able "to use the pronoun 'I'—the woman in the poem is always 'she.'" Still, dropping the initial capital letter in each line, increasing enjambment, using speech cadences in place of formal meters, limiting the use of rhyme, and varying stanza lengths increase the personal tone.

The "snapshots" center on a relationship in which a woman is bound by expectations that make her not only the passively wounded but also the active wounder of other women, as she identifies herself through masculine approval. The focus of consciousness in the poem is a young woman who is aware of the forces that limit her and other women; and there is a gradual progression from her feelings of restriction, helplessness, and subdued rage toward a hope for change. The poem begins with a picture of the mother, her "mind now, mouldering like wedding-cake," "crumbling to pieces under the knife-edge / of mere fact." The tone is a mixture of sympathy and outrage toward the woman who is an accomplice in this denial of her own life. In the next section the young woman realizes that she too is losing her personal identity, and her inner voice, the "angel," incites her to rebellion. Numbed by the endless round of meaningless tasks, however, she cannot heed the voice. Section three is a distressed recognition of the division of women against each other: ". . . all the old knives / that have rusted in my back, I drive in yours. . . ." Other sections show anger at the role of woman as object, which Rich sees as the imposed ideal of society; such devastating lines as "she shaves her legs until they gleam / like petrified mammoth-tusk," for instance, show the self as lifeless, extinct.

This stifling role leads to an urgent plea for all women to realize the demeaning effects of being praised for mediocrity, for "slattern thought styled intuition," that the accepted role promotes. Two sections recognize Emily Dickinson and Mary Wollstonecraft as women who, through remarkable courage, did not settle for mediocrity. These examples lead to a vision of the modern woman who will break out of the reductive pattern of relationships and expectations:

> Well,
> she's long about her coming, who must be
> more merciless to herself than history.
> Her mind full to the wind, I see her plunge
> breasted and glancing through the currents,
> taking the light upon her
> at least as beautiful as any boy
> or helicopter,
> poised, still coming,
> her fine blades making the air wince
> but her cargo
> no promise then:
> delivered
> palpable
> ours.

One senses in "Snapshots of a Daughter-in-Law" the relief of which Rich has spoken and the release into new concepts of form.

This poem also indicates the true beginning of her open treatment of relationships between women, a subject that becomes increasingly important for her. "A Woman Mourned by Daughters" deals with a natural relationship that Rich thinks has been subverted in a patriarchal society. In this poem the daughters bear a heavy burden of love and hate as the mother leaves them only "solid assertions" of herself: "teaspoons, goblets, / seas of carpet." "Sisters" combines the sense of estrangement with the recognition of past bonds. The focus in this collection, then, is a consciousness of the difficulty of a woman's maintaining a sense of personal identity or a sense of community with other women.

The poems are filled with the expression of pain and loss, but only occasionally do they lapse into self-pity or sentimentality, as in "Peeling Onions," in which the emotion seems somewhat contrived, with a note of facile cleverness that appears with less and less frequency in Rich's work. In several poems toward the end of the book, Rich begins to view her situation with more optimism but with no illusions about the risk involved in breaking out of old patterns. In "The Roofwalker," dedicated to

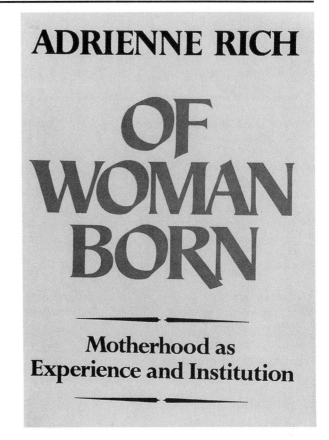

Dust jacket for Rich's 1976 prose work, which calls motherhood "the great mesh in which all human relationships are entangled"

the late Denise Levertov, Rich considers her condition (the woman is now "I"): "exposed, larger than life, / and due to break my neck"; then she questions: "Was it worth while to lay— / with infinite exertion— / a roof I can't live under?" There is a hint of exhilaration in the question itself, no matter what the implied answer may be. In "Prospective Immigrants Please Note" she proposes the definite alternatives of opening the door to discovering the self or of compromising with the existing situation; but "The door itself / makes no promises. / It is only a door." That Rich herself has chosen to open the door is evident in the poems of this collection. Albert Gelpi has called *Snapshots of a Daughter-in-Law* "the transitional book in Adrienne Rich's development. . . . Her themes—the burden of history, the separateness of individuals, the need for relationship where there is no other transcendence—begin to find their clarifying focus and center: what she is as woman and poet in late-twentieth-century America."

Rich's assurance in handling a new style is illustrated in her next collection, *Necessities of Life: Poems 1962–1965* (1966). In many of these poems she demonstrates a new acceptance of moments of release and celebration in ordinary, sensuous life—moments that lead to a reintegration of body and mind. The strong title poem describes this process of realizing the self:

> Piece by piece I seem
> to re-enter the world: I first began
>
> a small, fixed dot, still see
> that old myself, a dark-blue thumbtack
>
> pushed into the scene,
> a hard little head protruding
>
> from the pointillist's buzz and bloom.
> After a time the dot
>
> begins to ooze. Certain heats
> melt it.

Using an analogy to postimpressionist painting, Rich shows the gradual diffusion of the psyche, which is followed by the sense of having been "wolfed almost to shreds" by the lives of others. Then comes the beginning of reintegration through the senses, the ability

> now and again to lay
> one hand on a warm brick
>
> and touch the sun's ghost
> with economical joy,

which brings forth a promise to the self to "dare inhabit the world / trenchant in motion as an eel, solid // as a cabbage-head." These realistic images of eel and cabbage defy illusion but incorporate the hope that "practice" will make her "middling-perfect." "In the Woods" begins, "'Difficult ordinary happiness,' / no one nowadays believes in you," and ends with the speaker's amazement at her own ability to accept the moment of sensuous release: "If I move now, the sun / naked between the trees / will melt me as I lie." The release that brings body and mind together extends to the unconscious mind in "The Trees," with its compelling immediacy of dream imagery, as the struggle to become a part of the life-force continues: "The trees inside are moving out into the forest," and

> The leaves strain toward the glass
> small twigs stiff with exertion
> long-cramped boughs shuffling under the roof
> like newly discharged patients
> half-dazed, moving
> to the clinic doors.

Throughout her work, Rich battles against illusions but recognizes dreams as a deep part of reality. Yet the struggle to keep in touch with the elemental forces, the "necessities of life," is never easy, as the closing lines of "Like This Together" imply:

> Only our fierce attention
> gets hyacinths out of those
> hard cerebral lumps,
> unwraps the wet buds down
> the whole length of a stem.

As the opening up to life takes place, anger against forces that deny life increases, and Rich begins to speak her anger as well as her joy more openly. When this anger is directed through a sustained experience, such as that in "Night-Pieces: For a Child," it can be powerful, both emotionally and aesthetically. Less successful is "Open Air Museum," which begins with the question, "What burns in the dump today?" and is followed by a stream of images that do not coalesce in order to lead convincingly into lines such as "Oh my America / this then was your desire?" This collection also includes a group of translations of modern Dutch poems, and although these translations have been praised for their lively and sensitive qualities, the importance of the volume lies in Rich's original poems.

Reactions to her next book, *Leaflets: Poems 1965–1968* (1969), have been mixed. In fact, they range from the conviction that *Leaflets* marks a decline in Rich's career to high praise for her new vision of the changing world and self. The poems support both critical stances. The cover of the book, a collage of windblown and torn newspaper columns, photographs, tickets, and other "leaflets" of the time–concerning the Vietnam War, student unrest, Black Power, and so on–indicates the emphasis upon major issues of the 1960s. Rich's sense of conviction and urgency is strong, so strong that at times statement and moral judgment overpower aesthetic awareness. The long title poem, for example, is a pouring out of grief and anger in a rush of images that touch many specific issues. Strong images induce "this seasick neon / vision, this / division"; but the poem does not sustain this intensity and is marred by prosaic statements such as "your tears are not political / they are real water. . . ." The compulsion to break through the barriers to communication ("I want to hand you this / leaflet streaming with rain or tears / but the words coming clear," "I want this to reach you," "Tell me what you are going through") is the driving force of many poems in the book. Her sense of urgency for personal and political communication, however, increases her awareness of the inadequacy of language as an instrument for survival in a violent world.

Part 3 of *Leaflets,* Rich explains in an introductory note, was written after she had read translations of the *ghazals* of the Urdu poet Mirza Ghalib, who lived from 1797 to 1869 and was also "writing in an age of political and cultural break-up." Although she says that Ghalib's structure and metrics are stricter than hers, Rich has "adhered to his use of a minimum five couplets to a *ghazal,* each couplet being autonomous and independent of the others." They are, as are many other poems in the book, uneven in quality; but writing them helped Rich discover a new concept of juxtaposition, of circling around a thought (here the "political and cultural break-up"), in place of careful linear, logical progression.

The Will to Change: Poems 1968–1970 (1971) continues to combine personal and political commitment, centering on the pressing need for the act of will to change the self and the world. Again, aesthetic quality is uneven, but Rich's sense of identity is clearer. She says of the strong poem "Planetarium": "at last the woman in the poem and the woman writing the poem become the same person." Here, through the voice of the astronomer Caroline Herschel, Rich makes her own direct statement of commitment for her art as an instrument for change:

> I am an instrument in the shape
> of a woman trying to translate pulsations
> into images   for the relief of the body
> and the reconstruction of the mind.

She expresses her anguish about a language that has been used to support tyranny; in "The Burning of Paper Instead of Children," for instance, she spells out the contradiction that "this is the oppressor's language // yet I need it to talk to you" and, "there are books that describe all this / and they are useless." Rich turns hopefully to modern cinema as a model for the "reconstruction" of "the oppressor's language." She was fascinated with the movies of Jean-Luc Godard and other New Wave moviemakers who experimented with the handheld camera, fast zooms, rapid panning, freeze-frames, and jump cuts. With this freedom and flexibility, thematic meaning comes through rapid images that build to motifs, rather than through more traditional narrative. Rich adapts this filming method as a poetic form to express her concept of change, and she uses the metaphor of cinema itself extensively in the collection. In "Images for Godard," for example, she notes:

> the mind of the poet is the only poem
> the poet is at the movies

> dreaming the film-maker's dream but differently
> free in the dark as if asleep

> free in the dusty beam of the projector
> the mind of the poet is changing

> the moment of change is the only poem.

The long poem "Shooting Script" incorporates some techniques of modern cinema in an adapted form of the *ghazal.* Part one shows the tragic limitations of language, beginning with "We were bound on the wheel of an endless conversation" and concluding with the wounds of separation in this passionate rush of images:

> Picking apart the strands of pain; a warp of
> wool dipped in burning wax.

> When the flame strikes to a blue bead, there is
> danger; the change of light in a flickering
> situation.

> Stretched on the loom the light expands; the
> smell of a smell of burning.

> When the change leaves you dark, when the
> wax cools in the socket, when I thought I
> prayed, when I was talking to myself under the
> cover of my darkness.

> Someone who never said, "What do you feel?"

Part 2 sees hope for breaking out of the impasse of "a poetry of false problems, the shotgun wedding of the mind, the subversion of choice by language." The "alternative" is "to purge the room with light to feel the sun breaking in on the courtyard. . . ." Cinema has been a valuable tool, but it also has become too static, too far removed from reality:

> Whatever it was, the image that stopped you,
> the one on which you came to grief, projecting
> it over & over on empty walls.

> Now to give up the temptations of the
> projector; to see instead. . . .

> . . . the initial split, the filaments thrown out from that impasse.

In her next book Rich makes the direct plunge into experience, as the title *Diving into the Wreck: Poems 1971–1972* (1973) indicates. Rich begins the book with a restatement of the necessity for new language, new vision, and new action. In the opening poem she defines specifically what she sees as the root of the problem; in "Trying to Talk with a Man" language has become a destructive force, and his

ADRIENNE RICH

The Dream of a Common Language

Poems 1974-1977

Dust jacket for Rich's 1978 collection, poems that explore themes of communion and acceptance

"dry heat" "feels like power." In "When We Dead Awaken" the betrayal of the earth and the betrayal of women by this power become synonymous. What saves Rich's anger from being more bitter is that it so clearly comes out of her conviction that change is necessary for the benefit of all humanity. The poem includes an optimism about change brought about by the common language and love of women:

> . . . fellow-creature, sister,
> sitting across from me, dark with love,
> working like me to pick apart
> working like me to remake
> this trailing knitted thing, this cloth of darkness,
> this woman's garment, trying to save the skein.

She feels that "never have we been closer to the truth," but she refuses to see the truth in any devitalized, idealized way: "the faithfulness I can imagine would be a weed / flowering in tar, a blue energy piercing / the massed atoms of bedrock disbelief." Rich's consciousness rejects any temptation toward protective retreat or false compromise. As she says in "Waking in the Dark": it is "A man's world. But

finished. / They themselves have sold it to the machines." Her conviction of an ending opens up a vision of a new beginning:

> Clarity,
>   spray
> blinding and purging
> spears of sun striking the water
> the bodies riding the air
> . . . .
> the water opening
> like air
> like realization[.]

The full "realization" comes in the title poem, in which the dive is the controlling metaphor. The dive is into the unconscious to touch the dark, powerful, elemental forces of life and to bring the knowledge back into the conscious mind. Rich is aware of the difficulty and pain involved. The diver prepares with the standard equipment of the conscious mind: she reads the "book of myths" for directions and carries a camera for recording and a knife blade for protection. She is dressed in "body armor," but the "absurd flippers" and mask are armor for discovery, different from the burdensome mail of her earlier poem "The Knight." The diver must descend the ladder alone, crawling "like an insect," with no one to tell her "when the ocean / will begin. // First the air is blue and then / it is bluer and then green and then / black. . . ." She learns to turn her body "without force / in the deep element." After this relinquishing of the old self, she can see the wreck—the "damage" that has been done to the individual psyche and to the world:

> This is the place.
> And I am here, the mermaid whose dark hair
> streams black, the merman in his armored body
> We circle silently
> about the wreck
> we dive into the hold.
> I am she: I am he
>
> whose drowned face sleeps with open eyes[.]

She touches the primal forces of life and finds the "treasures" of full realization and commitment, as the conscious and unconscious parts of the mind are unified in the androgynous image. The diver accepts the side of herself that is part of the collective heritage of man, and the poem reaches the visionary power of a mind that has tapped the depths of the unconscious. The incantatory rhythms, repetitions, and multileveled imagery add to the mythic feeling.

Having integrated the psyche, Rich expresses both anguish and anger at distorted communication through poems such as "The Phenomenology of Anger":

I hate you.
I hate the mask you wear, your eyes
assuming a depth
they do not possess, drawing me
into the grotto of your skull
the landscape of bone[.]

After the full awakening, she cannot go on sharing the dry inner landscape; she says in "August":

His mind is too simple, I cannot go on
sharing his nightmares

My own are becoming clearer, they open
into prehistory[.]

In *Of Woman Born,* published in 1976, Rich traces the concept of motherhood as it has developed in a patriarchal society. Some critical reactions to the book are almost vehement, claiming Rich's perspective has been clouded by a rage that has led her into biased statements and a strident style. Others, who have read it with more sympathy, call it scholarly and well researched and insist that it should not be read quickly for polemics. Rich calls motherhood "the great mesh in which all human relationships are entangled, in which lurk our most elemental assumptions about love and power." Her style in *Of Woman Born* reveals her deep sincerity; she is speaking to a wide audience and with conviction. Throughout the book, passages from her journals support her thesis with the authority of personal experience combined with many examples based on extensive research.

Rich's exploration of the force of woman's anger and alienation, culminating in *Diving into the Wreck* and *Of Woman Born,* is supplanted more and more with works concerning possibility and connectedness, as in *The Dream of a Common Language: Poems 1974–1977* (1978). The male personae and distancing "she's" of the early poems and the strong personal "I" of later ones are both replaced by the communal "we" of shared love. For Rich the sense of communion has come through lesbian feminism, but her personal choice does not lead to any intent to impose it on others. Rather, it leads to a greater insistence upon each individual's freedom of choice in the discovery of personal fulfillment. With her choice has come the sense of joy in being alive, as a few lines from "Twenty-One Love Poems," the middle section in this book, show: "We want to live like trees, / sycamores blazing through the sulfuric air, / dappled with scars, still exuberantly budding, / our

animal passion rooted in the city." The image of the woman's hands that might "piece together / the fine, needle-like sherds of a great krater-cup" brings together the fragments of civilization:

such hands might carry out an unavoidable violence
with such restraint, with such a grasp
of the range and limits of violence
that violence ever after would be obsolete.

"Power," the first poem in the book, speaks of Madame Curie, who died from the effects of radium, "denying / her wounds / denying / her wounds   came   from the same source as her power." In "Phantasia for Elvira Shatayev" she thinks of the women's climbing team led by Shatayev and imagines their pain being transcended in a moment of total unity before their death by freezing: "A cable of blue fire ropes our bodies / burning together in the snow. . . ." Blue flame, symbolic here of creative unity, transforms death into a part of the life pattern. The speaker in "A Woman Dead in Her Forties" grieves over her former silence when, following the conventions of a society that makes death a fearsome and isolated experience and also forces silence about women's love for each other, she withholds this sense of communion: "In plain language: I never told you how I loved you / we never talked at your deathbed of your death."

"Sibling Mysteries" depicts a kind of psychic death—the denial of the elemental mysteries. Earth images are strong (as they are throughout the book) and frequently suggest erotic overtones. The daughters in the poem, as children, have been in touch with "the planetary rock." Later, they have "passed bark and root and berry / from hand to hand, whispering each one's power." The mother, however, has forfeited her own natural love and power and sends them "weeping into that law" where they will dwell in "two worlds / the daughters and the mothers / in the kingdom of the sons." In "Nights and Days," however, the possibility of change brings forth a vision: "The stars will come out over and over / the hyacinths rise like flames" as "the rivers freeze and burn. . . ." The vision must be fulfilled through gentleness, as the quality is defined in "Natural Resources":

. . . gentleness is active
gentleness swabs the crusted stump

invents more merciful instruments
to touch the wound beyond the wound[.]

Consistent with Rich's concept of form as a continuing language, the individual poems take on additional strength and meaning in the context of the book, where they become like strands, the images and ideas of which reinforce the pattern. "Transcendental Etude," the final piece, is an important poem in itself and attains even greater visionary strength in context. The poem begins quietly. A woman driving alone on an August evening startles a doe and her fawns and thinks about the fruitfulness of nature, her "nerves singing the immense / fragility of all this sweetness, / this green world" that "persists stubbornly." A "lifetime," she thinks, "is too narrow / to understand it all. . . ." Realizing how unprepared readers are for this study, Rich introduces the study of music as the metaphor for how to progress: to begin with the simplest exercises and slowly move to the hard ones, "practicing till strength / and accuracy became one with daring / to leap into transcendence. . . ." Rejecting, however, the temptation to become virtuosos, "competing / against the world for speed and brilliance," readers must cut away the "old force" and "disenthrall ourselves" because

> . . . the whole chorus throbbing at our ears
> like midges, told us nothing, nothing
> of origins, nothing we needed
> to know, nothing that could re-member us.

With the cutting away of useless knowledge there comes a new awareness of unity, "a whole new poetry beginning here."

In this composition Rich brings together the major images of her poetry, her concepts of language and form, and her feminine consciousness, with visionary power. Reviewers of *The Dream of a Common Language* recognize this power and praise the reconciliation that allows Rich to speak freely and compassionately in a language that is common to all. This important book combines vital thematic and aesthetic awareness.

The concerns of the essays in *On Lies, Secrets, and Silence: Selected Prose 1966–1978* (1979) overlap and reinforce those expressed in the poetry written during the same period. The most widely anthologized essay collected in this volume is "When We Dead Awaken: Writing as Re-Vision," which includes a critical self-examination and proclaims the need for female redefinition. Arguing that "Re-vision—the act of looking back, of seeing with fresh eyes, of entering an old text from a new critical direction—is for women more than a chapter in cultural history: it is an act of survival," Rich sets the stage for the subsequent wave of revisionary myth-making that aimed at revalidating and reinventing suppressed and forgotten female traditions and posi-

tions. Rich ends her essay with a call for action: "The creative energy of patriarchy is fast running out; what remains is its self-generating energy for destruction. As women, we have our work cut out for us." The purpose of her work at this time is "to define a female consciousness which is political, aesthetic, and erotic, and which refuses to be included or contained in the culture of passivity." While she continues the task of reclamation or repossession of her sources and foremothers, as in "Vesuvius at Home: The Poetry of Emily Dickinson" (first published in 1975), she sharpens her articulation of the goal of a feminist critique: to achieve "an end to male privilege and a changed relationship between the sexes."

Rich clarifies her concept of feminism, refusing "a shallow and trivial notion of feminism" as tokenism, equal rights, or the historically monolithic notion of female sameness, in favor of "a profound transformation of world society and of human relationships." She refines her critique of the patriarchy to focus on compulsory heterosexuality as a political institution. Represented in "It Is the Lesbian in Us . . ." (first published in 1976), "The Meaning of Our Love for Women Is What We Have Constantly to Expand" (first published in 1977), and the later essay "Compulsory Heterosexuality and Lesbian Existence" (first published in 1980 and collected in *Blood, Bread, and Poetry,* 1986), Rich increases her commitment to writing about lesbianism as the unspeakable, the unwritten text of women's lives. She notes, "If we have learned anything in our coming to language out of silence, it is that what has been kept unspoken, therefore *unspeakable,* in us is what is most threatening to the patriarchal order in which men control, first women, then all who can be defined and exploited as 'other.' All silence has a meaning." The lesbian and the woman of color, as the repressed "other," are the "beyond" of sex and race with which all women must connect in the effort to survive.

In the last two essays in *On Lies, Secrets, and Silence,* "Motherhood: The Contemporary Emergency and the Quantum Leap" and "Disloyal to Civilization: Feminism, Racism, Gynephobia," both published for the first time in 1978, Rich considers the goals of cultural transformation. It is utopian work, requiring a "quantum leap," "a leap of the imagination" to figure new relationships. She wants to make a leap to something "beyond," leaving the opposition that constructs sex-role polarization, racial dominance, and class oppression on the other side. She sees the separation from the other as a separation within the self; to address it requires a simultaneous, unending struggle with difference and identity.

The leap of Rich's new ethics demands that she position herself outside the conventional binary oppositions or, by negating it as she does with heterosexuality/lesbianism, that she formulate a highly controversial "lesbian continuum" of female bonding and resistance to patriarchal dominance along which each woman might plot her life at some time. In "Notes for a Magazine: What Does Separatism Mean?" (*Sinister Wisdom,* 1981) she turns the negative judgments of exclusion and forced separation into positive gestures of "claiming one's identity and community as an act of resistance." The subversive structure of the continuum connects women's difference, asks each woman to identify the difference within herself, and relates one to another. As the poems collected in *A Wild Patience Has Taken Me This Far: Poems 1978–1981* (1981) demonstrate, it is difficult to write beyond this point, to make this leap beyond the trap of the metalogic.

"The Images" explicitly undertakes the problem of refiguring "woman," given the realization that "no-man's-land does not exist," that separatism will neither reform nor displace the system of opposition. In another poem Rich writes her own account of "Culture and Anarchy," conspicuously stealing her title from Matthew Arnold's 1869 collection of essays and positioning herself at once in the culture of nineteenth-century women writers and in the anarchy of nature in August. Exposing the price of order, Rich presents a litany of the omissions culture requires to construct itself.

In "The Spirit of Place," Rich continues her struggle with the world "as it is," as it has been represented, as it might be. She unsettles singular identity, the sense that there is always a part of us "out beyond ourselves / knowing knowing knowing," but what that is—the identity, the knowledge—is never fully articulated. She locates it with the repressed and victimized of history, the unspeakable and silent "Other." Aware of the problematic nature of her project, Rich turns to the question of framing, what is seen under what circumstances, how position is a frame of vision. In "Frame" Rich reiterates the refrain of her own self-positioning: "I am standing all this time / just beyond the frame, trying to see." At the same time, she is always standing within the frame, too: "*I say I am there.*"

Rich's 1986 volume *Your Native Land, Your Life: Poems* develops the theme of standing on both sides of the frame, negotiating between self and other, between individuality and collectivity, as she defines her identity and place in her "native land." Rejecting, in Alice Templeton's words, "the false dichotomy" between multitude and solitude, *Your Native Land, Your Life* represents a quest for intersections between

Dust jacket for Rich's 1979 collection, in which she elaborates on her concepts of feminism and lesbianism

individual and collective consciousness, a quest that is reinforced by Rich's persistent use of *you,* the only English pronoun that is both singular and plural. Rich sees her multiplicity as an indicator of the world's and the world's as a reminder of her own. She lets her identity coexist and connect with others, but aware of her own internal division, she is careful not to lapse into a forced reconciliation or appropriation. In *Your Native Land, Your Life,* "the problem is . . . to connect" the multiple elements of which self, land, and life are composed. It is not to "resolve" and efface such multiplicity.

Published as a chapbook in 1983, "Sources," the first section in the collection, deals with various influences central to the formation of Rich's identity. In this thirteen-section poem, which may be read against her important autobiographical essay "Split at the Root: An Essay on Jewish Identity" (first published in 1982 and collected in *Blood, Bread, and Poetry*), she allows the past to enter her consciousness, speaking about her conflicted Jewish heritage and acknowledging her inextricable link to her family home, her late father, and her estranged and later deceased husband. Revealing and examining her heritage, Rich explores the ways in which she might complement and replace her roots so as to transform an imposed identity into a chosen identity. Because it is not only a coming to terms with the fragmentation of identity but also a celebration of the rich patchwork that self-chosen identity can provide, "Sources" is both a private and a public poem: in her self-examination, Rich reaches beyond the self into a social space from which she can speak to all those individuals who are also willing to construct their identities actively. Her mission is "to change the laws of history" and to know her place in the world "as a powerful and womanly series of choices."

A similar interplay between what, on the one hand, seems to be a commentary on Rich's personal circumstances only and what, on the other hand, proves to have implications for others is noticeable in "North American Time," the second section of *Your Native Land, Your Life.* For the first time, Rich almost completely distances herself from her "politics of asking women's questions," as she phrases it in *On Lies, Secrets, and Silence,* and turns to asking questions on behalf of Americans, both male and female. These poems argue that the context of a shared location and time, which Rich terms "North American Time," forces her readers and her to take into consideration lives and circumstances other than their own. The opening poem, "For the Record," sets the stage for Rich's concern with collective accountability. Wars, pollution, destitution, imprisonment, and illiteracy do not just happen; they are not unforeseeable natural catastrophes which one can only accept; instead, one must take responsibility and "Look around at all of it // and ask whose signature / is stamped on the orders. . . ."

Seeing everything as part of a larger whole leads Rich into her concern with maintaining the connection between her poetry and its intended context. In the poem "North American Time" Rich explores the transformation from the personal context in which a poem is written to the public context in which it is received:

> I am writing this in a time
> when anything we write
> can be used against those we love
> where the context is never given
> though we try to explain, over and over
> For the sake of poetry at least
> I need to know these things[.]

As the four-page struggle unfolds, it parallels Rich's lifelong conflict with an audience that has often resisted the politics of her poetry in favor of a context that she did not imply or intend. In both the poem and her career, the belief that readers ought to respect rather than appropriate her words gradually gives way to the realization that the interpretations of poetry cannot be contained and controlled by her personal intention. As the poem progresses, her desire to have the outside world look to her identity and politics as they respond to her poetry is gradually counterbalanced by a willingness to take into account the state of the outside world, to respond to and connect with "a certain North American pain."

Rich's endeavor to reach out to her surroundings and link them to her inner self is at its most literal in "Contradictions: Tracking Poems," the last section of *Your Native Land, Your Life.* Large parts of this sequence establish the difficulty and bleakness of the human condition in North America at the end of the twentieth century. She writes in the first of these poems, ". . . our lives will always be / a stew of contradictions," adding:

>   . . . and our bodies
> plod on without conviction
> and our thoughts cramp down before the sheer
> arsenal of everything that tries us:
> this battering, blunt-edged life[.]

Rich discusses a vast array of conflicts that are sometimes personal and sometimes public, but she always regards one type as just as urgent as the other and sees them as connected. She emphasizes this connection by speaking about her private bodily pain and by pointing out its interaction with the pain she witnesses in the world around her. To be "wired into pain," to be a "rider on the slow train," to live one's life "not under conditions" of one's "choosing" somehow implicates more people than an arthritic woman poet who has undergone several joint operations as well as spinal surgery. She is "signified by pain," but so is her native land. "The problem," she concludes, is "to connect, without hysteria, the pain / of any one's body with the pain of the body's world." She finds that connection is not easy but searching for it is worthwhile, as she states in a final address to the reader:

> Remember: the body's pain and the pain on the streets
> are not the same   but you can learn
> from the edges that blur   O you who love clear edges
> more than anything   watch the edges that blur[.]

The poems of *Your Native Land, Your Life* and the essays of *Blood, Bread, and Poetry* extend and deepen Rich's reflection on the relationships among art, politics, and personal experience, now in terms of an undeniably complex complicity. Like the poems in the section "North American Time" in *Your Native Land, Your Life,* four of the essays collected in *Blood, Bread, and Poetry* focus specifically on the de-

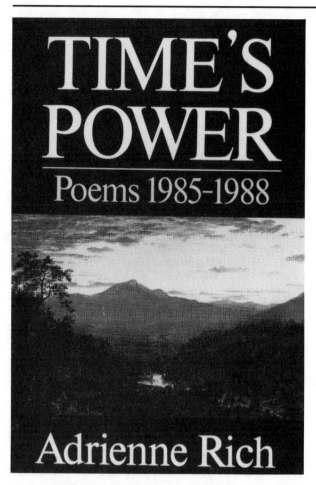

Dust jacket for Rich's twelfth volume of poetry (1989), in which she expresses her optimistic belief that "piece by piece, changes will come"

sire to deny complicity with murderous national policies and the need to acknowledge one's position of privilege. With "'Going There' and 'Being Here,'" "North American Tunnel Vision," and "Blood, Bread and Poetry: The Location of the Poet," all published in 1983, Rich pursues a line of inquiry that she follows through "Notes Toward a Politics of Location," first published in 1985. She wants to understand how she is affected by "*location*" as a Jewish lesbian feminist poet and writer in the United States, which, she sees in the second essay, entails a particular perspective on politics. Struggling with the definition of feminism, Rich asks if it is "something made only by white women, and only by women acknowledged as writers?" To test the limits of what she calls "North American Tunnel Vision," she traveled to Nicaragua in 1983. From her position in Nicaragua, Rich recognizes the inescapable influence of her "place" in North America on her identity. Nonetheless, she attempts to overcome this "tunnel vision" by moving toward greater inclusiveness and an increased attention to the particu-

larities of individual experience, setting the stage for a global phase that she develops in the poetry and prose following *Blood, Bread, and Poetry.*

Time's Power: Poems 1985–1988 (1989), Rich's twelfth collection of poetry, is more universal in focus than her previous work, contemplating the impact of the power of time on all humankind. Time, these poems argue, is all too often seen in terms of *passing* time, as a dwindling of opportunities. Although Rich shows awareness of the limitations time imposes, she mostly emphasizes time as a positive force. To Rich, time provides the opportunity to begin long-term change, to work gradually and partially toward a goal, to use negotiation as a method to make small steps forward, and to recover lost and misused memory so as to make it a usable part of the present. Time is a resource rather than a menace. To Rich, as she states in an interview with Molly McQuade, "it is important to possess a short-term pessimism and a long-term optimism—not to expect everything of any given 'campaign,' but to believe that, piece by piece, changes will come."

Memory, Rich implies in "The Slides" as well as in "Walking Down the Road," is often more like an amnesia, nostalgia, or denial. It frequently involves conjuring up and thriving on the clichés of the past, whereas it should be an unearthing of the reasons why "grains of the universe" began to flash "their angry tears." It should represent the less palatable aspects of history, such as "the razing of the spinal cord / by the polio virus," "the lung-tissue kissed by the tubercle bacillus," and "the cell that leaks anemia to the next generation." "Our story," as Rich writes in "For an Album,"

> . . . isn't a file of photographs
> faces laughing under green leaves
> or snowlit doorways, on the verge of driving
> away, our story is not about women
> victoriously perched on the one
> sunny day of the conference,
> nor lovers displaying love[.]

Far from embracing the tendency to remember selectively and romantically, Rich insists that

> Our story is of moments
> when even slow motion moved too fast
> for the shutter of the camera:
> words that blew our lives apart, like so,
> eyes that cut and caught each other,
> mime of the operating room
> where gas and knives quote each other
> moments before the telephone
> starts ringing. . . .

Unlike the happy photographs one might find in the attic, these realities "won't be quaint" as they are remembered. Rather, "they go on working; they still kill."

Memory, then, is an active agent connected as much to the present as to the past. It is a "Living Memory," as Rich argues in the poem that includes the title phrase of the collection, and it serves, above all, the living who remember. Memory may "still kill," but it exists for the living, not the dead. In this affirmation of life, time becomes a positive and necessary force. As Rich concludes, "Time's / power, the only just power—would you / give it away?"

Having contemplated time extensively in *Time's Power,* Rich turns to a meditation of place in *An Atlas of the Difficult World: Poems 1988–1991* (1991). In this book, Rich's thirteenth collection of poetry, her tendency toward a Whitmanian all-inclusiveness is reflected in both style and content. As her eye travels from coast to coast, her lines of poetry follow the movement, covering the pages almost entirely from left to right. The content, too, strives toward encompassing many areas, both physical and psychological. Rich moves from the United States to Europe to the Middle East and down to South Africa; from California to Vermont, Massachusetts, and New York; from Quebec to Mexico; from ocean to desert; from island to mainland; from sky to earth; and from dream to reality. Looking beyond the "North American tunnel vision," she asks herself repeatedly, "Where are we moored? / What are the bindings? / What behooves us?"

Of all the stylistic devices Rich employs to survey the world, contrast is among the most prominent. Contradictory observations placed side by side crowd her pages, making increasingly clear that her atlas is unable and unwilling to respect geographical and political boundaries. The contrast that most holds Rich's attention is "What can we control?" versus "What is beyond our control?" She wants to discern "the shapes of powerlessness and power." "Earthquake and drought followed by freezing followed by war,"—the California earthquake in 1989, the drought that lasted from 1984 to 1989, and the record-breaking freeze in December 1990 and January 1991—are, to be sure, beyond humans' control. Disasters like the outbreak of the Gulf War in mid-January 1991, however, are not. Man's "Sea of Indifference" is quite distinct from the indifferent Pacific. In man's sea of indifference, there are rivers whose water "we dare not taste"; there are deserts whose only growth are missiles "planted like corms"; and there are "suburbs of acquiescence" with "silence rising fumelike from the streets." That "there is talk of withering," Rich suggests, is far from beyond humans' control.

The poet is "bent on fathoming what it means to love my country." Such an investigation is a struggle, and the result is, as she says in an interview with David Trinidad, "one of the angriest books" that she has "ever written." She also reaches beyond the United States for global perspectives and interconnections. In the thirteen-section poem "Eastern War Time" she evokes victims of the Holocaust:

> A young girl knows she is young and meant to live
> taken on the closed journey
> her pockets drained of meaning
> her ankles greased in vomit and diarrhea
> driven naked across the yard
> . . . .
> thinking that she was pretty and that others would see it
> and not to bleed again and not to die
> in the gas but on the operating table
> of the famous doctor
> who plays string quartets with his staff in the laboratory[.]

The memory of the injustice done to Jews and other oppressed groups—such as the civil rights activists whose faces Rich has "seen / for thirty years under fire-hoses / walking through mobs to school / dragged singing from the buses / following the coffins"—becomes part of her present consciousness; it has "entered her connective tissue." This crime-ridden century, though "a blink in geological time," has been "heavy to those who had to wear it" or who, like Rich, have chosen to wear it. With its hypnotizing repetitions, "Final Notations," the closing poem in this volume, stresses both the urgency and the difficulty of upholding, repairing, and confronting all aspects of the world:

> it will not be simple, it will not be long
> it will take little time, it will take all your thought
> it will take all your heart, it will take all your breath
> it will be short, it will not be simple
> . . . .
> it will be short, it will take all your breath
> it will not be simple, it will become your will[.]

To exchange "pieces of our lives" and to go to "places never planned" is necessary, certain, and inevitable, as Rich's affirmative tone suggests. Her poem cannot reverse degradation and ruin, but it may contribute to repairing the damage done.

What Is Found There: Notebooks on Poetry and Politics (1993) consists of cultural and social criticism, defenses and definitions of poetry, autobiography, epistolary excerpts, and literary criticism. Rich writes:

I see the life of North American poetry at the end of the century as a pulsing, racing convergence of tributaries–regional, ethnic, racial, social, sexual–that, rising from lost or long-blocked springs, intersect and infuse each other while reaching back to the strengths of their origins.

Rich takes her title from William Carlos Williams's lines in "Asphodel, That Greeny Flower" (from *Journey to Love,* 1955): "It is difficult / to get the news from poems / yet men die miserably every day / for lack / of what is found there." She tries to show that the news that matters, that keeps individuals from dying miserably, can indeed be found in poetry. She argues that poetry breaks silences that had to be overcome; it "engage[s] with states that themselves would deprive us of language and reduce us to passive sufferers." If a poem can challenge seemingly self-evident propositions such as the "white noise" of corporate America, "the tranquil luxury of a complacent man," and "suburban separatism," then it provides life-preserving news. Finding "what is there," however, depends on "the active participant without whom the poem is never finished." After a poem has uncovered "desires and appetites buried under the accumulating emergencies of our lives," she states, "the task of acting on the truth, or making love, or meeting other needs, is ours."

Rich reiterates her belief that poetry itself, however radical and revolutionary, cannot change the world:

> A revolutionary poem will not tell you who or when to kill, what and when to burn, or even how to theorize. It reminds you . . . where and when and how you are living and might live–it is a wick of desire. . . .
> Any truly revolutionary art is an alchemy through which waste, greed, brutality, frozen indifference, "blind sorrow," and anger are transmuted into some drenching recognition of the *What if?*–the possible. *What if–?*–the first revolutionary question, the question dying forces don't know how to ask.

In a time that Rich calls "the worst . . . in this continent's history," much revolutionary art is still emerging. In order for poetry to trigger the desire for change and thus bring about change, however, poetry must be accessible. Rich's central questions are, "What kind of dialogue can exist between poets who are citizens of the United States and their countrypeople? What points of focus or connection exist? What could precipitate such a dialogue?" Rich continues:

> . . . most often someone writing a poem believes in, depends on, a delicate, vibrating range of difference, that an "I" can become a "we" without extinguishing others,

that a partly common language exists to which strangers can bring their own heartbeat, memories, images.

If poetry can reflect that "we are in the world and the world is in us," then a great deal can indeed "be found there," by everyone.

In *Dark Fields of the Republic: Poems 1991–1995* (1995) Rich displays a blend of optimism and pessimism similar to that in *What Is Found There.* Taken from a passage in F. Scott Fitzgerald's *The Great Gatsby* (1925), her title reflects her intention to conduct an end-of-the-century examination of the extent to which American ideals have been both realized and betrayed. Rich has committed her life to "Naming and mourning damage, keeping pain vocal so it cannot become normalized and acceptable," as she writes in *What Is Found There.* She has, as she elaborates in "And Now":

> . . . tried to listen to
> the public voice of our time
> tried to survey our public space
> as best I could
> –tried to remember and stay
> faithful to details, note
> precisely how the air moved
> and where the clock's hands stood
> and who was in charge of definitions
> and who stood by receiving them
> when the name of compassion
> was changed to the name of guilt
> when to feel with a human stranger
> was declared obsolete[.]

Having done all she can, wearing her "triple eye" as she walks "along the road / past, present, future all . . ." at her side, she turns to the public, insisting on their active participation in shaping history: "From you I want more than I've ever asked." She wants people to confront the uneasy question that serves as the title of both the first section and the first poem: "What Kind of Times Are These?"

To Rich "these times" are marked, on the one hand, by a "piercéd darkness" in which one may discern "Births arced into dumpsters" in New York City, "griefcrusted" streets, "the sexless swathed form lying in the doorway," and "Acceptable levels of cruelty, steadily rising." The country, she writes, is "moving closer to its own truth and dread, / its own ways of making people disappear." The time is "sick," and people resort to one form of escapism after another so as to avoid dealing with that realization.

If one persists in negotiating between national and individual afflictions, however, pain becomes "visionary," according to Rich. In the contemporary landscape, love is not extinct, for individuals are

Dust jacket for Rich's 1993 collection of essays, which includes some of her arguments about the functions of poetry

constantly "Sending Love," as the title of a further section of this volume suggests. Even if most of the heart will be consumed with despair about "the evening news, / fast-food miracles, ghostly revolutions," as she writes in "Miracle Ice Cream," "you can feel happy / with one piece of your heart." Faith, too, persists, however tentatively: "My testimony: yours: Trying to keep faith / not with each other exactly yet it's the one known and unknown / who stands for, imagines the other   with whom faith could be kept." Even beauty is attainable: "You can call on beauty still and it will leap / from all directions," and "with love," one can perhaps succeed in "trying to keep beauty afloat / on the bacterial waters."

The many changes throughout Rich's prolific career show that she resists easy categorization. Her self-revision is relentless, and readers are well advised to acknowledge her confrontational warning in her 1978 poem "Delta":

If you think you can grasp me, think again:
my story flows in more than one direction
a delta springing from the riverbed
with its five fingers spread[.]

Interviews:

Stanley Plumly, Wayne Dodd, and Walter Trevis, "Talking with Adrienne Rich," *Ohio Review: A Journal of the Humanities,* 13 (Fall 1971): 28–48;

David Kalstone, "Talking with Adrienne Rich," *Saturday Review: The Arts,* 4 (22 April 1972): 29–46;

Barbara Charlesworth Gelpi and Albert Gelpi, "Three Conversations (1974)," in *Adrienne Rich's Poetry,* edited by Gelpi and Gelpi (New York: Norton, 1975), pp. 105–122;

Blanche M. Boyd, "Interview," *Christopher Street,* 1 (January 1977): 9–16;

Elly Bulkin, "An Interview with Adrienne Rich," parts 1 and 2, *Conditions,* 1 (Spring 1977): 50–65; 2 (Fall 1977): 53–66;

"Adrienne Rich: An Interview by David Montenegro," *American Poetry Review,* 20 (January–February 1991): 7–14;

David Trinidad, "Adrienne Rich Charts a Difficult World: The Acclaimed Poet Talks of Art, Anger, and Activism," *Advocate,* 31 December 1991, pp. 82–84;

Patricia Kirkpatrick, "Look Around at All of It: An Interview with Adrienne Rich," *Hungry Mind Review* (Spring 1992): 56–59;

Molly McQuade, interview with Adrienne Rich, *Publishers Weekly* (29 November 1993): 44–45;

Matthew Rothschild, interview with Adrienne Rich, *Progressive,* 58 (January 1994): 31–35.

References:

Charles Altieri, *Self and Sensibility in Contemporary American Poetry* (New York: Cambridge University Press, 1984);

Thomas B. Byers, "Adrienne Rich: Vision as Rewriting," in *World, Self, Poem: Essays on Contemporary Poetry from the "Jubilation of Poets,"* edited by Leonard M. Trawick (Kent, Ill.: Kent State University Press, 1990), pp. 144–152;

Jane Roberta Cooper, ed., *Reading Adrienne Rich: Reviews and Re-Visions, 1951–81* (Ann Arbor: University of Michigan Press, 1984);

Helen M. Dennis, "Adrienne Rich: Consciousness Raising as Poetic Method," in *Contemporary Poetry Meets Modern Theory,* edited by Antony Easthope and John O. Thompson (Toronto: University of Toronto Press, 1991), pp. 177–194;

Myriam Díaz-Diocaretz, *Translating Poetic Discourse: Questions on Feminist Strategies in Adrienne Rich*

(Amsterdam & Philadelphia: John Benjamins, 1985);

Margaret Dickie, *Stein, Bishop, & Rich: Lyrics of Love, War, & Place* (Chapel Hill: University of North Carolina Press, 1997);

Peter Erickson, "Singing America: From Walt Whitman to Adrienne Rich," *Kenyon Review,* 17 (Winter 1995): 103–119;

Betsy Erkkila, *The Wicked Sisters: Women Poets, Literary History, and Discord* (New York: Oxford University Press, 1992);

Albert Gelpi and Jacqueline Voigt Brogan, eds., special issue on "'A Whole New Poetry Beginning Here': Adrienne Rich's Recent Poetry," *Women's Studies,* 27 (Spring 1998);

Barbara Charlesworth Gelpi and Albert Gelpi, *Adrienne Rich's Poetry and Prose: Poems, Prose, Reviews, and Criticism* (New York: Norton, 1993);

Gelpi and Gelpi, eds., *Adrienne Rich's Poetry: Texts of the Poems, The Poet on Her Work, Reviews and Criticism* (New York: Norton, 1975);

Roger Gilbert, "Framing Water: Historical Knowledge in Elizabeth Bishop and Adrienne Rich," *Twentieth Century Literature,* 43 (Summer 1997): 144–161;

Anne Herzog, "Adrienne Rich and the Discourse of Decolonization," *Centennial Review,* 33 (Summer 1989): 258–277;

Richard Howard, *Alone with America: Essays on the Art of Poetry in the United States Since 1950* (New York: Atheneum, 1969);

David Kalstone, *Five Temperaments: Elizabeth Bishop, Robert Lowell, James Merrill, Adrienne Rich, John Ashbery* (New York: Oxford University Press, 1977);

Claire Keyes, *The Aesthetics of Power: The Poetry of Adrienne Rich* (Athens: University of Georgia Press, 1986);

Marie-Christine Lemardeley-Cunci, *Adrienne Rich: Cartographies of Silence* (Lyon: Presses Universitaires de Lyon, 1990);

Janice Markey, *A New Tradition? The Poetry of Sylvia Plath, Anne Sexton, and Adrienne Rich: A Study of Feminism and Poetry* (Frankfurt am Main: Peter Lang, 1985);

Wendy Martin, *An American Triptych: Anne Bradstreet, Emily Dickinson, Adrienne Rich* (Chapel Hill: University of North Carolina Press, 1984);

James McCorkle, *The Still Performance: Writing, Self, and Interconnection in Five Postmodern American Poets* (Charlottesville: University Press of Virginia, 1989);

Kevin McGuirk, "Philoctetes Radicalized: 'Twenty-one Love Poems' and the Lyric Career of Adrienne Rich," *Contemporary Literature,* 34 (Spring 1993): 61–87;

Gretchen Mieszkowski, "No Longer 'by a miracle, a twin': Helen Vendler's Reviews of Adrienne Rich's Recent Poetry," *South Central Review,* 5 (Summer 1988): 72–86;

Carol Muske, "Backward into the Future," *Parnassus: Poetry in Review,* 7 (Spring–Summer 1979): 77–90;

Cary Nelson, *Our First Last Poets: Vision and History in Contemporary American Poetry* (Urbana: University of Illinois Press, 1981);

Alicia Ostriker, *Stealing the Language: the Emergence of Women's Poetry in America* (Boston: Beacon, 1986);

Ostriker, *Writing Like a Woman* (Ann Arbor: University of Michigan Press, 1983);

Marjorie Perloff, "Private Lives / Public Images," *Michigan Quarterly,* 22 (Winter 1983): 130–142;

Terrence des Pres, *Praises and Dispraises: Poetry and Politics, the 20th Century* (New York: Viking, 1988);

Sandra Runzo, "Adrienne Rich's Voice of Treason," *Women's Studies,* 18 (1990): 135–151;

Alan Shima, *Skirting the Subject: Pursuing Language in the Works of Adrienne Rich, Susan Griffin, and Beverly Dahlen* (Uppsala, Sweden: Acta Universitatis Upsaliensis, 1993);

Willard Spiegelman, *The Didactic Muse: Scenes of Instruction in Contemporary American Poetry* (Princeton: Princeton University Press, 1989);

Catharine Stimpson, "Adrienne Rich and Lesbian/Feminist Poetry," *Parnassus: Poetry in Review,* 12–13 (Spring/Summer/Fall/Winter 1985): 249–268;

Alice Templeton, *The Dream and the Dialogue: Adrienne Rich's Feminist Poetics* (Knoxville: University of Tennessee Press, 1994);

Helen Vendler, *Part of Nature, Part of Us: Modern American Poets* (Cambridge, Mass.: Harvard University Press, 1980);

Craig Werner, *Adrienne Rich: The Poet and Her Critics* (Chicago: American Library Association, 1988);

Liz Yorke, *Adrienne Rich: Passion, Politics, and the Body* (Thousand Oaks, Cal.: Sage Publications, 1997).

William Saroyan

This entry was updated from the entries by H. W. Matalene (University of South Carolina) in DLB 7: *Twentieth-Century American Dramatists, by Philip Bufithis (Shepherd College) in* DLB 9: *American Novelists, 1910–1945, and by Greg Keeler (Montana State University, Bozeman), in* DLB 86: *American Short-Story Writers, 1910-1945, First Series.*

See also the Saroyan entry in *DLB Yearbook 1981*.

BIRTH: Fresno, California, 31 August 1908, to Armenak and Takoohi Saroyan.

EDUCATION: Educated in Fresno public schools.

MARRIAGES: February 1943 to Carol Marcus (divorced, November 1949); remarried Carol Marcus, 1951 (divorced, 1952); children: Aram, Lucy.

AWARDS AND HONORS: O. Henry Award, 1934, for "The Daring Young Man on the Flying Trapeze"; Drama Critics Circle Award, 1940, for *The Time of Your Life;* Pulitzer Prize for drama, 1940, for *The Time of Your Life* (not accepted); Academy Award, 1943, for the screenplay *The Human Comedy;* California Literature Gold Medal, 1952, for *Tracy's Tiger;* inducted into New York City Theatre Hall of Fame, 1979; American Book Award nomination, 1980, for *Obituaries.*

DEATH: Fresno, California, 18 May 1981.

BOOKS: *The Daring Young Man on the Flying Trapeze and Other Stories* (New York: Random House, 1934; London: Faber & Faber, 1935);
Inhale & Exhale (New York: Random House, 1936; London: Faber & Faber, 1936);
Those Who Write Them and Those Who Collect Them (Chicago: Black Archer Press, 1936);
Three Times Three (Los Angeles: Conference Press, 1936);
Little Children (New York: Harcourt, Brace, 1937; London: Faber & Faber, 1937);
The Gay and Melancholy Flux (London: Faber & Faber, 1937)—comprises *Inhale & Exhale* and *Three Times Three;*
Love, Here Is My Hat (New York: Modern Age Books, 1938; London: Faber & Faber, 1938);
A Native American (San Francisco: George Fields, 1938);

William Saroyan, circa 1936 (photograph by DeMirjian)

The Trouble with Tigers (New York: Harcourt, Brace, 1938; London: Faber & Faber, 1939);
The Hungerers, A Short Play (New York & London: S. French, 1939);
Three Fragments and a Story (San Francisco: Little Man, 1939);
Peace, It's Wonderful (New York: Modern Age Books, 1939; London: Faber & Faber, 1940);
My Heart's in the Highlands: A Play (New York: Harcourt, Brace, 1939);
The Time of Your Life (New York: Harcourt, Brace, 1939);

Subway Circus (New York: S. French, 1940);

The Ping-Pong Game (New York: S. French, 1940);

Three Plays: My Heart's in the Highlands, The Time of Your Life, Love's Old Sweet Song (New York: Harcourt, Brace, 1940); republished as *The Time of Your Life and Two Other Plays* (London: Faber & Faber, 1942);

A Special Announcement, Crown Octavos, no. 7 (New York: House of Books, 1940);

My Name Is Aram (New York: Harcourt, Brace, 1940; London: Faber & Faber, 1941); revised edition (New York: Dell, 1966);

The Insurance Salesman, and Other Stories (London: Faber & Faber, 1941);

Jim Dandy (Cincinnati: Little Man Press, 1941); republished as *Jim Dandy, Fat Man in a Famine: A Play* (New York: Harcourt, Brace, 1947; London: Faber & Faber, 1948);

The People with Light Coming Out of Them (New York: Free Company, 1941);

Three Plays by William Saroyan: The Beautiful People, Sweeny in the Trees, Across the Board on Tomorrow Morning (New York: Harcourt, Brace, 1941); republished as *The Beautiful People and Other Plays* (London: Faber & Faber, 1943);

Saroyan's Fables (New York: Harcourt, Brace, 1941);

Best Stories of William Saroyan (London: Faber & Faber, 1942);

48 Saroyan Stories (New York: Avon, 1942)—comprises *Love, Here Is My Hat* and *Peace, It's Wonderful;*

Razzle-Dazzle (New York: Harcourt, Brace, 1942); revised as *Razzle Dazzle; the Human Opera, Ballet, and Circus* (London: Faber & Faber, 1945);

The Human Comedy (New York: Harcourt, Brace, 1943; London: Faber & Faber, 1943; revised edition, New York: Dell, 1966; London: Faber, 1975);

Some Day I'll Be A Millionaire: 34 More Great Stories (New York: Avon, 1943);

Thirty-One Selected Stories (New York: Avon, 1943);

Dear Baby (New York: Harcourt, Brace, 1944; London: Faber & Faber, 1945);

Get Away Old Man: A Play in Two Acts (New York: Harcourt, Brace, 1944; London: Faber & Faber, 1946);

Why Abstract? by Saroyan, Hilaire Hiler, and Henry Miller (New York: James Laughlin, 1945; London: Falcon Press, 1948);

The Adventures of Wesley Jackson (New York: Harcourt, Brace, 1946; London: Faber & Faber, 1947); enlarged as *The Twin Adventures: The Adventures of William Saroyan, a Diary; The Adventures of Wesley Jackson, a Novel* (New York: Harcourt, Brace, 1950);

The Saroyan Special: Selected Short Stories (New York: Harcourt, Brace, 1948);

Don't Go Away Mad: A Play in Three Acts (New York: S. French, 1949);

Hello Out There, a One Act Play (New York: S. French, 1949);

The Fiscal Hoboes (New York: Press of Valenti Angelo, 1949);

Sam Ego's House: A Play in Three Acts and Seven Scenes (New York: S. French, 1949);

Don't Go Away Mad and Two Other Plays: Sam Ego's House; A Decent Birth, A Happy Funeral (New York: Harcourt, Brace, 1949; London: Faber & Faber, 1951);

The Assyrian and Other Stories (New York: Harcourt, Brace, 1950; London: Faber & Faber, 1951);

Rock Wagram, a Novel (Garden City, N.Y.: Doubleday, 1951; London: Faber & Faber, 1952);

Tracy's Tiger (Garden City, N.Y.: Doubleday, 1951; London: Faber & Faber, 1952);

The Bicycle Rider in Beverly Hills (New York: Scribners, 1952; London: Faber & Faber, 1953);

The Laughing Matter: A Novel (Garden City, N.Y.: Doubleday, 1953); republished as *The Laughing Matter: A Serious Story* (London: Faber & Faber, 1954); republished as *A Secret Story* (New York: Popular Library, 1954);

Love, Lion Library Editions, no. 56 (New York: Lion Library Editions, 1955);

Mama I Love You (Boston & Toronto: Little, Brown / Atlantic Monthly, 1956; London: Faber & Faber, 1957);

The Whole Voyald and Other Stories (Boston & Toronto: Little, Brown / Atlantic Monthly, 1956; London: Faber & Faber, 1957);

Papa You're Crazy (Boston & Toronto: Little, Brown / Atlantic Monthly, 1957; London: Faber & Faber, 1958);

The Cave Dwellers: A Play (New York: Putnam, 1958; London: Faber & Faber, 1958);

The Slaughter of the Innocents: A Play in Two Acts (New York: S. French, 1958);

The William Saroyan Reader (New York: Braziller, 1958);

Once Around the Block; A Play in One Act (New York: S. French, 1959);

Sam, the Highest Jumper of Them All; or, The London Comedy (London: Faber & Faber, 1961);

Here Comes, There Goes, You Know Who (New York: Simon & Schuster / Trident, 1961; London: Davies, 1962);

Settled Out of Court: A Play in Three Acts, by Saroyan and Henry Cecil (London: S. French, 1962);

Boys and Girls Together (New York: Harcourt, Brace & World, 1963; London: Davies, 1963);

Me (New York: Crowell-Collier / London: Collier-Macmillan, 1963);

Not Dying (New York: Harcourt, Brace & World, 1963; London: Cassell, 1966);

After Thirty Years: The Daring Young Man on the Flying Trapeze (New York: Harcourt, Brace & World, 1964);

One Day in the Afternoon of the World (New York: Harcourt, Brace & World, 1964; London: Cassell, 1965);

Who is Varaz? (New York: Studio H. Gallery, 1965);

Horsey Gorsey and the Frog (Chippewa Falls, Wis.: Hale, 1965);

The Arabian Nights. Introduced for Young Readers (New York: Platt & Munk, 1966);

My Kind of Crazy and Wonderful People: Seventeen Stories and a Play (New York: Harcourt, Brace & World, 1966);

Short Drive, Sweet Chariot (New York: Phaedra, 1966);

Look at Us; Let's See; Here We Are; Look Hard, Speak Soft; I See, You See, We All See; Stop, Look, Listen; Beholder's Eye; Don't Look Now, but Isn't That You? (Us? U.S.?), text by Saroyan and photographs by Arthur Rothstein (New York: Cowles, 1967);

I Used to Believe I Had Forever Now I'm Not So Sure (New York: Cowles, 1968; London: Cassell, 1969);

The Dogs, or the Paris Comedy and Two Other Plays: Chris Sick, or Happy New Year Anyway, Making Money, and Nineteen Other Very Short Plays (New York: Phaedra, 1969);

Letters from 74 Rue Taitbout, or Don't Go, But If You Must, Say Hello to Everybody (New York & Cleveland: World, 1969); republished as *Don't Go, But If You Must, Say Hello to Everybody* (London: Cassell, 1970);

Days of Life and Death and Escape to the Moon (New York: Dial, 1970; London: Joseph, 1971);

Places Where I've Done Time (New York: Praeger, 1972; London: Davis-Poynter, 1973);

The Tooth and My Father (Garden City, N.Y.: Doubleday, 1974);

An Act or Two of Foolish Kindness: Two Stories (Lincoln, Mass.: Penmaen Press, 1976);

Morris Hirshfield (Parma: Franco Maria Ricci, 1976);

Sons Come and Go, Mothers Hang in Forever (New York, St. Louis & San Francisco: McGraw-Hill, 1976);

Chance Meetings: A Memoir (New York: Norton, 1978);

Assassinations; & Jim, Sam & Anna: Two Short Paris Summertime Plays of 1974 (Northridge: California State University Northridge Libraries/ Santa Susana Press, 1979);

Obituaries (Berkeley: Creative Arts, 1979);

Births, introduction by David Kherdian (Berkeley: Creative Arts, 1983);

An Armenian Trilogy: Three Plays About Armenian Life, edited by Dickran Kouymjian (Fresno: The Press at California State University, 1986);

Madness in the Family, edited by Leo Hamalian (New York: New Directions, 1988);

Warsaw Visitor; Tales from the Vienna Streets: The Last Two Plays of William Saroyan, edited, with an introduction, by Kouymjian (Fresno: Press at California State University, 1991).

Collections: *My Name is Saroyan,* edited by James H. Tashjian (New York: Coward, McCann & Geoghegan, 1983);

The New Saroyan Reader: A Connoisseur's Anthology of the Writings of William Saroyan, edited by Brian Darwent (San Francisco: D. S. Ellis / Berkeley: Creative Arts, 1984);

The Man with the Heart in the Highlands & Other Early Stories, introduction by Herb Caen (New York: New Directions, 1989);

Saroyan's Armenians: An Anthology, edited by Alice K. Barter (Huntington, W.V.: University Editions, 1992);

Fresno Stories (New York: New Directions, 1994);

Saroyan—Memoirs, edited, with an introduction, by Brian Darwent (London & Washington: Minerva Press, 1994).

PLAY PRODUCTIONS: *My Heart's in the Highlands,* New York, Guild Theatre, 13 April 1939;

The Time of Your Life, New York, Booth Theatre, 25 October 1939;

A Theme in the Life of the Great American Goof, New York, Center Theatre, 11 January 1940;

Love's Old Sweet Song, New York, Plymouth Theatre, 2 May 1940;

Sweeney in the Trees, Cape May, N.J., Cape Theatre, August 1940;

Across the Board on Tomorrow Morning, Pasadena, Pasadena Community Playhouse, 11 February 1941; New York, Theatre Showcase, March 1942; New York, Belasco Theatre, 17 August 1942;

The Beautiful People, New York, Lyceum Theatre, 21 April 1941;

Hello Out There, Santa Barbara, Lobero Theatre, 10 September 1941; New York, Belasco Theatre, 29 September 1942;

Jim Dandy, Princeton, N.J., Theatre Intime, November 1941;

Talking to You, New York, Belasco Theatre, 17 August 1942;

Get Away Old Man, New York, Cort Theatre, 24 November 1943;

The Hungerers, The Ping Pong Game, and *Hello Out There,* New York, Provincetown Playhouse, 23 August 1945;

Sam Ego's House, Hollywood, Circle Theatre, 30 October 1947;

Don't Go Away Mad, New York, Master Institute Theatre, 9 May 1949;

The Son, Hollywood, Circle Theatre, 31 March 1950;

Once Around the Block, New York, Master Institute Theatre, 24 May 1950;

Subway Circus, New York, Amato Opera Theatre, April 1952;

A Lost Child's Fireflies, Dallas, Round-up Theatre, 15 July 1954;

Opera, Opera, New York, Amato Opera Theatre, 21 December 1955;

The Slaughter of the Innocents, Nordmark-Landerstheater, Stadtheater Schleswig, 22 April 1955;

Ever Been in Love with a Midget, Berlin, Congress Hall, 20 September 1957;

The Cave Dwellers, New York, Bijou Theatre, 19 October 1957;

The Dogs: or, the Paris Comedy, Vienna, 17 February 1960;

Sam, The Highest Jumper of Them All: or, the London Comedy, London, Stratford East Theatre Royal, 6 April 1960;

Settled Out of Court, by Saroyan and Henry Cecil, London, Strand Theatre, 19 October 1960;

High Time along the Wabash, Lafayette, Purdue University Playhouse, 1 December 1961;

Ah Man, music by Peter Fricker, Suffolk, England, Aldeburgh Festival, 21 June 1962;

Bad Men in the West, Stanford, Stanford University, 19 May 1971;

People's Lives, by Saroyan and others, New York, Manhattan Theatre Club, August 1974;

The Rebirth Celebration of the Human Race at Artie Zabala's Off-Broadway Theatre, New York, Shirtsleeve Theatre, 10 July 1975;

Play Things: A Theatrical Lark, Vienna, English Theatre, 1978.

MOTION PICTURES: *The Good Job,* M-G-M, 1942; *The Human Comedy,* M-G-M, 1943.

TELEVISION: *The Oyster and the Pearl,* 1953;

Ah Sweet Mystery of Mrs. Murphy, Omnibus, NBC, 1 March 1959;

The Unstoppable Gray Fox, GE Theatre, CBS, 1962;

Making Money and Thirteen Other Very Short Plays, ETV, 12 November 1970.

RADIO: *Now Is the Time: A Sideshow of the World Today,* 1938;

Radio Play, Columbia Workshop, CBS, 1940;

The People with Light Coming Out of Them, Free Company, CBS, 1941;

There's Something I Got to Tell You, 1941.

OTHER: Al Hirschfeld, *Harlem as Seen by Hirschfeld,* text by Saroyan (New York: Hyperion Press, 1941), pp. 5-10;

Pauline Vinson, *Hilltop Russians in San Francisco,* text by Saroyan (Stanford University, Cal.: James Delkin, 1941), pp. 5-11;

George Jessel, *So Help Me, the Autobiography of George Jessel,* foreword by Saroyan (New York: Random House, 1943);

George Mardikian, *Dinner at Omar Khayyam's,* foreword by Saroyan (New York: Viking Press, 1944);

Khatchik Minasian, *The Simple Songs of Khatchik Minasian,* introduction by Saroyan (San Francisco: Colt Press/Grabhorn Press, 1950);

David Kherdian, *Six Poets of the San Francisco Renaissance: Portraits and Checklists,* introduction by Saroyan (Fresno, Cal.: Giligia Press, 1967);

Dentist and Patient and Husband and Wife, in *The Best Short Plays, 1968,* ed. Stanley Richards (Radnor, Pa.: Chilton Press, 1968);

A. J. Hacikyan, *Tomas: A Novel,* introduction by Saroyan (Montreal: Librairie Beauchemin / Fresno, Cal.: Giligia Press, 1970);

Kherdian, *On the Death of My Father, and Other Poems,* introduction by Saroyan (Fresno, Cal.: Giligia Press, 1970);

The New Play, in *The Best Short Plays, 1970,* edited by Richards (Radnor, Pa.: Chilton Press, 1970);

Arthur Tcholakian, *The Majesty of the Black Woman: Words and Pictures,* introduction by Saroyan (New York: Van Nostrand Reinhold, 1971).

SELECTED PERIODICAL PUBLICATIONS— UNCOLLECTED: "Once Around the Block," *American Mercury,* 69 (December 1949): 663-675;

The Oyster and the Pearl, Perspectives USA, 4 (Summer 1953): 86-104;

"The Time of My Life," *Theatre Arts,* 39 (January 1955): 22-24, 95;

Saroyan, circa 1920, when he was a telegraph messenger
(Collection of Aram Saroyan)

"Art for Man's Sake: A Minority View," *Nation,* 180 (23 April 1955): 364–366;

Cat, Mouse, Man, Woman, and The Accident, Contact 1: The San Francisco Journal of New Writing, Art and Ideas (1958);

Four Plays: The Playwright and the Public, The Handshakers, The Doctor and the Patient, This I Believe, Atlantic Monthly, 211 (April 1963): 50–52;

"The Funny Business of Marriage," *Saturday Evening Post,* 236 (5 October 1963): 44–45;

"I'll Tell You Who Joe Mannix Really Is: But First a Few Words about Muggerditch Muggerditchian, Krekor Ohanian and a Judge Named Denver Peckinpah," *TV Guide,* 22 (13 July 1974): 4–6;

"Something Else on My Mind," *New York Times,* 31 July 1974, p. 33;

"How to Write a Great Play," *TV Guide,* (6 March 1976): 2–5;

"Poetry for Profit," *New Republic,* 178 (4 March 1978): 29.

Growing up in an Armenian immigrant community in the San Joaquin Valley of California with both of his grandmothers as storytellers was a propitious circumstance for William Saroyan's career as a writer. Witnessing the behavior of an individualistic, free-spirited people who have endured for centuries the sadness of expatriation gave him immediately at hand the raw material of art. "I began to believe I was a writer when I was in the third grade at Emerson School in Fresno," Saroyan said, "and I began to be a writer when I was thirteen and had used up the better part of my first week's wages as a telegraph messenger in the buying of a secondhand upright Underwood typewriter."

Saroyan's father came to New York in 1905 from the mountainous Armenian-Kurdish town of Bitlis in eastern Turkey, eventually settling in Fresno, California, with its large population of Armenian-Americans. When Saroyan was three, his father, Armenak Saroyan, died, and William and his brother and two sisters had to leave their hometown of Fresno to live in an orphanage in Oakland. In 1915 they returned to Fresno, where they joined their mother, Takoohi Saroyan, then working as a domestic servant. Saroyan attended public schools and eventually got a job as a messenger boy for a telegraph company, a job that later became one of the major sources for his fiction and drama. After dropping out of high school he moved to San Francisco, where he worked at various jobs and eventually became a clerk, then a telegraph operator, for Postal Telegraph Company. In 1928 he published his first story in *Overland Monthly and Outwest Magazine* and took a trip to New York, having decided to make writing his career.

Despite a prolific career, Saroyan's reputation as short-story writer still rests largely on his first collection, *The Daring Young Man on the Flying Trapeze and Other Stories* (1934). As with many of his later writings, Saroyan dashed these stories off at an amazing speed, yet the manner of composition seemed to add to the urgency of his tone. When the title piece was published in *Story* magazine in February 1934, the public response was so favorable that in less than a year Random House had compiled the collection. Saroyan sets the tone of the volume in a preface, in which he advocates the abandonment of traditional short-story forms and asserts that the will of the author is the crucial element of unity. Thus, *The Daring Young Man on the Flying Trapeze* fit the literary vogue of the day both in its rebellious stance and in its advocacy of the individual.

As in many of his works, Saroyan's narrator in *The Daring Young Man on the Flying Trapeze* is a young writer, a thinly veiled representation of the author himself. The young man, unable to rationalize his position in a materialistic society, finds fulfillment only in death. He metaphorically carries the problems of a civilization on his back as he tries to find work, gets disgusted with the bureaucracy, gives up on physical sustenance, falls back on the literary fare that has sustained him psychically, and gives himself up to death: "Then swiftly, neatly, with the grace of the young man on the trapeze, he was gone from his body." In this story Saroyan establishes one of the main themes that permeates almost all of his subsequent writings—the brilliance and importance of life in the face of death—usually emphasized by Saroyan's direct, autobiographical narrative but often finding a more distinct, objective presentation.

Saroyan's next book, *Inhale & Exhale* (1936), is also a collection of stories. In mood and style they are of a piece with his first book, though now the focus moves from small-town boyhood to young manhood in the city and finally to travel abroad, for Saroyan was now prosperous and famous. He continued to fill his stories with authorial commentary, to such an extent in this book that readers and reviewers began to question the validity of the term story in connection with his work. What he called stories often seemed to be personal essays thinly disguised as fiction. He was turning his stories into podiums from which to affirm values that by now had become repetitive: the wonder and sacredness of life, the spiritual oneness that lies beneath individual variation, and the contradictory belief in the marvelous, irreducible, individualistic self.

Inhale & Exhale is the longest and perhaps the most divergent in style and quality of all of his works. Saroyan divided the stories into nine titled subdivisions that can be grouped into three unstated categories: stories of childhood, stories of young men, and stories of travel. Perhaps it is the stories of childhood that reveal most clearly both the worst and best in this stage of Saroyan's development.

The basic flaw in stories such as "The World and the Theater" (1935) stems from Saroyan's desire to load his narrative with emotional import rather than to let it develop within the text. The narrator, a young newsboy, through his perceptions of headlines on the papers he sells, conveys a picture of a national mind, yet his words and thoughts are obviously more mature, more Saroyan's; thus, the character and his situation are less believable.

"Five Ripe Pears" (1935), because of its adult perspective on a childhood experience, averts the confusion of adult speaking through child. The adult narrator has valuable hindsight on his childhood. He realizes the importance of nonownership as he recounts an incident where, as a child, he was punished for "stealing" pears which he thought should have been free by the mere strength of their beauty and his desire to have them. In retrospect the punishment still seems unfair, and the child's attitude is given an intensified validity through the mature narrator.

Whether in these stories of childhood or in those of young adulthood and travel, the strongest thematic development between *The Daring Young Man on the Flying Trapeze* and *Inhale & Exhale* concerns Saroyan's Armenian background. For it is in *Inhale & Exhale* that his optimistic themes of national identity and strong personal independence, first developed in the earlier collection, begin to solidify. To some critics this solidification of style, which led to the more objective, more tightly structured narratives of his later collections, was positive in that it was in keeping with the developing tenets of New Criticism, stressing an objectification of the narrative voice. To others, the solidification of his Armenian themes and the resulting traditional and highly crafted stories represented a diminishing of the original direct first-person voice used in *The Daring Young Man on the Flying Trapeze*. Instead of an improvement in craftsmanship, the stories of *Inhale & Exhale* revealed, to some critics, a departure from cynicism and independence toward triteness and sentimentality.

In stories such as "A Broken Wheel" (1935) Saroyan writes of his experiences in the Armenian community in Fresno with a narrative distance reinforced by the story's remote temporal setting. Saroyan's theme is implied, not forced, and the story's strength emerges in a single image: the narrator and his brother, Krikor, find a correlative for their Uncle Vahan's death in a broken bicycle wheel. The impact of the story thus comes from the imagery more than from any direct statement of theme, and yet "A Broken Wheel" depends heavily on a sense of nostalgia that, when combined with the emotional resolution, brings the story to the brink of sentimentality.

However, in the last story of *Inhale & Exhale*, "The Armenian and the Armenian" (1935), Saroyan reasserts his direct personal narrative style and thus eschews any sentimentality. Here, without subtlety and with the arrogance for which his young voice was so well known, Saroyan portrays the strength of the individual in the face of oblivion, of two Armenians in the face of extinction: "Go ahead, see if you can do anything about it. See if you can stop them from mocking the big ideas of the world. . . . go ahead and try to destroy them."

After Saroyan's brilliant and promising beginning with *The Daring Young Man on the Flying Trapeze*, most critics were disappointed with *Inhale & Exhale*: some thought it a boring continuation of the personal diatribes of the first collection; others wondered how long he could show promise without ful-

THE DARING
YOUNG MAN
on the flying
TRAPEZE

and other stories by
William Saroyan

Random House · New York

Dust jacket for Saroyan's first book, published in 1934

filling it. The volume includes some of the strongest stories Saroyan wrote and also some of the weakest. This polarization is perhaps due to Saroyan's attempt to answer the charges of critics concerned with the looseness of his narrative style yet preserve the integrity of his own voice.

Saroyan's next book, *Three Times Three* (1936), arose from a suggestion made by three university students who visited him while he was working on motion picture dialogue for B. P. Schulberg in Hollywood. Saroyan and the students, in an attempt to create an "uncommercial and easy-going" market for a book, created their own publishing company, The Conference Press. *Three Times Three* comprises nine stories and, to some degree, further marks Saroyan's progress toward more formal, belletristic narratives.

By becoming his own editor in this collection, Saroyan forced himself into a new role where he was responsible for the ultimate product. Because of this, he began to soften his hard, rebellious literary posture: "Critics are happiest with my stuff I think,

when I try for almost nothing, when I sit down and very quietly tell a little story. In a way I don't blame them. I myself enjoy writing and reading a very simple story, that is whole and with form." Thus, "The Man With the Heart in the Highlands" (1936), a fantasy about Fresno and Saroyan's Armenian background, finds its theme through the concrete language of its six-year-old narrator.

In the spring of 1939, when the work of Saroyan first reached the New York stage in the form of a one-act play based on this short story, *My Heart's in the Highlands,* Sidney B. Whipple of the *New York World-Telegram* accused Saroyan and his producers of conducting a "painful experiment . . . for one purpose—to test the I.Q. of the public and the critics." This response has considerable justice, for when the play was published, Saroyan included in the volume the perplexed and conflicting reviews of the play, and he added a preface in which he pilloried "A number of drama critics [who] sincerely regretted they couldn't understand this simple play, and a number [who] were bored by it." Children, he wrote, were better prepared to cope with him than were the Eastern cognoscenti. As Saroyan's subsequent plays were produced and published, he continued to surround them with autobiography and self-explanation, contemptuous of the social and cultural attitudes of his new Broadway public and of the critics shaping those attitudes.

Saroyan's play is a coherent and detailed statement of the most pervasive belief in his writing. This is the belief that human life takes on value and meaning through direct, hedonic excitation of the five senses by two classes of stimuli—those produced by people and those produced by nonhuman nature. In the former case Saroyan sees people, ideally, as constantly engaged in various kinds of direct exchanges that excite the love of life in the partners to these exchanges. For Saroyan a properly functioning economy includes exchanges not only of goods and specialized services but also of kindnesses and civilities. In the ideal exchange, Saroyan feels, the partners know what they need and like and feel in their bones that they are getting what they need from each other. Workers in the Saroyan economy perceive themselves as doing favors for one another and are constantly grateful not only for the gratifications others produce for them but also for the chances others give them to experience the sensuous joy of using the special, productive skills they have learned and refined. In Saroyan the social, the economic, the hedonistic, and the aesthetic, ideally, are one. This ideal unity is approached by the mutual regard which Saroyan finds in humble people such as the Armenians of Fresno, and he thinks it would be attained if established Western culture had not lost track of real, material value and invented the unattainable value of "greatness."

As the curtain is raised in *My Heart's in the Highlands,* the effects of the modern-art system's "advertising" for artificial value distinctions are instantly seen and heard. Johnny, a nine-year-old boy not yet contaminated by aspirations to culture as defined by established critics, is seen on the porch of the broken-down white house. He is "eagerly . . . trying to understand the meaning of . . . everything"—of a mournful train whistle, of "a small overjoyed but angry bird," and of "A fourteen-year-old boy on a bicycle, eating an icecream cone and carrying newspaper bags, [who] goes by . . . oblivious of the weight on his shoulders and of the contraption on which he is seated, because of the delight and glory of ice cream in the world." Meanwhile, inside the house, self-insulated from all the valuable sounds, sights, sensations, and tastes being soaked up outside by Johnny, his father, a poet, is heard struggling after the right alliteration in which to complain of "the long silent day" as it seems to his "sore solemn . . . lone lorn heart." Somehow he has lost track of sources of value obvious to the hedonistic young outside.

An old man named Jasper MacGregor enters, playing on a bugle "the loveliest and most amazing music in the world . . . 'My Heart's in the Highlands.'" Like Johnny's father, MacGregor wants to be a serious artist. He introduces himself as an actor who has done Shakespeare on the London stage, but Johnny's father alone honors MacGregor's impulse to pass for a serious artist. To Johnny and the neighbors, MacGregor is a folk musician whose bugle can increase the sensuous quality of life on San Benito Avenue, and it is not in exchange for Shakespearean gloom and bombast but for bugling to make them "weep, kneel, [and] sing the chorus" that Johnny and the neighbors are willing to honor MacGregor and bring him food.

For eighteen days MacGregor is happy to remain on San Benito Avenue as a working artist who makes survival enjoyable for other workers who make survival possible. But then he falls victim to his old ambition to succeed in the grimmer arts canonized not by hedonistic children and workers but by owners of money and power: the arts which replicate the miseries of real life and treat them as inevitable. The offer of a chance to play Lear—even in the annual show at the old people's home from which he has escaped—lures MacGregor back to its confines, and with him goes the musical competence he has been able to barter for enough of the neighbors'

food to keep him, and to keep the poet's family, in exchange for shelter in the poet's house.

Johnny begins to resent that he has again been reduced to begging food from the neighborhood grocer by a grown-up's addiction to serious art, expressive of personal pain, but his father remains hopeful. Concluding from MacGregor's success as a bugler that "The people love poetry but don't know it, that's all," Johnny's father writes new poems. But it is not to the people he goes with his new poems. Like MacGregor, Johnny's father still craves recognition from the cultural establishment, not from the friendly and supportive workers he knows on San Benito Avenue but from the distant editors of the *Atlantic Monthly* who "don't buy poetry, [but] scare you to death."

Only after the *Atlantic Monthly* rejects his new poems does the poet come to understand whom he is writing for and what his poems are really worth. He knows at last that the value of his poetry does not depend on its usefulness to an establishment of critics in the business of teaching people to yearn for experiences of value that the senses cannot feel. Accordingly, the poet takes his new poems to Mr. Kosak, the grocer from whom Johnny has been begging. He offers Mr. Kosak the poems not to cancel his debt for the groceries but to recognize the grocer's kindness. "Don't you see," he tells Mr. Kosak, "poetry must be read to be poetry." He goes on: "It may be that one reader is all that I deserve. If this is so, I want that reader to be you." Whereupon Mr. Kosak humbly accepts the poems. When he reads them, he and his little daughter are profoundly moved by a passage in which the poet acknowledges that his new writing is offered as his part in an exchange of kind remembrances by which people must sustain themselves amid the pain of living by artificial, socially imposed values, and in the face of death.

Thus does Saroyan's poet learn the real value of art, which (like all real values in Saroyan) is simply and immediately obvious to the uninstructed senses of a child and does not need to be "advertised" by an establishment of critics. With this, and all establishments, the poet makes no further attempt at accommodation. Behind with his rent, he agrees to move on, leaving the meager things with which he has furnished the broken-down house so that the next tenants, a poor young couple with a new baby, may use them. There is no work for anyone, and Mr. Kosak, after feeding the unemployed of San Benito Avenue on credit, is reduced to feeding his own family out of the dwindling stock of his grocery store. Johnny is now supporting the poet's household by bringing home fruit from the farms

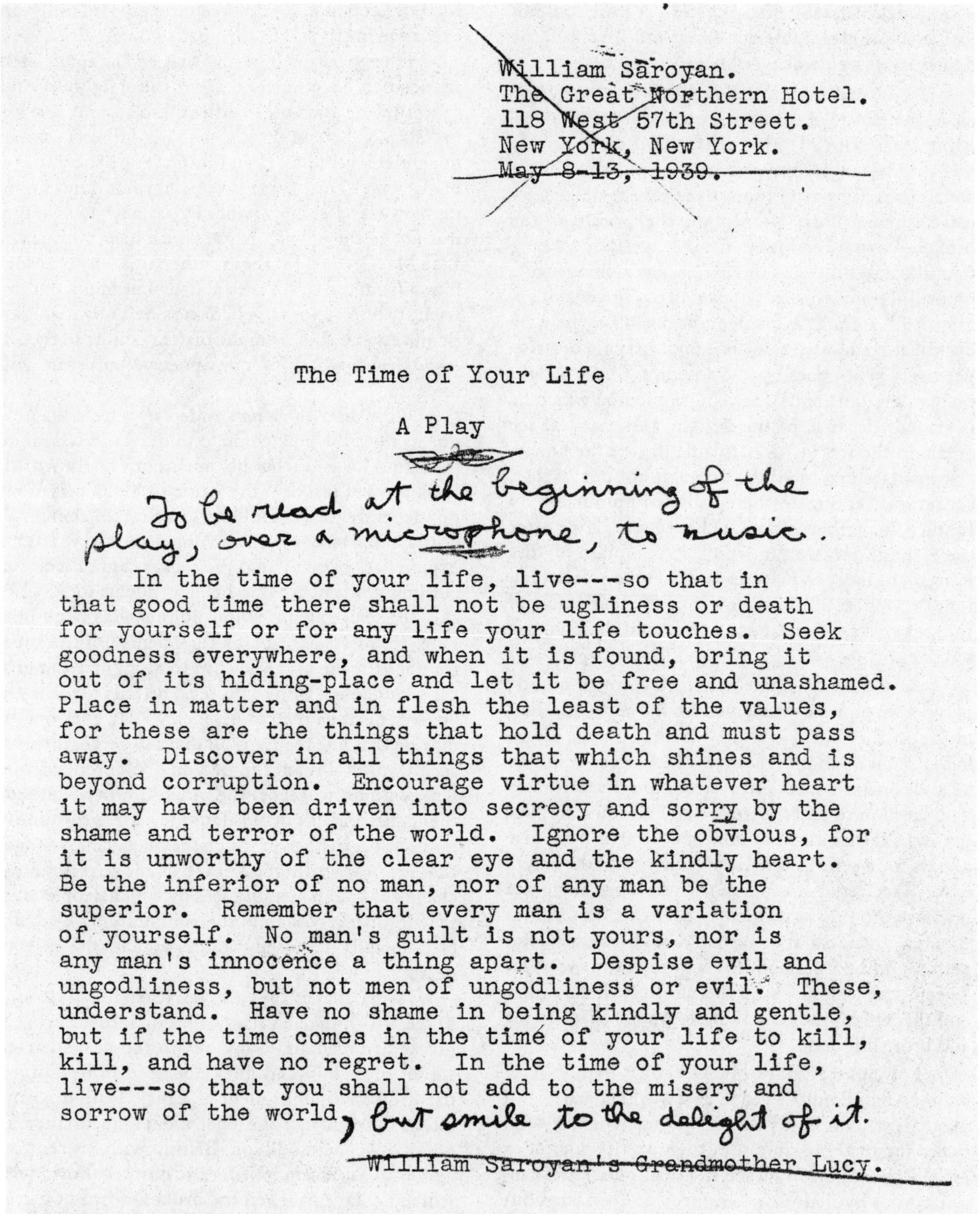

William Saroyan.
The Great Northern Hotel.
118 West 57th Street.
New York, New York.
May 8-13, 1939.

The Time of Your Life

A Play

To be read at the beginning of the play, over a microphone, to music.

In the time of your life, live---so that in
that good time there shall not be ugliness or death
for yourself or for any life your life touches. Seek
goodness everywhere, and when it is found, bring it
out of its hiding-place and let it be free and unashamed.
Place in matter and in flesh the least of the values,
for these are the things that hold death and must pass
away. Discover in all things that which shines and is
beyond corruption. Encourage virtue in whatever heart
it may have been driven into secrecy and sorry by the
shame and terror of the world. Ignore the obvious, for
it is unworthy of the clear eye and the kindly heart.
Be the inferior of no man, nor of any man be the
superior. Remember that every man is a variation
of yourself. No man's guilt is not yours, nor is
any man's innocence a thing apart. Despise evil and
ungodliness, but not men of ungodliness or evil. These,
understand. Have no shame in being kindly and gentle,
but if the time comes in the time of your life to kill,
kill, and have no regret. In the time of your life,
live---so that you shall not add to the misery and
sorrow of the world, *but smile to the delight of it.*

William Saroyan's Grandmother Lucy.

First page of the author's corrected typescript for Saroyan's second major play, with the introduction that Saroyan cut from the acting version of the play but restored to the published version (reproduced by permission of the Stanford University Libraries)

around Fresno. It is not stealing, the poet assures him, because "stealing is where there's unnecessary damage or cruelty to an innocent one, so that there may be undeserved profit or power to one who is not innocent." The implication is that most existing property arrangements, though legally sanctioned, are in reality no more than theft.

It is Johnny, as the family's provider, however, who (as always) is not permitted the self-indulgence of absolute high-mindedness. His father's notion of what is and is not stealing does not keep Johnny from fleeing home in guilt and terror and barricading his family in when he imagines that a fruit farmer and his dog are after him. And his troubles are not over when the man outside turns out not to be an angry farmer, but MacGregor, escaped again. The old man has been betrayed. At the old people's home, they tried to take away his bugle, and he has escaped to play a last, faltering solo and to die among his friends on San Benito Avenue.

While MacGregor plays, little Esther Kosak further involves Johnny in the problem of whether or not vulnerable innocence is, in fact, decent. In recognition of the poems her father has read to her, Esther gives Johnny money—her entire savings for Christmas—the cruel world's loathsome medium of exchange that inhibits the circulation of real empathy and real competence among people who know they need one another. Torn between the purity of Esther's purpose and the foulness of her coins, Johnny throws them against the wall, sobbing "Who the hell wants that stuff?"

In the end, however, Johnny himself wants Esther's money. Saroyan never makes the boy explain why he changes his mind about the coins he has flung away, but after a certain point in MacGregor's strange dying speech (which has verbal echoes of Lear's death speech), Johnny begins moving about the stage, picking Esther's coins up and looking at them closely, as if seeing them in a different, more favorable light. It is a gesture of accommodation with things as they are, and Saroyan leaves it to his audience to see that Johnny makes this gesture as a result of something MacGregor communicates to the boy.

It is as if Johnny, at first moved to empathy with MacGregor's failed aspirations, is suddenly warned off by the old man himself. The play therefore ends with Johnny's recognition that the poet's principled refusal to enter the economy and work for money, though validated as artistic integrity by the post-Romantic art system, is, in its way, an act of aggression in which the artist (though on a smaller scale) is as much of a parasite upon the worker as is the capitalist whom the self-expressive artist claims

to oppose. "I'm not mentioning any names, Pa," the boy says, accusingly, as the final curtain comes down, "but something's wrong somewhere."

Saroyan was unhappy with the set design for *My Heart's in the Highlands* and other aspects of the way the play was staged, but the play met with favorable reviews. The play had a modest run of forty-four performances, rather than the originally projected five; and when the Drama Critics Circle voted on the best New York play of the season of 1938–1939, John Mason Brown and George Jean Nathan voted for *My Heart's in the Highlands.*

According to Saroyan, these votes secured him an invitation to the annual dinner of the Drama Critics Circle, at the Algonquin, where he found himself across the table from the actor/impresario Eddie Dowling, who offered to buy, "sight unseen," any new Saroyan play. Within a week, Saroyan says, he had finished the draft of something he called "The Light Fantastic." With a changed title, it was to become the best known and most acted of Saroyan's plays, *The Time of Your Life* (1939). The playwright recalls its having been read and mentioned in *Newsweek* by George Jean Nathan, who suggested the title "Sunset Sonata," and he gratefully acknowledges that, true to his word, "Dowling drew up a contract with me and advanced me an enormous sum of money" for the new script at a time when he was "simply broke."

As with *My Heart's in the Highlands,* there were profound differences between the playwright and his company over the mounting of the new play. In recalling the production in "Opening Nights I Have Known" (1957), Saroyan acknowledges that the play went through four or five revisions after the speedy first draft. Moreover, there were other changes. A line and some stage business were suggested by actor William Bendix, who played Krupp, and when Saroyan's cousin Ross Bagdasarian came up from Fresno to San Francisco asking him to write a part into *The Time of Your Life* for him, the playwright obliged, sending young Bagdasarian along "to New York with the part and a letter." His cousin wired Saroyan "at the last minute that I had better have a look at the play right away because . . . it didn't look right." Saroyan reports that in New Haven, after one or two performances, he "took over the directing of the play," having learned, absolutely, that "a play is achieved or miscarried on the boards by its director." Less than three weeks later, on 25 October 1939, the play opened at the Booth Theatre in New York.

The published text of *The Time of Your Life,* in *Three Plays* (1940), begins with an explicit statement of the play's "moral," as if Saroyan were specifically guarding against the misinterpretation and mystification under which Broadway's thespians and critics had hidden *My Heart's in the Highlands* in interpreting it. Saroyan planned for this moral to be read over a loudspeaker before the curtain, but the plan was abandoned, and the moral survives only in print. It remains a touchstone for Saroyan's interpreters. It begins, "In the time of your life, live, so that in that good time there shall be no ugliness or death for yourself or for any life your life touches." To do this, Saroyan goes on to explain, one must "Be the inferior of no man, nor of any man . . . the superior." Moreover, one must put aside the conventional forms of materialism and fleshliness, from which "the obvious" in social life (its cruelty and inequality) results, and one must bring out the kindliness and gentleness of which man is also, obviously, capable, but which "have been driven into secrecy and sorrow by the shame and terror of the world." But even though one must encourage virtue during the only time in which one's moribund body has life, one may well be forced to kill, without regret, to resist the spread of "the obvious" against people too spontaneously kind to defend themselves against it. In 1976, in an interview (published in 1977 in the journal *Soviet Literature*), Saroyan was still essentially paraphrasing sentences from this statement when asked if he had "any kind of motto."

The plotting of *The Time of Your Life* is in keeping with the didactic impulse of this moral. At crucial junctures in *My Heart's in the Highlands,* such as MacGregor's death, Saroyan had trusted his audience to piece together the characters' motives and his judgments of their motives from actions which the characters themselves never explain. But in *The Time of Your Life* the playwright makes his characters state their motives or discuss the motives of others, thus providing *The Time of Your Life* with more verbal guides to interpretation than Saroyan had included in his first play.

The Time of Your Life is set in "Nick's . . . an American place: a San Francisco waterfront honkytonk." Despite his gruffness, Nick has a heart and an eye for artistic talent. He has hired Harry (first played by Gene Kelly), a dancing comic, and Wesley (played by Reginald Beane), a black piano player who has staggered in, fainting from hunger, in hopes only of a meal and a job as a cleaner. Among the other characters who staff or patronize Nick's bar is the expensively dressed, thoughtful, but "bored" figure of Joe. Like his presence in such a place, Joe's conduct is anomalous enough to demand explanation. He buys out a newsboy's remaining papers, but hardly reads them. He dictatorially sends the innocent, boyish Tom on "crazy" errands, but is acknowledged as a benefactor whose charity once saved Tom's life. He seems not to work, yet he is visibly well-off. When Kitty Duval, a prostitute with whom Tom is in love, enters, Joe alone treats her with respect. Still, when Kitty puts aside her initial defensiveness and asks Joe to dance, he refuses, almost in a panic. When Tom returns, Joe gives him five dollars and tells him to dance with Kitty.

At the beginning of the second act, however, Joe's contradictory toughness and fear of potential intimacies receives an explanation. Joe explains that for three years, he has "been trying . . . to find out if it's possible to live . . . a civilized life . . . a life that can't hurt any other life." Later, in act 5, Joe makes it clear that his strange charities are by way of atonement. He has been maimed by conventional success: "I earned the money I throw away, "he says. "I stole it like everybody else does. I hurt people to get it . . . I've got a Christian conscience in a world that's got no conscience at all . . . I'll always have money, as long as this world stays the way it is. I don't work. I don't make anything . . . I drink. . . . Well, you can't enjoy living unless you work. . . . There isn't anything I can do that won't make me feel embarrassed. Because I can't do simple, good things. I haven't the patience. And I'm too smart." Though he has money and does not write, Joe's predicament is, once again, that of the poor poet in *My Heart's in the Highlands.* He has been spiritually ruined—left stranded, without a means of valuing himself—after "maturing" normally in a stratified society that proliferates false values and does not value real satisfactions: the individual's capabilities for work, for love, and for guiltless aggression to protect work and love from the incursion of the false.

Nick's is "a good, low-down, honky-tonk American place that lets people alone," a sort of idealized microcosm of the world. Into this setting intrudes the "head of the lousy Vice Squad," Blick, who is "the sort of human being you dislike at sight . . . the strong man without strength . . . the weakling who uses force on the weaker." Blick bullies everyone, particularly Kitty, whom he tries to force to perform a strip-tease for him. When an old fraud named Kit Carson, who, throughout the play, has been exchanging tall tales about himself for drinks, comes to Kitty's defense, Blick beats him; when Wesley, the black piano player, also attempts to intervene, he too is beaten. Tom threatens to kill Blick, but Joe sends him and Kitty away, telling them to get married. Joe himself tries to kill Blick, who is offstage still beating Wesley, but his gun is not loaded. Soon after Blick is ejected by Nick, however, shots are heard outside. Nick runs out to investigate, and he

*Saroyan, in his U.S. Army Signal Corps uniform, and his wife, Carol Marcus,
in Dayton, Ohio, in 1943 at the time of their first marriage*

returns with the news that Blick is dead and the police are not bothering to investigate. Old Kit Carson
reenters just as Joe is leaving. The two "look at one
another knowingly." Carson, able to take himself seriously for the first time in his life, proudly takes
credit for Blick's death. His only regret is that he
"had to throw the beautiful revolver into the Bay."
Kit's new dignity apparently reassures Joe about the
worthiness of his own intent to kill Blick, and "with
great admiration and affection," Joe gives Kit the revolver that did not fire and leaves Nick's with a
hearty wave for all.

The play had an initial run of 185 performances, but it lost $25,000. Still, *The Time of Your Life*
was chosen best play of the 1939–1940 season by
the New York Drama Critics Circle, and, more important, in May of 1940 it also won a Pulitzer Prize,

which resulted in an immediate fall revival and an
eventual road tour.

The Pulitzer Prize carried not only great prestige but also an award of $1,000. Unlike the poet of
My Heart's in the Highlands, therefore, Saroyan, in
winning the Pulitzer, had been received at last in the
sanctum where canonizers scare poets to death and
admit plays to the status of "culture." In his two
Broadway successes, however, Saroyan had proclaimed his opposition to institutions that tell people
what to value beyond what they feel in life and in
art. Now, therefore, the sincerity of this opposition
was to be tested.

In a telegram to the Pulitzer judges at Columbia University, Saroyan rejected the prize. The playwright's wire reminds the board of his anticipatory
announcement that he would reject the prize if it

were offered him, and it explains that "I do not believe in prizes or awards in the realm of art, and have always been particularly opposed to material or official patronage of the arts by government, organization, or individual, a naive and innocent style of behavior which, nevertheless, I believe, vitiates and embarrasses art at its source." *My Heart's in the Highlands* had been concerned with the problem of eliminating canonizing middlemen from the "source" of art in direct dealings between artists and hedonistic perceivers who are not taught by prize committees what to feel and say about the work of artists. *The Time of Your Life* had, likewise, been specifically committed to encouraging people not to be ashamed of their impulses to value what immediately feels good and humane.

Hence, Saroyan's rejection of the Pulitzer Prize for his play was quite consistent with his notions about the political economy of art. For him, art was not to be one of the means of legitimizing "the obvious," but was rather to be one of the chief nonviolent antidotes to power and restorers of the damage done by critics and policers who do not respect what even children know in their bones that they need.

For a time it appeared as if Saroyan might hold his own in his rebellion against the official art system and have his way on the New York stage. But things eventually went against him, and in *Places Where I've Done Time,* a memoir published in 1972, he reports that "I used to like the theatre, . . . but [it] also has become something neither enjoyed nor needed." Nevertheless, five consecutive Broadway seasons, from 1939 until 1943, included productions of Saroyan's plays; and during these years, until he was inducted into the army in October of 1942, he himself produced his plays on the New York stage, as he had wished from the start.

In January 1940 his ballet, *A Theme in the Life of the Great American Goof,* opened, and in May of that year *Love's Old Sweet Song* began a run of forty-four performances at the Plymouth Theatre, produced, like *The Time of Your Life,* by Eddie Dowling and the Theatre Guild and (also like *The Time of Your Life*) much revised and largely directed by Saroyan himself while it was being prepared for Broadway. *Love's Old Sweet Song* carries on the themes and character types with which *My Heart's in the Highlands* and *The Time of Your Life* had been concerned. In revenge for a prank, a telegraph messenger and his brother forge a telegram to be delivered by their colleague, the unwitting prankster, to an attractive, middle-aged spinster named Ann Hamilton. The forged wire announces the return of one Barnaby Gaul, who claims to have briefly met Miss Hamilton

twenty-seven years before while whistling "Love's Old Sweet Song" in front of her house. In the wire this Barnaby Gaul also claims to have been nurturing his love for Miss Hamilton ever since. No such encounter had ever really occurred, but no sooner has Miss Hamilton's imagination been quickened by the forged telegram than a stranger arrives whose appearance roughly matches the wire's description of the fictitious Barnaby Gaul. The stranger is confused when the telegraph messenger and Miss Hamilton keep prompting him to remember her, but when the boy lets him read the wire he is supposed to have sent, the stranger instantly decides to take on Barnaby Gaul's identity and become the long-lost, unknown admirer Miss Hamilton obviously hopes he is.

In actuality Gaul (originally played by Walter Huston) is a traveling swindler–a medicine salesman, somewhat reminiscent of MacGregor in *My Heart's in the Highlands* or of Joe or Kit Carson in *The Time of Your Life*. He, too, has given himself over to living out hopeful lies, since the truth–"the obvious," as Saroyan had called it in the moral to *The Time of Your Life*–is such an insane, inhumane, body-violating guide to living. As Gaul tells Windmore, a subscription salesman for *Time* magazine and (hence) a purveyor of "the obvious": "I have studied the reasons for things: for disgrace, for wretchedness, for disease, for stupor. No man in the world knows better than I why these tragic things occur in that most miraculous and magnificent creation of the hand of God: the noble body which is man. You bring news of world-wide madness and horror to the living every Friday. You make of universal crime a topic for idle reading. You tell the people of foolishness everywhere, every week. That's fine. I bring hope to the people. I have here in these bottles a medicine. . . ." The problem faced by the messenger boy, Georgie Americanos, and his Greek immigrant family, is to keep the mountebank from backing out of his first really responsible act and abandoning the kindly impulse that had led him to bring real hope to Ann Hamilton by assuming the fictitious identity of Barnaby Gaul. It is again the problem of encouraging virtue not to be ashamed of itself, which is spelled out in the moral of *The Time of Your Life*. Some of the encouragement is supplied by Georgie's father, Stylianos Americanos, a wrestler and "World's Heavyweight Champion [of] Kern County," but in the end Gaul himself recognizes that his love for Ann Hamilton has been real–not just another swindle. He stops being afraid of his impulse to love her, and he proposes that Miss Hamilton join him in his travels.

A year after his debut as a playwright, Saroyan produced his finest collection of stories, *My Name Is Aram,* published 26 December 1940. It was as though he advanced his art by going back, for all the stories are set in the San Joaquin Valley where he grew up and told through the sensibility of a boy, Aram.

Some of the interrelated stories in *My Name Is Aram* feature the now familiar optimism bordering on sentimentality and nostalgia, while others retain the hard irreconcilability between the characters' illusions of life and the flat truth of the events that they confront. Of the former type are stories such as the first story in the collection, "The Summer of the Beautiful White Horse." On a summer morning just before daybreak his cousin Mourad taps on Aram's bedroom window. He is sitting on a beautiful white horse he has taken from a neighbor's barn. In the early dawn, while the world sleeps, the two boys ride the horse over streets and fields. As the world awakens, they hide the horse in an abandoned barn. Two weeks later the horse's owner encounters the boys on his horse. He studies the animal, knowing all the while that it is his, and says that it looks considerably like his own horse, yet he says it could not be because "the fame of your family for honesty is well known to me." Early the next morning the boys return the horse to its owner's barn: "My cousin Mourad put his arms around the horse, pressed his nose into the horse's nose, patted it, and then he went away." As in the other stories, innocence, freedom, and wishfulness are posed against the world of sense and practicality. Saroyan, however, does not focus on the implications of such a conflict or on Aram's growth in the face of it. The value of these stories lies in their tragicomic lyricism, in the wonder of the moment they evoke.

"The Three Swimmers and the Grocer from Yale" (1939) is representative of the stories of disillusionment in *My Name Is Aram.* These pieces, though sometimes not as vivid in their imagery, find a surer balance between the darker side of life and the glow of nostalgia. In "The Three Swimmers" Aram and his friends try to swim in a local ditch but end up waist deep in mud with rain pelting them. This slight, childish letdown finds a more serious parallel in the mind of a grocer who runs a store where the boys go for refuge. The grocer's fantasies interfere with the practicality required for being a successful businessman, so when the boys return to the store later, they find he has transformed himself into a dull clerk. The mud and rain find a more serious embodiment in a life of tedious necessity.

My Name Is Aram was well received. Some critics saw it as Saroyan's most accomplished collection of short fiction because of the sure themes and apparent ease yet conciseness with which the stories were crafted. However, this work can also be seen as a further compromise of the cold, hard insights promised behind the posturing and braggadocio of *The Daring Young Man on the Flying Trapeze. My Name Is Aram* comes close to realizing in more concrete, less personal, terms the unflinching stance between being and nonbeing that the first collection proposes, yet the warm nostalgia that makes it more generally palatable also causes it to retreat from the thematic standards of its predecessor.

While still writing short stories, Saroyan continued to focus most of his energies on the theater. Howard R. Floan reports that "For his next play, *The Beautiful People,* [Saroyan] took over the casting and directing himself and financed the play with money coming in from a successful road tour of *The Time of Your Life* and from wide sales of *My Name is Aram* in the stores and through the Book-of-the-Month Club." Saroyan himself reports that he put $11,000 into *The Beautiful People,* which opened at the Lyceum Theatre on 21 April 1941.

In *The Beautiful People* Saroyan again expresses his concerns for encouraging people to negate "the obvious" and to create a working economy in which people exchange real values—not only currency, advertised goods, and grimly contracted services but also civility, recognition of decent impulses, and love. Jonah Webster and his two youngest children, Agnes (seventeen years old) and Owen (fifteen years old), are living in an old house in San Francisco on a twenty-four-dollar pension check that keeps arriving in the mail every month for one Wilbur M. Stonehedge, now deceased. Jonah's oldest child, Harold, has gone to New York to become a musician. The old house in San Francisco is full of mice, for which Owen keeps setting traps; but Agnes, pitying the mice, keeps finding and burning the traps. She is "Saint Agnes of the Mice," Owen explains to a lady who has come looking for Jonah, and the mice keep praying for her and bringing her offerings—sometimes even spelling out her name, in flowers, across the floor. This "fairy-tale," as the lady calls it, turns out, however, to have a plausible, material explanation. Owen himself has been murmuring the mice's prayers and bringing the floral offerings, as Jonah explains to Father Hogan after Owen has fallen into the pipe organ at church while seeking to recognize and substantiate his sister's saintly fantasy by bringing home a mouse that she says has taken sanctuary there. "Father Hogan, if I do not encourage the imaginations of my children, I also do not hinder them. . . . It's not enough to make a record of the world—it's necessary to change it!

Saroyan on far left in Paris in 1945. His cousin Ross Bagdasarian, who acted in Saroyan's The Time of Your Life *(1957) and with whom he wrote the hit song "Come On-a My House" (1951) is the second from the right (Collection of Aram Saroyan).*

And you cannot begin to change it from the outside. The image of the good must first be real to the mind before it can inhabit substance and occupy space. . . . And my delight is my children. We are exactly the same as all other people, but I know we live better than the rich and better than the poor, because the values which make rich and poor are without image or reality, and the real values are the only values we recognize and cherish. . . ." Secretly, however, Jonah has been worrying that New York may have destroyed the goodness of his older son, Harold, whose cornet music the family often fancies can be heard across the continent. "I've lost faith," Jonah confesses to Father Hogan, "because I believed goodness was a coin for exchange more powerful than any coin minted by any government–the only coin. . . . My children must not know that what I have taught them may be useless in this world." But the end of *The Beautiful People* suggests that Jonah's teachings are holding their own. Prim, the vice president who has been sent to inform the Websters that the Stonehedge pension check will no longer be coming, has found a welcome with them anyway, and is moved to continue the checks with an additional ten dollars a month. And Harold returns, playing his cornet, and bringing with him a young man in need of a home. With this "miracle," the curtain falls.

With full control of the production, the playwright was able to confound Broadway by acting upon notions of the proper relationship between artist and spectator already suggested by his plays. With opening night less than one week away, Saroyan offered the public free tickets to dress rehearsals of *The Beautiful People.* On 15 April 1941 a large crowd consisting mostly of students, housewives, and aspiring thespians, quickly grabbed up the 850 tickets Saroyan had to offer. *The New York Times* reported that a thousand people were turned away and that many of the free tickets distributed were swapped, scalped, and gambled for, in an appropriately Saroyanesque manner, on the sidewalk outside the Lyceum Theatre. "Perfecting a play without an audience is like trying to improve an orchestra without musicians," Saroyan explained. *The Beautiful People* "in its present state is still an unfinished product and therefore not for sale."

Then, after the play had run for a little more than two months, on 2 July, Saroyan and his press agent, Leo Freedman, advertised that anyone who disliked *The Beautiful People* could have his money back, "just present the stub of your ticket to the boys in the box office and go home with every cent of your money—and no hard feelings." According to *The New York Times,* the offer remained in effect for two weeks, during which the Lyceum staff made bets on which spectators would ask for refunds and satisfied theatregoers sometimes rebuked those in line waiting to get back their money. In withdrawing the offer, Saroyan claimed that it had been unnecessary. He thanked the public for the overwhelming confidence in his work, which it had revealed by the fact that during the fortnight of the offer less than 2 percent of the receipts were refunded. Saroyan closed the play on 2 August, after a run of 120 performances, which Floan says "took it out of the red and encouraged Saroyan to consider further productions." In 1957 Saroyan reported that "I could have closed with my own money doubled, but I kept it going until the $11,000 had been used up."

Next, on Broadway, as the first of what he hoped would be a series of his productions of his plays, under the rubric of "The Saroyan Theatre," Saroyan produced and directed his two one-act plays, *Across the Board on Tomorrow Morning,* and *Talking to You* (both in 1942). *Across the Board on Tomorrow Morning* had had two prior productions, the first (in February 1941) at the Pasadena Playhouse in California, and the second in New York (in March 1942) at the Theatre Showcase. The Pasadena production, according to Floan, though not directed by Saroyan, still showed the playwright's interest in changing the norms under which audiences see plays. Saroyan specified that *Across the Board on Tomorrow Morning* was to be given twice in succession each evening so that spectators who wished to see it again might do so. For the Saroyan Theatre's production of *Across the Board on Tomorrow Morning,* the playwright again felt free, as he had done in casting *The Time of Your Life* and *The Beautiful People,* not to rely exclusively on professional actors. The cast included, as George Jean Nathan reported, "a hatcheck girl [from] the Stork Club, . . . a broke poet [from] Greenwich Village, and a couple of Filipinos [from] the Automat" who, by all accounts, stole the show. As Pablo and Pancho, two dishwashers in Callaghan's restaurant and bar, they emerge (like irate sociologists) from the kitchen to lecture Pinkerton, a Wall Street type who will not deign to speak with some of his fellow patrons, about his total ignorance of the plight of Filipino boys in America.

The playwright later recalled the fate of the Saroyan Theatre with some bitterness. In *Places Where I've Done Time,* he writes of closing his deal with Lee Schubert for the use of the Belasco Theatre. The memoir contrasts Schubert's sententious piety about the place as a shrine of the American theater with Saroyan's sense of it as "dusty, haunted by [the spirit of Belasco,] a fraud who never suspected so much, and by his banal ideas and his . . . insatiable capacity for enjoying the favors of . . . women [desperate to go on the stage]." Saroyan quotes Schubert as telling him "Any way that I can help, I am at your service. . . . Don't worry about business matters." Thus assured, Saroyan opened *Across the Board on Tomorrow Morning* and *Talking to You* on 17 August 1942.

As they had been over his direction of *The Beautiful People,* drama critics were divided over the playwright's work in mounting the two one-acts of the Saroyan Theatre. Stark Young, in the *New Republic,* had sensed a validity in Saroyan's refusal to allow Broadway to deck *The Beautiful People* in "wheezy old loads of stagecraft," snapping it up, stereotyping it, clipping and narrowing it. Young also saw "a certain elusive but fine [lyric] weaving and pressure of rhythms" that he did not think the established likes of Eddie Dowling could have brought "from the heart of" *Talking to You.* But the usually patronizing tone in which Brooks Atkinson wrote about Saroyan took on bluntness in treating his direction of the Saroyan Theatre. "Although Mr. Saroyan is an affable chap with an attractive slant on people, his [static and literal-minded] stage directions is like the compounding of a felony." Atkinson wrote. "He needs a professional director." According to Floan, Atkinson "echoed the judgment of many."

In 1972 Saroyan recalled that despite Lee Schubert's initial assurances, after eight performances Schubert gave notice that the Saroyan Theatre was to vacate the Belasco "by the end of the week when the terms of the written agreement were technically faulted" because box office receipts dropped below a certain weekly minimum. The failure of *Across the Board on Tomorrow Morning* and *Talking to You* marked the beginning of the end for Saroyan on Broadway.

Nevertheless, before 1942 was over, yet another Saroyan one-act play that had premiered a year earlier in California came to the New York stage. It was *Hello Out There,* a script for two performers, in which the roles were taken, on Broadway, by Eddie Dowling (who also directed) and Julie Haydon—the Joe and Kitty Duval of the first production of *The Time of Your Life. Hello Out There* opened on 29 September 1942 at the Belasco, as the curtain raiser for a revival of G. K. Chesterton's *Magic,* but the critics felt that Saroyan's piece was clearly the highlight of the evening. As Atkinson saw it, "Some professionals have taken hold of a short play by Saroyan and the results are stunning." It is possible, however, that New York critics were stunned by *Hello Out There* because it was the most conventional Saroyan script yet acted there.

The play is realistic, set in the jailhouse of a small town called Matador, Texas, where a young drifter, brought there, unconscious, for his own protection after having been accused of rape and beaten up in a nearby town, is tapping on the floor, as if in Morse code, with a spoon. "Hello—out there!" he begins calling; and after a while, he is answered by "A girl's voice, very sweet and soft." For fifty cents a day, it develops, she cleans the Matador jail and cooks for whatever inmates it may happen to have. Her father has eked out a living by stealing from her and by feigning a disability so as to collect "a little relief from the government." The townspeople have always laughed at her, but in his restless sleep while she was caring for him in the jailhouse, the prisoner said he liked her, and she hopes that this first evidence that someone might have feeling for her will continue after he begins recovering from his beating. From the moment he hears her voice, even before the sad facts of the girl's life are known, the prisoner recognizes a soul mate in the girl—someone "as lonesome as a coyote," as he is, himself. And through the bars of his cell, to which she cannot find the key, they exchange love and recognition, just as the poet of *My Heart's in the Highlands* had done in bringing his poems to Mr. Kosak in recognition of the grocer's kindness. Again, Saroyan is concerned with dramatizing people's basic capacity to exchange moral support, even in the face of "the obvious."

But "the obvious" has its way with the lovers of *Hello Out There.* The girl goes out for cigarettes, and while she is gone, the husband of the woman the prisoner is accused of having raped arrives at the head of a lynch mob, which waits outside while he enters the jail to confront his wife's alleged rapist alone. The desperate prisoner tells the husband that he "met her [the man's wife] at a lunch counter." The prisoner tells the husband that his wife seemed lonesome and that he spoke to her in simple recognition of her apparent loneliness. He admits that he walked the woman home and that he would have taken her to bed had she not then asked him for money and revealed to him that he had picked up not a kindred sufferer in need of comfort, but a prostitute out to profit from his own apparent suffering. The prisoner challenges the husband to call his wife in and confront her with these facts; but the husband draws a gun, shoots the caged prisoner three times and flees from the jail as his victim "falls to his knees," calling again, "Hello—out there!"

The girl comes running back, and hears the prisoner tell her "I'll be with you always—God damn it. Always!" as he dies. The husband reappears with two friends, one of whom unlocks the cell, and a woman, the alleged victim of the prisoner's rape, enters. She satisfies herself that the prisoner is, in fact, dead as "Her husband looks at her with contempt." When the husband and one of the other men begin to carry the body off, the girl, "suddenly, fiercely" tries to interfere, but the alleged rape victim "slaps the girl and pushes her to the floor," hissing "Listen to the little slut, will you?" The mob leaves with the body, and the curtain falls as the girl "looks straight out [at the audience], and whispers . . . Hello—out—there! Hello—out there!"—challenging the audience to support her resistance to "the obvious."

Floan follows the critical majority who look upon *Hello Out There* as Saroyan's "finest one-act play," remarking that it was written "with more unanswering singleness of purpose than Saroyan gave to any other play." But Saroyan has been his own best critic, and in 1955, in an essay entitled "Art for Man's Sake: A Minority View," published in the *Nation,* he repudiated *Hello Out There* as his own capitulation, in spite of himself, to the tradition that requires great art to replicate "the obvious." Writing that, "If [like Shakespeare] you're going to have murder and madness in art, then you're going to have them in life, too," Saroyan goes on to repent having "permitted" himself in *Hello Out There* "to write out of violent material, "confessing that "It was the easiest play I ever wrote,"and adding "I therefore consider the play worthless, if not in fact a mistake, the high opinion of others notwithstand-

Saroyan and his son, Aram, at a Los Angeles television studio in 1953 (Collection of Aram Saroyan)

ing." Saroyan said that "To report chaos and hate is not to put order into chaos or to banish hate," and he reaffirmed his constant position that "The potentials for order and love are inherent in human life and just as easy to achieve as their opposites—and certainly a lot more practical, if nothing else."

After acquiring a reputation as a short-story writer, and succeeding as a playwright, it was perhaps inevitable that Saroyan would turn to the novel. Since all the stories of *My Name Is Aram* have the same first-person narrator and take place in one general setting, they possess a greater unity than any of Saroyan's previous fiction, a unity that, in fact, resembles the novel. To look back on his youth was for Saroyan to strike the perfect balance between personal emotion and objectivity. He was writing about himself, but a self which was objectified by time. He used this strategy in his first novel, *The Human Comedy* (1943), the story of fourteen-year-old Homer Macauley of Ithaca, California, and the other members of his family: his four-year-old brother Ulysses; his older brother Marcus, who is overseas fighting in the U.S. Army; his widowed mother; and his teenaged sister Bess. Saroyan's choice of classical names for his characters suggests that he intends the meaning of the plot to extend beyond provincial life to the wider cultural context of

Western civilization. What happens to Homer and Ulysses is what happens to man and, it is implied, always will. The parochial life of *The Human Comedy* is meant to be microcosmic. Every scene possesses a gravity beyond its place in time. The reader senses the immortality of Homer's experiences: night-shift work in the telegraph office, delivering telegrams, philosophically pondering the nature of the world with Mr. Grogan, the alcoholic telegraph assistant, running the hurdles at high school, receiving news of the death of his brother Marcus. History is now, Saroyan is saying to the man from whom Homer takes his last name, the historian Thomas Babington Macaulay.

But Saroyan's theme of the universality and timelessness of human experiences is never developed. One scene follows another on a horizontal plane. Scenes do not grow out of one another. What happens to Homer in chapter 8 could just as well happen to him in chapter 4, and the death of Marcus at the end of the novel is mishandled. The family never internalizes it. Tobey George, Marcus's friend from the army, presents himself on the Macauley doorstep. He is welcomed into the family as a replacement for Marcus, and it is assumed he will marry Bess. Tobey assures the family that Marcus is not dead because he lives on in those who knew him. He says Marcus can never die. This smiling ending anesthetizes the reality of death–for the family and for the reader.

Saroyan's short-story collection *Dear Baby* (1944), though not as widely praised as *My Name Is Aram,* is perhaps as close as Saroyan's short fiction ever comes to the thematic standards proposed in *The Daring Young Man on the Flying Trapeze.* In these stories Saroyan combines the craftsmanship he learned over the years with the bright, original insights that emerged in his first collection. Much of the nostalgia has been stripped away from works more totally fabricated, yet perhaps more true to themselves, than the semi-autobiographical pieces which precede and follow *Dear Baby;* however, it does not completely measure up to the promise of his first short-story collection, for as bluntly as it deals with life and death it still relies on a level of sentimentality that the voice in *The Daring Young Man on the Flying Trapeze* might find inexcusable.

In the title piece, "Dear Baby" (1939), a boxer, Joe, and his wife decide to have a baby despite the wife's poor health. Using time shifts, Saroyan weaves the tragic events of the woman's death during childbirth into the boxer's struggles in the ring. The tragedy of death, the craftsmanship behind the time shifts, and the understatement of events all combine to give the title a sharp irony, yet at the end of "Dear Baby" Saroyan falls into the overstatement and sentimentality typical of much of his work: "The Phonograph was playing, and the fighter was sitting on the bed with his head in his hands and he was crying. . . . 'Dear Baby,' the fighter kept saying over and over again."

In his play *Get Away Old Man* (1944) Saroyan continues the analysis of the political economy of art begun in *My Heart's in the Highlands.* But rather than presenting that analysis from the viewpoint of an obscure, unpublished poet, Saroyan now presents it as a dramatic exposé of a recently concluded chapter in his own literary and theatrical success– his involvement with Hollywood in writing the screenplay for *The Human Comedy,* for which he received an Academy Award. As Floan reports, "In December, 1941, Saroyan moved into an office at Metro-Goldwyn-Mayer in Hollywood with the understanding that he would write 'a thoroughly American movie.' To the surprise of those who did not know him well, he declined to discuss contracts or salary until his scenario was ready."

Floan reports that when in February of 1942 Saroyan finished *The Human Comedy,* M-G-M paid him $60,000, "But at this point difficulties arose, for Saroyan had set his heart on directing the picture and the studio objected. . . . he tried to buy back the

script for eighty thousand dollars; but MGM refused. He gave vent to his anger and disappointment in an explosive article which appeared in *The Daily Variety,* a Hollywood trade paper: 'Why I am No Longer at Metro-Goldwyn-Mayer, or the California Shore-Bird in Its Native Habitat, or Brahms Double Concerto in A Minor.'" Apparently, he also retreated to San Francisco and, in no more than the six days in which he had completed the first draft of *The Time of Your Life,* he wrote *Get Away Old Man.*

The play dramatizes the conflict between a Hollywood producer named Patrick Hammer (played by Edward Begley) and a writer named Harry Bird (played by Richard Widmark). Hammer has made his way in the world by capitulating to "the obvious." He admits he is "a crook . . . But who isn't?," missing the constant Saroyan point that most people are not. For Hammer, "You can't survive in this world and live like a decent human being" without being "a crook." As a poor Dublin child, Hammer loved from afar a little rich girl, who spat at him when they finally met in the street. "I was murdered," Hammer complains, sentimentally, "as if they had put a knife in my heart." And he gloats of having had his revenge on the rich and powerful. "Their loveliest came to me . . . humiliated, seeking my favor, . . . their women hating me and pretending in their nakedness to love me." His mind a steady driveling of platitudes about the filmmaker's power and responsibility in the modern world, Hammer needs Harry Bird, who he says is like his son, to write the great film that will finally redeem the life Hammer has spent serving "the obvious." But Harry finds love and tells Hammer, "Get away, old man." The writer leaves with his girl, and the final curtain comes down as Hammer frantically telephones an aide to bring "the son of a bitch" back and arranges an assignation with the undiscovered actress he plans to introduce in Harry's unwritten motion picture.

In 1957 Saroyan recalled the premiere of *Get Away Old Man* as "the only opening night of any of my plays I have ever gone to." By the end of the second act, audience reactions had told him that the play was "a flop," and the experience convinced him that Broadway should see no more Saroyan unless it saw Saroyan as staged by its author. Explaining fourteen years of withdrawal from the Broadway stage, Saroyan writes that "From that year to this I have kept my plays away from Broadway, waiting for the time when I might produce them with my own money again. In May of this year [1957] I decided that I might never again be able to do that, and so I allowed another of my plays to appear on Broadway: 'The Cave Dwellers.'" *The Cave Dwellers*

(1957) was the last of Saroyan's plays to be produced on a Broadway stage during his lifetime.

Meanwhile, on 9 January 1943 Saroyan, who had been on active duty with the U.S. Army since 1942, was elected to the department of art and literature at the National Institute of Arts and Letters. He had reached the peak of his recognition as an American writer. On 24 February 1943, in Dayton, Ohio, where the thirty-four-year-old Saroyan was stationed with the U.S. Army Signal Corps, he married Carol Marcus, the eighteen-year-old daughter of a vice president of the Bendix Aviation Corporation. She was the former bridesmaid of Gloria Vanderbilt, and an actress who had made her Broadway debut in *Across the Board on Tomorrow Morning.*

Not every play Saroyan published during the 1940s was produced on Broadway. David Kherdian's *A Bibliography of William Saroyan 1934-1964* (1965) lists a total of twenty-four published plays, mostly one-acts, mostly unproduced on Broadway, from *The Man with the Heart in the Highlands,* in 1938, until *Get Away Old Man,* published in 1944. Three of these were broadcast as radio plays in 1940 and 1941.

Saroyan's Broadway years had not only been a period of serious literary and theatrical productivity. What Floan called "The Time of His Life"–the period of tremendous productivity in which Saroyan tried to mount a frontal assault on the content, forms, and institutions of the American stage–had also been a time for the good life: for world travel, for drinking, for wenching, and for gambling. He was a celebrity–"the fabulous Saroyan," Brooks Atkinson patronizingly called him–and he faced the temptations of celebrity. Rather than sheltering him from these temptations, his marriage (as he has several times written about it) drastically compounded them. The realization that he was in trouble seems to have begun setting in with a vengeance in 1947, the year in which he next published a play, *Jim Dandy, Fat Man in a Famine,* which had been acted in 1941. In the winter of 1947 the Saroyans, now including a son, Aram (born 25 September 1943), and a daughter, Lucy (born 17 January 1946), moved into a very fashionable rented house in Mill Neck, Long Island. "The arrangements of renting had been made," Saroyan writes in *Places Where I've Done Time,* "by the little woman's little mother . . . because [though exorbitantly expensive] it was perfect for the giving of parties." He adds, "I was broke and in debt, but . . . [Carol] and her little mother always believed–why, for that boy money is the easiest thing in the world to make, by the hundreds of thousands of dollars. . . . They were good at throwing around the titles of some of my

novels and plays in relation to various motion picture companies, producers, directors, actors, and actresses, but they spoke from ignorance. They had not read any of the plays or novels. . . ." Meanwhile, as Saroyan records in a *Saturday Evening Post* article titled "The Funny Business of Marriage," he became a roaring social lion, drinking too much, "going along at a good clip, writing 30 or 40 words a day like clockwork," and permitting himself to be endlessly talked at about "new books, new plays, new ideas, new liberalism, new ways to care about the poor people, the several minorities, the rejected, the despised [until] instead of writing 30 or 40 words a day I wrote only 15 or 20."

When the lease on the house in Mill Neck expired, the couple returned to San Francisco, where "the little bride" was miserable until, in 1948, they moved back again to New York. In April of 1949, the marriage broke up. Saroyan reports that he "wandered around [Europe] in a daze for three months," eventually going, via New York and San Francisco, "to Las Vegas, to establish residence in Nevada [for] the necessary six weeks in order to obtain a divorce." In Las Vegas, "drinking and gambling every day and all night," Saroyan lost $50,000–including a $36,000 advance from "a big publishing house [on] three books." During this troubled time, Saroyan had three more full-length plays published, all in 1949: *Don't Go Away Mad, Sam Ego's House,* and *A Decent Birth, A Happy Funeral.* Of these plays, Floan remarks that "they tend to repeat the weak points of his produced plays without adding any new dimensions." *Sam Ego's House,* produced in 1947, had opened in the round in Hollywood; and in 1949 an invited audience saw the Abbe Practical Workshop present *Don't Go Away Mad* Off Broadway at the Master Institute Theatre in New York.

Divorced in 1949, the Saroyans married a second time in 1951, but the union quickly ended once again in disaster. The playwright reached an emotional low point. "I was bankrupt," he writes, "in debt to the Tax Collector for about fifty thousand dollars, about half that much to others, most of them merchants" from whom his wife had purchased "stuff." At one point, he writes, he weighed his options: "Suicide was suicide, divorce was divorce. I flipped a coin." After his second divorce in 1952, Saroyan never remarried.

The Cave Dwellers, like *The Time of Your Life,* was written at the Great Northern Hotel in New York during a brief span of time (the first eight days of 1955), while Saroyan was in town for the City Center Theatre's revival of *The Time of Your Life.* On 19 October 1957, under the direction of Carmen

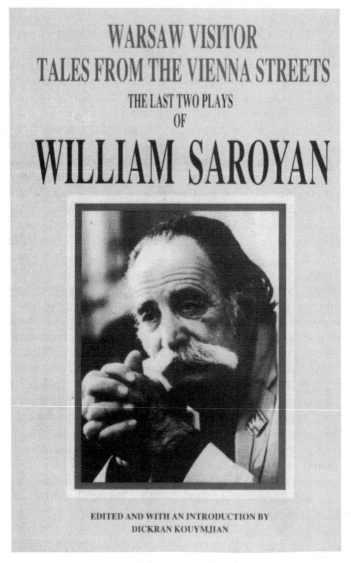

WARSAW VISITOR
TALES FROM THE VIENNA STREETS
THE LAST TWO PLAYS
OF
WILLIAM SAROYAN

EDITED AND WITH AN INTRODUCTION BY
DICKRAN KOUYMJIAN

*Cover for 1991 posthumous publication of two plays Saroyan wrote in
1979 and 1980*

Capalbo, *The Cave Dwellers* began a run of ninety-seven performances at the Bijou Theater, New York, with Wayne Morris, Susan Harrison, Eugenie Leontovich, and Barry Jones in the principal roles as the Duke, the Girl, the Queen, and the King, respectively.

Several of the play's critics have noted in *The Cave Dwellers* a new debt to the postwar theater of France, notably to Samuel Beckett's *Waiting for Godot* (1952). For Harold Clurman, in *The Nation,* "Its 'philosophy' might be called sugared existentialism": "We do not know why we are here, we cannot comprehend the universe we are in, we shall never understand the great pattern, if pattern there be, of life. No matter: there is goodness, there is love—even hate is love. We get up in the morning, go to bed at night, in between we play wondrously–and

that is enough." Briefly, *The Cave Dwellers* tells the story of various refugees from "the obvious" who take shelter in an abandoned theater, scheduled for demolition, and allegorically called "The World." The King is an old clown; the Queen is an old actress; the Duke is a former prizefighter; and they are joined at the beginning of the play by the Girl and later, by Gorky, a performing bear, and by the bear's trainer, his wife, and their newborn baby.

Outside, throughout the play, are heard the noises of demolition work going on in adjacent buildings. Each day the King goes forth to try to earn some sustenance for the cave dwellers by clowning in the street. One day the King returns, furious at having lost a shoe. He tells the Queen that he has tried to entertain the wrecking crew outside "after a whole day of failure." They have claimed that demolition gives them laughs enough, and when the King has offered to make them cry instead, they have bet him a coin from each of them against one of his shoes that he cannot bring one tear to even a single eye—and he has indeed failed. "What the devil's happened to the world? to the workers," the King asks. "Not one tear in one eye . . . they even offered me coins, but I refused them," he says. "You had no right to refuse coins," the Queen protests. "Did I have a right to fail?" he asks in response, and the scene ends with this important question unanswered. Clearly, the issues concerning the morality of art with which Saroyan had concerned himself at the close of *My Heart's in the Highlands,* when Johnny silently picks up the coins he has earlier flung against the wall, were once again very much on Saroyan's mind in his last Broadway play.

In the end, however, the King has not failed. The Boss of the wrecking crew and his black helper Jamie appear to plan the destruction of the theater. They are immediately sympathetic to the plight of those living in it, and the Boss directs his helper to have the crew call in sick for two days so that the cave dwellers will have time to find other accommodations. When the Queen asks the Boss why he is being so easy on them, he tells her that it is in recognition of the greatness of the performance in which the King lost his shoe that he is letting them stay in the doomed theater over the weekend. When the grace period is over and the play is about to end, the Boss returns, "Goes to the King, looks at him intently," and says, "Good luck, Father. Good luck, all." Thus does Saroyan's last Broadway venture end as another dramatization, like *The Time of Your Life,* of the possibility of refusing to capitulate to "the obvious" by refusing to be ashamed of one's equally obvious impulses to "pity and love."

Saroyan's gift as a playwright was not the gift for sentimental fantasy for which he has generally been tolerated. It was actually a gift for humane and rational analysis. Essentially, he was a pragmatist. His career-long habit of writing one-act plays (some of them are only minutes long) is evidence of Saroyan's analytic bent. *The Ping-Pong Game* (first published in 1940 and produced in 1945) analytically reduces to an actual, rule-structured game the way in which Western culture organizes exchanges of aggression between males and females. Similarly, *Making Money,* written in 1956, collected in 1968 in *I Used to Believe I Had Forever Now I'm Not So Sure,* and produced on public television in November of 1970, reduces his beliefs about money to the catechistic dialogue of an elementary school class. In the sketch called *Dentist and Patient* (one of thirty-one sketches in Saroyan's *Anybody and Anybody Else*), collected in

The Best Short Plays, 1968, Saroyan reveals the irony he has always seen in exchanging for money those things that really make life feel better. The patient in the play, "a millionaire, retired," has made far more money than the dentist. But he has made his money without doing anything but "cheating"—merely manipulating his investments among "gold, silver, paper, stocks, bonds, and . . . all the other forms [money] takes." Meanwhile, the dentist has been going through life making people's teeth better, unaware that others get away with charging a lot more money for dentistry.

Equally aware of the absurdity of existing political, economic, and social arrangements and of the grave moral risks of changing them, Saroyan at his best remained a prophet without honor in his country. From the beginning, however, he understood his situation clearly. "In fairness to my critics," he wrote in publishing *Love's Old Sweet Song* (1940), "I acknowledge the partial truth and validity of every charge brought against my work, against myself personally, and against my methods of making my work public." He goes on, "What is lacking in their criticism is the fullness and humanity of understanding which operates in myself, in my work, and in my regard for others. The essence of my work is honor, honesty, intelligence, grace, good humor, naturalness, and spontaneity, and these things do not appear to be nicely balanced in my critics. Consequently, it is difficult for them to make sense in themselves of that which is complicated and unusual for them." He goes on to deny, one by one, the most persistent charges made against him—those of "exhibitionism," "mindlessness," and "formlessness." On each count, his best writing for the stage supports these denials.

From 1958 until his death, Saroyan maintained an apartment in the Montmartre section of Paris. In 1964 he bought two adjacent "brand new and cheap" houses "across from a vineyard" in Fresno. In 1979 the San Francisco author Herbert Gold wrote of two decades of acquaintance with Saroyan in *The New York Times Book Review:* "He was dividing his time between Fresno—because the company of the Armenians there and the local melons were good—and Paris, with a few short visits a year to camp out with relatives in San Francisco." Gold also reported, "He was well into the process of disengagement from the literary scene," and quoted Saroyan as saying "I'm growing old! I'm falling apart! and it's VERY INTERESTING!"

Although he continued to publish plays, Saroyan largely separated himself from American theatrical production itself after the early 1960s. In 1960, *The Times* (London) reported that "Mr.

William Saroyan . . . moved into the Theatre Royal, [took] some two dozen of the regular company and proceeded to make up from scratch a play for, with and (spiritually speaking) about them." This play was *Sam, The Highest Jumper of Them All; or, The London Comedy*. In the same year he collaborated with Henry Cecil on an adaptation for the stage of a mystery story by Cecil, which was produced in London as *Settled Out of Court*. Also in 1960, a production of *The Dogs: or, the Paris Comedy* opened in Vienna. A year later Saroyan was writer in residence at Purdue University, and his *High Time along the Wabash,* a group of one-acts on the subject of racism in Indiana, was acted at the University Playhouse. In 1975, Saroyan was in New York for *The Rebirth Celebration of the Human Race at Artie Zabala's Off-Broadway Theatre*. At that time he told *The New York Times* that he lived in Paris for tax purposes, that he was always busy on five different writing projects at once, and that over the years he had lost $2 million gambling.

After the 1940s Saroyan wrote little of the short fiction that had first established him as a writer. The short fiction that he did publish frequently repeated the patterns he had set during his prolific period between *The Daring Young Man on the Flying Trapeze* and *Dear Baby*. Although he won the California Literature Gold Medal in 1952 for the novel *Tracy's Tiger* (1951), perhaps his finest postwar book is *The Whole Voyald and Other Stories* (1956), his first new collection of short stories since *Dear Baby* in 1944. By the 1950s Saroyan had become his own protagonist. Within ten years he wrote three autobiographies, all of them unstructured and discursive: *The Bicycle Rider in Beverly Hills* (1952), *Here Comes, There Goes, You Know Who* (1961), and *Not Dying* (1963). Three more followed in the 1970s: *Places Where I've Done Time* (1972), *Sons Come and Go, Mothers Hang in Forever* (1976) and *Chance Meetings: A Memoir* (1978). His last work published in his lifetime was a quasi-memoir, *Obituaries* (1979), a series of reminiscences about the show-business dead named in the 1976 edition of the annual *Variety* necrology—a sequel, *Births* (1983), was published posthumously. When Saroyan did turn his hand to fiction, his characters seemed less dramatic personae than deliberate substantiations of his own existence. His prose became increasingly loquacious, not as communicating but as a talking to himself—although he continued writing nearly every day until his death, he published less and less frequently, leaving many unpublished manuscripts.

Saroyan died of prostate cancer on 18 May 1981 at the Veterans Administration Hospital in Fresno, California. He had told almost no one of his illness, and had sought no treatment. Five days before his death, he told a reporter, "Everybody has got to die, but I have always believed an exception would be made in my case. Now what?"

The major charge against Saroyan's work can be expressed in a phrase—nostalgic sentimentality. The best of his writing leaves out the sentimentality and keeps the nostalgia. His style, when effective, conjures up the image of a musing, companionable raconteur. A central value that Saroyan invokes in all of his writing is that of human community. He rejects the authority of an age that insists that an individual's knowledge of other people and the world is no longer possible. Implicit in his writings is a magical relation with the world at large and the sad acknowledgment that it is languishing. Saroyan is therefore empathetic toward children because they take for granted the consanguinity of man and the world and remain free from guile and trends.

Throughout Saroyan's life his personal experiences were as diverse as the disparate genres through which his work ranges. His early success with the short story led to his interest in drama and the novel and to a fascination with film and television and even into the realm of popular music—his 1951 song "Come On-a My House," co-written with his cousin Ross Bagdasarian (and sung by Rosemary Clooney), was an international hit. It is probably in the theater that Saroyan made his most lasting mark, however. Hardly a year goes by in which professional actors somewhere in America do not revive *The Time of Your Life,* while *My Heart's in the Highlands* has been made into an opera and televised, and other Saroyan plays are occasionally featured on television. *My Heart's in the Highlands* and *The Time of Your Life* are collected in popular and school anthologies of American drama, and on the basis of those plays the place of William Saroyan in the history of the American theater still seems as secure as he always said it would be.

Interviews:

Annie Brierre, "William Saroyan à Paris," *Nouvelles Littéraires,* 1665 (30 July 1959): 5;

Budd Schulberg, "Saroyan: Ease and Unease on the Flying Trapeze," *Esquire,* 54 (October 1960): 85–91;

Zori Balayan, "Arguments for Soviet Power . . .," *Soviet Literature,* no. 12 (1977): 159–166;

Herbert Gold, "A 20-Year Talk with Saroyan," *New York Times Book Review,* 20 May 1979, pp. 7, 49–51.

Bibliography:
David Kherdian, *A Bibliography of William Saroyan 1934–1964* (San Francisco: Beacham, 1965).

Biographies:
Aram Saroyan, *Last Rites: The Death of William Saroyan* (New York: Morrow, 1982);

Saroyan, *William Saroyan* (San Diego: Harcourt Brace Jovanovich, 1983);

Lawrence Lee and Barry Gifford, *Saroyan : A Biography* (New York: Harper & Row, 1984);

Leo Hamalian, ed., *William Saroyan: The Man and the Writer Remembered* (Rutherford, N.J.: Fairleigh Dickinson University Press / London: Associated University Presses, 1987).

References:
Nona Balakian, *The World of William Saroyan* (Lewisburg, Pa.: Bucknell University Press, 1998);

David Stephen Calonne, *William Saroyan, My Real Work Is Being,* foreword by Dickran Kouymjian (Chapel Hill: University of North Carolina Press, 1983);

Frederic I. Carpenter, "The Time of William Saroyan's Life," *Pacific Spectator,* 1 (Winter 1947): 88–96;

William J. Fisher, "What Ever Happened to Saroyan?" *College English,* 16 (March 1955): 336–340, 385;

Elisabeth C. Foard, *William Saroyan: A Reference Guide* (Boston: G. K. Hall, 1989);

Howard R. Floan, *William Saroyan* (New York: Twayne, 1966);

Edward Halsey Foster, *William Saroyan* (Boise, Idaho: Boise State University, 1984);

Foster, *William Saroyan: A Study of the Short Fiction* (Boston: Twayne, 1991);

John Gassner, *The Theatre in Our Times* (New York: Crown, 1954), pp. 297–303, 443–445, 573–575;

James H. Justus, "William Saroyan and the Theatre of Transformation," in *The Thirties: Fiction, Poetry, Drama,* edited by Warren French (Deland, Fla.: Everett/Edwards, 1967), pp. 211–219;

Harry Keyishian, "Michael Arlen and William Saroyan: Armenian Ethnicity and the Writer," in *The Old Century and the New: Essays in Honor of Charles Angoff,* edited by Alfred Rosa (Rutherford, N.J.: Fairleigh Dickinson University Press, 1978), pp. 192–206;

Keyishian, ed., *Critical Essays on William Saroyan* (New York: G. K. Hall, 1995);

Edward Krickel, "Cozzens and Saroyan: A Look at Two Reputations," *Georgia Review,* 24 (Fall 1970): 281–296;

Lawrence Langner, *The Magic Curtain* (New York: Dutton, 1951), pp. 320–326;

William Peden, *The American Short Story: Continuity and Change 1940–1975* (Boston: Houghton Mifflin, 1975);

Thelma J. Shinn, "William Saroyan: Romantic Existentialist," *Modern Drama,* 15 (September 1972): 185–194;

Jon Whitmore, *William Saroyan: A Research and Production Sourcebook* (Westport, Conn.: Greenwood Press, 1994);

Edmund Wilson, *Classics and Commercials* (New York: Farrar, Straus, 1950), pp. 26–31, 327–330;

Stark Young, "Saroyan Directing, Note," *New Republic,* 104 (12 May 1941): 664;

Young, "Hello Out There," *New Republic,* 107 (12 October 1942): 466.

Papers:
The most substantial collection of William Saroyan's manuscripts is at the John M. Olin Library, Cornell University; the Department of Special Collections of the Stanford University Libraries holds two collections of Saroyan manuscripts and correspondence; the University of California Research Library, Los Angeles, has an extensive collection of letters; other collections of manuscripts, papers, and letters are in the William Saroyan Foundation collection, The Bancroft Library, University of California–Berkeley; the Fresno County Free Library, California; and The Harry Ransom Humanities Research Center, The University of Texas at Austin.

Amy Tan

*This entry was updated from the entry by Pin-chia Feng
(National Chiao-Tung University, Taiwan) in DLB 173:
American Novelists Since World War II, Fifth Series.*

BIRTH: Oakland, California, 19 February 1952, to John Yuehhan and Daisy Tu Ching Tan.

EDUCATION: B.A., San Jose State University, 1973; M.A., San Jose State University, 1974; postgraduate study at University of California, Berkeley, 1974–1976.

MARRIAGE: 6 April 1974 to Louis M. DiMattei.

AWARDS AND HONORS: Commonwealth Club Gold Award for fiction, Bay Area Book Reviewers Award for best fiction, American Library Association Best Book for Young Adults Award, nomination for National Book Critics Circle Award for best novel, and nomination for *Los Angeles Times* book award, all for *The Joy Luck Club,* 1989; *Booklist* Editor's Choice and nomination for Bay Area Book Reviewers Award for *The Kitchen God's Wife,* 1991; Best American Essays Award, 1991; honorary L.H.D., Dominican College, 1991.

BOOKS: *The Joy Luck Club* (New York: Putnam, 1989; London: Heinemann, 1989);
The Kitchen God's Wife (New York: Putnam, 1991; London: Collins, 1991);
The Moon Lady (New York: Macmillan, 1992; London: Hamilton, 1992);
The Chinese Siamese Cat (New York: Macmillan, 1994; London: Hamilton, 1994);
The Hundred Secret Senses (New York: Putnam, 1995; London: Flamingo, 1996).

MOTION PICTURE: *The Joy Luck Club,* screenplay by Tan and Ronald Bass, Hollywood Pictures, 1993.

Amy Tan (photograph © 1989 by Foothorap)

On the publication of her first novel, *The Joy Luck Club* (1989), Amy Tan became an instant star in the publishing world, and her second novel, *The Kitchen God's Wife* (1991), was a triumph as well. Tan's skillful renditions of mother-daughter relationships reach the hearts of millions of readers. Moreover, her work—which comes more than a dozen years after Maxine Hong Kingston's *The Woman Warrior* (1976)—has helped to create a renaissance of Chinese American writing. Tan's books also include two children's books and a third novel, *The Hundred Secret Senses* (1995).

Amy Tan's roots are in a sorrowful family history and painful personal traumas. Her father, John Tan, immigrated to the United States in 1947. He worked as an engineer and served as a Baptist minister. Amy's mother, Daisy, came to the United States in 1949, leaving behind three daughters from a previous marriage. When Amy was born in Oakland, California, her parents chose the Chinese name En-Mai, meaning Blessing of America. The blessing seemed inadequate when Amy's elder brother, Peter, died of brain cancer in 1967, and only months later John Tan died of the same disease. After consulting a Chinese geomancer, Daisy Tan decided to move to Europe with fifteen-year-old Amy and her younger brother, John, to cleanse the evil influence of their "diseased house" in Santa Clara. They went first to the Netherlands and finally found affordable housing in a hundred-year-old chalet set amid fourteenth-century houses in Montreux, Switzerland. Tan finished high school at the College Monte Rosa Internationale in Montreux, an outsider among the children of ambassadors, tycoons, and princes and still burdened by her losses and her anger. Because being good had not saved her father and brother, she decided to turn bad. She made friends with drug-dealing hippies and was arrested at sixteen. The nadir of her Montreux year came when she nearly eloped to Australia with a mental patient who claimed he was a deserter from the German army.

When the Tans returned to the United States, Amy enrolled at Linfield College in Oregon, majoring first in premed and later in English. After meeting Lou DiMattei on a blind date, eighteen-year-old Amy transferred to San Jose State University, where DiMattei was a law student, and put herself through college with the help of a scholarship and income from a job in a pizza parlor. She earned a B.A. in 1973 and married DiMattei in 1974, the same year she completed a master's degree in English and linguistics and enrolled in a doctoral program at the University of California, Berkeley. She quit in 1976, when the murder of her best friend brought back her sense of loss and anger. From 1976 to 1981 she worked as a language-development specialist for disabled children. She edited a medical journal from 1981 to 1983, and from 1983 to 1987 she was a technical writer specializing in corporate business proposals. Tan and her husband, a tax attorney, live in San Francisco and New York City.

Tan's work as a technical writer turned her into a workaholic who spent ninety hours a week at her job. In her late thirties, after an unsuccessful attempt at a cure through psychological counseling, Tan decided to cure herself by taking jazz piano lessons and joining the Squaw Valley Community of Writers, a weekly group, where she wrote her first fiction. At first she tried to write from a non-Chinese perspective because she thought that Chinese people could not get their work published in the United States. Later she realized that writing about the events of her own life could be therapeutic. In 1987 G. P. Putnam bought her short story "Rules of the Game" and the outline of a novel. Within four

months she finished the rest of the stories, which turned into *The Joy Luck Club*. The book made *The New York Times* best-seller list in the spring of 1989 and stayed on the list for nine months. It also won the 1989 Bay Area Book Reviewer Award for Best Fiction and the Best Book for Young Adults Award from the American Library Association.

Tan refuses to be pegged a mother-daughter expert, but both *The Joy Luck Club* and *The Kitchen God's Wife* center on the love and antagonism between Chinese immigrant mothers and their American daughters. In real life Tan and her mother experienced similar emotional turmoil. Daisy Tan had high expectations for her daughter. Amy Tan recalls that as a child she was expected to grow up to be a neurosurgeon by profession with the "hobby" of concert pianist. She also remembers her mother's disappointment when she changed her undergraduate major from premed to English. Like Waverly Jong in *The Joy Luck Club*, who always felt inadequate in the face of her mother, Amy Tan was pressured by Daisy Tan's standards. When *The Joy Luck Club* was fourth on *The New York Times* best-seller list, for instance, Daisy remarked that Amy should have aimed for first, explaining that Amy was so talented she deserved to be the best.

At first Tan thought of *The Joy Luck Club* as a collection of stories rather than a novel, but the arrangement of these stories created a formal wholeness. Tan carefully structured them into antiphonal exchanges among four pairs of mothers and daughters: Suyuan and Jing-mei "June" Woo, An-mei and Rose Hsu, Lindo and Waverly Jong, and Ying-ying and Lena St. Clair. Maternal voices can be heard in the four vignettes preceding the four main segments and in six of the sixteen stories. The first two segments, "Feathers from a Thousand Li Away" and "The Twenty-six Malignant Gates," cover the mothers' pasts in China and the daughters' childhoods in the United States. The third section, "American Translation," tells the stories of the adult daughters' struggles to resolve mother-daughter conflicts. The mothers again tell their stories in the final segment, "Queen Mother from the Western Skies," and achieve a kind of reconciliation with their daughters. Suyuan, the founder of the Joy Luck Club and the mother who passed away, has no narrative voice in the novel. Instead, June opens the novel by retelling her mother's stories, as well as replacing her in the mothers' mah-jongg game. Thus the daughters' stories are cradled by the two segments of maternal voices, with June's narrative providing a frame for all the others. This formal orchestration embodies the major theme of the novel: the continuation of the matriarchal line. An-mei Hsu visualizes this mat-

Dust jacket for Tan's first book, about the love and antagonism between Chinese immigrant mothers and their American daughters

rilineage when she observes the link among three generations of women in her family: "All of us are like stairs, one step after another, going up and down, but all going the same way." This apparently fatalistic statement reveals a sense of generational interconnectedness that brings eventual reconciliation and mother-daughter bonding. A complex ensemble of stories told by mothers and daughters, the novel, as Marina Heung argues, is an innovative variation of the traditional mother-daughter plot, which focuses on the daughter's perspective.

Tan acknowledges her own matrilineage by dedicating her first novel to her mother and maternal grandmother. *The Joy Luck Club* pays special homage to her grandmother, who before her suicide at thirty-nine was the number-three concubine to a wealthy man, much like An-mei Hsu's mother in the novel. This allusion to the grandmother hints at the theme of the female's triumph in the face of victimization. An-mei's mother represents all women who have been persecuted by rigid Chinese traditions. After her family has driven her away for her alleged violation of the rule of chastity, she is forced to serve a rapist as one of his concubines. Yet she returns as a dutiful daughter and sacrifices her own flesh to cook a soup for her dying mother. Instead of continuing as a silent victim of patriarchy, she de-

ploys her spiteful suicide to teach An-mei the power of language, thereby transforming her victimization into victory. An-mei in turn passes on this story of empowerment to her own daughter, Rose, who finds the voice and selfhood buried in her marriage. Both An-mei and Rose, therefore, benefit from the grandmother's suffering and strength. By dedicating her novel to her own grandmother, Tan suggests that, like An-mei and Rose, she owes part of her power of language to the inspiration of her grandmother.

Yet Tan wrote *The Joy Luck Club* mainly for Daisy, fulfilling a vow she made when her mother was hospitalized and nearly died of a heart attack in 1986, an event that forced Tan to face the possibility of losing her mother. In her dedication Tan writes, "You asked me once what I would remember. This, and much more," an effort to reassure her mother that she and her stories will not be forgotten. The Joy Luck Club mothers also fear oblivion and discontinuity of familial lineage. June detects it in her Joy Luck "aunties" when she claims not to have known Suyuan well enough to describe the dead mother to her half sisters:

They are frightened. In me, they see their own daughters, just as ignorant, just as unmindful of all the truths

408

and hopes they have brought to America. They see daughters who grow impatient when their mothers talk in Chinese, who think they are stupid when they explain things in fractured English. They see that joy and luck do not mean the same to their daughters, that to these closed American-born minds "joy luck" is not a word, it does not exist. They see daughters who will bear grandchildren born without any connecting hope passed from generation to generation.

In short, the immigrant mothers are afraid that the younger generations will lose their Chinese heritage and thereby forfeit their faith in joy and luck.

The true spirit of the Joy Luck Club is a hope against hopelessness and a battle to create one's own space. Suyuan describes the joy luck spirit when she tells June, "It is not that we have no heart or eyes for pain. We were all afraid. We all had our miseries. But to despair was to wish back for something already lost. Or to prolong what was already unbearable. . . . What was worse, we asked among ourselves, to sit and wait for our own deaths with proper somber faces? Or to choose our own happiness?" The women of the club choose to withstand physical hardship with their carnivalesque spirit. Both the Kweilin and San Francisco versions of the Joy Luck Club are more than social gatherings of women; they are support networks. Whereas in China the hope of joy holds back the fear of the war, in San Francisco it helps the immigrant women to survive the equally terrifying experiences of cultural transplantation. To the American daughters, however, the mah-jongg-playing Joy Luck Club seems to be, as June remarks, "a shameful Chinese custom, like the secret gathering of the Ku Klux Klan or the tom-tom dances of TV Indians preparing for wars." This association of her mother's invention with racist practices and stereotyping indicates June's misunderstanding and mistrust of her Chinese heritage. Only after her mother's death and a trip to China does June come to realize the significance of joy and luck.

Like June, Tan herself used to distrust joy and luck. In fact, for most of her life she felt "jinxed" because of all her tragic losses. She also felt dissatisfied with her Asian looks and with her mother's lack of "progress" in the New World. Like June, Tan had to make a trip to China to recognize fully the Chineseness inside her. In 1987, when she and her husband accompanied Daisy Tan on a visit to China, she experienced a magical moment of "homecoming": "It was just as my mother said: As soon as my feet touched China, I became Chinese." At the same time Tan realized how American she really was. No matter how she attempted to blend in, she always stood out among the Chinese. She emerged from the

trip better equipped than before to cope with her double heritage and hybrid identity.

This double heritage is evident in Tan's insertion of Mandarin words–such as *hulihudu* for confusion–in the American English prose. Tan admits that she can read and speak little Chinese. Yet her fine ear for the nuances of languages and her sensitivity as a linguist enable her to capture the spirit of Chinese phrases most of the time. Tan says that her mother speaks English as if it is a direct translation from Chinese, and her language has more imagery than English. Tan has also spent much time studying the rhythm of Chinese American speech. Her efforts are apparent in the language of the immigrant mothers in *The Joy Luck Club*. An-mei Hsu, for instance, refers to Rose's psychiatrist as "psycheatrick." In this case the effect of this creolized English is more than comic; it also carries a certain weight of truth. Heung identifies the mothers' "border" language as representing Tan's effort to reclaim language "as an instrument of intersubjectivity and dialogue, and as a medium of transmission from mothers to daughters." Instead of being "fractured English," the mothers' language becomes a location of cultural and generational communication. In a 1989 interview with Julie Lew, Tan explained her effort to "speak" to her mother: "I wanted her to know what I thought about China and what I thought about growing up in this country. And I wanted those words to almost fall off the page so that she could just see the story, that the language would be simple enough, almost like a little curtain that would fall away." She says the greatest compliment she has received for *The Joy Luck Club* came from Daisy Tan, who remarked how easy it was to read, a remark that serves as a confirmation of her success in integrating her imagined "maternal tongue" with perfect American English.

The ending of *The Joy Luck Club*–June's reunion with her Chinese sisters Chwun Yu (Spring Rain) and Chwun Hwa (Spring Flower)–also shows Tan's effort to integrate her Chinese and American heritages. On her 1987 visit to China, Tan met her three half sisters for the first time. June's reunion with her two Chinese sisters apparently draws on the emotional intensity of Tan's experience. The names of June and her sisters allude to the regenerative powers associated with the seasons of spring and summer. During the reunion scene in the 1993 movie version of the novel, for which Tan helped to write the screenplay, June momentarily sees the face of her mother in one of her sisters, highlighting the symbolic resurrection of the lost mother after the unification of her Chinese and American parts. With this hopeful note Tan demonstrates the double meaning of Suyuan, the mother's name. The reunion of her daughters fulfills her "Long-Cherished

AMY TAN

The KITCHEN GOD'S WIFE

PUTNAM

ISBN 0-399-13578-2

AMY TAN
author of *THE JOY LUCK CLUB*

The KITCHEN GOD'S WIFE

Dust jacket for Tan's second novel, a fictionalized account of her mother's life

Wish," and her "Long-held Grudge," the abandonment of her twin daughters, is finally resolved.

Tan's second novel, *The Kitchen God's Wife,* also focuses on generational conflicts and reconciliation, as well as female victimization and triumph. Instead of four pairs of mothers and daughters, however, Tan concentrates on one mother and daughter, Winnie Louie and Pearl, with Pearl's present-day narrative providing a frame for her mother's storytelling. Yet the novel is more than a traditional framed narrative. It appears to be dialogic, with two alternating narrative voices that hint toward the possibility of communication. It opens with Tan's familiar theme of mother-daughter conflict. At first Pearl appears reluctant to travel to Chinatown in San Francisco to visit her family, especially her mother, whom she calls "a Chinese version of Freud, or worse." As her first-person narrative unfolds, the reader learns that Pearl, who is suffering from multiple sclerosis and could soon become paralyzed, feels guilty for not telling her mother her secret. When she visits her mother, Winnie Louie unexpectedly reveals her other identity as Jaing Weili in China. In what appears to be a storytelling marathon, Winnie discloses a series of surprises about her past. She was the daughter of a Shanghai tycoon and his number-two

wife, who resisted the fate of concubinage and disappeared when Weili was six. To avoid family disgrace Weili was sent to live with her uncle's family on an island, and at eighteen she married a scheming brute who abused her physically and mentally. After suffering the loss of her three children during the Sino-Japanese War, she fell in love with a Chinese American soldier and tried to elope with him, but she was tried for "stealing" her husband's son and property and imprisoned for two years. She escaped China on the last flight from Shanghai before the Communist takeover and started her American life. The most shocking secret of the mother's past, however, is revealed as an afterthought. She tells Pearl that she is most likely the daughter of Winnie's sadistic first husband, Wen Fu, who raped Winnie just before her escape from China. After her mother's confession, Pearl finally feels free to talk about her medical condition. This talk around the kitchen table, a traditional place for female communion, becomes a ritual of secret sharing that bridges generations. Like *The Joy Luck Club, The Kitchen God's Wife* ends on a clear reconciliatory note: Winnie invents a new goddess, Lady Sorrowfree, who will grant Pearl a life of "happiness winning over bitterness, no regrets in the world."

The Kitchen God's Wife is the fictionalized life story of Daisy Tan. After the success of her first novel, Tan felt pressured by the fear that her second book would not be as good, or as well received, as her first. At first she tried to write something completely different from *The Joy Luck Club,* but after several false starts she again turned to her mother for inspiration. Having often complained that she had to tell every acquaintance that she was not the model for the mother in *The Joy Luck Club,* Daisy Tan wanted her true story told. In 1989, when she learned that her first husband had died, the past broke free and Daisy started telling her story. Her daughter videotaped her mother's storytelling and transformed it into a novel. Thus *The Kitchen God's Wife* is virtually a collaboration by Daisy and Amy. "My mother wanted me to write this book about her," Tan told Patti Doten in 1991. "She not only wanted to give me her story but I think she was looking for a way to release the pain and the anger over 'that bad man.'" Although many details are changed, the plot of *The Kitchen God's Wife* closely corresponds to the outlines of Daisy's life in China from before the Sino-Japanese War until she immigrated to the United States: "Everything from her horrible marriage to her children dying, to being in jail, to escaping right before the revolution in 1949." With her writing, moreover, Tan tried to uncover the reasons behind her mother's extraordinary endurance during a terrible first marriage that lasted twelve years, and she came to understand the oppressive patriarchal myths under which Chinese women have been governed for thousands of years, myths that had taught Daisy to suffer silently. The spirit of the 1989 student demonstrations in Tiananmen Square, Beijing, also finds its way into Tan's writing, as she attempts to capture the spirit of the students' resistance and to comprehend "what it is like to live a life of repression and to understand the fear that one has, and what you have to do to rise above that fear."

The Kitchen God's Wife is not only a fictionalized biography but also an effort to rewrite mythology. Like Kingston, Tan deliberately revises Chinese mythology, as in her creation of the new goddess Lady Sorrowfree. In telling the story of the Kitchen God, Tan exposes the poignant irony in the old myth: a wife abuser was apotheosized as a household deity and the guardian of kitchens, the space traditionally assigned to women. She also reveals the internalization of patriarchal values by traditional Chinese women, who have been educated to worship male oppressors such as the Kitchen God, whose story is a mythological parallel to that of Winnie's abusive first husband, who lives to an old

age and dies with honor. Tan regards the Kitchen God's story as a perfect metaphor for unquestioned governing myths, or the master plot, as Toni Morrison would term it. As Winnie says in the novel: "I was like that wife of Kitchen God. Nobody worshipped her either. He got all the excuses. He got all the credit. She was forgotten." Winnie's denial of the Kitchen God and her creation of a new goddess embody Tan's textual "revenge" for oppressed Chinese women. Sorrowfree is also a translation of the name of Winnie's stillborn daughter, Mochou, whose spirit Winnie symbolically resurrects in her reconciliation with Pearl. The final message of the novel, therefore, is one of forgiveness and hope, which leads to a "sorrowfree" life.

Besides replacing a patriarchal god with a female deity, Tan also supplants the patriarchal family structure with the circle of sisterhood. The most significant example of sisterhood is the commune of runaway wives, "an underground hiding place, filled with women and children." The matron of this house once colluded in forcing her daughter to suffer a dead-end marriage in silence and was "awakened" only after her daughter committed suicide—which, according to Tan, is the only way for a Chinese wife to free herself from such bondage. The commune provides an alternative for a suffering wife, and although it eventually dissolves, the novel clearly carries a message that sisterly support is a sanctuary against oppression and victimization.

This celebration of sisterhood is also revisionist because female friendship goes against the Confucian patriarchal master plot. Winnie confesses that she used to blame Wen Fu's mother for her misery, "And perhaps this was wrong of me, to blame another woman for my own miseries. But that was how I was raised—never to criticize men or the society they ruled, or Confucius, that awful man who made that society. I could blame only other women who were more fearful than I." Winnie's statement is a testimony of how internalization of patriarchal rules turns woman against woman. In *The Kitchen God's Wife,* however, women often support each other. For example, Aunt Du serves as a mother figure who partially compensates for Weili's loss of her mother. The friendship between Winnie and Helen, although interlaced with competition and tension, is sustaining and nourishing. Helen even initiates the process of communication between Winnie and Pearl. Only with the aid of her community of women can Winnie finally break away from her physical and mental imprisonment.

Tan's renditions of her mother's stories have been faulted as unauthentic and as stereotypical redactions of the "Orient" for the benefit of non-Asian

Dust jacket for Tan's third novel, set in rural southeastern China during the nineteenth century

readers. As with Kingston's works, the details of China and Chinese culture in Tan's books are often under critical scrutiny. Sau-ling Wong explains what she terms "the Amy Tan phenomenon," the enormous appeal and blockbuster success of Tan's fiction, by arguing that Tan's complex interplay of self-orientalizing and counterorientalist possibilities enables her to acquire a large readership. Yet, Wong charges, while "The nonintellectual consumer of Orientalism can find much in *The Joy Luck Club* and *The Kitchen God's Wife* to satisfy her curiosity about China and Chinatown; at the same time, subversions of naive voyeurism can be detected by the reader attuned to questions of cultural production." There is justice in Wong's critique. Nevertheless, Tan's ongoing feminist revisionist project has real significance.

In her best-selling third novel, *The Hundred Secret Senses,* Tan's portrayal of China is at its most questionable. Tan continues to concentrate on the conflicts and final reconciliation between mother and daughter figures as she again delves into Chinese history to contextualize her portrayal of Chinese American experiences. Her story is set in rural southeastern China during the nineteenth-century Taiping Rebellion and in the twentieth century in contemporary San Francisco. The war-torn, or Communist-ruled, Chinese village is juxtaposed with the postmodern metropolis of San Francisco. In a new twist Tan gives her American protagonist, Olivia, a Chinese half sister, Kwan, as the representative of Chinese culture and values. At six Olivia met the eighteen-year-old Kwan, then recently arrived from Communist China. At thirty-six Olivia and her estranged husband, Simon, are accompanied by Kwan on a trip to China. This venture is intended to save their marriage, but in a development unplanned by them, it settles business from another life. Instead of the revisionist mythmaking in her first two novels, Tan takes a step toward "Chinese superstitions" to embrace the concept of reincarnation. The result, if sensational, is also unbelievable and disappointing.

Tan's indulgence in implausible mysticism makes *The Hundred Secret Senses* unconvincing, and the many reincarnations in the novel appear whimsical and melodramatic. For example, it strains the reader's imagination to believe that the American yuppie couple Olivia and Simon are reincarnations of a nineteenth-century American woman, Miss Banner, and a Eurasian interpreter, Yiban, a pair of unfortunate lovers slaughtered by war-hysterical Manchu soldiers, and that Kwan was Miss Banner's maid and confidante, Nunumu, in her previous life. The body-snatcher story—in which Kwan has switched bodies with her drowned playmate in order to come back to keep her promise to Miss Banner—also lacks credibility. The sense of predestination that successfully set the mood of Tan's previous works overwhelms the plot in *The Hundred Secret Senses*.

Moreover, Tan becomes trapped in her schematic of binary opposition between Chinese and Chinese American values. As a Eurasian, Olivia is a racial and cultural hybrid. Yet Tan fails to develop the identity problems faced by such a character. Instead Tan repeats the familiar theme of American-born "daughter" entangled in a love-hate-guilt relationship with a mother figure. Kwan, who conveniently takes over the maternal role because of Olivia's irresponsible Caucasian mother, comes from a younger generation of Chinese women than the Joy Luck mothers and Winnie Louie; yet she appears little different from the older women. Whereas in her previous fiction Tan successfully created the sense of mother-daughter interconnectedness, in *The Hundred Secret Senses* her concept of reincarnation, which borders on mysticism, weakens the empathetic power of her mother-daughter plot.

Perhaps because of her own homecoming experience, Tan often uses China as a place to settle unresolved personal crises originating in the United States. In *The Hundred Secret Senses,* however, the American couple goes to China to do research for an essay on Chinese village cuisine to be written by Simon with photographs by Olivia. This project seems to objectify China as a site of Western tourist and anthropological interest, and Nunumu/Kwan's extreme devotion to Miss Banner/Olivia puts the former in a position of servitude to the latter—again suggesting a kind of unbalanced power relationship between the two cultures.

In both *The Joy Luck Club* and *The Kitchen God's Wife* Tan captures the culturally specific experiences of Chinese American women, having learned much from her mother about the lives of women who grew up in pre-Communist China. For Tan, growing up with a Chinese mother means constantly hearing three basic rules. As she told Susan Kepner in 1989: "First, if it's too easy, it's not worth pursuing. Second, you have to try harder, no matter what other people might have to do in the same situation—that's your lot in life. And if you're a woman, you're supposed to suffer in silence." She is willing to live by the first two dicta but refuses to accept the third decree. Speaking out against misogyny in traditional Chinese culture, Tan's novels have earned her riches and fame. For Tan, her most significant theme is mother-daughter communion. As she told Donn Fry in 1991, "My books have amounted to taking her stories—a gift to me—and giving them back to her. To me, it was the ultimate thing I ever could have done for myself and my mother." In her own way Tan has succeeded in speaking for and with her mother.

Interviews:

Susan Kepner, "Imagine This: The Amazing Adventure of Amy Tan," *San Francisco Examiner Focus,* May 1989, pp. 58–60, 161–162;

Julie Lew, "How Stories Written for Mother Became Amy Tan's Best Seller," *New York Times,* 4 July 1989, p. 23;

Mervyn Rothstein, "A New Novel by Amy Tan, Who's Still Trying to Adapt to Success," *New York Times,* 11 June 1991, pp. 13–14;

Patti Doten, "Sharing Her Mother's Secrets," *Boston Globe,* 21 June 1991, p. 63;

D. C. Denison, "Amy Tan," *Boston Sunday Globe,* 28 June 1991, p. 8;

Donn Fry, "The Joy and Luck of Amy Tan," *Seattle Times,* 7 July 1991;

Don Stanley, "Amy Tan Is Having Fun," *Sacramento Bee,* 14 July 1991;

Mark Morrison, "Joy, Luck—and a Movie Deal," *USA Weekend,* 10–12 September 1993, pp. 4–6.

References:

Marina Heung, "Daughter-Text/Mother-Text: Matrilineage in Amy Tan's *Joy Luck Club,*" *Feminist Studies,* 19 (Fall 1993): 597–616;

E. D. Huntley, *Amy Tan: A Critical Companion* (Westport, Conn.: Greenwood Press, 1998);

Amy Ling, *Between Worlds: Women Writers of Chinese Ancestry* (New York: Pergamon, 1990);

Malini Johar Schueller, "Theorizing Ethnicity and Subjectivity: Maxine Hong Kingston's *Tripmaster Monkey* and Amy Tan's *The Joy Luck Club,*" *Genders,* 15 (Winter 1992): 72–85;

Walter Shear, "Generational Differences and the Diaspora in *The Joy Luck Club,*" *Critique,* 34 (Spring 1993): 193–199;

Sau-ling Cynthia Wong, *Reading Asian American Literatures: From Necessity to Extravagance* (Princeton, N.J.: Princeton University Press, 1993);

Wong, "'Sugar Sisterhood': Situating the Amy Tan Phenomenon," in *The Ethnic Canon: Histories, Institutions, and Interventions,* edited by David Palumbo-Liu (Minneapolis & London: University of Minnesota Press, 1995), pp. 174–210.

Paul Theroux

Teresa F. O'Connor
City University of New York, College of Staten Island

See also the Theroux entry in *DLB 2: American Novelists Since World War II.*

BIRTH: Medford, Massachusetts, 10 April 1941, to Albert Eugene and Anne Dittami Theroux.

EDUCATION: Attended University of Maine, 1959-1960; B.A., University of Massachusetts, 1963; further study at Syracuse University, 1963.

MARRIAGE: 4 December 1967 to Anne Castle (divorced 1993); children: Marcel Raymond, Louis Sebastian.

AWARDS AND HONORS: Robert Hamlet one-act play award, 1960; *Playboy* Editorial Award, 1971, 1976; *The New York Times Book Review* "Editors' Choice" citation for *The Great Railway Bazaar: By Train through Asia,* 1975; American Academy and Institute of Arts and Letters Award for literature, 1977; American Book Award nominations for *The Old Patagonian Express: By Train through the Americas,* 1981, and for *The Mosquito Coast,* 1983; Thomas Cook Travel Book Prize, 1989; honorary degrees from Trinity College and Tufts University, both in 1980, and the University of Massachusetts–Amherst, 1988.

BOOKS: *Waldo* (Boston: Houghton Mifflin, 1967; London: Bodley Head, 1968);
Fong and the Indians (Boston: Houghton Mifflin, 1968; London: Hamilton, 1976);
Girls at Play (Boston: Houghton Mifflin, 1969; London: Bodley Head, 1969);
Murder in Mount Holly (London: Alan Ross, 1969);
Jungle Lovers (Boston: Houghton Mifflin, 1971; London: Bodley Head, 1971);
Sinning with Annie and Other Stories (Boston: Houghton Mifflin, 1972; London: Hamilton, 1975);
V. S. Naipaul: An Introduction to His Works (London: Deutsch, 1972; New York: Africana Publishing, 1972);
Saint Jack (Boston: Houghton Mifflin, 1973; London: Bodley Head, 1973);

Paul Theroux (photograph © Jerry Bauer, 1985)

The Black House (Boston: Houghton Mifflin, 1974; London: Hamilton, 1974);
The Great Railway Bazaar: By Train through Asia (Boston: Houghton Mifflin, 1975; London: Hamilton, 1975);
The Family Arsenal (Boston: Houghton Mifflin, 1976; London: Hamilton, 1976);
The Consul's File (Boston: Houghton Mifflin, 1977; London: Hamilton, 1977);
Picture Palace (Boston: Houghton Mifflin, 1978; London: Hamilton, 1978);
A Christmas Card (Boston: Houghton Mifflin, 1978; London: Hamilton, 1978);

London Snow: A Christmas Story (Wilton, Salisbury, Wiltshire: Michael Russell, 1979; Boston: Houghton Mifflin, 1980);

The Old Patagonian Express: By Train through the Americas (Boston: Houghton Mifflin, 1979; London: Hamilton, 1979);

World's End and Other Stories (Boston: Houghton Mifflin, 1980; London: Hamilton, 1980);

The Mosquito Coast (London: Hamilton, 1981; Boston: Houghton Mifflin, 1982);

The London Embassy (London: Hamilton, 1982; Boston: Houghton Mifflin, 1983);

The Kingdom by the Sea: A Journey around Great Britain (Boston: Houghton Mifflin, 1983); republished as *The Kingdom by the Sea: A Journey around the Coast of Great Britain* (London: Hamilton, 1983);

Sailing through China (Wilton, Salisbury, Wiltshire: Michael Russell, 1983; Boston: Houghton Mifflin, 1984);

Doctor Slaughter (London: Hamilton, 1984);

Half Moon Street: Two Short Novels (Boston: Houghton Mifflin, 1984)—includes *Doctor Slaughter* and *Doctor DeMarr;*

The Imperial Way: Making Tracks from Peshawar to Chittagong, by Theroux and Steve McCurry (Boston: Houghton Mifflin, 1985; London: Hamilton, 1985);

Patagonia Revisited, by Theroux and Bruce Chatwin (Wilton, Salisbury, Wiltshire: Michael Russell, 1985; Boston: Houghton Mifflin, 1986); republished as *Nowhere is a Place: Travels in Patagonia* (San Francisco: Sierra Club Books, 1992);

Sunrise with Seamonsters: Travels and Discoveries, 1964–1984 (Boston: Houghton Mifflin, 1985; London: Hamilton, 1985);

O-Zone (Franklin Center, Pa.: Franklin Library / New York: Putnam, 1986; London: Hamilton, 1986);

The White Man's Burden: A Play in Two Acts (London: Hamilton, 1987);

Riding the Iron Rooster: By Train through China (New York: Putnam, 1988; London: Hamilton, 1988);

My Secret History (New York: Putnam, 1989; London: Hamilton, 1989);

Doctor DeMarr (London: Hutchinson, 1990);

To the Ends of the Earth: The Selected Travels of Paul Theroux (New York: Random House, 1990); published in different form as *Travelling the World: The Illustrated Travels of Paul Theroux* (London: Sinclair-Stevenson, 1990);

Chicago Loop (London: Hamilton, 1990; New York: Random House, 1991);

The Happy Isles of Oceania: Paddling the Pacific (New York: Putnam, 1992; London: Hamilton, 1992);

Millroy the Magician (London: Hamilton, 1993; New York: Random House, 1994);

The Pillars of Hercules: A Grand Tour of the Mediterranean (New York: Putnam, 1995; London: Hamilton, 1995);

My Other Life (Boston: Houghton Mifflin, 1996; London: Hamilton, 1996);

The Collected Stories (New York: Viking, 1997; London: Hamilton, 1997);

Kowloon Tong (Boston: Houghton Mifflin, 1997; London: Hamilton, 1997);

The Collected Short Novels (London: Hamilton, 1998);

Sir Vidia's Shadow: A Friendship across Five Continents (Boston: Houghton Mifflin, 1998).

MOTION PICTURES: *Saint Jack,* by Theroux, Peter Bogdanovich, and Howard Sackler, New World Pictures, 1979;

Chinese Box, by Theroux, Wayne Wang, Jean-Claude Carrière, and Larry Gross, Trimark, 1998.

TELEVISION: *London Embassy,* by Theroux, T. R. Bowen, and Ian Kennedy Martin, London Television, 1987.

SELECTED PERIODICAL PUBLICATION–UNCOLLECTED: "Memory and Creation: Reflections at Fifty," *Massachusetts Review* (Fall 1991): 381–399.

Paul Theroux's novels, short stories, essays, and travel books, in which he often explores the expatriate experience and the postcolonial world of developing countries, have established his reputation as a prodigious and cosmopolitan man of letters. Critics compare his writing to the work of Evelyn Waugh, Graham Greene, Joseph Conrad, and V. S. Naipaul. Theroux's long-time residence as an outsider in Africa, Asia, and England has allowed him to bring global insight and a cultural perspective to his work. His prose is characterized by an ironic and detached wit; a concern with those who are "displaced"; an examination of the clashes that occur between cultures; and a vision that often verges on the apocalyptic. His writing, often described as realistic—and, at times, surrealistic—reveals, as Samuel Coale notes, Theroux's "own roots in traditional storytelling and plot structure." As the author of more than thirty volumes, Theroux ranks as an internationally acknowledged writer; his books have been translated into many languages. Jonathan Ra-

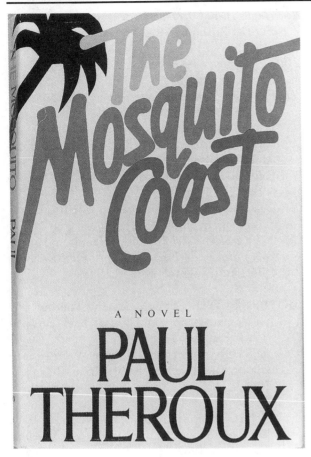

Dust jacket for the first American edition of Theroux's 1981 novel, which was nominated for an American Book Award

ban, writing in the *Saturday Review* (2 February 1982), has called Theroux "the most gifted, most prodigal writer of his generation."

Theroux has been made a fellow of the American Academy and Institute of Arts and Letters, the Royal Society of Literature, and the Royal Geographical Society. His first book of travel, *The Great Railway Bazaar: By Train through Asia* (1975), received several awards, including an American Academy and Institute of Arts and Letters Award for literature (1977), and *The Old Patagonian Express: By Train through the Americas* (1979) and *The Mosquito Coast* (1981) each received American Book Award nominations in 1981 and 1983, respectively.

Born in Medford, Massachusetts, on 10 April 1941, Paul Edward Theroux is the third of seven children of Albert and Anne Dittami Theroux. His French-Canadian grandfather came to the United States in the late nineteenth century, and his mother's Italian parents arrived in the early part of the twentieth century. Theroux has attributed to his large working-class family—and to the dreary town of Medford, where he grew up—the sources for his becoming a writer, an inveterate traveler, and a

sometime expatriate. He told James Atlas in 1978 that his parents had "no place, no influence, no money nor power," but to that statement he has added in a personal letter (10 March 1995) that they were a "good influence," being "highly ethical without being conservative." In the 1977 essay, "My Extended Family" (included in the 1985 collection *Sunrise with Seamonsters: Travels and Discoveries, 1964–1984*), he writes: "This family is a little like having a country; it is, in every way, like having a culture: art, literature, common memories, a private language. . . . For the first fifteen years of my life, or more, all my needs were met, all the society I required was available to me; practically and intellectually I was provided for within the family."

In a 1985 interview with Charles Ruas, Theroux notes that though his family is not "literary," it is "a family where there are a lot of ideas." Indeed, all of Theroux's brothers (but neither of his two sisters) share his interests in writing, in travel, or in both. His oldest brother, Eugene (divorced from the writer Phyllis Theroux), is an international lawyer who is an expert in Sino-American trade and has traveled extensively in China. Theroux's older brother, Alexander, is a novelist with a considerable reputation, and one of his two younger brothers is a travel writer, while the other, a former Peace Corps volunteer, has written of his experiences in Western Samoa. Theroux writes in "My Extended Family": "If I were not a part of an extended family I think it would have been impossible for me to travel or stay away for any length of time." In an unpublished interview Theroux told George Plimpton of *The Paris Review* that he had to leave home "in order for my imagination to catch fire."

While crediting his family for much, Theroux negates the value of his formal education in Medford and notes that his performance as a high-school student never suggested his future career. In his 1979 essay, "Traveling Home: High School Reunion" (included in *Sunrise with Seamonsters*), Theroux asks himself what he had been like during his school years. He writes: "None of us at the reunion had had a poor high school education, but for all of us it had been mediocre—non-intellectual rather than anti-intellectual. It had been decent, social, sporty, strict. . . . Who had I been all those years ago? The answer was easy. . . . I had been a punk." In the same essay he writes of his hometown: "I was nagged by one thought: the world was elsewhere. I left Medford the first chance I had, and Medford became part of the dark beyond, as I converted my memories into fiction."

In 1959 Theroux entered the University of Maine, where he wrote editorials against the

ROTC. After one year he transferred to the University of Massachusetts, from which he received a B.A. in 1963. Recalling his college years in the 1991 essay, "Memory and Creation: Reflections at Fifty," Theroux writes:

> My aim was never to excel but only to get it over with and move on. . . . My reading had given me a taste, not for more reading, nor writing, but for seeing the wider, and wilder, world. I had felt small and isolated living in the place where I had grown up. I had read to find out about the world; I knew that it was way beyond my home town; I wanted to leave.

Upon graduation Theroux joined the Peace Corps, serving as a teacher in the British protectorate of Nyasaland, a small and poor country in southeastern Africa that in 1964 became the independent nation of Malawi. In "Memory and Creation" Theroux describes his decision to go to Africa as "a lucky choice." In the same essay, referring to various representations of ethnic groups in the fiction of the 1950s and 1960s, he notes:

> In general I never recognized anything in fiction as resembling the world that I knew. . . . My own mongrel world had gone unreported. It was like being denied my own experience, and without a model—with nothing to imitate, with the mistaken notion that my own world might not even be worth writing about . . . I devised my own remedy, I fled—I went away—as far as I could: with the Peace Corps to Central Africa.

Theroux stayed in Malawi for two years, teaching and supplementing his income by writing pieces for the *Christian Science Monitor* and some African journals. Of these early African pieces, many of which have been reprinted in *Sunrise with Seamonsters,* Theroux writes in his introduction that he "was twenty-one or twenty-three, and if the prose is harshly old-fashioned, then so was the setting. I wrote most of the pieces in Africa—the old Africa." Theroux's presence in Africa coincided with the time when many former colonized areas began to emerge as independent nation states. It was a period of turmoil and instability, and in 1965 Theroux was hastily expelled from Malawi after the American Embassy was informed that Theroux was involved in an assassination attempt on the life of Hastings Bunda, the eventual "President for Life" of the new Malawi nation. If Theroux was not removed, the Embassy was advised, he would be imprisoned. Theroux was precipitously withdrawn from Malawi; transported to Washington, where he was questioned by the Peace Corps and the State Department; and then fined for "six months' unsatisfactory service." Theroux's version of this episode is re-printed in *Sunrise with Seamonsters,* in the 1971 essay, "The Killing of Hastings Bunda." Apparently Theroux had unwittingly been involved with members of an assassination group and had written articles for a German newsletter that may have been an organ of "the German version of the CIA."

Theroux nevertheless returned to Africa shortly after his expulsion from Malawi and taught English from 1965 to 1968 in the Department of Extra-Mural Studies at Makerere University in Kampala, Uganda. In Uganda, Theroux met his future wife, an English woman, Anne Castle (now a British broadcaster but at the time a teacher). They married on 4 December 1967, the same year Theroux published his first book, *Waldo,* a novel that traces its protagonist from the Booneville School for Delinquent Boys through a life of ceaseless activity as he tries to create order and meaning in his world. Though, as Coale notes, the book "reveals the self-conscious artifice of a first novel," it displays many of Theroux's "characteristic techniques and themes," including "the careful observation of detail, the encounters between past and present, the balanced structure and plot . . . , the 'deadpan' style with its ironic distance and precise one-liners."

Theroux completed *Waldo* at the age of twenty-five, just before the writer V. S. Naipaul came to Makerere University for several months. The two men became close, and Naipaul, almost a decade older than Theroux, became the young writer's literary mentor. In *Sunrise with Seamonsters* Theroux writes:

> He had woken me and made me think. . . . He was the first good writer I had ever met. . . . It is almost impossible for me to overestimate the importance of Naipaul's friendship then. . . . It was like private tuition—as if, at this crucial time in my life (I had just finished my first novel), he had come all the way to Africa to remind me of what writing really was and to make me aware of what a difficult path I was setting out on.

Naipaul also advised Theroux about practical career matters: the necessity of sending his work to "good magazines" rather than "little magazines"; the danger to a writer of doing other work such as teaching; and the need to be paid for one's writing. Clearly Theroux absorbed Naipaul's lessons, and he later expressed his admiration in his book *V. S. Naipaul: An Introduction to His Works* (1972).

In 1968 Theroux and his pregnant wife were attacked in their car by a mob. While neither was hurt, the episode convinced Theroux to leave Uganda. He, his wife, and their first son, Marcel, moved to Singapore, where he taught Jacobean drama for three years at the University of Singapore

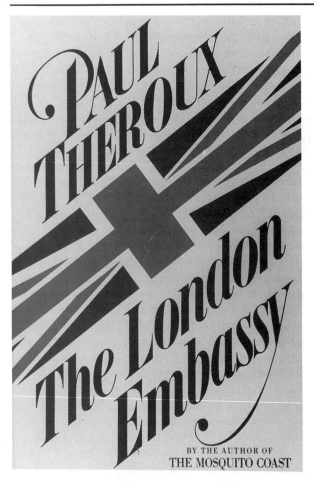

Dust jacket for the first American edition of Theroux's 1982 sequel to The Consul's File *(1977), taking the narrator from Malaysia to England*

and where his second son, Louis, was born. Theroux had discovered, as a developing writer of fiction, that travel and living in "foreign" places triggered his ability to "think creatively." In "Memory and Creation" he writes:

My need for external stimuli inspired in me a desire to travel—and travel, which is nearly always seen as an attempt to escape from the ego, is in my opinion the opposite: nothing induces concentration or stimulates memory like an alien landscape or a foreign culture. It is simply not possible . . . to lose yourself in an exotic place; much more likely is an experience of intense nostalgia, a harking back to an earlier stage of your life. . . . What makes the whole experience thrilling is the juxtaposition of the present and the past, Medford dreamed in Mandalay.

While living and teaching in Singapore, Theroux published three novels: *Fong and the Indians* (1968), *Girls at Play* (1969), and *Jungle Lovers* (1971), each of them set in postcolonial Africa and each dealing with protagonists who are alien and dislo-

cated. Sam Fong, a gentle Chinese Catholic grocer living in Africa and trying to eke out a living at the bottom of the social scale, experiences assaults from the groups that surround him—Americans, communists, Britons, and native Africans. He dreams of the destruction of the milk train, which will allow him to sell the milk he has in his store; the farcical novel concludes with the surreal image of the mangled remnants of the crashed train. Geoffrey Godsell, writing in the *Christian Science Monitor* (5 September 1968), described the novel as "outrageously funny, with a funniness that comes so close to the frequent tragedy of the human condition," and Constance Wagner in the *Saturday Review* (28 September 1968) asserted that the book is "a small masterpiece that . . . cuts so close to the bone of truth that anyone familiar with the 'developing nations' must regard it as selective and hilarious reportage."

In *Girls at Play* five foreign women (an Indian, three Englishwomen, and an American Peace Corps worker) teach at a girls' boarding school in Malawi. The novel ends in the demise of the school, the rape of two of the teachers, and the suicide of the American, whose naïveté and interference has precipitated the grim denouement. A reviewer in the *Times Literary Supplement* (12 June 1969) found the book "unremittingly depressing" but noted that its "power lies in Mr. Theroux's ability to instil an aura of seediness and decay, and a resultant tension, in which violence is a constant possibility."

Jungle Lovers involves two Americans in Africa, both of whom are also writers: an insurance salesman, Calvin Mullet, and a white revolutionary, Marai, who plans to "liberate" Malawi's people from their black dictator. The novel ends with no success for either man; Marai dies and Mullet plans to return to his hometown with his African lover and their son. L. J. Davis, alluding to Theroux's literary debt to Conrad, wrote in *Book World* (8 August 1971) that the novel "is an audacious attempt to tell the other half of *The Heart of Darkness*. . . . both sociologically and politically."

These novels examine the frustrations and difficulties in postcolonial African society and the inevitable problems that arise when "outsiders" attempt to intervene. The pattern of the composition of these and subsequent books follows one that James Atlas notes in *The New York Times Magazine:* Theroux's "practice is to situate each novel in the country where he last resided." Edward T. Wheeler, writing in *Commonweal,* comments that Theroux's "fiction seems to follow the travel, at least for locale and incident."

These early works by Theroux, published before he was thirty, received critical acclaim, particularly in England, and in 1971 Theroux, his wife, and their two sons moved to England, where Anne Theroux worked in broadcasting while Theroux devoted himself entirely to writing. In "A Love-Scene After Work: Writing in the Tropics" (1971; included in *Sunrise with Seamonsters*), Theroux describes his reasons for giving up teaching and for leaving Singapore: "A job . . . always menaces the novel. A job overseas is different; there are many advantages in being an expatriate worker, but there are more disadvantages, and after working abroad for nine years as a teacher in the seasonless monotony of three tropical countries I have decided to chuck the whole business and never take a job."

Soon after Theroux relocated to England, he published *Sinning with Annie and Other Stories* (1972), a diverse collection of pieces that Josephine Hendin, writing in *The New York Times Book Review* (16 November 1972), called "a finely written collection about the come-uppance of the mildly ruthless." Published in the following year, *Saint Jack* (1973) is a novel that examines the seamier side of Singapore through the life and aspirations of a middle-aged American drifter, Jack Fiori. A sometime pimp and panderer, Fiori dreams of writing a novel, though like many Theroux characters, he never succeeds. Yet Fiori manages to win the reader's affection by his exuberance and good heart. Coale describes Fiori as "Theroux's most joyous character, an adventurous, unpretentious soul assured only of his poverty and procrastination as promises of some ultimate reward." The book was well-received, and Theroux's reputation as a "new" novelist was growing. A review of *Saint Jack* in *The Times Literary Supplement* (27 April 1973) contended that "Theroux's style gets sadder, funnier and more distinctive with each novel." Many critics continued to praise Theroux's aptitude for exploring the expatriate experience, his ability to invoke atmosphere, and his wit (often manifested by his keen ear for the idiosyncrasies of individual speech and dialect).

Theroux's seventh novel, *The Black House* (1974), is a "ghost story" that reflects the reverse culture shock of an anthropologist who returns home after ten years in Uganda to retire with his wife in a rural British village. The novel reveals the isolation of Alfred Munday and, as with so many of Theroux's characters, the self-created loneliness to which he is doomed. Noting that the book is in part "a novel about the expatriate experience," Claire Tomalin, writing in *The New Statesman* (4 October 1974), commended Theroux for his skill in handling various themes and for the "level mastery of his writing."

After publication of *The Black House,* Theroux set out on the well-known railway trip that provided material for his first travel book, *The Great Railway Bazaar: By Train through Asia.* The book was a great success, providing Theroux with what he describes in an interview with Charles Ruas as "the first money" and catapulting him to fame as a travel writer. With the money earned from the book, Theroux purchased a house on Cape Cod and set up a pattern of residence that he followed for many years: most of the year spent in London and summers spent with his extended family on Cape Cod.

Though Theroux was already a respected writer who had published several volumes, this travel book established his reputation as a master of the genre. *The Great Railway Bazaar* recounts Theroux's four-month round-trip journey from London across Europe; to the Middle East, India, Southeast Asia, and Japan; through Siberia and Russia to Eastern Europe; and finally back to London. Theroux traveled almost exclusively by train on some of the most famous railways. At the conclusion of this seminal work, Theroux writes: "I had learned what I had always secretly believed, that the difference between travel writing and fiction is the difference between recording what the eye sees and discovering what the imagination knows."

Since the publication of *The Great Railway Bazaar,* Theroux has augmented his publication of fiction and essays with the publication of a long travel work every few years. As a travel writer he has gained a reputation for solitary travel in difficult circumstances and for bringing to his writing an ironic and detached humor that has delighted some readers and offended others. Often traveling by rail, Theroux is concerned with the "how" of the journey, with the intricacies and problems in the ordinary and the extraordinary. He eschews the moment of arrival, preferring to unfold the "poetry of departures" and, in reflective meditations on space and time, the theme of the individual alone in the world. His solitary narrator often reflects on the genre of travel writing, its evolution, and its relationship to fiction.

The connection between Theroux's travel, his travel writing, and his fiction has also interested critics. Elton Glaser remarks: "Like his friend and one-time mentor, V. S. Naipaul, Theroux seems to need the stimulation of travel, the glimpse of an alien life, in order to construct a fictional world." In a front-page review in *The New York Times Book Review* (24 August 1975), Robert Towers discussed *The Great Railway Bazaar* in conjunction with Theroux's fiction and commented on the continuity of theme and focus. He noted that Theroux, though an American,

Dust jacket for Theroux's 1986 novel, depicting American life in the future after a nuclear disaster

has "staked out for himself a fictional terrain that is generally thought of as British," and Towers placed *The Great Railway Bazaar* in the English tradition of the eccentric travel book whose origins, he said, date back to Laurence Sterne's *A Sentimental Journey* (1768). "If Theroux sees mainly decay, sloganism and impoverishment in the present," Towers wrote, "he is also mercilessly aware of the racial blindness, the stupidity, the arrogance and cruelty of the colonial past." Towers also pointed to an aspect of Theroux's writing that has been disparaged by many critics: "Unafraid of ethnic generalizations, he spares no one–African, Englishman, Chinaman, Indian, American–in his wildly absurd confrontations between the old and the new exploiters and the poor bastards caught in the middle; recklessly he juxtaposes the crumbling institutions of colonialism with some of the more bizarre outgrowths of the Third World." James Atlas articulates it another way, referring to "a disturbing racist edge" in Theroux's writing.

After *The Great Railway Bazaar* Theroux returned to fiction with *The Family Arsenal* (1976), a novel that examines the life of a disgraced American consul, Valentine Hood. While hiding in London from American authorities, Hood becomes enmeshed with members of a terrorist group and finally reaches a kind of dark redemption by murdering one of the terrorists and assuming the dead man's persona. Coale writes that "at times coincidences overwhelm the text [and] the reader can occasionally get lost in all the intricate maneuverings," but Coale also notes that the "intricate structure of the novel mirrors the juxtaposition and crosscutting between characters, indicating how firmly Theroux is in control of his material." In the following year, 1978, Theroux published *The Consul's File,* a collection of related short stories set in Malaysia that examines the ways in which uprooted individuals function and malfunction in colonial outposts. Several reviewers referred to W. Somerset Maugham's rendering of Malaysia, pointing to the similarities and differences between Theroux's and Maugham's work. Nicholas Delbanco, in *The New Republic* (10 September 1977), commended Theroux's "comic gift . . . his sense of incongruity," but Jeremy Treglown, writing in *The New Statesman* (17 June 1977), found that while Theroux's "robust expatriate snobbery is still amusing," his "plain style, generally alert in the novels, is often just bland and slack in this collection."

Theroux's tenth work of fiction, *Picture Palace* (1978), is narrated by Maude Coffin Pratt, a septuagenarian photographer famous for her pictures of celebrities. Her memories reveal her incestuous love for her dead brother, Orlando, and the temporary blindness she suffered after discovering that he was sexually involved with their sister. Though some critics found the treatment of incest in the book weak, many praised Theroux's ability to render the voice of an elderly female narrator and, as Vicki Goldberg wrote in the *Saturday Review* (8 July 1978), his "dexterous, energetic style." Goldberg added that the book is "inventive on the surface, deftly composed, full of minor revelations." In his appraisal of *Picture Palace* William H. Pritchard, writing in *The Hudson Review* (Autumn 1978), looked at Theroux's growing opus in retrospect and concluded: "*Picture Palace* is another impressive testimony that as a steadily producing writer of long and short fiction, travel books, essays and reviews–of 'letters' generally–no American writer matters more than this gifted and possessed word-man."

The Old Patagonian Express: By Train through the Americas, published in 1979, represents a return to travel writing for Theroux. The book traces Theroux's departure from his family home in Massachusetts for Patagonia, at the tip of South America in

Argentina. Theroux describes the impulse for starting his venture as similar to the impetus for *The Great Railway Bazaar*. He writes: "I was at a stage I had grown to recognize in my writing life. I had just finished a novel, two years of in-door activity. . . . I studied maps and discovered that there was a continuous track from my house in Medford to the Great Plateau of Patagonia in southern Argentina." Theroux's South American journey begins as he takes the "Boston commuter train" from his boyhood home of Medford and stays on as workers exit to go to their jobs. Theroux moves from the domestic, the mundane and familiar, to the foreign; as he travels further into unknown territory, he encounters the strange, the seedy, the "exotic," and finally, in Patagonia—"nothingness." The closing to *The Old Patagonian Express* encapsulates this existential journey: "I knew I was nowhere, but the most surprising thing of all was that I was still in the world after all this time, on a dot at the lower part of the map."

The Old Patagonian Express was hailed by critics as a welcome "sequel" to *The Great Railway Bazaar*. Paul Fussell, in a front-page article in *The New York Times Book Review* (26 August 1979), praised Theroux for his "sharp eye, which is capable of such shrewd perceptions." Fussell did not think that *The Old Patagonian Express* was as successful as Theroux's first travel book, however, asserting that "the reader gets little relief from the horrors and boredom. He misses the sheer joy of the anomalous, which surfaced frequently in *The Great Railway Bazaar*."

In the following year Theroux published *World's End and Other Stories* (1980), a collection of stories about characters who are, as Benjamin De-Mott wrote in *The New York Times Book Review* (24 August 1980), "travelers, truants and transplants." While DeMott pronounced much of the book "impressive," he concluded that "the book's preoccupation with uprootedness does become wearing before the end." Alan Hollinghurst, in *The New Statesman* (24 October 1980), asserted that the "short story with its emphasis on plot and its need for quick and shapely resolution is an ideal form for Theroux."

The Mosquito Coast (1981) is a novel that many readers consider to be one of Theroux's best. The story of Allie Fox, an obsessed, brilliant, and monomaniacal husband and father, is narrated by his worshipful thirteen-year-old son, Charlie. Allie decides to escape what he perceives as the doomed world of the United States, taking his family to an obscure section of Honduras, where he purchases his own village so that finally he can exercise complete control. At the end of the novel Allie dies, the victim of his own megalomania, in front of his disillusioned son. *The Mosquito Coast* was nominated for

an American Book Award and made into a movie starring Harrison Ford in 1986. Most reviews were laudatory, praising the book for its depth and universality. Jonathan Raban, in his 2 February 1982 *Saturday Review* article, saw the work as a milestone for Theroux, and Coale concludes:

The Mosquito Coast is the supreme example so far of Theroux's fiction, revealing the artist at the top of his form. Everything in it works, delights, and appalls exactly as it should. The querulous central character, the self wrestling with an alien landscape, the extraordinary detail of jungle and nightmare and sea . . . the use of doubling and paradox, the plot used not to contain inevitable collapse or shocks of recognition but to exploit them and make them seem inevitable. . . . *The Mosquito Coast* is an extraordinary novel and at this writing [1987] the apotheosis of Paul Theroux as a writer of fiction.

The London Embassy (1982) was written as a sequel to *The Consul's File*. The narrator, who has been promoted from his Malaysian position to the American Embassy in London, details the people he meets and with whom he works. Judith Chettle, writing in the *Christian Science Monitor* (11 March 1983), noted that though "each chapter could stand on its own as a self-contained short story . . . the changing seasons, a meeting with a beautiful and accomplished heroine, and the narrator's marriage to her at the end give the book the coherence of a novel." However, Robert Towers, in *The New York Review of Books* (2 June 1983), dismissed the collection as "essentially fluff" and asserted that the pieces lack "fictional power" and need to elicit "the reader's response from deeper levels of the imagination."

The Kingdom by the Sea: A Journey around Great Britain (1983) marks a departure in Theroux's travel writing. Instead of embarking on a journey in "underdeveloped" areas of the world, Theroux decided to explore the coast of England, a country in which he had been living for eleven years but much of which he had not seen. Deciding that he wanted to see and learn more about Britain, "the most written-about country in the world," he chose a coastal route for his itinerary. His trip of three months in the spring and summer of 1982 produces a depressing vision of a country rife with unemployment and of a coastline in grim decay, ruined by nuclear reactors, military installations, holiday villages, and trailer camps. The picture of decay and violence that figures so strongly in *The Kingdom by the Sea* connects to a doomsday, futuristic vision that continues to be a strong motif in Theroux's fiction as well.

Linking Theroux's negativity in *The Kingdom by the Sea* to the particulars of his biography, Au-

Dust jacket for Theroux's 1996 novel, which chronicles the adventures of a fictional Paul Theroux

beron Waugh wrote in *The New York Times Book Review* (20 October 1983): "It is hard not to suspect an element of perversity in his mission, even of revenge against a country that had begun to irritate him with its absurd assumption of superiority." This sense that Theroux's negative assessment may be linked to his experience as an American expatriate in London is also suggested by Wilfred Sheed, who wrote in *The Atlantic Monthly* (October 1983) that "Theroux represents a different stage of the American affair with England. It is very hard to keep the English myth going if you actually live there. . . . The moment a man is most likely to turn against an adopted country is when he feels himself becoming part of it."

Theroux published *Sailing through China* in 1983, the same year as *The Kingdom by the Sea.* A slim volume, it recounts Theroux's experience cruising 1,500 miles down the Yangtze River from Chongqing in southwest China to Shanghai on its east coast. The other members of this luxury cruise are primarily millionaires and mostly Americans. The book includes observations about the river and the locations where the boat makes land stops, and it details the often unattractive idiosyncrasies and, at

times, shocking wealth of Theroux's fellow passengers. *Sailing through China* also articulates the doomsday vision that Theroux describes in *The Kingdom by the Sea.*

In 1984 Theroux published two novellas, *Doctor DeMarr* and *Doctor Slaughter,* under the title *Half Moon Street;* in 1986 the latter was made into a movie starring Sigourney Weaver and Michael Caine. The two pieces deal with characters who lead a double life: in *Doctor DeMarr* the protagonist takes over his twin brother's life when he believes him dead, and in *Doctor Slaughter* an American woman on a study grant in England becomes a sexual decoy for an assassination plot. In *The New York Times Book Review* (28 October 1984) Alice McDermott dismissed the characters in both pieces as "figures in an adult cartoon," and Peter S. Prescott in *Newsweek* (22 October 1984) called the stories "rubbish of the very best sort," asserting that "they exemplify the victory of technique over substance."

Patagonia Revisited and *The Imperial Way: Making Tracks from Peshawar to Chittagong,* both brief volumes published in 1985, are further considerations of the sites of Theroux's first two books of travel. *Patagonia Revisited,* written with Bruce Chatwin (author of the 1977 travel book *In Patagonia*), is based on a dialogue between the two writers held at the Royal Geographic Society. Constituting a rather oblique discussion, the book alternates short pieces by Chatwin and Theroux concerning the effect of Patagonia on "the literary imagination." Chatwin begins by noting that he and Theroux went to Patagonia for different reasons but that if they "are travelers at all, . . . [they] are literary travelers," and that both of them are "fascinated by exiles."

The Imperial Way, a book that includes a brief introduction by Theroux and photographs by Steve McCurry, with whom Theroux traced the railway line from Peshawar to Chittagong in northern India in 1984, might be described as a coffee-table volume. Theroux notes that he had not been in the area for ten years and that the trip "was to be neither a vacation nor an ordeal, but rather a kind of sedentary adventuring—an imperial progress along the railways of the old Raj." He writes that one of the reasons for his trip was to see what had changed. When Theroux reaches Calcutta, he again returns to reflections articulated in *Sailing through China* and *The Kingdom by the Sea* of a futuristic world containing cities of devastation. He writes: "I am fascinated by Calcutta. It is one of the cities of the world that I associate with the future. This is how New York City could look, I think, after a terrible disaster—or simply in the fullness of time."

In 1985 Theroux published *Sunrise with Sea-monsters,* a collection of chronologically arranged essays and occasional pieces that spans the twenty-year period from 1964 to 1984. The collection, primarily comprised of previously published works, provides a useful overview of Theroux's career as a writer, traveler, and expatriate of two decades. This uneven collection includes autobiographical essays, appreciations of other writers, and short travel pieces. Almost all of the selections reveal the impressive extent of Theroux's reading and his pleasure in books.

Sunrise with Seamonsters is framed by Theroux's introduction, in which he outlines his conception of himself as a writer, and by his closing title essay, which provides a suitable and nostalgic coda to his career (up to 1985) as a writer of fiction and travel literature, as an intrepid traveler, and as a man deeply involved with his immediate and extended family. In the introduction Theroux says that he "always expected to be fairly paid" for his journalism and that his books saved him "from dropping back into the schoolroom, or into the even more dire profession of writing applications for grants and fellowships." Theroux also describes his writing habits: his need to write these shorter, journalistic pieces as well as his longer books. "I require a certain amount of undemanding interruption in order to maintain my concentration," he writes. "I start every day by writing letters, and even when I am working on a novel I answer the phone." Explaining the chronological arrangement of the volume, Theroux says that he has initially thought that the pieces could be categorized into "Travel, Photography, Books, Writers, Family, and Trains," but that he had to abandon that principle of organizing the pieces. He writes:

> I habitually mixed these topics together: travel was not only an experience of space and time, but had its literary and domextiv aspects as well. Travel is everything, and my way of traveling is completely personal. This is not a category—it is more like a whole way of life. And it is impossible to write about a subway [referring to a "travel" piece in the collection about New York subways] without alluding to *The Wasteland,* or to deal with Burma without mentioning Orwell. My piece about my family . . . owes a great deal to my having lived in Africa.

Though it is true that the concerns in the essays in *Sunrise with Seamonsters* overlap, several of them focus on travel and on a life away from "home." The earlier pieces, written when Theroux was a teacher in Africa, comment on expatriates there and on the local scene. In these essays one sees

many of the motifs that emerge in his later travel writings: the odd and eccentric native; the "ugly American" (or Westerner, European, colonist); and Theroux's attention to the body of literature that prefigures his current interests. Many of these early essays constitute his first travel writing and suggest its genesis in the necessity of the travel writer and novelist to be a careful observer. In "The Cerebral Snapshot" Theroux discusses the writer's charge—to find a way to express through words what he has seen and experienced: "If you really stand as innocent as you can, something of the movement, entering through your eyes, gets into your body where it continues to rearrange your senses. Also—and for a writer this bit of information is priceless—a picture is worth only a thousand or so words."

Theroux's next work, *O-Zone* (1986), is a novel that explores a grim futuristic America that bears some resemblance to the ugly "realities" he describes in *The Kingdom by the Sea* and *Sailing through China.* In Theroux's created world of post-nuclear disaster, O-Zone (formerly the Ozarks) is a nuclear wasteland, and cities such as New York are cordoned off from the rest of the country, which is inhabited by "aliens." Critical response to the book was mixed: Susan Fromberg Schaeffer, writing in *The New York Times Book Review* (14 September 1986), asserted that Theroux has failed "to create characters in whom we can take an interest." She reduced the plot to "a kidnaping, a rescue attempt and a 'surprising' resolution," saying it is "entirely predictable and repetitive." She concluded that "*O-Zone* tells us what we already know. But it does not tell us this well, or interestingly, or vividly." In *The New Statesman* (17 October 1986), however, John Clute says that "Theroux finally makes one able to believe in the seamy, fractured nightmare of his fascist America."

Theroux's second book about China, *Riding the Iron Rooster* (1988), is among his most spirited travel books, recounting his year of travel by train through almost every province in China. Departing London, he joins a group of tourists taking the Trans-Siberian Express to China. Hoping that they will not recognize him (none do), he remains part of the group until it leaves China after several weeks.

Though based on the brief observations of a traveler, Theroux's ability to characterize culturally different behavior is often remarkable, as with his description of Chinese farewells: "no lingering, no swapping of addresses, no reminiscence, nothing sentimental." His categorization throughout the book of various Chinese laughs and their incipient meanings also displays his knack of quickly summing up cultural behaviors. Though many critics

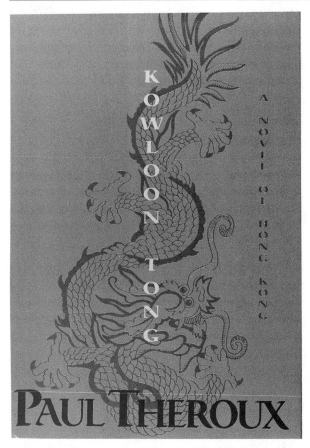

Dust jacket for Theroux's 1997 novel, set in Hong Kong at the time Great Britain returned it to China

have praised Theroux for his incisive and witty assessments, others criticize them as misanthropic generalizations based on a superficial view. For those whose judgment falls in the former camp, *Riding the Iron Rooster* is one of Theroux's funnier travel books, one in which, despite his discomforts and frustrations, the undaunted narrator seems to be thoroughly enjoying himself.

The 1989 novel *My Secret History* chronicles the adventures of Andre Parent, the details of whose life closely parallel Theroux's. The book incorporates many of the locations, experiences, and people significant in Theroux's own biography (including his family background, his Peace Corps work, his travel writing, and his wife and sons). Critics found the book well-written and entertaining. Writing in *The New Statesman* (30 June 1989), Sean French commented on Theroux's "skill at incorporating foreign locations," and R. Z. Sheppard noted in *Time* (22 May 1989) that the book will "undoubtedly cause the usual confusion about what is fact and what is fiction" but that Parent "is the author's best creation, a character who is honest enough to know that he wants it both ways: to be the lover and also the

solitary observer who betrays his loves by turning them into stories. Domestic contentment is not an end in itself, but a respite between difficult journeys."

In his next novel, *Chicago Loop* (1990), Theroux turns to a bleak Chicago landscape peopled by grim characters. Parker Jagoda, a successful architect, husband, and father, has a secret life—as a man who lures vulnerable women through the personal columns and finally murders one of them. As a form of retribution, Parker assumes the guise of the murdered woman and walks the streets at night, inviting attack. Clute, in the *Times Literary Supplement* (6 April 1990), criticized the "pervasive slackness of the imagination" in the novel, adding: "too much of Theroux's work (not excluding the virtuoso travel books) . . . [has] a kind of colonizing condescension. In *Chicago Loop* the colonizing is two-fold. The book seems to have been written in the assumption that . . . [a] tale of sexual pathology need not obey the normal courtesies of coherence; but more important than dropped plot-cues and fumbled sequences is the failure to render Parker Jagoda, and his pathology, with any real care."

Prior to the publication of *Chicago Loop,* Theroux and his wife separated (in 1990), and in 1993 they divorced. It was about this time that Theroux began extensive travel, often by kayak in the South Pacific—an odyssey that resulted in the book, *The Happy Isles of Oceania: Paddling the Pacific* (1992). The voice of *The Happy Isles* is markedly different in tone from Theroux's previous travel works. It is melancholic, more angry, and more personal. On his ambitious and hazardous journey Theroux travels to New Zealand, Australia, and to many of the islands of Melanesia, Polynesia, and Hawaii, often negotiating his way between and around islands in a collapsible kayak. Permeating his narrative is the public news of the Gulf War and the private sadness that Theroux feels, knowing that his marriage is over. Throughout his travels in the Pacific, Theroux often expresses a vituperative anger about the destruction of traditional ways of life among indigenous island peoples. He comments on their ignorance of fishing techniques or boat-building skills and their indifference to the waters that surround them. *The Happy Isles* is probably Theroux's most misanthropic and melancholy travel book.

Critics had a mixed response to *The Happy Isles,* some finding the book too prone to stereotyping, others declaring that it marked a transcendent stage in Theroux's travel writing. Eric Hansen commented in *The New York Times Book Review* (14 June 1992) that Theroux's "preoccupation with mocking strangers and passing hasty judgment severely limits his ability to transport the reader or capture the essence of the people he encounters along the way." He concluded that "Paul Theroux has long since mastered the craft of writing but, after finishing this book, I found myself wondering if he will ever master the fine art of travel." Conversely, Ronald Wright, discussing the book in the *Times Literary Supplement* (31 July 1992), declared it to be perhaps Theroux's best travel work and certainly "his most charming, candid, and adventurous." Wright points to "the undertow" of "personal loss [that] tugs at the book" and says that it "shows a writer letting go of his gimmicks and a man letting go of his life. It is a farewell to what has been and, in a way, a long letter to Anne Theroux" (the person to whom most of Theroux's books are dedicated.)

Theroux's 1993 satirical novel, *Millroy the Magician,* involves a teenaged runaway and Millroy, a magician who proselytizes about nutritious diets and vegetarianism. The novel, as a 20 November 1993 review in *The Economist* points out, is an "often disgusting [because of its concerns with control and manipulation of bodily functions], satire of American obsessions—self-serving evangelism, the need to be 'regular,' the role of television in society and so on." Writing in *The New Yorker* (14 March 1994), John Updike commended the novel, adding that it displays "a tenderness . . . and a jubilation, not hitherto conspicuous among this earnest and prolific author's qualities."

The Pillars of Hercules: A Grand Tour of the Mediterranean appeared in 1995. Dedicated to Theroux's father, who died toward the end of its composition, *The Pillars of Hercules* follows Theroux's peregrinations around and across the Mediterranean. Traveling for the most part "out of season, when the tourists were back home," Theroux begins his narrative at Gibraltar and ends in Tangiers, where he visits the writer Paul Bowles. Though he interrupts his journey for trips home, he spends more than a year traveling the Mediterranean area. Like Britain, the Mediterranean offers an explicit route. Theroux writes: "An inland sea is perfect for a journey, because the coastline determines the itinerary." Describing his proposed plan of travel, he writes:

> My idea was to begin in Gibraltar, and go to Spain, and keep going, hugging the coast, staying on the ground, no planes; to travel by train, bus, ferry, ship; to make a circuit of the sea from the Rock of Gibraltar all the way around to Ceuta [in Morocco], from one Pillar of Hercules to the other. To travel the whole shore, from the fish and chip shops of Torremolinos to the gun emplacements of Tel Aviv, by way of the war in Croatia and the nudist beaches of Crete.

Though Theroux eventually visits most of the places he intended, he is often forced to change his itinerary, back-tracking because of storms, unavailable ships, or the potential dangers of war and terrorism.

The book also "answers" the question of Theroux's failing marriage, left unresolved at the close of *The Happy Isles.* Theroux makes it clear that now, living in Hawaii, he has found a "new love," and for the first time in his travel writing he periodically interrupts his narrative of place to write about his personal life.

As Theroux's travel work became more personal and autobiographical, so did his fiction. In his novel *My Other Life* (1996) the central character is named Paul Theroux. Much of this character's background and accomplishments are exactly the same as Theroux's. For example, the fictional Paul Theroux is a well-known writer who has published books that bear the same titles as his creator's. When sections of this book were originally published in *The New Yorker,* many readers assumed that they were autobiographical essays; and Theroux, discussing the work at a public talk in New York on 17 October 1995, said that he wanted "to write something that looks like autobiography and it's all lies." Though referred to as a novel, the book reads more like a collection of related pieces, and reviewers found the various sections of uneven quality. Most critics found the book tremendously entertaining; Michael Gorra, writing in *The New York Times Book Review* (17 September 1996), asserted that the best pieces in the volume "must rank among the strongest things Mr. Theroux has ever written." Referring to Theroux's copious production of both travel works and fiction, Paul Gray, in *Time* (23 September 1996), said that Theroux has "moved consistently and successfully between the realms of fact and fiction. This time he roams the strange and, in his telling, enchanting territory in between."

In his next novel, *Kowloon Tong* (1997), Theroux returns to a more traditional mode of storytelling, though he roots his novel in the real 1997 return of Hong Kong to China. Neville (Bunt) Mullard, an Englishman born and raised in Hong Kong, and his mother try to deny the impending return of the colony, until Bunt becomes threatened by a Chinese from the mainland who menaces him in order to gain control of their family-owned factory. As Thomas Keneally wrote in *The New York Times Book Review* (8 June 1997): "Hong Kong on the eve of the takeover is itself a major character in this book, possessing both a Chinese and a British substance." In *Booklist* (1 March 1997) Donna Seaman summed up Theroux's accomplishment in this novel: "He has plunged into a completely fresh and vivifying realm, present day Hong Kong, and created a chilling, perfectly paced tale of insularity, coercion, and irrevocable change."

The appearance of *Sir Vidia's Shadow: A Friendship across Five Continents* in 1998 created a literary controversy because of its portrait of V. S. Naipaul (Sir Vidia), Theroux's one-time mentor and friend of more than thirty years. Theroux acknowledges his literary debt to Naipaul and reveals what Laura Shapiro, writing in *Newsweek* (10 August 1998) before the publication of the book, called "a creepy mixture of repulsion and thralldom." *Sir Vidia's Shadow* concludes with the disintegration of the friendship between Naipaul and Theroux; and while Naipaul's friends and acquaintances have criticized Theroux for publishing the book, Theroux was quoted in a 27 July 1998 article in *The New York Times* as saying that readers would be mistaken to focus on the ending: "This book is about the progress of a friendship and about the passage of time, not about the end of a friendship."

Theroux currently resides in Oahu, Hawaii, where his interests include beekeeping, kayaking, and cycling. The writer continues to spend part of the year on Cape Cod. When asked in 1995 about the impact of the move to Hawaii on his writing, Theroux replied in a personal letter: "I see a strong connection between the way I view my writing and the way a painter goes about his business. Painters are always busy sketching, experimenting, repeating themselves and now and then do an ambitious large canvas. They are immensely portable people, . . . the traveler artists. . . . They go to a place and soon the characters and motifs of that place begin to crop up in the work."

Theroux's prolific production of fiction, travel literature, reviews, and essays continues at the same tempo and with the same eclecticism. Since 1967 he has published more than thirty books (about two-thirds of them works of fiction) and hundreds of articles, reviews, and essays. His concerns continue to reflect the expatriate experience, the circumstances of developing countries in a postcolonial world, travel, global politics, and an escalating vision of apocalypse. As an American who has lived abroad for most of his professional life, he has achieved a distinctive reputation in the world of contemporary literature. While many critics have identified Theroux's work with British writers such as Graham Greene or with expatriate writers such as Joseph Conrad and Naipaul, Coale asserts that Theroux's outlook "coincides with that of most serious American fiction: the clash between various cultures . . .

[and] the traditional American faith in self-renewal and rebirth." Referring to Manichean conflicts in Theroux's writing, Coale compares Theroux's work to that of American writers such as Nathaniel Hawthorne, Herman Melville, John Gardner, Joyce Carol Oates, and William Styron.

While some critics have suggested that Theroux's writing is uneven and at times superficial in understanding, many consider him among the most important of contemporary American writers. Theroux, thus far, has not achieved the stature of some of the writers to whom he has been compared, but he remains a significant figure in the American and British literary landscape, one whose range and sheer productivity of serious and reflective writing is singular.

Interviews:
James T. Yenckel, "The Wanderlust World of Paul Theroux," *Washington Post,* 30 December 1984, pp. 1–3;

Charles Ruas, interview with Paul Theroux, in his *Conversations with American Writers* (New York: Knopf, 1985), pp. 244–264;

George Plimpton, unpublished interview with Theroux, on tape recording at Library of 92nd Street YMYWHA, New York (18 December 1989);

Sam Staggs, "Paul Theroux," *Publishers Weekly*, 241 (7 March 1994): 48–49;

Ray Suarez, "Talk of the Nation," National Public Radio (19 October 1995).

References:
James Atlas, "The Theroux Family Arsenal," *New York Times Magazine,* 30 April 1978, pp. 22–24, 49, 52, 54, 58, 60, 62, 64;

Terry Caesar, "The Book in the Travel: Paul Theroux's *The Old Patagonian Express,*" *Arizona Quarterly,* 46 (Summer 1990): 101–110;

Samuel Coale, *Paul Theroux* (Boston: Twayne, 1987);

Paul Fussell, "The Stationary Tourist," *Harper's,* 258 (March 1979): 31–38;

Elton Glaser, "Paul Theroux and the Poetry of Departures," in *Temperamental Journeys: Essays on the Modern Literature of Travel,* edited by Michael Kowalewski: (Athens & London: University of Georgia Press, 1992), pp. 153–163;

Mary Louise Pratt, *Imperial Eyes: Travel Writing and Transculturation* (London & New York: Routledge, 1992);

Edward T. Wheeler, "What the Imagination Knows: Paul Theroux's Search for the Second Self," *Commonweal,* 121 (20 May 1994): 18–22.

Anne Tyler

This entry was updated by Caren J. Town (Georgia Southern University) from her entry in
DLB 143: American Novelists Since World War II, Third Series.

See also the Tyler entries in *DLB 6: American Novelists Since World War II, Second Series,* and *DLB Yearbook 1982.*

BIRTH: Minneapolis, Minnesota, 25 October 1941, to Lloyd Parry and Phyllis Mahon Tyler.

EDUCATION: B.A., Duke University, 1961; graduate study at Columbia University, 1961–1962.

MARRIAGE: 3 May 1963 to Taghi Mohammed Modarressi (died 1997); children: Tezh, Mitra.

AWARDS AND HONORS: *Mademoiselle* award for writing, 1966; American Academy and Institute of Arts and Letters Award for literature, 1977; National Book Critics Circle fiction award nomination, 1980, Janet Heidinger Kafka prize, 1981, and American Book Award nomination in paperback fiction, 1982, all for *Morgan's Passing;* National Book Critics Circle fiction award nomination, 1982, American Book Award nomination in fiction, PEN/Faulkner Award for fiction, and Pulitzer Prize nomination for fiction, all 1983, for *Dinner at the Homesick Restaurant;* National Book Critics Circle Award and Pulitzer Prize nomination for *The Accidental Tourist,* 1985; Pulitzer Prize for *Breathing Lessons,* 1988.

BOOKS: *If Morning Ever Comes* (New York: Knopf, 1964; London: Chatto & Windus, 1965);
The Tin Can Tree (New York: Knopf, 1965; London: Macmillan, 1966);
A Slipping-Down Life (New York: Knopf, 1970; London: Severn House, 1983);
The Clock Winder (New York: Knopf, 1972; London: Chatto & Windus, 1973);
Celestial Navigation (New York: Knopf, 1974; London: Chatto & Windus, 1975);
Searching for Caleb (New York: Knopf, 1976; London: Chatto & Windus, 1976);
Earthly Possessions (New York: Knopf, 1977; London: Chatto & Windus, 1977);
Morgan's Passing (New York: Knopf, 1980; London: Chatto & Windus, 1980);

Anne Tyler (photograph © Diana Walker)

Dinner at the Homesick Restaurant (New York: Knopf, 1982; London: Chatto & Windus, 1982);
The Accidental Tourist (New York: Knopf, 1985; London: Chatto & Windus, 1985);
Breathing Lessons (New York: Knopf, 1988; London: Chatto & Windus, 1989);
Saint Maybe (New York: Knopf, 1991; London: Chatto & Windus, 1991);
Tumble Tower, illustrated by Mitra Modarressi (New York: Orchard Books, 1993; London: Julia MacRae, 1993);
Ladder of Years (New York: Knopf, 1995; London: Chatto & Windus, 1995);
A Patchwork Planet (New York: Knopf, 1998; London: Chatto & Windus, 1998).

OTHER: "Still Just Writing," in *The Writer and Her Work: Contemporary Women Writers Reflect on Their Art and Situation,* edited by Janet Sternburg (New York: Norton, 1980), pp. 3–16;

"Thank You, Marguerite Young," in *Marguerite Young: Our Darling: Tributes and Essays,* edited by Miriam Fuchs (Normal, Ill.: Salkey Archive Press, 1994).

SELECTED PERIODICAL PUBLICATIONS–UNCOLLECTED:

POETRY

"The Ice-Pond Alien," in "Have Yourself a Gorey Little Christmas," *New York Times Book Review,* 2 December 1980, pp. 16–18.

FICTION

"Laura," *Archive,* 71 (March 1959): 36–37;

"Lights on the River," *Archive,* 72 (October 1959): 5–6;

"The Bridge," *Archive,* 72 (March 1960): 10–15;

"I Never Saw Morning," *Archive,* 73 (April 1961): 11–14;

"The Baltimore Birth Certificate," *The Critic: A Catholic Review of Books and the Arts,* 21 (February–March 1963): 41–45;

"I Play Kings," *Seventeen,* 22 (August 1963): 338–341;

"The Street of Bugles," *Saturday Evening Post,* 236 (30 November 1963): 64–66;

"Nobody Answers the Door," *Antioch Review,* 24 (Fall 1964): 379–386;

"Dry Water," *Southern Review,* 1 (April 1965): 259–291;

"I'm Not Going to Ask You Again," *Harper's,* 231 (September 1965): 88–98;

"The Saints in Caesar's Household," *Archive,* 79 (September 1966): 18–21;

"As the Earth Gets Old," *New Yorker,* 42 (29 October 1966): 60–64;

"Two People and a Clock on the Wall," *New Yorker,* 42 (19 November 1966): 207–208;

"The Genuine Fur Eyelashes," *Mademoiselle,* 69 (January 1967): 102–103, 136–138;

"The Tea-Machine," *Southern Review,* 3 (January 1967): 171–179;

"The Feather Behind the Rock," *New Yorker,* 43 (12 August 1967): 26–30;

"A Flaw in the Crust of the Earth," *Reporter,* 37 (2 November 1967): 43–46;

"Who Would Want a Little Boy?" *Ladies Home Journal,* 85 (May 1968): 132–133, 156–158;

"The Common Courtesies," *McCall's,* 95 (June 1968): 62–63, 115–116;

"With All Flags Flying," *Redbook,* 137 (June 1971): 88–89, 136–139, 140;

"Outside," *Southern Review,* 7 (Autumn 1971): 1130–1144;

"The Bride in the Boatyard," *McCall's,* 99 (June 1972): 92–93;

"Respect," *Mademoiselle,* 75 (June 1972): 146;

"A Misstep of the Mind," *Seventeen,* 31 (October 1972): 118 ff.;

"The Base-Metal Egg," *Southern Review,* 9 (Summer 1973): 682–686;

"Spending," *Shenandoah,* 24 (Winter 1973): 58–68;

"Neutral Ground," *Family Circle,* 85 (November 1974): 36 ff.;

"Half-Truths and Semi-Miracles," *Cosmopolitan,* 177 (December 1974): 264 ff.;

"A Knack for Languages," *New Yorker,* 50 (13 January 1975): 32–37;

"The Artificial Family," *Southern Review,* 11 (Summer 1975): 615–621;

"The Geologist's Maid," *New Yorker,* 51 (28 July 1975): 29–33;

"Some Sign That I Ever Made You Happy," *McCall's,* 103 (October 1975): 90, 124–133;

"Your Place Is Empty," *New Yorker,* 52 (22 November 1976): 45–54;

"Holding Things Together," *New Yorker,* 52 (24 January 1977): 30–35;

"Average Waves in Unprotected Waters," *New Yorker,* 53 (28 February 1977): 32–36;

"Under the Bosom Tree," *Archive,* 89 (Spring 1977): 72–77;

"Foot-Footing On," *Mademoiselle,* 83 (November 1977): 82 ff.;

"Uncle Ahmad," *Quest/77,* 1 (November/December 1977): 76–82;

"Linguistics," *Washington Post Magazine,* 12 November 1978, pp. 38 ff.;

"Laps," *Parents' Magazine,* 56 (August 1981): 66–70;

"The Country Cook," *Harper's,* 264 (March 1982): 54–62;

"Teenage Wasteland," *Seventeen,* 42 (November 1983): 144–148;

"Rerun," *New Yorker,* 64 (4 July 1988): 20–32;

"A Woman Like a Fieldstone House," *Ladies Home Journal,* 106 (August 1989): 86 ff.;

"A Street of Bugles," *Saturday Evening Post,* 26 (July 1989): 54–57 ff;

"People Who Don't Know the Answers," *New Yorker,* 67 (26 August 1991): 26–36.

NONFICTION:

"Youth Talks About Youth: 'Will This Seem Ridiculous?'" *Vogue,* 145 (1 February 1965): 85, 206;

"Olives Out of a Bottle," *Archive,* 87 (Spring 1975): 70–90;

"Because I Want More Than One Life," *Washington Post,* 15 August 1976, sec. G, pp. 1, 7;

"Trouble in the Boys' Club: The Trials of Marvin Mandel," *New Republic,* 177 (30 July 1977): 16–19;

"Chocolates in the Afternoon and Other Temptations of a Novelist," *Washington Post Book World,* 4 December 1977, p. 3;

"Writers' Writers: Gabriel García Márquez," *New York Times Book Review,* 4 December 1977, p. 70;

"My Summer," *New York Times Book Review,* 4 June 1978, pp. 35–36;

"Please Don't Call It Persia," *New York Times Book Review,* 18 February 1979, pp. 3, 34–36;

"The Fine, Full World of Eudora Welty," *Washington Star,* 26 October 1980, sec. D, p. 1;

"A Visit with Eudora Welty," *New York Times Book Review,* 2 November 1980, pp. 33–34;

"Why I Still Treasure 'The Little House,'" *New York Times Book Review,* 9 November 1986, p. 5;

"Reynolds Price: Duke of Writers," *Vanity Fair,* 49 (July 1986): 82–85;

"Books Past, Present and to Come," *Washington Post Book World,* 6 December 1992, sec. G, p. 1 ff.

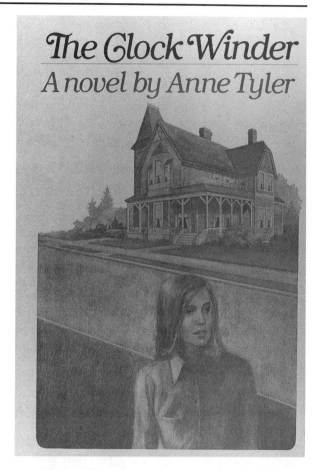

Dust jacket for Tyler's 1972 novel, about a young woman involved in the complex affairs of a large dysfunctional family for whom she works

"The real heroes to me in my books," Anne Tyler told interviewer Marguerite Michaels, "are first the ones who manage to endure and second the ones who somehow are able to grant other people the privacy of the space around them and yet still produce some warmth." Tyler herself has managed to endure—fourteen novels in thirty-five years—while demanding space around her (she steadfastly refuses teaching appointments, lectures, readings, and most interviews) and still producing a great deal of warmth. Her frequently appealing, often shy characters have endured in the minds of her readers as well, creating an enthusiastic following for this very private Baltimore writer.

Daughter of chemist Lloyd Parry Tyler and social worker Phyllis Mahon Tyler, Anne Tyler was born on 25 October 1941 in Minneapolis, Minnesota. From Minneapolis the family moved to Pennsylvania, Chicago, Duluth, Celo (a collective, experimental community in the North Carolina mountains), and finally to Raleigh, North Carolina. She finished her undergraduate work (in three years) at Duke University, during which time she was the student of writer Reynolds Price, published short stories in the school literary magazine, twice won the Anne Flexner Creative Writing Award, and graduated with a degree in Russian. She completed her graduate course work (but not the dissertation) in Russian at Columbia University and then worked as a Russian bibliographer at Duke.

In 1963 she married Iranian-born child psychologist (and novelist) Taghi Mohammed Modarressi. She and her husband moved to Montreal, where he completed his residency while she pub-

lished her first novels, *If Morning Ever Comes* (1964) and *The Tin Can Tree* (1965), and gave birth to their daughters—Tezh in 1965 and Mitra in 1967. The family then moved to Baltimore, where she still resides (she was widowed in 1997). In Baltimore, Tyler raised her daughters, managed her household, and published twelve additional novels, a children's book, more than fifty short stories, and many reviews. Barbara Dixson, who has studied Tyler's reviews, comments on the "astonishing range" of her reading and notes that she "produces reviews at an amazing rate." Her prolific output is in part due to the strictness with which she has maintained the divisions between her work and her family (when her daughters were school-aged, she did all writing between 8:05 a.m. and 3:30 p.m.) and ruthlessly protected her free time.

She is protective of her intellectual life as well, remaining, as Joseph C. Voelker says, "subtly evasive in all her nonfictional self-representations." She is as protective of her characters as she is of her own privacy: "I think that what I most fear," she commented to Wendy Lamb, "is intrusion, but it doesn't happen with those characters because on paper you control them, you guard against that intrusion." She protects her characters, not because she fears them—or for them—but, she says, because she likes them.

Her readers appear to like them as well. Since the publication of her first novel, Tyler has received predominantly favorable reviews; the enthusiastic attention of novelist John Updike, which began with her sixth novel, *Searching for Caleb* (1976), has increased her standing. Her recent novels have been commercially successful as well, with her ninth, *Dinner at the Homesick Restaurant* (1982), selling 60,000 copies in hardcover and more than 655,000 in paperback editions. *Breathing Lessons* (1988), her eleventh novel, was published in a hardcover edition of 100,000 and won the Pulitzer Prize for literature, and her most recent novels, *Ladder of Years* (1995) and *A Patchwork Planet* (1998), although puzzling to some critics, continue her popular success.

Tyler's popularity rests in part on the apparent ordinariness of her subjects: the power of family, the struggle for personal growth, the accumulation of possessions, and the influence of religion. Yet this ordinariness is not simplicity: she treats each common situation with a wry humor and fills each plot with eccentric characters and unconventional developments. For example, her attitude about religion, as Voelker says, "possesses no force of law. . . . has no concept of sin and no eschatology. . . . but . . . acknowledges as valid the Christian feeling of being out of place in the world, the spirit's restlessness." In this area as in many others, Tyler manages to maintain the spirit of an idea while still questioning many of its premises.

Her view of the family is similar. In nearly every novel her characters are both burdened with and supported by their families; for Tyler, families are something one simultaneously wants to escape and to re-create. Critics often point out the way in which Tyler disrupts conventional expectations about family and redefines the subject in her own terms. Doris Betts puts it well: "Tyler's homes are not merely broken but often crazed like a glass vessel but the vessels still hold; blood is still thicker than water."

Tyler is also interested in the growth and maturity of her characters, although drift and inaction frequently constitute a kind of progress. Her characters are often engaged in a struggle to cast off belongings and hold on to what is important: like Charlotte Emory in *Earthly Possessions* (1977), her female characters in particular remain at home, with their cosmetic cases packed and their sensible walking shoes on. For Tyler the most interesting moments in a person's life are not the grand gestures of repudiation or reconciliation but the day-to-day reality following such gestures—what happens to Cinderella after she marries (or divorces) her prince. As Betts says, Tyler's interest remains more in how "people survive and persist *beyond* crisis during the long, steady, three-meal-a-day aftermaths."

This attention to steady aftermaths is one of the reasons that Tyler's worlds are so full of objects. Margaret Morganroth Gullette notes that for Tyler's characters, decisions about accumulation are "momentous . . . because early on in life whether you can become an adult seems to hinge on it, and later, how you want your adulthood to be—whether you want it to be stationary (with a family, house and furniture), or whether you need it to be mobile and sparse." Some characters need it to be both; opposing forces operate in her novels between what Anne R. Zahlan identifies as "accumulating and gathering and clearing out and moving on." Tyler, too, finds herself drawn by these forces: "I build a house for them," she told Michaels about her characters, "and then I move on to the next house."

Her first house, occupied by Ben Joe Hawkes and his family in *If Morning Ever Comes,* is the prototypical Tyler home, cluttered with people and objects and becoming the place characters often leave and always miss. Ben Joe's leave-taking is fraught with difficulties, which Tyler establishes in the first lines of the novel: "When Ben Joe Hawkes left home he gave his sister Susannah one used guitar, six shelves of *National Geographic,* a battered microscope, and a foot-high hourglass. All of these things he began to miss as soon as he hit New York." Ben Joe, the only boy in a family of girls and the only man in the house after the desertion (and subsequent death) of their father, finds it hard to leave his things—and home—behind. His discomfort is echoed by later Tyler characters. Voelker notes astutely that Ben Joe is Tyler's first "gentle agoraphobic male," who later develops into such central characters as Jeremy Pauling in *Celestial Navigation* (1974) and Macon Leary in *The Accidental Tourist* (1985).

Ben Joe's family, however, does not find it hard to have him go; in fact, when he returns, supposedly to help with what he alone regards as the crisis his sister Joanne has caused by leaving her husband, "he suddenly saw how closed-off his family looked. They went peacefully on with what they were doing; Ben Joe, having vanished, might as well not exist." They continue on with their jobs, their quarrels, their lives, in apparent unconcern, but they are happier to have him back than is immediately apparent. Ben Joe comments, "You had to be a sort of detective with his mother; you had to search out the fresh-made bed, the flowers on the bureau, and the dinner table laid matter-of-factly with your favorite supper, and then you forgot her crisp manners." Like many mothers in Tyler's fiction, Ben Joe's mother is not expressively maternal; her care and concern have to be ferreted out.

Once home, the problem for Ben Joe becomes whether to remain trapped in old circumstances or to strike out for new territories. "Every place I go," he says, "I miss another place." Ben Joe starts to tell Joanne, who thinks returning to her husband would be "going backwards," that "sometimes it's not the same place when a person goes back to it, or not the same . . . " but then gives up on the argument. He ends up marrying his high-school sweetheart, Shelley, and taking her back to New York with him, effectively combining his past and his future, which he sees as "a long, deep rug, as real as the past or the present ever was." The important thing here, Voelker says, is that "Tyler imagines sane people who know that life is a trap, but that grace is a distinct possibility." Even in this first Tyler novel, Ben Joe Hawkes sees the trap—his home and family of women who appear to depend on him—and believes that in his marriage to Shelley he will find grace.

In *The Tin Can Tree,* Tyler's second novel, grace is harder to find, perhaps because the traps are deeper, the hold stronger, and the number of characters larger. As in *If Morning Ever Comes,* a death precedes this novel, but the death of six-year-old Janie Rose Pike plunges her mother, Lou, into a depression that causes her to neglect her remaining child, Simon. The accident reaches out to involve their neighbors as well—the Pikes' boarder and niece, Joan Pike; brothers James and Ansel Green; and elderly sisters Misses Faye and Lucy Potter, who share a three-family house with the Pikes and the Greens. Each of these groups is caught in its own trap as well: Joan can neither live with her parents, feel at home with the Pikes, nor progress in her relationship with James; James is unable to extricate himself from a destructive relationship with his hypochondriacal brother; and the maiden sisters are virtual prisoners of their fears and idiosyncrasies.

Photographs become emblematic of this stasis, as they do in many Tyler novels. Ansel calls James's pictures "very *remaining* things," but their ability to remain also causes him distress when he finds that James has accidentally captured an image of Janie Rose on film shortly before her death. His distress is similar to Simon's when he comments that "unliving things last much longer than living."

Yet while photographs "last longer" than the human lives they capture, they also reveal a solidity in people. After Simon, in the hope that his mother will notice him again, runs away to Ansel and

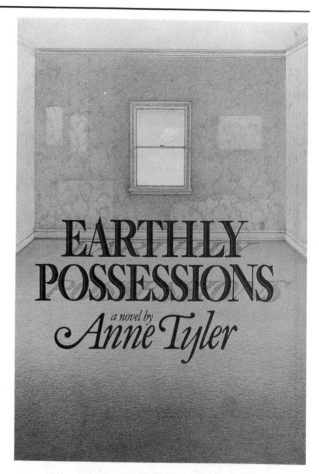

Dust jacket for Tyler's 1977 novel, in which the central character tries to help the bank robber who kidnaps her

James's family, and Joan returns after an abortive attempt to return home, the extended family has a party in the Potters' house, and James takes a picture. Joan thinks that "whole years could pass, they could be born and die, they could leave and return, they would marry or live out their separate lives alone, and nothing in this [camera view]finder would change. They were going to stay this way, she and all the rest of them, not because of anyone else but because it was what they had chosen, what they would keep a strong tight hold of." This keeping a "strong tight hold" becomes increasingly important in Tyler's fiction. Anne G. Jones poses the issue: "Tyler's novels present a meditation on mutability. How can identity persist if someone changes?" For the Pikes and the rest of their extended family, identity persists by keeping a "strong tight hold" of what matters—love, family, and neighbors.

For Evie Decker, the teenaged heroine of Tyler's next novel, *A Slipping-Down Life* (1970), who carves the name of her rock-star idol into her forehead, the question of identity is a crucial one. Fat, unattractive, trapped with a widowed father and an unsympathetic housekeeper, Evie thinks she finds what matters in Drum Casey, a local singer. Her self-mutilation gets Drum's attention, as well as that of his "manager" (and drummer), and Evie becomes part of their publicity. Drum proves to be as needy as Evie, and they marry. They are not well suited, in a typically Tyler way: Evie finds that the "importance of details seemed peaceful and lulling," but for Drum, "life is getting too cluttered." As Zahlan has said, "Opposed to the tendencies of accumulating and gathering in are the centrifugal forces of clearing out and moving on."

When her father dies, Evie returns to his home, leaving Drum behind. But just as for Ben Joe and the Pikes, there is the possibility that returning home is not giving up or moving backward. Drum asks her what she will say when people ask her why she has the name "Casey" on her forehead, and she says she will tell them it is her name, as it now is. Drum responds, "Now that you have done all that cutting . . . and endured through bleeding and police cars and stitches, are you going to say it was just for purposes of *identification?*" What Drum fails to realize is that it is for these very purposes that Evie, who is pregnant with his baby, has gone through all the trouble—she knows who she is; she has been identified. In this novel, to which Paul Binding accords "minor classic status," the growth from adolescence to adulthood involves enduring "bleeding and police cars and stitches" but ends with a clear sense of self.

Elizabeth Abbott, the main character in Tyler's fourth novel, *The Clock Winder* (1972), appears to lack this sense. When, after dropping out of college, she offers her help with odd jobs to widowed Mrs. Emerson, the older woman wonders "what kind of person would let herself get so sidetracked." On learning that Elizabeth has been looking for a job with another family, she asks, "Do you usually go at things in such a roundabout way?" Mrs. Emerson's son Timothy, who falls in love with Elizabeth and eventually kills himself (perhaps accidentally) out of jealousy, accuses her of "seeing life as some kind of gimmicky guided tour where everyone signs up for a surprise destination." Yet when Elizabeth finally realizes that he is talking about her attitude toward life, she smiles "as fondly and happily as if he had mentioned her favorite acquaintance."

Another of Mrs. Emerson's sons, Matthew, who also loves and eventually marries Elizabeth, thinks he will give her life direction and stability: "His life had solidified. He was a man in his thirties who lived by himself, encased in a comfortable set of habits and a plodding, easy-going job. He liked things the way they were. Change of any kind he

carefully avoided." But Elizabeth sees the flux in their (and every) relationship: "Life seemed to be a constant collision and recollision of bodies on the move in the universe; everything recurred. She would keep running into Emersons until the day she died; and she and Matthew would keep falling in love and out again." The only reality for Elizabeth is constant motion.

This novel also includes the first extended discussion of the internal dynamics of the family in Tyler's novels. All of Mrs. Emerson's seven children, she says, "are always moving away from me; I feel like the center of an asterisk. They *work* at moving away." Another of Tyler's apparently ambivalent mothers, she has a "way of summing up each child in a single word, putting a finger squarely on his flaw." Also, everything she says to her children is "attached to other things by long gluey strands, calling up other days, none of them good, touching off chords, opening doors." Yet her children are "split between wanting to defeat [their] mother's expectations and wanting to live up to them." Elizabeth sees Matthew's life—and hers within it—"as a piece of strong twine, with his mother and his brothers and sister knotting their tangled threads into every twist of it, and his wife another thread, linked to him and to all his family by long, frayed ropes."

Since she is not one of Mrs. Emerson's children yet, Elizabeth can still work free of the ropes, and she runs home to marry her former sweetheart, Dommie Whitehill. She bolts during the ceremony, however, and eventually ends up back at the Emersons' house, nursing Mrs. Emerson through a stroke, being shot by brother Andrew in retaliation for Timothy's death, marrying Matthew, having a series of children, and becoming thoroughly incorporated into the Emersons' troublesome domesticity.

Much of Elizabeth's transformation comes from a change in her attitude toward children. She has realized the amount of work it takes to raise children, in the process increasing her sympathy with Mrs. Emerson, her own family, and Matthew's desire to start his own family with her. "Human beings are born so helpless, and stay helpless so long," she tells Mrs. Emerson. "For every grownup you see, you know there must have been at least one person who had the patience to lug them around, and feed them, and walk them nights and keep them out of danger for years and years without a break." Early in the novel she seems so mismatched with her own parents that Timothy imagines a federal law that would require people to switch parents: "There would be a gigantic migration of children across the country, all cutting the old tangled threads and picking up new ones when they found the right niche,

free forever of other people's notions of them." Yet
Elizabeth has migrated to the Emersons and is completely transformed by them, with Mrs. Emerson
even giving her a new name, "Gillespie," which
turns her into "someone effective and managerial
who was summoned by her last name, like a WAC."

The novel ends with a vision of Elizabeth (now
calling herself Gillespie) with a baby at her breast
and dinner in the oven, smoothing over the usual
Emerson hysteria. This picture is not one of unmiti-
gated happiness. (Tyler told Clifford A. Ridley that
she thinks of this ending as sad and is surprised
when others do not.) Mrs. Emerson's youngest son
Peter has returned with his (as yet unannounced)
wife, P.J., who comments that his family is "depending on someone that is like the old-maid failure poor
relation you find some places, mending their screens
and cooking their supper and fixing their chimneys
and making peace–oh, she ended up worse off than
them."

But P.J. may not have the last word. When she
leaves, Peter is torn between wanting to go after his
wife and having Gillespie take care of him. "Maybe
they're right," he says to her, "You shouldn't hope
for anything from someone that much different
from your family." Gillespie responds, "You should
if your family doesn't *have* it," and goes to check the
oven; Peter goes after his wife. George (Matthew
and Gillespie's son) watches him go "absently, as if,
every day of his life, he saw people arriving and
leaving and getting sidetracked from their travels."
It seems that Gillespie/Elizabeth is not the only one
who has changed; the Emersons have become as
"sidetracked" as she. The last words come from
Mrs. Emerson and Andrew: when she asks, "Why
are my children always leaving?" he answers, "Why
are they always coming *back?* . . . Scratching their
heads and saying, '*What* was it you wanted me to
do?'"

Mary F. Robertson has noticed this movement: "Because the boundary between insiders and
outsiders is continually transgressed, the progress
of Tyler's novels is felt more as an expansion of narrative disorder than as a movement toward resolution and clarification." For Tyler, adding new members, getting sidetracked, and coming back home is
what families do.

Celestial Navigation, Tyler's fifth novel, and according to Voelker her "most theoretical book," addresses even more directly the issues of family disintegration and reformation. The novel opens, as do
six of Tyler's first twelve novels, with a death, this
time of artist Jeremy Pauling's mother. Jeremy has
no immediate family members in his house, but he is

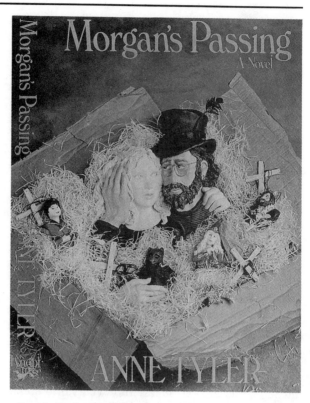

*Dust jacket for Tyler's 1980 novel, about a man whom Tyler
calls "the inveterate impostor"*

surrounded by a surrogate family of boarders.
Shortly after his mother's death, Jeremy takes in
Mary Tell and her four-and-a-half-year-old daughter, Darcy, who have left home in the company of a
man who promises to marry her but never does. In
their unfocused way, Jeremy and Mary fall in love
and raise a large family in the boardinghouse, always with the help and observation of their boarders. Theirs is clearly a complex and unusual love
story, as are all Tyler love stories.

Jeremy is severely agoraphobic, as well, unable to leave his block without having profound
anxiety attacks, but he is not primarily an object of
humor or pity. Voelker says that Tyler "recasts the
novelist's inventive processes in the guise of a consciousness so fragmentary and fleeting that it approaches autism" and calls *Celestial Navigation* "a
meditation on the connection between disorienta-
tion and insight." Jeremy thus becomes a figure for
the writer, and his character type is repeated in several novels, most particularly in Ezra Tull in *Dinner
at the Homesick Restaurant* and Macon Leary in *The Accidental Tourist,* as well as in many minor characters
throughout her work. Voelker says Tyler often sees
the "phobic moment as an initial imaginative conception."

Jeremy's attitude toward his collages and sculptures does seem analogous to Tyler's working strategies, in particular the absolute necessity of cutting himself off from life in order to re-create it. "All his eye for detail goes into cutting and pasting. There is none left over for real life," his sister Amanda says. When people look at him, he thinks, all they see is the artist; they never guess at "the cracks inside, the stray thoughts, tangents of memory, hours of idleness, days spent leafing through old magazines or practicing square knots on a length of red twine or humming under his breath while he tapped his fingers on the windowsill and stared down at the people on the street." After the breakup of his marriage (Mary tries to protect him from the outside world, and he thinks she no longer needs him), he realizes that "humanity was far more complex and untidy and depressing than it ever was in his pieces."

Yet for a while Jeremy's struggle to fit into his household and his family is the source of much of the tension in this novel. Alice Hall Petry points out that "Tyler's characters try to integrate the seemingly antithetical fragments of the world, rendering incongruous images, ideas, and events into meaningful wholes over which they, as artists, exert control." At first, integration seems impossible. He is "*always* himself. That's what's wrong with him," as Amanda says, and to him it seemed that "life was a series of hurdles that he had been tripping over for decades, with the end nowhere in sight." The boarder Miss Vinton notices that he "*lives* at a distance. He makes pictures the way other people make maps—setting down the few fixed points that he knows, hoping they will guide him as he goes floating through his unfamiliar planet. He keeps his eyes on the horizon while his hands work blind."

Still, he and Mary do manage to have children, and he comes to realize that she is more vulnerable, though also stronger than he is, because "the deepest pieces of herself were in those children and every day they scattered in sixty different directions and faced a thousand unknown perils; yet she sailed through the night without so much as a prayer. There was no way he could ever hope to match her." After their breakup he thinks "He had waited for love like a man awaiting salvation. The secret, the hidden key. Was it love that failed Jeremy, or was it Jeremy who failed love? Was there anything to hope for *after* love?" Mary, in self-imposed exile with her children in Jeremy's agent's waterfront cabin, decides that "all events, except childbirth, can be reduced to a heap of trivia in the end." Jeremy determines that "steadfast endurance" is what life is all about, and he continues to live out his life with his elderly boarders, recognizing that although "he had

heard that suffering made great art . . . in his case all it made was parched, measly, stunted lumps far below his usual standard." Without his family around him, no matter how difficult or painful their presence may have been at times, Tyler reveals, Jeremy is unable to create.

Marriage and family are not just two of the subjects of Tyler's sixth novel, *Searching for Caleb*; they are its lifeblood. In this novel Justine Peck marries her first cousin Duncan, reluctantly follows him in his attempted escape from the rigidities of life in the Peck family, and simultaneously helps her grandfather Daniel try to find his long-lost brother, Caleb, who did manage to escape the family. The reason someone even mildly unconventional would want to escape is fairly clear: the Pecks are a family united in their "perfect manners" and their disapproval of "sports cars, golf, women in slacks, chewing gum, the color chartreuse, emotional displays, ranch houses, bridge, mascara, household pets, religious discussions, plastic, politics, nail polish, transparent gems of any color," and on and on. This escape plan, however, is complicated by Justine and Duncan's daughter, Meg, who turns out to be afflicted with "total Peckness," and whose marriage to a man unlike her parents, but like the other Pecks, nevertheless makes her miserable.

Justine, too, has ambivalent feelings about the Pecks. She remembers childhood evenings at the Peck houses, where family members would piece together a memory, "each contributing his own little patch and then sitting back to see how it would turn out. Long after the children had grown calm and loose and dropped off to sleep, one by one, the grownups were still weaving family history in the darkness." Later, in self-imposed exile on a goat farm with her new husband, she is trimming grass around their electric fence when "the smell of cut grass swung her back over years and years and she found herself sitting on a twilit lawn, nestled between her parents, listening to the murmur of her family all around her." She has to be pried from the fence by Duncan, even though "the throb of electricity caused a distant, dull ache."

In an attempt to gain some control over her life, Justine turns to fortune-telling. When asked about whether people can choose their destiny, her mentor, Madame Olita, replies, "No, you can always choose to *some* extent. You can change your future a great deal. Also your past." Her grandfather, in his search for his brother, is engaged in trying to change the past, too, yet when he finally finds Caleb, he writes that "it appears that my ties to the present have weakened. I cannot feel that what happens today is of any real importance to me." Caleb tries a brief return but again cannot remain part of the Peck family. He runs away but remembers to send a bread-and-butter note, in the best Peck tradition. Most un-Peckishly, Justine and Duncan escape, too, by going off to join a carnival. Frank W. Shelton has considered the rebellion of Tyler's characters "against restrictive institutions, especially the family." The most successful of her heroes, Justine Peck among them, "balance distance and sympathy" in a struggle toward clarity and fulfillment.

Midway through Tyler's corpus, thematic connections such as the creation of family and identity, the passage of time, and the importance of details clearly emerge. Of even more interest is the connection between characters. The iron-willed orderliness of the Pecks (and the way the children flee from and return to it) recalls Mrs. Emerson in *The Clock Winder*. The "angular, slapdash lives" of Justine and Duncan look forward to Morgan Gower in *Morgan's Passing* (1980), and Justine's "lacking finality" foreshadows Muriel in *The Accidental Tourist*. The longing of Aunt Lucy for "her wing chair in which she could sit encircled, almost, with the wings working like a mule's blinders to confine her gaze to the latest historical romance" looks both forward and backward to Jeremy Pauling and Macon Leary, and the cooking ability of the long-lost brother Caleb, who shows his friendship not in words but by choosing "to cook them their favorite foods instead—the comfort foods that every man turns to when he is feeling low," anticipates Ezra Tull in *Dinner at the Homesick Restaurant*. Tyler appears to be trying out characters in minor roles before she lets them on stage for command performances.

Tyler's seventh novel, *Earthly Possessions*, directly tackles one of her most important issues: the relationship between people and their possessions. Charlotte Emory has decided to leave her husband Saul, a minister, but during a final visit to the bank she is taken hostage by a bank robber, Jake Simms, who takes her on a long car ride, first to pick up his pregnant girlfriend and then to visit an old jail buddy who he thinks can help him. Although Jake has the gun, Charlotte ends up supporting this mission, trying to patch up the relationship between Jake and Mindy, consoling him when his friend rejects him, and finally deciding when it is time for her to leave, even though Jake says he needs her to stay.

The road trip is interspersed with reflections on Charlotte's life. Like James in *The Tin Can Tree*, she is a photographer, albeit a reluctant one, having taken over her father's photography shop after his death. As a photographer, she says, "I was only a transient. My photos were limpid and relaxed, touched with that grace things have when you know

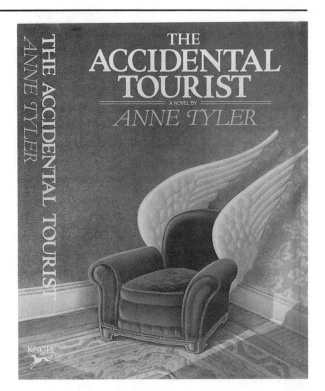

Dust jacket for Tyler's 1985 novel, about a reclusive travel writer who falls in love with an exuberant dog trainer

they're of no permanent importance." Charlotte thinks of herself as a transient in her entire life, although she longs, too, for the security of home. The twin worries of her life as a child, she says, were "that I was not their true daughter, and would be sent away" and "that I *was* their true daughter and would never, ever manage to escape to the outside world."

After her father's car accident, which cut short her college career, "it had hit finally where I was: home, trapped, no escape. My mother couldn't even sit him up without me there to help. I saw my life rolling out in front of me like an endless, mildewed rug." Charlotte felt "locked in a calendar; time was turning out to be the most closed-in space of all." In order to cope, especially after her marriage to Saul and all the physical possessions and human encumbrances he brings into her life, she "loosened her roots, floated a few feet off, and grew to look at things with a faint, pleasant humorousness that spiced my nose like the beginnings of a sneeze. After a while the humor became a habit; I couldn't have lost it even if I'd tried. My world began to seem . . . temporary. I saw that I must be planning to leave, eventually."

When her mother became ill with cancer, Charlotte spent time alone with her, asking questions. Unsatisfied with the answers, she could not "let loose of her yet. She was like some unsolvable math problem you keep staring at, worrying the edges of, chafing and cursing." Her husband tells her that he believes that "we're given the same lessons to learn, over and over, exactly the same experiences, till we get them right. Things keep circling past us."

Like Emily Meredith in *Morgan's Passing,* who always keeps a cosmetic bag packed for that day when she knows she must leave, and Delia Grinstead in *Ladder of Years,* who walks away from her family during a beach vacation, Charlotte says her whole life "has been a history of casting off encumbrances, paring down to the bare essentials, stripping for the journey." Charlotte has been ready for the trip she takes for her entire life, but after she returns she redefines, or makes metaphors of, her notion of travel. Her husband, perhaps suspecting that their marriage might not have been as perfect as he imagined, suggests they take a trip together. She declines, saying "We have been traveling for years, traveled all our lives, we are traveling still. We couldn't stay in one place if we tried. Go to sleep, I say."

The negative critical reaction to *Morgan's Passing* (1980) makes it unique among Tyler's early novels, except for the mixed response to *If Morning Ever Comes.* Shelton refers to it as "one of her most unruly and untidy novels," and *Morgan's Passing* appears only in a dismissive remark in Voelker's book. The critics' objections center around the main character, Morgan Gower, yet Tyler stressed in her interview with Wendy Lamb, given as she wrote *Morgan's Passing,* that she likes all her characters. She also told Patricia Rowe Willrich that Morgan's situation is "not unrelated to being a writer: the inveterate imposter, who is unable to stop himself from stepping into other people's worlds." Despite criticism, the book was nominated for the 1980 National Book Critics Circle Award. *Morgan's Passing* extends the characterization of the eccentric artist first seen in *Celestial Navigation;* this time, however, she takes him outside his house. She continues her treatment of the eccentric underachiever with Barnaby Gaitlin in *A Patchwork Planet,* a novel that was also negatively reviewed. Clearly Tyler has an affinity for the likable failure that some of her critics do not share.

The familiar Tyler issues are all here as well: the comfort and restrictions of family life, the urge to accumulate and to cast off the materials out of which one creates identity and direction. Morgan Gower has a fairly stable external identity: he is married to Bonny; has six daughters; lives in a large, old house; and works in a hardware store. Yet he also masquerades as a prospector, an explorer, and people of various nationalities, seemingly dis-

contented with the prospect of living just one kind of life.

Early in the book he performs a characteristic transformation: Emily Meredith, a young woman who puts on puppet shows for a living with her husband, Leon, goes into labor during one of their shows, and Morgan identifies himself as a doctor. Probably, he assumes he can bluff his way through this situation by merely offering comfort on the ride to the hospital, but the baby arrives quickly, and Morgan must actually assume his role. Later the Merediths wonder "if they had imagined the man—just conjured him up in time of need," because there seems to be something magical about him, as if he could be a "gnome" or "elf." Their sense of his unreality increases when Morgan takes to following them, attracted by what he perceives to be the bohemian simplicity of their lives. He thinks Emily, who wears only leotards, wrap skirts, and ballet slippers, "looked stark, pared down. She had done away with all the extras." Morgan feels "awed by the Merediths—by their austerity, their certitude, their mapped and charted lives."

As he becomes part of the baggage of the Merediths' lives, he begins to cast away encumbrances from his own life, even his children. "The trouble with fathering children," he thinks, "was, they got to know you so well. You couldn't make the faintest little realignment of the facts around them. They kept staring levelly into your eyes, eternally watchful and critical, forever prepared to pass judgment. They could point to so many places where you had gone permanently, irretrievably wrong." After a disastrous vacation at the beach (beach vacations often precipitate crises in Tyler novels), Morgan thinks his family could abandon him there: "He pictured how calm he would grow, at last. The breakers would act for him, tumbling about while he lay still. He would finally have a chance to sort himself out. It was *people* who disarranged his life."

Emily, too, is becoming dissatisfied with her life, feeling "the world [is] split in two: makers and doers. She was a maker and Leon was a doer. She sat home and put together puppets and Leon sprang onstage with them, all flair and action." In spite of the fact that Morgan, too, is a "doer," Emily and Morgan have an affair, and she gets pregnant. By the end of the novel they have decided, like Justine and Duncan Peck, to join the circus and give puppet shows, with Morgan assuming the role of Leon, both for the shows and for the proprietor, who doesn't know about the divorce. The novel ends with Morgan, ensconced in a trailer with the new baby and Emily, feeling "suddenly light-hearted. He started walking faster. He started smiling. By the time he reached Emily, he was humming. Everything he looked at seemed luminous and beautiful, and rich with possibilities." In order to enjoy what Anne Jones has called the "blessed profusion" of Tyler's novels, the reader must learn to see life as Morgan (and Tyler) do—as rich with a nearly unlimited variety of possibilities.

The variety of possibilities for constructing and reconstructing a family is the major concern of Tyler's ninth novel, *Dinner at the Homesick Restaurant*. This novel tells the story of the Tull family and the ways they each find to mend cracks formed when father Beck Tull, a salesman, leaves his wife and children, whose difficult situation is exacerbated by abuse from the abandoned mother, Pearl. Throughout most of the novel Beck is the "absent presence," the "invisible man" whose purpose seems to be (for Pearl) to "show how little importance a father has." Pearl, on her deathbed as the novel opens, spends the rest of the time she is alive trying to come to terms with her job as a single parent, wondering, when, if ever, she is going to be forgiven by her children.

Cody, the oldest son, seems obsessed by the past; he "catalogues grudges," as his sister Jenny says. Like many of Tyler's characters, he finds that photography is a useful metaphor for his attitude about the past: "Isn't it just that time for once is stopped that makes you wistful? If only you could turn it back, you think. If only you could change this or that, undo what you have done, if only you could roll the minutes the other way, for once," he says to his son, Luke. One of the things he may want to undo is stealing his brother Ezra's fiancée, Ruth, and marrying her himself. Not surprisingly, the marriage is vaguely unsatisfying, Cody says, because he's "always had the feeling it wasn't my marriage, anyhow. It was someone else's. It was theirs. Sometimes I seemed to enjoy it better when I imagined I was seeing it through someone else's eyes."

How one chooses to imagine the present—or the past—is vitally important to one's happiness in this novel. When Cody tells his son about his life, he always prefaces his remarks with "This really happened," but while the stories seem to him "unthinkable, beyond belief," his son finds that the stories "never seemed so terrible" to him. Beck returns for Pearl's funeral and remarks at the family dinner afterward that "it looks like this is one of those great big, jolly, noisy, rambling . . . why, *families!*" It is, of course. Cody's response is to try to set the record straight: "You think we're some jolly, situation-comedy family when we're in particles, torn apart, torn all over the place, and our mother was a witch."

Dust jacket for Tyler's 1988 novel, for which she received a Pulitzer Prize

The stories of Pearl's other children, Jenny and Ezra, while they do not necessarily prove Cody wrong, show him to be no more right than Beck: at times their mother was a witch, but they were also a family, or at least they have become a family. Middle child Jenny was afraid of her mother, dreaming that she "laughed a witch's shrieking laugh; dragged Jenny out of hiding as the Nazis tramped up the stairs; accused her of sins and crimes that had never crossed Jenny's mind. Her mother told her, in an informative and considerate tone of voice, that she was raising Jenny to eat her." Jenny also finds her family "too small," and too intense, so she marries in part for the "*angularity* of the situation—the mighty leap into space with someone she hardly knew." This marriage fails, but she ends up with that larger family she desires—her own daughter, the stepchildren of her new husband, Joe, and the children surrounding her daily in her job as a pediatrician. Her attitude has become what she tells her stepson Slevin's worried teacher: "I don't see the need to blame adjustments, broken homes, bad parents, that sort of thing. We make our own luck, right? You have to overcome your setbacks. You can't take them too much to heart."

The baby of the family, Ezra, makes his own luck, too, first by working in a restaurant run by Mrs. Scarlatti and then by feeding people himself in "a place where people come just like to a family dinner": the Homesick Restaurant. There he cooks "what people felt homesick for," and there he tries to feed his family. Cody, always the pessimist, notices that his family has never finished one of Ezra's dinners, and wonders why Ezra does not see it, why he cannot see "the theme" of his family, which is that "it was almost as if what they couldn't get right, they had to keep returning to." Ezra keeps trying, calling the family back, tracking down missing members, asking them, as at the funeral dinner, to "take up where we left off."

Pearl, the narrative and emotional focus of the book, also tries to make sense of her family. Her initial meditations lead her to the conclusion that "her family has failed. Neither of her sons is happy, and her daughter can't seem to stay married." At first she blames herself but then decides that "it's simply fate, and not a matter for blame at all." Her disappointment comes, Ezra realizes, because she "had imagined a perfectly wonderful plot—a significance to every chance meeting, the possibility of whirlwind courtships, grand white weddings, flawless bliss forever after." Yet she does find that she had at least one moment where she was "absolutely happy," and Ezra sees himself and his mother "traversing the curve of the earth, small and steadfast, surrounded by companions." Her last thoughts are of her version of a happy family, and she dies, being "borne away to the beach, where three small children ran toward her, laughing, across the sunlit sand."

Cody, too, comes to a kind of reconciliation with his past, including a pivotal memory of the day he accidentally shot his mother with an arrow:

> He remembered the archery trip, and it seemed to him now that he even remembered that arrow sailing in its graceful, fluttering path. He remembered his mother's upright form along the grasses, her hair lit gold, her small hands smoothing her bouquet while the arrow journeyed on. And high above, he seemed to recall, there had been a little brown airplane, almost motionless, droning through the sunshine like a bumblebee.

The elegiac quality of the last lines of the novel is intentional: each of the three children has created a satisfying surrogate family; Pearl has come to a final sense of her own identity; and even Beck has been reintegrated into the family. A novel that in other hands could have become a horrific chronicle of the violent legacy neglectful and cruel parents hand down to their children becomes instead a meditation on the ways people can produce sustaining families instead of reproducing destructive ones.

Both *Dinner at the Homesick Restaurant* and Tyler's next novel, *The Accidental Tourist,* create what Voelker calls a "utopian emotional state," in which characters achieve distance from the complex of emotions they have toward their families: "sickness for home (longing, nostalgia) but also sickness of it (the need to escape from the invasiveness of family) and sickness from it (the psychic wounds that human beings inevitably carry as a result of having had to grow up as children in families)." For Ezra, Voelker says, utopia is a "restaurant that is not a home but is as a home might be." For Macon Leary it is his winged armchair, the logo of his books for reluctant business travelers—a chair that both travels and "dream[s] of staying put."

Macon, who "above all else" is an "orderly man" who believes "that there must be an answer for everything, if only you knew how to set forth the questions," writes books that make travelers feel that they are traveling "in a capsule, a cocoon." Stunned by the violent death of his son, Ethan, and the sudden departure of his wife, Sarah, Macon holes up in his house, devising elaborate timesaving measures that threaten to turn him into a recluse and result eventually in a broken leg. His injury sends him back to live with his unmarried sister and brothers in the family house, where the favorite meal is baked potatoes and all the kitchen products are ruthlessly alphabetized.

Macon's reaction to this disruption is to feel "content with everything exactly the way it was. He seemed to be suspended, his life on hold." He even wonders if "he had engineered this injury—every elaborate step leading up to it—just so he could settle down safe among the people he'd started out with." He is jolted out of this safe suspension by Muriel Pritchett, an extravagant dog trainer who has offered her services, ostensibly for his unruly dog, Edward. The training of Edward becomes a retraining in life for Macon, and soon he and Muriel—and her young son, Alexander—are living together.

Things are not happily ever after, however, as they rarely are in Tyler's novels. Macon's brother Charles is worried about him: "You're not yourself these days and this Muriel person is a symptom. Everybody says so." Macon's response is, "I'm more myself than I've been my whole life long," to which his brother replies, "What kind of remark is that? It doesn't even make sense!"

Perhaps it does not—to someone who does not understand Tyler's notion of identity. Macon, like Jeremy Pauling (who is always himself), and like the children in *Dinner at the Homesick Restaurant,* try on roles, and partners, until they find ones that fit. They also chafe under their families' notions of who they have always been, as does Barnaby in *A Patch-work Planet*. Still, Macon is not sure he has made the right choice, fearing that he may have chosen a woman like his mother Alicia—"silly, vain, annoy-ing"—who "darted in and out of their lives leaving a trail of irresponsible remarks, apparently never con-sidering they might be passed on." He also realizes that "the world was divided sharply down the mid-dle: Some lived careful lives and some lived careless lives, and everything that happened could be ex-plained by the difference between them."

There is also the question of Muriel's son, Al-exander. Macon begins to care for him, easing the boy out of his mother's tight hold, comforting him when he is bullied by other children, buying him real-boy clothes. At one point he feels a "pleasant kind of sorrow seeping though him. Oh, his life had regained all its old perils. He was forced to worry once again about nuclear war and the future of the planet. He often had the same secret, guilty thought that had come to him after Ethan was born: *From this time on I can never be completely happy.* Not that he was before, of course."

In spite of this connection, he returns to Sarah after a trip to Canada, during which he has a crisis in identity, "pictur[ing] himself separating, falling into pieces, his head floating away with terrifying swiftness in the eerie green air of Alberta." Muriel, however, follows him on a subsequent trip to Paris, and then Sarah shows up after he hurts his back. Sarah's solicitous practicality smothers rather than consoles him, and he crawls from his bed and limps away to catch up with Muriel and her careless en-thusiasm for life. The final lines echo other Tyler endings: "A sudden flash of sunlight hit the wind-shield, and spangles flew across the glass. The span-gles were old water spots, or maybe the markings of leaves, but for a moment Macon thought they were something else. They were so bright and festive, for a moment he thought they were confetti." Like Jus-tine and Duncan, like Morgan and Emily, this un-likely couple walks out—not into a sunset—but into a celebration, a carnival, a circus.

Breathing Lessons, Tyler's eleventh novel, be-gins, as do many of her works, with a death—this time of Max, husband of the main character Mag-gie's best friend. Karin Linton says such opening cri-ses "eliminat[e] the safe and well-established rou-tines of life and jol[t] the temporal perspective of the main character." This jolt in time and perspective Tyler sees as positive, both for the characters and for the novelist. For example, what she most ad-mires about novelist Gabriel García Márquez, she says in *The New York Times Book Review* (4 December 1977), is that "he has somehow figured out how to

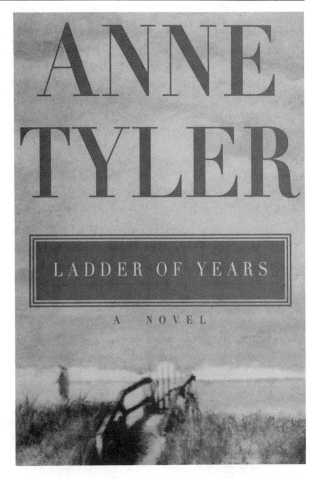

Dust jacket for Tyler's 1995 novel, in which the central character temporarily leaves her family in an effort to simplify her life

let time be in literature what it is in life: unpredict-able, sometimes circular, looped, doubling back, rushing through 60 years and then doddering over an afternoon, with glimmers of the past and future just beneath the surface." The story in *Breathing Les-sons* moves effortlessly between the present trip to the funeral, the past of Maggie's courtship and mar-riage to Ira, the recent past of the breakup of her son's marriage, and the future of his former wife and their child, as Maggie tries to combine them all into some meaningful whole.

Maggie's husband, Ira, although he loves her, cannot bear the disorganized way she goes about life, "how she refused to take her own life seriously. She seemed to believe it was a sort of practice life, something she could afford to play around with as if they offered second and third chances to get it right. She was always making clumsy, impetuous rushes toward nowhere in particular—side trips, random detours." She and her friend Serena disagree about the progress of life; Serena says that what life comes down to is "pruning and disposing . . . shucking off your children from the moment you give birth." Maggie's response is, "I don't feel like I'm letting go; I feel they're taking things away from me." Unlike Serena and Ira, Maggie wants to hold onto everything, no matter how cluttered and disorderly it makes her life.

The experience of traveling to the funeral has created a distanced perspective in Maggie that Serena describes: "Just to look around you one day and have it all amaze you—where you'd arrived at, who you'd married, what kind of person you'd grown into." What this distance leads Maggie to discover is that, although she might be easily classified by Ira as "teary and nostalgic," for example, "if she was locked in a pattern, at least she had chosen what the pattern could be. She felt strong and free and definite."

One of the patterns, she realizes, involves her marriage. In order to avoid being like her mother, Maggie avoids any man like her "bumbling and well-meaning and sentimental" father, whom she loved. But in comparison with her serious husband, she drinks, talks, eats, laughs, and cries too much; she finds she has turned into her father. At the funeral, however, she discovers that she has fallen in love with her husband again, the "convenience" of which pleases her "like finding right in her pantry all the fixings she needed for a new recipe."

She is not so lucky with her son, Jesse, whose marriage has failed and whose child is no longer a part of his life. No matter how hard she tries, she is unable to get Jesse, his wife, Fiona, and Leroy, the daughter, back together. She thinks perhaps that she is not "compatible" with Jesse. "All they had to rely on was luck—the proper personality genes turning up like dice. And in Jesse's case, maybe the luck had been poor."

Her new insight helps her to realize that "there was a single theme to every decision she had made as a parent: The mere fact that her children were children, condemned for years to feel powerless and bewildered and confined, filled her with such pity that to add any further hardship to their lives seemed unthinkable. She could excuse anything in them, forgive them everything. She would have made a better mother, perhaps, if she hadn't remembered so well how it felt to be a child."

Maggie's inability to effect any change in Jesse leads her to feel that her life has "forever repeated itself, and it was entirely lacking in hope." But this feeling does not last long. On the last page of the novel, as she and Ira are in bed trying to sleep prior to an early morning trip to take their daughter to college, "She felt a little stir of something that came over her like a flush, a sort of inner buoyancy, and

she lifted her face to kiss the warm blade of his cheekbone. Then she slipped free and moved to her side of the bed, because tomorrow they had a long car trip to make and she knew she would need a good night's sleep before they started."

Tyler's twelfth novel, *Saint Maybe* (1991), addresses most directly another important Tyler concern: religion. It is well known that Tyler has a skepticism about the premise of most religions: "It's not that I have anything against ministers," she told Wendy Lamb in a discussion about *Earthly Possessions,* "but that I'm particularly concerned with how much right anyone has to change someone, and ministers are people who feel they have that right." Still, she is interested in the subject, as she told Patricia Rowe Willrich about the genesis of *Saint Maybe:* "all I knew at the start was that I wondered what it must feel like to be a born-again Christian, since that is a kind of life very different from mine."

This emphasis on religion does not obscure the familiar Tyler issues—family, identity, marriage and children. Ian Bedloe, who is not born again until later in the novel, lives in his street's version of "the ideal, apple-pie household." The particular thing about his family is that they "believed that every part of their lives was absolutely wonderful." This belief wavers when Danny, the oldest son, brings home Lucy, a divorced woman with children, as his fiancée; falters when their baby is born "premature"; and finally is shattered when Danny runs his car into a wall after hearing from Ian that he suspects Lucy has been having an affair and that the child, Daphne, is not Danny's. Lucy dies shortly afterward, overdosing on sleeping pills, and Ian's family is left with the children—Agatha and Thomas from her first marriage, and Daphne.

Ian has an immediate connection to Daphne: "It seemed she had reached out and pulled a string from somewhere deep inside him. It seemed she *knew* him." Yet this feeling contrasts with his sense of "the monotony and irritation and confinement" of children. After he has taken over the child care, Ian feels that he is "travelling a treadmill, stuck with these querulous children night after night after night." Yet he also realizes the dual nature of his responsibility for them—his role in the loss of their father and mother and their helplessness. "Why being a child at all was scary," he realizes, "Powerlessness, outsiderness. Murmurs over your head about something everyone knows but you." The difficulties of both being a child and raising children have occupied Tyler at least since *Earthly Possessions* and continue to do so throughout her later novels.

The Church of the Second Chance gives Ian the other reason for taking care of the children: penance, a chance for forgiveness. While the church comforts him, Ian wonders: "Why didn't he, after all these years of penance, feel that God had forgiven him?" Yet he also realizes that what he is doing is not exactly penance, as the children were "all that gave his life color, and energy, and . . . well, life." Like all children, Daphne especially brings out in him "laughter and an ache." He realizes finally that he had to accept, for his children and others, "that the day would never arrive when [he] finally understood what they were all about," and this realization makes him "supremely happy."

Also there is the question of how the children—and his need to atone through them—are restricting the rest of his life. He wonders, "When is something philosophical acceptance and when is it dumb passivity? When is something a moral decision and when is it scar tissue?" After resuming a long-suspended romantic life with "clutter counselor" Rita diCarlo (a provider of unusual—but necessary—services reminiscent of Elizabeth Abbott's handyman, Muriel Pritchett's dog training, and finally, Barnaby's work for Rent-A-Back), he concludes that dramatic events, personal or religious—happiness, tragedy, sin, atonement, salvation—are really part of the fabric of life. Ian knows that the children have completely changed his life, but "People changed other people's lives every day of the year. There was no call to make such a fuss about it."

Ian Bedloe's situation at the end of this novel is not so different from that of Ben Joe Hawkes at the end of Tyler's first novel, or that of Maggie Moran, Ezra Tull, Charlotte Emory, Delia Grinstead, or several other Tyler characters: they hope, early or later in life, to escape from the burdens and responsibilities of their families, but they find that they are not really trapped and do not really want to escape. Daphne Bedloe, for example, when confronted with her sister Agatha's analogy that "living in a family is like taking a long, long, trip with people you're not very well acquainted with. At first they seem just fine, but after you've traveled awhile at close quarters they start grating on your nerves," responds, "Well, I guess I must not have traveled with them long enough, then."

Tyler's 1995 novel, *Ladder of Years,* offers her fullest statement yet on the significance of location. Wife and mother Delia Grinstead lives with her family in what was formerly her childhood home, a situation common to many Tyler characters. The large house is "shabby, its brown shingles streaked with mildew and its shutters snaggletoothed where the louvers had fallen out over the years." When Delia marries, she does not move away but "simply

install[s] her husband among her sweet-sixteen bedroom furniture." Once her father dies, however, her husband begins a massive renovation project, one that finds the house "groaning in distress—such a modest, mild house, so unprepared for change." Delia, too, is reluctant to change.

Her experience during her annual beach vacation is equally dissatisfying. In fact, her disappointment in the "dumpy little house on the inland side of Highway 1" precipitates the crisis of the novel: she walks out of her family's life while they play at the beach, acting out, as critic Dorothy Scura puts it, "a fantasy everyone has entertained for fleeting moments." Her search for simplicity continues on the road when she is given a ride in an RV. "I would make it my year-round home," Delia says, "Really! Who needs a big old house and all those extra rooms?"

Delia takes up her new life in Bay Borough and considers her family's reaction to her leaving: "An airy sense of exhilaration filled her chest. She felt so lightweight, all at once." She settles into her new room, which is "satisfyingly Spartan," and finds herself "reveling in its starkness." It also changes her sense of who she is. She walks up the steps to her room thinking, "*Here comes the executive secretary, returning from her lone meal to the solitude of her room.* It wasn't a complaint, though. It was a boast." Paring down, Delia discovers (as do many of Tyler's characters), more often leads to a loss of connection and complexity than to an increase in freedom and flexibility.

Her next job, as housekeeper and surrogate mother, however, threatens to become too close to the life she left behind. She is worried that she will become involved once again in others' lives, until she sees her room: "It was the sort of room where people were expected to spend no more than a night or two. The high double bed allowed barely a yard of space on either side. The nightstand bore a thoughtful supply of guest-type reading (more magazines, two books that looked like anthologies). The framed sample on the wall read WELCOME in six languages." The combination of temporariness and welcome is irresistibly appealing to Delia, and so she decides to stay.

Of course, this situation is too perfect to last, as Delia realizes when she finds herself becoming emotionally involved with the father and son for whom she works. This particular mix of love, duty, and guilt she can get at home, after all. Delia's eventual (and perhaps inevitable) return to her family is predicated by a visit to a doctor's office, which reminds her of her father. Returning home, however, she wonders (as do many of Tyler's other travelers)

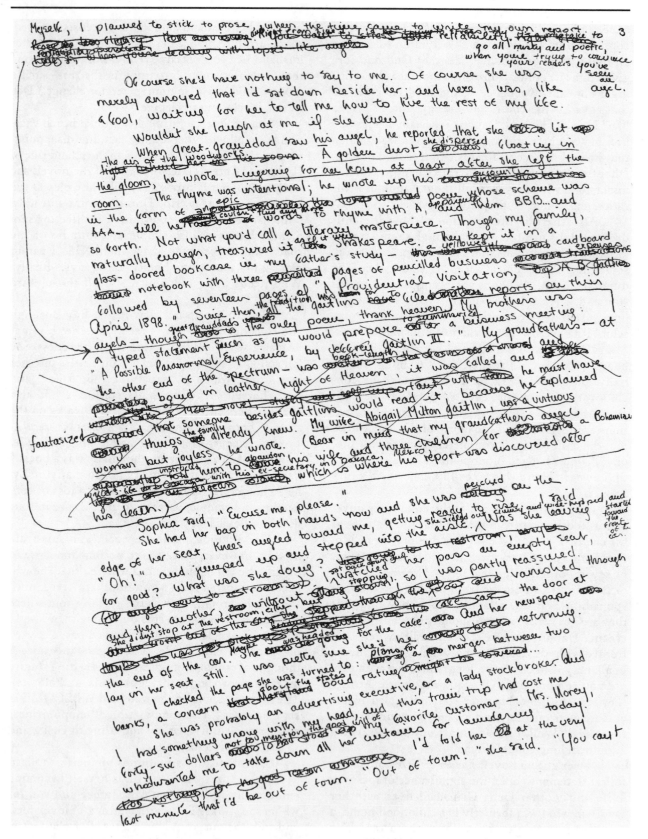

Page from the manuscript for Tyler's 1998 novel, A Patchwork Planet *(Perkins Library, Duke University)*

if her home was really worth returning to: "Was this how their house looked to strangers: so brown, so hunched, so forbidding?" But return she does, mingling her past and present lives—and the people in them.

In a late dinner scene reminiscent of those in several Tyler novels, Nat, part of Delia's newly extended family, describes a favorite picture, which shows a man (nineteenth-century Mormon photographer C. R. Savage) sitting alone at a perfectly laid table before his family arrives and the inevitable squabbling begins. "The table looked so beautiful," Nat says, "like somebody's dream of a table, and old Savage felt so happy and so—what's the word I want, so. . . . So anticipatory!" The image suggests an infinite regression: characters at dinner tables talking about photographs of dinner tables, recalling other dinners, disappointments, and anticipations in other lives, and other novels. But it also suggests, in this and other Tyler novels, the inevitability of both temporal change and familial return. As feminist critic Virginia Schaefer Carroll states, "By withdrawing, assessing and testing her new identity, Delia learns that she does not have to move to get somewhere."

One of only three Tyler novels with a first-person narrative (Charlotte narrates *Earthly Possessions; Celestial Navigation* has several narrators), *A Patchwork Planet* has its narrator, Barnaby Gaitlin, tell his readers on the first page, "I am a man you can trust, is how my customers view me." Whether or not readers will trust (and come to like) Barnaby is the main question of the novel. Reviewers' reactions have been mixed. Michiko Kakutani, writing for *The New York Times* (17 April 1998), says the novel is "strangely perfunctory and contrived," and Barnaby's characterization is merely "cute." Novelist Carol Shields, on the other hand, notes (also in *The New York Times,* 19 April 1998), "As in all her novels, Tyler is drawn here to the outsider, the perceived failure in our midst, the instinctual underdog who is sharply critical—but in a dreamy, unfocused and maddening way." The novel, she says, shows that "people make up their lives as they go along, a patchwork of good intentions and second guesses."

Barnaby seems terminally unclear about what role he will play in his family, the wealthy managers of the Gaitlin Foundation. He has assumed the role of black sheep since he was caught robbing neighbors at seventeen, but he is also drawn to the family history, which includes visitations by angels. In Barnaby's case, his angel is a rather plump and ordinary bank executive in an "angel coat" named Sophia Maynard, with whom he starts a romantic relationship. While Barnaby rejects a job with the foun-

dation, he nevertheless serves the public at Rent-a-Back, a company that provides physical work for the old and infirm (and one agoraphobic who resembles a female Jeremy Pauling)—a job that he admits is not for those who do not want to "get so tangled up in people's lives." Even when he was robbing people's homes, he was drawn to his victims' personal stories more than their valuables. Like many of Tyler's voyeurs, Barnaby "had a real thing about photo albums. The other kids who broke in along with me, they'd be hunting car keys and cigarettes and booze. They'd be tearing through closets and cabinets all around me, while I sat on the sofa poring over somebody's wedding pictures."

Barnaby appears to be searching for something his own family cannot provide, which is, not surprisingly for Tyler, expressed through the metaphor of the family dinner table. He wonders, "How come I always got the feeling that somebody was missing from our family table? I had thought so from the time I was little, toting up the faces at dinner every night: Mom, Dad, Jeff, Me . . . It was such a pitiful showing. We didn't make enough noise; we didn't seem busy enough, embroiled enough."

Throughout the novel Barnaby is torn between the desire to isolate himself from his family responsibilities and the need to become further "embroiled." He struggles to maintain the often difficult relationships with his former wife, Natalie, and daughter, Opal, whom he visits once a month and always disappoints. He also feels obligated to repay the money his parents spent to compensate neighbors for his juvenile burglaries and begins to save the money; but then he is accused by Sophia's aunt, for whom he works, of taking her money, which she has misplaced and forgotten. When Sophia replaces the lost money under the assumption that Barnaby took it, their relationship is strained. He tries to return her money and leaves her with the final message, "I am a man you can trust." Whether readers trust Barnaby or not, they do come to understand his twin needs for distance and involvement.

Even though their families smother them, force them into restrictive roles, and place unwanted obligations on them, Tyler's characters seem to want to stay part of some kind of family. Those who escape the confines of their original families—Morgan Gower and Emily Meredith, Duncan and Justine Peck, Jenny Tull, Elizabeth Abbott "Gillespie" Emerson—create new, improved families, although with responsibilities and problems of their own. Those who leave—Delia Grinstead, Charlotte Emory—return reconciled to the complex joys of family life. Finally, those who feel trapped at first by family—Maggie Moran, Ian Bedloe, Barnaby Gaitlin—come to realize its peculiar, quiet satisfactions. For Tyler it is not a question of never being able to go home again, or worse, never being able to leave home, but of creating a new home, remaking the old one into what you want it to be, or finding out that you never really wanted to leave after all. After more than thirty years of writing novels, Tyler continues to concentrate on the family, with insight, humor, and hope.

Interviews:

Clifford A. Ridley, "Anne Tyler: A Sense of Reticence Balanced by 'Oh, Well, Why Not?,'" *National Observer* (22 July 1972): 23;

Marguerite Michaels, "Anne Tyler, Writer 8:05 to 3:30," *New York Times Book Review*, 8 May 1977, pp. 42–43;

Bruce Cook, "A Writer—During School Hours," *Detroit News*, 6 April 1980, sec. E, p. 1ff.;

Wendy Lamb, "An Interview with Anne Tyler," *Iowa Journal of Literary Studies*, 3 (1981): 59–64;

Laurie L. Brown, "Interviews with Seven Contemporary Writers," *Southern Quarterly*, 21 (Summer 1983): 3–22.

Bibliographies:

Stella Ann Nesanovich, "An Anne Tyler Checklist, 1959–1980," *Bulletin of Bibliography*, 38 (April–June 1981): 53–64;

Elaine Gardiner and Catherine Rainwater, "A Bibliography of Writing by Anne Tyler," in *Contemporary American Women Writers: Narrative Strategies*, edited by Rainwater and William J. Sheick (Lexington: University Press of Kentucky, 1985), pp. 145–152;

Robert W. Croft, *Anne Tyler: A Bio-Bibliography* (Westport, Conn.: Greenwood Press, 1995).

References:

Doris Betts, "The Fiction of Anne Tyler," *Southern Quarterly*, 21 (Summer 1983): 23–27;

Paul Binding, "Anne Tyler," in his *Separate Country: A Literary Journey through the American South* (New York: Paddington Press, 1979);

Virginia Schaefer Carroll, "Wrestling with Change: Discourse Strategies in Anne Tyler," *Frontiers: A Journal of Women's Studies*, 19, no. 1 (1998): 86–109;

Barbara Dixson, "'A Quiet, Intelligent Voice': Thoughts on What Anne Tyler's Book Reviews Reveal about Anne Tyler," *Southern Quarterly*, 35 (Summer 1987): 81–86;

Elizabeth Evans, *Anne Tyler* (New York: Twayne, 1993);

Margaret Morganroth Gullette, *Safe at Last in the Middle Years: The Invention of the Midlife Progress Novel: Saul Bellow, Margaret Drabble, Anne Tyler, John Updike* (Berkeley: University of California Press, 1988);

Anne G. Jones, "Home at Last, and Homesick Again: The Ten Novels of Anne Tyler," *Hollins Critic*, 23 (April 1986): 1–14;

Karin Linton, *The Temporal Horizon: A Study of the Theme of Time in Anne Tyler's Major Novels* (Uppsala, Sweden: Acta Universitatis Upsalensis, 1989);

Stella Ann Nesanovich, "The Individual in the Family: Anne Tyler's *Searching for Caleb* and *Earthly Possessions*," *Southern Review*, 14 (Winter 1978): 170–176;

Alice Hall Petry, ed., *Critical Essays on Anne Tyler* (New York: G. K. Hall, 1992);

Petry, *Understanding Anne Tyler* (Columbia: University of South Carolina Press, 1990);

Mary F. Robertson, "Medusa Points and Contact Points," in *Contemporary American Women Writers: Narrative Strategies*, edited by Catherine Rainwater and William J. Sheick (Lexington: University Press of Kentucky, 1985), pp. 119–152;

Dale Salwak, ed., *Anne Tyler as Novelist* (Iowa City: University of Iowa Press, 1994);

Dorothy M. Scura, "Southern Women's Writing at the End of the Century: Five Recent Novels," *Southern Review*, 33 (Autumn 1997): 859–871;

Frank W. Shelton, "The Necessary Balance: Distance and Sympathy in the Novels of Anne Tyler," *Southern Review*, 20 (Autumn 1984): 851–860;

C. Ralph Stephens, ed., *The Fiction of Anne Tyler* (Jackson: University of Mississippi Press, 1990);

Joseph C. Voelker, *Art and the Accidental in Anne Tyler* (Columbia: University of Missouri Press, 1989);

Patricia Rowe Willrich, "Watching Through Windows: A Perspective on Anne Tyler," *Virginia Quarterly*, 68 (Summer 1992): 497–516;

Anne R. Zahlan, "Anne Tyler," in *Fifty Southern Writers After 1900: A Bio-Bibliographic Sourcebook*, edited by Joseph M. Flora and Robert Bain (New York: Greenwood Press, 1987), pp. 491–504.

Papers:

The Perkins Library at Duke University holds the manuscripts for three unpublished novels by Anne Tyler in addition to manuscripts and typescripts for several Tyler novels and short stories, as well as some of her correspondence, reviews, and newspaper clippings.

Yoshiko Uchida

Mary Jane Perna
University of California, Berkeley

and

Caroline C. Hunt
College of Charleston

BIRTH: Alameda, California, 24 November 1921, to Takashi ("Dwight") and Iku Umegaki Uchida.

EDUCATION: B.A. (cum laude), University of California, Berkeley, 1942; M.Ed., Smith College, 1944.

AWARDS AND HONORS: Ford Foundation research fellow in Japan, 1952; Children's Spring Book Festival honor award, *The New York Herald Tribune,* for *The Magic Listening Cap: More Folk Tales from Japan,* 1955; Notable Book citation, American Library Association, for *Journey to Topaz,* 1972; medal for best juvenile book by a California author, Commonwealth Club of California, for *Samurai of Gold Hill,* 1972; Award of Merit, California Association of Teachers of English, 1973; citation for outstanding contribution to the cultural development of society, Contra Costa chapter of Japanese American Citizens League, 1976; Morris S. Rosenblatt Award, Utah State Historical Society, for article "Topaz, City of Dust" (published in *Utah Historical Quarterly*), 1981; Distinguished Service Award, University of Oregon, 1981; California Japanese Alumni Association Award, 1982; Commonwealth Club of California Silver Medal for Excellence for *A Jar of Dreams,* 1982; award from Berkeley chapter of Japanese American Citizens League, 1983; *School Library Journal* Best Book of the Year citation, American Library Association Notable Book citation, and New York Public Library Best Book of the Year citation, all for *The Best Bad Thing,* 1983; Best Book of 1985 citation, Bay Area Book Reviewers, for *The Happiest Ending,* 1985; Children's Book of the Year citation, Child Study Association of America, for *The Happiest Ending,* 1985; Young Authors' Hall of Fame award, San Mateo and San Francisco Reading Associations, for *The Happiest Ending,* 1985; Friends of Children and Literature award for *A Jar of Dreams,* 1987; Japanese American of the Biennium

award, Japanese American Citizens Leagues, for outstanding achievement, 1988; Nikkei in Education Award, 1989.

DEATH: Berkeley, California, 21 June 1992.

BOOKS: *The Dancing Kettle, and Other Japanese Folk Tales* (New York: Harcourt, Brace, 1949);
New Friends for Susan (New York: Scribners, 1951);
We Do Not Work Alone: The Thoughts of Kanjiro Kawai (Kyoto, Japan: Folk Art Society, 1953);
The Magic Listening Cap: More Folk Tales from Japan (New York: Harcourt, Brace, 1955);
The Full Circle (New York: Friendship Press, 1957);
Takao and Grandfather's Sword (New York: Harcourt, Brace, 1958);
The Promised Year (New York: Harcourt, Brace, 1959);
Mik and the Prowler (New York: Harcourt, Brace, 1960);
Rokubei and the Thousand Rice Bowls (New York: Scribners, 1962);
The Forever Christmas Tree (New York: Scribners, 1963);
Sumi's Prize (New York: Scribners, 1964);
The Sea of Gold, and Other Tales from Japan (New York: Scribners, 1965);
Sumi's Special Happening (New York: Scribners, 1966);
In-Between Miya (New York: Scribners, 1967; London: Angus & Robertson, 1967);
Hisako's Mysteries (New York: Scribners, 1969);
Sumi & the Goat & the Tokyo Express (New York: Scribners, 1969);
Makoto, the Smallest Boy: A Story of Japan (New York: Crowell, 1970);
Journey to Topaz: A Story of the Japanese-American Evacuation (New York: Scribners, 1971);
Samurai of Gold Hill (New York: Scribners, 1972);
The Birthday Visitor (New York: Scribners, 1975);

Yoshiko Uchida (courtesy of the Bancroft Library, University of California, Berkeley)

The Rooster Who Understood Japanese (New York: Scribners, 1976);

Journey Home (New York: Atheneum, 1978);

A Jar of Dreams (New York: Atheneum, 1981);

Tabi: Journey through Time: Stories of the Japanese in America (El Cerrito, Cal.: Board of Christian Education, Sycamore Congregational Church, 1981);

Desert Exile: The Uprooting of a Japanese American Family (Seattle: University of Washington Press, 1982);

The Best Bad Thing (New York: Atheneum, 1983);

The Happiest Ending (New York: Atheneum, 1985);

The Two Foolish Cats: Suggested by a Japanese Folktale (New York: M. K. McElderry Books, 1987);

Picture Bride (Flagstaff, Ariz.: Northland Press, 1987);

The Terrible Leak (Mankato, Minn.: Creative Education, 1990);

The Invisible Thread: An Autobiography (Englewood Cliffs, N.J.: Messner, 1991);

Bird Song: Poems and Illustrations (Berkeley, Cal.: Privately printed, 1992);

The Bracelet (New York: Philomel, 1993);

The Magic Purse (New York: M. K. McElderry Books, 1993);

When the Sea Was Strangely Still (Scarborough, Ontario: Nelson Canada / Boston: Houghton Mifflin, 1993);

When Tricksters Won the Day (Scarborough, Ontario: Nelson Canada / Boston: Houghton Mifflin, 1993);

The Wise Old Woman (New York: M. K. McElderry Books, 1994).

Yoshiko Uchida almost single-handedly created a body of Japanese-American literature for children, where none existed before. As the first Nissei writer to devote an entire career to writing for young people about her own rich cultural heritage, she expanded the range of children's reading, with important results for young readers of all ethnic backgrounds.

Uchida was born in Alameda, California, on 24 November 1921, the second daughter of Takashi ("Dwight") and Iku Umegaki Uchida. Dwight Uchida immigrated to the United States from Japan in 1903 and worked for the San Francisco offices of Mitsui and Company, where he eventually became a manager. His daughter remembered him as a cheerful man with gregarious habits and a love of gardening. Iku Umegaki, the eldest daughter of a prefectural governor of Japan, immigrated to the United States in 1916 to marry Dwight Uchida. Both were graduates of Doshisha University, one of the early Christian universities of Japan, where relationships between students and teachers were exceptionally close; following the advice of two professors at Doshisha, Dwight and Iku began a year-long correspondence that culminated in their marriage.

Uchida and her older sister, Keiko, at ages three and five (courtesy of the Bancroft Library, University of California, Berkeley)

The Uchidas were early and active members of the Sycamore Congregational Church in El Cerrito, California.

Uchida and her older sister, Keiko ("Kay"), grew up in Berkeley, California. By Uchida's own account, her family was close-knit and supportive. The written word was important to Uchida's parents: her mother wrote poetry, using the thirty-one-syllable Japanese *tanka,* and her father was a prolific correspondent. Uchida's own interest in writing began early. At the age of ten, she wrote stories such as "Jimmy Chipmunk and His Friends" and "Willie the Squirrel" on brown wrapping paper. At twelve, graduating to white paper, she typed (and illustrated) her first "book," a seven-chapter tale called "Sally Jane Waters." Uchida attended Longfellow School in Berkeley and University High School in Oakland and graduated with honors from the University of California, Berkeley, in 1942 with a B.A. in English, philosophy, and history.

Uchida, however, was unable to attend her own graduation ceremony. After Japan bombed Pearl Harbor in December 1941 and the United States entered World War II, President Franklin D. Roosevelt issued Executive Order 9066, forcing the removal of all persons of Japanese descent (both American citizens and non-citizens) living on the western coast of the United States into centralized detention camps. Dwight Uchida was arrested, detained, and sent to a prisoner-of-war camp in Missoula, Montana. Uchida and her mother and sister had only ten days to pack all their possessions and vacate the house where they had lived for fifteen years. In May 1942 they were removed to the Tanforan Racetrack Relocation Center, where Uchida received her university diploma among the horse stalls that served as temporary barracks for the evacuees.

Eventually, Dwight Uchida was allowed to join his family at Tanforan, and in September 1942 the Uchida family was transferred to the Topaz Relocation Camp in the Utah desert. By June 1943 both Yoshiko and Kay were able to leave the relocation camp. Kay, who had a degree in child development, left to work in the nursery school of the department of education at Mount Holyoke College. Uchida, with the help of the National Student Relocation Council, left to attend Smith College, where she was awarded a graduate fellowship and received a master's degree in education in 1944. Dwight and Iku Uchida were eventually sponsored to leave Topaz for Salt Lake City and finally settled in Philadelphia before the end of the war.

After graduation from Smith, Uchida taught at the elementary level in a small Quaker school on the outskirts of Philadelphia. She found that she had no time to devote to writing and soon became ill with mononucleosis. She moved to New York City, where her sister was teaching in a private school, and worked as a secretary during the day to keep

Uchida with her grandmother (courtesy of the Bancroft Library, University of California, Berkeley)

her evenings free for writing. Uchida wrote short stories and submitted them to magazines but met with little success until she discovered her niche as a children's author. In 1949 her first book, *The Dancing Kettle, and Other Japanese Folk Tales,* was published—a competent though not particularly lively collection of folk stories. Uchida's solid judgment and clear language in the selection and retelling of these tales led to two later volumes, *The Magic Listening Cap: More Folk Tales from Japan* (1955) and *The Sea of Gold, and Other Tales from Japan* (1965).

In 1952 Uchida was awarded a Ford Foundation Foreign Study and Research Fellowship to Japan. While there, Uchida studied Japanese folk art with the three prominent men who founded the Japanese Folk Art Movement: the philosopher Soetsu Yanagi and the master potters Shoji Hamada and Kanjiro Kawai. Uchida wrote a series of feature articles about the Folk Art Movement for the *Nippon Times* in 1953 and 1954, as well as a monograph about Kanjiro Kawai. On her return to the United States, she served as the West Coast correspondent for *Craft Horizons* magazine, writing articles about weavers, jewelry makers, potters, and other artists.

Uchida settled in Oakland, California, to care for her parents, who were both in poor health. During this period she produced a series of children's books about Japanese characters: *Takao and Grandfather's Sword* (1958), *Rokubei and the Thousand Rice Bowls* (1962), and three Sumi books, *Sumi's Prize* (1964), *Sumi's Special Happening* (1966), and *Sumi &*

the Goat & the Tokyo Express (1969). These stories, along with *Makoto, the Smallest Boy: A Story of Japan* (1970) provided a picture of Japanese life and customs that had been lacking in American children's literature except for a few well-intentioned efforts by non-Japanese authors such as Lucy Fitch Perkins and Elizabeth Coatsworth.

Iku Uchida died in 1966, and Dwight Uchida followed in 1971. After her father's death, Uchida moved into her own apartment in Berkeley, where she lived and worked for the remainder of her life. Up until this point, her works had all concerned Japanese children, but none had addressed the special situation of Japanese Americans during the twentieth century. With *Journey to Topaz: A Story of the Japanese-American Evacuation,* published in the year of her father's death, Uchida discovered the central theme that resonated through her most important and successful books. *Journey to Topaz* relates the experiences of Yuki and her family as they travel to an internment camp and endure subhuman conditions there. In a sequel, *Journey Home* (1978), Uchida tackled the more difficult and subtle problems of the return of the evacuees after the war. Even Yuki's brother, a veteran of a Nisei unit, is a casualty, returning with a shattered leg and unresolved bitterness. *Journey to Topaz* was an American Library Association Notable Book, the first of Uchida's works to receive critical distinction on a national scale.

In *Desert Exile,* a nonfictional presentation starkly subtitled *The Uprooting of a Japanese American Family* (1982), Uchida adumbrated her post-1970 purpose in writing:

> I have tried in my writing not only to eradicate the stereotypic image of Japanese American still held by non-Asians, but I have also tried to evoke the strength and courage of the first generation Japanese whose survival over countless hardships is truly a triumph of the human spirit. I hope today's young people can learn from the Issei's sense of purpose, affirmation and hope in life, and will cherish the traditions and values of the past.

Desert Exile tells of the Uchida family's own experiences. Separated from Dwight Uchida, the mother and two daughters are sent first to Tanforan Racetrack for five months, then to Topaz, a "relocation center" of tarpaper shacks in the Utah desert. Excellent photographs from government and private collections document the Japanese Americans' plight first in horse stalls ("apartments"), then in unfinished and crude housing at "Topaz—Jewel of the Desert," as the internal camp newspaper styles it. Despite the grimness of their lives and prospects, the

*Uchida (at left) with her family as they left the Topaz Relocation Camp in Utah, 15 June 1943
(courtesy of the Bancroft Library, University of California, Berkeley)*

inhabitants of Topaz cope surprisingly well, even holding anniversary and birthday celebrations as well as conducting makeshift classes for the children. Uchida is careful to give a balanced picture of the non-Asians: her Swiss neighbors, for instance, invite the entire family over for a special dinner the night before the evacuation, and many friends come to visit them both at Tanforan and at Topaz.

Even when forced evacuation is not at the center of the plot, Uchida's post-1970 fiction always involves, to some degree, prejudice and its consequences. In a trilogy about Rinko Tsujimura, a Japanese American girl growing up during the Depression, Uchida touches on this issue deftly and effectively. The first Rinko book, *A Jar of Dreams* (1981), concerns the summer-long visit of Rinko's aunt Waka from Japan. During this summer, with Auntie Waka acting as a catalyst, major changes happen: Rinko's mother opens a laundry to help support the family; a rival white laundry owner sabotages her efforts and shoots the family dog; and both Rinko and her father stand up against this bullying. In a subplot, Rinko's brother, Cal (for California), nearly abandons his education but is induced to return to college, and Rinko herself learns a better acceptance of her difference from her white classmates. *A Jar of Dreams* received more critical attention than most of Uchida's previous writings and was awarded the Commonwealth Club of California Silver Medal for Excellence.

The second volume, *The Best Bad Thing* (1983), chronicles a month Rinko spends living with the eccentric Mrs. Hata and her two boys, Abu and Zenny. At first, Rinko has difficulty dealing with many aspects of her temporary home: Mrs. Hata's constant talking to the spirit of her dead husband; the endless pounds of cucumbers she raises to support the family; the shabby house without electricity; and the strange old lodger who makes beautiful kites. After a series of disasters, all turns out well and Mrs. Hata finds an excellent job through Rinko's father, thus staving off the unwelcome visits of an obnoxious welfare caseworker. Rinko continues to mature in this book, learning to accept more of the complexities of human behavior than she did earlier. *The Best Bad Thing* was an American Library Association Notable Book for 1983.

The concluding volume of the trilogy, *The Happiest Ending* (1985), shows a new side of Rinko, who at twelve is beginning to develop a romantic streak. Horrified that Auntie Hata's daughter, Teru, is to marry middle-aged Mr. Kinjo, Rinko determines to form a more perfect match between this young Japanese woman and a younger, more handsome boarder in the same house, run by Mrs. S., her Japanese language teacher. Uchida deals with some darker issues in this book: balanced against Rinko's preadolescent fantasy are the problems of Mrs. S.'s marriage, plagued by gambling and drunkenness, and the plight of the third boarder, Mr. Sad Higa, whose life savings are lost through Mr. S.'s gam-

449

bling. For problems as serious as these, the happy endings of the two previous books will not suffice. At the end, the relationship between Teru and Mr. Kinjo proves to be surprisingly strong, and a way is found to help Mr. Sad Higa return to Japan. *The Happiest Ending* won a Best Book citation in 1985 from the Bay Area Book Reviewers. Like its two predecessors, *The Happiest Ending* has an exceptionally handsome dust jacket: on the front, a delicate painting by Kinuko Craft; on the spine and around the painting, an elegant patterned motif; and on the back, a small oval surrounding a black-and-white drawing.

Like the Rinko books, Uchida's single novel for adult readers portrays the Issei and Nisei experience in California. In *Picture Bride* (1987), Hana leaves Japan for San Francisco in 1917, only to find that her Japanese American husband-to-be is far older and less successful financially than she expected. She also finds herself drawn to his younger, more handsome friend. As Hana makes some painful adjustments, the Depression and the shock of Pearl Harbor put everything she has worked for at risk. The novel is a straightforward, rather traditional narrative which did not receive a great deal of critical attention when first published (though it sold well enough to be republished by Simon and Schuster the following year). Because of its subject matter, however, *Picture Bride* has become more widely read since its initial appearance. A Japanese translation appeared in 1990, and the original English text has been republished twice more: once by a university press in 1997, and once that same year as part of a compendium called *Picture Bride and Related Readings,* which also includes excerpts from other Asian women writers. Presumably both of these republications are intended for the multicultural demands of the academic market.

Toward the end of her life, Uchida returned to the themes of racial division and forced relocation. In her memoir, *The Invisible Thread* (1991), she revisits her family's prewar life and her experiences at Tanforan and Topaz, already covered in *Desert Exile*. The memoir, however, understandably centers more on the developing mind and character of the writer herself and is a more personal and thus more coherent book than the former. It is also more artfully structured, from an opening squabble between sisters to the last paragraph in which the narrator takes a deep breath and announces to her first group of (non-Asian) students at Friends School, "My name is Miss Uchida, and I'm going to be your teacher." An epilogue describes Uchida's own growth in acceptance of her dual heritage:

> In my eagerness to be accepted as an American during my youth, I had been pushing my Japaneseness aside. Now at last, I appreciated it and was proud of it. I had finally come full circle.
>
> Now it was time for me to pass on this sense of pride and self-esteem to the third generation Japanese Americans—the Sansei—and to give them the kinds of books I'd never had as a child. The time was right, for now the world, too, was changing.

In her picture book, *The Bracelet* (1993), Uchida retold the story of the relocations for an even younger audience. Some critics felt that the book did not succeed because its intended readers had no way of knowing why the characters were in a sort of prison, could not follow the plot, and perhaps were too young for the subject. As she had said in *The Invisible Thread,* she still found the forced evacuations a painful subject but considered it essential to keep retelling the story to help prevent any future occurrences like it. Her task was not limited to her books: over the years Uchida gave many talks at schools, libraries, and professional conferences and answered hundreds of children's letters from throughout the world.

In addition to honors given to her individual books, Uchida received many awards, including the University of Oregon Distinguished Service Award, the California Japanese Alumni Association Award, the Japanese American of the Biennium Award, the Nikkei in Education Award, and the Morris S. Rosenblatt Award from the Utah State Historical Society. Uchida's growing reputation also led to the inclusion of her stories in textbooks and to the translation of several of her books into German, Dutch, and Japanese. She suffered from ill health during the later years of her life, which curtailed her writing and her public appearances. Uchida died in Berkeley on 21 June 1992.

Papers:

The Bancroft Library at the University of California, Berkeley, houses all Yoshiko Uchida's published books, manuscripts (partial), papers, and photographs. The University of Oregon Library, Eugene, Oregon, also has some early manuscripts, papers, and books.

Gore Vidal

This entry was updated by Susan Baker (University of Nevada, Reno) and Curtis S. Gibson from the entry by Robert F. Kiernan (Manhattan College) in DLB 152: American Novelists Since World War II, Fourth Series.

See also the Vidal entry in *DLB 6: American Novelists Since World War II, Second Series.*

BIRTH: West Point, New York, 3 October 1925, as Eugene Luther Gore Vidal, to Eugene Luther and Nina Gore Vidal.

EDUCATION: Graduate of Phillips Exeter Academy, 1943.

AWARDS AND HONORS: Edgar Allan Poe Award, Mystery Writers of America, 1955, for television drama; Screen Writers Annual Award nomination and Cannes Critics Prize, both for screenplay *The Best Man*, 1964; National Book Critics Circle Award for criticism for *The Second American Revolution and Other Essays (1976–1982)*, 1982; named honorary citizen, Ravello, Italy, 1983; Prix Deauville for *Creation*, 1983; National Book Award for nonfiction for *United States: Essays, 1952–1992*, 1993.

BOOKS: *Williwaw* (New York: Dutton, 1946; London: Panther, 1965); republished as *Dangerous Voyage* (New York: Signet/New American Library, 1953);

In a Yellow Wood (New York: Dutton, 1947; London: New English Library, 1967);

The City and the Pillar (New York: Dutton, 1948; London: Lehmann, 1949; revised and enlarged edition, New York: Dutton, 1965; London: Heinemann, 1965); revised and republished with *A Thirsty Evil* and a new preface by Vidal as *The City and the Pillar and Seven Early Stories* (New York: Random House, 1995);

The Season of Comfort (New York: Dutton, 1949);

Dark Green, Bright Red (New York: Dutton, 1950; London: Lehmann, 1950; revised edition, New York: Signet/New American Library, 1968; London: New English Library, 1968);

A Search for the King: A Twelfth-Century Legend (New York: Dutton, 1950; London: New English Library, 1967);

Death in the Fifth Position, as Edgar Box (New York: Dutton, 1952; London: Heinemann, 1954);

The Judgment of Paris (New York: Dutton, 1952; London: Heinemann, 1953; revised and abridged edition, New York: Ballantine, 1961; revised edition, Boston: Little, Brown, 1965; London: Heinemann, 1966);

Death Before Bedtime, as Edgar Box (New York: Dutton, 1953; London: Heinemann, 1954);

Death Likes It Hot, as Edgar Box (New York: Dutton, 1954; London: Heinemann, 1955);

Messiah (New York: Dutton, 1954; London: Heinemann, 1955; revised edition, Boston: Little, Brown, 1965; London: Heinemann, 1968);

A Thirsty Evil: Seven Short Stories (New York: Zero Press, 1956; London: Heinemann, 1958; enlarged edition, London: New English Library, 1967);

Visit to a Small Planet and Other Television Plays (Boston: Little, Brown, 1956);

Visit to a Small Planet: A Comedy Akin to a Vaudeville (Boston: Little, Brown, 1957; revised edition, New York: Dramatists Play Service, 1959);

The Best Man: A Play of Politics (Boston: Little, Brown, 1960; revised edition, New York: Dramatists Play Service, 1977);

On the March to the Sea: A Southron Tragedy (New York: Grove, n.d.; London: Heinemann, 1962);

Romulus: A New Comedy, Adapted from a Play by Friedrich Dürrenmatt (New York: Dramatists Play Service, 1962);

Rocking the Boat (Boston: Little, Brown, 1962; London: Heinemann, 1963);

Three Plays (London: Heinemann, 1962);

Julian: A Novel (Boston: Little, Brown, 1964; London: Heinemann, 1964);

Washington, D.C.: A Novel (Boston: Little, Brown, 1967; London: Heinemann, 1967);

Myra Breckinridge (Boston: Little, Brown, 1968; bowdlerized edition, London: Blond, 1968); revised and enlarged as *Myra Breckinridge & Myron* (New York: Random House, 1986);

Sex, Death and Money (New York & London: Bantam, 1968);

Weekend: A Comedy in Two Acts (New York: Dramatists Play Service, 1968);

Gore Vidal, 1992 (from Palimpsest: A Memoir, *1995)*

Reflections Upon a Sinking Ship (Boston: Little, Brown, 1969; London: Heinemann, 1969);

Two Sisters: A Memoir in the Form of a Novel (Boston: Little, Brown, 1970; London: Heinemann, 1970);

An Evening with Richard Nixon (New York: Random House, 1972);

Homage to Daniel Shays: Collected Essays, 1952–1972 (New York: Random House, 1972); published as *Collected Essays, 1952–1972* (London: Heinemann, 1974); republished as *On Our Own Now* (St. Albans, U.K.: Panther, 1976);

Burr: A Novel (New York: Random House, 1973; London: Heinemann, 1974);

Myron: A Novel (New York: Random House, 1974; London: Heinemann, 1975); enlarged as *Myra Breckinridge & Myron* (New York: Random House, 1986);

1876: A Novel (New York: Random House, 1976; London: Heinemann, 1976);

Matters of Fact and of Fiction: Essays 1973–1976 (New York: Random House, 1977);

Kalki: A Novel (New York: Random House, 1978; London: Heinemann, 1978);

Creation: A Novel (New York: Random House, 1981; London: Heinemann, 1981);

The Second American Revolution and Other Essays (1976–1982) (New York: Random House, 1982); republished as *Pink Triangle and Yellow Star, and Other Essays (1976–1982)* (London: Heinemann, 1982);

Duluth (New York: Random House, 1983; London: Heinemann, 1983);

Lincoln: A Novel (New York: Random House, 1984; London: Heinemann, 1984);

Vidal in Venice, edited by George Armstrong, photographs by Tore Gill (New York: Summit Books, 1985; London: Weidenfeld & Nicolson, 1985);

Armageddon? Essays, 1983–1987 (London: Deutsch, 1987); enlarged as *At Home: Essays 1982–88* (New York: Random House, 1988);

Empire: A Novel (New York: Random House, 1987; London: Deutsch, 1987);

The Best Man: A Screen Adaptation of the Original Play, edited by George P. Garrett and others (New York: Irvington, 1989);

Hollywood: A Novel of America in the 1920s (London: Deutsch, 1989; New York: Random House, 1990);

A View from the Diner's Club: Essays 1987–1991 (London: Deutsch, 1991);

The Decline and Fall of the American Empire (Berkeley, Cal.: Odonian Press, 1992);

Live from Golgotha (New York: Random House, 1992; London: Deutsch, 1992);

Screening History, The William E. Massey Sr. Lectures in the History of American Civilization

(Cambridge, Mass.: Harvard University Press, 1992; London: Deutsch, 1992);

United States: Essays, 1952–1992 (New York: Random House, 1993; London: Deutsch, 1994);

Palimpsest: A Memoir (New York: Random House, 1995; London: Deutsch, 1995);

Virgin Islands: A Dependency of United States: Essays 1992–1997 (London: Deutsch, 1997);

The American Presidency (Monroe, Maine: Odonian Press, 1998);

The Smithsonian Institution (New York: Random House, 1998).

PLAY PRODUCTIONS: *Visit to a Small Planet*, New York, Booth Theatre, 7 February 1957;

The Best Man, New York, Morosco Theatre, 31 March 1960;

On the March to the Sea: A Southron Comedy, Hyde Park, N.Y., summer 1960;

Romulus, New York, Music Box Theatre, 10 January 1962;

Weekend, New York, Broadhurst Theatre, 13 March 1968;

An Evening with Richard Nixon and . . . , New York, Schubert Theatre, 30 April 1972.

MOTION PICTURES: *The Catered Affair*, screenplay by Vidal, adapted from Paddy Chayefsky's teleplay, M-G-M, 1956;

I Accuse! screenplay by Vidal, M-G-M, 1958;

The Scapegoat, screenplay by Vidal and Robert Hamer, M-G-M, 1959;

Suddenly, Last Summer, screenplay by Vidal and Tennessee Williams, adapted from Williams's play, Columbia, 1959;

The Best Man, screenplay by Vidal, adapted from his play, United Artists, 1964;

Is Paris Burning? screenplay by Vidal and Francis Ford Coppola, adapted from the book by Gary Collins and Dominique Lapierre, Paramount, 1966;

The Last of the Mobile Hot-Shots, screenplay by Vidal, adapted from Tennessee Williams's *The Seven Descents of Myrtle*, Warner Bros., 1970.

TELEVISION: *Dark Possession*, teleplay by Vidal, *Studio One*, CBS, 15 February 1954;

Smoke, teleplay by Vidal, adapted from the story by William Faulkner, *Suspense*, CBS, 4 May 1954;

Barn Burning, teleplay by Vidal, adapted from the story by William Faulkner, *Suspense*, CBS, 17 August 1954;

A Sense of Justice, teleplay by Vidal, *Philco Television Playhouse*, NBC, 6 February 1955;

The Turn of the Screw, teleplay by Vidal, adapted from the novel by Henry James, *Omnibus*, CBS, 13 February 1955;

Stage Door, teleplay by Vidal, adapted from the drama by George S. Kaufman and Edna Ferber, *The Best of Broadway*, CBS, 6 April 1955;

Summer Pavilion, teleplay by Vidal, *Studio One*, CBS, 2 May 1955;

Visit to a Small Planet, teleplay by Vidal, *Goodyear Television Playhouse*, NBC, 8 May 1955;

A Farewell to Arms, teleplay by Vidal, adapted from the novel by Ernest Hemingway, *Climax*, CBS, 26 May 1955;

The Death of Billy the Kid, teleplay by Vidal, *Philco Television Playhouse*, NBC, 24 July 1955;

Dr. Jekyll and Mr. Hyde, teleplay by Vidal, adapted from the novel by Robert Louis Stevenson, *Climax*, CBS, 28 July 1955;

Portrait of a Ballerina, teleplay by Vidal as Edgar Box, adapted from his novel *Death in the Fifth Position*, CBS, 1 January 1956;

Honor, teleplay by Vidal, *Playwrights 56*, NBC, 19 June 1956;

The Indestructible Mr. Gore, teleplay and narration by Vidal, *Sunday Showcase*, NBC, 13 December 1959;

Dear Arthur, teleplay by Vidal, adapted from the drama by Ferenc Molnár, *Ford Startime*, NBC, 22 March 1960;

Dress Gray, teleplay by Vidal, adapted from the novel by Lucian K. Truscott IV, NBC, 9–10 March 1986;

Vidal in Venice, text and narration by Vidal, WNET, 30 June 1986;

Gore Vidal's Billy the Kid, teleplay by Vidal, adapted from his screenplay *The Death of Billy the Kid*, TNT, 10 May 1989.

OTHER: *Best Television Plays*, volume 1, edited by Vidal (New York: Ballantine, 1956);

Roloff Beny, *Roloff Beny in Italy*, epilogue by Vidal (New York: Harper & Row, 1974), pp. 408–409;

Great American Families, by Vidal and others (New York: Norton, 1975; London: Times Books, 1977), pp. 7–27;

"Reel History: Why John Quincy Adams Was the Hero of Amistad Affair," *New Yorker*, 73 (10 November 1997): 114–119.

"Gore Vidal wasn't what I set out to be . . . ," Gore Vidal quipped in the 18 November 1974 *Newsweek*, "but I don't mind what I've become." What he has become is one of America's preeminent novelists, a prolific writer whose novels and collections of essays have sold in excess of thirty million copies. His historical novels, especially the novels of the American Chronicles, are among the most accomplished and artful work in the genre by a living author. His Myra/Myron novels are classic works of camp sensibility, and his essays perfectly express his role of American cultural critic. These considerable achievements tend to be underestimated largely because of the variety of Vidal's writerly impulses, as if he had somehow failed to fix upon his essential being as a writer. He is viewed by Mitchell S. Ross as a "detoured politician," by Russell Jacoby as a "last intellectual," and by Bernard F. Dick as an "apostate angel." Such tags have their value, but Vidal has said that he is simply a professional writer, asserting in 1975 that he would like to be remembered as "the person who wrote the best sentences in his time."

Although Vidal styles himself a populist, he grew up in a patrician world that explains a great deal of who and what he is as a writer. His mother, Nina Gore Vidal Auchincloss Olds, was a Washington socialite who traced her American roots to the eighteenth century, and his father, Eugene Vidal, was an aviation expert who taught aeronautics at the United States Military Academy, founded several unsuccessful airlines, and from 1933 to 1937 served President Franklin D. Roosevelt as director of air commerce. Eugene Luther Gore Vidal was born on 3 October 1925, at the United States Military Academy at West Point, New York, but the family lived for the first ten years of his life in the Washington establishment of his maternal grandfather, Sen. Thomas Pryor Gore of Oklahoma. In the senator's parlors, the young Vidal became accustomed to such visitors as Huey Long and Eleanor Roosevelt.

After Vidal's parents divorced in 1935, his mother married the wealthy and socially prominent financier Hugh D. Auchincloss, and from 1936 until 1941 Vidal lived at the Auchincloss estate on the Potomac River when not at a succession of boarding schools, among them the spartan Los Alamos Ranch School in New Mexico. After separating from Vidal's mother, Auchincloss went on to marry Janet Lee Bouvier, the mother of Jacqueline Bouvier Kennedy Onassis, bringing Vidal into future orbit with the Kennedy family. Vidal apparently felt abandoned by his parents as a result of these several domestic upheavals and based his sense of family in Senator Gore. As a student at Phillips Exeter Academy in New Hampshire, he was an America Firster in imitation of his grandfather's populism, and by the time he graduated from Exeter in 1943 he had shortened his name to Gore Vidal. In 1959 he further commemorated his grandfather by scripting

and narrating a television play titled *The Indestructible Mr. Gore,* in which he played the role of himself.

Vidal's cynicism about American politics and the insider's perspective he likes to claim in writing about American history, as well as his taste for luxury and his stated pride in avoiding salaried employment, would all seem to have originated in his patrician background. To understand Vidal's political ideology, however, one must give special importance to the idiosyncratic populism of Senator Gore that Vidal adopted as his own. This populist legacy impelled him in 1960 to seek election to the House of Representatives from the heavily Republican Twenty-ninth Congressional District of New York on a platform of taxing wealth; to cofound with Dr. Benjamin Spock the short-lived New Party (later refounded briefly as the People's Party) at the Democratic National Convention of 1968; and to seek in 1982 a California Democratic nomination to the United States Senate on a platform that included taxing church income and nationalizing natural resources.

The advantages of a privileged youth ended for Vidal with graduation from Phillips Exeter Academy. Enlisting in the wartime army on 30 July 1943, he trained as an engineer and served in 1945 as a maritime warrant officer aboard a ship patrolling the Aleutian Islands. During this period he developed severe rheumatoid arthritis that led to his hospitalization. After demobilization, he worked as an editor for the firm of E. P. Dutton, which that same year published his first novel, *Williwaw* (1946). The novel was begun while Vidal was in uniform and tells the story of seven men caught up in a web of mutual antagonisms while they serve on an army transport vessel cruising the Aleutian waters during World War II. The novel is obviously influenced by Ernest Hemingway's style, and its central event is a storm (or williwaw), an echo of Stephen Crane's "The Open Boat" (1898). The men fail the test of camaraderie that the storm sets, and the novel thus deflates wartime clichés. If *Williwaw* is derivative and constituted something of a false start for Vidal, it bears remembering that he was a teenage author, nineteen years old when it was written. Surprisingly, the novel was well received. Indeed, encomiums in the *Saturday Review of Literature, The New York Times,* and *The New York Times Book Review* spoke of its palpable authenticity in such a way as to persuade the young editor to resign immediately his position at Dutton and to chance full-time in New York City the life of a literary wunderkind.

A second novel, *In a Yellow Wood* (1947), appeared quickly and drew upon Vidal's stint as a Dutton editor to tell the story of one day in the life of Robert Holton, a young veteran who chooses to embrace the dull routine of his days in a New York brokerage firm rather than to follow "the road not taken" in the yellow wood of Robert Frost's famous poem. While there are glimmers of artfulness in the novel, it is made tedious on the whole by Holton's unearned ennui. It received some favorable notice on its publication, but it was dismissed by its author in a 1974 interview with the *Paris Review* as "in limbo forever."

In his third novel, *The City and the Pillar* (1948), Vidal boldly told a story of homosexual self-discovery. A literary sensation in its day, it was generally considered to be of a piece with the Kinsey report, which came out the same year. The 10 January 1948 *New Yorker,* offended at words it thought proper to "a metropolitan police blotter," called it "tabloid writing." Other reviews called the novel a "social tract," and "clinical." The sensational plot traces a young man named Jim Willard and his adolescent homosexual passion for a friend he thinks of as a lost twin, until it culminates in a *crime passionnel*–murder in the first edition of the novel, homosexual rape in a 1965 revision. Reviewers found the plotting melodramatic and the tone inappropriately dispassionate, but particularly disturbing at the time was the depiction of Jim Willard as an all-American boy. Indeed, Willard is one of those boy-men almost prototypical in American literature, and his passion for his lost twin recalls not only Aristophanes' myth of creation in Plato's *Symposium* but also the mainstream pattern of Natty Bumppo's affection for Chingachgook, Ishmael's love for Queequeg, and Huck Finn's concern for Jim. Today, the novel is less striking for this audacious stance in relation to figures of the literary canon than for its authentic, unsentimental depiction of a coming-out experience in the 1940s. It survives the period of its writing better than any other American novel of comparable subject for the poise of its understandings and for the credibility of Jim Willard's confusions.

While residing primarily in Antigua, Guatemala, Vidal completed three more novels: *The Season of Comfort* (1949), *Dark Green, Bright Red* (1950), and *A Search for the King: A Twelfth-Century Legend* (1950). If none of these works has a claim to literary distinction, each can be understood as an incremental step toward Vidal's mature work. *The Season of Comfort* is something of an autobiographical self-indulgence, a novel about the psychic damage done young Bill Giraud in a dysfunctional Southern family whose personae correspond unmistakably to those of Vidal's own family. It attempts unsuccessfully the archness of tone that distinguishes much of

Dust jacket for Vidal's first novel (1946), about a storm that tests the crew of an army transport vessel

Vidal's mature work, but it is entirely successful in throwing off the Hemingway style that until then had straitjacketed Vidal's prose.

Dark Green, Bright Red is a quite different endeavor from *The Season of Comfort*. Inspired by Vidal's residence in Guatemala, it is a novel of tropical intrigue and failed revolution with a cast of characters adapted from the novels of Graham Greene and Joseph Conrad, among them Gen. Jorge Alvarez Asturias, a former president of the republic; José Alvarez, his playboy son; and Peter Nelson, an American mercenary. Like Greene and Conrad, Vidal envelops the adventure-story elements of his plot in a pervasive weltschmerz, but the novel is weakened by inadequate character development.

The most interesting and certainly the most narratively competent of these three novels is *A Search for the King,* a straightforward retelling of the thirteenth-century tale of the troubadour Blondel de Néel and his search for Richard the Lion-Hearted. If the straightforwardness of the novel points backward to the Hemingway manner, its historical elements point forward to the novels of Vidal's maturity. Its two central male figures, one of whom grounds his existence in the other, is an effective treatment of a twin motif that haunts Vidal's work.

The Judgment of Paris (1952) is the first work of Vidal's artistic maturity. Based on the incident in Greek mythology in which Paris is forced to choose among Hera, Athena, and Aphrodite, it depicts a young man sojourning in Europe who must choose among three women offering him variously a political career, an intellectual life, and physical intimacy. So entirely unimportant is this structure in the development of the novel, however, that one is compelled to wonder if Vidal is parodying the modernist tendency to find in mythology a gloss for every human situation. Far more interesting than the mythic parallel is the wealth of invention that Vidal expends on minor characters. Indeed, Vidal seems to have discovered in writing *The Judgment of Paris* the narrative power of anecdotes rendered wittily, of character sketches that approach caricature, and of a fine, enveloping insouciance—all hallmarks of his mature art. Presciently, the critic John W. Aldridge was moved to declare Vidal's long apprenticeship at an end.

Having purchased in 1950 an 1820 Greek Revival mansion in Barrytown, New York, Vidal was under increasing financial pressure. Three inconsequential if pleasant detective stories that he wrote under the pseudonym Edgar Box were the immediate result: *Death in the Fifth Position* (1952), *Death Before Bedtime* (1953), and *Death Likes It Hot* (1954). To augment his income further, Vidal began writing screenplays in the mid 1950s—some twenty or thirty, he avers, for television drama series such as *Omnibus* and *Studio One,* and about a dozen screenplays for Hollywood, among them *The Catered Affair* (1956), *I Accuse!* (1958), and an adaptation of Tennessee Williams's *Suddenly, Last Summer* (1959). His play *Visit to a Small Planet,* an engaging science-fiction fantasy, was successful in different versions on television in 1955 and on Broadway in 1957, where it ran for a respectable 338 performances. In the wake of its success, Vidal began to review stage productions as well as books, and he served in the late 1950s as a drama critic for the *Reporter.* *The Best Man* (1960), a topical election-year drama about character assassination in a presidential campaign, repeated the success of *Visit to a Small Planet* and enjoyed a Broadway run of 520 performances. Later works such as *Romulus* (1962), adapted from Friedrich Dürrenmatt's *Romulus der Grosse; Weekend* (1968); and *An Evening with Richard Nixon* (1972) did not gain large audiences. Briefly in the late 1950s, however, Vidal enjoyed a reputation as a scriptwriter superior to his reputation as a novelist. By

1960 he could command on occasion nearly five thousand dollars for a one-hour television script. "What became of our postwar hopes?" lamented the 29 July 1962 *New York Times Book Review,* believing that Vidal and other postwar writers had abandoned the novel.

Aside from a handful of short stories collected as *A Thirsty Evil* (1956), Vidal had published only one novel, *Messiah* (1954), in the decade preceding the *New York Times Book Review* lament. An undistinguished but in some ways seminal work, its putative subject is the origin of an imaginary messianic cult as recorded in a memoir and some diaristic passages set down in the year 2000 by Eugene Luther, a man who helped to launch the cult in the early 1950s. The real subjects of the novel are religious revisionism and the merchandising of messiahs—subjects to which Vidal would return several times in his career. Having discovered his best voice in *The Judgment of Paris,* Vidal discovered his best genre in *Messiah,* for the fictive memoir lends itself to Vidal's ideological revisionism and accommodates well his penchant for anecdote, quick character sketches, and incidental grotesquery.

These discoveries of voice and genre culminated in 1964 in *Julian,* a novel about the fourth-century Roman emperor known as Julian the Apostate in the Christian church, which the emperor rejected for Mithraism. Ostensibly Julian's autobiographical memoir and his private journal as written in the year of his death and introduced and annotated seventeen years later by the philosophers Libanius of Antioch and Priscus of Athens, the novel is a rich, many-layered tale of Julian the Christian becoming Julian the Apostate, of Julian the philosopher becoming Julian the warrior, and of Julian the heir-unapparent becoming Julian the emperor—all critiqued with entertaining volubility by Priscus and Libanius. The historical authenticity of the novel is impressive. Vidal had occupied himself for five years with voluminous source material on the emperor and for several more years with a general study of the fourth century, developing a discipline of serious research that he would bring to all of his historical fictions. *Julian* is also contemporaneously edged: Vidal's recent experiments in form and voice had provided him with a technique for turning the fourth-century triumph of Christianity over Mithraism into a diagnosis of present-day cultural ills. This latter achievement of the historicity of the novel was not generally recognized at the time. Critics tended to seek in Vidal's novel the high drama of Robert Graves's reconstructions of history but missed his effort to pinpoint in ancient history a moment of crisis for the modern world.

Vidal with Truman Capote and Tennessee Williams, 6 October 1948 (photograph by Jo Healey; from Palimpsest: A Memoir, *1995)*

Shortly after Vidal's unsuccessful bid for a congressional seat in 1960, he began to channel his political views into a series of articles for the magazine *Esquire*. Since then he has discoursed many times on politics and other cultural matters in the pages of the *New York Review of Books*, the *New Statesman*, and similar organs of opinion. A frequent guest on television talk shows since the early 1960s, he can be counted upon to turn the conversation to American politics, often in a confrontational way. Although not considered a weighty or original thinker, Vidal has earned considerable stature as a critic of the American establishment through his aphoristic style. The essays collected in *Reflections Upon a Sinking Ship* (1969), *Homage to Daniel Shays: Collected Essays, 1952–1972* (1972), and several other collections are in general less interesting for their large arguments than for their incidental disparagements and flashes of wit. The collection *United States: Essays, 1952–1992* (1993), however, represents the maturation of Vidal as essayist, and received the National Book Award for nonfiction in the year of its publication.

Julian led the way to the great endeavor of Vidal's maturity: a loosely coordinated, multivolume narrative that highlights figures and periods of American history. Not written or published in temporal sequence (not talked about at all and probably not conceived as a sequence until the mid 1970s), Vidal's chronicle of America includes to date the novels *Washington, D.C.* (1967), *Burr* (1973), *1876* (1976), *Lincoln* (1984), *Empire* (1987), and *Holly-*

wood: A Novel of America in the 1920s (1989). The sequence employs as an organizing motif an imaginary family dynasty, the Schuyler-Sanfords, but is not in any important sense a unified whole. The novels of the American Chronicles were creatively nourished, it would seem, by Vidal's selling his Barrytown mansion in the early 1960s and settling with his longtime companion Howard Austen in Rome and in Ravello, on the Amalfi coast in Italy. He quipped, in the epilogue to Roloff Beny's *Roloff Beny in Italy* (1974), that "a city which calls itself 'eternal' is obviously the best place to watch eternity go down the drain." James Tatum observes, in Jay Parini's 1992 work, that Vidal recovered the model for America as a second Rome in Italy and also recovered there a distinctively Roman way of attacking the American Rome.

Washington, D.C., the first-written, temporally last novel in Vidal's American Chronicles, is a comedy of political manners that unfolds between the years 1937 and 1956, with Pearl Harbor, Roosevelt's death, the McCarthy hearings, and the Korean War figuring prominently in the background. It focuses on the Washington families of James Burden Day, an influential senator, and of Blaise Sanford, owner of the *Washington Tribune*. It also traces the unscrupulous rise to power of Clay Overbury, a rise to power so ripely gothic that it imparts a humorous cast even to the seamiest aspects of political life. Vidal's spokesman for his own, seriocomic point of view is young Peter Sanford, who thrills to the melodrama of both familial and political life without losing his bearings in reality. He differs from Senator Day, whose overactive imagination leads him into madness, and from Overbury, who knows nothing of the thrill that gothic imaginings impart to Peter's life.

With little taste for the cynicism of *Washington, D.C.,* many reviewers were curtly negative. Josh Greenfeld wrote dismissively in the 30 April 1967 *New York Times Book Review* that "Vidal picks an assortment of on-target political themes, adds several pinches of off-beat sex, and cooks it all over a good melodramatically licking flame." Having achieved best-seller status with *Julian* and *Washington, D.C.,* Vidal decided to exploit the reputation as a cultural critic that he had begun to foster not only in his novels but also in his ideologically provocative essays. His novel *Myra Breckinridge* (1968) would outstrip in sexual daring *The City and the Pillar,* using the freedom of the form of the fictive journal, which had worked so well in *Julian,* to challenge the regnant culture like no other Vidal work.

An uninhibited disquisition by the eponymous Myra (who was Myron before a sex-change operation), *Myra Breckinridge* recounts Myra's establishment of herself in Hollywood, where she works as an instructor in an academy of drama and modeling. Like Vidal, she is a cinema enthusiast, erudite in Hollywood lore and unstinting in her esteem for the Golden Age of Hollywood. "*In the decade between 1935 and 1945, no irrelevant film was made in the United States,*" she boldly avers. Myra's goal is not only the inculcation in students of correct cinematic understandings; her psychosexual circumstances make her resolved as by a holy mission to realign the sexes. To that end she subjugates and finally rapes a virile young student. Myra also seduces his girlfriend.

It was immediately clear to aficionados of the genre that *Myra Breckinridge* is a masterpiece of camp, that form of humor that delights in the exaggerated and artificial sexuality celebrated by Myra both in her person and in her rhetoric. Fancying herself an archetypal femme fatale, even something of a goddess, she experiences a continual ravishment by her own beauty that is communicated in majestically allusive idiom. The effect is so rhetorically overripe that it belongs clearly to the realm of linguistic conceit on one level of understanding, to psychological pathology on another, while beggaring moral censure on both levels. Even the pornographic clichés of the novel have a kind of innocence in that they spring uncensured from Myra's hyperbolic consciousness of her mission. A segment of reviewers thought the novel in woeful taste, but

more than any previous Vidal novel it elicited widespread admiration.

Myra Breckinridge spawned a sequel in *Myron: A Novel* (1974), which finds the libidinous Myra and her repressed alter ego alternately possessing the Breckinridge psyche in dizzying convolutions of time and space. Accidentally transported back to the original M-G-M set of the 1948 Maria Montez film *Siren of Babylon,* Myra tampers creatively with the film and actually becomes Montez, while the Latin film star inhabits ten-year-old Myron. Myra does not shrink for a moment from altering history and attempts to save M-G-M from its future insolvency. A fervent Malthusian, she even finds the opportunity to reduce the 1973 population by attempting the 1948 castration of a young actor—in the midst of which Myron comes to the fore of the Breckinridge persona. The fun of such scenes is Myra's battling for dominance over Myron in a fireworks of invective, Myron's invective priggish and demotic, Myra's funky and garish. This stylistic élan of the novel falters only in Vidal's replacing references to genitalia with the names of the five Supreme Court justices who in 1973 linked obscenity to community standards—a gimmick eliminated in the 1986 revision.

As is usually the fate of sequels, *Myron* has been found inferior to *Myra Breckinridge,* although it is the more complexly imagined work of the two and Vidal's favorite. Whatever their relative merits, the two novels are an important pairing, as much a plateau of Vidal's art as the novels of his American Chronicles. If it is only occasionally observed that *Myra Breckinridge* and *Myron* include serious diagnoses of the relationship between power and sex and between politics and cinema—diagnoses that link the two novels to major themes of the American Chronicles and of the essays—it is because their unabashed campiness is triumphant over all else.

Having shared a stepfather with Jacqueline Kennedy, Vidal was briefly taken up by the Kennedys when they came to power in the White House. In the April 1967 *Esquire* Vidal asserts that he admired John F. Kennedy as "an ironist in a profession where the prize usually goes to the apparent cornball," but in an April 1975 interview he said he detested Robert Kennedy as "a child of Joe McCarthy, a little Torquemada." After a contretemps with the younger Kennedy at a White House reception in 1961, Vidal was no longer on good terms with the family. Of particular note from the period, therefore, are two iconoclastic essays Vidal subsequently wrote on the Kennedys titled "The Best Man, 1968" (*Esquire,* March 1963) and "The Holy Family" (*Esquire,* April 1967). There ensued also *Two Sisters*

(1970), a novel irreverent in incidental ways to the mystique of Jacqueline Kennedy.

Two Sisters is narrated by a Vidalian "V." who reminisces with a former mistress named Marietta Donegal about Eric and Erika Van Damm, twins whom they knew in Paris in the 1940s. At the heart of the novel is Eric's putative screenplay "Two Sisters of Ephesus," which concerns a rivalry of the fourth-century widows Helena and Artemisa and their efforts to outshine each other and their half-brother Herostratus on the great stage of the world—efforts with unmistakable relevance to the apparent relationship of Jacqueline Kennedy and her sister Lee Radziwill in the 1960s. Marietta is a gratuitous portrait of the diarist Anaïs Nin, who was once Vidal's confidante and who wrote indiscreetly of him in her 1944–1947 diary. Correspondences of all kinds proliferate in the novel in a postmodern interplay of reality with fiction and of fictions with fictions. The most undervalued of Vidal's novels, *Two Sisters* continues today to suffer critical neglect.

To many readers the publication of *Burr* in 1973 signaled Vidal's coming of age as a major novelist. Chronologically the first installment in the American Chronicles, the novel is set in the 1830s and is narrated by Charlie Schuyler, a junior law clerk employed by the aged Aaron Burr. When Schuyler is hired by others to write a scurrilous pamphlet alleging that Martin Van Buren is Burr's bastard son, he discovers ironically that he and Van Buren are both sons of the great man. More important than this secret of biological paternity is the scandal of national paternity that Schuyler discovers via a memoir that Burr has entrusted to him and that he presents in alternation with his own narrative. Indeed, Burr's memoir suggests that the founding fathers were despoilers of the infant republic and that Aaron Burr alone was innocent of their lust for empire. The actual Burr was probably guilty of that failing—some historians accept as fact Thomas Jefferson's charge that Burr attempted to separate the western territories from the Union in order to rule over them—but Vidal endorses the fictive Burr's self-image.

If the portraits of the founding fathers are revisionist good fun, the characterization of Burr as a charismatic and picaresque adventurer is the basis of considerable entertainment. Nothing is more central to Burr's charm than his verbal elegance. Of his impending death, he can say casually to Schuyler, "If you should hear that I have died in the bosom of the Dutch Reformed Church, you will know that either a noble mind was entirely overturned at the end or a man of the cloth has committed perjury." Such poise of mind and language vindicate charac-

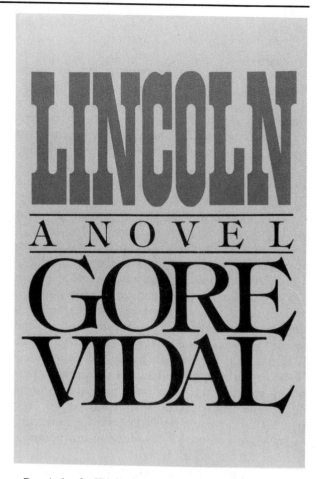

Dust jacket for Vidal's 1984 novel, a fictionalized portrait of the sixteenth American president

ter in the world of *Burr,* as in the world of *Myra Breckinridge* beforehand and in the Vidalian world at large. The great majority of critics found Burr an entertaining raconteur, and they were charmed by the incidental pleasures of the novel. Writing in the 28 October 1973 *New York Times Book Review,* John Leonard described Vidal admiringly as a craftsman "for whom wit is not a mechanical toy that explodes in the face of the reader but a feather that tickles the bare feet of the imagination."

With the publication of *1876* in America's bicentennial year, the American Chronicles began to take shape and to be promoted for the first time as an entity. The narrator of *1876* is once again Charlie Schuyler, now sixty-two years old and returning to New York from France for the first time in thirty-eight years. He is accompanied by his widowed daughter Emma, the Princess d'Agrigente, who eventually marries William Sanford and becomes the grandmother of Peter Sanford, Vidal's spokesman in *Washington, D.C.* The novel affects to be a workbook, a scribbled journal of impressions that Schuyler keeps from his arrival in New York until his death in 1877, in hopes, he says, of hacking from it "a monument or two to decorate the republic's centennial." Effectively, it is a Cook's tour of American life and politics in the centennial year, for the inconsequential plot of the novel functions almost entirely as scaffolding for a survey of the American scene and the satiric commentary that it occasions. Its satire of the year 1876 seemed to some readers to take on a contemporary edge with Samuel Jones Tilden functioning as a persona of George McGovern and Rutherford B. Hayes as a persona of Gerald Ford. Dark memories in 1876 of the Civil War, of the Lincoln assassination, and of the corrupt Grant administration seemed to foreshadow in 1976 memories of Vietnam, the Kennedy assassination, and the Watergate scandal of the Nixon presidency.

The tour through American life and politics in *1876* crystallized two ongoing questions about Vidal's art. To what extent, reviewers asked, can the reader's pleasure in Vidal's mandarin style and satiric eye compensate for the more ordinary novelistic pleasures of plot and character development? Vidal had proven himself able to create richly egocentric characters, but he seemed incapable of developing such characters in a workmanlike plot. Also, to what extent, some reviewers asked, can the historical novel tolerate Vidal's revisionism without vitiating its claim to historicity?

The popular successes of *Myra Breckinridge, Burr,* and *1876* might have persuaded Vidal that the fictive journal was his forte, the mode best able to convey his anecdotal virtuosity and flashes of incidental wit while demanding relatively little of his plotting skills. However, Vidal has never been one to impose self-limitations on his art, as he demonstrated with the 1978 publication of *Kalki,* an intricately-plotted if not well-received doomsday tale of a mad American Vietnam veteran who styles himself the incarnation of the Hindu deity Vishnu. Though the critical reception of *Kalki* was underwhelming, and perhaps not undeservedly so, Vidal's creation of the eponymous antihero seems remarkably prescient twenty years later.

Vidal purchased a home in Los Angeles in 1976, intending to live there half of each year in deference to new Italian tax laws. The purchase drew attention to what has come to be his love/hate relationship with Hollywood: love, because the movies are one of his great interests; hate, because he often remarks on the decline of Hollywood from the Golden Age of his youth. It had not improved Vidal's esteem for modern-day Hollywood that his screenplay for *The Last of the Mobile Hot-Shots* (1970), based on Tennessee Williams's *The Seven Descents of Myrtle,* was judged a "cruel parody" in the 15 Janu-

ary 1970 *New York Times.* Nor was he pleased that the disastrously tasteless films *Myra Breckinridge* (1970) and later *Caligula* (1979) were linked to his name even though he had nothing to do with them. Vidal was also displeased to discover in 1964 that *The Best Man,* a film he had thought wholly his own, was advertised at the Cannes Film Festival as "un film de Franklin Schaffner." Such irritations were vented in a 25 November 1976 *New York Review of Books* essay titled "Who Makes the Movies?" in which Vidal attacked the so-called auteur theory of filmmaking, a theory that asserts that a film has an author in the same way that a book does and that the author of a film is not the screenwriter but the director.

With the 510-page *Creation* (1981) Vidal returned to the form of the fictive historical memoir. His period is the fifth century B.C., and his protagonist is Cyrus Spitama, a putative grandson of Zoroaster, who dictates to his own grandson a disjointed memoir that details his career as a roving ambassador for Persia. The narrative encompasses four ancient civilizations—Athens, China, India, and Persia—but Cyrus's journeys are telescoped, and the landscapes through which he passes are barely sketched in deference to the conscription into the novel of such fifth-century notables as Confucius, Master Li, and Themistocles. In service to the title of the novel, Cyrus concerns himself intermittently with a quest for the secret of creation and inquires into the various creation myths of the East but never with a convincing show of interest. Like *1876, Creation* is essentially a Cook's tour of a remote world.

Much of the charm of *Creation* is the prosaism of Cyrus's point of view. The Buddha's bared teeth, he tells us, were "mottled and yellow, disconcertingly suggestive of fangs." Confucius he sums up as "a nag." "Protocol was particularly strict at the court of Darius," he recalls, "as it tends to be whenever a monarch is not born to the throne." Such observations take on at their best an aphoristic edge that is quintessentially Vidalian. "It is odd," Cyrus says, "—and charming—to talk to an intelligent woman who is not a prostitute." "For the Greek, what is not Greek is not," he quips. And like other Vidalian narrators, Cyrus is an observer of the emperor's new clothes. "At the core of the Buddhist system," he says, "there is an empty space which is not just the sought-after nirvana. It is perfect atheism." Elsewhere he says, "I have yet to know of a state that does not so misrepresent its military strength and wealth that, in time, the state ends by deceiving itself."

Such mordant observations crowd the pages of *Creation,* rendering the novel something of a sociological and ideological treatise as well as a geographical and historical travelogue. Cyrus is a camp follower of greatness who rarely sits at campfires with the camel drivers, only at the feet of kings and sages. Typically, he proclaims, "I have no intention of revealing to the Greeks *any* details of my journey to Cathay," a remark which has the advantage for Vidal of occasioning an ellipsis in the narrative that propels Cyrus expeditiously from one celebrity to the next. Reviewers found fault with several matters of historical accuracy and with the cardboard characterizations in the novel but tended to admire its compass. "As a novel of ideas, its ambition and its cast of characters could not possibly be bolder," observed Paul Theroux in the 29 March 1981 *New York Times Book Review*.

As a man who lives by the income from his writing, Vidal has not scrupled on occasion to publish work inferior to his best, but neither the Edgar Box novels nor the problematical *Kalki* prepared readers for *Duluth* (1983). One critic speculated that it was the world's first campaign-debt-retirement novel, its purpose to pay for the author's failed campaign in 1982 to win a senatorial nomination. Whatever its purpose, *Duluth* freewheelingly burlesques America as a land of yahoos—that is to say, a land of venal politicians, socially ambitious matrons, sadomasochistic police, angry blacks, and Chicanos whose barrios are "alive with mariachi music and joyous laughter because illegal aliens are essentially life-enhancing." Incidental objects of satire in the novel include Harlequin romances, racially balanced television news teams, and deconstructionist literary criticism as it approaches the millennium of "*après* post-structuralism." Suffice it to say that both critical and popular assessments of *Duluth* were remarkably divergent at the time of its publication and are likely to remain so.

Duluth is akin to *Myron* and to *Two Sisters* in its obsession with the octopus embrace of media and in its postmodern layering of realities with fictions, but its satire is far bleaker than that of the earlier novels—Swiftian, some have argued. The vast majority of critics found it mean-spirited in its humor where *Myron* is zestful and saw its narrative experimentation as plodding. A notable exception in a general chorus of disdain is Angela McRobbie, who wrote in the 6 May 1983 *New Statesman* that *Duluth* is "one of the most brilliant, most radical and most subversive pieces of writing to emerge from America in recent years."

Vidal wrote *Duluth* in two years while also occupied with research for the much more ambitious novel *Lincoln,* chronologically the second work in his American Chronicles. A daunting, 657-page study of the sixteenth American president from his

Dust jacket for the first American edition of Vidal's 1989 novel, one of the volumes in his historical sequence, the American Chronicles

inauguration in 1861 until his assassination in 1865, the novel depicts Lincoln from several different points of view: that of his wife Mary Todd Lincoln, of Secretary of State William H. Seward, of Secretary of the Treasury Salmon P. Chase, of the conspirator David Herold, and, most important, of the twenty-three-year-old John Hay, Lincoln's private secretary, to whom is given the climactic insight of the novel that Lincoln "not only put the Union back together again, but he made an entirely new country, and all of it in his own image." Refracted through these and other points of view, Lincoln is a shadowy figure, narratively only watched and judged, as around him swirl the politicians, the generals, and the bankers who constitute a sort of malarial miasma arising from the Potomac swampland.

Vidal's portrait of Lincoln is as respectful as it is compatible with his rendering him as a complete and accomplished politician, a self-mythologizer who encourages the legend of the naive rail-splitter while quietly subverting the Constitution in order to preserve the Union. Indeed, Vidal's Lincoln is the founder of what historians call the Imperial Presidency in that he broadly interprets the doctrine of the "inherent powers" of the presidency; empowers his secretary of the treasury with extraordinary latitude to raise funds for the war; and assists the decision of Maryland to remain in the Union by suspending several constitutional liberties, among them the rights of assembly and habeas corpus. Without giving the reader access to Lincoln's mind or heart and without challenging seriously the mystique of the sixteenth president, Vidal revives questions that historians have generally dismissed. Was Lincoln indulgent of his wife because he knew he had passed on to her a syphilitic infection that destroyed her mind and killed their sons? Did he superstitiously look to his own assassination as atonement for the terrible wartime slaughter of young men? In his transformation of the presidency, did Lincoln foresee and will into being what Vidal likes to call the American Imperium? Vidal does not applaud Lincoln's reinvention of the republic, certainly, but he admires the audacity of Lincoln's single-minded devotion to the Union in the same way that he admires the imperiousness of Myra Breckinridge.

The most interesting historical fictions are often those that illumine a moment in the past when the modern age or some dominant aspect of it came into existence. If *Julian* is marginally more successful as a novel than *Lincoln,* it is possibly for the reason that remote history lends its events and personae to fiction more readily than recent history, whose familiarity tends to inhibit a novelist's imagination. Such is a point made repeatedly by reviewers who found that Vidal's imagination had not adequately dominated the source material on Lincoln. Even enthusiastic reviewers such as Joyce Carol Oates in the 13 June 1984 *New York Times Book Review* found the novel thinly imagined: "*Lincoln,*" she noted, "is not so much an imaginative reconstruction of an era as an intelligent, lucid, and highly informative transcript of it."

The Schuyler-Sanford dynasty takes center stage again in *Empire,* chronologically the fourth installment in the American Chronicles. The central character of *Empire* is Caroline Sanford, a daughter of the French-born Emma of *1876.* In the course of the novel, Caroline is engaged to the son of John Hay from *Lincoln* and has an affair with James Burden Day from *Washington, D.C.* She also makes a success of a moribund newspaper by modeling it on the yellow journalism of the Hearst papers.

Vidal focuses in *Empire* on the years 1895–1906, a period during which the William McKinley and Theodore Roosevelt administrations indulged dreams of an empire with interventions in Cuba, the Philippine Islands, and Panama. It is a story without important villains as Vidal tells it—a story, rather, of political happenstance and journalistic mendacity. The aged John Hay views his "Open Door" pronouncement not as a logical capstone to the foreign policy of post-Civil War America but as a triumph of the imagination. William McKinley is simply perplexed by the consequences of what he has authorized in the Philippines. Theodore Roosevelt is a blustering boy elevated to the presidency by William Randolph Hearst. If there is any villain at all in the novel, it is Hearst, who boasts of the Spanish-American War as his creation, but Vidal seems to view Hearst less as an evil genius than as an imaginative force inseparable from the transformation of the republic. Indeed, reality surrenders increasingly to the inventions of the journalistic imagination in *Empire,* and Vidal links that surrender to the drift from isolationist republic to arrogant empire. This lack of meaningful villains adds to the tone of sadness in the novel. The reader might prefer to have a villain to blame for the lost honor of the republic, but *Empire* is an elegy, not a *J'accuse.*

After Vidal's tentative reach for the sublime in *Lincoln, Empire* seemed to some reviewers an unfortunate reversion to cynicism. "*Lincoln* has been Vidal's one concession that something other than tawdriness and hypocrisy might have been present in American political life," observed Andrew Delbanco; *Empire,* he said, "is one long expression of disgust." Some newspaper reviewers were put off by the conceit in the novel that newspapers invent national issues. "Surely Vidal blows his own cover," complained the reviewer for the 20 July 1987 *Christian Science Monitor:* "He spells out the Hearst formula. Sensationalism, scandal, invented news. And then he follows it himself." However, most reviewers found Vidal's mix of the fictive and the historical to be highly entertaining—a feast of confected and configured moments. Many reviewers were not at all put off by Vidal's confident cynicism. Richard Poirier went so far as to point out that "part of Vidal's originality derives from his attendant assurance that he can create and command the American history of his novels, as much as he can their imaginary components. No other American writer . . . has Vidal's sense of national proprietorship."

Vidal had ceased writing for television drama after the demise of its so-called Golden Age and did not return to the medium in a creative capacity until the mid 1980s. Still, he had not wholly spurned the medium he so often castigated in print. He wrote and narrated a television documentary titled *Vidal in Venice* (1986) and appeared on many television talk shows. Finally he was persuaded in 1986 to adapt for television Lucien K. Truscott IV's novel *Dress Gray,* a screenplay for which he won an Emmy nomination. In 1989 he adapted anew for Turner Network Television his early teleplay *The Death of Billy the Kid,* which was adapted with unhappy results for Warner Bros. as *The Left-Handed Gun* in 1955. The title of the third incarnation of the teleplay is *Gore Vidal's Billy the Kid.*

In *Hollywood,* temporally the fifth installment in the American Chronicles, Vidal deals with the years 1917 to 1923, a period dominated in American politics by World War I and the scandal-ridden administration of Warren G. Harding. The bit players in the novel comprise a veritable Who's Who of the age, including not only Woodrow Wilson and Harding but also the young Franklin and Eleanor Roosevelt, Alice Roosevelt Longworth, William Randolph Hearst and Marion Davies, W. D. Griffith, and such film stars as Douglas Fairbanks, Mary Pickford, Charlie Chaplin, and Fatty Arbuckle. There is even a cameo appearance by Vidal's grandfather Sen. Thomas Gore.

The major player and the author's narrative surrogate is once again Caroline Sanford. An owner of the influential *Washington Tribune,* she discovers still another realm of power in Hollywood, where she aids in recruiting the embryonic "photo play" industry to the war effort and where she discovers the ability of Hollywood not just to invent the news, like the Hearst newspapers, but actually to script reality. "Reality could now be entirely invented and history revised," she realizes with shock; "Suddenly, she knew what God must have felt when he gazed upon chaos, with nothing but himself upon his mind."

Its title notwithstanding, *Hollywood* focuses more on Washington than it does on the film industry. Organized around the fall in different ways of two markedly different presidents, *Hollywood* chronicles in detail the controversies that swirled around the proposed League of Nations, the course of Wilson's physical decline, the corruptions of the Harding administration, and the orchestrated rhetoric by which an America sympathetic toward Germany and hostile toward England had its sympathies precisely reversed. As much as in any novel of the series, the story in *Hollywood* is one of a nation too easily forced onto the paths of empire by the dream merchants of Washington and Hollywood and doomed to suffer too willingly its own corruption. Like his main characters, Vidal casts a cool eye on what Caroline knows to be "the prevailing fact of force in human affairs" but in this, his twenty-third

Vidal's house in Ravello, Italy, which he bought in 1972

novel, with less overt cynicism than heretofore toward all things American. "A wonderfully literate and consistently impressive work of fiction," opined Joel Conarroe in the 21 January 1990 *New York Times Book Review.* The general praise for *Hollywood* was tempered only by the commonplace criticism that Vidal's approach to writing novels indulges too many different impulses.

Among the several urgencies of Vidal's craft would seem to be a return periodically to messianic figures like Myra, Kalki, and Lincoln and a return periodically to Rabelaisian satire. The two impulses meet, not for the first time, in *Live from Golgotha* (1992), a freewheeling burlesque of the New Testament. Set near the close of the second millennium, the novel postulates that the technology exists for sending holograms, objects, and even persons into the past in such a way as to allow NBC to film the historical Crucifixion and to hire Timothy, the first bishop of Ephesus, to anchor the broadcast. At the same time, a computer virus orchestrated by a master hacker has corrupted the extant Gospels, making it imperative for Timothy to set down the "true" story of Judas crucified in lieu of Jesus even as the Crucifixion is so corrupted by contact with the future that Saint Paul, Shirley MacLaine, Oral Roberts, and Mary Baker Eddy are enabled to attend on Golgotha. There is in actuality no "true" story at all, for *Live from Golgotha* is a series of false bottoms. That the events occur only in Timothy's dream-life is a possibility Vidal keeps open.

The largest point of Vidal's satire would seem to be the corruptibility of religious texts, but that

"The American tradition of independent and curious learning is kept alive in the wit and great expressiveness of Gore Vidal's criticism."
—National Book Critics Circle
Award for Criticism

ISBN 0-679-41489-4

Dust jacket for Vidal's 1993 nonfiction collection, which received a National Book Award

point barely survives his crediting an undeveloped technology for so many of the actual corruptions in *Live from Golgotha*. Lesser points of Vidal's satire (for example, corrupt religious fund-raising, the idea that Saint Paul was homosexual) fail to shock. Wilfrid Sheed suggests in the 26 October 1992 *New Yorker* that such whimsies of the text are not blasphemies or even satire but only "roguish impieties."

The publication of Vidal's memoir *Palimpsest* in 1995 provided readers with a gossipy and frequently hilarious account of the writer's first thirty-nine years. Given that Vidal served as grandchild amanuensis to a United States senator, published a well-received novel at the age of nineteen, and lived in Hollywood with Joanne Woodward and Paul Newman as a young screenwriter, the range of his acquaintances was singularly wide early on. Never famous for reticence, Vidal settles some old scores with Truman Capote, Anaïs Nin, and his mother, among others, while expanding on the psychosexual theme set forth in Plato's *Symposium* as it applies to his own life. The author's one great love, apparently, was a schoolmate at the private boarding school of St. Albans, a boy named Jimmy Trimble who later died in the fighting on Iwo Jima.

That same Jimmy Trimble, fictionalized as the boy physics wizard "T," is the hero of Vidal's 1998

novel, *The Smithsonian Institution*. Plucked from St. Albans by an agreeably loopy cadre of American historical figures, including Charles Lindbergh, a brain-damaged Abraham Lincoln, and the philanthropist Smithson himself, T is charged with the task of saving America and the world from the impending World War II. Set in the castle of the Institution on the National Mall, where the figures in the dioramas come to life during closing hours, the novel employs several of the science-fiction devices Vidal used in his earlier "inventions" *Duluth* and *Live from Golgotha*—time travel, transmigrating souls, and the conceit of parallel universes—but to less successful comic effect. The resulting hybrid makes *The Smithsonian Institution* an ingenious and superior example of the "what if?" genre of historical fiction, but it also makes for middling Vidal.

Vidal is a writer, then, of uneven but substantial development. Throwing off early the influence of Hemingway and the modernists, he adapted to his own uses the genres of camp, historical fiction, and apocalyptic fantasy, and he helped to bring those genres into the literary mainstream by making them vehicles for his distinctive modes of auctorial audacity. In the best mode of that audacity, the indecorous and the demotic overlay his elegantly lucid prose. In another mode, a wit recognizably Vidalian underlies his artifices of time and person, tending to render such artifices a celebration of his authorial selfhood—which is to say, a celebration of his political and psychosexual agendas. It is generally recognized that these modes are both the limitation and the achievement of his art, irritating some readers while delighting others.

Interviews:

Eugene Walter, "Conversations with Gore Vidal," *Transatlantic Review,* 4 (Summer 1960): 5–17;

Eve Auchincloss and Nancy Lynch, "Disturber of the Peace: Gore Vidal," *Mademoiselle,* 53 (September 1961): 132–133, 176–179;

"*Playboy* Interview: Gore Vidal," *Playboy,* 16 (June 1969): 77–96, 238;

Daniel Halpern, "Interview with Gore Vidal," *Antaeus,* 1 (1971): 67–76;

Gerald Clarke, "Petronius Americanus: The Ways of Gore Vidal," *Atlantic,* 229 (March 1972): 44–51;

Clarke, "The Art of Fiction," *Paris Review,* 15 (Fall 1974): 130–165;

Arthur Cooper, "Gore Vidal on . . . Gore Vidal," *Newsweek,* 84 (18 November 1974): 97–99;

Michael S. Lasky, "The Complete Works on Gore Vidal: His Workings," *Writer's Digest,* 55 (March 1975): 20–26;

Ken Kelly, "*Penthouse* Interview: Gore Vidal," *Penthouse,* 6 (April 1975): 97–98, 104–106;

Diane Johnson, "Gore Vidal: Scorekeeper," *New York Times Book Review,* 17 April 1977, p. 47;

Michael Segell, "The Highbrow Railings of Gore Vidal," *Rolling Stone,* no. 317 (15 May 1980): 40–43;

Robert J. Stanton and Gore Vidal, *Views from a Window: Conversations with Gore Vidal* (Secaucus, N.J.: Lyle Stuart, 1980);

Charles Ruas, "Gore Vidal," in his *Conversations with American Writers* (New York: Knopf, 1985), pp. 57–74;

Claudia Dreifus, "Gore Vidal: The Writer as Citizen," *Progressive,* 50 (September 1986): 36–39;

Robert Katz, "Gore Goes to War," *American Film,* 13 (November 1987): 43–46;

Carole Mallory, "Mailer and Vidal: The Big Schmooze," *Esquire,* 15 (May 1991): 105–112;

Martha Duffy, "A Gadfly in Glorious, Angry Exile," *Time,* 140 (28 September 1992): 64–66;

David Hutchings, "Gospel According to Gore," *People,* 38 (2 November 1992): 103–106;

Jay Parini, "An Interview with Gore Vidal," in his *Gore Vidal: Writer Against the Grain* (New York: Columbia University Press, 1992), pp. 278–290;

Andrew Kopkind, "The Importance of Being Gore," *The Nation,* 257 (5 July 1993): 16–20;

Judy Wieder, "Vidal on Vidal," *Advocate,* 31 October 1995, pp. 34–41.

Bibliography:

Robert J. Stanton, *Gore Vidal: A Primary and Secondary Bibliography* (Boston: G. K. Hall, 1978).

References:

John W. Aldridge, "Gore Vidal: The Search for a King," in his *After the Lost Generation: A Critical Study of the Writers of the Two World Wars* (New York: McGraw-Hill, 1951), pp. 170–183;

Susan Baker and Curtis S. Gibson, *Gore Vidal: A Critical Companion* (Westport, Conn.: Greenwood Press, 1997);

Earl P. Bargainnier, "The Mysteries of Edgar Box (aka Gore Vidal)," *Clues: A Journal of Detection,* 2 (Spring–Summer 1981): 45–92;

David Barton, "Narrative Patterns in the Novels of Gore Vidal," *Notes on Contemporary American Literature,* 7 (September 1981): 3–9;

John Bayley, "Palimpsest," *New York Review of Books,* 44 (15 May 1997): 45–48;

Harold Bloom, "The Central Man," *New York Review of Books,* 31 (19 July 1984): 5–8;

Purvis E. Boyette, "'Myra Breckinridge' and Imitative Form," *Modern Fiction Studies,* 17 (Summer 1971): 229–238;

William F. Buckley Jr., "On Experiencing Gore Vidal," *Esquire,* 72 (August 1969): 108–113;

Walter Clemons, "Gore Vidal's Chronicle of America," *Newsweek,* 103 (9 June 1984): 74–75, 78–79;

Peter Conrad, "Hall of Mirrors: The Novels of Gore Vidal," *London Sunday Times,* 27 March 1977, p. 35;

Conrad, "Look at Us," *New Review,* 2 (July 1975): 63–66;

Conrad, "Re-inventing America," *Times Literary Supplement,* 26 March 1976, pp. 347–348;

Andrew Delbanco, "The Bad and the Ugly," *New Republic,* 197 (14 and 21 September 1987): 49–55;

Bernard F. Dick, *The Apostate Angel: A Critical Study of Gore Vidal* (New York: Random House, 1974);

Owen Dudley Edwards, "Fiction as History: On an Earlier President," *Encounter,* 64 (January 1985): 33–42;

Joseph Epstein, "What Makes Vidal Run," *Commentary,* 63 (June 1977): 72–75;

M. D. Fletcher, "Vidal's Duluth as 'Post-Modern' Political Satire," *Thalia: Studies in Literary Humor,* 9 (Spring–Summer 1986): 10–21;

Samuel M. Hines Jr., "Political Change in America: Perspectives from the Popular Historical Novels of Michener and Vidal," in *Political Mythology and Popular Fiction,* edited by Ernest J. Yanarella and Lee Sigelman (New York: Greenwood Press, 1988), pp. 81–99;

Russell Jacoby, *The Last Intellectuals: American Culture in the Age of Academe* (New York: Basic Books, 1987);

Michiko Kakutani, "Gore Vidal," in her *The Poet at the Piano: Portraits of Writers, Filmmakers, Playwrights, and Other Artists at Work* (New York: Times Books, 1988), pp. 89–92;

Roz Kaveney, "United States: Essays, 1952–1992," *New Statesman & Society,* 6 (8 October 1993): 33–34;

Robert F. Kiernan, *Gore Vidal* (New York: Ungar, 1982);

Seymour Krim, "Reflections on a Ship That's Not Sinking at All," *London Magazine,* new series 10 (May 1970): 26–43;

Marvin J. LaHood, "Gore Vidal: A Grandfather's Legacy," *World Literature Today,* 64 (Summer 1990): 413–417;

John Mitzel and Steven Abbot, *Myra & Gore: A New View of Myra Breckinridge and a Candid Interview with Gore Vidal. A Book for Vidalophiles* (Dorchester, Mass.: Manifest Destiny Books, 1974);

Mitzel and others, "Some Notes on Myra B," *Fag Rag,* 6 (Fall 1973): 21–25;

Anaïs Nin, *The Diary of Anaïs Nin, Volume IV, 1944–1947,* edited by Gunther Stuhlmann (New York: Harcourt Brace Jovanovich, 1971), pp. 106, 113, 121;

Jay Parini, ed., *Gore Vidal: Writer Against the Grain* (New York: Columbia University Press, 1992);

Chris Petrikin, "Heston and Vidal Tell Conflicting Tales," *Variety,* 16 October 1995, pp. 8–9;

Richard Poirier, "American Emperors," *New York Review of Books,* 34 (24 September 1987): 31–33;

Mitchell S. Ross, "Gore Vidal," in his *The Literary Politicians* (Garden City, N.Y.: Doubleday, 1978), pp. 247–300;

John Simon, "The Good and Bad of Gore Vidal," *Esquire,* 88 (August 1977): 22–24;

Catherine R. Stimpson, "My O My O Myra," *New England Review: Middlebury Series,* 14 (Fall 1991): 102–115;

Claude J. Summers, "'The Cabin and the River,' Gore Vidal's *The City and the Pillar,*" in his *Gay Fictions: Wilde to Stonewall: Studies in a Male Homosexual Literary Tradition* (New York: Continuum, 1990), pp. 112–129;

Ray Lewis White, *Gore Vidal* (Boston: Twayne, 1968);

John F. Wilhelm and Mary Ann Wilhelm, "'Myra Breckinridge': A Study of Identity," *Journal of Popular Culture,* 3 (Winter 1969): 590–599;

Theodore Ziolkowski, *Fictional Transfigurations of Jesus* (Princeton, N.J.: Princeton University Press, 1972), pp. 250–257.

Papers:
The largest collection of Gore Vidal's papers is held by the State Historical Society of Wisconsin at Madison. The libraries associated with the University of Florida, Yale University, Boston University, Syracuse University, and the University of Texas also have some of his papers.

E. B. White

This entry was updated from the entry by Edward C. Sampson (State University of New York College at Oneonta) in DLB 11: American Humorists, 1800–1950, *and the entry by Peter F. Neumeyer (San Diego State University) in* DLB 22: American Writers for Children, 1900–1960.

BIRTH: Mount Vernon, New York, 11 July 1899, to Samuel Tilly and Jessie Hart White.

EDUCATION: B.A., Cornell University, 1921.

MARRIAGE: 13 November 1929 to Katharine Sergeant Angell (died, 20 July 1977); child: Joel McCoun; stepchildren: Nancy Angell Stableford, Roger Angell.

AWARDS AND HONORS: Limited Editions Club gold medal for *One Man's Meat,* 1945; Newbery Honor Book, 1953, Lewis Carroll Shelf Award, 1958, George C. Stone Center for Children's Books Recognition of Merit Award, 1970, and the New England Round Table of Children's Libraries Award, 1973, all for *Charlotte's Web;* Page One Award, New York Newspaper Guild, 1954, and National Association of Independent Schools Award, 1955, both for *The Second Tree from the Corner;* National Institute of Arts and Letters gold medal for contribution to literature, 1960; Presidential Medal of Freedom, 1963; Laura Ingalls Wilder Award, American Library Association, for "a lasting contribution to children's literature," 1970; National Medal for Literature, National Institute of Arts and Letters, 1971; Pulitzer Prize for the body of his work, 1978; honorary degrees from Dartmouth College, University of Maine, and Yale University, all in 1948, Bowdoin College, 1950, Hamilton College, 1952, Harvard University, and Colby College, 1954.

DEATH: North Brooklin, Maine, 1 October 1985.

BOOKS: *The Lady Is Cold* (New York & London: Harper, 1929);
Is Sex Necessary? by White and James Thurber (New York: Harper, 1929);
Every Day Is Saturday (New York & London: Harper, 1934);
Farewell to Model T, as Lee Strout White (New York: Putnam, 1936);

E. B. White *(Gale International Portrait Gallery)*

The Fox of Peapack and Other Poems (New York & London: Harper, 1938);
Quo Vadimus? or The Case for the Bicycle (New York & London: Harper, 1939);
One Man's Meat (New York & London: Harper, 1942; London: Gollancz, 1943; enlarged edition, New York & London: Harper, 1944);
Stuart Little, illustrated by Garth Williams (New York & London: Harper, 1945; London: Hamilton, 1946);
The Wild Flag: Editorials from The New Yorker on Federal World Government and Other Matters (Boston: Houghton Mifflin, 1946);
Here Is New York (New York: Harper, 1949);
Charlotte's Web, illustrated by Garth Williams (New York: Harper, 1952; London: Hamilton, 1952);

The Second Tree from the Corner (New York: Harper, 1954; London: Hamilton, 1954);

The Points of My Compass (New York: Harper & Row, 1962; London: Hamilton, 1963);

An E. B. White Reader, edited by William W. Watt and Robert W. Bradford (New York: Harper & Row, 1966);

The Trumpet of the Swan, illustrated by Edward Frascino and one illustration by White (New York: Harper & Row, 1970; London: Hamilton, 1970);

Essays of E. B. White (New York: Harper & Row, 1977);

Poems and Sketches of E. B. White (New York: Harper & Row, 1981).

OTHER: James Thurber, *The Owl in the Attic,* introduction by White (New York & London: Harper, 1931);

Ho-Hum: Newsbreaks from The New Yorker, edited with tag lines by White (New York: Farrar & Rinehart, 1931);

Another Ho-Hum, edited with tag lines by White (New York: Farrar & Rinehart, 1932);

A Subtreasury of American Humor, edited by White and Katharine S. White (New York: Coward-McCann, 1941);

Roy E. Jones, *A Basic Chicken Guide for the Small Flock Owner,* introduction by White (New York: Morrow, 1944);

Don Marquis, *the lives and times of archy and mehitabel,* introduction by White (New York: Doubleday, 1950);

William Strunk Jr., *The Elements of Style,* revised, with an introduction and a new chapter, by White (New York: Macmillan, 1959; revised, 1972; revised again, 1979).

Generally recognized as one of the best essayists of the twentieth century, E. B. White was also a major force in the success of *The New Yorker* magazine, a writer of some of the best children's stories of our time, an inspiring advocate of world federalism, and, among other things, a spokesman for individualism and the right of privacy. He is, in E. M. Forster's sense of the word, one of the aristocracy of "the sensitive, the considerate and the plucky." Not a bohemian or an expatriate in the 1920s, nor a Marxist in the 1930s, not a joiner, and not easily classified, he is a true individualist. At the same time he has also been, although not exclusively so, a notable humorist.

White was born in Mount Vernon, New York; the youngest of six children to Samuel Tilly and Jessie Hart White, he grew up in a big Victorian house.

The family was well off, White's father having risen from somewhat humble beginnings to become president of Horace Waters and Company, a New York piano firm; but as White has stated, there was nothing "fashionable" about his background: "I was a middle class public school kid whose parents were not in the swim and didn't want to be." There were pianos and other instruments in the house and lots of music, performed with enthusiasm rather than professional dedication. White played the piano. In Mount Vernon High School, White was, as he called himself, a "writing fool." His poems, essays, and short stories were published in the Mount Vernon High School *Oracle,* and besides that, he was the class artist.

In the fall of 1917 White entered the Liberal Arts College at Cornell University. The beauty of the setting at Ithaca, the intellectual activity, the cosmopolitan student body, and the blend of the theoretical and the practical (engineering students surveying on the quadrangle as students went to literature classes), all had a broadening effect on White. He made the board of the *Cornell Daily Sun* his freshman year and became editor in chief at the end of his junior year. He wrote most of the *Sun* editorials from 5 April 1920 to 5 April 1921, and in early May 1920 he won first prize for an editorial submitted to the Convention of Eastern College Newspapers. Arthur Brisbane, editor of the *New York Evening Journal* awarded the prize; the editorial appeared in the *Sun* later that month. White was also a member of the Manuscript Club, an organization of several faculty members and about ten students. There he got practice writing in a variety of poetic forms, particularly the sonnet. For a brief time in the fall of 1918 White was a member of the Students' Army Training Corps. It was at Cornell that White was first called Andy (after Andrew D. White, the first president of Cornell; it was a traditional nickname for students at Cornell named White).

After he graduated from Cornell in 1921 with a B.A., White worked as a reporter for the United Press and briefly for the American Legion News Service. Then, in the spring of 1922, restless and unsettled, he set off in his Model T Ford with Howard Cushman, a college friend, on a journey across the United States that ended six months later in Seattle, Washington, where from the fall of 1922 until June of the next year White worked as a reporter for the *Seattle Times.* After that, White went to Alaska aboard the SS *Buford,* starting out in first class and ending as the firemen's mess boy. The somewhat delayed literary results of White's trips west and to Alaska were two of his best pieces: the beautifully detailed essay on Model T Fords, "Farewell, My

White and his sister Lillian, about 1903

Lovely!" (1936), and "The Years of Wonder" (1961), an account of his Alaska trip.

Back in New York in the fall of 1923, White was unemployed for a while, then worked in a couple of advertising agencies as production assistant and copywriter. He had no liking for the work, but he had to earn his living. He later wrote James Thurber that he hung on to his job in advertising because he had no confidence in his ability in the world of letters.

The New Yorker saved White. He started contributing small items to the magazine not long after it was founded in 1925; by 1926 he was working part-time there, and by 1927 he was working full-time, contributing a fair portion of the "Notes and Comment" department and writing tag lines for newsbreaks. He was beginning to find what he could do well and was doing it. For White, 1929 was the epochal year. It was not the stock market crash, however, that was important. In that year, his first two books—*The Lady Is Cold* and *Is Sex Necessary?* (with Thurber)—were published by Harper, and on 13 November he married Katharine Sergeant Angell, then and for many years one of the mainstays

of *The New Yorker*. Their son Joel was born on 21 December 1930.

The Lady Is Cold, White's first book, is a collection of poetry. Although most of White's poetry is light verse, his best poems are not always humorous, and his humorous ones often have an ironic twist or comment that gives them a serious tone. In most of the poems in this collection, White comments on the daily routine of city life, its minor conflicts, and its tensions. He describes late evening and early morning rambles, the chance appearance of a pretty face, and the brief contacts with people that bring a transient sense of unity. Taking a half-whimsical look at himself, he celebrates his minor victories and is amused by his weaknesses. He is restrained, modest, and perhaps too conscious of the danger of destroying his perceptions of life by putting them into words. As he says in "Words":

Words but catch the moment's tint,
Though their meaning rock you;
Never one shall fly to print
Will not live to mock you.

Thematically, the poems in *The Lady Is Cold* express many of White's basic ideas and views: his love of New York and his sharp awareness of the price one pays for living there, his nostalgic love of simplicity, his admiration for the stubborn endurance of natural life and beauty in an urban setting, his passion for freedom coupled with his need for love and responsibility, his sense of the transiency of life, and finally, his half-serious, ever-present fear of death. Yet there is little in these poems of permanent interest, aside from the insights they give into White's ideas and his development as a writer. Later on, White would write some better poems, but his strength was to be prose, not poetry.

Is Sex Necessary? made both White and Thurber well known. White's contributions were the foreword, chapters 2, 4, 6, and 8, and "Answers to Hard Questions." The book is a lighthearted spoof of the many books about sex that were being published in the 1920s; yet, beneath its humor it makes a serious point. There was a need for the work; the subject had been overburdened with glib books that pretended to speak with authority and with better books that did speak with authority. As White said later, paraphrasing Wolcott Gibbs, "the heavy writers had got sex down and were breaking its arm." Frederick J. Hoffman has noted that in the period "there were hundreds of popular summaries, expositions, and distortions of Freud's original works, together with a growing number of works allegedly presenting the psychologies of Jung, Adler and other psychoanalysts." In short, there was room for satire. "Kiss a girl," wrote White in "Notes and Comment" (23 March 1929) "and it reminds you of a footnote."

In *Is Sex Necessary?* both authors parody the serious writers on the subject, making light of complexities, taking a mock-serious attitude toward the obvious, delighting in reducing the case-history technique to an absurdity, and making fun of those writers who proceeded by definitions. "When I say love in this article," says White in chapter 2, "you will take it to mean *the pleasant confusion which we know exists.* When I say passion, I *mean* passion." Although some of the humorous gags of the 1920s have paled and the funny footnotes seem less funny now, the book has continued to be popular and, reprinted many times, it continues to amuse with its playful wit.

While the material in White's first two books was not written for *The New Yorker,* the majority of what he wrote from 1927 until 1938, when he left New York and went to Maine, was written for the magazine. In addition to writing the tag lines for newsbreaks (unintentionally humorous items from various newspapers and magazines) and a substantial part of "Notes and Comment," White wrote many sketches, articles, and short stories, most of which were published in *The New Yorker.* The best of the newsbreaks and their tag lines were collected in *Ho-Hum: Newsbreaks from The New Yorker* (1931) and *Another Ho-Hum* (1932); selections from "Notes and Comment" appear in *Every Day Is Saturday* (1934); and some of his sketches appear in *Quo Vadimus? or The Case for the Bicycle* (1939).

Many of these items are ephemeral. The tag lines, for example, date easily. Still, some classics remain, like the following news item: "LOST—Male fox hound, brown head, yellow legs, blue body with large black spots on left side, male. Also female, white with red head and spot on hip.—Fayette (Mo.) Democrat Leader." White's comment was, "Those aren't dogs, those are nasturtiums."

By 1932, however, a new seriousness appeared in White's writing. When Henry Ford, for example, had said something about the "normal processes of industry and business," White asked: "How do we know that two-million-men-idle isn't normal under our system of government by investigation, peace by appropriation, and happiness by aërial dissemination of dance music?" White actually wrote relatively little about the Great Depression; he was fortunate in not being deeply affected by it personally. Yet it certainly helped in leading him to think more deeply than he had about politics, religion, progress, the unrest in Europe, social and economic problems,

and particularly about the increasing complexity of American society.

It is customary to explain White's attitude toward simplicity and complexity in terms of Henry David Thoreau, whose writing without doubt had a strong influence on him. White likely read Thoreau in college (in his senior year at Cornell he took a survey course in American literature), and he speaks of buying a copy of *Walden, or Life in the Woods* (1854) in 1927. Yet even as a boy, White seemed to have been thinking of the simple life. In "Stratagem for Retirement," he says, "I find that I still hold to the same opinions that were mine when I was thirteen. I think a man should learn to swim in the pool of time, should tuck up his affairs so they fit into a canoe, and having snugged all down, should find out what bird is his eagle, and climb the tree."

In his early comments in *Every Day Is Saturday,* White remarks playfully about the complex life: when 100 clerks in an insurance office moved from one building to another, he asks incredulously, "And didn't any of the clerks escape?" In a later comment he notes that the healthiest countries in the world are "those in which men did the most tangible tasks."

In *Quo Vadimus?* White speaks with a clearer voice about complexity. Some of the sketches, from the late 1920s and early 1930s, represent the same playful attitude White had shown in *Every Day Is Saturday.* A later sketch, however, "The Family Which Dwelt Apart," though fanciful and humorous in part, has a seriousness that cannot be missed. (The sketch was later included in *A Subtreasury of American Humor,* 1941.) The parable, as White calls it, begins with a description of the simple life of the Pruitts, a family of fisherfolk living on a small island: "They liked the island and lived there from choice. In winter, when there wasn't much doing, they slept the clock around, like so many bears. In summer they dug clams and set off a few pinwheels and salutes on July 4th." One winter, alas, the water freezes: the marooned family cannot use a boat, and the ice is too treacherous to walk on. This would have been no misfortune—the Pruitts simply stay inside and play crokinole—but the outside world begins to worry about them, and help descends upon them like a plague. The army, the state police, Pathé news, reporters—all invade the island. Through a series of man-made disasters, the whole family but one is wiped out. The survivor, having buried his kin, leaves the island of his nativity.

The source of the parable was the partly bungled rescue attempt on Tangier Island in the Chesapeake Bay, where some 1,500 inhabitants had been in real need of supplies. The matter had been reported in *The New York Times,* 2–11 February 1936.

Other themes that White takes up in *Every Day Is Saturday* and *Quo Vadimus?* involve politics, religion, progress, and, briefly, internationalism. It would have been difficult for a person writing in the 1930s not to become concerned, if not involved with politics, and White was no exception. White, unlike many writers, belonged to no cults or groups; he was not a returning exile nor a writer on the left. One of his best qualities was that he could remain an objective commentator; he was a "committed" writer, but always on his own terms. "There is a lot of the cat in me" he once wrote, "and cats are not joiners."

He writes in 1931 that "we happen to be, in a small way, on the other side of the fence from Father Coughlin on all his points." On the other hand, about a year later, he chastises the members of the John Reed Club for bad manners in their attack on Diego Rivera for "turning reactionary on them." Capitalists, White adds, are at least polite. He could never accept the philosophy of "my country, right or wrong"; "We should like," he writes, "to be a good rebel, but it has always seemed to us difficult to be a rebel in this country, where there is nothing to rebel against except one's own stupidity in electing incompetent public officers and paying taxes on a standard of living far above the simple needs of life."

White was skeptical, too, about religion. He comments with mild irony on his feelings during a rare visit to church when Dr. Fosdick was preaching on the return of people to the Christian faith to do battle against atheism and agnosticism: "It stirred us to discover . . . that we were really part of a movement against irreligion, instead of just a mousy, faintly worried man, out wandering around the town on a Sunday morning." In "Dr. Vinton," a sketch in *Quo Vadimus?* White takes a less innocent poke at religious self-righteousness and complacency. Dr. Vinton, the sole survivor of a disaster at sea, finds in his rescue a confirmation of his own exalted sense of virtue: he is saved by Providence, in order, apparently, to preach a fatuous sermon with a sea gull as its motif. There is a *Candide* touch in the essay, and doubts as to the ultimate wisdom of Providence linger in the reader's mind, and White's.

In "The Wings of Orville," one of the most pleasant parables in *Quo Vadimus?* White, making fun of progress, tells of Orville, a New York City sparrow with an inspired but pointless urge to tow a wren from Madison Square to 110th Street; Orville succeeds. The story is told without comment; how-

Katherine Sergeant Angell shortly before her marriage to White in 1929

ever, in *Every Day Is Saturday* White had noted that "scientists assume that anything is progress just so long as it's never been accomplished before." "The Crack of Doom," a more explicit comment, describes how progress has gradually reduced the earth to a shambles—the elms and willows have disappeared, rainfall has increased, and tropical storms have broken out with great intensity. New manmade diseases emerge, and finally the earth, thrown off its course by the effect of radio waves, collides with a fixed star and goes up in flames. White concludes: "The light was noticed on Mars, where it brought a moment of pleasure to young lovers; for on Mars it is the custom to kiss one's beloved when a star falls."

On another note, "Farewell, My Lovely!" one of White's best-known essays, was published during this period, appearing first in *The New Yorker* on 16 May 1936; it was reprinted that same year in book form as *Farewell to Model T* and has been reprinted in collections and anthologies many times since, including in *The Second Tree from the Corner* (1954). Suggested to White by a manuscript submitted to *The New Yorker* by Richard L. Strout, the essay was published under the pseudonym Lee Strout White. It is essentially White's, however, and belongs in the canon of his works.

The essay, a product of White's experience with his Model T, expresses his nostalgia for the past, for the Model T Ford was important in American history as well as in White's. "My own generation," he writes, "identifies it with Youth, with its gaudy, irretrievable excitements." With White, the identification was not so much with the gaudy excitement of youth as with his own private search for a role in life—a search that had its trials, but its vigor too: "The days were golden, the nights were dim and strange."

The main part of the essay concerns two matters: first, the gadgets and attachments one could buy for a Model T; and, second, the almost mystic lore and legends associated with the car. For the first matter, Sears and Roebuck provided much; the Model T "was born naked as a baby, and a flourishing industry grew up out of correcting its rare deficiencies and combatting its fascinating diseases." Of the lore and legends, more can be said, and White obviously delights in saying it. Of special interest is the timer, "an extravagantly odd little device, simple in construction, mysterious in function." You could hit it, blow on it, oil it; or even, as White tried once, spit on it—"You see," he writes, "the Model T driver moved in the realm of metaphysics. He believed his car could be hexed." Beyond the fun, though, is accurate and close observation; White knew his car well, as a driver had to in those days.

White's second book of poems, *The Fox of Peapack and Other Poems* (1938), was a considerable improvement over *The Lady Is Cold*. Reviews were generally favorable; David McCord noted that White had come a long way since his earlier collection. One difference between the poems in this collection and those in the earlier one is that many of these begin with a newspaper comment and develop from it. The approach may tend to produce limited and topical poems, but it also suggests that White was moving closer to his material. *The Fox of Peapack* has fewer lyrical poems, fewer bits of whimsy; it has, on the other hand, stronger and more vigorous statements. Although there are, for example, references to advertising in *The Lady Is Cold,* they are light, scarcely critical; in "The Silence of the Gears" from *The Fox of Peapack* a different White speaks of the "whoring Voices of the reasonable air / In fifteen-minute lozenges of pleasure."

One of White's best poems was his response to the notorious comment by Vittorio Mussolini about bombing in Ethiopia: "I remember," said Mussolini, "that one group of horsemen gave me the impression of a budding rose as the bombs fell in their midst. It was exceptionally good fun." White, seeing in the comment an attitude that violated all decent respect for life, responds with strong feeling. The poem "Flying Over Ethiopian Mountain Ranges" begins thus:

Where horsemen's blood runs sickly
　To the absorbent earth,
The rose, unfolding quickly
　To give the canker birth,

Reveals a wormlike beauty
　To the new ranks of youth,
Their hands upraised in duty,
　Their heels unshod with ruth.

Equally effective, and probably better known, was "I Paint What I See," a poetic comment on the controversy over the Rivera murals in Rockefeller Center in New York City. Nelson Rockefeller had objected to some aspects of a mural that Rivera had been commissioned to paint, particularly to a portrait of Lenin that Rivera had included. Rivera offered to put in the head of Lincoln, or McCormick, though he was not willing to remove Lenin; White plays upon this nicely:

'I'll take out a couple of people drinkin'
'And put in a picture of Abraham Lincoln;
'I could even give you McCormick's reaper
'And still not make my art much cheaper
'But the head of Lenin has got to stay
'Or my friends will give me the bird today,
'The bird, the bird, forever.'

Another point Rockefeller had made, according to an account in *The New York Times,* was that Rockefeller Center was not a private house but a public building; in the poem, his objection becomes: "'For this, as you know, is a public hall, / 'And people want doves, or a tree in fall.'" The end of the poem may have been overly optimistic; when Rockefeller says, "And after all, / It's *my* wall," the last line has "'We'll see if it is,' said Rivera." White probably wrote the poem after the first news reports, for later, of course, Rivera lost his fight. The poem is one of White's happiest combinations of wit and seriousness. His refusal to take Rivera too seriously might seem to some a lack of commitment, but, by avoiding the role of either professional liberal or conservative, White in the long run may have spoken with his most effective voice.

The best case to be made for White's poetry is in Morris Bishop's introduction to *One Man's Meat* (1942). Speaking of the poems in White's two collections, Bishop notes that many of them are "mere trifles, amusing developments of small observations." However, Bishop continues, the best of White's poems should interest the critic: "For E. B. White and a few others are creating a new mid-form between Light Verse and Heavy Verse, between the determined comic conviction of the one and the pretentious obscurity of the other." These poets, says Bishop, "aim at lucidity, at the communication of their meaning to the large number of people who are responsive to poetic form and feeling but who are rebuffed by the hermetics of our time."

In the early part of 1938 White left New York for his farm on the Maine coast, where, except for a return to New York from 1943 to 1957, he lived until his death. He reduced considerably his contributions to *The New Yorker* and undertook to write a monthly essay for the "One Man's Meat" department of *Harper's* magazine. White liked the country, he liked animals, and he took farming seriously—at one point (October 1941), he was sending eighty dozen eggs a week to market. In his preface to the 1944 edition of *One Man's Meat*, White describes his book and his situation: "It is a collection of essays which I wrote from a salt water farm in Maine while engaged in trivial, peaceable pursuits, knowing all the time that the world hadn't arranged any true peace or granted anyone the privilege of indulging himself for long in trivialities. Although such a record is likely to seem incongruous, I see no harm in preserving it, the more so since I have begun to receive letters from soldiers overseas assuring me that there is a positive value to them in the memory of peace and home."

After reading *Quo Vadimus?* and *Every Day Is Saturday,* one is struck by White's greater sureness of material and expression, by his clearer thinking on many topics, and above all by his more penetrating moral purpose and his deeper conviction in attitudes and feelings in *One Man's Meat*. Not surprisingly he writes a good deal about his farming and such related matters in Maine as chickens, sheep, fertilizer, and the weather. He also writes about many of the topics he had approached, often tentatively, in his earlier work. White at times really does seem to come closer to something solid and honest than anything he had been able to find in New York. Although there is no single theme or pattern to the essays in *One Man's Meat,* certain topics turn up more than others: many of the essays concern war and its related problems; others are about domestic, social, and political matters. And some, like "Once More to the Lake," fit no simple category.

Certainly the coming war was on White's mind. In October 1938, in "Clear Days," he describes, among many other matters, roofing his barn; but like a counterpoint, Munich is on his mind: "I'm down now; the barn is tight, and the peace is preserved. It is the ugliest peace the earth

White and James Thurber at Sneden's Landing, New York, circa 1929

has ever received for a Christmas present." "Coon-Hunt" is another example of his use of counterpoint. Before describing the coon hunt itself, White talks about civil defense, and then he notes with some sharpness how the enemy had already made his presence felt. On Halloween some junk had been piled up in front of a Jewish merchant's store. "The enemy," says White, "slipped into town and out again, and I think there were hardly a dozen people who caught the glimpse of his coat tails. . . . There would never be a moment, in war or in peace, when I wouldn't trade all the patriots in the county for one tolerant man." These two essays, and many of the others, are made up of a variety of comments; some of his best, however, are on a single topic. Three of them are effective pieces of demolition: of the New York World's Fair ("The World of Tomorrow"), the Townsend Plan ("Camp Meeting"), and a review of Anne Morrow Lindbergh's book *The Wave of the Future* (1940).

The road to Tomorrow, writes White in the first of these, "leads through the chimney pots of Queens. It is a long, familiar journey, through Mulsified Shampoo and Mobilgas, through Bliss Street,

Kix, Ostring-O-Sol, and the Majestic Auto Seat Covers." White epitomizes the fair with a description of a giant automaton, located outside one of the girlie shows (where, with a neat compromise between morality and eroticism, the girls were allowed to expose one breast). Several girls sat on the robot's lap and were fondled by its huge rubber hands: "Here was the Fair, all fairs, in pantomime; and here the strange mixed dream that made the Fair: the heroic man, bloodless and perfect and enormous, created in his own image, and in his hand (rubber, aseptic) the literal desire, the warm and living breast."

In August 1939 White reported on a talk given by Dr. Francis E. Townsend on the Townsend Plan (a scheme, born of the Great Depression, to give a pension of $200 a month to all people over sixty by a tax of two percent on the gross business of the country; the money was supposed to be spent within a month by the pensioner). The first part of the report is a sympathetic account of Townsend's talk—its simple appeal, the artless approach. "Maybe this Plan was it," writes White; "I never heard a milder-mannered economist, nor one more fully convinced of the right and wisdom of his proposal." The shift in the report comes when White describes the question period after the talk: "It was at this point that Dr. Francis E. Townsend (of California) began quietly to come apart, like an inexpensive toy." With a combination of calm reporting, gentle irony, and understatement, White deflates Townsend: "It spoiled his afternoon to be asked anything. Details of Townsendism were irksome in the extreme—he wanted to keep the Plan simple and beautiful, like young love before sex has reared its head. And now he was going to have to answer a lot of nasty old questions."

Equally effective, and somewhat sharper in tone, is White's critical attack on Lindbergh's book *The Wave of the Future*. As in his treatment of Townsend, White is fair. Lindbergh, he says, "wants a good world, as I do," but "she has retreated into the pure realm of thought, leaving the rest of us to rassle with the bear." Her thesis was that the "wave of the future" was the new social and economic forces being exploited in Germany, Russia, and Italy. These forces had been used badly at times, she conceded; but they are the hope for a new world. White then moves in with more vigor than he had shown against Townsend, and with good reason—for the issue was far more important, the antagonist more formidable. These forces, says White, are not new at all: they are "the backwash of the past," and have "muddied the world for centuries." Lindbergh had argued that the new forces had emerged from the

distresses of the people and were therefore somehow good. White attacks this assumption:

> The fascist ideal, however great the misery which released it and however impressive the self-denial and the burning courage which promote it, does not hold the seed of a better order but of a worse one, and it always has a foul smell and a bad effect on the soil. It stank at the time of Christ and it stinks today, wherever you find it and in whatever form, big or little—even here in America, the little fascists always at their tricks, stirring up a lynching mob or flagellating the devil or selling a sex pamphlet to tired, bewildered old men. The forces are always the same—on the people's side frustration, disaffection; on the leader's side control of hysteria, perversion of information, abandonment of principle.

Careful not to accuse Lindbergh of being a fascist, White is bothered not only by what she has written but also by the popularity of her ideas; for this was a time when, in certain circles in England and America, fascism had disturbingly enthusiastic partisans. Many people had spoken of the book, White notes; they would say that, though they had reservations about it, "there's something to what she says just the same." This "something" White tries to find and cannot.

In the best essay in *One Man's Meat*, "Once More to the Lake," White recounts a weeklong visit he made with his son to a Maine lake where he himself had vacationed as a child with his parents. During this visit White walked and fished with his son, and in many ways lived again the days of his childhood: there was the same excitement at arrival, the same early mornings at the lake, the same cottage with partitions that did not go up to the ceiling, the same kind of farmhouse meals, the same lake, the same kind of people visiting, the same questions, the same thunderstorms, and the same swimming in the rain afterward.

The chief values of the essay lie partly in White's skillful evocation of past and present, as details of the past recur to him, sometimes blending harmoniously with the present and sometimes clashing; and partly they lie in his moving and almost obsessive feeling of duality as he becomes both himself and his son. There is a strong awareness of the circularity of time and of the joys of the past and the present: the pleasures of vacation then and now; but at the end, beautifully worked out, the tone suddenly shifts. White's son, going swimming during the rain, gets his dripping trunks from the line and puts them on: "I watched him, his hard little body, skinny and bare, saw him wince slightly as he pulled up around his vitals the small, soggy, icy garment. As he buckled the swollen belt suddenly my groin

The Whites' farmhouse in Brooklin, Maine

felt the chill of death." Age and death are present with frightening vividness, and time suddenly seems to reverse itself, for White is no longer young and in the past. Because the aura of death surrounds his son as well as himself, the generations are linked again, but in mortality, not in life.

Before White returned to New York, he completed another project: his editing, with the help of his wife, of *A Subtreasury of American Humor*. The anthology was popular: it was a Book-of-the-Month-Club selection; in abridged form, an Armed Services edition; and later, also in abridged form, a Pocket Book edition. The Whites interpreted the term *humor* broadly: the anthology included such selections as the first chapter of Sinclair Lewis's *Babbitt* (1922) and *The New Yorker* profile of evangelist Father Divine.

From the point of view of this study the most important part of *A Subtreasury of American Humor* was the preface by White. He explains the criteria for the selection of the items and talks about humor. The preface has been reprinted, in a slightly changed form, in *The Second Tree from the Corner* and in *An E. B. White Reader* (1966). In making the selections, says White, he and his wife rejected the goal of inclusiveness: "We asked simply that we be amused, now in 1941." Some areas of humor, White notes, were not represented at all: no joke-book stuff, radio humor, or comic-strip material.

White begins his discussion of the nature of humor with some valuable and original comments on dialect and illiteracies. Petroleum Nasby's misspellings for humorous effect, for example, pose a problem to White. Nasby uses "uv" for "of," and

"offis" for "office," to cite two examples. White notes that he pronounces "of" and "office" as if they were "uv" and "offis"; thus, he concludes, the humorous effect is not from the odd pronunciations but from the funny spellings themselves—as if the character involved were writing, not speaking; but then, as White says, no one who could write at all would write "uv." White also notes that in Edward Streeter's *Dere Mable* (1918), which clearly involves characters writing, not speaking, it is unlikely that anyone would consistently leave off the *g* in *-ing* words. White concludes that "the popularity of all dialect stuff derives in part from flattery of the reader—giving him a pleasant sensation of superiority which he gets from working out the intricacies of misspelling, and the satisfaction of detecting boorishness or illiteracy in someone else."

White is perfectly well aware that this "dialect stuff" is a surface matter; the real nature of humor lies deeper and has a certain "fragility, an evasiveness," that is beyond analysis. It is not that humorists are really sad people, sad clowns; rather, "there is a deep vein of melancholy running through everyone's life and . . . a humorist, perhaps more sensible of it than some others, compensates for it actively and positively." The humorist thus comes close to the truth of human experience, but there is an irony in being a humorist—the world patronizes him: "It decorates its serious artists with laurel, and its wags with Brussels sprouts." The humorist must learn to live with a kind of injustice; he must put up with his friends who will ask the question every humorist is asked: When are you "going to write something serious?" The real problem, however, is the conflict between high emotion and the temptation or danger of ending with a snicker: "Here, then, is the very nub of the conflict: the careful form of art, and the careless shape of life itself. What a man does with this uninvited snicker (which may closely resemble a sob, at that) decides his destiny. If he resists it, conceals it, destroys it, he may keep his architectural scheme intact and save his building, and the world will never know. If he gives in to it, he becomes a humorist, and the sharp brim of the fool's cap leaves a mark forever on his brow." Typical of White's critical writing, the preface is neither profound nor scholarly; yet, clear, refreshing, and funny at times, it probably comes as close to the truth as most of what has been written on the subject. The comments are perceptive and perhaps defensive; for White, more in his earlier days than later in his career, was considered to be primarily a humorist. He was that, but never exclusively so. Often he did give in to the temptation and throw his cap in the reader's face, but just as often he did not. Still, there is no great need to classify; it is possible to combine strong emotion and a deep moral purpose with a sense of humor—as Charles Dickens and Thomas Hardy have done.

White wrote his last "One Man's Meat" piece in January 1943 and later that year returned to New York. He did not give up his Maine farm (he went there off and on, returning to full-time residence in 1957), but he wanted to be closer to *The New Yorker* and to New York. He resumed active participation on *The New Yorker,* particularly as a writer for "Notes and Comment." Actually, he had started contributing extensively to the department in 1942—in 1941 he had written only two items; in 1942 he wrote more than fifty, and in 1943 sixty or so.

Many of those contributions were about war, peace, and the need for some sort of world government or world federalism; some were collected and published in *The Wild Flag: Editorials from The New Yorker on Federal World Government and Other Matters* (1946). These, comprising some of White's most serious writing, are, except for his children's stories, his most sustained efforts on a single topic. The book received mixed reviews, including a scathing notice in the *Nation.* The modern reader might view the work as naive and idealistic—and he would probably be right. Even if in some ways White lacked profundity, however, he made many good observations and made them clearly. Disarmament, security leagues, treaties—all these attempts at securing peace, he said, have been and will be futile. Unless men can achieve real union, unless each nation-state can agree to relinquish some of its sovereignty,

unless there can be a real basis for what we like to call international law and justice, unless, finally, men's loyalties can extend beyond those they feel for their own particular piece of territory, we have little hope. We have to have the worldview; the machinery can come later. White's own retrospective comment on *The Wild Flag* is an honest and valid summation: "The book was rather dreamy and uninformed, but it was good-spirited . . . and I still think that what I said was essentially sound, although I'm not sure the timing was right."

White wrote three children's books during his career. In an October 1964 interview with the *Cornell Daily Sun,* White explains why he wrote the first two of his children's books, *Stuart Little* (1945) and *Charlotte's Web* (1952) (the third, *The Trumpet of the Swan,* was not published until 1970): "I couldn't tell stories to children and they always were after me to tell them a story and I found I couldn't do it. So I had to get it down on paper." In an essay on children's books in *One Man's Meat,* White had expressed a mild distaste for the amount of geographical and linguistic information being purveyed to children that year (1938); *Stuart Little, Charlotte's Web,* and *The Trumpet of the Swan* are refreshingly free of studied attempts to improve young minds. What makes White's three books outstanding is that he has written them in the classical tradition of children's stories—the tradition of Lewis Carroll's *Alice's Adventures in Wonderland* (1865), Mary Molesworth's *The Cuckoo Clock* (1877), Kenneth Grahame's *The Wind in the Willows* (1908), and A. A. Milne's *Winnie the Pooh* (1926). There is much to be learned from White's stories, to be sure, but it is not geography, or science, or even the habits of mice and pigs. What the child does learn—and what children learn from the other fine children's books—is a great deal about loyalty, honesty, love, sadness, and happiness.

White's first two children's books have become classics. If in *Stuart Little* there were problems of unity, *Charlotte's Web* has a near-perfect structure. White has not been given to long works, but here he found a medium that was congenial to him, and it may well be that he will be longest remembered for these stories, particularly *Charlotte's Web.* In these stories White has written clearly and simply, as he has always done. His writing is free from the bondage of current events that has dated many of his pieces for *The New Yorker* and independent of the pressure of literary trends and fads.

Stuart Little is an episodic story of a quest, having for its protagonist a two-inch-tall picaresque hero. The book is episodic, perhaps because it had been so long coming—twenty-two years, by White's

Joel White in Brooklin, Maine, circa 1939, near the building where his father did much of his writing

account. White's reconstruction of the book's evolution, published in *The New York Times* (6 March 1966), tells the story: "Stuart Little . . . came into being as the result of a journey I once made. In the late Twenties, I took a train to Virginia, got out, walked up and down in the Shenandoah Valley in the beautiful springtime, then returned to New York by rail. While asleep in an upper berth, I dreamed of a small character who had the features of a mouse, was nicely dressed, courageous, and questing. When I woke up, being a journalist and thankful for small favors, I made a few notes about this mouse-child–the only fictional figure ever to have honored and disturbed my sleep."

In 1938, at the suggestion of his wife, White submitted *Stuart Little* to a publisher, who rejected the book. Seven years later, White recalls, "I was almost sure I was about to die, my head felt so queer. With death at hand, I cast about to discover what I could do to ease the lot of my poor widow, and again my thoughts strayed to Stuart Little." In the spring of 1945 White completed the book, and Harper accepted it for publication: "Stuart was off at last, after a pardonable delay of some fifteen years."

Stuart Little consists of fifteen loosely connected chapters concerning the hero, who is introduced in one of the more striking first sentences of modern literature: "When Mrs. Frederick C. Little's second son arrived, everybody noticed that he was not much bigger than a mouse." Whether, indeed, Stuart is a mouse remains open to speculation. White insisted that he was not, but the author

lapsed occasionally and called him one. In a letter to his editor, Ursula Nordstrom, shortly after publication of the book, White objected to Harper ads referring to Stuart as a "mouse." Wrote White, "this is inaccurate and probably better be abandoned. Nowhere in the book (I think I am right about this) is Stuart described as a mouse. He is a small guy who looks very much like a mouse, but he obviously is not a mouse. He is a second son." But then, alas, White was forced to add, in the same letter, "(I am wrong, Stuart is called a mouse on Page 36–I just found it. He should not have been.)"

Mouse or not, Stuart is a plucky fellow, just under two inches tall, whose somewhat random adventures show him to be brave, ingenious, enterprising, and of romantic inclination. For the first seven chapters–the sequence of which could be rearranged without damage to the tale–all these adventures evolve from Stuart's size, the logical consequences of which White has imaginatively extrapolated with all the ingenuity of Jonathan Swift plotting Gulliver's stay in Lilliput. Stuart sleeps in a little bed made out of four clothespins and a cigarette box; he is lowered down a bathtub drain to retrieve a ring Mrs. Little had dropped; he fetches grounded ping-pong balls; at some hazard, he crouches inside the piano to push up sticking keys when his brother, George Little, plays the piano. His life is beset with danger and obstacle: he must find means to shut off a water faucet the handle of which is larger than he is, and he must pay for a bus ride when the dime needed for fare is much too large an object for him

477

to manage. Danger lurks for him in the form of Snowbell, the great, sharptoothed family cat. He narrowly escapes disaster when he is whirled up into a rolling window shade. He demonstrates debonair insouciance and panache as he pilots a model sail boat, Wasp, through mountainous waves in a race on a pond in Central Park. Stuart emerges victorious for the ship's grateful owner, a "surgeon dentist" by the name of Dr. Paul Carey, who serves the story later by furnishing Stuart with the little automobile he needs to pursue his ideal beloved.

This beloved is the little bird Margalo, who, George Little thinks may be a "wall-eyed vireo," but who Mrs. Little thinks looks "more like a wren." After the introduction of Margalo, Stuart's adventures take on a measure of purposefulness and sequence as she, fearing Snowbell, disappears in the tenth chapter, and Stuart goes in pursuit of her. Like any knight errant, Stuart is tempted and distracted during this pursuit. On one occasion he takes over an elementary classroom for the sick teacher, Miss Gunderson, who, says the superintendent of schools, may be suffering from Rhinestones.

After the classroom interlude, Stuart is seriously diverted—tempted—from his path only once. He meets the lovely Harriet Ames, whose head came just above Stuart's shoulder, and for whose graceful appearance we have White's testimony in a letter he wrote to Garth Williams, the illustrator, that Harriet was taken from figure number twenty-one in the Montgomery Ward catalogue. After misadventures with a novelty-shop canoe in which Stuart had intended to take out Harriet, and after demonstrating to the cool young lady his classy crawl stroke, Stuart is left by Harriet "alone with his broken dreams and his damaged canoe."

"Stuart slept under the canoe that night," but the next morning he filled his little car with five drops of gasoline and set forth once again, driving till he encountered a telephone lineman who had seen many birds—but no Margalo. Still, as the lineman says, "a person who is heading north is not making a mistake, in my opinion," and Stuart agrees: "I rather expect that from now on I shall be traveling north until the end of my days." Stuart climbs into his car once again. "The sun was just coming up over the hills on his right. As he peered ahead into the great land that stretched before him, the way seemed long. But the sky was bright, and he somehow felt he was headed in the right direction."

The conclusion to *Stuart Little* may make the reader think of the end to Milton's *Paradise Lost*—the challenge of the brave new world to Adam and Eve as they venture out on their own responsibility—a parallel that White acknowledges. White always

uses established classic themes, and this use is a conscious one.

White gives his own testimony for the significance of Stuart's quest: "Stuart's journey symbolizes the continuing journey that everybody takes—in search of what is perfect and unattainable. This is perhaps too elusive an idea to put into a book for children, but I put it in anyway," White wrote in a 1955 letter.

The central question in this book, both for Stuart Little and for E. B. White, may well be the one that substitute teacher Stuart Little puts to his young fifth-grade charges: "How many of you know what's important?" One student, Henry Rackmeyer, has an impressive answer: "A shaft of sunlight at the end of a dark afternoon, a note in music, and the way the back of a baby's neck smells if its mother keeps it tidy." "Correct," says Stuart. "Those are the important things."

Finally, as splendid a character as White's Stuart Little is, the mock epic hero seen through the wrong end of the telescope, the picture of him would not be what it is without the contribution of the illustrator, Garth Williams. If Stuart becomes part of American folklore, it will be in the shape of Williams's line drawings, which continued with such extraordinary success in *Charlotte's Web*.

Phyllis McGinley wrote White that she had read the book and was having it reread to her by her husband. "I can't see why all the rest of the writers don't stop writing and let you do the country's books for a while. . . ." Her husband was proposing to adopt Stuart. Though periodical reviews were mixed, the *London Observer* agreed with McGinley, noting that "the only point of comparison it has with usual children's books is that the adults will never let their moppets get a chance to read it."

The one negative response was that of Anne Carroll Moore, head of the Children's Department of the New York Public Library, and, at the time, doyenne of children's books in the United States. Throughout 1939 Moore had written White impassioned letters praising his talent and expressing her joy at the prospect of his writing a children's book. After she had read the book in galleys, however, Moore wrote Katharine White a fourteen-page letter strongly advising that White withdraw the book from publication, and she urged Ursula Nordstrom and Harper not to publish it. As White wrote later to Frances Clarke Sayers (Moore's successor at the New York Public Library), however, Moore, out of regard for White, did not publish her view. Sayers also had reservations, writing White that she thought the "fantasy was not completely conceived, nor that it said anything positive to children." She

White in his New Yorker *office with his dog Minnie (Cornell University Library)*

spoke of feeling troubled at the thought of "the birth of Stuart to human parents, in this day when even the youngest child knows the facts of life," and she expressed similar views in *Tomorrow* magazine. Leonard Lyons, the gossip columnist, wrote his column in the *New York Post,* 23 November 1945, predicting "there will be a to-do about the New York Public Library's reluctance to accept *Stuart Little,* the children's book by E. B. White."

Since the time of those early teapot tempests, *Stuart Little* has established itself as one of the classics of American children's literature. Murmurs of dissatisfaction concerning Stuart's genesis are rare. He may not even be a mouse in the first place, after all—and this sophisticated age, one hopes, is more tolerant of a child who may just happen to look like a mouse.

White's second book for children, *Charlotte's Web,* unlike much of *Stuart Little,* has a bucolic setting. The Whites' removal to Brooklin, Maine, where in 1957 they set up full-time residence, is of central importance to the creation of *Charlotte's Web,* a book that is, among other things, a celebration of the seasons in a rural life. It is a book that moves between two levels of plot, both interwoven by significant, dominant themes. First, there is the tale of the title character, Charlotte, a spider, *Aranea cavatica,* and her friend, the somewhat lumpish pig, Wilbur,

born the runt of the litter. Wilber, originally to be slaughtered, is saved and weaned by eight-year-old Fern Arable and taken over then by Fern's uncle, the farmer Homer L. Zuckerman, who still plans to slaughter Wilbur. Zuckerman takes him first to the fair, where Wilbur's friend, Charlotte, miraculously saves him by weaving in a web above his pen the startling word "HUMBLE." After that "miracle," amusingly associated by the silly folk with the pig, Wilbur, rather than with the spinning spider, Wilbur is taken back to the farm to live a contented and pampered life; but Charlotte, alas, spins her last web and deposits eggs for her 514 offspring in Wilbur's crate at the barn, and then, at their birth, she dies. Wilbur, however, remains true to the promise he made Charlotte, pledging his friendship to her offspring "forever and ever."

The other plot, the plot that critic Roger Sale views (dubiously) as the plot for adults, is the story of Fern Arable, who, through the course of the story, grows up. For the first sixteen pages *Charlotte's Web* is a more or less distanced, realistic, third person account of Fern's saving Wilbur and of the doings in the barnyard. Beginning on page sixteen of the book, however, Wilbur speaks, is personified, and suffers more or less human emotions—fears, pangs, and even boredom. Like Wilbur, the other animals in the barnyard speak, too; the sheep and the geese foolishly and impoliticly about Wilbur's imminent demise; Charlotte about her past, about her arachnid nature (White had done extensive reading and had taken voluminous notes on spiders before writing the book) and about the plans she has for saving Wilbur's life. Not only do the barnyard animals speak, but Fern understands them as well, and she reports their conversation to her mother. Mrs. Arable is worried by her unusual daughter, and she takes her to Dr. Dorian, who reassures the mother, suggesting we all might hear more if only we had the ears to listen and suggesting what does come to pass—that Fern's barnyard fascinations will lessen. So it is that, precisely at the moment of Wilbur's glory, when he wins the prize at the fair, Fern is preoccupied with one young Henry Fussy. Fern wants nothing more at this moment than to sit with Henry in the gondola of the ferris wheel, looking far across the countryside. Sometime before this, already Fern's interest in the goings-on in the barnyard had slackened. No longer did she overhear the animals. In the last half of the book, she is no more than a silent bystander to the adventures and the drama of the rescue of Wilbur by his friend Charlotte.

Stuart Little, first conceived long before the Whites moved to Maine, includes passages in celebration of the city. *Charlotte's Web,* on the other hand, seems to have developed directly and exclusively out of White's joy in his own rural existence. He had observed spiders closely and had studied them intensely. The successive drafts of the opening of the story, all preserved in the Cornell archives, attest that in draft after discarded draft White had begun by dwelling lovingly on the coziness, the comfortableness, the mood, and the ambience of a barn. White's letters attest to his pleasure in the rural life; and, finally, the story of the almost slaughtered pig, Wilbur, was anticipated by White's essay "Death of a Pig," published first in the *Atlantic Monthly,* January 1948, and collected in *The Second Tree from the Corner.*

Charlotte's Web has prompted some bizarre overinterpretations, such as that of John Griffith, who perceives in Wilbur's plight "a desperate existential situation," and who sees in the extraordinarily realistic and unsentimental Charlotte, *Aranea cavatica,* a "fantastic character from fairyland," who dies "tired and alone."

Yet *Charlotte's Web* is unquestionably a rich and a contemplative book, deserving of the high praise given it by the distinguished critic and author Eleanor Cameron, who puts it on her shelf along with *Alice's Adventures in Wonderland, Little Women,* and *Pinocchio.* It is a book that sounds again, seriously

and eloquently, White's deep concerns and his basic and recurrent perceptions. Interwoven between the barnyard narrative of Charlotte and of Wilbur on the one hand, and the story of Fern's passage from childhood to preadolescence on the other is White's thematic preoccupation with friendship, with the warm glow of the pastoral, and with the cycle of the rural year.

White's second theme entails, specifically, the celebration of the barn and, on a larger scale, the celebration of the rural year. In a letter White himself has called the book "pastoral, seasonal . . . concerned with ordinary people. . . . " Of the nine successive surviving drafts of the story, several begin with descriptions of the barn and of the "dressing" in Wilbur's pen. These, however, are static openings, and as was his habitual wont, White eventually discarded the descriptive beginnings and substituted the fast-moving opening: "'Where's Papa going with that ax?' said Fern. . . . " The loving barn description was retained—merely moved to later in the book, becoming the opening of the third chapter. And throughout the book, White has interspersed similar celebrations of one aspect or another of the farm and of the whole round of the rural year, with its cycles of life and death.

The rural year, the sweet melancholy of death, and the final birth and the renewal out of the ashes—these are the timeless notes White sounds in this "simple" children's tale. Out of the winter earth comes, always, a new setting forth. The death of Charlotte means the life of her progeny. "We're leaving here on the warm updraft," the little spiders call to Wilbur as they rise on balloons they have spun for themselves. "This is our moment of setting forth." Repeatedly White's letters tell of his exasperation with those who would trivialize his noble theme for commercial purposes, making the story end happily, usually by eliminating the death of Charlotte. White knew perfectly well what he was about; as he wrote to a children's literature class in 1973, "Charlotte was a story of friendship, life, death, salvation."

Among the few negative responses to the book, the most puzzling may be that of Moore, who wrote in the *Horn Book Magazine,* "I may as well confess that I find *Charlotte's Web* hard to take from so masterly a hand. There is no one whose writing I more deeply regard in the adult field. *Stuart Little* disappointed me but thousands of people liked it." Specifically, Moore found Fern's mother offensively dumb. Of the other characters, she noted, "Fern, the real center of the book, is never developed. The animals never talk. They speculate. As to Charlotte, her magic and mystery require a different technique

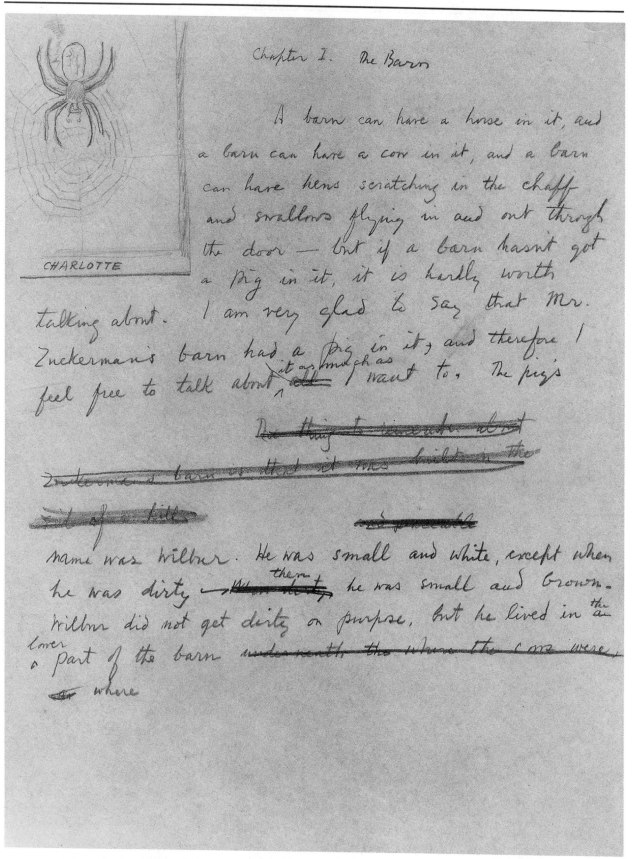

Chapter I. The Barn

A barn can have a horse in it, and a barn can have a cow in it, and a barn can have hens scratching in the chaff and swallows flying in and out through the door — but if a barn hasn't got a pig in it, it is hardly worth talking about. I am very glad to say that Mr. Zuckerman's barn had a pig in it, and therefore I feel free to talk about it as much as I want to. The pig's name was Wilbur. He was small and white, except when he was dirty then he was small and brown. Wilbur did not get dirty on purpose, but he lived in the lower part of the barn where

First page of an early draft for White's 1952 children's book, Charlotte's Web *(Cornell University Library)*

481

to create that lasting interest in spiders which controls childish impulse to do away with them."

If Moore's conclusions about *Charlotte's Web* seem eccentric, a happier summary statement is that of one of White's most distinguished colleagues and contemporaries. Writing in *The New York Times* in October 1952, Eudora Welty said:

> What the book is about is friendship on earth, affection, and protection, adventure and miracle, life and death, trust and treachery, pleasure and pain, and the passing of time. As a piece of work it is just about perfect, and just about magical in the way it is done. What it all proves—in the words of the minister in the story which he hands down to his congregation after Charlotte writes "Some Pig" in her web—is "that human beings must always be on the watch for the coming of wonders...."

From 1944, when White published the second edition of *One Man's Meat*, until 1954, when the next collection of his pieces, *The Second Tree from the Corner* was published, White wrote—in addition to *The Wild Flag* and his first two children's stories—*Here Is New York* (1949). He also continued writing tag lines for newsbreaks, contributed to "Notes and Comment," and wrote many poems, stories, and sketches, mostly for *The New Yorker*; some of these were later collected in *The Second Tree from the Corner*.

White's tribute to his city, *Here Is New York*, was first published in *Holiday* magazine (April 1949) and later that year in book form by Harper and Brothers. The book, or rather long essay—it is only forty-five pages—reveals as much about White as about New York: it helps to account for his love of New York, just as *One Man's Meat* does for his love of Maine. To the reader of White's poetry and his early pieces for *The New Yorker*, there are many familiar observations about the city in *Here Is New York*, and a few new ones. All are made with eloquence and in a kind of final form, for the book is not just an explanation of New York, but a plea for it—and a plea for peace, too; he ends the book with the observation that there is a willow tree in an interior garden near the United Nations headquarters: "Whenever I look at it nowadays, and feel the cold shadow of the planes, I think: 'This must be saved, this particular thing, this very tree.' If it were to go, all would go—this city, this mischievous and marvelous monument which not to look upon would be like death."

The willow tree symbol from the end of *Here Is New York* suggests the theme of a good many of the pieces in *The Second Tree from the Corner*, especially the more recent ones: the theme, that is, that deals with the paradox of modern man, the threats to his civilization, and the hope that something, at least, can be preserved of his culture. The selections in the book are uneven. Some, in the section "Notes on the City," are largely earlier sketches that show White to be a sensitive, warm, but somehow not fully involved observer of the city. Other sketches illustrate what White calls in the foreword his "tendency to revisit." One, "Speaking of Counterweights," goes back to his days on the *Seattle Times*, and a ride he took on an odd little car around the top of the building in preparation for a feature story.

The most successful pieces in *The Second Tree from the Corner* are those dealing with the quandary, the paradox, of modern man—those that show White's skepticism about science and progress. He had written on those matters before, but some of his strongest statements and his best work are in this book. Of these, "The Door" (first published in *The New Yorker*, 25 March 1939) has become White's most popular story. In it White makes extensive use of two matters recently discussed in articles in *The New York Times* (February and March 1939) and in *Life* (6 March 1939). The *Times* articles were reports about a model home exhibit in Rockefeller Center, and the one from *Life* about the effects of frustration in some experiments on rats. He also used some other briefer items from *Time* and *The New York Times*, as William R. Steinhoff has shown in a perceptive article on the story. White's use of contemporary material was characteristic, growing out of his long habit of using such material in his "Notes and Comment" for *The New Yorker*.

"The Door," with little plot in the conventional sense, has a structure that derives from White's sources. The central character is being shown through an exhibit of a model house (everything in the house had been tested and could be laundered); and, as he is taken through, he compares himself to rats in a laboratory. That the house was being exhibited in Rockefeller Center fits the theme of the story, for such a situation is as artificial and incongruous as modern life itself. The story opens with the sterile, artificial quality of the setting made explicit: "Everything (he kept saying) is something it isn't." The names of things were "tex," "koid," "duroid"—all artificial words with no antecedents or roots.

Having established the setting of the story, and having identified man's predicament with that of the rats in a laboratory, White becomes more specific about that predicament. Doors, literal in the rat's maze, are symbolic in man's own maze. "First," says the man, "they would teach you the prayers and the Psalms, and that would be the right door... and the long sweet words with the holy sound, and that would be the one to jump at to get where the food was." The doors will continue being changed; and man will still jump, for "nobody can not jump." Here man and the rats differ. Another door that man learns after the prayers and the psalms, and one that works for a while, is the one "with the picture of the girl on it (only it was spring), her arms outstretched in loveliness. . . ." One would go through the door "winged and exalted (like any rat) and the food would be there . . . and you had chosen the right door for the world was young." There is one cure for man, one ironic hope of escaping the unopening door–to have the prefrontal lobe removed. But then, man will cease to be man; the work of centuries will be removed: "The higher animal becomes a little easier in his mind and more like the lower one."

The man in the story achieves a kind of victory at the end, for he is still a man; he still keeps jumping: he goes to a door as he leaves the model house and faces the risk of a shattering bump. The door, however, opens for him–he had half expected to find "one of the old doors . . . the one with the girl her arms outstretched in loveliness and beauty before him." It was not so; still, he gets out, but not quite free, not quite untouched; the symptom of his tension, the projection of his inner turmoil to the world outside, meets him as he steps off the escalator, and "the ground came up slightly, to meet his foot." His, however, is only a partial triumph; the story ends with the final dislocation of the ground when it moves up to meet the foot. In fact, the man has achieved not victory, not health, but the kind of uneasy truce that modern life represented for White, the kind of uneasy truce that was New York City, or any large city. The inhabitants live close to the edge of collapse, and each day is survived, each jump at each door is made, with no more hope or confidence for the day to come than there was for the day just past.

The title story, "The Second Tree from the Corner," first published on 31 May 1947, has a clearer structure than "The Door," is lighter in tone, and is less pessimistic. It opens with Trexler, the main character, in a psychiatrist's office. To the doctor's question, "Ever have any bizarre thoughts?" he finally answers defensively, "No." He thinks: "What kind of thoughts except bizarre had he had since the age of two?" Eventually Trexler's problem becomes the doctor's problem, and neither one is getting from life what he wants. At the end, Trexler sees what he wants. Symbolized by a small tree he sees–the second tree from the corner–it is a momentary glimpse of truth that gives him courage. It cannot last, but Trexler "crossed Madison, boarded a

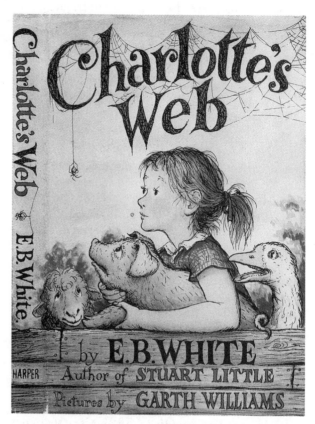

Dust jacket for White's second children's book, which he called "a story of friendship, life, death, salvation"

downtown bus, and rode all the way to Fifty-second Street before he had a thought that could rightly have been called bizarre." The point is basically the same as in "The Door": no permanent cure exists for the disease of life, for the fears it engenders, for the manipulations we must endure. Nevertheless, there is momentary relief, the tentative victory; and, doctor or patient, the hopeful man can find it and, like Trexler, glimpse "the flashy tail feathers of the bird courage."

Not all the pieces in *The Second Tree from the Corner* deal with such serious matters. White has written an amusing parody of Hemingway's *Across the River and into the Trees,* probably Hemingway's worst novel, and one that cries out for parody. In another piece, the endearing gem "Death of a Pig," White tells how, as his pig sickens and dies, he shifts from the farmer-butcher role he started with to become, suddenly, the physician and consoler of his pig. The death of the pig takes on an unexpected dignity, unmarred by any taint of civilization: there was "no stopover in the undertaker's foul parlor." Of the twelve poems in *The Second Tree from the Corner,* "Zoo Revisited," the longest, has considerable autobiographical significance. The best of the lot, however, is "Song of the Queen Bee"—a pleasant tribute to the freedom of nature; it ends with a happy refrain:

Oh, it's simply rare
In the beautiful air,
    And I wish to state
    That I'll always mate
With whatever drone I encounter.

The Points of My Compass (1962), the last published collection of White's hitherto uncollected pieces, includes material written from the summer of 1954 to March 1961. White published relatively little after that, and the collection includes his most personal and explicit statements on many matters; it also includes some of his best essays. During the period covered by The Points of My Compass White continued to write for "Notes and Comment," though on an increasingly reduced scale until, by 1960, he was contributing just a few items a year. He also continued to write the tag lines for newsbreaks, published many poems and sketches, and brought out in 1959 a revised edition of William Strunk's The Elements of Style, to which he added an introduction and a chapter about writing.

The Points of My Compass has a curious sort of circularity about it, ending with an essay that goes back to White's days in Seattle and Washington. There is a kind of geographical circularity about it too. The book is titled as it is because White datelined his essays from the four points of the compass, depending on what direction from The New Yorker office in Manhattan he happened to be when he wrote them. This "geographical distortion," as he calls it, seems to broaden the dimensions of the work; it also underlines the importance of New York City to White. It was for him a microcosm, a center, and the four corners of the world could almost be included within its emotional if not geographical limits. Geography was to White something of an emotional matter; it is, he says, "undergoing vast shifts anyway, with populations in turmoil and the weathercock spinning wildly as the wind veers." The essays represent the culmination of White's experience, the farthest point of navigation—not quite to the heart of darkness, perhaps, but certainly to the heart of his message to his readers. Part of that message has to do with politics, national and international. A lot had happened since The Wild Flag to temper some of White's hope and idealism: McCarthyism, nuclear testing, the Berlin wall and Communist control over Eastern Europe in general, and, among other things, the weaknesses that kept showing up in the United Nations. To these problems White had no clear solutions; what

he does, in part, is to reaffirm his view that a new international order must somehow evolve to match the new science of destruction. Some union of free nations is necessary—a union to which Communist and other totalitarian states will be admitted when they become eligible. He sums up in his essay "Unity" (written 4 June 1960): what is needed "is the evolution of community, community slowly and surely invested with the robes of government by the consent of the governed. We cannot conceivably achieve a peaceful life merely by relaxing the tensions of sovereign nations; there is an unending supply of them."

In another essay from The Points of My Compass, "A Slight Sound at Evening" (summer 1954), White pays a centenary tribute to Thoreau. Whenever White first read Thoreau, it seems clear that his real interest in him began in 1927, when he bought a World's Classics edition of Walden. Walden should be read, White says, at an age "when the normal anxieties and enthusiasm and rebellions of youth closely resemble those of Thoreau in that spring of 1845, when he borrowed an ax, went out to the woods, and began to whack down some trees for timber. Received at such a juncture, the book is like an invitation to life's dance." White himself had discovered Thoreau at such a time, and he quotes a critical sentence from Walden: "I learned this at least by my experiment: that if one advances confidently in the direction of his dreams, and endeavors to live the life which he has imagined, he will meet with a success unexpected in common hours." Then White adds: "The sentence has the power to resuscitate the youth drowning in his sea of doubt. I recall my exhilaration upon reading it, many years ago, in a time of hesitation and despair."

In another passage, the relevance of Thoreau to White is equally clear. To Thoreau's comment that, at a certain time of life, "we are accustomed to consider every spot as the possible site of a house," he replies, "There spoke the young man, a few years out of college, who had not yet broken away from home. He hadn't married, and he had found no job that measured up to his rigid standards of employment, and like any young man, or young animal, he felt uneasy and on the defensive until he had fixed himself a den." White might have been describing himself. White concludes that Thoreau was at once the companion and the chider (the "hair-shirt") of the "fellows who hate compromise and have compromised, fellows who love wildness and have lived tamely"; he was the man "who long ago gave corroboration to impulses they perceived were right and issued warnings against things they instinctively knew to be their enemies." This conclusion,

THE TALK OF THE TOWN

Notes and Comment

WE looked up Mr. Eustace Tilley this week, on the eve of his departure from the city—his "maiden" departure, as he pointed out. The elegant old gentleman was found in his suite at the Plaza, his portmanteau packed, his mourning doves wrapped in dotted swiss, his head in a sitz bath for a last shampoo. Everywhere, scattered about the place, were grim reminders of his genteel background: a cold bottle of Tavel on the lowboy, a spray of pinks in a cut-glass bowl, an album held with a silver clasp, and his social-security card copied in needlepoint and framed on the wall. We begged the privilege of an interview for The Talk of the Town (or what the French call "Murmures de la Ville"), and he reluctantly granted it.

When we inquired about his destination, Mr. Tilley was evasive. "I should prefer to be grilled on that," he remarked, bitterly.

So we grilled him, naming over all the fashionable watering places, without success.

"Would you say you were going to a spa?" we ventured.

"It has a little of the spa in it, a little of the gulch," replied the renowned fop.

"Oh, the White Mountains," we cried.

"Let it go. Ask me about things of moment, such as the ever-normal granary." Mr. Tilley pulled the plug in the sitz bath, sat down at a dressing table, and began to do his hair.

"Why are you leaving town?" we asked.

"I should say that my departure was in part a matter of temper, in part of expediency."

"You mean you're beating the purge?"

Mr. Tilley let the comb drop into his lap, and turned half around, his magnificent profile etched in light from the window.

"We live in a new world," he said. "St. Bernards are killing little girls. Books, or what pass for books, are being photographed on microfilm. There is a cemetery I want to see," he continued, "a grove where ancient trees shelter the graves and throw their umbrage on the imponderable dead. The branches of these trees, my dear young man, are alive with loudspeakers. I believe Upper Montclair is the place. That is one reason for my departure—I have certain macabre pilgrimages to make, while the lustiness is still in my bones. And besides, the other day I received a letter." He gave us a cryptic glance.

"You mean it contained a threat?" we asked.

"Oh my, no," said Tilley. "It came from the office of a division manager, and began: 'Dear Mr. Tilley, Take two pieces of metal and rub them together for a few seconds.' You see, it is time I took my leave." A waiter carrying a guinea fowl aspic entered the room and buzzed about Mr. Tilley. A fly buzzed about the waiter.

"And then, there are things I want to think about, things on which I can more readily concentrate when I am not in town. I want to think about the Will Rogers memorial."

"Why?" we inquired.

"I don't know why," said Tilley, petulantly. "I simply know what are the things I like to think about, and the Will Rogers memorial is one of them.

I want time to examine the new English divorce law, the ever-normal granary (which you forgot to ask me about), the new Knopf book about a man who had a good time, the grasshopper invasion, Hitler's ban on all art that he doesn't understand. I shall perhaps enter a putting tournament, using my old brassie, of course. And I have a strong desire to hear again the wildest sound in all the world."

"You mean timber wolves?" we said.

"I mean cockcrow," snapped Tilley, who by this time was becoming visibly agitated. "I want time to think about many people, alive and dead: Pearl White, Schoolboy Creekmore, Igor Sikorsky—I couldn't begin to name them. I want to think about the custom of skiing in summertime, want to hear a child play thirds on the pianoforte in midafternoon. I shall devote considerable time to studying the faces of motorists drawn up for the red light; in their look of discontent is the answer to the industrial revolution. Did you know that a porcupine has the longest intestine in Christendom, either because he eats so much wood or in order that he may? It is a fact. There must be something to be learned by thinking about that. Take a person employed by a broadcasting studio to close contracts with mountain people who sing folk songs over the air—what will such a person develop, in the course of time, to correspond to a porcupine's long intestine? Ah, well, it's time to be off."

The elderly eccentric rose, phoned

First page of White's 7 August 1937 contribution in The New Yorker, *written in the persona of Eustace Tilley (® and © 1937,* The New Yorker Magazine, Inc. *All rights reserved). The illustration by Otto Soglow shows Tilley's departure from the Plaza Hotel, at Fifty-ninth Street and Fifth Avenue in New York City.*

resembling Matthew Arnold's tribute to Ralph Waldo Emerson as the friend of those who live by the spirit, is at the core of White's feeling about modern life. Man does not want to live in a culture filled with gadgets and the "multiplicity of convenience"; he wants to live simply and naturally, but not in primitiveness or barbarity—for White was never ready to surrender all progress, all conveniences. Men should live so as to escape the charge that Thoreau once made when, in a passage White quoted, he describes a farmer fixing a hay baler: "This farmer is endeavoring to solve the problem of a livelihood by a formula more complicated than the problem itself."

Like "Once More to the Lake," the last essay in *The Points of My Compass,* "The Years of Wonder" (13 March 1961) has a circular quality, a feeling of duality about it, as White takes the reader back to his first years after college and particularly to his trip to Alaska—something White had only touched upon before. He tells us in the opening of "The Years of Wonder" that when Alaska achieved statehood, he looked into the journal he had kept while journeying to Alaska, "hoping to discover in its faded pages something instructive about the new state." As he says, a reader might not find much about Alaska in the account he wrote, but he might find something about White and about the 1920s. "The Years of Wonder" is, as White says, a "delayed account—some thirty-seven years late." In other essays White had returned to earlier times—his early dating, his unrest over what part to play in World War I, his recollections of childhood, his adolescent queries about sex. We see in these accounts White's sense of the transiency of life; we see also, from his half-belief in the cyclical quality of life, that he has faith, or something close to it, in permanency. *The Points of My Compass,* in its subject and structure, is a fitting and impressive summation. In space, it is a microcosm of his world; in time, it is a symbol of the unity and coherence of human experience, where youth and age, city and country, past and present, come together. The book is ultimately White's plea for a vital life where the means do not become ends, where gadgets do not create more problems than they solve, where the "advances" of science do not destroy all possibility of real advance because they have destroyed life itself.

On 15 July 1957 White wrote a sketch for *The New Yorker* titled "Will Strunk." Beginning as a rambling account of the mosquito problems in White's New York apartment, it turns into a nostalgic tribute to Prof. William Strunk Jr., late of Cornell University, and to Strunk's book on rhetoric, *The Elements of Style.* The essay, reprinted in *The Points of My Compass,* had unexpected repercussions. Strunk's work, a short, precise guide to writing, free of jargon and written with a respect for the reader's intelligence and needs, had been used at Cornell in White's day but had later passed out of circulation, the fate of most such books. The Macmillan Company, however, expressed an interest in reprinting the work and asked White to revise and amplify it. The task took White a year; when the book was published in 1959, it achieved an immediate and continuing popularity.

White's sketch for *The New Yorker* became, with a few changes, the introduction of the book; he made some revisions to the book itself and added a final chapter, "An Approach to Style." While giving much good advice to the student, White avoids the pitfall of considering style as something separable or isolated: "The beginner," he says, "should approach style warily, realizing that it is himself he is approaching." Many of his examples in this chapter are felicitous, and he generally manages to be precise and helpful, without being dogmatic. "Do not dress words up by adding *ly* to them, as though putting a hat on a horse," he writes, giving examples of "overly," "firstly," and "muchly."

Curiously, however, this chapter about style is not one of White's effective pieces. It is not always clear; it is sometimes inconsistent; and it is repetitious in a way rare for White. White was probably aware of some of these matters, for in the postscript to the sketch on Strunk in *The Points of My Compass,* he said that his work on *The Elements of Style* took him a lot longer than he had expected: "I discovered that for all my fine talk I was no match for the parts of speech—was, in fact, over my depth and in trouble. Not only that, I felt uneasy posing as an expert on rhetoric, when the truth is I write by ear, always with difficulty and seldom with any exact notion of what is taking place under the hood."

White's last children's book, *The Trumpet of the Swan,* was published in 1970. Its protagonist is a mute trumpeter swan, even though White had never seen such a bird. There is, in the White archives at Cornell, a rich and amusing correspondence between White and his old college friend Howard Cushman, a Philadelphian whom White asked to photograph and to observe closely the trumpeter swans at the Philadelphia Zoo, as well as to obtain other information about Philadelphia and about sentimental popular songs of a decade or two earlier, which the talented swan protagonist, Louis, named after Louis Armstrong, plays on his trumpet.

The first hint that the idea of *The Trumpet of the Swan* was beginning to form in White's mind is in an unpublished letter dated 21 July 1965. White wrote

Cushman, "If I get to Philly in the near future it will be because I am irresistibly drawn to your Zoo's bird park, where, as you probably don't know, a pair of Trumpeter Swans (with an assist from a second female) recently hatched five cygnets. I have never seen a Trumpeter Swan, and this would be my chance. The N.Y. Times had a lovely pix of them. . . ."

The story of *The Trumpet of the Swan,* in brief, is that eleven-year-old Sam Beaver, camping with his father in western Canada, sees a clutch of swan eggs hatching. Sam Beaver, as befits his last name, befriends the swans and stays in touch with them until the end of the story. Insofar as he is a child growing up, there is a parallel to the story of Fern in *Charlotte's Web.* On the other hand, unlike Fern, Sam does not grow alienated from the natural world. Near the end of the story, in fact, Sam is brought to the Philadelphia Zoo, where Louis the swan is negotiating with the Head Man in Charge of Birds to let his beloved female, Serena, fly back to Canada. Sam, having retained his love for animals, takes a job at the zoo, and in the last chapter, in sharp contrast to Fern, Sam, again camping at the same Canadian lake with his father, hears his beloved swans—and keeps the knowledge of them as his own.

Louis's adventures are episodic, in the vein of Stuart Little's, although not to the same degree. The story was written much more rapidly than that of Stuart, and perhaps, therefore, it is more integrated, even though the plot is not woven nearly as tightly as is the story of Wilbur. *The Trumpet of the Swan,* which would be a splendid accomplishment for a lesser writer, does not stand comparison with *Charlotte's Web,* or even with *Stuart Little,* particularly well. Nonetheless, the book is adventurous, imaginative, and it has some touching moments, such as the incident of Louis's care for Serena when she is driven into the zoo at night by a storm.

Perhaps the most significant praise came from John Updike, who wrote, "E. B. White's third novel for children joins the two others on the shelf of classics, . . . [This] is the most spacious and serene of the three, the most imbued with the author's sense of the precious instinctual heritage represented by wild nature. Its story most persuasively offers itself to children as a parable of growing, yet does not lack the simplicity that never condescends, the straight and earnest telling that happens upon, rather than veers into comedy."

The Trumpet of the Swan may be, however, the least plausible of White's children's books. *Charlotte's Web* violates the laws of nature with restraint, never gratuitously, but only and exclusively in further-

ance of its most basic plot. Stuart Little has adventures, car rides, boat races, and such, which exist for their own delightfulness, but which are not necessary—though certainly allowed—in furtherance of the plot. They do all together, however, help to create the picture of Stuart as the debonair character he is. In the case of Louis, however, plausibility is thrown to the winds. It is not even an issue. That, in itself, is not an evaluative judgment (after all, there is no universal law of aesthetics that says plots must be coherent, and that actions must arise organically out of plots). White, almost with bravado, it seems, throws down the gauntlet—a trumpet-playing swan who, without further ado, writes in English on a slate and who bargains with a human zoo keeper.

The Trumpet of the Swan is the only one of White's three children's books without the illustrations by Garth Williams. On the whole, however, the pictures by Edward Frascino (and one by White himself) were well received by reviewers, including Updike, who wrote that "drawings less vague than Frascino's might mar more illusion than they abet."

White's swan song is not an unfitting conclusion for the great contribution he has made to imaginative literature for children. This last book, as much as the first two, asks once again the question put by Stuart Little to the fifth graders, "How many of you know what's important?" The answer, as ever in White's writing, remains essentially the same: art (music, in this instance); friendship; nature; and growing up—or older—within time, within the circle of nature's seasons. Truly Charlotte's epitaph may be applied one last time: "It is not often that someone comes along who is a true friend and a good writer." For the children of the world, E. B. White was both.

White was widely honored during his career, with honorary degrees from many colleges. He received the Page One Award for Literature for *The Second Tree from the Corner* in 1954; the gold medal from the National Institute of Arts and Letters in 1960; the Presidential Medal of Freedom in 1963; the Laura Ingalls Wilder Award in 1970; the National Medal for Literature in 1971; and the William Allen White Children's Book Award for *The Trumpet of the Swan* in 1973. In 1978 White won a special Pulitzer Prize for the full body of his work. He has been important in American letters for another reason: his connection with *The New Yorker* magazine. In addition to the many stories, sketches, and essays he contributed to *The New Yorker* from 1927 to the late 1940s, he wrote more of the "Notes and Comment" department of the magazine than any other writer. That department became the heart of *The New Yorker* and helped set its tone. *Charlotte's Web,* the best of White's three children's stories, is a classic in that form—it may well turn out to be the longest remembered of his works. Certainly his writing has long been considered almost a definition of excellence in prose style.

Letters:

Letters of E. B. White, edited by Dorothy Lobrano Guth (New York: Harper & Row, 1976).

Biographies:

Scott Elledge, *E. B. White: A Biography* (New York: Norton, 1984);

Isabel Russell, *Katharine and E. B. White: An Affectionate Memoir* (New York: Norton, 1988).

References:

Lucien L. Agosta, *E. B. White: The Children's Books* (New York: Twayne, 1995);

Warren Beck, "E. B. White," *College English,* 7 (April 1946): 367–373;

J. W. Fuller, "Prose Style in the Essays of E. B. White," dissertation, University of Washington, 1959;

John W. Griffith, *Charlotte's Web: A Pig's Salvation* (New York: Twayne; Toronto: Maxwell Macmillan Canada; New York: Maxwell Macmillan International, 1993);

Louis Hasley, "The Talk of the Town and the Country: E. B. White," *Connecticut Review,* 5 (October 1971): 37–45;

Dale Kramer, *Ross and The New Yorker* (Garden City, N.Y.: Doubleday, 1951);

Peter F. Neumeyer, *The Annotated Charlotte's Web,* introduction and notes by Neumeyer, text by

White, pictures by Garth Williams (New York: Harper Collins, 1994);

Neumeyer, "What Makes a Good Children's Book? The Texture of *Charlotte's Web,*" *South Atlantic Bulletin,* 44 (May 1979): 66–75;

David Rees, "Timor mortis conturbat me: E. B. White and Doris Buchanan Smith," in *The Marble in the Water* (Boston: Horn Book, 1980), pp. 68–77;

Barbara J. Rogers, "E. B. White," in *American Writers: A Collection of Literary Biographies,* volume 5, edited by Leonard Unger (New York: Scribners, 1974), pp. 651–681;

Robert L. Root Jr., ed., *Critical Essays on E. B. White* (New York: Hall, 1994);

Roger Sale, *Fairy Tales and After: From Snow White to E. B. White* (Cambridge, Mass.: Harvard University Press, 1978), pp. 258–267;

Edward C. Sampson, *E. B. White* (New York: Twayne, 1974);

William R. Steinhoff, "'The Door': 'The Professor,' 'My Friend the Poet (Deceased),' 'The Washable House,' and 'The Man Out in Jersey,'" *College English,* 23 (December 1961): 229–232;

James Thurber, "E. B. W.," *Saturday Review of Literature,* 18 (15 October 1938): 8–9;

Thurber, *The Years With Ross* (Boston: Little, Brown, 1959).

Papers:

Most of White's papers are in the E. B. White Collection at Olin Library, Cornell University, with the exception of the manuscript for *The Trumpet of the Swan,* which is in the Pierpont Morgan Library, New York City.

Elie Wiesel

This entry was updated by Jack Kolbert (Susquehanna University)
from his entry in DLB 83: French Novelists Since 1960.

See also the Nobel Peace Prize entry in *DLB Yearbook 1986* and the Wiesel entry in *DLB Yearbook 1987*.

BIRTH: Sighet, Romania, 30 September 1928, to Shlomo and Sarah Feig Wiesel; immigrated to the United States, 1956; naturalized U.S. citizen, 1963.

EDUCATION: Attended Sorbonne, University of Paris, 1948–1951.

MARRIAGE: 1969 to Marion Erster Rose; child: Shlomo Elisha.

AWARDS AND HONORS: Prix Rivarol, 1963; Remembrance Award for *The Town beyond the Wall* and all other writings, 1965; William and Janice Epstein Fiction Award, Jewish Book Council, for *The Town beyond the Wall,* 1965; Jewish Heritage Award for excellence in literature, 1966; Prix Médicis for *Le Mendiant de Jérusalem,* 1969; Prix Bordin, French Academy, 1972; Eleanor Roosevelt Memorial Award, 1972; American Liberties Medallion, American Jewish Committee, 1972; Frank and Ethel S. Cohen Award, Jewish Book Council, for *Souls on Fire,* 1973; Martin Luther King Jr. Award, City College of the City University of New York, 1973; Faculty Distinguished Scholar Award, Hofstra University, 1973–1974; Joseph Prize for Human Rights, Anti-Defamation League of B'nai B'rith, 1978; Zalman Shazar Award, State of Israel, 1979; Jabotinsky Medal, State of Israel, 1980; Prix Livre-International, 1980, and Prix des Bibliothécaires, 1981, both for *Le Testament d'un poète juif assassiné;* Anatoly Scharansky Humanitarian Award, 1983; Congressional Gold Medal of Achievement, 1984; Humanitarian Award, International League for Human Rights, 1985; Freedom Cup award, Women's League of Israel, 1986; Nobel Peace Prize, 1986; Special Christopher Book Award, 1987; achievement award, Artists and Writers for Peace in the Middle East, 1987; Profiles of Courage award, B'nai B'rith, 1987; Human Rights Law Award, International Human Rights Law Group, 1988; Presidential Medal, Hofstra University, 1988; Bicentennial

Elie Wiesel (Boston University Photo Services)

Medal, Georgetown University, 1988; Janus Korczak Humanitarian award, NAHE, Kent State University, 1989; Count Sforza Award in Philanthropy, Interphil, 1989; Lily Edelman Award for excellence in continuing Jewish education, B'nai B'rith International, 1989; George Washington Award, American Hungarian Foundation, 1989; Bicentennial Medal, New York University, 1989; Humanitarian Award, Human Rights Campaign Fund, 1989; International Brotherhood Award, C.O.R.E., 1990; Frank Weil Award for distinguished contribution to the advancement of North American Jewish culture, Jewish Community Centers Association of North America, 1990; first Raoul Wallenberg Medal, University of Michigan, 1990; Award of Highest

Honor, Soka University, 1991; Facing History and Ourselves Humanity Award, 1991; La Medaille de la Ville de Toulouse, 1991; Fifth Centennial Christopher Columbus Medal, City of Genoa, 1992; first Primo Levi Award, 1992; Literature Arts Award, National Foundation for Jewish Culture, 1992; Ellis Island Medal of Honor, 1992; Guardian of the Children Award, AKIM USA, 1992; Bishop Francis J. Mugavero Award for religious and racial harmony, Queens College, 1994; Golden Slipper Humanitarian Award, 1994; Humanitarian Award, Interfaith Council on the Holocaust, 1994; Crystal Award, Davos World Economic Forum, 1995; first Niebuhr Award, Elmhurst College, 1995; named Humanitarian of the Century, Council of Jewish Organizations; Freedom Award, National Civil Rights Movement, Memphis, Tennessee, 1995; Golden Plate Award, American Academy of Achievement, 1996; Guardian of Zion Award, Ingeborg Rennert Center for Jerusalem Studies, Bar-Ilan University, 1997; Canterbury Medalist, The Becket Fund for Religious Liberty, 1998; Rabbi Marc H. Tanenbaum Award for the Advancement of Interreligious Understanding, 1998; Yitzhak Rabin Peacemaker Award, Merrimack College, 1998; recipient of many honorary degrees; honors established in his name include the Elie Wiesel Award for Holocaust Research, University of Haifa; Elie Wiesel Chair in Holocaust Studies, Bar-Ilan University; Elie Wiesel Endowment Fund for Jewish Culture, University of Denver; Elie Wiesel Distinguished Service Award, University of Florida; Elie Wiesel Awards for Jewish Arts and Culture, B'nai B'rith Hillel Foundations; and the Elie Wiesel Chair in Judaic Studies, Connecticut College.

BOOKS: *Un di Velt Hot Geshvign* (Buenos Aires: Central Farbond Fun Poylishe Yidn in Argentina, 1956); revised and abridged as *La Nuit* (Paris: Editions de Minuit, 1958); *La Nuit* translated by Stella Rodway as *Night* (New York: Hill & Wang, 1960; London: MacGibbon & Kee, 1960);

L'Aube (Paris: Seuil, 1960); translated by Anne Borchardt as *Dawn* (New York: Hill & Wang, 1961); translated by Frances Frenaye (London: MacGibbon & Kee, 1961);

Le Jour (Paris: Seuil, 1961); translated by Borchardt as *The Accident* (New York: Hill & Wang, 1962);

La Ville de la chance (Paris: Seuil, 1962); translated by Stephen Becker as *The Town beyond the Wall* (New York: Holt, Rinehart & Winston, 1964; London: Robson, 1975);

Les Portes de la forêt (Paris: Seuil, 1964); translated by Frenaye as *The Gates of the Forest* (New York: Holt, Rinehart & Winston, 1966; London: Heinemann, 1967);

Les Juifs du silence (Paris: Seuil, 1966); translated from the original Hebrew by Neal Kozodoy as *The Jews of Silence: A Personal Report on Soviet Jewry* (New York: Holt, Rinehart & Winston, 1966; London: Valentine Mitchell, 1968);

Les Chants des morts (Paris: Seuil, 1966); translated by Steven Donadio as *Legends of Our Time* (New York: Holt, Rinehart & Winston, 1968);

Zalmen ou la folie de Dieu (Paris: Seuil, 1968); translated by Nathan Edelman and adapted for the stage by Marion Wiesel as *Zalmen, or The Madness of God* (New York: Random House, 1974);

Le Mendiant de Jérusalem (Paris: Seuil, 1968); translated by Lily Edelman and Elie Wiesel as *A Beggar in Jerusalem* (New York: Random House, 1970; London: Weidenfeld & Nicolson, 1970);

Entre deux soleils (Paris: Seuil, 1970); translated by Lily Edelman and Elie Wiesel as *One Generation After* (New York: Random House, 1970; London: Weidenfeld & Nicolson, 1971);

Célébration hassidique: Portraits et légendes (Paris: Seuil, 1972); translated by Marion Wiesel as *Souls on Fire: Portraits and Legends of Hasidic Masters* (New York: Random House, 1972; London: Weidenfeld & Nicolson, 1972);

Le Serment de Kolvillàg (Paris: Seuil, 1973); translated by Marion Wiesel as *The Oath* (New York: Random House, 1973);

Ani Maamin: Un Chant perdu et retrouvé (Paris: Seuil, 1973); bilingual edition, with translation by Marion Wiesel, published as *Ani Maamin: A Song Lost and Found Again* (New York: Random House, 1973);

Célébration biblique: Portraits et légendes (Paris: Seuil, 1975); translated by Marion Wiesel as *Messengers of God: Biblical Portraits and Legends* (New York: Random House, 1976);

Un Juif aujourd'hui (Paris: Seuil, 1977); translated by Marion Wiesel as *A Jew Today* (New York: Random House, 1978);

Four Hasidic Masters and Their Struggle Against Melancholy (Notre Dame, Ind.: University of Notre Dame Press, 1978);

Le Procès de Shamgorod (tel qu'il se déroula le 25 février 1649) (Paris: Seuil, 1979); translated by Marion Wiesel as *The Trial of God (as it was held on February 25, 1649, in Shamgorod)* (New York: Random House, 1979);

Images from the Bible: The Paintings of Shalom of Safed, the Words of Elie Wiesel (Woodstock, N.Y.: Overlook Press, 1980);

Le Testament d'un poète juif assassiné (Paris: Seuil, 1980); translated by Marion Wiesel as *The Testament* (New York: Summit, 1981; London: Allen Lane, 1981);

Five Biblical Portraits (Notre Dame, Ind.: University of Notre Dame Press, 1981);

Contre la mélancolie: Célébration hassidique II (Paris: Seuil, 1981); translated by Marion Wiesel as *Somewhere a Master: Further Hasidic Portraits and Legends* (New York: Summit, 1982);

Paroles d'étranger (Paris: Seuil, 1982);

The Golem: The Story of a Legend as Told by Elie Wiesel (New York: Summit, 1983);

Le Cinquième Fils (Paris: Grasset, 1983); translated by Marion Wiesel as *The Fifth Son* (New York: Summit, 1985);

Against Silence: The Voice and Vision of Elie Wiesel, 3 volumes, edited by Irving Abrahamson (New York: Holocaust Library, 1985);

Signes d'Exode (Paris: Grasset & Fasquelle, 1985);

Job ou Dieu dans la tempête (Paris: Grasset & Fasquelle, 1986);

Discours d'Oslo (Paris: Grasset & Fasquelle, 1987);

The Night Trilogy: Night, Dawn, The Accident (New York: Farrar, Straus & Giroux, 1987);

A Song for Hope, a Cantata (New York: 92nd Street Y, 1987);

Le Crépuscule au loin (Paris: Grasset & Fasquelle, 1987); translated by Marion Wiesel as *Twilight* (New York: Summit Books, 1988);

The Six Days of Destruction: Meditations toward Hope, by Wiesel and Albert H. Friedlander (Oxford, U.K. & New York: Pergamon Press, 1988);

L'Oublié: roman (Paris: Seuil, 1989); translated by Stephen Becker as *The Forgotten* (New York: Summit, 1992);

Silences et mémoire d'hommes (Paris: Seuil, 1989);

From the Kingdom of Memory: Reminiscences (New York: Summit, 1990);

A Journey of Faith, by Wiesel and John Cardinal O'Connor (New York: Donald I. Fine, 1990);

Célébration talmudique: portrait et légendes (Paris: Seuil, 1991); portions translated by Marion Wiesel as *Sages and Dreamers: Biblical, Talmudic, and Hasidic Portraits and Legends* (New York: Summit, 1991);

A Passover Haggadah, English and Hebrew as commented upon by Elie Wiesel and illustrated by Mark Podwal, English edited by Marion Wiesel (New York: Simon and Schuster, 1993);

Semprún, Wiesel: se taire est impossible, by Wiesel and Jorge Semprún (Paris: Arte éditions/Editions Mille et une nuits, 1995);

Tous les fleuves vont à la mer: mémoires (Paris: Seuil, 1994); translated as *All Rivers Run to the Sea: Memoirs* (New York: Knopf, 1995);

Mémoire à deux voix, by Wiesel and François Mitterand (Paris: Jacob, 1995); translated by Richard Seaver and Timothy Bent as *Memoir in Two Voices* (New York: Arcade, 1996);

Et la mer n'est pas remplie: mémoires II (Paris: Seuil, 1996);

Célébration prophétique: Portraits et légendes (Paris: Seuil, 1998).

OTHER: "The Holocaust as Literary Imagination," in *Dimensions of the Holocaust: Lectures at Northwestern University* (Evanston, Ill.: The University, 1977).

SELECTED PERIODICAL PUBLICATIONS–UNCOLLECTED: "From Exile to Exile," *Nation,* 202 (25 April 1966): 494–495;

"Will Soviet Jewry Survive?" *Commentary,* 43 (February 1967): 47–52;

"Arts and Culture After the Holocaust," *Crosscurrents,* 261 (Fall 1976): 258–269;

"Why I Write: Making No Become Yes," *New York Times Book Review,* 14 April 1985, pp. 13–14.

The work of a survivor of Auschwitz and Buchenwald, Elie Wiesel's literature, most of which he wrote in French, is rooted in the horror of the Holocaust and devoted to the examination of the most fundamental moral issues. Although he has depicted events in the lives of those who outlived Hitler's gas chambers, Wiesel's novels, plays, short stories, lectures, and philosophical texts do more than serve as archives for those who suffered or perished and more than attest to the resiliency of the Jewish people. "This is what I demand for literature," Wiesel once wrote, "a moral dimension. Art for art's sake is gone. . . . Just to write a novel, that's why I survived?" Elsewhere he noted, "I have always felt that words mean responsibility. I try to use them not against the human condition but for humankind; never to create anger but to attenuate anger, not to separate people but to bring them together." In 1986 Wiesel received the Nobel Peace Prize, cited for his "commitment, which originated in the suffering of the Jewish people, [and] has been widened to embrace all oppressed people and races."

Wiesel's parents were Shlomo and Sarah Feig Wiesel. He was born Eliezer Wiesel on 30 September 1928, in Sighet, Romania, a well-known center

Dust jacket for the American edition of Wiesel's 1964 novel,
Les Portes de la forêt, *the story of a concentration camp
survivor who seeks to understand why God
allows such suffering*

of Jewish culture, in the region of Transylvania.
Shlomo Wiesel, a grocer and storekeeper, represented for the young Elie the spirit of learning and
Hebrew education. He always encouraged his son to
study Hebrew and Yiddish languages and their literatures. Wiesel's mother, Sarah, inculcated in him
a respect for mysticism and faith and a fascination
with the ancient teachings of the Torah and Tal-
mud. Possibly the most influential force in the boy's
life was his maternal grandfather, Dodye Feig, an
old Hasid, who fired the child's imagination with
tales of Hasidic inspiration. Indeed many of Wiesel's works of fiction depict an ancient storyteller
who recounts similar tales to an inspired young listener.

What for Wiesel was a traditional and idyllic
boyhood in an orthodox Jewish family came to a
dramatic end with the arrival of the Nazi armies during the spring of 1944. All of Sighet's approximately
fifteen thousand Jews were arrested and deported
by train to Auschwitz, Poland. Wiesel was separated
by the SS guards from his mother and three sisters,

Tzipora, Hilda, and Batya, although he was able to
remain with his father. When Soviet troops neared
Auschwitz in early 1945, these two were moved to
Buchenwald. Wiesel's father perished from starvation and dysentery at Buchenwald, while his mother
and Tzipora were murdered in the gas chambers of
Auschwitz. Well after the liberation in 1945, Wiesel
learned of the survival of his older sisters, Hilda and
Batya. His best-known work, *La Nuit* (1958; translated as *Night,* 1960), was written as a memorial to
his parents and his younger sister.

During his period of imprisonment in the
camps, the adolescent Wiesel suffered every kind of
indignity imaginable: torture, hunger, filth, intense
cold, illness, and the terror of facing the constant
threat of execution. These experiences are the substance of *La Nuit* and continue to reverberate in his
later works.

On 11 April 1945 Wiesel was liberated at
Buchenwald by the United States Third Army. His
initial desire was to move to the then-British man-
date of Palestine, but immigration restrictions made
this impossible. To be repatriated to his native
Transylvania was unthinkable. He consented to go
to Belgium with hundreds of other Jewish orphans,
but his train was rerouted to France at the insistence
of Gen. Charles de Gaulle, who wished France to
become a haven for the homeless. Initially Wiesel
was sent to Normandy, where the Œuvres du Se-
cours aux Enfants, a charitable children's aid society, provided him with nourishment and shelter.
Later he moved to Paris, where from 1948 to 1951
he studied at the Sorbonne and mastered the French
language, which eventually became his preferred
medium of literary expression. His principal areas
of study were philosophy, literature, and psychology. At the same time, he supported himself by
working at a variety of jobs, including choir director, part-time teacher of Hebrew and the Jewish Bible, translator of Hebrew into French, and summer-
camp counselor.

Under the influence of the philosopher Gustave Wahl of the Sorbonne, Wiesel studied the texts
of the French classical era and those of Greco-
Roman antiquity with the same dedication he had
demonstrated in his boyhood analyses of the Tal-
mud and the Hasidic texts. During his Sorbonne
days Wiesel became a journalist for the French-
Jewish periodical *Arche* and was assigned to cover
the early days of the State of Israel. By 1952 he was
working for the Tel Aviv daily newspaper *Yediot
Ahronot.* Sent to cover a story in India, Wiesel realized that he would need to learn English as well as
French. Although he never completed his Sorbonne
studies, he did acquire proficiency in English, and in

1956 he went to America to cover the United Nations for the Tel Aviv paper. He was struck by a taxicab in New York and for nearly a year was forced to remain in America, in a wheelchair. Since his French travel documents were expiring, he decided to apply for United States citizenship. Wiesel has been an American citizen since 1963, and his French books have been translated into English almost immediately following their publication in Paris. On Passover eve 1969, he married Marion Erster Rose; their son, Shlomo Elisha, was born in 1972. Since the early 1970s Marion Wiesel has served as the translator of her husband's books.

In 1957 Wiesel joined the staff of the *Jewish Daily Forward,* but he dreamed of writing more than the journalistic work he had been producing. As a child he had written a book (never published) about the Jewish Bible. He felt that the sincerest source of inspiration for him was his rich knowledge of old Jewish folk tales. He also felt that because he had personally witnessed the most tragic era in human history, he should somehow recapture his experiences in durable literary form. Yet in 1945 he had taken a vow not to speak or write of his experiences in the camps for ten years. He wondered how to break his silence, how to find the right words, if indeed any existed. How could one use language, a refined and orderly system of signs developed by civilized society, to express experiences that were totally antithetical to civilization—events that were in all regards supreme manifestations of chaos and disorder? For a whole decade Wiesel pondered these questions and wondered as well whether he had the stamina to relive, even in literature, the horror of the Holocaust. In a 1984 interview in *Paris Review,* he told John S. Friedman: "I didn't want to use the wrong words. I was afraid that words might betray it [the Holocaust]. I waited. I waited. I'm still not sure that it was the wrong move, or the right move, that is, whether to choose language or silence. . . . Sometimes you don't have to speak in order to be heard, not when the message is so powerful." Ultimately, however, Wiesel realized that his message must be expressed in words.

Wiesel chose in his first major book to deal with the Holocaust. In 1954 *Yediot Ahronot* assigned him to interview the 1952 Nobel Laureate in literature, the well-known Catholic novelist François Mauriac. Fascinated by Wiesel's memories of the Holocaust, Mauriac discussed at length with him the question of Christian responsibility, even complicity, in the Holocaust. During this painful discussion Mauriac persuaded Wiesel that it was his solemn obligation to speak, to terminate his silence and write of his experiences as a witness of the concentration camps. Feeling more at home with his native Yiddish language than with his acquired French, Wiesel wrote his first book, about Auschwitz and Buchenwald, in Yiddish, calling it *Un di Velt Hot Geshvign* (And the World Remained Silent, 1956). This enormous tome (eight hundred pages in manuscript) was published initially in Buenos Aires, but its success was limited. In order to have the work accepted for publication in Paris, Wiesel drastically reduced the scope of the original to a 127-page volume, which, thanks to the intercession of Mauriac, was published in 1958 under the title *La Nuit.* The publisher was Editions de Minuit, which had become prominent for including among its authors well-known *nouveaux romanciers* such as Michel Butor.

A work that has sold well since its original publication, *La Nuit* has been translated into all of the major languages. In 1960, superbly translated by Stella Rodway, it appeared in the United States and Great Britain as *Night.* The foreword, by Mauriac, adds a significant dimension to *La Nuit.* Because in this work one sees a youthful commentator describing the terror of life in the Nazi universe, many critics have compared Wiesel's book with Anne Frank's *Diary of a Young Girl* (1947), despite the fact that the two are fundamentally different in tone and subject matter. *La Nuit* is a personal record of a child's life in a world of barbed wire, starvation, and gas chambers. It recounts his innermost anxieties as he struggles to remain alive and as he clings to the last remaining vestige of his earlier life, his slowly declining father. Written in the starkest, most naked literary style, *La Nuit* seethes with powerful scenes. It is difficult to imagine a work that is more barren of literary adornment and at the same time so rich in intensity of human experience.

Once Wiesel had learned that it was possible to verbalize, at least partially, the world of the death camps, he transformed himself, in several compact, partly autobiographical novels, from a witness of death to a person who had experienced survival. Along with *Night,* the first two of these novels form Wiesel's *Night Trilogy: Night, Dawn, The Accident,* published in a single volume under that title in 1987. *L'Aube* appeared in Paris in 1960 and was translated as *Dawn* in 1961. It deals with the desire of a death-camp survivor to join the underground Jewish movement just prior to the creation of the State of Israel in 1948. Having lived through the reign of terror in the camps, he now must gather enough courage to kill the enemies of the hoped-for Jewish state. One year later, in 1961, there appeared another short novel, *Le Jour* (literally, Day; freely translated into English under the title *The Accident,* in 1962), a novel about a young survivor who is hit by an automobile in New York and who considers committing suicide because of guilt from having lived through the Holocaust. After weeks of moral crisis, hovering between life and death, this young survivor realizes that his accident was not accidental, but rather an unconscious desire to do away with himself. Although he can barely endure the memories of his past, he must choose life.

In 1962 Wiesel published *La Ville de la chance* (translated as *The Town beyond the Wall,* 1964), a novel in which he portrays a spectator who watches in silence through his windows in Sighet as the Jews of that town, his neighbors, are led through the streets toward the trains that will deport them to Auschwitz. The theme is silence, or rather the guilt of those who are silent and indifferent. Movingly, the author recaptures in the final scene the emotion of a survivor who returns to Sighet and sees a similar face staring at him through a window. The novel received the Prix Rivarol in 1963.

Wiesel's subsequent volume, *Les Portes de la forêt* (1964; translated as *The Gates of the Forest,* 1966), includes his most penetrating analysis of the relationship between people suffering through the Holocaust and their God. In the novel, Gregor, a young Hungarian Jew separated from his family, survives in a camp and later fights with the partisans in the forest. After the war he seeks safety in America, but there he is devoured by the moral crisis of how the God of the Jews could have allowed His people to suffer so tragically. Accusations are interspersed with passages of remorse, but in the end Gregor chooses life, and love: "It's inhuman," one of the key utterances in the novel holds, "to wall yourself up in pain and memories as if in a prison. Suffering must open us up to others. It must not cause us to reject them."

Wiesel's next work was a pause in his series of semi-autobiographical novels, presenting a nonfictional, firsthand report on the Jews in the Soviet Union. A series of articles originally appearing in Hebrew in *Yediot Ahronot* is the basis of *Les Juifs du silence,* published in French and in English translation (as *The Jews of Silence*) in 1966. The English version of this documentary work is enriched by the historical afterword by Neal Kozodoy, who translated it from Hebrew. According to Wiesel's preface to *Les Juifs du silence:* "The pages that follow are the report of a witness. Nothing more and nothing else. Their purpose is to draw attention to a problem about which no one should remain unaware." Henceforth Wiesel assumed the role of champion of the persecuted Soviet Jews. In *Les Juifs du silence* Wiesel underscores the fact that as the world remained silent during the early days of Auschwitz and Buchenwald, so too there has been silence—even among his fellow Jews—in the face of anti-Semitism in Russia.

Twenty years following his deportation from Sighet, Wiesel returned there for a visit in 1964. This visit was the basis for *Les Chants des morts,* published in 1966 in Paris and translated as *Legends of Our Time* in 1968. A loosely knit collection, it comprises philosophical essays, short stories, and autobiographical episodes. In this same vein he wrote *Entre deux soleils,* which appeared in French and in English translation (as *One Generation After*) in 1970, the twenty-fifth anniversary of Wiesel's liberation from Buchenwald.

Le Mendiant de Jérusalem (1968; translated as *A Beggar in Jerusalem,* 1970), Wiesel's next novel after *Les Portes de la forêt,* may be, along with *La Nuit,* his most successful literary undertaking to date. It received the Prix Médicis in Paris and was a best-seller on both sides of the Atlantic. A fictional transposition of the Israeli-Arab Six Day War of June 1967, Wiesel's novel treats the heady days of this Jewish victory as a pivotal moment in the history of his people. It is probably Wiesel's most jubilant work of fiction.

Despite the hopefulness expressed in *Le Mendiant de Jérusalem,* in a work of the same period Wiesel took up again the theme he had enunciated in *Les Juifs du silence.* This time he chose for the first time to write a play, *Zalmen ou la folie de Dieu,* in which he dramatized his moral outrage at what was taking place in Russia. In 1968 the French version of the play was published; in 1974 the English translation, *Zalmen, or The Madness of God,* adapted for the stage by Wiesel's wife, Marion, was produced at the Arena Stage in Washington, D.C. and published in the United States. Suffering from wordiness and from a not-always-successful attempt by Wiesel to blend symbolism with realism, the play nonetheless was widely viewed when public television broadcast the Arena Stage production, also in 1974. The play depicts a visit by American Jews to a small-town Russian synagogue during Yom Kippur services. The strongest character in the plot, Zalmen, is an eloquent and perceptive town idiot who serves to dramatize the plight of Soviet Jewry. Zalmen is one example of Wiesel's frequent use of the town idiot, or someone who is often wrongly perceived as mad, as a person who manifests greater insight into human destiny than those who regard themselves as rational and who refuse to see the truth as it really is.

Célébration hassidique: Portraits et légendes (1972) was Wiesel's next major work following *Le Mendiant de Jérusalem.* It received the Prix Bordin de l'Académie Française and was translated by Marion Wiesel as *Souls on Fire: Portraits and Legends of Hasidic Masters* (1972). Drawing on the heritage of Hasidic tales that he had heard from his grandfather, the author recounts a set of stories about how the Hasidic Jews lived, their relationships with their legendary rabbis, and the warmth and joy permeating the life of the Hasidic home. *Célébration hassidique* is Wiesel's best work on this rich historical movement in Judaism. Many critics have found in this work reverberations of Camusian existentialism, especially in Wiesel's insistence that man, despite the overwhelming odds of human destiny, must reject despair and continue to live with hope.

Of all of Wiesel's works, perhaps the most unusual is *Ani Maamin* (1973), subtitled *Un Chant perdu et retrouvé* (A Song Lost and Found Again) and published first in France and then in the United States in an attractive bilingual volume in 1973. Written as the libretto for a cantata by Darius Milhaud, *Ani Maamin: Un Chant perdu et retrouvé* is a song of exaltation of the Messianic spirit in Jewish history. Composed in blank verse, the poetry is laden with tensions and rhythms that carry the reader from one crescendo to another.

One of Wiesel's most powerful novels is *Le Serment de Kolvillàg* (1973; translated as *The Oath*, 1973), an epic narrative that depicts the character type of the madman who understands more clearly than so-called people of reason the dangerous course of an insane world. The theme of silence is again central, as Azriel, a typical Wieselian character, tries to keep a young man from committing suicide by telling him a story he had been sworn (thus the "oath" of the title) never to relate to any living being: how all the Jews, except him, had been slaughtered by their gentile neighbors in the Hungarian village of Kolvillàg because they were accused of being Christ-killers. Of the work Wiesel once stated, "Take *The Oath,* a novel set at the beginning of the century, about a village and a ritual murder, nothing about the Holocaust. But then on another level, it is the Holocaust—not of the Jews but of the world. That's why I called the village Kolvillàg. Villàg in Hungarian means world, and Kol in Hebrew means all—the entire world." *Le Serment de Kolvillàg* is in this way typical of Wiesel's novels, with the exception of *La Nuit.* As the author once noted: "I have never spoken about the Holocaust except in one book, *Night . . .* where I tried to tell a tale directly, as though face to face with that experience." However, if one penetrates beyond Wiesel's plots, one finds the ubiquitous presence of the Holocaust. Mankind lives under the threat of renewed genocides and in the shadow of previous ones.

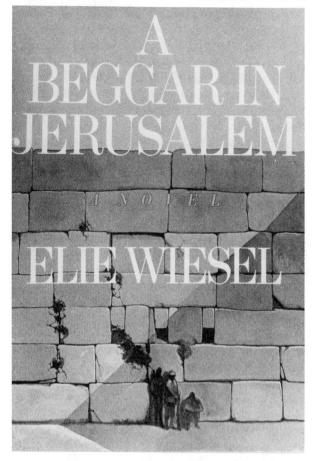

Dust jacket for the American edition of Wiesel's 1968 novel, Le Mendiant de Jérusalem, *about the Israeli-Arab Six-Day War in 1967*

With *Célébration biblique: Portraits et légendes* (1975; translated as *Messengers of God: Biblical Portraits and Legends,* 1976), Wiesel produced a volume in the same vein as *Célébration hassidique,* except that in this collection of tales and legends, the main characters are not Hasidic rabbis but the patriarchs themselves. Seeking to make Abraham, Isaac, Adam, and Job more meaningful for post-Holocaust mankind, Wiesel makes the patriarchs relive their own personal tragedies. Demythifying these biblical figures, the author transforms them into almost contemporary people. They are like Albert Camus's Sisyphus, who chooses perseverence and life over despair and death. The work constitutes for Wiesel a supreme reaffirmation of faith and hope.

In *Un Juif aujourd'hui* (1977; translated as *A Jew Today,* 1978) Wiesel assembled his third collection of essays, tales, fragments, and dialogues. Here he expands his concern beyond the Jewish destiny in order to include Palestinian Arabs and other oppressed peoples around the world, in South Africa, Biafra, Cambodia, Vietnam, and Bangladesh. In the late 1970s and early 1980s Wiesel wrote two

English-language volumes, *Four Hasidic Masters and Their Struggle Against Melancholy* (1978) and *Five Biblical Portraits* (1981), both in the tradition of *Célébration hassidique* and *Célébration biblique*.

In 1979 Wiesel published his second play, *Le Procès de Shamgorod (tel qu'il se déroula le 25 février 1649)*, translated the same year as *The Trial of God (as it was held on February 25, 1649, in Shamgorod)*. The drama concerns a Jewish innkeeper and three Jewish troubadour-like wanderers who put God on trial for allowing the massacre of their coreligionists in a pogrom. In act 2 they seek an appropriate prosecutor and defense attorney. Act 3 presents the trial in which, with Job-like passion, Wiesel's characters accuse their God of indifference. In reality it is not God who is on trial, but rather the faith of those who would prosecute Him. The play has been performed before enthusiastic audiences by professional theaters in Paris, Oslo, and West Germany as well as by many campus groups at American universities.

Le Testament d'un poète juif assassiné (1980), a novel which received the Prix Livre-International and the Prix des Bibliothécaires, continues Wiesel's concern with the suffering of the Soviet Jews. Written as the confessional diary of a Jewish poet, Paltiel Kossover, who was murdered under the Stalin regime in 1952, the novel describes how this poet's only son, Grisha, seeks to rediscover and to comprehend the life of his father through the diary. The circumstances under which the diary was written and the way in which it comes to Grisha are important. Paltiel, imprisoned by the KGB, is told to write his autobiography. Although he never leaves the prison, the document eventually finds its way to his son. The analogy Wiesel implicitly draws between Stalin's mass murders and Hitler's is clear. The work, acclaimed with virtually unanimous applause in the Parisian press, was translated and published in English in 1981 as *The Testament*.

Wiesel's 1983 novel, *Le Cinquième Fils* (translated as *The Fifth Son*, 1985), is set for the most part in New York City and portrays a son who devotes his life to unraveling the mysterious past of his parents. Eventually the young man, Ariel, learns that he had a brother, also named Ariel, who was killed by the SS during World War II. He also discovers that his father had participated in an attempt to assassinate the SS leader in his native town but that the attempt was unsuccessful. A witness relates to the young New Yorker the nightmarish experiences that his parents had endured, stressing that they are psychologically incapable of sharing these experiences with their son. Ariel departs on a trip to Europe to seek vengeance against the Nazi SS officer who had persecuted his parents and who has since assumed a mask of respectability as a high-ranking corporate executive in one of West Germany's most successful businesses. In keeping with Wiesel's visions, however, the vengeance does not take place.

Le Crépuscule au loin (1987; translated as *Twilight*, 1988), is among the most complex of Wiesel's novels. Metaphysical in character, it deals with a problem that has ceaselessly preoccupied Wiesel: madness and sanity. For Wiesel, the insane are those who see the truth, while the sane commit the most horrible atrocities. Set almost entirely in an institution for the insane located in upstate New York, *Le Crépuscule au loin* depicts a typically Wieselian character, Raphael. He searches for a long-lost friend, Pedro, who, he has reason to believe, has disappeared into the catacombs of madness. Raphael has encounters with several madmen who imagine that they are biblical personages: Cain, Adam, Abraham, even God himself. As Raphael searches for his friend he slowly, meticulously unravels the mysteries of the past—his past—and also gains greater insight into human nature, at its loftiest and basest levels of conduct. As in so many Wiesel novels, past and present are confusingly, hauntingly interlaced.

In 1989 Wiesel published his highly popular and well-received novel *L'Oublié* (translated as *The Forgotten*, 1992). Once again his central theme is memory. The main character is a young American boy, Malkiel, who, like Wiesel's own son Elisha, is the son of a Holocaust survivor. Indefatigably the young man in the novel struggles to find his own identity by pressing his aging father to reveal his tragic experiences in the concentration camp and to explain the circumstances of the death of the boy's mother. Badly scarred physically and psychologically by the Holocaust, Malkiel's father has gradually been losing his ability to remember and especially to speak to his son. Eventually the latter is able to extract from the ashes of his father's tragic past enough data so that he can travel to the Old Country, visit the town where his father and mother had resided before their deportation by the Nazis, and eventually undergo a spiritual rebirth as he finally begins to appreciate the tribulations experienced by his parents.

By far the major literary undertaking by Wiesel during the 1990s was the completion of his memoirs, a massive two-volume compendium of his personal recollections, trials, tribulations, and triumphs of life. For his titles Wiesel borrows from the poetic language of the Book of Ecclesiastes in the Hebrew Bible: volume one is titled *Tous les fleuves vont à le mer: mémoires*, published in 1994 and translated as *All Rivers Run to the Sea: Memoirs* (1995); volume two is titled *Et la mer n'est pas remplie: memoires II* (And the Sea is not Full), published in 1996 and not yet translated into English. In the first volume Wiesel retraces his happy childhood

Dust jacket for the American edition of Wiesel's 1973 novel, Le Serment de Kolvillàg, *in which a sole survivor tells the story of his destroyed village*

in Sighet, his painful imprisonment in the death-camps, and the decade he spent in Paris, where he could reinvigorate his life by discovering his passion for writing. He also recounts his earliest literary successes and finally recaptures the scene of his marriage with Marion Wiesel in an ancient synagogue located in the Old City of Jerusalem.

In the second volume he reveals himself as a surprisingly feisty, even combative personality who expresses his disappointments with some of the people he knew well. Especially significant is his relationship with François Mitterrand, the late president of the French Republic, a relationship that, after five years of mutual admiration, culminated in a bitter rift after Wiesel had learned of Mitterrand's earlier involvement with a prominent French collaborator during the Nazi occupation of France. When the French president stubbornly refused to express his regret over this involvement, Wiesel candidly admitted his disillusionment with his former friend. With similar disapproval Wiesel describes his dismay that American president Ronald Reagan refused to be deterred, during a state visit to Germany, from visiting the Cemetery of Bitburg, a place where many Nazi SS stormtroopers were buried. Wiesel also betrays his keen disappointment with Simon Wiesenthal, the well-known Nazi hunter, who had steadfastly supported the cause of Kurt Waldheim, the former Austrian president and former secretary-general of the United Nations, who had been accused of cooperating with the Nazis in their campaign to destroy thousands of Jews from the Balkan region. Yet another former friend, Polish head of state Lech Walesa, did not do enough, in Wiesel's

judgment, to combat anti-Semitism in Poland. On a more cheerful note, the writer describes the great satisfaction felt by him during the ceremony in Oslo, Norway, when he received the Nobel Peace Prize.

In *Célébration prophétique: Portraits et légendes,* (Celebrating the Prophets: Portraits and Legends, not yet translated into English), published in 1998, the author provides his readers with a collection of chapters devoted to most of the major Jewish prophets in the Bible. Instead of dealing with these men and women as icons, Wiesel paints them as fairly ordinary human beings whose main uniqueness came from their ability to enter occasionally into face-to-face encounters with their God, especially as He ordered them to perform some sort of mission or deed that ultimately affected the destiny of the Jewish people.

One of the great events in Wiesel's life took place in July 1995 at the International Cultural Center of the chateau of Cerisy-La-Salle, Normandy, where a distinguished assemblage of Wiesel scholars and admirers gathered to read papers in Wiesel's presence concerning his many contributions as one of the world's leading messengers of human values. The week-long ceremony took place to commemorate the fiftieth anniversary of Wiesel's liberation from the Nazi concentration camps. The proceedings of the colloquium have since been published by Philippe-Michael de Saint-Cheron, the organizer of this multinational gathering.

Wiesel, whose residence is in New York City, continues to write and to study ancient Hebraic texts and classics of French literature. From 1972 to 1976

Wiesel and his wife, Marion, who has translated many of his books into English (Rosen/Sipa)

he taught Judaic studies at the City University of New York. He has spoken at forums and on university campuses around the world. Since 1976 Wiesel has been the Andrew Mellon Professor in the Humanities at Boston University and commutes every week between New York and Boston.

Among the many prizes he has received are the Martin Luther King Jr. Award; the William and Janice Epstein Fiction Award and the Frank and Ethel S. Cohen Award, both from the Jewish Book Council; the Remembrance Award; the National Jewish Book Award; and the Jewish Heritage Award for excellence in literature. In 1984 he was awarded the Congressional Gold Medal of Achievement. He has also been named commander of the French Légion d'Honneur. He has received honorary doctorates from many institutions, including Hebrew Union College, Manhattanville College, the Jewish Theological Seminary, Yeshiva University, Bar-Ilan University (Israel), Boston University, Hofstra University, Marquette University, and Yale University. He served presidents Jimmy Carter and Ronald Reagan as the chairman of the U.S. Holocaust Memorial Council.

If Wiesel had written only *La Nuit,* it would be sufficient to guarantee him a lasting place among the writers of the post-World War II era. A tiny classic, *La Nuit* is a tautly written, tensely expressed, yet glowingly human work that ranks with such books as Vercors's *Le Silence de la mer* (The Silence of the Sea, 1942). Yet Wiesel has since written more than forty other works—novels, essays, short stories, chronicles, testimonies—many of which are literary works of high or-

der. His novels, essays, and stories include resonances of Camus, André Malraux, and to a lesser extent, Jean-Paul Sartre and Mauriac. In his direct, relatively image-free, concise language, rich with meaning, he resembles the French classicists. Wiesel told John S. Friedman:

> I reduce nine hundred pages to one hundred sixty pages. I also enjoy cutting. I do it with a masochistic pleasure although even when you cut, you don't. Writing is not like painting where you add. It is not what you put on the canvas that the reader sees. Writing is more like sculpture where you remove, you eliminate in order to make the work visible. Even those pages you remove somehow remain.

Wiesel has not remained unaffected by the bold experiments that have taken place in French narrative writing since the advent of the *nouveaux romanciers.* Some of his novels depart from traditional chronological narrative to move forward and backward in time; they also include fragments of poetry, incantations, and often-dramatic shifts of points of view.

A compelling speaker, Wiesel leaves an indelible mark on all who have heard him. As chairman of the Nobel Committee, Egel Aarvik noted in naming Wiesel recipient of the 1986 Peace Prize: "Elie Wiesel has emerged as one of the most spiritual leaders and guides in an age when violence, repression and racism continue to characterize the world. . . . Wiesel is a messenger to Mankind. His message is one of peace, atonement, and human dignity. His belief that the forces fighting evil in the world can be victorious is a hard-won belief."

Interviews:

Gene Koppel and Henry Kaufmann, *Elie Wiesel: A Small Measure of Victory* (Tucson: University of Arizona Press, 1974);

Harry James Cargas, *Harry James Cargas in Conversation with Elie Wiesel* (New York: Paulist Press, 1976);

John K. Roth, *A Consuming Fire: Encounters with Elie Wiesel and the Holocaust* (Atlanta: John Knox, 1979);

John S. Friedman, "The Art of Fiction LXXIX: Elie Wiesel," *Paris Review,* 26 (Spring 1984): 130–178;

Brigitte-Fanny Cohen, *Elie Wiesel–Qui êtes-vous?* (Paris: La Manufacture, 1987);

Philippe-Michael de Saint-Cheron, *Le mal et l'exil: Rencontre avec Elie Wiesel* (Paris: Nouvelle Cité, 1988) translated by Jon Rothschild as *Evil and Exile* (Notre Dame, Ind.: University of Notre Dame Press, 1990);

David Patterson, *In Dialogue and Dilemma with Elie Wiesel* (Wakefield, N.H.: Longwood Academic, 1991);

Cargas, *Conversations with Elie Wiesel* (South Bend, Ind.: Justice Books, 1992);

Saloman Malka, *Monsieur Chouchani: L'énigme d'un maître du Xième siècle: entretiens avec Elie Wiesel*, (Paris: J. C. Lattaes, 1994).

Bibliography:

Molly Abramowitz, *Elie Wiesel: A Bibliography* (Metuchen, N.J.: Scarecrow Press, 1974).

Biography:

Philippe-Michael de Saint-Cheron, *Elie Wiesel: Pèlerin de la mémoire* (Paris: Plon, 1994).

References:

David Banon, *Présence d'Elie Wiesel* (Geneva: Editions Labor et Fides, 1990);

Michael Berenbaum, *Vision of the Void: Theological Reflections on the Works of Elie Wiesel* (Middletown, Conn.: Wesleyan University Press, 1979);

Robert McAfee Brown, *Elie Wiesel: Messenger to All Humanity* (Notre Dame, Ind.: University of Notre Dame Press, 1983);

Brown, "The Holocaust as a Problem in Moral Choice," in *Dimensions of the Holocaust: Lectures at Northwestern University* (Evanston, Ill.: The University, 1977), pp. 47–83;

Harry James Cargas, ed., *Responses to Elie Wiesel: Critical Essays by Major Jewish and Christian Scholars* (New York: Persea Books, 1978);

Cargas, ed., *Telling the Tale: A Tribute to Elie Wiesel on the Occasion of His 65th Birthday: Essays, Reflections, and Poems* (Saint Louis, Mo.: Time Being Books, 1993);

Colin Davis, *Elie Wiesel's Secretive Texts* (Gainesville: University Press of Florida, 1994);

Denis Diamond, "Elie Wiesel: Reconciling the Irreconcilable," *World Literature Today,* 57 (Spring 1983): 228–233;

Ted L. Estess, *Elie Wiesel* (New York: Frederick Ungar, 1980);

Ellen S. Fine, *Legacy of Night: The Literary Universe of Elie Wiesel* (Albany: State University of New York Press, 1982);

S. G. Freedman, "Bearing Witness: The Life and Work of Elie Wiesel," *New York Times Magazine,* 23 October 1983, pp. 32–36;

Joë Friedmann, *Le Rire dans l'univers tragique d'Elie Wiesel* (Paris: Nizet, 1982);

Maurice Friedman, *Abraham J. Heschel and Elie Wiesel, You are my Witnesses* (New York: Farrar, Straus & Giroux, 1987);

Christopher J. Frost, *Religious Melancholy or Psychological Depression: Some Issues Involved in Relating Psychology and Religion as Illustrated in a Study of Elie Wiesel* (Lanham, Md.: University Press of America, 1985);

Mary Jean Green, "Witness to the Absurd; Elie Wiesel and the French Existentialists," *Renascence,* 29 (Summer 1977): 170–184;

Carol Greene, *Elie Wiesel, Messenger from the Holocaust* (Chicago: Children's Press, 1987);

Irving Halperin, *Messengers from the Dead* (Philadelphia: Westminster Press, 1970), pp. 65–106;

Samuel H. Joseloff, "Link and Promise: The Works of Elie Wiesel," *Southern Humanities Review,* 8 (Spring 1974): 163–170;

Lawrence Langer, *The Holocaust and the Literary Imagination* (New Haven: Yale University Press, 1975), pp. 75–89;

Caroline Lazo, *Elie Wiesel* (New York: Dillon Press, 1994);

N. McCain, "Elie Wiesel: The Struggle to Reconcile the Reality of Evil with Faith in God," *Chronicle of Higher Education,* 13 April 1983, pp. 21–22;

Michael Pariser, *Elie Wiesel: Bearing Witness* (Brookfield, Conn.: Millbrook Press, 1994);

Wladimir Rabi, "Elie Wiesel: Un Homme, une oeuvre, un public," *Esprit,* no. 9 (1980): 79–92;

Carol Rittner, ed., *Elie Wiesel: Between Memory and Hope* (New York: New York University Press, 1990);

Alvin H. Rosenfeld and Irving Greenberg, eds., *Confronting the Holocaust: The Impact of Elie Wiesel* (Bloomington: Indiana University Press, 1978);

Philippe-Michael de Saint-Cheron, ed., *Autour de Elie Wiesel: Une parole pour l'avenir: Colloque de Cerisy* (Paris: Jacob, 1996);

Michael Schuman, *Elie Wiesel: Voice from the Holocaust* (Hillside, N.J.: Enslow, 1994);

Simon P. Sibelman, *Silence in the Novels of Elie Wiesel* (New York: St. Martin, 1995);

Ellen N. Stern, *Elie Wiesel: Witness for Life* (Hoboken, N.J.: Ktav, 1982);

Stern, *Elie Wiesel: A Voice for Humanity* (Philadelphia: Jewish Publication Society, 1996);

Graham B. Walker Jr., *Elie Wiesel: A Challenge to Theology* (Jefferson, N.C.: McFarland, 1988).

Richard Wilbur

This entry was updated by Richard J. Calhoun (Clemson University) from his entry in
DLB 169: American Poets Since World War II, Fifth Series.

See also the Wilbur entry in *DLB 5: American Poets Since World War II.*

BIRTH: New York, New York, 1 March 1921, to Lawrence Lazear and Helen Ruth Purdy Wilbur.

EDUCATION: A.B., Amherst College, 1942; A.M., Harvard University, 1947.

MARRIAGE: 20 June 1942 to Mary Charlotte Hayes Ward; children: Ellen Dickinson, Christopher Hayes, Nathan Lord, Aaron Hammond.

AWARDS AND HONORS: Harriet Monroe Memorial Prize, *Poetry* magazine, 1948 and 1978; Oscar Blumenthal Prize, *Poetry* magazine, 1950; honorary M.A., Amherst College, 1952; Guggenheim Fellowships, 1952–1953 and 1963; Prix de Rome fellowship, American Academy of Arts and Letters, 1954; Edna St. Vincent Millay Memorial Award, Pulitzer Prize for poetry, and National Book Award for poetry, all for *Things of This World,* 1957; Boston Festival Award, 1959; Ford Foundation fellowship for drama, 1960; Melville Cane Award, 1962; co-recipient, Bollingen Prize for translation, Yale University Library, for *Tartuffe,* 1963, and for poetry, for *Walking to Sleep,* 1971; Sarah Josepha Hale Award, 1968; Creative Arts Award, Brandeis University, 1971; Prix Henri Desfueilles, 1971; Shelley Memorial Award, 1973; *Book World* Children's Spring Book Festival award for *Opposites: Poems and Drawings,* 1973; PEN translation prize for *Moliere: Four Comedies,* 1983; St. Botolph's Club Foundation Award, 1983; Drama Desk Award, 1983; Chevalier, Ordre des Palmes Academiques, 1983; named Poet Laureate of the United States, Library of Congress, 1987–1988; Taylor Poetry Award, *Sewanee Review* and University of the South, 1988; Bunn Award, 1988; Washington College Literature Award, 1988; National Book Critics Circle Award nomination, 1988, *Los Angeles Times* Book Prize, 1988, and Pulitzer Prize for poetry, 1989, all for *New and Collected Poems;* St. Louis Literature Award, 1988; Gold Medal for poetry, American Academy and Institute of Arts and Letters, 1991; Edward MacDowell

Richard Wilbur (*photograph © 1986 Stathis Orphanos*)

medal, 1992; National Arts Club Medal of Honor for Literature, 1994; PEN/Manheim Medal for Translation, 1994; Milton Center prize, 1995; Robert Frost medal, Poetry Society of America, 1996; honorary degrees include L.H.D., Lawrence College (now Lawrence University of Wisconsin), 1960, Washington University, 1964, Williams College, 1975, University of Rochester, 1976, Carnegie-Mellon University, 1980, State University of New York, Potsdam, 1986, Skidmore College, 1987, University of Lowell, 1990; Litt.D., Amherst College, 1967, Clark University, 1970, American International College, 1974, Marquette University, 1977, Wesleyan University, 1977, and Lake Forest College, 1982.

BOOKS: *The Beautiful Changes and Other Poems* (New York: Reynal & Hitchcock, 1947);

Ceremony and Other Poems (New York: Harcourt, Brace, 1950);

Things of This World (New York: Harcourt, Brace, 1956);

Poems 1943–1956 (London: Faber & Faber, 1957);

Advice to a Prophet, and Other Poems (New York: Harcourt, Brace & World, 1961; London: Faber & Faber, 1962);

Loudmouse (New York: Crowell-Collier / London: Collier-Macmillan, 1963);

The Poems of Richard Wilbur (New York: Harcourt, Brace & World, 1963);

Walking to Sleep, New Poems and Translations (New York: Harcourt, Brace & World, 1969);

Opposites (New York: Harcourt Brace Jovanovich, 1973);

The Mind-Reader (New York & London: Harcourt Brace Jovanovich, 1976);

Responses, Prose Pieces: 1953–1976 (New York: Harcourt Brace Jovanovich, 1976);

New and Collected Poems (New York: Harcourt Brace Jovanovich, 1988);

More Opposites (New York: Harcourt Brace Jovanovich, 1991);

A Game of Catch (San Diego: Harcourt, Brace, 1994);

Runaway Opposites (San Diego: Harcourt, Brace, 1995);

The Catbird's Song: Prose Pieces, 1963–1995 (New York: Harcourt, Brace, 1997);

The Disappearing Alphabet (San Diego: Harcourt, Brace, 1998).

OTHER: "The Genie in the Bottle," in *Mid-Century American Poets,* edited by John Ciardi (New York: Twayne, 1950), pp. 1–13;

A Bestiary, compiled by Wilbur (New York: Spiral Press for Pantheon Books, 1955);

Candide: A Comic Operetta Based on Voltaire's Satire, lyrics by Wilbur (New York: Random House, 1957);

Poe: Complete Poems, edited, with an introduction, by Wilbur (New York: Dell, 1959);

Emily Dickinson: Three Views, by Wilbur, Archibald MacLeish, and Louise Bogan (Amherst, Mass.: Amherst College Press, 1960);

Paul Engle and Joseph Langland, eds., *Poet's Choice,* includes comment and poems by Wilbur (New York: Dial Press, 1962);

William Shakespeare, *Poems,* edited by Wilbur and Alfred Harbage (Baltimore: Penguin, 1966); revised and republished as *The Narrative Poems and Poems of Doubtful Authenticity* (Baltimore: Penguin, 1974);

Witter Bynner, *Selected Poems,* edited, with an introduction, by Wilbur (New York: Farrar, Straus & Giroux, 1978).

TRANSLATIONS: Molière, *The Misanthrope* (New York: Harcourt, Brace, 1955; London: Faber & Faber, 1958);

Molière, *Tartuffe: Comedy in Five Acts* (New York: Harcourt, Brace & World, 1963; London: Faber & Faber, 1964; bilingual edition, New York: Harcourt, Brace, 1997);

Molière, *The Misanthrope and Tartuffe* (New York: Harcourt, Brace & World, 1965);

Molière, *The School for Wives* (New York: Harcourt Brace Jovanovich, 1972);

Molière, *The Learned Ladies* (New York: Harcourt Brace Jovanovich, 1978);

Jean Racine, *Andromache* (New York: Harcourt Brace Jovanovich, 1982);

The Whale and Other Uncollected Translations (Brockport, N.Y.: Boa Editions, 1982);

Racine, *Phaedra: A Tragedy in Five Acts. 1677* (San Diego: Harcourt Brace Jovanovich, 1986);

Molière, *The School for Husbands: Comedy in Three Acts, 1661* (New York: Dramatists Play Service, 1991);

Molière, *The Imaginary Cuckold, or, Sganarelle* (New York: Dramatists Play Service, 1993);

Molière, *Amphitryon* (New York: Harcourt, Brace, 1995).

SELECTED PERIODICAL PUBLICATIONS–UNCOLLECTED: "Elizabeth Bishop," *Ploughshares,* 7 (1980): 1–14;

"Ash Wednesday," *Yale Review,* 78 (Winter 1989): 215–217.

Richard Wilbur has always been recognized as a major literary talent and as an important man of letters–poet, critic, translator, editor–even if he has never quite been ranked as one of the two or three best contemporary American poets. Early in his career he was overshadowed as a poet by Robert Lowell, who won the Pulitzer Prize for *Lord Weary's Castle* in 1947 (the year Wilbur's first book of poems, *The Beautiful Changes and Other Poems,* was published) and whose *Life Studies* (1959) was given principal credit for important new directions in poetry that Wilbur chose not to take. In the 1960s comparisons between Lowell and Wilbur as important new poets became comparisons between Lowell and James Dickey as the country's most important poets. Since the 1970s more critical attention has been given to such poets as John Ashbery, A. R. Ammons, James

Wright, W. S. Merwin, and James Merrill than to Wilbur.

For more than four decades Wilbur's poetry has remained much as it has always been—skilled, sophisticated, witty, and impersonal. In 1949, when Philip Rahv in *Image and Idea* divided American writers into two camps—"Palefaces," elegant and controlled, and "Redskins," intense and spontaneous—Wilbur was clearly a "Paleface." After Lowell made his break in 1959 with modernist impersonality in poetry, he revised Rahv's distinction in his National Book Award comments by specifying American poets as either "cooked" or "raw." Wilbur's "marvelously expert" poetry was undeniably one of the choice examples of "cooked" poetry. In *Waiting for the End* (1964), at a time when poetic styles were moving away from impersonality, Leslie A. Fiedler, one of the advocates of the reemergence of the "I" at the center of the poem and of a neo-Whitmanesque rejection of objectivity, found the influence of T. S. Eliot's formalistic theories especially strong on Wilbur: "There is no personal source anywhere, as there is no passion and no insanity; the insistent 'I,' the asserting of sex, and the flaunting of madness considered apparently in equally bad taste."

Wilbur has seldom likened his poetry to that of his contemporaries. Instead, in "On My Own Work," an essay collected in *Responses, Prose Pieces: 1953-1976* (1976), he described his art as "a public quarrel with the aesthetics of E. A. Poe," a writer on whom he has written some significant literary criticism. In Wilbur's view, Poe believed that the imagination must utterly repudiate the things of "this diseased earth." In contrast, Wilbur contends it is within the province of poems to make some order in the world while not allowing the reader to forget that there is a reality of things. Poets are not philosophers: "What poetry does with ideas is to redeem them from abstraction and submerge them in sensibility." Consequently, Wilbur's main concern is to maintain a difficult balance between the intellectual and the emotive, between an appreciation of the particulars of the world and their spiritual essence. If he is explicit in his prose about his quarrel with Poe, it might also be said that he had an implicit quarrel with the "raw" poetry in Donald Allen's *New American Poetry 1945-60,* an anthology recognized in the 1960s as a manifesto against the "academy," and also with the extremely personal, seemingly confessional poetry of Lowell, W. D. Snodgrass, and Anne Sexton. Wilbur as a poet clearly accepts the modernist doctrine of impersonality and does not advertise his personal life in his poetry. "I vote for obliquity and distancing in the use of one's own life, because I am a bit reserved and because I think these produce

Cover for Wilbur's first book, in which he expresses the need for a poet to have not only imagination but also contact with the physical world

a more honest and usable poetry," he commented in a 1967 questionnaire included in *Conversations with Richard Wilbur* (1990).

Richard Purdy Wilbur was born in New York City, one of two children of Lawrence Lazear and Helen Ruth Purdy Wilbur. His father was a portrait painter. When Wilbur was two years old, the family moved into a pre-Revolutionary War stone house in North Caldwell, New Jersey. Although not far from New York City, he and his brother, Lawrence, grew up in rural surroundings that, Wilbur later speculated, led to his love of nature.

Wilbur showed an early interest in writing, which he has attributed to his mother's family because her father was an editor of the *Baltimore Sun* and her grandfather was both an editor and a publisher of small papers aligned with the Democratic Party. At Montclair High School, from which he graduated in 1938, Wilbur wrote editorials for the school newspaper. At Amherst College he was editor of the campus newspaper, the *Amherst Student*. He also contributed stories and poems to the Amherst student magazine, the *Touchstone,* and considered a career in journalism.

Immediately after his college graduation in June 1942, Wilbur married Mary Charlotte Hayes Ward of Boston, an alumna of Smith College. Having joined the Enlisted Reserve Corps in 1942, he went on active duty in the army in 1943 in the midst of World War II. He served with the Thirty-sixth "Texas" Division in Italy at Monte Cassino and Anzio and then in Germany along the Siegfried Line. It was during the war that he began writing poems, intending, as he said in a 1964 interview with *The Amherst Literary Magazine* (borrowing Robert Frost's phrase), "a momentary stay against confusion" in a time of world disorder. When the war ended, he found himself with a drawer full of poems, only one of which had been published.

Wilbur went to Harvard for graduate work in English to become a college teacher. As he recalled in his 1964 Amherst interview, Wilbur decided to submit additional poems for publication only after a French friend read his manuscripts, "kissed me on both cheeks and said, 'you're a poet.'" In 1947, the year he received his A.M. from Harvard, his first volume of poems, *The Beautiful Changes and Other Poems,* was published.

The Beautiful Changes includes the largest number of poems (forty-two) and the smallest number of translations (three) of any of his collections. Although he began writing his poetry to relieve boredom while he was in the army, there are actually only seven war poems; and they are more poetic exercises on how to face the problems of disorder and destruction than laments over the losses occasioned by war, as in the traditions of the World War I British poet Wilfred Owen and the World War II American poet Randall Jarrell.

The first of Wilbur's war poems, "Tywater," presents the paradox of the violence illustrated in a Texas corporal's skill in killing the enemy–"The violent, neat, and practiced skill / Was all he loved and all he learned"–contrasted with the quietness of his death–"When he was hit, his body turned / To clumsy dirt before it fell." The compassion of Jarrell's war poetry is clearly missing. Instead there is an ironic detachment somewhat like John Crowe Ransom's but without the meticulous characterization that distinguishes Ransom's best poems:

And what to say of him, God knows.
Such violence. And such repose.

Another war poem, "First Snow in Alsace," suggests the theme implied by the title of the volume, *The Beautiful Changes.* The beautiful can change

man even in times of duress. War is horrible because man permits it in spite of such simple childlike pleasures as a night sentry on being "the first to see the snow." "On the Eyes of an SS Officer" is a poetic exercise on the extremes of fanaticism. Wilbur compares the explorer Roald Amundsen, a victim of the northern ice that he desired to conquer, and a "Bombay saint," blinded by staring at the southern sun, with an SS officer, a villain of the Holocaust. The SS officer in his fanaticism combines what is evident in the eyes of the first two fanatics, ice and fire, for his eyes are "iced or ashen." The persona stays detached and does not explicitly condemn this terrible kind of fanaticism. The poem ends a bit tamely with his request to "my makeshift God of this / My opulent bric-a-brac earth to damn his eyes."

If there is a prevailing theme in Wilbur's first volume, it is how the power of the beautiful to change can be used as a buttress against disorder. The initial poem, "Cicadas," suggests the necessity for and the beauty of mystery in nature. The song of the *cigale* (better known as the cicada) can change those who hear it, but the reason for the song is beyond the scientist's analytical abilities to explain. It is spontaneous, gratuitous, and consequently a mystery to be appreciated as an aesthetic experience and described by a poet in a spirit of celebration.

"Water Walker" postulates an analogy between man and the caddis flies, or "water walkers," which can live successfully in two elements, air and water. A human equivalent would be the two lives of Saint Paul, described as "Paulsaul." He serves as an example of a "water walker," a person who was converted from service in the material world to service in the spiritual but who remained capable of living in both. The speaker in this poem desires a similar balance between two worlds, material and spiritual; but he is kept from transcendence, like the larva of the caddis held in the cocoon, by the fear that he might be unable to return to the material world.

In his first book imagination is a creative force necessary to the poet, but Wilbur also touches on an important theme developed more thoroughly in his later poetry, the danger that the imagination may lead to actions based entirely on illusions. His interpretation of Eugène Delacroix's painting, the subject of the poem "The Giaour and the Pacha," seems to be that in his moment of victory the giaour realizes that by killing his enemy he will lose his main purpose in life, which has been based on a single desire that proves valueless and illusory.

Another poem, "Objects," stresses what is to become a dominant theme for Wilbur, the need for contact with the physical world. Unlike the gulls in the poem, the poet cannot be guided by instincts or imagination alone. His imagination requires something more tangible, physical objects from the real world. The poet must be like the Dutch realist painter Pieter de Hooch, who needed real objects for his "devout intransitive eye" to imagine the unreal. It is only through being involved in the real world that the "Cheshire smile" of his imagination sets him "fearfully free." The poet, like the painter, must appreciate the "true textures" of this world before he can imagine their fading away.

One of the best lyrics in the collection is "My Father Paints the Summer." It has an autobiographical basis because Wilbur's father was a painter, but it is not a personal poem. The lyric develops the second meaning implied by the title *The Beautiful Changes*—the existence of change, mutability. It praises the power of the artist to retain a heightened vision in a world of mutability. The last stanza begins with the kind of simple, graceful line that is to become characteristic of Wilbur at his best: "Caught Summer is always an imagined time." Again the concern is balance in the relationship of the imagination and the particulars, the physical things of this world. The imagination needs the particulars of a summer season, but the artist needs his imagination for transcendence of time, "to reach past rain and find / Riding the palest days / Its perfect blaze."

The title poem of the volume is also the concluding poem and serves at this stage of Wilbur's poetic career as an example of his growing distrust of Poe-like romantic escapes into illusion and of his preference for a firm grasp of reality enhanced by the imagination. In "The Beautiful Changes" Wilbur gives four examples of how the beautiful can change: the effect of Queen Anne's lace on a fall meadow, the change brought about by the poet's love, a chameleon's change in order to blend in with the green of the forest, and the special beauty that a mantis, resting on a green leaf, has for him. The beautiful changes itself to harmonize with its environment, but it also alters the objects that surround it. The ultimate change described is the total effect of the changes of nature on the beholder, worded in Wilbur's most polished lyric manner:

> it turns
> Dry grass to a lake, as the slightest shade of you
> Valleys my mind in fabulous blue Lucernes.

Wilbur's first volume was generally well received by the reviewers, and it was evident that a new poet of considerable talent had appeared on the postwar scene. Many of his first poems had a common motive, the desire to stress the importance of

Cover for Wilbur's third volume of poetry, in which he continues to emphasize the poet's need for connection to reality

finding order in a world where war had served as a reminder of disorder and destruction. There were also the first versions of what was to become a recurring theme: the importance of a balance between reality and dream, of things of this world enhanced by imagination.

Wilbur spent three years between the publication of his first volume of poetry in 1947 and the appearance of his second in 1950 as a member of the Society of Fellows at Harvard, working on studies of the dandy and Poe that he never completed. What he did complete, though, was *Ceremony and Other Poems* (1950), continuing his concern with the need for a delicate balance between the material and the spiritual, the real and the ideal. In finding order in a world of disorder, poetry as celebration of nature is a "Ceremony," something aesthetically and humanly necessary. The concept of mutability, secondary in his first volume, is now primary, leading to a consideration of death, both as the ultimate threat of disorder and chaos and as motivation for creating order in the human realm. One of the poems concerned with facing death has come to be among Wilbur's most frequently anthologized poems, "The Death of a Toad." Wilbur finds in the toad a symbol for primal life energies accidentally and absurdly castrated by a tool of modern man, a power mower. The toad patiently and silently awaits his death with his "wide and antique eyes" observing this world that has cost him his heart's blood. His antiquity mocks a modern world that is already in decline.

"Year's-End," another poem on the threat of death, even more clearly contrasts the death of natural things, in their readiness to accept it, and the incompleteness and discord that death brings in the human realm. A dog that "slept the deeper as the ashes rose" is contrasted with "the loose unready eyes / of men expecting yet another sun / To do the shapely thing they had not done." This poem demonstrates Wilbur's skill in describing objects but also reveals his sometimes functional, sometimes not, desire to pun. Some reviewers found the first line of the poem to be Wilbur close to his worst: "Now winter downs the dying of the year." In contrast, his description of winter is Wilbur near his best:

> I've known the wind by water banks to shake
> The late leaves down, which frozen where they fell
> And held in ice as dancers in a spell
> Fluttered all winter long into a lake.

"Lament" is a poem about death, about expressing regret that the particulars of the world, what is "visible and firm," must vanish. This time a pun is functional: "It is, I say, a most material loss." "Still, Citizen Sparrow" is one of Wilbur's best known poems and, along with "Beowulf," introduces a new and important theme: whether heroism is possible in a world of disorder. In "Beowulf" the stress is on the loneliness and isolation of the hero. In "Still, Citizen Sparrow," in contrast to the common citizens (the sparrows), the hero appears as "vulture," a creature the sparrows must learn to appreciate. The poem is tonally complex, beginning as an argument between Citizen Sparrow and the poet over a political leader as a vulture and ending with an argument for seeing the faults of leaders in a broader perspective because they perform essential services, accept the risks of action, and are capable of dominating existence. The "vulture" is regarded as heroic because he is capable of heroic action: he feeds on death, "mocks mutability," and "keeps nature new." Wilbur concludes: "all men are Noah's sons" in that they potentially have the abilities of the hero if they will take the risks.

Another poem, "Driftwood," illustrates what some of Wilbur's early reviewers saw as a possible influence of Marianne Moore: finding a symbol or emblem in something so unexpected that the choice seems whimsical. In this poem the driftwood becomes an emblem for survival with an identity. It has "long revolved / In the lathe of all the seas." It is isolated but has retained its "ingenerate grain."

In Wilbur's second volume, as in his first, the need for a balance between the real and the ideal that avoids illusions and escapism is a significant theme. In "Grasse: The Olive Trees" the town in its abundance exceeds the normal and symbolizes reaching beyond the usual limits of reality, the overabundance of the South, that can become enervating and illusionary:

> and all is full
> Of heat and juice and a heavy jammed excess.
>
> Whatever moves moves with the slow
>   complete
> Gestures of statuary.

Only the "unearthly pale" of the olive represents the other pole of the reality principle and "Teaches the South it is not paradise."

"La Rose des Vents" is the first dialogue poem for Wilbur, a dialogue between a lady and the poet in a format reminiscent of Wallace Stevens's "Sunday Morning." The lady argues for the sufficiency of accepting the reality of objects, while the poet desires symbols removed from reality. In Wilbur's version the lady has the last word:

> Forsake those roses
> Of the mind
> And tend the true,
> The mortal flower.

"'A World without Objects Is a Sensible Emptiness'" is a poem with perhaps the quintessential Wilbur title. Visions, illusions, and oases are the objects of quests for people in a wasteland world, but the questing spirit, "The tall camels of the spirit," must also have the necessary endurance to turn back to the things of this world as a resource:

> Turn, O turn
> From the fine sleights of the sand, from the long
>   empty oven
> Where flames in flamings burn
>
>   Back to the trees arrayed
>   In bursts of glare, to the halo-dialing run
> Of the country creeks, and the hills' bracken
>   tiaras made
> Gold in the sunken sun[.]

Extravagant claims are made for visions that are firmly based on life. A supernova can be seen "burgeoning over the barn," and "Lampshine blurred in the steam of beasts" can be "light incarnate."

In *Ceremony* Wilbur exhibits greater versatility than is evident in his first book. He can now express his major themes in lighter poems, even in epigrams. The importance of a delicate balance between idealism and empiricism, speculation and skepticism, is concisely and wittily expressed in the two couplets of "Epistemology." Samuel Johnson is told to "Kick at the rock" in his rejection of Berkeleyan idealism, but the rock is also a reminder of the molecular mysteries within it: "But cloudy, cloudy is the stuff of stones." Man's occasional denials of the physical world he so desperately needs are mocked in the second couplet:

> We milk the cow of the world, and as we do
> We whisper in her ear, "You are not true."

With the appearance of his second book of poems, Wilbur was appointed an assistant professor of English at Harvard, where he remained until 1954, living in Lincoln, Massachusetts, with his wife and four children—Ellen Dickinson, Christopher Hayes, Nathan Lord, and Aaron Hammond. He spent the academic year of 1952–1953 in New Mexico on a Guggenheim Fellowship to write a poetic drama. When his attempts at a play did not work out to his satisfaction, he turned to translating Molière's *Le Misanthrope* instead, beginning his distinguished career as a translator. A grant of $3,000, the Prix de Rome, permitted Wilbur to live at the American Academy in Rome in 1954. After his return to America his translation, *The Misanthrope* (1955), was published and performed at the Poets' Theatre in Cambridge, Massachusetts.

In 1954 Wilbur was appointed an associate professor of English at Wellesley College, where he taught until 1957. His third volume of poetry, *Things of This World,* was published in 1956. In his September 1956 review of the collection for *Poetry* magazine, Donald Hall concluded: "The best poems Wilbur has yet written are in this volume." His judgment was confirmed, as the collection remains Wilbur's most honored book; it received the Edna St. Vincent Millay Memorial Award, the National Book Award, and the Pulitzer Prize. The same year the musical version of Voltaire's *Candide* (1759), with lyrics by Wilbur, book by Lillian Hellman, and a score by Leonard Bernstein, was produced at the Martin Beck Theatre in New York City.

Three poems in *Things of This World* should certainly be ranked among Wilbur's best, "A Baroque Wall-Fountain in the Villa Sciarra," "Love Calls Us to the Things of This World," and "For the New Railway Station in Rome." The last two reveal the influence of his year spent in Rome. As the title would suggest, there is even a greater stress on the importance of the use of the real in the poems in this volume. If the imagination does create a world independent of objects, it is made clear in "Love Calls Us to the Things of This World" that love always brings one back to the world of objects. Even nuns move away from pure vision back to the impure, "keeping their difficult balance."

It is not always the simpler forms that are the most inspiring. Wilbur remarked in the anthology *Poet's Choice* (1962) that "A Baroque Wall-Fountain in the Villa Sciarra" was based on his daily observation of a "charming sixteenth- or seventeenth-century fountain that appeared to me the very symbol or concretion of Pleasure." The elaborate baroque fountain is described as an artistic embodiment of the pleasure principle. Human aspiration may be more clearly seen in the simpler Maderna fountains, but the elaborate forms on the baroque fountain:

> They are at rest in fulness of desire
>   For what is given, they do not tire
> Of the smart of the sun, the pleasant water-douse
>
>   And riddled pool below,
> Reproving our disgust and our ennui
>   With humble insatiety.

It is indicative of Wilbur's penchant for impersonality that he ends the poem not by indicating the personal delight he feels in the fountain but by imagining what Saint Francis of Assisi might have seen in the fountain: "No trifle, but a shade of bliss."

The final poem in the volume is one of the best, "For the New Railway Station in Rome." The impressive new station becomes a symbol of how man's mind must continually work on things of this world for the imagination to have the power to recreate and to cope with disorder:

> "What is our praise or pride
> But to imagine excellence, and try to make it?
>   What does it say over the door of Heaven
>   But *homo fecit*?"

Donald L. Hill has said of Wilbur's early poetry that he has seemingly taken William Carlos Williams's slogan "No ideas but in things" and altered it to "No things but ideas." Beginning with his third volume, *Things of This World,* Wilbur still recognizes the importance of the imagination, but his emphasis has clearly shifted toward Williams's concept in his stress on the need for things of this world, both for effective endurance in a world of death and disorder and for creativity.

In 1957 Wilbur began a twenty-year tenure as professor of English at Wesleyan University and as adviser for the Wesleyan Poetry Series. He also received a Ford Foundation grant in drama and worked with the Alley Theater in Houston. *Advice to a Prophet, and Other Poems,* his fourth book of poetry, was published in 1961. It is a larger volume of poetry than *Things of This World,* with thirty-two poems, including four translations and a passage translated from Molière's *Tartuffe* (1664), as well as "Pangloss's Song" from the comic-opera version of Voltaire's *Candide.* The collection received favorable comments from such critics as Babette Deutsch, Dudley Fitts, M. L. Rosenthal, William Meredith, and Reed Whittemore. However, the praise for *Advice to a Prophet* was tempered by criticisms that it had an academic, privileged, even ivory-tower perspective. The title poem is vaguely topical, suggesting the threat of the ultimate atomic holocaust that became a near reality in October 1962 with the Cuban Missile Crisis. Even here Wilbur might be accused of aesthetic detachment: his poem is not humanistic in its concerns but aesthetic and phenomenological, envisioning a world without its familiar objects, without things rather than without people:

> Nor shall you scare us with talk of the death of the race.
> . . . .
> Ask us, ask us whether with the worldless rose
> Our hearts shall fail us[.]

Perhaps still showing the influence of Marianne Moore's passion for oddities, Wilbur stresses in this volume what the imagination can do with apparently mundane things. In "Junk" he suggests that intimations of the ideal can be found in the rubbish, the junk of the world, and in "Stop," in the grim everyday objects at a train stop. In "A Hole in the Floor" Wilbur even compares the potentials of his discoveries in the floor with those of a great archeologist: "As Schliemann stood when his shovel / Knocked on the crowns of Troy."

In "A Grasshopper" Wilbur adds to the poetic bestiary that he had collected in his volume *A Bestiary* (1955). He admires the grasshopper for having achieved a delicate balance between stasis in its pause on a chicory leaf and action in its springs from the leaf. Hall in his *Contemporary American Poetry* (1962) calls the poem "a minor masterpiece," but some reviewers believed that Wilbur seemed too content with "minor masterpieces," both in form and in subject matter. He showed an unwillingness to undertake major experi-

ments in form or to introduce new and socially relevant subject matter at a time when that was becoming expected. To some reviewers and critics, he seemed a poet reluctant to take risks of any sort. In fairness one must say that Wilbur does experiment with "new" lines in his poetry, such as his use of the Anglo-Saxon alliterative line in "Junk." However, in comparison with what such poets as Lowell and John Berryman were then doing, the experimentation is comparatively minor.

Wilbur seemed almost to be writing his poems in a cultural and political vacuum. By the time of the publication of *Advice to a Prophet* the tremendous impact that Lowell had made in *Life Studies* by apparently confessing disorder in his own family life had been felt. Two years after *Life Studies* Wilbur opened his volume with what he intended to be a dramatic poem, "Two Voices in a Meadow," a dialogue between two objects from the world of the mundane, a milkweed and a stone. The drama in this poem and in the title poem, "Advice to a Prophet," seemed humanly insignificant compared to Lowell's more personal approach. Wilbur seemed to fail in his attempts to indicate more dramatically and more positively how order might be restored and what his personal "stays against confusion" are, much as Robinson Jeffers's attempt at a tragic poetry had failed before, because he seems too exclusively concerned with symbolic things rather than with people. Wilbur's message appears to be that when man becomes more familiar with the world's own change, he can deal with his own problems as something related to the reality of things. Wilbur calls those who do not respond to the things of this world, those who prefer their dreams and who move to illusions, "the Undead"–vampires.

In "Shame" Wilbur defines the kind of human behavior that disturbs him–irresoluteness, a failure to deal with reality. He attempts to provide positive examples of heroic behavior, but he fails to create convincing examples as Lowell does with his symbol of the mother skunk, "refusing to scare," in "Skunk Hour." In Wilbur's dialogue poem "The Aspen and the Stream," the aspen is the positive heroic example because it seems to escape its existence by delving into flux, experience–symbolized by the dream–even if the result is only "a few more aspen-leaves."

It was eight years before Wilbur's fifth volume of poetry, *Walking to Sleep,* appeared in 1969. In the interim he published a children's book, *Loudmouse* (1963); his collected poems, *The Poems of Richard Wilbur* (1963); and his translation of Molière's *Tartuffe* (1963), which earned him an award as corecipient of the Bollingen Prize for translation. The Lincoln Center Repertory Theatre brought his translation of *Tartuffe* to the stage in New York City in 1964. *Walking to*

Sleep is a slim collection, with fewer original poems (only twenty-two) and more translations (eleven) than in previous collections. What overall unity there is in the four sections of the volume is suggested by the title: these are poems on the subject of how to "walk"–symbolically, how to live before sleep and death.

As in "Junk," Wilbur experiments with the Anglo-Saxon alliterative line divided by a caesura. In "The Lilacs" the flowers are used as a symbol of the cycle of death and rebirth, the "pure power" of nature perhaps compensating for the "depth" of death. The poem concludes:

> These lacquered leaves
> > where the light paddles
> And the big blooms
> > buzzing among them
> Have kept their counsel,
> > conveying nothing
> Of their mortal message,
> > unless one should measure
> The depth and dumbness
> > of death's kingdom
> By the pure power
> > of this perfume.

A kind of balance between life and death may be seen if one can appreciate "the pure power" of life. "In the Field," the title poem of the first section, also suggests that the power in life may be sufficient to compensate for the ultimate disorder, death. Wilbur finds in the field "the heart's wish for life, . . . staking here / In the least field an endless claim." And he believes that the same principle is in man. It "is ourselves, and is the one / Unbounded thing we know."

Wilbur also believes that in man's desires lies the answer to his questions. "Running" is, like "In the Field," a longer poem than Wilbur usually writes. It is divided into three parts and describes the act of running at three different times in the poet's life. The poem is intended not only as an affirmative statement about human aspiration but also as an assertion of the ultimate meaning of human activities. Wilbur's running becomes a symbol of aspiration at different stages in life. What keeps man running? It is human aspiration:

> What is the thing which men will not surrender?
> It is what they have never had, I think,
> Or missed in its true season[.]

"Running" is by Wilbur's own admission one of his most personal poems. It also implies the middle-aged poet's belief that his own life is satisfying and worthwhile.

Wilbur in the 1960s

The title poem, "Walking to Sleep," begins with a discussion of going to sleep that soon becomes a meditation on how to live and a warning against a life of illusion. It is also an argument for accepting death without illusions by literally staring it down. This piece might be regarded as a climactic poem on a major thematic concern. What is recommended is once again a balance, a life in which reality and "strong dream" work together.

One of the few poems in the volume to be almost immediately anthologized, "Playboy" describes the imaginative response of an adolescent stockboy to the impact of a centerfold in *Playboy* showing a beautiful naked woman. "High on his stockroom ladder like a dunce," he examines "her body's grace," engrossed in "how the cunning picture holds her still / At just that smiling instant when her soul, / Grown sweetly faint, and swept beyond control, / Consents to his inexorable will."

Other poems are also atypical of Wilbur's usual themes. He even includes a protest poem addressed to President Lyndon Johnson; the occasion is not the Vietnam War but Johnson's refusing the official portrait painted by the artist Peter Hurd. The protest is more artistic than political. The poem makes a contrast between Johnson and the culture of Thomas Jefferson, with his Rotunda and "Palestrina in his head."

Although the poems were published in the midst of the Vietnam vortex, Wilbur is once again primarily concerned with maintaining "a difficult balance" between reality and the ideal as the way to personal fulfillment.

Wilbur's sixth volume of poetry, *The Mind-Reader* (1976), includes twenty-seven new poems (nine previously published in *The New Yorker*) and nine translations. The reviews were again mixed, with some reviewers praising his craftsmanship and defending him from what they regarded as unfair attacks on his conservatism as a poet; others found his new volume to be simply more of the same and lamented his not taking risks by seeking new directions. The translations provide new examples of Wilbur's superb ability to translate from the French and the Russian, especially the poems by Andrei Voznesensky.

There are new things in the volume, especially in Wilbur's clearly discernible movement toward simpler diction and more-direct poems. Except for the title poem, there are no long poems in this book. Wilbur seems to enjoy working with shorter poems, as in the six-line, three-couplet "To the Etruscan Poets," on the theme of mutability exemplified by the Etruscan poets, who "strove to leave some line of verse behind / . . . / Not reckoning that all could melt and go."

Some reviewers found "Cottage Street, 1953" to be provocative. It is an account of Wilbur's meeting a young Sylvia Plath and her mother at the home of his mother-in-law, Edna Ward. A contrast is made between Plath's destructive tendencies and Ward's power of endurance. A few reviewers read the poem as if it were a personal attack on Plath by a poet hostile to confessional poetry. The poem is undoubtedly intended as a variation on Wilbur's theme of a need for balance, which he later came to realize that Plath had always lacked. He opposes love as a principle of order to the "brilliant negative" of Plath in her life. What makes this poem exceptional is that Wilbur is dealing with real people characterized rather brilliantly:

> And Edna Ward shall die in fifteen years,
> After her eight-and-eighty summers of
> Such grace and courage as permit me no tears,
> The thin hand reaching out, the last word *love*,
>
> Outliving Sylvia, who, condemned to live,
> Shall study for a decade, as she must,
> To state at last her brilliant negative
> In poems free and helpless and unjust.

In this poem Wilbur deals with the human problem of survival and death without his usual detachment and with a directness his poems usually lack.

More representative of his usual type of poem is "A Black Birch in Winter." It could have appeared in any of Wilbur's first five volumes. A symbol (the black birch) is found for nature's ability to survive and grow to greater wisdom each year. Except for slightly simpler diction, the poem is a variation on a usual theme, and the conclusion seems a parody of the conclusion of Alfred Tennyson's "Ulysses":

> Old trees are doomed to annual rebirth,
> New wood, new life, new compass, greater girth,
> And this is all their wisdom and their art—
> To grow, stretch, crack, and not yet come apart.

One poem would seem on the surface to be atypical, Wilbur taking the unusual risk of involving his poetry in the political protest against the war in Vietnam. "For the Student Strikers" was written for the Wesleyan Strike News at the time of the Kent State shootings. Wilbur's support is not, however, for student protests but for their canvassing programs, house-to-house visits to discuss the student point of view about the war. Typically, he urges dialogue—order—instead of protests—disorder:

> It is not yet time for the rock, the bullet, the blunt
> Slogan that fuddles the mind toward force.
> Let the new sound in our streets be the patient sound
> Of your discourse.

There is an evident difference in emotional perspective, in dramatic intensity, and in contemporary relevance between Wilbur in this poem and Lowell in *Notebook 1967–68*.

Whereas Lowell, Sexton, Snodgrass, Plath, and even Dickey have told much about their families, until *The Mind-Reader* Wilbur did not mention his family. Two poems about his children mark a change. His son Christopher's wedding is described indirectly in "A Wedding Toast," and "The Writer" is one of Wilbur's most personal poems and perhaps one of his best. As a father and as a writer he empathizes with his daughter's attempts to write a story. He describes her creative struggles "In her room at the prow of the house," and he is reminded of another struggle that he saw before at the same window:

> I remember the dazed starling
> Which was trapped in that very room, two years ago;
> How we stole in, lifted a sash
>
> And retreated, not to affright it;
> And how for a helpless hour, through the crack of the door,
> We watched the sleek, wild, dark
>
> And iridescent creature
> Batter against the brilliance, drop like a glove
> To the hard floor, or the desk-top.

14

The opposite of *robber*? Come,
You know the answer. Don't be dumb!
While robbers *take things* for a living,
Philanthropists are fond of *giving.*
"And yet," you say, "that's not quite true;
Philanthropists are takers, too,
And often have been very greedy
Before they thought to help the needy."

Well, let's be obvious, then: the op-
Posite of *robber* is a *cop.*

Page from More Opposites *(1991), one of Wilbur's volumes of light verse, with illustrations by Wilbur*

Wilbur's slightly more personal approach is apparent in a few other poems. The engaging persona Wilbur creates in the title poem, "The Mind-Reader," helps that poem achieve more dramatic intensity than is apparent in much of his earlier work. He seems to be seeking even firmer and more affirmative statements of the need for order and responsibility, and his tone in these poems is more confident, as if he is assured that his own artistic life has been worthwhile, that he has himself maintained a balance between reality and imagination. Wilbur's perspective is concisely stated in "C-Minor," a poem about switching off "Beethoven at breakfast" to turn back to the reality of the day:

There is nothing to do with a day except to live it.
Let us have music again when the light dies
(Sullenly, or in glory) and we can give it
    Something to organize.

In 1977 Wilbur moved to Smith College, where he remained as writer in residence until his retirement in 1986. While continuing his translating of Molière's work, he also produced translations of Jean Racine's *Andromache* (1982) and *Phaedra* (1986). In 1987 Wilbur was honored by an appointment as poetry consultant at the Library of Congress and poet laureate.

New and Collected Poems (1988) earned Wilbur the Pulitzer Prize for poetry in 1989. The new poems include twenty-six short lyrics and "On Freedom's Ground," the lyrics for a five-part cantata by William Schuman. This long poem was a joint project written to mark the refurbishing of the Statue of Liberty on its centennial in 1987. Wilbur may have had in mind memories of Robert Frost's impromptu reciting of "The Gift Outright" at the John F. Kennedy inauguration, for he offers a variation of Frost's theme that Americans have gradually become worthy of the land:

> We are immigrants still, who travel in time,
> Bound where the thought of America beckons;
> But we hold our course, and the wind is with us.

In several of the newly collected poems Wilbur creates a persona who ruminates on his life and achievement. He clearly has Frost in mind in "The Ride," an extension of "Stopping by Woods on a Snowy Evening" in which the journey of the rider and his horse continues through the night: "The horse beneath me seemed / To know what course to steer / Through the horror of snow I dreamed, / And so I had no fear." The poem seems a consummation of a life-journey of creating and drawing on intuitions and dreams that one must believe in or fall victim to the grief that comes from thinking "there was no horse at all." "Leaving" is an indictment of the comforts in modern life. The people at a garden party resemble the stone figures that border the scene. The question raised is whether or not knowledge of the future would have influenced the people's decisions in life:

> Filling our selves as sculpture
> Fills the stone.
> We had not played so surely,
> Had we known.

"For W. H. Auden" is a poem written earlier and published only when Wilbur thought it was finished. It is an impressive poem on lost moments in memory as much as a personal lament for Auden:

> Of all these noted in stride and detained in memory
> I now know better that they were going to die,
>
> Since you, who sustained the civil tongue
> In a scattering time, and were poet of all our cities,
> Have for all your clever difference quietly left us,
> As we might have known that you would, by that common
>   door.

In "Lying" Wilbur begins by lightly invoking a "dead party," where a white lie "can do no harm" to one's reputation. The poem evolves more seriously as the speaker explores the nature of lying and

reality, the imagination and illusionary truth: "What is it, after all, but something missed?" Wilbur offers John Milton's Satan as the

> arch-negator, sprung
> From Hell to probe with intellectual sight
> The cells and heavens of a given world
> Which he could take but as another prison[.]

He then turns the poem to the ordinary experiences of a summer's day metaphorically likened to all days: "It is a chant / Of the first springs, and it is tributary / To the great lies told with the eyes half-shut / That have the truth in view." The poem concludes by alluding to *The Song of Roland,* implying the superiority of the lie of the romance to the ordinary fact of history, as Roland "Was faithful unto death, and shamed the Devil."

Wilbur's long tenure in academia is still evident in some poems. "A Finished Man" is a portrait, perhaps wryly autobiographical, of a man who has completed his career and is being honored by the university. The enemies, friends, and colleagues who knew his fears and faults now either dead or fading in his memory, the honoree is nearly "finished"–"If the dead die, if he can but forget, / If money talks, he may be perfect yet." "Icarium Mare" is clearly an academic poem, with arcane references to the mythical figure Icarus, the Greek astronomer Aristarchus of Samos, and St. John the Divine's "geodic skull."

The short poems in the "New Poems" section often seem to be merely sketches, but there is always depth to a Wilbur surface. "Wyeth's Milk Cans" records the lucid simplicity of an Andrew Wyeth scene but at the same time raises doubts about the beauty of the landscape. "Shad-Time" examines two events, the spawning of shad and the blooming of the shadblow tree along the banks of a river, and raises the old question anew of how to make sense of nature's bounty and waste. The critic Bruce Michelson judges this poem to be proof that Wilbur could produce a postmodernist poem that goes beyond skillful play and raises uncomfortable questions about the self and the world.

Despite Wilbur's achievement as a poet and his many awards, including the Gold Medal for poetry from the American Academy and Institute of Arts and Letters in 1991, many critics would argue that he has not become the major poet he seemed destined to be when *Things of This World* was so celebrated. Even if this arguable judgment is accepted, Wilbur's poetry alone is not the measure of his significance as a man of letters. For a balanced view of his literary importance it should be acknowledged that he is a discerning critic and an accomplished translator of poetry and drama in verse. Wilbur's view of translating is unquestionably an extension of his poetry writing. Viewing translation as a craft, he has consistently set for himself the goal of authenticity in translating not just the language but the verse forms as well. The importance of including Wilbur's translations in an evaluation of his talents as a poet has been neatly summed up by Raymond Oliver: "His degree of accuracy is almost always very high and his technical skill as a poet is just about equal to that of the people he translates." Wilbur's versions of Molière's works not only read well as verse but also have been staged with great success. He has followed success in comedy with highly regarded translations in the 1980s of two of Racine's tragedies.

Wilbur has also had considerable importance as a literary critic. He has written perceptively on his poetic opposite, Edgar Allan Poe, and he has delivered a major essay on Emily Dickinson. He has edited the poems of Poe and coedited the poems of William Shakespeare. The sixteen reviews and critical essays collected in *Responses, Prose Pieces: 1953–1976* (1976) and the interviews and conversations in *Conversations with Richard Wilbur* show Wilbur's perception of other writers as well as of his own work. His insights into his own work compare in quality, if not quite in quantity, with Dickey's attempts in *Self-Interviews* (1970) and *Sorties* (1971) to describe his own creativity.

If Wilbur has been fittingly acclaimed as a lyric poet and as an outstanding translator of French drama into readable and stageworthy English, his 1997 collection of prose pieces, *The Catbird's Song,* validates what the 1976 volume, *Responses,* should have suggested. Wilbur should now be acknowledged as one of the few remaining accomplished poet-critics, perhaps the best since Jarrell. His critical volumes are not collections of formal essays but rather what used to be called miscellanies. They are literally responses to requests, "prose products of a poet's life." The sixteen items in the first volume and the twenty-two in the later include reviews, explications, introductions, a symposium statement, an interview, and "the anecdotal letter." Wilbur's introductions to his translations of Molière and Racine are not reprinted here, but he does include two substantial essays on the art of translation. He also adds to his reputation as a Poe scholar and critic by continuing his "quarrel'" with Poe in an explication of the 1842 story "Eleonora" and in a perceptive commentary on "the art of suggestion" in Poe. His comments on May Swenson, John Ciardi, and Robert Francis might make the reader wish that

Wilbur had written more about his contemporaries. He does include an interview about "Cottage Street, 1953," his sensitive poem on his encounter with Plath. The descriptive title of *The Catbird's Song* suggests responses from "the catbird's seat," a position of prominence anticipated for a man of letters.

Certainly, a trenchant defense of Wilbur as a poet is to be made on the grounds that many critics have overlooked the stylistic and tonal complexities of his poetry, much as the New Critic formalists had earlier failed to recognize complexities in Frost, a poet Wilbur has always admired. Wilbur has evidenced a craftsman's interest in a wide variety of poetry—dramatic, lyric, meditation, and light verse. His wit, especially his skillful rhymes and the puns found even in his serious poetry, has not always been treated kindly by critics, but it has often captivated readers. He has been recognized by children's literature specialists for his volumes of light verse—*Loudmouse, Opposites* (1973), *More Opposites* (1991), and *Runaway Opposites* (1995)—all written with grace, wit, and humor.

The Disappearing Alphabet (1998) is Wilbur's most notable contribution to children's literature, featuring a felicitous blend of instruction and humor. Before book publication Wilbur offered individual poems at public readings with appreciable success, providing a change of pace from lyric seriousness to witty wordplay. Like the best of children's verse, these poems were distinctly not intended to be enjoyed only by children. The twenty-six poems, one for each letter of the alphabet, pose an engaging question: what would be the loss for meaningful communication if the alphabet began to disappear letter by letter? The response is that humans as verbal creatures are dependent on words and ultimately on each letter of the alphabet for verbal communication. As read, these poems verified Wilbur's linguistic dexterity; as a book, they offer further evidence of his versatility and skill as a composer of children's verse.

In "The Genie in the Bottle," published in Ciardi's *Mid-Century Poets* (1950), Wilbur identified what has remained his constant goal as a poet, whatever type of poem he has written: "The poem is an effort to articulate relationships not quite seen, to make or discover some pattern in the world. It is conflict with disorder." Wilbur's confrontation with disorder has led him to be satisfied with established patterns and traditional themes, old ways to solve old problems. Consistently a poet of affirmation, he has reacted against the two extremes of disorder: chaos and destruction on the one hand and illusions and escapism on the other. His response as both poet and humanist is to maintain a firm focus on re-

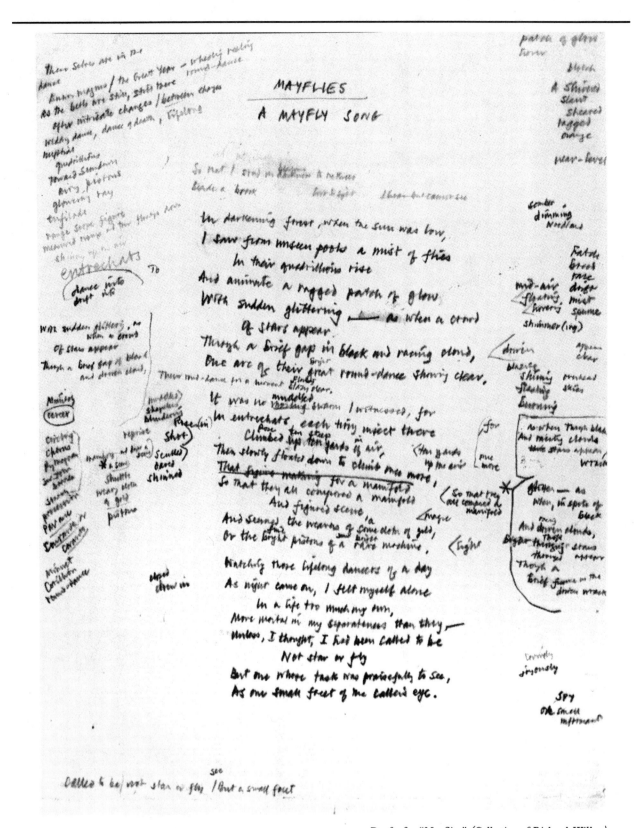

Drafts for "Mayflies" (Collection of Richard Wilbur)

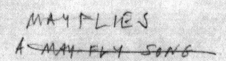

MAYFLIES
A ~~MAY-FLY SONG~~

In somber forest, when the sun was low,
I saw from unseen pools a mist of flies
    In their quadrillions rise
And animate a ragged patch of glow
With sudden glittering — as when a crowd
      Of stars appear
Through a brief gap in black and driven cloud,
One arc of their great round-dance showing clear.

It was no muddled swarm I witnessed, for
In *entrechats* each tiny insect there
     Rose ten steep yards in air,
Then slowly floated down to climb once more,
So that they all composed a manifold
      And figured scene,
And seemed the weavers of some cloth of gold,
Or the fine pistons of some bright machine.

Watching these lifelong dancers of a day
As night closed in, I felt myself alone
     In a life too much my own,
More mortal in my separateness than they —
Unless, I thought, I had been called to be
    Not fly or star
But one whose task was joyfully to see
How fair the fiats of the caller are.

(marginal notes)

Austere

burning,
flashing,
~~shining~~

weird
fragile
fluttering
< one steep yard
< two steep yards

fine / bright

Nuptial many / in nuptial joy

light rare

whose task is

god bright rare
brave

ality as represented by objects, by the things of this world. As a poet he must be modestly heroic, see more, and range further than the ordinary citizen. Wilbur writes in "Objects," a poem from his first collection:

> I see afloat among the leaves, all calm and
>   curled,
> The Cheshire smile which sets me fearfully free.

Nevertheless, the question raised earlier in Wilbur's career in regard to his development remains in the 1990s: Does his adherence to formalist principles preclude his consideration as a major poet during a postmodernist period in which poets were expected to respond to a changing social and literary landscape?

In *Wilbur's Poetry: Music in a Scattering Time* (1991) Michelson avoids reviving all the old arguments about formalism versus experimentation, closed versus open forms, and academic poetry versus postmodernism, from which Wilbur emerges as a reactionary, if not a heavy. Michelson goes instead directly to the poems to argue not only for evidence of the stylistic range and variety of Wilbur's artistry but also to affirm his sensitivity to the major moral and aesthetic crises of his times. As Lionel Trilling found in Frost, Michelson finds in Wilbur a darker side. He is to be redeemed as not only the acknowledged master of light verse but also of some less acknowledged dark, meditative poems. Michelson does not find Wilbur to be a "terrifying poet" as Trilling did Frost but rather reckons him "a serious artist for an anxious century." He identifies in many of the poems not just "safe creeds and certainties" but, significantly, a tone of "skeptical virtuosity" that has gone largely unrecognized.

If one is satisfied to judge Richard Wilbur in terms of his intentions, he has achieved them well. Nonetheless it is clear he has not been a poet for all decades. In the 1950s his view of poetic creation was compatible with that of the dominant critical view of his generation of emerging poets, the "rage for order view" of creativity promulgated by the formalistic New Criticism. By the 1960s formalism was no longer the dominant critical approach, and man's rage for order was balanced by an interest in man's rage for chaos. In the 1970s modernism had been supplanted by a neo-Romantic postmodernism. Critics discovered the virtues of political correctness by the 1980s, and Wilbur seemed relatively lackluster as a poet who was neither politically correct nor notably incorrect.

What Wilbur's critics and his readers must not disregard is his mild irony, sophisticated wit, effec-

tive humor, and, as Michelson has appended, seriousness. His craftsmanship and skill with words and traditional poetic forms should also be considered. Wilbur is a formalist who at his best manages to make formalism seem continually new. For many readers, his poetic art always was, and still is, sufficient. In 1996 Wilbur received the Robert Frost medal from the Poetry Society of America. This award pays just tribute to Wilbur both as a spokesman for Frost and as the significant New England poet of his own generation.

Interviews:

William Butts, *Conversations with Richard Wilbur* (Jackson: University Press of Mississippi, 1990).

Bibliographies:

John P. Field, *Richard Wilbur: A Bibliographical Checklist* (Kent, Ohio: Kent State University Press, 1971);

Frances Bixler, *Richard Wilbur: A Reference Guide* (New York: Macmillan, 1991).

References:

Louise Bogan, *Achievement in American Poetry* (Chicago: Regnery, 1951), pp. 133–134;

Robert Boyers, "On Richard Wilbur," *Salmagundi,* 12 (Spring 1970): 76–82;

James E. B. Breslin, "The New Rear Guard," in *From Modern to Contemporary American Poetry, 1945–1965* (Chicago: University of Chicago Press, 1984), pp. 23–52;

Paul F. Cummins, *Richard Wilbur: A Critical Essay* (Grand Rapids, Mich.: Eerdmans, 1971);

James Dickey, *Babel to Byzantium: Poets and Poetry Now* (New York: Farrar, Straus & Giroux, 1968), pp. 170–172;

Rodney Stenning Edgecombe, *A Reader's Guide to the Poetry of Richard Wilbur* (Tuscaloosa: University of Alabama Press, 1995);

Frederic E. Faverty, "Well-Open Eyes; or, the Poetry of Richard Wilbur," in *Poets in Progress,* edited by Edward Hungerford (Evanston, Ill.: Northwestern University Press, 1962), pp. 59–72;

Leslie A. Fiedler, *Waiting for the End* (New York: Dell, 1964), pp. 218–221;

Walter Freed, "Richard Wilbur," in *Critical Survey Poetry,* edited by Frank Magill (Englewood Cliffs, N.J.: Salem Press, 1982), pp. 3091–3100;

John Gery, *Nuclear Annihilation and Contemporary American Poetry: Ways of Nothingness* (Gainesville: University of Florida Press, 1996);

Donald Hall, *Contemporary American Poetry* (Baltimore: Penguin, 1962), pp. 17–26;

Hall, "The New Poetry: Notes on the Past Fifteen Years in America," in *New World Writing* (New York: New American Library, 1955), pp. 231–247;

Peter Harris, "Forty Years of Richard Wilbur: The Loving Work of an Equilibrist," *Virginia Quarterly Review,* 66 (Summer 1990): 412–425;

William Heyen, "On Richard Wilbur," *Southern Review,* 9 (July 1973): 617–634;

Donald L. Hill, *Richard Wilbur* (New Haven: College & University Press, 1967);

John B. Hougon, *Ecstasy Within Discipline: The Poetry of Richard Wilbur* (Atlanta: Scholars Press, 1994);

Randall Jarrell, *Poetry and the Age* (New York: Vintage, 1953), pp. 227–240;

Kenneth Johnson, "Virtues in Style, Defect in Content: The Poetry of Richard Wilbur," in *The Fifties: Fiction, Poetry, and Drama,* edited by Warren G. French (Deland, Fla.: Everett/Edwards, 1970), pp. 209–216;

Brad Leithauser, "Reconsideration: Richard Wilbur—America's Master of Formal Verse," *New Republic,* 181 (24 March 1982): 28–31;

Bruce Michelson, *Wilbur's Poetry: Music in a Scattering Time* (Amherst: University of Massachusetts Press, 1991);

Ralph J. Mills Jr., *Contemporary American Poetry* (New York: Random House, 1965), pp. 160–175;

Raymond Oliver, "Verse Translation and Richard Wilbur," *Southern Review,* 11 (April 1975): 318–330;

Anthony Ostroff, ed., *The Contemporary Poet as Artist and Critic: Eight Symposia* (Boston: Little, Brown, 1964), pp. 1–21;

David Perkins, *A History of Modern Poetry* (Cambridge, Mass.: Belknap/Harvard University Press, 1987), pp. 383–386;

M. L. Rosenthal, *The Modern Poets: A Critical Introduction* (New York: Oxford University Press, 1960), pp. 253–255;

Rosenthal, *The New Poets: American and British Poetry Since World War II* (New York: Oxford University Press, 1967), pp. 328–330;

Wendy Salinger, ed., *Richard Wilbur's Creation* (Ann Arbor: University of Michigan Press, 1983);

Donald Barlow Stauffer, *A Short History of American Poetry* (New York: Dutton, 1974), pp. 385–387;

Hyatt H. Waggoner, *American Poets: From the Puritans to the Present* (Boston: Houghton Mifflin, 1968), pp. 596–604;

A. K. Weatherhead, "Richard Wilbur: Poetry of Things," *English Literary History,* 35 (December 1968): 606–617;

Philip White, "'Walking to Sleep' and Richard Wilbur's Quest for a Rational Imagination," *Twentieth Century Literature,* 41 (Winter 1995): 249–265.

Papers:

Most of Richard Wilbur's papers are in the Robert Frost Library, Amherst College. Additional manuscripts, mostly early works, are in the Poetry Collection, Lockwood Memorial Library, State University of New York at Buffalo.

Thornton Wilder

This entry was updated from the entries by Sally Johns (University of South Carolina)
in DLB 7: Twentieth-Century American Dramatists and
by Richard H. Goldstone (City College of New York)
in DLB 9: American Novelists, 1910–1945.

See also the Wilder entry in *DLB 4: American Writers in Paris, 1920–1939, Part 2.*

BIRTH: Madison, Wisconsin, 17 April 1897 to Amos Parker and Isabella Thornton Niven Wilder.

EDUCATION: Attended Oberlin College, 1915–1917; A.B., Yale University, 1920; attended American Academy in Rome 1920–1921; A.M., Princeton University, 1926.

AWARDS AND HONORS: Pulitzer Prize for *The Bridge of San Luis Rey,* 1928, for *Our Town,* 1938, and for *The Skin of Our Teeth,* 1943; Chevalier, Legion of Honor, 1951; Gold Medal for Fiction, American Academy of Arts and Letters, 1952; Friedenspreis des Deutschen Buchhandels (Frankfurt on the Main, West Germany), 1957; Sonderpreis des Oesterreichischen Staatspreises, 1959; Goethe-Plakette, 1959; Brandeis University Creative Arts Award for theater and film, 1959–1960; Edward MacDowell Medal (first time presented), 1960; Century Association Art Medal; Medal of the Order of Merit (Peru); Order Pour le Merite (Bonn, West Germany); invited by President Kennedy's cabinet to present reading, 1962; Presidential Medal of Freedom, 1963; National Book Committee's National Medal for Literature (first time presented), 1965; National Book Award for *The Eighth Day,* 1968; honorary degrees from New York University, Yale University, Kenyon College, College of Wooster, Harvard University, Northeastern University, Oberlin College, University of New Hampshire, University of Zurich.

DEATH: Hamden, Connecticut, 7 December 1975.

BOOKS: *The Cabala* (New York: A. & C. Boni, 1926; London: Longmans, Green, 1926);
The Bridge of San Luis Rey (London: Longmans, Green, 1927; New York: A. & C. Boni, 1927);
The Angel That Troubled the Waters and Other Plays (New York: Coward-McCann, 1928; London:

Thornton Wilder

Longmans, Green, 1928)—includes *Nascunter Poetae, Proserpina and the Devil, Fanny Otcott, Brother Fire, The Penny That Beauty Spent, The Angel on the Ship, The Message and Jehanne, Childe Roland to the Dark Tower Came, Centaurs, Leviathan, And the Sea Shall Give Up Its Dead, Now the Servant's Name Was Malchus, Mozart and the Gray Steward, Hast Thou Considered My Servant Job? The Flight into Egypt,* and *The Angel That Troubled the Waters;*

The Woman of Andros (New York: A. & C. Boni, 1930; London: Longmans, Green, 1930);

The Long Christmas Dinner & Other Plays in One Act (New York: Coward-McCann / New Haven: Yale University Press, 1931; London: Longmans, Green, 1931)–includes *The Long Christmas Dinner, Queens of France, Pullman Car Hiawatha, Love and How to Cure It, Such Things Only Happen in Books,* and *The Happy Journey to Trenton and Camden;*

Lucrece, adapted from André Obey's *Le Viol de Lucèrce* (Boston & New York: Houghton Mifflin, 1933; London: Longmans, Green, 1933);

Heaven's My Destination (London, New York & Toronto: Longmans, Green, 1934; New York & London: Harper, 1935);

Our Town (New York: Coward-McCann, 1938; London: Longmans, Green, 1956);

The Merchant of Yonkers (New York & London: Harper, 1939);

The Skin of Our Teeth (New York & London: Harper, 1942; London: Longmans, Green, 1958);

Our Century (New York: Century, 1947);

The Ides of March (New York & London: Harper, 1948; London: Longmans, Green, 1948);

The Drunken Sisters (New York, Hollywood, London & Toronto: S. French, 1957);

The Matchmaker (New York, Hollywood, London & Toronto: S. French, 1957);

Three Plays: Our Town, The Skin of Our Teeth, The Matchmaker (New York: Harper, 1957; London: Longmans, Green, 1958);

Plays for Bleecker Street, 3 volumes (New York: S. French, 1960–1961)–includes Infancy, Childhood, and Someone from Assisi;

The Eighth Day (New York, Evanston, Ill. & London: Harper & Row, 1967; London: Longmans, 1967);

Theophilus North (New York, Evanston, Ill. & San Francisco & London: Harper & Row, 1973; London: Allen Lane, 1974);

The Alcestiad (New York, Hagerstown, Md., San Francisco & London: Harper & Row, 1977);

American Characteristics and Other Essays, edited by Donald Gallup (New York, Hagerstown, Md., San Francisco & London: Harper & Row, 1979);

The Journals of Thornton Wilder, 1939–1961, edited by Donald Gallup (New Haven, Conn.: Yale University Press, 1985).

PLAY PRODUCTIONS: *The Trumpet Shall Sound,* American Laboratory Theatre, New York, 10 December 1926;

Lucrece, translated and adapted from André Obey's *Le Viol de Lucèrce,* Belasco Theatre, New York, 20 December 1932;

A Doll's House, translated and adapted from Henrik Ibsen's play, Morosco Theatre, New York, 27 December 1937;

Our Town, Henry Miller's Theatre, 4 February 1938, New York;

The Merchant of Yonkers, Guild Theatre, New York; revised as *The Matchmaker,* 28 December 1938, Royale Theatre, New York, 5 December 1955;

The Skin of Our Teeth, Plymouth Theatre, New York; 18 November 1942;

Our Century, Century Association, New York, 26 April 1947;

The Happy Journey to Trenton and Camden, Cort Theatre, New York, 9 February 1948;

A Life in the Sun, Assembly Hall, Edinburgh, Scotland, 25 August 1955;

The Wreck of the 5:25 and *Bernice,* Congresshalle Theater, West Berlin, West Germany, 20 September 1957;

Das Lange Weihnachtsmal (opera version of *The Long Christmas Dinner*), libretto by Wilder, music by Paul Hindemith, National Theatre, Manheim, West Germany, 17 December 1961;

Plays for Bleecker Street (*Infancy, Childhood,* and *Someone from Assisi*), Circle in the Square, New York, 11 January 1962;

Die Alkestiade (opera version of *A Life in the Sun*), libretto by Wilder, music by Louise Talma, Stadische Buhnen, Frankfurt, West Germany, 1 March 1962;

Pullman Car Hiawatha, Circle in the Square, New York, 3 December 1964;

Thornton Wilder's Triple Bill (*The Long Christmas Dinner, Queens of France,* and *The Happy Journey to Trenton and Camden*), Cherry Lane Theatre, New York, 6 September 1966;

The Drunken Sisters, Spencer Memorial Church, Brooklyn Heights, New York, 28 June 1970.

MOTION PICTURES: *Our Town,* by Wilder, Frank Craven, and others, United Artists, 1940;

Shadow of a Doubt, Universal, 1943.

OTHER: Introduction to *Narration: Four Lectures,* by Gertrude Stein (Chicago: University of Chicago Press, 1935);

Introduction to *The Geographical History of America,* by Stein (New York: Random House, 1936);

"Some Thoughts on Playwriting," in *The Intent of the Artist,* edited by Augusto Centeno (Princeton,

The Wilder family, 1911: Isabel, Amos, Isabella, Janet, Thornton, and Charlotte (Thornton Wilder Archive, Collection of American Literature, Beinecke Rare Book and Manuscript Library, Yale University)

N.J.: Princeton University Press, 1941), pp. 83–98.

SELECTED PERIODICAL PUBLICATIONS–
UNCOLLECTED: *The Trumpet Shall Sound, Yale Literary Magazine,* 85 (October–December 1919, January 1920): 9–26, 78–92, 128–146, 192–207;

"A Diary: First and Last Entry," *S4N,* 32 (February 1924): 7–11;

"Three Sentences," *Double Dealer,* 4 (September 1924): 110;

"Playgoing Nights: From a Travel Diary," by Wilder and Isabel Wilder, *Theatre Arts Monthly,* 13 (June 1929): 411–419;

"James Joyce (1882–1941)," *Poetry: A Magazine of Verse,* 62 (March 1941): 370–374;

"Toward an American Language," *Atlantic Monthly,* 190 (July 1952): 29–37;

"The American Loneliness," *Atlantic Monthly,* 190 (August 1952): 65–69.

On the strength of only three full-length plays and a bare handful of one-acts, Thornton Wilder ranks among the top half dozen playwrights in the history of American theater. The modest volume of his dramatic work is not the result of a limitation of talent or interest; rather, it is due to his abilities and inclinations being multifocused, without becoming diffused. His career is marked with superior achievement in three fields: academics, fiction, and drama. Beginning as a schoolmaster for young boys, he eventually held the Charles Eliot Norton Professorship of Poetry at Harvard. His fiction was rewarded with both the Pulitzer Prize and the National Book Award. In the field of drama, *Our Town* (1938) not only won the Pulitzer Prize but also has become the best-known and most-produced play in the United States. *The Skin of Our Teeth* (1942), another Pulitzer Prize winner, expanded Wilder's reputation to international status; the play continues to be held in high esteem in both the United States and Europe, particularly in Germany. His light farce *The Matchmaker* (1957), designed as a spoof of conventional theater, survives in transformation as America's most popular musical comedy, *Hello, Dolly!* A classicist and humanist with a profound interest in the past—both ancient and recent—Wilder has always appealed to the sentimental; yet his works skillfully avoid sentimentality. His literary career, punctuated by the crests of awards and renown, also survived momentarily devastating attacks: a lambasting for elitism amid proletarian suffering at the beginning of the Great Depression and an accusation that *The Skin of Our Teeth* was plagiarized. His achievement in American drama lies in his employment of innovative, unconventional theatrical techniques to affirm conventional, humanistic values.

Thornton Niven Wilder was born on 17 April 1897 in Madison, Wisconsin, a surviving twin. His siblings included Amos, two years his senior, who later became a distinguished professor, theologian, and writer; Charlotte, born in 1898; Isabel, born in 1900, herself a writer who devoted most of her adult life to serving as Wilder's confidante, traveling companion, correspondence secretary, and general buffer against the world; and Janet, born in 1910. He was named for his mother, the former Isabella Thornton Niven, daughter of a Presbyterian minister. His father, Amos Parker Wilder, had earned a doctorate in political science and at the time of Wilder's birth was working as editor of the *Wisconsin State Journal*. Both this man's personality and his career were important influences on shaping his young son. Amos Wilder was a robust, stern, morally upright man who placed exacting demands on himself and his family, and Thornton Wilder's critics and biographers agree that the playwright sensed strongly that his interests and achievements–both as a child and later as an adult–never won his father's approval. In addition, Amos Wilder's decision in 1906 to enter the foreign service had a profound effect on the entire family. He accepted the post of consul general in Hong Kong; though Isabella and the children accompanied him, after six months they returned to the United States, and although they would again live in the same city, the entire family never again shared a household. Though Amos Wilder was a hemisphere away, his presence was continuously felt: through correspondence he kept abreast of his children's progress in school, constantly urging superior achievement and admonishing them when their marks fell below his expectations.

Because of his father's career, Wilder's early formal education came from a variety of institutions. After being uprooted from Wisconsin at the age of nine, he attended a German school in Hong Kong for six months before moving with his mother and siblings to Berkeley, California, where he was enrolled in public school. In 1909 his father was transferred to Shanghai, where the family rejoined him and the children were placed in boarding schools. After a brief period in a German school, fourteen-year-old Thornton was sent to the China Inland Mission School at Chefoo. He did not fare well at the mission school, which was run like an English public school, and after a little more than a year his father sent him to join his older brother at the Thatcher School in Ojai, California. He withdrew after a year, joining his mother and sisters, who were resituated in Berkeley, and in 1915 he graduated from Berkeley High School. During his

two years at Berkeley High he frequented the Liberty Theater in Oakland, participated in some of the dramatic productions of the school, and dreamed of attending his father's alma mater, Yale University.

Perhaps fearing the negative influence of Yale's worldliness, Amos Wilder instead enrolled his disappointed son in Oberlin College, far more isolated in location and religious in atmosphere. Despite his initial chagrin, young Wilder, who had up to this time been rather withdrawn, found at Oberlin an acceptance that he had never before enjoyed at an academic institution. He participated in student theatrics, studied the classics with Professor Charles H. A. Wager (according to Wilder, "the greatest lecturer I have ever heard"), and saw several of his writings published in the *Oberlin Literary Magazine* (some of which were later included in his volume of brief plays, *The Angel That Troubled the Waters and Other Plays,* 1928). After two years, however, he was again uprooted by his father, who had settled in New Haven, Connecticut, as executive director of Yale-in-China. Though Yale had previously been his supreme goal, Wilder was less than enthusiastic over the transfer, for he had thrived in the intimate and stimulating atmosphere of Oberlin. Though he never became part of the inner circle at Yale (he was lacking in athletic ability, masculine good looks, and social prominence), he did make a place for himself through his increasing gregariousness and his literary abilities. When World War I came, Wilder, like most of his classmates, was eager to participate, but nearsightedness prevented his acceptance by various branches of service. He finally entered the Coast Artillery Corps in September 1918, serving briefly at Fort Adams, Rhode Island, before being discharged in time to return to Yale in January 1919. Before his graduation in 1920, he was elected to the literary group Pundits and served on the editorial board of the *Yale Literary Magazine,* which published several of his short plays and essays and–in serialized form–his first long play, *The Trumpet Shall Sound* (1926).

Though Wilder knew upon his graduation that he wanted to be a writer, his father had other plans for the son he considered less than competent: a schoolmaster's wages, though meager, would provide a steady and stable income for the family, should they need to rely upon him as a source of support. Bowing to duty, Wilder acquiesced, agreeing to spend a preparatory year as a resident visitor studying archaeology at the American Academy in Rome. In addition to attending classes and participating in expeditions, he learned Italian and pursued the classics, with which he had become fascinated when studying with Professor Wager at Oberlin. He also began to collect material for "Memoirs of a Roman Student" (the working title of *The Cabala*, 1926). After several months his idyll was interrupted by a cable from his father—still firmly holding the reins—announcing that he had secured for his son a position teaching French at the Lawrenceville School in Princeton, New Jersey. For four years Wilder remained at the select preparatory school for boys, teaching French and serving as assistant master of Davis House. In the time he could find to write, he continued work on "Memoirs of a Roman Student," an excerpt from which was published in the September 1924 issue of *Double Dealer*. Additionally, the February 1924 issue of *S4N* included "A Diary: First and Last Entry," Wilder's last short story published in a commercial periodical. His summers were spent escorting young students to Europe, their parents providing the passage he could not otherwise afford. On one such voyage he met drama critic Stark Young, who in 1924 introduced him to Edith Isaacs, editor of *Theatre Arts Monthly*. Impressed with his readings from "Memoirs of a Roman Student," she recommended him for a scholarship at the MacDowell Colony in Peterborough, New Hampshire; the summer of 1924 was the first of several he spent at this mountain encampment for artists. She also commissioned him (in the temporary absence of John Mason Brown) to review for *Theatre Arts Monthly* the fifteen or so New York theater openings in early 1925.

Encouraged by a former Yale classmate, Lewis Baer, who had become a partner in the new publishing firm Albert & Charles Boni, Wilder turned his attention to completing the novel begun in Rome. In order to have more time for writing, he resigned his position at Lawrenceville to enroll in the master's program in French at Princeton. After spending the summer tutoring at a camp for boys preparing for college boards (a source of income to which he would return several times), he began his studies at Princeton and, despite periodic writer's block, completed his first book. The fictitious memoirs of a young American among a wealthy and socially prominent coterie in Rome, the volume was retitled *The Cabala* and published in the spring of 1926 to a small but generally favorable reception.

In addition to the publication of his first novel, the year 1926 brought two other events of significance to Wilder's life: he was awarded an A.M. in French, and the first of his plays was professionally produced. On the recommendation of Edith Isaacs, Richard Boleslavsky produced *The Trumpet Shall Sound* (which Wilder had written while a student at Yale) at the American Laboratory Theatre. Trained

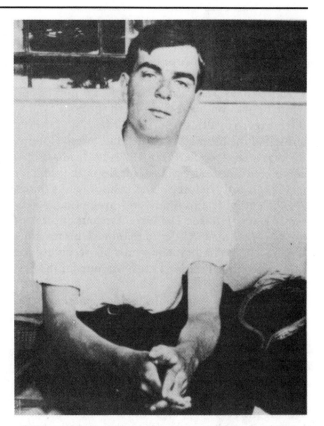

Wilder at Oberlin College, September 1916 (Thornton Wilder Archive, Collection of American Literature, Beinecke Rare Book and Manuscript Library, Yale University)

by Stanislavsky at the Moscow Art Theatre, Boleslavsky was intrigued with the nonrealistic approach of the play. A lengthy allegory, it presents a master who leaves his servants in charge of his house, returns to find that his maid has rented out the rooms of his mansion to a collection of undesirables, "sounds the trumpet" to place each of them in judgment, and ultimately forgives them for their wickedness. The link between the master of the mansion and God, who in his mercy forgives even the worst of sinners, is overly obvious. Except for bits of dialogue that ring true to conversational speech, the play is undistinguished, and the production was not a success.

Wilder himself was not involved with the premiere staging of his dramatic work. During the fall of 1926 he was touring Europe (again in the employ of the parents of a bored adolescent) where, in Paris, he began a seemingly unlikely friendship with Ernest Hemingway. Wilder's biographer Richard H. Goldstone surmises that in addition to a common interest in writing, the two were attracted to each other as complementary opposites: "Wilder respected Hemingway's athleticism, his bravado, his openness, his professionalism; and Hemingway, in turn, admired Wilder's cultivation, his taste, his wit, his detachment."

During the European tour Wilder began his second novel, *The Bridge of San Luis Rey,* in winter 1925–1926, as *The Cabala* was being set in type and while he was on leave from Lawrenceville. Using the meager royalties from *The Cabala* and availing himself of the hospitality of the MacDowell Colony, Wilder, after a further year (1926–1927) in Europe, completed *The Bridge of San Luis Rey* in the summer of 1927, shortly before resuming his teaching duties at Lawrenceville, this time with a promotion to master of Davis House. The instantaneous success of the novel enabled Wilder to relinquish his teaching post in 1928, simultaneous with his receiving the first of his three Pulitzer Prizes, this one for the best fictional work of 1927.

Though he had published one novel and was certain of the publication of a second, he could not realistically expect a living income from royalties, so he unenthusiastically returned to teaching. During the fall term his gloom increased, and his depression was compounded by appendicitis that necessitated serious surgery and a long convalescence. During his recovery, on vacation in Miami Beach, he introduced himself to Gene Tunney, whose title as world heavyweight boxing champion had made him an international celebrity. There began another of Wilder's celebrated incongruous relationships; the press would later have a heyday with the friendship between the diminutive, unathletic writer and the world-championship boxer with a taste for books.

The novel that Wilder had completed the previous summer was published in late 1927, and its reception came as a total surprise to its author. By early 1928 *The Bridge of San Luis Rey* had earned a monumental stack of favorable reviews; by spring its author had become a bona fide celebrity; and in May it was awarded the Pulitzer Prize. The novel is actually three separate stories, threaded together loosely through plot but tightly through theme, set within a rather obtrusive and unnecessary frame. The setting is early-eighteenth-century Peru. A friar witnesses the collapse of a slat-and-vine bridge, sending its five travelers plunging to their deaths in the gorge far below. This friar's examination of the lives of the victims, in order to determine God's purpose in allowing them to die, provides the frame that opens and closes the novel; the three episodes within trace the lives of those who have perished. Their stories reveal a common theme: each had focused obsessively on an object of affection who either could not or did not reciprocate, and the extensiveness of the obsession resulted in spiritual isola-

tion from the rest of humanity. Shortly before traveling over the bridge, each had awakened to the folly of such an obsession and had set out in a new direction, attempting to make recompense. An expression of Wilder's Christian humanism, the novel presents a concept that recurs in *Our Town:* there is wastefulness—sinfulness, even—in failure to examine and appreciate every experience. Though the book has been read by many for its "inspirational" value, it is unsentimental in its valuation of vigorous participation in life; it in no way encourages neglect of earthly experience in favor of promises of an afterlife. Wilder's prose style, influenced by his study of the classics, achieves a simple elegance that is neither ornate nor archaic. In addition to winning high critical acclaim, the novel has remained Wilder's most popularly successful work of fiction.

The book brought its author the financial security that allowed him to resign his position at Lawrenceville and sail to England in the summer of 1928. He was soon joined by Gene Tunney for a "walking tour" of Europe that brought him even wider press coverage than his Pulitzer Prize-winning novel. After the summer he extended his stay for several months, traveling with his sister Isabel and working on a third novel. While he was in Europe, in November 1928, *The Angel That Troubled the Waters and Other Plays* was published. The volume includes sixteen brief works (its title was at one time to have been "Three-Minute Plays for Three Persons") composed over a twelve-year period beginning during Wilder's high school days. Though the short pieces exhibit the scope of Wilder's knowledge of literature, history, and philosophy, they fall short as dramatic works. Their brevity precludes any sort of development, and many of them include actions or events totally impossible to stage ("Suddenly the thirty pieces of silver are cast upward from the revolted hand of Judas. They hurtle through the skies, flinging their enormous shadows across the stars and continue falling forever through the vast funnel of space"). However, what appears to be blatant disregard for the realities of theatrical production may in fact be the early (perhaps unconscious) rebellion against conventional staging by a playwright whose later innovations would supersede many of these limitations. Elements of some of the plays do prefigure later works: *Proserpina and the Devil,* for instance, combines past and present, as well as Christianity and Roman mythology, foreshadowing the omnidimensional world created so effectively in *The Skin of Our Teeth.* Also noteworthy is Wilder's foreword, in which he comments on the nature of the budding artist: "Authors of fifteen and sixteen years of age spend their time drawing up

Wilder (right) with Gene Tunney, hiking in Switzerland, September 1928 (Thornton Wilder Archive, Collection of American Literature, Beinecke Rare Book and Manuscript Library, Yale University)

title-pages and adjusting the tables of contents of works they have neither the perseverance nor the ability to execute." He straightforwardly voices the point of view he espouses: "Almost all the plays in this book are religious, but religious in that dilute fashion that is a believer's concession to a contemporary standard of good manners."

After returning to the United States in early 1929, Wilder set out on the first of several lecture tours. Though *The Bridge of San Luis Rey* had been a tremendous financial success, he felt that it would be imprudent to rely on his writing as a continuous source of income. By this time a failed venture in the newspaper business had broken his father both physically and financially, leaving the second son responsible for the support of his parents and his younger sisters. (The older son, Amos, had gone into the ministry, a choice of profession that had won his father's unqualified support, despite its lack of financial rewards.) Thus Wilder felt pressed to combine gainful employment with his writing efforts. In addition to the lecture tours, he accepted a post at the University of Chicago that allowed him to teach only part of the year, therefore freeing him to travel or concentrate on writing the remainder of the time.

In early 1930 his third novel, *The Woman of Andros,* was published. Based on the Roman playwright Terence's comedy *Andria,* the book received reviews that, although mixed, were gener-

ally favorable, and so seemed destined for moderate success. Then in October 1930, to Wilder's complete surprise and dismay, a critical attack was launched that would temporarily demolish the reputation *The Bridge of San Luis Rey* had achieved for him. Michael Gold, a Communist journalist writing in the *New Republic,* lambasted Wilder as the "Prophet of the Genteel Christ" and the religious stance of his novel as a "daydream of homosexual figures in graceful gowns moving archaically through the lilies." America had been plunged into the Great Depression, and Gold, a leader of the proletarian school of criticism, was enraged that in the midst of immediate social crisis Wilder, instead of using his art to champion reform, had chosen to display his New Humanist ideas in a setting as far removed as ancient Greece. He labeled Wilder's Jesus Christ "the First British Gentleman" and his religion "Anglo-Catholicism, that last refuge of the American literary snob." Though in retrospect the blatant vituperativeness of Gold's piece clearly nullifies it as criticism, in 1930 it created a literary controversy from which Wilder could not emerge totally unscathed, although he was ably defended in print by such notables as Edmund Wilson. Realizing that the fabric of American culture was indeed changing, he maintained his humanistic concepts but turned his talents in new directions, leaving behind temporarily both fiction and the past.

The publication of *The Long Christmas Dinner & Other Plays in One Act* in 1931 marks the beginning of Wilder's successful career as an American dramatist. If Gold's attack had forced his attentions to the subject matter of his own time and place, his European travels and experiences with European experiments in nonrealistic theater had also profoundly influenced his approach. While this volume may be considered the workshop in which he refined the techniques so highly lauded in the plays to follow, *Our Town* and *The Skin of Our Teeth,* it is no mere testing ground; it includes some of his finest dramatic works.

The title work deals with one of Wilder's favorite subjects—time. Several conventional elements unify the play: its setting is the dining room of an American household, with the long table set for Christmas dinner, and its characters are the family members. However, the action of the one-act play spans a period of ninety years, its characters changing as one generation passes on and another replaces it. As the play opens, a young couple celebrating their first Christmas in a newly built house share the festivities with the husband's mother, who remembers girlhood experiences "on this very ground." As the play progresses, characters exit through a portal representing death and enter through an opposite door representing birth, suggesting the ebb and flow of life. As babies are born and grow to adulthood, other family members quietly leave through death's portal—some dying of old age, one a victim of war, and one a baby who died at birth. The rhythm is gentle and smooth, sustained through the constant situation of the family Christmas dinner. Wilder's dialogue is simple and believable; as in *Our Town,* the focus is on the commonplace—the weather, the Christmas sermon, a parent's aspirations for a child—but here the time frame allows for an effective use of repetition. As the generations pass, the same comments are echoed and reechoed as "Mother" is tempted with "just another sliver of white meat" and the head of the family toasts "the ladies" with a glass of wine. Thus Wilder masterfully fuses the recognizable, the ordinary of American life, with an innovative nonrealistic theatrical technique.

Queens of France, though also consistent with Wilder's philosophy of celebrating the ordinary, is more conventionally realistic in technique. Set in New Orleans in 1869, it presents an unscrupulous lawyer who preys on the spiritual poverty of naive women. Convincing each that she is the long-lost successor to the French throne, he persuades her to "purchase" various royal artifacts, thereby providing funds necessary for locating documents that will prove the authenticity of her claim. Though Cahusac, the lawyer, is clearly a swindler, he inadvertently brings a new vigor to these women's lives. As one of the women, upon abandoning hope that proof will be discovered, observes dreamily, "It was so beautiful while it lasted. It made even schoolteaching a pleasure." Though the external conditions of her life had remained unchanged, and the belief that she was in fact a monarch had been kept a secret between the lawyer and herself, by perceiving herself as uncommon, she had experienced greater appreciation of her singular life.

Pullman Car Hiawatha (1964) is the most technically ambitious of the collection. Virtually plotless, the play represents a slice of life (radiating from the narrow to the cosmic) on a train journeying from New York to Chicago on the evening of "December twenty-first, 1930." Wilder employs several of the devices used by the German expressionists and their American followers, but to a significantly different end. The travelers are types rather than fully developed characters—a maiden lady, a young couple, a middle-aged doctor, an insane woman—and cities, fields, planets, and even units of time are personified by actors: "The minutes are gossips; the hours are philosophers; the years are theologians." However, unlike the works of expressionists who seek to demonstrate the dehumanization and insignificance of man, Wilder's panorama displays a vast but ordered cosmos of which man is an integral part. Presiding over the presentation is the Stage Manager (employed most famously in the later *Our Town*), who introduces the audience to the characters and setting (represented by chairs placed within chalk-marked areas of an otherwise bare stage), takes various roles within the action, and provides commentary throughout.

Love and How to Cure It, in the vein of *Queens of France,* is conventional in presentation technique. Three performers—a young ballerina, a comedian, and a soubrette—await a rehearsal on the bare stage of a Soho music hall in 1895. Linda, the "beautiful, impersonal, remote, almost sullen" dancer, is plagued by an undesired suitor, a young student who she is convinced is about to shoot her because she refuses to return his affections. The older soubrette and the comedian invite the student to share their supper, secretly unloading the gun he has hidden in his cape. After putting the young man at ease with casual, friendly conversation, the comedian tells him gravely that he does not know what to make of newspaper accounts of "people who shoot the persons they love." He suspects that they want to be noticed, and for those who must shoot to get noticed, "it's themselves they love." Confessing that he had

Wilder and director Max Reinhardt going over the script for The Merchant of Yonkers, *New York, 1938 (Thornton Wilder Archive, Collection of American Literature, Beinecke Rare Book and Manuscript Library, Yale University)*

planned to shoot himself rather than his love, the young man apologizes to Linda, thanks the older pair for their kindness, concludes that "just loving isn't wasted," remarks on his own youth, and takes his leave. The young girl is still unmoved, but the older soubrette patiently notes, "Well, young lady, you're only sixteen. Wait 'til your turn comes. We'll have to take care of you."

Such Things Only Happen in Books is also a realistic drama; though it was removed by Wilder when the collection was reprinted, it is an effectively ironic piece. Set in a young couple's combination library/study/living room in a New Hampshire village, it comments on the major details of life that may be missed by its unobservant participants. The husband, a writer, plays solitaire while his wife sews. He comments that the card game is "like fiction. You have to adjust the cards to make a plot. In life most people live along without plots." Through the course of the play the audience learns that the couple's house is filled with "plots": their maid, Katie, who is suffering from serious burns, actually received her injuries while harboring her brother, an escaped prisoner, in the kitchen; the wife is having an affair with the doctor who treats the maid; and two rather mysterious visitors are in fact the former inhabitants of the house who probably murdered their father. Holding fast to the notion that the excitement of fiction seldom touches real life, the un-

suspecting husband maintains that "when you come down to it, the rank and file—rich and poor—live much as we do. Not much plot. Work and a nice wife and a nice house and a nice Katie."

The Happy Journey to Trenton and Camden (1948) is the most frequently anthologized and most frequently performed of the plays in the volume. In tone and technique it strongly prefigures *Our Town*. Its plot line is simple: Ma and Pa Kirby, along with their children Arthur and Caroline, take an automobile trip to visit their married daughter. Again a Stage Manager appears, but he offers no comment on the action; instead, he plays various supplementary roles—a neighbor bidding the family goodbye, a gas station attendant—reading his lines from a typescript. Wilder again employs no scenery; four chairs suffice for the automobile, and all the props are imaginary. The focus is on the commonplace: as the lower-middle-class family ride through the countryside, they admire the scenery, read from billboards, eat hot dogs, bicker mildly, and eagerly anticipate their visit. Only in a moving scene after they arrive does the audience learn the full reason for the trip: the married daughter is recovering from a difficult childbirth in which her baby died. Emerging as the most strongly developed character is Ma Kirby, whose mundane aphorisms indicate a simple but clear and solid philosophy of life based on a positive outlook, appreciation of natural beauty, sincere devotion to family, and patient acceptance of a divine plan beyond human understanding. Of the six plays in this collection, this one best rebuts Michael Gold's charge that Wilder was incapable of writing an "American" work.

Although all of the plays in the volume were staged before the end of 1931 (on bills of various combinations at Yale, Vassar, the University of Chicago, and Antioch), and their stock productions soon began to provide Wilder with modest royalty checks, none was given a professional Broadway production until several years later. In 1948 Wilder's *The Happy Journey to Trenton and Camden,* on a bill with Jean-Paul Sartre's *The Respectful Prostitute,* ran for 318 performances at the Cort Theatre. *Pullman Car Hiawatha* was produced in 1964 at Circle in the Square, and Wilder's *Triple Bill (The Long Christmas Dinner, Queens of France,* and *The Happy Journey to Trenton and Camden)* appeared at the Cherry Lane Theatre in 1966. An operatic version of *The Long Christmas Dinner (Das Lange Weihnachtsmal),* with libretto by Wilder and music by Paul Hindemith, was presented in Germany in 1961.

Wilder's next writing for the theater was a translation and adaptation of André Obey's *Le Viol de Lucrèce (The Rape of Lucrece).* A vehicle for Katharine Cornell, the production (titled simply *Lucrece*) marked the first appearance on Broadway of a Wilder work. Despite a stellar list of collaborators (direction by Guthrie McClintic, music by Deems Taylor, choreography by Martha Graham), it was a failure. It opened in December 1932 at the Belasco Theatre, received unfavorable notices, and closed after only thirty-one performances.

During the early and mid 1930s Wilder's half-year position at the University of Chicago allowed him time to pursue interests beyond teaching and writing. His friendship with Alexander Woollcott provided him with an entrée to the New York theater circles that had long fascinated him. Although he was regarded by some as an academic unversed in the realities of professional theater, he enjoyed an easy social relationship with many of New York's luminaries and established more-important friendships with a few of them. One was Jed Harris, a former Yale classmate who had become a successful producer; impressed with the volume of one-act plays, a few years later he produced Wilder's first Broadway success, *Our Town.* Another contemporary was actress Ruth Gordon, whose genuine friendship continued long after Wilder had parted ways with most of the other celebrities he reveled in socializing with during this period. The novel he was working on at this time was published in late 1934. *Heaven's My Destination,* a comic-spirited pica-resque, presents the journey of a naïve religious fanatic book salesman through the skeptical Midwest of the 1930s. Though the book's reputation has increased with time, on publication it met with generally unfavorable reviews. The stimulation provided by Wilder's theatrical friends, coupled with his dwindling success in the world of fiction, prompted him once again to turn his focus toward writing for the stage.

Among those few who lauded *Heaven's My Destination*—and her praise was high indeed—was Gertrude Stein, who called it *the* American novel. Though he had been familiar with her writings, Wilder did not meet her until the mid 1930s when she visited Chicago as part of an American lecture tour. They began to correspond, and when she returned to conduct a lecture series at the University of Chicago, he gave up his apartment to her and Alice B. Toklas. The friendship that developed was one of the most enriching of Wilder's life. Something of an isolate as a child, he later developed a gregariousness and social self-confidence that made him entertaining company, and he took great pleasure in various types of socializing. However, despite his sincere conviviality, he remained essentially a private person emotionally. Whenever questioned as to why he had never married, he responded that the emotional energy required by his writing precluded such a relationship. The consistent answer was only a half-truth, for he was a homosexual; however, his life included no long-term emotional relationship with a male. He never spoke publicly of his homosexuality, and his sexual preference was kept so private that even many people who were closely acquainted with him assumed that he was neither homosexual nor heterosexual, but asexual. He formed few strong emotional attachments. Throughout his life, however, he enjoyed several friendships with women (often older than he), among them Lady Sibyl Colefax, the celebrated London hostess whom he had met during the 1920s, and actress Ruth Gordon. The relationship with Gertrude Stein was the most important friendship with a woman (perhaps with anyone) of his entire life. Besides stimulating him intellectually, she nurtured him artistically and influenced him philosophically and aesthetically. Their visits and correspondence continued until her death in 1946.

By the spring of 1936 Wilder had become quite tired of his teaching duties, and he used the occasion of his father's serious illness and ultimate death to resign his post at the University of Chicago. Though his schedule still included lecture tours, he found himself free to travel, visit friends, and work on several long plays (some of which were never completed). He translated and adapted Ibsen's *A Doll's House* for a late 1937 production starring Ruth Gordon. Both the production (which ran for 142 performances) and the translation were reviewed favorably, encouraging producer Jed Harris to maintain his interest in the playwright's talents; for several years Harris had insisted that Wilder would someday write a play of real significance, and he wanted to produce it. His opportunity came with the work that ultimately sent Wilder's reputation back to the peak from which it had plummeted with Gold's 1930 attack in the *New Republic*.

Our Town, possibly America's most read and most produced play, opened in February 1938. Despite his confidence in both Wilder's script and the production he had mounted, producer and director Jed Harris experienced some uneasiness in anticipation of the critics' reaction to a play encompassing so many unusual elements. The out-of-town tryouts were met with a cool reception, but the New York critics—spearheaded by Brooks Atkinson—gradually built up a favorable response matched by public enthusiasm that resulted in a run of 336 performances. The success of the play notwithstanding, the reviewers did not award it the New York Drama Critics Circle Award (which went instead to *Of Mice and Men*), but it won for Wilder his second Pulitzer Prize.

In *Our Town* Wilder combines in a full-length work several of the experimental elements employed in the collection of one-act plays. As in *Pullman Car Hiawatha* and *The Happy Journey to Trenton and Camden,* an omniscient Stage Manager—with comfortable casualness and wry humor—provides exposition, narration, and commentary, occasionally playing a brief role as well. His verbal descriptions and the actors' pantomimed business create the imaginary props and scenery on an essentially bare stage set. Like *Pullman Car Hiawatha,* this play begins with the specific details of specific lives and then expands to place those lives within a cosmic context. Wilder fuses his theatrical techniques with Gertrude Stein's notions of the relationship between the individual and eternity, as well as his own belief (echoed from, among other works, *The Bridge of San Luis Rey*) in the inestimable value of appreciating human experience.

In the first act, called "Daily Life," the Stage Manager introduces the audience to Grover's Corners, New Hampshire, on 7 May 1901. The action encompasses the events of a single ordinary, decidedly unspectacular day. The town's inhabitants meander in and out of the action, going about their daily routines of delivering newspapers, preparing

The original 1942 cast for Wilder's The Skin of Our Teeth: *Tallulah Bankhead, Florence Eldridge, Fredric March, Frances Heflin, and Montgomery Clift (Thornton Wilder Archive, Collection of American Literature, Beinecke Rare Book and Manuscript Library, Yale University)*

breakfast, gossiping about the town drunk, and walking home from choir practice. The focus is on two families, the Webbs and the Gibbeses, and particularly on the oldest child of each family. Emily Webb and George Gibbes, high-school students, are next-door neighbors whose collaboration on homework is obviously evidence of a budding romance. Although the townspeople's dialogue has the aura of verisimilitude, both the presence of the Stage Manager and the absence of scenery maintain the play's anti-illusionary effect. At the end of the first act, as Emily's father whistles "Blessed Be the Tie That Binds," George's younger sister effectively links the events of the day to a larger perspective by telling her brother of the remarkable address on a letter a sick friend had received from her minister—Jane Crofut, The Crofut Farm, Grover's Corners, Sutton County, New Hampshire, United States of America, Continent of North America, Western Hemisphere, the Earth, the Solar System, the Universe, the Mind of God—"And the postman brought it just the same." The Stage Manager closes the act with a characteristically casual remark directly to the audience: "That's the end of the First Act, friends. You can go and smoke now, those that smoke."

Act 2 is called "Love and Marriage." Wilder points out in his preface to a 1957 volume including *Our Town* that "the recurrent words in this play (few have noticed it) are 'hundreds,' 'thousands,' and 'millions.'" He maintains that in the face of multiplicity of such magnitude, "each individual's assertion to an absolute reality can only be inner, very inner." The Stage Manager points up the vastness of the continuum of all human experience as he introduces the second act, set three years after the first: he speaks in terms of the sun having "come up over a thousand times" and elderly couples who over a lifetime have "eaten over fifty thousand meals" together. In the first act he demonstrated his omniscience; here he exhibits his control over conventional time. It is George and Emily's wedding day, and several minutes of dialogue present the early morning events of that day: meditativeness, nostalgia, and anxiousness characterize the parents of the bride and groom. Then the Stage Manager interrupts to turn back the scene to the events leading up to the marriage: "I'm awfully interested in how big things like that begin." George and Emily reenact a conversation in the drugstore (with the Stage Manager playing the druggist), just before their senior year of high school, during which they discuss the future and shyly but sincerely declare their affection for each other. Then time is returned to the present, and the act concludes with their wedding ceremony, officiated by the Stage Manager.

Act 3 takes place nine years later. Titled "Death," it is set in the little town's cemetery, represented simply by rows of ordinary chairs on which the actors are seated. According to the stage directions, "The dead do not turn their heads or their eyes to right or left, but they sit in a quiet manner without stiffness. When they speak their tone is matter-of-fact, without sentimentality and, above all, without lugubriousness." The occasion is the funeral of Emily Webb Gibbes, who has died in childbirth. As the mourners arrive, the dead note their presence and reminisce not unkindly, but with a detachment that indicates their transcendence of both earthly pains and earthly pleasures. As one comments, "I'm always uncomfortable when *they're* here." Despite strong warnings that she will regret her mistake, newcomer Emily insists on going back to relive a time in the past. She chooses her twelfth birthday, and as she and the Stage Manager verbally create the scenery on the bare stage, she returns to the home and family of her childhood. She quickly discovers that the warnings were well-founded, for the experience is impossibly painful. Knowing the future, she attempts to savor the moments, to express her love to her mother who is preparing breakfast. Breaking into sobs, realizing in frustration that "It goes so fast. We don't have time to look at one another," she requests permission to say goodbye to the world she has known before rejoining the dead.

Recognizing too late the value of her everyday experiences, she bids farewell to her parents, Grover's Corners, clocks ticking, newly ironed dresses—a list whose commonplaceness brings her to the awareness that human beings never "realize life while they live it." As she calmly takes her seat and George mourns silently at her grave, the Stage Manager quietly closes the play with a conversational monologue that combines comments on sleepy Grover's Corners at eleven o'clock (most everyone is asleep, someone has heard a train go by, and "at the livery stable somebody's setting up late and talking") with remarks about the heavenly bodies, particularly "this one," which is "straining away all the time to make something of itself. The strain's so bad that every sixteen hours everybody lies down and gets a rest." Winding his watch, he bids the audience good night with, "You get a good rest, too."

The play established for Wilder a permanent place in American theater. Since its opening in 1938, scarcely a day has passed that *Our Town* has not been performed somewhere in this country—in productions ranging from professional revivals to little theaters to colleges and high schools. The original production brought the playwright an opportunity shared by few others: temporarily replacing actor Frank Craven as the Stage Manager, for two weeks in September 1938 he starred on Broadway in his own highly successful show. (He subsequently appeared in stock productions of *Our Town* and, somewhat less successfully, as Mr. Antrobus in *The Skin of Our Teeth*.) Additionally, the acclaim awarded the New York production boosted sales of the published version of the play, thus significantly increasing Wilder's financial rewards.

His next Broadway production was initially far less successful. *The Merchant of Yonkers,* based on Johann Nestroy's *Einen Jux will er sich Machen* (1842), opened 28 December 1938 and closed after only thirty-nine performances. Wilder had turned the direction over to Max Reinhardt, whose work he had admired for several years, but the critical consensus was that the production suffered from what Harold Clurman called the Viennese Reinhardt's "unfamiliarity with American theatre custom." The later success of the play substantiates the notion that the director, rather than the script, may have been at fault: after highly acclaimed runs at the Edinburgh Festival and in London, it was brought back in a slightly revised form to the New York stage in 1955 in a production that ran for 486 performances. Director Tyrone Guthrie's light touch and rapid pace set off Wilder's farce (retitled *The Matchmaker*) to its best advantage. *Hello, Dolly!* the adaptation by Michael Stewart, with words and music by Jerry Her-

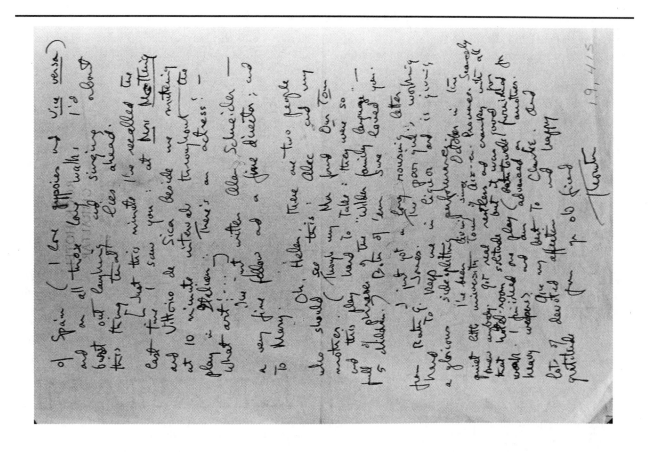

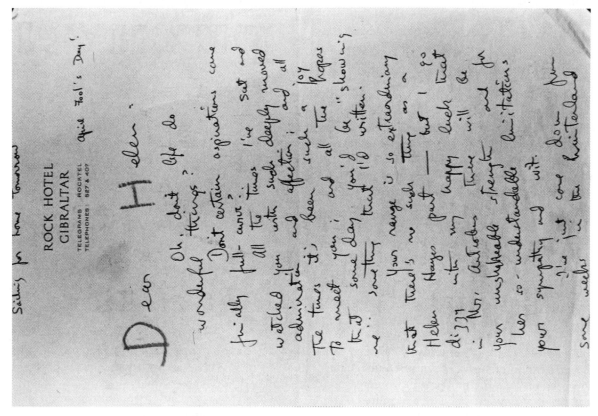

Letter from Wilder to Helen Hayes regarding her accepting a part for the 1955 revival of The Skin of Our Teeth *in Paris*
(The New York Public Library at Lincoln Center, Astor, Lenox, and Tilden Foundation)

man, opened in 1964; that production's run of almost 3,000 performances, a smash hit film version, and a later Broadway revival with an all-black cast have made it one of America's most successful and most popular musical comedies of all times.

Because *The Matchmaker* is essentially the same script as *The Merchant of Yonkers,* its discussion properly follows *Our Town* in a chronological examination of Wilder's career. The alterations of the earlier version involve only minor changes in dialogue and the addition of a closing monologue to point up the theme; the most significant difference is in the title change, which marks a shift in focus from one character to another. The appearance of something so close to a well-made play at this point in Wilder's career might appear peculiar, for all his efforts thus far had clearly countered the box-set, representational, realistic traditional conventions. However, as he states in his preface to the later *Three Plays* (1957), "One way to shake off the nonsense of the nineteenth-century staging is to make fun of it." As Wilder critics point out, he significantly chooses "to make fun of" rather than "to satirize." Thus the piece is a skillfully crafted bit of light entertainment, a farce that—true to the nature of its genre—delights and amuses but challenges neither the emotions nor the intellect of its audience.

The Yonkers merchant is Horace Vandergelder, a sixty-year-old miser who is more grumpy than villainous. In amassing his wealth he has consciously turned his back on human feelings and emotions. He has absolutely no patience with his lovesick niece, Ermengarde, for the object of her affections, Ambrose Kemper, is an artist; he regards the choice of either love or art above money as total foolishness. Also suffering from his stinginess are his clerks, Cornelius and Barnaby, two provincials who long for adventure in the big city. Their love interests are provided by a young and pretty widowed milliner, Irene Molloy, and her giddy assistant, Minnie Fay. The focal character is Mrs. Dolly Levi, an older widow whose philosophy of life is the exact opposite of Vandergelder's: "Money is like manure; it's not worth a thing unless it's spread about encouraging young things to grow." Her goal is to marry the miser so she can live more comfortably and do good with his money. Barnaby and Cornelius, determined that life will not pass them by, rebelliously blow up their employer's canned tomatoes and head into New York City. Vandergelder is also in the city, so their adventure is increased by the necessity to avoid him. The plot relies on traditional farcical conventions, such as madcap chases, mistaken identities, females dressed in male clothing, and collapsing screens. As both the day of ad-

venture and the play come to a close, Mrs. Levi's matchmaking has paid off: the four couples—Ermengarde and Ambrose, Cornelius and Irene, Barnaby and Minnie Fay, Dolly Levi and Horace Vandergelder—are happily joined. Those who sought excitement have found it, the misanthropic merchant is on the road to reform, and Barnaby (as the "youngest person here") is summoned to the footlights by Mrs. Levi to "tell us what the moral of the play is": "Oh, I think it's about . . . I think it's about adventure. The test of an adventure is that when you're in the middle of it, you say to yourself, 'Oh, now I've got myself into an awful mess; I wish I were sitting quietly at home.' And the sign that something's wrong with you is when you sit quietly at home wishing you were out having lots of adventure. . . . " The work is both lighthearted and lightweight, but its continued popularity attests to the playwright's mastery of stage-worthy farce; and its celebration of experience and "adventure" echoes Wilder's humanistic philosophy.

When his next play, *The Skin of Our Teeth,* opened in November 1942, its author was a captain in the U.S. Army Air Force. After the failure of *The Merchant of Yonkers,* Wilder had traveled extensively, including an unsuccessful sojourn in Mexico, where he had hoped to find the perfect climate for writing. A trip to Europe included a visit with Gertrude Stein and Alice B. Toklas in France, where he tried in vain to warn them of the impending war and to persuade them to return to America. Among his literary interests were the works of James Joyce, upon whose death he wrote a memorial piece for the March 1941 issue of *Poetry.* He also devoted some of his time to writing film scripts, the most notable of which was *Shadow of a Doubt* (1943) for Alfred Hitchcock. At the request of the State Department, he made a goodwill tour of Latin America in the spring of 1941; his mission was to foster favorable feelings toward the United States among the cultural and intellectual circles of the countries he visited. A growing patriotism and sympathy for the Allied forces prompted him, at the age of forty-five, to enlist in the U.S. Army Air Force; his commission in Intelligence led to his service for three years, first in Africa and later Italy, and a promotion to lieutenant colonel before his separation from the military in 1945.

The Skin of Our Teeth made a much greater impact, both positive and negative, than *The Merchant of Yonkers.* Its topicality no doubt contributed to its success: it celebrates the human race's ability to survive disaster, an optimistic notion enthusiastically embraced by audiences in the middle of World War II. Despite the misgivings of several producers and actors who hesitated to align themselves with a play so unconventional in approach, neophyte producer Michael Myerberg, then-untried director Elia Kazan, and an experienced cast headed by Tallulah Bankhead (Sabina), Fredrich March (Mr. Antrobus), and Florence Eldridge (Mrs. Antrobus) combined forces to yield a production that won immediate critical and popular acclaim.

In previous works Wilder had tampered with conventional concepts of time. In *The Long Christmas Dinner* events occur sequentially, but the chronology is selective and compressed. The Stage Manager in *Our Town* exhibits both omniscience and an ability to control time: he is able to allow Emily to relive part of her twelfth birthday, implying that the past continues to exist, but past and present are clearly separate entities. *The Skin of Our Teeth* represents an even further departure, for here major events of the entire history of the human race occur simultaneously. As the play opens, the setting is modern-day Excelsior, New Jersey, but its inhabitants are suffering the perils of the Ice Age. Act 2, spotlighting a convention on the Boardwalk of Atlantic City, ends with Mr. Antrobus loading a boat with his family and two of each kind of animal, preparing for the onslaught of the Great Flood. In the third act the characters are back in Excelsior, trying to put back together the pieces of civilization after surviving a seven-year war.

To further compound the violation of traditional perceptions of time, the illusion created by conventional realistic theater is constantly broken. The play opens with a slide show that includes projections of the theater in which the drama is being performed. Sabina, the maid, periodically drops her character, assuming the role of an actress playing the maid (Miss Somerset), to confide to the audience her misgivings about a script that she does not understand. The house area several times becomes part of the set, and at the end of the first act, in an effort to collect firewood for warmth against the impending glacier, Sabina entreats the audience to "Pass up your chairs, everybody. Save the human race." Act 3 opens with a rehearsal of production staff volunteers who will fill in for actors stricken with a digestive disorder, and later the actors playing Mr. Antrobus and his son abandon their characters to discuss events in their own lives and facets of their own personalities that make it difficult for them to play a father-son confrontation scene. The Stage Manager occasionally discusses interpretation of action with other characters, but his function differs from his predecessors' functions in the one-act plays and *Our Town:* he is given a name (Mr. Fitzpatrick), and he clearly is in charge of overseeing the production. His more conventional stage mana-

ger's role includes rehearsing the stand-ins, settling differences between actors, and cajoling Miss Somerset back into her role of Sabina in her recalcitrant moments—albeit this typically "behind the scenes" action takes place as part of the play, in view of the audience. Although these devices are encompassed in the onstage action, they serve as constant reminders to the audience that they are in fact watching a play, rather than observing an enactment of real life, an anti-illusionary Brechtian technique that promotes intellectual rather than emotional involvement and response.

The characterizations also contribute to the effect of melding all of human history. George and Maggie Antrobus are at once Adam and Eve, the archetypical Everyman and Everywoman, and the average modern middle-class couple. Mr. Antrobus, the inventor of the alphabet, the lever, and the wheel, commutes across the Hudson River and serves as president of his fraternal order. Through glacier, flood, and war his primary concern is preserving for future generations the advances civilization has made: as the ice approaches and temperatures drop, he offers refuge to Moses, Homer, and the Muses. When he returns from the war, he is anxious to be assured that his books have not been lost. Mrs. Antrobus is a further development of Ma Kirby from *The Happy Journey to Trenton and Camden,* elevated to the next social class. An inventor herself (of, among other things, the apron), she keeps as her watchword "Save the Family." She faces disaster with energy, determination, and resourcefulness. Sabina describes her as a fine woman who lives only for her children: "If it would be any benefit to her children she'd see the rest of us stretched out dead at her feet without turning a hair,—and that's the truth. If you want to know anything more about Mrs. Antrobus, just go and look at a tigress, and look hard."

Like their parents, the Antrobus children are allegorical figures. In the first act Gladys is admonished to "Put down your dress!!" and scolded for painting her face with makeup. Despite her mother's constant exhortations that she be a lady and make her father proud of her, the daughter becomes more and more sluttish. She shocks her parents by appearing on the Boardwalk in a pair of probably ill-gotten red stockings, and by the end of the war she is the mother of an illegitimate baby. Her brother Henry has a penchant for throwing stones; his name has been changed from Cain (his hair is combed forward in an effort to hide the mark on his forehead), and his parents are still pained by the "accident" in which he killed his brother. In the third act, after he has been identified as the enemy against whom the war has been fought, the stage directions indicate that in the confrontation with his father "Henry is played, not as a misunderstood or misguided young man, but as a representation of strong unreconciled evil."

The adjunct to the Antrobus family who as often as possible places herself at the center of the action is Lily Sabina, a combination of Lilith and the Sabine women (supposedly Mr. Antrobus has "raped" her and brought her home to insult his wife). In the first act she appears as the family's good-natured but less than efficient maid. As she introduces the other characters, she prattles to the audience (both in and out of character) about the confusion in the world around her. Her low-level panic in the face of adversity is in opposition to Mrs. Antrobus's firm resolve. On the Boardwalk in act 2, after she has won the bathing beauty contest (under the name Lily Fairweather—but Mrs. Antrobus recognizes her for who she really is), she makes a concerted but unsuccessful effort to lure Mr.Antrobus away from his wife. In the final act she has resumed her former position with the family; she goes about her duties "out of *habit*" but without conviction, for after so many disasters she holds little faith in new beginnings. Her character provides much of the comedy in the play, and both the role and Tallulah Bankhead's performance in it were given large credit for the success of the premiere production.

Taken as a whole, the play is a delightfully nontraditional comedy with substantial seriousness that provides ballast without overweighting it into pretentiousness. Wilder's vision is again affirmative, but because he encapsulates the whole of human history simultaneously rather than sequentially, and because the play cyclically ends where it begins (Sabina's curtain speech duplicates her entrance in act 1, with the whole world "at sixes and sevens"), he offers no traditional "happy ending" with all troubles vanquished and all problems resolved. Instead, he presents the human race—faced with disasters of the highest magnitude, some natural and some man-made—exhibiting the ability to survive, keeping intact the contributions of the past as well as a strong desire to make some slight advances for the future. The play's engaging theatrical, anti-illusionary technique—complete with slides and newsreels, walls that first totter and then disappear into the loft, actors who drop their roles to voice their apprehensions and opinions to the audience and each other, and ludicrously costumed animals who parade through the audience—provides an opportunity for entertainment, surprise, and intellectual challenge.

Scarcely three months after the play's opening, amid critical acclaim and popular success, Joseph Campbell and Henry M. Robinson launched an attack in the *Saturday Review of Literature* that was reminiscent of Michael Gold's 1930 onslaught in its effect on Wilder's literary reputation. In an article titled "The Skin of Whose Teeth?" (1942) they noted the similarities in theme and technique between Wilder's play and James Joyce's *Finnegans Wake;* although they avoided a direct accusation, the implication was that Wilder had plagiarized. The effect of the charge was compounded by the fact that at that time, the number of Americans, even among the literati, with firsthand knowledge of Joyce's work (published in 1939) was small. Wilder himself did little to abate the controversy; refusing to take a stand, he suggested that those in doubt should read both works and make up their own minds. (Not until years later did he publicly respond to the charge; in the preface to *Three Plays* he acknowledges a debt to Joyce, commenting that he would be pleased if future authors should feel similarly indebted to him. "Literature has always more resembled a torch race than a furious dispute among heirs.") Several critics of the day adopted the view that has prevailed in retrospect: that Wilder, as most artists do, was making legitimate use of another's work for his own purposes, and that (as phrased by *Time*) the attackers, who were "trying to make headlines out of footnotes, were confusing influences with imitations."

The clamor did little damage to the popular success of the play (it ran for 355 performances), but among literary critics the taint of possible plagiarism was slow to die. The work was voted down for the New York Drama Critics Circle Award (which went to Sidney Kingsley's *The Patriots*), reportedly on the basis of the unrefuted plagiarism charge. However, three weeks later it was awarded the Pulitzer Prize. The play subsequently enjoyed a successful run in Britain, and a production in postwar Germany engendered an enthusiasm for Wilder's work that, though somewhat diminished, remains strong today; in fact, his work has generated more academic scholarship in Germany than it has in the United States.

For several years after World War II, Wilder's literary career leaned in the directions of fiction and academia. In June 1947 he was awarded an honorary doctorate by Yale University. Later that year he wrote a three-scene burlesque, *Our Century,* in celebration of the centenary of the Century Association of New York, of which he was a member. Because the production was not reviewed, and the distribution of the published version was limited, the short work did little to advance his career as a dramatist.

Wilder in Paris, 1950, with Sylvia Beach (left) and Alice B. Toklas (right)

The Ides of March, a fictionalized account of the last days of Julius Caesar, was published in 1948. The book displays the influence of—in addition to Wilder's previous concerns with history, ancient literature, and the notions of Gertrude Stein—the existentialism of Jean-Paul Sartre. Eliminating the narrator, Wilder presents a randomly ordered collection of letters and journal entries almost entirely of his own creation. Although the novel was warmly received in England, American critics, balking at both the unconventional format and Wilder's alterations of historical facts, responded unfavorably. (A stage adaptation several years later, authored by Jerome Kilty with Wilder's unofficial but enthusiastic collaboration, was also a failure.) In 1950–1951 Wilder held the Charles Eliot Norton Professorship of Poetry at Harvard, lecturing on nineteenth-century American writers in a series titled "The American Characteristics in Classic American Literature." His scholarly publications included works on, among others, Emily Dickinson and Lope de Vega. In 1952 he was awarded the American Academy of Arts and Letters Gold Medal for Fiction.

Wilder's dramatic career in the 1950s was marked primarily by revivals, revisions, and foreign productions. *The Matchmaker,* the revision of *The Merchant of Yonkers,* was performed at the Edinburgh Festival in Scotland (August 1954) and in England before its successful run in New York. French productions of *The Skin of Our Teeth* and *The Matchmaker* increased his international reputation. His only

original dramatic work of the period was *The Alcestiad,* a play based on Euripides' *Alcestis* on which he had worked for almost a decade. It was first performed in August 1955 at the Edinburgh Festival under the title *A Life in the Sun;* as *Die Alkestiade* it was produced in Germany in 1959, and a German operatic version, with libretto by Wilder and music by Louise Talma, opened in Frankfurt in March 1962. Though it saw German production, at the time only the fourth act, a satyr play titled *The Drunken Sisters,* was published in English (both in the *Atlantic Monthly* and under its own cover in 1957); the complete work was not published in Wilder's language until 1977, two years after his death. The satyr play was performed in Brooklyn Heights in June 1970, but as yet neither it nor the full-length work has been given a Broadway production.

Two other plays that received only German stagings were the one-act plays *The Wreck of the 5:25* and *Bernice.* Performed in September 1957 as part of the dedication ceremonies for the new Congress Hall in West Berlin, both works exhibit a gloomy outlook uncharacteristic of Wilder's vision. The first focuses on a commuter who, even though he claims to have examined his life closely and determined to value it more highly, has in fact been averted from a suicide that would have eradicated a world he had cynically rejected. The second presents the alienation of an embezzler just released from prison; rather than being reunited with his daughter, who represents the society from which he has become estranged, he has her sent away, choosing to remain in permanent isolation. Unfavorably received in West Berlin, the two plays remain unpublished.

Bernice was written as the "Pride" selection of a proposed cycle to be titled "The Seven Deadly Sins"; "The Seven Ages of Man" was planned as a companion group. Neither cycle was completed, but works from each were performed together at Circle in the Square in January 1962. Billed as *Plays for Bleecker Street,* the José Quintero production marks the final premiere of a Wilder drama. The first two *Plays for Bleecker Street* belong to "The Seven Ages of Man." *Infancy,* in which grown men appear in the roles of babies, extols the virtues of the young in a world marred by the errors of their elders. In *Childhood,* the most widely praised of the three, a father is allowed to become a participant in the enactment of his children's fantasies, and the ensuing mood of communication and harmony was likened by critics to that of *Our Town.* The "Lust" episode of the proposed "Seven Deadly Sins" cycle, *Someone from Assisi,* which focuses on a rejected lover of Saint Francis, was found unnatural and pretentious, in the mode of the early three-minute plays. Favorable response to the other two works, however, sustained the run through 349 performances.

Although Wilder was to produce no further dramatic works, his literary career had not come to an end. Later in 1962 he was invited to Washington by President Kennedy's cabinet to present a reading from his works titled "An Evening with Thornton Wilder," and in 1963 he was awarded the U.S. Presidential Medal of Freedom. Having retired to the Arizona desert to write in seclusion, he did not appear in person to receive the award. In 1965 he was honored with the National Medal of Literature, and in 1967 *The Eighth Day,* the book he went into isolation to complete, was published.

The Eighth Day, lauded as a novel encompassing the best in theme and technique from his entire career, won the National Book Award in 1968. Like all of Wilder's novels, it incorporates Wilder's religious and philosophical speculations, but in addition it attempts to define or at least describe the uniqueness of American traditions, values, and behavior. The work reflects Wilder's essential perceptions about man's struggles to build and survive, about the American spirit, about universality and eternity. Published weeks before Wilder reached his seventieth birthday, the book represented his final statement. Older critics such as Malcolm Cowley, Granville Hicks, and Clifton Fadiman applauded the work and Edmund Wilson privately viewed the novel as Wilder's masterpiece. The newer genera-

tion of critics, however, either attacked the book or ignored it. In short, they consigned Wilder and all of his work to what Wilder's longtime detractor Dwight Macdonald dubbed Mid-Cult.

The Eighth Day is Wilder's longest and most intricately plotted novel. In its skeletal structure it describes the interaction between two families living in a small town in southern Illinois. The head of one of the families, John Ashley, is convicted of fatally shooting his friend and neighbor Breckenridge Lansing. The novel begins with Ashley's fleeing from justice after being sentenced to death, and half the narrative deals with Ashley's several months as a fugitive. The remainder of the novel is devoted to the impact of his escape upon both the Ashley and Lansing families, attempting to survive without a head of household.

Although *The Eighth Day* was in Wilder's view a critical disappointment, it was widely read. Aware that his reading public had become greater than it had ever been, Wilder at seventy began what was to be his final work: a series of fictional autobiographical short stories that were finally published as a novel. A first-person account of a man who has just resigned a job at a prep school for boys, the work was found somewhat wanting for the author's insufficient detachment. *Theophilus North* (1973) purported to be the adventures of Wilder's alter ego. (Wilder, the survivor of twins, told an interviewer that *Theophilus North* was what his brother might have lived to become.) Despite what appear to be autobiographical clues and what have been often interpreted as such, the volume reveals less than it conceals about the private life of its author. It might, in fact, have been subtitled "A Puritan Swan Song." The collection, while stylistically up to the high standard Wilder always set for himself, is a work that he never would have indulged himself in when he was at the height of his powers.

By this time Wilder, back in New Haven, was suffering the infirmities of age—failing eyesight, chronic back problems, a disposition that was becoming more waspish. However, rather than seeing his reputation fade as he grew older, he enjoyed the security of knowing that he had become an American institution. When he died in 1975, he was recognized as a novelist, dramatist, and man of letters.

Letters:

Wilder and Gertrude Stein, *The Letters of Gertrude Stein and Thornton Wilder,* edited by Edward Burns and Ulla E. Dydo, with William Rice (New Haven, Conn.: Yale University Press, 1996).

Bibliographies:

J. M. Edelstein, *A Bibliographical Checklist of the Writings of Thornton Wilder* (New Haven, Conn.: Yale University Library, 1959);

Heinz Kosok, "Thornton Wilder: A Bibliography of Criticism," *Twentieth Century Literature,* 9 (1963): 93–100.

Biographies:

Richard H. Goldstone, *Thornton Wilder, An Intimate Portrait* (New York: Saturday Review Press/ Dutton, 1975);

Linda Simon, *Thornton Wilder: His World* (Garden City, N.Y.: Doubleday, 1979).

References:

Carl Balliet Jr., "The Skin of Whose Teeth: Part III," *Saturday Review of Literature,* 26 (2 January 1943): 11;

Martin Blank, ed., *Critical Essays on Thornton Wilder* (New York: G. K. Hall / London: Prentice Hall International, 1996);

Rex Burbank, *Thornton Wilder* (New York: Twayne, 1961);

Joseph Campbell and Henry M. Robinson, "The Skin of Whose Teeth? The Strange Case of Mr. Wilder's Play and *Finnegans Wake*," *Saturday Review of Literature,* 25 (19 December 1942): 3–4;

Campbell and Robinson, "The Skin of Whose Teeth: Part II, The Intention Behind the Deed," *Saturday Review of Literature,* 26 (13 February 1943): 16–18;

Robert W. Corrigan, "Thornton Wilder and the Tragic Sense of Life," *Educational Theater,* 13 (October 1961): 167–173;

Malcolm Cowley, "The Man Who Abolished Time," *Saturday Review of Literature,* 39 (6 October 1956): 13–14, 50–52;

Joseph J. Firebaugh, "The Humanism of Thornton Wilder," *Pacific Spectator,* 4 (Fall 1950): 426–428;

Four Quarters, Special Wilder issue, 16 (May 1967);

Michael Gold, "Wilder: Prophet of the Genteel Christ," *New Republic,* 24 (22 October 1930): 266–267;

Malcolm Goldstein, *The Art of Thornton Wilder* (Lincoln: University of Nebraska Press, 1965);

Richard Goldstone, "An Interview with Thornton Wilder," *Paris Review,* 15 (Winter 1957): 36–57;

Bernard Grebanier, *Thornton Wilder* (Minneapolis: University of Minnesota Press, 1965);

Tyrone Guthrie, "The World of Thornton Wilder," *New York Times Magazine* (27 November 1955): 26–27, 64, 66–68;

Donald Haberman, *The Plays of Thornton Wilder* (Middletown, Conn.: Wesleyan University Press, 1967);

Katie de Koster, ed., *Readings on Thornton Wilder* (San Diego, Cal.: Greenhaven Press, 1998);

Mildred Christophe Kuner, *Thornton Wilder: The Bright and the Dark* (New York: Crowell, 1972);

Paul Lifton, *Vast Encyclopedia: The Theatre of Thornton Wilder* (Westport, Conn.: Greenwood Press, 1995);

Helmut Papajewski, *Thornton Wilder* (New York: Ungar, 1968);

Harrison Smith, "The Skin of Whose Teeth: Part II," *Saturday Review of Literature,* 25 (26 December 1942): 12.

Papers:

Portions of Wilder's papers are held by the libraries of Yale University, Kent State University, and the University of Virginia.

Herman Wouk

This entry was updated by Laurence W. Mazzeno (Alvernia College)
from the entry by Mark J. Charney (Clemson University)
in DLB Yearbook 1982.

BIRTH: New York, New York, 27 May 1915, to Abraham Isaac and Esther Levine Wouk.

EDUCATION: B.A., with honors, Columbia University, 1934.

MARRIAGE: 9 December 1945 to Betty Sarah Brown; children: Abraham Isaac (died 1951), Nathaniel, Joseph.

AWARDS AND HONORS: Richard H. Fox Prize, 1934; Pulitzer Prize in fiction for *The Caine Mutiny: A Novel of World War II,* 1952; Columbia University Medal of Excellence, 1952; Alexander Hamilton Medal, Columbia College Alumni Association, 1980; American Book Award nomination for *War and Remembrance,* 1981; Ralph Waldo Emerson Award, International Platform Association, 1981; University of California–Berkeley Medal, 1984; Golden Plate Award, American Academy of Achievement, 1986; Washingtonian Book Award for *Inside, Outside,* 1986; U.S. Naval Memorial Foundation Lone Sailor Award, 1987; Tel Aviv University Guardian of Zion Award, 1988; Yad Vashem KaZetnik award, 1990; honorary degrees include L.H.D., Yeshiva University, 1955; LL.D., Clark University, 1960; Litt.D., American International University, 1979; Ph.D., Bar-Ilan University, 1990, Hebrew University, 1997; D.S.T., Trinity College, 1998.

BOOKS: *Aurora Dawn* (New York: Simon & Schuster, 1947; London: Barrie, 1947);
The City Boy (New York: Simon & Schuster, 1948; London: Cape, 1956);
The Traitor (New York: S. French, 1949);
The Caine Mutiny: A Novel of World War II (Garden City, N.Y.: Doubleday, 1951; London: Cape, 1951);
The Caine Mutiny Court-Martial (Garden City, N.Y.: Doubleday, 1954; London: Cape, 1955);
Marjorie Morningstar (Garden City, N.Y.: Doubleday, 1955; London: Cape, 1955);

Herman Wouk

Slattery's Hurricane (New York: Permabooks, 1956; London: New English Library, 1965);
Nature's Way (Garden City, N.Y.: Doubleday, 1958);
This Is My God (Garden City, N.Y.: Doubleday, 1959; London: Cape, 1960);
Youngblood Hawke (Garden City, N.Y.: Doubleday, 1962; London: Collins, 1962);
Don't Stop the Carnival (Garden City, N.Y.: Doubleday, 1965; London: Collins, 1965);
The Lomokome Papers (New York: Pocket Books, 1968);
The Winds of War (Boston: Little, Brown, 1971; London: Collins, 1971);
War and Remembrance (Boston: Little, Brown, 1978; London: Collins, 1978);

Inside, Outside (Boston: Little, Brown, 1985; London: Collins, 1985);
The Hope (Boston: Little, Brown, 1993; London: Hodder & Stoughton, 1994);
The Glory (Boston: Little, Brown, 1994; London: Hodder & Stoughton, 1994).

PLAY PRODUCTIONS: *The Traitor*, New York, Forty-Eighth Street Theatre, 4 April 1949;
The Caine Mutiny Court-Martial, New York, Plymouth Theatre, 20 January 1954;
Nature's Way, New York, Coronet Theatre, 15 October 1957;
Don't Stop the Carnival, libretto by Wouk, music and lyrics by Jimmy Buffett, Miami, Coconut Grove Playhouse, 19 April 1997.

MOTION PICTURE: *Slattery's Hurricane*, Twentieth Century-Fox, 1949.

TELEVISION: *The Winds of War*, ABC, 6–13 February 1983;
War and Remembrance, ABC, 13–23 November 1988, 7–14 May 1989.

Herman Wouk, novelist and dramatist, has written twelve novels and four plays. Though the critical response to his works varies as much as the subject matter, at least eight of the novels were best-sellers and two of his plays were popular and critical successes. A reading of his works makes the reasons for their popularity apparent: each displays his expertise at composing a compelling narrative.

Born in New York City on 27 May 1915, Herman Wouk is the son of Abraham Isaac and Esther Levine Wouk, both Russian-Jewish immigrants. His father began as a three-dollar-per-week laundry laborer and became the owner of a laundry chain. Wouk spent most of his youth in the Bronx and attended Townsend Harris High School from 1927 to 1930. He majored in comparative literature and philosophy at Columbia University, and in 1934 he received a bachelor of arts degree with general honors. At Columbia, Wouk began his writing career. He edited the college humor magazine, *Columbia Jester,* and wrote two popular varsity shows.

In 1935 Wouk accepted a job as a radio comedy writer but was disillusioned to find that his "first literary task was copying old jokes out of tattered comic magazines on to file cards." Between 1936 and 1941, however, Wouk took on more responsibilities and began assisting Fred Allen with his weekly radio scripts. In June 1941 he began to write and produce radio shows promoting war bonds for the United States Treasury. He kept this job until 1942, when he enlisted in the navy and served as a deck officer on the destroyer/ minesweeper USS *Zane* in the Pacific for three years.

In 1943, during this tour of duty aboard the *Zane,* Wouk began his first novel, a humorous attack on radio and advertising, in order "to relieve the tedium of military service at sea in wartime." He did not complete the first part of the novel, *Aurora Dawn* (1947), until he became an executive officer on the USS *Southard* at Okinawa in 1945, and he did not finish the book until May 1946 while he was in Northport, Long Island.

On 9 December 1945, before the completion of *Aurora Dawn,* Wouk married Betty Sarah Brown, a convert to Judaism. The Wouks had three children—Abraham Isaac, Nathaniel, and Joseph—the first of whom died just short of the age of five in 1951.

Wouk's first novel follows the adventures and loves of Andrew Reale, who is convinced that "the road to happiness lay in becoming rich very quickly." Though the book was not received favorably by the critics, several reviewers recognized Wouk's future potential, and the Book-of-the-Month Club chose it as a featured selection in May 1947. Spencer Klaw of the *New York Herald Tribune Weekly Book Review* called *Aurora Dawn* "a delightfully fresh and funny satire on radio advertising that never descends to mere burlesque and is all the more effective because the author—a former radio writer—refrains from grinding any personal axes," while Percy Atkinson of the *Saturday Review of Literature* appreciated Wouk's "good-natured banter and philosophic discursiveness."

Though both Klaw and Atkinson cited some of the positive qualities of *Aurora Dawn,* Wouk's exploration of the advertising world was criticized for its highly stylized manner. Russell Maloney of *The New York Time Book Review* said the novel had "no more authority than a lace valentine." Indeed, though Wouk's parody in the eighteenth-century style is fun, it fails to achieve the primary purpose of works of this kind. Whatever important social criticisms Wouk hoped to make are lost within the patterned, overly stylized, superficial story of one man's comic series of successes and failures within a farcical representation of the world of advertising and radio broadcasting. As in Henry Fielding's *Tom Jones* (1749), a narrator attempts to manipulate, entertain, and instruct the reader with comic diversions and witty discourse; but Wouk's diversions are either too didactic ("There is a school of philosophy which holds that there is no such thing in the world as evil, but only the absence of Being where Being should be") or too obvious ("Every novel

Humphrey Bogart as Captain Queeg in the 1954 movie version of Wouk's 1951 novel, The Caine Mutiny *(Columbia Pictures)*

nowadays is supposed to have a purpose . . . of correcting a specific social disorder such as capitalism, deforestation, inadequate city planning, war or . . . religion"). Although it is predictable, *Aurora Dawn* does reveal Wouk's ability to keep his reader entertained.

Wouk's second novel was published in 1948. *The City Boy* is a maturation tale about the adventures of a plump, eleven-year-old Jewish boy from the Bronx named Herbie Bookbinder, who learns the meaning of responsibility and the joys of first love while spending a summer at camp. The theme and structure of *The City Boy* have sometimes been favorably compared to those of Mark Twain's *Tom Sawyer* (1876), and indeed Wouk does acknowledge a great fondness for Twain's novels. In the foreword to the 1969 edition of *The City Boy,* Wouk admits that Herbie is possibly his "favorite creation to this day," but when the book was published, "it slid off the plank, and with scarcely a ripple went bubbling down."

The reviews of *The City Boy,* however, were somewhat more positive than those for *Aurora Dawn.* Marc Brandel wrote in *The New York Times Book Review* that *The City Boy* made "delightful reading," and Joseph Henry Jackson of the *San Francisco*

Chronicle praised the novel for being "affectionately written, enormously entertaining." Critics who disapproved of the novel, such as R. B. Gehman of the *Saturday Review of Literature,* concentrated upon Wouk's failure to achieve fully rounded characters because he was imitating the styles of other authors such as Booth Tarkington, Sinclair Lewis, and, of course, Twain.

In spite of the mixed reviews he received for his first two novels, Wouk was becoming well known within literary circles. Eloise Perry Hazard, in a *Saturday Review* article titled "First Novelists of 1947" (14 February 1948), characterized Wouk as "tall, handsome, a good speaker, a deft writer, [who] has known from the first where he was going." In 1949 Wouk finished his first play, *The Traitor,* a melodrama; starring Lee Tracy and Walter Hampden, it opened on Broadway on 4 April 1949 to mixed reviews. Harold Clurman in the *New Republic* noted the similarity between the plot of *The Traitor* and the events of the Klaus Fuchs atom-spy case: "This is an effort to cash in on a topicality that is related to the audience's mental confusion—compounded of prejudice, indecision, and *Reader's Digest* information or ignorance." The play, which focuses upon the decisions of a scientist to release atomic

538

bomb secrets to the enemy in the hope of gaining world peace, is often difficult to believe; nevertheless, other critics, such as Wolcott Gibbs of *The New Yorker,* found the play "continuously entertaining" in spite of its naive nature.

One of Wouk's greatest successes, *The Caine Mutiny: A Novel of World War II* (1951) is his third novel. Obviously borrowing from his experience at sea, Wouk provides a suspenseful plot and a firm thematic base. Wouk's story of young Willie Keith's fated meeting with the paranoid Captain Queeg and the events that lead to Lieutenant Maryk's eventual court-martial for assuming Queeg's command in a time of crisis creates an array of themes. Though in this book and in both of Wouk's previous novels the protagonists have matured and learned from their mistakes, in *The Caine Mutiny* Keith's maturation process is handled with much more subtlety and honesty. Willie Keith, a Princeton graduate in comparative literature and a "mama's boy" who "is somewhat chubby, and good looking, with curly red hair and an innocent, gay face," is believably transformed into the final commander of the *Caine*—a perceptive, sensitive, responsible individual who realizes on coming home the changes the navy has made in his character: "he had felt his military personality dissolving, drifting away into the sea air like vapor, leaving a residue which was only Willie Keith. . . . He was no longer a naval officer—but he was no longer Willie Keith, either."

In *The Caine Mutiny* Wouk offers much more than just a maturation story. Because of Wouk's intelligent depiction of the unstable Queeg, the book raises questions about the nature of sanity and man's responsibility to man. In the brilliantly conceived and executed court-martial scenes, Wouk skillfully shifts the reader's opinions from dislike of Queeg to pity for him, forcing the reader to examine his own judgments about the importance of appearances and the nature of cowardice.

The Caine Mutiny was warmly received by critics and the public. Edward Weeks of the *Atlantic Monthly* felt that it had "scope and the skill to reveal how men are tested, exposed, and developed under the long routine of war," and Kelsey Guilfoil of the *Chicago Sunday Tribune* praised *The Caine Mutiny* for being a real story, not a drab and wearisome account of the extracurricular activities of the service man." Most reviewers also pointed to Wouk's stylistic improvement in his third book. W. K. Harrison wrote in *Library Journal* that "superb writing and deft characterization make this the most exciting sea story since *Mutiny on the Bounty*," and E. L. Acken of the *New York Herald Tribune Book Review* called *The Caine Mutiny* "a provocative book, full of authentic

people and atmosphere." The only notable fault of the novel is the consistently sentimental shallow romance between Willie and Mae Wynn. Because Wouk spends so little time defining Willie and Mae's relationship and because Mae never shares the important experiences that Willie encounters, their relationship remains undeveloped. *The Caine Mutiny* won the Pulitzer Prize for literature. It was also on *The New York Times* best-seller list for more than two and a half years.

After seeing a production of George Bernard Shaw's *Don Juan in Hell* (first performed in 1907), Wouk decided to adapt *The Caine Mutiny* into a play, *The Caine Mutiny Court-Martial* (1954). The Broadway play, with Henry Fonda, John Hodiak, and Lloyd Nolan, was extremely well received. The play remains a favorite both in the United States and abroad; one major production ended a two-year run in the major cities of France in 1997.

In 1953 Wouk accepted a visiting professorship in English at Yeshiva University, where he stayed until 1957. In 1955, while he was at the university, Wouk's next major novel was published. *Marjorie Morningstar* is about the aspirations of a young, beautiful Jewish girl in New York, and the many relationships that help her to reach womanhood and to understand her heritage. More than a maturation story, *Marjorie Morningstar* also presents the conflicts inherent in attempting to live by both Jewish and American standards and the struggle young American Jews experience in coming to terms with the traditions of their elders. Like Wouk's previous novels, *Marjorie Morningstar* is immensely readable, and it became an immediate best-seller.

Despite its popularity, critics disagreed over the worth of this novel. F. H. Bullock of the *New York Herald Tribune Book Review* termed *Marjorie Morningstar* a "modern Jewish Vanity Fair . . . spacious, abundantly peopled, shrewd, observant, humane," and Meyer Levin of the *Saturday Review* generously called it "Herman Wouk's most solid achievement to date." While most critics felt the novel was much too long and that the tedious, repetitive conflicts dragged, few were as wholly negative as Nora Nagid of the *New Republic,* who wrote, "*Marjorie Morningstar* is a soap opera with psychological and sociological props," or the reviewer for *The New Yorker* who called it "a damp and endless tale."

Wouk's long novel may seem melodramatic and endless because of Marjorie's patterned, moralistic conflicts, but its subtle characterization and clear prose reveal Wouk's development as a fiction writer. For example, the first sentence in the book reflects a control of style and purpose: "Customs of

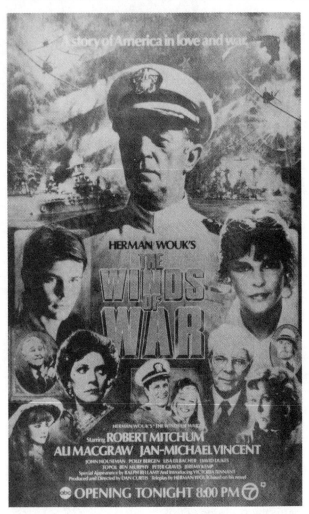

Advertisement for the 1983 miniseries Wouk adapted from his 1971 epic novel about World War II

courtship vary greatly in different times and places, but the way the thing happens to be done here and now always seems the only natural way to do it." Although at first glance *Marjorie Morningstar* appears to be a predictable soap opera, a closer look shows that Wouk achieved his primary purpose: to write in an honest, interesting manner of customs, traditions, and the conflicts of maturity.

Wouk's third play, *Nature's Way*, was produced in 1957; it is his least successful dramatic work. *Nature's Way* is a farce about the problems of a young married songwriter who decides to leave his "too" newly pregnant wife for a while and accompany a homosexual friend to Italy in order to save his marriage and his career. Wouk's overly moralistic tone both condemns and laughs at such subjects as premarital sex, greed, and homosexuality. His inconsistent approach to these subjects prevents any humor that could be derived from the situation of the characters. Wolcott Gibbs of *The New Yorker*

summed up the opinions of most reviewers when he said that "The whole enterprise, I guess, is a demonstration of the sad fact that strong moral indignation unassisted by a real detachment of urbanity, can easily be the deadly enemy of humor."

Wouk's religious faith is expressed in *This Is My God* (1959), an informal but detailed account of Judaism for "the many Jews who do not observe the religion, who yet would like to know a lot more about it." Obviously a "labor of love," *This Is My God* succeeds in providing the reader with an account of Jewish symbols, beliefs, customs, festivals, and holy days. It also effectively defines the conflicts that Jewish immigrants met in America and the constant struggle Jews still meet in continuing to practice the traditions that sometimes seem outdated and difficult; and these explanations are easily understood by the interested layman.

In 1962 one of Wouk's most important novels, *Youngblood Hawke,* was published; it became an immediate best-seller. A sprawling tale about a talented Southern writer's struggles to succeed in a world of publishers, theater agents, and tax collectors, *Youngblood Hawke* attacks the business policies and compromises associated with publishing works of artistic merit.

Obviously borrowing from experiences in his own life and from incidents in Thomas Wolfe's, Wouk intended for his novel to examine the pressures connected with publishing and achieving fame; but the book lapses too often into the protagonist's melodramatic struggles with his true love, his mistress, and his overbearing mother. During the final one-third of the novel, with tax collectors and moneylenders demanding payment, *Youngblood Hawke* descends into triteness and oversentimentality. The critical reception was largely unfavorable. David Boroff of the *Saturday Review,* for example, found that *Youngblood Hawke* possessed "an elaborate plot, a vast gallery of characters, enormous length, and a persuasive air of unreality," and W. J. Smith of *Commonweal* maintained that Wouk "plods. Sometimes he plods so doggedly that you begin to admire him more for his stamina than his story telling. . . ." Stanley Kauffman of the *New Republic* chided Wouk for characterization "constructed with the knit-browed, honest concentration of a child working with a Meccano set," while the reviewer for *Time* took offense at the obvious parallels between Youngblood Hawke and Thomas Wolfe: "Wouk has borrowed almost everything from Wolfe but his cuff links."

Youngblood Hawke, however, is not without merit. The characters, though somewhat stereotypical, are interesting and the plot, though sometimes predictable, manages to keep the reader's interest—especially in those sections of the novel that describe the devotion, doubts, and insecurities the writing profession entails.

Wouk lived with his family in the Virgin Islands from 1958 until 1964, and those years provided much of the experience leading to his novel *Don't Stop the Carnival*. Critics generally consider this book Wouk's weakest novel, although it continues to sell well in the Caribbean resort world. Published in 1965, it tells the story of a married Broadway press agent, Norman Paperman, who, tired of the pressures of New York, decides to purchase a resort hotel in a mythical Caribbean island Wouk calls Amerigo. The novel traces Paperman's minor successes and failures with the hotel until a love interest and the death of a friend force Paperman to reevaluate his life and return to New York. The thematic line, which deals with man meeting his responsibilities and his dreams, remains vague and unclear because *Don't Stop the Carnival* is replete with type characters and predictable situations. Haskel Frankel of the *Saturday Review* pointed out that Paperman moves in "a land of labels—Jew, gentile, white, Negro, homosexual." Samuel L. Simon of the *Library Journal* wrote that "*Don't Stop the Carnival* is a shoddy and absurd novel. . . . The problems are so exaggerated and comic as to border on slapstick." When entire chapters focus upon whether the cistern in the hotel will be repaired, the reader loses interest.

Wouk's next novel, another best-seller titled *The Winds of War* (1971), took nine years to write and much longer to research than any of his previous novels. The novel about World War II, as seen through the eyes of the Henry family, is a sprawling, detailed epic that gives an accurate account of the moods and insecurities of both America and Europe from the early months of 1939 to the bombing of Pearl Harbor on 7 December 1941. It has been recognized as Wouk's best literary achievement since *The Caine Mutiny*.

The Winds of War has two distinct narrative lines. First, Wouk examines the lives and loves of the Henry family: Pug (a middle-aged naval attaché whose job brings him into contact with Roosevelt, Hitler, Goering, Stalin, and Churchill), his wife, his two sons, and his daughter. Through their eyes, Wouk provides diverse views and reactions to historical situations and also heightens the theme he identifies in the foreword to the sequel, *War and Remembrance* (1978): "Either war is finished or we are."

The second narrative line is a translation by the character Pug Henry of a book called *World Empire Lost* by General Armin Von Roon, "a fictitious German staff officer fictitiously imprisoned for

twenty years by the very real Nuremburg Tribunal." The device of interspersing parts of the "translation" within the text of the novel provides transitions between historical events and furnishes detailed information about the German's opinions of Hitler and the war. Henry's translation of Von Roon's book also gives an account of several of the specific battles that are not included within the rest of the narrative. This interesting device, although a bit contrived, keeps the adventures of the Henrys in historical perspective.

L. R. Andrews of the *Library Journal* congratulated Wouk for his "well-executed plot as well as believable characters acting against a fascinating background of social history," and the reviewer of the *Economist* stated the "*The Winds of War* is as serious a contribution to the literature of our time as *War and Peace* was to that of the nineteenth century." Though Granville Hicks pointed out in *The New York Times Book Review* that "the failures of Wouk's style betray the failures of his imagination," he admitted that Wouk has the "gift of compelling narrative." Wouk's style may be undemanding, but his stylistic inadequacies do not detract from the power of his narrative or the effectiveness of his extensive research. *The Winds of War* provides the reader with a compelling, informative, honest picture of the brooding, threatening times, and this picture, in itself, is an achievement.

War and Remembrance, Wouk's sequel to *The Winds of War,* was written after Wouk served as a scholar in residence at the Aspen Institute of Humanistic Studies from 1973 to 1974. Published in 1978 and also an immediate best-seller, Wouk's sequel lacks the sense of balance and freshness that its predecessor has. In the foreword to *War and Remembrance,* Wouk gives the purpose for his sequel: "It is the main tale I had to tell. While I naturally hope that some reader, even in this rushed age, will find the time for both novels, *War and Remembrance* is a story in itself, and can be read without the prologue." Unfortunately, this claim does not hold true. Though Wouk awkwardly attempts to provide sufficient background material at the beginning of the sequel, the characters' motives or intentions are difficult to understand without the fully rounded characterization the earlier book supplies, and the reader who has read *The Winds of War* might be bored by the repetitive exposition. Moreover, the sequel is weighed down with interruptions for exposition of history through another fictitious book, *World Holocaust,* by General Armin Von Roon. Paul Fussell, reviewing *War and Remembrance* for the *New Republic,* said of *World Holocaust* that "the quality of the military reasoning in this document—the whole

Wouk in Jerusalem, on the wall of the Old City, at the time his 1994 novel, The Glory, *was published (photograph by David Hume Kennedy)*

comprises about 122 pages—is impressive, and so is Wouk's scholarship in contemporary history." However, Wouk's accounts of technicalities of war, though impressive, interrupt the narrative line rather than support it as they do in *The Winds of War*. Because these constant interruptions break the suspense, the narrative line and the military history together do not unify the novel.

Walter Clemons of *Newsweek* stated that the strongest point in *War and Remembrance* is that it makes the reader "feel the Holocaust afresh." Wouk is at his best in *War and Remembrance* when he uses descriptive passages to serve as detailed, all-too-realistic reminders of the suffering war brings:

> It may have been the worst siege in the history of the world. It was a siege of Biblical horror; a siege like the siege of Jerusalem, when, as the Book of Lamentations tells, women boiled and ate their children. When the war began, Leningrad was a city of close to three million. By the time Victor Henry visited it, there were about six hundred thousand people left. Half of those who were gone had been evacuated; the other half had died.

Passages such as this one work to heighten Wouk's purpose: to move men to prevent further warfare through a careful examination of the past.

The success of Wouk's war epic attracted executives at ABC, and a deal was struck to produce a miniseries based on the novels. In 1983 Wouk wrote a script for *The Winds of War*. The show was im-

mensely popular, becoming the second highest-rated miniseries, behind Alex Haley's *Roots* (televised in 1977). An all-star cast headed by Robert Mitchum as Pug Henry had much to do with the series' success.

When Wouk had completed his epic about World War II, he returned to the second theme that had interested him throughout his professional life: the place of the Jew in American society. In *Inside, Outside,* published in 1985, he combines large doses of fictionalized autobiography with an examination of America's efforts to stave off further conflict between the State of Israel and its Arab neighbors.

Wouk's hero, David Goodkind, is a successful lawyer who, despite his liberal leanings, ends up working for Richard Nixon as a political adviser. During the months leading up to the 1973 Arab-Israeli war, he serves as a special envoy negotiating with Israeli prime minister Golda Meir; his behind-the-scenes efforts result in American aid being provided to Israel at this crucial time in its history.

Surprisingly, however, Goodkind finds he has hours to idle away at the White House, and he spends them writing a memoir of his childhood. The intellectually gifted child of Russian emigres, he was pampered by his family and sent to Columbia, where he had an affair with a Gentile woman. Upon graduation, he disappointed everyone by postponing law school in favor of a career as a writer for radio comedians. Only after experiencing the lifestyle of mainstream America did he return to his Jewish roots, enroll in law school, and finally embark on the career that led him to the side of his embattled president in a time of national crisis.

The interweaving of these two stories, sometimes in alternating chapters, builds dramatic interest in the novel and provides Wouk many opportunities to expound once again on the values of Conservatism and Orthodox Judaism. The narrative of Goodkind's early life is the most highly autobiographical work that Wouk has produced. He portrays vividly the distinctions between living "inside" the Jewish community in New York City and negotiating with the "outside" forces of modern American society. By making his hero a writer, Wouk is able to use *Inside, Outside* as a forum for literary criticism as well. Goodkind engages in a lifelong rivalry with fellow Jew Peter Quat, a popular novelist with a large readership—distinctly reminiscent of real-life Jewish writer Philip Roth. Wouk attacks Roth and other Jewish writers who he believes have exploited their heritage and mocked the values of Judaism, and who have moved the novel away from its traditional concern with social issues into the realm of psychological analysis.

Like virtually every Wouk novel published since 1948, *Inside, Outside* achieved best-seller status. Just as typically, reviews were mixed. Wouk's friend Arnold Beichman, writing in the *National Review,* calls the book yet another example of the novelist's "ability to relate social history to individual destiny." In *The New York Times Book Review,* James Michener (himself a novelist whose reputation among critics has been checkered) praises Wouk for his true-to-life portrait of Jewish-American customs, but gently chides him for succumbing to contemporary tendencies to use graphic sexual language. That criticism might not be fair if leveled at another writer, but Wouk had, in a short preface to *The Caine Mutiny,* obliquely criticized novelists who find it necessary to use foul language as a means of gaining readership. Several critics were less kind. R. Z. Sheppard, reviewing the novel for *Time,* is typical of a group who have repeatedly taken Wouk to task for faulty characterization, contrived plotting, and heavy-handed philosophizing. Noting that Wouk has one of his characters remark that "Hammering out a style takes work," Sheppard remarks that "if you hammer too long, you get pulp."

Wouk's next major project was the development of a television screenplay for *War and Remembrance.* Extremely satisfied with the success achieved by *The Winds of War* as a television miniseries in 1983, executives at ABC decided to take a chance on dramatizing the second part of Wouk's war epic. This time collaborating with other writers, Wouk

turned his one-thousand-page manuscript into a thirty-hour series in which many of the actors from *The Winds of War* reprised their roles. The first half of the series, however, which aired during sweeps week in the fall of 1988, did not achieve the high ratings garnered by *The Winds of War;* network executives delayed airing the second half until late in the rating season, in May 1989.

The success of *The Winds of War* and *War and Remembrance,* as well as his lifelong interest in Judaic issues, which he had exploited in *Inside, Outside,* shaped the focus of Wouk's next two novels. Using the technique that had proven successful in his saga about World War II, Wouk produced two independent but closely related novels about the struggles of Israel to achieve and maintain statehood. In *The Hope* (1993) he steps back in time to the years after World War II when an intrepid band of freedom fighters ousted the British from Palestine and forced the world to recognize the emergence of the State of Israel. Carefully weaving together the lives of several fictional characters with the real-life heroes and heroines of the new Jewish state, Wouk retells the story of the 1948 War of Independence, the struggles of leaders such as David Ben-Gurion and Moshe Dayan to form a coalition among the disparate Zionist groups in the country, and the stunning victory of the Israelis over their Arab enemies in the Six-Day War of 1967. In *The Glory* (1994), which must certainly be regarded as a sequel, Wouk continues the story of the Israeli people, placing his fictional characters beside figures such as Golda Meir, Arik Sharon, and Menachim Begin during the struggles leading up to the Camp David Peace Accords.

As he does in *The Winds of War* and *War and Remembrance,* Wouk creates several families whose lives are affected by events in Israel during these turbulent decades: the Baraks, the Nitzans, the Pasternaks, and the Lurias. Through their professional and personal relationships Wouk is able to introduce other characters whose stories give a human face to the historical period he attempts to bring to life. The role of the unconquerable hero—who clearly stands as a symbol of Israel itself—falls to a fearless front-line fighter whose comrades dub him "Don Kishote." This Quixotic figure emerges from battle scarred but not daunted, living to fight another day against formidable odds.

Wouk is careful to plead in the "Historical Notes" appended to *The Hope* that he has made "no attempt" to "caricature, distort, or defame" the Arabs portrayed in these novels. Unfortunately, he is often lax in developing his characters and too quick to resort to stereotypes in creating his fictional Israelis. One reviewer dismisses his characters as flat, "undermined by too much talk and too little action." David B. Green in *The New York Times Book Review* (9 January 1994) bemoans the fact that these fictional men and women never "leap from the page to take root in the reader's mind." Wouk continues, in the words of Marcia Dorey in *Library Journal* (1 November 1993), to treat women merely as "handmaidens of men." John Skow, reviewing *The Hope* in *Time* (6 December 1993), finds the complex historical themes of the novel treated with "only slightly more subtlety than a grade-school Thanksgiving pageant." The mainstream reviews for *The Glory* reflect these general sentiments.

In 1995 Librarian of Congress James Billington named Wouk's five historical novels—*The Winds of War; War and Remembrance; Inside, Outside; The Hope;* and *The Glory*—as "works of national significance." Butler Library at Columbia University, the repository of Wouk's archival material, agreed to transfer the papers and manuscripts for these novels at the request of the Library of Congress. On 15 May 1995, his eightieth birthday, Wouk formally presented these archives to the Library of Congress on the occasion of a symposium on the historical novel, held in his honor and attended by historians, novelists, publishers, and critics. Among the participants were Robert Caro, Martin Gilbert, David McCullough, George Garrett, Daniel Boorstin, and Mary Lee Settle.

It seems ironic that, in the latter part of his professional career, Wouk found himself returning to one of his least successful novels, *Don't Stop the Carnival,* to collaborate in a most unusual project. Singer Jimmy Buffett, known for popularizing the carefree lifestyle of southern Florida and the Caribbean, discovered in that novel the germ of an idea for a musical comedy. Wouk agreed to work with him on the libretto. The show opened in Florida in 1997 to standing-room-only audiences.

Wouk once said that "setting aside the years at war, I have had no other aim of occupation than that of writing; and it is the ambition I had when I was a boy." Like Trollope and the Victorians, he admits to being an "over-writer," refusing to labor over cuts until the end of a novel. He is a man inseparably devoted to both his profession and his faith. Maxwell Geismar writes of this devotion in *American Moderns from Rebellion to Conformity* (1958), placing the novels of Herman Wouk "in a curious realm between art and entertainment." Though some of his efforts such as *The City Boy* and *Marjorie Morningstar* may be artistically flawed because they rely too heavily on Wouk's expertise as a storyteller, his best novels, *The Caine Mutiny* and *The Winds of War,* achieve both literary and thematic merit.

References:

Arnold Beichman, *Herman Wouk: The Novelist as Social Historian* (New Brunswick, N.J.: Transaction Books, 1984);

Richard R. Bolton, "*The Winds of War* and Wouk's Wish for the World," *Midwest Quarterly,* 16 (July 1975): 389–408;

William Darby, *Necessary American Fictions: Popular Literature of the 1950s* (Bowling Green, Ohio: Bowling Green State University Popular Press, 1987), pp. 43–55;

Maxwell Geismar, *American Moderns from Rebellion to Conformity* (New York: Hill & Wang, 1958), pp. 38–45;

Laurence Mazzeno, *Herman Wouk* (New York: Twayne, 1994);

B. R. McElderry, "The Conservative as Novelist: Herman Wouk," *Arizona Quarterly,* 15 (Summer 1959): 128–136.

Papers:

The repositories of Herman Wouk's papers are the Butler Library at Columbia University and the Library of Congress.

James Wright

This entry was updated from the entry by Andrew Elkins (Chadron State College)
in DLB 169: American Poets Since World War II, Fifth Series.

See also the Wright entry in *DLB 5: American Poets Since World War II, First Series.*

BIRTH: Martins Ferry, Ohio, 13 December 1927, to Dudley and Jessie Wright.

EDUCATION: B.A., Kenyon College, 1952; M.A., University of Washington, 1954; Ph.D., University of Washington, 1959; also studied with John Crowe Ransom and Theodore Roethke.

MARRIAGE: 1952 to Liberty Kardules (divorced 1962); children: Franz Paul, Marshall John; 1967 to Edith Anne Runk.

AWARDS AND HONORS: Fulbright Fellowship in Austria, 1952–1953; Robert Frost Poetry Prize, 1952; Borestone Mountain Poetry Award, 1954 and 1955; Eunice Tietjens Memorial Prize, 1955, and Oscar Blumenthal Award, 1968, both from *Poetry;* Yale Series of Younger Poets award for *The Green Wall,* 1957; *Kenyon Review* fellowship in poetry, 1958; National Institute of Arts and Letters grant in literature, 1959; Ohioana Book Award, for *Saint Judas,* 1960; Guggenheim Fellowship, 1964 and 1978; Creative Arts Award, Brandeis University, 1970; Academy of American Poets fellowship, 1971; Melville Cane Award, Poetry Society of America, 1972; Pulitzer Prize in poetry, for *Collected Poems,* 1972.

DEATH: New York, New York, 25 March 1980.

BOOKS: *The Green Wall* (New Haven: Yale University Press, 1957; London: Oxford University Press, 1957);
Saint Judas (Middletown, Conn.: Wesleyan University Press, 1959);
The Lion's Tail and Eyes: Poems Written Out of Laziness and Silence, by Wright, Robert Bly, and William Duffy (Madison, Minn.: Sixties Press, 1962);
The Branch Will Not Break (Middletown, Conn.: Wesleyan University Press, 1963; London: Longmans, Green, 1964);

James Wright (courtesy of the Lilly Library, Indiana University)

Shall We Gather at the River (Middletown, Conn.: Wesleyan University Press, 1968; London: Rapp & Whiting, 1969);
Collected Poems (Middletown, Conn.: Wesleyan University Press, 1971);
Two Citizens (New York: Farrar, Straus & Giroux, 1973);
Moments of the Italian Summer (Washington, D.C. & San Francisco: Dryad Press, 1976);
To a Blossoming Pear Tree (New York: Farrar, Straus & Giroux, 1977);
Leave It to the Sunlight (Durango, Colo.: Logbridge-Rhodes, 1981);

A Reply to Matthew Arnold (Durango, Colo.: Logbridge-Rhodes, 1981);

The Summers of James and Annie Wright: Sketches and Mosaics, by Wright and Annie Wright (New York: Sheep Meadow Press, 1981);

This Journey (New York: Random House, 1982);

Collected Prose of James Wright, edited by Anne Wright (Ann Arbor: University of Michigan Press, 1983);

A Secret Field: Selections from the Final Journals of James Wright, edited by Anne Wright (Durango, Colo.: Logbridge-Rhodes, 1985);

Above the River: The Complete Poems (New York: Farrar, Straus & Giroux, 1990).

TRANSLATIONS: René Char, *Hypnos Waking: Poems and Prose,* translated by Wright and others (New York: Random House, 1956);

George Trakl, *Twenty Poems of George Trakl,* translated by Wright and Robert Bly (Madison, Minn.: Sixties Press, 1961);

César Vallejo, *Twenty Poems of César Vallejo,* translated by Wright, Bly, and John Knoepfle (Madison, Minn.: Sixties Press, 1962);

Theodor Storm, *The Rider on the White Horse* (New York: Signet, 1964);

Jorge Guillén, *Cantico: A Selection* (Boston: Little, Brown, 1965);

Pablo Neruda, *Twenty Poems of Pablo Neruda,* translated by Wright and Bly (Madison, Minn.: Sixties Press, 1968);

Herman Hesse, *Poems* (New York: Farrar, Straus & Giroux, 1970);

Neruda and Vallejo, *Selected Poems,* translated by Wright, Bly, and Knoepfle (Boston: Beacon Press, 1971);

Hesse, *Wanderings: Notes and Sketches* (New York: Farrar, Straus & Giroux, 1972).

Often remembered as one of the strongest of post-World War II American poets, James Wright was one of a group of young writers who, after establishing themselves with early books of prosodically conservative poetry, broke away from the mainstream traditions to experiment with looser form, freer rhythms, and bolder images. The verse in Wright's first two books, *The Green Wall* (1957) and *Saint Judas* (1959), is characterized by its use of traditional forms and shows the influence of such established poets as Robert Frost and Edwin Arlington Robinson. Much of Wright's middle verse, however, features the use of what some critics, using Robert Kelly's term of 1961, have called *deep imagery*. A subjective imagery that is purportedly drawn from a poet's unconscious, such imagery was used in this period in a reaction to what Wright considered the too analytical, too cerebral, perhaps spiritually enervated poetry that he and his older peers had been producing. Seeking a method of composition that would allow him to establish common ground with the reader and be understood immediately, but a method that would also allow him to abandon what he considered the restrictive tradition of predominantly iambic, logical, discursive verse, Wright began to write what Robert Bly called "leaping poetry," poetry that "leaps" from conscious to unconscious material, that eschews obvious, logical links between images and semantic units, and that prefers, instead, the bold jump from one image or statement to another, with the artist's and the reader's imaginations working in concert to supply the missing links. The source of such deep imagery, or leaping poetry, is assumed to be in a preconscious or unconscious state of mind that is shared by all people and can therefore be accessed by the reader for clues to the poet's vision. According to this theory of poetics, the writer is able to abandon traditional forms while not losing the audience comprehension that working within such recognizable forms normally facilitates. Such poetry dominates Wright's output beginning with his third volume, *The Branch Will Not Break* (1963).

To describe the literary movement in which Wright properly fits and the type of poetry for which he is most likely to be remembered—to understand him exclusively as a deep image poet or a leaping poet or a poet of the emotive imagination—is to minimize the breadth and power of this important poet's work. Wright's poetry expresses his lifelong confrontation with the urgent problems of living and writing in mid- and late-twentieth-century America, and it possesses a relevance that far transcends its dynamic character as one tributary of a stream of consciousness verse produced during one period of American literary history. Indeed, Wright is a poet who asks the deepest and most fundamental questions that most people are forced to confront as they live in a bewildering phase of history; and his verse will likely be remembered and returned to whenever readers find themselves asking such basic, compelling questions as who they are, why they do what they do, and what value their lives have in the social and cosmic order. Wright's poetic career was a continuing quest to find answers to such questions—particularly to find his own most fully human, fully responsive and creative self. His career also became a method and strategy for enabling that especially valued self to live in the contemporary world.

His body of work might be compared to an epic poem, one which can be divided chronologically into three stages, characterized respectively by rejection and denial, then doubt and fear, and finally acceptance and affirmation. What begins perhaps as an adolescent's identity crisis in verse becomes, in the poet's mature work, a profound search for answers to the major philosophical questions of life. What does it mean, he asks himself repeatedly, to be "a good man" in contemporary America; and why should one, in this age of information saturation, write poetry, which makes nothing happen and perhaps only adds to the inane babel that characterizes the commercial culture? Such questions take the poet's entire lifetime to answer; meanwhile, the careful reader may profit greatly from witnessing and imaginatively participating in the struggle being fought and the quest being undertaken.

James Arlington Wright was born on 13 December 1927 into a working-class family in Martins Ferry, Ohio, an industrial town on the banks of the Ohio River. His father, Dudley, was employed for fifty years at the Hazel-Atlas Glass Company, which later, in the son's poetry, became a symbol of the oppressive, mind-numbing place and way of life that the young poet hoped to escape. His mother, Jessie, left school at fourteen to work in the White Swan Laundry; she later raised the Wright children (James had two brothers and an adopted sister). Neither parent went to school beyond the eighth grade. Their son James was a writer who began his literary career early. In a 1980 *American Poetry Review* interview, Wright recalls first writing poetry when he was about eleven years old. While in high school in 1943 he suffered a nervous breakdown and missed a year of school. When he graduated in 1946, a year late, he joined the U.S. Army and served as a clerk typist with the occupation forces in Japan after World War II. After his honorable discharge he did his undergraduate work at Kenyon College, where he studied poetry with John Crowe Ransom and graduated cum laude and Phi Beta Kappa in 1952, the same year he won his first poetry award, the Robert Frost Poetry Prize.

From Ransom, Wright learned to think of poetry as an intelligent, consciously crafted, formal art. In his *American Poetry Review* interview he says that Ransom taught him "the ideal, what elsewhere I've called the Horatian ideal, the attempt finally to write a poem that will be put together so carefully that it does produce a single unifying effect." Others who knew him in these days remember him as already being a serious poet, not just one who wrote poems, but one for whom writing poetry was the

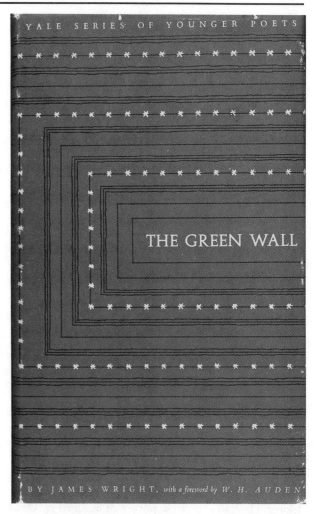

Cover for Wright's first book, which includes poems that show the influence of Robert Frost and Edwin Arlington Robinson

definition of himself. Writing in 1990 in *The Gettysburg Review*, E. L. Doctorow, at Kenyon during the same period as Wright, remembers that Wright had a "high and richly timbered voice, like a tenor's. His conversation was intense, opinionated, heavy with four-letter words, but what made it astonishing is that it was interwoven with recitations of poetry. . . . He would glide from ordinary speech to verse without dropping a beat." Doctorow recalls that "Wright always carried with him the verses he was working on in stiff, black, clamp binders. . . . You'd find him at the Village Inn, sitting alone with a cigarette and a cup of coffee, or in front of a beer at Jean Valjean's, and he'd be hunched in a booth revising a typed draft in his round, grade-school hand."

After graduating from Kenyon College, Wright married another Martins Ferry native, Liberty Kardules, and the two traveled to Austria, where, on a Fulbright Fellowship, the poet studied the works of Theodor Storm and Georg Trakl at the

University of Vienna. The couple's first son was born in Austria in March 1953. Wright returned to the United States and did his graduate work in English at the University of Washington, earning his M.A. degree in creative writing in 1954 ("I took the Master's in creative writing to get it the hell out of the way," he explains in his 1975 *Paris Review* interview) and his Ph.D. in English in 1959, after writing a dissertation on Charles Dickens, "The Comic Imagination of Charles Dickens." While at Washington he studied poetry with Theodore Roethke and Stanley Kunitz and published his first book, *The Green Wall;* this book, the fifty-third volume in the Yale Series of Younger Poets, was selected and introduced by W. H. Auden. The book, Wright admits, was influenced by the work of Frost and Robinson. When asked by Peter A. Stitt in the 1975 interview what he had learned from Frost, Wright responded, "Well, first of all I think that there is his profound, terrifying, and very tragic view of the universe, which seems to me true." During these early years he also received the Borestone Mountain Poetry Award (1954 and 1955) and the Eunice Tietjens Memorial Prize from *Poetry* magazine (1955).

Wright held his first academic position at the University of Minnesota, where he worked as an English professor from 1957 to 1964. Writing in the *American Poetry Review* in 1982, James Breslin, a graduate student at Minnesota when Wright was a professor there, remembers the poet as "a striking figure. He had the thick, powerful body of an Ohio State fullback, but he wore horn-rimmed glasses and a three-button suit: a football player squeezed into the uniform of an English professor." Breslin recalls that Wright was intense, quoted long passages of poetry, and drank heavily. According to Stitt, in 1963 Wright "was denied tenure at the University of Minnesota" because "the senior members of the English Department (including poet Allen Tate) unanimously opposed Wright's candidacy, citing the excessive drinking that was causing him to miss some of his classes." Denied tenure at Minnesota, Wright taught at Macalaster College in Saint Paul from 1963 to 1965. During the same period that his academic career seemed doomed, his marriage deteriorated; he and his wife separated several times, and the two finally divorced in 1962. While the darkness in Wright's early poetry cannot be attributed solely to his personal problems—he was also a harsh social critic and seemed driven nearly to despair by his aversion to the materialism and conformism of the prevailing culture—certainly his personal demons contributed to the black mood one notes in the poet's first four books, published between 1957 and 1968.

One productive result of his time at Minnesota was that Wright met Robert Bly. According to Wright in his *Paris Review* interview, "I was in despair at the time"; but, after reading Bly's magazine *The Fifties,* Wright was so impressed by a translation of George Trakl that he wrote Bly a letter, "sixteen pages long and single spaced." Bly's response was simple: "Come on out to the farm." Robert and Carol Bly owned a farm in western Minnesota at the time; Wright accepted the invitation, and a lifelong friendship began. The two poets later collaborated on translations of the poetry of Trakl, César Vallejo, and Pablo Neruda. In Bly, Wright found a kindred soul, one who shared his political and poetical attitudes at a time when he was, if his poetry is any indication, feeling the profound pain of loneliness, alienation, and self-doubt.

In 1965 Wright went to Europe for a year on a Guggenheim Fellowship. Returning in 1966, he took a position in the English department of Hunter College of the City University of New York, where he was employed until his death in 1980. In 1967 he married his second wife, the former Edith Anne Runk. The two traveled to and worked in Hawaii and Europe, and Wright became especially fond of Paris, Verona, and Tuscany, all of which appear in his later poems. In 1978 Wright won a second Guggenheim, and he and Anne traveled in Europe for nine months in 1979. A persistent sore throat, noticed by the poet while abroad, was diagnosed as cancer of the tongue when the Wrights returned to New York; Wright died in the spring of 1980.

During his writing career Wright won many poetry prizes, including the *Kenyon Review* Poetry Fellowship (1958–1959), a National Institute of Arts and Letters grant in literature (1959), the Longview Foundation Award (1959), a prize from *Chelsea* magazine in 1960, the Ohioana Award in poetry for *Saint Judas* (1960), the Oscar Blumenthal Award from *Poetry* (1968), the Creative Arts Award from Brandeis University (1970), the Fellowship of the Academy of American Poets (1971), and the Poetry Society of America's Melville Cane Award (1972). His *Collected Poems* (1971), a collection of the work from his first four books that included a selection of new poems, won the 1972 Pulitzer Prize.

Wright was a poet whose life may be seen as a quest for answers to essential and, for him, fiercely urgent questions, questions about identity, ethics, and human suffering. The first stage of his quest for answers, expressed in his first two books, *The Green Wall* and *Saint Judas,* dramatizes the young rebel's cry of disappointment and disillusionment with the mainstream culture. It also conveys his avowal of loyalty to those whom Auden, in his introduction to

The Green Wall, called "social outsiders"–that is, those on the margins of society–the derelicts, drunks, and criminals. Evidently feeling himself psychologically and spiritually disenfranchised, Wright identifies with and celebrates those who are truly outside the prevailing American culture of the work ethic, capitalist acquisition, conformity, and middle-class values. As a college professor Wright was economically mainstream, but the poet in him imaginatively–and occasionally literally–roamed the cold streets of Ohio and Minnesota with the homeless, listened with prisoners as guards locked cell doors for the night, and wandered the beach with the mother who had lost her child to the waves of an indifferent sea while indifferent "harly-charlies" partied nearby. His cultural criticism has a political dimension, of course, expressing as it does a disdain for those who place material values above human values; but his criticism is motivated more by his human sympathy for the outcast and dejected than by any abstract philosophical principles of good government. He sees suffering and his heart goes out. He identifies the major cause of the suffering as a system that counsels that, above all, the gears of the industrial machine must be kept moving smoothly, a system that judges individuals by their income and class status. He believes that the poor and the suffering, those "dark" figures in his poetry associated with the "lower" world, must be written about, must be given a voice, and, in doing so, he finds himself condemning those whom he identifies as their tormentors, those of the "light" or "upper" world. Wright's hometown of Martins Ferry and the Ohio River figure prominently in his early work, serving as symbols of what the poet finds wrong with the culture into which he has been born: the willingness, even eagerness, of Americans to despoil what is beautiful–frequently symbolized by the Ohio River and the ravaged Ohio landscape–in the interest of wealth, economic development, and an industrial notion of progress. In Wright's Ohio the beautiful woods struggle for survival against the relentless onslaught of the ugly factories and strip mines. In his early work the poet wonders if he, too, is one of the beautiful misfits that must be destroyed to satisfy the culture's appetite.

In the first stage of Wright's struggle, the poet attempts to escape and dissociate himself from the realm of the "ugly," which includes those who proceed passively through their lives, the timid and the conventional, those who bulldoze trees to erect chiropractors' offices, who pollute Wright's beloved Ohio River, and who otherwise participate, wittingly or unwittingly, in what the poet characterizes as a culture of death and destruction. By so partici-

Cover for Wright's 1963 collection of antitraditional poems characterized by doubt and fear

pating, they not only perpetuate the culture, but they also lose their souls. These characters are anonymous figures who seem to be everywhere: the old fishermen whose twine has "gone slack" and whose blood has "gone dumb"; the glum cop whose "flat face and empty eyes" are perfectly adapted to the "pale town"; the "two stupid harly-charlies" who lure a drunken and blameless girl to her death by drowning. The "ugly" are also recognizable or identifiable figures of the time: President Dwight D. Eisenhower; industrialist Mark Hanna; FBI director J. Edgar Hoover; the owners of Hazel-Atlas Glass Company; and all the policemen, bankers, businessmen, and wardens of the world. These are "the rising dead who fear the dark," those who rise in the morning to greet the solid assurance of another day but who fear the dark of their own souls. They lead, in Henry David Thoreau's famous phrase, "lives of quiet desperation," but they have no clue to their own predicament. Wright decisively rejects both the characters and the culture they serve or accept.

By contrast, Wright's early work celebrates figures whom he considers heroic correctives to those who meekly accept the culture, figures who are instinctive, antirational, sensual, and innocent;

these are celebrated by the poet in such characters as a prostitute named Betty; a woman in the insane asylum; a little girl on her way to school; Judas; and, perhaps Wright's most controversial hero, George Doty, the executed Ohio murderer. All the unconventional, the rebellious, the losers, the outcasts, the aliens in their own land are celebrated. They are children, lunatics, murderers, prostitutes, homeless poor, amputees, and poets—hunted by the ugly, lured to their deaths, or forced to repress their central desires and impulses. They are sensuous, untamed, primeval, and, above all, innocent—even if they are felons—because they have at least listened to their instincts, the dark murmurings of the heart that bring news of their real identity that exists somehow beyond, below, above, or behind society's prescriptions for good behavior. Whatever else they may be, they are innocent of self-betrayal.

In *The Green Wall* Wright provides the reader with several examples of his innocents. One is the female mental patient in "She Hid in the Trees from the Nurses." When the woman's attendants whistle for her, she prefers not to respond, choosing instead to enjoy her freedom,

> And dabble her feet in the damp grass,
> And lean against a yielding stalk,
> And spread her name in dew across
> The pebbles where the droplets walk.

The woman prefers to listen to the rhythms deep within herself, which are attuned to the natural world around her, rather than to the attendants' oppressive whistles, symbols of the order that humankind logically imposes on the psyche's freedom. The insane woman is sane in Wright's inverted moral world, where the society that establishes such places as mental hospitals is indicted for insisting upon whistles and chimes, symbols of conformity and the suppression of natural desires.

Another innocent is Betty, the black prostitute of "Morning Hymn to a Dark Girl." Betty lives beneath a bridge, under and apart from the world of conventional commerce. In that upper world, men become "stone," "flat," and "empty," while Betty is a perfect exemplar of the character Wright wants to celebrate, the sensuous, uninhibited human beyond convention:

> Betty, burgeoning your golden skin, you poise
> Tracing gazelles and tigers on your breasts,
> Deep in the jungle of your bed you drowse.

Other exemplary characters are the schoolgirl of "A Little Girl on Her Way to School" who understands the language of the birds and stones and the female speaker of "Sappho," condemned for her homosexual love by the "sly voices" of the town but insistent on her innocence, despite having violated conventional standards: "They cannot tear the garden out of me, / Nor smear my love with names." The woman's strength comes from her deeper knowledge, discovered in pain, the source of which is deeper than logic or social convention:

> There is a fire that burns beyond the names
> Of sludge and filth of which the world is made.
> Agony sears the dark flesh of the body,
> And lifts me higher than the smoke, to rise
> Above the earth, above the sacrifice.

To be "above the earth, above the sacrifice" is the position many of Wright's early heroes and heroines seek, a position above society's restrictions that serve conformity and production.

The radicalness of his position is illustrated by the most controversial poem in his first volume, "A Poem About George Doty in the Death House," in which the poet idolizes a real-life murderer, a taxi driver from Ohio who one night killed one of his passengers with a tree branch when she refused a pass he made. In the words of the poet:

> A month and a day ago
> He stopped his car and found
> A girl on the darkening ground,
> And killed her in the snow.

Despite acknowledging Doty's guilt, Wright declares that he "will mourn no soul but his," not even the soul of "the homely girl whose cry / Crumbled his pleading kiss." The poem does not entirely convince one that Doty's is the soul that most deserves the reader's sympathy. Wright's poetic goal, as he explains it in his *American Poetry Review* interview, is nevertheless a valid one: "Many people in that community thought [Doty] was terribly wicked, but he did not seem to me wicked. He was just a dumb guy who suddenly was thrust into the middle of the problem of evil and he was not able to handle it." That statement summarizes the human condition as Wright understands it early in his career: we are all "dumb" humans "thrust into the middle of the problem of evil," who daily have to ask ourselves how to "handle it." The poet's sympathy extends in *The Green Wall* to those who struggle honestly and unconventionally, albeit unsuccessfully, with this problem, but not to those who simply accept the solutions others have forged for them.

The same theme underlies the poet's second volume, *Saint Judas,* in which Wright announces, on the cover, his desire to discover "exactly what is a good and humane action" and "why an individual should perform such an act." The most noticeable example of the poet's struggling with the problem of the human confrontation with good and evil is found in the volume's best-known poem, the title poem, in which Wright canonizes the figure of Judas, a bolder move perhaps than idolizing George Doty. Having already that day betrayed Christ, Judas in this sonnet "slipped away" from the crowds, determined to kill himself. Instead, he "caught / A pack of hoodlums beating up a man" and, "for nothing" this time, "held the man . . . in my arms." Judas is another "dumb guy," like Doty, caught in the trap of evil, who has to decide how to act in a world well beyond his limited understanding. On the record he is the greatest of traitors, but, in this off-the-record glimpse, he is revealed by Wright to be a man still capable of compassion. In his first two books Wright insistently identifies with life's losers and victims, those who find themselves overwhelmed by the problem of evil, which is frequently symbolized by the men in the gray flannel suits (or, in the case of "Saint Judas," Roman soldiers). The poet's simplified moral stance is the product of his refusal to accept and sympathize with his own flawed humanity, his fear that he is the ugly one, the impure soul, the "dumb guy" no one wants to admit to being. As Bly suggests in an article originally published in *The Sixties* under the pseudonym Crunk, "the most profound emotion in *Saint Judas* is guilt." Wright suspects and fears his own sin, the sin that all are guilty of, the sin of being merely human, and deludes himself with the thought that he might escape his inevitable human failings by identifying with the beautiful—who are not of this world—and distancing himself from the ugly—who are too much of this world. His affirmation or gathering of all souls, beautiful and ugly, must await what the Puritan preacher Thomas Hooker called "a true sight of one's sin," a recognition of the ugly within himself.

The poet's struggle to avoid his own humanity provides the drama of the second stage of his poetry, which begins in *The Branch Will Not Break* and culminates in *Shall We Gather at the River* (1968), the darkest book of Wright's career. Like Milton's Satan, Wright discovers that "I myself am hell." Or, as he says, "I am the dark / Bone I was born to be." Having tried to purify his world by pushing away the ugly, Wright discovers that it is his own inner sphere that is corrupted, the very recognition he hoped to escape by pushing the others away. The youthful arrogance of the two early volumes, in which the poet dares to tell others how to live, thinking himself qualified to do so by his innocence and vitality, becomes the self-pity, self-loathing, and flirtation with suicide in *The Branch Will*

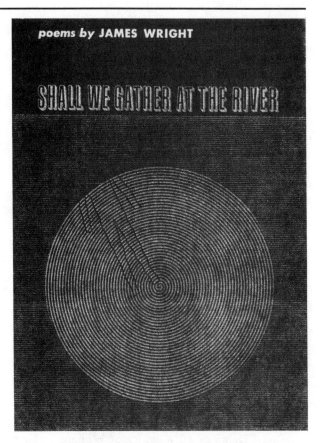

Cover for Wright's 1968 book, poems suggesting a desire to cross from one existence to another

Not Break and *Shall We Gather at the River,* volumes characterized by doubt and fear and by a looser form and relaxed rhythms. The first-person speaker replaces the persona of earlier poems; the dominant iambic meter of Wright's first two books is less common; stanzas and lines show no consistent or predictable length; ambiguous pronouns tease the reader; the poems often begin in medias res; and the normal discursive links are omitted or blurred. The stylistic changes are actually thematic: they suggest confusion, the difficulty of making sense of the world, and the need for confrontation with the world's data before drawing conclusions. In this light the style, while it may seem a break from earlier work, is really an extension of the themes of that work, now in a more appropriate frame, a frame that is part of the theme itself. Some critics originally thought that the change in style marked a revolution in Wright's work, but it is now clear that it was part of an evolution that began as early as 1952, when Wright was in Europe on a Fulbright Fellowship. He himself describes accidentally wandering into a University of Vienna classroom in which Trakl was reading his poetry. "It was as though the sea had entered the class at the last moment," Wright says in his introduction to his translation of

Trakl's poetry. "For this poem was not like any poem I had ever recognized." His later translations of Trakl, Vallejo, Neruda, and René Char show that, well before the publication of *The Branch Will Not Break,* he had been fascinated with verse that is antitraditional in form. His own work had bothered him as early as 1958, when, in a letter to Roethke, Wright complained that "My stuff stinks. . . . I am trapped by the very thing—the traditional technique—which I labored so hard to attain."

The occasionally hopeful tone of some poems in *The Branch Will Not Break* sometimes obscures the true darkness of the volume. Again and again, Wright longs for escape, wants to get out, says that life is too hard, as in these lines from "Having Lost My Sons, I Confront the Wreckage of the Moon: 1960":

> I am sick
> Of it, and I go on,
> Living alone, alone,
> Past the charred silos, past the hidden graves
> Of Chippewas and Norwegians.

The quest for deliverance, combined with images of stasis and petrifaction, dominates *The Branch Will Not Break.* The most often anthologized poem in the volume, "Lying in a Hammock at William Duffy's Farm in Pine Island, Minnesota," concludes with these famous lines:

> I lean back, as the evening darkens and comes on.
> A chicken hawk floats over, looking for home.
> I have wasted my life.

Critics argue whether the final line has been adequately prepared for by the series of images that precedes it. The more important point is that the final line has been prepared for by all of Wright's preceding poetry. He has abandoned his home but, being human, has not been able to find a replacement residence among the hawks or horses of the world. He is lost and unable to save himself. He lies in his hammock suspended, passive, and alone.

The other anthology piece from the book, "A Blessing," narrates an encounter between "my friend and me" and "two Indian ponies" in a field "just off the highway to Rochester, Minnesota." The horses accept the two humans' presence, and for a moment the speaker feels he has found a home in nonhuman nature. His exultant ending, however, reveals the limitation of such a hope:

> Suddenly I realize
> That if I stepped out of my body I would break
> Into blossom.

This is a joyous conclusion, but in order to feel the joy of the encounter with the peaceful horses, the speaker has to imagine losing his human identity, stepping out of his body. There seems to be no real salvation at this stage in Wright's quest; but every quest has its peaks and valleys, and these two books, *The Branch Will Not Break* and *Shall We Gather at the River,* present Wright's psychological nadir.

If possible, *Shall We Gather at the River* is even darker than *The Branch Will Not Break,* unrelentingly darker. There is irony in this further bleakness. Wright has been pursuing his immaculate self, free of the influences of others; but, having freed himself, he finds only loneliness and pain. In "Before A Cashier's Window in a Department Store" he writes:

> I am hungry. In two more days
> It will be spring. So this
> Is what it feels like.

Wright has exiled himself, and "this / is what it feels like." Spring promises no rejuvenation for the poet. The controlling image cluster of the book—rivers, boats, water, shores—suggests a passage from one life into another, a movement across the boundaries separating this existence from the next. The desire to make that move, to die as the person James Wright and be delivered as something else, anything else, is strong in *Shall We Gather at the River.*

At the end of "The Minneapolis Poem," for example, Wright says,

> I want to be lifted up
> By some great white bird unknown to the police,
> And soar for a thousand miles and be carefully hidden
> Modest and golden as one last corn grain. . . .

These lines suggest the poet's belief that he is unable to deliver himself and yet he longs to be nonhuman, because to be human, he has discovered, is enormously difficult. The conflict in the book is concisely summarized by one line from "A Christmas Greeting": "It hurts to die, although the lucky do." To die might mean deliverance, but it certainly means pain; to live means pain, also. Mired in a dilemma apparently without solution, the poet hits bottom in "To the Muse," the final poem of *Shall We Gather at the River.* The poem finds the speaker poised on the bank of the Ohio River, the polluted symbol of the destruction that the ugly leave behind them. The poet stands at the river's edge, seeing his own sins clearly ("I admit everything"), not at all sure whether he should step forward into oblivion and peaceful death or step back-

*Cover for Wright's 1973 book, in which the poet explores the
offering of undeserved love*

ward to his Ohio shore into continued, painful life.
"I wish to God I had made this world, this scurvy /
And disastrous place," he cries, "but I didn't, I can't
bear it." Staying alive is so painful that "It hurts," he
says, "like nothing I know." Dying also hurts, and
that fact immobilizes him.

At this point, the darkest in his poetry,
Wright chooses life—but how and on what terms?
He steps away from the edge of death in time to understand that to live necessitates "gathering" the
ugliness that is inside and outside himself. Staying
alive means forgiving the ugly thing he has discovered himself to be and offering mercy to himself for
being merely human. To live means backing up,
joining the others, accepting his country, his fellow
humans, and himself, with all the attendant flaws,
disfigurements, warts, and crimes intact. The point
is not to purify falsely what is ugly, but to gather it
in all its ugliness after he has gathered himself.
This is the process of "gathering" that he begins in
his fifth major book, *Two Citizens* (1973), the truly
transitional volume in Wright's career. The key

verb in *Two Citizens* is *gather,* and, by repeatedly using it, trying it out, the poet nudges himself from
the precarious perch he occupied in "To the Muse"
into the position he occupies at the end of his final
volume, *This Journey* (1982)—on the side of a mountain at daybreak, "on top of the sunlight."

"Gathering" in *Two Citizens* and in Wright's
later poetry is the literal or imaginative act of
reaching toward the other, a sympathetic extending beyond oneself to another. Wright extends
himself in early poems, but always selectively, embracing only various outcasts and rebels. Those are
embraced because they deserve to be. The key to
"gathering" is that it is an extension of one's sympathy, which begins in *Two Citizens* as simple tolerance, to others without reference to their merits.
Like God, Wright chooses to offer his grace even if
it is not, or cannot be, deserved or earned. He
chooses to make a commitment despite judgment
because he moves toward gathering even those he
continues to judge. He struggles in *Two Citizens* and
subsequent volumes toward offering the miracle of

undeserved love, extending his hand to those same Philistines he earlier denounced, without changing his rational or moral judgment of them, simply choosing to embrace them as part of the depraved human species of which he is one dark member. "Gathering," then, is the act of offering human love gratuitously, an act that is a kind of grace, mercy, and beauty. Arnold Bennett, in his *Journal* (1932–1933), argues that "the essential characteristic of the really great novelist is a Christlike, all-embracing compassion." This is precisely what Wright struggles toward in *Two Citizens* and what he achieves in his last two books.

One reaches that point by small steps, the first of which is a candid recognition of one's own sinfulness; this step is followed by forgiving oneself for being part of the imperfect human race and loving oneself, anyway. These steps are followed by learning to offer that love to others. That last and most difficult lesson is initially taught to Wright by nature, specifically, by a herd of deer that appear in "A Secret Gratitude," from the "New Poems" section of *Collected Poems*. In the poem one is told several unpleasant things, one of which is that "Man's heart is the rotten yolk of a blacksnake egg / Corroding, as it is just born, in a pile of dead / Horse dung." Given this understanding of human nature, not surprisingly the poet concludes that humans deserve neither grace nor mercy nor beauty. He asks:

Why should any mere multitude of the angels care
To lay one blind white plume down
On this outermost limit of something that is probably no more
Than an aphid.

The answer, the poet suggests, is that there is no good reason at all why any angel should deign to look upon such pitiful wretches as humans. Yet the men in the poem, these "chemical accidents of horror," as he calls them, "capable of anything," are soon blessed when five deer, "those fleet lights," emerge from the woods and momentarily do not flee the men's presence. There is the wonder—that these wretched men are allowed into the presence of beauty at all. Perhaps in a world in which this is possible, against all odds and contrary to all logic or justice, perhaps, if men who are undeserving are allowed to stumble across beauty occasionally, then one should, in turn, offer his love and what little beauty he has to other undeserving souls.

The lesson is completed, however, only when learned from other humans, as happens in *Two Citizens*. In that book Wright says that his wife Anne "gave me the strength to come to terms with things which I loved and hated at the same time." As he did

in "A Secret Gratitude," he finds himself loved despite considering himself undeserving of that love, discovers himself the recipient of love offered for nothing. The next step is to turn his mercy outward, to love or "gather" those "things which I loved and hated at the same time" (a phrase that comes from the poem "Paul"), all those things he has seen (America's culture, destructive Americans, himself) that are also undeserving. The acts of accepting his own ugliness, falling in love with "a beautiful woman," being charitable toward others, and discovering "my native place" are all analogous forms of gathering the other, who is at times as repugnant as she, they, it, or oneself is alluring. "Though love can be scarcely imaginable hell," as he writes in "The Art of the Fugue: A Prayer," still, "By God, it is not a lie," and so, he accepts it; although he himself is "the rotten yolk of a blacksnake egg," he has to accept himself; although America is "a brutal and savage place," he says, "I still love" it. Americans are still depicted as defacers of the beautiful (for example, in "Names Scarred at the Entrance to Chartres"), yet they are his only heritage and his rightful companions. Therefore, even though "Dolan" and "Doyle" scratch their names at the entrance to Chartres Cathedral, Wright painfully admits that they are, they must be, his companions: "I have no way to go in / Except only / In the company of two vulgars. . . . "

His struggle for innocence has shown him his guilt. To reject the guilty is thus to deny part of himself, which is precisely what he wants not to do. Recognizing his own sin and seeing himself the beneficiary of Anne's undeserved love, he gains the power to extend his own hand to others equally undeserving. To refuse to gather the ugly would be to commit the sin of Nathaniel Hawthorne's Young Goodman Brown and to end as Brown did: "a stern, a sad, a darkly meditative, a distrustful, if not a desperate man," unable to have faith in anything except his own false purity. To refuse to have faith in the beauty of others, even while knowing they are also ugly, is to react to the inevitable confrontation with darkness as George Doty, who committed murder, did—by placing one's faith in evil; ultimately, it is also to die, as Brown did, "a hoary corpse," separated from what Hawthorne calls the "universal throb," having voluntarily cut oneself off from "the magnetic chain of humanity." Wright's mature recognition and perspective, begun in *Two Citizens,* is completed in *To a Blossoming Pear Tree* (1977) and in *This Journey.*

Reviewers noted the new understanding that was present in *To a Blossoming Pear Tree,* the last volume published during Wright's lifetime. The remarks of Peter Serchuk, writing in 1978 in the *Hud-*

son Review, are typical of the praise the book received: "What perhaps most distinguishes Wright's voice in this book from that of his previous collections is its authority of middle age, its active acceptance of a tottering world along with the well-seasoned understanding that among the rubbled debris there is always some sustaining beauty to be found, however difficult it may be to recognize." That "active acceptance of a tottering world" is the goal toward which Wright's poetry, seen in perspective, has been moving since *The Green Wall.* Finally, having recognized the futility of hoping to exile himself from the realm of the ugly by writing poems in which the forces of the beautiful and the ugly battle to a standoff, Wright now composes poems in which, in Linda Pastan's words in the *Library Journal* in 1977, "the brutal and the beautiful mysteriously illuminate each other."

Wright begins *To a Blossoming Pear Tree* with some of his old bitterness toward Ohio and a hint of the paranoia the reader expects from one of the self-proclaimed pure people ("somebody / Is wondering right at this moment / How to get rid of us, while we sleep," he writes in "Redwings"), but he moves beyond that self-destructiveness to shower the reader with images of what it means "To drink, to live" in the poem "Hell." His deliverance is effected by a brutal self-awareness: ten times in the book he reminds the reader of the necessity of facing oneself, of literally looking unflinchingly into one's own or another's face, and, as he does, one notices the preponderance of images of light—secret light, dazzles, brilliances, candlelight, sunlight, light of every variety—whereas images of darkness had earlier prevailed.

Even when darkness enters the poem, it does not prevent the speaker from seeing clearly. In "With the Shell of a Hermit Crab," a poem often anthologized, the speaker examines a crab that has been forced out of its shell and has died. The observation might in previous volumes have prompted the poet to conclude that one must remain armored. He reaches the opposite conclusion in *To a Blossoming Pear Tree,* and he reaches it in the darkness:

> I reach out and flick out the light.
> Darkly I touch his fragile scars,
> So far away, so delicate,
> Stars in a wilderness of stars.

Scars become stars. The pains one bears provide one's illumination. Darkness and light do, as Pastan says, "mysteriously illuminate each other."

"Beautiful Ohio," the final poem in *To a Blossoming Pear Tree,* is the best illustration in the volume

Dust jacket for Wright's 1977 book, poems in which he found beauty even in ugliness

of Wright's mature vision. Sitting on a railroad tie above the Martins Ferry sewer main, the poet watches as "a shining waterfall" of waste spews out of the pipe. He says:

> I know what we call it
> Most of the time.
> But I have my own song for it,
> And sometimes, even today,
> I call it beauty.

Ohio in this poem is "beautiful"; Martins Ferry is "my home, my native place"; and even the waste of the culture, for the moment, is "beauty." The ugliness of the sewer is incorporated undiluted into the singer's song. Wright here sees the beauty *in* the ugliness, not merely the beauty *and* the ugliness. The "secret light" that he has been searching for was supposed to be pure, beautiful, innocent, undefiled, the opposite of the "perilous black," the ugliness that he spent so many poems defining and rejecting. Discovering that the secret light actually resides in the "perilous black" and can only be discovered there moves him not toward despair but toward fulfillment. He does not turn his back to the waste but chooses to "call it beauty," chooses to see, recognize, and identify the ugliness around him as part of the beautiful. To "call" it beauty implies a choice. He has wanted beauty to overwhelm him, to jump across the subject-object divide and grab him. It will not do that, and the poet now accepts his duty as poet, which is also his uniquely human power: to call into consciousness the beauty that lies enveloped in ugliness.

Wright began his poetic career trying to diminish what cannot be diminished—specifically, humankind's flaws, including greed, selfishness, willful destruction, and complacent ignorance. He succeeded in changing nothing around him, but he did change himself, and in so doing, he changed his reaction to the ugly facts of life from one of rejection and despair to one of acceptance and hope. This acceptance so strengthened the poet as a poet that he was able to face life's horrors while simultaneously singing life's joys. The result is a continuous consciousness of life's wonders, undiminished by—in fact, made more profound by—the equally sharp awareness of life's brutality.

This hard-won perspective shines through in the amazing posthumous volume *This Journey*. Many critics have noted what Robert Shaw in 1982 called in *The Nation,* "Wright's awareness of approaching death." Critics have also noticed, again quoting Shaw, "a heightened sensitivity to the pulse of vitality everywhere around him." Death and vitality meet, and one is not surprised, because that is exactly what should happen in the work of a poet finally capable of "gathering" all the world to him. Any longing for escape or vague transcendence is gone. Reality is sufficient; meaning inheres in life's cicadas, hawks, and humans. Fantastic images are often related in a deadpan tone because life is a series of amazing moments, and no one should be surprised to see beauty thrust in front of him or her at any moment, in the form of lightning bugs, diminutive blue spiders, jagged pieces of ice, or the outstretched hands of strangers. Salvation comes from knowing enough to gather the inexplicable gratefully. "Come, Look Quietly" is the title of one of these final poems and a final statement of Wright's epistemology and ethics. The world holds life-giving, life-sustaining, and meaningful moments, and to overlook them would be immoral, to dwell exclusively on ugliness: "Sheep eat everything," the poet tells us in "Sheep in the Rain," "All the way down to the root"; and, as a result of this appetite for all that life offers, sheep have all that anyone can rightly ask, "a good life of it, / While it lasts." The

point is to live, to gather, rather than to waste one's brief time finding fault: "The trouble with me is / I worry too much about things that should be / Left alone," Wright observes in "Leave Him Alone."

Moral exemplars in earlier volumes taught the poet to resist, protest, and create a life outside the mainstream where most people live. Exemplars in *This Journey,* such as the sheep, teach the poet to embrace what sustenance the world offers. In "Come, Look Quietly," he writes:

> The plump Parisian wild bird is scoring a light breakfast at the end of December. He has found the last seeds left in tiny cones on the outcast Christmas tree that blows on the terrace.

Finding himself in *The Green Wall* in what he diagnosed as a dead land, the poet saw no hope except escape, which threatened to result in his own death. Now his characters take life from death, without compromising their integrity: the plump bird remains "wild." This way of life suggests that reality may be beneficent, if given a chance, and that the world offers miracles, if one takes the time to attend to them. One such small miracle occurs in "Against Surrealism." The poet and his wife buy some chocolate penguins at a Parisian confectionery:

> We set them out on a small table above half the rooftops of Paris. I reached out to brush a tiny obvious particle of dust from the tip of a beak. Suddenly the dust dropped an inch and hovered there. Then it rose to the beak again.
> It was a blue spider.

Omit the chocolate penguins, and many readers may remember having encountered spiders in this manner; and many may have crushed them or flicked them away. Wright has converted himself into Emerson's and Whitman's poet, the "seer" who is also and inevitably the "sayer." He searches for what he encounters accidentally, notes it, and gives it back to the reader as a gift, as the world has given it to him, without egotism, as an act of humility rather than achievement:

> Many men
> Have searched all over Tuscany and never found
> What I found there, the heart of the light
> Itself shelled and leaved, balancing on filaments themselves falling.

Instead of continuing to long for escape or an otherworldly transcendence, Wright reveals his faith in the plenitude and sufficiency of reality.

Wright comes nearest to a direct statement of his philosophy in *This Journey* in the last stanza of "The Journey":

> The secret
> Of this journey is to let the wind
> Blow its dust all over your body,
> To let it go on blowing, to step lightly, lightly,
> All the way through your ruins, and not to lose
> Any sleep over the dead, who surely
> Will bury their own, don't worry.

Wright counseled passivity in *The Branch Will Not Break* and *Shall We Gather at the River* because he feared that activity was by its nature aggressive and too closely allied with the culture of conquest beyond which he was trying to move. Here he admits the possibility of a morality that is simultaneously active and respectful rather than aggressive: "step lightly, lightly."

Such a philosophy is easy to articulate but difficult to live. The right to perceive the plenitude and sufficiency of reality, however, was not a simple gift. Through years of honest struggle Wright earned the right to contend, implicitly, and despite William Butler Yeats's imagery of chaos and dissolution in his poem "The Second Coming," that the center, in fact, does hold. This contention is not the expression of a naive simplicity but, rather, the result of a deep understanding of life wrought by years of anguish and poetic labor. As Thoreau says in *Walden*, "darkness bear[s] its own fruit"; and Wright in "A Winter Daybreak Above Venice," the final poem in his final volume, is not seen as the "hoary corpse" that Goodman Brown became and that the poet had seemed doomed to become, but is seen at daybreak, "on top of the sunlight," taking all he can from "the only life I have."

Letters:

In Defense against This Exile: Letters to Wayne Burns, edited by John R. Doheny (Seattle, Wash.: Genitron Press, 1985);

The Delicacy and Strength of Lace: Letters between Leslie Marmon Silko and James Wright, edited by Anne Wright (St. Paul, Minn.: Graywolf Press, 1986).

Interviews:

Michael André, "An Interview with James Wright," *Unmuzzled Ox,* 1 (February 1972): 3–18;

William Heyen and Jerome Mazzaro, "Something to Be Said for the Light: A Conversation with James Wright," *Southern Humanities Review,* 6 (1972): 134–153;

Peter A. Stitt, "The Art of Poetry, XIX: James Wright," *Paris Review,* 16 (Summer 1975): 34–61;

Bruce Henricksen, "Poetry Must Think," *New Orleans Review,* 6, no. 3 (1978): 201–207;

David Smith, "An Interview with James Wright: The Pure Clear Word," *American Poetry Review,* 9, no. 3 (1980): 19–30.

Bibliographies:

Belle M. McMaster, "James Arlington Wright: A Checklist," *Bulletin of Bibliography and Magazine Notes,* 31 (April/June 1974): 71–82, 88;

William H. Roberson, *James Wright: An Annotated Bibliography* (Lanham, Md.: Scarecrow Press, 1995).

References:

Roger Blakeley, "Form and Meaning in the Poetry of James Wright," *South Dakota Review,* 25 (Summer 1987): 20–30;

Edward Butscher, "The Rise and Fall of James Wright," *Georgia Review,* 28 (Spring 1974): 257–268;

"Crunk" [Robert Bly], "The Work of James Wright," *Sixties,* 8 (Spring 1966): 52–78;

Madeline DeFrees, "James Wright's Early Poems: A Study in 'Convulsive' Form," *Modern Poetry Studies,* 2 (1979): 241–251;

David C. Dougherty, *James Wright* (Boston: Twayne, 1987);

Andrew Elkins, *The Poetry of James Wright* (Tuscaloosa: University of Alabama Press, 1991);

Nicholas Gattuccio, "Now My Amenities of Stone Are Done: Some Notes on the Style of James Wright," *Scape: Seattle, New York,* 1 (1981): 31–44;

Michael Graves, "Crisis in the Career of James Wright," *Hollins Critic,* 22 (December 1985): 1–9;

Graves, "A Look at the Ceremonial Range of James Wright," *Concerning Poetry,* 16, no. 2 (1983): 43–54;

Victoria Harris, "James Wright's Odyssey: A Journey from Dualism to Incorporation," *Contemporary Poetry: A Journal of Criticism,* 3, no. 3 (1978): 56–74;

Richard Howard, *Alone with America: Essays on the Art of Poetry in the United States since 1950,* enlarged edition (New York: Atheneum, 1980), pp. 662–678;

Howard, "James Wright's Transformations," *New York Arts Journal,* 8 (February/March 1978): 22–23;

Cor van den Huevel, "The Poetry of James Wright," *Mosaic,* 7 (Spring 1974): 163–170;

Ironwood, special Wright issue, 10 (1977);

G. A. M. Janssens, "The Present State of American Poetry: Robert Bly and James Wright," *English Studies,* 51 (Spring 1970): 112–137;

Walter Kalaidjian, "'Many of Our Waters': The Poetry of James Wright," *Boundary 2: A Journal of Postmodern Literature,* 9, no. 2 (1981): 101–121;

Paul A. Lacey, "That Scarred Truth of Wretchedness," in his *The Inner War: Forms and Themes in Recent American Poetry* (Philadelphia: Fortress Press, 1972), pp. 57–81;

Edward Lense, "'This Is What I Wanted': James Wright and the Other World," *Modern Poetry Studies,* 11, nos. 1–2 (1982): 19–32;

George S. Lensing and Robert Moran, *Four Poets of the Emotive Imagination: Robert Bly, James Wright, Louis Simpson, and William Stafford* (Baton Rouge: Louisiana State University Press, 1976);

Laurence Lieberman, "James Wright: Words of Grass," in his *Unassigned Frequencies: American Poetry in Review, 1964–77* (Urbana: University of Illinois Press, 1977), pp. 182–189;

Saundra Maley, *Solitary Apprenticeship: James Wright and German Poetry* (Lewiston, N.Y.: Mellen University Press, 1996);

William Matthews, "The Continuity of James Wright's Poems," *Ohio Review,* 18 (Spring/Summer 1977): 44–57;

Jerome Mazzaro, "Dark Water: James Wright's Early Poetry," *Centennial Review,* 27 (Spring 1983): 135–155;

Ralph J. Mills Jr., "James Wright's Poetry: Introductory Notes," *Chicago Review,* 17, nos. 2–3 (1964): 128–143;

Charles Molesworth, "James Wright and the Dissolving Self," in *Contemporary Poetry in America: Essays and Interviews,* edited by Ralph Boyers (New York: Schocken Books, 1974), pp. 267–278;

William S. Saunders, "Indignation Born of Love: James Wright's Ohio Poems," *Old Northwest: A Journal of Regional Life and Letters,* 4 (December 1978): 353–369;

Saunders, *James Wright: An Introduction* (Columbus: State Library of Ohio, 1979);

James Seay, "A World Immeasurably Alive and Good: A Look at James Wright's Collected Poems," *Georgia Review,* 27 (Spring 1973): 71–81;

Peter Serchuk, "On the Poet James Wright," *Modern Poetry Studies,* 10, nos. 2–3 (1981): 85–90;

Dave Smith, ed., *The Pure Clear Word: Essays on the Poetry of James Wright* (Urbana: University of Illinois Press, 1982);

Kevin Stein, *James Wright, the Poetry of a Grown Man: Constancy and Transition in the Work of James Wright* (Athens: Ohio University Press, 1989);

Stephen Stepanchev, *American Poetry Since 1945: A Critical Survey* (New York: Harper & Row, 1965), pp. 180–184;

Randall Stiffler, "The Reconciled Vision of James Wright," *Literary Review,* 28, no. 1 (1984): 77–92;

Peter A. Stitt, "The Garden and the Grime," *Kenyon Review,* 6, no. 2 (1984): 76–91;

Stitt, "The Poetry of James Wright," *Minnesota Review,* 2 (Spring 1972): 13–29;

Stitt and Frank Graziano, eds., *James Wright: The Heart of Light* (Ann Arbor: University of Michigan Press, 1990).

Paul Zindel

This entry was updated by Jack Forman (San Diego Mesa College) from the entries by Ruth L. Strickland (University of South Carolina) in DLB 7: Twentieth-Century American Dramatists, and by Theodore W. Hipple (University of Tennessee) in DLB 52: American Writers for Children Since 1960.

BIRTH: Staten Island, New York, 15 May 1936, to Paul and Beatrice Mary Frank Zindel.

EDUCATION: B.S., Wagner College, 1958; M.S., Wagner College, 1959.

MARRIAGE: 25 October 1973 to Bonnie Hildebrand; children: David Jack, Lizabeth Claire.

AWARDS AND HONORS: Ford Foundation grant for drama, 1967; *Boston Globe-Horn Book* Award for text for *The Pigman*, 1969; Outstanding Children's Book of the Year citations from *The New York Times Book Review* for *My Darling, My Hamburger*, 1969, for *I Never Loved Your Mind*, 1970, for *Pardon Me, You're Stepping on My Eyeball!* 1976, for *The Undertaker's Gone Bananas*, 1978, and for *The Pigman's Legacy*, 1980; Obie Award for best new American play from the *Village Voice*, New York Drama Critics Circle Award for best American play of the year, and *Variety* Award for most promising playwright, all 1970, and Pulitzer Prize in drama, New York Critics Award, and Vernon Rice Drama Desk Award for the most promising playwright, all 1971, all for *The Effect of Gamma Rays on Man-in-the-Moon Marigolds;* American Library Association (ALA) Best Books for Young Adults citations for *The Effect of Gamma Rays on Man-in-the-Moon Marigolds*, 1971, for *The Pigman*, 1975, for *Pardon Me, You're Stepping on My Eyeball!* 1976, for *Confessions of a Teenage Baboon*, 1977, for *The Pigman's Legacy*, 1981, and for *To Take a Dare*, 1982; *Media & Methods* Maxi Award for *The Pigman*, 1973; New York Public Library "books for the teen age" citations for *Confessions of a Teenage Baboon*, 1980, for *The Effect of Gamma Rays on Man-in-the-Moon Marigolds*, 1980, 1981, for *A Star for the Latecomer*, 1981, 1982, and for *The Pigman's Legacy*, 1981, 1982; honorary Doctorate of Humanities from Wagner College, 1971.

BOOKS: *The Pigman* (New York: Harper & Row, 1968; London: Bodley Head, 1969);
My Darling, My Hamburger (New York: Harper & Row, 1969; London: Bodley Head, 1970);

Paul Zindel, 1982

I Never Loved Your Mind (New York: Harper & Row, 1970; London: Bodley Head, 1971);
And Miss Reardon Drinks a Little (New York: Dramatists Play Service, 1971; New York: Random House, 1972);
The Effect of Gamma Rays on Man-in-the-Moon Marigolds (New York: Harper & Row, 1971);
Let Me Hear You Whisper and The Ladies Should Be in Bed (New York: Dramatists Play Service, 1973);
The Secret Affairs of Mildred Wild (New York: Dramatists Play Service, 1973);
Let Me Hear You Whisper (New York: Harper & Row, 1974);
I Love My Mother (New York: Harper & Row, 1975);

Pardon Me, You're Stepping On My Eyeball! (New York: Harper & Row, 1976; London: Bodley Head, 1976);

Confessions of a Teenage Baboon (New York: Harper & Row, 1977; London: Bodley Head, 1978);

Ladies at the Alamo (New York: Dramatists Play Service, 1977);

The Undertaker's Gone Bananas (New York: Harper & Row, 1978; London: Bodley Head, 1979);

A Star for the Latecomer, by Zindel and Bonnie Zindel (New York: Harper & Row, 1980; London: Bodley Head, 1980);

The Pigman's Legacy (New York: Harper & Row, 1980; London: Bodley Head, 1980);

The Girl Who Wanted a Boy (New York: Harper & Row, 1981; London: Bodley Head, 1981);

To Take a Dare, by Zindel and Crescent Dragonwagon (New York: Harper & Row, 1982);

Harry and Hortense at Hormone High (New York: Harper & Row, 1984; London: Bodley Head, 1985);

When a Darkness Falls (New York: Bantam, 1984);

The Amazing and Death-Defying Diary of Eugene Dingman (New York: Harper & Row, 1987; London: Bodley Head, 1987);

A Begonia for Miss Applebaum (New York: Harper & Row, 1989; London: Bodley Head, 1989);

Amulets Against the Dragon Forces (New York: Dramatists Play Service, 1989);

The Pigman and Me (London: Bodley Head, 1991; New York: HarperCollins, 1992);

Attack of the Killer Fishsticks (New York: Bantam, 1993); republished as *Attack of the Killer Fishfingers* (London: Random House, 1993);

David & Della (New York: HarperCollins, 1993; London: Bodley Head, 1994);

Fright Party (New York: Bantam, 1993; London: Red Fox, 1993);

Fifth Grade Safari (New York: Bantam, 1993); republished as *City Safari* (London: Random House, 1994);

Loch (New York: HarperCollins, 1994; London: Red Fox, 1995);

The 100% Laugh Riot (New York: Bantam, 1994; London: Red Fox, 1994);

The Doom Stone (New York: HarperCollins, 1995; London: Bodley Head, 1996);

Reef of Death (New York: HarperCollins, 1998);

Raptor (New York: Hyperion, 1998).

PLAY PRODUCTIONS: *Dimensions of Peacocks,* New York, 1959;

Euthanasia and the Endless Hearts, New York, Take 3, 1960;

A Dream of Swallows, New York, Jan Hus House, 14 April 1964;

The Effect of Gamma Rays on Man-in-the-Moon Marigolds, Houston, Texas, Alley Theatre, 12 May 1965; New York, Mercer-O'Casey Theatre, 7 April 1970 (transferred 11 August 1970 to the New Theatre);

And Miss Reardon Drinks a Little, Los Angeles, Mark Taper Forum, 1967; New York, Morosco Theatre, 25 February 1971;

The Secret Affairs of Mildred Wild, New York, Ambassador Theatre, 14 November 1972;

Ladies at the Alamo, New York, Actors Studio, 29 May 1975.

MOTION PICTURES: *Up the Sandbox,* adapted from Anne Roiphe's novel, First Artist Films, 1972;

Mame, adapted from Patrick Dennis's *Auntie Mame,* Warner Brothers, 1974;

Maria's Lovers, screenplay by Zindel, Gérard Brach, Andrei Konchalovsky, and Marjorie Rand, Cannon Films, 1984;

Runaway Train, adapted from a screenplay by Akira Kurosawa, screenplay by Zindel, Djordje Milicevic, and Edward Bunker, Cannon Films, 1985.

TELEVISION: *Let Me Hear You Whisper,* NET, 1969;

Alice in Wonderland—Through the Looking Glass, CBS, 1985;

Babes in Toyland, NBC, 1986;

A Connecticut Yankee in King Arthur's Court, NBC, 18 December 1989.

SELECTED PERIODICAL PUBLICATIONS—UNCOLLECTED: "Interview with Edward Albee," by Zindel and Loree Yerby, *Wagner [College] Literary Magazine,* 3 (1962): 1-10;

"The Theater is Born Within Us," *New York Times,* 26 July 1970, sec. 2, pp. 1, 3.

Critics of adolescent literature generally cite four novels of the late 1960s as helping this subgenre break its ties with its past formulaic romanticism and move dramatically into a much more realistic mode: *The Outsiders* (1967) by S. E. Hinton, *The Contender* (1967) by Robert Lipsyte, *Mr. and Mrs. Bo Jo Jones* (1967) by Ann Head, and *The Pigman* (1968) by Paul Zindel. Before these works appeared, literature for young adults seemed almost an extension of the grade-school primers, with Dick and Jane as teenagers and Spot replaced by an Irish setter. After these books, however, came a flood of novels—

which are still coming–that placed young adult novels squarely in a new realistic tradition. Much of the credit for this long overdue change must go to these authors, and especially to Zindel, who has kept the movement flourishing with a steady stream of novels that explore teenagers' lives in realistic ways.

Paul Zindel was born on 15 May 1936 on Staten Island. His policeman father (also named Paul Zindel) deserted his family when Paul was two years old and his sister, Betty, was four. Zindel has said that he only saw his father about ten times before his death in 1957 and that he deeply resents growing up fatherless. His mother, who was a practical nurse, took many kinds of strange jobs to make ends meet–and as a result moved her family almost every year while Zindel was growing up. When his mother died of cancer in 1968, Zindel had been teaching high-school chemistry for ten years on Staten Island. He was then ending a sabbatical from his teaching position during which he served as a playwright in residence in Houston, and he had just published his groundbreaking first novel, *The Pigman*. After he quit teaching, Zindel focused on writing plays and young adult novels, and in 1971 he was awarded the Pulitzer Prize for his emotional and electrifying play *The Effect of Gamma Rays on Man-in-the-Moon Marigolds*. While helping to produce the play in Cleveland, he met Bonnie Hildebrand, the playhouse publicity director, and in 1973 he married her.

Gamma Rays is Zindel's best-known play. It is essentially a domestic melodrama, with an occasional lapse into sentimentality, about a family composed of the mother, Beatrice Hunsdorfer, and her two teenage daughters, Ruth and Tillie. Beatrice, known in her youth as "Betty the Loon," is the dominant character in the play. She is a bitter widow, cynical and half-mad, who dreams of opening a tea room but who lives in chaos and is paid to care for Nanny, an elderly woman who can neither speak nor hear. Beatrice fears the ridicule of the world, so she makes her daughters dependent upon her and vents her rage and frustration upon them.

Everyone in the untidy house is psychically wounded. Nanny has been abandoned by a daughter who finds her existence a burden. Ruth, untidy and wanton, has seizures brought on by memories of her mother's boarders' deaths and by her mother's threats of cruelty. Tillie, a shy, plain girl, bestows her affection on a rabbit given to her by her science teacher. Ruth longs to have the rabbit for herself, and Beatrice threatens daily to chloroform the pet. Tillie, however, has found an even more important release from her squalid environment–science. She is fascinated by the structure of atoms,

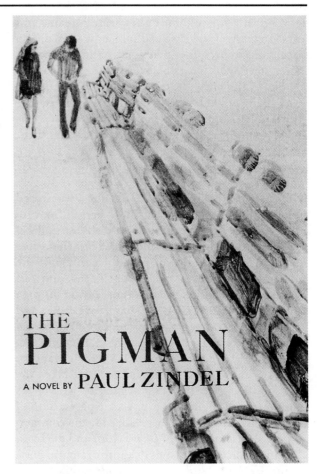

Dust jacket for the 1968 novel that launched Zindel's career as a writer for young adults

and her science teacher has given her marigold seeds to grow that have been exposed to varying degrees of radiation. At the science fair, where she wins first prize, she describes the results of her experiment, showing how some of the seeds gave forth normal plants, while others bore mutations with double blooms or giant stems, and still others died. She ends her speech by expressing her belief that some of the "mutations will be good ones–wonderful things beyond our dreams–and . . . THE DAY WILL COME WHEN MANKIND WILL THANK GOD FOR THE STRANGE AND BEAUTIFUL ENERGY FROM THE ATOM."

The message is clear: Tillie is the mutant who has emerged from a horrifying environment with faith and potential intact–she is the double bloom. Life has bypassed Beatrice, and Ruth is a victim of her mother's despair. Tillie is Zindel's synthesis of the brutal and the beautiful. Zindel's own background was his source: Beatrice, he has told a *Time* reporter, is his mother in "nightmarish exaggeration." In the introduction to the 1971 published version of *Gamma Rays,* Zindel writes of his mother: "In her own way she told me of her secret dreams and fears—so many of which I had somehow sensed, and discovered written into that manuscript next to my typewriter, many years before." While Tillie is the heroine of the play, Beatrice, misfit par excellence, is the character who lives in the playgoer's memory.

Zindel's other plays include *And Miss Reardon Drinks a Little* (first performed in 1967), about three sisters, all schoolteachers, who have been psychologically maimed by a domineering, neurotic mother, now deceased; *The Secret Affairs of Mildred Wild* (first performed in 1972), about a frustrated and eccentric woman who excludes herself from society, living a vicarious life through movies; and *Ladies at the Alamo* (first performed in 1975), about five strong women in a power play for control of the most important theater complex in Texas. Many of the characters combine traits Zindel saw in his own mother (sexual fixation, sexual repression, and paranoia) with elements from Tennessee Williams's tragic female protagonists (alcoholism, romantic isolation, and a huge capacity to create fantasy worlds). There is leavening humor that takes the edge off these portraits of negativity as well as sharp, witty dialogue that propels the plays. Both of these strengths were major reasons for the commercial and critical success of *Gamma Rays* and the overall critical success of Zindel's most dramatic playscript, *And Miss Reardon Drinks A Little*. While Zindel has not fulfilled his early promise as a playwright after *Gamma Rays,* he has continued to explore the recurrent themes of loneliness, eccentricity, isolation, and escapism.

Zindel wrote *The Pigman* in 1968, largely at the prodding and encouragement of Charlotte Zolotow, the senior editor of the Harper and Row juvenile books department. Zolotow had seen a local educational production of *Gamma Rays* and immediately recognized that Zindel possessed an accurate ear for incisive dialogue and an eye for honest and unusual personal relationships. She knew that these qualities were lacking but much needed in fiction for teenagers, so she convinced Zindel to write a novel for adolescents. Zindel felt he knew the territory because of his high-school teaching experience. He was also primed to weave his own life into his stories: a virtually fatherless childhood; a turbulent relationship with a paranoiac mother; a feeling of worthlessness; and an absence of long-term friendships, caused in part by his mother's proclivity to move often.

The story of *The Pigman* is essentially a tragic one. Through a telephone hoax, high-school sophomores John Conlan and Lorraine Jensen meet Mr. Angelo Pignati, an aged widower with a zest for life

and a passion for the assortment of model pigs he and his wife had been collecting. John and Lorraine become friends with Pignati (whom they call "the Pigman"); they go to the zoo with him, drink his homemade wine, and develop a deep affection for him. When Pignati is hospitalized after a mild heart attack, the two teenagers use his house to host a party that gets out of control, resulting in serious damage to Pignati's property and the complete destruction of the glass- and clay-pig collection. The old man returns home at the height of the chaos, finds the devastation more than he can stand, and dies a short time later of a second, more severe heart attack. John and Lorraine are left wondering to what degree they had played a part in his death.

The two teen protagonists alternate as first-person narrators, a technique that affords some insight into Zindel's skillful use of language. John swears; Lorraine does not. Her sentences are longer than his. Hers is the more sentimental voice; his, the more matter-of-fact. This first novel anticipates Zindel's later work in several ways. Dialogue plays a major role in carrying the action of the novel. In *The Pigman* lies Zindel's first treatment of teenage alienation, principally from parental authority. Rarely does Zindel feature teenagers who have solid, normal relationships with both parents. More typical are John, who labels his father "the Bore," and Lorraine, whose divorced mother tries to convince her that all men are sex maniacs. Often, Zindel's novels include autobiographical details; for instance, his mother was a practical nurse who boarded the terminally ill, as is Lorraine's; in *Confessions of a Teenage Baboon* (1977), Chris Boyd's mother works as a live-in nurse for the dying. In addition, school in a Zindel novel is more a place where teens meet than where they learn. In the opening paragraph of *The Pigman* John says, "I hate school," a message implied if not actually echoed by many later Zindel characters.

In *The Pigman's Legacy* (1980), a sequel written twelve years and many literary successes after the first novel, John and Lorraine, now juniors in high school, happen to return to the Pigman's house, only to discover that it is lived in—"squatted in"—by an old recluse whom they call "the Colonel" and who, they later learn, is dying of cancer. They become the Colonel's friends; accompany him to Atlantic City, where John gambles away the old man's savings; and arrange a deathbed marriage for the old man with Dolly, a worker in their school cafeteria. The feelings that Dolly and the Colonel share help John and Lorraine learn that the legacy left them by the Pigman was not shame or sorrow or regret; it was love. Although many aspects of *The Pig-*

man's *Legacy* mirror scenes in its predecessor, one new development is that Lorraine finally discovers the love she had been seeking–her friend John. It has taken the deaths of the two old men, both of whom they loved and both of whom loved them, to show John and Lorraine the strength of their own love for each other.

Between the two Pigman novels Zindel wrote seven highly successful novels for teenagers. *My Darling, My Hamburger* (1969) continues the trend toward realism begun in *The Pigman*. Zindel portrays two couples–popular and confident Sean and Liz, and shy and uncertain Maggie and Dennis. The provocative title of the book, a Zindel trademark, points out the absurdity of a teacher's advice to Liz that she deflect Sean's sexual advances by asking him out for a hamburger. Given such inane guidance, and saddled with an overstrict stepfather, Liz succumbs to Sean's pressures and becomes pregnant. Sean, encouraged by his selfish and insensitive father, reneges on his promise to marry Liz. Maggie secretly accompanies Liz to a then-illegal abortionist, who botches the operation and almost kills the teenager. The novel ends with the four teens going their separate ways, matured and embittered by their experiences.

In this novel Zindel reiterates themes established in *The Pigman*–Sean and Liz have mutually destructive relationships with their parents, and school is merely tolerated–yet Zindel also continues to break new ground for adolescent fiction. High schoolers are seen smoking and drinking. They have sex and they get pregnant and go to illegal abortionists. However, Zindel does not generalize his characters. Maggie and Dennis are endearing in their self-consciousness. Dennis spends four times the required fifteen seconds gargling mouthwash and still worries about bad breath. On their first date Maggie fears that her attempt to get a share of the armrest in the movie theater may be mistaken as a signal that she really wants Dennis to move his arm and put it around her. Both miss most of the movie because of their concern about a later goodnight kiss.

In many ways *My Darling, My Hamburger* is one of Zindel's best novels for adolescents. Its characters, though unusual, are not bizarre themselves or placed in bizarre situations. Moreover, what happens in the novel, though it ranges from first-date behavior to a butchered abortion, is well within the experience of teenagers. Although Zindel provides no definitive solutions–indeed, he properly avoids such presumptions–his insights in this novel are informative in positive ways.

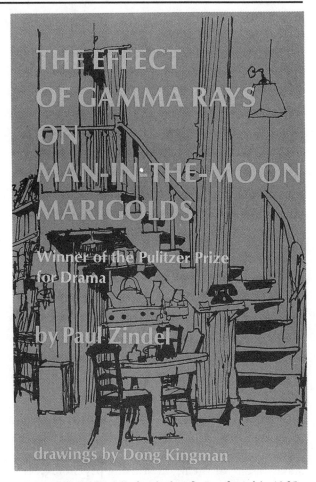

THE EFFECT
OF GAMMA RAYS
ON
MAN-IN-THE-MOON
MARIGOLDS

Winner of the Pulitzer Prize
for Drama

by Paul Zindel

drawings by Dong Kingman

Dust jacket for Zindel's fourth play, first performed in 1965 and published in 1971, about a domineering mother and her two daughters

In 1975 Zindel wrote a book for young children. *I Love My Mother,* a picture book illustrated by John Melo, tells in the first person how much a little boy loves his mother. The fatherless boy, about six years old, tells the reader that his mother says "Absolutely not" when he wants to drive the car and "Have a good time" when he threatens to run away to Miami; but when he says "I miss my father," she hugs him and tells him that his father misses him, too. Zindel has created a fantasy view of a perfect mother.

Zindel's next three novels for adolescents satirically portray teenagers and adults. In *I Never Loved Your Mind* (1970), Dewey, a seventeen-year-old dropout, meets Yvette Goethals in the autopsy room of the hospital where they both work. An eighteen-year-old flower child, Yvette steals everything she can from the hospital, eats broccoli sandwiches for lunch, and sleeps "nonsexually" in the same bed with a drummer from a rock band, although she and Dewey do share a sexual relationship. Dewey's involvement with her is interrupted when Yvette and the band are forced from their rented home because the landlord objects to their keeping horses in the living room. Dewey eventually rejects Yvette's aimless, self-destructive lifestyle and decides to go to medical school.

"Marsh" Mallow and Edna Shinglebox share the protagonist's role in *Pardon Me, You're Stepping On My Eyeball!* (1976). Marsh, who carries a live raccoon in his coat pocket, engages Edna in a search for his father. From Marsh's alcoholic mother, Edna learns that Marsh's father is dead, and she subsequently helps Marsh accept this fact. In so doing, she breaks from her own mother's protective hold on her life and declares her independence. Minor characters, such as Mr. Meizner, the self-absorbed school psychiatrist who thinks the classroom is a playground for group sensitivity sessions, and God Boy, a teenage "evangelist" whose exaltations about the human body turn a teen party into a Roman orgy, are also well developed.

Confessions of a Teenage Baboon is the story of fifteen-year-old Chris Boyd, who lives with his mother (a nurse who cares for terminally ill patients) and carries around the overcoat of his deceased father. Chris and his mother live temporarily in the home of an older woman named Mrs. Dipardi, who is dying of cancer. Her son, Lloyd, takes fatherless boys like Chris under his wing and tries to make "men" of them, often using psychologically brutal methods. For example, in an effort to give the hapless and passive Chris some support, Lloyd tries to shame the boy by calling him a "nurd," "out of it," and "retarded." After receiving a thinly veiled accusation of homosexuality and getting beaten by local police, Lloyd commits suicide, which Chris witnesses. In the aftermath of this tragedy, Chris frees himself from the domination of his mother and comes to terms with his father's death.

Despite its characteristically bizarre title, *The Undertaker's Gone Bananas* (1978) represents a sharp departure from Zindel's earlier novels. The book is a mystery in which two friends, Bobby and Lauri, accuse an undertaker in their apartment complex of murdering his wife. When she appears, the charge is dropped, and when the two teenagers bring it up again, the police accuse them of crying wolf. Lauri and Bobby eventually risk their lives and solve the mystery, discovering that the undertaker had killed his girlfriend and then murdered his wife. Both Bobby and Lauri have supportive, normal parents—for the first time in a Zindel novel. Other features common to Zindel's books do appear: Bobby and Lauri are each other's best friends, a reprise of the John-Lorraine relationship in *The Pigman* and the Marsh-Edna duo of *Pardon Me, You're Stepping On My*

Eyeball! Bobby, like other male Zindel protagonists, is not liked by his peers, in his case because he is too smart and too outspoken. Also apparent is Zindel's careful sense of place, his awareness that teens often define themselves by their parties and their hangouts.

In 1980 Zindel's wife Bonnie wrote with him a moving young adult novel titled *A Star for the Latecomer*. The first Zindel story to feature a girl as its protagonist, this novel presents Brooke Hillary, who attends a fine-arts school in order to pursue a dancing career that is more her mother's goal than her own. Brooke loves her mother and is especially reluctant to disappoint her when she learns her mother has terminal cancer. In helping her mother come to terms with her impending death, Brooke is able to shed the guilt and ambivalence she feels about asserting her own needs.

In *The Girl Who Wanted a Boy* (1981) Zindel again uses a female protagonist—Sibella Cametta, daughter of divorced parents and younger sister of the popular and sophisticated Maureen. Sibella can tolerate her parents and her sister (the latter barely) but not the fact that she does not have a boyfriend. When she sees a picture of Dan in the newspaper, she immediately decides that he is the one she wants. So she finds him and falls in love, although Dan does not reciprocate. When Dan leaves her, Sibella decides that love is for later—at least beyond fifteen years old. Zindel's lively dialogue and portrayal of the spunky Sibella carry this thin, stereotypical story. Marijuana and beer replace the more common cigarettes and Cokes of earlier novels, and sex is referred to as almost a given of teenage life.

Zindel wrote *To Take a Dare* (1982) with Crescent Dragonwagon. In this book, Chrysta Perretti, a thirteen-year-old runaway, takes to the road as a hitchhiker and experiences three years of assorted adventures before ending up in a small Arkansas town. There she meets Luke, who becomes her lover. She undergoes a hysterectomy and becomes a surrogate parent for Dare, a fourteen-year-old dyslexic runaway boy. The novel is about her relationship with the boy and how this experience makes her wiser and more mature, enabling her to forgive her parents for their neglect. Dare eventually runs away again, but Chrysta has learned never to run away.

Zindel returns to his earlier literary strategy of a male and a female protagonist in *Harry and Hortense at Hormone High* (1984). Harry and Hortense resemble John and Lorraine of the Pigman novels, including the penchant for meeting unusual characters. Jason Rohr, a classmate of Harry and Hortense, believing himself a reincarnation of Icarus, tries to be-

YOU WILL ALSO ENJOY
PAUL ZINDEL'S
LOCH
*A 1995 Recommended Book for the
Reluctant YA Reader (ALA)*

"Zindel draws on his scientific background in this story of Luke Perkins, 15,
nicknamed 'Loch' after claiming to see a
lake monster as a little boy. He and his
younger sister, Zaidee, join their ocean-
ographer father on an expedition searching
for enormous prehistoric creatures sighted
in Lake Alban in Vermont. Their leader,
Cavanger, is a ruthless despot who would
just as soon annihilate as preserve the
Plesiosaurs, water beasts thought to be
extinct for over 10 million years. The
gruesome attacks by Plesiosaurs on some
humans are gory and grisly enough to
satisfy even the blood-thirstiest of middle
schoolers." —*School Library Journal*

"The Loch Ness Monster lives in this latest
adventure by award-winning author Zindel.
Fast, furious, and masterful." (A pointer
review)
—*Kirkus Reviews*

"A good, rip-roaring, kids-know-best
adventure."
—*Bulletin of the Center for
Children's Books*

Dust jacket for Zindel's 1995 novel, in which the protagonists must thwart an utterly evil creature

come the hero they believe their forsaken high
school badly needs. Jason posts circulars attacking
the school and its administration on the bulletin
boards and signs them "Icarus, a God." However,
his imagination overtakes this mentally unstable
teen, and soon he believes he is indeed Icarus and
can fly. His death is predictable, but he leaves a legacy of wisdom and philosophy for Harry and Hortense.

*The Amazing and Death-Defying Diary of Eugene
Dingman* (1987) is in effect the highly fictionalized diary of Zindel himself. Dingman, like Zindel, has endured an egoless childhood, avoiding confrontations whenever he could. He meets a girl whom he
believes he loves. However, he has competition
from Bunker, a much bigger and meaner adversary.
Eugene wins his battle against Bunker by using his
wits rather than his strength, but the girl leaves him,
and he is finally forced to face the demons of his
childhood and establish an identity for himself as an
adult. The diary format personalizes Eugene's up-
beat story, and it simulates the first-person alternate
narratives of John and Lorraine in the Pigman novels.

In 1989, Zindel wrote *A Begonia For Miss Applebaum,* a cathartic story about two high-school students whose beloved biology teacher is dying of cancer. In this moving, deeply felt story laced with teen
innocence and humor, Zindel confronts the painful
death of his mother from cancer twenty years earlier.

It is not surprising that at this point in his literary life, Zindel published an entertaining autobiographical account of the roots of some of his literary
characters. He titled it *The Pigman and Me* (1991) because it shows how the various characters within the
Pigman stories evolved from Zindel's childhood experiences. While many readers of Zindel's novels
may have wanted more information about his life
than what appears in this account, Zindel satisfies
their curiosity about how his often bizarre characters relate to his own life.

Zindel's loosely structured novel *David & Della*
(1993) is one of his more forgettable stories. It is
about a repressed young man named David who aspires to be a playwright (like Zindel) and his meeting with an idiosyncratic, alcoholic young actress.

They try to help each other, but the meandering story never seems to focus on a plot.

After this novel, Zindel changed his literary formula, creating mystery/horror stories involving monsters. In his play *Let Me Hear You Whisper* (televised in 1969), Zindel had dramatized the ethical problems of using dolphins to further military power, with scientists cast as the villains. In 1994 he published *Loch,* a novel with three young heroes who try to save a romanticized and benign baby sea monster named "Wee Beastie" (whose father eats people in self-defense) from the clutches of exploitative bounty hunters. Protagonist Loch, his girlfriend, Sarah, and his younger sister, Zaidee, conspire against evil adult antagonists whose motives are entirely self-seeking and immoral.

Things turn somewhat darker in *The Doom Stone* (1995). Instead of an ocean freak, there is a dangerous, malevolent life-form that attacks people with no warning. The creature is called "Skull Face," and fifteen-year-old Jason and a female friend named Alma join forces with Jason's resolute Aunt Sarah to unlock the mystery of the Skull Face. However, unlike all of his other novels, Zindel ends this story with a strong hint that all is not well. Although the creature has been rendered powerless for the moment, there is a clear indication the life-form will raise its ugly head in the future.

Zindel has also written a series of books for younger readers, featuring a group of intrepid fifth-graders known as the "Wacky Facts Lunch Bunch": *Attack of the Killer Fishsticks* (1993), *Fright Party* (1993), *Fifth Grade Safari* (1993), and *The 100% Laugh Riot* (1994). *Raptor* (1998) is another monster book, this time for younger readers; and *Reef of Death* (1998) is his third young-adult mystery/horror story, about a secret and a monster hidden in an Australian coral reef. Roger Leslie, writing in *Booklist* (1 March 1998), states that "Few YA writers can spin a tale of terror with the deftness and macabre humor of Zindel," and adds that the antagonist in *Reef of Death,* the sadistic Dr. Ecanbarger, "is the most delectable villain since Cruella DeVil."

Without doubt, Zindel's understanding of adolescent concerns, his sense of the absurd, his sense of humor, and his skill at writing clear, believable dialogue are major factors in the success of his novels with teenage readers. Further, his influence on the creation and early development of the realistic young adult novel is pivotal. In the best of his works, teens see a reflection of themselves communicated in a language they instinctively understand and appreciate.

Interviews:

Tom Prideaux, "Man with a Bag of Marigold Dust," *Life,* 69 (4 July 1970): 8–9;

"Prizewinning Marigolds," *Time,* 97 (17 May 1971): 66;

Aidan Chambers, "An Interview with Paul Zindel," *Times Literary Supplement,* September 1973, pp. 55ff.;

Patricia Bosworth, "The Effect of Five Actresses on a Play-in-Progress," *New York Times,* 3 April 1977, section 2, pp. 1, 8, 9;

Paul Janeczko, "In Their Own Words: An Interview with Paul Zindel," *English Journal* (October 1977): 20–21;

Jean Mercier, "Paul Zindel," *Publishers Weekly,* 212 (5 December 1977): 6–7;

Audrey Eaglen, "Of Life, Love, Death, Kids, and Inhalation Therapy: An Interview with Paul Zindel," *Top of the News* (Winter 1978): 178–185.

References:

Crescent Dragonwagon, "Under a Good Star: Working with Paul Zindel," *ALAN Review* (Spring 1982): 1–3;

Jack Jacob Forman, *Presenting Paul Zindel* (Boston: Twayne, 1988);

Beverly A. Haley and Kenneth Donelson, "Pigs and Hamburgers, Cadavers and Gamma Rays: Paul Zindel's Adolescents," *Elementary English* (October 1974): 941–945;

James T. Henke, "Six Characters In Search of the Family: The Novels of Paul Zindel," in *Children's Literature,* volume 5 (Philadelphia: Temple University Press, 1976), pp. 130–140;

Stanley Hoffman, "Winning, Losing, but Above All Taking Risks: A Look at the Novels of Paul Zindel," *Lion and the Unicorn* (Fall 1978): 78–88;

Lou Willet Stanek, "The Junior Novel: A Stylistic Study," *Elementary English* (October 1974): 947–953.

Contributors

Ruth M. Alvarez..University of Maryland

Susan Z. Andrade ....University of Pittsburgh

Susan Baker ....University of Nevada, Reno

Earl F. Bargainnier ....Wesleyan College

Marleen Barr ....Virginia Polytechnic Institute and State University

Samuel I. Bellman.......................California State Polytechnic University, Pomona

Kimberly D. Blockett.......................................University of Wisconsin–Madison

Lynn Z. Bloom ....Virginia Commonwealth University

Ashley Brown..University of South Carolina

Philip Bufithis ....Shepherd College

Richard J. Calhoun..Clemson University

Agnes Toloczko Cardoni................................King's College, Wilkes-Barre

Mark J. Charney..Clemson University

David Cowart ....University of South Carolina

Alice A. Deck................................University of Illinois, Urbana–Champaign

Anne Day Dewey................................Saint Louis University, Madrid, Spain

Paul A. Doyle .... Nassau Community College

Andrew Elkins ....Chadron State College

Pin-chia Feng.......................National Chiao-Tung University, Taiwan

Jack Forman..San Diego Mesa College

Robert A. Foster ....Glen Mills, Pennsylvania

Curtis S. Gibson..Reno, Nevada

Sam B. Girgus..University of New Mexico

Joan Givner..University of Regina

Richard H. Goldstone..City College of New York

P. Jane Hafen ....University of Nevada, Las Vegas

Darren Harris-Fain..Shawnee State University

Linnea Hendrickson..University of New Mexico

Sylvia Henneberg ....Morehead State University

Theodore W. Hipple..University of Tennessee

Lillie P. Howard ....Wright State University

Caroline C. Hunt..College of Charleston

Sally Johns ....University of South Carolina

Dan R. Jones ....University of Houston

Kirkland C. Jones ....Lamar University

Victor H. Jones ....Indiana State University

John D. Kalb ....Salisbury State University

Greg Keeler..Montana State University, Bozeman

Marilyn Kern-Foxworth..Florida A & M University

Robert F. Kiernan..Manhattan College

Reese Danley Kilgo................................University of Alabama, Huntsville

Jack Kolbert ....Susquehanna University

Lotta M. Lofgren ....University of Virginia

Carol A. MacCurdy..*University of Southwestern Louisiana*

Christopher MacGowan...*College of William and Mary*

H. W. Matalene ....*University of South Carolina*

Laurence W. Mazzeno ....*Alvernia College*

James L. McWilliams III ....*University of Texas at Austin*

Katherine M. Mellen ....*Yale University*

Elizabeth Meese ....*University of Alabama*

Laurence Miller ....*Western Washington University*

Mozella G. Mitchell ....*University of South Florida*

Keith A. Morgan ....*North Carolina State University*

Thomas Myers...*Saint Norbert College*

Peter F. Neumeyer ....*San Diego State University*

Anne Newman ....*University of North Carolina at Charlotte*

David O'Connell ....*Georgia State University*

Teresa F. O'Connor....................................*City University of New York, College of Staten Island*

Donald E. Palumbo ....*East Carolina University*

Mary Jane Perna...*University of California, Berkeley*

Carolyn and Ernest Rhodes ....*Old Dominion University*

Pat Salomon...*Bowling Green State University*

Edward C. Sampson..*State University of New York College at Oneonta*

William J. Scheick...*University of Texas at Austin*

Matthias Schubnell...*University of the Incarnate Word*

Ruth L. Strickland..*University of South Carolina*

Rodger L. Tarr ....*Illinois State University*

Caren J. Town ....*Georgia State University*

Gioia Woods ....*University of Nevada, Reno*

Thomas Daniel Young...*Vanderbilt University*

Laura M. Zaidman ....*University of South Carolina, Sumter*

Concise Dictionary of American Literary Biography Cumulative Index

Cumulative Index

Evans, Donald   III:259

Evans, Ernestine   VII:312, 315

Evans, Mari   IV:154; VII:21, 81

Evans, Walker   V:3, 4, 6

Everett, Alexander H.   I:187

Evers, Medgar   V:51; VII:76

Everson, William (Brother Antonius)   III:115, 117; V:202, 207, 426

Fabre, Michael   IV:403

Fadiman, Clifton   III:150, 155; VII:534

Fagin, N. Bryllion   II:329

Fairbanks, Douglas   II:246; VII:463

Fairbanks, Mary Mason   II:71

Falcoff, Mark   VI:79

Falk, Signi Lenea   VII:239, 241, 242

Falkner, Dean   IV:116, 128

Falkner, John Wesley Thompson   IV:116

Falkner, Maud Butler   IV:113

Falkner, Murry Cuthbert   IV:113, 116

Falkner, Murry   IV:116

Falkner, William Clark   IV:116

Fancher, Edwin   VI:167

Fanon, Frantz   VII:82

Farmer, James   V:196

Farr, Florence   III:220

Farrand, Max   I:113

Farrar, Geraldine   II:42

Farrell, James T.   IV:75, 180; V:32, 35, 37, 86, 142, 235; VI:162, 165

Fast, Howard   V:372

Fatout, Paul   II:32

Faulkner, Jill   IV:124, 129

Faulkner, Lida Estelle Oldham Franklin   IV:113, 116, 117, 122

Faulkner, William   I:150; II:88, 226; III:2, 4, 12, 107, 108, 155, 164, 174, 178; IV:5, 8, 112, 113, 220, 224, 268, 284, 290, 291, 308, 367, 373, 398, 404, 418; V:49, 82, 99, 188, 201, 235, 346, 399, 403, 492, 494, 498, 500, 504; VI:68, 70, 84, 86, 96, 104, 110, 113, 165, 197, 200, 213, 216, 260, 263, 265, 280, 284; VII:48, 50, 171, 269, 274, 275, 284

Fauquier, Francis   I:202

Faure, Elie   IV:176

Fauset, Jessie   III:282; IV:158, 160

Fawcett, Edgar   II:94

Fay, Monsignor Cyril Sigourney Webster   III:50, 53

Fay, Theodore S.   I:313

Faÿ, Bernard   III:257, 266, 270

Feiden, Margo   VI:310

Feig, Dodye   VII:492

Feldstein, Albert   VI:22

Felgar, Robert   IV:395

Felton, Cornelius   I:217

Felton, Verna   V:278

Fenelon, Fania   V:380

Fenollosa, Ernest   III:225, 232

Fenton, J. O.   I:254

Ferber, Edna   IV:155

Ferguson, Moira   VII:163

Ferguson, Suzanne   V:308

Ferling, Charles   V:198

Ferling, Clemence Mendes-Monsanto   V:198

Ferlinghetti, Julie   V:198

Ferlinghetti, Lawrence   V:198–214, 230, 233, 423, 426, 427, 430, 431; VII:199

Ferlinghetti, Lorenzo   V:198

Ferlinghetti, Selden Kirby-Smith   V:198, 202

Fern, Fanny (see Parton, Sara Payson Willis)   I:386

Ferrar, Nicholas   IV:105

Ferrer, Jose   VII:326

Ficke, Arthur Davison   III:200, 202, 205, 207, 212

Fiedler, Leslie   V:37, 152, 303, 317, 456, 474, 475, 485, 486; VI:187; VII:126

Fiedler, Leslie A.   VII:502

Field, Betty   V:278

Field, Leslie   IV:377, 379

Fielding, Henry   I:179, 183; II:202; III:106; VII:64, 298, 537

Fielding, Mildred   II:125

Fields, Annie Adams   II:221, 363, 365

Fields, James T.   I:148, 156, 159, 161, 163; II:193, 194, 221

Fields, Joseph   V:502

Fillmore, Millard   III:192

Filsinger, Ernst   II:259

Finch, Jean Louise   V:323

Finney, Charles G.   I:130, 134; VI:28

Firestone, Bruce M.   VI:75

Firmage, George   IV:53

Fischel, Eric   VII:164

Fischer, William C.   V:66

Fish, Jr., Hamilton   IV:72

Fisher, Dorothy Canfield   II:38; IV:404

Fisher, Eleanor   V:249

Fisher, Margery   VII:144

Fisher, Rudolph   VII:148

Fishkin, Shelly Fisher   VII:191

Fitch, Clyde   II:198; IV:245, 314

Fitch, George Hamlin   II:276

Fitts, Dudley   IV:49; VII:507

Fitzgerald, Annabel   III:52

Fitzgerald, Edward   III:50, 52

Fitzgerald, F. Scott   II:88, 285, 382, II:50–67, 88, 91, 108, 146, 148–151, 154, 155, 178, 253, 258; III:50–67; IV:62, 64, 174, 214, 220, 224, 290, 341, 357, 369, 370, 373, 375, 389; V:9, 34, 448, 535; IV:68, 77, 263, 266; VII:140, 232, 235, 284, 351

Fitzgerald, Karen   VII:173

Fitzgerald, Mollie McQuillan   III:50, 52

Fitzgerald, Philip   VII:265

Fitzgerald, Robert   V:3–5, 303, 399, 400, 403, 405, 407; VII:217, 219

Fitzgerald, Sally   V:399, 405

Fitzgerald, Zelda Sayre   III:50, 53, 54, 57, 58, 61, 64, 108, 148, 151, 154; IV:62; V:535

Flanagan, John T.   II:246, 299

Flanagan, William   V:14

Flaubert, Gustave   II:36, 52, 62, 89, 214, 221, 224, 306; III:107, 248, 256, 277; IV:11, 217, 360, 363, 374; V:128, 130, 136; VI:200, 242, 264

Flavin, James   VII:48

Fleming, Anne Taylor   V:135

Harte, Catherine Bret   II:174, 175
Harte, Eliza   II:174, 175
Harte, Elizabeth Ostrander   II:173–175
Harte, Ethel   II:173, 177
Harte, Francis King   II:173, 178
Harte, Griswold   II:173, 178
Harte, Henry (father)   II:173–175
Harte, Henry (son)   II:174
Harte, James D.   II:308
Harte, Jessamy   II:173, 183
Harte, Margaret   II:174, 175
Harte, Mrs. Francis King   II:177
Hartpence, Alanson   III:299
Harvey, Anne Gray   V:461
Harvey, Mary Gray Staples   V:460, 461, 467, 468
Harvey, Ralph Churchill   V:460, 461
Hastings, Selina, Countess of Huntingdon   I:366, 367, 369, 374
Haskell, Frankel   VI:204
Hass, Robert   IV:126, 128
Hassan, Ihab   V:131, 132, 134, 138, 210, 456
Hasse, Henry   VI:20
Hathorne, Daniel   I:150
Hathorne, Elizabeth Clarke Manning   I:149
Hathorne, John   I:150
Hathorne, William   I:150
Havens, Lila   VII:248
Havilland, Olivia de   IV:348
Hawkes, John   V:89, 399, 406, 407
Hawkins, Willis   II:101
Hawks, Howard   IV:112, 126
Hawthorne, Elizabeth   I:151, 152
Hawthorne, Julian   I:149, 156, 158
Hawthorne, Nathaniel   I:12, 33, 53, 74, 120, 122, 148–167, 172, 176, 214, 222, 229, 231, 252, 261, 264, 266, 270, 272, 328, 337, 343, 348, 357, 384, 391, 402; II:5, 26, 36, 112, 113, 154, 161, 191, 193, 195, 200, 214, 226, 227, 238, 307; III:22, 79; IV:127, 239; V:131, 134, 143, 261, 327, 346, 399, 403; VI:79, 94, 216, 276, 279, 280, 284, 286, 295; VII:106, 216, 221, 223, 295, 426, 554
Hawthorne, Rose   I:149
Hawthorne, Sophia Amelia Peabody   I:149, 153–156, 162, 266
Hawthorne, Una   I:149, 155, 158, 160, 162
Hay, John   II:159, 197, 221, 225, 232; VII:461, 462
Hayden, Erma Morris   V:260
Hayden, Julie   V:515
Hayden, Maria   V:260
Hayden, Robert   V:259–269
Hayden, Sue Ellen Westerfield   V:260, 261
Hayden, William   V:260, 261
Haydn, Franz Joseph   IV:9, 210
Haydn, Hiram   V:304; VI:264, 269; VII:339
Haydon, Julie   VII:398
Hayes, Christopher   VII:506
Hayes, Helen   V:511
Hayes, Marvin   VI:61, 62
Hayes, Rutherford B.   I:70; II:183, 196; IV:85; VII:460
Hayes, Paul Hamilton   II:196
Haynes, Mabel   III:256

Haywood, Big Bill   VI:89
Hazard, Eloise Perry   VII:538
Hazen, Brig. Gen. William   II:23
Head, Ann   VII:560
Head, Bessie   VI:326
Healy, George P. A.   I:160
Hearn, Lafcadio   V:425
Hearst, William Randolph   II:20, 24, 26, 27, 104; IV:70; VII:462, 463
Heartman, Charles F.   I:368
Hebestreit, Ludwig   V:187
Hecht, Anthony   VI:14; VII:343
Hecht, Ben   V:35
Hedge, Frederic Henry   I:84
Hedges, William L.   I:187
Hegel, Georg Friedrich Wilhelm   V:90; VI:6
Heidegger, Martin   III:252; IV:406; V:98
Heilman, Robert   V:181
Heine, Heinrich   II:186, 192
Heinlein, Robert   VI:16, 20; VII:116
Heiserman, Arthur   V:456
Heitzer, Lore   VII:275
Heitzer, Regina   VII:275
Hejinian, Lyn   III:253
Helburn, Theresa   IV:251; V:512; IV:251
Heller, Joseph   IV:370; VII:298
Hellman, Lillian   III:107; IV:119, 136, 146, 165, 185; VII:506
Helprin, Eleanor Lynn   VII:100
Helprin, Lisa Kennedy   VII:100
Helprin, Mark   VII:99–111
Helprin, Morris   VII:100
Helvetius, Anne-Catherine de Ligniville   I:103, 110
Hemenway, Robert   VII:147, 148, 153, 155, 159
Hemingway, Clarence Edmonds   III:89–91
Hemingway, Ernest   I:41; II:44, 75, 88, 272; III:2, 4, 9, 13, 50, 58, 88–111, 155, 159, 173, 174, 178, 214, 217, 234, 235, 243, 244, 248, 253, 263; IV:20, 56, 58, 62, 72, 74, 115, 126, 141, 165, 174, 214, 220, 222, 224, 290, 291, 301, 341, 373, 389; V:31, 37, 42, 50, 80, 82, 84, 88, 144, 188, 201, 329, 472, 479, 535; VI:19, 34, 37, 68, 70, 78, 79, 96, 100, 104, 114, 162, 165, 176, 280, 284; VII:63, 128, 141, 232, 235, 282, 284, 286, 287, 291, 454, 455, 464, 483, 521
Hemingway, Grace Hall   III:89, 90
Hemingway, Gregory Hancock   III:89, 91
Hemingway, Hadley Richardson   II:89–91, 95, 107, 108
Hemingway, John Hadley Nicanor ("Bumby")   III:89, 91, 108
Hemingway, Martha Gellhorn   III:89, 92, 102
Hemingway, Mary Welsh   III:89, 92, 103, 108
Hemingway, Patrick   III:89, 91
Hemingway, Pauline Pfeiffer   III:89, 91, 92
Hemphill, Samuel   I:104
Henderson, Alice Corbin   II:348, 353
Henderson, Annie   VII:6, 8, 13
Henderson, Archibald   II:329
Henderson, Katherine   VI:82
Henderson, R. W.   V:325
Hendin, Josephine   VII:419
Hendricks, King   II:289

Hendricks, Newell   VII:209
Henri, Robert   II:252, 253
Henry, Arthur   II:126, 127
Henry, Maude Wood   II:126
Henry, O.   IV:336, 340
Hepburn, Katharine   V:7
Herbert, Brian   VII:114, 123
Herbert, Eugenia W.   I:102, 103, 114, 115
Herbert, Frank   VII:112–124
Herbert, George   I:103; VI:2, 4; VII:197
Herbst, Josephine   IV:365; V:89; VII:315, 316, 320, 322, 326
Hergesheimer, Joseph   II:88
Herman, Charlotte   III:298
Herman, Jerry   VII:528
Herdon, William   II:300
Herne, James A.   II:198; IV:245, 246
Herold, David   VII:461
Herr, Michael   VII:285
Herring, Eliza   I:342
Herring, Henry   I:342
Herschel, Caroline   VII:371
Hersey, Ann   VII:128
Hersey, Baird   VII:128
Hersey, Barbara Kaufman   VII:128
Hersey, Brook   VII:128
Hersey, Frances Cannon   VII:128
Hersey, Grace Baird   VII:128
Hersey, John   V:10; VII:125–136
Hersey, John Jr.   VII:128
Hersey, Marie   III:52
Hersey, Martin   VII:128
Hersey, Roscoe   VII:128
Hesoid   I:3
Hesse, Herman   VI:326
Heubsch, B. W.   III:8, 11, 12
Heuffer, Ford Madox (see Ford, Ford Madox)
Hewes, Henry   V:249
Hewett, Mrs. Mary   I:337
Hewlett, Maurice   III:220
Heyen, William   V:114
Heyman, Katherine   III:220, 222, 237
Hibben, Paxton   IV:70
Hicks, Elias   I:381
Hicks, Granville   IV:67, 392, 399, 415; V:49, 81, 172, 325; VII:58, 534, 541
Hidalgo, Luis   VII:316
Higginson, Thomas Wentworth   I:120, 128; II:110, 115–117, 339; IV:5
Hill, Arthur   V:254
Hill, Donald L.   VII:506
Hill, Hamlin   I:103
Hill, Herbert   V:316
Hillsborough, Earl of   I:109
Hillyer, Robert   III:38, 43, 44, 241; IV:40, 60; V:437
Himes, Chester   IV:405, 416; VII:158
Hindemith, Paul   VII:526
Hinkley, Eleanor   IV:87, 90
Hinman, Wilbur   II:96
Hinton, Beverly   VII:138
Hinton, Grady P.   VII:138

Hinton, S. E.   VII:137–145, 560
Hippatia   I:9
Hirsch, Sidney Mttron   VII:343, 346, 347
Hirst, Henry   I:338
Hirst, Robert H.   II:82
Hiss, Alger   V:333
Hitchcock, Alfred   VII:530
Hitler, Adolf   III:125, 126, 211, 238; IV:165, 278, 346, 376; V:454; VII:237, 239, 324, 326, 491, 496, 541
Hoagland, Edward   V:111
Hobbes, Thomas   I:3; VII:59
Hobhouse, Janet   III:266
Hodiak, John   VII:539
Hoffa, Jimmy   IV:76
Hoffman, Abbie   V:238
Hoffman, Daniel   V:180
Hoffman, Dustin   V:380
Hoffman, Frederick J.   III:170; IV:5, 7, 183; V:308; VII:469
Hoffman, Josiah   I:180
Hoffman, Matilda   I:180, 182
Hoffmann, Camille   VII:172
Hoffmann, Joseph   VII:172
Hofmannsthal, Hugo von   IV:201
Hogan, Ernest   II:163; III:133
Hogarth, William   II:219
Hoge, Warren   VI:79
Hoheb, George   III:292
Hohoff, Tay   V:323
Hokusai, Katsuskika   VII:275
Holbein, Hans   II:48; IV:13
Holbrook, Carrie   VII:265
Holden, William   V:278
Holiday, Billie   VI:7
Holland, Josiah G.   II:110, 113
Holland, Willard   V:511
Hollander, John   V:217
Hollindale, Peter   VII:145
Hollinghurst, Alan   VII:421
Hollo, Anself   V:206
Holman, C. Hugh   IV:377
Holman, Hugh   II:317
Holmes, Abiel   I:167
Holmes, Amelia Jackson   I:167
Holmes, Amelia Lee Jackson   I:167
Holmes, Edward Jackson   I:167
Holmes, George F.   II:366
Holmes, John Clellon   V:181, 217, 218, 221, 226, 227, 242, 312, 317, 459, 461, 464; VI:110, 111
Holmes, Oliver Wendell Jr.   I:167
Holmes, Oliver Wendell   I:33, 80, 162, 166–175, 192, 252, 254, 270, 395; II:73, 74, 182, 193, 194, 221
Holmes, Sarah Wendell   I:167
Holt, Henry   III:77; IV:50
Homer   VII:217, 225, 226, 283, 284, 531
Homer, Louise   II:42
Homer   I:3, 34, 203, 301, 364, 370, 384; III:115, 228; IV:88; V:427; VI:184, 302
Hong, Tom   VII:182, 183, 189
Hooch, Pieter de   VII:504
Hood, Thomas   I:271; II:23

Johnson, Grace Nail   III:131, 134, 135, 142
Johnson, Greer   V:353
Johnson, Guy B.   IV:162
Johnson, Helen Louise Dillet   III:131, 132
Johnson, Hillary   VI:478
Johnson, James   III:131, 132
Johnson, James Weldon   I:376; II:154, 165, 169; III:38,
    40, 44, 130–145; IV:159, 160, 162; V:188, 190, 191;
    VII:6, 148, 152
Johnson, John Rosamond   III:130, 132, 141
Johnson, Joyce   V:312
Johnson, Lionel   III:220, 221
Johnson, Lyndon   IV:278; V:196, 342; VII:221, 223,
    508
Johnson, Martyn   IV:41
Johnson, Mary   II:256, 258, 259
Johnson, Owen   IV:224
Johnson, Richard M.   I:321
Johnson, Richard   V:289
Johnson, Samuel   I:114, 179, 180, 258; V:114, 394, 469;
    VII:223, 506
Johnson, Stanley   VII:343, 347
Johnson, Thomas   II:117
Johnson, Vivian Baxter   VII:5, 6
Johnston, Carol   IV:379
Johnston, John   I:395
Jones, Anna Lois Russ   V:61–63
Jones, Anne G.   VII:431
Jones, Barry   VII:402
Jones, Coyette Le Roy   V:61–63
Jones, David   III:313
Jones, Emma Berdis   V:41
Jones, Gayl   VI:200
Jones, George Frederic   II:371, 372
Jones, Helen Elizabeth   VII:366
Jones, Howard Mumford   I:204; IV:402
Jones, James   V:45, 479; VI:260; VII:282
Jones, John Paul   I:269
Jones, LeRoi (see Baraka, Amiri)
Jones, Lucretia Rhinelander   II:371, 372
Jones, Margo   V:273
Jones, Quincy   VI:332; VII:93
Jones, Robert Edmond   IV:245
Jones, Sandra Elaine   V:63
Jonson, Ben   II:342; V:110, 157; VII:226
Joost, Nicholas   VII:58
Joplin, Scott   VI:89
Jordan, June   VII:21, 366
Jordan, Vernon   VII:95
Joseffy   II:351
Joseloff, Samuel H.   V:484
Josephson, Matthew   VII:316, 318, 320
Joubert, Jean   VII:205
Joyce, James   III:8, 9, 23, 32, 88, 90, 107, 214, 217, 224,
    227, 229, 230, 233, 234, 253, 263, 271, 288, 300,
    306, 313; IV:56, 80, 96, 108, 112, 190, 195, 201,
    317, 360, 364, 365, 395, 417, 426, 444, 452, 454;
    VI:86, 115, 173, 231, 248, 263; VII:163, 220, 232,
    284, 295, 530, 532
Judd, Gerritt P.   I:259
Julian the Apostate   VII:456

Jung, Carl Gustav   II:276, 288, 289; IV:188, 268, 334;
    V:299, 351, 433, 441; VI:89, 148; VII:61, 469
Justice, B. Martin   II:168
Justice, Donald   V:111
Juvenal   VII:215, 223, 224
Kafka, Franz   IV:406; V:6, 217, 420, 421; VI:216, 219,
    235, 236, 242, 249, 252; VII:275
Kahane, Jack   IV:179, 181, 182
Kahane, Maurice   IV:179
Kahn, Herman   VII:100
Kahn, Otto   III:25, 32
Kaiser, Ernest   V:196
Kakutani, Michiko   VII:54, 443
Kaltonborn, H. V.   III:237
Kakutani, Michiko   VI:195, 197
Kamehameha III, King   I:259
Kamin, Martin   IV:364
Kandinsky, Vassily   III:107
Kant, Immanuel   I:77
Kaplan, Charles   V:456
Kapstein, Isadore   IV:362, 364
Kardules, Liberty   VII:547
Karenga, Maulana Ron   V:60, 77, 124
Karp, David   V:48
Kasabian, Linda   VI:77
Kasper, John   III:242
Kastor, Elizabeth   VII:41
Katsimbalis, George   IV:172, 172
Kauffmann, Stanley   IV:238; VII:540
Kaufman, Bob   V:206, 207
Kaufman, George S.   III:146, 150; IV:294
Kawai, Kanjiro   VII:448
Kaye, Marilyn   VII:144
Kazan, Elia   IV:70, 76, 302, 303; V:49, 51, 270, 273, 372,
    525, 526; VII:531
Kazin, Alfred   IV:78, 145, 185, 220; V:84, 87, 88, 90, 94,
    138; VI:71
Kazuko, Shiraishi   V:432
Keach, Stacy Jr.   VI:107
Keaton, Buster   V:7
Keats, John   I:11, 31; II:157; III:35, 38, 43, 50, 288, 294,
    315; IV:39, 52, 188, 313, 333; V:234, 261, 341;
    VII:197, 199, 201
Keen, Edwin H.   II:165
Keil, Charles   V:71
Keimer, Samuel   I:99–101, 107
Keith, Gov. William   I:100
Kelley, John   V:207
Kelly, Gene   VII:392
Kelly, Robert   VII:546
Kemble, Edward Windsor   II:160, 166
Kemble, Fanny   II:223
Kemler, Edgar   III:191
Kemphis, Thomas à   V:282
Keneally, Thomas   VII:425
Kennedy, Daniel Edwards   I:20
Kennedy, Jacqueline   VII:454, 458, 459
Kennedy, John F.   III:68, 82, 84; VI:223, 251, 256;
    VII:14, 76, 79, 80, 136, 458, 460, 511, 534
Kennedy, John Pendleton   I:298, 310, 312, 313, 316, 359
Kennedy, Richard S.   IV:377, 378, 380

Melvill, Maria   I:253
Melville, Elizabeth Knapp Shaw   I:253, 257, 258, 272, 275
Melville, Elizabeth   I:253, 265, 268
Melville, Frances   I:253, 268
Melville, Gansevoort   I:256
Melville, Herman   I:41, 44, 52, 57, 75, 148, 150, 154, 157, 163, 193, 222, 234, 252–279, 316, 385; II:112, 113, 226, 238, 270, 286; III:23, 30, 79, 81; IV:17, 248; V:206, 230, 314; VI:162, 280, 284, 295, 296; VII:51, 63, 106, 217, 221, 223, 226, 282, 288, 293, 307, 426
Melville, Malcolm   I:253, 268, 272
Melville, Stanwix   I:253, 268, 272
Mencius   III:240
Mencken, Anna Abha   III:183, 185
Mencken, August (Jr.)   III:185
Mencken, August   III:183, 185, 186
Mencken, Charles   III:185
Mencken, Gertrude   III:185
Mencken, H. L.   I:235; II:27, 44, 122, 128–130, 211; III:50, 54, 141, 146, 148, 154, 162, 170, 182–199, 232, 237, 241, 263; IV:8, 61, 139, 360, 363, 393, 396; VI:298
Mencken, Sara Powell Haardt   III:183, 188, 196
Mendelssohn, Jacob Ludwig Felix   III:138
Mendes-Monsanto, Emily   V:201
Menken, Alan   VI:310
Mennes, Sir John   I:103
Menuhin, Yehudi   II:50
Mercer, Dr. Mary   V:354
Meredith, Burgess   IV:356
Meredith, Hugh   I:101
Meredith, James   V:50
Meredith, William   II:113; VII:507
Merlo, Frank   V:521–535
Merrill, James   VI:11; V:237, 240, 243; VII:502
Merrill, Thomas   V:237, 240, 243
Mershon, Katharine   VII:155
Merwin, W. S.   V:106; VII:502
Metternich, Prince Klemens von   IV:72
Meyer, Annie Nathan   VII:149
Meyerowitz, Patricia   III:271
Mérimée, Prosper   II:220
Michelangelo   I:305; IV:88
Michaels, Marguerite   VII:429
Michelson, Bruce   VII:511, 515
Michener, James   VII:543
Mielziner, Jo   V:358, 364
Miles, Josephine   V:180, 426
Milford, Nancy   III:58, 64
Milhaud, Darius   VII:495
Millay, Cora Buzzelle   III:201, 202, 207
Millay, Edna St. Vincent   III:40, 43, 200–213; IV:117; V:261
Millay, Henry Tolman   III:201, 202
Millay, Norma   III:203
Miller, Barbara   IV:173, 175
Miller, Amassa   IV:285
Miller, Arthur   IV:267; V:15, 244, 273, 282, 358–385, 510; VI:242

Miller, Augusta Barnett   V:359
Miller, Beatrice Sylvas Wickens   IV:173, 175, 176
Miller, Daniel   V:359
Miller, Edith Smith Mansfield (June)   IV:173, 176, 181
Miller, Eve McClure   IV:173, 181, 182, 184, 185
Miller, Heinrich   IV:173, 175
Miller, Henry   I:349, 396; II:272; III:4; IV:172–188; V:200, 201, 203, 316, 426; VI:162, 175, 176
Miller, Hiroko Tokuda   IV:173, 185
Miller, Isidore   V:359
Miller, James E.   V:456, 457
Miller, James   III:53
Miller, Jane   V:359
Miller, Janina Martha Lepska   IV:173, 183–185
Miller, Joaquin   I:391
Miller, Marie Louise Nieting   IV:173
Miller, Mary Grace Stattery   V:359, 361, 372, 373
Miller, Rebecca   V:359
Miller, Robert   V:359
Miller, Tony   IV:173, 185
Miller, Valentine   IV:173, 185
Millet, Fred B.   V:156
Millet, Jean François   IV:202
Millet, Kate   VI:174, 175
Mills, Florence   IV:158
Millstein, Gilbert   V:316
Milne, A. A.   VII:476
Milnes, Richard Monckton (Lord Houghton)   II:224
Milosz, Czeslaw   VII:209
Milton, Edith   VI:272
Milton, Evon Easley   VII:98
Milton, John   3, 94, 138, 238, 243, 314, 362, 365, 370, 400; II:252, 329, 330; III:116, 203, 224, 294; IV:104, 114, 193, 293; V:378; VII:163, 217, 226, 307, 478, 511, 551
Mims, Edwin   VII:343, 346
Miner, Julia   II:30
Mingus, Charlie   V:65
Minter, David   IV:129
Mirandola, Pico della   III:222
Misakian, Jo Ellen   VII:138
Mitchell, Donald Grant   II:117
Mitchell, Eugene   VII:262
Mitchell, Margaret   VII:262–266
Mitchell, Maria   I:273
Mitchell, O. M.   I:384
Mitchell, Samuel L.   I:182
Mitchell, Stephens   VII:266
Mitchell, Stewart   IV:39, 40
Mitchell, Tennessee   II:295, 298
Mitchum, Robert   VII:542
Mitterand, François   VII:497
Mizener, Arthur   III:61, 63
Modarressi, Mitra   VII:429
Modarressi, Taghi Mohammed   VII:429
Modarressi, Tezh   VII:429
Moeller, Philip   IV:245, 262
Molesworth, Mary   VII:476
Molette, Carlton   V:53
Molière   VII:506, 507, 510, 512
Momaday, Brit   VII:269

Snodgrass, W. D. V:111, 302, 459, 461; VII:220, 502, 509

Snow, C. P. V:176

Snyder, Albert VI:272

Snyder, Gary 64-66, 202, 207, 214, 229, 237, 241, 312, 314, 316, 423, 426, 427, 429, 430, 432; VII:202

Snyder, Ruth VI:272

Sobiloff, Hy IV:18

Socrates I:94, 114; VII:286

Soete, Mary VI:230

Solomon, Carl V:206, 214, 221-223, 230, 232

Solomons, Leon III:255

Somer, John VI:309

Sontag, Susan VI:81

Sophocles II:337; III:112, 118, 243; V:365, 371, 372; VI:267

Sorel, Georges III:295

Sorrentino, Gilbert V:65-67

Soupault, Philippe III:306

South, Eudora Lindsay II:247, 248

Southey, Robert I:274

Sowter, John I:104

Spacks, Patricia Meyer V:470

Spann, Marcella III:242, 243

Spark, Muriel VI:295

Speare, M. E. III:240

Speiser, Lawrence V:203

Spellman, A. B. V:63, 69

Spencer, Anne VII:39, 43

Spencer, Hazelton II:266

Spencer, Herbert II:52, 122, 126, 133, 224, 270, 275, 276, 280, 284, 316, 317, 370, 375; VI:293

Spencer, Theodore III:237; IV:50

Spender, Stephen II:237; IV:100; V:178, 297, 309, 443

Spengler, Oswald III:62, 63

Spenser, Edmund I:3, 271; III:294; V:110

Spielberg, Steven VI:332

Spillane, Mickey IV:216

Spiller, Robert E. II:283

Spingarn, Amy IV:159

Spingarn, Arthur II:151

Spingarn, Joel E. III:140

Spinoza, Baruch III:117

Spinoza, Benedict de IV:87, 182

Spivack, Charlotte VI:154, 157

Spock, Dr. Benjamin V:238; VII:454

Spooner, Alden I:381, 383

Spooner, Edwin B. I:383

Spoto, Donald V:535

Springarn, Arthur IV:150, 159, 162

Springer, Haskell 185

Springsteen, Bruce VII:250

Squire, J. C. II:262

Squires, Radcliffe III:117

Stade, George VI:93; VII:62

Stael, Anne Louise Germaine Necker de I:271

Stafford, Jean VII:215, 218

Stalin, Joseph VII:496, 541

Stanard, Jane Stith I:301

Stanard, Robert I:301

Stanberry, Henry I:389

Standish, Miles I:220

Stanford, Ann I:9

Stanford, Leland II:24

Stanislavsky, Konstantin IV:76; VII:521

Stanley, George V:65

Stanley, Henry M. II:160

Stanton, Elizabeth Cady II:368

Staples, Samuel I:352

Stapleton, Laurence IV:194

Starbuck, George V:459, 461; VI:10, 14

Starr, Mary (Mary Devereaux) I:308

Starr, Menroe V:298

Starr, Sara V:298

Starr, Zaro V:298

Stavros, George V:121-123

Stead, Christina V:302, 308

Stedman, E. C. II:194, 197

Stedman, Edmund Clarence I:375, 386, 395

Steele, E. L. G. II:26

Steele, Lloyd V:274

Steele, Richard I:94, 98, 104, 180

Steger, Henry Peyton II:322

Stegner, Page VII:174

Stegner, Wallace VI:111; VII:174

Steichen, Edward II:348, 351, 352, 355, 357, 358

Steichen, John Carl II:358

Steichen Karlen Paula II:358

Stein, Allan III:270

Stein, Amelia Keyser III:249, 253

Stein, Bertha III:255

Stein, Daniel III:249, 253-255

Stein, Gertrude III:2, 9, 15, 88, 90, 91, 94, 96, 108, 248-273; IV:40, 194, 341, 392, 398, 405; V:201, 426; VII:526, 527, 530, 533

Stein, Leo III:252, 254-256, 259

Stein, Michael III:252, 255, 257

Stein, Sarah III:252, 257

Stein, Simon III:255

Steinbeck, Carol Henning IV:281, 283, 284

Steinbeck, Elaine Scott IV:281, 294, 299, 304

Steinbeck, Gwyndolyn Conger IV:281, 290

Steinbeck, Johann Ernst II IV:281, 283

Steinbeck, John II:317; III:4; IV:214, 280-309, 401; V:452, 479; VI:84, 165, 166, 220

Steinbeck, John (father) IV:281, 292

Steinbeck, Olive Hamilton IV:281, 283

Steinbeck, Thom IV:281, 292

Steinem, Gloria VI:320; VII:162

Steiner, George V:388

Steiner, Wendy III:268

Steinhoff, William R. VII:482

Steinmetz, Charles Proteus IV:70

Stendahl (Marie Henri Beyle) III:107

Stephen, Leslie II:224

Stephens, Annie Fitzgerald VII:265

Stephens, James II:246; IV:285

Stephens, Sir Leslie I:226

Stepto, Robert III:136

Sterling, George II:20, 27, 270, 281, 284; III:112

Sterling, John II:219

Stern, Richard V:99

Sterne, Laurence I:17; III:253; V:109; VII:322, 420

ISBN 0-7876-1695-8

90000